CONSERVATION DIRECTORY

1989

34TH EDITION

A list of organizations, agencies, and officials
concerned with natural resource use and management

Published by

Working for the Nature of Tomorrow.

NATIONAL WILDLIFE FEDERATION
1400 Sixteenth Street, N.W., Washington, D.C. 20036-2266
(703) 790-4000

Printed on 100% Recycled Paper

Copyright 1989, National Wildlife Federation
Library of Congress Catalog Card Number 70-10646
ISSN 0069-9 11X
ISBN 0-945051-00-X

The Conservation Directory, item no. 79556, may be purchased
for $15.00 per copy, plus $3.25 shipping charge per order.
Please send check or purchase order to:

NATIONAL WILDLIFE FEDERATION
1400 Sixteenth Street, N.W., Washington, D.C. 20036-2266

TABLE OF CONTENTS

United States Congress. 1

International, National, and Interstate Commissions. 34

International, National, and Interstate Organizations 37

State and Territorial Agencies, Citizens' Groups 114

*National Wildlife Federation Affiliate

Canadian Government Agencies and National Citizens' Groups. 236

Canadian Provincial Territorial Agencies and Citizens' Groups 242

Colleges and Universities in the United States and Canada 252
Fish and Game Commissioners and Directors of the United States
and Canada 268

Editor's Note: The state abbreviations which are used throughout this publication are the two-letter form:

Alabama	AL	Kentucky	KY	Ohio.	OH
Alaska	AK	Louisiana	LA	Oklahoma	OK
Arizona	AZ	Maine	ME	Oregon	OR
Arkansas	AR	Maryland	MD	Pennsylvania	PA
California	CA	Massachusetts	MA	Puerto Rico	PR
Colorado	CO	Michigan	MI	Rhode Island	RI
Connecticut	CT	Minnesota	MN	South Carolina	SC
Delaware	DE	Mississippi	MS	South Dakota	SD
District of Columbia	DC	Missouri	MO	Tennessee	TN
Florida	FL	Montana	MT	Texas	TX
Georgia	GA	Nebraska	NE	Utah	UT
Guam	GU	Nevada	NV	Vermont	VT
Hawaii	HI	New Hampshire	NH	Virgin Islands	VI
Idaho	ID	New Jersey	NJ	Virginia	VA
Illinois	IL	New Mexico	NM	Washington	WA
Indiana	IN	New York	NY	West Virginia	WV
Iowa	IA	North Carolina	NC	Wisconsin	WI
Kansas	KS	North Dakota	ND	Wyoming	WY

UNITED STATES CONGRESS

(Considering environmental and natural resource legislation)

SENATE COMMITTEES AND SUBCOMMITTEES

COMMITTEE ON AGRICULTURE, NUTRITION AND FORESTRY,
Rm. 328-A, Russell Bldg., Washington, DC 20510 (202, 224-2035)
Chairman: PATRICK LEAHY (VT)
Ranking Minority Member: RICHARD G. LUGAR (IN)
Concerned with agriculture and agricultural commodities; inspection of livestock, meat and agricultural products; animal industry and diseases of animals; pests and pesticides; agricultural extension services and experiment stations; forestry, forest reserves and wilderness areas other than those created from the public domain; agricultural economics and research; human nutrition; home economics; extension of farm credit and farm security; rural development, rural electrification and watersheds; agricultural production and marketing and stabilization of prices of agricultural products; crop insurance and soil conservation; school nutrition programs; food stamp programs; food from fresh waters; plant industry, soils, and agricultural engineering; such committee shall also study and review, on a comprehensive basis, matters relating to food, nutrition and hunger, both in the U.S. and in foreign countries, and rural affairs and report thereon from time to time.

Subcommittees
Agricultural Production and Stabilization of Prices; Domestic and Foreign Marketing and Product Promotion; Agricultural Credit; Rural Development and Rural Electrification; Nutrition and Investigations; Agricultural Research and General Legislation; Conservation and Forestry.
Staff: CHARLES RIEMENSCHNEIDER, Chief of Staff; JAMES M. CUBIE, Chief Counsel; CHARLES F. CONNER, Minority Staff Director; CHRISTINE SARCONE, Chief Clerk

COMMITTEE ON APPROPRIATIONS, SD-136, Dirksen Senate Office Building, Washington, DC 20510 (202, 224-3471)
Chairman: JOHN C. STENNIS (MS)
Concerned with all proposed legislation, messages, petitions, memorials, and other matters relating to appropriation of the revenue for the support of the government.

Subcommittees
Agriculture, Rural Development, Related Agencies; Defense; District of Columbia; Foreign Operations; HUD-Independent Agencies; Interior and Related Agencies; Labor, Health and Human Services, and Education; Legislative; Military Construction; Energy and Water Development; Commerce, Justice, State and Judiciary; Transportation and Related Agencies; Treasury, Postal Service, and General Government.

COMMITTEE ON COMMERCE, SCIENCE AND TRANSPORTATION, U.S. Senate, SD-508, Washington, DC 20510 (202, 224-5115)
Chairman: ERNEST F. HOLLINGS (SC)
Concerned with interstate commerce; transportation; regulation of interstate common carriers, including railroads, buses, trucks, vessels, pipelines, and civil aviation; merchant marine and navigation; marine and ocean navigation, safety and transportation, including navigational aspects of deepwater ports; Coast Guard; inland waterways, except construction; communications; regulation of consumer products and services, except for credit, financial services and housing; the Panama Canal, except for maintenance, operation, administration, sanitation and government, and interoceanic canals generally; standards and measurement; highway safety; science, engineering and technology research and development and policy; nonmilitary aeronautical and space sciences; transportation and commerce aspects of Outer Continental Shelf lands; marine fisheries; coastal zone management; oceans, weather and atmospheric activities; sports.

Subcommittees
Aviation; Communications; Consumer; Merchant Marine; Science, Technology and Space; Surface Transportation; Business, Trade and Tourism; National Ocean Policy Study.

COMMITTEE ON ENERGY AND NATURAL RESOURCES, Rm. SD-364, Dirksen Bldg., Washington, DC 20510 (202, 224-4971)
Chairman: J. BENNETT JOHNSTON (LA)
Ranking Minority Member: JAMES A. McCLURE (ID)

Subcommittees
Coal Production, Distribution, and Utilization; Energy Policy; Energy Regulation and Conservation; Energy Related Aspects of Deepwater Ports; Energy Research and Development; Extraction of Minerals from Oceans and Outer Continental Shelf Lands; Hydroelectric Power, Irrigation, and Reclamation; Mining Education and Research; Mining, Mineral Lands, Mining Claims, and Mineral Conservation; National Parks, Recreation Areas, Wilderness Areas, Wild and Scenic Rivers, Historical Sites, Military Parks and Battlefields, and on the Public Domain, Preservation of Prehistoric Ruins and Objects of Interest; Naval Petroleum Reserves in Alaska; Nonmilitary Development of Nuclear Energy; Oil and Gas Production and Distribution; Public Lands and Forests, Including Farming and Grazing Thereon, and Mineral Extraction Therefrom; Solar Energy Systems; Territorial Possessions of the United States, Including Trusteeships.

COMMITTEE ON ENVIRONMENT AND PUBLIC WORKS, Rm. SD-458, Dirksen Bldg., Washington, DC 20510 (202, 224-6176)
Chairman: QUENTIN N. BURDICK (ND)
Committee on Environment and Public Works, to which shall be referred all proposed legislation, messages, petitions, memorials, and other matters relating to the following subjects: environmental policy; environmental research and development; ocean dumping; fisheries and wildlife; environmental aspects of Outer Continental Shelf lands; solid waste disposal and recycling; environmental effects of toxic substances, other than pesticides; water resources; flood control and improvements of rivers and harbors, including environmental aspects of deepwater ports; public works, bridges, and dams; water pollution; air pollution; noise pollution; nonmilitary environmental regulation and control of nuclear energy; regional economic development; construction and maintenance of highways; public buildings and improved grounds of the United States generally, including federal buildings in the District of Columbia. Such committee shall also study and review, on a comprehensive

basis, matters relating to environmental protection and resource utilization and conservation, and report thereon from time to time.

Subcommittees
Water Resources; Transportation and Infrastructure; Environmental Protection; Hazardous Waste and Toxic Substances; Superfund and Environmental Oversight; Nuclear Regulation.

COMMITTEE ON LABOR AND HUMAN RESOURCES, Dirksen Bldg., Rm. SD-428, Washington, DC 20510 (202, 224-5375)
Chairman: EDWARD M. KENNEDY (MA)
Jurisdiction: all proposed legislation, messages, petitions, memorials, and other matters relating to the following subjects are referred to the Committee on Labor and Human Resources: measures relating to education, labor, health and public welfare; labor standards and labor statistics; wages and hours of labor; child labor; mediation and arbitration of labor disputes; convict labor and the entry of goods made by convicts into interstate commerce; regulation of foreign laborers; handicapped individuals; equal employment opportunity, occupational safety and health, including the welfare of miners; private pension plans; aging; railway labor and retirement; public health; arts and humanities; Gallaudet College, Howard University, and Saint Elizabeth's Hospital; biomedical research and development; student loans; agricultural colleges; and domestic activities of the American Red Cross. The committee also studies and reviews, on a comprehensive basis, matters relating to health, education and training, and public welfare.

Subcommittees
Aging; Children, Family, Drugs, and Alcoholism; Education, Arts and Humanities; Employment and Productivity; Handicapped; Labor.

HOUSE OF REPRESENTATIVES COMMITTEES AND SUBCOMMITTEES

COMMITTEE ON AGRICULTURE, Rm. 1301, Longworth House Office Bldg., Washington, DC 20515 (202, 225-2171)
Chairman: E. (Kirka) de la GARZA (TX)
Consists of 43 members: adulteration of seeds, insect pests, and protection of birds and animals in forest reserves; agriculture generally; agricultural and industrial chemistry; agricultural colleges and experiment stations; agricultural economics and research; agricultural education extension services; agricultural production and marketing and stabilization of prices of agricultural products; animal industry and diseases of animals; crop insurance and soil conservation; dairy industry; entomology and plant quarantine; extension of farm credit and farm security; forestry in general, and forest reserves other than those created from the public domain; human nutrition and home economics; inspection of livestock and meat products; plant industry, soils, and agricultural engineering; rural electrification; commodities exchanges and rural development.

Subcommittees
Cotton, Rice, and Sugar; Livestock, Dairy, and Poultry; Forests, Family Farms, and Energy; Wheat, Soybeans, and Feed Grains; Tobacco and Peanuts; Conservation, Credit, and Rural Development; Domestic Marketing, Consumer Relations, and Nutrition; Department Operations, Research, and Foreign Agriculture.

COMMITTEE ON APPROPRIATIONS, Rm. H-218, Capitol Bldg., Washington, DC 20515 (202, 225-2771)
Chairman: JAMIE L. WHITTEN (MS)

Consists of 57 members: appropriation of the revenue for the support of the government, rescissions of appropriations contained in appropriation acts, and transfers of unexpended balances.

Subcommittees
Agriculture, Rural Development, and Related Agencies; Commerce, Justice, State, and the Judiciary; Defense; District of Columbia; Energy and Water Development; Foreign Operations; Housing and Urban Development, Independent Agencies; Interior and Related Agencies; Labor, Health, and Human Services, Education; Legislative; Military Construction; Transportation; Treasury, Postal Service, and General Government.

COMMITTEE ON EDUCATION AND LABOR, 2181 Rayburn House Office Bldg., Washington, DC 20515 (202, 225-4527)
Chairman: AUGUSTUS F. HAWKINS (CA)
Jurisdiction: measures relating to education or labor generally; child labor; Gallaudet College; Howard University; convict labor and the entry of goods made by convicts into interstate commerce; labor standards; labor statistics; mediation and arbitration of labor disputes; regulation or prevention of importation of foreign laborers under contract; food programs for children in schools; United States Employees' Compensation Commission; vocational rehabilitation; wages and hours of labor; welfare of miners; and work incentive programs.

Subcommittees
Elementary, Secondary, and Vocational Education; Postsecondary Education; Health and Safety; Labor-Management Relations; Labor Standards; Human Resources; Select Education; Employment Opportunities.

COMMITTEE ON ENERGY AND COMMERCE, 2125 Rayburn House Office Bldg., Washington, DC 20515 (202, 225-2927)
Chairman: JOHN D. DINGELL (MI)
Staff Director: WILLIAM MICHAEL KITZMILLER
Jurisdiction: interstate and foreign commerce generally; national energy policy generally; measures relating to the exploration, production, storage, supply, marketing, pricing, and regulation of energy resources, including all fossil fuels, solar energy, and other unconventional or renewable energy resources; measures relating to the conservation of energy resources; measures relating to the commercial application of energy technology; measures relating to energy information generally; measures relating to: (A) the generation and marketing of power (except by federally chartered or federal regional power marketing authorities), (B) the reliability and interstate transmission of, and ratemaking for, all power, and (C) the siting of generation facilities (except the installation of interconnections between government waterpower projects); interstate energy compacts; measures relating to general management of the Department of Energy, and the management and all functions of the Federal Energy Regulatory Commission; inland waterways; railroads, including railroad labor, railroad retirement and unemployment, except revenue measures related thereto; regulations of interstate and foreign communications; securities and exchanges; consumer affairs and consumer protection; travel and tourism; public health and quarantine; health and health facilities, except health care supported by payroll deductions; biomedical research and development. The committee shall have the same jurisdiction with respect to regulation of nuclear facilities and of use of nuclear energy as it has with respect to regulation of nonnuclear facilities and of use of nonnuclear energy.

Subcommittees

Commerce, Consumer Protection, and Competitiveness; Energy and Power; Health and the Environment; Oversight and Investigations; Telecommunications and Finance; Transportation, Tourism, and Hazardous Materials.

COMMITTEE ON INTERIOR AND INSULAR AFFAIRS, Rm.

1324, Longworth House Office Bldg., Washington, DC 20515 (202, 225-2761)

Chairman: MORRIS K. UDALL (AZ)

Consists of 41 members: forest reserves and national parks created from the public domain; national parks lands; forfeiture of land grants and alien ownership, including alien ownership of mineral lands; geological survey; interstate compacts relating to apportionment of waters for irrigation purposes; irrigation and reclamation, including water supply for reclamation projects, and easements on public lands for irrigation projects, and acquisition of private lands when necessary to complete irrigation projects; measures relating to the care and management of Indians, including the care and allotment of Indian lands and general and special measures relating to Indian claims ; measures (including funding measures) relating generally to the U.S. territories, commonwealths, and successor governments of the Trust Territory of the Pacific Islands, except measures concerning the federal tax system and federal appropriations; military parks and battlefields; national cemeteries administered by the Secretary of the Interior, and parks within the District of Columbia; mineral land laws and claims and entries thereunder; mineral resources of the public lands; mining interests generally; mining schools and experimental stations; petroleum conservation on the public lands and conservation of the radium supply in the U.S.; preservation of prehistoric ruins and objects of interest on the public domain; public lands generally, including entry, easements, and grazing thereon; relations of the U.S. with the Indians and the Indian tribes; regulation of the domestic nuclear energy industry, including regulation of research and development of reactors and nuclear regulatory research. Also special oversight functions with respect to all programs affecting Indians and nonmilitary nuclear energy and research and development, including the disposal of nuclear waste.

Subcommittees and Other Offices

Energy and the Environment; Water and Power Resources; Mining and Natural Resources; National Parks and Public Lands; Insular and International Affairs; General Oversight and Investigations; Office of Indian Affairs (full committee).

COMMITTEE ON MERCHANT MARINE AND FISHERIES, Rm.

1334, Longworth House Office Bldg., Washington, DC 20515 (202, 225-4047)

Chairman: WALTER B. JONES (NC)

Consists of 42 members: merchant marine generally; oceanography and marine affairs, including coastal zone management; Coast Guard, including lifesaving service, lighthouses, lightships, and ocean derelicts; fisheries and wildlife, including research, restoration, refuges, and conservation; measures relating to the regulation of common carriers by water (except matters subject to the jurisdiction of the Interstate Commerce Commission) and to the inspection of merchant marine vessels, lights and signals, lifesaving equipment, and fire protection on such vessels; Merchant Marine officers and seamen; navigation and the laws relating thereto, including pilotage, Panama Canal and the maintenance and operation of the Panama Canal consistent with the treaty with Panama and the implementation legislation enacted pursuant to such treaty; and interoceanic canals generally; primary oversight jurisdiction over the Outer Continental Shelf Lands Act and legislative jurisdiction over any proposed amendments. Registering and licensing of vessels and small boats; rules and international arrangements to prevent collisions at sea; United States Coast Guard, Merchant Marine Academies, and State Maritime Academies; international fishing agreements.

Subcommittees

Oversight and Investigations; Coast Guard and Navigation; Fisheries and Wildlife Conservation and the Environment; Merchant Marine; Oceanography; Panama Canal/Outer Continental Shelf.

Staff: EDMUND B. WELCH, Chief Counsel; BARBARA L. CAVAS, Chief Clerk; GEORGE D. PENCE, Minority Staff Director; DUNCAN C. SMITH III, Chief Minority Counsel

COMMITTEE ON PUBLIC WORKS AND TRANSPORTATION,

Rm. 2165, Rayburn House Office Bldg., Washington, DC 20515 (202, 225-4472)

Chairman: GLENN M. ANDERSON (CA)

Consists of 52 members: flood control and improvement of rivers and harbors; measures relating to the Capitol building and the Senate and House Office buildings; measures relating to the construction or maintenance of roads and post roads, other than appropriations thereof; but it shall not be in order for any bill providing general legislation in relation to roads to contain any provision for any specific road, nor for any bill in relation to a specific road to embrace a provision in relation to any other specific road; measures relating to the construction or reconstruction, maintenance, and care of the buildings and grounds of the Botanic Gardens, the Library of Congress, and the Smithsonian Institution; measures relating to the purchase of sites and construction of post offices, customhouses, federal courthouses, and government buildings within the District of Columbia; oil and other pollution of navigable waters; public buildings and occupied or improved grounds of the United States generally; public works for the benefit of navigation, including bridges and dams (other than international bridges and dams); water power; transportation, including civil aviation except railroads, railroad labor, and pensions; roads and the safety thereof; water transportation subject to the jurisdiction of the Interstate Commerce Commission; related transportation regulatory agencies (except (A) the Interstate Commerce Commission as it relates to railroads, (B) Federal Railroad Administration, and (C) Amtrak).

Subcommittees

Aviation; Economic Development; Investigations and Oversight; Public Buildings and Grounds; Surface Transportation; Water Resources.

COMMITTEE ON RULES, Rm. H-312, Capitol Bldg.,

Washington, DC 20515 (202, 225-9486)

Chairman: CLAUDE PEPPER (FL)

Consists of 13 members: grants rules outlining conditions for floor debate on legislation reported by regular standing committees, which includes granting emergency waivers under the Congressional Budget Act of 1974; has legislative authority to create committees, change the rules of the House, and provide order of business of the House.

ENVIRONMENTAL AND ENERGY STUDY CONFERENCE, House

Annex II, Rm. 515, Washington, DC 20515 (202, 226-3300)

A congressionally certified, bipartisan legislative service organization with a membership of more than 335 Senators and Congressmen. The conference does not serve as an advocate, it provides balanced research and analyses of environmental, energy, and natural resources issues for its members. Founded: 1975.

Co-Chairmen: REP. BILL GREEN (R-NY); SEN. ALBERT GORE, JR. (D-TN)

Co-Vice-Chairmen: REP. BOB WISE (D-WVA); SEN. JOHN McCAIN (R-AR)

Staff Director: LINDA CARTWRIGHT

Executive Assistant: DAN RIEDINGER

Publication: *Weekly Bulletin*

Editor: ROBERT LIVERNASH

MEMBERS, UNITED STATES CONGRESS

Listings are by state, with Senators first and then, by District, Representatives. One may contact a Senator by writing: The Honorable _____, U.S. Senate, Washington, DC 20510. One may contact a member of the House of Representatives by writing: The Honorable _____, U.S. House of Representatives, Washington, DC 20515. Listings as of November 11, 1988. Contact the Clerk for changes: House: (D): (202, 225-7330), (R): (202, 225-7350); Senate: (D): (202, 224-8541), (R): (202, 224-6391)

ALABAMA

Senators: HOWELL HEFLIN; RICHARD C. SHELBY.
Representatives: 1st, SONNY CALLAHAN; 2nd, WILLIAM L. DICKINSON; 3rd, BILL NICHOLS; 4th, TOM BEVILL; 5th, RONNIE G. FLIPPO; 6th, BEN ERDREICH; 7th, CLAUDE HARRIS.

ALASKA

Senators: TED STEVENS; FRANK MURKOWSKI.
Representative: At large, DON YOUNG.

ARIZONA

Senators: DENNIS DeCONCINI; JOHN McCAIN.
Representatives: 1st, JOHN J. RHODES; 2nd, MORRIS K. UDALL; 3rd, BOB STUMP; 4th, JON L. KYL; 5th, JIM KOLBE.

ARKANSAS

Senators: DALE BUMPERS; DAVID PRYOR.
Representatives: 1st, BILL ALEXANDER; 2nd, TOMMY F. ROBINSON; 3rd, JOHN PAUL HAMMERSCHMIDT; 4th, BERYL ANTHONY, JR.

CALIFORNIA

Senators: ALAN CRANSTON; PETE WILSON.
Representatives: 1st, DOUGLAS H. BOSCO; 2nd, WALLY HERGER; 3rd, ROBERT T. MATSUI; 4th, VIC FAZIO; 5th, NANCY PELOSI; 6th, BARBARA BOXER; 7th, GEORGE MILLER; 8th, RONALD V. DELLUMS; 9th, FORTNEY H. (Pete) STARK; 10th, DON EDWARDS; 11th, TOM LANTOS; 12th, TOM J. CAMPBELL; 13th, NORMAN Y. MINETA; 14th, NORMAN D. SHUMWAY; 15th, TONY COELHO; 16th, LEON E. PANETTA; 17th, CHARLES PASHAYAN, JR.; 18th, RICHARD H. LEHMAN; 19th, ROBERT J. LAGOMARSINO; 20th, WILLIAM M. THOMAS; 21st, ELTON GALLEGLY; 22nd, CARLOS J. MOORHEAD; 23rd, ANTHONY C. BEILENSON; 24th, HENRY A. WAXMAN; 25th, EDWARD R. ROYBAL; 26th, HOWARD L. BERMAN; 27th, MEL LEVINE; 28th, JULIAN C. DIXON; 29th, AUGUSTUS F. HAWKINS; 30th, MATTHEW G. MARTINEZ; 31st, MERVYN M. DYMALLY; 32nd, GLENN M. ANDERSON; 33rd, DAVID DREIER; 34th, ESTEBAN EDWARD TORRES; 35th, JERRY LEWIS; 36th, GEORGE E. BROWN, JR.; 37th, ALFRED A. (Al) McCANDLESS; 38th, ROBERT K. DORNAN; 39th, WILLIAM E. DANNEMEYER; 40th, CHRISTOPHER COX; 41st, BILL LOWERY; 42nd, DANA ROHRABACHER; 43rd, RON PACKARD; 44th, JIM BATES; 45th, DUNCAN HUNTER.

COLORADO

Senators: WILLIAM L. ARMSTRONG; TIMOTHY E. WIRTH.
Representatives: 1st, PATRICIA SCHROEDER; 2nd, DAVID E. SKAGGS; 3rd, BEN NIGHTHORSE CAMPBELL; 4th, HANK BROWN; 5th, JOEL HEFLEY; 6th, DAN SCHAEFER.

CONNECTICUT

Senators: JOE LIEBERMAN; CHRISTOPHER J. DODD.
Representatives: 1st, BARBARA B. KENNELLY; 2nd, SAMUEL GEJDENSON; 3rd, BRUCE A. MORRISON; 4th, CHRISTOPHER SHAYS; 5th, JOHN G. ROWLAND; 6th, NANCY L. JOHNSON.

DELAWARE

Senators: WILLIAM V. ROTH, JR.; JOSEPH R. BIDEN, JR.
Representative: At large, THOMAS R. CARPER.

FLORIDA

Senators: BUDDY MacKAY; BOB GRAHAM.
Representatives: 1st, EARL HUTTO; 2nd, BILL GRANT; 3rd, CHARLES E. BENNETT; 4th, BILL CHAPPELL, JR.; 5th, BILL McCOLLUM; 6th, CLIFFORD B. STEARNS; 7th, SAM GIBBONS; 8th, C.W. BILL YOUNG; 9th, MICHAEL BILIRAKIS; 10th, ANDY IRELAND; 11th, BILL NELSON; 12th, TOM LEWIS; 13th, PORTER J. GOSS; 14th, HARRY A. JOHNSTON III; 15th, E. CLAY SHAW, JR.; 16th, LARRY J. SMITH; 17th, WILLIAM LEHMAN; 18th, CLAUDE PEPPER; 19th, DANTE B. FASCELL.

GEORGIA

Senators: SAM NUNN; WYCHE FOWLER, JR.
Representatives: 1st, ROBERT LINDSAY THOMAS; 2nd, CHARLES HATCHER; 3rd, RICHARD RAY; 4th, BEN JONES; 5th, JOHN LEWIS; 6th, NEWT GINGRICH; 7th, GEORGE (Buddy) DARDEN; 8th, J. ROY ROWLAND; 9th, ED JENKINS; 10th, DOUG BARNARD, JR.

HAWAII

Senators: DANIEL K. INOUYE; SPARK M. MATSUNAGA.
Representatives: 1st, PATRICIA F. SAIKI; 2nd, DANIEL K. AKAKA.

IDAHO

Senators: JAMES A. McCLURE; STEVE D. SYMMS.

Representatives: 1st, LARRY E. CRAIG; 2nd, RICHARD H. STALLINGS.

ILLINOIS

Senators: ALAN J. DIXON; PAUL SIMON.
Representatives: 1st, CHARLES A. HAYES; 2nd, GUS SAVAGE; 3rd, MARTY RUSSO; 4th, GEORGE SANGMEISTER; 5th, WILLIAM O. LIPINSKI; 6th, HENRY J. HYDE; 7th, CARDISS COLLINS; 8th, DAN ROSTENKOWSKI; 9th, SIDNEY R. YATES; 10th, JOHN EDWARD PORTER; 11th, FRANK ANNUNZIO; 12th, PHILIP M. CRANE; 13th, HARRIS W. FAWELL; 14th, J. DENNIS HASTERT; 15th, EDWARD R. MADIGAN; 16th, LYNN MARTIN; 17th, LANE EVANS; 18th, ROBERT H. MICHEL; 19th, TERRY L. BRUCE; 20th, RICHARD J. DURBIN; 21st, JERRY COSTELLO; 22nd, GLEN POSHARD.

INDIANA

Senator: RICHARD G. LUGAR.
Representatives: 1st, PETER J. VISCLOSKY; 2nd, PHILIP R. SHARP; 3rd, JOHN HILER; 4th, DAN COATS; 5th, JIM JONTZ; 6th, DAN BURTON; 7th, JOHN T. MYERS; 8th, FRANK McCLOSKEY; 9th, LEE H. HAMILTON; 10th, ANDREW JACOBS, JR.

IOWA

Senators: CHARLES E. GRASSLEY; TOM HARKIN.
Representatives: 1st, JIM LEACH; 2nd, THOMAS J. TAUKE; 3rd, DAVID R. NAGLE; 4th, NEAL SMITH; 5th, JIM ROSS LIGHTFOOT; 6th, FRED GRANDY.

KANSAS

Senators: ROBERT DOLE; NANCY LANDON KASSEBAUM.
Representatives: 1st, PAT ROBERTS; 2nd, JIM SLATTERY; 3rd, JAN MEYERS; 4th, DAN GLICKMAN; 5th, ROBERT WHITTAKER.

KENTUCKY

Senators: WENDELL H. FORD; MITCH McCONNELL.
Representatives: 1st, CARROLL HUBBARD, JR.; 2nd, WILLIAM H. NATCHER; 3rd, ROMANO L. MAZZOLI; 4th, JIM BUNNING; 5th, HAROLD ROGERS; 6th, LARRY J. HOPKINS; 7th, CARL C. PERKINS.

LOUISIANA

Senators: J. BENNETT JOHNSTON; JOHN B. BREAUX.
Representatives: 1st, BOB LIVINGSTON; 2nd, LINDY (Mrs. Hale) BOGGS; 3rd, W.J. (Billy) TAUZIN; 4th, JIM McCRERY; 5th, JERRY HUCKABY; 6th, RICHARD H. BAKER; 7th, JAMES A. HAYES; 8th, CLYDE C. HOLLOWAY.

MAINE

Senators: WILLIAM S. COHEN; GEORGE J. MITCHELL.
Representatives: 1st, JOSEPH E. BRENNAN; 2nd, OLYMPIA J. SNOWE.

MARYLAND

Senators: PAUL S. SARBANES; BARBARA A. MIKULSKI.
Representatives: 1st, ROY DYSON; 2nd, HELEN DELICH BENTLEY; 3rd, BENJAMIN L. CARDIN; 4th, C. THOMAS McMILLEN; 5th, STENY H. HOYER; 6th, BEVERLY B. BYRON; 7th, KWEISI MFUME; 8th, CONSTANCE A. MORELLA.

MASSACHUSETTS

Senators: EDWARD M. KENNEDY; JOHN F. KERRY.
Representatives: 1st, SILVIO O. CONTE; 2nd, RICHARD E. NEAL; 3rd, JOSEPH D. EARLY; 4th, BARNEY FRANK; 5th, CHESTER G. ATKINS; 6th, NICHOLAS MAVROULES; 7th, EDWARD J. MARKEY; 8th, JOSEPH P. KENNEDY II; 9th, JOE MOAKLEY; 10th, GERRY E. STUDDS; 11th, BRIAN J. DONNELLY.

MICHIGAN

Senators: DONALD W. RIEGLE, JR.; CARL LEVIN.
Representatives: 1st, JOHN CONYERS, JR.; 2nd, CARL D. PURSELL; 3rd, HOWARD WOLPE; 4th, FREDERICK S. UPTON; 5th, PAUL B. HENRY; 6th, BOB CARR; 7th, DALE E. KILDEE; 8th, BOB TRAXLER; 9th, GUY VANDER JAGT; 10th, BILL SCHUETTE; 11th, ROBERT W. DAVIS; 12th, DAVID E. BONIOR; 13th, GEORGE W. CROCKETT, JR.; 14th, DENNIS M. HERTEL; 15th, WILLIAM D. FORD; 16th, JOHN D. DINGELL; 17th, SANDER M. LEVIN; 18th, WM. S. BROOMFIELD.

MINNESOTA

Senators: DAVID DURENBERGER; RUDY BOSCHWITZ.
Representatives: 1st, TIMOTHY J. PENNY; 2nd, VIN WEBER; 3rd, BILL FRENZEL; 4th, BRUCE F. VENTO; 5th, MARTIN OLAV SABO; 6th, GERRY SIKORSKI; 7th, ARLAN STANGELAND; 8th, JAMES L. OBERSTAR.

MISSISSIPPI

Senators: TRENT LOTT; THAD COCHRAN.
Representatives: 1st, JAMIE L. WHITTEN; 2nd, MIKE ESPY; 3rd, G.V. (Sonny) MONTGOMERY; 4th, MIKE PARKER; 5th, LARKIN SMITH.

MISSOURI

Senators: JOHN C. DANFORTH; CHRISTOPHER S. BOND.
Representatives: 1st, WILLIAM (Bill) CLAY; 2nd, JACK BUECHNER; 3rd, RICHARD A. GEPHARDT; 4th, IKE SKELTON; 5th, ALAN WHEAT; 6th, E. THOMAS COLEMAN; 7th, MEL HANCOCK; 8th, BILL EMERSON; 9th, HAROLD L. VOLKMER.

MONTANA

Senators: CONRAD BURNS; MAX BAUCUS.
Representatives: 1st, PAT WILLIAMS; 2nd, RON MARLENEE.

NEBRASKA

Senators: J. JAMES EXON; BOB KERREY.
Representatives: 1st, DOUG K. BEREUTER; 2nd, PETER HOAGLAND; 3rd, VIRGINIA SMITH.

NEVADA

Senators: RICHARD BRYAN; HARRY REID.
Representatives: 1st, JAMES H. BILBRAY; 2nd, BARBARA F. VUCANOVICH.

NEW HAMPSHIRE

Senators: GORDON J. HUMPHREY; WARREN RUDMAN.
Representatives: 1st, ROBERT C. SMITH; 2nd, CHARLES G. DOUGLAS III.

NEW JERSEY

Senators: BILL BRADLEY; FRANK R. LAUTENBERG.
Representatives: 1st, JAMES J. FLORIO; 2nd, WILLIAM J. HUGHES; 3rd, FRANK PALLONE, JR.; 4th, CHRISTOPHER H. SMITH; 5th, MARGE ROUKEMA; 6th, BERNARD J. DWYER; 7th, MATTHEW J. RINALDO; 8th, ROBERT A. ROE; 9th, ROBERT G. TORRICELLI; 10th, DONALD PAYNE; 11th, DEAN A. GALLO; 12th, JIM COURTER; 13th, H. JIM SAXTON; 14th, FRANK J. GUARINI.

NEW MEXICO

Senators: PETE V. DOMENICI; JEFF BINGAMAN.
Representatives: 1st, STEVEN H. SCHIFF; 2nd, JOE SKEEN; 3rd, BILL RICHARDSON.

NEW YORK

Senators: DANIEL PATRICK MOYNIHAN; ALFONSE M. D'AMATO.
Representatives: 1st, GEORGE J. HOCHBRUECKNER; 2nd, THOMAS J. DOWNEY; 3rd, ROBERT J. MRAZEK; 4th, NORMAN F. LENT; 5th, RAYMOND J. McGRATH; 6th, FLOYD H. FLAKE; 7th, GARY L. ACKERMAN; 8th, JAMES H. SCHEUER; 9th, THOMAS J. MANTON; 10th, CHARLES E. SCHUMER; 11th, EDOLPHUS TOWNS; 12th, MAJOR R. OWENS; 13th, STEPHEN J. SOLARZ; 14th, GUY V. MOLINARI; 15th, BILL GREEN; 16th, CHARLES B. RANGEL; 17th, TED WEISS; 18th, ROBERT GARCIA; 19th, ELIOT L. ENGEL; 20th, NITA M. LOWEY; 21st, HAMILTON FISH, JR.; 22nd, BENJAMIN A. GILMAN; 23rd, MICHAEL R. McNULTY; 24th, GERALD B. H. SOLOMON; 25th, SHERWOOD L. BOEHLERT; 26th, DAVID O'B. MARTIN; 27th, JAMES T. WALSH; 28th, MATTHEW F. McHUGH; 29th, FRANK HORTON; 30th, LOUISE McINTOSH SLAUGHTER; 31st, WILLIAM PAXON; 32nd, JOHN J. LaFALCE; 33rd, HENRY J. NOWAK; 34th, AMORY HOUGHTON, JR.

NORTH CAROLINA

Senators: JESSE HELMS; TERRY SANFORD.
Representatives: 1st, WALTER B. JONES; 2nd, TIM VALENTINE, JR.; 3rd, H. MARTIN LANCASTER; 4th, DAVID E. PRICE; 5th, STEPHEN L. NEAL; 6th, HOWARD COBLE; 7th, CHARLES ROSE; 8th, W.G. (Bill) HEFNER; 9th, J. ALEX McMILLAN; 10th, CASS BALLENGER; 11th, JAMES McCLURE CLARKE.

NORTH DAKOTA

Senators: QUENTIN N. BURDICK; KENT CONRAD.
Representative: At Large, BYRON L. DORGAN.

OHIO

Senators: JOHN H. GLENN; HOWARD M. METZENBAUM.
Representatives: 1st, THOMAS A. LUKEN; 2nd, WILLIS D. GRADISON, JR.; 3rd, TONY P. HALL; 4th, MICHAEL G. OXLEY; 5th, PAUL E. GILMORE; 6th, BOB McEWEN; 7th, MICHAEL DeWINE; 8th, DONALD E. LUKENS; 9th, MARCY KAPTUR; 10th, CLARENCE E. MILLER; 11th, DENNIS E. ECKART; 12th, JOHN R. KASICH; 13th, DONALD J. PEASE; 14th, THOMAS C.

SAWYER; 15th, CHALMERS P. WYLIE; 16th, RALPH S. REGULA; 17th, JAMES A. TRAFICANT, JR.; 18th, DOUGLAS APPLEGATE; 19th, EDWARD F. FEIGHAN; 20th, MARY ROSE OAKAR; 21st, LOUIS STOKES.

OKLAHOMA

Senators: DAVID LYLE BOREN; DON NICKLES.
Representatives: 1st, JAMES M. INHOFE; 2nd, MIKE SYNAR; 3rd, WES WATKINS; 4th, DAVE McCURDY; 5th, MICKEY EDWARDS; 6th, GLENN ENGLISH.

OREGON

Senators: MARK O. HATFIELD; BOB PACKWOOD.
Representatives: 1st, LES AuCOIN; 2nd, ROBERT F. (Bob) SMITH; 3rd, RON WYDEN; 4th, PETER A. DeFAZIO; 5th, MICHAEL J. KOPETSKI.

PENNSYLVANIA

Senators: JOHN HEINZ; ARLEN SPECTER.
Representatives: 1st, THOMAS M. FOGLIETTA; 2nd, WILLIAM H. GRAY, III; 3rd, ROBERT A. BORSKI, JR.; 4th, JOSEPH P. KOLTER; 5th, RICHARD T. SCHULZE; 6th, GUS YATRON; 7th, CURT WELDON; 8th, PETER H. KOSTMAYER; 9th, BUD SHUSTER; 10th, JOSEPH M. McDADE; 11th, PAUL E. KANJORSKI; 12th, JOHN P. MURTHA; 13th, LAWRENCE COUGHLIN; 14th, WILLIAM J. COYNE; 15th, DON RITTER; 16th, ROBERT S. WALKER; 17th, GEORGE W. GEKAS; 18th, DOUG WALGREN; 19th, WILLIAM F. GOODLING; 20th, JOSEPH M. GAYDOS; 21st, THOMAS J. RIDGE; 22nd, AUSTIN J. MURPHY; 23rd, WILLIAM F. CLINGER, JR.

RHODE ISLAND

Senators: CLAIBORNE PELL; JOHN H. CHAFEE.
Representatives: 1st, RONALD K. MACHTLEY; 2nd, CLAUDINE SCHNEIDER.

SOUTH CAROLINA

Senators: STROM THURMOND; ERNEST F. HOLLINGS.
Representatives: 1st, ARTHUR RAVENEL, JR; 2nd, FLOYD SPENCE; 3rd, BUTLER DERRICK; 4th, ELIZABETH J. PATTERSON; 5th, JOHN SPRATT, JR.; 6th, ROBIN TALLON.

SOUTH DAKOTA

Senators: LARRY PRESSLER; THOMAS A. DASCHLE.
Representative: At Large, TIM JOHNSON.

TENNESSEE

Senators: JAMES SASSER; ALBERT GORE, JR.
Representatives: 1st, JAMES H. (Jimmy) QUILLEN; 2nd, JOHN J. DUNCAN; 3rd, MARILYN LLOYD; 4th, JIM COOPER; 5th, BOB CLEMENT; 6th, BART GORDON; 7th, DON SUNDQUIST; 8th, JOHN S. TANNER; 9th, HAROLD E. FORD.

TEXAS

Senators: LLOYD BENTSEN; PHIL GRAMM.
Representatives: 1st, JIM CHAPMAN; 2nd, CHARLES WILSON; 3rd, STEVE BARTLETT; 4th, RALPH M. HALL; 5th, JOHN BRYANT; 6th, JOE BARTON; 7th, BILL ARCHER; 8th, JACK

FIELDS; 9th, JACK BROOKS; 10th, J.J. PICKLE; 11th, MARVIN LEATH; 12th, JIM WRIGHT; 13th, BILL SARPALIUS; 14th, GREG LAUGHLIN; 15th, E. de la GARZA; 16th, RONALD D. COLEMAN; 17th, CHARLES W. STENHOLM; 18th, MICKEY LELAND; 19th, LARRY COMBEST; 20th, HENRY B. GONZALEZ; 21st, LAMAR S. SMITH; 22nd, TOM DELAY; 23rd, ALBERT G. BUSTAMANTE; 24th, MARTIN FROST; 25th, MICHAEL A. ANDREWS; 26th, RICHARD ARMEY; 27th, SOLOMON P. ORTIZ.

UTAH

Senators: JAKE GARN; ORRIN G. HATCH.
Representatives: 1st, JAMES V. HANSEN; 2nd, WAYNE OWENS; 3rd, HOWARD C. NIELSON.

VERMONT

Senators: JIM JEFFORDS; PATRICK J. LEAHY.
Representative: At Large, PETER P. SMITH.

VIRGINIA

Senators: JOHN WILLIAM WARNER; CHARLES ROBB.
Representatives: 1st, HERBERT H. BATEMAN; 2nd, OWEN B. PICKETT; 3rd, THOMAS J. BLILEY, JR.; 4th, NORMAN SISISKY; 5th, LEWIS F. PAYNE, JR.; 6th, JAMES R. (Jim) OLIN; 7th, D. FRENCH SLAUGHTER JR.; 8th, STAN PARRIS; 9th, RICK BOUCHER; 10th, FRANK R. WOLF.

WASHINGTON

Senators: SLADE GORTON; BROCK ADAMS.
Representatives: 1st, JOHN MILLER; 2nd, AL SWIFT; 3rd, JOLENE UNSOELD; 4th, SID MORRISON; 5th, THOMAS S. FOLEY; 6th, NORMAN D. DICKS; 7th, JIM McDERMOTT; 8th, ROD CHANDLER.

WEST VIRGINIA

Senators: ROBERT C. BYRD; JAY ROCKEFELLER, IV.

Representatives: 1st, ALAN B. MOLLOHAN; 2nd, HARLEY O. STAGGERS, JR.; 3rd, ROBERT E. WISE, JR.; 4th, NICK JOE RAHALL II.

WISCONSIN

Senators: HERBERT KOHL; ROBERT W. KASTEN, JR.
Representatives: 1st, LES ASPIN; 2nd, ROBERT W. KASTENMEIER; 3rd, STEVEN GUNDERSON; 4th, GERALD D. KLECZKA; 5th, JIM MOODY; 6th, THOMAS E. PETRI; 7th, DAVID R. OBEY; 8th, TOBY ROTH; 9th, F. JAMES SENSENBRENNER, JR.

WYOMING

Senators: MALCOLM WALLOP; ALAN K. SIMPSON.
Representative: At large, DICK CHENEY.

DISTRICT OF COLUMBIA

Delegate: WALTER E. FAUNTROY.

GUAM

Delegate: BEN BLAZ.

PUERTO RICO

Resident Commissioner: JAIME B. FUSTER.

VIRGIN ISLANDS

Delegate: RON DE LUGO.

AMERICAN SAMOA

Delegate: FOFO I.F. SUNIA.

UNITED STATES GOVERNMENT—EXECUTIVE BRANCH

COUNCIL ON ENVIRONMENTAL QUALITY, 722 Jackson Pl., NW, Washington, DC 20503 202, 395-5750)
Established by Public Law 91-190, January 1, 1970, to assist and advise the President, with authoritative information concerning the conditions and trends in the quality of the environment; review and appraise the various programs and activities of the federal government; develop and recommend to the President national policies to foster and promote the improvement of environmental quality; document and define changes in the natural environment; make and furnish such studies, reports thereon, and recommendations with respect to matters of policy and legislation as the President may request.
Chairman: A. ALAN HILL (395-5080)
Members: WILLIAM L. MILLS (395-3742); JACQUELINE E. SCHAFER (395-3742)
Public Information: (395-5750)
General Counsel: DINAH BEAR (395-5754)
Deputy General Counsel: LUCINDA LOW SWARTZ (395-5754)

DEPARTMENT OF AGRICULTURE

14th St. and Independence Ave., SW, Washington, DC 20250 (202, 44 plus extension; information: (202, 447-2791)
Created by Congress in 1862 to acquire and diffuse 'useful' information on subjects connected with agriculture in the most general and comprehensive sense of that word, and to procure, propagate and distribute among the people new and valuable seeds and plants.' Today, in addition to managing the national forests and grasslands, USDA manages a variety of research, regulatory, domestic and foreign marketing, food and nutrition, and many other programs.
Secretary: RICHARD E. LYNG (Ext. 73631)
Deputy Secretary: PETER C. MYERS (Ext. 76158)
Under Secretary, International Affairs and Commodity Programs: DANIEL G. AMSTUTZ (Ext. 73111)
Under Secretary (Acting), Small Community and Rural Development: LA VERNE AUSMAN (Ext. 74581)
Assistant Secretary for Natural Resources and Environment: GEORGE S. DUNLOP (Ext. 77173)
Assistant Secretary for Science and Education: ORVILLE G. BENTLEY (Ext. 75923)
Assistant Secretary for Marketing and Inspection: KENNETH A. GILLES (Ext. 74256)
Assistant Secretary for Food and Consumer Services: JOHN W. BODE (Ext. 77711)
Assistant Secretary for Economics: EWEN M. WILSON (Ext. 74164)
Assistant Secretary for Governmental and Public Affairs: WILMER D. MIZELL (Ext. 77977)
Assistant Secretary for Administration: JOHN J. FRANKE, JR. (Ext. 73291)

AGRICULTURAL STABILIZATION AND CONSERVATION
SERVICE, P.O. Box 2415, Washington, DC 20013 (202, 44 plus extension; information: Ext. 447-5237)
Administers the following nationwide or regional programs: Conservation Reserve Program, Agricultural Conservation Program, Emergency Conservation Program, Emergency Feed Assistance Program, Water Bank Program, Rural Clean Water Program, Forestry Incentives Program, and various commodity programs, including feed grains, wheat, cotton, rice, wool, etc.
Administrator: MILTON J. HERTZ (Ext. 73467)
Associate Administrator: VERN NEPPL (Ext. 76215)
Director, Conservation and Environmental Protection Division: JAMES R. MCMULLEN (Ext. 76221)
Deputy Director: D. REX WRIGHT (Ext. 75295)
Branch Chiefs: VINCENT GRIMES, Conservation Programs (Ext. 77333); GEORGE T. DENLEY, Planning and Evaluation (Ext. 73264); JACK L. WEBB, Land Retirement and Water Quality (Ext. 76825)
Director, Information Division: M. RAY WAGGONER (Ext. 75237)
Deputy Director: ROLAND OLSON (Ext. 75238)

ANIMAL AND PLANT HEALTH INSPECTION SERVICE,
Washington, DC 20250 (202, 44 plus extension; information: 301, 436-7799)
Administrator: DR. JAMES W. GLOSSER (Ext. 73668)
Associate Administrator: LARRY B. SLAGLE (Ext. 73861)
Director, Legislative and Public Affairs: JOHN P. DUNCAN III (447-2511)
Director, Biotechnology and Environmental Coordination Staff: TERRY MEDLEY (436-7602)
Deputy Administrator for Management and Budget: ROBERT L. BUCHANAN (Ext. 75213)
Associate Deputy Administrator for Management and Budget: WILLIAM S. WALLACE (Ext. 72463)

Plant Protection and Quarantine, Federal Center Bldg., Hyattsville, MD 20782 (301, 43 plus extension)
Enforces federal quarantines affecting importation of plants, fruits, vegetables, plant products, animal products, and byproducts from foreign countries. Regulates the movement of such plant and plant products between U.S. possessions and the mainland, and regulates importation and interstate movement of plant pests. Inspects and certifies plants and plant products being exported to meet foreign import requirements. Administers cooperative plant protection and domestic quarantine programs with states to control and eradicate insects, diseases, weeds, and nematodes of economic importance.
Deputy Administrator: WILLIAM F. HELMS (202, 447-5601)
Associate Deputy Administrator: DONALD F. HUSNIK (202, 447-4441)
Assistant Deputy Administrator for National Programs: RICHARD R. BACKUS (202, 447-5283)
Assistant Director, National Programs: CHARLES HALL (301, 436-6365)
Assistant Deputy Administrator for International Programs: Vacant (202, 447-7021)
Assistant Director, International Programs: D. SCOT CAMPBELL (301, 436-8892)
Director, Program Planning and Development Staff: ROBERT L. WILLIAMSON (301, 436-8261)
Associate Director, Program Planning and Development Staff: EDWIN A. THOMAS (301, 436-8261)

Regional Directors
Northeastern Region: JAMES O. LEE, JR., 505 South Lenola Rd., Moorestown, NJ 08057 (609, 235-9120)
South-Central: ALFRED S. EDLER, Suite 360, 3505 Boca Chica Blvd., Brownsville, TX 78521 (512, 542-7231)

Southeastern: B. WAYNE GRANBERRY 3505 25th Ave., Bldg. I, North Gulfport, MS 39501 (601, 863-1980)

Western: B. GLEN LEE, 9580 Micron Ave., Suite I, Sacramento, CA 95827 (916, 551-3220)

Latin American (Mexico): ED L. AYERS, JR., American Embassy, Reforma 305, Col. Cuauhtemoc, 06500, Mexico, D.F. (21I-0042, Ext. 3480)

Veterinary Services, Federal Center Bldg., Hyattsville, MD 20782 (301, 436 plus extension)

Enforces quarantines affecting importation of animals, poultry or birds, and animal semen from foreign countries, and interstate movement of such animals and birds. Inspects and certifies animals being exported to make sure they meet foreign import requirements. Administers cooperative federal-state programs to control and eradicate animal pests and diseases.

Deputy Administrator: DR. LONNIE J. KING (202, 447-5193)

Associate Deputy Administrator: DR. BILLY G. JOHNSON (202, 447-6835)

Assistant Deputy Administrator, International Programs: Vacant (202, 447-7593)

Assistant Director, International Programs: DR. JOHN WYSS (301, 436-8441)

Chief Staff Veterinarian, International Programs Support Staff: Vacant (436-5986)

Assistant Deputy Administrator, Domestic Programs: DR. CLAUDE NELSON (436-8093)

Assistant Director, Domestic Programs: DR. R.L. RISSLER (436-5286)

Assistant Director, Domestic Programs: DR. G.P. COMBS (436-8097)

Chief Staff Veterinarian, Animal Care Staff: DR. W.C. STEWART (436-7833)

Chief Staff Officer, Compliance and Enforcement Staff: A.J. WILSON (436-8684)

Chief Staff Veterinarian, Domestic Program Support Staff: DR. D.F. SCHWINDAMAN (436-8438)

Chief Staff Veterinarian, National Emergency Field Operations: DR. M.A. MIXSON, (436-8073)

Chief Staff Veterinarian, Import-Export Operations Staff: DR. D.E. HERRICK, (436-8590)

Assistant Deputy Administrator, Program Planning and Development: DR. S.T. WILSON, JR. (436-8721)

Chief Staff Officer, Animal Health Information Staff: PHILLIP B. LADD, (436-8087)

Chief Staff Veterinarian, Import-Export and Emergency Planning Staff: DR. R.D. WHITING (436-8695)

Chief Staff Veterinarian, Program Planning Staff: DR. G.H. FRYE (436-8711)

Chief Staff Veterinarian, Regulatory Communications and Compliance Policy Staff: DR. W.E. KETTER (436-8565)

Chief Staff Veterinarian, Veterinary Biologics Staff: DR. D.A. ESPESETH (436-8245)

Director, National Veterinary Services Laboratories: DR. R.M. NERVIG, Ames, IA (515, 232-0250)

Director, Resource Management Staff: G.H. McFADEN, JR. (301, 436-8511)

Regional Directors

Northern Region: DR. GEORGE P. PIERSON, Bldg. 12, GSA Depot, Scotia, NY 12302 (518, 370-5026)

Western Region: DR. R. HARRINGTON, JR., P.O. BOX 3857, 317 Inverness Way South, Englewood, CO 80112 (303, 796-6850)

Southeastern Region: DR. L.D. KONYA, 700 Twiggs St., Tampa, FL 33601 (813, 228-2952)

Central Region: DR. A.L. STRATING, Ft. Worth, TX 76102 (817, 885-5566)

ECONOMIC RESEARCH SERVICE, 1301 New York Ave., NW, Rm. 1226, Washington, DC 20005-4788 (202, 786-1504)

Provides a program of agricultural economic, economic, and social research and analysis, statistical programs, technical consultation, planning assistance, and associated services. Conducts research and staff work relating to natural resources and environmental quality including supplies, uses, and projected future requirements for land and water; effects of environmental quality improvement measures on agricultural production and agricultural resource use; achievement of environmental goals in rural areas; ownership and control of land and water resources; methods for natural resource planning; and evaluation of natural resource plans and projects.

Administrator: JOHN E. LEE, JR. (786-3300)

Director, Natural Resource Economics Division: JOHN MIRANOWSKI (786-1455)

Research Information Branch: JAMES R. SAYRE (786-1512)

Information Director: BENJAMIN BLANKENSHIP (786-1504)

Publications: *Major Uses of Land in the United States; Handbook of Agricultural Charts;* various research monographs on natural resources use, pest control, and agricultural inputs.

FOREST SERVICE, P.O. Box 96090, Washington, DC 20013-6090 (202, 447-3957)

Administers national forests and national grasslands and is responsible for the management of their resources. Cooperates with federal and state officials in the enforcement of game laws on the National Forests and in the development and maintenance of wildlife resources; cooperates with the state and private owners in the application of sound forest management practices, in protection of forest lands against fire, insects, diseases, and in the distribution of planting stock. Conducts research in the entire field of forestry and wildland management. NOTE: Please see the state listing for National Forests on page 278.

Chief: F. DALE ROBERTSON (447-6661)

Associate Chief: GEORGE M. LEONARD (447-7491)

Deputy Chief, Programs and Legislation: JEFF M. SIRMON (447-6663)

Deputy Chief, State and Private Forestry: ALLAN J. WEST (447-6657)

Deputy Chief, National Forest System: JAMES C. OVERBAYY (447-3523)

Deputy Chief, Administration: WILLIAM L. RICE (447-6707)

Director of Wildlife and Fisheries: ROBERT D. NELSON (703, 235-8015)

Deputy Director: HAL SALWASSER (703, 235-8015)

Wildlife Program Manager: HUGH C. BLACK (703, 235-8015)

Fisheries Program Manager: MIKE DOMBECK (703, 235-8015)

Planning Program Manager: JACK CAPP (703, 235-8015)

Endangered Species Program Manager: GLEN CONTRERAS (703, 235-8015)

Wildlife Coordinator: RANDY LONG (703, 235-8015)

Deputy Chief, Research: JERRY A. SESCO (447-6665)

Director of Forest Inventory and Economics: H. FRED KAISER, JR. (703, 447-2747)

Wildlife and Fish Habitat Research: FRED A. STORMER (703, 235-1071)

Range Research: GALE L. WOLTERS (703, 235-1071)

Director of Forest Insect and Disease Research: JAMES L. STEWART (703, 235-8065)

Director of Public Affairs Office: SUSAN B. HESS (447-3760)

Regional Foresters

Region 1, Northern: JOHN W. MUMMA, Federal Bldg., P.O. Box 7669, Missoula, MT 59807 (406, 329-3316)

  Director of Wildlife and Fisheries: KIRK M. HORN (406, 329-3520); DAVID P. GARBER (406, 329-3291); DON K. BARTSCHI (406, 329-3287)

Region 2, Rocky Mountain: GARY E. CARGILL, 11177 W. 8th Ave., Box 25127, Lakewood, CO 80255 (303, 236-9427)

  Director of Range, Wildlife, Fisheries, and Ecology: GLEN E. HETZEL (303, 236-9526)

  Threatened and Endangered Species, Waterfowl, Animal Damage Control, and Non-Game Habitat: DALE L. WILLS

  Terrestrial Wildlife Habitat Management: Vacant (303, 236-9529)

Region 3, Southwestern: SOTERO MUNIZ, Federal Bldg., 517 Gold Ave., SW, Albuquerque, NM 87102 (505, 476-3300)

  Director of Wildlife Management: WILLIAM D. ZEEDYK (505, 476-3260)

  Wildlife Management Biologist: Vacant

  NM Zone Biologist: JERRY STEFFERUD

Region 4, Intermountain: STAN TIXIER, Federal Office Bldg., 324 25th St., Ogden, UT 84401 (801, 625-5605)

  Director of Wildlife Management: WM. R. BURBRIDGE (801, 625-5669)

  Wildlife Habitat Management: PAUL W. SHIELDS (801, 625-5665)

  Aquatic Habitat Management, Fisheries: DONALD A. DUFF (801, 625-5662)

Region 5, California: PAUL F. BARKER, 630 Sansome St., San Francisco, CA 94111 (415, 556-4310)

  Director of Fisheries and Wildlife Management: RANDALL C. LONG (415, 556-1584)

Region 6, Pacific Northwest: JAMES F. TORRENCE, 319 SW Pine St., Box 3623, Portland, OR 97208 (503, 221-3625)

  Director of Fish and Wildlife Management: HUGH BLACK, JR. (503, 221-3418)

Region 8, Southern: JOHN E. ALCOCK, Suite 800, 1720 Peachtree Rd., NW, Atlanta, GA 30367 (404, 347-4177)

  Director of Fisheries, Wildlife and Range: JERRY P. McILWAIN (404, 347-7397)

  Wildlife Management: TOM L. DARDEN (404, 347-4081)

  Fisheries: JAMES C. LLOYD (404, 347-4082)

Region 9, Eastern: FLOYD J. MARITA, 310 W. Wisconsin Ave., Milwaukee, WI 53203 (414, 291-3693)

  Director of Recreation, Range, Wildlife & Landscape Management: BRUCE HRONEK (414, 291-3615)

  Wildlife: ROBERT E. RADTKE (414, 291-3612)

  Fisheries Biologist: ROBERT W. HOLLINGSWORTH (414, 291-1749)

Region 10, Arkansas: MICHAEL A. BARTON, Federal Office Bldg., Box 21628, Juneau, AK 99802-1628 (907, 586-8863)

  Director of Wildlife and Fisheries: PHIL JANIK (907, 586-8752)

Station Directors of Forest and Range Experiment Stations

Intermountain: LAURENCE E. LASSEN, 324 25th St., Ogden, UT 84401 (801, 625-5412)

North Central: RONALD D. LINDMARK, 1992 Folwell Ave., St. Paul, MN 55108 (612, 642-0249)

Northeastern: DENVER P. BURNS, 370 Reed Rd., Broomall, PA 19008 (215, 690-3008)

Pacific Northwest: CHARLES W. PHILPOT, P.O. Box 3890, Portland, OR 97208 (503, 294-5640)

Pacific Southwest: RONALD E. STEWART, 1960 Addison St., Box 245, Berkeley, CA 94704 (415, 486-3292)

Rocky Mountain: CHARLES M. LOVELESS, 240 W. Prospect St., Ft. Collins, CO 80526-2098 (303, 224-1126)

Southeastern: J. LAMAR BEASLEY, 200 Weaver Blvd., Asheville, NC 28802 (704, 259-0758)

Southern: THOMAS H. ELLIS, T-10210 U.S. Postal Service Bldg., 701 Loyola Ave., New Orleans, LA 70113 (504, 589-6787)

Forest Products Laboratory: JOHN R. ERICKSON, One Gifford Pinchot Dr., Madison, WI 53705-2398 (608, 264-5717)

Northeastern Area Director, State and Private Forestry: THOMAS N. SCHENARTS, 370 Reed Rd., Broomall, PA 19008 (215, 690-3125)

Grey Towers National Historic Landmark and Pinchot Institute for Conservation: RITA A. WILLIAMS, Director, Milford, PA 18337 (717, 296-6401)

SCIENCE AND EDUCATION

Agricultural Research, S&E, Rm. 217-W, Washington, DC 20250

Conducts research in watershed engineering, soil management, water management and air pollution control.

Administrator: R.D. PLOWMAN (202, 447-3656)

Associate Administrator: M.E. CARTER (202, 447-3658)

Deputy Administrator, NPS: GARY R. EVANS (301, 344-3084)

Associate Deputy Administrator, NPS: WALDEMAR KLASSEN (301, 344-3252)

Erosion: Vacant (301, 344-4034)

Dryland Agricultural and Soil Fertility: J.R. PARR (301, 344-4281)

Soil Atmosphere: W.D. KEMPER (301, 344-4034)

Water Management: DALE A. BUCKS (303, 226-9425)

Water Quality: D.A. FARRELL (301, 344-4246)

Area Directors

North Atlantic Area: DR. HERBERT L. ROTHBART, USDA-ARS, 600 East Mermaid Ln., Philadelphia, PA 19118 (FTS: 489-6593/215, 233-6593)

Beltsville Area: EDWARD B. KNIPLING, USDA-ARS, Rm. 227, B-003 BARC-West, Beltsville, MD 20705 (FTS: 344-3078)

South Atlantic Area: DR. ERNEST L. CORLEY, USDA-ARS, Russell Agr. Res. Center, P.O. Box 5677, College Station Rd., Athens, GA 30613 (FTS: 250-3311/404, 546-3311)

Mid South Area: PAUL A. PUTNAM, USDA-ARS, P.O. Box 225, Stoneville, MS 38776 (FTS: 497-2265/601, 686-2311)

Southern Plains Area: DR. FLOYD HORN, USDA-ARS, 1812 Welsh St., Suite 130, College Station, TX 77840 (FTS: 527-1346/409, 260-9346)

Midwest Area: DR. GERALD E. CARLSON, USDA-ARS, 1815 North University St., Peoria, IL 61604 (FTS: 360-4602/309, 685-4011)

Pacific West Area: WILLIAM G. CHACE, USDA-ARS, 800 Buchanan St., Albany, CA 94710 (FTS: 449-3227/415, 486-3227)

Northern Plains Area: THOMAS J. ARMY, USDA-ARS, Drake Executive Plaza, 2625 Redwing Rd., Suite 350, Fort Collins, CO 80526 (FTS: 323-5557/303, 229-5557)

Cooperative State Research Service, Washington, DC 20250 (202, 44 plus extension; information: 202, 655-4000)

Administers federal-grant funds for research in agriculture, forestry, resource conservation, and rural life made available to state agricultural experiment stations and forestry schools in the 58 state and territorial agricultural experiment stations; 17 colleges of 1890, including Tuskegee University; 28 schools of forestry; and 29 colleges of veterinary medicine.

Administrator: JOHN PATRICK JORDON (Ext. 74423)

Associate Administrator: CLARE I. HARRIS (Ext. 77441)

Deputy Administrator (Acting), Plant and Animal Sciences: EDWARD M. WILSON (Ext. 74329)

Program Coordinator, Plant Sciences: DANIEL R. TOMPKINS (74202)

Program Coordinator, Animal Sciences: HOWARD S. TEAGUE (Ext. 73847)

Deputy Administrator, Natural Resources, Food and Social Sciences: CHARLES B. RUMBURG (Ext. 73555)

Deputy Administrator (Acting), Regional Research and Special Grants: JOHN NAEGELE (Ext. 74587)

Operations Manager: KAY HATCH (Ext. 76845)

Coordinator, Organic Farming: CHARLES SMITH (Ext. 72039)

1890 Coordinator: McKINLEY MAYES (Ext. 75620)

State Agricultural Experiment Station Directors

Director: PEMERIKA L. TAUILIILI, Agricultural Experiment Station, American Samoa Community College, P.O. Box 2609, Pago Pago, American Samoa 96799 (684, 639-9155)

Director: ISHMAEL LEBEHN, Agricultural Research Station, College of Tropical Agriculture and Life Sciences, College of Micronesia, Drawer F, Kolonia, Ponape, Eastern Caroline Islands 96941

AL: LOWELL T. FROBISH, Director, Auburn University, Auburn 36849 (205, 826-4840)

AK: JAMES V. DREW, University of Alaska, Fairbanks 99775-0080 (907, 474-7188)

AZ: EUGENE G. SANDER, University of Arizona, Tucson 85721 (602, 621-3859)

AR: GERALD J. MUSICK, University of Arkansas, Fayetteville 72701 (501, 575-4446)

CA: WILFORD R. GARDNER, University of California, Berkeley 94720 (415, 642-7171)

    Oakland: KENNETH R. FARRELL, University of California, Oakland 94612 (415, 987-0060)

    Davis: C.E. HESS, Dean and Associate Director, College of Agricultural and Environmental Sciences, University of California, Davis 95615 (916, 752-1605)

    Riverside: IRWIN W. SHERMAN, Dean and Associate Director, Citrus Research Center, College of Natural and Agricultural Sciences, Riverside 92521 (714, 787-3101)

CO: ROBERT D. HEIL, Colorado State University, Fort Collins 80523 (303, 491-5371)

CT: New Haven: JOHN H. ANDERSON, Agricultural Experiment Station, P.O. Box 1106, New Haven 06504 (203, 789-7214)

    Storrs: KIRVIN L. KNOX, University of Connecticut, Storrs 06268 (203, 486-2917)

DE: D.F. CROSSAN, University of Delaware, Newark 19717-1303 (302, 451-2501)

DC: EMORY M. LEVANT, Interim Director, University of the District of Columbia, 4200 Connecticut Ave., NW, Washington, DC 20008 (202, 282-7322)

FL: GERALD ZACHARIAH, University of Florida, Institute of Food and Agricultural Sciences, Gainesville 32611 (904, 392-1971)

GA: Athens: CLIVE DONOHO, JR, University of Georgia, Athens 30602 (404, 542-2151)

    Experiment: GERALD F. ARKIN, Associate Director, Georgia Station, Experiment 30212 (404, 228-7263)

    Tifton: GALE A. BUCHANAN, Associate Director, Coastal Plain Station, Tifton 31793 (912, 386-3338)

GUAM: JOSE T. BARCINAS, Dean and Director (Acting), College of Agriculture and Life Sciences, University of Guam, Mangilao, Guam 96913 (734-2579)

HI: NOEL P. KEFFORD, Dean and Director, College of Tropical Agriculture and Human Resources, University of Hawaii at Manoa, 3050 Maile Way, Rm. 202, Honolulu 96822 (808, 948-8234)

ID: GARY A. LEE, Director, University of Idaho, Moscow 83843 (208, 885-7173)

IL: DONALD A. HOLT, University of Illinois, Urbana 61801 (217, 333-0240)

IN: B.R. BAUMGARDT, Purdue University, West Lafayette 47907 (317, 494-8360)

IA: DAVID G. TOPEL, Agriculture and Home Economics Experiment Station, Iowa State University, Ames 50011 (515, 294-2518)

KS: WALTER R. WOODS, Director, Kansas State University, 113 Waters Hall, Manhattan 66506 (913, 532-6147)

KY: C. ORAN LITTLE, University of Kentucky, Lexington 40506-0091 (606, 257-4772)

LA: MACON FAULKNER, Louisiana State University and A&M College, Drawer E, University Station, Baton Rouge 70893-0905 (504, 388-4181)

ME: WALLACE C. DUNHAM, University of Maine, Orono 04469 (207, 581-3202)

MD: CRAIG OLIVER, Director (Acting), Agricultural Experiment Station, University of Maryland, College Park 20742 (301, 454-3707)

MA: Director: E. BRUCE MacDOUGALL, University of Massachusetts, Amherst 01003 (413, 545-2771/2058)

MI: ROBERT G. GAST, Director, Michigan State University, East Lansing 48824-1039 (517, 355-0123)

MN: Director: RICHARD SAUER, University of Minnesota, St. Paul Campus, St. Paul 55208 (612, 625-4211)

MS: VERNER G. HURT, Director, Agricultural and Forestry Experiment Station, Mississippi State University, Mississippi State 39762 (601, 325-3006)

MO: ROGER L. MITCHELL, University of Missouri, Columbia 65211 (314, 882-3846)

MT: JAMES WELSH, Montana State University, Bozeman 59717-0002 (406, 994-3681)

NE: DALE VANDERHOLM, Interim Dean and Director, University of Nebraska, Lincoln 68583-0704 (402, 472-2045)

NV: BERNARD M. JONES, University of Nevada, Reno 89557 (702, 784-6611)

NH: THOMAS P. FAIRCHILD, Director, University of New Hampshire, Durham 03824 (603, 862-1450)

NJ: STEPHEN J. KLEINSCHUSTER, Executive Director, Rutgers University, P.O. Box 231, New Brunswick 08903 (201, 932-9447)

NM: DAVID W. SMITH, New Mexico State University P.O. Box 3BF, Las Cruces 88003 (505, 646-3125)

NY: Ithaca: NORMAN R. SCOTT, Cornell University, Cornell Station, Ithaca 14853 (607, 255-5420)

    Geneva: ROBERT A. PLANE, Director, Agricultural Experiment Station, State Station, Geneva 14456 (315, 787-2211)

NC: RONALD J. KUHR, Director of Research, North Carolina State University, Box 7601, Raleigh 27695-7601 (919, 737-2718)

ND: H.R. LUND, North Dakota State University, State University Station, Fargo 58105 (701, 237-7654)

OH: Columbus: KIRKLYN KERR, Director, Ohio Agricultural Research and Development Center, Ohio State University, Columbus 43210 (614, 292-3897)

    Wooster: KIRKLYN KERR, Director, Ohio Agricultural Research & Development Center, Wooster 44691 (216, 263-3703)

OK: CHARLES BROWNING, Oklahoma State University, Stillwater 74078-0500 (405, 624-5398)

OR: THAYNE R. DUTSON, Director, Oregon State University, Corvallis 97331 (503, 754-4251)

PA: LAMARTINE F. HOOD, Director, Pennsylvania State University,

229 Agr. Admin. Bldg., University Park 16802 (814, 865-2541)

PR: JORGE L. RODRIGUEZ, Dean and Director (Acting), University of Puerto Rico, Mayaquez 00708 (809, 834-4040)

RI: G.A. DONOVAN, University of Rhode Island, Kingston 02881 (401, 792-2474); ANTONIA A. SANTOS, Community College of Northern Mariana Islands, Saipan, CM 96950 (234-8567)

SC: JAMES FISCHER, Dean and Director, Clemson University, Clemson 29634-0351, (803, 656-3141)

SD: R.A. MOORE, South Dakota State University, Brookings 57006 (605, 688-4149)

TN: DON O. RICHARDSON, Dean, University of Tennessee, P.O. Box 1071, Knoxville 37901-1071 (615, 974-7121)

TX: N.P. CLARKE, Texas A&M University, College Station 77843 (409, 845-8484)

UT: D.J. MATTHEWS, Utah State University, Logan 84322 (801, 750-2215)

VT: DONALD L. McLEAN, Director, University of Vermont, Burlington 05405 (802, 656-2980)

VA: J.R. NICHOLS, Virginia Polytechnic Institute & State University, Blacksburg 24061 (703, 961-6337)

VI: D.S. PADDA, RR 2-10,000, University of the Virgin Islands, Kingshill, St. Croix 00850 (809, 778-0246)

WA: JAMES J. ZUICHES, Director, Washington State University, Pullman 99164 (509, 335-4563)

WV: ROBERT H. MAXWELL, West Virginia University, Morgantown 26506-6108 (304, 293-2395)

WI: LEO WALSH, University of Wisconsin, Madison 53706 (608, 262-4930)

WY: C. COLIN KALTENBACH, University of Wyoming, University Station, Box 3354, Laramie 82071 (307, 766-3667)

Research Directors 1890 Institutions and Tuskegee Institute

AL: JAMES W. SHUFORD, Alabama A&M University, Normal 35762 (205, 859-7244); WALTER HILL, Tuskegee Univesity, Tuskegee 36088 (205, 727-8246)

AR: ARTHUR ALLEN, University of Arkansas, Pine Bluff 71601 (501, 541-6868)

DE: U.S. WASHINGTON, JR., Delaware State College, Dover 19901 (302, 736-4929)

FL: SUNIL K. PANCHOLY, Florida A&M University, Tallahassee 32307 (904, 599-3594)

GA: MELVIN E. WALKER, JR., Fort Valley State College, Fort Valley 31030 (912, 825-6320)

KY: DR. HAROLD R. BENSON, Kentucky State University, Frankfort 40601 (502, 227-6174)

LA: BOBBY RAY PHILLS, Southern University, Baton Rouge 70813 (504, 771-3660)

MD: MORTIMER H. NEUFVILLE, University of Maryland-Eastern Shore, Princess Anne 21853 (301, 651-2200/Ext. 632)

MS: SAMUEL L. DONALD, Alcorn State University, Lorman 39096 (601, 877-6137)

MO: JOHN WARREN, Lincoln University, Jefferson City 65101 (314, 636-6321)

NC: BURLEIGH C. WEBB, North Carolina A&T State University, Greensboro 27411 (919, 379-7665)

OK: OCLERIS SIMPSON, Langston University, Langston 73050 (405, 466-3833)

SC: LEON G. CHAVOUS, South Carolina State College, Orangeburg 29117 (803, 534-6916)

TN: TROY WAKEFIELD, JR. (Acting), Tennessee State University, Nashville 37203 (615, 320-3337/3718)

TX: ALDEN REINE, Prairie View A&M University, Prairie View 77446-2886 (409, 857-2811)

VA: P.S. BENEPAL, Virginia State University, Petersburg 23803 (804, 520-5151/5635)

Cooperating Forestry School Administrators

AK: JAMES V. DREW, A-TR M-S, University of Alaska, Fairbanks 99701

AL: LOWELL T. FROBISH, A-TR M-S Program, Auburn University, Auburn 36849

AZ: EUGENE G. SANDER, A-TR M-S, University of Arizona, Tucson 85721; LAWRENCE GARRETT, Dean, School of Forestry, Northern Arizona University, Flagstaff 86001

AR: GERALD J. MUSICK, Director (Acting), A-TR M-S Program, University of Arkansas, Fayetteville 72701

CA: KENNETH R. FARRELL, A-TR M-S Program, University of California, Oakland 94612-3560; RICHARD L. RIDENHOUR, A-TR M-S Program, Humboldt State College, Arcata 95521; LARK CARTER, School of Agriculture, California Polytechnia State University, San Luis Obispo 93407

CO: JAY M. HUGHES, Dean, College of Forestry and Natural Resources, Colorado State University, Ft. Collins 80523

CT: LOUIS J. PIERRO, University of Connecticut, Storrs 06268; JOHN F. ANDERSON, A-TR M-S Program, Connecticut Agricultural Experiment Station, New Haven 06504

DE: DONALD F. CROSSAN, Director, Agricultural Experiment Station, College of Agriculture Sciences, University of Delaware, Newark 19711

FL: GERALD ZACHARIAH, University of Florida, Gainesville 32611

GA: LEON HARGREAVES, JR., Dean, School of Forest Resources, University of Georgia, Athens 30602

GU: JOSE T. BARCINAS, A-TR M-S Program, University of Guam, UOG Station, Mangilao 96913

HI: N.P. KEFFORD, Director, College of Tropical Agriculture and Human Resources, University of Hawaii, Honolulu 96822

ID: JOHN C. HENDEE, Dean, College of Forestry, Wildlife, and Range Sciences, University of Idaho, Moscow 83843

IL: DONALD A. HOLT, University of Illinois, Urbana 61801; D.W. McCURDY, Chairman, Dept. of Forestry, Southern Illinois University, Carbondale 62901

IN: B.R. BAUMGARDT, Purdue University, West Lafayette 47907

IA: DAVID G. TOPEL, Iowa State University, Ames 50011

KS: KURT C. FELTNER, Kansas State University, Manhattan 66506

KY: MILTON SHUFFETT, University of Kentucky, Lexington 40506

LA: DR. J. LAMAR TEATE, Director, School of Forestry, Louisiana Tech University, Ruston 71272; MACON FAULKNER, Director, Louisiana State University, Baton Rouge 70893-0905

MD: CRAIG OLIVER, Director (Acting), Agricultural Experiment Station, University of Maryland, College Park 20742

ME: FRED B. KNIGHT, Associate Director (Acting), University of Maine, Orono 04469

MA: RICHARD A. ROHDE, University of Massachusetts, Amherst 01003

MI: DR. JAMES E. CROWFOOT, Dean, School of Natural Resources, University of Michigan, Ann Arbor 48109; ROBERT G. GAST, Michigan State University, East Lansing 48824; WARREN E. FRAYER, Michigan Technological University, Houghton 49931

MN: R.A. SKOK, Dean, College of Forestry, University of Minnesota, St. Paul 55108

MS: WARREN THOMPSON, Dean, School of Forest Resources, Mississippi State University, Mississippi State 39762

MO: W.H. PFANDER, University of Missouri, Columbia 65211

MT: SIDNEY S. FRISSELL, Dean, University of Montana, Missoula 59812 JAMES R. WELSH, Montana State University, Bozeman 59715-0002

NE: DALE VANDERHOLM, Interim Director, University of Nebraska, Lincoln 68583

NV: BERNARD M. JONES, Associate Director, University of Nevada, Reno 89557

NH: JAMES A. STEWART, Associate Director, University of New Hampshire, Durham 03824

NJ: STEPHEN J. KLEINSCHUSTER, Director, Rutgers University, New Brunswick 08903

NM: DINUS M. BRIGGS, Associate Director and Dean, Agricultural Experiment Station, New Mexico State University, Las Cruces 88003

NY: HELMUTH RESCH, State University of New York, College of Environmental Science and Forestry at Syracuse University, Syracuse 13210; NORMAN R. SCOTT, Director, Cornell University, Ithaca 14853

NC: ERIC L. ELLWOOD, Dean, School of Forest Resources, North Carolina State University, Raleigh 27695

ND: H. RONALD LUND, North Dakota State University, Fargo 58105

OH: KIRKLYN KERR, Director, Ohio Agricultural Research and Development Center, Ohio State University, Columbus 43210

OK: CHARLES B. BROWNING, Oklahoma State University, Stillwater 74074

OR: CARL STOLTENBERG, Dean, College of Forestry, Oregon State University, Corvallis 97331

PA: C.R. KRUEGER, Pennsylvania State University, University Park 16802

PR: JESSE ROMAN, Director, University of Puerto Rico, P.O. Box H, Mayaguez 00708

RI: GERALD A. DONOVAN, Director, Agricultural Experiment Station, University of Rhode Island, Kingston 2881

SC: BENTON H. BOX, Dean, College of Forest and Recreation Resources, Clemson University, Clemson 29631

SD: R.A. MOORE, South Dakota State University, Brookings 57007

TN: DON O. RICHARDSON, Dean, P.O. Box 1071, University of Tennessee, Knoxville 37901

TX: NEVILLE P. CLARKE, Director, Texas A&M University System, University Station, College Station 77843; KENT T. ADAIR, Dean, Box 6109, Stephen F. Austin State University, Nacogdoches 75962

UT: THADIS W. BOX, Director, College of Natural Resources, Utah State University, Logan 84322

VT: LAWRENCE K. FORCIER, Dean, School of Natural Resources, University of Vermont, Burlington 05405

VA: DR. JOHN F. HOSNER, Head, School of Forestry and Wildlife Resources, Virginia Polytechnic Institute, Blacksburg 24061

VI: D.S. PADDA, Director, University of the Virgin Islands, P.O. Box L, Kingshill, St. Croix 00850

WA: DAVID B. THORUD, Dean, College of Forest Resources, University of Washington, Seattle 98195; JAMES J. ZUICHES, Director, Agricultural Research Center, Washington State University, Pullman 99164

WV: JACK COSTER, Assistant Director, The West Virginia Agricultural and Forestry Experiment Station, West Virginia University, Morgantown 26506

WI: STEPHEN C. SMITH, Associate Dean, School of Natural Resources, University of Wisconsin, Madison 53706

WY: C. COLIN KATENBACH, Agricultural Experiment Station, University of Wyoming, Laramie 82071

Extension Service, Washington, DC 20250 (202, 447 plus extension)

The Extension Service, created by legislation in 1914, has an office at each state land-grant university and over 3,000 local offices, with total staff of 15,000. The agency has the responsibility for and leadership in all general educational programs of the Department of Agriculture. Administrative and technical personnel serve as liaison between departmental research and action agencies and the administrative and extension technical staffs at land-grant universities in the 50 states, District of Columbia, Micronesia, American Samoa, Puerto Rico, Virgin Islands, and Guam. County extension agents, located in nearly all counties, make available to farmers, homemakers, youth, and others the results of research and management conducted by the Department of Agriculture, land grant institutions, and other state and federal agencies. Results include information on the management and utilization of natural resources, including fish, wildlife, forage, timber, recreation, soil and water for owners, managers, processors, and users.

Administrator for Extension: DR. MYRON D. JOHNSRUD (Ext. 3377)

Associate Administrator: DR. DENZIL O. CLEGG (Ext. 3381)

Natural Resources and Rural Development Unit: JOHN A. VANCE, Deputy Administrator (Ext. 7947)

Wood Products Marketing National Program Leader: DONALD E. NELSON (Ext. 5119)

Aquaculture Program Leader: MERYL L. BROUSSARD (Ext. 5468)

Wildlife and Fisheries National Program Leader: JAMES E. MILLER (Ext. 5468)

Soil and Water Conservation National Program Leader: E. WAYNE CHAPMAN (Ext. 5004)

Forest Resource Management National Program Leader: FRED J. DENEKE (Ext. 5119)

Natural Resources and Marine Extension National Program Leader: ANDREW J. WEBER (Ext. 2506)

Range Management National Program Leader: JOHN L. ARTZ (Ext. 2506)

Economic Development National Program Leader: BETH WALTER HONADLE (Ext. 7185)

Community Services and Facilities National Program Leader: MARVIN E. KONYHA (Ext. 2602)

Local Government: THEODORE J. MAHER (Ext. 7185)

Community Communications and Public Affairs National Program Leader: DONALD L. NELSON (Ext. 2602)

Leadership Development and Community Decision-Making National Program Leader: W. ROBERT LOVAN (Ext. 2805)

Food Security Act-Information and Education National Leader: DWIGHT M. TREADWAY (Ext. 4946)

Water Resources Management National Program Leader: FRED SWADER (Ext. 5369)

Environmental Management of Agricultural Chemicals National Program Leader: CYNTHIA GARMAN-SQUIER (Ext. 5245)

Integrated Pest Management and Alternative Agriculture National Program Leader: DAVID C. McNEAL (Ext. 4481)

SOIL CONSERVATION SERVICE, P.O. Box 2890, Washington, DC 20013 (202, 447 plus extension; Information: 447-4543)

Local offices provide technical and educational assistance through conservation districts with watershed projects, flood protection, water supply/management, recreation and wildlife habitat. Directs multi-county Resource Conservation and Development and Great Plains Conservation programs, publishes soil surveys and other resource information. Provides on-site assistance to urban and rural residents. Organized: 1935.

Chief: WILSON SCALING (Ext. 4525)

Associate Chief: MANLY S. WILDER (Ext. 4531)

Deputy Chief for Programs: GALEN S. BRIDGE (Ext. 4527)

Assistant Chief, South: COY A. GARRETT (Ext. 2322)

Deputy Chief for Technology: ROBERT R. SHAW (Ext. 4630)

Assistant Chief, West: FRANCIS C.H. LUM (Ext. 4514)

Associate Deputy Chief for Programs: GARY A. MARGHEIM (Ext. 3587)

Director, Project Development and Maintenance Division: HOWARD C. TANKERSLEY (Ext. 3527)

Director of Land Treatment Programs: PETER M. TIDD (382-1870)

Director, Information Resources Management: GERALD D. SEINWILL (475-4047)

Special Assistant for Science and Technology: KLAUS W. FLACH (Ext. 5195)
Director of Engineering: DONALD L. BASINGER (Ext. 2520)
Director of Basin and Area Planning: EDWARD G. RIEKERT (Ext. 8766)
Director of Soil Survey: RICHARD W. ARNOLD (382-1819)
Director, Midwest National Technical Center: AUGUST F. DORNBUSCH, JR., Lincoln, NE (402, 471-5346)
Director, South National Technical Center: PAUL F. LARSON (817, 334-5253)
Deputy Chief for Administration: JOHN W. PETERSON (Ext. 6297)
Associate Deputy Chief for Administration: WILLIAM E. GARDNER, JR. (Ext. 7847)
Assistant Chief, Northeast: RICHARD L. DUESTERHAUS (Ext. 2241)
Director, Ecological Sciences: JAMES B. NEWMAN (Ext. 2587)
National Biologist: BILLY M. TEELS (Ext. 5991)
Director (Acting), Public Information: HENRY C. WYMAN (Ext. 4543)
National Recreation Specialist (Acting): CLARENCE M. MAESNER Federal Bldg., Rm. 209, NW Broadway, Portland, OR 97209-3489
Assistant Chief, Midwest: DENNIS G. BURNS (Ext. 4514)

Regional Biologists
Northeast: ROBERT W. FRANZEN, 160 E. 7th St., Chester, PA 19013
South: Vacant, Federal Center, Bldg. 23, Felix & Hemphill Sts., Fort Worth, TX 76115
Midwest: MIKE W. ANDERSON, 100 Centennial Mall North, Federal Bldg., Lincoln, NE 68508-3866
West: DAVID E. CHALK, Federal Bldg., 511 NW Bdwy., Portland, OR 97209-2826

Field Biologists
AL: ROBERT E. WATERS, P.O. Box 311, 665 Opelika Rd., Auburn 36830
AK: DEVONY LEHNER-WELCH, 201 East 9th, Suite 300, Anchorage 99501
AZ: JOHN C. YORK, 201 East Indianola, Suite 200, Phoenix 85025
AR: PAUL M. BRADY, Federal Office Bldg., 700 W. Capitol Ave., Federal Bldg., Little Rock 72201
CA: RONALD F. SCHULTZE, 2121-C Second St., Davis, 95616
CO: ELDIE W. MUSTARD, JR., 2490 W. 26th Ave., Rm. 309, Denver 80211
DE, MD: ANNE M. LYNN, 4321 Hartwick Rd., Rm. 522, College Park, MD 20740
FL: JOHN F. VANCE, JR., 401 SE 1st Ave., Gainesville 32601
GA: LOUIS A. JUSTICE, Federal Bldg., Box 13, 355 Hancock Ave., Athens 30601
ID: FRANK J. FINK, JR., 304 N. 8th St., Rm. 345, Boise 83702
IL: STEPHEN J. BRADY, Springer Federal Bldg., 301 N. Randolph St., Champaign 61820
IN: JAMES D. McCALL, Corporate Square-West, 5610 Crawfordsville Rd., Indianapolis 46224
IA: BILL D. WELKER, 693 Federal Bldg., 210 Walnut St., Des Moines 50309
KS: ROBERT J. HIGGINS, 760 S. Broadway, Salina 67401
KY: Vacant, 333 Waller Ave., Lexington 40504
LA: BILLY R. CRAFT, 3737 Government St., Alexandria 71302
ME: ROBERT J. WENGRZYNEK, JR., USDA Bldg., University of Maine, Orono 04473
MD: (See DE)
MA: Vacant, 451 West St., Amherst 01002

MI: LYNN C. SAMPSON, 1405 S. Harrison Rd., Rm. 101, East Lansing 48823-5202
MN: GEORGE L. POLLARD, 316 N. Robert St., 200 Federal Bldg. and U.S. Courthouse, St. Paul 55101
MS: HARVEY G. HUFFSTATLER, Federal Bldg., Suite 1321, 100 W. Capitol St., Jackson 39269
MO: JOHN P. GRAHAM, 555 Vandiver Dr., Columbia 65202
MT: RONALD F. BATCHELOR, 10 E. Babcock, Federal Bldg., Bozeman 59715
NE: MIKE W. ANDERSON, Rm. 345, Federal Bldg., 100 Centennial Mall, Lincoln 68508-3866
NV: LESIA A. YOUNG, Rm. 219, 1201 Terminal Way, Reno 89505
NH: ALAN P. AMMAN, Federal Bldg., Durham 03824
NJ: DAVID L. SMART, 1370 Hamilton St., Somerset 08873
NM: EDWIN A. SWENSON, JR., 517 Gold Ave., SW, Albuquerque 87102
NY: ROBERT E. MYERS, James M. Hanley Federal Bldg., 100 South Clinton St., Syracuse 13260
NC: JOHN P. EDWARDS, 310 New Bern Ave., Federal Bldg., Raleigh 27601
ND: DAVID DEWALD, Rossner Avenue and Third St., Federal Bldg., P.O. Box 1458, Bismarck 58502
OH: JEROME MYSZKA, Federal Bldg., 200 N. High St., Columbus 43215
OK: STEPHEN R. TULLY, USDA-Agricultural Center Bldg., Stillwater 74074
OR: CLYDE A. SCOTT, Federal Office Bldg., 1220 SW Third Ave., Portland 97204
PA: BARRY ISSACS, Box 985, Federal Square Station, 228 Walnut St., Harrisburg 17108
SC: LAWRENCE H. ROBINSON, Strom Thurmond Federal Bldg., 1835 Assembly St., Columbia 29201
SD: CONNIE M. VICUNA, Federal Bldg., 200 Fourth St., SW, Huron 57350
TN: GERALD L. MONTGOMERY, 675 Estes Kefauver, FB-USCH, 801 Broadway, Nashville 37203
TX: JAMES HENSON, GARY L. VALENTINE, W.R. Poage Bldg., 101 S. Main St., Temple 76501-7682
UT: ROBERT SENNETT, 125 So. State St., Salt Lake City 84138
VA: GREGORY H. MOSER, Federal Bldg., 400 N. 8th St., Richmond 23240
VT: Vacant, 69 Union St., Winooski, Burlington 05404
WA: IVAN L. LINES, JR., 360 U.S. Courthouse, West 920 Riverside Ave., Spokane 99201
WV: GARY A. GWINN, 75 High St., Morgantown 26505
WI: THOMAS P. THRALL, 4601 Hamersley Rd., Madison 53711
WY: RICHARD C. RINTAMAKI, Federal Office Bldg., 100 East B St., Casper 82601

State Conservationists
AL: ERNEST V. TODD, 665 Opelika Rd., Auburn 36830 (205, 821-8070)
AK: BURTON L. CLIFFORD, Suite 300, 201 E., 9th Ave., Anchorage 99501-3687 (907, 271-2420)
AZ: Vacant, Suite 200, 201 E. Indianola Ave., Phoenix 85012 (602, 261-2247)
AR: ALBERT E. SULLIVAN, Federal Office Bldg., 700 West Capitol Ave., Little Rock 72201 (501, 378-5445)
CA: E.E. ANDREUCCETTI, 2121-C 2nd St., Suite 102, Davis 95616-5475 (916, 449-2848)
CO: SHELDON G. BOONE, 2490 West 26th Ave., Diamond Hill, Bldg. A, Denver 80211 (303, 964-0292)
CT: PHILIP H. CHRISTENSEN, 16 Professional Park Rd., Storrs 06268-1299 (203, 487-4011)
DE: DOUGLAS E. HAWKINS, 9 East Loockerman St., Dover 19901-7377 (302, 678-0750)

FL: JAMES W. MITCHELL, Federal Bldg., 401 SE First Ave., Rm. 248, Gainesville 32601 (904, 377-0946)

GA: B. CLAYTON GRAHAM, Federal Bldg., 355 E. Hancock Ave., Athens 30601 (404, 546-2273)

HI: RICHARD N. DUNCAN, 300 Ala Moana Blvd., Honolulu 96850 (808, 546-2601)

ID: PAUL H. CALVERLEY, 3244 Elder St., Rm. 124, Boise 83705 (208, 334-1601)

IL: JOHN J. ECKES, Federal Bldg., 301 N. Randolph St., Champaign 61820 (217, 398-5267)

IN: ROBERT L. EDDLEMAN, 5610 Crawfordsville Rd., Indianapolis 46224 (317, 248-4350)

IA: J. MICHAEL NETHERY, 693 Federal Bldg., 210 Walnut St., Des Moines 50309 (515, 284-4261)

KS: JAMES N. HABIGER, 760 S. Broadway, Salina 674021 (913, 823-4565)

KY: RANDY W. GIESSLER, 333 Waller Ave., Lexington 40504 (606, 233-2749)

LA: HORACE J. AUSTIN, 3737 Government St., Alexandria 71302 (318, 473-7751)

ME: CHARLES WHITMORE, USDA Bldg., University of Maine, Orono 04473 (207, 866-2132)

MD: PEARLIE S. REED, Rm. 522, Hartwick Bldg., 4321 Hartwick Rd., College Park 20740 (301, 344-4180)

MA: REX O. TRACY, 451 West St., Amherst 01002 (413, 256-0441)

MI: HOMER R. HILNER, 1405 S. Harrison Rd., East Lansing 48823-5202 (517, 337-6702)

MN: GARY R. NORDSTROM, 200 Federal Bldg., 316 North Robert St., St. Paul 55101 (612, 290-3675)

MS: LOUIE P. HEARD, Suite 1321, Federal Bldg., 100 W. Capitol St., Jackson 39269 (601, 965-5205)

MO: RUSSELL C. MILLS, 555 Vandiver Dr., Columbia 65202 (314, 875-5214)

MT: RICHARD J. GOOBY, 10 E. Babcock, Federal Bldg., Bozeman 59715 (406, 587-6813)

NE: RONALD E. HENDRICKS, Federal Bldg., 100 Centennial Mall, N., Lincoln 68508-3866 (402, 471-5300)

NV: CHARLES R. ADAMS, Rm. 219, 1201 Terminal Way, Reno 89505 (702, 784-5863)

NH: DAVID L. MUSSULMAN, Federal Bldg., Durham 03824 (603, 868-7581)

NJ: BARBARA OSGOOD, 1370 Hamilton St., Somerset 08873 (201, 246-1662)

NM: RAY T. MARGO, JR., 517 Gold Ave., SW, Albuquerque 87102-3157 (505, 766-2173)

NY: PAUL A. DODD, Federal Bldg., 100 S. Clinton St., Syracuse 13260 (315, 423-5521)

NC: BOBBYE J. JONES, Federal Bldg., 310 New Bern Ave., Raleigh 27601 (919, 856-4210)

ND: RONNIE L. CLARK, Federal Bldg., Rosser Ave. and 3rd St., Bismarck 58502-1458 (701, 783-4421/Ext. 421)

OH: JOSEPH C. BRANCO, Rm. 522, 200 North High St., Columbus 43215 (614, 469-6962)

OK: C. BUDD FOUNTAIN, Agriculture Bldg., Farm Rd. and Brumley St., Stillwater 74074 (405, 624-4360)

OR: JACK P. KANALZ, Federal Office Bldg., 1220 SW 3rd. Ave., Portland 97204 (503, 221-2751)

PA: JAMES H. OLSON, Federal Square Station, Box 985, Harrisburg 17108 (717, 782-2202)

Puerto Rico and U.S. Virgin Islands (Caribbean Area): Vacant, G.P.O. Box 4868, San Juan 00936 (809, 753-7665)

RI: ROBERT J. KLUMPE, 46 Quaker Ln., West Warwick 02893 (401, 828-1300)

SC: BILLY R. ABERCROMBIE, Federal Bldg., 1835 Assembly St., Columbia 29201 (803, 765-5681)

SD: BILLY W. MILLIKEN, 200 Fourth St., SW, Federal Bldg., Huron 57350 (605, 352-8651, ext. 333)

TN: JERRY S. LEE, U.S. Court House, Rm. 675, 801 Broadway St., Nashville 37203 (615, 251-5471)

TX: HARRY W. ONETH, W.R. Poage Bldg., 101 S. Main St., Temple 76501-7682 (817, 774-1214)

UT: FRANCIS T. HOLT, 4012 Federal Bldg., 125 S. State St., Salt Lake City 84138 (801, 524-5050)

VT: JOHN C. TITCHNER, 69 Union St., Winooski 05404 (802, 951-6795)

VA: GEORGE C. NORRIS, Federal Bldg., Rm. 9201, 400 N. 8th St., Richmond 23240 (804, 771-2455)

WA: LYNN A. BROWN, 360 U.S. Courthouse, W. 920 Riverside Ave., Spokane 99201 (509, 456-3711)

WV: ROLLIN N. SWANK, 75 High St., Morgantown 26505 (304, 291-4151)

WI: CLIFFTON A. MAGUIRE, 4601 Hammersley Rd., Madison 53711 (608, 264-5577)

WY: FRANK S. DICKSON, JR., Federal Office Bldg., 100 East B St., Casper 82601 (307, 261-5201, ext 3217)

DEPARTMENT OF COMMERCE

HCH Building, Rm. 5862, 14th St. between Constitution Ave. and E St., NW, Washington, DC 20230 (202, 377 plus extension; information: 202, 377-2000)

Secretary of Commerce: C. WILLIAM VERITY (Ext. 2112)

Deputy Secretary: CLARENCE J. BROWN (Ext. 4625)

Director of Public Affairs: B. JAY COOPER (Ext. 2067)

ECONOMIC DEVELOPMENT ADMINISTRATION, Washington, DC 20230 (202, 377-5113)

Conducts programs to help stimulate private enterprise and create permanent jobs in economically distressed areas of the nation. Provides public works grants, business loan guarantees and planning and technical assistance in areas with high unemployment or low median family income.

Assistant Secretary of Commerce for Economic Development: ORSON G. SWINDLE III

Deputy Assistant Secretary For Economic Development: STANLEY M. McGEEHAN, JR.

Deputy Assistant Secretary for Grant Programs: JAMES L. PERRY, JR.

Deputy Assistant Secretary for Loan Programs: STEVEN BRENNEN

Special Assistant for Public Affairs (Acting): JONATHAN H. MERTZ

NATIONAL OCEANIC AND ATMOSPHERIC ADMINISTRATION, Rockville, MD 20852 (301, 443-8910)

NOAA was created within the U.S. Department of Commerce in 1970 to improve the comprehension and uses of the physical environment and oceanic life. It is a major Federal environmental management agency and a source of objective information on the effects which human actions may have on environmental quality.

Under Secretary for Oceans and Atmosphere and Deputy Administrator of NOAA: DR. WILLIAM E. EVANS

Assistant Secretary for Oceans and Atmosphere and Deputy Administrator of NOAA: B. KENT BURTON (202, 377-3436)

Chief Scientist: DR. MELVIN N.A. PETERSON (202, 377-8565)

Office of Public Affairs: A. JOSEPH LACOVEY, Director (202, 377-4190)

Assistant Administrator, National Marine Fisheries Service: JAMES W. BRENNAN (202, 634-7283)

Assistant Administrator, Oceanic and Atmospheric Research: DR. JOSEPH O. FLETCHER (301, 443-8344)

Assistant Administrator, National Environmental Satellite, Data and Information Service: THOMAS N. PYKE, JR. (301, 763-7190)

Assistant Administrator, National Weather Service: DR. ELBERT W. FRIDAY (301, 427-7689)

Assistant Administrator, National Ocean Service: THOMAS J. MAGINNIS (202, 377-4699)

Director, NOAA Corps: Radm. FRANCIS D. MORGAN (301, 443-2383)

Naval Deputy to the Administrator: Como., ADM. RICHARD PITTENGER, JR. USN (202, 632-5355)

General Counsel: TIMOTHY R.E. KEENEY (202, 377-4080)

Director, Office of Legislative Affairs: PATRICK LINK, Deputy (202, 377-4981)

Comptroller: RODNEY WEIHER

Director, Office of Administration: DENNIS F. GEER (202, 377-8900)

Environmental Research Laboratories, Director: DR. VERNON E. DERR (303, 497-6357)

Atlantic Oceanographic and Meteorological Laboratories, Director: DR. HUGO BEZDEK (305, 361-4300)

Pacific Marine Environmental Research Laboratory, Director: DR. EDDIE N. BERNARD (206, 526-6239)

Great Lakes Environmental Research Laboratory, Director: DR. EUGENE J. AUBERT (313, 769-7100)

Office of Sea Grant and Extramural Programs: DR. NED OSTEUSO (301, 443-8923)

Western Administrative Support Center, Director: KELLY C. SANDY

Mountain Administrative Support Center: CURTIS T. HILL (303, 497-6431)

Central Administrative Support Center: ARLENE D. SCHLEY (816, 374-2050)

Eastern Administrative Support Center: ROBERT SMITH (804, 441-6864)

National Marine Fisheries Service, U.S. Dept. of Commerce, NOAA, 1335 East-West Highway, Silver Spring, MD 20910 (301, 427-2239)

A component of the National Oceanic and Atmospheric Administration. Provides management, research, and services for the protection and rational use of living marine resources for their aesthetic, economic, and recreational value. Determines the consequences of the natural environment and human activities on living marine resources and provides knowledge and services to achieve efficient and judicious domestic and international management, use, and conservation of the resources.

Assistant Administrator for Fisheries: JAMES W. BRENNAN (Ext. 2239)

Deputy Assistant Administrator: JAMES E. DOUGLAS, JR. (Ext. 2239)

Executive Director: WILLIAM MATUSZESKI (Ext. 2239)

General Information: (Ext. 5828)

Regional Offices

Northwest, Director: ROLLAND A. SCHMITTEN, NMFS, 7600 Sand Point Way, NE, BIN C15700. Bldg. 1, Seattle, WA 98115-0070 (206, 526-6150)

Science and Research, Director: DR. RICHARD J. BERRY, NMFS, 7600 Sand Point Way, NE, BIN C15700, Bldg. 4, Seattle, WA 98115-0070 (526-4000)

Southwest, Director: E. CHARLES FULLERTON, NMFS, 300 South Ferry St., Terminal Island, CA 90731 (213, 514,-6196)

Science and Research, Director: DR. IZADORE BARRETT, NMFS, P.O. Box 271, La Jolla, CA 92038 (619, 453-2820)

Northeast, Director: RICHARD ROE, 14 Elm St., Federal Bldg., Gloucester, MA 01930 (617, 281-3600)

Science and Research, Director: ALLEN E. PETERSON, JR., NMFS, Wood Hole, MA 02543 (548-5123)

Southeast, Director (Acting): DR. JOSEPH W. ANGELOVIC, NMFS, 9450 Koger Blvd., St. Petersburg, FL 33702 (813, 893-3141)

Science and Research, Director (Acting): DR. BRADFORD E. BROWN, NMFS, 75 Virginia Beach Dr., Miami, FL 33149 (305, 361-4284)

Alaska, Director (Acting): JAMES E. BROOKS, NMFS, P.O. Box 1668, Juneau, AK 99802 (907, 586-7221)

Science and Research, Director: DR. WILLIAM ARON, NMFS, 7600 Sand Point Way, NE, BIN C15700, Seattle, WA 98115 (206, 526-4000)

National Sea Grant College Program, 6010 Executive Blvd., Rockville, MD 20852 (301, 443-8923)

A component of the National Oceanic and Atmospheric Administration. Administers and directs the National Sea Grant College Program, which provides support for the development of marine resources through grants to universities, colleges, and laboratories for research, education, and advisory/extension services.

Director: DR. NED A. OSTENSO (443-8923)

Deputy Director: ROBERT D. WILDMAN (443-8925)

Associate Director, Extension and External Affairs: ROBERT J. SHEPHARD (443-8886)

Assistant Director, Program Development: DAVID B. DUANE (443-8894)

Assistant Director, Grants Management: WILLIAM F. GRAHAM (443-8926)

Assistant Director, Program Review: RICHARD C. KOLF (443-8977)

Program Director, Marine Advisory Services: BERNARD L. GRISWOLD (443-8886)

Ocean Pollution Data and Information Network, National Environmental Satellite, Data and Information Service (NESDIS/NOAA), 1825 Connecticut Ave., NW, Washington, DC 20235 (202, 673-5539)

A component of the National Oceanic and Atmospheric Administration. The OPDIN is operated by the Central Coordination and Referral Office, established within the National Oceanographic Data Center in May 1981 to improve the dissemination of marine pollution data and information obtained from federally funded research, development and monitoring programs. Network participation is principally from national and regional offices of the federal agencies involved in marine pollution activities.

Manager (Acting): JAMES BERGER (673-5539)

Director: GREGORY W. WITHEE (673-5594)

Director, NOAA's National Marine Pollution Program Office: AMOR LANE (301, 443-8823)

Office of Ocean and Coastal Resource Management, 1825 Connecticut Ave., NW, Suite 700, Washington, DC 20235 (202, 673 plus extension)

A component of the National Oceanic and Atmospheric Administration and serves as a granting agency to coastal states for planning and management of coastal areas. Provides coordination and advice to all levels of government and organizations involved in coastal zone management.

Director, Office of Ocean and Coastal Resource Management: Vacant (Ext. 5111)

Chief, Coastal Programs Division: JAMES BURGESS (Ext. 5158)

Chief, Ocean Minerals and Energy Division: JAMES P. LAWLESS (Ext. 5121)

Chief, Policy Coordination Division: VICKIE ALLIN (Ext. 5110)

Chief, Marine and Estuarine Management Division: Management: JOSEPH URAVITCH (Ext. 5122)

Information Center: SALLIE P. CAUCHON (Ext. 5115)

DEPARTMENT OF DEFENSE

The Pentagon, Office of the Secretary, Washington, DC 20301-8000 (202, 545-6700)
Responsible for the security of the U.S. through establishment of integrated military policies and procedures relating to national defense. Programs to abate pollution, enhance the environment, and manage the natural resources on military lands are promulgated and monitored by the Department of Defense.
Secretary of Defense:
Assistant Secretary of Defense (Production and Logistics): JACK KATZEN
Deputy Assistant Secretary of Defense (Environment): WILLIAM H. PARKER (695-7820)
Deputy Director, Environmental Planning: CHRISTINA RAMSEY (325-2215)
Executive Director, Armed Forces Pest Management Board: COL. ROBERT CLEGERN, USAF (427-5191)

DEPARTMENT OF THE AIR FORCE

Washington, DC 20330
A comprehensive multiple-use natural resource program involving fish and wildlife, forestry, soil and water conservation and outdoor recreation has been conducted on Air Force lands since the mid-1950s. Current policy requires all installations with suitable land and water areas to develop as part of the overall land management plan a continuing program for the management and conservation of renewable natural resources.
Deputy Assistant Secretary of the Air Force for Environment, Safety and Occupational Health (SAF/RQ): GARY D. VEST (202, 697-9297)
Director of Engineering and Services (AF/LEE): MAJ. GEN. GEORGE E. ELLIS, HQ US Air Force, Washington, DC 20330 (202, 697-9221)
Chief, Environmental Division (AF/LEEV): COL. DONALD A. KANE, HQ USAF/LEEV, Bolling AFB, Washington DC 20332 (202, 767-4180)
Deputy Chief, Environmental Division: ERVIN J. BEDKER (202, 767-6240)
Chief, Natural Resources Branch (AF/LEEVN): DR. A. LUDLOW CLARK, HQ USAF/LEEV, Bolling AFB, Washington, DC 20332 (202, 767-3639)
Chief, Bird Aircraft Strike Hazard (BASH) Team: MAJ. RONALD L. MERRITT, HQ USAF/LEEV, Bolling AFB, Washington, DC 20332 (202, 767-9267)
BASH Team Ecologists: CAPT. ROBERT DEFUSCO (202, 767-9267); CAPT. ROBERT DOGAN (202, 767-9267); 2nd LT. SHELLEY ZUEHLKE (202, 767-9267)
Senior Staff Biologist: LTC. JAMES D. RIPLEY (202, 767-6242)
Senior Staff Agronomist: WAYNE FORDHAM (202, 767-3668)
Senior Staff Forester: DR. HAMP W. ECHOLS (202, 767-3668)
Senior Staff Entomologist: LT. COL. NEIL LAMB, HQ AFESC/DEMM, Tyndall AFB, FL 32403 (904, 283-6166)
Air Force Regional Civil Engineer: Eastern Region, Atlanta, GA 30303 (404, 331-6776); Chief, Environmental Planning Division: THOMAS SIMS, Central Region, Dallas, TX 75242 (214, 556-6439); Chief, Environmental Planning Division: LT. COL. JOHN MILLER, Western Region, San Francisco, CA 94111 (415, 556-6439); Chief, Environmental Planning Division: PHILLIP LAMMI

Major Air Commands:
Strategic Air Command, Offutt AFB, NE, Chief of Natural Resources: MICHAEL NEUZIL; Biologist: MICK SANDINE (402, 294-6324); Tactical Air Command, Langley AFB, VA, Natural Resources Manager: ROY BARKER (804, 764-4430); Forester: ERNEST LOONEY (804, 764-2071); Air Force Logistics Command, Wright-Patterson AFB, OH, Entomologist: MICHEAL CORNELIUS (513, 257-6939); Air Force Reserves, Robins AFB, GA, Community Planner: DEBBIE HOWARD-MARTINJAK (912, 926-5598); Air Training Command, Randolph AFB, TX, Agronomist: CLIFFORD NOVOSAD (512, 652-2594); Air Force Systems Command, Andrews AFB, MD, Natural Resources Planner: ERNEST LAGIMONIERE (301, 981-6341); Alaskan Air Command, Elmendorf AFB, AK, Chief, Environmental Planning: JAMES HOSTMAN (907, 552-4151); Military Airlift Command, Scott AFB, IL, Environmental Protection Specialist: PATRICIA CALLIOTT (618, 256-5764); Air Force Academy, CO, Chief of Natural Resources: MIKE BABLER; Biologist: Vacant (719, 472-3336); Pacific Air Forces, Hickam AFB, HI, Entomologist: JONATHAN T. KAJIWARA (808, 449-9824); Air Force Space Command, Peterson AFB, CO, Chief, Environmental Planning: GARY MAHER; (719, 554-5187); Air National Guard, Andrews AFB, MD, Planner: RICHARD MASSE (301, 981-4048)

Installations:
Anderson AFB, Guam, Biologist: BRUCE REINHARDT, Arnold Engineering Development Center, TN (671, 366-2101); Forester: MARK MORAN (615, 454-3230); Avon Park AFR, FL; Chief of Natural Resources: PAUL EBERSBACH (813, 452-4119); Wildlife Biologist: BOB PROGULSKE; Range Conservationist: SCOTT PENFIELD; Foresters: KURT OLSEN; SAM VAN HOOK; Barksdale AFB, LA, Chief of Natural Resources: JOHN HAYGOOD (318, 456-3353); Forester: BRUCE HOLLAND; Beale AFB, CA, Range Manager: JOHN THOMPSON, Davis-Monthan AFB, AZ (916, 634-4485); Biologist: JOHN A. THOMPSON (602, 748-4885); Eielson AFB, AK, Natural Resources Planner: GERALD VON RUEDEN (907, 377-5182); Elmendorf AFB, AK, Natural Resources Planner: ALLEN RICHMOND (907, 552-2282); Edwards AFB, CA, Natural Resources Planner: MICHAEL PHILLIPS (805, 277-8092); Eglin AFB, FL, Chief of Natural Resources: RICK McWHITE; Wildlife Biologist: CARL PETRICK (904, 882-4164); Goodfellow AFB, TX, Biologist: LYNDAL FISHER (915, 657-3470); Griffiss AFB, NY, Landscape Architects: BRUCE MERO, MIKE BAMBERGER (315, 330-2098); Hickam AFB, HI, Agronomist: TATSUO SAITO (808, 449-1831); Landscape Architect: WAYNE IWAMDT (808, 449-1662); Hill AFB, UT, Biologists: MURRAY SANT, MIKE KING (801, 777-2065); Keesler AFB, MS, Agronomist: LOUIS LANG (601, 377-2548); Kirtland AFB, NM, Range Conservationist: ROBERT DOW (505, 844-0951); Lackland AFB, TX, Biologist: LT. CHRIS FORMAN (512, 671-2901); Langley AFB, VA, Biologist: TOM WITTKAMP; Loring AFB, ME, Forester: DAVID STRAINGE (207, 999-2257); Lowry AFB, CO, Agronomist: THEODORE RUPLE (719, 370-3315); McChord AFB, WA, Forester: ROBERT MacDONALD (206, 984-3268); McClellan AFB, CA, Biologist: JERRY WILSON (916, 643-1250); McGuire AFB, NJ, Biologist: MARTIN EISENHART (609, 724-2770); Moody AFB, GA, Planner: CARLTON CRENSHAW (912, 333-3069); Mountain Home AFB, ID, Natural Resources Planner: JOHN EISEMAN (208, 828-2750); Myrtle Beach AFB, SC, Natural Resources Planner: Vacant; Nellis AFB, NV, Biologist: LES MONROE (702, 643-4287); New Boston AFB, NH, Forester: JOHN MITCHELL (603, 472-3911); Norton AFB,

CA, Natural Resources Planner: ROBERT ANDERSON (714, 382-3909); Osan AB,XR, Landscape Architect: OK MUX KWON (284-6601); Patrick AFB, FL, Agronomist/Entomologist: CLAY GORDON (305, 494-7288); Pease AFB, NH, Landscape Architect: DAVID NYLUND (603, 430-2586); Robins AFB, GA, Agronomist: BOBBY ELLIS (912, 926-6037); SARPMA, San Antonio, TX, Agronomist: JOHN MALENKY (512, 221-6274); Scott AFB, IL, Natural Resources Planner: WAYNE SIEFERT (618, 256-2092); Sheppard AFB, TX, Agronomist: LT. HYNIE (817, 851-2001); Travis AFB, CA, Natural Resources Planner: ROBERT HOLMES (707, 438-2264); Tinker AFB, OK, Planner: WARREN JONES (405, 734-3201); Tyndall AFB, FL, Forester: ROBERT BATES (904, 283-2641); Wildlife Biologist: Vacant; Vandenberg AFB, CA, Chief Natural Resources Planner: JAMES JOHNSTON (805, 866-1921); Natural Resources Planner: ALLAN NAYDOL (805, 866-9687); Natural Resources Planner: RICHARD NICHOLS; Wildlife Biologist: CAROLYN PALERMO; Range Conservationist: JEFFERY LINN; Ecologist: MIKE McELLIGOTT; Wright-Patterson AFB, OH, Natural Resources Planner: TERRI LUCAS (513, 257-6260); Yokota AB, JA, Landscape Architect: YUJI YAMAGUCHI (255-8123)

DEPARTMENT OF THE ARMY

Pentagon, Washington, DC 20310
Assistant Secretary of the Army, Installations, Logistics: JOHN W. SHANNON (202, 695-6527)
Deputy for Environment, Safety and Occupational Health: LEWIS D. WALKER (695-7824)

ARMY CORPS OF ENGINEERS, Office of the Chief of Engineers, Pulaski Bldg., 200 Mass Ave., NW, Washington, DC 20314
Chief of Engineers: LT. GEN. JOSEPH K. BRATTON (202, 272-0001)
Deputy Chief of Engineers: MAJ. GEN. RICHARD M. WELLS (202, 272-0002)
Chief, Public Affairs Office: COL. DONALD E. WILLIFORD (202, 272-0010)
Deputy Chief, Public Affairs Office: WARREN J. PAPIN (272-0011)
Assistant, Conservation Liaison: LU DUCHARME (202, 272-0011)

Civil Works
Director of Civil Works: M.G. JOHN WALL (272-0099)
Assistant Director, Environmental Programs: LT. COL. RONALD G. KELSEY (272-0104)
Chief Advisor of Environmental Policy: DR. BILL BURRIS (272-0104)
Recreation-Resource Management Branch Chief: DARRELL E. LEWIS (272-0247)
Natural Resource Management Section Chief: Vacant (272-0247)
Environmental Resources Branch:
    Chief, JOHN C. BELSHE (272-0131)
    Endangered Species Coordinator: JOHN B. BUSHMAN (272-0131)

Division and District Offices
Lower Mississippi Valley: P.O. Box 80, Vicksburg, MS 39180 (District Offices: 668 Federal Office Bldg., Memphis, TN 38103; P.O. Box 60267, New Orleans, LA 70160; 210 N. 12th St., St. Louis, MO 63101; P.O. Box 60, Vicksburg, MS 39180)
Missouri River: P.O. Box 103, Downtown Station, Omaha, NE

68101 (District Offices: 700 Federal Office Bldg., Kansas City, MO 64106; 6014 U.S. Post Office and Courthouse, Omaha, NE 68102)
New England: 424 Trapelo Rd., Waltham, MA 02154
North Atlantic: 90 Church St., New York, NY 10007 (District Offices: P.O. Box 1715, Baltimore, MD 21203; 26 Federal Plaza, New York, NY 10007; 803 Front St., Norfolk, VA 23510; U.S. Custom House, Philadelphia, PA 19106)
North Central: 536 S. Clark St., Chicago, IL 60605 (District Offices: 1776 Niagara St., Buffalo, NY 14207; 219 S. Dearborn St., Chicago, IL 60604; P.O. Box 1027, Detroit, MI 48231; Clock Tower Bldg., Rock Island, IL 61201; 1135 U.S. Post Office and Customhouse, St. Paul, MN 55101)
North Pacific: P.O. Box 2870, Portland, OR 97208 (District Offices: P.O. Box 7002, Anchorage, AK 99510; P.O. Box 2946, Portland, OR 97208; 4735 East Marginal Way South, Seattle, WA 98134; Bldg. 602, City-County Airport, Walla Walla, WA 99362)
Ohio River: P.O. Box 1159, Cincinnati, OH 45201 (District Offices: P.O. Box 2127, Huntington, WV 25721; P.O. Box 59, Louisville, KY 40201; P.O. Box 1070, Nashville, TN 37202; Federal Bldg., 1000 Liberty Ave., Pittsburgh, PA 15222)
Pacific Ocean: Bldg. 230, Ft. Shafter, HI, APO San Francisco, CA 96858
South Atlantic: 510 Title Bldg., Atlanta, GA 30303 (District Offices: P.O. Box 919, Charleston, SC 29402; P.O. Box 4970, Jacksonville, FL 32201; P.O. Box 2288, Mobile, AL 36628; P.O. Box 889, Savannah, GA 31402; P.O. Box 1890, Wilmington, NC 28402)
South Pacific: 630 Sansome St., San Francisco, CA 94111 (District Offices: P.O. Box 2711, Los Angeles, CA 90053; 650 Capitol Mall, Sacramento, CA 95814; 211 Main St., San Francisco, CA 94105)
Southwestern: 1114 Commerce St., Dallas, TX 75242 (District Offices: P.O. Box 1580, Albuquerque, NM 87103; P.O. Box 17300, Fort Worth, TX 76102; P.O. Box 1229, Galveston, TX 77553; P.O. Box 867, Little Rock, AR 72203; P.O. Box 61, Tulsa, OK 74102)

Military Construction
Director, Military Programs: MAJ. GEN. AMES S. ALBRO, JR. (693-6495)
Chief of Engineers' Environmental Advisory Board: Chairman, Dean, GERALD J. McLINDON, School of Environmental Design, Louisiana State University, Baton Rouge, LA 70803; DR. LAURENCE R. JAHN, Wildlife Management Institute, 1000 Vermont Ave., Washington, DC 20005; DR. NICHOLAS L. CLESCERI, Professor, Civil & Environmental Engineering, Rensselaer Polytechnic Institute

Waterways Experiment Station (WES), P.O. Box 631, Vicksburg, MS 39180-0631 (601, 634-3111)
Established in 1929, WES is a complex of six research laboratories employing over 1,500 and is the largest R&D facility of the U.S. Army Corps of Engineers. WES conducts research in a wide variety of areas, including environmental engineering, hyraulic engineering, coastal engineering, water resources, water quality, dredging operations, aquatic plant control, recreation, wetlands, environmental impacts, fisheries, wildlife management, hazardous wastes, analytical chemistry, land use management, applied remote sensing, and other areas.
Commander and Director: COL. DWAYNE LEE
Deputy Commander amd Director: LT. COL. JACK STEPHENS
Technical Director: DR. ROBERT WHALIN

ARMY TRAINING AND DOCTRINE COMMAND
Natural Resources Specialist: ROBERT L. ANDERSON, DCSENGR, U.S. Army Training and Doctrine Command, ATEN-FN, Fort Monroe, VA 23651 (804, 727-3335)
Forester: JAMES A. SABO, DCSENGR, U.S. Army Training and Doctrine Command, ATEN-FN, Fort Monroe, VA 23651 (804, 727-2265)

HQS U.S. ARMY EUROPE AND SEVENTH ARMY
Agronomist: JERRY L. HOUGH, P.O. DCSENGR, Attn: AEAEN-FE-E, APO 09403-0108

U.S. FORCES COMMAND
Forester: ROBERT DUCKWORTH, Office of the Engineer (ATTN: FCEN-RDF, ENGR. FORSCOM, Fort McPherson, GA 30330-6000 (404, 362-7143)

DEPARTMENT OF THE NAVY

NAVAL FACILITIES ENGINEERING COMMAND, Headquarters, 200 Stovall St., Alexandria, VA 22332-2300 (202, 325 plus extension)
Provides overall program management for natural resources on Navy lands.
Commander: REAR ADM. B.F. MONTOYA, CEC, USN (Ext. 0400)
Head, Natural Resources Branch and Navy Natural Resources Program Manager: LEWIS R. SHOTTON (Ext. 0427)
Forester: MARK E. DECOT (Ext. 0427)
Wildlife Biologist: Vacant
Soil Conservationist: LORRI A. SCHWARTZ (Ext. 0427)
Natural Resources Specialist: ANN L. ANDERSON (Ext. 0427)

Field Divisions
Northern Division, Natural Resources Branch Head: WILLIAM J. SUMMERS
Wildlife Biologist: CARL J. KELLER
Forester: HOWARD J. SCHLEGEL
Landscape Architect: Vacant
Naval Facilities Engineering Command, Code 243, Philadelphia, PA 19112 (215, 897-6207/6208)
Chesapeake Division, Natural Resources Branch Head: JOSEPH HAUTZENRODER
Forester: DWIGHT FIELDER
Soil Conservationist: JERI BERC
Wildlife Biologist: Vacant
Naval Facilities Engineering Command, Code 243, Washington Navy Yard, Bldg., 57, Washington, DC 20374 (202, 433-3586)
Atlantic Division, Fish and Wildlife Administrator: LARRY ADAMS (Ext. 2369)
Soil Conservationists: ARLA STRASSER (Ext. 2371)
Forester: GRAY N. LEINBACH (Ext. 2370)
Natural Resources Specialist: JEFFREY BOSSART (Ext. 2363)
Naval Facilities Engineering Command, Code 242, Norfolk, VA 23511 (804, 445 plus extension)
Southern Division, Natural Resources Branch Head: JAMES P. CLINE (Ext. 0588)
Wildlife Biologist: TOM BURST (Ext. 0590)
Soil Conservationists: JAMES A. COX (Ext. 0593); ANDY D. JOHNSON (Ext. 0589)
Foresters: WAYNE HOWARD (Ext. 0594); ELWYN A. SPENCE (Ext. 0591)
Naval Facilities Engineering Command, Code 243, P.O. Box 10068, Charleston, SC 29411-0499 (803, 743 plus extension)

Western Division, Natural Resources Branch Head: MICHAEL C. STROUD
Forester: Vacant
Wildlife Biologists: STEVEN D. KOVACK; PATRICIA WORTHING; DOUGLAS POMEROY
Soil Conservationists: JOHN LLOYD-REILLEY; RICHARD RUGEN; EDIE JACOBSON; MITCH PERDUE
Naval Facilities Engineering Command, Code 243, P.O. Box 727, San Bruno, CA 94066 (415, 877-7608/7609)
Pacific Division, Natural Resources Branch Head: THOMAS EGELAND
Wildlife Biologist: TIMOTHY SUTTERFIELD
Soil Conservationist: Vacant
Natural Resources Specialist: BRUCE D. EILERTS
Naval Facilities Engineering Command, Code 24B, Pearl Harbor, HI 96860 (808, 471-3217)
Naval Installation Personnel:
AFETA Camp Peary, VA: LEE ALLEN, Natural Resources Technician; DONALD SEAL, Natural Resources Technician; KENNETH AMOS, Natural Resources Technician
NWS Charleston, SC: CLIFF J. TOWNSEND, Natural Resources Manager; JAMES E. MOORE, Forestry Technician
NWC China Lake, CA: THOMAS McGILL, Environmental Branch Head; JERRY BOGGS, Environmental Resources Management Branch Head; BEVERLY KOHFIELD, Biologist; CAROLYN SHEPHERD, Environmental Protection Specialist; TOM CAMPBELL, Environmental Specialist; WILLIAM ECKHARDT, Archeologist
NWC Dahlgren, VA: THOMAS WRAY, Natural Resources Manager
NAEC Lakehurst, NJ: JOHN JOYCE, Soil Conservationist
NAS Lemoore, CA: THOMAS CLARK, Natural Resources Specialist
NAS Meridian, MS: CHARLES B. CUSHING, Forester; RUFUS A. RAWSON, Forest Technician
NAS Miramar, CA: MICHAEL SCOTT, Ecologist
NAS Cecil Field, FL: THOMAS G. SILCOX, Forester; STEVEN J. TAYLOR, Forestry Technician
NAS Chase Field, TX: C.L. WINSLETTE, Recreational Director
NSC Cheatham Annex, VA: WALTER E. FEUER, Natural Resources Technician
NAS Fallon, NV: LARRY JONES, Natural Resources Specialist
NES St. Inigoes, MD: Vacant, Natural Resources Manager
NOS Indian Head, MD: RICHARD LeCLERC, Forester
NWS Earle, Colts Neck, NJ: THOMAS GENTILE, Forester
NSB Bangor, WA: ART SCHICK, Forester; THOMAS JAMES, Wildlife Biologist
NSB Kings Bay, GA: ELIZABETH BISHOP, Wildlife Biologist; THOMAS REDDICK, Forestry Technician
NUWES Keyport, WA: DONALD MORRIS, Biologist
OICC Southwest San Diego, CA: MERRILY SEVERENCE, Natural Resources Specialist
NCBC Gulfport, MS: JAMES CLUFF, Environmental Engineer
NAS North Island, CA: JAN K. LARSON, Natural Resources Manager; ANDY YATSKO, Archeologist; LARRY SALADA, Biologist
NTC Orlando, FL: WILLIAM RASPIT, Environmentalist
NWSC Crane, IN: LYNN ANDREWS, Natural Resources Manager; TERRY HOBSON, Forester
NAS Patuxent River, MD: KYLE RAMBO, Natural Resources Manager; MIKE BRYANT, Wildlife Biologist; JIM SOBRACK, Forestry Technician
NAS Pensacola, FL: MARK GIBSON, Natural Resources Manager
PMTC Point Mugu, CA: RON DOW, Head, Environmental Section; MATT KLOPE, Biologist; JOE DiVITTORIO, Botanist

NS San Diego, CA: E. LOWELL MARTIN, Landscape Architect/Natural Resources Specialist

NWS Seal Beach, CA: JESSICA JOHNSON, Environmental Engineer

NWS Yorktown, VA: DAVID G. SHIELD, Special Assistant for Natural Resources; CHARLES WILSON, Forester

NAB Little Creek, VA: WILKIE DIN, Natural Resources; SHARON WALIGORA, Environmental Protection Specialist; JIM ADAIR, Game Warden

NAS Whidbey Island, WA: SHIELA ASHTON, Environmental and Natural Resources Coordinator

NWS Concord, CA: RANDY SCOTT, Natural Resources Coordinator

NSGA Northwest Chesapeake, VA: MIKE BRADBURY, Outdoor Recreation Specialist

NAS Oceana, VA: TERRY BERGLAND, Environmental/Energy Engineer; JEFF CHYZIK, Environmental/Energy Engineer

FCTC Dam Neck, VA: JIMMI BONAVITA, Park Technician

NOS Louisville, KY: LEE OGDEN, Energy/Environmental Engineer

NS Roosevelt Roads, PR: WINSTON MARTINEZ, Vieques Land Manager

U.S. MARINE CORPS, Headquarters, Washington, DC 20380-0001 (202, 697-1890/1891/1904/1909)
Natural Resources Management Officer: MARLO ACOCK (697-1904)
Program Analyst: THOMAS CODA
Marine Corps Installations:

MCDECFD Quantico, VA: JAMES MARSH, Director, Natural Resources and Environmental Affairs; BRUCE FRIZZELL, Base Forester; BILL CROSS, Assistant Forester; JOHN GIANNICO, Forestry Technician; TIM STAMPS, Wildlife Manager; MAC GARNER, Game Warden

MCB Camp Lejeune, NC: JULIAN I. WOOTEN, Natural Resources and Environmental Affairs Director; DANNY SHARPE, Supervisory Ecologist; SAMMY GWYNN, Environmental Protection Specialist; PETER E. BLACK, Base Forester; DANIEL BECKER, Assistant Base Forester; CHARLES D. PETERSON, Supervisory Biological Technician; ALBERT HENRY, Wildlife Biologist; THOMAS BARBE, Environmental Protection Specialist

MCAS Cherry Point, NC; DOUGLAS R. NELSON, Supervisory, Environmental Engineer; JOHN C. MEASE, Station Forester; WILLIAM ROGERS, Fish and Wildlife Manager; JAMES MANSFIELD, Forestry Technician

MCLB Albany, GA: VICKI DAVIS, Environmental/Natural Resources Specialist

MCAS Beaufort, SC: MIKE HERBAUGH, Natural Resources and Environmental Affairs Officer

MCRD Parris Island, SC: H.R. GARNETT, Natural Resources and Environmental Affairs Officer; GARY DUKES, Environmental Protection Specialist

MCB Camp Pendleton, CA: TIM BURR, Director, Natural Resources Office; SLADER BUCK, Wildlife Biologist/Game Warden; CLARK WINCHELL, Wildlife Biologist; DAWN LAWSON, Soil/Range Conservationist; LARRY CARLSON, Geologist

MCAS Yuma, AZ: CARL JOHNSON, Environmental and Natural Resources Coordinator

MCAGCC Twentynine Palms, CA: ROGER TWITCHELL, Natural Resources Manager; GARY ROBERTSON, Environmental Protection Specialist

MCAS Kaneohe Bay, HI: DIANE DRIGOT, Environmental Protection Specialist

DEPARTMENT OF EDUCATION

400 Maryland Ave., SW, Washington, DC 20202 (202, 732-4576)

DEPARTMENT OF ENERGY

Forrestal Bldg., 1000 Independence Ave., SW, Washington, DC 20585
Provides the framework for a comprehensive and balanced national energy plan through the coordination and administration of the energy functions of the federal government. The department is responsible for long-term, high-risk research and development of energy technology; the marketing of federal power; energy conservation; the nuclear weapons program; energy regulatory programs, and a central energy data collection and analysis program. Established by the Department of Energy Organization Act: 1977.
Secretary: JOHN S. HERRINGTON (202, 586-6210)
Deputy Secretary: WILLIAM F. MARTIN
Under Secretary: JOSEPH F. SALGADO
Assistant Secretary, Conservation and Renewable Energy: DONNA R. FITZPATRICK
Assistant Secretary, Environment, Safety and Health: MARY L. WALKER
Assistant Secretary (Acting), Fossil Energy: DONALD L. BAUER
Assistant Secretary (Acting), Nuclear Energy: JAMES W. VAUGHAN
Administrator, Energy Information Administration: HELMUT A. MERKLEIN

FEDERAL ENERGY REGULATORY COMMISSION, 825 N. Capitol St., NE, Washington, DC 20426 (202, 357 or 376 plus extension)
Established October 1, 1977, pursuant to the Department of Energy Organization Act of 1977, the Federal Energy Regulatory Commission regulates the interstate aspects of the electric power and natural gas industries and establishes rates for transporting oil by pipeline. The commission issues and enforces licenses for construction and operation of non federal hydroelectric power projects. The FERC also advises federal agencies on the merits of proposed federal multiple-purpose water development projects.
Chairman: MARTHA O. HESSE (357-8200)
Commissioners: CHARLES A. TRABANDT (357-8366); CHARLES G. STALON (357-8388)
Executive Director: Vacant (357-8300)
Secretary (Acting): LOIS D. CASHELL (357-8400)
Director of External Affairs: ROGER W. GALE (357-8004)
General Counsel: CATHERINE C. COOK (357-8000)
Director, Office of Economic Policy: DOUGLAS R. BOHI (357-8100)
Director, Office of Electric Power Regulation: J. STEVEN HEROD (376-9232)
Director (Acting), Hydropower Licensing: FRED E. SPRINGER (376-1768)
Director, Office of Pipeline and Producer Regulation: RICHARD P. O'NEILL (357-8500)

DEPARTMENT OF HEALTH AND HUMAN SERVICES

200 Independence Ave., SW, Washington, DC 20201
Secretary: OTIS R. BOWEN, M.D. (202, 245-7000)
Assistant Secretary for Health: ROBERT WINDOM (245-7694)

Assistant Secretary for Human Development Services (Acting): JEAN K. ELDER (245-7246)

Assistant Secretary for Public Affairs: STEPHANIE LEE-MILLER (245-1850)

Under Secretary: DON M. NEWMAN (245-7431)

Inspector General: RICHARD P. KUSSEROW (472-3148)

General Counsel: RONALD ROBERTSON (245-7741)

Visitors-Information Center: (245-6296)

Commissioner, Social Security Administration: DORCAS HARDY (245-6764)

Administrator, Health Care Financing Administration: WILLIAM ROPER, M.D. (245-6726)

FOOD AND DRUG ADMINISTRATION, 5600 Fishers Ln., Rockville, MD 20857 (301, 443 plus extension; information: Ext. 1544)

Protects the health of American consumers by enforcing federal laws which require that foods must be safe, pure and wholesome; human and veterinary drugs, biologies and therapeutic devices must be safe and effective; cosmetics and radiation-emitting products must be harmless; and that all these products must be honestly and informatively labeled and packaged.

Commissioner: FRANK E. YOUNG, M.D., Ph.D. (Ext. 2410)

Deputy Commissioner: JOHN NORRIS (Ext. 2400)

Associate Commissioner for Regulatory Affairs: JOSEPH P. HILE (Ext. 1594)

Associate Commissioner for Health Affairs (Acting): STUART NIGHTINGALE, M.D. (Ext. 6143)

Associate Commissioner for Management and Operations: GERALD F. MEYER (Ext. 3370)

Associate Commissioner for Public Affairs: JACK W. MARTIN

Director, Press Relations Staff, Office of Public Affairs: (Ext. 4177) WILLIAM M. GRIGG (Ext. 4177)

Associate Commissioner for Planning and Evaluation: GERALD L. BARKDOLL (Ext. 4230)

Associate Commissioner for Legislative Affairs: HUGH C. CANNON (Ext. 3793)

Associate Commissioner for Consumer Affairs: ALEX GRANT (Ext. 5006)

Executive Director of Regional Operations: DONALD HEALTON (Ext. 6230)

Director, Office of Public Affairs: Communications Staff, ROGER W. MILLER (Ext. 3220)

DEPARTMENT OF HOUSING AND URBAN DEVELOPMENT

451 7th St., SW, Washington, DC 20410 (202, 755 plus extension; information: Ext. 5111)

Secretary: SAMUEL R. PIERCE, JR. (Ext. 6417)

Under Secretary: CARL D. COVITZ (Ext. 7123)

Assistant Secretary for Community Planning and Development: Vacant (Ext. 6270)

Office of Environment and Energy: RICHARD H. BROUN, Director (Ext. 7894)

Deputy Under Secretary (Acting), Field Coordination: EDMUND R. DAVIS (Ext. 7426)

Assistant Secretary, Administration: JUDITH L. HOFMANN (Ext. 6940)

Assistant Secretary, Housing FHA Commissioner: THOMAS T. DEMERY (Ext. 6600)

Assistant Secretary, Police Dev. and Research: KENNETH BEIRNE (Ext. 5600)

Assistant Secretary, Fair Housing and Equal Opportunity: JUDITH Y. BRACHMAN (Ext. 7252)

Director for Public Affairs: JAYNE GALLAGHER (Ext. 6980)

Inspector General: PAUL A. ADAMS (Ext. 6430)

Assistant Secretary (Acting), Public and Indian Housing: JAMES E. BAUGH (Ext. 0950)

DEPARTMENT OF THE INTERIOR

Interior Bldg., C St. between 18th and 19th, NW, Washington, DC 20240 (202, 343 plus extension; information: Ext. 1100)

Secretary: DONALD PAUL HODEL (Ext. 7351)

Executive Assistant: DONALD H. PEARLMAN

Assistant to the Secretary and Director, Office of Public Affairs: DAVID PROSPERI

Assistant to the Secretary and Director, Office of Congressional and Legislative Affairs: J. STEPHEN BRITT

Under Secretary: Vacant

Principal Deputy to the Under Secretary: Vacant

Deputy Under Secretaries: J. LISLE REED

Director, Office for Equal Opportunity: CARMEN R. MAYMI

Director, Office of Hearings and Appeals: PAUL T. BAIRD

Solicitor: RALPH W. TARR

Deputy Solicitor: HOWARD H. SHAFFERMAN

Associate Solicitor (Acting), General Law: TIMOTHY S. ELLIOTT

Associate Solicitor, Conservation and Wildlife: Vacant

Associate Solicitor, Indian Affairs: TIMOTHY A. VOLLMANN

Associate Solicitor, Energy and Resources: Vacant

Associate Solicitor, Surface Mining: CHRISTOPHER CANNON

Associate Solicitor, Audit and Inspections: MAURICE O. ELLSWORTH

Assistant Secretary, Indian Affairs: ROSS O. SWIMMER

Deputy Assistant Secretary, Indian Affairs: Vacant

Director (Acting), Office of Administration: RONAL EDEN

Director, Office of Indian Education Programs: HENRIETTA WHITEMAN

Director, Office of Indian Services: HAZEL ELBERT

Director, Office of Trust Responsibilities: FRANK RYAN

Assistant Secretary for Fish, Wildlife, and Parks: WILLIAM P. HORN

Deputy Assistant Secretary: SUSAN RECCE

Director, United States Fish and Wildlife Service: FRANK H. DUNKLE

Director, National Park Service: WILLIAM PENN MOTT

Assistant Secretary, Land and Minerals Management: STEVEN GRILES

Deputy Assistant Secretaries: LEONA A. POWER, Commissioner, Bureau of Reclamation; C. DALE DUVALL

Director, Bureau of Land Management: ROBERT BURFORD

Deputy Assistant Secretary, Water and Science: Vacant

Director, Bureau of Mines: Vacant

Director, Geological Survey: DALLAS PECK

Director, Office of Surface Mining Reclamation and Enforcement: JED CHRISTENSEN

Assistant Secretary, Policy, Budget and Administration: Vacant

Deputy Assistant Secretaries: JOSEPH E. DODDRIDGE, JR.; JOSEPH W. GORRELL

Director, Office Information Resources Management: REED PHILLIPS

Chief, Office of Aircraft Services: JACK WILSON

Director, Office of Administrative Services: ALBERT C. CAMACHO

Director, Acquisition and Property Management: RONALD W. PIASECKI

Director, Office of Budget: ANTHONY L. ITTEILAG

Director, Office of Environmental Project Review: BRUCE BLANCHARD

Inspector General: JAMES R. RICHARDS

Chief, Division of Information and Library Services: PHILLIP M. HAYMOND

Director, Office of Youth Programs: DOYLE A. HUGHES

Director, Office of Personnel: MORRIS A. SIMMS

Director, Office of Policy Analysis: MARTIN L. SMITH

Assistant Secretary for Territorial and International Affairs: Vacant

Deputy Director Office of Administrative Services: ALBERT C. CAMACHO

Director, Minerals Management Service: WILLIAM D. BETTENBERG

BUREAU OF INDIAN AFFAIRS, 1951 Constitution Ave., NW, Washington, DC 20245 (202, 343-5116)

An agency in the federal government charged with carrying out the major portion of the trust responsibility of the United States to Indian tribes. This trust includes the protection and enhancement of Indian lands and natural resources through technical assistance in the fields of forest management, fish and wildlife management, water rights, range management, irrigation, soil and moisture conservation and management, and mineral resource management. Bureau created in War Department 1824; transferred to Department of the Interior 1949.

Assistant Secretary for Indian Affairs: ROSS O. SWIMNER (343-7163)

Deputy Assistant Secretary for Indian Affairs (Operations): WILLIAM P. RAGSDALE (343-5116)

Deputy to the Assistant Secretary for Indian Affairs (Trust and Economic Development) (Acting): RICHARD WHITESELL (343-5831)

Trust Resource Program Managers

Forestry: MARSHALL M. CUTSFORTH (343-6067)

Fish, Wildlife and Recreation: GARY L. RANKEL (343-4088)

Environment Services: GEORGE R. FARRIS (343-4541)

Water Resources: JOHN S. BUSHMAN (343-5893)

Energy and Minerals: DON AUBERTIN (Acting) (343-2792)

Soil Conservation: H.B. SIMPSON (343-3598)

Range Management: SAM MILLER (343-4004)

BUREAU OF LAND MANAGEMENT, U.S. Department of Interior, 18 and C Sts., NW, Rm 5600, Washington, DC 20240 (202, 343-5717 for information)

Administers the public lands which are located primarily in the western states and which amount to about 48 percent (over 272 million acres) of all federally owned lands. These lands and resources are managed under multiple-use principles, including outdoor recreation, fish and wildlife production, livestock grazing, timber, industrial development, watershed protection, and onshore mineral production. Organized: 1946. NOTE: Please see the state listing for Bureau of Land Management Districts on page 283.

Director: ROBERT F. BURFORD (343-3801)

Deputy Director: ROLAND G. ROBINSON (343-6731)

Director, Office of External Affairs: W. TIMOTHY LOCKE (343-1913)

Chief, Division of Public Affairs: Vacant (343-9435)

Assistant Director, Lands and Renewable Resources: DEAN STEPANEK (343-4896)

Chief, Division of Wildlife: J. DAVID ALMAND (653-9202)

Program Manager, Habitat: NEAL R. MIDDLEBROOK (653-9202)

Program Manager, Fisheries: MIKE KRAUS (653-9202)

Threatened and Endangered Species Coordinator: Vacant (653-9202)

Assistant Director, Energy and Mineral Resources: ROBERT H. LAWTON (343-4201)

Assistant Director, Support Services: Vacant (343-3897)

Assistant Director, Management Services: TOM ALLEN (343-4864)

Boise Interagency Fire Center

BLM Director: JACK F. WILSON, 3905 Vista Ave., Boise, ID 83705 (208, 334-9421)

Denver Service Center

Provides certain technical and administrative support to state offices.

Director: ROBERT MOORE, Denver Federal Center, Bldg. 50, Denver, CO 80225 (303, 236-6452)

State Directors

AK: MICHAEL J. PENFOLD, 701 C St., Box 13, Anchorage 99513 (907, 271-5076)

AZ: D. DEAN BIBLES, 3707 N. 7th St., P.O. Box 16563, Phoenix 85011 (602, 241-5501)

CA: EDWARD L. HASTEY, Federal Office Bldg., Rm. E-2841, 2800 Cottage Way, Sacramento 95825 (916, 978-4743)

CO: NEIL F. MORCK, 2850 Youngfield St., Lakewood 80215 (303, 236-1721)

ID: DELMAR D. VAIL, 3380 Americana Terr. Boise 83706 (208, 334-1401)

MT: Vacant, 222 N. 32nd St., P.O. Box 36800, Billings 59107 (406, 657-6461)

NV: EDWARD F. SPANG, 850 Harvard Way, P.O. Box 12000, Reno 89520 (702, 784-5451)

NM: LARRY WOODARD, Joseph M. Montoya Federal Bldg., South Federal Place, P.O. Box 19449, Santa Fe 87504 (505, 988-6030)

OR: CHARLES W. LUSCHER, 825 N.E. Multnomah St., (P.O. Box 2965), Portland 97208 (503, 231-6251)

UT: ROLAND G. ROBISON, JR., 324 South State St., Salt Lake City 84111-2303 (801, 524-5311)

WY: HILLARY ODEN, 2515 Warren Ave., (P.O. Box 1828), Cheyenne 82003 (307, 772-2326)

Eastern States: G. CURTIS JONES, JR., 350 S. Pickett St., Alexandria, VA 22304 (703, 274-0180)

BUREAU OF MINES, 2401 E St., NW, Washington, DC 20241 (202, 634 plus extension; information: Ext. 1004)

Conducts programs aimed at developing the information and technology essential to supplying the nation's mineral and material needs while minimizing harm to the environment, and to the workers involved. Pursues programs involving the acquisition and analysis of minerals data on a worldwide basis, and research to make mining and mineral processing safer, more productive, and more compatible with the effective use of all the nation's resources.

Director, Bureau of Mines: T.S. ARY

Deputy Director: DAVID S. BROWN

Chief Staff Officer: JOHN D. MORGAN, JR.

Chief, Office of Public Information: DAVID BARNA

Associate Director, Information and Analysis: Vacant

Associate Director, Research: DAVID R. FORSHEY

Research Director, Twin Cities Research Center: LEWIS V. WADE

Research Director, Rolla Research Center: DANTON L. PAULSON

Research Director, Reno Research Center: ARTHUR F. COLOMBO

Research Director, Albany Research Center: GEORGE J. DOOLEY III

Research Director, Tuscaloosa Research Center: Vacant

Research Director, Salt Lake City Research Center: STEPHEN D. HILL

Research Director, Pittsburgh Research Center: JOHN N. MURPHY

Research Director, Denver Research Center: EDWARD HOLLOP

Research Director, Spokane Research Center: DOUGLAS D. BOLSTAD

Associate Director, Finance and Management: ROBERT F. FAGIN

Assistant Director, Helium Operations: ARMOND A. SONNEK

BUREAU OF RECLAMATION, Washington, DC 20240 (202, 343-4991)

The U.S. Department of the Interior's Bureau of Reclamation was created by the Reclamation Act of 1902 to reclaim arid lands in the 17 western states. Through the development of such facilities as the Columbia Basin Project in Washington and the Central Valley Project in California, today, Reclamation provides water to more than 10 million acres of land. In addition, Reclamation projects provide municipal and industrial water, hydroelectric power, recreational opportunities, and fish and wildlife enhancement.

Commissioner, Washington Office: C. DALE DUVALL (343-4157)

Environment and Planning Branch: DICK PORTER (343-5501)

Assistant Commissioner, Administration and Liaison: W.C. KLOSTERMEYER (343-8081)

Director, Office of Public Affairs: CARL GAGLIARDI (343-4662)

Denver Office, Bldg. 67, Denver Federal Center, Denver, CO 80225 (303, 236 plus extension)

Deputy Commissioner: JOE D. HALL (236-9208)

Assistant Commissioner, Engineering and Research: DARRELL W. WEBBER (Ext. 6985)

Assistant Commissioner, Resources Management: TERRY P. LYNOTT (343-3289)

Director, Public Affairs Technical Services: Vacant

Public Affairs Specialist: LINDA K. WOODWORTH (Ext. 7000)

Chief (Acting), Ecological Resources Division: GEORGE H. WALLEN (Ext. 6778)

Regional Directors and Officials

Pacific Northwest Region:

Regional Director: JOHN W. KEYS III, P.O. Box 043, U.S. Court House, 550 W. Fort St., Boise, ID 83724 (208, 334-1908)

Regional Public Affairs Officer: STEPHEN WADE (208, 334-1938)

Regional Environmental Officer: DOUG JAMES (208, 334-1207)

Mid-Pacific Region:

Regional Director: DAVID G. HOUSTON, Federal Office Bldg., 2800 Cottage Way, Sacramento, CA 95825 (916, 978-5135)

Special Assistant to the Regional Director, Regional Public Affairs Officer: JASON PELTIER (916, 978-4919)

Regional Environmental Officer: RODERICK M. HALL (916, 978-5130)

Lower Colorado Region:

Regional Director: EDWARD M. HALLENBECK, P.O. Box 427, Boulder City, NV 89005 (702, 293-8411)

Regional Public Affairs Officer: JULIAN RHINEHART (702, 293-8419)

Regional Environmental Officer: WILLIAM E. RINNE (702, 293-8560)

Upper Colorado Region:

Regional Director: CLIFFORD I. BARRETT, P.O. Box 11568, Salt Lake City, UT 84147 (801, 524-5592)

Regional Public Affairs Officer: BARRY WIRTH (801, 524-5403)

Regional Environmental Officer: HAROLD N. SERSLAND (801, 524-5580)

Missouri Basin Region:

Regional Director: B.E. MARTIN, P.O. Box 36900, Billings, MT 59107-6900 (406, 657-6214)

Regional Public Affairs Officer: RODNEY J. OTTENBREIT, P.O. Box 36900, Billings, MT 59107-6900 (406, 657-6218)

Regional Environmental Affairs Officer: ROBERT L. SCHROEDER (406, 657-6558)

GEOLOGICAL SURVEY, U.S., National Center, Reston, VA 22092 (703, 648-4000)

This research agency of the Interior Department publishes and distributes maps and reports covering our nation's physical features and its mineral, fuel and water resources. Responsibilities include activities in topographic mapping, geology, water, energy and mineral resources and natural hazards. Personnel are stationed in Reston, Va., and at more than 300 field offices and two major regional centers in Denver, CO, and Menlo Park, CA. Established: 1879.

Director: DALLAS L. PECK (648-7411)

Associate Director: DOYLE G. FREDERICK (648-7412)

Public Affairs Officer: DONOVAN KELLY (648-4460)

NATIONAL PARK SERVICE, Interior Bldg., P.O. Box 37127, Washington, DC 20013-7127 (202, 343 plus extension; Information: Ext. 6843)

Administers parks, monuments, and other administrative classifications of national significance for their recreational, historic and natural values. Manages landmarks programs for natural and historic properties; coordinates Wild and Scenic Rivers System and National Trail System; administers study and grants programs. NOTE: Please see the state listing of National Parks on page 281, and the National Seashores on page 282.

Director: WILLIAM PENN MOTT, JR. (Ext. 4621)

Deputy Director: DENIS P. GALVIN (Ext. 5081)

Associate Director, Park Operations: ROBERT G. STANTON (Ext. 5651)

Associate Director, Natural Resources: DR. F. EUGENE HESTER (Ext. 5193)

Associate Director, Policy, Budget and Administration: EDWARD L. DAVIS (Ext. 6741)

Deputy Associate Director, Policy, Budget and Administration: DANIEL SALISBURY (Ext. 2002)

Assistant Director, Personnel and Administrative Services: RICHARD E. POWERS (Ext. 8855)

Office of Legislative and Congressional Affairs: G. ROBERT WALLACE (Ext. 5883)

Associate Director, Planning and Development: GERALD D. PATTEN (Ext. 6741)

Chief, Office of Public Affairs: GEORGE J. BERKLACY (Ext. 6843)

Chief, Division of Media Information: DUNCAN MORROW (Ext. 7394)

Associate Director, Cultural Resources: JERRY L. ROGERS (Ext. 7625)

Assistant Director, Archeology: BENNIE C. KEEL (Ext. 1878)

Manager, Harpers Ferry Center: DAVID G. WRIGHT (304, 535-6588)

Manager, Denver Service Center: Vacant (303, 234-8729)

Regional Directors

Mid-Atlantic: JAMES W. COLEMAN, 143 S. Third St., Philadelphia, PA 19106 (215, 597-7013)

North Atlantic: HERBERT S. CABLES, JR., 15 State St., Boston, MA 02109 (617, 223-3769)

Southeast: ROBERT W. BAKER, 75 Spring St., SW, Atlanta, GA 30303 (404, 221-5185)

Midwest: DON H. CASTLEBERRY, 1709 Jackson St., Omaha, NE 68102 (402, 221-3431)

Southwest: JOHN E. COOK, Old Santa Fe Trail, P.O. Box 728, Santa Fe, NM 87501 (505, 988-6388)

Rocky Mountain: L. LORRAINE MINTZMYER, P.O. Box 25287, Denver, CO 80225 (303, 236-8700)

Western: STANLEY T. ALBRIGHT, 450 Golden Gate Ave., P.O. Box 36063, San Francisco, CA 94102 (415, 556-4196)

Pacific Northwest: CHARLES ODEGAARD, 1920 Westin Bldg., 2001 Sixth Ave., Seattle, WA 98121 (206, 442-5565)

National Capital: MANUS J. FISH, 1100 Ohio Dr., SW, Washington, DC 20242 (202, 426-6612)

Alaska: BOYD EVISON, 2525 Gambell St., Rm. 107, Anchorage 99503 (907, 261-2690)

OFFICE OF SURFACE MINING RECLAMATION AND ENFORCEMENT, 1951 Constitution Ave., NW, Washington, DC 20240

Established by the Surface Mining Control and Reclamation Act of 1977 to administer the nationwide program to protect society and the environment from adverse side effects of coal mining operations, to establish national standards for regulating the surface environmental effects of coal mining, to support state implementation of such regulatory programs, and to promote reclamation of previously mined areas.

Director: JED CHRISTENSEN (202, 343-4006)

Deputy Director for Administration and Finance: ROBERT BOLDT (343-4222)

Deputy Director for Operations and Technical Services: JAMES WORKMAN (343-2107)

Special Assistant to the Director: KATHY BROCATO (343-4006)

Assistant Director, Program Operations: BRENT WAHLQUIST (343-4264)

Assistant Director, Eastern Field Operations: CARL CLOSE (412, 726-2828)

Assistant Director, Western Field Operations: RAY LOWRIE (303, 844-2459)

Assistant Director, Budget and Administration: CARSON CULP (343-4293)

Assistant Director, Finance and Accounting: ROBERT EWING (343-2160)

Assistant Director (Acting), Information Systems Management: MARK BOSTER (343-1150)

Chief, Congressional Liaison: NANCY SMITH (343-2165)

Chief, Public Affairs: ALAN COLE

UNITED STATES FISH AND WILDLIFE SERVICE, Washington, DC 20240 (202, 343 plus extension)

Effective July 1, 1974, an act of Congress (Public Law 93-271, April 22, 1974) renamed the Bureau of Sport Fisheries and Wildlife, the United States Fish and Wildlife Service, under the Assistant Secretary for Fish and Wildlife and Parks. The service is the lead federal agency in the conservation of the nation's migratory birds, endangered species, certain mammals, and sport fishes. This includes application of research findings in the development and management of a system of national wildlife refuges for migratory birds and endangered species; operation of a system of fish hatcheries; management of populations of migratory game birds through regulation of time, degree, and manner of taking; acquisition and application of technical knowledge necessary for perpetuation and enhancement of fish and wildlife resources; biological monitoring of development projects; enforcement of several laws including the Endangered Species Act, the Lacey Act, the Marine Mammal Protection Act, and the Migratory Bird Treaty Act. The service administers federal aid to state governments; provides technical assistance to state and foreign governments; serves as lead federal agency in international conventions on wildlife conservation; and operates a program of public affairs and environmental education to inform the public of the status of America's fish and wildlife resources. NOTE: Please see the state listing for National Wildlife Refuges on page 273.

Director: FRANK H. DUNKLE (Ext. 4717)

Deputy Director: STEVE ROBINSON (Ext. 4545)

Office of Human Resources, Chief: JEROME M. BUTLER (Ext. 3195)

Assistant Director, Fish and Wildlife Enhancement: RALPH O. MORGENWECK (Ext. 4647)

Deputy Assistant Director, Fish and Wildlife Enhancement: ROBERT P. SMITH (Ext. 4646)

Division of Endangered Species and Habitat Conservation: WILLIAM E. KNAPP (Ext. 3245)

Division of Environmental Contaminants, Chief (Acting): JOHN BLANKENSHIP (Ext. 5685)

Division of Federal Aid, Chief: CONLEY MOFFETT (703, 235-1526)

Office of Management Authority, Chief: MARSHALL JONES (703, 235-1937)

Assistant Director, Refuges and Wildlife: MARVIN L. PLENERT (Ext. 5333)

Deputy Assistant Director (Acting), Refuges and Wildlife: JOHN ROGERS (Ext. 5333)

Division of Refuge Management, Chief: Vacant (Ext. 4311)

Division of Realty, Chief: WILLIAM F. HARTWIG (653-7650)

Division of Law Enforcement, Chief: CLARK R. BAVIN (Ext. 9242)

Office of Migratory Bird Management, Chief: DR. ROLLIN D. SPARROWE (254-3207)

Assistant Director (Acting), Fisheries: H. DALE HALL (Ext. 6394)

Deputy Assistant Director (Acting): LYNN STARNES (Ext. 4266)

National Fisheries Academy: WENDELL S. OGDEN, Superintendent, Box 700, Kearneysville, WV 25430 (304, 725-8461)

Division of National Fish Hatcheries, Chief: JOSEPH WEBSTER (653-8746)

Division of Fish and Wildlife Management Assistance, Chief (Acting): DANIEL BUMGARNER (632-7463)

Assistant Director, External Affairs: JOSEPH (Sam) MARLER (343-2500)

Office of Public Affairs, Chief: PHIL MILLION (Ext. 4131)

Office of International Affairs, Chief: LAWRENCE N. MASON (5188)

Office of Legislative Services, Chief: OWEN AMBUR (Ext. 5403)

Assistant Director, Policy, Budget, and Administration: JAY L. GERST (Ext. 4888)

Deputy Assistant Director (Acting), Policy, Budget, and Administration: JAMES C. LEUPOLD (Ext. 4329)

Division of Budget and Analysis, Chief: KATHLEEN F. TYNAN (Ext. 2444)

Division of Policy and Directives Management, Chief: JOHN R. CARACCIOLO (Ext. 4633)

Division of Finance, Chief: H. HOWARD HULBERT (Ext. 8991)

Division of Personnel, Chief: EDWARD CYNAR (Ext. 6104)

Division of Information Resources Management, Chief: PHILLIP DAWSON (202, 653-8770)

Office of Safety, Security, and Aircraft Management, Chief: FREEMAN WALKER, JR. (653-7912)

Division of Contracting and General Services, Chief: JOEL G. GREENSTEIN (653-8703)

FWS Finance Center, Chief: JOHN O'GRADY, Denver Federal Center, P.O. Box 25207, Denver, CO 80225-0207 (303, 236-2331)

Northwest Regional Office (CA, HI, ID, NV, OR, WA), 500 NE Multnomah St., Suite 1692, Portland, OR 97232

Regional Director (Acting), Region 1: GARY EDWARDS (503, 231-6118)

Deputy Regional Director: ERWIN W STEUCKE (503, 231-6122)

Associate Regional Director: LAWRENCE W. DeBATES (503, 231-6122)

Assistant Regional Director, Public Affairs: DIANE HOOBLER (503, 231-6121)

Assistant Regional Director (Acting), Refuges and Wildlife: JOHN DOEBEL (503, 231-6214)

Assistant Regional Director, Fishery Resources: WILLIAM F. SHAKE (503, 231-5967)

Assistant Regional Director, Fish and Wildlife Enhancement: DAVID F. RILEY (503, 231-6159)

Assistant Regional Director, Administration: DON WEATHERS (503, 231-6115)

Assistant Regional Director, Law Enforcement: DAVID L. McMULLEN (503, 231-6125)

Southwest Regional Office (AZ, NM, OK, TX), 500 Gold Ave., SW, Rm. 3018, Albuquerque, NM 87102

Regional Director, Region 2: MICHAEL J. SPEAR (505, 766-2321)

Deputy Regional Director: RUSSELL D. EARNEST (505, 766-2322)

Assistant Regional Director, Public Affairs: THOMAS M. SMYLIE (505, 766-3940)

Assistant Regional Director, Refuges and Wildlife: JOSEPH P. MAZZONI (505, 766-2324)

Assistant Regional Director, Fishery Resources and Federal Assistance: CONRAD A. FJETLAND (505, 766-2323)

Assistant Regional Director, Fish and Wildlife Enhancement: JAMES A. YOUNG (505, 766-2324)

Assistant Regional Director, Administration: PAT LANGLEY (505, 766-1888)

Assistant Regional Director, Law Enforcement: JOHN E. CROSS (505, 766-2091)

Great Lakes Regional Office (IA, IL, IN, MI, MN, MO, OH, WI), Federal Bldg., Fort Snelling, Twin Cities, MN 55111

Regional Director, Region 3: JAMES C. GRITMAN (612, 725-3563)

Deputy Regional Director: MARVIN E. MORIARTY (612, 725-3503)

Assistant Regional Director, Public Affairs: GEORGE SURA (612, 725-3519)

Assistant Regional Director, Refuges and Wildlife: JOHN R. EADIE (612, 725-3507)

Assistant Regional Director, Fisheries and Federal Aid: JOHN S. POPOWSKI (612, 725-3505)

Assistant Regional Director, Fish and Wildlife Enhancement: GERALD R. LOWRY (612, 725-3510)

Assistant Regional Director, Budget and Administration: THOMAS J. KERZE (612, 725-3568)

Assistant Regional Director, Law Enforcement: LARRY L. HOOD (612, 725-3530)

Southeast Regional Office (AL, AR, FL, GA, KY, LA, MS, NC, PR, SC, TN, VI), Richard B. Russell Federal Bldg., 75 Spring St., SW, Rm. 1200, Atlanta, GA 30303

Regional Director, Region 4: JAMES W. PULLIAM, JR. (404, 331-3588)

Deputy Regional Director: DAVID B. ALLEN (404, 331-3588)

Assistant Regional Director, Public Affairs: DONALD W. PFITZER (404, 331-3594)

Assistant Regional Director, Refuges and Wildlife: HAROLD W. BENSON (404, 331-0833)

Assistant Regional Director, Fisheries and Federal Aid: JOHN T. BROWN (404, 331-3576)

Assistant Regional Director, Fish and Wildlife Enhancement: W.T. OLDS, JR. (404, 331-6343)

Assistant Regional Director, Budget and Administration: FRANCIS J. PRATT (404, 331-3591)

Assistant Regional Director, Law Enforcement: DANNY M. SEARCY (404, 331-5872)

Northeast Regional Office (CT, DC, DE, MA, MD, ME, NH, NJ, NY, PA, RI, VA, VT, WV), One Gateway Ctr., Suite 700, Newton Corner, MA 02158 (617, 965-5100 plus extension)

Regional Director, Region 5: RONALD E. LAMBERTSON (Ext. 200)

Deputy Regional Director: JAMES F. GILLETT (Ext. 200)

Assistant Regional Director, Public Affairs: INEZ E. CONNOR (Ext. 206)

Assistant Regional Director, Refuges and Wildlife: DONALD YOUNG (Ext. 222)

Assistant Regional Director, Fisheries and Federal Assistance: JAMES E. WEAVER (Ext. 208)

Assistant Regional Director, Fish and Wildlife Enhancement: RALPH PISAPIA (Ext. 217)

Assistant Regional Director, Administration: DALE COGGESHALL (Ext. 235)

Assistant Regional Director, Law Enforcement: A. EUGENE HESTER (Ext. 254)

Rocky Mountain Regional Office (CO, KS, MT, ND, NE, SD, UT, WY), 134 Union Blvd., P.O. Box 25486, Denver Federal Ctr., Denver, CO 80225

Regional Director, Region 6: GALEN L. BUTERBAUGH (303, 236-7920)

Deputy Regional Director: JOHN L. SPINKS, JR. (303, 236-7920)

Associate Regional Director: KRIS LAMONTAGNE (303, 236-7909)

Assistant Regional Director, Public Affairs: JACK HALLOWELL (303, 236-7904)

Assistant Regional Director, Refuges and Wildlife: NELSON B. KVERNO (303, 236-8145)

Assistant Regional Director, Fisheries and Federal Aid: WILLIAM E. MARTIN (303, 236-8154)

Assistant Regional Director, Fish and Wildlife Enhancement: ROBERT D. JACOBSEN (303, 236-8189)

Assistant Regional Director, Budget and Administration: ELLIOTT N. SUTTA (303, 236-7917)

Assistant Regional Director, Law Enforcement: TERRY L. GROSZ (303, 236-7540)

Alaska Regional Office (AK), 1011 E. Tudor Rd., Anchorage, AK 99503

Regional Director, Region 7: WALTER O. STIEGLITZ (907, 786-3542)

Deputy Regional Director: DAVID L. OLSEN (907, 786-3543)

Assistant Regional Director, Public Affairs: BRUCE T. BATTEN (907, 786-3486)

Assistant Regional Director, Refuges and Wildlife: JOHN P. ROGERS (907, 786-3538)

Assistant Regional Director, Fish and Wildlife Enhancement: ROWAN GOULD (907, 786-3522)

Assistant Regional Director, Administration: EDWARD R. WHITE (907, 786-3489)

Assistant Regional Director, Law Enforcement: R. DAVID PURINTON (907, 786-3311)

Research and Development Regional Office: 18th and C Streets, NW, Washington, DC 20240

Regional Director, Region 8: RICHARD N. SMITH (202, 653-8791)

Deputy Regional Director: DR. JOHN D. BUFFINGTON (202, 653-8791)

Office of Scientific Authority, Chief: DR. CHARLES W. DANE (653-5948)

Office of Extension Education and Publications: DUNCAN MacDONALD (653-8787)

Wildlife Research Laboratories

Patuxent Wildlife Research Center: HAROLD O'CONNOR, Director, Laurel, MD 20708 (301, 498-0300)

Northern Prairie Wildlife Research Center: DR. REY C. STENDELL, Director, P.O. Box 2096, Jamestown, ND 58402 (701, 252-5363)

National Fisheries Research Center-Leetown: JAN RIFFE, Director, Box 700, Kearneysville, WV 25430 (304, 725-8461)

National Fisheries Research Center, La Crosse: DR. FRED P. MEYER, Director, P.O. Box 818, La Crosse, WI 54601 (608, 783-6451)

National Fisheries Contaminant Research Center: DR. RICHARD A. SCHOETTGER, Director, R.D. 1, Columbia, MO 65202-0818 (314, 875-5399)

National Fisheries Research Center, Seattle; DR. ALFRED C. FOX, Director, Bldg. 204, Naval Station, Seattle, WA 98115-5007 (206, 526-6282)

National Fisheries Research Center, Great Lakes: DR. JON G. STANLEY, Director, 1451 Green Rd., Ann Arbor, MI 48105 (313, 994-3331)

National Wildlife Health Research Center: DR. MILTON FRIEND, Director, 6006 Schroeder Rd., Madison, WI 53711 (608, 271-4640)

Alaska Fish and Wildlife Research Center: A.W. PALMISANO, Director, 1011 E. Tudor Rd., Anchorage, AK 99503 (907, 786-3512)

Cooperative Fish and Wildlife Research Unit Center: EDWARD P. LaROE, Director, Matomic Bldg., MS: Rm. 527, Washington, DC 20240 (202, 653-8718)

National Ecology Research Center: Director, Vacant, 2627 Redwing Rd., Creekside One, Ft. Collins, CO 80526 (303, 226-9230)

National Fisheries Research Center, Gainesville: JAMES A. McCANN, Director, 7920 NW 71st St., Gainesville, FL 32606 (904, 378-8181)

National Wetlands Research Center: ROBERT E. STEWART, JR., Director, NASA--Slidell Computer Complex, 1010 Gause Blvd., Slidell, LA 70458 (504, 646-7295)

NOTE: Cooperative research units are listed under the states in which they are located.

DEPARTMENT OF JUSTICE

Land and Natural Resources Division, Rm. 2143, 10th St. and Constitution Ave., NW, Washington, DC 20530 (202, 633 2701)

The responsibilities of the Land and Natural Resources Division include litigation involving the protection and enhancement of the American environment and wildlife resources; the acquisition, administration and disposition of public land, water and mineral resources; and the safeguarding of Indian rights and property.

Assistant Attorney General: ROGER J. MARZULLA (633-2701)

Deputy Assistant Attorney General: JAMES L. BYRNES (633-3237)

Deputy Assistant Attorney General: RICHARD J. LEON (633-5242)

Deputy Assistant Attorney General: MYLES E. FLINT (633-2718)

Executive Assistant: GARY PETERSON (272-9888)

Appellate Section, Chief: PETER R. STEENLAND (633-2748)

Indian Resources Section, Chief: HANK MESHORER (272-4111)

Wildlife and Marine Resources Section, Chief: DONALD CARR (633-1811)

Environmental Defense Section, Chief: MARGARET N. STRAND (633-2219)

Land Acquisition Section, Chief: WILLIAM J. KOLLINS (272-6776)

Policy, Legislation and Special Litigation Section, Chief: ANNE SHIELDS (633-2714)

General Litigation Section, Chief: WILLIAM M. COHEN (272-6851)

Environmental Enforcement Section, Chief: DAVID T. BUENTE (633-5271)

Environmental Crimes Section, Chief: JUDSON W. STARR (272-9877)

DEPARTMENT OF LABOR

200 Constitution Ave., NW, Washington, DC 20210 (202, 523-6666)

Secretary: ANNE McLAUGHLIN (202, 523-8271)

Deputy Secretary: DENNIS WHITFIELD

Mine Safety and Health Administrator (Acting): DAVID C. O'NEAL

JOB CORPS, Employment and Training Administration, Frances Perkins Bldg., 200 Constitution Ave., NW, Washington, DC 20210

Authorized by the Job Training Partnership Act, the program includes conservation centers known as Civilian Conservation Centers, located primarily in rural areas and operated for the Department of Labor by the Departments of Agriculture and Interior conservation agencies. In addition to providing training and other assistance to young people, the programs of work experience, training, and remedial education are focused upon activities to conserve, develop, or manage public resources or public recreational areas or to assist in developing community projects in the public interest.

Director: PETER E. RELL (202, 535-0550)

Senior Community Service Employment Program, Employment and Training Administration, Frances Perkins Bldg., 200 Constitution Ave., NW, Washington, DC 20210

Provides part-time subsidized employment for older adults past 55 years of age. Program participants are employed by nonprofit or public agencies. Much of the work is beautification and conservation work in rural areas.

Administrator: PAUL A. MAYRAND (535-0500)

MINE SAFETY AND HEALTH ADMINISTRATION, 4015 Wilson Blvd., Arlington, VA 22203 (703, 235-1452)

Objectives are to administer the Federal Mine Safety and Health Act, thereby promoting safety and health in the mining industry, preventing disasters, and protecting the health and safety of the nation's miners.

Assistant Secretary: ALAN C. McMILLAN (235-1385)

Deputy Assistant Secretary: THOMAS J. SHEPICH (235-2600)

Office of Standards, Regulations and Variances: PATRICIA W. SILVEY (235-1910)

Office of Information and Public Affairs: WAYNE E. VENEMAN, Director (235-1452)

Administrator, Coal Mine Health and Safety: JERRY L. SPICER (235-9423)

Administrator, Metal and Nonmetal Mine Health and Safety: ROY L. BERNARD (235-1565)

Director, Educational Policy and Development: JOHN C. ENGLISH (235-1515)

Director of Administration and Management: MARGE BURTON (235-1383)

Office of Congressional and Legislative Affairs: HARRISON J. COMBS, Chief (235-1392)

DEPARTMENT OF STATE

2201 C St., NW, Washington, DC 20520 (202, 634-3600)
Secretary: JAMES BAKER
Under Secretary for Security Assistance, Science, and Technology: EDWARD J. DERWINSKI

Bureau of Oceans and International Environmental and Scientific Affairs
Has principal responsibility for formulating and implementing policies and proposals for the scientific and technological aspects of U.S. relations with other governmental and international organizations and for dealing with a broad range of foreign policy issues relating to oceans, fisheries, environment, tropical forests, biological diversity, wildlife population, nuclear energy, new energy technology, space and other fields of advanced technology.
Assistant Secretary: FREDERICK M. BERNTHAL (Ext. 1554)
Principal Deputy Assistant Secretary: RICHARD J. SMITH (Ext. 1555)
Coordinator of Population Affairs: NANCY OSTRANDER (Ext. 3472)
Deputy Assistant Secretary for Oceans and Fisheries Affairs: EDWARD E. WOLFE (Ext. 2396)
Office of Ocean Affairs, Director: TUCKER R. SCULLY (Ext. 3262)
Office of Fisheries Affairs, Director: LARRY L. SNEAD (Ext. 2335)
Deputy Assistant Secretary for Environment, Health and Natural Resources: WILLIAM A. NITZE (Ext. 2232)
Director, Office of Ecology, Health and Natural Resources: WALTER LOCKWOOD (Ext. 2418)
Deputy Director, Office of Ecology, Health and Natural Resources: CHARLES CISSEL (Ext. 3367)
International Wildlife Officer: MARK WILLIS (Ext. 4824)
Deputy Assistant Secretary for Nuclear Energy and Energy Technology Affairs: RICHARD J.K. STRATFORD (Ext. 4360)
Deputy Assistant Secretary for Science and Technology Affairs: PETER JON de VOS (Ext. 3004)

DEPARTMENT OF TRANSPORTATION

400 7th St., SW, Washington, DC 20590 (202, 366-4000)
Composed of these main elements: the United States Coast Guard, Federal Aviation Administration, Federal Highway Administration, Federal Railroad Administration, Maritime Administration, St. Lawrence Seaway Development Corporation, National Highway Traffic Safety Administration, Urban Mass Transportation Administration, and Research and Special Programs Administration. Major objectives are to develop and improve a coordinated national transportation system consistent with other national objectives such as environmental protection, and to stimulate technological advances in the industry, preserving the nation's free enterprise transportation network. Employees: approximately 96,000. Established: April 1, 1967.
Secretary: JAMES BURNLEY (366-1111)
Deputy Secretary: Vacant (366-2222)
Assistant Secretary for Governmental Affairs: REBECCA RANGE (366-4573)
Office of Technology and Planning Assistance, Director: ALFONSO B. LINHARES (366-4208)
Assistant Secretary for Public Affairs: DALE PETROSKEY (366-4570)
Assistant Secretary for Policy and International Affairs: MATTHEW V. SCOCOZZA (366-4544)
Office of Economics: RICHARD WALSH, Director (366-4416)

Office of Transportation Regulatory Affairs: JOSEPH CANNY, (366-4220)
Environmental Division: EUGENE L. LEHR, Chief (366-4366)
Assistant Secretary for Budget and Programs: JANET HALE (366-9191)
General Counsel: WAYNE VANCE (366-4702)
Assistant Secretary for Administration: JON H. SEYMOUR (366-2332)
Inspector General: JOHN W. MELCHNER (366-1959)

COAST GUARD, U.S. Coast Guard, 2100 2nd St., SW, Washington, DC 20593-0001 (202, 267-2229)
Commandant: ADM. PAUL A. YOST (267-2390)
Vice Commandant: VADM. CLYDE T. LUSK, JR. (267-2385)
Chief of Staff: RADM. A BRUCE BERAN (267-1642)
Chief, Office of Acquistion: RADM. ERNEST B. ACKLIN (267-2007)
Resource Director/Comptroller: RADM. MARSHALL E. GILBERT (267-1088)
Chief, Office of Engineering: RADM. ROBERT L. JOHANSON (267-1844)
Office of the Chief Counsel: RADM. JOSEPH E. VORBACH (267-1616)
Chief, Office of Merchant Marine Safety Security and Environmental Protection: RADM. JOEL D. SIPES (426-2200)
Chief, Office of Operations: RADM. HOWARD B. THORSEN (267-0977)
Chief, Office of Health Services: EDWARD F. BLASSER, USPHS (366-0852)
Chief, Office of Navigation Safety and Waterways Services: RADM. ROBERT T. NELSON (267-2267)
Chief, Office of Personnel and Training: RADM. THOMAS T. MATTESON (267-0905)
Chief, Office of Command, Control and Communications: RADM. RONALD M. POLANT (755-2767)
Chief, Office of Readiness and Reserve: RADM. PAUL A. WELLING (267-2350)

FEDERAL AVIATION ADMINISTRATION, 800 Independence Ave., SW, Washington, DC 20591 (202, 267-3484)
Charged with regulating air commerce to foster aviation safety; promoting civil aviation and a national system of airports; achieving efficient use of navigable airspace; and developing and operating a common system of air traffic control and air navigation for both civilian and military aircraft.
Administrator: T. ALLAN McARTOR (267-3111)
Deputy Administrator: BARBARA BARRETT McCONNELL (267-8111)
Associate Administrator for Administration: BROOKS C. GOLDMAN (267-8078)
Associate Administrator for Human Resource Management: HERBERT R. McLURE (267-3456)
Associate Administrator for Policy and International Aviation: Vacant (267-9110)
Federal Air Surgeon: ROBERT McMEEKIN (267-3535)
Associate Administrator for Airports: ROBERT L. DONAHUE (267-9471)
Assistant Administrator for Public Affairs: KATHLEEN HARRINGTON (267-3883)
Chief Counsel: GREGORY WALDEN (267-3222)
Director of Environment and Energy (Acting): JAMES E. DENSMORE (267-3576)

FEDERAL HIGHWAY ADMINISTRATION, Washington Headquarters, 400 7th St., SW, Washington, DC 20590
Charged with carrying out the Department of Transportation responsibilities concerned with the highway mode of land transport,

has the primary missions of ensuring that the nation's highway transportation system is safe, economic, and efficient with respect to the movement of people and goods, while giving full consideration to the highway's impact on the environment and social and economic conditions.

Administrator: ROBERT E. FARRIS (202, 366-0650)
Deputy Administrator: LOWELL B. JACKSON (366-2240)
Executive Director: RICHARD D. MORGAN (366-2242)
Chief Counsel: ANTHONY J. McMAHON (366-0740)
Director, Office of Public Affairs: GARY HOITSMA (366-0660)
Director, Office of Civil Rights: EDWARD W. MORRIS, JR. (366-0693)
Associate Administrator for Policy: RICHARD B. ROBERTSON (366-0585)
Associate Administrator for Administration: GEORGE S. MOORE, JR. (366-0604)
Associate Administrator for Safety Second Operations: MARSHALL JACKS, JR. (366-2149)
Associate Administrator for Right-of-Way and Environment: ANTHONY R. KANE (366-0100)
Associate Administrator for Engineering and Program Development: RONALD E. HEINZ (366-0371)
Associate Administrator for Research, Development, and Technology: DAVID K. PHILLIPS (703, 285-2051)
Associate Administrator for Motor Carriers: RICHARD P. LANDIS (366-2519)

FEDERAL RAILROAD ADMINISTRATION, 400 7th St., SW, Washington, DC 20590 (202, 366-0881)

The Federal Railroad Administration promulgates and enforces rail safety regulation, administers financial assistance programs for certain railroads, conducts research and development in support of improved railroad safety and national rail transportation policy, provides for the rehabilitation of Northeast Corridor rail passenger service, and consolidates government support of rail transportation activities.

Administrator: JOHN RILEY (366-0710)
Deputy Administrator: SUSAN M. COUGHLIN (366-0857)
Chief Counsel: S. MARK LINDSEY (366-0767)
Executive Director: WILLIAM E. LOFTUS (366-2257)
Associate Administrator for Safety: JOSEPH W. WALSH (366-0895)

NATIONAL HIGHWAY TRAFFIC SAFETY ADMINISTRATION, 400 7th St., SW, Washington, DC 20590 (202, 366-0123); Hotline (Toll free: 800, 366-9393); Metropolitan Washington: (366-0123)

Administrator: DIANE K. STEED
Deputy Administrator: JEFFREY R. MILLER
Managing Director: HOWARD M. SMOLKIN
Associate Administrator for Enforcement: GEORGE L. PARKER
Associate Administrator for Rulemaking: BARRY FELRICE
Chief Counsel: ERIKA Z. JONES
Associate Administrator for Traffic Safety Programs: GEORGE REAGLE
Associate Administrator for Administration: BARBARA D. KERNAN
Associate Administrator for Plans and Policy: ADELE SPIELBERGER
Associate Administrator for Research and Development: MICHAEL FINKELSTEIN

SAINT LAWRENCE SEAWAY DEVELOPMENT CORPORATION, 400 7th St., SW, Washington, DC 20590 (202, 366-0091)

Administrator: JAMES L. EMERY
Associate Administrator: ERMAN J. COCCI, Saint Lawrence Seaway

Development Corporation, P.O. Box 520, Massena, NY (315, 764-3200)
Director, Public Affairs: DENNIS E. DEUSCHL, P.O. Box 44090, Washington, DC 20026-4090 (202-366-0110)

URBAN MASS TRANSPORTATION ADMINISTRATION, 400 7th St., SW, Washington, DC 20590 (202, 366-4043)

Seeks to improve the environmental standards of American cities through grant programs which extend and modernize existing urban mass transit equipment and facilities and which study, develop, and test new equipment and concepts in urban mass transit applications and operations.

Administrator: ALFRE A. DELLIBOVI
Deputy Administrator: MATTHEW M. WIRGAU (366-4325)
Associate Administrator for Administration: THOMAS M. HUNT (366-4007)
Chief Counsel: Vacant
Deputy Chief Counsel: THEODORE A. MUNTER (366-4063)
Director of Public Affairs: JAMES L. BYNUM (366-4043)
Director: Vacant
Deputy Director: RICHARD CENTNER (366-4043)
Associate Administrator for Grants Management: ROBERT H. McMANUS (366-4020)
Associate Administrator for Budget and Policy: BRIEN G. BENSON (366-4050)
Associate Administrator for Technical Assistance: LAWRENCE L. SCHULMAN (366-4052)
Director of Civil Rights: ROBERT OWENS (366-4018)
Director of Executive Secretariat: KEVIN MORSE (366-9788)
Director of Financial Management (Acting): JOHN SPENCER (366-2918)

DEPARTMENT OF THE TREASURY

15th St. and Pennsylvania Ave., NW, Washington, DC 20220 (202, 566-2000)
Secretary: NICHOLAS F. BRADY
Assistant Secretary of the Treasury (Management): JOHN F. W. ROGERS (566-8585)

U.S. CUSTOMS SERVICE, 1301 Constitution Ave., NW, Washington, DC 20229 (202, 566-2416)

The United States Customs Service is responsible for the enforcement of the U.S. laws regarding the importation and exportation of injurious and endangered species.

Commissioner: WILLIAM von RAAB
Assistant Commissioner, Enforcement: WILLIAM ROSENBLATT
Director, Smuggling Investigations Division: BONNI TISCHLER

Regional Offices

Northeast Region (Boston)
DONALD S. DONOHUE, Assistant Regional Commissioner, Enforcement, 10 Causeway St., Boston, MA 02222 (617, 565-6250)

Region (New York)
DAVID J. RIPA, Assistant Regional Commissioner, Enforcement, U.S. Customs Service, 6 World Trade Center, New York, NY 10048 (212, 466-5641)

Southeast Region (Miami)
LEON W. GUINN, Assistant Regional Commissioner, Enforcement, 99 SE 5th St., Miami, FL 33131 (305, 536-5952)

South Central Region (New Orleans)

LAWRENCE A. LA DAGE, Assistant Regional Commissioner, Enforcement, R.D. 1, Office of Regional Director, Investigations, Suite 2440, Canal-Lasalle Bldg., 423 Canal St., New Orleans, LA 70130 (504, 589-6499)

Southwest Region (Houston)

JOHN BURNS, Assistant Regional Director, Enforcement, 5850 San Felipe, Suite 500, Houston, TX 77057 (713, 953-6802)

Pacific Region (Los Angeles)

JOHN HENSLEY, Assistant Regional Commissioner, Enforcement, Suite 7542, N. Los Angeles St., Los Angeles, CA 90053 (213, 894-4692)

North Central Region (Chicago)

DONALD WATSON, Assistant Regional Commissioner, Enforcement, 55 E Monroe St., Suite 1423, Chicago, IL 60603 (312, 886-9596)

UNITED STATES GOVERNMENT - INDEPENDENT AGENCIES

ADVISORY COUNCIL ON HISTORIC PRESERVATION, 1100 Pennsylvania Ave., NW, #809, The Old Post Office Bldg., Washington, DC 20004 (202, 786-0503)

An independent federal agency, the Advisory Council on Historic Preservation is the primary policy advisor to the President and Congress on historic preservation matters, and guides other federal agencies to ensure their actions do not result in unnecessary harm to the nation's historic properties. The council—established by the National Historic Preservation Act of 1966—is made up of the heads of 7 federal departments whose actions regularly affect historic properties; 8 members, a governor and a mayor appointed by the President; and representatives of the National Trust for Historic Preservation and the National Conference of State Historic Preservation Officers. The council is supported by a small professional staff; offices are in Washington and Denver.

Council Chairman: JOHN F.W. ROGERS

Council Vice-Chairman: ROBERT O. JOHNS, D.P.M.

Professional Staff: ROBERT D. BUSH, Executive Director; JOHN M. FOWLER, Deputy Executive Director and General Counsel; THOMAS F. KING, Director, Cultural Resource Preservation; DON KLIMA, Chief, Eastern Division of Project Review (786-0505); ROBERT FINK, Chief, Western Division of Project Review (303, 236-2682) Denver; MARCIA AXTMANN SMITH, Publications Director

ENVIRONMENTAL PROTECTION AGENCY, 401 M St., SW, Washington, DC 20460 (202, 382-2090)

Charged with mounting a coordinated attack on the environmental problems of air and water pollution, management of solid and hazardous wastes, cleanup of hazardous wastes under Super Fund, regulation of pesticides, toxic substances, and some aspects of radiation. The organization of EPA in 1970 placed under one roof programs which had been scattered throughout several agencies of the federal government. Functions include: setting and enforcing environmental standards; conducting research on the causes, effects, and control of environmental problems; assisting states and local governments.

Administrator: LEE M. THOMAS (382-4700)

Deputy Administrator (Acting): JOHN A. MOORE (382-4711)

International Activities: SHELDON MEYERS, Associate Administrator (Acting) (382-4870)

Regional Operations: ROBERT S. CAHILL, Associate Administrator (382-4719)

Administrative Law Judges: GERALD HARWOOD, Chief Judge (382-4860)

Civil Rights: NATHANIEL SCURRY, Director (382-4575)

Small and Disadvantaged Business Utilization: JOHN M. ROPES, Director (557-7777)

Science Advisory Board: DONALD G. BARNES, Director (382-4126)

Administration and Resources Management

Assistant Administrator: CHARLES L. GRIZZLE (382-4600)

Comptroller: DAVID P. RYAN (475-9674)

Director, Administration: JOHN C. CHAMBERLIN (475-8400)

Director, Information Resources Management: EDWARD J. HANLEY (382-4465)

Administration and Resources Management, Research Triangle Park, NC, Director: WILLIS GREENSTREET (919, 629-2258)

Administration, Cincinnati, OH, Director: WILLIAM J. BENOIT (513, 684-7911)

Human Resources Management, Director: KEN DAWSEY (382-4467)

Enforcement and Compliance Monitoring

Assistant Administrator: THOMAS L. ADAMS, JR. (383-4134)

Air Enforcement: MICHAEL S. ALUSHIN, Associate Enforcement Counsel (383-2820)

Water Enforcement: GLEN L. UNTERBERGER, Associate Enforcement Counsel (457-8180)

Hazardous Waste Enforcement: STEVEN L. LEIFER, Associate Enforcement Counsel (Acting) (382-3050)

Pesticides and Toxic Substances Enforcement: FREDERICK F. STIEHL, Associate Enforcement Counsel (382-4544)

Criminal Enforcement Counsel: PAUL R. THOMSON, JR., Deputy Assistant Administrator, Criminal (382-4539)

National Enforcement Investigations Center, Denver, CO: THOMAS P. GALLAGHER, Director (303, 776-5100)

General Counsel (Acting): LAWRENCE J. JENSEN (475-8040)

Air and Radiation Division: ALAN W. ECKERT, Associate General Counsel (382-7606)

Water Division: SUSAN LEPOW, Associate General Counsel (383-7700)

Pesticides and Toxic Substances Division: MARK A. GREENWOOD, Associate General Counsel (382-7505)

Solid Waste and Emergency Response Division: LISA K. FRIEDMAN, Associate General Counsel (382-7706)

Inspector General Division: CRAIG B. ANNEAR, Associate General Counsel (475-6660)

Grants, Contracts and General Law Division: HOWARD F. CORCORAN, Associate General Counsel 382-5320)

Policy, Planning and Evaluation

Assistant Administrator: LINDA J. FISHER (382-4332)

Policy Analysis: RICHARD D. MORGENSTERN, Director (382-4034)

Standards and Regulations: THOMAS E. KELLY, Director (382-4001)

Managment Systems and Evaluation: BRUCE T. BARKLEY, Director (382-4028)

External Affairs

Assistant Administrator: JENNIFER JOY WILSON (382-5654)

Community and Intergovernmental Relations: PEGGY HARLOW KNIGHT, Director (382-4454)

Federal Activities: RICHARD E. SANDERSON, Director (382-5053)

Congressional Liaison: PATRICK QUINN, Director (382-5200)

Legislative Analysis: A. HENRY SCHILLING, Director (382-5414)

Public Affairs: R. AUGUSTUS EDWARDS, Director (Acting) (382-4361)

Inspector General: JOHN C. MARTIN (382-3137)

Audit: ERNEST E. BRADLEY III, Assistant Inspector General (382-4106)

Investigations: JOHN E. BARDEN, Assistant Inspector General (382-4109)

Management and Technical Assessment: ANNA HOPKINS, Assistant Inspector General (382-4912)

Air and Radiation

Assistant Administrator (Acting): DON R. CLAY (382-7400)

Air Quality Planning and Standards: GERALD EMISON, Director (919, 541-5615)

Radiation Programs: RICHARD J. GUIMOND, Director (557-9710)
Mobile Sources: RICHARD D. WILSON, Director (382-7645)

Water

Assistant Administrator (Acting): REBECCA W. HANMER (382-5700)
Drinking Water: MICHAEL COOK, Director (382-5543)
Water Enforcement and Permits: JAMES ELDER, Director (475-8488)
Water Regulations and Standards: MARTHA G. PROTHRO, Director (382-5400)
Municipal Pollution Control: MICHAEL QUIGLEY, Director (382-5850)
Marine and Estuarine Protection: TUDOR T. DAVIES, Director (475-8580)
Ground-Water Protection: MARIAN MLAY, Director (382-7077)
Wetlands Protection: DAVID DAVIS, Director (382-7946)

Research and Development

Assistant Administrator: VAUN A. NEWILL (382-7676)
Environmental Engineering and Technology Demonstration: JOHN SKINNER, Director (382-2600)
Acid Deposition, Environmental Monitoring and Quality Assurance: MATTHEW BILLS, Director (Acting) (382-5767)
Environmental Processes and Effects Research: COURTNEY RIORDAN, Director (382-5950)
Health Research: KEN SEXTON, Director (Acting) (382-5900)
Health and Environmental Assessment: WILLIAM N. FARLAND, Director (382-7317)

Pesticides and Toxic Substances

Assistant Administrator (Acting): VICTOR KIMM (382-2902)
Pesticide Programs: DOUGLAS D. CAMPT, Director (557-7090)
Toxic Substances: CHARLES L. ELKINS, Director (382-3813)
Compliance Monitoring: AUGUSTINE E. CONROY, Director (382-3807)

Solid Waster and Emergency Response

Assistant Administrator: J. WINSTON PORTER (382-4610)
Waste Programs Enforcement: BRUCE DIAMOND, Director (382-4814)
Emergency and Remedial Response: HENRY L. LONGEST, Director (382-2180)
Solid Waste: SYLVIA LOWRANCE, Director (382-4627)
Underground Storage Tanks: RONALD BRAND, Director (382-4517)
Federal Facilities Hazardous Waste Compliance Office: CHRISTOPHER GRUNDLER, Director

Regional Administrators

Region 1

Administrator: MICHAEL DELAND, John F. Kennedy Federal Bldg., Boston, MA 02203 (617, 565-3400)
Public Affairs: BROOKE CHAMBERLAIN-COOK, Director 617, 565-3424)

Region 2

Administrator: CHRISTOPHER DAGGETT, 26 Federal Plaza, New York, NY 10278 (212, 264-2525)
External Programs: JAMES MARSHALL, Director (212, 264-2515)

Region 3

Administrator: JAMES M. SEIF, 841 Chestnut St.,, Philadelphia, PA 19107 (215, 597-9814)
Public Affairs: JANET VINISKI, Director (212, 597-9370)

Region 4

Administrator: GREER C. TIDWELL, 345 Courtland St., NE, Atlanta, GA 30365 (404, 257-4727)
Congressional and External Affairs: FRANK REED, Director (404, 257-2013)

Region 5

Administrator: VALDAS V. ADAMKUS, 230 S. Dearborn, Chicago, IL 60604 (312, 353-2000)
Public Affairs: JON GRAND, Director (312, 353-2072)

Region 6

Administrator: ROBERT LAYTON, 1445 Ross Ave., Dallas, TX 75202 (214, 655-6444)
External Affairs: PHILIP CHARLES, Director (214, 655-2200)

Region 7

Administrator: MORRIS KAY, 726 Minnesota Ave., Kansas City, KS 66101 (913, 236-2800)
Public Affairs: ROWENA MICHAELS, Director (913, 236-2803)

Region 8

Administrator: JAMES SCHERER, 999 18th St., Suite 500, Denver, CO 80202 (303, 293-1603)
External Affairs: Vacant, Director (303, 293-1692)

Region 9

Administrator: DANIEL W. McGOVERN, 215 Fremont St., San Francisco, CA 94105 (415, 974-8073)
External Affairs: DEANNA M. WIEMAN, Director (415, 974-8071)

Region 10

Administrator: ROBIE G. RUSSELL, 1200 Sixth Ave., Seattle, WA 98101 (206, 442-5810)
Public Affairs: BOB JACOBSON, Director (206, 399-1465)

GENERAL SERVICES ADMINISTRATION, 18th and F Sts., NW, Washington, DC 20405 (202, 566-1231)
Concerned with the conveyance of surplus real property for wildlife conservation purposes to the Secretary of Interior or to a state, pursuant to Public Law 537, 80th Congress.
Administrator (Acting): RAY KLINE
Federal Property Resources Service, Commissioner (Acting): EARL E. JONES (535-7210)
Director, Eastern Division: NORMAN C. MILLER (535-7062)
Director, Western Division: JOHN V. NEALE (535-7052)
Director, Special Programs Division: JAMES H. PITTS (535-7067)
Environmental Staff Officer: Vacant (535-7074)
Assistant Commissioner, Real Property (Acting): JAMES J. BUCKLEY (535-7084)
Director, Technical Services and Surveys Division: B. MICHAEL O'HARA (535-7074)
Information Officer: PATRICK H. McKELVEY (523-1209)

NATIONAL SCIENCE FOUNDATION, Washington, DC 20550 (202, 357-9498)
Responsible for the initiation and support of scientific research and the development of science education programs. Policy is set by the National Science Board, which is composed of 25 members appointed by the President, with the consent of the Senate, and includes the Director of the Foundation. Founded: 1950.
Director: ERICH BLOCH (357-7748)
Deputy Director: JOHN H. MOORE (357-9443)
Chairman, National Science Board: MARY L. GOOD (357-9582)
Public Affairs and Publications Group Director: KAREN LEBOVICH (357-9498)

NATIONAL TRANSPORTATION SAFETY BOARD, 800 Independence Ave., SW, Washington, DC 20594 (202, 382-6500)
Chairman: JIM BURNETT

NUCLEAR REGULATORY COMMISSION, Washington, DC 20555 (301, 492-7000)
Five-member commission responsible for regulating all commercial uses of nuclear energy to protect the health and safety of the public and the environment. Established: Jan. 19, 1975.
Chairman: LANDO W. ZECH, JR., (202, 634-1481)
Commissioners: THOMAS M. ROBERTS (301, 492-1800); KENNETH M. CARR (492-1820); KENNETH C. ROGERS (492-1855); JAMES R. CURTISS (492-1875)
Advisory Committee on Reactor Safeguards, Chairman: WILLIAM KERR (492-4516); Vice-Chairman: FORREST J. REMICK (492-4516); Executive Director: RAYMOND F. FRALEY (492-4516)
Chief Administrative Judge, Atomic Safety and Licensing Board: B. PAUL COTTER, JR. (492-7814)
Deputy Chief Administrative Judge: ROBERT M. LAZO (492-7842)
Chairman, Atomic Safety and Licensing Appeal Panel: CHRISTINE N. KOHL (492-7662)
Chairman, Advisory Committee on Nuclear Waste: DADE W. MOELLER
Director, Office of Inspector and Auditor: SHARON R. CONNELLY (492-7301)
Director, Office of Enforcement: JAMES LIEBERMAN (492-0741)
Director, Office of Investigation: BEN B. HAYES (492-0373)
Deputy Director, Office of Investigations: ROGER A. FORTUNA (492-3476)
General Counsel: WILLIAM C. PARLER (492-1743)
Deputy General Counsel for Licensing and Regulation: MARTIN G. MALSCH (492-1740)
Deputy General Counsel for Hearings and Enforcement: JAMES P. MURRAY (492-1740)
Secretary of the Commission: SAMUEL J. CHILK (492-1969)
Director, Office of Governmental and Public Affairs: HAROLD R. DENTON (492-1780)
Director, Public Affairs: JOSEPH J. FOUCHARD (492-0240)
Director, Congressional Affairs: JOHN C. BRADBURNE (492-1776)
Director, International Programs: JAMES R. SHEA (492-0347)
Director, State, Local and Indian Tribe Programs: CARLTON KAMMERER (492-0321)
Executive Director for Operations: VICTOR STELLO, JR. (492-7500)
Deputy Executive Director for Operations: JAMES M. TAYLOR (492-1705)
Director, Office of Consolidation: MICHAEL L. SPRINGER (492-1500)
Director, Office of Administration and Resources Management: WILLIAM G. McDONALD (492-4303)
Deputy Director: PATRICIA G. NORRY (492-7335)
Director, Office for Analysis and Evaluation of Operational Data: EDWARD L. JORDAN (492-4848)
Deputy Director: CLEMENS J. HELTEMES, JR. (492-7361)
Director, Office of Special Projects: JAMES G. PARTLOW (492-3295)
Director, Office of Personnel: PAUL E. BIRD (492-4661); Deputy Director, JAMES F. MCDERMOTT (492-4661); Associate Director, Employee Development and Training, PETER J. GOLDMAN (492-4661)
Director, Office of Small and Disadvantaged Business Utilization and Civil Rights: WILLIAM B. KERR (492-4665)
Director, Office of Nuclear Regulatory Research: ERIC S. BECKFORD (492-3700)

Deputy Director: DENWOOD F. ROSS (492-3720)
Director, Division of Engineering: GUY A. ARLOTTO (492-3800)
Director, Division of Regulatory Applications: BILL M. MORRIS (492-3750)
Director, Division of Safety Issue Resolution: ROBERT W. HOUSTON (492-3900)
Director, Division of Systems Research: BRIAN W. SHERON (492-3500)
Director, Office of Nuclear Material Safety and Safeguards: HUGH L. THOMPSON, JR. (492-3352)
Deputy Director: ROBERT M. BERNERO (492-3326)
Director, Special Issues Group: WILLARD B. BROWN
Director, Division of Safeguards and Transportation: ROBERT F. BURNETT (492-3365)
Director, Division of Industrial and Medical Nuclear Safety: RICHARD E. CUNNINGHAM (492-3426)
Director, Division of High Level Waste Management: ROBERT E. BROWNING (492-3404)
Director, Division of Low Level Waste Management and Decommissioning: MALCOLM R. KNAPP (492-3340)
Director, Office of Nuclear Reactor Regulation: THOMAS E. MURLEY (492-1270)
Deputy Director, Office of Nuclear Reactor Regulation: JAMES H. SNIEZEK (492-1272)
Director, Program Management, Policy Development and Anal. Staff: FRANCIS P. GILLESPIE (492-1275)
Associate Director, Projects: Vacant
Director, Division of Reactor Projects I/II: STEVEN A. VARGA (492-1403)
Director, Division of Reactor Project III-V and Special Projects: DENNIS M. CRUTCHFIELD (492-1354)
Associate Director, Insp. and Tech. Asst.: FRANK J. MIRAGLIA (492-1274)
Director, Division of Eng. and System Technology: LAWRENCE C. SHAO (492-0884)
Director, Division of Operational Events Assessment: CHARLES E. ROSSI
Director, Division of Reactor Insp. and Sfgds.: BRIAN K. GRIMES (492-0903)
Director, Division of Radiation Protection and Emer. Prep.: FRANK J. CONGEL (492-1088)
Director, Division of License Performance and Qual. Eval.: JACK W. ROE (492-1004)

Regional Administrators

Region 1
WILLIAM T. RUSSELL, Administrator, 475 Allendale Rd., King of Prussia, PA 19406 (215, 337-5299)
Deputy Administrator: JAMES M. ALLAN

Region 2
MALCOLM L. ERNST, Administrator (Acting), 101 Marietta St., Suite 3100, Atlanta, GA 30303 (404, 331-5500)
Deputy Administrator (Acting): J.P. STOHR

Region 3
A. BERT DAVIS, Administrator, 799 Roosevelt Rd., Glen Ellyn, IL 60137 (312, 790-5681)
Deputy Administrator: CARL J. PAPERIELLO

Region 4
ROBERT D. MARTIN, Administrator, 611 Ryan Plaza Dr., Suite 1000, Arlington, TX 76011 (817 860-8225)
Deputy Administrator: JOHN M. MONTGOMERY

Region 5
JOHN B. MARTIN, Administrator, 1450 Maria Ln., Suite 210, Walnut Creek, CA 94596 (415, 943-3707)
Deputy Administrator: BOBBY H. FAULKENBERRY

TENNESSEE VALLEY AUTHORITY, 400 West Summit Hill Dr., Knoxville, TN 37902 (615, 632-2101)
Concerned with the development of the natural resources within the Tennessee Valley Region, in Tennessee, Kentucky, Mississippi, Alabama, Georgia, Virginia, and North Carolina. Its dam and reservoir system regulates the Tennessee River and major tributaries for flood control, navigation, power production, and other purposes. TVA has developed the Land Between The Lakes as a major demonstration project for outdoor recreation, environmental education, and wildlife.

Board of Directors: MARVIN RUNYON, Chairman; C.H. DEAN, JR., Director; JOHN B. WATERS, Director
Executive Vice-President and Chief Operating Officer: WILLIAM F. WILLIS
General Counsel: EDWARD S. CHRISTENBURY (615, 632-2241)
Director of Public Affairs: ALAN CARMICHAEL (615, 632-8018)
Washington Representative: BILL PHILLIPS, 412 First St., SE, Washington, DC 20444 (202, 245-0101)
Senior Vice-President, Resource Development: JOHN T. SHIELDS, Muscle Shoals, AL (205, 386-2598)

INTERNATIONAL, NATIONAL, AND INTERSTATE COMMISSIONS

(Also see listings under U.S. Government-Independent Agencies)

APPALACHIAN REGIONAL COMMISSION, 1666 Connecticut Ave., NW, Washington, DC 20235 (202, 673-7893)
To promote the economic and social development of the region and to provide a framework for joint federal and state efforts. Includes AL, GA, KY, MD, MS, NY, NC, OH, PA, SC, TN, VA, WV. Established: 1965.
Federal Co-Chairman: WINIFRED A. PIZZANO (673-7856)
States' Co-Chairman: GOV. CARROLL A. CAMPBELL, JR.
Alternate Federal Co-Chairman: JACQUELINE PHILLIPS (673-7856)
States' Washington Representative: MICHAEL R. WENGER (673-7842)
Executive Director: FRANCIS E. MORAVITZ (673-7874)
Public Information: ANN ANDERSON (673-7968)

ATLANTIC STATES MARINE FISHERIES COMMISSION, 1400 Sixteenth St., NW, Washington, DC 20036 (202, 387-5330)
Established by the Atlantic States Marine Fisheries Compact to promote the better utilization of the fisheries, marine, shell and anadromous, of the 15 Atlantic seaboard states, Maine to Florida, through the development of a joint program for the promotion and protection of such fisheries, and by the prevention of physical waste of the fisheries from any cause. Organized: 1942.
Chairman: ROBERT A. JONES, Connecticut Department, Bureau of Fisheries
Vice-Chairman: DUANE HARRIS, Georgia Department of Natural Resources, Coastal Resources Division
Executive Director: IRWIN M. ALPERIN

COMMISSION ON NATIONAL PARKS AND PROTECTED AREAS, IUCN Headquarters, 1196 Gland, Switzerland
Carries out activities concerning national parks and other categories of protected lands and related subjects for the parent International Union for Conservation and Natural Resources (IUCN). Technical Advisor on Natural Sites for UNESCO'S World Heritage Convention. Administers International Park Valor Award. Organized: 1958.
Chairman: H.K. EIDSVIK, 135 Dorothea Dr., Ottawa, Ontario K1V 7C6, Canada
Executive Officer: JIM THORSELL, IUCN, 1196 Gland, Switzerland (022-64-71-81)

GREAT LAKES COMMISSION, The Argus II Bldg., 400 S. Fourth St., Ann Arbor, MI 48103-4816 (313,665-9135)
Recommendatory and advisory agency for the eight Great Lakes states in regional water resource matters. Great Lakes Compact ratified by Great Lakes states' legislatures 1955; Congressional consent: 1968.
Chairman: THOMAS D. MARTIN, Lansing, MI
Vice-Chairman: HENRY G. WILLIAMS, Albany, NY
Executive Director: DR. MICHAEL J. DONAHUE
Natural Resources Management Specialist: THOMAS CRANE
Transportation and Economic Development Specialist: STEPHEN J. THORP
Communications Specialist: CATHY CHOWN

Publications: *The Advisor Newsletter;* periodic reports and issue papers

GREAT LAKES FISHERY COMMISSION, 1451 Green Rd., Ann Arbor, MI 48105 (313, 662-3209)
The 1955 Canada-U.S. Convention on Great Lakes Fisheries established the commission to advise governments on ways to improve the then-devastated fisheries, to develop and coordinate fishery research programs, and to develop measures and implement programs to manage sea lamprey.
Commission Members: PIERRE ASSELIN, Ottawa, Ontario, Canada; GEORGE WHITNEY, Toronto, Ontario, Canada; SUSAN RECCE, Washington, DC; CHUCK C. KRUEGER, Ithaca, NY; HENRY A. REGIER, Toronto, Ontario, Canada; JAMES M. RIDENOUR, Indianapolis, IN; PAUL H. SUTHERLAND, Winnipeg, Manitoba, Canada; JAMES M. CADY, Peterson, MN
Executive Secretary: CARLOS M. FETTEROLF, JR.
Assistant Executive Secretary: ARRNE K. LAMSA
Administrative Officer: BARBARA S. STAPLES

GULF STATES MARINE FISHERIES COMMISSION, P.O. Box 726, Ocean Springs, MS 39564 (601, 875-5912) (Semi-annual meetings: third week March, third week October)
An interstate compact of the states of Alabama, Florida, Louisiana, Mississippi, and Texas. The compact was signed in July 1949. The commission has 15 members, three from each of its member states. Of these three members, one is the chairman of his state's Conservation Board, one is a state legislator, and the third is a representative of industry and the general public. The purpose of the compact is to promote proper utilization of the fisheries common to the seaboard of the Gulf Coast states.
Executive Director: LARRY B. SIMPSON
Commission Chairman: TAYLOR F. HARPER, AL

INTER-AMERICAN TROPICAL TUNA COMMISSION, c/o Scripps Institution of Oceanography, La Jolla, CA 92093 (619, 546-7100)
Charged with the investigation and conservation of the tuna and dolphin resources of the eastern Pacific Ocean. Member nations: U.S., France, Japan, Nicaragua, Panama. Established by convention between the U.S. and Costa Rica: 1949.
Commission Members: U.S.: HENRY R. BEASLEY, Washington, D.C.; WYMBERLEY COERR, San Francisco, CA; ROBERT C. MacDONALD, Astoria, OR; JACK GORBY, Los Angeles, CA; France: DOMINIQUE PINEY; SERGE GARACHE; Panama: ARMANDO MARTINEZ; CARLOS ICAZA; Japan: TAKEHISA NOGAMI; KAZUO SHIMA; YAMATO UEDA; Nicaragua: ABELINO AROSTEGUI VALLAARDES
Director: JAMES JOSEPH (546-7019)
Publications: *Bulletin of the Inter-American Tropical Tuna Commission; Annual Report; Special Report of the Inter-American Tropical Tuna Commission*
Editor: WILLIAM H. BAYLIFF (619, 546-7025)

INTERNATIONAL JOINT COMMISSION, 2001 S St., NW, Second Fl., Washington, DC 20440 (202, 673-6222); 100 Metcalfe St., Ottawa, Ontario K1P 5M1 (613, 995-2984); Regional Office: Suite 800, 100 Ouellette Ave., Windsor, Ontario N9A 6T3 (519, 256-7821/313, 226-2170)
Established by the Boundary Waters Treaty of 1909 between the

United States and Great Britain for the purpose of preventing disputes regarding the use of the waters on the U.S.-Canadian Boundary. Regional Office monitors, evaluates, and reports on compliance with the Great Lakes Water Quality Agreement of November 22, 1978. Commission functions in quasi-judicial, investigative, and coordination capacities.

Commissioners: U.S. Chairman: ROBERT C. McEWEN (202, 673-6222); L. KEITH BULEN (202, 673-6222); DONALD L. TOTTEN (202, 673-6222)

Canadian Chairmen: P. ANDRE BISONNETTE (613, 995-2984); E. DAVIE FULTON (613, 995-2984); ROBERT WELCH (613, 995-2984)

Secretary, U.S. Section: DAVID A. LaROCHE (202, 673-6222)

Secretary, Canadian Section: DAVID G. CHANCE (613, 995-2984)

Director, Regional Office: DR. AL DUDA (519, 256-7821/313, 226-2170)

Publication: *Focus*

Editor: SALLY COLE-MISCH, Regional Office

INTERNATIONAL NORTH PACIFIC FISHERIES COMMISSION,
6640 NW Marine Dr., Vancouver, British Columbia, Canada V6T 1X2 (604, 228-1128)

Established by convention between Canada, Japan, and the U.S. in 1952 for the conservation of the fisheries resources of the North Pacific Ocean.

Executive Director: B.E. SKUD

Assistant Director: KATSUMA HANAFUSA

Chairman: KENJIRO NISHIMURA (Japan)

Vice-Chairman: C.V. TILLION (U.S.)

Secretary: P. ASSELIN (Canada)

INTERNATIONAL PACIFIC HALIBUT COMMISSION, P.O. Box 95009, Seattle, WA 98145-2009 (206, 634-1838)

Scientific investigation and management of the Pacific halibut resource. Established in 1923 by a convention between Canada and the United States.

Commissioners: DENNIS N. BROCK, Chairman (613, 993-0097); JIM BROOKS, Commissioner (Acting) (907, 586-7221); SEN. RICHARD ELIASON (907, 747-6276); DR. GEORGE WADE (206, 282-4370); GARY T. WILLIAMSON (604, 531-1788); LINDA J. ALEXANDER (604, 248-4171)

Director: DONALD A. McCAUGHRAN

Publications: Scientific reports; technical reports; annual reports

INTERNATIONAL WHALING COMMISSION, The Red House, 135 Station Rd., Histon, Cambridge CB4 4NP England (022023 3971) (Annual Meeting: June/July)

Established under the International Convention for the Regulation of Whaling, 1946, to provide for the conservation of whale stocks and the orderly development of the whaling industry. Member Nations: U.S., Antigua and Barbuda, Argentina, Australia, Brazil, Chile, People's Republic of China, Costa Rica, Denmark, Egypt, Finland, France, Federal Republic of Germany, Iceland, India, Ireland, Japan, Kenya, Republic of Korea, Mexico, Monoco, Netherlands, New Zealand, Norway, Oman, Peru, Saint Lucia, Saint Vincent and the Grenandines, Senegal, Seychelles, Solomon Islands, South Africa, Spain, Sweden, Switzerland, Uruguay, U.S.S.R., and United Kingdom.

Chairman: S. IRBERGER (Sweden)

Vice-Chairman: L.A. FLEISCHER (Mexico)

Secretary: DR. R. GAMBELL (at Cambridge address)

Executive Officer: M. HARVEY (at Cambridge address)

U.S. Commissioner: DR. W.E. EVANS, NOAA, Dept. of Commerce, Washington, DC 20230, USA

Publications: Annual reports of the Commission (including reports and papers of the Scientific Committee); Special Issues Series on specialist cetacean subjects

Editor: G.P. DONOVAN

INTERSTATE COMMISSION ON THE POTOMAC RIVER BASIN,
6110 Executive Blvd., Suite 300, Rockville, MD 20852-3903 (301, 984-1908)

Interstate compact, established in 1940 by Maryland, Pennsylvania, Virginia, West Virginia, and the District of Columbia. Coordinates tabulates, and summarizes existing data on condition of streams in Potomac Watershed; promotes uniform legislation; disseminates information; cooperates in studies; promotes coordination of program in Basin states. Areas of interest are water quality, water supply and land resources associated with the Potomac and its tributaries.

Executive Director: L.E. ZENI

Associate Director, Technical Services: CARLTON HAYWOOD

Associate Director, Public Affairs: BEVERLY G. BANDLER

Associate Director, Administration: MARY- ELLEN WEBSTER

Associate Director, Water Resources and Director CO-OP: DR. ROLAND C. STEINER

Publications: *Potomac Basin Reporter; In The Anacostia Watershed*

MARINE MAMMAL COMMISSION, 1625 I St., NW, Washington, DC 20006 (202, 653-6237)

Established by the Marine Mammal Protection Act of 1972, P.L. 92-522, in consultation with the Committee of Scientific Advisors on Marine Mammals, to periodically review the status of marine mammal populations; to manage a research program concerned with their conservation; and to develop, review, and make recommendations of federal activities and policies which affect the protection and conservation of marine mammals.

Commissioners: WILLIAM W. FOX, JR., Ph.D., Chairman, Miami, Fl; ROBERT ELSNER, Ph.D., Fairbanks, AK; FRANCIS H. FAY, Ph.D., Fairbanks, AK

Committee: ROBERT L. BROWNELL, JR., Ph.D., San Simeon, CA; DOUGLAS G. CHAPMAN, Ph.D., Seattle, WA; DANIEL GOODMAN, Ph.D, Bozeman, MT; MURRAY L. JOHNSON, M.D., Committee Chairman, Tacoma, WA; JACK W. LENTFER, Juneau, AK; GEORGE A. LLANO, Ph.D., Naples, FL; WILLIAM MEDWAY, D.V.M., Ph.D., Philadelphia, PA; JANE M. PACKARD, Ph.D., College Station, TX; FORREST G. WOOD, San Diego, CA

Executive Director: JOHN R. TWISS, JR.

Scientific Program Director: ROBERT J. HOFMAN, Ph.D.

Policy and Program Analyst: DAVID W. LAIST

General Counsel: MICHAEL L. GOSLINER

Publication: *Annual Report*

MIGRATORY BIRD CONSERVATION COMMISSION, Interior Bldg., Washington, DC 20240 (202, 653-7653)

Considers, passes upon, and fixes the prices for lands recommended by the Secretary of the Interior for purchase or lease by him under the Migratory Bird Conservation Act of February 18, 1929, as amended, as migratory bird refuges in the National Wildlife Refuge System. Established: 1929.

Chairman:

Secretary of the Interior, DONALD PAUL HODEL

Commission Members: Secretary of Agriculture, RICHARD LYNG; Secretary of Transportation, JAMES BURNLEY IV; U.S. Senate, THAD COCHRAN, DAVID H. PRYOR; House of Representatives, SILVIO O. CONTE, JOHN D. DINGELL

Secretary: WILLIAM F. HARTWIG

MINNESOTA-WISCONSIN BOUNDARY AREA COMMISSION,
619 2nd St., Hudson, WI 54016 (612, 436-7131 or 715, 386-9444)

To conduct studies, develop recommendations, and coordinate planning for protection, use, and development in the public interest of lands, river valleys, and waters that form the boundary between Minnesota and Wisconsin, principally on the St. Croix and Mississippi rivers. Also serves as service center for Upper and Lower St. Croix National Riverways. Founded: 1965 under interstate compact.

Executive Director: JAMES M. HARRISON
Associate Executive Director: DANIEL W. McGUINESS
Director, Mississippi River Program: ALAN ROBBINS-FENGER
Secretary: ROSETTA M. HERRICKS

Commission Members
Minnesota: RICHARD COOL, 16233 5th St. S., Lakeland, MN 55043 (612, 436-8664); RANDY SCHUMACHER, 23110 Melanie Trail, Scadia, MN 55073 (612, 464-5568); MARY SWANGER, Island View Dr., R.R. 1, Wabasha, MN 55981 (612, 565-3859); EILEEN A. MARTIN, Winona County Historical Society, 160 Johnson St., Winona, MN 55987 (507, 454-2723); Wisconsin: GREG EGAN, P.O. Box 786, La Crosse, WI 54602 (808, 784-8310); WILLIAM HOWE, P.O. Box 149, Prairie du Chien, WI 53821 (608, 326-2441); SYLVESTER CLEMENTS, RR 1, Coon Valley, WI 54623 (608, 788-6954); ROBERT M. BOCHE, Rt. I, Box 421, Star Prairie, WI 54026 (715, 248-3919); JAMES P. GOKEY, 205 5 Ave. S., P.O. Box 1626, LaCrosse, WI 54602-1626 (608, 784-5678)

NEW ENGLAND INTERSTATE WATER POLLUTION CONTROL COMMISSION, 85 Merrimac St., Boston, MA 02114 (617, 367-8522)

Coordinates the work of the member states in the control of pollution of interstate waters; establishes water quality standards and approves and enforces stream classifications; trains waste treatment plant operators, and develops public information and education programs. Compact ratified July 31, 1947.

Chairman: N. BRUCE HANES, Winchester, MA (617, 381-3211)
Treasurer: JOHN B. CASAZZA, Newbury, MA (617, 462-7323)
Executive Director: RONALD F. POLTAK, Director, New England Regional Wastewater Institute: KIRK LAFLIN, S. Portland, ME (207, 767-2539)
Publications: *Newsletter; Technical Report Series; Annual Report*

NORTH-EAST ATLANTIC FISHERIES COMMISSION, Rm. 336, Great Westminster House, Horseferry Rd., London, SW 1P 2AE. England (01, 216-6102)

To promote the conservation and optimum utilization of the fishery resources in the northeast Atlantic, within a framework appropriate to the regimes of contracting parties' own jurisdiction over fisheries in their waters; and to encourage international cooperation and consultation with respect to these resources. Founded in 1959 and reconstituted in 1980.

President: DR. W. RANKE
Vice-President: CAPT. BOAVIDA
Secretary: P.J. OGDEN
Publications: *Annual Report; Handbook of Basic Texts*

NORTHEASTERN FOREST FIRE PROTECTION COMMISSION

International forest fire protection mutual aid organization composed of three commissioners each from CT, ME, MA, NH, RI, VT, NY, and Canadian Provinces of Quebec and New Brunswick. Uniform fire organization planning and suppression technique training carried out annually by the members. The Northeastern Interstate Forest Fire Protection Compact is the governing document that established the organization.

Executive Director: RICHARD E. MULLAVEY, 10 Ladybug Ln., Concord, NH 03301 (603, 224-6966)

OHIO RIVER VALLEY WATER SANITATION COMMISSION, 49 E. Fourth St., Suite 815, Cincinnati, OH 45202 (513, 421-1151)

An interstate agency representing Illinois, Indiana, Kentucky, New York, Ohio, Pennsylvania, Virginia, and West Virginia for control of water pollution in the Ohio River Valley Compact District. Established: 1948.

Executive Director and Chief Engineer: ALAN H. VICORY, JR., P.E.
Chairman: PATRICK L. STANDING, VA
Vice-Chairman: PASQUALE V. SCARPINO, Ph.D., OH
Secretary: GORDON R. GARNER, KY
Treasurer: RICHARD L. HERD, JR.
Publications: *ORSANCO Quality Monitor; Annual Report;* publications of general or technical interest, such as Ohio River fish populations, trace chemicals, and monitoring programs.
Editor: JEANNE JAHNIGEN ISON

PACIFIC MARINE FISHERIES COMMISSION, 2000 SW 1st Ave., Suite 170, Portland, OR 97201 (503, 294-7025)

Organized in 1947, the commission serves the Pacific states of Alaska, California, Idaho, Oregon, and Washington to promote conservation, development, and management of marine and anadromous fisheries of mutual concern through a coordinated regional approach to fisheries research, monitoring, and utilization.

Executive Director: GUY THORNBURGH

SUSQUEHANNA RIVER BASIN COMMISSION, Interior Bldg., Washington, DC 20240 (202, 343-4091)

Conservation and development of water resources and water-related resources in the river basin, comprising parts of Maryland, New York, and Pennsylvania.

Secretary of the Interior and Federal Member: DONALD P. HODEL, Rm. 6151, Dept. of the Interior, Washington, DC 20240
United States Commissioner: WARNER M. DEPUY, Rm. 5113, 1100 L St., N.W., Dept. of Interior Bldg., Washington, DC 20240 (202, 343-4091)
Executive Director: ROBERT J. BIELO, 1721 N. Front St., Harrisburg PA 17102 (717, 238-0422)
Publication: *Annual Report*

UNITED STATES NATIONAL COMMITTEE FOR THE MAN AND THE BIOSPHERE PROGRAM (MAB), U.S. MAB Secretariat, OES/ENR/MAB, Dept. of State, Washington, DC 20520

The U.S. MAB program's objective is to provide practical and policy-relevant information through a program of interdisciplinary research, education, and training concerning man's interaction with, and management of, the environment. The program's principal foci are (1) management and restoration of human-impacted ecosystems; (2) ecosystem functioning under different intensities of human impact; (3) human investment and resource use; (4) human response to environmental stress; (5) the implementation of the biosphere reserve action plan; (6) biodiversity; and (7) global and environmental change.

Chairman: SAMUEL McKEE
Executive Director, U.S. MAB: DR. ROGER E. SOLES (202, 632-2786/2816)

UPPER COLORADO RIVER COMMISSION, 355 S. 4th East St., Salt Lake City, UT 84111 (801, 531-1150)

An administrative agency, composed of commissioners appointed by the states of the Upper Division of the Colorado River—CO, NM, UT, and WY—and by the President of the U.S. Created: 1949.

Chairman: JACK F. ROSS, 707 17th St., Suite 3500. Denver, CO 80202
Executive Director and Secretary: GERALD R. ZIMMERMAN
Treasurer: RONALD A. SCHULTHIES

INTERNATIONAL, NATIONAL, AND INTERSTATE ORGANIZATIONS*

1

ACCORD ASSOCIATES, 5500 Central Ave., Boulder, CO
80301 (303, 444-5080)
Accord Associates, formerly ROMCOE, is a private, nonprofit
organization founded in 1968 to act as an intermediary in
environmental disputes. "Environment" is defined to include the
economic, political, social, cultural and physical elements of our
surroundings. The Board of Directors represents diverse interests
including industry, public interest groups, government and academia. Accord's conflict management services, which range from
conflict anticipation to mediation, are used to resolve disputes over
policy issues and site-specific controversies. The experienced staff
designs and manages conflict management efforts, offers training
programs, and provides advice and consultation about conflict
management alternatives, nationally and, occasionally, internationally.
Executive Director: W. JOHN D. KENNEDY
Publication: *Accord*

2

ACID RAIN INFORMATION CLEARINGHOUSE (ARIC), 33 S.
Washington St., Rochester, NY 14608 (716, 546-3796)
Provides comprehensive on-call reference and referral, current
awareness and educational services to scientists, educators, gov-
ernment agency staff policy makers, business and industry manag-
ers, and public interest groups. Maintains special library collection.
(Annual Conference - November or December, near or in Washing-
ton, D.C.); sponsors conferences and seminars; produces topical
bibliographies. Founded: 1982.
Executive Director: ELIZABETH THORNDIKE
Director of Library and Information Services: FREDERICK W.
STOSS
Publications: *Acid Precipitation Digest; Monthly Current Awareness
Bulletin; Proceedings of Annual Conferences*
Editor: DR. ROBERT PRATT, R.D. 1, Box 185, Valley Falls, NY
12185 (518, 753-7838)

3

AFRICAN WILDLIFE FOUNDATION, 1717 Massachusetts Ave.,
NW, Washington, DC 20036 (202, 265-8393)
Finances and operates wildlife conservation projects in Africa in
cooperation with African Governmental Ministries; maintains an
international office in Nairobi, Kenya, which includes wildlife
management, scientific and education experts; provides technical
assistance to national parks and carries out conservation education
programs in schools.
Honorary Chairman of the Board: KERMIT ROOSEVELT
Chairman of the Board: JOHN H. HEMINWAY, JR.
Vice-Chairman of the Board: GEORGE C. HIXON
President: PAUL T. SCHINDLER
Vice-President: DIANA E. McMEEKIN
Secretary: JENNIFER INSKEEP
Treasurer: HENRY P. McINTOSH, IV
Assistant Secretary Treasurer: ELIZABETH McCORKLE
Publication: *African Wildlife News*
Editor: DIANA E. McMEEKIN

4

AIR POLLUTION CONTROL ASSOCIATION, H3W Gateway
Bldg., Pittsburgh, PA 15222; Mailing Address: P.O. Box
2861, Pittsburgh, PA 15230 (412, 232-3444)
A nonprofit, nongovernmental technical association whose activi-
ties are directed to the collection and dissemination of authoritative
information about air pollution control and hazardous waste
management. Membership: 8,350. Founded: 1907.
President: GALE F. HOFFNAGLE, TRC Environmental Consultants,
Hartford, CT
Executive Vice-President: MARTIN E. RIVERS
Publication: *The International Journal of Air Pollution Control and
Hazardous Waste Management (JAPCA)*
Editor: HAROLD M. ENGLUND

5

ALLIANCE FOR ENVIRONMENTAL EDUCATION, INC., Box
1040, 3421 M St., NW, Washington, DC 20007 (202,
797-4530)
A consortium of business, labor, educational, and environmental
organizations dedicated to raising the level and quality of environmental literacy in the United States through its National Network
for Environmental Education and other national projects. Founded:
1972.
President: DR. RALPH H. LUTTS, Blue Hills Trailside Museum
Education Alliance, 1904 Canton Ave., Milton, MA 02186
Past President: THOMAS LEVERMANN, U.S. Soils Conservation
Services, P.O. Box 2890, Washington, DC 20013
President-Elect: STEVEN C. KUSSMANN, American Gas Associa-
tion, 1515 Wilson Blvd., Arlington, VA 22209
Secretary: BECKY WILSON, Keep America Beautiful, 9 West Broad
St., Stamford, CT 06902
Treasurer: JOHN J. PADALINO, Pocono Environmental Education
Center, R.F.D. #1, Box 268, Dingmans Ferry, PA 18328
Director, National Network for Environmental Education: JOHN R.
PAULK, c/o TVA, IB35 Old City Hall Bldg., Knoxville, TN 37902
Publication: *Alliance Exchange Newsletter*

6

AMERICA THE BEAUTIFUL FUND, 219 Shoreham Bldg.,
Washington, DC 20005 (202, 638-1649)
Gives recognition, technical support, small seed grants, gifts of free
seeds and national recognition awards to volunteers and community groups to initiate new local action projects improving the quality
of the environment, including design, land preservation, local food
production, arts, historical and cultural preservation, and horticul-
tural therapy. Organized: 1965.
President: JOSHUA PETERFREUND, 4D Weavers Hill, Greenwich,
CT 06830
Secretary: PAUL BRUCE DOWLING, 219 Shoreham Bldg., Washington, DC 20005 (202, 638-1649)
Treasurer: CAL KLAUSNER, 5454 Wisconsin Ave., NW, Suite
1040, Washington, DC 20815
Executive Director: PAUL BRUCE DOWLING
Project Director: NANINE BILSKI (1-800-522-3557)
Publications: *Old Glory; Better Times*

*****Subject Index for organizations listed in this section appears on p. 331**

7

AMERICAN ALLIANCE FOR HEALTH, PHYSICAL EDUCATION AND RECREATION AND DANCE, 1900 Association Dr., Reston, VA. 22091 (703, 476-3488)

A voluntary professional organization for educators in the fields of physical education, sports and athletics, dance, health and safety, recreation, and outdoor and environmental education. Its purpose is the improvement of education through such professional services as consultation, periodicals and special publications, conferences and workshops, leadership development, determination of standards, and research. Membership: 50,000.

President: JEAN PERRY, San Francisco State, San Francisco, CA

President-Elect: JOEL MEIER, University of Montana, Science Complex 465, Missoula, MT 59812

Executive Vice-President: CHARLES H. HARTMAN

Publications: *Journal of Physical Education, Recreation and Dance; Health Education; Research* Quarterly; *AAHPERD Update; Strategies*

Editors: FRAN ROWAN; PATRICIA STEFFAN; LINDA TOPPER; DEBRA LEWIN

District Representatives:

Central: CHARLES SPENCER, University of South Dakota, Dept. of P.E., Vermillion, SD 57069 (605, 677-5336)

Eastern: JAMES KENT, University of Delaware, CSB, Newark, DE 19716 (302, 451-2261)

Midwest: BILL DOUGLAS, West Virginia University, School of P.E., Morgantown, WV 26506 (304, 293-3823)

Northwest: ROGER WILEY, Washington State University, Department of Physical Education, Sport and Leisure Study, Pullman, WA 99164-1410 (509, 335-4261)

Southern: GENE EZELL, University of Tennessee, HPER Department, MacLellan Gym, Chattanooga, TN 37403 (615, 755-4194)

Southwestern: ROBERT DOERING, 3035 Charlotte Dr., Thousand Oak, CA 91320 (W: 805, 492-2411; H: 499-4498)

Public Information, Advertising Coordinator: LISA CLOUGH

8

AMERICAN ASSOCIATION FOR THE ADVANCEMENT OF SCIENCE, 1333 H St., NW, Washington, DC 20005 (202, 326-6400) (Annual Meeting: 1989, January 14-19, San Francisco, CA)

Objectives are to further the work of scientists, to facilitate cooperation among them, to foster scientific freedom and responsibility, to improve the effectiveness of science in the promotion of human welfare, and to increase public understanding and appreciation of the importance and promise of the methods of science in human progress. Membership: 132,000. Founded: 1848.

Chairman of the Board: SHEILA E. WIDNALL

President: WALTER E. MASSEY

Treasurer: WILLIAM T. GOLDEN (212, 425-0333)

Executive Officer: ALVIN W. TRIVELPIECE (202, 326-6639)

Publication: *Science*

Editor: DANIEL E. KOSHLAND, JR. (202, 326-6505)

9

AMERICAN ASSOCIATION OF BOTANICAL GARDENS AND ARBORETA, INC., P.O. Box 206, Swarthmore, PA 19081 (215, 328-9145)

Dedicated to all aspects of research and education as they relate to botanical gardens and arboreta of North America. Represents institutions and individuals devoted to preserving and enhancing the environment for the benefit of mankind. Organized: 1949.

Membership: 1,400 individuals, institutions, organizations and corporations.

President: CHARLES A. HUCKINS, Rochambeau Farm, 10618 Old Colchester Rd., Mason Neck, VA 22070 (703, 339-8221)

Vice-President: HADLEY OSBORN, P.O. Box 223128, Carmel, CA 93922 (408, 624-5458)

Secretary-Treasurer: WILLIAM E. BARRICK, Director of Gardens, Callaway Gardens, Pine Mountain, GA 31822 (404, 663-5154)

Executive Director: SUSAN H. LATHROP, AABGA National Office, P.O. Box 206, Swarthmore, PA 19081 (215, 328-9145)

Directors: R. ROY FORSTER, Vandusen Botanical Garden, 5251 Oak St., Vancouver, British Columbia V6M 7HI (604, 266-7194); JONATHAN SHAW, Bok Tower Gardens, P.O. Drawer 3810, Lake Wales, FL 33859 (813, 676-1408); GREGORY ARMSTRONG, University of Wisconsin Arboretum, 1207 Seminole Highway, Madison, WI 53711 (608, 262-2746); ARTHUR H. ODE, Nebraska Statewide Arboretum, 112 Forestry Sciences Laboratory, University of Nebraska-Lincoln, Lincoln, NE 68583-0823 (402, 472-2971); C.W. ELIOT PAINE, Director, The Holden Arboretum, 9500 Sperry Rd., Mentor, OH 44060 (216, 946-4400); JUDITH ZUK, Scott Arboretum of Swarthmore College, Swarthmore, PA 19081 (215, 328-8025)

Publications: *The Public Garden; AABGA Newsletter*

Editor: SHARON LEE, AABGA, P.O. Box 206, Swarthmore, PA 19081 (215, 328-9145)

10

AMERICAN ASSOCIATION OF ZOOKEEPERS, INC., National Headquarters, 635 Gage Blvd., Topeka, KS 66606 (913, 272-5821)

An international, nonprofit organization of animal keepers and other persons interested in quality animal care and in promoting animal keeping as a profession. Chapters are active at many zoos throughout the country. Various chapters currently sponsor speakers bureaus, behind-the-scenes tours, movies and other fundraising projects. Membership: 2,380. Organized: 1967.

Board of Directors: FRANK KOHN, President, Dept. Zoological Research, National Zoological Park, Washington, DC 20008 (202, 673-4753); OLIVER CLAFFEY, Vice-President, Metro Toronto Zoo, Box 280, Westhill, Ontario, Canada M1E 4R5 (416, 284-8181); BRINT SPENCER, Minnesota Zoological Garden, 12101 Johnny Cake Ridge Rd., Apple Valley, MN 55124 (612, 431-9200); SUSAN BARNARD, Zoo Atlanta, 800 Cherokee Ave., SE, Atlanta, GA 30315 (404, 624-5618); BOB DEBETS, Assiniboine Park Zoo, 2355 Corydon Ave., Winnipeg, Manitoba, Canada R3P OR5; BARBARA MANSPEAKER, Administrative Secretary, National Headquarters

Publication: *Animal Keepers Forum*

Editor: SUSAN CHAN

11

AMERICAN ASSOCIATION OF ZOOLOGICAL PARKS AND AQUARIUMS, Oglebay Park, Wheeling, WV 26003 (304, 242-2160)

Strives to promote the welfare of zoological parks and aquariums and their advancement as public educational institutions, as scientific centers, as natural science and wildlife exhibitions and conservation agencies, and as cultural and recreational establishments dedicated to the enrichment of human and natural resources. Conservation of wildlife and the preservation and propagation of endangered and rare species are vital programs. Membership: 5,000. Organized: 1924.

President: PALMER E. KRANTZ, Director, Riverbanks Zoological Park, Columbia, SC 29210 (803, 779-8717)

President-Elect: CHARLES HOESSLE, Director, St. Louis Zoological Park, St. Louis, MO 63110 (314, 781-0900)
Executive Director: ROBERT O. WAGNER (304, 242-2160)
Publications: *AAZPA Newsletter; Directory-Zoological Parks and Aquariums in the Americas*
Editor: LINDA J. BOYD

12
AMERICAN BASS ASSOCIATION, INC., 886 Trotters Trail, Wetumpka, AL 36092 (205, 567-6035)
A nonprofit, tax-exempt national association dedicated to protecting and enhancing America's fishery resources; to promoting bass fishing as a major sport; and to teaching young people the fun of fishing and instilling in them an appreciation of the life-giving waters of America. Founded: 1985. Membership: 20,000.
President: BOB BARKER
Director, Eastern Region: GARY CLARK, 12 Woodhaven Cir., Merrimack, NH 03054
Director, Southern Region: KEN JAMES, 18139 Cherrywood Dr., Catlettsburg, KY 41129-8929
Director, Northern Region: WAYNE J. HOOD, JR., 450 Losey Ct., LaCrosse, WI 54601
Director, Central Region: EARL McKEITHAN, Rt. I, Box 131-B, Richland Springs, TX 76871
Director, Western Region: AUDREY BARNETT, 1201 Bohmen, Pubelo, CO 81006
Publication: *American Bass News*
Editor: BOB BARKER

13
AMERICAN CAMPING ASSOCIATION, INC., Bradford Woods, Martinsville, IN 46151 (317, 342-8456)
A nationwide, nonprofit, nonsectarian organization of people interested in organized camping for children and adults. Also includes 2,500 camps, directors, camp owners, camp staff members, educators, and others associated with the operation of camps. Membership: 5,600. Organized: 1910 as Camp Directors' Association.
President: EDIE KLEIN, Department of Recreation Studies, University of Georgia, #1 Peabody Hall, Athens, GA 30602
Vice-Presidents: TED S. HALPERN, Pine Forest Camps, 407 Benson East, Jenkintown, PA 19046; MARY FAETH CHENERY, 5285 Nectar Way, Eugene, OR 97405; JOAN W. FINCUTTER, G.S. of USA, 830 Third Ave., New York, NY 10022
Executive Vice-President: JOHN A. MILLER
Publications: *Camping Magazine; Guides to Accredited Camps*
Editors: ROBERT BAIRD; DON CHELEY, P.O. Box 6525, Denver, CO 80206; JACK PEARSE, 274 Shakespeare Dr., Waterloo, Ontario, Canada N2L 2T6

14
AMERICAN CANAL SOCIETY, INC., 809 Rathton Rd., York, PA 17403 (717, 843-4035)
A nonprofit organization dedicated to historic canal research, preservation and parks. Membership: 850. Organized: 1972.
President: WILLIAM E. TROUT III, Ph.D., 35 Towana Rd., Richmond, VA 23226 (804, 288-1334)
Secretary-Treasurer: CHARLES W. DERR, JR., 117 Main St., Freemansburg, PA 18017 (215, 691-0956)
Publications: *American Canals, American Canal Guides #1, #2, #3; Best From American Canals #1, #2, #3 Journal*
Editor: WILLIAM H. SHANK, P.E.

15
AMERICAN CAVE CONSERVATION ASSOCIATION, 131 Main and Cave St., P.O. Box 409, Horse Cave, KY 42749 (502, 786-1466)
The ACCA is a national organization formed to protect and preserve caves and karstlands, and natural resources associated with them. Primary objectives are to provide information, technical assistance, and public education and training programs; and to establish an endowment and a national cave and karst educational center and museum. Established: 1977.
Executive Director: DAVID G. FOSTER
President: GEORGE N. HUPPERT (608, 787-0499)
Vice-President: CHARLES RICE (703, 628-6292)
Publications: *American Caves; Newsletter*

16
AMERICAN CETACEAN SOCIETY, P.O. Box 2639, San Pedro, CA 90731-0943 (213, 548-6279)
A nonprofit organization, which has a threefold aim: conservation, education, and research. While concerned primarily with marine mammals, especially whales, dolphins, and porpoises, we recognize the interdependence of all marine life and take concerted action to protect it. Membership: 2,000. Established: 1967.
President: DR. DONALD PATTEN
Vice-President: THOMAS LEWIS
Membership Secretary: LAURA OSTEEN
Secretary: JEANE O'BRIEN
Treasurer: LINDA LEWIS
Executive Director: PATRICIA WARHOL
Publications: *Whalewatcher: Journal of the American Cetacean Society; Whale News; ACS National Newsletter*
Editors: SHERRYL TAYLOR, SUE LAFFERTY, PATRICIA WARHOL

17
AMERICAN CHEMICAL SOCIETY, 1155 16th St., NW, Washington, DC 20036 (202, 872-4600)
A nonprofit scientific and educational association of professional chemists and chemical engineers. "To encourage in the broadest and most liberal manner the advancement of chemistry in all its branches; the promotion of research in chemical science and industry; and the improvement of the qualifications and usefulness of chemists through high standards of professional ethics, education and attainments." Membership: 137,000. Founded: 1876.
Chairman of the Board: ERNEST L. ELIEL (919, 962-6198)
President: GORDON G. NELSON (601, 266-4868)
Executive Director: DR. JOHN K. CRUM (202, 872-4534)
Head, Department of Government Relations and Science Policy: KATHLEEN A. REAM (202, 872-4474)
Publications: *Chemical and Engineering News; Environmental Science and Technology*
Editors: MICHAEL HEYLIN (202, 872-4501); STANTON S. MILLER, Managing Editor (202, 872-4581)

18
AMERICAN COMMITTEE FOR INTERNATIONAL CONSERVATION, INC., c/o Mike McCloskey, Sierra Club, 330 Pennsylvania Ave. SE, Washington, DC 20003 (202, 547-1144)
An association of nongovernmental organizations concerned with international conservation. Promotes but does not fund research; assists international conservation activities; stimulates coordination of members' overseas activities; and assists activities of IUCN.
Chairman: DAVID J. RUNNALS, International Institute for Environment and Development (462-0900)
Vice-Chairman: GEORGE RABB, Chicago Zoological Society (312, 485-0263)

Treasurer: DR. JOHN GRANDY IV, Humane Society of U.S. (202, 452-1100)

Secretary: J. MICHAEL McCLOSKEY, Sierra Club (202, 547-1141)

NOTE: Members, which are listed separately, include: African Wildlife Leadership Foundation; National Wildlife Federation; World Wildlife Fund (US)/RARE; Caribbean Conservation Corporation; National Audubon Society; Defenders of Wildlife; New York Zoological Society; Natural Resources Defense Council; Nature Conservancy; Sierra Club; International Association of Fish and Wildlife Agencies; National Parks and Conservation Association; The Conservation Foundation; International Institute for Environment and Development; Humane Society of the United States; Massachusetts Audubon Society; Chicago Zoological Society; Wildlife Preservation Trust; Oceanic Society; Wildfowl Trust; School of Natural Resources, Univ. of Michigan; World Resources Institute; Global Tomorrow Coal.; The Wildlife Society, Inc.

19

AMERICAN CONSERVATION ASSOCIATION, INC., 30 Rockefeller Plaza, Rm. 5402, New York, NY 10112 (212, 649-5600)

A nonmembership, nonprofit, educational and scientific organization formed to advance knowledge and understanding of conservation and to preserve and develop natural resources for public use. Founded: 1958.

Honorary Co-Chairman: Vacant

Honorary Trustee: LAURANCE ROCKEFELLER

Chairman of the Board: LAURANCE S. ROCKEFELLER

Executive Vice-President: GEORGE R. LAMB

Vice-President: GENE W. SETZER

Secretary: FRANKLIN E. PARKER

Treasurer and Assistant Secretary: RUTH C. HAUPERT

Assistant Treasurer: CARMEN REYES

Trustees: JOHN H. ADAMS; FRANCES G. BEINECKE; NASH CASTRO; CHARLES M. CLUSEN; WILLIAM G. CONWAY; DANA S. CREEL; HENRY L. DIAMOND; MRS. LYNDON B. JOHNSON; FRED I. KENT III; GEORGE R. LAMB; W. BARNABAS McHENRY; PATRICK F. NOONAN; STORY CLARK RESOR; LAURANCE ROCKEFELLER; DAVID S. SAMPSON; GENE W. SETZER; CATHLEEN DOUGLAS STONE; RUSSELL E. TRAIN; WILLIAM H. WHYTE, JR.; CONRAD L. WIRTH

20

AMERICAN FARM BUREAU FEDERATION, 225 Touhy Ave., Park Ridge, IL 60068 (312, 399-5700); 600 Maryland Ave., SW, Suite 800, Washington, DC 20024 (202, 484-3600)

A free, independent, nongovernmental, voluntary organization of farm and ranch families united for the purpose of analyzing their problems and formulating action to achieve educational improvement, economic opportunity and social advancement and, thereby, to promote the national well-being. The federation is local, statewide, national, and international in its scope and influence. Member families: 3,500,000. Founded: 1919.

President: DEAN KLECKNER

Administrative Assistant: DAVID P. CONOVER

Treasurer: WILLIAM BRODERICK

Director, Natural and Environmental Resources Division: DON E. RAWLINS

Publication: *American Farm Bureau Official News Letter*

21

AMERICAN FARMLAND TRUST, 1920 N St., NW, Suite 400, Washington, DC 20036 (202, 659-5170)

Informs Americans about the issues posed by rapid depletion of the nation's agricultural land base, the harmful effects of soil erosion, and other threats to agricultural viability. AFT undertakes projects, directly and through cooperating organizations, which demonstrate farmland retention techniques, and assists policy and legislative/land use initiatives by local, state and federal government. Organized: 1980. Membership: 40,000.

President: RALPH E. GROSSI

Director of Policy Development: DAVID R. DYER

Counsel: EDWARD THOMPSON, JR.

Director of Development and Administration: CAROL B. WAITE

Director of Field Operations: JAMES RIGGLE

Director of Membership and Communications: STACEY BERG

Director of Land Conservation: MICHAEL A. DINKIN

Western Field Office Director: WILL SHAFROTH (415, 543-2098)

Northeastern Field Office Director: BOB WAGNER (413, 586-9330)

Midwestern Field Office Director: JIM PETERS (312, 478-8917)

Executive Assistant: EMILY BEAVER (202, 659-5170)

Board of Directors: PATRICK F. NOONAN, Chairman; MASON WALSH, JR., Vice-Chairman; STEPHEN S. ADAMS; DWAYNE ANDREAS; ROBERT B. ANDERSON; LOUIS R. BENZAK; ROBERT CHINN; DOYLE CONNER; WILLIAM M. DIETEL; GILBERT M. GROSVENOR; EDWARD H. HARTE; THOMAS L. LYON; WILLIAM K. REILLY; MRS. DAVID ROCKEFELLER; RICHARD E. ROMINGER; MORGAN SMITH; FREDERIC WINTHROP, JR.

Publications: *Farmland; AFT Update*

Editor: STACEY BERG

22

AMERICAN FEDERATION OF MINERALOGICAL SOCIETIES, INC., Central Office, 920 SW 70th St., Oklahoma City, OK 73139

To promote popular interest and education in the various earth sciences, in particular, the subjects of geology, mineralogy, paleontology, lapidary and other related subjects, and to sponsor and provide means of coordinating the work and efforts of all persons and groups interested therein; to sponsor and encourage the formation and international development of societies and regional federations and by and through such means to strive toward greater international goodwill and fellowship. Membership: 69,000. Organized: 1945.

President: Vacant

Publications: *American Federation Newsletter; AFMS Safety Manual; AFMS Uniform Rules* booklets

Editor: JEAN REYNOLDS, 107 Tuttle Ave., Clarendon Hills, IL 60514

23

AMERICAN FISHERIES SOCIETY, 5410 Grosvenor Ln., Bethesda, MD 20814 (301, 897-8616)

A professional society to promote the conservation, development and wise utilization of fisheries, both recreational and commercial. Membership: 8,500. Organized: 1870.

President: STANLEY A. MOBERLY (907, 789-0024)

President-Elect: DR. ROBERT G. WHITE (406, 994-3491)

1st Vice-President: JOE G. DILLARD (314, 449-3761)

2nd Vice-President: LARRY A. NIELSEN (703, 961-6959)

Executive Director: CARL R. SULLIVAN

Publications: *Transactions of the American Fisheries Society; Fisheries; North American Journal of Fisheries Management; The Progressive Fish-Culturist; Homopiscis Rusticus*
Editors: DR. ROBERT L. KENDALL, Managing Editor, P.O. Box 1150, Columbia, MD 21044; CARL R. SULLIVAN, American Fisheries Society, 5410 Grosvenor Ln., Bethesda, MD 20814; DR. ROBERT F. CARLINE, Cooperative Fish and Wildlife Research Unit, Pennsylvania State University, University Park, PA 16802; ROBERT G. PIPER, P.O. Box 3706, Bozeman, MT 59722; DR. VICTOR S. KENNEDY, Horn Pt. Environmental Labs, University of Maryland, Cambridge, MD 21613; DR. J. FRANCES ALLEN, Meeker Hollow Rd., Roxbury, NY 12474
Northeastern Division:
President: ANGELO INCERPI, Vermont Fish and Game Department, 103 S. Main St., Waterbury, VT 05676 (802, 244-7331)
North Central Division:
President: HAROLD KLAASSEN, Department of Biology, Kansas State University, Manhattan, KS 66506 (913, 632-6654)
Southern Division:
President: DAVID K. WHITEHURST, Virginia Department of Game and Inland Fisheries, Box 11104, Richmond, VA 23230 (804, 257-1000)
Western Division:
President: ALVIN D. MILLS, 615 E. Center St., Orem, UT 84057 (801, 377-5780)
Fish Culture Section:
President: H. RANDALL ROBINETTE, Wildlife and Fisheries, Mississippi State University, P.O. Drawer LW, Mississippi State, MS 39762 (601, 325-3133)
Fish Health Section:
President: RONALD P. HEDRICK, Bodega Marine Laboratory, University of California-Davis, P.O. Box 247, Bodega Bay, CA 94923 (707, 875-3662)
Fisheries Administrators Section:
President: BRUCE SHUPP, Box 278, Chestertown, NY 12817 (518, 457-5420)
Water Quality Section:
President: CHARLES COUTANT, 120 Miramar Cir., Oak Ridge, TN 37830 (615, 574-7386)
Education Section:
President: JAMES REYNOLDS, Alaska Cooperative Fish Research Unit, 138 AHRB-University of Alaska, Fairbanks, AK 99775 (907, 474-7661)
Early Life History Section:
President: JOAN HOLT, Marine Science Institute, University of Texas, Port Aransas, TX 78373 (512, 749-6716)
Marine Fisheries Section:
President: GENE HUNTSMAN, NMFS Beaufort Laboratory, SE Fisheries Ctr., Beaufort, NC 28516 (919, 728-4595)
Introduced Fish Section:
President: NICK PARKER, 503 Bibb St., Marion, AL 36756 (205, 683-6175)
Fisheries Management Section:
President: DONALD A. DUFF, U.S. Forest Service, 324 Twenty-fifth St., Ogden, UT 84401 (801, 625-5662)
Bioengineering Section:
President: WAYNE DALY, Box 123, Rolling Bay, WA 98061 (206, 447-5300)
Socioeconomics Section:
President: DANIEL D. HUPPERT, 2603 Angell Ave., San Diego, CA 92122 (619, 453-2820)
Computer User Section:
President : RICHARD KEISER, 32 Stillway Ct., Cockeysville, MD 21030 (301, 428-0414)
Fish Genetics Section:

President: ROBERT J. WATTENDORF, Game and Fresh Water Fish Commission, 620 S. Meridian St., Tallahassee, FL 32301 (305, 391-6409)
International Fish Section:
President: TAPAN BANERJEE, U.S. Department of Commerce, Rm. 3130, Washington, DC 20230 (202, 377-3922)

24
AMERICAN FOREST COUNCIL, 1250 Connecticut Ave., NW, Washington, DC 20036 (202, 463-2459)
A nonprofit, nonpolitical, information, policy, and education organization, supported by the nation's forest products industries to promote the development and productive management of the nation's commercial forest lands by government, industry and private landowners. Organized: 1941.
President: LAURENCE D. WISEMAN
Vice-President, Communications: LUKE POPOVICH
Vice-President, Policy: SCOTT BERG
Vice-President, Forest Resources: LESTER A. DeCOSTER
Vice-President, Allied Audience Programs: CARLTON N. OWEN
Publication: *American Tree Farmer*

Regional Managers
South: DON SMITH, 2900 Chamblee Tucker Rd., Bldg. 5, Atlanta, GA 30341 (404, 451-7106)
New England: JANE DIFLEY, 415 River St., Troy, NY 12181 (518, 272-0062)
Mid-Atlantic: JOHN H. HERRINGTON, 415 River St., Troy, NY 12181 (518, 272-0062)
Western: JOHN E. BENNETH, 10580 SW McDonald St., Tigard, OR 97223 (503, 620-8990)

25
AMERICAN FORESTRY ASSOCIATION, THE, 1516 P St., NW, Washington, DC 20005 (202, 667-3300)
Objective: advancement of intelligent management and use of forests, soil, water, wildlife, and all other natural resources. Seeks to create an enlightened public appreciation of these resources and the part they play in the social and economic life of the nation. Created: 1875.
President: R. SCOTT WALLINGER
Vice-President: RICHARD W. BEHAN
Vice-President: RICHARD M. HOLLIER
Immediate Past President: PERRY R. HAGENSTEIN
Board of Directors: DURWARD L. ALLEN; ROBERT L. ANDERSON; MOLLIE H. BEATTIE; PAUL O. BOFINGER; BARBARA G. CLARK; CHARLES A. CONNAUGHTON; ARTHUR A. DAVIS; LYNN W. DAY; PAUL M. DUNN; SUSAN L. FLADER; VOIT GILMORE; JOHN C. GORDON; ROBERT W. HARRIS; LEE W. HINDS; LUTHER H. HODGES, Jr.; JOHN R. McGUIRE; CARL H. REIDEL; THOMAS H. RIPLEY; ROBERT W. SKIERA; CHARLES M. TARVER; WILLIAM D. TICKNOR; HESTER L. TURNER; FRANK H. WADSWORTH; PETER F. WATZEK; WILFRED R. WOODS
Executive Vice-President: R. NEIL SAMPSON
Programs Director: GARY MOLL
Regional Representatives: HENRY W. DE BRUIN; JAMES P. JACKSON; NOEL K. SHELDON
Publications: *American Forests; Resource Hotline*
Editors: BILL ROONEY; FRANCES HUNT

26
AMERICAN FUR RESOURCES INSTITUTE AND AMERICAN FUR RESOURCES FOUNDATION, 1825 K St., NW, Suite 711, Washington, DC 20006 (703, 281-0207)
Companion nonprofit organizations created to promote and protect the heritage of trappers and various entities within the fur industry

in North America through principles of sound and scientific wildlife management. AFRI is engaged in activities in the legislative, administrative and legal forums on a state and national level. AFRF is concerned with public education and scientific research.

Chairman of the Board: PARKER L. DOZHIER

Treasurer: VIVIAN F. PRYOR

Washington Counsel: STEPHEN S. BOYNTON

Directors: PARKER L. DOZHIER, 1 Trapper Trail, Bigelow, AR 72016 (501, 333-2516); GERRY BLAIR, 3941 North Paradise Rd., Flagstaff, AZ 86001 (602, 744-6913); ROD HARDER, 93601 Pope Rd., Blachly, OR 97412 (505, 925-3732); JOHN T. FOUKE, JR., P.O. Box 207, Greer, SC 29651 (803, 879-7849); RUSS CARMEN, New Milford, PA 18834, (717, 278-1276); WILLARD MAGEE, P.O. Box 37, Eolia, MO 63344; DR. MAJOR L. BODDICKER, P.O. Box 999, LaPorte, CO 80535 (303, 484-2768); VIVIAN F. PRYOR, P.O. Box 186, Newington, GA 30446 (912, 857-4562)

27

AMERICAN GEOGRAPHICAL SOCIETY, 156 Fifth Ave., Suite 600, New York, NY 10010 (212, 242-0214)

The AGS has sponsored research projects, held symposia and lectures, and published scientific and popular books, periodicals, and maps. Its publications bring accurate, up-to-date information on man and the land to more than 8,000 fellows and subscribers in over 100 countries. Founded: 1851.

President: JOHN E. GOULD

Secretary: JOHN R. MATHER

Treasurer: PATRICK H. O'NEILL

Director: MARY LYNNE BIRD

Publications: *Geographical Review; Focus*

Editors: DOUGLAS R. McMANIS; HILARY LAMBERT RENWICK

28

AMERICAN HIKING SOCIETY, 1015 Thirty-first St., NW, Washington, D.C. 20007 (703, 385-3252)

A nonprofit organization formed to educate the public in the appreciation of hiking and the use of foot trails and to provide for and protect the interests of hikers.

President: LOUISE MARSHALL

Vice-Presidents: TOM FLOYD; HULET HORNBECK

Volunteer Vacations Director: KAY BEEBE (617, 545-7019)

Publications: *American Hiker; Helping Out in the Outdoors*

29

AMERICAN HORSE PROTECTION ASSOCIATION, INC., 1038 31st St., NW, Washington, DC 20007 (202, 965-0500)

A national nonprofit, tax-exempt organization dedicated entirely to the welfare of horses, both wild and domestic. Works for the enforcement of all humane legislation for both wild and domestic horses. Founded: 1966.

President and Chairman, Board of Directors: WILLIAM L. BLUE

Vice-Presidents: NANCY A. MURRAY; SUSAN L. WEST

Secretary: Vacant

Treasurer: DOROTHY SAMSON

General Counsel: RUSSELL GASPAR

Directors: SUSAN L. WEST; DOROTHY SAMSON; GENE C. LANG; NANCY A. MURRAY; MRS. WILLIAM ELSAESSER; DR. MELVIN MYERS; KARL YENSER

Executive Director: ROBIN C. LOHNES

Publications: Newsletter; Special Bulletins

30

AMERICAN HUMANE ASSOCIATION, THE, 9725 E. Hampden, Denver, CO 80231 (303, 695-0811)

A federation of more than 3,500 local humane organizations, representing approximately 350,000 individuals and serving as the central agency in the U.S. for collection and dissemination of humane materials and methods. Nationwide programs deal with problems of child abuse and neglect, and cruelty to animals. Maintains close liaison with related interest groups to protect small animals, livestock, and wildlife. Founded: 1877.

President: DONALD H. ANTHONY, Humane Society of Missouri, 1210 Macklind Ave., St. Louis, MO 63110 (314, 647-8800)

Vice-President: HORTENSE LANDAU, 200 East 66th St., New York, NY 10021 (212, 233-5500)

Treasurer: CHARLES W. ENNIS, 1217 Two United Bank Center, 1700 Broadway, Denver, CO 80290 (303, 861-4100)

Executive Director: LAWRENCE C. BROWN

Publications: *Shoptalk; Advocate*

Editor: SUSAN W. HALBERSTADT

31

AMERICAN INSTITUTE OF BIOLOGICAL SCIENCES, INC., 730 11th St., NW, Washington, DC 20001-4584 (202, 628-1500) (Annual Meeting: 1989, August 6-10, University of Toronto, Toronto, Canada)

A national organization for biology and biologists, combining an individual membership organization with the federation principle. Operates educational, advisory, liaison, informational, publication and editorial programs to serve biologists, promote unity and effectiveness of effort, and apply knowledge of biology to human welfare. Membership: 10,000 individuals and 42 societies, and laboratories representing an additional 80,000 biologists. Organized: 1947.

President: JOHN PATRICK JORDAN, Cooperative State Research Service, US Department of Agriculture, Washington, DC 20250

Past President: BOYD R. STRAIN

Secretary-Treasurer: PAUL A. OPLER

Executive Director: CHARLES M. CHAMBERS

Board of Directors: GARY W. BARRETT; LAURENCE D. MOORE; PAUL G. RISSER; DONALD R. McLEAN; WILLIAM L. STERN; ELIZABETH F. WELLS; J. WAYNE CAMPBELL; G. HERB WARD

Publication: *BioScience Forum*

Editor: JULIE ANN MILLER

32

AMERICAN INSTITUTE OF FISHERY RESEARCH BIOLOGISTS, NOAA/NMFS, S. Ferry Rd., Narragansett, RI 02882 (401, 789-9326)

The institute was founded to advance the science of fishery biology and to promote conservation and proper use of fishery resources. It serves that goal primarily by being concerned with the professional development and performance of its members, and recognition of their competence and achievement. Founded: 1957. Members: 1,200.

President: JOHN R. HUNTER, NOAA/NMFS, P.O. Box 271, La Jolla, CA 92038

Secretary of Membership: SAMMY RAY, Marine Biology Bldg., Texas A&M University, Fort Crockett, Galveston, TX 77550 (409, 766-3325)

Secretary: HERBERT LAWLER, 501 Crescent, Winnipeg, MB Canada R3T 2N6 (204, 949-5117

Treasurer: CHARLES F. COLE, 2021 Coffey Rd., Ohio State University, Columbus, OH 43210 (614, 422-0908)

Publication: *Briefs*

Editor: DR. OLIVER B. COPE, 15 Adamswood Rd., Asheville, NC 28803 (704, 274-7773)

33

AMERICAN LITTORAL SOCIETY, Sandy Hook, Highlands, NJ 07732 (201, 291-0055)

A national organization of professionals and amateurs interested in the study and conservation of coastal habitat, barrier beaches, wetlands, estuaries, and near-shore waters, and their fish, shellfish, bird, and mammal resources. Publishes scientific and popular material. Conducts field trips, dive and study expeditions, and a fish tag-and-release program. Special activities for scuba divers and underwater photographers. Members and contributors: 10,000. Founded: 1961.

President: THOMAS DICK

Vice-Presidents: GEORGE KOWALLIS; WILLIAM FEINBERG; EUGENIE CLARK

Secretary: EUGENE GEER

Treasurer: ELIAS BALTIN

Executive Director: D.W. BENNETT

Publications: *Underwater Naturalist; Coastal Reporter*

Regional Offices:

Florida: SYDNEY CRAMPTON, SARAH MITCHELL, c/o Mote Marine Lab, City Island, Sarasota, FL 33509 (813, 388-3301); ALEXANDER STONE, 75 Virginia Beach Blvd., Key Biscayne, Miami, FL 33149 (305, 361-4200)

Water Shed Association of The Delaware River (WADR) Delaware Riverkeeper: 9A Church St., Lambertville, NJ 08530 WADR: (609, 397-4410); Riverkeeper: (609, 397-3077)

New York: DONALD RIEPE, 28 West 9th Rd., Broad Channel, NY 11693 (718, 634-6467)

New England: WILLIAM SARGENT, P.O. Box 331, Woods Hole, MA (617, 548-2673)

34

AMERICAN LUNG ASSOCIATION, 1740 Broadway, New York, NY 10019 (212,315-8700)

Formerly known as the National Tuberculosis and Respiratory Disease Association, founded in 1904, a voluntary agency concerned with prevention and control of lung disease and aggravating factors, including air pollution. National Air Conservation Commission and local and state air conservation committees work with citizenry and other groups for effective air pollution control. Informational material available from national, state and local lung associations.

Managing Director: JAMES A. SWOMLEY (315-8701)

Air Conservation Manager: RONALD WHITE (315-8720)

Publication: *American Review of Respiratory Disease*

Editor: REUBEN M. CHERNIACK, M.D.

35

AMERICAN MUSEUM OF NATURAL HISTORY, Central Park West at 79th St., New York, NY 10024 (212, 769-5000)

Conducts research in anthropology, astronomy, entomology, herpetology, ichthyology, invertebrates, mammalogy, mineral sciences, ornithology and vertebrate paleontology using museum collections and field studies. Publishes scientific and popular material. Instructs the public, especially its over 2.5 million yearly visitors, in natural sciences, including living and extinct animals, ecological relationships, evolution of earth and life, development of human cultures, and astronomy. Gives formal instruction to 200,000 children and adults yearly. Membership: 500,000. Founded: 1869.

President: ROBERT G. GOELET (769-5010)

Director: THOMAS D. NICHOLSON (769-5020)

Publications: *Natural History; Bulletin of the American Museum of Natural History; American Museum Novitates;* anthropological papers; *Catalogue of Foraminifera; Catalogue of Ostracoda; Catalogue of Diatoms; Micropaleontology Press;* special publications; *The Bibliography and Index of Micropaleontology; Catalogue of Planktonic Foraminifera; Curator*

Editors: ALAN P. TERNES (769-5500); JOHN A. VAN COUVERING (769-5656); BRENDA JONES (769-5470)

36

AMERICAN NATURE STUDY SOCIETY, 5881 Cold Brook Rd., Homer, NY 13077 (607, 749-3655)

Promotes environmental education and avocation by conducting meetings, workshops and field excursions, producing and distributing publications and contributing to publications of other agencies; cooperates with organizations with allied interests, and, through membership in Alliance for Environmental Education, encourages members to contribute consultant services; assists in training nature lay leaders. Membership: 800. Founded: 1908.

President: FRANK KNIGHT, NYS DEC, Rm. 504, 50 Wolf Rd., Albany, NY 12233 (518, 457-3720)

President-Elect: PAUL SPECTOR, Holden Arboretum, 9500 Sperry Rd., Mentor, OH 44060 (216, 946-4400)

1st Vice-President: ALAN SEXTON, Bucks County Int. Unit # 22, Rts. 611 and 313, Doylestown, PA 18901

Secretary: MARY D. HOUTS, 70 Hillymede Rd., Hummelstown, PA 17036

Treasurer: JOHN A. GUSTAFSON (607, 749-3655)

Publications: *ANSS Newsletter; Nature Study, A Journal of Environmental Education and Interpretation*

Editors: KERRY PFLUGH, 70 Lenape Tr., Washington, NJ 07882; HELEN ROSS RUSSELL, 44 College Dr., Jersey City, NJ 07305 (201, 432-1053)

37

AMERICAN ORNITHOLOGISTS' UNION, INC., National Museum of Natural History, Smithsonian Institution, Washington, DC 20560

Aims to advance ornithological science through its publications, annual meetings, committees and membership. Members: 5,000.

President: GLEN WOOLFENDEN, Department of Biology, University of South Florida, Tampa, FL 33620 (813, 974-2242)

Vice-President: DENNIS M. POWER, Santa Barbara Museum Natural History, 2559 Puesta Del Sol Rd., Santa Barbara, CA 93105 (805, 682-4711)

President-Elect: BURT L. MONROE, JR., Department of Biology, University of Louisville, Louisville, KY 40292 (502, 588-6771)

Secretary: STEPHEN M. RUSSELL, Dept. of Ecology and Evolutionary Biology, University of Arizona, Tucson, AZ 85721 (602, 621-1026)

Treasurer: MARION JENKINSON, Museum of Natural History, University of Kansas, Lawrence, KS 66045 (913, 864-3897)

Chairman, Conservation Committee: DANIEL W. ANDERSON, Division of Wildlife and Fisheries, University of California, Davis, CA 95616 (916, 752-3576)

Publications: *The Auk; Ornithological Monographs*

Editors: ALAN H. BRUSH, Biological Sciences Group, University of Connecticut, Storrs, CT 06268; DAVID W. JOHNSTON, 5219 Concordia St., Fairfax, VA 22032

38

AMERICAN PEDESTRIAN ASSOCIATION, P.O. Box 624, Forest Hills Station, Forest Hills, NY 11375

Independent, nonprofit pedestrian environmental interest group working for spatial, environmental, conservational, planning, safety, mobility, health, and urban needs and interests of all pedestrians,

primarily nonmotorist pedestrians. Works for park and recreational and urban needs against vehicular encroachments of varied forms. Works to improve and advance the environment of the American pedestrian to a point where the fears, insecurities, dangers and vehicular encroachments of all types to the pedestrian environment will so diminish that the new freedoms and advances and progress of the pedestrian and the pedestrian environment will herald new attitudes and policies concerned with and be protective of pedestrian environmental interests. First pedestrian group in the U.S.
Original Founder: JOAN VICKIES
Temporary President (Honorary): M. CARASSO
Vice-President: LEO WILENSKY
Secretary: M. WERBER
Treasurer: M. SPACK
Publication: *Pedestrian Research*
Editor: LEO WILENSKY

39

AMERICAN PETROLEUM INSTITUTE, 1220 L St., NW, Washington, DC 20005 (202, 682-8000)
The major, national, nonprofit trade association of the petroleum industry. Membership includes all branches of the industry and is concerned with the development of business and technical skills to best serve the public and the industry. It affords a means of cooperation with the government and the conservation community in matters of national concern, including the wise use of energy and its compatibility with a quality environment.
President: CHARLES J. DiBONA (682-8100)
Chief Operating Officer: WILLIAM F. O'KEEFE (682-8300)
Vice-President, Health and Environment: TERRY F. YOSIE (682-8090)
External Liaison Director: DAVID A. SCOTT (682-8280)

40

AMERICAN RECREATION COALITION, 1331 Pennsylvania Ave., NW, #726, Washington, DC 20004 (202, 622-7420)
ARC is a \national, nonprofit tax-exempt federation of more than 100 recreation-related trade associations, corporations, and enthusiasts organizations that provides a unified voice for American recreation interests to ensure their full participation in government policy-making on such issues as energy and public lands and waters management. ARC also initiates and supports partnerships between public and private recreation providers and conducts meetings, seminars and activities to improve public awareness of recreation opportunities. Founded: 1979.
President: DERRICK A. CRANDALL
Chairman: DAVID J. HUMPHREYS, RVIA, P.O. Box 2999, Reston, VA 22090 (703, 620-6003)
Vice-Chairmen: CHARLES MCILWAINE, The Coleman Company, P.O. Box 1762, Wichita, KS 67201 (316, 261-3211); JEFF W. NAPIER, National Marine Manufacturers Association, 401 N. Michigan Ave., Chicago, IL 60611 (312, 836-4747); ROBERT W. RASOR, American Motorcyclist Association, P.O. Box 6114, Westerville, OH 43081-6114 (614, 891-2425)

41

AMERICAN RESOURCES GROUP, Suite 210, Signet Bank Bldg., 374 Maple Ave., East, Vienna, VA 22180 (703, 255-2700)
A nonprofit organization engaged in educational, monitoring, research, and related activities to promote the wise use of America's natural resources. Provides forestry, environmental inventory, conservation support services, and land acquisition assistance to public agencies, associations, and landowners. Organized: 1981.

President: DR. KEITH A. ARGOW
Vice-President, Forestry: DAVID A. TICE, P.O. Box 6777, Charlottesville, VA 22906 (804, 293-TREE)
Vice-President, Conservation Lands: Vacant
Publications: *National Woodlands; Conservation News Digest*
Editors: DR. JOHN D. SCHULTZ; DR. KEITH A. ARGOW

42

AMERICAN RIVERS (formerly American Rivers Conservation Council), 801 Pennsylvania Ave., SE, Suite 303, Washington, DC 20003 (202, 547-6900)
National organization dedicated to the preservation of America's remaining free-flowing rivers. Works on legislation aimed at protection of wild and scenic rivers at the federal and state level. Strives to prevent destructive and wasteful water resources projects. Provides assistance to groups and individuals concerned with river conservation. Organized: 1973.
President: W. KENT OLSON
Conservation Director: KEVIN J. COYLE
Administrative Director: RON VLASKAMP
Chairman of Board of Directors: RALPH LUKEN, Washington, DC; SCOOTCH PANKONIN, Secretary, Washington, DC; JOHN WILLIAMS, Treasurer, Washington, DC
Publications: *American Rivers; Hydropower Handbook*
Editor: RON VLASKAMP

43

AMERICAN SOCIETY FOR ENVIRONMENTAL HISTORY, Department of History, Oregon State University, Corvallis, OR 97331 (503, 754-3421)
A nonprofit international society that seeks understanding of human ecology through the perspectives of history and the humanities. Founded: 1976. Membership: 500.
President: JOHN RICHARDS, Department of History, Duke University, Durham, NC 27708 (916, 684-3966)
Vice-President: SAMUEL P. HAYS, Department of History, University of Pittsburgh, Pittsburgh, PA 15260 (412, 624-5515)
Treasurer: CARYN DAVIS BERNART, Department of History, Oregon State University, Corvallis, OR 97331
Publication: *Environmental Review*
Editor: WILLIAM G. ROBBINS

44

AMERICAN SOCIETY OF ICHTHYOLOGISTS AND HERPETOLOGISTS
To advance the science of study of fishes, amphibians, and reptiles. Membership: 2,700.
President: DR. HERBERT C. DESSAUER, Department of Biochemistry, Louisiana State University School of Medicine, 1901 Perdido St., New Orleans, LA 70112 (504, 568-4734)
President-Elect: CLARK HUBBS, Department of Biology, University of Texas, Austin, TX (504, 568-4734)
Secretary: DR. CARTER GILBERT, Florida State Museum, Department of Biology, University of Florida, Gainesville, FL 32611 (904, 392-1721)
Treasurer: DR. JOHN C. BRIGGS, Department of Marine Sciences, University of South Florida, 830 First St. South, St. Petersburg, FL 33701 (813, 893-9130)
Chairman of Committee on Environmental Quality: DR. WALTER R. COURTENAY, JR., Department of Biological Sciences, Florida Atlantic University, Boca Raton, FL 33431 (305, 395-5100, Ext. 2725)
Secretary: DR. JAMES HANKEN, Department of EPO Biology, University of Colorado, Boulder, CO 80302 (303, 492-5676)
Publication: *Copeia*
Managing Editor: DR. ROBERT K. JOHNSON, College of Charleston, Charleston, SC (312, 922-9410)

45

AMERICAN SOCIETY OF LANDSCAPE ARCHITECTS, 1733
Connecticut Ave., NW, Washington, DC 20009 (202, 466-
7730) (Annual Meeting: 1989, November 17-21, Orlando,
FL)
To advance knowledge, education and skill in the art and science of
landscape architecture as an instrument of service in the public
welfare. Authorized by Department of Education and Council on
Post-Secondary Education to accredit programs of landscape
architecture at U.S. colleges and universities. Membership:
10,000. Founded: 1899.
President: BRIAN S. KUBOTA, Peters, Kubota and Glen, P.A., 2500
West 6th St., Suite A, Lawrence, KS 66044 (913, 843-5554)
Past-President: CHERYL BARTON, ASLA, EDAW, Inc., 1725 Mont-
gomery St., San Francisco, CA 94111
President-Elect: GERALD D. PATTEN, FASLA, 429 No. St., SW,
#209, Washington, DC 20024 (202, 343-1264)
Executive Vice-President: DAVID BOHARDT
Director, Government Affairs and Public Relations: BETSY A.
CUTHBERTSON, ESQ.
Consultant, Government Affairs: RAYMOND L. FREEMAN
Director, Education: KAREN NILES
Vice-Presidents: GRANT R. JONES, FASLA, Jones and Jones, 105
S. Main St., Seattle, WA 98104 (206, 624-5702); ROBERT W.
ROSS, JR., 2719 Fort Dr., Alexandria, VA 22303 (202, 447-
7754); HELEN M. QUACKENBUSH, FASLA, 110 So. St.,
Harrisburg, PA 17101 (717, 938-9337); DARREL MORRI-
SON, University of Georgia, Department of Environmental
Design, 609 Caldwell Hall, Athens, GA 30602 (404, 542-
1816)
Publications: *Landscape Architecture Magazine; Garden Design;
Landscape Architecture News Digest (Land)*
Editors: JIM TRULOVE; KAREN FISHER

46

**AMERICAN SOCIETY OF LIMNOLOGY AND OCEANOGRAPHY,
INC.**
President: RICHARD T. BARBER, Monterey Bay Aquarium Research
Institute, P.O. Box 20, Pacific Grove, CA 93950
Secretary: POLLY A. PENHALE, College of William and Mary,
Virginia Institute of Marine Science, Gloucester Point, VA
23062 (804, 642-7242)
Treasurer: JOHN G. STOCKNER, Canada Fisheries and Oceans,
West Vancouver Laboratory, 4160 Marine Dr., West Vancouver,
B.C. V7V 1N6 Canada (604, 922-6225)
Publication: *Limnology and Oceanography*
Editor: PETER A. JUMARS, School of Oceanography, WB-10,
University of Washington, Seattle, WA 98195

47

AMERICAN SOCIETY OF MAMMALOGISTS
Encourages research and learning in all phases of mammalogy and
by holding annual meetings for presentation and discussion of the
results of research dealing with mammals, through issuing periodicals and other publications, and by giving advice on matters
pertaining to mammals, particularly conservation issues. Membership: 3,600. Founded: 1919.
President: ELMER C. BIRNEY, Bell Museum of Natural History,
University of Minnesota, Minneapolis, MN 55455 (612, 624-
0578)
Vice-Presidents: JAMES L. PATTON, lst Vice-President, Museum of
Vertebrate Zoology, University of California, Berkeley, CA
94720 (415, 642-3567); JAMES H. BROWN, Department of
Biology, University of New Mexico, Albuquerque, NM 87131
(505, 277-9337)

Secretary-Treasurer: H. DUANE SMITH, Department of Zoology,
Brigham Young University, Provo, UT 84602 (801, 378-2492)
Chairman, Committee on Conservation of Land Mammals: GARY A.
HEIDT, Division of Biological Sciences, University of Arkansas at
Little Rock, Little Rock, AR 72204 (501, 569-3000)
Chairman, Committee on Marine Mammals: JEANETTE A.
THOMAS, Naval Ocean Systems Center, Code 512, P.O. Box
997, Kailua, HI 96734 (808, 471-7110)
Chairman, Committee on Legislation and Regulations: PETER D.
WEIGL, Department of Biology, Wake Forest University, Win-
ston-Salem, NC 27109 (919, 761-5314)
Publications: *Journal of Mammalogy; Mammalian Species;* Special
Publications of American Society of Mammalogists
Managing Editor: CLYDE JONES, The Museum, Texas Tech Univer-
sity, Lubbock, TX 79409 (806, 742-2442)

48

AMERICAN SOCIETY OF ZOOLOGISTS, 104 Sirius Cir.,
Thousand Oaks, CA 91360 (805, 492-3585)
The association of professional zoologists for the presentation,
discussion and public dissemination of new or important facts and
concepts in the area of animal biology. Supports the adoption of
measures that will advance the zoological sciences. Membership:
4,500. Founded: 1890.
President: STEVEN A. WAINWRIGHT, Department of Zoology, Duke
University, Durham, NC 27706 (919, 684-3592)
Secretary: WILLIAM D. HUMMON, Department of Zoological and
Biomedical Sciences, Ohio University, Athens, OH 45701 (614,
593-2993)
Treasurer: NANCY B. CLARK, Department of Physiology and
Neurobiology, University of Connecticut, Storrs, CT 06268
(203, 486-4563)
Executive Officer: MARY ADAMS-WILEY, 104 Sirius Cir., Thousand
Oaks, CA 91360 (805, 492-3585)
Publication: *The American Zoologist*
Managing Editor: MILTON FINGERMAN, Department of Biology,
Tulane University, New Orleans, LA 70118 (504, 865-5546)

49

AMERICAN WATER RESOURCES ASSOCIATION, 5410
Grosvenor Ln., Suite 220, Bethesda, MD 20814 (301,
493-8600)
A nonprofit scientific organization to advance water resources
research, planning, development and management; to establish a
common meeting ground for engineers and physical, biological and
social scientists concerned with water resources; to collect, orga-
nize and disseminate information in the field of water resources
science and technology. Members: 3,700. Established: 1964.
President: JERRY R. ROGERS
President-Elect: WARREN VIESSMAN, JR.
Secretary: S. DHAMOTHARAN
Treasurer: DAVID W. MOODY
Executive Director: KENNETH D. REID, CAE
Publications: *Water Resources Bulletin; Hydata-News and Views;
Symposium Proceedings*
Editors: RICHARD H. McCUEN; N. EARL SPANGENBERG

50

AMERICAN WILDERNESS ALLIANCE, 7600 E. Arapahoe Rd.,
Suite 114, Englewood, CO 80112 (303, 771-0380)
A national nonprofit organization dedicated primarily to promoting
the conservation and wise use of the nation's wilderness, wildlife

habitat and wild river resources. Founded: 1977. Membership: 3,500.

President: SALLY A. RANNEY
Vice-President: W. MITCHELL
Secretary-Treasurer: DR. BERNARD SHANKS
Executive Director: CLIFTON R. MERRITT
Director, Marketing: TOM ELLIS
Publications: *Wild America; On the Wild Side Bulletin; It's Time to Go Wild*
Executive Editor: SALLY A. RANNEY
Editor: CLIFTON R. MERRITT

51

AMERICANS FOR THE ENVIRONMENT, 322 Fourth St., NE, Washington, DC 20002 (202, 547-8000)

A national, nonprofit, nonpartisan educational institution which serves as the political skills training arm of the environmental community. AFE works closely with national, regional and local conservation groups and individual activists.

Board of Directors: ALDEN M. MYER, Chair, League of Conservation Voters, 320 4th St., NE, Washington, DC 20002 (547-7200); DAVID BAKER, Vice-Chair, Friends of the Earth, 530 7th St., SE, Washington, DC 20003 (543-4312); WILLIAM PAINTER, Secretary, Defenders of Wildlife, 1244 19th St., NW, Washington, DC 20036 (659-9510); HOLLY SCHADLER, Treasurer, Sierra Club, 330 Pennsylvania Ave., SE, Washington, DC 20003 (547-1141); SOPHIE ANN AOKI, Clean Water Action Project, 317 Pennsylvania Ave., SE, Washington, DC 20003 (547-1196); DAN BECKER, Environmental Action, 1525 New Hampshire Ave., NW, Washington, DC 20036 (745-4870); MARTHA BROAD, Natural Resources Defense Council, 1350 New York Ave., NW, Washington, DC 20005 (783-7800); PETER CARLSON, Environmental Policy Institute, 218 D St., SE, Washington, DC 20003 (544-2600); AMY CHAPMAN, League of Conservation Voters, 320 4th St., NE, Washington, DC 20002 (547-7200); CHARLES CLUSEN, THe Wilderness Society, 1400 Eye St., NW, 10th Fl., Washington, DC 20005 (842-3400); LESLIE DACH, National Audubon Society, 645 Pennsylvania Ave., SE, Washington, DC 20003 (547-9009); SCOTT MARTIN, League of Conservation Voters, 320 Fourth St., NE, Washington, DC 20002; JOHN McCOMB, Sierra Club, 330 Pennsylvania Ave., SE, Washington, DC 20003; JOAN MOODY, Fund for Renewable Energy and the Environment (formerly the Solar Lobby), 1001 Connecticut Ave., NW, Washington, DC 20036 (466-6350); SHARON NEWSOME, National Wildlife Federation, 1412 Sixteenth St., NW, Washington, DC 20036 (797-6800); MICHAEL SCOTT, The Wilderness Society, 1400 Eye St., NW, Washington, DC 20005 (842-3400); GEOFF WEBB, Friends of the Earth, 530 7th St., SE, Washington, DC 20003 (543-4312)

52

ANIMAL PROTECTION INSTITUTE OF AMERICA, P.O. Box 22505, 6130 Freeport Blvd., Sacramento, CA 95822 (916, 422-1921)

A nonprofit organization whose goal is to eliminate or alleviate fear, pain and suffering among all animals—domestic livestock, pets, native and exotic wildlife—through humane education and membership action. Membership: 180,000. Founded: 1968.

Executive Director: DUF FISCHER
Chairman of the Board: KENNETH GUERRERO
Vice-Presidents: BRUCE WEBB; VERNON WEIR
Creative Services: TED CRAIL
Publication: *Mainstream*
Editor: TIM MANOLIS

53

ANIMAL WELFARE INSTITUTE, P.O. Box 3650, Washington, DC 20007 (202, 337-2333)

Active in improvement of conditions for laboratory animals, protection of endangered species, Save the Whales campaign, and humane education. Albert Schweitzer award is presented for outstanding contributions to animal welfare. Membership: 8,000. Founded: 1951.

President: CHRISTINE STEVENS (337-2332)
Vice-President: CYNTHIA WILSON (833-3892)
Secretary: MARJORIE COOKE (401, 849-2249)
Treasurer: ROGER STEVENS (254-3606)
Executive Assistant: Vacant
Whale Campaign Coordinator: LYNNE HUTCHISON (703, 941-5343)
Research Associate: CATHY LISS (337-2332)
Research Assistant: LOUISE WRIGHT
Administrative Assistant: LAURA SWEDBERG
Publications Coordinator: JESSIE DESPARD
Editorial Consultant: PATRICK ALLEN (337-2332)
Publication: *Animal Welfare Institute*
Editor: CHRISTINE STEVENS

54

APPALACHIAN MOUNTAIN CLUB, 5 Joy St., Boston, MA 02108 (617, 523-0636)

Sponsors program of recreational service in the northeastern states including trail and shelter maintenance, conservation, research, outdoor education, publication of guidebooks and maps, operation of nine-unit public hut system, camp grounds, varied activities and educational programs for members and nonmembers. Membership: 30,000. Founded: 1876.

President: FRANK KELLIHER
Executive Director: THOMAS S. DEANS
Assistant Executive Director: THOMAS J. MARTORELLI
Conservation Director: DAVID HOSKINS
Northern New England Regional Office, Pinkham Notch Camp, P.O. Box 298, Gorham, NH 03581 (603, 466-2721)
Huts Manager: MICHAEL TORREY
Research Director: KENNETH KIMBALL
Trails Director: REUBEN RAJALA
Education Director: WALTER GRAFF
Connecticut Appalachian Trail Coordinator: PETER JENSEN (203, 435-0243)
Field Representatives:
    Catskills: DENNIS REGAN (914, 889-4100)
    New York City: CLAUDIA MAUSNER (212, 684-3683)
Publications: *Appalachia; Appalachia Bulletin; AMC Guidebooks*

55

APPALACHIAN TRAIL CONFERENCE, P.O. Box 807, Harpers Ferry, WV 25425 (304, 535-6331)

Coordinates preservation and management of the Appalachian Trail, a 2,100-mile footpath and protective corridor generally following the crest of the Appalachian Mountains from Maine to Georgia. Prepares and distributes trail guidebooks and other user information. Membership: 20,000. Organized: 1925.

Chairman: RAYMOND F. HUNT, 4524 Stagecoach Rd., Kingsport, TN 37664 (615, 228-5182)
Vice-Chairpersons: COLIN TAIT, 290 Litchfield Rd., Norfolk, CT 06058 (203, 542-5378); DAVID L. RAPHAEL, 230 E. Hartswick Ave., State College, PA 16803 (814, 238-1835); MARGARET C. DRUMMOND, 1351 Springdale Rd., Atlanta, GA 30306 (404, 378-9557)
Secretary: DAVID B. FIELD
Executive Director: DAVID N. STARTZELL

Treasurer: KENNETH OSTERMANN
Publications: *Appalachian Trailways News; Newsletter; The Register*
Editor: JUDY JENNER

56

ARCHAEOLOGICAL CONSERVANCY, THE, 415 Orchard Dr.,
Santa Fe, NM 87501 (505, 982-3278)
Nonprofit membership organization dedicated to the permanent preservation of the most significant prehistoric sites in the United States, usually through acquisition. Cooperates with government, universities, museums and private conservation organizations to acquire lands for permanent archaeological preserves. Organized: 1979.
Chairman of the Board: STEWART L. UDALL
President: MARK MICHEL
Southwest Regional Director: JAMES B. WALKER
Eastern Regional Office: WILLIAM KERRIGAN, Director, 1500 Chiquita Center, 250 E. 5th St., Cincinnati, OH 45202
Directors: TIMOTHY ATKESON; JANE E. BUIKSTRA; HELEN MICHAELIS; BETTY MITCHELL; EDMUND J. LADD; JACK and PAT McCREERY; JAY T. LAST; EDWARD M. NICHOLAS; JAMES JUDGE; GEORGE B. HARTZOG, JR.
Publication: *The Archaeological Conservancy Newsletter*

57

ARCTIC INSTITUTE OF NORTH AMERICA, THE, University Library Tower, 2500 University Dr., NW, Calgary, Alberta, Canada T2N 1N4 (403, 220-7515); Rasmuson Library, University of Alaska 99775-1000
A nonprofit, research organization dedicated to acquisition, interpretation, and dissemination of knowledge of the polar regions. Sponsors student research. Membership: 2,350. Organized: 1945.
Executive Director: MICHAEL ROBINSON
Director, Administration: G.J. THOMPSON
Executive Secretary, U.S. Corporation: DAVID W. NORTON
Publications: *Arctic Journal;* Newsletter
Editor: GORDON W. HODGSON, Calgary

58

ARCTIC INTERNATIONAL WILDLIFE RANGE SOCIETY
An associate member organization of the National Wildlife Federation.
President: NANCY R. LEBLOND, 917 Leovista Ave., North Vancouver, British Columbia VTR 1R1 (604, 986-0586)
Director: DR. A.R. THOMPSON
Director: GEORGE L. COLLINS, 37 E. Ashland Ave., Phoenix, AZ 85004

59

ASSOCIATION FOR CONSERVATION INFORMATION, INC.
Facilitates free exchange of ideas, materials, techniques, experiences, and procedures bearing on conservation information and education and establishes media furthering such exchange; promotes public understanding of basic conservation principles; informs states, territories, and provinces that do not have conservation education programs of their desirability and assists them in setting up conservation education, information and public relations programs. Organized: 1938.
President: ROD GREEN, Missouri Department of Conservation, 408 S. Polk, Albany, MO 64402 (816, 726-3677)
Vice-President: DAVE RICE, Nevada Department of Wildlife, Box 10678, Reno, NV 89520 (702, 789-0500)
Secretary: BOB CAMPBELL, South Carolina Wildlife and Marine Resources Department, Box 12559, Charleston, SC 29412 (803, 795-6350)

Treasurer: DAVID L. WATTS, Mississippi Department of Wildlife Conservation, Box 451, Jackson, MS 39205 (601, 961-5369)
Immediate Past-President: HUGH M. BURTS, Louisiana Department of Wildlife and Fisheries, 2156 Wooddale Blvd., Suite 900, Baton Rouge, LA 70806 (504, 922-0247)
Directors: ROY EDWARDS, VA; BRADY MAYO, TX; JOHN WILSON, KY; JEFF BUTLER, CO; NORRIS McDOWELL, MI; DAVID WARREN, OK; MIKE COX, KS; GAIL GENDLER, MN; GARY THOMAS, IL
Publication: *The Balance Wheel*
Editor: SARA ANN HARRIS, Louisiana Department of Wildlife and Fisheries, 2156 Wooddale, Suite 900, Baton Rouge, LA 70806

60

ASSOCIATION FOR FISH AND WILDLIFE ENFORCEMENT TRAINING
The goal of the association is to promote and enhance professional standards of training in fish and wildlife enforcement. The objectives are: (1) to promote officer safety and a safer working environment; (2) to promote uniform training standards and exchange training information; (3) to promote law enforcement research and development by determining training requirements, conducting training research and developing training strategies; (4) to encourage cost-effective trainining programs; (5) to act as a repository to catalogue agency training personnel and materials; and (6) to host annual workshop to facilitate the exchange of training information. Open to Canadian and United States agencies.
President: RED HASAY, Alberta Fish and Wildlife, Main Fl., North Tower, Petroleum Plaza, 9945 - 108 St., Edmonton, Alberta, Canada T5K 2G6 (403, 427-6735)
Vice-President: RUSS FILLMORE, Department of Renewable Resources, Box 2703, Whitehorse, Yukon, Canada Y1A 2C6 (403, 667-5786)
Secretary-Treasurer: JOHN C. SMITH, Conservation Officer Service, 2162 Esplanade, Victoria, British Columbia, Canada (604, 387-9402)

61

ASSOCIATION FOR VOLUNTARY SURGICAL CONTRACEPTION, 122 E. 42nd St., New York, NY 10168 (212, 351-2500)
To ensure through education, research, and service, that men and women everywhere have access to safe and effective voluntary contraceptive sterilization. Founded: 1943.
Chair: JOSEPH E. DAVIS, M.D.
Executive Director: HUGO HOOGENBOOM
Director of International Programs: TERRENCE JEZOWSKI
Director of National Programs: LIBBY ANTARSH
Director, Medical Division: DOUGLAS HUBER, M.D.
Director, Finance and Administration: GEORGE WOODRING
Publications: *AVSC News; BioMedical Bulletin*
Publications Manager: PAMELA B. HARPER
Manager of Public Information: JANEL H. HALPERN

62

ASSOCIATION OF AMERICAN GEOGRAPHERS, 1710 16th St., NW, Washington, DC 20009 (202, 234-1450)
To further professional investigations in geography and encourage the application of geographic findings in education, government, and business. Membership: 5,800.
President: DAVID WARD, Geography, Science Hall, University of Wisconsin, Madison, WI 53706 (608, 262-1453)
Vice-President: SAUL B. COHEN, The Governor's School and Business Alliance, 11 W. 42nd St., 21st Fl., New York, NY 10036 (212, 790-2490)

Secretary: RICHARD H. SKAGGS, Geography, University of Minnesota, Minneapolis, MN 55455 (612, 625-6080)

Treasurer: DAVID A. LANEGRAN, Department of Geography, Macalester College, St. Paul, MN 55105 (612, 696-6504)

Executive Director: DR. ROBERT T. AANGEENBRUG, Association of American Geographers, 1710 16th St., NW, Washington, DC 20009 (202, 234-1450)

Publications: *The Annals; The Professional Geographer; AAG Newsletter*

Editors: STANLEY D. BRUNN; JEANNE and PAUL KAY; VONDA WITMAN

63
ASSOCIATION OF CONSERVATION ENGINEERS, (Annual Meeting: Autumn)

To encourage and broaden the educational, social, and economic interests of conservation engineering practices; to promote recognition of the importance of sound engineering practices in fish, wildlife, and recreation development; to enable each member to take advantage of the experience of other states. Membership: 185. Organized: 1961.

President: WILLIAM F. LUECKENHOFF, Missouri Department of Conservation, P.O. Box 180, 2901 West Truman Blvd., Jefferson City, MO 65102 (314, 751-4115)

Secretary-Treasurer: WILLIAM ALLINDER, Alabama Department of Conservation and Natural Resources, Engineering Section, 64 North Union St., Montgomery, AL 36130

Publications: *A.C.E. Newsletter;* handbook; conference proceedings; informational brochure

64
ASSOCIATION OF FIELD ORNITHOLOGISTS, INC.

To promote the study of birds and their habitats, especially by means of bird-banding, and dissemination of the information obtained from this study. Organized: 1922.

President: DR. WILLIAM E. DAVIS, JR., College of Basic Studies, Boston University, Boston, MA 02215 (617, 353-2886)

Vice-President: DR. PETER CANNELL, Division of Birds, National Museum of Natural history, Smithsonian Institution, Washington, DC 20560 (202, 357-2031)

Secretary: SARAH B. LAUGHLIN, Vermont Institute of Natural Science, Woodstock, VT 05091 (802, 457-2779)

Treasurer: SCOTT SUTCLIFFE, Laboratory of Ornithology, Ithaca, NY 85018 (607, 256-4288)

Publication: *Journal of Field Ornithology*

Editor: DR. EDWARD H. BURTT, JR., Department of Biology, Ohio Wesleyan University, Delaware, OH 43015 (614, 369-4431)

65
ASSOCIATION OF MIDWEST FISH AND WILDLIFE AGENCIES

Includes commissioners and directors of 18 agencies throughout the Midwest, including the Canadian provinces of Manitoba, Ontario and Saskatchewan. Objectives are to gather and disseminate information, exchange ideas and lend helpful cooperation in all matters of administration and investigation pertinent to the protection, preservation, restoration and management of our fish and wildlife.

President: LARRY SHANNON, Chairman, Minnesota Department of Natural Resources, 500 Lafayette Rd., St. Paul, MN 55146

Vice-President: JOHN URBAIN, Wildlife Division, Michigan Department of Natural Resources, P.O. Box 30028, Lansing, MI 48909

66
ASSOCIATION OF MIDWEST FISH AND GAME LAW ENFORCEMENT OFFICERS

To promote law enforcement cooperation among members, develop efficient cooperative law enforcement practices, establish a medium for disseminating information relating to illegal game law practices, devise legislative or regulatory changes for improving and standardizing law enforcement, and encourage the highest possible standards and practices of law enforcement among member organizations. Organized: 1944.

President: ROBERT ADAMS, Fish and Game Division, L.E., 8th Fl., 5th Tower, Petroleum Plaza, 9915-108th St., Edmonton, Alberta, Canada T5K 2J5

Executive Secretaries: G.I. HOILIEN; DONALD L. HASTINGS, Midwest Fish and Game Law Enforcement Officers, P.O. Box 653, Edwardsville, IL 62025 (618, 656-4090)

67
ASSOCIATION OF STATE AND TERRITORIAL HEALTH OFFICIALS, 6728 Old McLean Village Dr., McLean, VA 22101 (703, 556-9222)

An organization composed of all state and territorial health authorities, whose objective is to facilitate communication among the state health departments and their relationships with the federal government. Founded: 1942.

President: THOMAS VERNON, M.D., Department of Health, 4210 East IIth Ave., Denver, CO 80220

Director, Washington Office: GEORGE K. DEGNON

68
ASSOCIATION OF UNIVERSITY FISHERIES AND WILDLIFE PROGRAM ADMINISTRATORS

Meets biannually at the North American Wildlife and Natural Resources Conference and the annual meeting of the American Fisheries Society. The purpose is to foster improved communications among members and between other agencies, organizations, and the general public in order to provide a unified voice for academic fisheries and wildlife programs. Organized: 1979.

Chairman: DR. RICHARD L. NOBLE, Fish and Wildlife Program Coordinator, North Carolina State University, Campus Box 7617, Raleigh, NC 27695 (919, 737-2741)

Chairman-Elect: DAVID J. SCHMIDLY, Head, Department of Wildlife and Fisheries Science, Texas A & M University, College Station, TX 77843 (409, 845-1261)

Immediate Past Chairman: DR. ROBERT S. COOK, Head, Department of Fishery and Wildlife Biology, Colorado State University, Fort Collins, CO 80523 (303, 491-5020)

69
ATLANTIC CENTER FOR THE ENVIRONMENT, THE, 39 S. Main St., Ipswich, MA 01938 (508, 356-0038/Fax: 508, 356-7322)

A regional conservation organization promoting public involvement in resource management through year-round education, policy, and research programs in Atlantic Canada, eastern Quebec, and northern New England (the Atlantic Region). It conducts most of its programs through an intern work force, which it recruits from colleges and universities across North America. The Atlantic Center also facilitates the exchange of ideas between its region and others. It has an active exchange program with organizations in the Caribbean, Appalachia, and Great Britain. The Atlantic Center is a division of the Quebec-Labrador Foundation.

Director: LAWRENCE B. MORRIS

Director, Research and Education: KATHLEEN BLANCHARD

Field Director: THOMAS F. HORN (802, 457-2818)

Director, Inter-Regional Exchange and Policy: JESSICA BROWN

Director, Program Operations: JULIE EARLY
Director, Special Projects: BRENT MITCHELL
Administrative Assistant: LINDA MITTON
Publications: *Nexus; Atlantic Naturalist*

70

ATLANTIC SALMON FEDERATION, International Headquarters, P.O. Box 429, St. Andrews, N.B., Canada E0G 2X0 (506, 529-8889/Fax: 506, 529-4438)

The largest international nonprofit organization dedicated to the preservation and wise management of the Atlantic salmon and its habitat. It was established in 1982 upon consolidation of two leading salmon organizations, The Atlantic Salmon Association and The International Atlantic Salmon Foundation. ASF programs are directed toward research, conservation, education and international cooperation. The federation supports a network of regional groupings of local salmon conservation and other organizations which address a variety of salmon issues. ASF is totally dependent on contributions from individuals, foundations and corporations in Canada, the United States and overseas. Membership inquiries are welcomed. Membership and affiliates 500,000.

Executive Vice-President: WILFRED M. CARTER, D.Sc.
Vice-President, Operations: JOHN M. ANDERSON, Ph.D.
Chief Scientist, Salmon Genetics Research Program: GERRY W. FRIARS, Ph.D.
Vice-President, Finance and Administration: BERTHA DAY
Manager, Affiliate and Public Information Services: BILL TAYLOR
Director of Membership Services: LINDA N. WALSH
Executive Director (Canada): ALEX T. BIELAK, Ph.D., 1435 St. Alexandre, Suite 1030, Montreal, P.Q. H3A 2G4 (514, 842-8059)
President, Atlantic Salmon Federation (U.S.) (New York Office): JOSEPH F. CULLMAN, 3rd, 100 Park Ave., New York, NY 10017 (212, 880-3604)
President, Atlantic Salmon Federation (Canada) (Montreal Office): LUCIEN ROLLAND, 1435 St. Alexandre, Suite 1030, Montreal, P.Q. Canada H3A 2G4
Executive Director, (U.S.A.): JOHN C. PHILLIPS, P.O. Box 684, Ipswich, MA 01938 (617, 356-0717)
Publications: *The Atlantic Salmon Journal; Salar*
Editors: NOREEN RODRIGUES, TERRY DAVIS, 1435 St. Alexandre, Suite 1030, Montreal, Quebec, Canada H3A 2G4 (514, 842-8059)

71

AUDUBON NATURALIST SOCIETY OF THE CENTRAL ATLANTIC STATES, INC., 8940 Jones Mill Rd., Chevy Chase, MD 20815 (301, 652-9188)

One of the original independent Audubon societies active in public education, conservation issues, and natural science studies in the greater Washington metropolitan area for over 90 years. The society is headquartered at Woodend, a 40-acre wildlife sanctuary in suburban Maryland. Membership: 9,500. Founded: 1897.

President: FLOYD MURDOCH
Vice-President: ANTHONY WHITE
Secretary: DAVID COTTINGHAM
Treasurer: ELTING ARNOLD
Executive Director: HOBSON CALHOUN
Publications: *Naturalist News; Atlantic Naturalist; Naturalist Review*
Editor: KATHRYN RUSHING

72

BASS ANGLERS FOR CLEAN WATER, INC., P.O. Box 17900, Montgomery, AL 36141 (205, 272-9530)

A nonprofit organization dedicated to educating the American public on the conditions of pollution nationwide and to the danger of the failure to halt the pollution of the streams, rivers and lakes of the United States and to promote, educate and inform the American public of the need for conservation of our natural resources. Founded: 1970.

President: HELEN SEVIER
Vice-President, Communications: BOB COBB
Vice-President, Finance: KARL DABBS
Publication: *B.A.S.S. Times*
Editor: KATHY KAMBURIS

73

BASS ANGLERS SPORTSMAN SOCIETY, #1 Bell Rd., Montgomery, AL 36117 (205, 272-9530)

Organized in 1968 to fight pollution, assist state and national conservation agencies in their efforts and teach the young people of our country good conservation practices. Dedicated to the realistic conservation of our water resources.

President: HELEN SEVIER, Bass Anglers Sportsman Society
President: RAY W. SCOTT, JR.
Environmental Coordinator: JOHN KNOTT
Publications: *Bassmaster Magazine; Southern Outdoors; Saltwater Magazine; B.A.S.S. Times; Fishing Tackle Retailer*

74

BASS RESEARCH FOUNDATION, 1001 Market St., Chattanooga, TN (615, 756-2514)

A nonprofit, tax deductible, public foundation organized to promote and encourage results-oriented research aimed at improving both the quantity and quality of America's bass fishery resources. Works to provide the angler with a better understanding of scientific bass management and to provide the bass manager with a better understanding of the needs and desires of the angler. Incorporated: 1973.

Executive Director: H. WILLIAM BUCHER
Board of Directors: STU BELL, Quincy, IL; LARRY BOST, Starkville, MS; LOREN HILL, Norman, OK; BARRY CARIS, Waukegan, IL; RON PEDDERSON, Milwaukee, WI (414, 354-2322);
Coordinator of Chapter Services: ANN DAHL
Publications: *BRF Report; Bass Life*

75

BAT CONSERVATION INTERNATIONAL, P.O. Box 162603, Austin, TX 78716 (512, 327-9721)

A nonprofit organization with members in 35 countries. BCI is dedicated to the conservation and protection of bats and their habitats worldwide. Major efforts are: education to promote awareness and understanding of the importance of bats in maintaining healthy ecosystems; gaining protection for designated bat populations and their habitats, and conservation science. Membership: 6,500. Founded: 1982.

Chairman: MRS. ALFRED A. KING
Secretary: MRS JOHN C. PHILLIPS
Treasurer: DONALD D. GRANTGES
Executive Director and Associate Director of Science (Acting): DR. PAUL B. ROBERTSON
Founder and Director, Science: DR. MERLIN D. TUTTLE
Publication: *BATS*

76

BIO-INTEGRAL RESOURCE CENTER, P.O. Box 7414, Berkeley, CA 94707 (415, 524-2567)

A nonprofit organization dedicated to providing information on least-toxic pest control. Members receive the *IPM Practitioner,* or the less technical *Common Sense Pest Control,* plus help on solving any pest problem. Formed: 1979.

Executive Director: SHEILA DAAR
Technical Director: WILLIAM OLKOWSKI
Membership Director: HELGA OLKOWSKI

77

BOLTON INSTITUTE FOR A SUSTAINABLE FUTURE, INC., 4
Linden Square, Wellesley, MA 02181-4709 (617, 235-
5320)
An independent organization for research and public education
about the values which lie back of our choices about limits-to-
growth issues. Founded: 1972.
Co-Directors: ELIZABETH and DAVID DODSON GRAY (235-5320)
Publication: List available on request.

78

BOONE AND CROCKETT CLUB, 241 S. Fraley Blvd.,
Dumfries, VA 22026 (703, 221-1888)
A tax-exempt, nonprofit organization that works for conservation of
the wild animal life of North America, and, so far as possible,
encourages appropriate governmental and private actions to
further that end. Sponsors graduate level wildlife research and
workshops to result in comprehensive summaries of big game
species (examples: *The Wild Sheep in Modern North America,*
1975 and *The Black Bear in Modern North America,* 1979.)
Maintains the official records keeping for native North American
big game mammals and publishes the book *Records of North
American Big Game.* Assists in supporting the existing laws and
educating the American public in the importance of modern wildlife
management. Organized: 1887.
President: JAMES H. DUKE, JR.
Secretary: JOHN P. POSTON
Treasurer: SHERMAN GRAY
Executive Director: W. HAROLD NESBITT
Conservation Committee: GEORGE C. HIXON
Big Game Records Committee: WALTER H. WHITE
Editorial and Historical Committee: GEORGE V. COE

79

BOONE AND CROCKETT CLUB FOUNDATION, INC., 2225
11th Ave., Suite 21, Helena, MT 59601 (406, 442-6350)
Nonprofit foundation that owns and operates the Theodore Roosevelt Memorial Ranch, a 6,000-acre big-game wintering area on the
east front of the Rocky Mountains, near Dupuyer, MT. The TRMR is
operated as both a wildlife research area and a working cattle ranch
to provide a testing ground for management plans to enhance
wildlife values of privately-owned lands of the future.
Board of Directors: OTIS CARNEY; WESLEY M. DIXON, JR.; JOHN
W. HANES, JR.; GEORGE C. HIXON; ROBERT D. MARCOTTE,
SR.; JACK S. PARKER; JOHN P. POSTON; FREDERICK C.
PULLMAN; WILLIAM I. SPENCER
President: WILLIAM L. SEARLE (312, 291-0546)
Secretary: EDWIN W. OBRECHT, JR. (301, 363-3191)
Treasurer: SHERMAN GRAY (516, 676-6507)
TRMR Manager: THOMAS STIVERS (406, 472-3380)

80

BOUNTY INFORMATION SERVICE, Stephens College Post
Office, Columbia, MO 65215 (314, 876-7186)
Promotes the removal of bounties in North America by publishing
Bounty News and studies of the bounty system and by coordinating
activities and legal aspects. Founded: 1966.
Director and Editor: H. CHARLES LAUN
Publication: *Bounty News*

81

BOY SCOUTS OF AMERICA, National Office, P.O. Box
152079, 1325 Walnut Hill Ln., Irving, TX 75015-2079
(214, 580-2000)
To supplement and enlarge established modern educational facili-
ties for activities in the out-of-doors, to better develop physical
strength and endurance, self-reliance, and powers of initiative and
resourcefulness, all for the purpose of establishing through the
youth of today the very highest type of American citizenship.
Organized: 1910. Chartered by Congress: 1916.
President: HAROLD S. HOOK
Chief Scout Executive: BEN H. LOVE
Treasurer: FRANK W. GAY
Assistant Treasurer: H.L. HEMBREE III
Conservation Director: LAWRENCE R. THIBAULT

Regional Executives
Southeast Region: C. HOYT HUNT, P.O. Box 440728, Kennesaw,
GA 30144 (404, 955-2333)
East Central Region: M. GENE CRUSE, 230 W. Diehl Rd., Naperville,
IL 60540 (312, 983-6730)
North Central Region: J. THOMAS FORD, JR., P.O. Box 29140,
Overland Park, KS 66201
South Central Region: RICHARD O. BENTLEY, P.O. Box 152325,
Irving, TX 75015 (214, 580-2471)
Western Region: RICHARD R. HARRINGTON, P.O. Box 3464,
Sunnyvale, CA 94088-3464 (408, 735-1201)
Northeast Region: RUDOLPH FLYTHE, P.O. Box 350, Dayton, NJ
08810 (201, 821-6500)

82

BROOKS BIRD CLUB, INC., THE, 707 Warwood Ave.,
Wheeling, WV 26003
A nonprofit organization formed to encourage the study and
conservation of birds and other phases of natural history. Members
in thirty-eight states, Canada and eight foreign countries. Named in
honor of A.B. Brooks, naturalist. Membership: 1,000. Founded:
1932.
Intermediate Past-President: WILLIAM B. MURRAY, P.O. Box 944,
New Cumberland, WV 26047
President: NEVADA LAITSCH, 1203 East Park Blvd., East Liver-
pool, OH 43920
President-Elect: ROBERT S. HOGAN, Rt. 11, Box 203, Roanoke, VA
24019
Vice-President: CHARLES D. PIERCE, Rt. HC 38, Box 372,
Winchester, VA 22601
Secretary: JoANN GRAHAM, R.D. I, Box 543, Industry, PA 15052
Treasurer: RICHARD L. HOGG, SR., 39 Warwood Terr., Wheeling,
WV 26003
Membership Chairman: HELEN B. CONRAD, Rt. 1, Box 116,
Triadelphia, WV 26059
Administrator: HELEN B. CONRAD, Rt. I, Box I16, Triadelphia, WV
26059
Publications: *The Redstart; The Mail Bag*
Editors: DR. A.R. BUCKELEW, JR., Box J, Bethany, WV 26032;
ROBERT RINE, 157 Beacon Dr., Weirton, WV 26062

83

BROTHERHOOD OF THE JUNGLE COCK, INC., THE, P.O. Box
576, Glen Burnie, MD 21061
Seeks to teach youth the true meaning of conservation. Primary
interest is the preservation of American game fishes, placing great
emphasis on adult responsibility of personal instruction along those
lines.

President: BILL HAMPT

1st Vice-President: GENE HIGDON

Administrator: BOSLEY WRIGHT (301, 761-7727)

Assistant Executive Vice-President: GENE HIGDON, 7846 Hillsway Ave., Baltimore, MD 21234 (823-8906)

Secretary: EDWARD T. LITTLE, 6623 Kenwood Ave., Baltimore, MD 21237 (682-4631)

Treasurer: M.H. DAY, 706 Orchard Way, Silver Spring, MD 20904

84

CAMP FIRE CLUB OF AMERICA, THE, 230 Camp Fire Rd., Chappaqua, NY 10514 (914, 941-0199)

Works to preserve forests and woodland; to protect and conserve the wildlife of our country; to sponsor and support all reasonable measures to the end that present and future generations may continue to enjoy advantages and benefits of life in the great outdoors. Organized: 1897.

Committee on Conservation of Forests and Wildlife

Chairman: PETER ROEMER

Deputy Chairman: LLOYD B. MORGAN

Publication: *The Backlog*

Editor: MARK F. BECK

85

CAMP FIRE CONSERVATION FUND, INC., 230 Camp Fire Rd., Chappaqua, NY 10514 (914, 941-2800)

A tax-exempt membership organization dedicated to the preservation of wildlife and their habitat. To coordinate the efforts of sportsmen's and conservation organizations; to inform the general public and governmental agencies with regard to intelligent use of our natural resources; and to support and promote conservation research. Founded: 1977.

President: HENRY F. AYRES, JR. (203, 869-8310)

Vice-President: GEORGE R. LAMB

Treasurer: MOTTELL D. PEEK

Secretary: WALTER C. KEHM

Directors: FRANK W. KIEPER; PETER ROEMER; L.R. WALDVOGEL, JR.; THOMAS J. FISHER; ALFRED S. REED; WALTER C. KEHM; CHARLES J. SPIES, JR.; JOSEPH KARCZMIT, JR.; WILLIAM C. PARKER; JAMES S. TROY; HENRY F. AYRES, JR.; WILLIAM W. BUCHER; GEORGE R. LAMB; LLOYD B. MORGAN; MOTTELL D. PEEK

86

CAMP FIRE, INC., 4601 Madison Ave., Kansas City, MO 64112 (816, 756-1950)

Open to boys and girls from birth to 21 years of age, without regard to race, creed, ethnic origin, sex, or income level. Provides a program of informal education that focuses on developing skills in interpersonal relationships, decision-making, leadership, creativity, citizenship, community service, and individual growth. Membership: 500,000. Founded: 1910.

National President: CHARLES A. HEINRICH

National Executive Director: DAVID W. BAHLMANN

Director, Program Department: CONNIE COUTELLIER

87

CANADA-UNITED STATES ENVIRONMENTAL COUNCIL

Nongovernmental organization sponsored by major Canadian and American conservation and environmental groups. Established in 1974 to facilitate interchange of information and cooperative action on questions of concern in the two nations.

Coordinating Committee Co-Chairmen:

United States: JAMES G. DEANE, Defenders of Wildlife, 1244 19th St., NW, Washington, DC 20036 (202, 659-9510)

Canada: PAUL GRISS, Canadian Nature Federation, 75 Albert St., Ottawa, Ontario K1P 6G1 (613, 238-6154)

88

CANVASBACK SOCIETY, THE, P.O. Box 101, Gates Mills, OH 44040 (216, 443-2340)

A nonprofit, tax-exempt organization established to conserve, restore and promote the increase of the canvasback species of duck on the North American continent. Founded: 1975.

Chairman of the Board: KEITH C. RUSSELL

President: OAKLEY V. ANDREWS (621-0200)

Vice-President and Secretary: R. DUGALD PEARSON (696-4640)

Treasurer: OAKLEY V. ANDREWS (621-0200)

Publication: *The Canvasbacker*

89

CARIBBEAN CONSERVATION ASSOCIATION, Savannah Lodge, The Garrison, St. Michael, Barbados; (Tel. 809, 426-5373/426-9635)

An associate member organization of the National Wildlife Federation. Ascertains and coordinates the conservation needs of the area, encourages the creation of national and other conservation organizations in each island and country, and helps to foster in the people of the Caribbean a greater awareness of the value of their natural and cultural resources. Founded: 1967.

President: YVES RENARD

Executive Director: MICHAEL I. KING

Secretary: DR. FRANK WADSWORTH

Treasurer: DR. MELVIN GOODWIN

Publication: *Caribbean Conservation News*

Editor: CALVIN HOWELL

90

CARIBBEAN CONSERVATION CORPORATION, P.O. Box 2866, Gainesville, FL 32602 (904, 373-6441)

A nonprofit international membership organization founded in 1959 to support research and conservation of marine turtles in the Caribbean and throughout the world. In addition to conservation activities, it operates a research station at Tortuguero, Costa Rica--the site of the largest green turtle nesting colony in the Caribbean Sea--and maintains a semi-natural impoundment for sea turtles on Great Inagua Island in the Bahamas.

Chairman of the Board of Directors: CHARLES D. WEBSTER, P.O. Box 196, Islip, NY 11751 (516, 581-0965)

President: COLIN S. PHIPPS, P.O. Box 14206, Tallahassee, FL 32317 (904, 893-3514)

Secretary: DAVID CARR

Treasurer: WILLIAM H. LANE, P.O. Box 3048, Tallahassee, FL 32315 (904, 893-6666)

Executive Director: DAVID CARR

Publication: *Velador*

Editor: DAVID CARR

Costa Rica Office

GUILLERMO CRUZ B., Apartado Postal 6975-1000, San Jose, Costa Rica (506, 33-80-69)

91

CASCADE HOLISTIC ECONOMIC CONSULTANTS (CHEC), P.O. Box 3479, Eugene, OR 97403 (503, 686-CHEC)

Nonprofit, tax-exempt consultant firm providing low cost technical and educational services to forestry conservation groups, specializing in public forest planning and management. Founded: 1974.

Director, Forester and Economist: RANDAL O'TOOLE

Wildlife Biologist: DIETER MAHLEIN

Publications: *Forest Watch Magazine; Reform! Newsletter;* research papers

Editor: ANAE BOULTON

92

CENTER FOR ENVIRONMENTAL EDUCATION, INC., 1725 DeSales St., NW, Suite 500, Washington, DC 20036 (202, 429-5609)

A nonprofit, tax-exempt organization dedicated to conservation of endangered and threatened species and their marine habitats. The center sponsors several special programs: The Whale Protection Fund, Seal Rescue Fund, and Sea Turtle Rescue Fund. The Marine Habitat Program, and the Endangered Species Project. Program efforts focus on research, policy analysis, education, and public information and involvement. Membership: 110,000. Founded: 1972.

Chairman of the Board: WILLIAM Y. BROWN

Board of Directors: LARRY BARRETT; GORDON WOOD; NORMAN ROBERTS; MICHAEL FRANKEL; BONNIE COHEN; ANTHONY LAPHAM; CAMERON SANDERS; STEVEN MELANDER-DAYTON; VAUGHAN BROWN

President: ROGER E. McMANUS

Publications: *The CEE Report;* list of additional publications on request.

93

CEIP FUND, INC., THE, 68 Harrison Ave., Boston, MA 02111 (617, 426-4375)

A nonprofit, educational organization operating regional offices throughout the country. The regional offices work with government, corporations, and citizens groups on a wide variety of environmental issues. It matches over 300 advanced-level college and graduate students seeking professional paid experience. Career planning management along with conferences and workshops are provided through its professional development services.

President: JOHN R. COOK, JR.

Treasurer: JERRY TONE

Northeast Office: MARLA MEYER, Regional Director, 68 Harrison Ave., 5th Fl., Boston, MA 02111

California Office: ELIZABETH ECKL, Regional Director, 512 Second St., San Francisco, CA 94107 (415, 543-4400)

Great Lakes Office: LEE P. DeANGELIS, Regional Director, Professional Development Services, 332 The Arcade, Cleveland, OH 44114 (216, 861-4545)

Pacific Northwest Office: ANDREA HALLECK, Regional Director, 731 Securities Bldg., Seattle, WA 98101 (206, 625-1750)

94

CENTER FOR INTERNATIONAL DEVELOPMENT AND ENVIRONMENT OF THE WORLD RESOURCES INSTITUTE, THE (CIDE) (formly International Institute for Environment and Development, 1717 Massachusetts Ave., NW, Suite 302, Washington, DC 20036 (202, 462-0900)

CIDE is a nonprofit center providing services for developing countries in the sustainable management of natural resources. It focuses on the connections between human needs, the environment and economic development. Current programs include: developing non-governmental groups; forestry and land use; sustainable agriculture and environmental planning. Sister organizations in London and Buenos Aires. Established: January 1971.

Executive Director: THOMAS H. FOX

95

CENTER FOR PLANT CONSERVATION, INC., 125 Arborway, Jamaica Plain, MA 02130 (617, 524-6988)

A national network of 19 botanical gardens and arboreta dedicated to the conservation and study of rare and endangered U.S. plants. The center establishes conservation collections of endangered species in regional gardens and seed banks as a resource for conservation and research efforts: The National Collection of Endangered Plants.

Executive Director: DONALD A. FALK

Program Directors: DR. KERRY S. WALTER; DR. LINDA R. McMAHAN

Publication: *Plant Conservation* Newsletter

Editor: LINDA R. McMAHAN

96

CENTER FOR SCIENCE IN THE PUBLIC INTEREST, 1501 16th St., NW, Washington, DC 20036 (202, 332-9110)

National consumer advocacy organization that focuses on health and nutrition issues. CSPI informs the public of its findings through a variety of publications, press releases, speeches, media appearances, and initiates legal actions. The center has an intern program throughout the year. Membership: 90,000. Founded: 1971.

Executive Director: MICHAEL F. JACOBSON, Ph.D.

Publications: *Nutrition Action Healthletter;* reports, posters, and software

97

CENTRAL STATES RESOURCE CENTER, 809 S. Fifth, Champaign, IL 61820 (217, 344-2371)

A regional conservation organization primarily concerned with water policy, solid, hazardous, and radioactive waste issues. Organizational and research assistance is provided to persons and organizations involved in related activities. Founded: 1972.

Executive Director: JOHN W. THOMPSON (356-6210)

President: BRUCE M. HANNON (352-3646)

Secretary: ROBERT BALES (896-2297)

Treasurer: ANNE EHRLICH (352-8818)

Publications: *Rivers; Roads; Toxic Wastes*

98

CHARLES A. LINDBERGH FUND, INC., THE, Drawer O, Summit, NJ 07901 (201, 522-1392)

The Charles A. Lindbergh Fund will promote and advance Charles Lindbergh's vision by offering grants to individuals working for a better balance between technological progress and the preservation of our human and natural environment to achieve a better quality of life for all. Established: 1977 in New York City. Associate membership information is available by writing the president.

President: CHARLES G. HOUGHTON III

Vice-President: REEVE LINDBERGH TRIPP

Secretary: JAMES W. LLOYD

Treasurer: DR. SYLVIA A. EARLE

Grants and Awards Administrator: GLORIA S. PERKINS

Chairperson, Grants Selection Committee: REEVE LINDBERGH TRIPP

Chairperson, Award Committee: DR. SYLVIA A. EARLE

Publication: *The Charles A. Lindbergh Fund Newsletter*

Editor: GENE BRATSCH

99

CHELONIA INSTITUTE, P.O. Box 9174, Arlington, VA 22209 (703, 524-4900)

A private operating foundation with ecological concerns focused primarily on the conservation of marine turtles. The institute undertakes a broad range of programs including land acquisition, technical publications, and so on, and works cooperatively with many other organizations. Founded: 1977.

Trustees: ROBERT W. TRULAND, ALICE O. TRULAND

Director: ROBERT W. TRULAND

Assistant Director: MARY W. TRULAND

Program Director: DR. PETER PRITCHARD

100

CHIHUAHUAN DESERT RESEARCH INSTITUTE, P.O. Box
1334, Alpine, TX 79831 (915, 837-8370)
Nonprofit organization formed to promote human understanding
and appreciation of the Chihuahuan Desert through scientific
research and public education. Current studies include life history
related studies, systematic zoology, systematic botany, desert
ecology, anthropology, archeology, geology, and theoretical ecology. Founded: 1974.
President: JAMES F. SCUDDAY, Ph.D.
Vice-President: JACK POPE, JR.
Secretary: THOMAS BRUNNER
Treasurer: DAVID MOORE
Executive Director: DENNIS J. MILLER
Publications: *CDRI Contributions; The Chihuahuan Desert Discovery; Chihuahaun Newsbriefs*

101

CHILDREN OF THE GREEN EARTH, Box 95219, Seattle, WA
98145
A growing worldwide association of individuals committed to re-
greening the Earth by helping young people plant and care for trees
and forests. The organization publishes educational materials, a
period newsletter, and promotes tree planting efforts by young
people worldwide. A partnership program involves groups in
Germany, India, Lesotho, South Africa, Senegal, and Nepal. Founded in 1980, by the late Dr. Richard St. Barbe Baker, and friends at
the United Nations. We assist others in becoming involved through
work in their own local communities.
Board of Directors: MICHAEL SOULE (206, 781-0852); DOROTHY
CRAIG (754-7842)
Publication: Newsletter, *Tree Song,* Reprints, send for sample and
list.
Editor: HOLLY KOTTEN

102

CLEAN WATER ACTION PROJECT, 317 Pennsylvania Ave.,
SE, Washington, DC 20003 (202, 547-I196)
A national citizen organization working for clean and safe water at
an affordable cost, control of toxic chemicals and the protection of
our nation's natural resources. Works to influence public policy
decisions at all levels of government through advocacy, education,
technical assistance, grassroots organizing, and lobbying. Conducts
summer and year-round intern programs. Organizes coalitions of
diverse economic and political constituencies. Conducts voter
education programs. Membership: 400,000. Founded: 1971.
Board of Directors: SOPHIE ANN AOKI; DAVID GRUBB; PETER
LOCKWOOD; PETER MONTAGUE; PATRICIA SCHIFFERLE;
DAVID ZWICK
Executive Director: DAVID ZWICK
Science Director: DR. HENRY COLE
Campaigns Director: ERIC DRAPER
National Canvass Coordinator: GARY STEINBERG
Publications: *Clean Water Action News;* information on other
publications and reports, etc. is available upon request.

Regional Offices

Chesapeake (MD, VA): JOHN KABLER, Director, 2500 N. Charles
St., Baltimore, MD 21218 (301, 235-8808)
Other Chesapeake Offices: 217 West Grace St., Richmond, VA
23220 (804, 649-9075); 201 Granby St., Rm. 510, Norfolk,
VA 23510 (804, 623-4784)
Mid-Atlantic (DE, NJ, PA): (Clean Water Action's New Jersey
chapter is in the New Jersey Environmental Federation). KEN
BROWN, Director, 46 Bayard St., Rm. 309, New Brunswick, NJ
08901 (201, 846-4224)

Other Mid-Atlantic Offices: 921 Main St., 2nd Fl., Belmar, NJ
07719 (201, 280-8988); 606 Bloomfield Ave., 2nd Fl.,
Bloomfield, NJ 07003 (201, 680-8446); 37 South 13th St.,
5th Fl., Philadelphia, PA 19107 (215, 557-8044); 4 Smithfield St., 6th Fl., Pittsburgh, PA 15222 (412, 765-3053)
Midwest (IA, MN, MI, ND, WI): DIANE JENSEN, Co-Director, 2395
University Ave., St. Paul, MN 55114 (612, 645-0961)
Other Midwest Offices: 2904 West 3rd St., Duluth, MN 55804
(218, 628-0391); 122 South Grand Ave., Lansing, MI 48933
(517, 487-0900)
New England (MA, ME, NH, RI, VT): AMY GOLDSMITH, Director,
186 A South St., Boston, MA 02111 (617, 423-4661)
Other New England Offices: 15 Pray St., Amherst, MA 01002
(413, 549-7450)
South/Southwest (TX): ERIC MENDELMAN, Staff Director, 610
Brazos St., Suite 101, Austin, TX 78701 (512, 474-0605)

103

CLEAN WATER FUND, National Office, 317 Pennsylvania Ave.,
SE, 3rd Fl., Washington, DC 20005 (202, 547-2312)
A national nonprofit, tax-exempt, research and educational organization that began operating in 1978. Primary goals are to advance
environmental and consumer protections (with a special focus on
water pollution, toxic hazards, and natural resources) and develop
the grassroots strength of the environmental movement. The Clean
Water Fund specializes in helping to build strong ongoing citizen
leadership, organizations, and coalitions for more effective grassroots participation in policy debates. The Fund shares office space,
and some staff resources with Clean Water Action, a closely-
cooperating grassroots organization.
Executive Director: DAVID R. ZWICK
Board of Directors: SOPHIE ANN AOKI; PETER LOCKWOOD ;
BERNARD NAGELVOORT; DAVID BORDEN; GINA GLANTZ;
MICHAEL GRAVITZ; DAVID ZWICK
Publications: Information on publications and reports, etc. is
available upon request.

Regional Offices

Chesapeake (MD, VA): JOHN KABLER, Director, 2500 North
Charles St., Baltimore, MD 21218 (301, 235-8808)
Mid-Atlantic (DE, NJ, PA): KEN BROWN, Director, 46 Bayard St.,
Rm. 309, New Brunswick, NJ 08901 (201, 846-4224)
Midwest (IA, MN, MI, ND, WI): DIANE JENSEN, Co-Director, 2395
University Ave., St. Paul, MN 55114 (612, 645-0961)
New England (MA, ME, NH, RI, VT): AMY GOLDSMITH, Director,
186 A South St., Boston, MA 02111 (617, 423-4661)
South/Southwest (TX): DAVID ZWICK, Director (Acting), 610
Brazos St., Suite 101, Austin, TX 78701 (512, 474-0605)

104

COALITION FOR SCENIC BEAUTY, 218 D St., SE,
Washington, DC 20003 (202, 546-1100)
To fight billboard blight and other forms of visual pollution,
preserve scenic resources, and promote scenic highways. To
achieve these goals, the coalition provides educational material,
information and technical assistance to local government and
citizen groups interested in sign control, scenic highways and other
landscape protection measures.
President: CARROLL SHADDOCK (713, 226-1200)
Vice-Presidents: MARION F. BROWN, ME (207, 363-5289); RICK
MIDDLETON (804, 977-4090); JOHN C. MILLER, CA (415,
948-0893)
Executive Director: EDWARD McMAHON (202, 546-1100)
Secretary/Treasurer: RUTH H. BECKER, PA (215, 565-9131)
Publication: *Sign Control News*

105

COASTAL CONSERVATION ASSOCIATION, INC., 4801
   Woodway, Suite 220 West, Houston, TX 77056 (713,
   626-4222)
A national, nonprofit corporation organized exclusively for the
purpose of promoting and advancing the preservation, conserva-
tion and protection of the marine, animal and plant life both
onshore and offshore along the coastal areas of the United States
for the benefit and enjoyment of the general public. Membership:
35,000. Organized: 1977.
Chairman of the Board: WALTER W. FONDREN III, Houston, TX
Vice-Chairman: MAUMUS CLAVERIE, JR., New Orleans, LA
President: J. MANNING McPHILLIPS, Mobile, AL
Vice-Presidents: ALEX JERNIGAN, JR., Islamorada, FL; JACK
   LAWTON, JR., Sulphur, LA
Executive Director: RANDY O. BRIGHT, Houston, TX
Assistant Directors: BRUCE CARTWRIGHT, Houston, TX; JEFFER-
   SON P. SELLERS, Houston, TX
Secretary: KARL WICKSTROM, Miami, FL
Treasurer: JOHN MILNE, Houston, TX
Publication: *The Tide*
Editor: JOE RICHARD, Houston, TX

106

COASTAL SOCIETY, THE, 5410 Grosvenor Ln., Suite 110,
   Bethesda, MD 20814 (301, 897-8616)
An international nonprofit organization dedicated to promoting the
understanding and wise use of coastal environments. Through
conferences, workshops, and publications, the society seeks to
foster improved interdisciplinary communication, promote wise use
of resources consistent with natural processes, and further public
understanding and knowledge of the coast. Organized: 1975.
President: WILLIAM QUEEN, East Carolina University, Institute for
   Coastal amd Marine Resources, Greenville, NC 27834 (919,
   757-6779)
Treasurer: LAURIE McGILVRAY, NOAA, Office of Ocean and
   Coastal Resource Management (202, 673-5130)
Secretary: DARCEY ROSENBLATT, Technical Resources, Inc., Rock-
   ville, MD 20852 (301, 231-5250)
Directors: VIRGINIA TIPPIE; THOMAS BIGFORD; SHIRLEY FISKE;
   WILLIAM WISE; SUSAN ESSIG
Publication: *The Coastal Society Bulletin*
Editors: THOMAS E. BIGFORD; ELLEN GORDON

107

COLORADO RIVER FISH AND WILDLIFE COUNCIL, 241 North
   Vine St., East 401, Salt Lake City, UT 84103-1962
Formed to coordinate the protection and management of fish and
wildlife resources of the Colorado River. The council consists of
representatives of the wildlife agencies of the seven states located
on the Colorado River Drainage: Arizona, California, Colorado,
Nevada, New Mexico, Utah and Wyoming. A professional technical
committee advises the council. The council is active in encouraging,
promoting, advising and coordinating sound fisheries management,
planning, laws, and regulations. Founded: 1957.
Chairman: TEMPLE REYNOLDS, 2222 W. Greenway Rd., Phoenix,
   AZ 85023 (602, 942-3000)
Secretary: RODERICK STONE, 241 North Vine St., East 401, Salt
   Lake City, UT 84103 (801, 355-8714)
Chairman Technical Committee: JOSEPH JANISH, 2222 W. Green-
   way Rd., Phoenix, AZ 85023 (602, 942-3000)
Publications: *Endemic Fishes of the Colorado River System;
   Endemic Amphibians and Reptiles of the Colorado River System*

108

COLUMBIA BASIN FISH AND WILDLIFE AUTHORITY, 2000
   SW First Ave., Suite 170, Portland, OR 97201-5346 (503,
   294-7031)
A regional association of all the fish and wildlife agencies (two
federal, five state) and Indian tribes (13) in the Columbia River
Basin (Idaho, Montana, Oregon, and Washington). Established to
coordinate planning and implementation of the fish and wildlife
provisions of the Pacific Northwest Electric Power Planning and
Conservation Act and for oversight of fish and wildlife requirements
under the Fish and Wildlife Coordination Act and other authorities.
Originally organized: 1982; current charter: 1987.
Chairman: RANDY FISHER, Oregon Department of Fish and Wildlife, P.O. Box 59, Portland, OR 97207 (503, 229-5406)
Executive Secretary: JOHN R. DONALDSON
Water Budget Manager: MICHELE DeHART, Fish Passage Center,
   825 NE 20th Ave., Suite 336, Portland, OR 97232-2295
   (230-4288)

109

COMMITTEE FOR NATIONAL ARBOR DAY, THE
To establish a unified national observance date on the last Friday in
April. Organized: 1936.
Honorary National Chairman: MRS. EDWARD H. SCANLON, P.O.
   Box 38247, Olmsted Falls, OH 44138
National Chairman: HARRY J. BANKER, 640 Eagle Rock Ave., West
   Orange, NJ 07052

110

CONCERN, INC., 1794 Columbia Rd., NW, Washington, DC
   20009 (202, 328-8160)
A nonprofit, tax-exempt organization which provides environmental
information to individuals and groups. Concern's publications give
an overview of the issue and include guidelines to encourage and
aid citizen participation in the community and in policy decisions at
the local, state, and federal levels of government. Founded: 1970.
Executive Director: SUSAN BOYD
Treasurer: MARY P. SLAYTON
Chairman of the Board: BURKS LAPHAM
Publications: *Community Action Guides on Groundwater, Pesticides, and Drinking Water* (each revised 1987); *Farmland: A
   Community Issue* (1987); *Waste: Choices for Communities*
   (1988)

111

CONNECTICUT RIVER WATERSHED COUNCIL, INC.,
   Headquarters, 125 Combs Rd., Easthampton, MA 01027
   (413, 584-0057)
A member-supported, nonprofit organization, CRWC is the only
regional voice for improvement and protection of surface and
ground water resources throughout the 11,260 square-mile, four-
state river basin of Vermont, New Hampshire, Massachusetts, and
Connecticut. CRWC participates in relevant environmental and
resource allocation issues through its land conservancy, water
quality improvement, and watershed stewardship programs. Land
conservancy revolving loan fund. Conservation education and
research grant fund. Membership: 2,500. Established: 1952.
Chairman: ASTRID T. HANZALEK
Vice-Chairmen: RUSSELL L. BRENNEMAN, Esq., Hartford, CT; ANN
   Q. SOUTHWORTH, Longmeadow, MA; GEORGE W. MOULTON,
   Charlestown, NH; PETER RICHARDSON, Norwich, VT
Executive Director: PHILIP H. KLOTZ
Secretary-Treasurer: FRANKLIN P. KEARNEY

Field Office, Regional Directors: GEOFFREY G. DATES, 312 First New Hampshire Bank Bldg., Lebanon, NH 03766 (603, 448-2792); CT, 118 Oak St., Hartford, CT 06103 (203, 293-0227)
Publications: *The Valley Newsletter; Currents and Eddies; The Complete Boating Guide to The Connecticut River*

112

CONSERVATION AND RESEARCH FOUNDATION, INC., THE

To promote the conservation of renewable natural resources; to encourage study and research in the biological sciences; and to deepen understanding of the intricate relationship between man and the environment that supports him. Founded: 1953.
President: RICHARD H. GOODWIN, Connecticut College, New London, CT 06320 (203, 873-8514)
Treasurer: RICHARD H. GOODWIN, JR., Cabin John, MD (301, 229-8598)
Clerk: JOHN R. JOHNSTON, Warner and Stackpole, Rm. 1600, 28 State St., Boston, MA 02109 (617, 725-1400)
Secretary: MARY G. WETZEL, 7317 Broxburn Ct., Bethesda, MD 20817 (301, 229-6025)
Trustees: WALLACE D. BOWMAN, Falls Church, VA (703, 256-8606); WINSLOW R. BRIGGS, Stanford, CA (415, 325-1521); BELTON A. COPP, Old Lyme, CT (203, 434-7805); SARAH M. B. HENRY, Concord, NH (603, 228-1068); HUBERT W. VOGELMANN, Burlington, VT (802, 656-2930); ALEXANDER T. WILSON, Brattleboro, VT (802, 257-0019)

113

CONSERVATION DISTRICTS FOUNDATION, INC., Conservation Film Service, Davis Conservation Library, 404 E. Main, P.O. Box 776, League City, TX 77574-0776 (713, 332-3404)

Directed by the Conservation Districts Foundation, Inc., an adjunct of the National Association of Conservation Districts. Collects, catalogs, and loans materials pertinent to the social, economic, and political aspects of the conservation movement in America. Dedicated to the memory of Waters S. Davis, Past President of NACD. Organized: 1962.
Executive Vice-President: ERNEST SHEA, NACD, 509 Capitol Ct., NE, Washington, DC 20002

114

CONSERVATION EDUCATION ASSOCIATION

Encourages local, state, and national conservation education programs by disseminating news, ideas, and suggestions on conservation education through annual conferences and reports, a newsletter, other publications, special projects, and cooperation with organizations and agencies active in this field. Organized: 1953.
President: ROBERT RYE, Conservation Education Center, R.R. #1, Box 53, Guthrie Center, IA 50115
1st Vice-President: HOLLIS CRAWFORD, Missouri Department of Conservation, P.O. Box 180, Jefferson City, MO 65102
2nd Vice-President: ALICE STEINBACH, 70 Cedar Lake, Chelsea, MI 48118
Executive Secretary: DAN SEBERT, Oklahoma Conservation Commission, 2800 N. Lincoln Blvd., Suite 160, Oklahoma City, OK 73105
Past President: KEN FRAZIER, 518 6th St., Boone, IA 50036
Publication: Newsletter
Editor: CELE BURNETT, Story County Conservation Board

115

CONSERVATION FOUNDATION, THE, 1250 24th St., NW, Washington, DC 20037 (202, 293-4800)

Affiliated with World Wildlife Fund-U.S., is a nonprofit research and public education organization promoting wise use of the earth's resources. Conducts research and/or provides technical assistance in land use (including a field program called successful communities), toxic substances, risk assessment, water resources, environmental dispute resolution, environmental issues in developing countries, and reports periodically on environmental conditions and trends. Founded: 1948.
Chairman of the Board: RUSSELL E. TRAIN
President: WILLIAM K. REILLY
Executive Vice-President: J. CLARENCE DAVIES III
Vice-President for Planning and Evaluation: JOHN H. NOBLE
Vice-President for Finance and Administration: PAIGE K. MacDONALD
Vice-President for Development: JANEEN WALLACE STOUT
Vice-Presidents: EDWIN H. CLARK II; GAIL BINGHAM; H. JEFFREY LEONARD
Vice-President, Communications: JULIA A. MOORE
General Counsel: MICHAEL MANTELL
Senior Associates: FRANCES H. IRWIN; RICHARD A. LIROFF; PHYLLIS MYERS; SUZANNE GOULET ORENSTEIN; WILLIAM E. SHANDS
Senior Fellows: HOWARD S. BELLMAN; RICHARD E. BENEDICK; BLAIR BOWER; RICHARD Z. DONOVAN; BENJAMIN C. DYSART III; JOHN E. EARHART; DANIEL J. FIORINO; JOSEPH FISHER; ROBERT G. HEALY; JANET MENDELSOHN; V. ALARIC SAMPLE; KONRAD VON MOLTKE; THOMAS E. WADDELL
Director of Publications: ROBERT J. McCOY
Librarian: BARBARA K. RODES
Publications: *Conservation Foundation Letter; Resolve; Successful Communities;* books, films, reports, and conferences; publications catalog available.

116

CONSERVATION FUND, THE, 1800 North Kent St., Suite 1120, Arlington, VA 22209 (703, 525-6300)

A national nonprofit organization dedicated to advancing land and water conservation with creative ideas and new resources; establishes partnerships with other nonprofit organizations, public agencies and the private sector. Provides specialized services ranging from land planning and acquisition to ecological assessment and communications support. Collaborates with public and private partners to conserve land. Programs: Giftlands, Conservation 100, Greenways for America, Spring and Groundwater Resources Institute, Conservation Leadership Project, Conservation Enterprise and Conservation Partnership awards. Organized: 1985.
President: PATRICK F. NOONAN
Vice-President, Development: KIKU HOAGLAND HANES
Treasurer: HADLAI HULL
Legal Counsel: RICHARD L. ERDMANN
Associate Director, Development: DAVID TREVETT
Senior Associates: JOSEPH C. DAVIS; WILLIAM deBUYS; KEITH HAY; DOUGLAS HORNE; DOUGLAS LUDINGTON; JACK LYNN; TOM MACY; ROBERT PUTZ; JON ROUSH; DAVE SUTHERLAND

117

CONSERVATION LAW FOUNDATION OF NEW ENGLAND, INC., (CLF), 3 Joy St., Boston, MA 02108 (617, 742-2540)

A nonprofit, environmental law organization dedicated to improved resource management, environmental protection, and public health in New England. Work includes: energy conservation and utility regulation; environmental health; water resource protection; public and private land preservation; legal assistance in environmental matters; and marine resources protection. Founded: 1966. Membership: 5,000.
Chairman of the Board: HON. FRANCIS W. HATCH, JR.
Vice-Chairman of the Board: DR. JOHN M. TEAL

Secretary-Treasurer: DAVID F. CAVERS, JR.
Executive Director: DOUGLAS I. FOY
Publications: *Power to Spare* (energy conservation opportunities in New England); *A Silent and Costly Epidemic* (costs of childhood lead poisoning); *Annual Report;* Newsletter
Editor: JEAN PENDLETON

118

COOLIDGE CENTER FOR ENVIRONMENTAL LEADERSHIP, 1675 Massachusetts Ave., Suite 4, Cambridge, MA 02138-1836 (617, 864-5085)
The center organizes programs for future leaders of developing countries on environment and sustainable development; supports efforts in universities of New England and New York relating to environment and development; has a library on sustainable development; sponsors special programs for the general public; and provides information on organizations and individuals working on these subjects. Established 1983 in honor of Harold J. Coolidge.
Chairman of Board: PETER J. AMES
Executive Director: BRUCE J. STEDMAN
Program Director: CLARE HILLIKER
Program Associates: POONAN MUHREJA; CATHY CRUMBLEY

119

COOPER ORNITHOLOGICAL SOCIETY, Department of Biology, University of California, Los Angeles, CA 90024-1606
Observation and cooperative study of birds; the spread of interest in bird study; the conservation of birds and wildlife in general; the publication of ornithological knowledge. Founded: 1893. Membership: 2,200.
President: DR. RUSSELL P. BALDA, Department of Biological Science, Northern Arizona University, Flagstaff, AZ 86011 (602, 523-4307)
President-Elect: JARED VERNER, Forestry Science Lab., 2081 E. Sierra Ave., Fresno, CA 93710 (209, 487-5588)
Secretary: DR. MICHAEL L. MORRISON, Department of Forestry and Resource Management, University of California, Berkeley, CA 94720 (415, 642-5344)
Treasurer: ROBERT SZARO, USDA Forest Service, Forestry Sciences Lab., Arizona State University, Tempe, AZ 85287-1304
Publications: *The Condor; Studies in Avian Biology*
Editors: DR. MARTIN L. MORTON, DR. JOSEPH R. JHEL, JR.

120

COUSTEAU SOCIETY, INC., THE, Headquarters: 930 W. 21st St., Norfolk, VA 23517 (804, 627-1144); 425 East 52nd St., New York, NY 10022 (212, 826-2940); 8440 Santa Monica Blvd., Los Angeles, CA 90069 (213, 656-4422); 25 Wagram, F75017 Paris, France (14-766-02-46)
A nonprofit, membership-supported environmental education organization dedicated to the protection and improvement of the quality of life; believing that an informed and alerted public can best make the choices for a more productive way of living, it produces television films, research, lectures, books, and other publications. Membership: 250,000. Created: 1973.
President and Chairman of the Board: JACQUES-YVES COUSTEAU
Executive Vice-President: JEAN-MICHEL COUSTEAU
Vice-President, European Business Affairs: HENRI JACQUIER
Vice-President, Science and Technology and International Affairs: JACQUES CONSTANS
Vice-President, Business Affairs: CHARLES W. VINICK
Vice-President, Finance: ROBERT L. STEELE
Vice-President, Science and Education: RICHARD C. MURPHY
Publications: *Calypso Log; Dolphin Log*
Editors: PAMELA STACEY; MARY BATTEN

121

CRAIGHEAD ENVIRONMENTAL RESEARCH INSTITUTE, Box 156, Moose, WY 83012 (307, 733-3387)
A nonprofit, professional organization of scientists, dedicated to exploring the cause-and-effect relationships of man and his environment. Activity includes research, education, and conservation, with emphasis on ecological studies and interdisciplinary approach. Originally the Outdoor Recreation Institute. Staff Members: 6. Founded: 1955.
President: FRANK C. CRAIGHEAD, JR.
Program Director: FRANK L. CRAIGHEAD
Media Director: CHARLES S. CRAIGHEAD (307, 739-9527)

122

J.N. (DING) DARLING FOUNDATION, INC., c/o RALPH SCHLENKER, Treasurer, P.O. Box 657, Des Moines, IA 50303 (515, 281-2371)
To initiate, coordinate, guide, and expedite programs, research, education and to provide educational grants for students in fish, wildlife, conservation and environmental courses that will bring about conservation and sound management of our country's natural resources of water, woods, and soil; restore and preserve historical sites; create and assist in wildlife management plans; improve and assure outdoor recreational opportunities for present and future generations.
President, Board of Trustees and Chairman Executive Committee: CHRISTOPHER KOSS

123

DEFENDERS OF WILDLIFE, 1244 19th St., NW, Washington, DC 20036 (202, 659-9510)
A national nonprofit organization whose goal is to preserve, enhance, and protect the natural abundance and diversity of wildlife including the integrity of natural wildlife ecosystems. Defenders recognizes the intrinsic value of wildlife, the importance of its humane treatment and the many benefits of wildlife to society. Defenders seeks to achieve its goals through education and reasoned advocacy of appropriate public policies. Membership: 80,000. Founded: 1947.
President: DR. M. RUPERT CUTLER
Board-Chair: BRENDA T. MOORMAN
Vice-Chair: DR. BERNARD SHANKS
Secretary: MAXINE F. McCLOSKEY
Treasurer: ALAN W. STEINBERG
Public Information Director: DANIEL C. SMITH
Controller: CHRISTOPHER F. CARR
Development Director: JAMES K. HICKEY
Assistant Development Director: SUSAN ALPERN FISCH
Conservation Director: GAY MacKINTOSH
Associate Conservation Director for Government Relations: KATHRYN R. TOLLERTON
Senior Staff, Wildlife Biologist: ALBERT M. MANVILLE II
Washington Representative for Wildlife Protection: SUSAN P. HAGOOD
Washington Representative for Endangered Wildlife: GINGER MERCHANT MEESE
Counsel for Wildlife Policy: JOHN M. FITZGERALD
Activist Coordinator: CINDY SHOGAN
Regional Program Director: SARA VICKERMAN, 0434 SW Iowa, Portland, OR 97201 (503, 293-1433)

Regional Representatives
KAREN WOODSUM, Northeast, P.O. Box 2820, R.F.D. 1, Wayne, ME 04284 (207, 685-9442)
HANK FISCHER, Northern Rockies, 1534 Mansfield Ave., Missoula, MT 59801 (406, 549-0761)

AUBREY STEPHEN JOHNSON, Southwest, 13795 N. Como Dr., Tucson, AZ 85741 (602, 297-1434)

RICHARD SPOTTS, California, Nevada, 5604 Rosedale Way, Sacramento, CA 95822 (916, 442-6386)

Publications: *Defenders; Activist Network News; Newsletter; Saving Endangered Wildlife*

Editor: JAMES G. DEANE

124

DESERT BIGHORN COUNCIL, P.O. Box 521, Winnemucca, NV 89445

International organization established to promote the advancement of knowledge concerning the desert bighorn sheep, and the long-range welfare of these animals in Mexico and the United States. Membership: 128. Organized: 1957.

Chairman: JERRY L. WOLFE, 2771 Cheyenne Dr., Grand Junction, CO 81503

Vice-Chairman: ALLEN COOPERRIDER, P.O. Box 558, La Porte, CO 80535

Secretary-Treasurer: DONALD J. ARMENTROUT, P.O. Box 521, Winnemucca, NV 89445

Technical Staff Chairman: RICHARD A. WEAVER, P.O. Box 1383, Loomis, CA 95650

Publication: *Desert Bighorn Council Transactions*

Editor: PAUL R. KRAUSMAN, 325 Biological Sciences E., University of Arizona, Tucson, AZ 85721

125

DESERT FISHES COUNCIL, 407 W. Line St., Bishop, CA 93514 (619, 872-1171)

A nationwide representation of state, federal, and university scientists and resource specialists, and private conservation groups to provide for the exchange and transmittal of information on the status, protection, and management of the endemic fauna and flora of North American desert ecosystems. Organized: 1969.

Chairman: GAIL C. KOBETICH, Sacramento Endangered Species Office, U.S. Fish and Wildlife Service, 2800 Cottage Way, Rm. E-1823, Sacramento, CA 95825 (916, 978-4866)

Chairman Elect: PAUL HOLDEN, Bio and West, Inc., P.O. Box 3226, Logan, UT 84321 (801, 752-4202)

Executive Secretary: EDWIN P. PISTER, Department of Fish and Game, 407 W. Line St., Bishop, CA 93514

Publication: *Proceedings of the Desert Fishes Council*

Editor: EDWIN P. PISTER

126

DESERT PROTECTIVE COUNCIL, INC., THE, P.O. Box 4294, Palm Springs, CA 92263

To safeguard by wise and reverent use those desert areas that are of unique scenic, scientific, historical, spiritual, and recreational value; to educate children and adults to better understand the desert so that it may be preserved. Organized: 1954.

President: BILL NEILL, 4900 Glenview, Anaheim, CA 92807 (714, 779-2099)

Vice-President: GLENN VARGAS, 85-159 Ave. 66, Thermal, CA 92274 (619, 397-4264)

Secretary: GLORIA NEILL, 4900 Glenview Ave., Anaheim, CA 92807 (714, 779-2099)

Treasurer: LYLE GASTON, 3648 Mt. Vernon, Riverside, CA 92507 (714, 686-0248)

Executive Director: MARY SWEDELIUS, 3941 Clark St., San Diego, CA 92103 (619, 295-5096)

Publication: Quarterly Newsletter, *El Paisano*

Editor: HARRIET ALLEN, 3750 El Canto Dr., Spring Valley, CA 92077 (619, 670-7127)

127

DESERT TORTOISE COUNCIL, 5319 Cerritos Ave., Long Beach, CA 90805 (213, 422-6172)

Organized in 1975 to assure the continued survival of viable populations of the desert tortoise, *Gopherus agassizi*, which is endemic to Arizona, California, Nevada, and Utah.

Co-Chairmen: JAMES ST. AMANT, 5319 Cerritos, Long Beach, CA 90805

Recording Secretary: TED CORDERZ, 5319 Cerritos Ave., Long Beach, CA 90805

Secretary: EVELYN ST. AMANT, 5319 Cerritos Ave., Long Beach, CA 90805

Treasurer: MIKE COFFEEN

128

DESERT TORTOISE PRESERVE COMMITTEE, INC., P.O. Box 453, Ridgecrest, CA 93555 (619, 377-4904)

A nonprofit organization formed to promote the welfare of the Desert Tortoise in the Southwestern United States and to establish a preserve as a natural area in a portion of the Upper Mojave Desert known to be ideal habitat. Founded: 1974.

President: GEORGE E. MONCSKO, 218 Primrose, Ridgecrest, CA 93555 (619, 375-9593)

Corresponding Secretary: JEAN E. JONES, 339 W. 25th St., San Bernardino, CA 92405 (714, 882-7825)

Treasurer: MARY TROTTER, 1835 Klauber Ave., San Diego, CA 92114 (619, 264-3352)

Publications: Newsletter; *Tortoise T-R-A-C-K-S*

Editor: JEAN E. JONES

129

DUCKS UNLIMITED, INC., One Waterfowl Way, Long Grove, IL 60047 (312, 438-4300) (Annual Meeting: 1989, May 3-May 7, Boston, MA)

Nonprofit, nonpolitical membership corporation, organized to perpetuate waterfowl and other wildlife on the North American continent, principally by development, preservation, restoration, management, and maintenance of wetland areas on the Canadian primary breeding grounds, which produce the majority of continental waterfowl; in prime waterfowl nesting, resting, and wintering areas of the U.S.; and, in the nesting and wintering areas of Mexico. Establishes, promotes, assists, and contributes to conservation, restoration and management of waterfowl habitat. Membership: 575,000. Organized: 1937.

President: HARRY D. KNIGHT, 100 Kingsmill Rd., Williamsburg, VA 23185 (804, 253-3950)

Chairman of the Board: HAZARD K. CAMPBELL, 3737 Marine Midland Center, Buffalo, NY 14203 (716, 849-3851)

Chairman of the Executive Committee: PETER H. COORS, Adolph Coors Company, Golden, CO 80401 (303, 277-3109)

Executive Vice-President: MATTHEW B. CONNOLLY JR., One Waterfowl Way, Long Grove, IL 60047 (312, 438-4300)

Counsel, Legal Committee Chairman: JAMES P. CONROY, c/o Porter, Wright, Morris and Arthur, Euclid Ave., Cleveland, OH 44115 (216, 443-9000)

Chairman Emeritus: E. HERRICK LOW, 975 Barriolhet Ave., Hillsborough, CA 94010 (415, 348-3556)

Flyway Senior Vice-Presidents

North Atlantic Flyway: RANDOLPH A. MARKS, 70 Sayre St., P.O. Box 981, Buffalo, NY 14240 (716, 879-6705)

South Atlantic Flyway: THOMAS L. WILLIAMS III, P.O. Box 1577, Thomasville, GA 31799 (912, 226-4300)

Northeast Mississippi Flyway: JOHN A. TOMKE, 2006 Wilmington, Midland, MI 48640 (517, 636-3671)

Northwest Mississippi Flyway: JEFF CHURAN, P.O. Box 787, Chillicothe, MO 64601 (816, 646-1330)
South Mississippi Flyway: RICHARD D. PHILLIPS, P.O. Box 41291, Memphis, TN 38174 (901, 526-7631)
North Central Flyway: HAROLD W. ANDERSEN, World Herald Square, Omaha, NE 68102 (402, 444-1000)
South Central Flyway: JOHN E. WALKER, 6608 Stewart Rd., Suite 412, Galveston, TX 77551 (409, 935-8606)
Pacific Flyway: JOSEPH O. HALL, 5303 Pacific Highway East, Fife, WA 98424 (206, 922-6815)

Senior Vice-Presidents (Advisory to the President)
Development: ROBERT D. MARCOTTE, 3568 Dodge St., Omaha, NE 68131 (402, 342-4175)
Membership: STEPHEN L. SCHUETZ, 155 N. Market, #800, Wichita, KS 67202 (316, 264-0616)
Conservation Programs: OMER W. LONG, 5 Upper Newport Plaza, Newport Beach, CA 92660 (714, 851-2460)
Special Projects: EDSON GALLAUDET II, 1263 Souter Blvd., Troy, MI 48083 (313, 585-6100)
Secretary: PETER N. PUND, 1020 Cedar Ave., St. Charles, IL 60174 (312, 584-7677)
Executive Secretary: KENNETH V. McCREARY, One Waterfowl Way, Long Grove, IL 60047 (312, 438-4300)
Treasurer: WILLIAM G. MECKLENBURG, 615 Laurie Ln., Northfield, IL 60093 (312, 446-7797)
Assistant Treasurers: WYNDHAM HASLER, Lake Forest, IL; STANLEY W. KOENIG, SR., Elgin, IL; PATRICK J. MULLADY, Lake Forest, IL; EDWARD M. PULS, Long Grove, IL; RICHARD T. SCHROEDER, Chicago, IL
Publication: *Ducks Unlimited Magazine*
Publisher: MATTHEW B. CONNOLLY, JR.
Editor-in-Chief: LEE D. SALBER

Regional Vice-Presidents
Northeast Atlantic: MAURICE A. HARVEY, Charlotte, VT
North Atlantic: CHARLES F. KANE, Boston, MA
North Central Atlantic: JOHN T. O'BRIEN, Batavia, NY
South Central Atlantic: LARRY LEESE, Ocean City, MD
South Atlantic: MARVIN N. DAVANT, Columbia, SC
North Mississippi: J. DANIEL BAASEN, Minneapolis, MN
East Central Mississippi: EDWARD J. MOXLEY, Vickery, OH
Mid-Central Mississippi: FRANKLIN H. PETERSOHN, Evansville, IN
West Central Mississippi: JOHN R. BELZ, St. Louis, MO
South Central Mississippi: KEITH WILLIAMS, Harrods Creek, KY
South West Mississippi: BARRE C. TANGUIS, Monroe, LA
South Mississippi: EDWIN H. ROBERTS, Oxford, MS
North Central: MAYNARD ISAACSON, Sioux Falls, SD
Northwest Central: SCOTT LIVENGOOD, Billings, MT
Mid-Central: ROBERT H. HAWKINS, Broken Arrow, OK
South Central: KENT VAN METER, McKinney, TX
Pacific Intermountain: STEPHEN G. DENKERS, Ogden, UT
North Pacific: CLARK SPRINGER, Fairbanks, AK
South Pacific: ROBERT J. SCIUTTO, Orinda, CA

National Staff
Executive Vice-President: MATTHEW B. CONNOLLY JR.
Executive Group Manager/Fiscal Officer: EDWARD M. PULS
Executive Secretary: KENNETH V. McCREARY
Group Manager, Conservation Programs: DAVID E. WESLEY, Ph.D.
Group Manager, Communications: CHARLOTTE RUSH
Group Manager, Fiscal Operations: K. RAY LIGGETT
Director, Government Relations: MICHAEL E. BERGER, Ph.D.
Director, Development: HUNTINGTON ELDRIDGE JR.
Director, Habitat Inventory and Evaluation: GREGORY T. KOELN, Ph.D.

Director, Special Projects: JONATHAN KRONSBERG
Membership Services Manager: CAROL J. MAIER
Director, Field Operations: BRENT MANNING
Director, MARSH Programs: JEFFREY W. NELSON
Director, Personnel: HANS SCHILLER
Director, Membership Development: CLIFFORD J. SCHULTZ
Internal Auditor: GRAEME STEWART
Director, Information and Education: RICHARD V. WENTZ

MARSH Coordinators
Atlantic Flyway: RALPH A. BITELY, Rt. 1, Box 179, Queenstown, MD 21658 (301, 827-7793)
Mississippi Flyway: DONALD W. THOMPSON, II Sylwood Pl., Jackson, MS 39209 (601, 982-5226)
Central Flyway: B.J. ROSE, 14937 N St., Omaha, NE 68137 (402, 895-1005)
Pacific Flyway: JOHN NAGEL, 9823 Old Winery Pl., Suite 16, Sacramento, CA 95827 (916, 363-8257)

Great Plains Regional Office
6115 E. Main Ave., Bismarck, ND 58501 (701, 258-5599)
Regional Operations Supervisor: ROBERT L. MEEKS, Ph.D.

Western Regional Office
9823 Old Winery Pl., Suite 16, Sacramento, CA 95827 (916, 363-8257)
Field Operations Supervisor, Pacific Flyway: JAMES WARE
Regional Operations Supervisor: JOHN NAGEL

Pacific Flyway Field Operations Supervisor
JAMES WARE, Sacramento, CA

Regional Supervisors
N. California-Hawaii-Oregon: JEROME CAWTHON, Los Banos, CA
S. California-Arizona-Nevada: HUGH THOMAS, Paso Robles, CA
Idaho-Utah-Washington: DAVID URBAN, Jerome, ID

Regional Directors
California South: RONALD A. ALEXANDER, Carlsbad, CA
California Valley: KENNETH D. BOETTCHER, Santa Rosa, CA
East Washington-North Idaho: BERNARD F. BROWN, Wenatchee, WA
California Island: GEORGE A. COUGHRAN, JR., Camarillo, CA
Northwest Washington: CHRIS EDER, Arlington, WA
North Oregon: DAVID EISENHAUER, Beaverton, OR
Arizona: ROBERT B. GOODE, Sedona, AZ
South Oregon: BRENT LAWS, Bend, OR
Southwest Washington: FRANK R. LOCKARD, Olympia, WA
Nevada: JOHN LUDWIG, Ph.D., Reno, NV
California North: STEVEN A. SCHULTZ, Fort Bragg, CA
Alaska: LARRY C. VAN RAY, Soldotna, AK
Utah: PHILLIP WAGNER, Kaysville, UT

Central Flyway Field Operations Supervisor
TAL LOCKWOOD, Custer, SD

Regional Supervisors
Montana-North Dakota-South Dakota: THOMAS L. KUCK, Aberdeen, SD
Nebraska-Kansas: LELAND M. QUEAL, Pratt, KS
Wyoming-Colorado-New Mexico: JOHN SCHMIDT, Ph.D., Fort Collins, CO
Texas-Oklahoma: JIM STEVENS, Valley Mills, TX

Regional Directors
Montana: STEVE R. BAYLESS, Helena, MT
North Colorado: HARVEY BRAY, Pueblo, CO
Western South Dakota: K.L. COOL, Pierre, SD
East Oklahoma: FARRELL COPELIN, Edmond, OK
South Texas: JAMES H. DUNKS, Austin, TX
Wyoming: BARRY FLOYD, Sundance, WY
North Dakota: CONRAD N. HILLMAN, Bismarck, ND
West Nebraska: JAMES HURT, Kearney, NE
East Nebraska: JOSEPH M. HYLAND, Lincoln, NE
Southeast Texas: ROY B. JOHNSON JR., League City, TX
East Kansas: LARRY E. KRAMER, Paola, KS
New Mexico-Southern Colorado: G. PATRICK O'BRIEN, Albuquerque, NM
Western Texas-Western Oklahoma: LARRY TATOM, Clyde, TX

Northeast Mississippi Flyway Field Operations Supervisor
DAVID D. KENNEDY, Anna, IL

Regional Supervisors
Ohio-Michigan: FRED ABRAHAM, Navarre, OH
Indiana-Illinois: BILL R. WILLSEY, Nashville, IN

Regional Directors
Southwest Michigan: WILLIAM FUCHS, Newaygo, MI
Southeast Michigan: FRED K. HINGST, Clio, MI
North Indiana: ROBERT A. KOCH, Michigan City, IN
South Ohio: DOUGLAS N. LASHER, Pataskala, OH
North Illinois: JOHN E. MEDEMA, Antioch, IL
North Michigan: JAMES H. RUBIN, Buckley, MI
South Illinois: JAMES M. SHANK, Brighton, IL
Central Illinois: JAMES WEST

Northwest Mississippi Flyway Field Operations Supervisor
CAL BARSTOW, Stoddard, WI

Regional Supervisors
Minnesota: BILL ALLEN, Wabasha, MN
Iowa-Michigan: ROCK BRIDGES, Lake Mills, IA
Wisconsin: BRUCE GRUTHOFF, Wisconsin Rapids, WI

Regional Directors
North Missouri: GEORGE K. BRAKHAGE, Columbia, MO
Southern Minnesota: JOSEPH BREIDENBACH, New Ulm, MN
Southwest Wisconsin: RONALD H. NICKLAUS, Genoa, WI
Southeast Wisconsin: DANIEL G. OLSON, DePere, WI
West Minnesota: WILLIAM C. PEABODY, Alexandria, MN
Northern Wisconsin: WILLIAM F. RICHIE, Shell Lake, WI
South Missouri: MITCHELL J. ROGERS, Clinton, MO
South Iowa: Vacant
Northeast Minnesota: DICK WETTERSTEN, Ogilvie, MN

South Mississippi Flyway Field Operations Supervisor
BILLY JOE CROSS, Clinton, MS

Regional Supervisors
Alabama-Mississippi: DAN GARDNER, Ph.D., Auburn, AL
Tennessee-Kentucky: JOHN C. KRUZAN, Carthage, TN
Arkansas-Lousiana: EARL D. NORWOOD, JR., Ruston, LA

Regional Directors
Kentucky: BEN R. BURNLEY, Henderson, KY
North Arkansas: R. KEVIN CAUGHMAN, Russellville, AR
South Mississippi: WILLIAM C. EARNEST, Clinton, MS
South Arkansas: STEVEN W. FRICK, Russellville, AR
North Mississippi: CURTIS R. HOPKINS, Ph.D., Grenada, MS

North Alabama: GEORGE HORTON, Ph.D., Heflin, AL
South Louisiana: CHARLES M. SMITH, Walker, LA

North Atlantic Flyway Field Operations Supervisor
KEITH RUBIN

Regional Supervisors
Maine-Massachusetts-Connecticut-New Hampshire-Rhode Island-Vermont: COLTON H. BRIDGES, Grafton, MA
Pennsylvania-New Jersey: DAVID C. DOHNER, Harrisburg, PA
New York: AL STARLING, Union Springs, NY

Regional Directors
New Jersey: PETER G. BROWN, Cape May Court House, NJ
West Pennsylvania: GEORGE M. KELLY, Ph.D., Boyers, PA
Southeast New York: CRAIG WILLIAM KESSLER, Stony Brook, NY
Eastern Pennsylvania: STEPHEN A. MILLER, Hummelstown, PA
Connecticut-Rhode Island: ROBERT F. SAMPSON JR., Preston, CT
Massachusetts: DUNBAR SEAMONS, Grafton, MA
New Hampshire-Vermont-Maine: PHILIP D. WARREN, Charlestown, NH
North New York: GARY B. WILL, Hamilton, NY

South Atlantic Flyway Field Operations Supervisor
DONALD J. MANLEY, Clinton, NC

Regional Supervisors
North Carolina-South Carolina: CLIFFORD L. BAMPTON, Pittsboro, NC
Georgia-Florida: DAN DENTON, Redan, GA
Maryland-Delaware-Virginia-West Virginia: JOSEPH F. ROWAN, Queenstown, MD

Regional Directors
East Virginia: DAN E. CANTNER, Culpepper, VA
Central Georgia: CECIL DAVIS , Griffin, GA
East South Carolina: CURTIS WOOTEN
Southwest Georgia-North Florida: O. EARLE FRYE JR., Ph.D., Tallahassee, FL
South Florida: SONNY E. MOWBRAY, Estero, FL
West Virginia-Western Virginia: GERALD A. THOMAS, Elkins, WV
Eastern North Carolina: STEPHEN A. THOMAS, New Bern, NC
West North Carolina-West South Carolina: DANIEL O'NEAL

130
EAGLE FOUNDATION, INC., THE, 300 E. Hickory St., Apple River, IL 61001 (815, 594-2259)
A nonprofit organization whose goal is to preserve vital eagle habitat and develop awareness and sensitivity on the part of the public as to why natural areas should be preserved. Membership: 1,200. Founded: 1972.
President and Executive Director: TERRENCE N. INGRAM, 8384 N. Broadway, Apple River, IL 61001 (312, 594-2592)
Vice-President: EUGENE SMALL, 4049 N. Long, Chicago, IL 60641 (312, 545-7036)
Secretary: CARROLL RUDY, W. 3866 Highway H., Chilton, WI 53014 (414, 849-9021)
Treasurer: BILLIE D'ENTREMONT, 1318 S. King, Janesville, WI 53545 (608, 756-2582)
Office Manager: Vacant
Administrative Secretary: Vacant
Director of Captive Breeding: BRETT MANDERNACK, P.O. Box 37, Glen Haven, WI 53810 (608, 794-2373)

131

EARTHSCAN, 3 Endsleigh St., London, WC1H ODD
An international, nonprofit publishing house for global resource, environment, and development issues. Serves as a resource to journalists, nongovernmental organizations, and government and development agencies with concise, readable information on major environment and development issues, including water and sanitation, the contribution of wildlife and wild genetic resources, desertification, energy, health, Third World housing issues, and the links between environmental problems and natural disasters.
Director, Earthscan Books Ltd., London: NEIL MIDDLETON

132

ECOLOGICAL SOCIETY OF AMERICA, THE
As North America's professional society of ecologists, encourages the scientific study of organisms in relation to their environment and promotes the exchange of ideas among those interested in ecology. ESA opened its Washington Office of Public Affairs in 1983 to provide ecological perspective on issues of public policy.
Membership: 6,200. Organized: 1915.
President: DR. HAROLD A. MOONEY, Department of Biology, Stanford University, Stanford, CA 94305 (415, 723-1179)
Vice-President: DR. JANE LUBCHENCO, Department of Zoology, Oregon State University, Corvallis, OR 97331 (503, 754-3705)
Secretary: DR. HAZEL R. DELCOURT, Department of Botany, University of Tennessee, Knoxville, TN 37996 (615, 974-3094)
Treasurer: DR. REBECCA R. SHARITZ, Savannah River Ecology Laboratory, Drawer E, Aiken, SC 29801 (803, 725-2472)
Business Manager: DR. DUNCAN T. PATTEN, Center for Environmental Studies, Arizona State University, Tempe, AZ 85281 (602, 965-3000)
Director, Office of Public Affairs: DR. MARJORIE M. HOLLAND, The Ecological Society of America, 730 11th St., NW, Suite 400, Washington, DC 20001-4584 (202, 393-5566)
Publications: *Ecology; Ecological Monographs; Bulletin of the Ecological Society of America.*
Managing Editor: DR. LEE MILLER, The Ecological Society of America, Corson Hall, Cornell University, Ithaca, NY 14853 (607, 255-3221)

133

EDUCATIONAL COMMUNICATIONS, INC., P.O. Box 35473, Los Angeles, CA 90035 (213, 559-9160) (Annual Meeting: September, generally in Idyllwild, CA)
Established in 1958, to create and to promote educational and scientific purposes for the public welfare focusing on environmental concerns and media productions. Founded in 1972, the Ecology Center of Southern California, a regional conservation organization serving a fifteen million-person area; sponsors since 1977, the award-winning ENVIRONMENTAL DIRECTIONS, weekly national and international radio series; and since 1984, the two-time EMMY-nominated ECONEWS, weekly television series distributed nationally to broadcast and cablecast outlets; shows cover all ecological issues; producers of award-winning programs including ACE-nominated special 'Gem in the Heart of the City,' award-winning public service announcements, and ENVIRONMENTAL REPORTS AND ENVIRONMENTAL VIEW POINTS columns and features.

134

ELM RESEARCH INSTITUTE, Harrisville, NH 03450 (603, 827-3048; 1-800-FOR-ELMS)
A nonprofit organization, which funds research for the control of Dutch elm disease and the preservation of the American elm; supplies equipment and information concerning specialized elm care and treatment of Dutch elm disease. Propogate a disease-resistant American Liberty Elm and distribute under the auspices of a program called, 'Johnny Elmseed' which was adopted by Boy Scouts of America in 1985. Membership: 3,500. Organized: 1967.
Executive Director: JOHN P. HANSEL
Assistant Director: BARBARA J. O'BRIEN
Educational Director: YVONNE SPALTOFF
Publications: Specialized Elm Care Brochure; Progress Report; News Bulletins; Educational Film; *Preserving a Heritage; The American Elm*

135

ELSA CLUBS OF AMERICA, 3201 Tepusquet Canyon Rd., Santa Maria, CA 93454 (805, 937-5640)
Sponsored by ELSA WILD ANIMAL APPEAL, a nationwide, nonprofit, tax-exempt organization. A unique national network of youth-oriented conservation awareness groups, largely in classrooms or similar situations, reaching and involving young people (primary through upper grades, secondary grades) in learning about and acting to constructively protect the natural environment and our diminishing wildlife heritage on a local, national and international level. Provides activities, projects, educational games and other involving ideas. Provides Wildlife Kits on wild animal subjects to Club Sponsors as part of membership. Available Kits include NORTH AMERICAN PREDATORS, PREDATORS OF THE WORLD (Part 1), PREDATORS OF THE WORLD (Part 2), MARINE MAMMALS OF THE WORLD, AMERICA'S ENDANGERED WILDLIFE. Founded: 1974. Membership: 3,000.
Education Director: KAREN OLIN JOHNSTON
Publication: *Elsa's Echo*
Editor: KAREN OLIN JOHNSTON,

136

ELSA WILD ANIMAL APPEAL, P.O. Box 4572, North Hollywood, CA 91607 (818, 761-8387)
A nonprofit, tax-exempt wildlife organization founded by BORN FREE author, Joy Adamson, and dedicated to the conservation of all wildlife, protection of endangered species and the natural environment, establishment of wildlife sanctuaries, and support of educational and research projects to benefit our environment. An effective and diversified program of activities exists to research and disseminate education pertaining to wildlife and habitat, humane treatment of animals, and educational projects to actively involve adults and young people on a local, national and international level. An active Conservation Committee acts in an advisory capacity, working with the various governmental agencies on all levels to assure that protection of wildlife and habitat is effectively carried out. Affiliated on an international level with E.W.A.A. branches in Kenya, United Kingdom, Japan and Canada. Sponsors ELSA CLUBS OF AMERICA. Founded: 1969.

Regional Representatives
Louisiana: LAURA LANZA, 1540 Chateau Cr., Lake Charles, LA 70605;
California (Headquarters): A. PETER RASSMUSEN JR.
Southern California: EVE RATTNER, 3139 Coachman Ct., Oceanside, CA 92054
New Hampshire: PAMELA CLARK, Laconia, NH 03246
Illinois: DONALD A. ROLLA, 994 S. Saylor Ave., Elmhurst, IL 60126
President: DONALD A. ROLLA
Vice-President: HARVEY M. FISCHER
Secretary: LEO M. LOBSENZ
Treasurer: EVE RATTNER

Directors: DONNA FISHER; DONALD A. ROLLA; BEVIN ANNE SMITH; LEO M. LOBSENZ; KAREN OLIN; A. PETER RASMUSSEN JR.

Honorary Directors: EDWARD ASNER; AMANDA BLAKE; GLORIA DE HAVEN; TIPPI HEDREN; JUNE FORAY; MARGOT HENKE; EARL HOLLIMAN; CAROL PERKINS; LORETTA SWIT; KRISTINA WAYBORN; BETTY WHITE; GRETCHEN WYLER

General Manager: A. PETER RASMUSSEN JR.

Publications: *Born Free News;* Action Alerts

Editor: A.P. RASMUSSEN JR.

137

ENVIRONMENTAL ACTION FOUNDATION, INC., 1525 New Hampshire Ave., Washington, DC 20036 (202, 745-4870)

A nonprofit, tax-exempt, public foundation formed to develop research and conduct broad educational programs on complex environmental issues. Working closely with the lobbying, membership organization, Environmental Action, Inc.. Programs include electric utilities, energy conservation, safe energy, toxic waste, solid waste alteratives (including recycling), and citizen action. On April 4, 1988, the Environmental Task Force merged with Environmental Action Foundation. Established: 1970.

Principal staff: JEANNE WIRKA; SCOTT HEMPLING; MORGAN GOPNIK; NICK FEDORUK; DRU PERKINS; MEG NAGLE; JIM PIERCE; CAROL DANSEREAU; NANCY HIRSH

Director: RUTH CAPLAN

Pollution Project: CAROL DANSEREAU

Energy Project: SCOTT HEMPLING

Publication: *Power Line*

Editor: Vacant

138

ENVIRONMENTAL ACTION, INC., 1525 New Hampshire Ave., NW, Washington, DC 20036 (202, 745-4870)

A membership-based nonprofit, non-tax deductible, lobbying organization, formed after organizing 'Earth Day 1970'. Political and social change group covering many environmental issues, including: nuclear power, energy conservation, acid rain, solid waste, deposit legislation, and others. EA's Political Action Committee (Enact/PAC) elects good environmentalists to Congress by training volunteers to be campaign organizers using environmental issues as a way to win votes. Has research and educational arm called Environmental Action Foundation. Established: 1970.

Principal Staff: RUTH CAPLAN; BILL ASP; NICK FEDORUK; SCOTT HEMPLING; HAWLEY TRUAX

Publication: *Environmental Action*

Co-Editors: ROSE AUDETTE; HAWLEY TRUAX

139

ENVIRONMENTAL AND ENERGY STUDY INSTITUTE, 122 C St., NW, Washington, DC 20001 (202, 628-1400)

A nonpartisan, nonprofit, tax-exempt public policy research, analysis, and education organization launched in 1985 by the leaders of the Congressional Environmental and Energy Study Conference and other national leaders. The Institute works closely with the conference to educate national policymakers; identify, define and analyze critical issues; develop and evaluate policy options; promote creative public policy solutions; and serve as a convener, catalyst and consensus-builder.

Executive Director: KEN MURPHY

Directors: RICHARD L. OTTINGER, Chairman; JOAN Z. BERNSTEIN; ROBERT O. BLAKE; LESTER BROWN; CARLETON D. BURTT, Secretary-Treasurer; GERALD R. DECKER; CAROL E. DINKINS; THOMAS B. EVANS, Vice-Chairman; JOSEPH L. FISHER; S. DAVID FREEMAN; GILBERT GUDE; JOHN HEINZ; THOMAS C. JORLING; C. PAYNE LUCAS; PAUL N. McCLOSKEY, Jr.; ED-MUND S. MUSKIE; RUTH PATRICK; FRANK M. POTTER; JOHN R. QUARLES; ROGER W. SANT; JOHN F. SEIBERLING; JOHN J. SHEEHAN; JAMES GUSTAVE SPETH; ELVIS J. STAHR; RAUL R. TAPIA; VICTORIA J. TSCHINKEL; LARRY YOUNG

140

ENVIRONMENTAL DEFENSE FUND, INC., Headquarters, 257 Park Avenue South, New York, NY 10010 (212, 505-2100); 1616 P St., NW, Suite 150, Washington, DC 20036 (202, 387-3500); 5655 College Ave., Oakland, CA 94618 (415, 658-8008); 1405 Arapahoe, Boulder, CO 80302 (303, 440-4901); 1108 E. Main St., Richmond, VA 23219 (804, 780-1297); 128 E. Hargett St., Raleigh, NC 27601 (919, 821-7793)

A nationwide public interest organization of lawyers, scientists, and economists dedicated to protecting and improving environmental quality and public health. EDF pursues responsible reform of public policy in the fields of energy and resource conservation, toxic chemicals, water resources, air quality, land use and wildlife, working through research and public education, and judicial, administrative, and legislative action. Public membership of 60,000. Incorporated in 1967 as a tax-exempt, nonprofit organization.

Chairman, Board of Trustees: FRANK E. LOY

Executive Director: FREDERIC D. KRUPP

Publication: *EDF Letter*

Editor: NORMA H. WATSON (212, 505-2100)

141

ENVIRONMENTAL EDUCATION COALITION, Pocono Environmental Education Center, Box 1010, Dingmans Ferry, PA 18328 (717, 828-2319)

The purpose of the coalition is to enhance the role of member organizations in bettering education in, for, and about the environment throughout the United States. The central focus of the coalition is on how member organizations can best act in concert. The aims of the coalition are: to help upgrade the status and competence of teachers; to help improve environmental experiences of students; to help increase citizen literacy in environment; and to help inform the political system as it formulates policies that affect environment, schooling and education in America.

Co-Chairman: JOHN J. PADALINO, Congress Coordinator, Pocono Environmental Education Center, RD 1, Box 1010, Dingmans Ferry, PA 18328

Co-Chairman: JOHN PAULK, Congress Program Chairman, TVA Forestry Bldg., Norris, TN 37828

President: KATHLEEN BLANCHARD, American Nature Study Society, Atlantic Center for the Environment, 39 South Main St., Ipswich, MA 01938-2321

President: ROBERT RYE, Conservation Education Association, R.R. # I, Box 59, Guthrie Center, IA 50115

Congress Practices Chairman: TALBERT SPENCE, Director of Education, New York Academy of Sciences, 2 East 63rd St., New York, NY 10021

142

ENVIRONMENTAL LAW INSTITUTE, THE, 1616 P St., NW, Suite 200, Washington, DC 20036 (202, 328-5150)

A unique, nonprofit national center for research and education on environmental law and policy. Activities include research into the law of environmental protection and natural resources use, design of new institutional arrangements to carry out environmental policy, environmental management including private sector programs, improvement of institutional ability to implement existing law, provision of information on environmental law, a publications program, and educational undertakings. Founded: 1969.

President: J. WILLIAM FUTRELL
Chairman: JAMES ROGERS
Secretary-Treasurer: JEFFREY MILLER
Directors: ALVIN ALM; TIMOTHY ATKESON; T. LOUIS AUSTIN, JR.;
BARBARA BLUM; DAVID CHALLINOR; CAROL DINKINS; NICHO-
LAS YOST; RICHARD DEWLING; F. HENRY HABICHT II; GRO-
VER WRENN; NANCY MALOLEY; ANTHONY CELEBREZZE, JR.;
DAVID ZOLL; CRAIG MATHEWS; LANGDON MARSH; ERNEST
GELLHORN; JOAN BERNSTEIN; FRANK FRIEDMAN; NELSON
TALBOTT; RICHARD MERRILL; OWEN OLPIN; EDMUND MUSK-
IE; NANCY NORD; B. SUZI RUHL; DAVID SIVE; J. GUSTAVE
SPETH; HELEN PETRAUSKAS; ANN POWERS; JOHN QUARLES;
DAVID HAWKINS ALLEN SMITH; ROGER STRELOW
Publications: *The Environmental Law Reporter; National Wetlands
Newsletter; The Environmental Forum; Law of Environmental
Protection*
Editors: BARRY BREEN; CAROLE PARKER; ANNE SOUTHWORTH;
LYNN STEWART

143
ENVIRONMENTAL POLICY INSTITUTE, 218 D St., SE,
Washington, DC 20003 (202, 544-2600)
An independent, nonprofit public interest advocacy organization
dedicated to influencing national and international public policies
affecting natural resources through research, public education,
lobbying, litigation, and organization of coalitions which are economically, politically and geographically diverse. Helps citizens
influence policies by informing them how their views can be most
effectively voiced in Washington. Primary areas of focus: energy,
water, agriculture, toxics, national security as affected by natural
resources, and public health. Integrated areas of concentration:
energy and water conservation; protection of groundwater, rivers,
farmland, wetlands, Chesapeake Bay, coasts and oceans; air, water,
toxics, pesticides and strip mining pollution control; genetic
diversity and biotechnology in agriculture; public lands; transportation; nuclear waste; nuclear insurance; nuclear power; nuclear
weapons production and testing; health effects of radiation; gas; oil;
coal; international water, energy, and agricultural projects. Found-
ed: 1972. Merged with Environmental Policy Center: 1982.
Chair: HERMAN WARSH
Vice-Chair, Board of Directors: FRANCES CLOSE HART
Treasurer: LINDA KAMM
Secretary: CLARENCE DITLOW III
President: MICHAEL S. CLARK
Vice-President for Policy: BRENT BLACKWELDER
Directors: ROBERT ALVAREZ; BRENT BLACKWELDER; ROBERT
CAHN; MARION EDEY; ALVIN JOSEPHY, JR.; LINDA HELLER
KAMM; WILLIAM KLINEFELTER; HELEN MILLS; KATHARINE B.
MOUNTCASTLE; DR. JOSEPHINE L. MURRAY; ROBERT RED-
FORD; MARIE RIDDER; DAVID ZWICK
Publications: *EPI Update;* A complete list of EPI's publications is
available upon request.

144
ENVIROSOUTH, INC., P.O. Box 11468, Montgomery, AL
36111 (205, 277-7050)
Private, nonprofit, environmental public information service organi-
zation, working in Alabama to create an environmentally literate
citizenry within the state and to tailor a balanced growth through a
practical application of the region's many resources.
President: MARTHA McINNIS
Publication: *EnviroSouth*
Editor: MARTHA McINNIS

145
FEDERAL CARTRIDGE COMPANY, 900 Ehlen Dr., Anoka, MN
55303 (612, 422-2577)
Manager, Conservation Activities: WILLIAM STEVENS

146
FEDERATION OF FLY FISHERS, P.O. Box 1088, W.
Yellowstone, MT 59758 (406, 646-9541)
To promote international fly fishing as a most enjoyable and
sportsmanlike method of fishing and to preserve all species of fish
in all classes of waters through local stream and fishery restoration
projects, conservation grants, audiovisual programs, public educa-
tion, and international committees. The Federation of Fly Fishers
has built its classroom of the future in West Yellowstone, Montana.
The International Fly Fishing Center is open to the public May 25-
September 30. Features a fly fishing museum and gallery of angling
art. Founded: 1965.
President: AL WILKIE, 6325 Shady Brook Ln., #2120, Dallas, TX
75206 (214, 691-4137)
Senior Vice-Presidents, Conservation: GEORGE JOHNSON, Rt. 2,
Box 576, Pullman, WA 99163 (509, 334-3135); CARRIE J.
CHRISTIANSEN, Office Manager (406, 646-9541); DON OB-
LANDER, 1708 S. Tyler Rd., St. Charles, IL 60174 (312, 228-
0602); MARY BLACK, FFF Development, 1017 East 49th,
Tulsa, OK 74105 (918, 742-7601); IRA HENDON, Education,
1851 Park Noll Ln., Port Washington, WI 53074-l131 (414,
284-5806)
Treasurer: KEITH GROTY, 3496 Josephine Ln., Mason, MI 48854
(517, 676-4255)
Publication: *The Flyfisher*
Editor: DENNIS BITTON, 1387 Cambridge, Idaho Falls, ID 83401
(208, 523-7300)
Salt Water Fly Fishing Group: B. BOULDIN (713, 782-2708)
Warm Water Fisheries Group: FRED STEVENSON (205, 881-
2754)
Atlantic Salmon Committee: D. EGAN (203, 457-1178)
Whitlock Vibert Box Chairman: D. DAVIS (207, 353-4879)

147
FEDERATION OF WESTERN OUTDOOR CLUBS
Forty-two clubs banded together for mutual service and promotion
of the proper use, enjoyment, and protection of America's scenic,
wilderness, and outdoor recreation resources. Organized: 1932.
President: JACK WALKER, 431 Green Glen Way, Mill Valley, CA
94941 (415, 388-7888)
Secretary: WINCHELL HAYWARD, 208 Willard No., San Francisco,
CA 94118
Treasurer: VIRGINIA DANKE, E. 1103-14th, Spokane, WA 99202
Northwest Conservation Representative: JIM BLOMQUIST, 1516
Melrose, Seattle, WA 98122
Washington, DC Representative: BROCK EVANS, 645 Pennsylvania
Ave., SE, Washington, DC 20003
Publication: *Outdoors West*
Editor: HAZEL WOLF, 512 Boylston Ave., E., #106, Seattle, WA
98102 (206, 322-3041)

148
FELICIDADES WILDLIFE FOUNDATION, INC., Box 490,
Waynesville, NC 28786 (704, 926-0192)
A nonprofit, tax-exempt organization devoted to the care and
rehabilitation of native wildlife; the education of youth in the areas
of wildlife protection, preservation and wise use of all natural
resources, the aesthetic as well as biological benefits of wildlife in
relation to man; the promotion of conservation of wildlife and all
natural resources. Conducts wildlife rehabilitation workshops,
presents slide lectures.

President: GEORGE R. COLLETT, JR., 150 Fox Run Rd., Waynesville, NC 28786 (704, 926-0192)
Secretary-Treasurer: ROSEMARY K. COLLETT

149

FISH AND WILDLIFE REFERENCE SERVICE, 5430 Grosvenor Ln., Bethesda, MD 20814 (301, 492-6403/4/800-582-3421)

A computerized information retrieval system and clearinghouse, providing selected published and unpublished fish and wildlife management research reports. Operated under a contract with the U.S. Fish and Wildlife Service to provide access to reports produced by the Federal Aid in Fish and Wildlife Restoration Program, the Cooperative Fishery and Wildlife Research Units Program, and the Anadromous (sport) Fish Conservation Program. Literature searches produced. Customized computer generated bibliographies. Organized: 1965.
Project Leader: MARY J. NICKUM
Publication: *Fish and Wildlife Reference Service Newsletter*
Editor: MARY J. NICKUM

150

FOOD AND AGRICULTURE ORGANIZATION OF THE UNITED NATIONS, Via delle Terme di Caracalla, Rome 00100, Italy (Telephone: 57971)

A specialized agency of the UN family established to raise levels of nutrition and standard of living of people, to improve efficiency in the production and distribution of all food and agricultural products, including fishery and forestry products, to improve the conditions of rural populations, and thus contribute toward an expanding world economy and ensure humanity's freedom from hunger. Membership: 158 governments. Established: 1945.
Director-General: EDOUARD SAOUMA
Publications: *The State of Food and Agriculture; FAO Plant Protection Bulletin; Animal Health Yearbook; Yearbooks of Production, Trade, Forest Products, Fisheries Statistics, and Fertilizer*

151

FOREST FARMERS ASSOCIATION, INC., Suite 120, 4 Executive Park East, NE, P.O. Box 95385, Atlanta, GA 30347 (404, 325-2954)

Nonprofit forestry organization of timberland owners, primarily small owners, in 15 southern states seeking to give private timberland owners and related interests a greater voice in matters affecting their business. Organized: 1941.
President: A. KENT VAN CLEAVE, Buffalo Wood, Inc., Box 576, Centreville, MS 39631
President-Elect: ELEY C. FRAZER III, President, Fish and Wildlife Forestry Services, Box 3610, Albany, GA 31706
Executive Vice-President: B. JACK WARREN
Regional Vice-Presidents: NOLL A. VAN CLEAVE, Valley Wood, Inc., P.O. Box 127, Richland, GA 31825; A.C. EDWARDS, Manager, Wood Procurement, Westvaco Corp., P.O. Box 5207, North Charleston, SC 29406; A. FELTON ANDREWS, 741 Galloway, Memphis, TN 38105; BRUCE R. MILES, Director, Texas Forest Service, College Station, TX 77843; RONALD M. BOST, Vice-President, Forestry, Crescent Land and Timber Corporation, P.O. Box 30817, Charlotte, NC 28230
Publications: *Forest Farmer Magazine; Forest Farmer Manual*
Editorial Consultant: LEON S. BROWN

152

FOREST HISTORY SOCIETY, INC., 701 Vickers Ave., Durham, NC 27701 (919, 682-9319)

A nonprofit, educational institution, the Forest History Society is dedicated to the advancement of historical understanding of man's interaction with the forest environment--forest industries, forestry, conservation, and other forms of use and appreciation. A membership organization, it sponsors programs in research, publication, archives-library, and professional service. Membership: 1,900. Established: 1946.
President: HERBERT I. WINER
Vice-President: WILLIAM R. SIZEMORE
Executive Director: HAROLD K. STEEN
Librarian: MARGARET S. BRILL
Publications: *Journal of Forest History; Forest History Cruiser Newsletter*
Editor: ALICE E. INGERSON

153

FOREST TRUST, P.O. Box 9238, Santa Fe, NM 87504-9238 (505, 983-8992)

A nonprofit organization seeking to protect and improve forest ecosystems and resources by providing innovative land management techniques for private landowners, communities, and land management agencies. Involved in national forest planning, land stewardship, land trust services, and forestry development for rural communities. Founded: 1984.
Director: HENRY H. CAREY
Executive Assistant to the Director: KATHRYN BREWER
Environmental Forester, Mora Forestry Center: DANNY GOMEZ, P.O. Box 1625, Las Vegas, NM 87701 (505, 387-5752)
Senior Forester: HARRY SEVERTSON

154

FOUNDATION FOR NORTH AMERICAN WILD SHEEP, 720 Allen Ave., Cody, WY 82414 (Annual Convention: February 24-27, 1988, Reno, NV)

A nonprofit organization whose purposes are to: promote the management of and safeguard against the extinction of all species of wild sheep native to the continent of North America; promote the protection and intensive management of the remaining wild sheep populations and their habitat; and promote the re-establishment of wild sheep populations in suitable historic habitat in North America. The foundation funds wild sheep research, wildlife studies, improves habitat, finances sheep transplants, and supports hunting and game management policies based on sound, proven principles. Founded: 1977. Members: More than 5,000.
Office Manager: KATHY MUFICH (307, 527-6441)
President: ARNIE JOHNS, Box 135, Stockholm, WI 54769
President-Elect: HARVEY KADLEC, 16970 Crocus St., Andover, MN 55304
Secretary: DICK GUNLOGSON, Box 193, Willow, AK 99688
Treasurer: MARTIN NIELSEN, P.O. Box 27048, Las Vegas, NV 89126
Publication: *Wild Sheep*

155

FRESHWATER FOUNDATION, 2500 Shadywood Rd., Box 90, Navarre, MN 55392 (612, 471-8407)

The FF is an international, nonprofit organization established in 1968, to support research and education. The foundation encourages proper use and management to keep surface water and groundwater usable for human consumption, industry and recreation. Through publications, conferences, media and other information programs, the foundation seeks to help people understand water issues and their environmental, political, social and economic impact. Individual, professional, corporate and organization memberships are available.
Chairman: DANIEL C. CHABOT
President and CEO: H. MARTIN JESSEN

Director, Development: LYNN SLIFER
Manager, Publications and Conferences: LINDA SCHROEDER
Manager, Environmental Health Programs: BARBARA SCOTT MUR-
DOCK
Publications: *Journal of Freshwater; Facets of Freshwater Newsletter; Health and Environment Digest; U.S. Water News;* various special reports

156
FRIENDS OF AFRICA IN AMERICA, 330 S. Broadway, Tarrytown, NY 10591 (914, 631-5168)
A nonprofit educational organization promoting understanding of Africans in development, and support for wildlife, primarily in East Africa. Founded: 1963.
President: CLEMENT E. MEROWIT
Vice-President: HERMAN W. KITCHEN (212, 865-6201)
Secretary: BARBARA THOMPSON (914, 478-0727)
Treasurer: EUGENE C. NEWMAN (203, 264-6632)

157
FRIENDS OF ANIMALS, INC., 11 W. 60th St., New York, NY 10023 (212, 247-8120)
An international animal protection organization dedicated to the elimination of human brutality to animals. Membership: 120,000. Founded: 1957.
President: PRISCILLA FERAL
Vice-President: HARRISON MAAS, Esq.
Secretary-Treasurer: SALLY LEINER
Directors: SUE CONN ; VAL RINTOUL; HARRISON MAAS; ZEPHYR CARLYLE; KEVIN MALANGA; SALLY LEINER; LYNN WELLEN-KAMP; PRISCILLA FERAL
Publication: *Act'ionLine*
Editor: PRISCILLA FERAL

158
FRIENDS OF THE EARTH, 530 Seventh St., SE, Washington, DC 20003 (202, 543-4312)
Committed to the preservation, restoration, and rational use of the earth. Affiliated Friends of the Earth organizations are active in France, West Germany, Sweden, Poland, Ghana, The Netherlands, Australia, Ireland, New Zealand, Canada, Switzerland, Belgium, Italy, Mexico, Spain, Austria, Greece, Japan, Malaysia, England, Scotland, Cyprus, Portugal, Sri Lanka, Papua New Guinea, Brazil, Hong Kong, and Argentina. Membership: 15,000. Founded: 1969.
Chairman of the Board: DANIEL B. LUTEN, Berkeley, CA
President: ALAN GUSSOW, Congers, NY
Secretary: ELIZABETH RAISBECK, Washington, DC
Treasurer: Vacant
Directors: DANIEL B. LUTEN; LYNDA TAYLOR; RICK SUTHER-LAND; ESTELLA LEOPOLD; MARK TERRY; ELIZABETH RAIS-BECK; PAUL D. BURKS; WES JACKSON; ALAN GUSSOW; EDWIN S. MATTHEWS, JR.; ANN C. ROOSEVELT; CHARLES BRADLEY; JANET BROWN; HERMAN DALY; JOHN SIMPSON
Seattle Office: DAVID ORTMAN, Director, Field Operations, 4512 University Way, NE, Seattle, WA 98105 (206, 633-1661)
Conservation Director: GEOFFREY WEBB, 530 7th St., SE, Washington, DC 20003 (202, 543-4312)
Executive Director: CYNTHIA WILSON, 530 7th St., SE, Washington, DC 20003 (202, 543-4312)
Office Manager: ERICA WALZ, 530 7th St., SE, Washington, DC 20003 (202, 543-4312)

Regional Representatives
Northwest: DAVID ORTMAN, 4512 University Way, NE, Seattle, WA 98105 (206, 633-1661)

Water Resources Specialist: CAROLYN JOHNSON, 286 S. Gilpin, Denver, CO 80209
Publication: *Not Man Apart*
Editor: KENNEDY MAIZE

159
FRIENDS OF THE EARTH FOUNDATION, INC., 1045 Sansome St., San Francisco, CA 94111 (415, 433-7373)
To conduct a scientific, educational, and literary program for the preservation, restoration, and rational use of the earth. Program includes research, publishing, holding symposia, conferences, and workshops to improve the human environment. Organized: 1972.
Chairman of the Board: DAVID R. BROWER
President: ALAN GUSSOW
Vice-Presidents: STEPHEN Q. SCHAFER; AMORY B. LOVINS
Secretary: AVIS OGILVY (212, 675-5911)
Treasurer: DANIEL GABEL
Executive Director: KARL F. WENDELOWSKI
Financial Secretary: DEBORAH OGDEN
Directors: MICHAEL SLATER; CHARLES BEAR; EDWIN S. MAT-THEWS Jr.; DAVID SIVE; THOMAS LLOYD
Directors Emeritus: STEWART M. OGILVY; PHILIP BUCHANAN

160
FRIENDS OF THE RIVER, INC., Friends of the River Foundation, Bldg. C, Fort Mason Ctr., San Francisco, CA 94123 (415, 771-0400)
A nonprofit membership organization dedicated to protection of our rivers and streams and to conservation of our water and energy resources. Through research, political action, public education, lobbying, publicity, and legal activities, the group works on state and national wild and scenic river efforts and implementation of conservation-oriented state and federal water and energy policies. Founded: 1974. Membership: 9,000.
Board of Directors: LARRY ORMAN, Chair, Friends of the River
Executive Director: DAVID BOLLING, Friends of the River Foundation
Executive Director: DAVID BOLLING, Friends of the River Foundation
Publication: *Headwaters*
Editor: ROBERT BRUCE
Advertising: EMILY TIBBOTT

161
FRIENDS OF THE UNITED NATIONS ENVIRONMENT PROGRAMME (FUNEP), 2013 Que St., NW, Washington, DC 20009 (202, 234-3600)
A nonprofit support group for the UN Environment Programme, FUNEP generates public awareness both of global environmental issues, including ozone layer depletion, the greenhouse effect, and the transport of hazardous chemicals, and UNEP's response to these issues. Through a Cooperator system, FUNEP links UNEP to environmental groups across the US.
Executive Director: RICHARD A. HELLMAN
Publication: *FUNEP Focus*
Editor: ANDREA NEIGHBOURS

162
FUND FOR ANIMALS, INC., THE, 200 W. 57th St., New York, NY 10019 (212, 246-2096)
National, nonprofit animal protection organization whose purpose is to preserve wildlife, save endangered species, and promote humane treatment for all animals. Primarily serves as an advocacy group and information and education agency to help animals, domestic and wild, and to see to it that the government fulfills its

responsibilities to protect animals. Membership: 250,000. Founded: 1967.
President: CLEVELAND AMORY
Vice-President: LEWIS REGENSTEIN
Vice-Chairman: GRETCHEN WYLER
Secretary: MARIAN PROBST
Treasurer: WINTHROP WADLEIGH
Legal Counsel: EDWARD J. WALSH, JR., Vedder Price Kaufman Kammholz and Day, I Dag Hammarskjold Plaza, New York, NY 10005 (212, DI9-4141)
Field Officers: MARGARET ASPROYERAKAS, 642 W. Buckingham Pl., Chicago, IL 60657 (312, 943-6700); CYNTHIA BRANIGAN, 21 Stoney Hill Rd., New Hope, PA 18938 (215, 862-5031); GEORGE CAMPBELL, 4069 Coquina Dr., Sanibel Island, FL 33954 (813, 472-2825); GLENN CHASE, 1506 19th St., NW, Suite 3, Washington, DC 20036 (202, 234-4002/03); DORIS DIXON, 2841 Colony Rd., Ann Arbor, MI 48104 (313, 971-4632); CAROLINE GILBERT, Rt. 2, Box 559, Simponsville, SC 29681 (803, 963-4389); GREGORY GORNEY, 2160 Marlow Rd., Toledo, OH 43613 (419, 474-9805); DONNA GREGORY, 6354 Van Nuys Blvd., Suite 444, Van Nuys, CA 91401 (213, 789-1190); VIRGINIA HANDLEY, Fort Mason Center, Bldg. 310, San Francisco, CA 94123 (415, 474-4020); JOAN JENRICH, P.O. Box 1780, St. Petersburg, FL 33731 (813, 821-7804); RICHARD KENLY, 701 15th St., Fairlawn, NJ 07410 (201, 791-7935); MARLENE LAKIN, 2335 Lakeshore Blvd., Apt. 715, Toronto, Ontario, Canada M8V 1B9 (416, 251-4571); Vacant, Hinson Island, Hamilton, Bermuda (809, 292-7751); SID and CAROLYN ROSENTHAL, P.O. Box 10676, Jefferson, LA 70181 (803, 834-5010); LEWIS REGENSTEIN, 4290 Raintree Ln., Atlanta, GA 30327; DOROTHY SCHMITT, 7116 Pippin Rds., Cincinnati, OH 45215 (513, 521-1134); DORIT STARK-RIEMER, 98 Woodlawn Ave., Albany, NY 12208 (518, 438-6369); SHERRI TIPPIE, 1291 Gaylord, Denver, CO 80219 (303, 333-8294); PAUL WATSON, P.O. Box 48446, Bentall Center, Vancouver British Columbia, Canada V7X 1A2 (604, 688-7325); JERRY and BARBARA ZELL, P.O. Box 427, Spring Park, MN (612, 471-9305); PAULA VAN ORDEN, 3536 East Colorado Blvd., Pasadena, CA 91107; BILL SAXON, Manager, Black Beauty Ranch, P.O. Box 367, Murchison, TX 75778; CHUCK TRAISI, Manager, Animal Trust Santuary, 18740 Highland Valley Rd., Ramona, CA 92065

163

FUTURE FISHERMAN FOUNDATION, 1 Berkley Dr., Spirit Lake, IA 51360 (1-800, 237-5539; 712, 336-1520)
A nonprofit organization dedicated to promoting the participation and education in fishing as well as the enhancement and protection of the aquatic resources.
Executive Director: Vacant

164

GAME CONSERVATION INTERNATIONAL, P.O. Box 17444, San Antonio, TX 78217 (512, 824-7509)
Nonprofit organization of hunter conservationists that participates in wildlife conservation projects relating to protection of habitat, anti-poaching programs and translocation of game animals. Membership: 1,500. Founded: 1967.
President: HARRY L. TENNISON (817, 335-1942)
Secretary-Treasurer: ED R.L. WROE, JR.
Executive Director: PAULA C. McGEHEE
Publication: *Game Coin*
Editor: PAULA C. McGEHEE

165

GARDEN CLUB OF AMERICA, THE, 598 Madison Ave., New York, NY 10022 (212, 753-8287)
A national, nonprofit organization with member clubs from coast to coast and in Hawaii. Dedicated to conservation of natural resources, protection of the environment, control of pollution, wise land use, historic preservation. Active support of billboard and sign control. Distributes widely an educational packet called "The World Around You." Founded: 1913.
President: MRS. CHARLES G. WARD, JR.
Corresponding Secretary: MRS. EDWARD S. ELLIMAN
Conservation Chairman: MRS. ROBERT W. FREITAG
National Affairs and Legislation Committee: MRS. RUSSELL SCHILLING WEHRLE
Horticulture Chairman: MRS. HENRY S. STREETER

166

GENERAL FEDERATION OF WOMEN'S CLUBS, 1734 N St., NW, Washington, DC 20036 (202, 347-3168)
The GFWC has 10 million members worldwide, with 400,000 members in the United States. GWFC unites women's clubs to work on volunteer service projects throughout the world in areas of conservation, education, home life, international affairs, public affairs, and the arts. Founded: 1890.
President: ALICE C. DONAHUE
President-Elect: PHYLLIS A. DUDENHOFFER
1st Vice-President: ANN L. HOLLAND
2nd Vice-President: JEANNINE C. FAUBION
Recording Secretary: FAYE Z. DISSINGER
Treasurer: MAXINE SCARBRO

Conservation Department
Chairman: ELIZABETH ANDERSON, 4687 Westhampton Dr., Tucker, GA 30084
Junior Chairman: BONNIE TODD, 10143 W. Pierson Rd., Flushing, MI 48433
Beautification: CAROLINE STADLER, Rt. #1, Box 80, Axtill, NE 68924
Conservation of Natural Resources: VI THORNBURG, P.O. Box 1797, Auburndale, FL 33823
Environmental Education Division: MARGARET ENGLAND, P.O. Box 696, 103 Maple, Sparta, TN 38583
Publication: *General Federation Women's Clubs Clubwoman*
Editor: JUDITH WALTER MAGGRETT

167

GEORGE MIKSCH SUTTON AVIAN RESEARCH CENTER, INC., P.O. Box 2007, Bartlesville, OK 74005 (918, 336-7778)
A nonprofit, tax-exempt research center initiated in 1983 to conduct scientific studies, conservation projects and educational programs regarding avian species worldwide. Areas of particular interest include the restoration of nesting populations of bald eagles in the southeastern U.S., Andean condor surveys in Argentina, avian captive breeding, and public educational programs.
Board Chairman: JOHN A. BROCK
Vice-Chairman: KENNETH L. WIRE
Secretary: HERBERT S. BEATTIE
Treasurer: HOWARD R. BURMAN
Executive Director: STEVE K. SHERROD

168

GIRL SCOUTS OF THE UNITED STATES OF AMERICA, 830 3rd Ave., New York, NY 10022 (212, 940-7500)
The national organization offers an informal education and recreation program designed to help each girl develop her own values and sense of worth as an individual. It provides opportunities for

girls to experience, to discover, and to share planned activities that meet their interests. These activities encourage personal development through a wide variety of projects in social action, environmental action, wildlife values education, youth leadership, career exploration, and community service. Membership includes more than two and a half million girls and about half a million adults. Founded: 1912.

President: BETTY F. PILSBURY (940-7702)

National Executive Director: FRANCES R. HESSELBEIN (940-7700)

Director, National Program Department: SHARON WOODS HUSSEY (940-7730)

Director, Outdoor Education: CAROLYN L. KENNEDY (940-7735)

Program Specialist: DONNA L. NYE (940-7416)

Washington Representative: MARY FRANCES PETERS, 1625 I St., NW, Suite 612, Washington, DC (202, 659-3780)

Publication: *Girl Scout Leader*

Editor: CAROLYN CAGGINE (940-7813)

169

GLOBAL TOMORROW COALITION, INC., 1325 G St., NW, Suite 915, Washington, DC 20005-3104 (202, 628-4016)

A national alliance of organizations and individuals dedicated to fostering broader public understanding in the U.S. of the long-term significance of interrelated global trends in population, resources, environment, and development; and to helping promote informed and responsible public choice among alternative futures for the U.S. and alternative roles for the nation within the international community. Membership: 115 organizations with combined memberships of over 8,000,000. Founded: 1981.

Executive Director: DONALD R. LESH

Deputy Director: DIANE G. LOWRIE

President: JAN HARTKE, Hartke & Hartke, Attorneys at Law, 7637 Leesburg Pike, Falls Church, VA 22043 (703, 734-2810)

Secretary: JOAN MARTIN-BROWN, United Nations Environment Programme, 1889 F St., NW, Ground Fl., Washington, DC 20006 (202, 289-8456)

Treasurer: FRANK L. MORRIS, SR., Associate Professor, School of Graduates Studies, Morgan State University, Cold Spring Lane and Hillen Road, Baltimore, MD 21239 (301, 444-3185)

Board Chair: DR. FRED O. PINKHAM, Associate Director, Institute for Population and Resource Studies, Box 9281, Stanford University, Stanford, CA 94305 (415, 723-7517)

Publications: *Interaction; Action Letter on Global Issues; Citizen's Guide to Global Issues; Global Issues Teacher packets; Contact Directory*

170

GOPHER TORTOISE COUNCIL, Florida Museum of Natural History, University of Florida, Gainesville, FL 32611 (904, 392-1721) (Annual meeting: October-November)

A nonprofit organization formed to assure the continued survival of viable populations of the gopher tortoise, *Gopherus polyphemus,* throughout its existing range in the southeastern United States. Membership: 222. Founded: 1978.

Co-Chairmen: RAY ASHTON, 611 NW 79th Dr., Gainesville, FL 32607; EDWARD WESTER, General Biology, 101 Cary Hall, Auburn University, Auburn, AL 36849

Secretary: RHODA J. BRYANT, Florida Museum of Natural History, University of Florida, Gainesville, FL 32611

Treasurer: SUSANNE WAHLQUIST, 1346 Arlene Ct., Lilburn, GA 30247

Publication: *The Tortoise Burrow Newsletter*

Editor: ELLEN NICOL, Rt. 1, Box 1367, Anthony, FL 32617

171

GRASSLAND HERITAGE FOUNDATION, 5450 Buena Vista, Shawnee Mission, KS 66205 (913, 677-3326)

A tax-exempt, nonprofit organization created to advance public understanding and appreciation of cultural, historical and scientific value of native American grassland; more specifically, to acquire and preserve representative tracts of native prairie and to produce educational materials for schools and the general public. Membership: 1,300. Founded: 1976.

Executive Director: Vacant

President: PHILLIP S. BROWN

Director/Naturalist: WENDELL MOHLING

Publications: Newsletter; Membership Brochure; *Gifts of Land for Conservation; Prairie Center News*

172

GREAT BEAR FOUNDATION, P.O. Box 2699, Missoula, MT 59806 (406, 721-3009)

Nonprofit tax-exempt corporation established for the conservation of bears. The top priority currently is grizzly bears. Memberships: approx. 750 from eight nations.

President: LANCE OLSEN

Publication: *Bear News*

173

GREAT LAKES SPORT FISHING COUNCIL, 8244 N. Monticello, Skokie, IL 60076 (312, 677-7683)

A nonprofit confederation of organizations throughout the Great Lakes states and provinces whose members are concerned with the present and future of sport fishing in the Great Lakes and adjoining waters. The Council, which acts as a clearinghouse for the exchange of information among members, also seeks to protect the Great Lakes against pollution and exploitation by commercial, individual, or other interests. Membership: Nearly 50 U.S. and Canadian organizations with a combined membership of more than 25,000 families. Established: 1973.

President: SHERWIN S. SCHWARTZ

Vice-President: JOHN REINKE, Rt. 1, Box 147 M, Marinette, WI 54143 (715, 732-0718)

Secretary: MIKE RATTER, 1554 Shirley Dr., Calumet City, IL 60409 (312, 862-0348)

Treasurer: RICHARD REUSS, 12813 S. Maple Ave., Blue Island, IL 60406 (312, 385-3261)

Publication: *Inland Seas Angler*

Editor: BOB SCHMIDT, 4608 N. Elston Ave., Chicago, IL 60630 (312, 283-7871)

174

GREAT LAKES UNITED, State University College at Buffalo, Cassety Hall, 1300 Elmwood Ave., Buffalo, NY 14222 (716, 886-0142); Canadian Address: P.O. Box 548, Station A, Windsor, Ontario, Canada N9A 6M6

An international coalition of environmental, sportsmen, union, government and small business organizations, and individuals throughout the eight Great Lakes states and two Canadian Provinces. GLU is dedicated to the protection, conservation and proper management of the Great Lakes-St. Lawrence River system.

President: FREDERICK L. BROWN, Ph.D., Michigan United Conservation Clubs, 488 Ashby Rd., Rt. 5, Midland, MI 48640 (517, 835-9625)

Vice-President: SR. MARGEEN HOFFMANN, O.S.F., Ecumenical Task Force of the Niagara Frontier, 259 Fourth St., Niagara Falls, NY 14303 (716, 284-0026)

Secretary: GLENDA DANIEL, Lake Michigan Federation, 8 South Michigan Blvd., Suite 2010, Chicago, IL 60603 (312, 263-5550)

Treasurer: JOSHUA WUNSCH, Michigan Association of Conservation Districts, 16888 Wunsch Rd., Traverse City, MI 49684

Canadian Treasurer: RICK CORONADO, Windsor and District Clean Water Alliance, P.O. Box 3303, Tecumseh, Ontario, Canada N8N 2M4 (519, 735-3574)

Executive Director: DAVID J. MILLER, Great Lakes United, State University College at Buffalo, Cassety Hall, 1300 Elmwood Ave., Buffalo, NY 14222 (716,886-0142)

Regional Directors

Region I (Superior): SCOT STEWART, Upper Peninsula Environmental Coalition, P.O. Box 1014, Marquette, MI 49855 (906, 225-4323)

Region II (Huron): JOHN WITZKE, Saginaw Bay Advisory Council, 1023 Brissette Beach, Kawkawlin, MI 48631 (H-517, 686-4408; W-636-3141)

Region III (Michigan): JOE FINKBEINER, Capitol Area Audubon, 13750 Hardenburg Trail, Eagle, MI 48822 (517, 626-6680)

Region IV (Erie): PAM LEISINGER, UAW, Conservation Department, 8000 East Jefferson Ave., Detroit, MI 48214 (313, 926-5269)

Region V (Ontario): SARAH MILLER, Canadian Environmental Law Association, 243 Queen St., West, 4th Fl., Toronto, Ontario, Canada M5V 1Z4 (416, 977-2410)

Region VI (St. Lawrence): CAMILLA SMITH, Save the River, 96 Grand Ave., New York, NY 10013 (212, 226-2088)

Directors-at-Large: JOHN JACKSON, Ontario Toxic Waste Research Coalition, 139 Waterloo St., Kitchener, Ontario, Canada N2H 3V5 (519, 744-7503); WILLIAM NEUHAUS, Racine-Kenosha UAP CAP Council, 1101 136th Ave., Union Grove, WI 53182 (414, 859-2549); PETER LEMON, City of Owen Sound, 808 2nd Avenue East, Owen Sound, Ontario, Canada N4K 2H4 (W: 519, 376-9431; H: 519, 371- 0746); KEN LOUNSBURY, Ontario Federation of Anglers and Hunters, 465 Hixon St., Beamsville, Ontario, Canada L0R 1B0 (416, 688-4440); RICHARD KUBIAK, Ph.D., Pennsylvania Sportsman Federation, 2534 East 33rd St., Erie, PA 16510 (H-814, 899-9676/W-825-0345); JOHN HICKEY, Ph.D., Cortland County Environmental Management Council, 73 Greenbush St., Cortland, NY 13045 (607, 756-2336); DANIEL GREEN, Societe pour Vaincre la Pollution, C.P. 65 Place D'Arme, Montreal, Quebec, Canada H2Y 3E9 (514, 844-5477); PAT LUPO, O.S.B., Erie County Environmental Coalition, 6101 East Lake Rd., Erie, PA 16511 (814, 899-0614); PAUL MULDOON, Energy Probe, 225 Caroline St., South, Hamilton, Ontario, Canada L8P 3L5 (416, 978-5856); DR. WILLIAM L. ROBINSON, Upper Penninsula Environmental Coalition, 410 East Crescent St., Marquette, MI 49855 (906, 227-2812)

Publications: *The Great Lakes United; GLU Action updates*

175

GREAT SWAMP RESEARCH INSTITUTE, Office of the Dean, College of Natural Sciences and Math, Indiana University of Pennsylvania, 305 Weyandt Hall, Indiana, PA 15705 (412, 357-2609)

A tax-exempt, research and educational membership organization dedicated to protecting, preserving and maintaining our environment. The institute seeks new and innovative solutions to deal with the daily pressures society is placing on the environment, particularly the ecological component of the environment; and attempts to represent the environment when seeking environmental solutions. Founded: 1981.

President: ANNE HARRIS KATZ

Director: HARVEY M. KATZ

Publication: *Environmental Chronicle*

176

GREATER YELLOWSTONE COALITION, P.O. Box 1874, 420 West Mendenhall, Bozeman, MT 59715 (406, 586-1593) (Annual meeting: May 1989, Old Faithful Lodge, Yellowstone National Park)

A nonprofit, tax-exempt organization to preserve and protect the Greater Yellowstone ecosystem by enhancing the ecosystem concept, raising the national public consciousness about the Greater Yellowstone ecosystem, and combining the political effectiveness of the coalition's 2,000+ individual members and 50 national and regional member organizations. Founded: 1983.

President: THOMAS McNAMEE (212, 627-1409)

1st Vice-President: DON STREUBEL (208, 236-2207)

2nd Vice-President: JIM SCHMITT (406, 586-3118)

Secretary-Treasurer: JOHN WINSOR (303, 444-6805)

Executive Director: EDWARD M. LEWIS

Publication: *Greater Yellowstone Report Newsletter*

Editor: LOUISA WILLCOX

177

GREEN MOUNTAIN CLUB, INC., THE, P.O. Box 889, 43 State St., Montpelier, VT 05602 (802, 223-3463)

A nonprofit organization organized to build the Long Trail, a footpath completed in 1931 that follows the crest of the Green Mountains from Massachusetts to the Canadian border. The Club operates field programs and publishes guidebooks, maps, and educational materials in its efforts to maintain and protect the 440-mile Long Trail system. Founded: 1910. Membership: 4,500.

President: BRIAN T. FITZGERALD, P.O. Box 298, Gorham, NH 03581

Vice-President: SMITH EDWARDS, R.R. 2, Box 3850, Stowe, VT 05672

Secretary: BEN DAVIS, 206 East Rd., Colchester, VT 05446

Treasurer: KIM SIMPSON, 17 Gary Cir., Westboro, MA 01581

Executive Director: HARRY T. PEET, JR.

Publication: *The Long Trail News*

Editor: CLEO BILLINGS

178

GREENPEACE USA, INC., 1436 U St., NW, Washington, DC 20009 (202, 462-1177)

A nonprofit organization dedicated to preserving the earth and the life it supports. Greenpeace works to halt the needless slaughter of whales, dolphins, seals, and other endangered animals; to protect the environment from nuclear and toxic pollution, and to stop the threat of nuclear war. Founded: 1970. Active supporters: 850,000.

Executive Director: PETER BAHOUTH

Secretary: TRULY A. WEBB

Administrative Director: J.R. YEAGER

Campaign Coordinators: DAVE RAPAPORT, Toxics; ANNE DINGWALL, Ocean Ecology; DAMON MOGLEN, Nuclear Disarmament; LAUREN PREZIOSE, Merchandise (415, 474-6767); VICKEY MONREAN, Development; TERESA MACIOCHA, Donor Services; NEVILLE WILLIAMS, Media

Publication: *The Greenpeace Magazine*

Editor: ANDRE CAROTHERS

179

GULF AND CARIBBEAN FISHERIES INSTITUTE, 4600 Rickenbacker Causeway, Miami, FL 33149 (305, 361-4191)

Promotes fishery research by holding an annual meeting at which

scientists, members of the fishing industry, and administrators can discuss status of various fisheries of the region; assists countries of the Caribbean in development and management of their fisheries; and makes information available on fisheries of the region, and on research findings, through the publication of the proceedings of the annual meeting. Membership: 600. Founded: 1948.
Executive Secretary: DR. MELVIN GOODWIN

180

HARDWOOD RESEARCH COUNCIL, P.O. Box 34518, Memphis, TN 38184-0518 (901, 377-1824)
A nonprofit organization of the hardwood-using industry, its interdependent suppliers, landowners and others interested in promoting research and education in hardwood forest management and utilization. Organized in 1953 as the Furniture, Plywood and Veneer Council of the North Carolina Forestry Association but broadened to include anyone interested in hardwoods. Became affiliated with the National Hardwood Lumber Association in 1986. Membership: 1,290.
Director: JOHN A. PITCHER
Publications: *Hardwood Forestry Bulletin; Proceedings, Annual Hardwood Symposium;* Technical Reports
Editor: JOHN A. PITCHER

181

HAWK MIGRATION ASSOCIATION OF NORTH AMERICA
A nonprofit organization whose purpose is to advance the knowledge of bird-of-prey migration across the continent, to monitor raptor populations as an indicator of environmental health, to study further the behavior of raptors, and to contribute to greater public understanding of birds of prey. Membership: 1,000. Founded: 1974.
Chairman: DIANN MacRAE, 22622 - 53rd Ave., SE, Bothell, WA 98021 (206, 481-2797)
Vice-Chairman: SETH KELLOGG, 377 Loomis St., Southwick, MA 01077 (413, 569-3335)
Treasurer: RICHARD A. MORTON, 604 Windsor Pl., Moorestown, NJ 08057 (609, 235-6796)
Secretary: MYRIAM MOORE, Box 3482, Lynchburg, VA 24503 (804, 847-7811)
Membership Secretary: JOYCE ANN G. HOLT, 3094 Forest Acre Trail, Salem, VA 24153 (703, 384-6674)
Publications: *The Newsletter; The Journal;* Conference Proceedings
Editors: JEFFREY DODGE, 432 Manitou Beach Rd., Hilton, NY 14468; MICHAEL HARWOOD, Box 51, Washington, CT 06095

182

HAWK MOUNTAIN SANCTUARY ASSOCIATION, Rte. 2, Box 191, Kempton, PA 19529 (215, 756-6961)
A nonprofit organization formed to maintain the 2,200-acre Hawk Mountain Sanctuary and to foster the conservation of birds of prey and other wildlife. Program includes public education, research on birds and forest ecology, and involvement with policy issues affecting birds of prey. Membership: 7,500. Founded: 1934.
Executive Director: STANLEY E. SENNER
President: JOSEPH WILLIAM TAYLOR
Vice-President: WILLIAM H. PARKS
Secretary: MICHAEL HARWOOD
Treasurer: ALAN CRAWFORD, JR.
Curator: JAMES J. BRETT
Publication: *Hawk Mountain News*

183

HAWK TRUST, THE, c/o Birds of Prey Section, London Zoo, Regent's Park, London NW1 4RY, England
The Hawk Trust aims to conserve birds of prey, including owls, and

encourage the appreciation of them. Current projects: Nationwide Barn Owl Survey and Merlin study group. Founded: 1969.
Chairman: JANE FENTON
President: LORD TWEEDSMUIR
Publications: *Annual Report;* Newsletters
Hon. Editor: ANTHONY BOOSEY

184

HIGH DESERT MUSEUM, THE, 59800 S. Highway 97, bend, OR 97702 (503, 382-4754)
Created to broaden the knowledge and understanding of the natural and cultural history and resources of the high desert country for the purpose of promoting thoughtful management decisions that will sustain the region's natural and cultural heritage. It is a 'living,' participation-oriented museum which focuses on the Intermountain West -- portions of eight Western states and the Canadian province of British Columbia. Membership: 2,070. Founded: 1974. Opened to the public: 1982.
President of the Board of Trustees: MICHAEL P. HOLLERN
Executive Director: DONALD M. KERR
Assistant Director, Operations: JERRY N. MOORE
Assistant Director, Communications: SUSAN E. FISHER
Curator: CARYN TALBOT THROOP
Education Services Coordinator: KATHLEEN RONNING
Development Assistant: LAURA JOHNSON
Publication: *The High Desert Museum Newsletter*
Editor: SUSAN E. FISHER
Earle A. Chiles Award: Annual $10,000 cash award presented to an individual whose accomplishments lead to a better understanding of the high desert region.

185

HOLLY SOCIETY OF AMERICA, INC., 304 Northwind Rd., Baltimore, MD 21204
National, nonprofit organization dedicated to bringing together persons interested in any phase of holly culture. Collects and disseminates information about holly; studies methods of conservatively cutting and marketing holly; promotes research and hybridization, publishes research papers and popularizes the use of holly as a landscape material. Membership: 1,000. Incorporated: 1947.
President: HAROLD L. ELMORE
Executive Vice-Presidents: LLOYD C. HAHN; ELWIN R. ORTON, JR.
Secretary: CATHERINE RICHARDSON
Treasurer: B. M. BAUERS, SR.
Publications: *Holly Society Journal* (including the Proceedings); H.S.A. Books
Editor: MRS. RUSSELL E. MARKS, 52 Constitution Hill West, Princeton, NJ 08540

186

HUMAN ECOLOGY ACTION LEAGUE, INC., THE, P.O. Box 66637, Chicago, IL 60666 (312, 665-6575)
A international nonprofit volunteer organization, dedicated to increasing awareness of environmental conditions which are hazardous to human health. It serves as an information clearinghouse on chemical sensitivities and related disorders; works toward minimizing the indiscriminate use of harmful chemicals; and establishes local chapters which provide emotional support for members and educate their communities. Membership: 5,000. Founded: 1977.
President: VIRGINIA CARLSON
Vice-President and Treasurer: MARIANNE SAMS
Directors: MARY LAMIELLE; LOUISE KOSTA; BEATRICE TRUM HUNTER; JUNE LARSON; VERA REA; LINDA DAVIDOFF, Ph.D.; LESLIE PEICKERT-KROKER, R.N.
Advisory Board: NATALIE GOLOS; JOSEPH T. MORGAN, M.D.;

THERON G. RANDOLPH, M.D.; WILLIAM J. REA, M.D.; PHYLLIS SAIFER, M.D.; FRANCIS SILVER
Publication: *The Human Ecologist*
Editor: MARY BUCHELE

187

HUMAN ENVIRONMENT CENTER, 1001 Connecticut Ave.,
NW, Suite 829, Washington, DC 20036 (202, 331-8387)
Nonprofit organization providing education, information, and services to encourage integration of environmental organizations, and promotion of joint activities among environmental and social equity groups. Serves as a clearinghouse and technical assistance center for youth conservation and service corps programs and operates a recruitment and placement service for minority environmental interns and profesionals. Other concerns include urban parks and recreation, minority environmental issues and multi-interest coalition development. Founded: 1976.
Co-Chair of the Board: DAVID BURWELL (202, 797-5400)
Co-Chair: SHIRLEY MALCOM (202, 326-6680)
Executive Director: MARGARET ROSENBERRY
Publications: *Human Environment Center NEWS; Conservation and Service Corps Profiles; Conservation and Service Corps Workbook; Urban Conservation Corps Resource Reports*

188

HUMANE SOCIETY OF THE UNITED STATES, THE, 2100 L
St., NW, Washington, DC, 20037 (202, 452-1100)
A nonprofit organization dedicated to the protection of animals, both domestic and wild. Professional staff experienced in animal control, cruelty investigation, publications, humane education, federal and state legislative activities, wildlife protection and laboratory animal welfare, offer resources to local organizations, government, media, and the general public. Constituency: 600,000. Organized: 1954.
Chairman of the Board: K. WILLIAM WISEMAN
Chairman Emeritus: COLEMAN BURKE, Esq.
Vice-Chairman: O.J. RAMSEY, Esq.
Secretary: DR. AMY FREEMAN LEE
President: JOHN A. HOYT
Executive Vice-President/Treasurer: PAUL G. IRWIN
Senior Vice-President: PATRICIA FORKAN
Vice-President, General Counsel: MURDAUGH S. MADDEN
Vice-President, Wildlife and Environment: DR. JOHN W. GRANDY
Vice-President, Companion Animals: PHYLLIS WRIGHT
Vice-President, Farm Animals and Bioethics: DR. MICHAEL W. FOX
Director, National Association for the Advancement of Humane Education: PATRICIA A. FINCH
Regional Directors: SANDY ROWLAND; WILLIAM MEADE III; NINA AUSTENBERG; JOHN J. DOMMERS; MARC PAULHUS; WENDELL MADDOX; CHARLENE DRENNON; FRANTZ DANTZLER
Publications: *HSUS News; Kind News; Children and Animals: Shelter Sense*

189

INFORM, 381 Park Ave. South, New York, NY 10016 (212, 689-4040)
A nonprofit, tax-exempt, research, and public education organization that identifies and reports on practical actions for the conservation and preservation of natural resources. Members: 1,500. Founded: 1973.
Chairman of the Board: KENNETH F. MOUNTCASTLE, JR.
Executive Director: JOANNA D. UNDERWOOD
Publication: *INFORM Reports*

190

INLAND BIRD BANDING ASSOCIATION, R.D. 2, Box 26,
Wisner, NE 68791 (402, 529-6679)
Promotes cooperation among its members and other organizations, with state, federal, or other officials or individuals engaged in bird banding or other scientific work with birds; informs the public of the purposes and results secured by banding. Organized: 1922.
President: JOHN J. FLORA, 3636 Williams, Dearborn, MI 48124
Secretary: CAROL RUDY, W. 3866 Hwy. H, Chilton, WI 53084
Treasurer: C. HOLMES SMITH, 6305 Cumberland Rd., SW, Sherrodsville, OH 44675
Membership Secretary: AL VALENTINE, 17403 Oakington Ct., Dallas, TX 75252
Publications: *North American Bird Bander; Inland Bird Banding Newsletter*
Editors: DAN KRAMER, 3451 Co. Rd. 256, Victory, OH 43464; WILLETTA LUESHEN, R. 2, Box 26, Wisner, NE 68791

191

INSTITUTE FOR CONSERVATION LEADERSHIP, 1400
Sixteenth St., NW, Washington, DC 20036-2266 (202, 797-6656)
The Institute serves to increase the number and effectiveness of volunteer conservation leaders and their organizations through training and research. Using a variety of programs, the institute exists to serve the entire conservation community. Programs are offered on several levels including training for individual leaders, boards of directors, and setting up state networking conferences.
Director: ED EASTON
Assistant Director: DIANNE RUSSELL

192

INSTITUTE FOR EARTH EDUCATION, THE, Box 288,
Warrenville, IL 60555 (312, 393-3096)
The Institute for Earth Education develops and disseminates focused educational programs that will help people build an understanding of, appreciation for, and harmony with the earth and its life. The institute conducts workshops, provides a seasonal journal, hosts an international conference, supports regional branches, and publishes books and program materials. Members: I,000. Founded: 1974.
Chair: STEVE VAN MATRE
Coordinator: DAVE WAMPLER
Publication: *Talking Leaves Journal*

193

INTERNATIONAL ASSOCIATION FOR BEAR RESEARCH AND MANAGEMENT, Box 3129, Station B, Calgary, Alberta, Canada T2M 4L7
A professional organization of biologists and animal or land managers with an interest or involvement in bear research and management. The association encourages and monitors research and management by the various agencies or university research groups and sponsors the International Conference on Bears: Their Biology and Management, publishes the proceedings of the conferences, and sponsors or aids a world network of regional bear workshops, groups, and committees and the IUCN Bear Groups.
President: DR. STEPHEN HERRERO, Faculty of Environmental Design, University of Calgary, Calgary, Alberta, Canada T2N 1N4 (403, 220-6605)
Vice-President: GARY ALT, R.D. 5, Box 65B, Moscow, PA 18444 (717, 842-2771)
Secretary-Treasurer: DR. BRIAN L. HOREJSI, Western Wildlife

Environments Consulting Ltd., Box 3129, Station B, Calgary, Alberta, Canada T2M 4L7 (403, 246-9328)
Council: AL LECOUNT (Arizona); DR. FRANCISCO PEREZ-TREJO (Venezuela); DR. CHARLES JONKEL (Montana); DR. TOSHIKI AOI (Japan); DR. FRED DEAN (Alaska); HARRY REYNOLDS (Alaska); OLE JACOB SORENSON (Norway)
Publications: *IAB Newsletter, Conference Proceedings*

194

INTERNATIONAL ASSOCIATION OF FISH AND WILDLIFE AGENCIES, 444 North Capitol St., NW, Suite 534, Washington, DC 20001 (202, 624-7890)
Association of states or territories of the United States, provinces of Canada, the Commonwealth of Puerto Rico, the United States Government, the Dominion Government of Canada, and governments of countries located in the western hemisphere as well as individual associate members whose principal objective is conservation, protection and management of wildlife and related natural resources.
President: JAMES H. PATTERSON, Director, Wildlife Conservation, Wildlife Habitat Canada, 1704 Carling Ave., Ottawa, Ontario, Canada K2A IC7
1st Vice-President: WILLIAM A. MOLINI, Director, Nevada Department of Wildlife, P.O. Box 10678, Reno, NV 89520
2nd Vice-President: STEVEN A. LEWIS, Oklahoma Department of Wildlife Conservation, 1801 N. Lincoln, P.O. Box 53465, Oklahoma City, OK 73152
Executive Vice-President: R. MAX PETERSON
Legislative Counsel: GORDON C. ROBERTSON
Resource Specialist: MARK J. REEFF
Habitat Coordinator: J. MITCHELL KING
Secretary-Treasurer: CHESTER F. PHELPS, 107 Canal St., Williamston, NC 27892
General Counsel: GLENN BOWERS, 221 Mountain Rd., Dillsburg, PA 17019
Counselor Emeritus: JACK H. BERRYMAN, Fairfax, VA
Executive Committee:
Chairman: PETER S. DUNCAN, Executive Director, Pennsylvania Game Commission, 2001 Elmerton Ave., Harrisburg, PA 17110-9797
Vice-Chairman: STEVEN N. WILSON, Director, Arkansas Game and Fish Commission, #2 Natural Resources Dr., Little Rock, AR 72205
Members: DONALD E. MacLAUCHLAN, Annapolis, MD; LARRY R. SHANNON, St. Paul, MN; JERRY M. CONLEY, Boise, ID; LARRY WILSON, Des Moines, IA; WILLIAM GEER, Salt Lake City, UT
Executive Committee Ex-Officio Members: JOSE DOMINGO GONZALEZ, Director General, Direccion General de Conservacion Ecologica de Los Recursos Naturales, Mexico; ROBERT R. ANDREWS, Edmonton, Alberta
Executive Committee Ex-Officio Regional Presidents:
Northeast: ROBERT L. MILES, WV
Southeast: DON R. McCORMICK, KY
Midwest: LARRY R. SHANNON, MN
Western Association: CURT SMITCH, WA
Legal Counsel: PAUL A. LENZINI, Washington, DC
Publications: Newsletter; Annual Proceedings
Editors: MARK J. REEFF; KEN SABOL

195

INTERNATIONAL ASSOCIATION OF NATURAL RESOURCE PILOTS, 200 Patrick St., SW, Vienna, VA 22180 (703, 560-1271)
Performs aviation and aircrew conservation related responsibilities for federal and state game and fish divisions and departments of natural resources throughout the U.S. and for their counterparts in the Canadian provinces. Additional membership includes a variety of aviation-oriented corporations and advanced technological suppliers of equipment used in the performance of the aviation missions. Membership: 200.
President: JOHN W. WINSHIP, United States Fish and Wildlife Service, P.O. Box 1306, Albuquerque, NM 87103 (H-505, 876-1764; W-505, 766-8042)
Vice-President: FLOYD D. SWANT, Chief Pilot, Ontario Ministery of Natural Resources, Box 310, 747 Queen St., Sault Ste Marie, Ontario, Canada P6A 5L8 (W-705, 942-1800/Ext. 151; H-705, 949-7539)
Secretary-Treasurer: ROBERT C. FOSTER, U.S. Fish and Wildlife Service, Federal Building Fort Snelling, Twin Cities, MN 55111 (612, 725-3313)
Public Affairs Officer/Newsletter Editor: FRANCIS N. SATTERLEE, Maj. USAF Retired, 200 Patrick St., SW, Vienna, VA 22180 (703, 560-1271)
Publication: *Conservation Aviation*

196

INTERNATIONAL COUNCIL FOR BIRD PRESERVATION, 32 Cambridge Rd., Girton, Cambridge CB3 OPJ, United Kingdom, (0223) 277318
Determines status of bird species throughout the world and compiles data on all endangered species; identifies conservation problems and priorities; and initiates, promotes and coordinates conservation projects and international conventions. National sections and representatives in 100 countries. Founded: 1922.
President Emeritus: PROF. S. DILLON RIPLEY, U.S.A.
Hon. President: ROGER TORY PETERSON
President: RUSSELL W. PETERSON, U.S.A.
Director: DR. CHRISTOPH IMBODEN, U.K.
Executive Assistant to the President: FRANCES SPIVY-WEBER, National Audubon Society, 801 Pennsylvania Ave., SE, Washington, DC 20003 (202, 547-9009)

U.S. Section
Chairman: STANLEY E. SENNER, Hawk Mountain Sanctuary Association, Rt. 2, Box 191, Kempton, PA 19529
Vice-Chairman: RON NAVEEN, 2378 Rt. 97, Cooksville, MD 21723
Secretary: KATHLEEN ANDERSON, 22 Winter St., Middleboro, MA 02396
Treasurer: FRANCES SPIVY-WEBER, National Audubon Society, 801 Pennsylvania Ave., SE, Washington, DC 20003

Pan American Section
Includes representatives of leading scientific and conservation societies in Argentina, Bolivia, Brazil, Canada, Chile, Colombia, Costa Rica, Cuba, Guatemala, Ecuador, Mexico, Panama, Paraguay, Peru, Suriname, U.S., Uruguay, and Venezuela.
Chairman: MERCEDES S. FOSTER, United States Fish and Wildlife Service Lab, Division of Birds, National Museum of Natural History, Washington, DC 20560
Secretary: FRANCES SPIVY-WEBER, National Audubon Society, 801 Pennsylvania Ave., SE, Washington, DC 20003
Treasurer: MARSHALL HOWE, Patuxent Wildlife Reserve Center, Laurel-Bowie Rd., Laurel, MD 20708

197

INTERNATIONAL COUNCIL FOR OUTDOOR EDUCATION, P.O. Box 17255, Pittsburgh, PA 15235 (412, 372-5992)
A nonprofit organization created to emphasize development and implementation of education programs in conservation and outdoor recreation. Programs serve all age levels, and are used by

governmental agencies, school systems, community centers, and other public and private organizations throughout North America. ICOE's programs promote maintenance of a quality natural environment. Incorporated: 1976.

President (Acting): JOHN F. EVELAND
Executive Vice-President: JOHN F. EVELAND
Vice-President, Administration: ROBERT M. MILLS
Vice-President, Finance: MICHAEL J. SCHUMAKER
Board of Directors: DR. JAMES S. LINDZEY, Chairman; DR. JAMES E. CONKLIN; RALPH F. EBERLE; JOHN F. EVELAND; MARTYN I. GEFSKY; ROGER E. LATHAM; ROBERT M. MILLS; LEIGH H. PERKINS; MARK L. RUTLEDGE; ROBERT W. SCHLEMMER; MICHAEL J. SCHUMAKER; JAMES H. SCOTT
Publications: List of outdoor education materials available upon request.

198

INTERNATIONAL COUNCIL OF ENVIRONMENTAL LAW,

D 53 Bonn', Federal Republic of Germany, Adenaueralle 214 (49-228-269240)
A nonprofit, private international organization with elected membership, structured in ten regions worldwide, for the purpose of exchange of information on international environmental law, policy and administration and mutual assistance among members. Founded: 1969.

Executive Governors: W.E. BURHENNE, Federal Republic of Germany; NAGENDRA SINGH, India
Publications: *Environmental Policy and Law; References* Newsletter; *Directory of Members*
Editor: MARLENE JAHNKE, Ireland

199

INTERNATIONAL CRANE FOUNDATION, E-11376, Shady Lane

Rd., Baraboo, WI 53913-9778 (608, 356-9462)
Preservation of cranes through research, conservation, captive propagation, restocking, and public education. Founded: 1973. Membership: 4,000.

Board of Trustees: GEORGE ARCHIBALD; ABIGAIL AVERY; MARY BURKE; VICTORIA COHEN; JOHN DAY; JOHN HENRY DICK, Honorary; THOMAS DONNELLEY; C.P. FOX; OWEN GROMME, Honorary; JAMES KUEHN; FRANK LARKIN; MARK LEFEBVRE; CHARLES NELSON; FRED OTT; DOROTHY PAIN, Honorary; GEORGE A. RANNEY, SR.; NORMAN SAUEY; DONALD SAUEY; LEONARD A. SHELTON; JEFFREY SHORT, JR.; PATRICIA STEDMAN; ANN TISDALE; MARY WICKHEM; BELINDA WRIGHT
Board of Advisors: TSO-HSIN CHENG; WILLIAM CONWAY; KAI CURRY-LINDAHL; WILLIAM DILGER; RAY ERICKSON; VLADIMIR FLINT; FATESINGHRAO P. GAEKWAD; KIM HON KYU; THOMAS E. LOVEJOY; TIMOTHY C. MOERMOND; CECILY NIVEN; S. DILLON RIPLEY; PETER SCOTT; STANLEY A. TEMPLE; LAWRENCE WALKINSHAW; WON PYONG-OH; YOSHIMARO YAMASHINA; THOMAS M. YUILL
Curator of Birds: CLAIRE MIRANDE
Assistant Curator: SCOTT SWENGEL
Administrator: JOAN FORDHAM
Research Staff: GEORGE ARCHIBALD
Education: JAMES HARRIS
Development: ROBERT HALLAM
Site Manager: DAVID CHESKY
Publications: *The ICF Bugle; Cranes, Cranes, Cranes; Crane Research Around the World; Proceedings of The 1983 International Crane Workshop*
Editor: JAMES HARRIS

200

INTERNATIONAL ECOLOGY SOCIETY (IES), 1471 Barclay St.,

Saint Paul, MN 55106-1405 (612, 774-4971)
International organization dedicated to the protection of the environment and the encouragement of better understanding of all life forms. Efforts include Save the Whales, prohibition of the leghold trap, wetland protection, urban natural areas protection, campaigns against primate research, acid rain, prohibitions on rodeo cruelties, alternatives to live animal testing, repeal of pound animal seizure laws, hazardous/toxic wastes, protection of Alaskan lands, protection of endangered wilderness, preservation of wild fur bearers, Canadian harp seal preservation, protection of all dove species in North America, clean air and water, marine mammals, national wildlife refuges, energy, domestic animal welfare, research and prohibitions on pesticides, herbicides, insecticides found harmful, nongame wildlife programs, protection of the Eastern timber wolf, raptor protection, preservation of endangered species, prohibition of trophy hunting, research on cruelty in fur ranching, bobcat, lynx, river otter, coyote, and black bear protection, control of all types of pollution, and the humane treatment of animals. Protection of land and wildlife in Belize, Central America. Supporters: 6,000. Founded: June 1975. Member of Pigs Eye Coalition (lake area), League to Save Lake Tahoe, Minnesota Committee to Protect the Mourning Dove, Antarctic and Southern Ocean Coalition, Minnesota Coalition on Uranium Mining, Voyageurs National Park Coalition, Alaska Coaliion, Coast Alliance, and Citizens National Forest Coalition.

President: R.J.F. KRAMER, 1471 Barclay St., Saint Paul, MN 55106-1405
Board members: MARJORIE J. EBENSTEINER; RICHARD J. EBENSTEINER; ROSEMARY A. KRAMER; SARAH L. KRAMER; MARY E. MARANDA; ROSEMARY N. MARANDA; TOM TUFT
Educational Director: RICHARD J. EBENSTEINER
Great Plains Representative: JEANNINE P. JOHNSON, 906 Ginny, Apt. #49, Bellevue, NE 68005
North East Representative: BINA ROBINSON, Swain, NY 14884
Belize, Central America Representative: RICHARD J. EBENSTEINER, Personalized Services, P.O. Box 1158, Belize City, Belize, Central America
Dakota Territory: MAGGIE WARREN, Rt. #2, Box #51, Hermosa, SD 57744
Project Assistants: JOYCE TALLEY ASCHITTINO; BLAKE TALLEY; PEGGY GREER; CATHLEEN CASEY
Publications: *Eco-Humane Letter;* Action Alerts Brochures: IES, Outlaw Cruel Leghold Traps (poster)
Editor: R.J.F. KRAMER

201

INTERNATIONAL FUND FOR ANIMAL WELFARE, P.O. Box

193, Yarmouth Port, MA. 02675. (508, 362-4944)
An international, nonprofit, tax-exempt organization in the U.S. dedicated to the protection of wild and domestic animals. Current issues include harp and hood seals in Canada, fur seals in Alaska, vicuna in Peru, monarch butterflies in U.S., swans in Great Britain, dog and cat abuse in Asia, and whales and other marine mammals around the world. Founded: 1969. International membership: 550,000.

Founder: BRIAN D. DAVIES
Executive Director: RICHARD MOORE
UK Office: JULIE WARTENBERG, Office Manager, Tubwell House, New Rd., Crowborough, E. Sussex TN6 2QH
Holland Office: JETTY TAK, Office Manager, Sterrenweg 3B, 2651 HZ Berkel en Rodenrijs
Canadian Office: ROSLYN CHAMBERLAIN, Office Manager, P.O. Box 556, Station T, Toronto, Ontario M6B 4C2

German Office: SUE OESTMANN, Office Manager, Mohlmanweg 2, D2000 Hamburg 55

202

INTERNATIONAL GAME FISH ASSOCIATION, 3000 E. Las Olas Blvd., Ft. Lauderdale, FL 33316-1616 (305, 467-0161)

A nonprofit, tax-deductible organization which maintains and promotes ethical international angling regulations and compiles world game fish records for saltwater, freshwater and fly fishing. Also represents and informs recreational fishermen regarding research, conservation and legislative developments related to their sport. Encourages and supports game fish tagging programs and other scientific data collection efforts. Sponsers "Annual IGFA Fishing Contest" and "Annual Marine Recreational Fisheries Symposium" in conjunction with other organizations. In September 1984, IGFA sponsored the first International Game Fish Association World Angling Conference in France. Maintains International library on angling literature and history. There are over 212 international representatives and 1,500 affiliated fishing clubs. Membership open to interested persons and organizations. Founded: 1939.

President: ELWOOD K. HARRY
Vice-Presidents: JOHN W. ANDERSON II; GEORGE G. MATTHEWS
Treasurer: OGDEN M. PHIPPS
Secretary: ROY E. NAFTZGER

Board of Trustees:

Chairman, ELWOOD K. HARRY; JOHN W. ANDERSON II; DANIEL H. BRAMAN, JR.; PIERRE CLOSTERMANN; PETER S. FITHIAN; WALTER W. FONDREN III; CURT GOWDY; ARTHUR HALL; RICHARD J. KOTIS; GEORGE G. MATTHEWS; A.J. McCLANE; ROY E. NAFTZGER; ERNEST W. PALMER; OGDEN M. PHIPPS; STEPHEN SLOAN; JOHN F. WILLITS
Publications: *World Record Game Fishes; The International Angler; Rule Book for Freshwater; Saltwater and Fly Fishing*

203

INTERNATIONAL OCEANOGRAPHIC FOUNDATION, 3979 Rickenbacker Causeway, Virginia Key, Miami, FL 33149 (305, 361-5786)

Nonprofit foundation organized to encourage the extension of human knowledge by scientific study and exploration of the oceans in all their aspects and to acquaint and educate the general public concerning the vital role of the oceans to all life on this planet. Founded: 1953. Membership: 25,000.

President: EDWARD T. FOOTE II
Vice-President: LUIS GLASER
Secretary: CYRUS M. JOLLIVETTE
Vice-President: DAVID A. LIEBERMAN
Treasurer: DERINDA S. PELL
Publication: *Sea Frontiers*
Editors: GILBERT L. VOSS; JEAN BRADFISCH; FAITH SCHAEFER

204

INTERNATIONAL OSPREY FOUNDATION, INC., THE, P.O. Box 250, Sanibel, FL 33957 (813, 472-5218)

A nonprofit, tax-exempt organization dedicated to studying the problem of restoring osprey numbers to a stable population, making recommendations to enhance the continued survival of the osprey and initiating educational programs. Founded: 1981.

President: DAVID LOVELAND
Vice-President: ANNE MITCHELL
Treasurer: MARK WESTALL
Secretary: PATTEE LOVELAND
Publication: *TIOF Newsletter*

205

INTERNATIONAL PRIMATE PROTECTION LEAGUE, P.O. Box 766, Summerville, SC 29484 (803, 871-2280)

A nonprofit, international organization devoted to the conservation and protection of nonhuman primates. Founded: 1974.

Chairperson: DR. SHIRLEY McGREAL
Secretary: MARJORIE DOGGETT, 1 Toh Heights, Singapore 1750
Treasurer: DIANE WALTERS
Publication: *International Primate Protection League Newsletter*

206

INTERNATIONAL SOCIETY OF ARBORICULTURE, P.O. Box 908, 303 W. University Ave., Urbana, IL 61801 (217, 328-2032)

To promote and improve the care and preservation of shade and ornamental trees through research and education. Membership: 5,000. Founded: 1924.

President: CLAUDE DESJARDINS, Quebec, Canada
President-Elect: DR. MICHAEL WALTERSCHEIDT, College Station, TX
Vice-President: DR. DONALD HAM, Clemson, SC
Executive Director: BILL KRUIDENIER
Publications: *Journal of Arboriculture; Valuation of Landscape Trees, Shrubs, and Other Plants; Tree and Shrub Transplanting Manual;* VHS Video Tapes on Construction Damage to Trees on Wooded Lots
Editor: DR. DAN NEELY, Illinois Natural History Survey, Natural Resources Bldg., Urbana, IL 61801

207

INTERNATIONAL SOCIETY OF TROPICAL FORESTERS, INC., 5400 Grosvenor Ln., Bethesda, MD 20814 (301, 897-8720)

A nonprofit organization founded with the objective of providing an information exchange for members involved in the management, protection, and use of tropical forests. Membership of over 1,700 in 106 countries. Founded: 1980.

President: WARREN T. DOOLITTLE (USA)
Vice-President: FREDERICK OWINO (Kenya)
Secretary: KHUBCHAND TEJWANI (India)
Treasurer: BJORN LUNDGREN (Kenya)
Director (Latin America): RONNIE de CAMINO V. (Costa Rico)
Director (Africa): FREDERICK OWINO (Kenya)
Director (Asia): KHUBCHAND TEJWANI (India)
Directors at Large: S. DENNIS RICHARDSON (New Zealand); JEFFERY BURLEY (United Kingdom)
Consultants (Headquarters): M.B. DICKERMAN; CLIFFORD S. SCHOPMEYER
Publications: *ISTF News; ISTF Noticias*
Editor: FRANK H. WADSWORTH

208

INTERNATIONAL UNION FOR CONSERVATION OF NATURE AND NATURAL RESOURCES (IUCN), Avenue du Mont-Blanc, CH-1196 Gland, Switzerland (022.64 71 81) (Telex: 22618 IUCN CH; Telefax: 022. 644615; Cable: IUCNATURE GLAND)

An independent body to promote scientifically based action for the conservation of wild living resources. Six hundred and thirty-four voting members in 120 countries: 61 states, 128 government agencies and 416 non-governmental organizations. Also 29 non-voting affiliate members. Maintains a global network of more than 3,000 scientists and professionals organized into 6 commissions. Founded: 1948.

President: MONKOMBU S. SWAMINATHAN, India
Vice-Presidents: WALTER LUSIG I, Kenya; WILLIAM E. REILLY, U.S.A.; ALVARO UMANA, Costa Rica; YURI YAZAN, U.S.S.R.
Chairman of the Bureau: MONKOMBU S. SWAMINATHAN, India
Treasurer: RICHARD STEELE, U.K.
Director General: MARTIN W. HONDGATE, U.K.
Director, Conservation Policy: JEFFREY A. McNEELY, U.S.A.
Director, Administration and Management: MICHAEL J. COCKE-RELL
Director, Conservation Monitoring Centre, Cambridge (U.K.): ROBIN PELLEW, U.K.
Head, Environmental Law Centre, Bonn, F.R.G.: FRANCOISE BURHENNE-GUILMIN, Belgium

Commission on Ecology
Chairman: JOSE I. FURTADO, Singapore

Commission on Education and Training
Chairman: M.A. PARTHA SARATHY, India

Commission on Sustainable Development
Chairman: PETER JACOBS, Canada

Commission on Environmental Policy, Law and Administration (CEPLA)
Chairman: WOLFGANG E. BURHENNE, F.R.G.

Commission on National Parks and Protected Areas (CNPPA)
Chairman: HAROLD K. EIDSVIK, Canada

Species Survival Commission (SSC)
Chairman: GRENVILLE LUCAS, U.K.

Publications: *IUCN Bulletin; Red Data Books* (describing threatened species of mammals, amphibia and reptilia, invertebrates and plants); *United Nations List of National Parks and Protected Areas;* Books on conservation and development, land and freshwater animals, marine and coastal ecology and management, national parks and other protected areas, and regional conservation; Environmental Policy and Law Papers; *World Conservation Strategy: Living Resource Conservation for Sustainable Development*

209
INTERNATIONAL WILD WATERFOWL ASSOCIATION, R.F.D. #1, James Farm, Durham, NH 03824
Works toward protection, conservation and reproduction of any species of wild waterfowl considered in danger of eventual extinction; encourages breeding of well known and rare species in captivity. Established Avicultural Hall of Fame. Sponsors annual conference and gives grants in field. Membership: 500. Founded: 1958.
President: WALT STURGEON, R.F.D. #1, James Farm, Durham, NH 03824
1st Vice-President: EDWARD ASPER, Vice-President, Sea World, 7007 Sea World Dr., Orlando, FL 32821
2nd Vice-President: PAUL DYE, 10114 54th Pl., NE, Everett, WA 98205
Secretary-Treasurer: WENDI SCHENDEL, 217 Ridge Tr., Bozeman, MT 59715

210
ISLAND RESOURCES FOUNDATION, Red Hook Center, Box 33, St. Thomas, Virgin Islands 00802 (809, 775-6225); Webster House, Suite T-4, 1718 P St., NW, Washington, DC, 20036 (202, 265-9712)
An independent center for the study of island systems, dedicated to improved resources management, comprehensive eco-development planning and the conservation of cultural, physical and natural resources of islands. Founded: 1972.
President and Executive Director: DR. EDWARD L. TOWLE
Vice-President: HENRY U. WHEATLEY
Secretary: CHARLES W. CONSOLVO
Treasurer: JUDITH A. TOWLE

211
IZAAK WALTON LEAGUE OF AMERICA, INC., THE, 1401 Wilson Blvd., Level B, Arlington, VA 22209 (703, 528-1818)
Promotes means and opportunities for educating the public to conserve, maintain, protect and restore the soil, forest, water, air and other natural resources of the U.S. and promotes the enjoyment and wholesome utilization of those resources. Membership: 50,000.
Chairman, Executive Board: DONALD L. FERRIS, Hamilton, OH
Honorary President: HELENE D. KENT, Rockville, MD
President: STANFORD ENSBERG, Toronto, SD
Vice-President: DONALD C. FREEMAN, Waverly, IA
Secretary: FERN ELLIOTT, Myrtle Beach, SC
Treasurer: GLADYS L. HARRIS, Front Royal, VA
Regional Governors: LES KING, Anaheim, CA; HELEN STAMMEN, Colorado Springs, CO; MAYNARD PIPER, Clear Lake, SD; DAN SPALINK, Grand Rapids, MI; NELSON ROSS, Jefferson City, TN; AUDREY LEWIS, Westmoreland, NY
Executive Director: JACK LORENZ
Director of Development: ERIC SWANSON
Associate Executive Director-Conservation Director: MAITLAND S. SHARPE
Conservation Associates: DAVID DICKSON; MARCHANT WENTWORTH
Publications: *Outdoor America; Outdoor Ethics Newsletter; Splash*
Editors: KEVIN KASOWSKI; JACK LORENZ; KRISTIN MERRIMAN
Upper Mississippi Regional Office: 6601 Auto Club Rd., Minneapolis, MN 55438 (612, 941-6654)
Regional Representative: PAUL HANSEN

212
IZAAK WALTON LEAGUE OF AMERICA ENDOWMENT, P.O. Box 824, Iowa City, IA 52244 (319, 351-7037)
Organized in 1943 to help rebuild Outdoor America by the acquisition, for governmental agencies, of unique natural areas for the use of future generations. Membership: Members of the Izaak Walton League of America.
Honorary President: HOWARD WHITE, 302 S. Mckinley St., Havana, IL 62644 (309, 543-4391)
President: WENDELL P. HALEY, 1840 NE 92nd Ave., Portland, OR 97220 (503, 253-9749)
Vice-President: EDWARD SCHEKELHOFF, 512 N. Sandusky St., Tiffin, OH 44883 (419, 447-7716)
Secretary: DR. L.C. SMITH, 636 Ridgewood Rd., Huntington, WV 25701 (304, 525-4410)
Treasurer: J. MICHAEL BORDEN, P.O. Box 591, Janesville, WI 53547 (608, 756-1241)
President Emeritus: SEN. ALDEN J. ERSKINE, 2315 Patterson, Sioux City, IA 51106 (712, 276-1109)
Executive Secretary: ROBERT C. RUSSELL, P.O. Box 824, Iowa City, IA 52244 (319, 351-7037)

213

JACKSON HOLE PRESERVE, INC., 30 Rockefeller Plaza, Rm. 5402, New York, NY 10112 (212, 649-5600)
Nonprofit, charitable, and educational organization, established to conserve areas of outstanding primitive grandeur and natural beauty and to provide facilities for their use and enjoyment by the public. Founded: 1940.
President: LAURANCE S. ROCKEFELLER
Executive Vice-President: GEORGE R. LAMB
Vice-President: GENE W. SETZER
Secretary: FRANKLIN E. PARKER
Treasurer and Assistant Secretary: RUTH C. HAUPERT
Assistant Treasurer: CARMEN REYES
Trustees: NASH CASTRO; C. WESLEY FRYE, JR.; CARLISLE H. HUMELSINE; MRS. LYNDON B. JOHNSON; LAURANCE S. ROCKEFELLER; GENE W. SETZER; FRED SMITH; CONRAD L. WIRTH; HENRY L. DIAMOND; GEORGE R. LAMB; FRANKLIN E. PARKER; HOWARD PHIPPS, JR.; LAURANCE ROCKEFELLER

214

JOHN MUIR INSTITUTE FOR ENVIRONMENTAL STUDIES, INC., 743 Wilson St., Napa, CA 94559 (707, 252-8333)
A nonprofit research organization founded in 1968 to identify and study environmental problems which are not receiving adequate attention; conduct research which will fill information gaps in natural resource management; identify and evaluate options in policy and practice; constructively analyze programs and practices of institutions which are environmentally significant. Tax-deductible contributions used to develop new projects which are then funded by government agencies, foundations and industry.
President: MAX LINN, Napa, CA
Vice-President: DIANA TODD, Pacific Palisades, CA
Secretary: PETER R. TAFT, Los Angeles, CA
Treasurer: LEO KRULITZ, Columbus, IN
Administrator: JULIA N. HILLIS, J.D., Napa, CA; LEE BROWN, Ph.D., Albuquerque, NM; GARY D. WEATHERFORD, Director, Water Program, Berkeley, CA
Members of the Board: ROBERT and PATRICIA CAHN, Leesburg, VA; MAX LINN, Napa, CA; DAVID SIVE, New York, NY; PETER R. TAFT, Los Angeles, CA; LEO M. KRULITZ, Columbus, IN; CHARLES L. DRAKE, Ph.D., Hanover, NH; NATHANIEL WOLLMAN, Ph.D., Albuquerque, NM

215

KEEP AMERICA BEAUTIFUL, INC., 9 West Broad St., Stamford, CT 06902 (203, 323-8987)
A national, nonprofit, public education organization dedicated to improving waste handling practices in American communities. Manages the Keep America Beautiful System, a local-level behaviorally-based approach to improved waste handling. Sponsors a National Awards Program, annual Keep America Beautiful Month, Public Lands Day, and a national public service advertising campaign. Established: 1953.
Chairman of the Board: RICHARD D. HOFMANN, Consultant
President: ROGER W. POWERS
Director, Training and Program Development: SUSIE HARPHAM
Western Regional Field Director: THERESA G. CREECH
Publication: *Vision Newsletter*

216

KEYSTONE CENTER, THE, P.O. Box 606, Keystone, CO 80435 (303, 468-5822)
A nonprofit national center for environmental negotiation, training, and education. Conducts national policy dialogues on environmental, energy, and science/technology issues; assists in environmental decisionmaking and regulatory negotiations; provides environmental mediation services; provides training and organizational development services in environmental conflict resolution; and operates a year-round residential environmental education program on a 16-acre campus in the Rocky Mountains (Arapahoe National Forest) under lease from the U.S. Forest Service. Founded: 1975.
Chairman: PAUL A. DOWNEY
Vice-Chairmen: KEITH R. McKENNON; JOHN M. SOMMER; GEORGE S. STRANAHAN
President: ROBERT W. CRAIG
Program Directors: JOHN R. EHRMANN; MICHAEL T. LESNICK; DAN McBRIDE
Trustees: C.L. BLACKBURN; EDWARD BLEIER; JAMES BONNER; RONNIE BROOKS; HAROLD BRUNO; FLETCHER L. BYROM; ALVIN L. COHEN; DOUGLAS M. COSTLE; WILLIAM DANFORTH; PAUL DOWNEY; LOUIS FERNANDEZ; JOHN T. FILES; WILLIAM FUTRELL; JAY D. HAIR; LADONNA HARRIS; N. BERNE HART; CHARLES HOUSTON; MARTIN JISCHKE; JERRY JONES; MARVIN H. KOSLOW; WILLIAM W. LOWRANCE; JOAN MANLEY; ROBERT A. MAYNARD; HARRIS D. SHERMAN; BRIAN E. URQUHART; ARNOLD WEBER
Publication: *Consensus Newsletter*
Editor: PHYLLIS C. MARTINEZ

217

LABORATORY OF ORNITHOLOGY, Cornell University, 159 Sapsucker Woods Rd., Ithaca, NY 14850 (607, 254-2473)
A center for the study and cultural appreciation of birds, with a membership of scientists and bird enthusiasts of all kinds. Organized: 1955.
Executive Director: CHARLES WALCOTT (254-2410)
Director, Special Projects: CHARLES R. SMITH (Ext. 2445)
Executive Staff Assistant: JANE HANCE WOOD (Ext. 2411)
Assistant Director for Operations: DIANE E. JOHNSON (Ext. 2471)
Director, Bioacoustics: CHRISTOPHER CLARK (Ext. 2405)
Curator, Library of Natural Sounds: GREGORY BUDNEY (Ext. 2406)
Director, Bird Population Studies: GREGORY S. BUTCHER (Ext. 2414)
Director, Public Affairs: SCOTT A. SUTCLIFFE (Ext. 2424)
Publication: *The Living Bird*
Editor: JILL M. CRANE (Ext. 2443)

218

LAKE ERIE CLEANUP COMMITTEE, INC.
To stop pollution of Lake Erie and of all fresh water lakes and streams and to inform the public of the need for greater pollution controls to prevent the return to the old methods of the past and to encourage industry do more research. "Our Great Lakes are a fragile part of our ecosystem and we must continue to protect them." Membership includes representatives of Michigan and Ohio citizen groups. Organized: 1959.
President: JOHN CHASCSA, 3568 Brewster Rd., Dearborn, MI 48120 (313, 271-8906)
Secretary: IRENE FINCK
Vice-President: RICHARD G. MICKA, 47 E. Elm, Monroe, MI 48161 (313, 242-0909)

219

LAKE MICHIGAN FEDERATION, 8 South Michigan Ave., Suite 2010, Chicago, IL 60603 (312, 263-5550)
A coalition of citizens and citizen organizations in Wisconsin, Illinois, Indiana, and Michigan dedicated to protection of Lake Michigan through community action and research. Supported by foundation and corporate grants and member contributions. Founded: 1970.
President of the Board of Directors: HENRY T. CHANDLER

Executive Director: GLENDA L. DANIEL
Administrative Assistant: MARY DURKIN
Publications: *The Lake Michigan Monitor; New Wave; Great Lakes Toxic Hotspots: A Citizen's Action Guide; Restoring Lake Michigan's Ecosystem* (poster)

220

LAND TRUST EXCHANGE, 1017 Duke St., Alexandria, VA 22314 (703, 683-7778)
A national network and service center that is improving the effectiveness and capacity of local and regional land conservation groups. Enables these organizations to share experiences and lessons learned; helps them gain access to needed, specialized expertise; assists them in coordinating efforts on issues and projects of common concern. Founded: 1982. Membership: l,000.
President/Executive Director: JEAN W. HOCKER
Chairman: MARK C. ACKELSON, Iowa Natural Heritage Foundation, Des Moines, IA
Vice-Chairman: JOHN R. COOK, JR., The CEIP Fund, Boston, MA
Secretary: HANS NEUHAUSER, The Georgia Conservancy, Savannah, GA
Treasurer: JUDITH STOCKDALE, Chicago Community Trust, Chicago, IL
Counsel: KINGSBURY BROWNE
Associate Director: KATHERINE BARTON
Coordinator, Information and Education: SYLVIA K. BATES
Office Manager: ELIZABETH STEENROD
Publications: *Exchange Journal; The Conservation Easement Handbook; Appraising Easements; The Federal Tax Law of Conservation Easements; For the Common Good: Preserving Private Lands with Conservation Easements; National Directory of Local and Regional Land Conservation Organizations*

221

LEAGUE OF CONSERVATION VOTERS, 2000 L St., NW, Suite 804, Washington, DC 20036 (202, 785-8683)
A nonpartisan, national political campaign committee to promote the election of public officials who will work for a healthy environment. Also evaluates environmental records of Congressmen, Senators and Presidential candidates. Researches and publishes Congressional voting records on important environmental legislation.
Board of Directors: JIM MADDY, Executive Director, Washington, DC; BRENT BLACKWELDER, Chairman, Washington, DC; RAFE POMERANCE, Washington, DC; RICHARD AYRES, Washington, DC; FRANCES BEINECKE, New York, NY; THE HON. ROBERT O. BLAKE, Washington, DC; RUTH CAPLAN, Washington, DC; SHARON FRANCES, Charlestown, NH; TINA HOBSON, Washington, DC; WILLIAM HOWARD, Washington, DC; JOHN HUNTING, Washington, DC; FREDRIC D. KRUPP, New York, NY; EDWARD M. NORTON, JR., Washington, DC; PAUL PRITCHARD, Washington, DC; AUDREY C. RUST, Menlo Park, CA; DOUGLAS SCOTT, San Francisco, CA; MAITLAND SHARPE, Arlington, VA; GEORGE H. SHELDON, Washington, DC; LYNDA TAYLOR, Albuquerque, NM; CHARLES WARREN, New York, NY; CYNTHIA WILSON, Washington, DC; DAVID ZWICK, Washington, DC; DOUGLAS SCOTT; CHARLES CLUSEN, Washington, DC; LOUISE DUNLAP, Washington, DC; ALLEN SMITH, Washington, DC; BROCK EVANS, Washington, DC; V. CRANE WRIGHT, Seattle, WA

Publications: *Annual Voting Chart (through the 100th Congress): How Congress Voted on Energy and the Environment; The Presidential Candidates: What they say, what they do on Energy and the Environment; Election Report; Support State*

222

LEAGUE OF WOMEN VOTERS OF THE U.S., 1730 M St., NW, Washington, DC 20036 (202, 429-1965)
Nonpartisan organization of 110,000 members located in all 50 states, the District of Columbia, Puerto Rico and the Virgin Islands, working to promote political responsibility through informed and active participation of citizens in government. Takes political action on water and air quality, solid and hazardous waste management, land use and energy. The League of Women Voters Education Fund carries out educational projects, publishes materials and arranges conferences on these natural resource issues.
President: NANCY M. NEUMAN
Executive Director: GRANT P. THOMPSON
Director, Natural Resources: DAVID GRAY LOVELAND
Publication: *The National Voter*
Editor: DEBRA DUFF

223

LEAGUE TO SAVE LAKE TAHOE, P.O. Box 10110, S. Lake Tahoe, CA 95731 (916, 541-5388)
A private, nonprofit corporation dedicated to preserving the environmental balance, scenic beauty and recreational opportunities of the Lake Tahoe Basin. Membership: 3,500. Founded: 1965.
President: GRAHAM B. MOODY, Mill Valley, CA
Vice-Presidents: JAMES W. BRUNER, JR.; WILLIAM V. REGAN; RICHARD H. WARD; JAMES E. WICKERSHAM
Secretary: KAREN B. NILSON
Treasurer: ADOLPHUS ANDREWS, JR., 600 Montgomery St., 35th Fl., San Francisco, CA 94111 (415, 981-1750)
Executive Director: THOMAS A. MARTENS
Publication: *Keep Tahoe Blue*

224

MANOMET BIRD OBSERVATORY, P.O. Box 936, Manomet, MA 02345 (617, 224-6521)
Nonprofit, membership-supported research and education institute dedicated to promoting informed conservation policy through long-term research on natural systems. Studies range throughout the Americas, including long-term monitoring of migrant songbird populations and ecology, international shorebird migration and identification of critical wetlands habitats, populations and distributions of seabirds and marine mammals in the northwest Atlantic, and tropical forest ecology. Conducts college-accredited Field Biology Training Program for hands-on training in field research; undergraduate and beginning graduate students can apply for spring, summer, and fall courses. Education program develops elementary and secondary school environmental curricula. Founded: 1969. Members: 2,200.
Chairman: WILLIAM S. BREWSTER
Director: LINDA E. LEDDY
Director, Field Biology Training Program: ELIZABETH P. MALLORY, Ph.D.
Education Specialist: JANIS ALBRIGHT

225

MARINE TECHNOLOGY SOCIETY, 2000 Florida Ave., NW, Suite 500, Washington, DC 20009 (202, 462-7557)
A professional society seeking to promote the exchange of information on marine-related subjects through its interdisciplinary structure; coordinates activities on important public and technical issues such as coastal zone management, marine mineral and

energy resources, marine environmental protection and economic potential of the oceans. Membership: 3,000.
President: RICHARD M. SHAMP
General Manager: MARTIN J. FINERTY, JR.
Publications: *Marine Technology Society Journal; MTS Newsletter; Currents; Various Proceedings*
Managing Editor: MARY BETH HATEM

226
MARK TRAIL/ED DODD FOUNDATION, P.O. Box 2807, Gainesville, GA 30503 (404, 532-4274)
A nonprofit public foundation dedicated to the conservation ideals and teachings of comic strip character Mark Trail and his creator Ed Dodd. The foundation teaches today's children/tomorrow's leaders to make sound environmental decisions, and also teaches these children to communicate these choices skillfully. Founded: 1986. Membership: 450. New members are welcome.
Executive Director: ROSEMARY DODD
Foundation Director: JIM HILLEGAS
Chairman: PETER MILLER

227
MAX McGRAW WILDLIFE FOUNDATION, P.O. Box 9, Dundee, IL 60118 (312, 741-8000)
Conducts wildlife and fisheries research and management and conservation education projects; cooperates with other conservation agencies and institutions.
Directors: LEONARD W. BUSSE; FREDERICK G. ACKER; MARSHALL FIELD; SCOTT M. ELROD; ROBERT P. GWINN; ROBERT L. MILLIGAN; STANLEY KOENIG; WALTER A. CLEMENTS; RICHARD S. PEPPER; HAROLD T. PERRY; GOFF SMITH; ALLAN L. MACA; M.P. VENEMA; DAVID REWICK; THOMAS E. DONNELLEY II
General Manager: GEORGE V. BURGER, Ph.D.
Publications: Descriptive brochure; Wildlife Management Notes Series

228
MEN'S GARDEN CLUBS OF AMERICA, INC., 5560 Merle Hay Rd., Johnston, IA 50131 (515, 278-0295)
A nonprofit organization of men and women interested in gardening. One hundred and sixty chapters located throughout the U.S. that sponsor Gardening from the Heart, a nationwide program for mentally, emotionally, physically disadvantaged youth and adults; youth gardening; Big Pumpkin - Giant Sunflower Contest. Membership: 9,000. Founded: 1932.
President: LARRY J. JASKOVIAK
1st Vice-President: CHRIS CHRISTENSEN
2nd Vice-President: ROBERT SCHWARZ
3rd Vice-President: JAMES TRACY
Treasurer: ALBERT J. MILLER
Publication: *The Gardener/National Newsletter*
Editor/Executive Committee: NANCY D. GORDEN

229
MID-ATLANTIC COUNCIL OF WATERSHED ASSOCIATIONS, 2955 Edge Hill Rd., Huntingdon Valley, PA 19006 (215, 657-0830)
Promotes exchange of ideas on citizen watershed association activities and advises any group wishing to start a new watershed association.
President: BRUCE McNAUGHT, Honey Hollow Watershed Association, Box 263A R.D. 1, New Hope, PA 18938 (297-5677)
Secretary: ROBERT STRUBLE, JR., Brandywine Valley Association, Inc., 1760 Unionville-Wawaset Rd., West Chester, PA 19382 (793-1090)
Treasurer: DAVID WITWER

230
MONITOR, 1506 19th St., NW, Washington, DC 20036 (202, 234-6576)
A nonprofit consortium founded in 1972 as a coordinating center and information clearing-house on endangered species and marine mammals for its 35 member conservation, environmental and animal welfare organizations. By assisting in the development and presentation of consensus positions by a maximum number of participating organizations, Monitor helps increase the impact of each.
Executive Vice-President: CRAIG VAN NOTE
President: DR. JOHN W. GRANDY (202, 452-1100)
Vice-President: BARBARA BRITTEN (703, 920-0076)
Secretary: CHRISTINE STEVENS (202, 337-2332)
Treasurer: LEWIS REGENSTEIN (404, 252-9176)
Board Members: FRED DAVIS (617, 522-5055); BILL PAINTER (202, 659-9510); JOHN FRIZELL (202, 332-4042); ROBERT HUGHES (609, 292-2080); BRIAN DAVIES (617, 362-4944)

231
MUSKIES, INC., 2301 7th St., No., Fargo, ND 58102 (701, 232-9544)
A nonprofit organization dedicated to establishing hatcheries and introduce the Muskellunge into suitable waters, abate water pollution, promote a high quality muskellunge sport fishery, support selected conservation practices, promote muskellunge research, disseminate muskellunge information, maintain records of habits, growth and range, and promote good fellowship and sportsmanship. Founded: 1966. Membership: 5,532.
President: BILL DAVIS, 679 Greenbriar Ln., Lake Forest, IL 60045 (312, 234-3915)
1st Vice-President: AL SKAAR, R. 5, Box 240A, Alexandria, MN 56308 (612, 763-3939)
2nd Vice-President: JIM BUNCH, 5757 Stewart Ln., Chippewa Falls, WI 54729 (715, 723-8343)
Secretary: MIKE BRANDT, R.R. 7, Box 7650, Hayward, WI 54843 (715, 462-3563)
Treasurer: FRANK SCHNEIDER, JR., 770 Cottage Ave., W., St. Paul, MN 55117 (612, 489-7341)
Administrative Secretary: PAT JOHNSON, 2301 7th St., North, Fargo, ND 58102 (701, 232-9544)
Publications: *Muskie*
Editor: KEITH OGDEN, P.O. Box 189, Cavalier, ND 58220 (701, 265-8023)

232
NATIONAL ARBOR DAY FOUNDATION, 100 Arbor Ave., Nebraska City, NE 68410 (402, 474-5655)
A nonprofit membership organization, sponsors National Arbor Day, Tree City USA, and Conservation Trees educational programs. It also manages the J. Sterling Morton Orchard and Tree Farm in Nebraska City, a national historic landmark. The Foundation publishes "Grow Your Own Tree" and "Trees are Terrific" instructional units for grade schools. Its public-service advertising messages for TV, radio, and magazines are endorsed by the Advertising Council. Steinhart Lodge, the foundation's educational and conference center in Nebraska City, is available for use for workshops, conferences, retreats, and meetings by conservation and other groups. Organized: 1971.
Board of Trustees: President, SUSAN SEACREST; Vice-President and President-Elect, DR. JAMES O'HANLON; Secretary, CHARLES CHACE; Treasurer, DR. GARY HERGENRADER; Executive Director, JOHN ROSENOW, Suite 501, 211 N. 12th St., Lincoln, NE 68508

Honorary Trustees: Chairman, STEWART UDALL; Resource Chairman, F. DALE ROBERTSON
Publications: *Arbor Day; Tree City USA Bulletin; Conservation Trees* booklet; *Celebrate Arbor Day* booklet
Editor: JOHN ROSENOW

233

NATIONAL ASSOCIATION OF BIOLOGY TEACHERS, 11250 Roger Bacon Dr., #19, Reston, VA 22090 (703, 471-1134) (Annual Meeting 1988: November 16-20, Chicago, IL)
The only national association specifically organized to assist teachers in the improvement of biology teaching. NABT offers teachers an opportunity to develop professionally through its journal, annual convention, summer workshops, and other publication programs. Membership: 6,000. Organized: 1938.
President: JANE ABBOTT, Dwight-Englewood School, 315 East Palisade Ave., Englewood, NJ 07631 (H: 201, 871-1725)
Vice-President: JOHN PENICK, Science Education Center, University of Iowa, Iowa City, IA 52242 (319, 335-1183)
Secretary/Treasurer: EDWARD FRAZIER, Speedway High School, 5357 West 25th St., Speedway, IN 46224 (317, 244-7238)
Executive Director: PATRICIA J. McWETHY
Publications: *The American Biology Teacher; News and Views*
Editor: RANDY MOORE, Department of Biology, Wright State University, Dayton, OH 45435 (817, 755-2911)
Managing Editor: MICHELLE ROBBINS

234

NATIONAL ASSOCIATION OF CONSERVATION DISTRICTS, 509 Capitol Ct., NW, Washington, DC 20002 (202, 547-6223)
Serves as the national instrument of its membership - 3,000 local districts and 52 state and territorial associations. Conservation districts, local subdivisions of state government, work to conserve and develop land, water, forests, wildlife, and related natural resources. Organized: 1946.
President: CLARENCE DURBAN, 15558 Robinson Rd., Plain City, OH 43064
Vice-President: ROBERT WETHERBEE, Rt. 1, Box 320, Fairmount, ND 58030
Secretary-Treasurer: GERALD B. DIGERNESS, 5155 Rock Rd., Sumas, WA 98295
Executive Vice-President: ERNEST C. SHEA, 509 Capitol Ct., NW, Washington, DC 20002
Manager, Service Department: DAVID SCHOVAJSA, Box 855, League City, TX 77574 (713, 332-3402)
Director of Communications: RONALD G. FRANCIS, Box 855, League City, TX 77574 (713, 332-3402)
Director of Governmental Affairs: STEVEN MEYER, 509 Capitol Ct., NW, Washington, DC 20002 (202, 547-6223)
State Programs Specialist: EUGENE LAMB, 509 Capitol Ct., NW, Washington, DC 20002 (202, 547-6223)
CTIC Coordinator: JOHN BECHERER, 1220 Potter Dr., Rm. 170, Purdue Research Park, West Lafayette, IN 47906 (317, 494-9555)
Northeastern Representative: MALCOLM P. CROOKS, Rt. 263, P.O. Box 297, Solebury, PA 18963 (215, 297-5676)
Southern Representative: DAVID L. FIROR, P.O. Box 606, Athens, GA 30603 (404, 546-1003)
North Central Representative: WILLIAM J. HORVATH, 1052 Main St., Stevens Point, WI 54481 (715, 341-1022)
Western Representative: ROBERT E. RASCHKE, Suite 113, 9150 W. Jewell, Lakewood, CO 80226 (303, 988-1810)
Pacific Representative: ROBERT BAUM, Suite 207, 831 Lancaster Dr., NE, Salem, OR 97301 (503, 363-0912)

Publications: *Tuesday Letter; America's Conservation Districts; Guide to Conservation Careers;* Environmental Film Service Catalogue

235

NATIONAL ASSOCIATION OF INTERPRETATION, Central Business Office, 6700 Needwood Rd., Derwood, MD 20855 (301, 948-8844)
A professional organization serving 1,300 members, employed by agencies and organizations concerned with natural and cultural resources, conservation and management, and in the interpretation of the natural and cultural environment as a service to the public. Founded: 1961.
Executive Manager: Vacant
President: Vacant
Vice-President: Vacant
Secretary: JANN YOUNG
Treasurer: KARIN HOSTETTER

Regional Directors
Region I: BOB BUDLINGER (303, 545-9114)
Region II: ROSS ZITO
Region III: DOUG WEEKS
Region IV: FRED WOOLEY
Region V: ALAN CAPELLE
Region VI: BOB JENNINGS
Region VII: CHAN BIGGS
Region VIII: Vacant
Region IX: MIKE NICHOLSON
Region X: NEIL HAGADORN
Publications: *NAI Newsletter; NAI Journal Interpretation; Interpretive Research*
Editors: Vacant

236

NATIONAL ASSOCIATION OF SERVICE AND CONSERVATION CORPS, 1001 Connecticut Ave., Suite 827, Washington, DC 20036 (202, 331-8387)
Nonprofit education association made up of conservation and service corps operating in states and cities. Serves as information exchange network for members concerning conservation corps administration and management, promotes conservation and service values among staff and corpsmembers, offers technical assistance to those interested in launching new corps, and promotes establishment of federal, state and local programs. NASCC sponsors an annual national conference and regional seminars and workshops for youth corps advocates and related youth service programs. Founded: May, 1985.
Board President: ROBERT BURKHARDT (415, 928-7322)
Vice-President: SCOTT IZZO (603, 826-7732)
Executive Director: MARGARET ROSENBERRY
Publication: *The Reading*

237

NATIONAL ASSOCIATION OF STATE DEPARTMENTS OF AGRICULTURE, Suite 704, 1616 H St., NW, Washington, DC 20006 (202, 628-1566)
Composed of the executive heads of departments of agriculture of the 50 states and the trust territories for betterment of American agriculture and the general welfare of the people; promotes unity and efficiency in the administration of all agricultural statutes and regulations; develops, through teamwork, cooperation between the departments and persons interested or engaged in agriculture.
President: THOMAS W. BALLOW, Reno, NV
Secretary-Treasurer: S. MASON CARBAUGH, Richmond, VA
Executive Secretary: JAMES B. GRANT
Asst. Executive Secretary: ROBERT AMATO, Washington, DC

238

NATIONAL ASSOCIATION OF STATE FORESTERS

Composed of state foresters whose agencies are the legally constituted authorities for conducting public forestry work within the states. In cooperation with Federal and private agencies and individuals, undertakes to conduct and strengthen all activities in forestry and conservation programs.

President: JAMES B. ROBERTS, State Forester, Forest, Park and Wildlife Service, 580 Taylor Ave., Annapolis, MD 21501-2351 (301, 269-3776)

Vice-President: JAMES E. HUBBARD, State Forester, Colorado

Secretary: JOHN E. SARGENT, Director, Division of Forests and Lands, Box 856, Prescott Park, 105 Loudon Rd., Concord, NH 03301 (603, 271-2214)

Treasurer: JOHN MIXON, Director, Georgia Forestry Commission, P.O. Box 819, Macon, GA 31298-0001 (912, 744-3237)

Area Representatives: STANLEY F. HAMILTON, Idaho, Western Representative; HARRY LAYMAN, North Carolina Southeastern Representative; JOHN E. SARGENT, New Hampshire Northeastern Representative

Washington, D.C. Representative: MELINDA COHEN, 444 No. Capitol St., NW, Washington, DC 20001 (202, 624-5415)

239

NATIONAL ASSOCIATION OF STATE OUTDOOR RECREATION LIAISON OFFICERS

Advisory group working with the National Park Service, Department of the Interior to strengthen the nation's total outdoor recreation program. Represents state and local interests in administration of the Land and Water Conservation Fund Program, which provides money for acquisition and development of recreation land and facilities. Organized: 1967.

President: HELEN C. FENSKE, Dept. of Environmental Protection, CN 402, Trenton, NJ 08625 (609, 292-3541)

Vice-President: JO LUCK WILSON, Dept. of Parks and Tourism, 1 Capitol Mall, Little Rock, AR 72201 (501, 371-2535)

Secretary: DOUGLAS EIKEN, Parks and Recreation Dept., 1424 West Century Ave., Suite 202, Bismarck, ND 58501 (701, 224-4887)

Executive Director: ART BUEHLER, Dept of Conservation and Historic Resources, Washington Bldg., Capitol Square, Richmond, VA 23219 (804, 786-2556)

240

NATIONAL ASSOCIATION OF STATE PARK DIRECTORS

Works to unite the states on a common ground for the development of park systems to meet the intensive public demand for out-of-doors recreational opportunities; to promote the exchange of ideas regarding the development of state park systems; to encourage and develop professional leadership; and to expand and improve park policies and practices. Membership: 50. Founded: 1962.

President: WILLIAM C. WALTERS, Director, Division of State Parks, Department of Natural Resources, 616 State Office Bldg., Indianapolis, IN 46204 (317, 232-4136)

Secretary-Treasurer: DALE R. BREE, Assistant Director, Nebraska Game and Parks Commission, P.O. Box 30370, Lincoln, NE 68503 (402, 464-0641)

241

NATIONAL ASSOCIATION OF STATE RECREATION

PLANNERS, 205 Butler St., SE, Suite 1352, Atlanta, GA 30334 (404, 656-2753)

A nonprofit organization involved in the exchange of recreation planning information among the states, participates in national recreation concerns, promotes improvements in the state-of-the-art of recreation planning and professionalism among its members and acts as an advocate for conservation and recreation opportunities for the future. The core group of members are those persons in each state and territory who are responsible for meeting the planning requirements of the Federal Land and Water Conservation Fund Act.

President: TERRI YEARWOOD, GA

Vice-President: BRUCE KENNEDY, CA

Secretary: SUSAN BULMER, AZ

Treasurer: ROBERT OWENS, SC

Publications: *NASRP Newsletter; Compendium of State Planning Projects*

242

NATIONAL AUDUBON SOCIETY, 950 Third Ave., New York, NY 10022 (212, 832-3200)

One of the nation's oldest and largest conservation organizations, Audubon carries out a balanced program of research, education and action. Its prime objective is the long term protection and wise use of land, water, wildlife and other natural resources. Through its study of bird life the society has come to believe that all forms of life are interdependent. Membership: 550,000. Founded: 1905.

Chairman of the Board: DONAL C. O'BRIEN, JR.

Vice-Chairmen: HELEN ENGLE; NOEL LEE DUNN; NATHANIEL P. REED

National Office Staff: (212, 832-3200 /212, 546-9100)

President: PETER A.A. BERLE

Senior Vice-Presidents: Publications, LES LINE; Regional and Governmental Affairs, ELIZABETH RAISBECK; Development, SUSAN P. MARTIN; Science and Sanctuaries, J.P. MYERS; Controller, JAMES A. CUNNINGHAM

Vice-Presidents: Office of the President and Director, MARY JOY BRETON; Public Affairs, ROBERT SANGEORGE; Membership, CARMINE BRANAGAN; Conservation Information, CHRIS WILLE

Senior Staff Scientist, Environmental Policy Analysis: DR. JAN BEYEA

Publications: *Audubon; American Birds; Audubon Wildlife Report; Audubon Adventures; Audubon Activist*

Editors: LES LINE; SUSAN DRENNAN; CHRIS WILLE

Washington, DC Office, 801 Pennsylvania Ave., SE, Suite 301, Washington, DC 20003 (202, 547-9009)

Vice-Presidents: Government Relations, Vacant; National Issues, BROCK EVANS; Television, CHRISTOPHER N. PALMER; Counsel, HOPE BABCOCK

Education Division (headquarters), Rt. 1, Box 171, Sharon, CT 06069 (203, 364-0520)

Vice-President: MARSHAL T. CASE

Field Research and Ornithological Research (headquarters), 115 Indian Mound Tr., Tavernier, FL 33070 (305, 852-5092)

Vice-President: ALEXANDER SPRUNT IV

Sanctuaries

Vice-President and Director: FRANK M. DUNSTAN, R.R. 1 Box 294, Sharon, CT 06069 (203, 364-0048)

Regional Activities and Field Offices

Mid-Atlantic (DE, MD, NJ, PA, VA, WV): WALT POMEROY, Vice-President, 1104 Fernwood Ave., Suite 300, Camp Hill, PA 17011 (717, 763-4985)

Northeast (CT, ME, MA, NH, NY, RI, VT): Vacant, Sr. Vice-President, 950 Third Ave., New York, NY 10022 (212, 546-9220)

Vermont: STEVE YOUNG, Representative, Fiddler's Green, Box 9, Waitsfield, VT 05673 (802, 496-5727)

Southeast (AL, FL, GA, KY, MS, NC, SC, TN): LARRY THOMPSON, Vice-President, 928 N. Monroe St., Tallahassee, FL 32303 (904, 222-2473)

Great Lakes (IL, IN, MI, MN, OH, WI): DAVID NEWHOUSE, Vice-President, 7 North Meridian St., #400, Indianapolis, IN 46204 (317, 631-2676)

Minnesota: TOM McGUIGAN, State Representative, 730 Hennepin Ave., Suite 330, City Place, Minneapolis, MN 55403 (612, 375-9140)

West Central (AR, IA, KS, MO, NE, ND, OK, SD): RON KLATASKE, Vice-President, 200 Southwind Pl., #205, Manhattan, KS 66502 (913, 537-4385)

Southwest (LA, NM, TX, Mexico, Panama): DEDE ARMENTROUT, Vice-President, 2525 Wallingford, #1505, Austin, TX 78736 (512, 327-1943)

New Mexico: DAVID HENDERSON, Representative, P.O. Box 9314, Santa Fe, NM 87504 (505, 983-4609)

Rocky Mountain (AZ, CO, ID, MT, UT, WY): ROBERT TURNER, Vice-President, 4150 Darley, Suite 5, Boulder, CO 80303 (303, 499-0219)

Western (CA, HI, NV, OR, WA, Guam): GLEN OLSON, Vice-President, 555 Audubon Pl., Sacramento, CA 95825 (916, 481-5332)

Washington: PAM CROCKER DAVIS, State Representative, P.O. Box 462, Olympia,WA 98507 (206, 786-8020)

ALASKA (AK): DAVID CLINE, Vice-President, 308 'G' St., Suite 219, Anchorage, AK 99501 (907, 276-7034)

243

NATIONAL CAMPERS AND HIKERS ASSOCIATION, INC., 7172 Transit Rd., Buffalo, NY 14221 (716, 634-5433)

An organization dedicated to the education of the public concerning the need for conservation of natural resources. Membership: 50,000 families.

President: RICHARD DeCABOOTER, 26655 Campau Ln., Mt. Clemens, MI 48045 (313, 468-3707)

National Conservation Directors: THOMAS and HELEN KIRKLAND, 301 Byck Ave., Garden City, GA 31408

National Wildlife Refuge Directors: BEN and SUSAN KINSEY, 1695 Otto Rd., Charlotte, MI 48813

244

NATIONAL CENTER FOR URBAN ENVIRONMENTAL STUDIES, 516 N. Charles St., Suite 501, Baltimore, MD 21201 (301, 727-6212)

A nonprofit, public interest organization dedicated to providing a program of research, training, technical assistance and information dissemination for governments, organizations and institutions involved in the development of aging, energy, and health urban environmental strategies.

President: LARRY YOUNG

Publications: *Results; Minority Energy Watch;* Complete listing available upon request.

245

NATIONAL COALITION AGAINST THE MISUSE OF PESTICIDES, 530 7th St., SE, Washington, DC 20003 (202, 543-5450)

Nonprofit membership organization committed to assisting individuals, organizations and communities with useful information on pesticides and their alternatives. NCAMP's information clearinghouse provides material on a wide range of both agricultural and urban issues concerning farm workers' safety, lawn care safety, groundwater problems, and alternatives to pesticides as well as legislation. Founded: 1981.

National Coordinator: JAY FELDMAN

Staff Toxicologist: DIANE BAXTER Administrative Assistant: SARAH SULLIVAN

Information Coordinator: TOM OATES

Staff Entomologist: KEVIN THORPE, Ph.D.

Research Associate: ERIK JANSSON

Publications: *Pesticides and You Newsletter; NCAMP's Technical Report; Pesticide Safety:* Myths and Facts brochure; Pest Control Without Toxic Chemicals brochure; *Pesticide Review* (Series)

Editors: JAY FELDMAN; DIANE BAXTER

246

NATIONAL COALITION FOR MARINE CONSERVATION, P.O. Box 23298, Savannah, GA 31403 (912, 234-8062)

A nonprofit, privately supported organization devoted exclusively to the conservation of ocean fish and the protection of the marine environment. Promotes public awareness of marine conservation issues, stimulates the formulation of responsible public policy with respect to such issues, and shapes the implementation of such policy. Membership: 5,000. Founded: 1973.

President: CHRISTOPHER M. WELD, One Post Office Square, Boston, MA 02109 (617, 338-2909)

Chairman: JOHN M. GREEN, P.O. Box 2095, Beaumont, TX 77704

Vice-Chairman: FRANK E. CARLTON

Executive Director: KEN HINMAN

Publication: *Marine Bulletin*

Editor: KEN HINMAN

247

NATIONAL COUNCIL FOR GEOGRAPHIC EDUCATION, 16A Leonard Hall, Indiana University of Pennsylvania, Indiana, PA 15705 (412, 357-6290)

To promote and advance geographic and environmental education in the public schools and colleges of the U.S. and Canada. Membership: 3,500. Organized: 1915.

President: ROBERT MORRILL

Vice-President: DOROTHY DRUMMOND

Secretary: SANDRA PRITCHARD

Treasurer: DIXIE PEMBERTON

Executive Director: RUTH I. SHIREY

Publications: *Journal of Geography;* List of other publications available upon request.

Editor: ROBERT S. BEDNARZ, Department of Geography, Texas A&M University, College Station, TX 77843-3147

248

NATIONAL COUNCIL OF STATE GARDEN CLUBS, INC., 4401 Magnolia Ave., St. Louis, MO 63110 (314, 776-7574)

Coordinates and furthers the interests and activities of the State Federations of Garden Clubs, together with similar organizations in the U.S. and foreign countries; aids in the protection and conservation of natural resources; protects civic beauty and encourages the improvement of roadsides and parks; encourages and assists in establishing and maintaining botanical gardens and horticultural centers; and advances art of gardening, of landscape design, and study of horticulture. Members: 365,430. Organized: 1929.

President: MRS. CARROLL O. GRIFFIN, 839 Riverbend Blvd., Longwood, FL 32779

1st Vice-President: MRS. C. MANNING SMITH, P.O. Box 450, Charles Town, WV 25414

2nd Vice-President: MRS. JAMES DAWSON, 165 Olive St., Elmhurst, IL 60126

Corresponding Secretary: MRS. J.B. LAWTON, III, 1114 Meadows Ave., Orlando, FL 32804

Treasurer: MRS. EDWARD J. NEUNER, 17945 Wild Horse Creek Rd., Chesterfield, MO 63017

Office Manager: MRS. CHARLES MANTLER (776-7574)

Environmental Education: MRS. RICHARD J. HARLEY, 9744 Trilobi Dr., Indianapolis, IN 46236

Publication: *The National Gardener*

Editor: MRS. WILLIAM V. DONNAN, 995 Kirkham, St. Louis, MO 63122

249

NATIONAL EDUCATION ASSOCIATION, 1201 16th St., NW, Washington, DC 20036 (202, 833-4000)

Works to elevate the character and advance the interests of the teaching profession and to promote the cause of education in the U.S. Membership: 1,800,000. Organized 1857.

President: MARY H. FUTRELL

Vice-President: KEITH GEIGER

Secretary-Treasurer: ROXANNE E. BRADSHAW

Executive Director: DON CAMERON

250

NATIONAL ENVIRONMENTAL HEALTH ASSOCIATION, 720 S. Colorado Blvd., South Tower, 970, Denver, CO 80222 (303, 756-9090)

The NEHA is a member nonprofit organization dedicated to the enhancement of health through environmental control. It is the largest society of environmental health practitioners in the nation today numbering over 5,000 members and growing. Membership is comprised of individuals from the public and the private sector which includes academia. Founded: 1937.

Executive Director: NELSON E. FABIAN

Publications: *Journal of Environmental Health; Environmental Health Trends Report; Self Paced Learning Modules; NEHA Newsletter*

251

NATIONAL FARMERS UNION, Denver, CO 80251 (303, 337-5500) (Annual Convention 1989: March 5-8, Little Rock, AR)

Believes that the soil, water, forest and other natural resources of the nation should be used and conserved in a manner to pass these resources on undiminished to future generations and that publicly and privately owned land and resources should be administered in the interest of all the public. Organized: 1902.

President: LELAND H. SWENSON

Vice-President: JACK KELSEY

Treasurer: WILLIAM OWEN

Secretary: DAVID CARTER

Director of Legislative Services: MICHAEL V. DUNN, 600 Maryland Ave., SW, Suite 202W, Washington, DC 20024 (202, 554-1600)

Publication: *National Farmers Union Washington Newsletter*

Editor: MILTON D. HAKEL, 600 Maryland Ave., SW, Suite 202W, Washington, DC 20024

252

NATIONAL FIELD ARCHERY ASSOCIATION, 31407 Outer I-10, Redlands, CA 92373 (714, 794-2133)

A nonprofit national membership headquarters for field archers. Membership: 20,000.

President: JOHN SLACK, I1658 Mulhall, El Monte, CA 91732

Executive Secretary: Vacant

Publication: *Archery Magazine*

Editor: Vacant

253

NATIONAL FISH AND WILDLIFE FOUNDATION, Main Interior Bldg., 18th and C Streets, NW, Rm. 2725, Washington, DC 20240 (202, 343-1040)

A private, nonprofit organization established by the U.S. Congress in 1984. Encourages and administers private sector contributions for the benefit of, or in connection with, the programs of the U.S. Fish and Wildlife Service, and promotes other innovative public and private partnerships to enhance the conservation and management of the nation's fish, wildlife and plant resources.

Executive Director: CHARLES H. COLLINS

Director of Policy: AMOS S. ENO

Chairman of the Board: BEATRICE C. PICKENS

Members of the Board: EUGENE A. BAY, JR.; JOHN F. BOOKOUT; FRANK H. DUNKLE; WILLIAM A. MOLINI; THOMAS G. McMILLIAN; JAMES D. RANGE; MICHAEL H. SHLAUDEMAN; KENNETH HOFMANN; CHARLES E. YEAGER

254

NATIONAL FLYWAY COUNCIL

Chairman: DALE STRICKLAND, Assistant Game Warden, Wyoming Game and Fish Dept., Cheyenne, WY 82002 (307, 777-7604)

Flyway Councils

Atlantic Flyway (CT, DE, FL, GA, ME, MD, MA, NH, NJ, NY, NC, PA, RI, SC, VT, VA, WV, DC, Puerto Rico, Ontario, Quebec, New Brunswick, Nova Scotia, Prince Edward Island, Newfoundland) Chairman: KENNETH WICH, Director, Division of Fish and Wildlife, Department of Environmental Conservation, 50 Wolf Rd., Albany, NY 12233 (518, 457-5690)

Mississippi Flyway (AL, AR, IL, IN, IA, KY, LA, MI, MN, MS, MO, OH, TN, WI, Ontario, Manitoba, Saskatchewan) Chairman: WILLIAM GRAVES, Director, Division of Wildlife, Dept. of Fish and Wildlife Resources, #I Game Farm Rd., Frankfort, KY 40601

Central Flyway (CO, KS, MT, NB, NM, ND, OK, SD, TX, WY) Chairman: DALE STRICKLAND, Assistant Game Warden, Wyoming Game and Fish Department, Cheyenne, WY 82002

Pacific Flyway (AZ, CA, ID, NV, OR, UT, WA, AK, MT, WY, CO, NM, Alberta, British Columbia) Chairman: RON MARCOUX, Associate Director, Montana Dept. of Fish and Wildlife, and Parks, 1420 E 6th Ave., Helena, MT 59620 (406, 444-3186)

255

NATIONAL FUTURE FARMERS OF AMERICA ORGANIZATION, P.O. Box 15160, National FFA Center, Alexandria, VA 22309 (703, 360-3600) (Annual Meeting: National Convention, November, Kansas City, MO)

The FFA is a national organization of high school agriculture students in public secondary schools. Congress granted the organization a federal charter in 1950, making it an integral part of the high school agriculture program. Major aims are to provide activities that will stimulate students to higher achievement in the study of production agriculture, agriscience, agribusiness and agrimarketing, and give them opportunities through student-planned programs for leadership and self-development. The organization has award programs in farm business management, livestock judging, meats judging, poultry judging, extemporaneous and prepared public speaking, chapter safety, national chapter, building our american communities and many others. Membership: 416,000. Founded: 1928, Kansas City, MO.

Advisor: DR. LARRY D. CASE (202, 732-2425)

Executive Secretary: C. COLEMAN HARRIS (703, 360-3600)

Treasurer: DAVID A. MILLER, Regional Coordinator for Vocational Education, State Dept. of Education, Baltimore, MD (301, 659-2568)

Publications: *The National Future Farmer Magazine; Between Issues Newsletter; Update Newsletter*
Editor-in-Chief: WILSON W. CARNES (703, 360-3600)

256

NATIONAL GARDENING ASSOCIATION, 180 Flynn Ave., Burlington, VT 05401 (802, 863-1308)
A 200,000 member-supported organization established in 1972, dedicated to helping people be successful gardeners at home, in community groups, and in institutions. We believe that gardening adds joy and health to living while improving the environment, and encouraging an appreciation for the proper stewardship of the earth.
Board of Directors: JOHN KERR; CHARLES SCOTT, President, NGA; CHRISTOPHER GILBERT; JOAN DYE GUSSOW, Chair; MARY BUDD ROWE; EDWARD N. ROBINSON; JACKSON W. ROBINSON; ROBERT B. THOMSON
President: CHARLES SCOTT
Secretary: BARBARA GODFREY
Treasurer: GAYE SYMINGTON
Accountant: BETSY BOGNER
Membership Analyst: SUE MARCHANT
Member Services Coordinator: VICKI GAYLORD
Grow Lab Program Coordinator: EVE FANCIS
Market Research: BRUCE BUTTERFIELD
Radio Program Producer: JULIA GILBERT
Advertising Sales Manager: JOHN SIMINGOR
Educational Products Manager: LARRY SOMMERS
Education Programs: TIM PARSONS, Director; SUE DIXON, Grant and Corporate Associates Coordinator
Advertising and Publications: CHERYL DORSCHNER, Director
Marketing: BETSY BRADBURY, Director; NANCY FLINN, Public Relations
Publications: *National Gardening Magazine; The Youth Gardening Book; The Community Garden Book; National Gardening Survey; Gardening; Gardeners' Questions Answered; Directory of Seed and Nursery Catalogs; Yardening Video Series; Grow Lab: A Complete Guide to Gardening in the Classroom; Ruth Page's Gardening Journal*
Editor-in-Chief: KIT ANDERSON
Managing Editor: EMILY STETSON
Horticultural Editor: WARREN SCHULTZ
Senior Editor: JACK RUTTLE
Horticulturalist: CHARLIE NARDOZZI

257

NATIONAL GEOGRAPHIC SOCIETY, 17th and M Sts., NW, Washington, DC 20036 (202, 857-7000)
For the increase and diffusion of geographic knowledge. Membership: 10,600,000. Founded: 1888.
Chairman of the Board: GILBERT M. GROSVENOR
President: GILBERT M. GROSVENOR
Executive Vice-President: OWEN R. ANDERSON
Editor, National Geographic: WILBUR E. GARRETT
Vice-President and Treasurer: ALFRED J. HAYRE
Vice-Presidents: ROBERT L. BREEDEN; FREDERICK C. GALE; LEONARD J. GRANT; JOSEPH B. HOGAN; ADRIAN L. LOFTIN; LEWIS P. LOWE; RAYMOND T. McELLIGOTT, JR.; ROBERT B. SIMS
Secretary: EDWIN W. SNIDER

Publications: *National Geographic; National Geographic Research; National Geographic World magazine* (for children); *National Geographic Traveler;* Books; Atlases; Maps; Filmstrips; Documentary Films

258

NATIONAL GRANGE, THE, 1616 H St., NW, Washington, DC 20006 (202, 628-3507)
Farm organization with additional interests in community service and family projects. Membership: 365,000. Founded: 1867.
Master: ROBERT E. BARROW, Washington, DC office
Secretary: JOANNE O. PASSMORE, 630 Taylor's Bridge Rd., Townsend, DE 19734
Legislative Director: ROBERT M. FREDERICK, Washington, DC Office
Information Director: JUDY TAYLOR MASSABNY, Washington, DC Office
Executive Committee: JACK SILVERS, Chairman, Seattle, WA; LESTER WALLACE, Secretary, Beloit, WI; JEANNE DAVIES, Denver, CO; ROLAND WINTER, Haslett, MI; KERMIT RICHARDSON, Barre, VT; ROBERT E. BARROW, (Ex-Officio)

259

NATIONAL HUNTERS ASSOCIATION, THE, P.O. Box 16, Eagle Rock, NC 27523 (919, 365-9289/7157)
The National Hunters Association, Inc. was incorporated under the laws of NC in 1976 to protect your hunting rights in the US and around the world. We are dedicated to hunter safety, the preservation of the rights of the individual sportsman to pursue the sport of hunting and the preservation of an adequate supply of game for the sportsman to hunt -- now and in the future. Our organization conducts hunter educational camps for young people to give them a quality outdoor learning experience in establishing wilderness survival courses where people of all ages learn to handle themselves in the wild. The NHA is there with a comprehensive organization of professionals experts in their fields, to meet all your hunting and outdoor needs.
President: D.V. SMITH
Vice-Presidents: JIM (Catfish) HUNTER; RICHARD CHILDRESS; CHARLES (Pink) ATKINS; FRANK GRAINGER
Secretary-Treasurer: FAYE M. SMITH
Publication: *NHS Newsletter*

260

NATIONAL INSTITUTE FOR URBAN WILDLIFE (formerly the URBAN WILDLIFE RESEARCH CENTER, INC.), 10921 Trotting Ridge Way, Columbia, MD 21044-2831 (301, 596-3311) (Annual Meeting: May)
Established as a private, nonprofit national organization to conduct research on the relationship between man and wildlife in urban and developing areas, to discover and disseminate practical procedures for maintaining or enhancing wildlife populations and controlling certain wildlife species in urban areas, and to improve the quality of life in communities. Founded: 1973.
President: GOMER E. JONES
Chairman of the Board: DR. JOSEPH P. LINDUSKA (301, 778-5369)
Vice-Chairman of the Board: H.J. YOUNG (202, 778-6400)
Treasurer: PAUL H. WENDLER
Vice-President for Research: DR. LOWELL W. ADAMS
Senior Scientist: DR. DANIEL L. LEEDY
Publication: *Urban Wildlife News, Urban Wildlife Manager's Notebook*
Editor: LOUISE E. DOVE, Wildlife Biologist

261
NATIONAL MILITARY FISH AND WILDLIFE ASSOCIATION

A nonprofit organization established in 1983 to improve fish and wildlife management on Department of Defense lands throughout the nation. Membership is primarily comprised of professional natural resources personnel within the Department of Defense. The association conducts an annual training session for its members.

President: LARRY ADAMS, Code 241B, Atlantic Division, NAVFA-CENGCOM, Norfolk, VA 23511-6287 (804, 445-2369)

Immediate Past President: TOM WARREN, Attn: AFZC-DEH, Fort Carson, CO 80913-5000 (303, 579-4828)

Vice-President: SLADER BUCK, Marine Corps Base, Natural Resources Office, Building 25154, Camp Pendleton, CA 92055 (619, 725-3528)

Secretary-Treasurer: RICHARD GRIFFITH, PMPMD, USAEHA, Aberdeen Proving Ground, MD 21010-5422 (301, 671-3015)

Board of Directors At-Large Members: SCOTT KLINGER, Directorate of Facilities Engineering, Fort Riley, KS 66442-5036 (913, 239-6211); KIM MELLO, Attn: AFZR-DFE, Fort McCoy, Sparta, WI 54656 (608, 388-2252); DONALD PROGULSKE, 56 CSS/DEN, Avon Park, FL 33825 (813, 452-4119); TOM WRAY, Naval Surface Weapons Center, Public Works Office, Dahlgren, VA 22448 (703, 663-8695)

Program Chairman: GENE STOUT, Fish and Wildlife Branch, DEH, Fort Sill, OK 73503-5100 (405, 352-4324)

Publication: *Fish And Wildlife News*

Editor: CHESTER O. MARTIN, Environmental Laboratory, USAE Waterways Experiment Station, P.O. Box 631, Vicksburg, MS 39180-0631 (601, 634-3958)

262
NATIONAL ORGANIZATION FOR RIVER SPORTS, 314 N.
20th St., P.O. Box 6847, Colorado Springs, CO 80934 (719, 473-2466)

A nonprofit organization dedicated to education about whitewater river sports, including kayaking, rafting, and canoeing; to preserving rivers; and to protecting river access rights of river runners. Founded: 1979. Membership: 10,000.

President: GARY LACY

Vice-President: BEN HARDING

Secretary-Treasurer and Executive Director: ERIC LEAPER

Board Members: FLETCHER ANDERSON; EARL PERRY

Membership Director: MARY McCURDY

Development Director: JENNIE GOLDBERG

Publication: *Currents*

Editor: ERIC LEAPER

263
NATIONAL PARK FOUNDATION, P.O. Box 57473, Washington,
DC 20037 (202, 785-4500)

A private, nonprofit organization chartered by the U.S. Congress, which provides imaginative private-sector support for the enhancement and improvement of the National Park system in ways not generally possible through government processes. The foundation seeks contributions to carry out its programs of publications, grants for innovative park programs, improvement of visitor services, the development of educational materials about the National Parks, and the acquisition of key, irreplaceable tracts of land to be added to America's system of National Parks.

President: JOHN L. BRYANT, JR.

Chairman: DONALD PAUL HODEL, Secretary of the Interior

Vice-Chairman: WILLIAM B. GRAHAM

Treasurer: GORDON P. STREET, JR.

Secretary, Director of the National Park Service: WILLIAM PENN MOTT, JR.

Publication: *The Complete Guide to America's National Parks*

264
NATIONAL PARKS AND CONSERVATION ASSOCIATION,
1015 31st St., NW, Washington, DC 20007 (202, 944-8530)

A private, nonprofit, membership organization, whose role is the preservation, promotion, and improvement of our nation's park system. NPCA has been an advocate as well as a constructive critic of the National Park Service. NPCA has focused on the health of the entire system-from specific sites and programs to the processes of planning, management, and evaluation. Members and contributors: 70,000. Established: 1919.

Chairman of Executive Committee and Board of Trustees: STEPHEN MATHER McPHERSON

Vice-Chairmen: GORDON T. BEAHAM III; A. JAMES MATSON; CHARLES W. SLOAN

Secretary: SUSAN HANSON

Treasurer: DONALD S. DOWNING

President: PAUL C. PRITCHARD

Vice-President, Conservation Policy: T. DESTRY JARVIS

Vice-President, Operations: KAREN B. KRESS

Director of Federal Activities: WILLIAM C. LIENESCH

Director of Citizen Involvement: LAURA LOOMIS

Southwest/California Regional Office: RUSSELL D. BUTCHER, Box 67, Cottonwood, AZ 86326

Rocky Mountain Regional Office: TERRI MARTIN, Box 1563, Salt Lake City, UT 84110-1563

New York Chapter Office: RICHARD WHITE-SMITH, P.O. Box 309, Albany, NY 12201

Media Coordinator: THOMAS M. MILLER

Publication: *National Parks Magazine*

Editor: MICHELE STRUTIN

265
NATIONAL RECREATION AND PARK ASSOCIATION, 3101
Park Center Dr., Alexandria, VA 22302 (703, 820-4940)

A nonprofit service, education and research organization dedicated to the improvement of park and recreation leadership, programs and facilities. The association attempts to build public understanding that leisure programs and environments are indispensable to the well-being of a nation and its citizens. Membership: 18,500.

Chairman of the Board: ANNE S. CLOSE, Fort Mill, SC

Chairman, Executive Committee: MICK POPE, Elmhurst, IL

President: MICK POPE, Elmhurst, IL

Vice-President: PETER KOUKOS, Highland Park, IL

Executive Director: R. DEAN TICE

Secretary: MARVIN F. BILLUPS, JR., Charlotte, NC

Director of Governmental Affairs: BARRY TINDALL

Publications: *Parks & Recreation Magazine; Journal of Leisure Research; Therapeutic Recreation Journal; Recreation & Parks Law Reporter; Park Practice Program; Dateline: NRPA*

Regional Directors

Pacific: JANE HIPPS ADAMS, Suite 202, 3031 F St., Sacramento, CA 95816 (916, 441-0445)

Western: FRANK COSGROVE, 3500 Ridge Rd., P.O. Box 6900, Colorado Springs, CO 80934 (303, 632-7031)

Great Lakes: WALTER JOHNSON, 650 W. Higgins, Hoffman Estates, IL 60195 (312, 843-7529)

Northeast: Vacant, 1800 Silas Deane Highway, Suite 1, Rocky Hill, CT 06067 (203, 721-1055)

Southeast: W. TOM MARTIN, JR., 4319 Covington, Rm. 209, Decatur, GA 30035 (404, 284-5826)

266

NATIONAL RESEARCH COUNCIL, NATIONAL ACADEMY OF SCIENCES, NATIONAL ACADEMY OF ENGINEERING, INSTITUTE OF MEDICINE, 2101 Constitution Ave., NW, Washington,DC 20418 (202, 334-2000)

An independent advisor to the federal government on scientific and technical questions of national importance. Jointly administered by the National Academies of Sciences and Engineering and the Institute of Medicine. Organized: 1916.

Chairman: FRANK PRESS

Executive Officer: PHILIP M. SMITH

Director, Office of News and Public Information: GAIL PORTER

Publications: Catalogue available upon request.

267

NATIONAL RIFLE ASSOCIATION OF AMERICA, 1600 Rhode Island Ave., NW, Washington, DC 20036 (202, 828-6000)

A nonprofit organization dedicated to protect and defend the Constitution of the United States especially the right to possess and use arms; to promote public safety, law and order, and the national defense; to train members of law enforcement agencies, the armed forces, the militia and people of good repute in marksmanship and the safe handling and efficient use of small arms; to foster and promote the shooting sports, including the advancement of amateur competitions in marksmanship at the local, state, regional, national, and international levels; to promote hunter safety, and to promote and defend hunting as a shooting sport and as a viable and necessary method of fostering the propagation, growth, conservation, and wise use of our renewable wildlife resources. Membership: 3,000,000. Organized: 1871.

President: JOE FOSS

Executive Vice-President: J. WARREN CASSIDY

1st Vice-President: RICHARD RILEY

2nd Vice-President: WAYNE ROSS

Secretary: WARREN L. CHEEK

Treasurer: WILLIAM B. BINSWANGER

Executive Director, General Operations: GARY L. ANDERSON

Executive Director, Institute for Legislative Action: WAYNE R. LAPIERRE, JR.

Hunter Services Division: JAMES M. NORINE, Director;

Publications: *American Rifleman; American Hunter*

Executive Director of Publications: GEORGE MARTIN

268

NATIONAL SCIENCE TEACHERS ASSOCIATION, 1742 Connecticut Ave., NW, Washington, DC 20009 (202, 328-5800)

A nonprofit educational organization for all who are interested in improving the teaching of science, pre-school through college. NSTA is an affiliate of the American Association for the Advancement of Science.

President: LaMOINE L. MOTZ (313, 858-1992)

President-Elect: HANS O. ANDERSEN (812, 335-8658)

Executive Director: BILL G. ALDRIDGE

Publications: *Science and Children; The Science Teacher; Journal of College Science Teaching; Energy & Education Newsletter; NSTA Report; Science Scope*

Editors: PHYLLIS MARCUCCIO; DR. JULIANA TEXLEY; DR. LESTER PALDY; JANE PONTON; STEVEN RAKOW

269

NATIONAL SHOOTING SPORTS FOUNDATION, INC., 555 Danbury Rd., Wilton, CT 06897 (203, 762-1320)

Nonprofit, educational, trade-supported association intended to create in the public mind a better understanding of and a more active participation in the shooting sports and in practical conservation. Founded: 1960.

Executive Director: ROBERT T. DELFAY

Director, Marketing: DOUGLAS PAINTER

270

NATIONAL SPELEOLOGICAL SOCIETY, INC., Cave Ave., Huntsville, AL 35810

A nonprofit membership organization dedicated to the exploration, study, and conservation of America's caves and caverns, related features and the ecology of caves. Membership: 8,000. Organized: 1941.

President: JOHN SCHELTENS, 303 North River St., Hot Springs, SD 57747

Conservation Chairpersons: JANET THORNE, 473 Crescent Blvd., Coraopolis, PA 15108, United States; JEANNE GURNEE, International

Publications: *NSS News;* Bulletin

271

NATIONAL TRAILS COUNCIL, Box 493, Brookings, SD 57006

A nonprofit organization formed in 1971 to promote and support the planning, development and maintenance of trails systems on public and private land. It is composed of all types of trail clubs, agencies, individuals, and landowners interested in trails. Informs public about trail issues at federal, state, and local level and giving information about trails.

President: PAUL E. NORDSTROM, Box 493, Brookings, SD 57006

Vice-President: ROBERT RASOR, P.O. Box 141, Westerville, OH 43081

Secretary: VIVIAN (Vie) OBERN, 4140 Marina Dr., Santa Barbara, CA 93110

Treasurer: JOE PAYNE, JR., Rt. 2, Box 36, Whitetown, IN 46075

Publication: *Trail Tracks*

Editor: Vacant

272

NATIONAL TRAPPERS ASSOCIATION, INC., 216 N. Center St., P.O. Box 3667, Bloomington, IL 61702 (309, 829-2422)

A national trappers organization dedicated to promoting sound conservation legislation; to conserving the nation's natural resources; to assisting in implementing environmental educational programs and to promoting a continued annual furbearer harvest as a necessary wildlife management tool. Founded: 1959.

President: SCOTT HARTMAN, R.R. 1, Box 43, New Martinsville, WV 26155

Vice-President: WILLIS KENT, P.O. Box 645, Lewistown, MT 59457

Executive Director: KEN SEYLER

Conservation Director: MARVIN D. MILLER, 29201 Rainbow Hill Rd., Golden, CO 80401

Secretary: CHRIS GROCE

Membership Secretary: KAREN LAVALLIER

Advertising Manager: TOM KRAUSE, P.O. Box 513, Riverton, WY 82501

General Organizer: JOE CALLAHAN, R.R. 1, Onaga, KS 66521

Publication: *Voice of the Trapper*

Editor: TOM KRAUSE

273

NATIONAL TRUST FOR HISTORIC PRESERVATION, 1785 Massachusetts Ave., NW, Washington, DC 20036 (202, 673-4000)

Private, nonprofit membership organization chartered by Congress in 1949 to encourage the public to participate in the preservation of America's historic and cultural heritage. Through advocacy, education, technical assistance, financial aid and demonstration programs, helps nonprofit groups, public agencies and individuals to preserve the built environment. Membership: over 200,000 individuals and 3,000 organizations.

Chairman, Board of Trustees: ROBERT M. BASS

President: J. JACKSON WALTER

Public Affairs: RUTH LYN THOMPSON (673-4141)

Mid-Atlantic Regional Office: LINDA ELLSWORTH, Director, 6401 Germantown Ave., Philadelphia, PA 19144 (215, 438-2886)

Northeast Regional Office: VICKIE SANDSTEAD, Director, Old City Hall, 45 School St., 2nd Floor, Boston, MA 02108 (617, 523-0885)

Mountains/Plains Regional Office: CLARK STRICKLAND, Director, 511 16th St., Suite 700, Denver, CO 80202 (303, 623-1504)

Southern Regional Office: SUSAN KIDD, Director (Acting), 456 King St., Charleston, SC 29403 (803, 722-8552)

Midwest Regional Office: TIM TURNER, Director, 53 West Jackson Blvd., Suite 1135, Chicago, IL 60604 (312, 939-5547)

Western Regional Office: KATHRYN BURNS, Director, One Sutter St., Suite 700, San Francisco, CA 94104 (415, 956-0610)

Publications: *Preservation News; Historic Preservation Magazine; Preservation Law Reporter; Preservation Forum*

274

NATIONAL WATER RESOURCES ASSOCIATION, 955 L'Enfant Plaza, North, SW, #1202, Washington, DC 20024 (202, 488-0610)

Promotes development, conservation and management of the water resources of 17 western state associations, including cities, counties, conservation districts and individual members.

President: RAYMOND R. RUMMONDS, 81-713 Highway III, Indio, CA 92201

Executive Vice-President: THOMAS F. DONNELLY

Publication: *National Water Line*

275

NATIONAL WATER WELL ASSOCIATION, THE, 6375 Riverside Dr., Dublin, OH 43017 (614, 761-1711)

The NWWA is the nation's leading organization committed to the study of the occurrence, development and protection of ground-water. The association annually sponsors more than 70 educational programs dealing with a wide variety of water issues, including toxic substances, solid waste, and water pollution. Founded: 1948.

President: RICHARD HENKLE, Box 639, Garden City, KS 67846

Secretary: WAYNE WESTBERG, P.O. Box 10-378, Anchorage, AK 99511

Treasurer: WORTH PICKARD, P.O. Box 1085, 110 Maple Ave., Sanford, NC 27330

Executive Director: JAY H. LEHR, 6375 Riverside Dr., Dublin, OH 43017

Affiliated Publications: *Water Well Journal; Groundwater Monitoring Review; Journal of Groundwater*

276

NATIONAL WATERWAYS CONFERENCE, INC., 1130 17th St., NW, Washington, DC 20036 (202, 296-4415) (Annual Meeting 1989: September 20-22, St. Louis, MO)

To promote a better understanding of the public value of water resource and water transportation programs and their importance to the total environment. Membership: 500. Founded: 1960.

Chairman: SHELDON L. MORGAN, Senior Vice-President, First Alabama Bank, P.O. Box 2527, Mobile, Al 36622 (205, 690-1595)

Vice-Chairman: BERDON LAWRENCE, President, Hollywood Marine, Inc., P.O. Box 1343, Houston, TX 77001 (713, 868-1661)

President: HARRY N. COOK

Vice-President: J.D. LAMAN, Manager, Marine Transportation, Dow Chemical USA, P.O. Box 4384, Houston, TX 77210 (713, 978-2031)

Secretary: H. NELSON SPENCER, III, Publisher, The Waterways Journal, 319 North Fourth St., #666, St. Louis, MO 63102 (314, 241-7354)

Treasurer: HOWARD D. MARGRAFF, President, St. Louis Terminals Corporation, No. I North Market St., St. Louis, MO 63102 (314,436-7000)

Publication: Newsletter

Editor: HARRY N. COOK

277

NATIONAL WETLANDS TECHNICAL COUNCIL, 1616 P St., NW, Suite 200, Washington, DC 20036 (202, 328-5150)

An independent council of leading wetlands scientists organized to provide scientific assistance in the nation's wetlands conservation efforts. The council advises federal agencies and other national institutions on wetlands policy and research priority matters through consultation, meetings, and publications. Founded: 1977.

Chairman: DR. JOSEPH S. LARSON

Administrative Assistant: ANNE D. SOUTHWORTH

Council Members: JOHN R. CLARK; ROBERT T. HUFFMAN; ORIE L. LOUCKS; JESSOP LOW; ARIEL E. LUGO; WILLIAM A. NIERING; RICHARD P. NOVITZKI; WILLIAM H. PATRICK, JR.; J. HENRY SATHER; ARNOLD VAN DER VALK; MILTON W. WELLER; JOY B. ZEDLER

Council Advisor: JON A. KUSLER

278

NATIONAL WILD TURKEY FEDERATION, INC., THE, Wild Turkey Bldg., P.O. Box 530, Edgefield, SC 29824-0530 (803, 637-3106)

A nonprofit organization dedicated to the wise conservation and management of the American Wild Turkey. Comprised of over 274 state and local affiliates, and 50,000+ members. Supports annual grants and aid programs. Founded: 1973.

Executive Vice-President: ROB KECK

Director of Research and Management: DR. JAMES EARL KENNAMER

Director of Chapter and Membership Development: CARL BROWN

Director of Marketing: GARY WEST

Treasurer: EARL T. GROVES, 1515 Heatherlock Dr., Gastonia, NC 28052 (704, 864-3201)

Chairman of the Board: RON FRETTS, R.D. #1, Box 235-A, Scottdale, PA 15683 (412, 547-6600)

President: GENE DENTON, Rt. 2,Box 90-D, Perryville, AR 72126 (501, 562-2244)

Secretary: PETER BROMLEY, Ph.D., Rt. 1, Box 253, Elliston, VA 24087 (703, 961-5087)

Board of Directors: SHAUN VIGUERIE, Vice-President, 14 Nassau Dr., Metarie, LA 70005 (504, 588-2811); A. LEWIS YOUNT, 409 Richardson Cir., NW, Hartsville, SC 29550 (803, 383-7650); GLENN HARRELSON, 3112 Champaign St., Charlotte, NC 28210 (704, 597-1100); AL HUESMANN, East Madison St., Caledonia, MO 55921 (507, 724-3333); CLAIBOURNE DARDEN, JR., c/o Darden Research Corporation, 1534 North Decatur Rd., NE, Atlanta, GA 30307 (404, 377-9294); CHARLES DAVIS, Rt. #I, Box 180-A, Whipple, OH 45788 (614, 373-5896); GEORGE CLARK, 1437 Polk, Chillicothe, MO 64601 (816, 646-3663); JERRY ANTLEY, Rt. #2, Box 236, Downsville, LA 71234 (318, 368-9762); CHARLES PETERSON, 104 Elizabeth St., Richlands, NC 28574 (919, 451-2195); WILLIAM D. ZEEDYK, P.O. Box 284, Albuquerque, NM 87103 (505, 766-2981)

Publications: *Turkey Call; Turkitat and Pinfeathers*
Editors: GENE SMITH; MARY KENNAMER

279

NATIONAL WILDFLOWER RESEARCH CENTER, 2600 FM 973
North, Austin, TX 78725 (512, 929-3600)
A nonprofit organization devoted to conservation and preservation
of native plants by promoting their use in public and private
landscape designs. Conducts field research to learn more about
proper cultivation, propagation, and botanical properties of wild-
flowers and native plants. Serves as a national clearinghouse of
information providing sources of native plants, educational materi-
als, and information on appropriate resource organizations and
agencies. Sponsors educational seminars, programs, and tours.
Established: December, 1982.
Founder: MRS. LYNDON B. JOHNSON
Executive Director: DR. DAVID NORTHINGTON
Research Director: DR. JOHN AVERETT
Development Director: MAE DANILLER
Research Botanist: KATY KRAMER-McKINNEY
Horticulturist: ELINOR CRANK
Resource Botanists: ANNIE PAULSON; BETH ANDERSON
Publications: *WILDFLOWER Newsletter; WILDFLOWER: Journal of
the National Wildflower Research Center*

280

NATIONAL WILDLIFE FEDERATION, 1400 Sixteenth St., NW,
Washington, DC 20036-2266 (202, 797-6800); Laurel
Ridge Conservation Education Center, 8925 Leesburg Pike,
Vienna, VA 22180-0001 (703, 790-4000) (Annual
Meeting 1989: March 16-19, Gateway Marriott, Crystal
City, Arlington, VA.)
A nonprofit conservation education organization dedicated to
creating and encouraging an awareness among the people of the
world of the need for wise use and proper management of those
resources of the earth upon which our lives and welfare depend:
soil, air, water, forests, minerals, plant life, and wildlife. Undertakes
a comprehensive conservation education program, distributes
numerous periodicals and educational materials, sponsors outdoor
education programs in conservation and litigates environmental
disputes in an effort to conserve natural resources and wildlife.
Members and supporters: 5,100,000. Organized: 1936.
Chairman of the Board: LEONARD A. GREEN, PA
Vice-Chairmen: ROBERT H. GARDINER, JR., ME (Eastern Region);
GEORGE H. HULSEY, OK (Central Region); PHILLIP W.
SCHNEIDER, OR (Western Region)
Honorary Presidents: THOMAS L. KIMBALL; CLAUDE MOORE

Regional Directors

Region 1 (CT, ME, MA, NH, RI, VT): CARL REIDEL, Hollow Rd.,
North Ferrisburgh, VT 05473 (802, 425-2329)
Region 2 (DE, MD, NJ, NY, PA): RALPH W. ABELE, Box 267,
Millerstown, PA 17062 (717, 589-3929)
Region 3 (NC, SC, VA, WV): JOHN F. LENTZ, P.O. Box 527, Ellerbe,
NC 28338 (919, 652-5061)
Region 4 (AL, FL, GA, MS, PR, VI): DELANO DEEN, Rt. 1, Box 50,
Alma, GA 31510 (912, 383-4356, Ext. 209)
Region 5 (AR, KY, MO, TN): DON F. HAMILTON, 3800 Capitol
Tower Bldg., Little Rock, AR 72201 (501, 375-9151)
Region 6 (IL, IN, OH): EMILY M. KRESS, R.R. I, Box 465, Parker
City, IN 47368 (317, 468-7410)
Region 7 (MI, MN, WI): GORDON G. MEYER, 735 E. Crystal Lake
Rd., Burnsville, MN 55337 (612, 774-6600)
Region 8 (LA, OK, TX): GENE G. STOUT, 3101 Northeast
Kingsbriar Cir., Lawton, OK 73507 (405, 351-3453)

Region 9 (IA, KS, NE, ND, SD): RAYMOND L. LINDER, 625 Elm
Ave., Unit D, Brookings, SD 57006 (605, 692-6748)
Region 10 (AZ, CO, NM, UT): SHELDON M. EPPICH, 2110 E. 6025
South, Ogden, UT 84403 (801, 777-7594)
Region 11 (AK, OR, WA): JAMES E. HEMMING, c/o National
Wildlife Federation Alaska Natural Resources Center, 750 West
Second Ave., Suite 200, Anchorage, AK 99501 (907, 562-
3366)
Region 12 (CA, HI, NV): RUDY J. H. SCHAFER, 2820 Echo Way,
Sacramento, CA 95821 (916, 323-2602)
Region 13 (ID, MT, WY): DAN E. CUNNINGHAM, 714 Sun Valley
Dr., Cheyenne, WY 82001 (307, 777-6564)

Directors-At-Large

VIRGINIA B. BALL; MARY F. BERRY; DEAN L. BUNTROCK; BUR-
NETT C. DAHL; MAURICE K. GODDARD; CHARLES T. HASKELL;
HENRY LYMAN; ELIZABETH W. MEADOWCROFT; CLARENCE A.
SCHOENFELD

Ex-Officio Directors

CARL N. CROUSE; BENJAMIN C. DYSART III

National Office Staff (202, 797-6800; 703, 790-4000)
President and Chief Executive Officer: JAY D. HAIR
General Counsel and Secretary: JOEL T. THOMAS
Senior Vice-President, Administration: ALRIC H. CLAY
Senior Vice-President, Conservation Programs: WILLIAM W. HO-
WARD, JR.
Vice-President, Financial Affairs and Treasurer: FRANCIS A.
DICICCO
Vice-President, Resources Conservation: LYNN A. GREENWALT
Vice-President, Development: JOHN W. JENSEN
Vice-President, Research and Education: S. DOUGLAS MILLER
Vice-President, Promotional Activities: KENNETH S. MODZELEW-
SKI
Vice-President, Affiliate and Regional Programs: LARRY J.
SCHWEIGER
Vice-President, Public Affairs: STEPHANIE C. SKLAR
NWF Natural Resources Centers: THOMAS D. LUSTIG, Counsel,
NWF Rocky Mountain Natural Resources Clinic, Campus Box
401, Fleming Law Bldg., Boulder, CO 80309 (303, 492-
6552); RUDY ROSEN, Director, NWF Southeastern Natural
Resources Center, 1718 Peachtree St., NW, Suite 592, Atlanta,
GA 30309 (404, 876-8733); THOMAS M. FRANCE, Counsel,
NWF Northern Rockies Resources Center, 240 N. Higgins,
Missoula, MT 59801 (406, 721-6705); BRUCE APPLE, Direc-
tor, NWF Pacific Northwest Natural Resources Center, 606
Dekum Bldg., 519 SW 3rd Ave., Portland, OR 97204 (503,
222-1429); MARK VAN PUTTEN, Director, NWF Great Lakes
Natural Resources Center, 802 Monroe, Ann Arbor, MI 48104
(313, 769-3351); ANN ROTHE, Regional Representative, NWF
Alaska Natural Resources Center, 750 West Second Ave., Suite
200, Anchorage, AK 99501 (907, 258-4800); WAYNE BAR-
ON, Director, Prairie Wetlands Resource Center, 1605 E.
Capitol Ave., Bismarck, ND 58501 (701, 222-2442)

Regional Executives

New England (ME, MA, NH, RI, VT): E. WARNER SHEDD, East
Calais, VT 05650 (802, 456-8985)
Eastern Great Lakes (CT, NJ, NY, PA): ANGIE BERCHIELLI, Rt. I,
Box 75, Westerlo, NY 12193 (518, 797-3747)
Mid-Atlantic (DE, MD, VA, WV): JACQUELYN BONOMO, 1400
Sixteenth St., NW, Washington, DC 20036 (202, 797-6693)
Southeast (FL, GA, NC, SC): CHARLES R. SHAW, Box 12081,
Raleigh, NC 27605 (919, 828-6720)

Carribean (PR, VI): EDWARD EASTON, 1400 Sixteenth St., NW, Washington, DC 20036 (202, 797-6823)

Western Great Lakes (IL, IN, KY, OH,): DAVID L. HERBST, Rt. 7, Box 377, Rochester, IN 46975 (219, 223-3251)

Michigan: MARK VAN PUTTEN, 802 Monroe, Ann Arbor, MI 48104 (313, 769-3351)

North Central (MN, ND, SD, WI): WAYNE BARON, 1605 East Capitol Ave., Bismarck, ND 58501 (701, 222-2442)

Central (IA, KS, MO, NE, OK): RUSSELL R. HYER, 2510 Alabama, Lawrence, KS 66604 (913, 843-9198)

South Central (AL, AR, LA, MS, TN, TX): ROBERT E. APPLE, Rt. 1, Box 255, Dardanelle, AR 72834 (501, 576-4213)

Northern Rockies: (ID, MT): CHARLES J. GRIFFITH, 12 Gardner Park Dr., Bozeman, MT 59715 (406, 586-8641)

Central Rocky Mountain (CO, NM, WY): THOMAS J. DOUGHERTY, Campus Box 401, Fleming Law Bldg., Boulder, CO 80309 (303, 492-1256)

Pacific Northwest (AK, OR, WA): BRUCE N. APPLE, 606 Dekum Bldg., 519 SW 3rd Ave., Portland, OR 97204 (503, 222-1429)

Western (AZ, CA, HI, NV): DALE T. GASKILL, P.O. Box 368, Gardnerville, NV 89410 (702, 265-3700)

Regional Representatives

North Central: DAVID NOMSEN, 1605 E. Capitol Ave., Bismarck, ND 58501 (701, 222-2442)

Alaska: ANN ROTHE, 750 West Second Ave., Suite 200, Anchorage, AK 99501 (907, 258-4800)

Publications: *International Wildlife, National Wildlife*, LRCEC (703, 790-4510)

Executive Editor: ROBERT STROHM

Ranger Rick Magazine, LRCEC (703, 790-4277)

Editor: GERALD BISHOP

Executive Editor: ROBERT L. DUNNE

Other Publications: *Your Big Backyard* (Preschool); *NatureScope* (Educator's Activity Guide); Wildlife Conservation Stamps and Albums; *Conservation '89; Conservation Directory; The Leader* (Affiliate Newspaper); conservation education pamphlets; catalog of nature-related materials, the *EYAS* Newsletter, publications catalog available on request.

NOTE: Please see individual state listings for National Wildlife Federation's affiliated organizations, including Puerto Rico and the Virgin Islands. They are identified by the federation's logo.

281

NATIONAL WILDLIFE FEDERATION ENDOWMENT, INC., 1400 Sixteenth St., NW, Washington, DC 20036-2266 (703, 790-4321)

Established to finance conservation education and resource management programs through the National Wildlife Federation. Gifts and bequests are held inviolate; only the income from the sums invested is used.

Chairman: VIRGINIA B. BALL, 1707 Riverside Ave., Muncie, IN 47303

Vice-Chairman: PHILLIP W. SCHNEIDER

Secretary-Treasurer: J.A. BROWNRIDGE

Assistant Secretary: JOEL T. THOMAS

Assistant Treasurer: FRANCIS A. DICICCO

Board of Trustees: ROBERT H. GARDINER, JR.; LEONARD A. GREEN, Ex-Officio; T. HALTER CUNNINGHAM; CHARLES T. HASKELL; WILLIAM F. PILES

282

NATIONAL WILDLIFE REFUGE ASSOCIATION, P.O. Box 124, Winona, MN 55987 (507, 454-5940)

A nonprofit organization dedicated to protecting the integrity of the National Wildlife Refuge System and to increasing public understanding and appreciation of the National Wildlife Refuge System. Membership open to interested persons, organizations, institutions. Organized: 1975.

President: CHARLES A. HUGHLETT, 61500 Lobo Rd., Montrose, CO 81401 (303, 249-8717)

Past President: FORREST A. CARPENTER, 16096 Creekwood Rd., Prior Lake, MN 55372 (612, 447-5586)

Vice-President: DONALD V. GRAY, 67 E. Howard St., Winona, MN 55987 (507, 454-5940)

Secretary: LESTER H. DUNDAS, 4657 Deerwood Dr., Hopkins, MN 55343 (612, 935-7138)

Treasurer: DOROTHY L. GRAY, 67 E. Howard St., Winona, MN 55987 (507, 454-5940)

Regional Representatives

Alaska: CALVIN J. LENSINK, 13541 Jarvi Dr., Anchorage, AK 99515 (907, 345-3096)

Pacific: RICHARD RODGERS, 34793 SE Kelso Rd., Boring, OR 97009 (503, 668-5948)

California, Nevada: ROBERT G. PERSONIUS, 3510 Dalton Common, Fremont, CA 94536 (415, 796-9002)

Southwest: LAWRENCE S. SMITH, 1525 Cedar Ridge, NE, Albuquerque, NM 87112 (505, 293-0454)

North Central: FORREST A. CARPENTER, 16096 Creekwood Rd., Prior Lake, MN 55372 (612, 447-5586)

North Dakota: LYLE J. SCHOONOVER, Rt. I, Box 176, Bismarck, ND 58501 (701, 258-4547)

Southeast: HANS NEUHAUSER, 711 Sandtown Rd., Savannah, GA 31410 (912, 897-6462)

Northeast: RICHARD E. GRIFFITH, Washington Dr., Washington, NH 03280 (603, 495-3174)

Denver Region: CHARLES A. HUGHLETT, 61500 Lobo Rd., Montrose, CO 81401 (303, 249-8717)

Washington D.C.: MARCUS C. NELSON, 4216 Downing St., Annandale, VA 22003 (703, 256-3566)

Publication: *Blue Goose Flyer*

Editor: RUSSEL W. CLAPPER, P.O. Box 1453, Anahuac, TX 77514 (409, 252-3346)

283

NATIONAL WILDLIFE REHABILITATORS ASSOCIATION, 708 Riverside Ave., S., Sartell, MN 56377 (618, 372-3083)

The NWRA is an organization for people concerned about wildlife. Primarily structured for active rehabilitators, the NWRA also attracts state and federal agency personnel, conservationists, educators, naturalists, researchers, veterinarians, zoo and humane society staff, and many others interested in improving their knowledge of wild animals and in assuring the survival of wildlife.

President: ELAINE M. THRUNE

Vice-Presidents: WALTER C. CRAWFORD, JR.; JAMES M. FITZPATRICK; SALLY JOOSTEN

Treasurer: ADELE MOORE

Secretary: DANIEL R. LUDWIG, Ph.D.

284

NATIONAL WOODLAND OWNERS ASSOCIATION, 374 Maple Ave., E., Suite 204, Vienna, VA 22180 (703, 255-2300)

A nonprofit nationwide association of woodland owners united to foster wise management of their non-industrial private forest lands. Working together with cooperating and affiliated state woodland owner/forestry associations, the association is a voice for private landowners on forestry, wildlife, and resource conservation issues. Sponsors the Federation of Woodland Owner Associations with 22 state affiliates. Membership: 27,000. Founded: 1983.

Chairman: BERT W. UDELL, Lebanon, OR (503, 258-6643)

President and CEO: DR. KEITH A. ARGOW, Washington, DC
Publications: *Woodland Report; News from National Woodland Owners Assocation*
Editor: DR. KEITH A. ARGOW,

285

NATURAL AREAS ASSOCIATION, 320 S. Third St., Rockford, IL 61108 (815, 964-6666)
A nonprofit organization of professional and active workers in natural area identification, preservation, protection, management, and research. Aims to provide a medium of exchange and coordination and to advance the public understanding and appreciation of natural areas and other elements of natural diversity. Founded: 1978.
President: GLENN JUDAY, Institute of Northern Forestry, 308 Tanana Dr., Fairbanks, AK 99775-5500 (907, 474-7443)
Vice-President: SARAH GREENE, Forest Science Laboratory, 3200 Jefferson Way, Corvallis, OR 97331 (503, 757-4429)
Secretary-Treasurer: LYDIA S. MACAULEY, 1721 Calle de Cinco, La Jolla, CA 92037 (619, 459-8793)
Publication: *Natural Areas Journal*
Editor: GREG IFFRIG, 3074 E. Avalon Dr., Springfield, MO 65804

286

NATURAL RESOURCES COUNCIL OF AMERICA, 1015 31st St., NW, Washington, DC 20007 (202, 333-8498 or 8595)
An association of major national and regional organizations concerned with the sound management of natural resources in the public interest. Exists for the purpose of providing member organizations with information on actions by Congress and the Executive Branch, by making available to them scientific data on conservation problems, and by facilitating communication and cooperation among member organizations. It is not itself an action organization, nor does it represent or attempt to control the policies and actions of its member organizations. Membership: 51 national and regional conservation and scientific and organizations. Organized: 1946.
Chairman: GILBERT C. RADONSKI, Sport Fishing Institute
Vice-Chairman: PAUL C. PRITCHARD, National Parks and Conservation Association
Secretary: ROBERT L. HERBST, Trout Unlimited
Executive Director: ANDREA J. YANK, 1412 16th St., NW, Washington, DC 20036 (202, 639-8596
NOTE: Members, all of which are listed separately, include: Alliance for Environmental Education, Inc.; American Committee for International Conservation; American Farmland Trust; American Fisheries Society; American Forestry Association; American Land Resource Association; American Society of Landscape Architects; Appalachian Mountain Club; Appalachian Trail Conference; Association of Interpretive Naturalists; Audubon Naturalist Society (Central Atlantic States); Boone and Crockett Club; Boy Scouts of America High Adventure and Conservation Service; Camp Fire Club of America; Conservation Foundation; World Wildlife Fund-U.S.; J. N. "Ding" Darling Foundation, Inc.; Defenders of Wildlife; Environmental Defense Fund; Federation of Western Outdoor Clubs; Georgia Conservancy; International Association of Fish and Wildlife Agencies; Izaak Walton League of America; Land Trust Exchange; League of Women Voters of the United States; National Association of Conservation Districts; National Association of State Foresters; National Audubon Society; National Fish and Wildlife Foundation; National Institute for Urban Wildlife; National Parks and Conservation Association; National Recreation and Park Association; National Rifle Association of America; Hunter Services Division; National Wildlife Federation; National Wildlife Refuge Association; Natu-

ral Areas Association; Natural Resources Defense Council (includes Public Lands Institute); Nature Conservancy; North American Wildlife Foundation; Population-Environment Balance; Rachel Carson Council, Inc.; Rails to Trails Conservancy; Renewable Natural Resources Foundation; Sierra Club; Society of American Foresters; Society for Range Management; Soil Conservation Society of America; Sport Fishing Institute; Trout Unlimited; Wilderness Society; Wildfowl Foundation; Wildlife Management Institute; Wildlife Society; Zero Population Growth.

287

NATURAL RESOURCES DEFENSE COUNCIL, INC., 122 E. 42nd St., New York, NY 10168 (212, 949-0049); 1350 New York Ave., NW, Washington, DC 20005 (202, 783-7800); 90 New Montgomery, San Francisco, CA 94105 (415, 777-0220)
Nonprofit membership organization dedicated to protecting America's endangered natural resources and to improving the quality of the human environment. Combines interdisciplinary legal and scientific approach in monitoring government agencies, bringing legal action and disseminating citizen information. Areas of concentration: Air and Water Pollution, Global Warming, Nuclear Safety, Land Use, Urban Environment, Toxic Substances Control, Resource Management, Wilderness and Wildlife Protection, International Environment, Alaska, Coastal Zone Management, Energy Conservation, Agriculture, and Forestry. Membership: 85,000. Founded: 1970.
Executive Director: JOHN H. ADAMS (212, 949-0049)
Chairman of the Board: ADRIAN W. DEWIND (212, 949-0049)
Publications: *The Amicus Journal; Natural Resources Defense Council Newsline;* A complete list of NRDC's books and reports is available upon request.
Editors: PETER BORRELLI; CATHERINE DOLD

288

NATURAL SCIENCE FOR YOUTH FOUNDATION, 130 Azalea Dr., Roswell, GA 30075 (404, 594-9367)
Provides counseling to community groups in the planning and development of environmental and natural science centers and museums and native animal parks which are designed particularly to meet the needs and interests of children and young people. Conducts an annual conference as part of its widespread effort to promote professional excellence in environmental and natural science centers and museums.
Chairman of Board: JOHN RIPLEY FORBES
President: DR. ELEANOR K. DAVIS
Executive Director: DICK TOUVELL
Publications Director: OWEN D. WINTERR
Secretary: KATHY S. COOLEY
Treasurer: JOHN L. HAMMAKER
Publications: *Directory of Natural Science Centers; Natural Science Center News; Opportunities Bulletin*

289

NATURE CONSERVANCY, THE, 1815 North Lynn St., Arlington, VA 22209 (703, 841-5300 FAX: 841-1283)
National nonprofit membership organization committed to preserving biological diversity by protecting natural lands, and the life they harbor; cooperates with educational institutions, public and private conservation agencies. Works with states through "natural heritage programs" to identify ecologically significant natural areas. Manages a system of over 1,000 nature sanctuaries nationwide. Organized: 1951. Membership: 436,000
Chairman of the Board: DAVID L. HARRISON
President: FRANK D. BOREN
Director, U.S. Operations: JOHN R. FLICKER

Administration: BRADFORD C. NORTHRUP
Communication: LYNNE C. MURPHY
Controller: THOMAS J. FITZGERALD
Development: MIKE NOLAN
Finance: JOHN W. BOLTON
Heritage Programs: ROBERT M. CHIPLEY
Information Systems: PETER D. WHITFORD
Land Acquisition: DAVID E. MORINE
Legal: MICHAEL DENNIS
Legislative Liaison: NATHANIEL E. WILLIAMS
Membership/Development: MARY-ELLEN KIRKBRIDE
Membership Services: JOSEPHINE JOHNSON
Personnel/Administration: ANITA H. ALLEN
Publications: SUE E. DODGE
Science: ROBERT E. JENKINS
Stewardship: JOHN HUMKE
Trade Lands: RICH FRIEDMAN
Resources: KELVIN TAKETA; RAY M. CULTER

International Program, 1785 Massachusetts Ave., NW,
    Washington, DC 20036 (202, 483-0231)
Director: GEOFFREY S. BARNARD

Regional Offices
Eastern Regional Office: 294 Washington St., Rm. 740, Boston, MA
    02108 (617, 542-1908)
    Vice-President: DENNIS B. WOLKOFF
    CT: LES COREY (203, 344-0716); Lower Hudson, NY: OLIVIA
    MILLARD (914, 666-5365); ME: J. MASON MORFIT (207,
    729-5181); MD/DE: STEVEN T. HAMBLIN (301, 656-8673);
    MA/RI: LAURA JOHNSON (617, 423-2545); NY: MARTIN
    CARAVANO (518, 869-6959); PA: ROBERT T. COOK (215,
    925-1065); NJ: BRUCE RUNNELS (201, 439-3007); VT:
    ROBERT J. KLEIN (802, 229-4425); VA: GEORGE FENWICK
    (804, 295-6106); WV: EDWARD F. MAGUIRE, II (304, 345-
    4350)
Midwest Regional Office: 1313 5th St., SE, Minneapolis, MN
    55414 (612, 379-2207)
    Vice-President: RUSS VAN HERIK
    IL: ALBERT PYOTT (312, 346-8166); IN: DENNY McGRATH
    (317, 923-7547); IA: WILLIAM W. CREWS (515, 244-5044);
    MI: THOMAS M. WOIWODE (517, 332-1741); MN: MARGARET
    KOHRING (612, 379-2134); MO: G. RODNEY MILLER (314,
    968-1105); OH: WILLIAM POSSIEL (614, 486-6789); WI:
    BRENT M. HAGLUND (608, 251-8140)
Southeast Regional Office: P.O. Box 270, Chapel Hill, NC 27514
    (919, 967-5493)
    Vice-President: CHUCK BASSETT
    AR: NANCY DeLAMAR (501, 372-2750); FL: JOHN COOK
    (305, 628-5887); KY: JAMES ALDRICH (606, 291-8585);
    NC: KATHERINE SKINNER (919, 967-7007); LA: NANCY JO
    CRAIG (504, 342-4602); OK: HERB BEATTIE (918, 585-
    1117); SC: LABRUCE ALEXANDER (803, 254-9049); TN:
    JEFFREY SINKS (615, 242-1787); TX: DAVID BRAUN (512,
    224-8774)
Western Regional Office: 785 Market St., 3rd Floor, San Francisco,
    CA 94103 (415, 777-0541)
    Vice-President: LAUREL MAYER
    AZ: DAN CAMPBELL (602, 327-4478); CA: STEVE
    McCORMICK (415, 777-0487); CO: SYDNEY S. MACY (303,
    444-2950); HI: Vacant (808, 537-4508); MT/WY: ROBERT J.
    KIESLING (406, 443-0303); NM: BILL WALDMAN (505, 242-
    2015); OR: RUSSELL S. HOEFLICH (503, 228-9561); WA:
    ELLIOT L. MARKS (206, 728-9696)
Publication: *The Nature Conservancy Magazine*
Editor: SUE E. DODGE

290
**NEW ENGLAND ASSOCIATION OF ENVIRONMENTAL
    BIOLOGISTS (NEAEB),** 25 Nashua Rd., Bedford, NH
    03102 (603, 472-5191)
A professional society of environmental scientists, engineers and
planners from industry and state and federal agencies in the
northeast working to coordinate and enhance environmental pro-
grams in each state. The organization advances technical informa-
tion on environmental research, planning and management and
evaluates the effectiveness of environmental regulations for protec-
tion of water quality. Established: 1976.
Executive Committee:
Industry: DR. TOM ABBOTT
Connecticut: ERNEST PIZZUTO
Maine: MATTHEW SCOTT
Massachusetts: PETER NOLAN; EBEN CHESEBROUGH
New Hampshire: ROBERT ESTABROOK
New York: ROBERT BODE
Rhode Island: ROBERT RICHARDSON
Vermont: DOUGLAS BURNHAM
Information Officer: HOWARD DAVIS, EPA, 60 Westview St.,
    Lexington, MA 02173 (617, 861-6700)

291
NEW ENGLAND FORESTRY FOUNDATION, INC., 85 Newbury
    St., Boston, MA 02116 (617, 437-1441)
The 44-year old NEFF manages over 13,000 acres of forest land in
the region through its Memorial Forest Program. Over 72 Memorial
Forests demonstrate the benefits of self-sustaining conservation,
including support of the local tax base and the provision of an
enhanced environment for wildlife and passive recreationists. Along
with recruiting new woodland donors, the foundation's twenty-three
Consulting Forestry centers combine education on sound forestry
practices with woodlot management techniques for private woodland owners in five states.
Executive Director: HUGH PUTNAM, JR.
Publications: *Foundation Newsletter; New England Forestry Foun-
    dation Service Report; New England Forestry Foundation--A
    History*

292
NEW ENGLAND NATURAL RESOURCES CENTER, 200 Lincoln
    St., Boston, MA 02111 (617, 451-3670)
A nonprofit trust organized to provide a focal point for discussion
and resolution of regional natural resource and environmental
issues. Current projects of the center are The Fund for New
England (a regional natural resources philanthropy) and The New
England Environmental Mediation Center (a dispute resolution
project specializing in negotiated solutions to land use, energy, and
environmental problems). Founded: 1970. 15-member Board of
Trustees.
Chairman: PERRY HAGENSTEIN, Box 44, Wayland, MA 01778
Vice-Chairman: RUSSELL L. BRENNEMAN, Murtha, Cullina, Richter
    & Pinney, 101 Pearl St., Hartford, CT 06102
Clerk: DONALD J. ZINN
Executive Director: PERRY R. HAGENSTEIN
Associate Executive Director, New England Environmental Media-
    tion Center: JAMES ARTHUR (508, 283-1153)

293
NEW ENGLAND WILD FLOWER SOCIETY, INC., "Garden in
    the Woods," Hemenway Rd., Framingham, MA 01701
    (617, 237-4924 or recorded information and events: 877-
    6574)
Nonprofit organization established in 1922 to promote the appre-
ciation, knowledge, and conservation of native plants. Holds field

trips, classes and events for adults, children, naturalists, and professionals. Maintains library of 3,000 volumes and collection of 20,000 colored slides. Is clearinghouse for native plant projects in New England region. Plays activist role in promoting protective legislation for native plants and critical habitats. Owns 438 acres of sanctuaries protecting rare native plants. Garden in the Woods is the largest landscaped botanical collection of native plants in the Northeast, Membership: 3,500. Founded: 1922.
President: GERALDINE PAYNE
Vice-President: EDWARD N. DANE
Secretary: ELLEN BENNETT
Treasurer: JOHN MYERS
Executive Director: DAVID BLANCHARD
Garden Director: DAVID LONGLAND
Education Director: ELLYN M. MEYERS
Propagator: WILLIAM BRUMBACK
Public Relations Director: BARBARA F. PRYOR
Publications: *Wildflower Notes;* Newsletters; Programs and Events; Native Plant Sources; Cultivation; Propagation
Editor: ELLYN M. MEYERS

294

NEW YORK-NEW JERSEY TRAIL CONFERENCE, INC., 232 Madison Ave., New York, NY 10016 (212, 685-9699)
A nonprofit organization which coordinates the efforts of hiking and outdoor groups in New York and New Jersey to build and maintain over 750 miles of foot trails and whose purpose is to protect and conserve open space, wildlife, and places of natural beauty and interest. Membership: 70 organizations, 6,000 individuals. Founded: 1920.
President: H. NEIL ZIMMERMAN
1st Vice-President: JANE LEVENSON
2nd Vice-President: DONALD DERR
Secretary: DANIEL CHAZIN, c/o NY-NJ Trail Conference
Treasurer: HOWARD DASH
Executive Director: MADELINE DENNIS
Directors: ANN G. LOEB; STELLA J. GREEN; GEORGE PERTEN; DIANE JUKOFSKY; GEORGE G. NEFFINGER
Chairman, Map Committee: MATHEW VISCO
Chairman, Membership Committee: ANNE COTTAVOZ
Publications: *Trail Walker; New York Walk Book; Guide to the Appalachian Trail in New York and New Jersey; Day Walker Guide To The Long Path;* Catskill Trails Map Set

295

NEW YORK ZOOLOGICAL SOCIETY, The Zoological Park, Bronx, NY 10460 (212, 220-5100)
A nonprofit membership organization which operates the New York Zoological Park Bronx Zoo , the New York Aquarium, the Osborn Laboratories of Marine Sciences, Wildlife Survival Center and Wildlife Conservation International. Purposes are to promote zoological research; to increase public understanding of zoology and the environment through publications, operation of educational programs, and establishment of zoological parks; to support and promote wildlife conservation. Funds an international program of wildlife conservation, research, development of wildlife management plans and establishment of parks and reserves. This program includes over 60 projects in more than 29 countries. Founded: 1895.
Honorary Chairman, Board of Trustees: LAURANCE S. ROCKEFELLER
President: HOWARD PHIPPS, JR.
General Director: WILLIAM CONWAY
New York Aquarium & Osborn Laboratories Director: GEORGE D. RUGGIERI, S.J.
Conservation Director: GEORGE B. SCHALLER

General Curator, Zoo: JAMES G. DOHERTY
Comptroller: JOHN HOARE
Administrative Services Director: JOHN McKEW
Deputy Director of Operations: DAVID COLE
Curator of Ornithology: DONALD BRUNING
Curator of Herpetology: JOHN BEHLER
Associate Curator of Mammalogy: FRED KOONTZ
Curator of Education: ANNETTE R. BERKOVITS
Deputy Director of Administration: TIMOTHY O'SULLIVAN
Director of Public Affairs: JAMES MEEUWSEN
Wildlife Survival Center Curator: JOHN IADEROSA
Director, City Zoos Project: RICHARD LATTIS
Publications: *Animal Kingdom; Annual Report*
Editor Curator of Publications: EUGENE J. WALTER, JR.

296

NORTH AMERICAN ASSOCIATION FOR ENVIRONMENTAL EDUCATION, P.O. Box 400, Troy, OH 45373 (513, 698-6493) (Annual Meeting: 1988, Orlando, FL)
Established to assist and support the work of individuals and groups engaged in environmental education, research, and service. NAEE promotes the analysis and understanding of environmental issues and questions as the basis for effective education, problem-solving, policy-making, and management. Organized: 1971.
President: ED McCREA
Treasurer: AGUSTO Q. MEDINA
Executive Vice-President: JOAN C. HEIDELBERG
Publications: *The Environmental Communicator; Annual Conference Proceedings; Recent Graduate Works in Environmental Education and Communications Monograph Series*

297

NORTH AMERICAN BENTHOLOGICAL SOCIETY, c/o The Allen Press, Inc., 1041 New Hampshire St., Lawrence, KS 66044
The society is an international scientific organization whose purpose is to promote better understanding of the biotic communities of lake and stream bottoms and their role in aquatic ecosystems. The society provides media for disseminating results of scientific investigations and other information to aquatic biologists and to the scientific community at large. Founded: 1953. Membership: I,500.
President: DR. ARTHUR C. BENKE (205, 348-1799)
Treasurer: DR. VIRGINIA R. TOLBERT (615, 574-7288)
Secretary: DAVID D. HERLONG (919, 362-3285)
Publications: *Journal of the North American Benthological Society; Bulletin of the North American Benthological Society; Current and Selected Bibliography of Benthic Biology*
Editors: DR. ROSEMARY J. MacKAY, Dept. of Zoology, University of Toronto, Ontario, Canada M55 IAI; DR. PENNY FIRTH, Lockheed Life Sciences Programs Office, 600 Maryland Ave., SW, Suite 600, Washington, DC 20024; DR. DONALD W. WEBB, Illinois Natural History Survey, 607 E. Peabody St., Champaign, IL 61820

298

NORTH AMERICAN BLUEBIRD SOCIETY, P.O. Box 6295, Silver Spring, MD 20906 (301, 384-2798)
A nonprofit organization concerned with increasing the populations of the three species of bluebirds on this continent, and to educating the public about the importance of preserving these singular creatures in their native environment. Founded: 1978. Membership: 6,000.
President: MRS. SADIE DORBER, Underwood Dr., R.R. #4, Vestal, NY 13850

Vice-President: THOMAS M. TAIT, 11021 Oakwood St., Silver Spring, MD 20901

Treasurer: DELOS C. DUPREE, 6002 Hunt Club Rd., Elkridge, MD 21227 (301, 796-1080)

Recording Secretary: SUE PENNELL, 13291-C Kalnica Ln., Fairfax, VA 22033 (H: 703, 830-0467)

Corresponding Secretary: JOSEPH G. TAIT, 13011 Ivy Dr., Beltsville, MD 20705

Executive Director: MARY D. JANETATOS, 2 Countryside Ct., Silver Spring, MD 20904

Publication: *Sialia*

Editor: JOANNE K. SOLEM, 10617 Graeloch Rd., Laurel, MD 20810

299

NORTH AMERICAN FALCONERS ASSOCIATION

A nonprofit fraternal organization with the following purposes: improve and encourage competency in the practice of falconry; urge recognition of falconry as a legal field sport; promote scientific study, conservation, and welfare of birds of prey with an appreciation of their value in nature. An associate member organization of the National Wildlife Federation. Founded: 1962.

President: RALPH R. ROGERS, P.O. Box 63, Winifred, MT 59489 (406, 462-5487)

Secretary: LARRY MILLER, 305 Long Ave., North Aurora, IL 60542 (312, 892-4556)

Publications: *Hawk Chalk;* Journal

Editors: WILLISTON SHOR, 318 Montford Ave., Mill Valley, CA 94941; DAN CECCHINI, JR., 7220 Burgess Rd., Colorado Springs, CO 80908 (303, 495-4506)

300

NORTH AMERICAN FAMILY CAMPERS ASSOCIATION, P.O. Box 328, Concord, VT 05824 (802, 695-2563)

International organization of family campers with four-sided program of camper education, campground development, conservation concern, and legislative alertness. Seeks to improve camping conditions, promote good outdoor manners, serve as voice of and foster fellowship among family campers. Membership: 4,000.

President: HAROLD COAKLEY, P.O. Box 328, Concord, VT 05824

Treasurer: DONALD MASON, 67 Manor Rd., Denville, NJ 07834

Publication: *Campfire Chatter*

Editor: PATRICK & MARY O'MALLEY, 223 Pleasant St., Lunenburg, MA 01462

301

NORTH AMERICAN GAMEBIRD ASSOCIATION, INC. P.O. Box 2105, Cayce West, Columbia, SC 29171 (803, 796-8163)

To promote educational work and develop interest in game bird breeding and hunting preserves (nonprofit); to afford a means of cooperation with the federal and state governments in all matters of concern to the industry; and to encourage study of the sciences connected with the live production, preparation for markets, and marketing of game bird eggs and game birds. Membership: 1,937 in July, 1987. Founded: 1932.

President: CHARLES R. PHILLIPS, Mahantongo Game Farms, Box 5, Pillow, PA 17080 (717, 758-8911)

Ist Vice-President: BILL WHALEN, Whistling Wings, Inc., 113 Washington St., Hanover, IL 61041 (815, 591-3512)

Treasurer: MARY S. WALKER

Secretary: WALTER S. WALKER

Information Officer and Editor: JOHN M. MULLIN, Fee-Consultant for hunting resorts, P.O. Box 96, Goose Lake, IA 52750 (319, 242-3046)

Publications: *Wildlife Harvest Magazine; Game Cookbook; Game Bird Propagation Book;* List of Hunting Resort Members.

302

NORTH AMERICAN LAKE MANAGEMENT SOCIETY, 1000 Connecticut Ave., NW, Suite 202, Washington, DC 20036 (202, 833-3382); P.O. Box 217, Merrifield, VA 22116

A nonprofit organization dedicated solely to protecting, restoring and managing lakes and reservoirs and their watersheds. A network of limnologists, lake managers and associations, and concerned citizens, NALMS' purpose is educational. Sponsors annual conferences and regional workshops; publishes bimonthly newletter, a peer-reviewed conference proceedings/journal, and citizen booklets. Organized: 1980.

President: RON RASCHKE, U.S. EPA Southwest Water Lab., Bailey Rd., Athens, GA 30601

Treasurer: HARVEY OLEM, TVA, 248 401 Bldg., Chattanooga, TN 37401

Secretary: JOSEPH H. WLOSINSKI, P.O. Box 631, WES ES-Q, Vicksburg, MS 39180-0631

National Office Staff (202, 833-3382)

Executive Secretary: JUDITH F. TAGGART

Development Coordinator: JUDITH B. MORTON

Publications: *Lake and Reservoir Management; Annual Conference Proceedings /Journal-1988; Lake Line Newsletter*

Editors: JUDITH F. TAGGART; GARTH REDFIELD

303

NORTH AMERICAN LOON FUND, R.R. 4, Box 240C, Meredith, NH 03253 (603, 279-6163)

A nonprofit organization established to sponsor loon conservation, public education and scienific research projects across the U.S. and Canada. Sponsors annual grant program, and organizes annual research conference. Established: 1978.

Chairman: RAWSON L. WOOD

Vice/Chairman: SCOTT SUTCLIFFE

Clerk: GUY A. SWENSON

Treasurer: JANE ARBUCKLE

Executive Director: DAVID S. SEVERANCE

Publications: *Loon Call Newsletter;* Loon's Feather Gift Catalog

304

NORTH AMERICAN NATIVE FISHES ASSOCIATION, 123 W. Mt. Airy Ave., Philadelphia, PA 19119

Membership includes ichthyologists, students, sportsmen, amateur naturalists, and aquarists who seek to promote the study, research, and conservation of North American native fishes. Goals are to promote the restoration and protection of habitat and to distribute information about native fishes. Membership: 450. Organized: 1972.

President: BRUCE GEBHARDT (215, 247-0384)

Vice-President: KONRAD P. SCHMIDT (612, 458-3159)

Treasurer: ROBERT E. SCHMIDT (518, 325-7265)

Publication: *American Currents Magazine*

Editor: BRUCE GEBHARDT

305

NORTH AMERICAN WILDLIFE FOUNDATION, 102 Wilmot Rd., Suite 410, Deerfield, IL 60015 (312, 940-7776)

Operates the Delta Waterfowl and Wetlands Research Station and its research programs concerning the breeding grounds of the continental waterfowl resource, enhancing the understanding of wetlands ecology and improving marsh management, determining the importance of wintering grounds and their management and facilitating the transfer of scientific information to user and managers.

President: P.A.W. GREEN

Executive Committee Chairman: P.A.W. GREEN

Vice-President/ Secretary: CHARLES S. POTTER, JR.

Treasurer: RICHARD T. SCHROEDER

Vice-Presidents: CECIL H. BELL; RICHARD A. N. BONNYCASTLE; EDSON I. GAYLORD; FRANK B. WILLIAMS

306

NORTH AMERICAN WILDLIFE PARK FOUNDATION, INC.,
Battle Ground, IN 47920

A nonprofit organization which operates a Wolf Park; continuous behavior research programs; offers lectures and a teaching program; monitors legislation on predators; provides research opportunities for scientists and students. Membership: 1,000. Founded: 1972.

President and Treasurer: ERICH KLINGHAMMER, Ph.D., Battle Ground, IN 47920

Assistant Treasurer and Assistant Secretary: ALBERT W. ZIMMERMANN, Suite 418, 3320 N. Meridian St., Indianapolis, IN 46204

Vice-President: SUZANNE C. KLINGHAMMER, J.D., Battle Ground, IN 47920

Publication: *Wolf Park News*

Editor: ERICH KLINGHAMMER

307

NORTH AMERICAN WOLF SOCIETY, 6461 Troy Pike,
Versailles, KY 40383 (606, 873-6450)

Nonprofit, tax-exempt, volunteer organization dedicated to the wise stewardship of the wolf and other wild canids found in North America. Reports to members on all facets of subjects affecting North American wild canids including: reintroduction potential, current research, population status/prospects, historical concepts, available literature/art, legislation, national/regional updates, and activities of related organizations. Organized: 1973.

President: ANNE K. RUGGLES, 1409 Bentwood, Austin, TX 78723 (512, 459-5139)

Secretary-Treasurer: CURT BLACK, 1409 Bentwood, Austin, TX 78723 (512, 459-5139)

Publications: *Journal of the North American Wolf Society; LYKOS Newsletter*

Editors: SANDRA GRAY THACKER; ANNE RUGGLES; CURT BLACK

308

NORTHEAST ASSOCIATION OF FISH AND WILDLIFE RESOURCE AGENCIES

Consists of heads of fish and game agencies in 11 northeastern states, Canadian Maritime Provinces, Newfoundland, Ontario, and Quebec. Meets at least yearly to review progress, consider mutual problems, coordinate programs on a regional basis, and promote sound fish and game management programs.

President: KENNETH WICH, Director, Division of Fish and Wildlife, Department of Environmental Conservation, 50 Wolf Rd., Albany, NY 12233 (518, 457-5691)

Vice-President: PETER DUNCAN, III, Executive Director, Pennsylvania Game Commission, P.O. Box 1567, Harrisburg, PA 17105-1567 (717, 787-3633)

Secretary-Treasurer: DR. DONALD NORMANDEAU, Executive Director, Fish and Game Department, 34 Bridge St., Concord, NH 03301 (603, 271-3421)

309

NORTHEAST CONSERVATION LAW ENFORCEMENT CHIEFS' ASSOCIATION (CLECA),

President: ALLAN McGROARY, Director, Division of Law Enforcement, 100 Nashua St., Boston, MA 02114 (617, 727-3190)

1st Vice-President: CAPT. BRUCE A. DAWSON, Assistant Director, Law Enforcement DN, Vermont Fish and Wildlife Department, 103 South Main St., Waterbury, VT 05676 (802, 244-7331)

2nd Vice-President: STEVEN HERB, Chief, Department of Environmental Law Enforcement Protection, Division of Fish, Game and Wildlife, CN 400, Trenton, NJ 08625 (609, 292-9430)

Secretary-Treasurer: J.R. FAGAN, Director of Law Enforcement, Pennsylvania Game Commission, 2001 Elmerton Ave., Harrisburg, PA 17110 (717, 787-5743)

310

NORTHERN PLAINS RESOURCE COUNCIL, 419 Stapleton
Bldg., Billings, MT 59101 (406, 248-1154)

Regional coalition of farmers, ranchers, and other citizens concerned about proposed development of Montana coal deposits, hard rock minerals and preservation of a family farm-based agricultural economy in Montana. Members live primarily in Montana. The council's goal is to help the people of the Northern Plains make their voices heard in decisions affecting the use of their mineral and water resources, land and air. Founded: 1971. Members and Contributors 6,000.

Staff Director: TERESA ERICKSON

311

NORTHWEST ATLANTIC FISHERIES ORGANIZATION (NAFO),
P.O. Box 638, Dartmouth, Nova Scotia, Canada B2Y 3Y9 (902, 469-9105)

For the investigation, protection, and conservation of the fish stocks of the Northwest Atlantic and management of those occurring outside of the 200-mile limit. Contracting Parties: Bulgaria, Canada, Cuba, Denmark for the Faroes and Greenland, European Economic Community, German Democratic Republic, Iceland, Japan, Norway, Poland, Romania, and U.S.S.R. Established by convention: December 31, 1978.

Executive Secretary: JOAQUIM C. ESTEVES CARDOSO

President: F. HARTUNG (GDR)

Constituent Bodies of NAFO, General Council-Chairman: F. HARTUNG (GDR)

Vice-Chairman: K. HOYDAL (Denmark, Faroes)

Scientific Council, Chairman: J. BECKETT (Canada)

Scientific Council, Vice-Chairman: SV. AA. HORSTED (EEC)

Fisheries Commission, Vice-Chairman: K. YONEZAWA (Japan)

Fisheries Commission, Vice-Chairman: J. ZIGMANOWSKI (Poland)

Publications: *Annual Report; Journal of Northwest Atlantic Fishery Science; Statistical Bulletin; Scientific Council Studies; Sampling Yearbook;* List of Fishing Vessels; Index of Meeting Documents; NW Atlantic Catch Statistics

312

OCEANIC SOCIETY, THE, Executive Offices, 1536 16th St.,
NW, Washington, DC 20036 (202, 328-0098)

A national, nonprofit, membership organization working to protect and preserve the marine environment for the people and wildlife who depend on it for life, livelihood and enjoyment. The society analyzes public policy initiatives and practices from an environmental perspective, advocating research, education and conservation initiatives that will ensure the protection and wise use of ocean, coastal, and estuarine resources. Founded: 1969. Membership: 40,000.

President: CLIFTON E. CURTIS

Publication: *Ocean Watch*
Editor: JOHN G. CATENA

Long Island Sound Taskforce
President: KATHRYN CLARKE, Stamford Marine Center, 185 Magee Ave., Stamford, CT 06902 (203, 327-9786)

Los Angeles Chapter
President: LILA PETERSEN, 1415 3rd St., Suite 300A, Santa Monica, CA 90401

San Francisco Bay Chapter
President: JOSEF COOPER, Fort Mason Ctr., Bldg. E, San Francisco, CA 94123 (415, 441-5970)
Executive Director: MARGARET ELLIOT

313
ORGANIZATION OF WILDLIFE PLANNERS, Box 7921, Madison, WI 53707 (307, 777-7461) (Annual meeting: May 22-26, 1989 Duluth, MN).
A nonprofit, tax-exempt organization comprised of professional state and federal fish and wildlife resource planners, natural resources educators, professional conservationists and associated interests dedicated to improving, through education and training, the quality of state level resource management and planning. The focus of the organization is on current experienced professionals consisting of other state resource planners in developing both the necessary tools and skills to conduct effective planned management system. Formed: 1978.
President: HARRY LIBBY, Wisconsin Department of Natural Resources, Box 7921, Madison, WI 53707
President-Elect: WAIT GASSON, Wyoming Game and Fish Department, 5400 Bishop Blvd., Cheyenne, WY 82002
Secretary/Treasurer: DWIGHT GUYNN, Montana Department of Fish, Wildlife, and Parks, 1420 East 6th, Helena, MT 59620
Immediate Past-President: JAMES C. FISHER, Missouri Department of Conservation, Jefferson City, MO 65102
Publication: Newsletter
Editors: PATTY MOE, WALT GASSON, Wyoming Game and Fish Department, Cheyenne, WY 82002

314
OUTBOARD BOATING CLUB OF AMERICA, 2550 M St., NW, Suite 425, Washington, DC 20037 (202, 296-4588)
Activities include promotion of the interests of those who use boats for fishing, water skiing, cruising and other forms of water sports. Membership: 5,000. Organized: 1945.
Executive Director: RON STONE
Public Relations: KEVIN KEARNEY
Publications: *Legislative Ledger;* Assorted Safety Materials
Editor: RON STONE

315
OUTDOOR WRITERS ASSOCIATION OF AMERICA, INC., 2017 Cato Ave., Suite 101, State College, PA 16801 (814, 234-1011) (Annual Conference 1988: May 22-26, Marco Island, FL)
We strive to improve ourselves in the art and media of our craft and to increase our knowledge and understanding in supporting the conservation of our natural resources. To this end we pledge ourselves to maintain the highest ethical standards in the exercise of our craft. Membership: 1,800. Founded: 1927.
Chairman, Board of Directors: THAYNE SMITH, Rt. I, Box 493A, Oakcliff Acres, Wagoner, OK 74467
President: C. BOYD PFEIFFER, 14303 Robcaste Rd., Phoenix, MD 21131

Vice-Presidents: JOEL M. VANCE, 525 Aurora St., Jefferson City, MO 65101; BILL HILTS, SR., 5115 Bear Rd., Pen-Rod Acres, Sanborn, NY 14132; LONNIE WILLIAMSON, 410 Point Mary, Fairhaven, MD 20754
Secretary-Treasurer: DON L. JOHNSON, 35875 Parry Rd., Oconomowoc, WI 53066
Executive Director: SYLVIA G. BASHLINE
Publication: *Outdoors Unlimited*
Editor: CAROL KERSAVAGE

316
PACIFIC FISHERY MANAGEMENT COUNCIL, Metro Center, Suite 420, 2000 SW, Ist Ave., Portland, OR 97201 (503, 221-6352)
Nonprofit organization established by the Magnuson Fishery Conservation and Management Act of 1976. Develops management plans for fisheries off the coasts of Washington, Oregon and California. Thirteen voting and five nonvoting members are appointed by the Secretary of Commerce and include state and federal fishery agency managers and representatives of user groups.
Council Members: DONALD COLLINSWORTH, Juneau, AK; JERRY CONLEY, Boise, ID; ROGER THOMAS, Sausalito, CA; RANDY FISHER, Portland, OR; ROBERT FLETCHER, Chairman, Sacramento, CA; CLYDE E. ROBBINS, Vice-Admiral, USCG, Alameda, CA; GEORGE J. EASLEY, Astoria, OR; GUY THORNBURGH, Portland, OR; ROLLAND SCHMITTEN, Seattle, WA; JERRY THOMAS, Eureka, CA; WILLIAM SHAKE, Portland, OR; RICHARD SCHWARZ, Vice-Chairman, Idaho Falls, ID; FRANK WARRENS, Portland, OR; JIM HARP, Taholah, WA; PHILIP ANDERSON, Westport, WA; BOB FORD, Department of State, Washington, DC; DAVE DANBOM, Moss Landing, CA; JOSEPH BLUM, Olympia, WA
Executive Director: LAWRENCE D. SIX
Administrative Officer: GERALD L. FISHER
Staff Officer-Marine: JAMES W. GLOCK
Staff Officer-Salmon: JOHN COON
Staff Officer-Economist: JAMES L. SEGER

317
PACIFIC SEABIRD GROUP, Box 321, Bolinas, CA 94924 (405, 868-1434)
An international organization to promote the knowledge, study and conservation of Pacific seabirds. Membership: 415. Founded: 1972.
Chairman: DANIEL W. ANDERSON, Dept. of Wildlife and Fisheries, University of California, Davis, CA 95616
Chairman-Elect: LAURA LESCHNER, Washington Dept. of Game, 9209-180th NW, Stanewood, WA 98292
Secretary: SUSAN E. QUINLAN, P.O. Box 82115, Fairbanks, AK 99708
Treasurer: DOUGLAS SIEGAL-CAUSEY, Museum of Natural History, Dyche Hall, University of Kansas, Lawrence, KS 66045
Regional Representatives: ANTHONY DEGANGE; DEE BOERSMA; ROBERT BOEKELHEIDE; STEWART I. FEFER; KEES VERMEER; DANIEL VAROUJEAN; JEFF B. FROKE; ENRIQUETA VELARDE; JEAN H. BEDARD; ERICA H. DUNN; DAVID N. NETTLESHIP
Publication: *Pacific Seabird Group Bulletin*
Editor: JOSEPH G. STRAUCH, 7892 Greenbriar Cir., Boulder, CO 80301

318
PACIFIC WHALE FOUNDATION, P.O. Box 1038, Kihei, Maui, HI 96753
A nonprofit, tax-exempt organization comprised of scientists, conservationists and volunteers dedicated to conducting research,

conservation and education programs involving whales, dolphins, porpoises and other marine mammals. The focus of the foundation's work is primarily concerned with population dynamics and reproductive biology of humpback whales. Foundation conducts research in Hawaii, American Samoa, Tonga, Australia and Alaska. Founded: 1980.

President: GREGORY DEAN KAUFMAN
Vice-President: KRISTI F. KAUFMAN
Secretary: LEE JONES
Treasurer: SHERRY RAILEY
Staff Members: CAROL HART; JERRY MELLINGER; JAMES HOUSH; LESLIE HAGEN; LORRAINE PALELLA
Publications: *Fin and Fluke; Soundings*
Editor: CAROL HART

319

PEREGRINE FUND, INC., THE, 5666 West Flying Hawk Ln., Boise, ID 83709 (208, 362-3716)
A publicly supported, nonprofit organization for the study and preservation of falcons and other birds of prey.
Chairman of Board: DR. TOM J. CADE
President: DR. WILLIAM A. BURNHAM
Vice-President: BRIAN WALTON, Lower Quarry, University of California, Santa Cruz, CA 95064 (408, 429-2466)
Treasurer: CARTER R. MONTGOMERY, 5430 LBJ Freeway, Dallas, TX 75240
Secretary: JOE TERTELING, P.O. Box 4127, Boise, ID 83704
Publications: *The Peregrine Fund Newsletter*
Editors: TOM J. CADE; PHYLLIS R. DAGUE

320

PHEASANTS FOREVER, P.O. Box 75473, St. Paul, MN 55175 (612, 481-7142)
Pheasants Forever is a nonprofit conservation organization formed in response to the continuing decline of ringnecked pheasants. The lifeblood of Pheasants Forever is the county chapter, which retains most of the money raised at annual banquets and uses those funds for local habitat projects. Membership: 46,000. Organized: August 5, 1982.
President: GARY C. MOLITOR
Vice-Presidents: ROBERT C. BRENGMAN; DR. JOHN P. WHITTEN
Secretary: ROBERT P. LARSON
Executive Director: JEFFREY S. FINDEN
Publication: *Pheasants Forever*
Editor: DENNIS M. ANDERSON

321

PLANNED PARENTHOOD FEDERATION OF AMERICA, INC., 810 Seventh Ave., New York, NY 10019 (212, 541-7800)
Federated, voluntary, nonprofit health and advocacy agency joining 183 affiliates, which operate 786 medically supervised clinics providing family planning services and information to 3.6 million Americans, and including an international division serving 3.5 people in the developing world.
Chairperson: ANNE M. SAUNIER
1st Vice-Chairperson: MARY A. GREFE
2nd Vice-Chairperson: ROBERT J. PHILLIPS
Treasurer: MARITZA GOMEZ
Secretary: DARLEE CROCKETT
President: FAYE WATTLETON
Vice-Presidents: DAVID J. ANDREWS; LAWRENCE BROADWELL; NORMA CLEVENGER; WINSTON FORREST, JR.; DOUGLAS GOULD; JANE JOHNSON; EVE PAUL; LOUISE TYRER, M.D.; DANIEL WEINTRAUB

322

POPULATION CRISIS COMMITTEE, Main Office: Suite 550, 1120 19th St., NW, Washington, DC 20036 (202, 659-1833)
Develops worldwide support for international population and family planning programs through public education, policy analysis, and liaison with international leaders and organizations, as well as through direct funding of private family planning projects overseas. Founded: 1965.
Founder: WILLIAM H. DRAPER, JR. (1894-1974)
National Co-Chairmen: ROBIN CHANDLER DUKE; JOSEPH D. TYDINGS; ROBERT B. WALLACE
President: J. JOSEPH SPEIDEL, M.D., M.P.H.
Vice-President: SHARON L. CAMP
Secretary: PHYLLIS T. PIOTROW
Treasurer: LOUIS J. MULKERN
Publications: population briefing sheets; country status reports; legislative and policy updates; *Annual Report* of activities
Director of Publications: PATRICIA G. BARNETT

323

POPULATION-ENVIRONMENT BALANCE, INC, 1325 G St., NW, Suite 1003, Washington, DC 20005 (202, 879-3000)
A national, nonprofit, membership organization. The purpose of Balance is to impress upon the American public and policymakers the significant relationship between population growth and distribution in the United States and our national well-being, and to champion a national commitment to a stable population, a strong economy, sustainable resource use and an ecologically diverse, pleasant and healthful environment for all Americans. Activities include a community growth management strategies information clearinghouse, public policy research and advocacy, case studies of the impact of population growth, media campaigns and publications. Membership: 5,000. Established: 1973. Name changed from The Environmental Fund to Balance in 1986.
Chairman of the Board: DAVID F. DURHAM
Executive Director (Acting): ROBERT J. GRAY
Publications: *Balance Report; Have You Heard; BALANCEdata;* monographs; case studies; action alerts; brochures
Editor: ANNELISE DUNMIRE

324

POPULATION INSTITUTE, THE, 110 Maryland Ave., NE, Washington, DC 20002 (202, 544-3300)
To enlist and motivate key leadership groups to participate in the effort to bring population growth into balance with resources by means consistent with human dignity and freedom; works in communications and with mass membership organizations, educational leaders and policy leaders. Founded: 1969.
Chairperson of the Board: STEPHEN KEESE (202, 544-3300)
Vice-Chairperson: JOHN KAREFA-SMART, M.D.
President: WERNER FORNOS (202, 544-3300)
Secretary: JOYCE CRAMER
Treasurer: JACK BRANDENBURG
Publications: *POPLINE - World Population News Service; Annual Report; Development News*

325

POPULATION REFERENCE BUREAU, INC., 777 14th St., NW, Suite 800, Washington, DC 20005 (202, 639-8040)
A private, nonprofit educational organization which gathers, interprets, and publishes information on the social, economic, and environmental implications of U.S. and international population dynamics. Its divisions include Demographic Research and Public Information, which develops substantive backup for other organiza-

tional activities; a Library Information Service, which responds to public information requests; a Population Education Program, which prepares learning materials for classroom use; a Public Information Program, which produces a variety of publications and provides specialized information services for the lay public. Membership: 6,000. Founded: 1929.

Chairman of the Board: JOSEPH L. FISHER
President: THOMAS W. MERRICK
Secretary: FRANCES GARCIA
Treasurer: BERT T. EDWARDS
Technical Information Specialist in Charge, Library, Information Service: DENISE DODWELL
Director, Education: KIMBERLY CREWS
Director, Demographic and Public Information: CARL HAUB
Director, Policy Studies: WILLIAM O'HARE
Publications: Population Bulletins; *Population Today,* Newsletter; Population Education materials, occasional Population Trends and Public Policy reports; List available on request.

326
PRAIRIE CLUB, THE, Suite 603A, 10 S. Wabash Ave., Chicago, IL 60603 (312, 236-3342)
Organized for the promotion of outdoor recreation in the form of walks, outings, camping and canoeing; the establishment and maintenance of permanent and temporary camps; and the encouragement of the love of nature. Membership: 900. Incorporated: 1911.
President: JESS T. SPURGIN
1st Vice-President: JOHN LONK
2nd Vice-President: CARL VON MEDING
Secretary: GEORGE BURTON
Treasurer: HENRY GRAEF
Chairman, Conservation Committee: HELEN STRZELECKI
Publication: *The Bulletin*
Editor: MARLENE SHALES

327
PRAIRIE GROUSE TECHNICAL COUNCIL, Michigan Department of Natural Resources, Rt. 2, Box 2555, Manistique, MI 49854
Comprises federal, state, and private agency biologists or administrators concerned with the status, research, and management of the prairie-chicken and sharp-tailed grouse in North America. Membership: 150.
Executive Committee: GREGG D. STOLL, Chairman (906, 341-6917); DONALD M. CHRISTISEN, Missouri Dept. of Conservation, 1110 College Ave., Columbia, MO 65201 (314, 442-0001); ROGER WELLS, Quail Unlimited, P.O. Box 26, Americus, KS 66835 (316, 443-5642)
Publications: Newsletter and Proceedings

328
PROFESSIONAL BOWHUNTERS SOCIETY, P.O. Box 5275, Charlotte, NC 28225 (704, 536-6009)
Created in 1963 as an organization of dedicated bowhunters interested in promoting a high level of ethics in the taking of wild game with bow and arrow. To provide training for others in safety, shooting skill and hunting techniques. To practice and promote the wise use of our natural resources and conservation of wildlife. Current membership around 2,500.
President: DOUG BORLAND, P.O. Box 272, Marysville, WA 98270 (206, 485-7461)
Vice-President: FRED RICHTER, 89 Orchard Ln., Wheeling, WV 26003 (304, 242-9737)
Secretary-Treasurer: JACK SMITH
Councilmen: BILL LITAKER, P.O. Box 1205, Mt. Pleasant, NC

28124 (704, 436-2262); VERNON STRUBLE, P.O. Box 1402, Corvallis, OR 97339 (503, 754-8200); TIM REED, P.O. Box 60, Valley Grove, WV 26060 (304, 336-7277)
Publication: *The Professional Bowhunter Magazine*
Editor: JACK SMITH

329
PROJECT LIGHTHAWK, P.O. Box 8163, Santa Fe, NM 87504 (505, 982-9656)
Nonprofit organization which brings the power of flight to conservation. The only flying operation of its kind, Lighthawk has flown thousands of missions from Alaska to Central America. In full-time operation since 1980, Lighthawk not only saves time and money - it often makes the difference between winning and losing a critical resource battle. Lighthawk is a membership organization.
Executive Director: MICHAEL M. STEWARTT
Publication: *Lighthawk Newsletter*

330
PUBLIC ENVIRONMENT CENTER, INC., One Milligan Pl., NY 10011 (212, 691-4877)
A nonprofit tax-exempt organization engaged in research studies and information programs about critical regional planning, city planning, urban design, and environmental policies and issues--in particular, those related to open space preservation, land development, and transportation. The center is a coalition of environmentalists, urban planners, and architects. Founded: 1981.
President: H. ALAN HOGLUND
Directors: JOSEPH A. ARONSON, Townsend Hollow, NY; L. LEE HARRISON, Williamstown, MA; JOAN ROTH, NY; MAREK ZAMDMER, NY

331
PUBLIC INTEREST RESEARCH GROUP, 215 Pennsylvania Ave., SE, Washington, DC 20003 (202, 546-9707)
A public interest group engaged in research, investigation, and administrative action. Established: 1970.
Founder: RALPH NADER

332
PURPLE MARTIN CONSERVATION ASSOCIATION, Institute for Research and Community Services, Edinboro University of Pennsylvania, Edinboro, PA 16444 (814, 732-2610)
An international nonprofit organization dedicated to the conservation of the Purple Martin (Progne subis) species of bird through scientific research, state-of-the-art wildlife management techniques, and public education. The PMCA's scientific staff conducts research on all aspects of martin biology throughout the bird's North, South, and Middle American breeding, wintering, and migratory ranges. The organization functions as a centralized data-gathering and information source on the species, serving both the scientist and the martin enthusiast. Its major mission is educating martin enthusiasts in the proper techniques for managing this human-dependent species. Founded: 1987. Membership: 3,000.
Director: JAMES R. HILL III
Publication: *Purple Martin* Update
Editor: JAMES R. HILL III

333
QUAIL UNLIMITED, INC., P.O. Box 10041, Augusta, GA 30903 (803, 637-5731)
A national, nonprofit conservation organization dedicated to improving quail and upland game bird populations through habitat management and research. Organized to reestablish and manage suitable upland game habitat, both public and private lands across

the country, and to educate the public to the needs for wildlife habitat management. Membership: 34,000. Organized: 1981.

President: M. McNIELL HOLLOWAY, P.O. Box 1590, Thomson, GA (404, 595-5946)

Executive Vice-President: JOSEPH R. EVANS, 3012 Sussex Rd., Augusta, GA 30909 (404, 738-0692)

Secretary-Treasurer: KEITH S. HENRY, 1800 Peachtree St., NW, Atlanta, GA 30367-8301

Publication: *Quail Unlimited* Magazine

Editor: GEORGE CONRAD

334

RACHEL CARSON COUNCIL, INC. (formerly Rachel Carson Trust for the Living Environment, Inc.), 8940 Jones Mill Rd., Chevy Chase, MD 20815 (301, 652-1877)

An international clearinghouse of information on ecology of the environment for both scientists and laymen, in relation to chemical contamination, especially pesticides, through publications, conferences, and response to specific questions. Founded: 1965.

President: DR. SAMUEL S. EPSTEIN, School of Public Health, University of Illinois, P.O. Box 6998, Chicago, IL 60680 (312, 996-2296)

Vice-President: VICTOR MULLER, 6478 Gildar St., Alexandria, VA 22310 (703, 971-9065)

Secretary and Executive Director: SHIRLEY A. BRIGGS, 7605 Honeywell Ln., Bethesda, MD 20814 (301, 652-1877)

Treasurer: DAVID B. McGRATH, 3115 Chain Bridge Rd., NW, Washington, DC 20016

Advisory Committee: DR. F. RAYMOND FOSBERG; DR. JOHN L. GEORGE; DR. WILLIAM LIJINSKY; DR. DAVID B. PEAKALL; ESTHER PETERSON; DR. ROBERT L. RUDD

Board of Directors: DR. NORMAN A. BERG; DR. AARON BLAIR; DR. DAVID CHALLINOR; ANN CORNELL; JAY FELDMAN; DR. PETER S. GOLD; DR. ROBERT E. HARRIS; CHARLES HORWITZ; ELIZABETH DALE JOHNSON; DR. THOMAS E. LOVEJOY III; DR. WILLIAM MEGGS; VICTOR MILLER; DR. FREDERICK W. PLAPP, JR.; DR. DIANA POST; MARJORIE SMIGEL; CLAIRE PIKE SMITH; MARTHA HAYNE TALBOT; DR. MARK TICEHURST; DR. JOSEPH K. WAGONER

Publications: List of current publications on pesticides available on request.

335

RAILS-TO-TRAILS CONSERVANCY, 1400 Sixteenth St., NW, Suite 300, Washington, DC 20036 (202, 797-5400)

A national, nonprofit, membership organization working with local recreation and conservation agencies to preserve our national built rail system for conservation and recreational uses through public education, advocacy, and technical assistance to grass-roots organizations. Membership: 16,000. Founded: 1985.

Board of Directors: EDWARD M. NORTON, JR., Chair; DOUGLAS COSTLE; HENRY DIAMOND; CHARLES H. MONTANGE; JEANETTE FITZWILLIAMS; JAY D. HAIR; DAVID INGEMIE; DAVID DAWSON; JOHN SEIBERLING; RALPH BENSON; JOEL HORN

President: DAVID G. BURWELL

Director of Programs: PETER HARNIK

Director, Administration and Development: PEGGY ROBINSON

Publication: *TRAILBLAZER*

336

RAINFOREST ACTION NETWORK, 300 Broadway, Suite 28, San Francisco, CA 94133 (415, 398-4404)

RAN works internationally in cooperation with other environmental organizations on major campaigns to protect rainforests using direct actions: letter writing campaigns, boycotts and demonstrations against corporations and lending agencies contributing to rainforest destruction. RAN also produces materials on rainforest issues, a teachers' packet, and a how-to booklet for community organizers. Formed: 1984.

Director: RANDALL HAYES

Treasurer: JAMES HUPP

Secretary: VIVIENNE VERDON-ROE

Publications: *World Rainforest Report; Action Alert*

337

RAPTOR EDUCATION FOUNDATION, INC., 21901 East Hampden Ave., Aurora, CO 80013 (303, 680-8500)

A nonprofit charitable educational organization utilizing non-releasable raptors in a special series of lecture programs illustrating the importance of raptors (predators) in the balance of nature. Lectures travel nationwide. Also working on creating a National Raptor Collection of all indigenous species in North America. Live non-releasable examples (according to availability) for educational uses and the establishment of a gene pool. Founded: 1980.

President: PETER RESHETNIAK

Vice-Presidents: ROBERT P. KOEHLER ; WILLIAM F. GREVE, JR.

Secretary: JUDITH BARATTA

Publications: *Talon; Talon Supplement; Eagles, Hawks, Falcons, and Owls of America,* a coloring album; *Castings* (volunteer newsletter)

Editors: JUDY BARATTA; PETER RESHETNIAK

338

RAPTOR RESEARCH FOUNDATION, INC.

A nonprofit corporation formed to stimulate and coordinate the dissemination of information on the biology and management of birds of prey and their habitats. Areas of particular interest include raptor banding, behavior, captive breeding, conservation, ecology, research techniques, management, migration, population monitoring, pathology, and rehabilitation. Incorporated: 1966.

President: DR. GARY E. DUKE, Department of Veterinary Biology, University of Minnesota, St. Paul, MN 55108 (612, 624-4702)

Vice-President: DR. RICHARD CLARK, York College of Pennsylvania, Country Club Rd., York, PA 17405 (717, 846-7788, Ext. 405)

Secretary and Membership Information: DR. JIM FRASER, Dept. Fish and Wildlife Science, V.P.I. & S.U., Blacksburg, VA 24061 (703, 961-6064)

Treasurer: JIM FITZPATRICK, Carpenter Nature Center, 12805 St. Croix Tr., Hastings, MN 55033 (612, 437-4359)

Publication: *The Journal of Raptor Research*

Editor: JIMMIE PARRISH, Dept. of Zoology, 161 WIDB, Brigham Young University, Provo, UT 84602 (801, 378-4860)

339

RARE, INC., 19th and the Parkway, Philadelphia, PA 19103 (215, 299-1182)

The conservative education affiliate of World Wildlife Fund—U.S. Works to advance the protection of endangered species and habitat, through environmental education with special emphasis on tropical rain forests and the oceans. Technical and financial aid concentrated on developing countries. Supported by contributions from the general public.

President: KENNETH BERLIN

Vice-Presidents: DAVID O. HILL; ROBERT S. RIDGELY

Secretary: FAITH HALTER

Treasurer: ALAN CRAWFORD, JR.

Executive Director: GEORGE S. GLENN, JR.

Administrator Director: JOHN GUARNACCIA

Board of Trustees: WILLIAM BELTON; KENNETH BERLIN; ELISE BOEGER; DONALD CARR; ALAN CRAWFORD, JR.; JOHN E. EARHART; VICTOR EMANUEL; AMOS ENO; FRANK B. GILL;

FAITH HALTER; DAVID O. HILL; CHARLES A. MINN III; J. PETERSON MYERS; ROGER F. PASQUIER; ROBERT McC PECK; GEORGE V.N. POWELL; ROBERT S. RIDGELY; CHARLOTTE RUSH; JOHN TERBORGH; GUY TUDOR; MARTHA WALSH; DAVID T. WASHBURN; MINTURN T. WRIGHT

340
REMINGTON FARMS, R.D. #2, Box 660, Chestertown, MD 21620 (301, 778-1565)
Operated by Remington Arms Co., Inc., since 1956 to demonstrate through wise land use how wildlife habitat can be improved in a manner compatible with normal farm operation. Operates a wildlife research program, primarily through research fellowships to graduate students.
Manager, Wildlife Management: E. HUGH GALBREATH
Assistant Manager, Wildlife Management: EDWARD C. SOUTIERE

341
RENE DUBOS CENTER FOR HUMAN ENVIRONMENTS, THE
100 East 85th St., NY 10028 (212, 249-7745)
A nonprofit education and research organization founded by Rene Dubos to help the general public and decision makers formulate policies for the resolution of environmental conflicts, and for the creation of new environmental values. Its programs emphasize the creative aspects of human interventions into nature and include: organizing and conducting Dubos Forums; developing educational resources; and maintaining the Dubos library/archives. Founded: 1977.
Executive Director: RUTH A. EBLEN
Board of Trustees: President, WILLIAM R. EBLEN; JOHN CAIRNS, JR.; BENJAMIN C. DYSART III; KERRY MARK JOELS; JAMES F. MATHIS; JEAN S. MEDAWAR; NORTON NELSON; CHARLES A. NORRIS; GLENN PAULSON; JAMES A. PERKINS; GERALD PIEL; PHILIP ROBBINS; JONAS SALK; KEITH E. SIMPSON
Publications: *Thinking Globally, Acting Locally Newsletter;* forum proceedings and reports; books, films, video and audio cassettes and other educational resources.

342
RENEW AMERICA, 1001 Connecticut Ave., NW, Suite 719, Washington, DC 20036 (202, 466-6880)
A nonprofit, tax-exempt organization created to move America toward a sustainable society. It replaces the Solar Lobby and its educational arm, the Center for Renewable Resources. Renew America addresses the need for increased natural resource efficiency, including renewable energy, sustainable agricultual practices, water conservation, and the recycling of refined materials. Renew America will also design a state and local action program and will continue to conduct legislative oversight on Capitol Hill through the Renew America Scorecard.
Executive Director: TINA C. HOBSON
Management Director: TINA C. HOBSON
Publications: *Renewable Energy at the Crossroads; Electricity: New Consumer Choices; Alternative Energy: A Guide to Free Information for Educators; The Hidden Costs of Energy; The Annual State of the States Report*

343
RENEWABLE NATURAL RESOURCES FOUNDATION, 5430 Grosvenor Ln., Bethesda, MD 20814 (301, 493-9101)
A public, nonprofit, operating foundation. Conducts conferences and symposia on renewable natural resource subjects and public policy alternatives. Fosters interdisciplinary cooperation among its member organizations. Developer of the Renewable Natural Resources Center, an office park complex for natural resource and other nonprofit organizations. Member organizations: American Fisheries Society, American Geophysical Union, American Society for Photogrammetry and Remote Sensing, American Society of Landscape Architects, American Water Resources Association, Association for Conservation Information, Association of American Geographers, Ecological Society of America, Resources for the Future, Society for Range Management. The Coastal Society, The Nature Conservancy, and The Wildlife Society. Established: 1972.
Board of Directors: Chairman, CARL R. SULLIVAN, (AFS); Vice-Chairman: CLARE W. HENDEE, (Public Interest Member); Executive Director; ROBERT D. DAY, ROBERT T. AANGEEN-BRUG, (AAG) JOHN C. BILLING, (ASLA); MICHAEL DENNNIS, (TNC); HARDIN R. GLASCOCK, JR., (Public Interest Member); HARRY E. HODGDON, (TWS); RAYMOND M. HOUSLEY, (SRM); DENNIS A. JOHNSON, (ACI); WILLIAM S. OSBURN, JR., (ESA); LAWRENCE R. PETTINGER, (ASPRS); KENNETH D. REID, (AWRA); ROGER A. SEDJO, (RFF); A.F. SPILHAUS, JR., (AGU); VIRGINIA K. TIPPIE, (TCS)
Administrative Assistant: CLAREMARIE SCHOTTHOEFER
Director, Administration and Finance: NANCY HILL
Publication: *Renewable Resources Journal*
Associate Editor: WATSON FENIMORE

344
RESOURCES FOR THE FUTURE, 1616 P St., NW, Washington, DC 20036 (202, 328-5000)
Works to advance research and education in the development, conservation, and use of natural resources including the quality of the environment. Most of its programs are carried on by the resident staff; a few are supported by grants to outside nonprofit institutions. Organized: 1952.
Board of Directors: Chairman, CHARLES E. BISHOP; ANNE P. CARTER; WILLIAM T. CRESON; HENRY L. DIAMOND; JAMES R. ELLIS; LAWRENCE E. FOURAKER; ROBERT W. FRI; JOHN H. GIBBONS; BOHDAN HAWRYLYSHYN; THOMAS J. KLUTZNICK; FREDERIC D. KRUPP; HENRY R. LINDEN; RICHARD W. MANDERBACH; WILLIAM T. McCORMICK, JR.; LAURENCE I. MOSS; WILLIAM D. RUCKELSHAUS; LEOPOLDO SOLIS; CARL H. STOLTENBERG; BARBARA S. UEHLING; ROBERT M. WHITE; MACAULEY WHITING; FRANKLIN H. WILLIAMS
Honorary Directors: HUGH L. KEENLEYSIDE; EDWARD S. MASON; WILLIAM S. PALEY; JOHN W VANDERWILT
President: ROBERT W. FRI (328-5020)
Vice-President: JOHN F. AHEARNE (328-5019)
Secretary-Treasurer: EDWARD F. HAND (328-5029)
Director, Energy and Natural Resources Division: DOUGLAS R. BOTTI (328-5072)
Director, Quality of the Environment Division: RAYMOND J. KOPP (328-5059)
Director, National Center for Food and Agricultural Policy: GEORGE E. ROSSMILLER (328-5124)
Director, Center for Risk Management: PAUL R. PORTNEY (328-5093)
Director, Publications and Communication: JAMES M. BANNER, JR.
Public Affairs: K. STORCK (328-5006)
Publication: *Resources*
Senior Editor: ELAINE KOERNER (328-5113)

345
ROCKY MOUNTAIN ELK FOUNDATION, P.O. Box 8249, Missoula, MT 59802 (406, 721-0010)
Nonprofit, apolitical, wildlife organization dedicated to the conservation and management of elk and elk habitat. The Foundation's primary course of action is to raise funds from private sources to support on-the-ground projects which benefit elk, other wildlife, and their habitats. Projects funded by RMEF include research,

management, habitat improvement, and habitat acquisition. Founded: 1984. Membership: 35,000

President: WALLACE PATE, Georgetown, SC

Vice-President: AARON JONES, Eugene, OR

Secretary: LEO SMITH, Chama, NM

Treasurer: CHARLIE DECKER, Libby, MT

Publications: *BUGLE Magazine; WAPITI Newsletter*

Directors: DAN BOES, Chehalis, WA; RON BOGH, McMinnville, OR; DALE BURK, Stevensville, MT; BOB BUTTON, Flagstaff, AZ; MIKE CUPEL, Glendale, AZ; LYLE DOREY, Rocky Mountain House, AB; RAY GOFF, St. Louis, MO; DR. HUGH HOGLE, Salt Lake City, UT; JIM KILMER, Arlington, WA; JIM RICE, Durango, CO; ARNIE SCHAID, Moscow, ID; DWIGHT SCHUH, Nampa, ID; JIM ZUMBO, Cody, WY

National Staff

Executive Director: ROBERT MUNSON

Administrative Services: VICKI MUNSON

Advertising/Distribution: DWIGHT VAN BRUNT

Field Operations: GARY J. WOLFE, Ph.D.

Marketing: DAN WALKER

North American Habitat Fund: J. KEVIN LACKEY

Publications: LANCE SCHELVAN

Field Staff

GARY BURNETT (AB, ID, MT), 1017 South Willson, Bozeman, MT 59715 (406, 587-2212)

TERRY W. CLOUTIER (Midwest, U.S.), 602 E. Ottawa, Paola, KS 66071 (913, 294-9106)

MARTY HOLMES (CO, NM, WY), 2642 Hatch Cir., Colorado Springs, CO 80918 (719, 599-8798)

GEORGE KAMINSKI (AZ, CA, NV, UT), P.O. Box 378, Chino Valley, AZ 86323 (602, 636-5594)

WAYNE VAN ZWOLL (AK, BC, OR, WA), 109 Highland Dr., Bridgeport, WA 98813 (509, 686-9051)

RON WHITE, 1323 Robert E. Lee Ln., Brentwood, TN 37027 (615, 370-0370)

346

RUFFED GROUSE SOCIETY, THE, 1400 Lee Dr., Coraopolis, PA 15108 (412, 262-4044)

Nonprofit conservation organization dedicated to improving the environment for ruffed grouse, woodcock and other forest wildlife through maintenance, improvement and expansion of their habitat. Assists private industrial, county, state, and federal landholders in forest wildlife habitat improvement programs. Membership: 21,000. Founded: 1961.

President: DAVID V. UIHLEIN, Milwaukee, WI

Executive Vice-President: WILLIAM C. HELSLEY, Oil City, PA

Vice-President: MARK L. RUTLEDGE, Pittsburgh, PA

Executive Director: DR. SAMUEL R. PURSGLOVE, JR.

Secretary: MRS. PETER FLANIGAN, Purchase, NY

Treasurer: ALFRED S. WARREN, JR., Detroit, MI

Directors: T. STANTON ARMOUR, Chicago, IL; JOHN A. MILLINGTON, Greenwich, CT; ROBERT M. JAMES, JR., West Falls, NY; R. R. BARRETT, JR., Grafton, VT; ROY D. CHAPIN, JR., Grosse Pointe Farms, MI; ALBERT H. SCHWARTZ, Pittsburgh, PA; GORDON W. GULLION, Cloquet, MN; TORRENCE M. HUNT, SR., Pittsburgh, PA; D.W. JACOBSON, SR., Grand Rapids, MN; DONALD C. SHEPARD, Neenah, WI; WILLARD F. ROCKWELL, JR., Honorary Director, Pittsburgh, PA; JOE R. IRWIN, Pittsburgh, PA

Honorary Directors: GEORGE L. FORD, Palm Beach, FL; BRUCE R. RICHARDSON, Monterey, VA; HAROLD A. VOGEL, JR., New York, NY; SALLY SEARLE, Lake Forest, IL; LEIGH H. PERKINS,

SR., Manchester, VT; STANLEY R. DAY, Grosse Pointe, MI; ED GRAY, South Hamilton, MA

Regional Representatives

Eastern Mid-Atlantic: WILLIAM H. GOUDY (717, 745-7313)

Eastern Great Lakes: DONALD G. CHILCOTE (517, 631-3993)

Western Great Lakes: LOUIS S. GEORGE; DANIEL R. DESSECKER, Assistant, Habitat (608, 782-6479)

New York and New England: B. WILLIAM HUNYADI (518, 854-9665)

Western Mid-Atlantic States: CHARLES A. SAUER (614, 587-2653)

Director of Information and Education: PAUL E. CARSON

Publication: *The Drummer*

Editor: PAUL E. CARSON

347

SAFARI CLUB INTERNATIONAL, 4800 West Gates Pass Rd., Tucson, AZ 85745 (602, 620-1220)

Nonprofit organization formed to promote good fellowship and communication among sportsmen conservationists. To promote conservation of the wildlife of the world as a valuable, renewable resource in which hunting is one management tool among many. To assist wildlife management and research projects. To further conservation education for the public. To preserve public hunting and to protect the rights of hunters.

Chairman of the Board: C.J. MCELROY

President: VERN EDEWAARD, 75 E. 33rd St., Holland, MI 49423 (616, 396-1525)

Vice-Presidents: BRUCE KELLER, Box 718, 148 Quanset Rd., South Orleans, MA 02662 (508, 240-0870); LEN VINING, 4050 Broadmoor SE, Grand Rapids, MI 49508 (616, 698-9000); DON J. KIRN, 1801 SW Sampson Rd., Lee's Summit, MO 64082 (816, 363-4169); WARREN PARKER, lst Vice-President, 804 N. 7 Highway, Blue Springs, MO 64015 (816, 229-8899); DAVE LAUZEN, 105 West Jackson, Naperville, IL 60566 (312, 357-0202); AUDREY MURTLAND, 11901 Brookfield Ave., Livonia, MI 48151 (313, 427-2270); MARY PARKER, 804 N. 7 Highway, Blue Springs, MO 64015 (816, 229-8899)

Secretary: WAYNE POCIUS, 1340 Zipp Rd., Pennsburg, PA 18073 (215, 538-0450)

Treasurer: PAUL C. BROUN, M.D., Rt. 2, Box 12A, Americus, GA 31709 (912, 924-8318)

Executive Director: HOLT BODINSON

Publications: *Safari Magazine; Worldwide Hunting Annual; Record Book of Trophy Animals; The Sheep Special; The Deer Special; The African Special; North of the 48*

Publications Director: BILL QUIMBY

348

SAFARI CLUB INTERNATIONAL CONSERVATION FUND, 4800 West Gates Pass Rd., Tucson, AZ 85745 (602, 620-1220)

To stimulate conservation education programs, curriculum materials, and teacher training workshops emphasizing the wise use and management of renewable natural resources. Sponsors wildlife management research, field projects, and emergency game animal relief programs. Annually operates the American Wilderness Leadership School.

Chairman of the Board: C.J. MCELROY

President: VERN EDEWAARD, 75 E. 33rd St., Holland, MI 49423 (616, 396-1525)

Vice-Presidents: WARREN PARKER, 804 North 7 Highway, Blue Springs, MO 64015 (816, 229-8899); BRUCE KELLER, Box 718, 148 Quanset Rd., South Orleans, MA 02662 (508, 240-

0870); DON KIRN, 1801 SW Sampson Rd., Lee's Summit, MO 64082 (816, 363-4169); DAVE LAUZEN, 105 West Jackson, Naperville, IL 60566 (312, 357-0202); AUDREY MURTLAND, 11901 Brookfield Ave., Livonia, MI 48151 (313, 427-2270); LEN VINING, 4050 Broadmoor SE, Grand Rapids, MI 49508 (616, 698-9000); MARY PARKER, 804 N. 7 Highway, Blue Springs, MO 64015 (816, 229-8899)

Secretary: WAYNE POCIUS, 1340 Zipp Rd., Pennsburg, PA 18073 (215, 538-0450)

Treasurer: PAUL C. BROUN, M.D., Rt. 2, Box 12A, Americus, GA 31709 (912, 924-8318)

Education Director: DON BROWN

Publications: *Environmental Respect Manual; Outdoor Education Curriculum Units; Profile*

349

SAFE ENERGY COMMUNICATION COUNCIL, 1717 Massachusetts Ave., NW, Washington, DC 20036 (202, 483-8491)

A coalition of national environmental, safe energy, and public interest media groups. SECC produces broadcast and print ads and studies to respond to the nuclear industry and utility campaigns and helps groups develop media skills.

Director: SCOTT DENMAN

Research Associate: ALEX ANTYPAS

President (Acting): ANDREW SCHWARTZMAN

Secretary (Acting): TINA HOBSON

Treasurer: CHRIS BEDFORD

Publications: *ALERT; MYTHBusters* Series, *Viewpoint*

350

SAVE THE DOLPHINS PROJECT, Earth Island Institute, 300 Broadway, Suite 28, San Francisco, CA 94133 (415, 788-3666/1-800, 3-DOLFIN)

Devoted to ending the slaughter of dolphins by the international tuna industry. Activities include: research and dissemination of educational materials, coordination of a national canned tuna boycott, lawsuit to force implementation of the Marine Mammal Protection Act, organization of local activities to end the slaughter through involvement of individuals and organizations in their communities, including letter writing to local representatives and senators, and literature distribution.

Contacts: DAVID PHILLIPS; TODD STEINER; CARRIE STEWART; LINDA BLACKNER

351

SAVE THE DUNES COUNCIL, P.O. Box 114, Beverly Shores, IN 46301 (219, 879-3937)

Dedicated to the establishment and preservation of the Indiana Dunes National Lakeshore for public use and enjoyment. Concerned with protecting the ecological values of the dunes region, preserving Lake Michigan, and combating air, water, and hazardous waste pollution. Membership: 2,000. Established: 1952 by Dorothy Buell.

President: THOMAS SERYNEK, 1001 North Warrick, Gary, IN 46403 (219, 938-5410)

1st Vice-President: GARY HICKS, 702 Washington St., Valparaiso, IN 46383 (462-8129)

2nd Vice-President: RUTH H. OSANN, 92 West Rd., Dune Acres, Chesterton, IN 46304 (219, 879-3937)

Treasurer: DON SQUIRES, 598 Graham Dr., Chesterton, IN 46304 (219, 926-2198)

Executive Director: CHARLOTTE J. READ

Publication: Newsletter

Editors: CHARLOTTE J. READ; ANNE BAYLESS

352

SAVE-THE-REDWOODS LEAGUE, 114 Sansome St., Rm. 605, San Francisco, CA 94104 (415, 362-2352)

Established in 1918 to rescue from destruction representative areas of our primeval forests; to cooperate with the California State Park Commission, the National Park Service, and other agencies in establishing redwood parks and other parks and reservations; to purchase redwood groves by private subscription; to support reforestation and conservation of our forest areas.

President: BRUCE S. HOWARD

Vice-President: R.A.L. MENZIES

Treasurer: WILLIAM P. WENTWORTH, P.O. Box 44614, San Francisco, CA 94144

Secretary and Executive Director: JOHN B. DEWITT

Chairman of the Board: RICHARD M. LEONARD

Assistant Secretary: BRADLEE S. WELTON

353

SCIENTISTS' INSTITUTE FOR PUBLIC INFORMATION, 355 Lexington Ave., New York, NY 10017 (212, 661-9110)

Seeks out, informs, and enlists scientists and other experts of all disciplines in public information programs for the media relevant to a variety of scientific, technological, environmental and educational public policy issues. Organized: 1963.

Chairman: LEWIS THOMAS, M.D., President Emeritus, Memorial Sloan-Kettering Cancer Center

Vice-Chairman: DAVID BALTIMORE, Director, Whitehead Institute for Biomedical Research

Secretary-Treasurer: LAWRENCE J. GOLDSTEIN, Executive Vice-President, Petroleum Industry Research Foundation

President: ALAN McGOWAN

Other Members of Board of Trustees: ALICE ARLEN, Screenwriter; IVAN L. BENNETT, JR., M.D., Professor, School of Medicine, New York University; JERRY GREY, Ph.D., Publisher, Aerospace America; WILLIAM D. CAREY (Retired); JOHN DYSON, Chairman, Wakefield National, Inc.; JERRY W. FRIEDHEIM, President, American Newspaper Publishers Association; JOHN R. PARTEN, President, Farmers Oil Company; CHARLES E. GLOVER, Editor-in-Chief, Cox Enterprises, Inc.; ROBERT E. POLLACK, Ph.D., Dean of Columbia College, Columbia University; WILLIAM T. GOLDEN, President, Board of Governors, New York Academy of Sciences; HENRY A. GRUNWOLD, Ambassador, Austria; WILLIAM R. HEARST III, Publisher, San Francisco Examiner; MARK N. KAPLAN, Esq., Skadden, Arps, Slate, Meagher and Flom; JONATHAN LASH, Commissioner, Department of Water Resources, State Office Bldg., Montpelier, VT; MATHILDE KRIM, Co-Chair, American Foundation for AIDS Research; GEN. EDWARD C. MEYER, USA, (Retired); HOMER A. NEAL, Ph.D., Professor, Department of Physics, University of Michigan; DAVID PERLMAN, Associate Editor, San Francisco Chronicle; THOMAS B. ROSS, Senior Vice-President, News, NBC; WILLIAM D. RUCKELSHAUS, Perkins, Coie, Stone, Olsen, and Williams; FREDERICK SEITZ, President Emeritus, The Rockefeller University; GRANT P. THOMPSON, Senior Associate Conservation Foundation; PAUL C. SHEELINE, Chairman, Vale Energy Corporation; EDWARD E. DAVID, JR., Past-President, Exxon Research and Engineering Company; HOWARD A. SLACK (Retired); EDWARD T. THOMPSON (Retired); RUSSELL E. TRAIN, Chairman of the Board, World Wildlife Fund and The Conservation Foundation; PATRICIA WOOLF, Department of Sociology, Princeton University

Publication: *SIPISCOPE*

354

SEA SHEPHERD CONSERVATION SOCIETY, P.O. Box 7000-S, Redondo Beach, CA 90277 (213, 373-6979)
An international marine conservation action organization, currently involved with field campaigns and education campaigns directed towards the conservation and protection of marine wildlife. Special projects for 1988 are campaigns against illegal whaling, grey seals off Ireland and Scotland and a continued campaign to prevent the re-establishment of the commercial Canadian harp seal hunt. Education campaigns include the creation of the Whaling Walls, life-size whale murals around the world. Also involved with organizing and directing Project WOLF, a coalition to oppose the aerial hunting of wolves in British Columbia and the slaughter of caribou in Quebec. The society owns and operates two conservation ships named "Sea Shepherd". A nonprofit organization. Incorporated: 1977. International Membership: 15,000.
President: SCOTT TRIMINGHAM
Vice-President: CAPT. PAUL WATSON
Field Offices:
USA: SCOTT TRIMINGHAM, (CA), P.O. Box 7000-S, Redondo Beach, CA 90277; PETER WALLERSTEIN, (CA)
Canada: STARLET LUM, (British Columbia), P.O. Box 48446, Vancouver, B.C. Canada V7X 1A2
Ireland and Great Britain: SARAH HAMBLY, P.O. Box 114, Plymouth PL1 1DR UK
Publications: *Sea Shepherd Log; Cry Wolf; Sea Shepherd-My Fight for Whales and Seals*
Editors: PAUL WATSON; ROBERT HUNTER

355

SIERRA CLUB, 730 Polk St., San Francisco, CA 94109 (415, 776-2211)
To explore, enjoy, and protect the wild places of the earth; to practice and promote the responsible use of the earth's ecosystems and resources; to educate and enlist humanity to protect and restore the quality of the natural and human environment; and to use all lawful means to carry out these objectives. With 57 chapters, and 340 groups coast-to-coast, the club's nonprofit program includes work on legislation, litigation, public information, publishing, wilderness outings, and conferences. Membership: 450,000. Founded: 1892 by John Muir.
President: RICHARD CELLARIUS
Vice-President: ROBERT HOWARD
Secretary: RUTH FREAR
Treasurer: DENNY SHAFFER
Fifth Officer: SUSAN MERROW
Other Members, Board of Directors: FREEMAN ALLEN; DAVID BROWER; LAWRENCE DOWNING; RICHARD FIDDLER; VIVIEN LI; MICHELE PERRAULT; SALLY REID; SHIRLEY TAYLOR; SANDY TEPFER; EDGAR WAYBURN
Chairman: J. MICHAEL McCLOSKEY
Executive Director: MICHAEL L. FISCHER
Conservation Director: DOUGLAS W. SCOTT
Deputy Conservation Director: CARL POPE
Director of Conservation Field Services: BRUCE HAMILTON
Assistant Conservation Director: GENE COAN
Public Affairs Director: JOANNE K. HURLEY
Publications: *Sierra; National News Report;* National Issue Committee Newsletters; Chapter and Group Newsletters
Editor-in-Chief: JONATHAN F. KING
Publisher, Books: JON BECKMANN

Washington, DC Office, 408-412 C St., NE, Washington, DC 20002 (202, 547-1144)
Legislative Director: DAVID GARDINER
Washington Representatives: TIMOTHY MAHONEY; BLAKE EARLY; DANIEL WEISS; LARRY WILLIAMS; BROOKS YEAGER; DEBBIE SEASE; JIM BLOMQUIST, NANCY LIGHT, Media Relations Representative

Field Offices

Alaska Representatives: JACK HESSION, EMILY BARNETT, MICHAEL MATZ, 241 E. 5th Ave., #205, Anchorage, AK 99501 (907, 276-4048)
Southern California-Nevada Representatives: BOB HATTOY, JEFF WIDEN, 3550 W. 6th St., #323, Los Angeles, CA 90020 (213, 387-6528)
Midwest Representatives: JANE ELDER, LEANNE KLYZA-LINCK, CARL ZICHELLA, 214 N. Henry St., Suite 203, Madison, WI 53703 (608, 257-4994)
Northeast Representative: CHRIS BALLANTYNE, 360 Broadway, Saratoga Springs, NY 12866 (518, 587-9166)
Northern Plains Representative: LARRY MEHLHAFF, 23 N. Scott, Rm. 25, Sheridan, WY 82801 (307, 672-0425)
Northwest Representatives: BILL ARTHUR, BARBARA BOYLE, 1516 Melrose Ave., Seattle, WA 98122 (206, 621-1696)
Northern California-Nevada Representative: SALLY KABISCH, 5428 College Ave., Oakland, CA 94618 (415, 654-7847)
Southwest Representatives: MAGGIE FOX, 1240 Pine St., Boulder, CO 80302 (303, 449-5595); LAWSON LEGATE, 177 E. 900 South #102, Salt Lake City, UT 84111 (801, 355-0509) ROB SMITH, 3201 N. 16th St., #6-A, Phoenix, AZ 85016 (602, 277-8079)
Southern Plains Representative: BETH JOHNSON, 6220 Gaston, #609, Dallas, TX 75214 (214, 824-5930)
Southeast Representatives: JAMES PRICE, P.O. Box 11248, Knoxville, TN 37939-1248 (615, 588-1892); THERESA WOODY, 50 South Military Trail, Rm. 211-K, West Palm Beach, FL 33415 (407, 471-3449)
Appalachian Representatives: KEN GERSTEN, JOY OAKES, P.O. Box 667, Annapolis, MD 21404-0667 (301, 268-7411)

356

SIERRA CLUB FOUNDATION, THE, 730 Polk St., San Francisco, CA 94109 (415, 776-2211)
A nonprofit, tax-deductible, public foundation established in 1960 to finance the educational, literary, and scientific projects of groups working on national and international environmental problems. Special regional or interest funds may be established by individuals or groups.
President: JOHN HOOPER
Vice-President: ROBERT B. FLINT, JR.
Treasurer: J. FRED WEINTZ, JR.
Secretary: JOSEPH FONTAINE
Fifth Officer: MARK GORDON
Trustees: MIRIAM HAMILTON KEARE; PHILIP BLUMENTHAL; RICHARD CELLARIUS; ANN S. DUFF; MAURICE E. HOLLOWAY; ROBERT B. FLINT, JR.; RONALD P. KLEIN; ROBERT GIRARD; BERT FINGERHUT
Director: STEPHEN M. STEVICK

357

SIERRA CLUB LEGAL DEFENSE FUND, INC., 2044 Fillmore St., San Francisco, CA 94115 (415, 567-6100)
A nonprofit, tax-deductible corporation created to support lawsuits brought on behalf of citizens' organizations to protect the environment. As such, provides lawyers from its own staff to bring

environmental cases. SCLDF also engages in administrative proceedings before federal, state and, occasionally, local agencies.
Executive Director: FREDRIC P. SUTHERLAND
Coordinating Attorney: VAWTER PARKER
Staff Attorneys: JULIE E. McDONALD; STEPHAN C. VOLKER; WILLIAM S. CURTISS; LAURENS H. SILVER; MICHAEL R. SHERWOOD; DEBORAH S. REAMES
Counsel: EARL M. BLAUNER
Rocky Mountain Office:
Staff Attorneys: LORI POTTER; FERN SHEPHERD; DOUGLAS L. HONNOLD, 1600 Broadway St., Suite 1600, Denver, CO 80202 (303, 863-9898)
Seattle Office:
Staff Attorneys: VICTOR SHER; TODD TRUE, 216 1st Ave., Suite 330, Seattle, WA 98104 (206, 343-7340)
Washington, DC, Office:
Staff Attorneys: HOWARD I. FOX; DURWOOD J. ZAELKE, JR.; ROBERT G. DREHER; ERIC P. JORGENSEN
Counsel: RONALD J. WILSON, 1531 P St., NW, Suite 200, Washington, DC 20005 (202, 667-4500)
Southeast Alaska Office:
Staff Attorneys: LAURI J. ADAMS, 325 4th St., Juneau, AK 99801 (907, 586-2751); ARNOLD LUM, Arcade Bldg., 212 Merchant St., Honolulu, HI 96813 (808, 599-2436)
Publications: *Annual Report; In Brief*
Editor: TOM TURNER, SCLDF, 2044 Fillmore St., San Francisco, CA 94115

358

SMALLMOUTH, INC., 260 Crest Rd., Edgefield, SC 29824 (803, 637-5722)
Organized in 1984 to promote research, education, restoration, and conservation of the smallmouth bass fishery in North America. Represents the interest of smallmouth fishermen everywhere.
Membership: 10,000.
President: TOM RODGERS (808, 637-5722)
Chief Consultants: BILLY WESTMORLAND; JERRY McKINNIS; HARRY MURRAY; BILL HUNTLEY; BILL NICHOLS; JIM RIVERS; TONY BEAN; CHARLIE BREWER; BOB PINGEL
Publication: *SMALLMOUTH Magazine*
Managing Editor: JENNIE RODGERS

359

SMITHSONIAN INSTITUTION, 1000 Jefferson Dr., SW, Washington, DC 20560 (202, 357-1300)
A trust instrumentality of the United States, established in 1846 for the "increase and diffusion of knowledge among men." Mission accomplished by: field investigations; the development of the national collections in natural history and anthropology and their preservation for study, reference, and exhibition; scientific research and publications; programs of national and international cooperative research, conservation, education, and training; answering inquiries from the general public and educational and scientific organizations.
Secretary: ROBERT McCORMICK ADAMS
Assistant Secretary for Research: ROBERT HOFFMANN
Director (Acting), Office of Public Affairs: MADELEINE JACOBS (202, 357-2627)

Smithsonian Institution Press, 955 L'Enfant Plaza, Suite 2100, Washington, DC 20560 (202, 287-3728)

Publications: Research in various fields is reported in continuing series of publications by the Smithsonian Institution Press under the following general headings: Smithsonian Contributions to Anthropology; Smithsonian Contributions to Astrophysics; Smithsonian Contributions to Botany; Smithsonian Contributions to the Earth Sciences; Smithsonian Contributions to the Marine Sciences; Smithsonian Contributions to Paleobiology; Smithsonian Contributions to Zoology; Smithsonian Studies in Air and Space; Smithsonian Studies in History and Technology; Smithsonian Studies in Folklife. Information on history, art and science research, presented in less technical style, appears in non-Press publications *Smithsonian Institution Research Reports,* issued three times a year by the Office of Public Affairs (202, 357-2627); *Smithsonian* Magazine (202, 357-2600)
Director, Smithsonian Institution Press: FELIX LOWE

National Museum of Natural History/National Museum of Man, 10th St. and Constitution Ave., NW, Washington, DC 20560 (202, 357-1300)
A center for the study of plants, animals, fossil organisms, terrestrial and extraterrestrial rocks and minerals, and man himself.
Director: FRANK HAMILTON TALBOT

Office of Fellowships and Grants, Smithsonian Institution, L'Enfant Plaza, SW, Rm. 7300, Washington, DC 20560 (202, 287-3271)
Oversees all Smithsonian fellowships and supports a wide range of research activities. It also provides program and administrative assistance for cooperative teaching arrangements between the Institution and local universities in American history, museum studies, and other areas.
Director: ROBERTA RUBINOFF

International Center, Smithsonian Institution, S. Dillon Ripley Center, 1100 Jefferson Dr., SW, Washington, DC 20560 (202, 357-4795)
Supports the research activities of American institutions of higher learning through grants in U.S.-owned local currencies.
Director (Acting): FRANCINE BERKOWITZ

National Zoological Park, 3000 Connecticut Ave., NW, Washington, DC 20008 (Public: 202, 357-2700; Press: 673-4789)
Concentrates research on a better understanding of animal behavior and health, particularly endangered species. Through the operation of the Front Royal Center (VA), the NZP is developing a program of animal propagation which will aid in the survival of threatened and endangered species. Undertakes a number of programs overseas to develop new methodology and increase knowledge of species in the wild.
Director: MICHAEL HILL ROBINSON

Smithsonian Tropical Research Institute, APO Miami 34002-0011 (Balboa 62-3049)
A center for advanced studies in tropical biology. Ecology, behavior and evolution are the primary research interests of the staff. The reserve and laboratories on Barro Colorado Island as well as marine facilities on both coasts are available to visiting scientists and students.
Director: IRA RUBINOFF

Smithsonian Environmental Research Center, P.O. Box 28, Edgewater, MD 21037 (301, 261-4190)
The SERC measures physical, chemical, and biological interactions in the environment and determines how these interactions control

biological responses. This research is carried out in a 2,600-acre facility in Edgewater, MD, where the ecology of land and water interactions is studied for an estuary and its adjacent watersheds.
Director (Acting): DAVID L. CORRELL

Marine Station at Link Port, Rt. 1, Box 194-C, Fort Pierce, FL 33946 (407, 465-6632)
Concentrates on marine studies aimed at understanding the ecological function of inland waterways and their relationship to land use policy.
Scientist-In-Charge: MARY E. RICE

360
SOCIETY FOR ANIMAL PROTECTIVE LEGISLATION, P.O. Box 3719, Georgetown Station, Washington, DC 20007 (202, 337-2334)
Nonprofit organization which keeps its 16,000 correspondents apprised of current developments in legislation for the protection of animals. Has been instrumental in obtaining enactment of 14 federal laws. Founded: 1954.
President: MADELEINE BEMELMANS (201, 782-3520)
Vice-President: JOHN F. KULLBERG (212, 876-7700)
Secretary: CHRISTINE STEVENS (202, 337-2334)
Treasurer: ROGER L. STEVENS (202, 254-3606)
Executive Secretary: JOHN GLEIBER (202, 337-2334)

361
SOCIETY FOR CONSERVATION BIOLOGY, Biology Dept., Montana State University, Bozeman, MT 59717 (406, 994-4548)
A professional society dedicated to providing the scientific information and expertise for the protection of biological diversity. Incorporated as a tax-exempt (509(c)3) scientific organization, the society has an international advisory counsel and a Board composed of scholars, government personnel, and administrators of scientific and conservation organizations. Established: 1985; Membership: 2,000.
President: MICHAEL E. SOULE (313, 763-1312)
Secretary/CFO: PETER F. BRUSSARD (406, 994-4548)
Publication: *Conservation Biology*
Editor: DAVID EHRENFELD, 104 Blake Hall, Cook College, Rutgers University, New Brunswick, NJ 08903

362
SOCIETY FOR MARINE MAMMALOGY, THE,
To promote the educational, scientific, and managerial advancement of marine mammal science; gather and disseminate scientific, technical and management information, through publications and meetings, to members of the society, the public, and public and private institutions; and promote the wise conservation and management of marine mammal resources. Founded: 1981. Membership: 1,000.
President: ROBERT L. BROWNELL, JR., U.S. Fish and Wildlife Service, P.O. Box 70, San Simeon, CA 93452 (805, 927-3893)
President-Elect: CHRISTINA LOCKYER, c/o Southwest Fisheries Center, P.O. Box 271, La Jolla, CA 92083 (619, 546-7090)
Secretary: RANDALL W. DAVIS, Sea World Research Institute, 1700 South Shores Rd., San Diego, CA 92109 (619, 226-3877)
Treasurer: BRUCE R. MATE, Oregon State University, Hatfield Marine Science Center, Newport, OR 97365 (503, 867-3011)
Members-at-Large: PETER J.H. REIJNDERS, Research Institute for Nature Management, Department of Estuarine Ecology, P.O. Box 59, 1790 AB Den Burg, The Netherlands; RANDALL R.

REEVES, 27 Chandler Ln., Box 1096, R.R. I, Hudson, Quebec, Canada J0P 1H0 (514, 458-7383)
Chairman, Membership Committee: JEANETTE A. THOMAS, Naval Ocean Systems Center, P.O. Box 997, Kailua, HI 96734 (808, 257-1654)
Chairman, Conservation and Policy Committee: SHEILA S. ANDERSON, Sea Mammals Research Unit, Madingley Rd., High Cross, Cambridge, UK CB3 0ET
Chairman, Conference Committee: BERND WURSIG, Moss Landing Marine Laboratories, P.O. Box 450, Moss Landing, CA 95039 (408, 633-3304)
Chairman, Board of Editors: DOUGLAS WARTZOK, Department of Biological Sciences, Purdue University, Fort Wayne, IN 46805-1499 (219, 481-6304)
Publication: *Marine Mammal Science*
Managing Editor: GARY J.D. SMITH, Department of Pathology, Ontario Veterinary College, University of Guelph, Guelph, Ontario N1G 2W1 (519, 823-8800 Ext. 4659)

363
SOCIETY FOR RANGE MANAGEMENT, 1839 York St., Denver, CO 80206 (303, 355-7070)
Professional society which promotes understanding of rangeland ecosystems and their management and use for tangible products and intangible values; reports new findings and techniques in range science; promotes public appreciation of rangelands and benefits derived from them; promotes professional development of members. Membership: 5,000. Organized: 1948.
President: THOMAS E. BEDELL, Oregon State University, Corvallis, OR 97331
Past President: WILLIAM A. LAYCOCK, Department of Range Management, Box 3354, Laramie, WY 82071
1st Vice-President: REX CLEARY, 705 Hall St., Susanville, CA 96130
Executive Vice-President and Managing Editor: PETER V. JACKSON III
Representative (Washington, DC): RAY M. HOUSLEY, 6512 Orland St., Falls Church, VA 22043 (703, 536-8139)
Directors: MARILYN J. SAMUEL, High Plains Grassland Res. Sta., 8408 Hildreth Rd., Cheyenne, WY 82009; KENNETH D. SANDERS, 1330 Filer Avenue East, University of Idaho Extension System, Twin Falls, ID 83301; KENDALL JOHNSON, University of Idaho, Moscow, ID; ED NELSON, Box 206, Stavely, Alberta, Canada T0L IZO; TOMMY G. WELCH, 1516 Foxfire, College Station, TX 77840; GARY DONART, Department of Animal and Range Science, New Mexico State University, Las Cruces, NM 88001
Publications: *Journal of Range Management; Rangelands*
Technical Editors: DR. PAT SMITH; GARY FRASIER, 780 W. Cool Dr., Tucson, AZ 85704

364
SOCIETY OF AMERICAN FORESTERS, 5400 Grosvenor Ln., Bethesda, MD 20814 (301, 897-8720)
The national organization representing all segments of the forestry profession and the accreditation authority for professional forestry education in the U.S. Objectives are to advance the science, technology, education, and practice of professional forestry and to use the knowledge and skills of the profession to benefit society. Membership: 21,000. Organized: 1900.
President: CARL H. STOLTENBERG
Vice-President: JAY H. CRAVENS
Past President: J. WALTER MYERS, JR.
Executive Vice-President: WILLIAM H. BANZHAF

Publications: *Journal of Forestry; Forest Science; Southern Journal of Applied Forestry; Northern Journal of Applied Forestry; Western Journal of Applied Forestry*
Editor: BARBARA RICHMAN

Staff Members
Director of Finance and Administration: KENNETH M. BEAM
Director, Resource Policy: E. THOMAS TUCHMANN
Director, Science and Education: CHARLES H. HARDEN
Director, Member Services and Development: GENE W. GREY
Director, Publications: Vacant
Associate Director, Educational and Professional Standards: P. GREGORY SMITH
Director, Public Affairs: PAULA TARNAPOL
Associate Director, Continuing Education and Meetings: Vacant

Council Members
WILLIAM J. BARTON, 304 McLaws St., Savannah, GA 31405; HARRY W. CAMP, 603 Silver Lake Dr., Danville, CA 94526; F. BRYAN CLARK, 4205 Hoborn Ave., Annandale, VA 22003; MAX R. CRAIGHEAD, 1119 West Eskridge Pl., Stillwater, OK 74075; JAMES E. WILKINSON, 125 Tremont St., Barre, VT 05641; FREDERICK W. EBEL, Region Timber Manager, WTD Industries, N 222 Wall St., Suite 302, Spokane, WA 99201; THOMAS W. OSTERMANN, 224 Bradley Dr., Fort Collins, CO 80524; LEONARD A. KILIAN, JR., State Forester, South Carolina Forestry Commission, 5500 Broad River Rd., Box 21707, Columbia, SC 29221; JAMES B. HULL, JR., Associate Director, Texas Forest Service, College Station, TX 77843-2136; GERALD A. ROSE, 7486 Upper 20th St., Oakdale, MN 55119; DONALD R. THEOE, 5932 87th St., E, Puyallup, WA 98371

365
SOCIETY OF TYMPANUCHUS CUPIDO PINNATUS LTD., 930 Elm Grove Rd., Elm Grove, WI 53122 (414, 782-6333)
Nonprofit organization dedicated to the preservation of the Prairie Chicken. Habitat acquired to date: 11,000 acres. Membership: 1,200. Organized: 1961.
President: BERNARD J. WESTFAHL
Vice-Presidents: WILLIAM H. EMORY, Klug and Smith Company, 4425 W. Mitchell, Milwaukee, WI 53214; RICHARD A. STEINMAN, Steinman Lumber Company, P.O. Box 338, Germantown, WI 53022
Secretary: ALLAN D. ROBERTSON, 6055 N. 91st St., Milwaukee, WI 53225
Treasurer: LAWRENCE N. DeLEERS, JR., P.O. Box 572, Newburg, WI 53060
Publication: *Boom*

366
SOIL AND WATER CONSERVATION SOCIETY (formerly Soil Conservation Society of America), 7515 NE Ankeny Rd., Ankeny, IA 50021-9764 (515, 289-2331)
To advance the science and art of good land and water use worldwide. Creates a variety of multidisciplinary forums to identify, analyze, and formulate workable recommendations on land and water management policies and issues. Membership: 12,500. Organized: 1945.
President: DAVID R. CRESSMAN, Ecologistics Ltd., 50 Westmount Rd. North, Suite 225, Waterloo, Ontario, Canada N2L 2R5
Vice-President: RICHARD L. DUESTERHAUS, 2220 Malraux Dr., Vienna, VA 22180
Treasurer: RON HICKS, River Basin Planner, 1068 Parker Dr., Sherwood Park, Alberta, Canada T8A 3Y2
Executive Vice-President: ALAN C. EPPS
Administrative Assistant: LARRY D. DAVIS

Program Assistant: TIMOTHY J. KAUTZA
Publication: *Journal of Soil and Water Conservation*
Editor: MAX SCHNEPF
Managing Editor: JAMES L. SANDERS
Assistant Editor: EILEEN WILLIAMS

Board Members
Northeastern: RAYMOND N. BROWN, JR., 2 Fletcher Ln., Shelburne, VT 05482
Southeastern: R. HUGH CALDWELL, USDA-SCS, Rm. 106, Lexington County Memorial Bldg., Lexington, SC 29072
South Central: ROBERT L. BLEVINS, Agronomy Department, University of Kentucky, Lexington, KY 40546
East North Central: PAUL B. HOSKINS, 124 Parkview Ave., Circleville, OH 43113
West North Central: WILLIAM J. BRUNE, 3923 76th St., Des Moines, IA 50322
Northern Plains: GERALD E. SCHUMAN, USDA-ARS, High Plains Grasslands Research Station, 8408 Hildreth Rd., Cheyenne, WY 82009
Southwestern: DONALD G. BARTOLINA, USDA-SCS, 1000 West Wilshire, Suite 223-A, Oklahoma City, OK 73116
Western: JAN JININGS, 3160 Elder St., Suite A, Boise, ID 83705
Canadian: RONALD J. HICKS, 1068 Parker Dr., Sherwood Park, AB, Canada T8A 3Y2
Student Representative: JEANNE SISSON, c/o Royce Lambert, Advisor, CA Poly/Soil Science, San Luis Obispo, CA 93407

367
SOUNDS CONSERVANCY, INC., THE, P.O. Box 266, 43 Main St., Essex, CT 06426 (203, 767-1933)
A nonprofit organization to conserve, protect, and restore the natural resources of the marine region of southern New England comprising Long Island, Fishers Island, Block Island, Rhode Island, Vineyard and Nantucket Sounds, and the adjacent coastline of Connecticut, New York, Rhode Island and Massachusetts. Founded 1984.
President: CHRISTOPHER PERCY, 41 New Shore Rd., Waterford, CT 06385
Chairman: DR. G.C. MATTHIESSEN, 41 Mill Pond Ln., Old Lyme, CT 06371
Secretary: MRS. I.H. DEITRICK, Lyme St., Old Lyme, CT 06371
Treasurer: CALVIN C. COBURN, 24 Bank Ln., Essex, CT 06426
Chairman, Resource Advisory Committee: DR. G.C. MATTHIESSEN, 41 Mill Pond Ln., Old Lyme, CT 06371
Publication: Special Report
Editor: CHRISTOPHER PERCY

368
SOUTHEASTERN ASSOCIATION OF FISH & WILDLIFE AGENCIES
To protect the best interests of the southeastern states by maintaining their right of jurisdiction over their wildlife resources on public and private lands, by supporting or opposing state and federal wildlife legislation, and by making recommendations on federal programs involving aid. Serves as a clearinghouse for the exchange of ideas concerning wildlife management and research techniques.
President: DON R. McCORMICK, Commissioner, Kentucky Department of Fish and Wildlife Resources, #1 Game Farm Rd., Frankfort, KY 40601 (502, 564-3400)
Vice-President: ROBERT L. MILES, Chief, Wildlife Resources West Virginia Department of Natural Resources, 1800 Washington St., East, Charleston, WV 25305 (304, 348-2771)
Secretary-Treasurer: JAMES A. REMINGTON, Executive Director, Virginia Department of Game and Inland Fisheries, 4010 West

Broad St., Box 11104, Richmond, VA 23230 (804, 367-1000)

Executive Secretary-Treasurer: JOE L. HERRING, 1021 Rodney Dr., Baton Rouge, LA 70808 (504, 766-0519)

369

SOUTHEASTERN COOPERATIVE WILDLIFE AND FISHERIES STATISTICS PROJECT, Institute of Statistics, North Carolina State University, Box 8203, Raleigh, NC 27695-8203. (919, 737-2531)

Objective is to provide statistical and computational expertise to member wildlife agencies in the southeast. This joint state organization was founded in 1959 and is sponsored by the Southeastern Association of Fish and Wildlife Agencies. Participating agencies: AL, AR, FL, GA, LA, MD, NC, SC, TN, VA, plus the Southeastern Cooperative Wildlife Disease Study and the U.S. Virgin Islands.

Director: DAVID W. TURNER

370

SOUTHEASTERN COOPERATIVE WILDLIFE DISEASE STUDY, College of Veterinary Medicine, University of Georgia, Athens, GA 30602 (404, 542-1741)

The first regional diagnostic and research service in the U.S. for the specific purpose of investigating wildlife diseases. This joint-state organization was founded in 1957 and currently is sponsored by the Southeastern Association of Fish and Wildlife Agencies; Veterinary Services of APHIS, USDA; and the Fish and Wildlife Service, of USDI. Participating states: AL, AR, FL, GA, KY, LA, MD, MS, NC, SC, TN, VA, WV.

Director: VICTOR F. NETTLES

371

SOUTHEASTERN FISHES COUNCIL, Department of Biology, Roanoke College, Salem, VA 24153 (703, 375-2463)

Objectives are to provide for the pursuit and transmittal of information on the status and protection of southeastern fishes and their habitats and to promote the perpetuation of rich natural assemblages of fishes and their habitats as well as the localized unique forms and their habitats.

Chairman: DR. ROBERT E. JENKINS

Chairman-Elect: FRANKLIN F. SNELSON, JR., Dept. of Biological Sciences, University of Central Florida, Orlando, FL 32816 (305, 275-2141)

Past Chairman: ROBERT C. CASHNER, Dept. of Biological Sciences, University of New Orleans, New Orleans, LA 70124 (504, 286-6589)

Secretary-Treasurer: WERNER WIELAND, Dept. of Biological Sceinces, Mary Washington University, Fredericksburg, VA 22401 (703, 899-4697)

Publication: *Proceedings of the Southeastern Fishes Council*

Editor: MICHAEL M. STEVENSON, Dept. of Biological Sciences, University of New Orleans, New Orleans, LA 70148 (504, 286-7057)

372

SPORT FISHERY RESEARCH PROGRAM, Suite 100, 1010 Massachusetts Ave., NW, Washington, DC 20001 (202, 898-0771)

To help finance the graduate-level training of promising fishery scientists and to support critically needed ecological research on aquatic ecosystems, water quality requirements of aquatic life, and recreational fisheries resources conservation. Organized: 1962.

President: D.F. MYERS

Secretary: GILBERT C. RADONSKI

Treasurer: PETER HENNING

373

SPORT FISHING INSTITUTE, Suite 100, 1010 Massachusetts Ave., NW, Washington, DC 20001 (202, 898-0770)

Based on the philosophy that "the quality of fishing reflects the quality of living," works through an integrated program of ecological research, fish conservation education, and aquatic sciences advisory service to help insure optimum productivity of marine and freshwater ecosystems, together with abundant high-quality recreational fishing opportunities. Incorporated 1949.

Chairman of the Board: D.F. MYERS, Waukegan, IL

Vice-Chairmen: T. DYER, Eufaula, AL; N.L. OLDRIDGE, Wilmington, DE; DON STURDEVANT, Columbia, SC

President: GILBERT C. RADONSKI

Vice-President: NORVILLE S. PROSSER

Secretary: DR. DAVID B. ROCKLAND

Director of Development: SUSAN M. EVANS

Research Specialist: RICHARD T. CHRISTIAN

Treasurer: DR. PETER HENNING, Plano, IL

Publication: *SFI Bulletin*

Editor: GILBERT C. RADONSKI

374

STATE AND TERRITORIAL AIR POLLUTION PROGRAM ADMINISTRATORS AND THE ASSOCIATION OF LOCAL AIR POLLUTION CONTROL OFFICIALS (STAPPA and ALAPCO), 444 North Capitol St., NW, Suite 306, Washington, DC, 20001 (202, 624-7864)

The national associations of air pollution control agencies in the states, territories, and major metropolitan areas. The associations' members have primary responsibility for ensuring healthy air quality for our citizens and represent the technical expertise behind the implementation of our nation's air pollution control laws and regulations. Associations established: Mid-sixties; Washington office created: 1980. STAPPA membership: 54; ALAPCO membership: 150.

Executive Director: S. WILLIAM BECKER

Publications: *Toxic Air Pollutants: State and Local Regulatory Policies, 1984; Air Permit and Emissions Fees, 1987; Washington Update Newsletter*

375

STEAMBOATERS, THE, P.O. Box 176, Idleyld Park, OR 97447

An associate member organization of the National Wildlife Federation.

President: JOE FERGUSON (503, 747-4917)

Secretary: Vacant

376

STRIPERS UNLIMITED, INC., P.O. Box 3045, South Attleboro, MA 02703 (508, 761-7983)

Nonprofit organization formed to promote, conserve and protect striped bass and to protect and restore its environment. Promotes and encourages research on striped bass in order to preserve it as a natural resource and to increase its areas of reproduction. Members in 21 states and two Canadian provinces. Founded: 1965.

President: JOSEPH A. JUFFRE, II Newport Ave., Pembroke, MA 02359 (294-7853)

Executive Secretary: AVIS E. BOYD, P.O. Box 3166, South Attleboro, MA 02703 (761-4627)

Treasurer: ROBERT B. POND, P.O. Box 3045, South Attleboro, MA 02703 (761-7983)

Executive Director: ROBERT B. POND

Publication: Newsletter

Editor: AVIS E. BOYD

377

STUDENT CONSERVATION ASSOCIATION, INC., National
  Headquarters: Box 550, Charlestown, NH 03603 (603,
  826-5206); Northwest Regional Office: P.O. Box 31989,
  Seattle, WA 98103 (206, 547-7380); Southwest Regional
  Office: P.O. Box 7329, Boulder, CO 80306 (303, 443-
  6803)
This nonprofit membership corporation conducts and operates the
Student Conservation Program in cooperation with the National
Park Service, U.S. Forest Service, The Bureau of Land Management,
U.S. Fish and Wildlife Service, state and local resource agencies.
The program, one of work and conservation education for youth,
enlists the voluntary services of conservation-minded students,
high school, college, and graduate men and women, to work and
learn during their summer vacations. Fall, winter and spring
positions are offered to persons at least 18 years old who have
completed high school. Membership: 3,500. Founded: 1964.
Chairman of the Board: JOHN R. TWISS, JR.
Founding President: ELIZABETH C. TITUS
President: HENRY S. FRANCIS, JR.
Vice-President: SCOTT D. IZZO
Secretary: DAVID C. DAVENPORT, JR.
Treasurer: B. JANE SHERWIN
Director, Field Programs: SCOTT C. WEAVER
Membership: JANET WARREN
Publication: *Job Scan*
Editor: LINDA ROUNDS

378

SUSQUEHANNA RIVER TRI-STATE ASSOCIATION, Rm. 441,
  Stark Learning Center, Wilkes College, Wilkes-Barre, PA
  18702 (717, 824-5193)
Nonprofit association of New York, Pennsylvania and Maryland
citizens, corporate and individual, dedicated to the orderly develop-
ment and management of the water and related resources of the
Susquehanna River Basin. Undertakes programs and activities
devoted to ensuring public awareness and participation in the
planning and management of the economic, environmental and
cultural future of the 27,500 square mile basin. Founded in 1962.
President: R.C. RICHERT G.P.U. Service Corporation, Reading, PA
Executive Director: WILLIAM TOOTHILL
Publications: *SRTSA Newsletter; SRTSA Bulletin; SRTSA Summary
  Report;* and other periodic notices and announcements.

379

TAHOE REGIONAL PLANNING AGENCY, 195 U.S. Highway
  50, P.O. Box 1038, Zephyr Cove, NV 89448-1038 (702,
  588-4547)
To establish and implement land use and environmental plans and
regulations in the Lake Tahoe Region. Established by Public Law
No. 91-148, December 1969, amended by Public Law No. 96-
551, December 1980.
Chairman: CHESTER A. GIBBS
Executive Director: WILLIAM A. MORGAN
Legal Counsel: SUSAN SCHOLLEY

380

TALL GRASS PRAIRIE ALLIANCE, THE, P.O. Box 557,
  Topeka, KS 66601 (913, 357-4681)
The Tallgrass Prairie Alliance, formerly Save The Tallgrass Prairie,
Inc., is dedicated to the preservation of the remaining segments of
the tallgrass prairie ecosystem where its historic character, beauty
and significance can be appreciated by future generations. Only
one percent of this principal biotic community is left with the few
large tracts found in the Flint Hills of Kansas and Osage Hills of
Oklahoma. Projects focus on education, working towards federal,
state and private means of protecting prairie, development of a
prairie inventory, networking with all interested parties along with
future plans for nature centers and purchase of land and easements.
President: DR. ROGER BOYD, P.O. Box 379, Baldwin City, KS
  66006 (H:913, 594-3172/W:594-6459) Baker University
Vice-President: DR. DWIGHT PLATT, Rt #2, Box 209, (H:316,
  283-6708/W:283-2500 ext. 215) Bethel College
National Honorary Chairman: DR. KARL MENNINGER
Publications: *Tallgrass Prairie News;* Membership brochure, bulletins, action alerts, position papers, maps, slide/tape program,
  film. List of other items available on request.

381

THORNE ECOLOGICAL INSTITUTE, 5370 Manhattan Cir.,
  Boulder, CO 80303 (303, 499-3647)
A public, tax-exempt, unendowed, educational institute dedicated
to the application of ecological principles to the stewardship of
natural resources and enhancement of the human environment.
Conducts seminars on ecology bringing together adults from
diverse professions and interests. Offers ecological research
services to business and government agencies on environmental
problems arising from natural resource development. Runs Boulder
Natural Science School for children. Founded: 1954.
President: DR. OAKLEIGH THORNE II
Chairman of the Board: JAMES E. FREEMAN
Executive Director: SUSAN Q. FOSTER
Trustees: JAMES E. FREEMAN, Chairman; WILLIAM E. COBB;
  EDWARD HARVEY, Secretary; MICHAEL HART, Treasurer; DR.
  DENNIS DONALD; ROBERT GOLTON; ROGER HANSEN; CAROL
  HARLOW; DR. SPENSER HAVLICK; KENNETH HUBBARD; LAR-
  RY JOHNSON; DR. GREG McARTHUR; SILVER MILLER; CRAIG
  SUMMERS; REBECCA VORIES; DR. OAKLEIGH THORNE II,
  President; RON WALTERS; DR. BEATRICE WILLARD

382

**THRESHOLD, INC., International Center for Environmental
  Renewal,** Drawer CU, Bisbee, AZ 85603 (602, 432-7353)
An independent, nongovernmental, nonprofit, and international
center serving to improve mankind's understanding of and relationship to the environment at five levels: individual/home, neighbor-
hood, city, bioregion, national and international. Projects involve
environmental research, case studies, planning, education, communication, conferencing and demonstration activities. A major focus
is on the development of ecologically sound alternatives for
practical application in human society. Tropical forests protection,
acid rain reduction, solar energy, international park planning,
wilderness solo retreats (Nature Quests), community sacred parks,
pollution control, bioregional education, and river basin studies are
other major activities. Established: 1972.
Chairman: JOHN P. MILTON (602, 432-5814)
Vice-Chairman: GEORGE A. BINNEY; (602, 398-9163)
Secretary: GEORGE A. BINNEY
Treasurer: KATHRYN DAILY (602, 432-7353)
Administrative Officer, Arizona Office: KATHRYN DAILY (432-
  7353)
Director, San Francisco Office: JOHN DIAMANTE (415, 986-
  0999)
Director, New York Office: JAMES GEORGE (201, 852-9171)
Director, Washington, DC Office: JAMES N. BARNES (202, 232-
  2015)
Board of Trustees: JOHN P. MILTON; GEORGE A. BINNEY; CLAIR
  REINIGER; JAMES GEORGE; DR. RAYMOND F. DASMANN;
  EDWARD GOLDSMITH

383

TRAFFIC (U.S.A.), 1250 24th St., NW, Washington, DC
20037 (202, 293-4800)
Trade Records Analysis of Flora and Fauna in Commerce is a
scientific information-gathering program that monitors the trade in
wild animals and plants and the products made from them. It is a
program of World Wildlife Fund and is a part of an international
network of TRAFFIC offices.
Director: GINETTE HEMLEY
Staff Biologists: JORGEN B. THOMSEN; ANDREA GASKI; LILI
SHEELINE
Administrative Assistant Secretary: EVA ECKENRODE
Publications: *TRAFFIC (U.S.A.) Newsletter;* Special Reports

384

TROUT UNLIMITED, National Headquarters, 501 Church St.,
NE, Vienna, VA 22180 (703, 281-1100)
A nonprofit, tax deductible, international conservation organization
dedicated to the protection of clean water and the enhancement of
trout and salmon fishery resources. Founded: 1959. Membership:
58,000.
Chairman of the Board: C.C. PITTACK, 1721 N. Aurora, East
Wenatchee, WA 98801 (509, 884-5173)
President: STEPHEN LUNDY, 240 St. Paul St., Suite 310, Denver,
CO 80206 (303, 320-4327)
Ist Vice-President: G. RICHARD MODE, 206 Woodlawn Dr., Morgan-
ton, NC 28655 (704, 433-I162)
Secretary: TERRY BOONE, P.O. Box 910, White River Junction, VT
05001 (802, 295-3093)
Treasurer: RICHARD NICOLO, 1225 Charles St., North Providence,
RI 02904 (401, 723-3800)
Executive Director: ROBERT L. HERBST
Administrative Director: BERNARD C. NAGELVOORT
Resource Director: PAMELA K. McCLELLAND
Special Projects Director: SALVATORE L. PALATUCCI
Membership Development and Services Director: WENDY NEW-
MAN
Development Director: MARY ANN KRICKUS
Regional Vice-Presidents:
New England: STEVE MESSIER, 104 Sharon Ave., Pawtucket, RI
02860 (401, 724-0655)
Northeast: HOWARD GUSTAFSON, 41 Vine St., Port Alleghany,
PA 16743 (814, 642-2882)
Southeast: ALEN BAKER, 13400 Hiwassee Rd., Huntersville,
NC 28078 (704, 875-1505)
Midwest: ALLEN PIENKOWSKI, 830 Merton Rd., #102, Detroit,
MI 48203 (313, 341-1915)
Rocky Mountains: DAVE TAYLOR, 3189 Redstone Ln., Boulder,
CO 80303 (303, 837-1908)
West Coast: GENE WINN, 4069 W. Mercer Way, Mercer Island,
WA 98040 (206, 232-0270)
Publication: *TROUT Magazine*
Editor: THOMAS R. PERO, P.O. Box 6225, Bend, OR 97708 (503,
382-2327)

385

TRUMPETER SWAN SOCIETY, THE, 3800 County Rd. 24,
Maple Plain, MN 55359 (612, 476-4663) (Biennial
Meeting: September, 1989, Minneapolis, MN)
International scientific and educational organization to promote
research into ecology and management of the trumpeter swan, to
restore the trumpeter swan in its original range, and to provide a
framework for exchange of knowledge about the species. Membership: 400. Founded: 1968.
President: R.W. McKELVEY, Canadian Wildlife Service, P.O. Box

340, Delta, British Columbia, Canada V3K 3K4 (604, 946-
8546)
Vice-President: LAURENCE N. GILLETTE, Hennepin Parks, 3800
County Road 24, Maple Plain, MN
Executive Secretary-Treasurer: DAVID K. WEAVER, Hennepin
Parks, 3800 County Rd. 24, Maple Plain, MN 55359 (559-
6705)
Directors: HAROLD H. BURGESS, Weslaco, TX; BRUCE CONANT,
Juneau, AK; MARTHA JORDAN, Snohomish, WA; KENNETH K.
KALENAK, Saginaw, MI; DAVE C. LOCKMAN, Smoot, WY;
HARRY G. LUMSDEN, Maple, Ontario; BARRY REISWIG, Lake-
view, MT; BETH SHEEHAN, Grande Prairie, Alberta
Directors-At-Large: DAVID HARTWELL, Long Lake, MN; C.A. HUGH-
LETT, Montrose, CO
Publication: *The Trumpeter Swan Society Newsletter*
Editor: DAVID K. WEAVER

386

TRUST FOR PUBLIC LAND, THE, 82 Second St., San
Francisco, CA 94105 (415, 495-4014)
A private, nonprofit land conservation organization working to
acquire scenic, recreational, urban, rural, and wilderness lands.
Started January, 1973.
President: MARTIN J. ROSEN
Vice-President, Finance & Chief Financial Officer: ROBERT W.
McINTYRE
Northwest Regional Manager: KIM MILLER, 625 Commerce,
#330D, Tacoma, WA 98402 (206, 627-7774)
Executive Vice-President and General Counsel: RALPH W. BENSON
Vice-President, Land Trust Program: JENNIE GERARD
Vice-President, Southeast Regional Manager: CAROLYN RUESCH,
322 Beard St., Tallahassee, FL 32303 (904, 222-9280)
Vice-President, Southwest Regional Manager: PHILLIP WALLIN,
P.O. Box 2383, Santa Fe, NM 87504 (505, 988-5922)
Vice-President, Urban Land Program: PETER R. STEIN, 666
Broadway, New York, NY 10012 (212, 677-7171)
Vice-President, Washington Liaison: HARRIET BURGESS, San Fran-
cisco, CA
Publications: *Annual Report;* Newsletter
Editor: BRYAN HOLLEY

387

UNION OF CONCERNED SCIENTISTS, 26 Church St.,
Cambridge, MA 02238 (617, 547-5552)
A nonprofit organization which conducts policy and technical
research, public education, and legislative advocacy on issues
concerning advanced technologies. A coalition of scientists, engi-
neers and other professionals concerned with health, safety,
environmental and national security problems posed by the coun-
try's nuclear programs. Founded: 1969. Sponsorship: over
100,000.
Executive Director: HOWARD RIS
Counsel: ELLYN WEISS (202, 296-5600)
Legislative Director: CHARLES MONFORT (202, 332-0900)
Nuclear Safety Engineer: ROBERT POLLARD (202, 332-0900)
Senior Arms Analyst: PETER CLAUSEN
Publication: Newsletter: *NUCCEUS*
Editor: STEVEN KRAUSS (617, 547-5552)

388

UNITED NATIONS ENVIRONMENT PROGRAMME, P.O. Box
30552, Nairobi, Kenya; New York North American Office,
United Nations, Rm. DC2-0803, New York, NY 10017
(212, 963-8138); UNEP Washington Office, 1889 F St.,
NW, Washington, DC 20006 (202, 289-8456)
The United Nations Environment Programme (UNEP) was estab-

lished by the UN General Assembly in 1972 to encourage and help coordinate global environmental efforts. Working with other UN agencies, national governments and nongovernmental organizations, UNEP reports regularly on environmental problems and helps develop new approaches to better management of our resources. World Environment Day designated as June 5 each year.

Executive Director: MOSTAFA K. TOLBA
Deputy Executive Director: WILLIAM H. MANSFIELD
Assistant Executive Director for Environment Fund: Vacant
Assistant Executive Director, Bureau of the Programme: GENADY N. GOLUBEV
Director: DR. NOEL J. BROWN, North American Office
Senior Liaison Officer: JOAN MARTIN BROWN, Washington Office
Publication: *UNEP North American News*

389

UNITED STATES CHAMBER OF COMMERCE, 1615 H St., NW, Washington, DC 20062

Created to provide business representation on major national issues. Membership includes 2,700 chambers of commerce, 1,300 trade and professional associations, and 180,000 business firms. Organized: 1912.
President: DR. RICHARD L. LESHER

Resources Policy Department

Program objective: To seek equitable solutions to the problems involving multiple use and development of the nation's energy, agriculture, natural resources and public lands, and to attain fair strategies for achieving the nation's environmental goals.
Department Manager: DR. HARVEY ALTER (202, 463-5533)
Policy Managers: SUSAN MOYA, Energy and Natural Resources Policy, (463-5533); MARY BERNHARD, Environment Policy (463-5533); DR. STUART HARDY, Food & Agriculture Policy (463-5533); WILLIAM KELLEHER, Community Resources (463-5533)

390

UNITED STATES TOURIST COUNCIL, Drawer 1875, Washington, DC 20013-1875

A nonprofit association of conservation concerned individuals, industries and institutions who travel or cater to the traveler. Emphasis is on historic and scenic preservation, wilderness and roadside development, ecology through sound planning and education, and support of scientific studies of natural wilderness.
Chairman, Board of Trustees and Executive Director: STANFORD WEST, Ph.D.
Trustees: ALLEN H. FARNSWORTH, Ph.D.; CHARLES A. KELLEY, Ph.D.; COL. W.H. JOHNSON

391

UPPER MISSISSIPPI RIVER CONSERVATION COMMITTEE, 1830 Second Ave., Rock Island, IL 61201 (309, 793-5800)

Promotes preservation, development, and wise use of the natural and recreational resources of the Upper Mississippi River and formulates policies, plans, and programs for conducting cooperative studies. Members: state conservation departments of Illinois, Iowa, Minnesota, Missouri, and Wisconsin. Organized: 1943.
Chairman: LEE KERNEN, Wisconsin Department of Natural Resources, P.O. Box 7921, Madison, WI 53707 (608, 267-7502)
Secretary-Treasurer: WILLIS FERNHOLZ, Wisconsin Department of Natural Resources, 3550 Mormon College Rd., 108 State Office Bldg., Lacrosse, WI 54601
Coordinator: GAIL A. CARMODY

Publications: *Annual Proceedings;* Newsletter; and miscellaneous technical reports

392

WATER POLLUTION CONTROL FEDERATION, 601 Wythe St., Alexandria, VA 22314-1994 (703, 684-2400)

An international, nonprofit organization devoted to the development and dissemination of technical information concerning the preservation and enhancement of water quality, water resources, and the relationship of those resources to the total environment. The federation has held as an integral part of its mandate the pledge to act as a source of education to the general public as well as to individuals engaged in the field of water pollution control. Founded: 1928. Membership: 34,000.
President: JAMES E. ABBOTT
President-Elect: ARTHUR W. SAARINEN, JR.
Vice-President: CHARLES B. KAISER, JR.
Executive Director: DR. QUINCALEE BROWN
Treasurer: KARL W. MUELDENER
Publications: *Journal Water Pollution Control Federation; Highlights; Operations Forum*
Editor: PETER J. PIECUCH

393

WATER RESOURCES ASSOCIATION OF THE DELAWARE RIVER BASIN, Box 867, Davis Rd., Valley Forge, PA 19481 (215, 783-0634)

Nonprofit federation of businesses, industries, citizens, and citizen organizations which serves to advise of and advocate the need for adequate water supplies through the orderly conservation, development and equitable use and reuse of the water and related land resources of the Delaware River Basin. Organized: 1959.
President: JAMES A. SHISSIAS
Executive Director: BRUCE E. STEWART

394

WELDER WILDLIFE FOUNDATION, P.O. Box 1400, Sinton, TX 78387 (512, 364-2643)

Established by the will of the late Rob Welder, the foundation is dedicated to the cause of conservation through research and education in wildlife ecology and management and closely related fields. Operates through a small staff, and research fellowships to graduate students. Founded: 1954.
Director: JAMES G. TEER
Assistant Director: D. LYNN DRAWE

395

WESTERN ASSOCIATION OF FISH AND WILDLIFE AGENCIES

A regional organization including 18 fish and wildlife agencies of 13 states and three provinces. Meets annually to consider mutual problems and provide a forum for exchange of information at both administrative and technical levels.
President: CURT SMITCH (206, 753-5700)
1st Vice-President: JERRY M. CONLEY (208, 334-5259)
2nd Vice-President: LES COOKE (403, 427-6749)
3rd Vice-President: TEMPLE REYNOLDS (602, 942-3000)
Secretary-Treasurer: SANDRA J. WOLFE, Dept. of Fish & Game, 1416 9th St., Sacramento, CA 95814 (916, 445-9880)

396

WESTERN BIRD BANDING ASSOCIATION, 3975 N. Pontatoc, Tucson, AZ 85718 (602, 299-1287)

Works to advance ornithology by studies that employ the banding of birds. Membership: 470. Organized: 1925.
President: DR. ROBERT C. TWEIT, 4100 N. Romero Rd., SP 108, Tucson, AZ 85705

1st Vice-President: DR. STEPHEN M. RUSSELL, Dept. Ecology and Evolution Biology, University of Arizona, Tucson, AZ 85721

2nd Vice-President: ROBERT E. GILL, JR., 3014 Knik Ave., Anchorage, AK 99503

Secretary: DR. MARTHA H. BALPH, Dept. of Wildlife Science, UMC 52, Utah State University, Logan, UT 84322

Treasurer: SHIRLEY SPITLER, 3975 N. Pontatoc, Tucson, AZ 85718

Publication: *North American Bird Bander* (co-publ. with Eastern and Inland Bird Banding Associations)

Editor: DR. WILLIAM B. QUAY, 2003 Ida St., Napa, CA 94558

397

WESTERN FORESTRY AND CONSERVATION ASSOCIATION, 4033 SW Canyon Rd., Portland, OR 97221 (503, 226-4562)

Promotes the practice of forestry and the development of forest conservation on all forest land in the western U.S. and western Canada, provides a medium for exchanging and disseminating forestry and conservation information, and fosters cooperation between federal, state, provincial, and private forest agencies. Organized: 1909.

Past-President: MORRIS BERGMAN, Albany, OR (503, 926-7771)

President: STAN HUMANN, Eatonville, WA (206, 832-6534)

Vice-Presidents: JIM BENTLEY, Milltown, MT (406, 258-5511); WILLIAM ATKINSON, Corvallis, OR (503, 754-4952); GILBERT MURRAY, Chester, CA; MILT KOPPANG, Orofino, ID (208, 476-5612); JOHN CUTHBERT, Victoria, British Columbia (604, 387-3912)

Secretary: BRUCE DEVITT, Vancouver, British Columbia (406, 728-1710)

Treasurer: DAVE COX, Portland, OR

Executive Director: RICHARD ZABEL

398

WESTERN INTERPRETERS ASSOCIATION, P.O. Box 28366, Sacramento, CA 95828

A nonprofit professional organization dedicated to promoting the welfare of historical, recreational, archeological, anthropological, and natural history interpretation. Assists in the development of the profession and the professionals that provide interpretive services. Organized: 1967.

President: JIM COVEL, 2934 Grinnel Dr., Davis, CA 95616 (916, 421-7275)

Vice-President: ROBERT FLASHER, 1406 Josephine St., Berkeley, CA 94703 (526-6626)

Secretary: KAREN HARDESTY, 1842 South Pierson Ct., Lakewood, CO 80226 (303, 659-1160)

Executive Manager: DOUG BRYCE, P.O. Box 28366, Sacramento, CA 95828 (916, 381-4620)

Treasurer: LINDA YEMOTO, Tilden Nature Area, Berkeley, CA 94708 (415, 525-2233/339-3425)

Publications: *The Interpreter; WIA Newsletter*

Editors: GREG STARYPAN, 4921 North 11th St., Tacoma, WA 98406 (206, 832-6116); ALLAN D. CAPELLE, 1276 East Wincrest, Winona, MN 55987 (507, 454-1971)

399

WESTERN REGIONAL ENVIRONMENTAL EDUCATION COUNCIL, c/o DON MacCARTER, New Mexico Game and Fish, State Capitol Bldg., Santa Fe, NM 87503 (505, 827-7911)

Membership includes department of education and resource management personnel from 13 western states. Works to advance state and regional level formal and nonformal environmental education programs in cooperation with public and private agencies. Conducts materials development and in-service training activities, and provides consultant services to various organizations developing environmental education materials and programs. Produced Project WILD and Project Learning Tree, interdisciplinary, supplemental environmental education programs for use in grades K-12.

President: DON MacCARTER

Past-President: JOHN GAHL, Idaho Department of Fish and Game (208, 334-3747)

President-Elect: PEGGY COWAN, Alaska Department of Education (907, 465-2841)

Executive Director: RUDY SCHAFER, California Department of Education (916, 323-2602)

Fiscal Manager: CLIFF HAMILTON (503, 229-5423)

400

WETLANDS FOR WILDLIFE, INC., P.O. Box 344, West Bend, WI 53095

Advocates and participates in promotion, preservation and acquisition of wetlands and wildlife habitat in the U.S. which will be transferred to federal, state or county agencies exclusively for public purposes and to be so maintained and managed. Organized: 1960.

President: LAMBERT NEUBURG, 164 Freiss Lake Rd., Hubertus, WI 53033 (414, 628-1060)

President Emeritus, Inland Wetlands: EUGENE MAUCH, 333 N. German St., Mayville, WI 53050

Vice-President: THOMAS McNULTY, 817 Mill St., Delafield, WI 53018

Secretary-Treasurer: FRANK LORD, 242 N. 7th Ave., West Bend, WI 53095 (334-0327)

Trustees: RALPH JONES, 4964 Brown St., Oconomowoc, WI 53066; JEROME BRUCHERT, R. 1 Box 252, Theresa, WI 53091; JOE WALTER, 4174 Arthur Rd., Slinger, WI 53086; CHUCK O'MEARA, 622 Elm St., West Bend, WI 53095; GREG THATCHER, 3843 E. Ramsey Ave., Cudahy, WI 53110; STEVE PAULOSKI, 113 Luther Ave., Oconomowoc, WI 53066; DICK BERGHOEFFER, 715 S. 111th St., West Allis, WI 53214

Financial Advisor: KEVIN GRIFFIN, 237 N. Main St., West Bend, WI 53095 (414, 338-6136)

Publication: *Wetlands for Wildlife News Letter*

Associate Editor: Vacant

401

WHALE CENTER, 3929 Piedmont Ave., Oakland, CA 94611 (415, 654-6621)

A nonprofit organization working for whales and their ocean habitat through conservation, education, research and advocacy. The Whale Center has been instrumental in achieving the moratorium on commercial whaling. Whale Center programs include: the "WhaleBus" mobile classroom; whalewatching and other nature trips and educational activities; protection of endangered whale species; reducing ocean pollution; protecting whales and marine life from entanglement in nets; and promoting whalewatching. Founded: 1978.

President: THOMAS JOHNSON

Vice-President: RONN STORRO-PATTERSON

Treasurer: MARILYN DOONAN

Secretary: J. WALLACE OMAN

Director: THOMAS SOUTHWORTH

Executive Director: MARK I. PALMER

WhaleBus Director: VALERIE WELSH

Librarian: ANTHONY PETTINATO

Publications: Newsletter; Research Reports; Fact Sheets

Editor: ANTHONY PETTINATO

402

WHITETAILS UNLIMITED, INC., P.O. Box 422, Sturgeon Bay, WI 54235. (414, 743-6777)
A national, nonprofit organization dedicated to promote sound management and conservation of the white-tailed deer for today and future generations. WTU emphasizes public education through specialized environmental programs, and financially aids wildlife research and habitat improvement projects. Founded: June, 1982. Membership: 15,000.
Executive Board: PETER J. GERL, 1629 Texas Pl., Sturgeon Bay, WI 54235; JEFF SCHINKTEN, 812 Fremont St., Algoma, WI 54201; WILLIAM E. GERL, JR., 1638 Superior Ct., Sturgeon Bay, WI 54235
President: JEFFREY B. SCHINKTEN (Ext. 2)
Vice-President, Finance: WILLIAM E. GERL, JR.
Vice-President, Marketing: DAVID HAWKEY
Chief Executive Officer: PETER J. GERL

District Representatives
Illinois: LARRY YOAKUM, R.R. 2, Box 331, Athens, IL 62613
New York: GERALD HUDSON, 74 Mohawk St., Fort Plain, NY 13339
Wisconsin: JACK EMNOTT, JR., Neenah, WI; MARLIN LAIDLAW, Marshfield, WI; LeROY SCHULTZ, Lake Mills, WI; JAMES WESOLOSKI, Sturgeon Bay, WI
Mid-West Indiana: TERRY TIMBERMAN, Brazil, IN
Publications: *The Deer Trail Magazine; WTU Insider Newsletter*
Editor: DALE G. DECKMAN, 9479 Lake Canyon Rd., Santee, CA 92071
Assistant Editors: ED ELSNER, Rt. 3, Delavan, WI 53115; KEVIN NAZE, Box 233, Algoma, WI 54201

403

WHOOPING CRANE CONSERVATION ASSOCIATION, INC., 3000 Meadowlark Dr., Sierra Vista, AZ 85635 (602, 458-0971)
A scientific and educational organization, international in scope, working to prevent the extinction of the whooping crane and save wetland habitats. Membership: 600. Founded: 1961.
President: R. LORNE SCOTT, Indian Head, Saskatchewan
Vice-President: LAWRENCE S. SMITH, Albuquerque, NM
Secretary: JEROME J. PRATT
Board of Trustees: WILLIAM S. HUEY, Santa Fe, NM; C. EUGENE KNODER, Elgin, AZ
Publication: *Grus Americana*

404

WILD CANID SURVIVAL AND RESEARCH CENTER/WOLF SANCTUARY, P.O. Box 760, Eureka, MO 63025 (314, 938-5900)
Nonprofit organization which maintains endangered wolves for possible use in reestablishment efforts and for gene pool stock, and which serves as a research, educational, and informational facility to promote the preservation and restoration of threatened and endangered species, particularly the wolf, and their natural habitat. Membership: 2,100. Organized: 1971.
President: GARY SCHOENBERGER
Administrative Director: VICKI O'TOOLE (938-5900)
Publications: Bulletin; Alerts

405

WILD HORSE ORGANIZED ASSISTANCE, INC., (WHOA), P.O. Box 555, Reno, NV 89504 (702, 323-5908)
Directs efforts toward the welfare of wild horses and burros; implementation of federal efforts in carrying out terms of the management, protection and control program for their welfare;

student projects pertaining to all phases of our heritage. Members: 12,000. Incorporated: 1971.
Executive Director and Chairman of the Board: DAWN Y. LAPPIN (851-4817)
Vice-Chairman: DAVID R. BELDING (786-7600)
Secretary: JACK C. McELWEE (323-5908)
Treasurer: GORDON W. HARRIS (322-4567)
Publications: Newsletter; News Bulletin

406

WILDERNESS FLYERS, Seaplane Pilots Association, 421 Aviation Way, Frederick, MD 21701 (301, 695-2082)
A unit formed to provide seaplane services, to agencies and environmental groups involved in forest fire detection, search and rescue, wildlife surveys, pollution patrols and other related environmental and ecological projects. Founded: 1972. Membership: 4,000.
Executive Director: ROBERT A. RICHARDSON
President: DAVE QUAM (914, 986-4631)
Vice-Presidents: STANLEY HAWKINS (416, 461-8111); WALTER WINDUS (408, 434-6900)
Secretary: JOHN S. YODICE (202, 479-4053)
Publications: *Water Flying; Water Flying Annual; WaterLanding Directory*

407

WILDERNESS SOCIETY, THE, 1400 I St., NW, 10th Fl., Washington, DC 20005 (202, 842-3400)
A nonprofit membership organization devoted to preserving wilderness and wildlife, protecting America's prime forests, parks, rivers and shorelands, and fostering an American land ethic. The society welcomes membership inquiries, contributions and bequests. Membership: 220,000. Organized: 1935.
Chair: ALICE RIVLIN, Washington, DC
Counselor: GAYLORD NELSON
President: GEORGE T. FRAMPTON, JR.
Vice-Presidents: PETER COPPELMAN; ALLEN SMITH, Finance and Administration; SYDNEY J. BUTLER, Conservation; PETER M. EMERSON, Resources Planning and Economics (RP/E); REBECCA R. WODDER, Membership and Development; MARY F. HANLEY, Public Affairs
Program Directors: KARIN SHELDON, Sr. Counsel, RP/E; TERRY SOPHER, BLM Issues; STEVE WHITNEY, National Parks Issues; WILLIAM C. REFFALT, Deputy Conservation, National Wildlife Refuge Issues; STEVE RICHARDSON, Forest Wilderness Program; RANDALL SNODGRASS, Alaska Programs

Field Representatives
Alaska Region: SUSAN ALEXANDER, 519 W. 8th Ave., Suite 205, Anchorage, AK 99501 (907, 272-9453)
Inter-Mountain (MT, WY, ID): CRAIG GEHRKE, 413 W. Idaho St., Suite 102, Boise, ID 83702 (208, 343-8153)
CA, NV: PATRICIA SCHIFFERLE, 116 New Montgomery, Suite 526, San Francisco, CA 94105 (415, 541-9144)
Southeast Region (AL, AR, GA, KY, LA, MS, NC, OK, SC, TN, East TX, WV): PETER KIRBY, 1819 Peachtree Rd., NE, Suite 714, Atlanta, GA 30309 (404, 355-1783)
Colorado Region (CO): DARRELL KNUFFKE, 777 Grant St., Suite 606, Denver, CO 80206 (303, 839-1175)
Northwest Region (WA, OR): JEAN DURNING, 1424 Fourth St., Rm 813, Seattle, WA 98101 (206, 624-6430)
Utah Region (UT): MIKE MEDBERRY, 436 East Alameda, Salt Lake City, UT 84111 (801, 355-4742)
Northeast Region (MA, VT, NH, ME, CT, RI, NJ, NY): MICHAEL KELLETT, 20 Park Plaza, #536, Boston, MA 02116 (617, 350-8866)

Southwest Region (AZ, NM, West TX): JAMES NORTON, 234 N. Central Ave., Phoenix, AZ 85004 (602, 256-7921)

Florida Region (FL): JAMES D. WEBB, 4055 Ponce de Leon Blvd., Coral Gables, FL 33146 (305, 448-3636)

Northern Rockies (MT, WY): MICHAEL SCOTT, 105 W. Main St., Suite E, Bozeman, MT 59715 (406, 586-1600)

Publication: *Wilderness*

Editor: T.H. WATKINS

408

WILDERNESS WATCH, P.O. Box 782, Sturgeon Bay, WI 54235 (414, 743-1238)

Dedicated to the sustained use of America's sylvan lands and waters, placing ecological considerations foremost. Decisions are based upon the advice of a scientific advisory staff of experts in the behavioral and the physical sciences. Founded: 1969.

President-Treasurer: DR. JERRY GANDT

Vice-Presidents: THOMAS C. GOODALE, Ph.D., Ottawa, Canada; DONALD F. QUINN, Washington Island, WI;

Secretary: M. WILLIAM YUNKER, Baileys Harbor, WI

Director of Scientific Advisory Staff: ROBERT B. DITTON, Ph.D., College Station, TX (713, 845-5412)

Director, Legal Staff: GREGORY CONWAY, Green Bay, WI (414, 432-7781)

Publication: *Watch It*

409

WILDFOWL FOUNDATION, INC., 2111 Jefferson Davis Highway, 605-S, Arlington, VA 22202 (703, 979-2626)

A tax-exempt, nonprofit organization dedicated to advancing the conservation of ducks, geese and swans of the world by international cooperation in scientific research and education. Founded: 1956.

President: C.R. GUTERMUTH (Ext. 2626)

Vice-President: J.S. GOTTSCHALK, National Wildlife Federation, 1400 16th St., NW, Washington, DC 20036

Treasurer: THOMAS M. BEERS

Secretary: LAURENCE R. JAHN

410

WILDFOWL TRUST OF NORTH AMERICA, INC., THE, P.O. Box 519, Grasonville, MD 21638 (301, 827-6694)

A nonprofit, tax-exempt organization dedicated to fostering a sense of public stewardship toward wetlands and their highly visible waterfowl through programs in education, recreation, and research. The trust operates Horsehead Sanctuary, a 310-acre wetland reserve, as a headquarters, providing trails, blinds, a visitor center and a collection of resident waterfowl for public use. Founded: 1979. Membership: 600.

President: DR. PETER CROWCROFT

Vice-Presidents: NAJEEB HALABY; F. PHILLIPS WILLIAMSON

Secretary: BROUGHTON EARNEST

Treasurer: ARTHUR KUDNER

General Manager: BENEDICT J. HREN

Publication: Newsletter

Editors: EMILY RUSSELL; JEAN ROBERTS

411

WILDLIFE CONSERVATION INTERNATIONAL (WCI), New York Zoological Society, 185th St., and So. Blvd., Bldg. A, Bronx, NY 10460 (212, 220-5155)

The international conservation program of the New York Zoological Society, supports a full-time staff of field scientists as well as short-term projects; strives to obtain a better understanding of the biology of endangered species and the structure, functioning, and stability of large ecosystems and to apply this understanding to

conservation. The program is the oldest of its kind in America. Established: 1895.

Director and Resource Ecologist (Acting): DR. DAVID WESTERN

Director, Science: DR. GEORGE B. SCHALLER

Assistant Directors: DR. MARY C. PEARL; WILLIAM WEBER

Regional Coordinator: DR. ARCHIE CARR III

Research Zoologist: DR. THOMAS STRUHSAKER

Staff Zoologist: DR. PATRICIA MOEHLMAN

Associate Research Zoologists: DRS. TERESE AND JOHN HART DR. J.C. HILLMAN; DR. CHARLES MUNN; DR. ALAN RABINOWITZ; DR. STUART STRAHL

Publication: *Wildlife Conservation International Newsletter*

412

WILDLIFE DISEASE ASSOCIATION, P.O. Box 886, Ames, IA 50010 (515, 233-1931)

An international nonprofit organization of scientists interested in advancing knowledge of the effects of infectious, parasitic, toxic, genetic, and physiologic diseases and environmental factors upon the health and survival of free-living and captive wild animals, and upon their relationships to man. Membership: 1,500. Founded: 1951.

President: DR. ROBERT E. LANGE, JR.

Secretary: DR. LOUIS N. LOCKE

Treasurer: DR. ALAN KOCAN

Business Managers: DICK DALE; DOROTHY GERBER

Publication: *Journal of Wildlife Diseases*

Editors: DR. D.B. PENCE, Dept. of Pathology, Texas Tech. Univ., Lubbock, TX 79430; HARRY W. HUIZINGA, Ph.D., Dept. Biological Science, Illinois State University, Normal, IL 61761

413

WILDLIFE INFORMATION CENTER, INC., 629 Green St., Allentown, PA 18102 (215, 434-1637)

A nonprofit organization whose purpose is to secure and disseminate wildlife conservation, education, recreation, and scientific research information. Programs include in-service teacher training courses and other public education activities; research and preparation of conservation-education papers and reports on significant wildlife issues; maintaining a Wildlife Conservation Registry of Fame; maintaining wildlife issues archives of magazine and newspaper clips; sponsoring and conducting long-term hawk migration field studies at Bake Oven Knob, PA.; sponsoring wildlife conferences on selected topics; and advocating nonkilling uses of wildlife including observation, photography, sound recording, drawing and painting, and wildlife tourism. Founded: 1986.

President: DONALD S. HEINTZELMAN (434-1637)

Vice-President: PRISCILLA N. COHN, Ph.D. (525-2957)

Secretary: MARYANNE C. COATES, Esq. (424-4777)

Treasurer: Vacant

Executive Director: DONALD S. HEINTZELMAN (434-1637)

Publications: *Educational Hawkwatcher; Wildlife Book Review; Wildlife Conservation Reports; Wildlife Activist*

Editor: DONALD S. HEINTZELMAN (434-1637)

414

WILDLIFE LEGISLATIVE FUND OF AMERICA, THE, AND WILDLIFE CONSERVATION FUND OF AMERICA, THE, 50 W. Broad St., Columbus, OH 43215 (614, 221-2684); National Affairs Office, 1000 Connecticut Ave., NW, Suite 1002, Washington, DC 20036 (202, 466-4407)

Companion nonprofit organizations established to protect the heritage of the American sportsman to hunt, fish and trap and to protect scientific wildlife management practices. The WLFA is the legislative and political arm. The WCFA is the legal defense, information, public education and research arm. Through their

associated organizations, WLFA and WCFA represent an aggregate membership of 750,000. Incorporated: 1978.
Chairman of the Board: DANIEL M. GALBREATH
Vice-Chairman: DR. VINCENT SHIEL
President (CEO): JAMES H. GLASS
Treasurer: MRS. GILBERT W. HUMPHREY
Senior Vice-President/Secretary: JAMES W. GOODRICH
Vice-President for Programs and Public Relations: RICK STORY
Director of Resources and Systems: WILLIAM R. CHRISTENSEN
Director of State Services: THOMAS B. ADDIS
General Counsel: JAMES R. HANSON
Director of National Affairs: CAROL A. PORTER
Director of Communications: T. ALLAN WOLTER
Directors/Trustees: THOMAS E. BASS, Flying TB Ranch, Rt. 6, Box 396, Gainesville, TX 76240 (817, 665-1437); HENRY FONER, 275 Seventh Ave., 18th Flr., New York, NY, 10001 (212, 242-5450); DANIEL M. GALBREATH, 180 E. Broad St., 9th Flr., Columbus, OH, 43215 (614, 460-4444); JAMES H. GLASS, 50 West Broad St., Columbus, OH 43215 (614, 221-2684); JAMES W. GOODRICH, 50 W. Broad St., Columbus, OH 43215 (614, 221-2684); J. HIBBARD ROBERTSON, SR., 69 N. Locust St., Lititz, PA 17543 (717, 626-2125); B.H. HARDAWAY III, P.O. Box 1360, Columbus, GA 31902 (404, 322-3274); WILLIAM E. MOFFETT, 102 Rockwood Dr., Pittsburgh, PA 15238 (412, 963-0622); MRS. GILBERT W. HUMPHREY, Woodfield Springs, Miccosukee, FL 32309 (904, 893-2808); DR. EDWARD L. KOZICKY, 817 Southmoor Dr., R.R. 3, Godfrey, IL 62035 (618, 466-3156); DAVID B. MELTZER, Olympia Center, 161 Chicago Ave., East, Chicago, IL 60611 (312, 855-2120); DR. VINCENT W. SHIEL, 474 South Beach Rd., Hobe Sound, FL 33455 (305, 546-8128); PETER H. COORS, Adolph Coors Company, Golden, CO 80401 (303, 277-3109)

415

WILDLIFE MANAGEMENT INSTITUTE, Suite 725, 1101 14th St., NW, Washington, DC 20005 (202, 371-1808)
(Sponsor, 54th North American Wildlife and Natural Resources Conference, 1989: March 17-22, Washington, DC)
National, nonprofit, private, membership organization, supported by industries, groups, and individuals, promoting better use of natural resources for the welfare of the nation.
President: LAURENCE R. JAHN
Vice-President: LONNIE L. WILLIAMSON
Secretary and Publications Director: RICHARD E. McCABE
Resource Associate: ERIC W. SCHENCK
Publications: *Outdoor News Bulletin; Transactions North American Wildlife and Natural Resources Conference*

Field Representatives, CHESTER A. McCONNELL, Rt. 6, Box 212, Lawrenceburg, TN 38464 (615, 762-7718); KEITH W. HARMON, 421 Pioneer Ct., Hickman, NE 68372 (402, 792-2559)

416

WILDLIFE PRESERVATION TRUST INTERNATIONAL, INC., 34th St. and Girard Ave., Philadelphia, PA 19104 (215, 222-3636; Cable: DODO Philadelphia)
Supports the preservation of endangered species through captive propagation, including research, education and fieldwork. Awards grants internationally in these areas. Affiliated with the Jersey Wildlife Preservation Trust, Jersey, Channel Islands, Incorporated: 1971. Membership: 7,000.
Honorary Chairman: GERALD M. DURRELL
Chairman: THOMAS E. LOVEJOY
Secretary: PETER D. LEDERER

Treasurer: META P. BARTON
Executive Director: WILLIAM R. KONSTANT
Publications: *On the Edge; The Dodo; Dodo Dispatch; Annual Report*

417

WILDLIFE SOCIETY, THE, 5410 Grosvenor Ln., Bethesda, MD 20814 (301, 897-9770)
International scientific and educational organization of professionals and students engaged in wildlife research, management, education, and administration. Dedicated to sound stewardship of wildlife resources and the environments upon which wildlife and humans depend; undertakes an active role in preventing human-induced environmental degradation; increases awareness and appreciation of wildlife values; and seeks the highest standards in all activities of the wildlife profession. Membership: over 8,200; Organized: 1937.
President: JAMES G. TEER, Rob and Bessie Welder Wildlife Foundation, P.O. Drawer 1400, Sinton, TX 78387 (512, 364-2643)
Vice-President: OLLIE TORGERSON, 2700 Lola Dr., Jefferson City, MO 65101 (314, 449-3761)
Past-President: LYTLE H. BLANKENSHIP, HCR 34, Box 979, Uvalde, TX 78801
Executive Director: HARRY E. HODGDON
Field Director: THOMAS M. FRANKLIN
Publications: Serial Publications: *The Journal of Wildlife Management;* Wildlife Monographs; *Wildlife Society Bulletin; The Wildlifer*

Section (Regional) Representatives

Northeast Section: WILLIAM M. HEALY, P.O. Box 225, Leverett, MA 01054 (413, 549-0520)
Southeastern Section: JAMES E. MILLER, Natural Resources and Rural Development Unit, USDA, Rm. 3871, South Bldg., Washington, DC 20250 (202, 447-5468)
North Central Section: ERIK K. FRITZELL, School of Forestry, Fisheries and Wildlife, 112 Stephens Hall, University of Missouri, Columbia, MO 65211 (314, 882-3436)
Central Mountains and Plains Section: CLAIT E. BRAUN, Wildlife Research Center, 317 W. Prospect, Fort Collins, CO 80526 (303, 484-2836)
Southwest Section: NOVA J. SILVY, Department of Wildlife and Fisheries Sciences, Texas A&m University, College Station, TX 77843 (409, 845-5777)
Northwest Section: LEWIS NELSON, JR., Dept. of Fish and Wildlife, University of Idaho, Moscow, ID 83843 (208, 885-7323)
Western Section: DONALD J. ARMENTROUT, P.O. Box 521, Winnemucca, NV 89445 (702, 623-3676)

418

WILSON ORNITHOLOGICAL SOCIETY
To advance the science of ornithology and to secure cooperation in measures tending to this end. Membership: 3,100. Organized: 1888.
President: MARY H. CLENCH, Department of Internal Medicine, Division of Gastroenterology, University of Texas Medical Branch, Galveston, TX 77550
1st Vice-President: JON C. BARLOW, Department of Ornithology, Royal Ontario Museum, Toronto, Ontario, Canada M5S-2C6
Secretary: JOHN L. ZIMMERMAN, Division of Biology, Kansas State University, Manhattan, KS 66506
Treasurer: ROBERT D. BURNS, Department of Biology, Kenyon College, Gambier, OH 42022 (614, 427-2244)

Publication: *The Wilson Bulletin*
Editor: CHARLES R. BLEM, Department of Biology, Virginia Commonwealth University, Richmond, VA 23284

419

WINCHESTER GROUP, NILO, Olin Corporation, East Alton, IL 62024 (618, 258-3133)
Director, Distribution and NILO: C.E. BECKER (618, 258-3500)

420

WOMAN'S NATIONAL FARM AND GARDEN ASSOCIATION, INC.
Main goals are to stimulate an active interest in the conservation of our natural resources, to help women through scholarships to be trained in agriculture, horticulture and related professions and to promote better understanding among women of the world. Membership: 7,200. Organized: 1914.
President: MARIAN B. RENAUD, Glens of Whitehills, 1223 Windgate Ln., East Lansing, MI 48823
Recording Secretary: JESSIE WINK, 3907 Isabella Ave., Allison Park, PA 15101
Corresponding Secretary: JEANNE WATSON, 1927 Kingstree Ct., Rochester, MI 48063
Conservation Committee Chairman: BEA PETERSON, P.O. Box 41, Cherry Plain, NY 12040
Ecology and Rural Urban Committee Chairman: BEA PETERSON
Publication: *Woman's National Farm and Garden Magazine*
Editor: ELINOR BURGHER, 3739 Cotton Tail Ln., Utica, MI 48087

421

WORLD ENVIRONMENT CENTER, INC., 419 Park Ave., Suite 1403, New York, NY 10016 (212, 683-4700)
A nonprofit, non-advocacy organization whose mission is to serve as a bridge between industry and governments aimed at strengthening environmental management and industrial safety worldwide through exchange of information and technical expertise; to foster cooperation instead of confrontation between industry and governments to achieve mutually beneficial goals; to provide channels of communication and a range of management training and environmental and safety audits to developing countries using volunteers from industry, trade associations, government and international agencies, and private individuals; and to provide international public recognition for outstanding industry accomplishments, thus encouraging the growth of corporate environmental responsibility worldwide. Established: January, 1974.
President: WHITMAN BASSOW, Ph.D.
Vice-President and Director of Technical Assistance: ANTHONY G. MARCIL
Publications: *Network News; The World Environment Handbook*

422

WORLD FORESTRY CENTER, 4033 SW Canyon Rd., Portland, OR 97221 (503, 228-1367)
The World Forestry Center is a nonprofit conservation education organization, designed to improve understanding of the importance of well-managed forests and related resources and is dedicated to the establishment, protection and management of forests, soils, waters, wildlife, and other renewable resources through scientific research, demonstration and dissemination of forestry information. Established: 1971.
Education Coordinator: CAROL SMART
Publication: *Forest World*

423

WORLD NATURE ASSOCIATION, INC., P.O. Box 673, Silver Spring, MD 20901 (301, 593-2522)
Founded in 1969, the association with a membership of 250 supports educational and conservation projects in various parts of the world. We seek out small projects that are not able to be funded by other means and are often the work of a few individuals. We also sponsor a scholarship for young educators.
President: DR. DONALD H. MESSERSMITH, 10418 Brookmoor Dr., Silver Spring, MD 20901 (593-5942)
Vice-President: WINIFRED WALKER-JONES, 1250 Irving St., NE, Washington, DC 20017
Secretary: THELMA SCHMITT, 74 Pasture Ln., Bryn Mawr, PA 19010
Treasurer: RUDOLPH SCHMITT, 74 Pasture Ln., Bryn Mawr, PA 19010
Publication: *World Nature News*
Editor: MARTHA Z. BELOTE, 708 Valley Rd., Upper Montclair, NJ 07043 (201, 744-6070)

424

WORLD PHEASANT ASSOCIATION, P.O. Box 5, Child Beale Wildlife Trust, Lower Basildon, Reading, Berks, England RG8 9PF (07357-5140)
Aims are to develop, promote and support conservation of all species of the order Galliformes with initial emphasis on the family Phasianidae. Formed: 1975.
President: PROF. CHENG TSO-HSIN
Chairman: KEITH C.R. HOWMAN (0932-566591)
Publications: Annual Journal; Newsletters
Editor: DR. PETER ROBERTSON, The Game Conservancy, Fordingbridge, Hampshire SP6 1EF (0425-52381)

425

WORLD PHEASANT ASSOCIATION OF U.S.A., INC., c/o Brookfield Zoo, 3300 Golf Rd., Brookfield, IL 60513 (312, 485-0263/449)
A nonprofit, tax-exempt membership organization devoted to support of research, education, propagation and conservation of galliform birds throughout the world. Participates in the development of a World Conservation Strategy for the galliformes and serves in collaboration with other national chapters as the I.C.B.P./I.U.C.N. Specialist Group on galliform birds. Founded: 1982.
President: EDWARD C. SCHMITT
Chairman of Executive Committee: MICHAEL BARRETT
Board of Directors: MICHAEL BARRETT; DAVID J. CALVIN; DR. SCOTT R. DERRICKSON; JESUS L. ESTUDILLO; JAMES D. GUNDERSON; KEITH HOWE; K.C.R. HOWMAN; C. EUGENE KNODER; EDWARD C. SCHMITT; HARRY W. (Pete) SQUIBB
Vice-President: DAVID J. CALVIN
Secretary-Treasurer: EDWARD C. SCHMITT
General Counsel: JAMES D. GUNDERSON
Honorary President: DIDY GRAHAME
Publications: *WPA Newsletter;* Annual Journal; *Annual Report*
Editors: IAIN GRAHAME; DAVID HILL; G.E.S. ROBBINS

426

WORLD RESOURCES INSTITUTE, 1735 New York Ave., NW, Washington, DC 20006 (202, 638-6300)
A policy research center created in late 1982 with funding from the John D. and Catherine T. MacArthur Foundation and others, to help governments, international organizations, the private sector and others address vital issues of environmental integrity, natural

resource management, economic growth, and international security.
President: JAMES GUSTAVE SPETH
Vice-President, Research and Policy Affairs: MOHAMED T. EL ASHRY
Corporate Secretary and Treasurer: WALLACE D. BOWMAN
Publications: *Policy Studies Series; Research Report Series; World Resources Report*

427

WORLD SOCIETY FOR THE PROTECTION OF ANIMALS, **(WSPA)** Formerly: International Society for the Protection of Animals (ISPA), 29 Perkins St., P.O. Box 190, Boston, MA 02130 (617, 522-7000)
International organization formed in January 1981 by merger of the International Society for the Protection of Animals and the World Federation for the Protection of Animals, to undertake and promote conservation and protection of animals both domestic and wild. Field staff are deployed to aid animals during disasters and/or advise animal welfare societies and governments in any part of the world. Maintains offices in London, Boston, Toronto, Colombia, Costa Rica, Italy, and New Zealand. In addition to individual members, 312 animal protection and conservation organizations in 63 countries have membership with WSPA. Incorporated: 1981.
President: JOHN HOYT
Director General: TREVOR H. SCOTT
Treasurer: ROBERT CUMMINGS
Regional Director: JOHN C. WALSH
Publication: *Animals International*

428

WORLD WILDLIFE FUND-U.S., 1250 24th St., NW, Washington, DC 20037 (202, 293-4800)
Affiliated with The Conservation Foundation, WWF is the largest private U.S. organization working worldwide to protect endangered wildlife and wildlands--especially in the tropical forests of Latin America, Asia, and Africa. WWF has helped protect some 180 national parks and nature reserves; supports scientific investigations; monitors international trade in wildlife; promotes ecologically sound development; assists local groups to take the lead in needed conservation projects; and seeks to influence public opinion and the policies of governments and private institutions to promote conservation of the earth's living resources. Membership: 500,000. Founded: 1961
Chairman of Board: RUSSELL E. TRAIN
Chairman of Executive Committee: MELVIN B. LANE
President: WILLIAM K. REILLY
Secretary: ANNE P. SIDAMON-ERISTOFF
Treasurer: DOUGLAS F. WILLIAMSON, JR.
Executive Vice-President: KATHRYN S. FULLERS
General Counsel: MICHAEL MANTELL
Vice-President, Latin America Program: CURTIS H. FREESE
Vice-President, Science: RUSSELL A. MITTERMEIER
Vice-President, Finance and Administration: PAIGE K. MacDONALD
Vice-President, Development: JANEEN WALLACE STOUT
Vice-President, Communications: JULIA A. MOORE
Vice-President, Planning and Evaluation: JOHN H. NOBLE
Senior Vice-President, Public Policy and T.R.A.F.F.I.C.: E.U. CURTIS BOHLEN
Vice-President, Grant Services: NANCY E. HAMMOND
Vice-President, Wildlands and Human Needs: R. MICHAEL WRIGHT
Vice-President, The Osborn Center: H. JEFFERY LEONARD
Publication: *FOCUS*

429

WORLDWATCH INSTITUTE, 1776 Massachusetts Ave., NW, Washington, DC 20036 (202, 452-1999)
A nonprofit research organization concerned with identifying and analyzing emerging global problems and trends and bringing them to attention of opinion leaders and the general public. Issues covered in first sixteen years include: energy, population growth and migration, food, changing roles of women, recycling, global economy, environment, impact of technology, soil erosion, nuclear power, toxic wastes, deforestation, and energy efficiency. Formed: 1974.
President: LESTER R. BROWN
Director of Outreach: STEPHEN R. DUJACK
Publications: Worldwatch Papers; State of the World series; *WorldWatch Magazine*
Editor: STEPHEN R. DUJACK

430

WORLDWIDE, 1250 24th St., NW, Suite 500, Washington, DC 20037 (202, 331-9863)
An international membership organization established to strengthen the role of women in developing and implementing sound policies for managing the environment and natural resources. The WORLDWIDE goals are: (1) to educate the public and policymakers as to how women are affected when natural systems are destroyed or contaminated, and to put forth their perspectives on these issues; and (2) to increase the inclusion of women and their environmental perceptions in the design and implementation of development policies and programs. Founded: 1982.
Board of Directors: SUSAN ABBASI; CYNTHIA HELMS, President; YOLANDA KAKABADSE; JOAN MARTIN-BROWN, Chair; WANGARI MAATHAI, Ph.D.; WAAFAS OFOSU-AMAAH; HIND SADEK-KOOROS, Ph.D.; KATHY SREEDHAR; JANE PRATT, Ph.D.; SHELLY WEINSTEIN; DIANE WOOD
Publications: *Worldwide News* (International Newsletter); *Worldwide Directory of Women in Environment*

431

XERCES SOCIETY, THE, 10 SW Ash St., Portland, OR 97204 (503, 222-2788)
A nonprofit, international organization with two goals: habitat protection for rare or endangered invertebrates, especially butterflies; and enhancing the public's positive feelings for insects by emphasizing their beneficial roles in natural ecosystems. Founded: 1971. Membership: 1,100.
President: JEFF GLASSBERG, Lifecodes Corp., Sawmill River Rd., Valhalla, NY 10595 (914, 592-4122)
Vice-President: PAUL OPLER, 5100 Greenview Ct., Ft. Collins, CO 80525 (303, 226-2433)
Executive Director: MELODY ALLEN, 10 SW Ash St., Portland, OR 97204 (503, 222-2788)
Secretary: ED GROSSWILER, Director of Government Affairs, 920 SW 6th Ave., Portland, OR 97204 (503, 464-5770)
Treasurer: DR. DAVID FURTH, Dept. of Entomology, Peabody Museum, Yale University, New Haven, CT 06520 (203, 432-5001)
Publications: *Journal ATALA: Journal of Invertebrate Conservation; Wings* (membership magazine)
Editors: DR. LAWRENCE F. GALL, Dept. of Entomology, Peabody Museum, Yale University, New Haven, CT 06520 (203, 436-8847); MARY TROYCHAK, 10 SW Ash St., Portland, OR 97204 (503, 222-2788)

432
ZERO POPULATION GROWTH, INC., 1601 Connecticut Ave., NW, Washington, DC 20009 (202, 332-2200)
A national, nonprofit, grassroots organization which works to achieve a balance among people, resources and environment by advocating population stabilization in the United States and worldwide. Activities include citizen action projects, school-based population-education curricula, public policy advocacy, media campaigns and publications. Membership: 15,000. Chapters: 15. Established: 1968.

Honorary President: PAUL R. EHRLICH, Ph.D. (415, 497-3171)
President: JUDITH JACOBSEN (303, 494-6616)
Executive Director: SUSAN WEBER
Directors: DEBORAH BROUSE, Population Education; MARK ESHERICK, Public Policy; ELYSE CHILAND, Communications; GLENN HOFFMAN, Administration
Political Representatives: SUSAN WEBER; MARK ESHERICK
Publications: *ZPG Reporter; ZPG Activist; Media Targets; Teachers' PET Term Paper;* Action Alerts, Factsheets, and Brochures
Editor: ELYSE CHILAND

STATE AND TERRITORIAL AGENCIES AND CITIZENS' GROUPS

ALABAMA

GOVERNMENT AGENCIES

GOVERNOR: HAROLD GUY HUNT, Governor of Alabama, State Capitol, Montgomery 36130 (205, 261-7100)

ALABAMA COOPERATIVE FISH AND WILDLIFE RESEARCH UNIT, USDI, 331 Funchess Hall, Auburn University, Auburn 36849 (205, 826-4796)
The unit is sponsored by the U.S. Fish and Wildlife Service, Alabama Department of Conservation and Natural Resources, Division of Game and Fish, Auburn University and the Wildlife Management Institute. Fish and wildlife research, graduate education and technical assistance are the units' primary purposes. Established by merger: July 2, 1984.
Leader: DR. NICHOLAS R. HOLLER
Assistant Leaders: DR. DANIEL W. SPEAKE, Wildlife; DR. MARK B. BAIN, Aquatic Resources

DEPARTMENT OF AGRICULTURE AND INDUSTRIES, The Richard Beard Bldg., P.O. Box 3336, Montgomery 36193 (205, 261-2650)
Commissioner: ALBERT McDONALD

DEPARTMENT OF CONSERVATION AND NATURAL RESOURCES, 64 N. Union St., Montgomery 36130 (205, 261-3486)
Commissioner: JAMES D. MARTIN (261-3486)
Assistant Commissioner: M.N. (Corky) PUGH (261-3487)
Director, Division of Game and Fish: CHARLES D. KELLEY (261-3465)
Director, Division of Lands: ROBERT A. MACRORY (261-3484)
Director, Division of State Parks: GARY LEACH (261-3334)
Director, Division of Marine Police: WILLIAM B. GARNER (261-3673)
Director, Division of Marine Resources: HUGH A. SWINGLE, P.O. Box 189, Dauphin Island 36528 (861-2882/261-3346)
Chief Legal Counsel: OTIS J. GOODWYN (261-3165)
Chief, Accounting Section: CURTIS PARRISH (261-3260)
Chief, Engineering Section: CLURIN B. REED, JR. (261-3476)
Chief (Acting), Personnel and Payroll Section: FAYE DAVIS (261-3501)
Chief, Information and Education Section: BETTINA WOOD (261-3151)
Property Inventory Manager: JOHN F. DAVIS (261-2574)
Publications: *Alabama Conservation Magazine; Conservation Employee Newsletter; Conservation Update Newsletter*
Editor: BETTINA WOOD (261-3151)

DEPARTMENT OF ENVIRONMENTAL MANAGEMENT, 1751 Congressman W.L. Dickinson Dr., Montgomery 36130 (205, 271-7700)
To respond in an efficient, comprehensive, and coordinated manner to environmental problems, thereby assuring for all citizens of the state a safe, healthful, and productive environment. Encompasses water quality, public water supply, underground injection control, solid waste, hazardous waste, air pollution control, water well standards, operator certification, and coastal area functions. Founded: 1982.
Chairman: STANLEY L. GRAVES
Director: LEIGH PEGUES
Deputy Director: JAMES W. WARR
Land Division: DANIEL E. COOPER
Water Division: CHARLES HORN
Air Division: RICHARD GRUSNICK
Field Operations: E. JOHN WILLIFORD

FORESTRY COMMISSION, 513 Madison Ave., Montgomery 36130 (205, 240-9300)
The FC was created by the 1969 regular session of the Alabama Legislature and is charged by law with protecting, extending and developing Alabama's most bountiful resource—her forests. A seven-member board is the policy-making body of the commission. The State Forester is Chief Administrative Officer. Fire prevention and suppression, educational programs and materials, and free forest management assistance are some of the services which the commission offers to the general public.
Commission Members: G.A. GIBBS, Chairman; JOHN GOODSON; JAMES B. NEIGHBORS; JACK HOPPER, Vice-Chairman; CLAUDE S. SWIFT; RICHARD PORTERFIELD; HOMAJEAN GRISHAM
State Forester: C.W. MOODY (240-9304)
Assistant State Forester: C.A. PIGG (240-9369)
Director, Forest Resource Protection Division: RICHARD H. CUMBIE (240-9335)
Director, Productivity Division: DAVID FREDERICK (240-9346)
Director, Forest Resource Development Division: TIM BOYCE (240-9367)
Director, Administration Division: JOHN KUMMEL (240-9333)
Treasured Forest Coordinator/Wildlife Biologist: FREDERICK A. BUSCH
Publication: *Alabama's TREASURED Forests*
Editor: CYNTHIA K. PAGE (240-9349)

SEA GRANT PROGRAM
Director, MS/AL Sea Grant Consortium: JAMES I. JONES, Ph.D., Caylor Bldg., Gulf Coast Research Lab., P.O. ox 7000, Ocean Springs, MS 39564-7000 (601, 875-9341)
Program Coordinator, State Marine Advisory Programs: WILLIAM HOSKING, Ph.D., Alabama Sea Grant Extension Service, 3940 Government Blvd., #5, Mobile 36609 (205, 661-5004)
Leader, Mississippi Sea Grant Advisory Services: C. DAVID VEAL, Ph.D., 4646 W. Beach Blvd., Suite 1-E, Biloxi 39531 (601, 388-4710)

STATE EXTENSION SERVICES
Director and Vice-President, Cooperative Extension Service: DR. ANN E. THOMPSON, Auburn University 36849 (205, 826-4444)
Forester and Coordinator, Extension Forestry Programs: LARKIN H. WADE, (826-5330)
Wildlife Specialist: DR. H. LEE STRIBLING (826-4850)
Fisheries Specialist: DR. JOHN W. JENSEN (826-4786)
Forest Economist: Vacant
Forester, Wood Products: Vacant
Forest Management Specialist: Vacant
Program Associate—Forestry: DR. A.R. GILMORE (826-5330)
Program Associate—Timber Harvesting: Vacant
Forest Herbicide Specialist: Vacant

CITIZENS' GROUPS

ALABAMA WILDLIFE FEDERATION, 46 Commerce St., P.O. Box 2102, Montgomery 36102 (205, 832-9453)
A representative statewide organization, affiliated with the National Wildlife Federation, primarily devoted to the wise use, conservation, aesthetic appreciation, and restoration of wildlife and other natural resources. Organized: 1937.
President: ROSS SELF, Rt. 7, Box 326-E, Talladega 35160
Executive Director: DOUG SCHOFIELD
Affiliate Representative: JOHN C. MIMS, Box 74032, Birmingham 35253 (205, 933-6935)
Alternate: MICKEY EASLEY, P.O. Box 158, Hurtsboro 36860
Publication: *Alabama Wildlife*
Editor: DOUG SCHOFIELD

ALABAMA ASSOCIATION OF CONSERVATION DISTRICTS, INC.
President: CHARLES HOLMES, Rt. 1, Box 260, Marion 36756
Vice-President: ZERREL SMALLEY, Rt. 5, Box 16, Arab 35016
Secretary-Treasurer: CHARLES W. RITTENOUR, JR., 713 Alamo Dr., Montgomery 36111

ALABAMA BASS CHAPTER FEDERATION
An organization of Bassmaster Chapters, affiliated with the Bass Anglers Sportsman Society, to fight pollution, assist state and national conservation agencies in their efforts and teach the young people of our country good conservation practices. Dedicated to the realistic conservation of our water resources.
President: JERRY PENDERGRASS, 3717 Sola Cir., Ft. Payne 35967 (205, 845-1441/3044)

ALABAMA CONSERVANCY, THE, 2717 7th Ave. South, Suite 201, Birmingham 35233 (205, 322-3126)
Dedicated to the preservation of Alabama's environment on all fronts: air, water, land, and wildlife. Membership: 1,200 individuals, 100 organizations. Founded: 1967.
President: DR. ED PASSERINI (348-4600)
Vice-President for Administration: LEE LAECHELT (663-4138)
Director, Recycling: LARRY CRENSHAW (591-I110)
Vice-President for Conservation: JIM TAYLOR (348-8941)
Vice-President for Membership: TERRY BISHOP (687-5741)
Treasurer: DR. ROBERT E. BURKS (967-0367)
Secretary: JERI MARTIN (322-3126)
Executive Director: KYLE CRIDER
Publications: *ACT;* other alerts on urgent issues
Editor: KYLE CRIDER

WILDLIFE SOCIETY ALABAMA CHAPTER
President: RHETT JOHNSON, Rt. 7, Box 131, Andalusia 36420 (205, 222-7779)
President-Elect: GEORGE HORTON, P.O. Box 365, Heflin, AL 36264 (205, 463-7570)
Secretary-Treasurer: DOREEN MILLER, 2025 Joe Quick Rd., New Market 37561

ALASKA

GOVERNMENT AGENCIES

GOVERNOR: STEVE COWPER, Governor of Alaska, P.O. Box A, Juneau 99811 (907, 465-3500)

ALASKA COOPERATIVE FISHERY RESEARCH UNIT, 138 Arctic Health Research Bldg., University of Alaska, Fairbanks 99701 (907, 474-7661)
The unit is sponsored jointly by the U.S. Fish and Wildlife Service, the Alaska Department of Fish and, Game and the University of Alaska, Fairbanks. Its purpose is to conduct education and research programs on the structure and function of aquatic ecosystems, with emphasis on interior and arctic Alaska. Founded: 1978.
Leader: DR. JAMES B. REYNOLDS
Assistant Leader: JACQUELINE D. LAPERRIERE

ALASKA COOPERATIVE WILDLIFE RESEARCH UNIT, University of Alaska, Fairbanks 99775-0990 (907, 474-7673)
Sponsored jointly by the University of Alaska, the Alaska Dept. of Fish and Game, the U.S. Fish and Wildlife Service, and the Wildlife Management Institute, the unit functions through the University to undertake research and provide graduate training in wildlife ecology and management. Founded: 1950.
Leader: DR. DAVID R. KLEIN

ALASKA SEA GRANT COLLEGE PROGRAM
Director: RONALD K. DEARBORN, Alaska Sea Grant College Program, University of Alaska, 138 Irving II, Fairbanks 99775-5040 (907, 474-7086)
Leader, Marine Advisory Program: DONALD E. KRAMER, University of Alaska, Carlton Trust Bldg., #220, 2221 E. Northern Lights Blvd., Anchorage 99508-4143 (274-9691)

DEPARTMENT OF ENVIRONMENTAL CONSERVATION, P.O. Box O, Juneau 99811-1800 (907, 465-2600)
Created in 1971 by the Seventh Alaska Legislature to protect the quality of the state's natural resources and the health and quality of life of its people. The department has broad regulatory authority in the areas of water quality, air quality, land, and subsurface pollution, pesticides, and radiation. The department also has programs for construction of water, sewer, and solid waste facilities in Alaskan cities and villages.
Commissioner: BILL ROSS (465-2600)
Deputy Commissioner: AMY KYLE (465-2600)
Director, Division of Environmental Quality: KEITH KELTON (465-2640)
Director, Division Environmental Health: DOUG DONEGAN (465-2696)
Director, Division Facilities Construction & Operations: GARY HAYDEN (465-2610)
Director, Division of Administrative Service: BILL PUBLICOVER (465-2621)
Supervisor, Southeast Regional Office: DEENA HENKINS (789-3151)
Supervisor, Southcentral Regional Office: BILL LAMOREAUX (274-2533)
Supervisor, Northern Regional Office: DOUGLAS LOWERY (452-1714)
Publication: *Alaska Environment*
Editor: JOE FERGUSON (465-2606)

DEPARTMENT OF FISH AND GAME, P.O. Box 3-2000, Juneau 99802 (907, 465-4100)

A research and management agency whose mission is to develop and organize its technical, human and fiscal assets to maintain, rehabilitate and enhance the fish and wildlife resources of the State and to provide for their sustained optimum use consistent with the social, cultural, environmental, and economical needs of the public.

Commissioner: DON W. COLLINSWORTH

Deputy Commissioner: NORMAN COHEN

Assistant Commissioner: WARREN WILEY

Director, Administration Division: BEVERLY D. REAUME (465-4120)

Director, Commercial Fish Division: KENNETH P. PARKER (465-4210)

Director, Fisheries Rehabilitation Enhancement and Development Division: BRIAN ALEE (465-4160)

Director, Game Division: W. LEWIS PAMPLIN (267-2179)

Director, Sport Fish Division: NORVAL NETSCH (465-4180)

Director, Habitat Protection Division: FRANK RUE (465-4147)

Director, Subsistence Division: STEVE BEHNKE (465-4147)

Director, Division of Boards: BETH STEWART (465-4110)

Board of Fisheries: GARY SLAVEN, Chairman, Petersburg; JOE DEMMERT, JR., Vice-Chairman, Ketchikau; VAL ANGASAN, Dillingham; ERNEST C. CARTER, Fairbanks; BUD HODSON, Anchorage; BOB LOCHMAN, Kodiak; JESSE FOSTER, Quinhagak

Board of Game: BRENDA JOHNSON, Chairman, Nome; SARAH SCANLON, Vice-Chairman, Anchorage; SAMANTHA CASTLE, Fairbanks; SIDNEY HUNTINGTON, Galena; JOEL BENNETT, Juneau; NICK JACKSON, Gakona; JAY MASSEY, Girdwood

Publication: *Alaska Fish and Game*

Editor: SHEILA NICKERSON (465-4113)

DEPARTMENT OF NATURAL RESOURCES, 400 Willoughby, Juneau 99801 (907, 465-2400)

Commissioner: JUDITH M. BRADY

Deputy Commissioner: LENNIE BOSTON GORSUCH

Division of Land and Water Management: GARY GUSTAFSON, Director, P.O. Box 107005, Anchorage 99510-7005 (762-2692)

Division of Forestry:

State Forester (Acting): TOM HAWKINS (762-2483)

Division of Agriculture: FRANK MIELKE, Director (Acting), P.O. Box 949, Palmer 99645-0949 (745-7200)

Division of Parks and Outdoor Recreation: NEIL JOHANNSEN, P.O. Box 107001, Anchorage 99510-7001 (762-2600)

Division of Management: SHARON BARTON, Director (465-2406)

Division of Oil and Gas: JAMES EASON, Director (762-2547)

Division of Geological and Geophysical Surveys: DR. ROBERT FORBES, Director, 3700 Airport Way, Fairbanks 99709 (451-2761)

Division of Mining: GERALD GALLAGHER, Director, P.O. Box 107016, Anchorage 99510-7016 (762-2165)

DEPARTMENT OF PUBLIC SAFETY, 450 Whittier St., Juneau 99801 (907, 465-4322); Division of Fish and Wildlife Protection, 5700 E. Tudor Rd., Anchorage 99507 (907, 269-5532)

Responsible for enforcing all of the Fish and Game laws and regulations of the state.

Commissioner: ARTHUR ENGLISH

Deputy Commissioner: GAYLE A. HORETSKI

Director of Fish and Wildlife Protection: COL. JACK JORDAN, Department of Commerce and Economic Development, Guide Control Board, Division of Occupational Licensing, Box D, Juneau 99811 (465-2542)

Chairman: RAY MCNUTT

Enforcement Commander: CAPT. PHILLIP V. GILSON

Operations Commander: CAPT. CONRAD G. SEIBEL

Board Members: BEN G. BALLENGER; CHARLES WEIR; ARTHUR L. CLARK; STANLEY FROST; PETER BUIST

STATE EXTENSION SERVICES

Director (Acting), Cooperative Extension Service: DR. IRVIN W. SKELTON, 103 Arctic Health Bldg., University of Alaska, Fairbanks 99775-5200 (907, 474-7246)

Chairman (Acting), Land Resource: JERRY PURSER

CITIZENS' GROUPS

 WILDLIFE FEDERATION OF ALASKA, 750 West Second Ave., Suite 200-B, Anchorage 99501 (907, 274-3388)

Organized: 1984.

President: *JIM JACKSON,* 15301 Elmore Rd., Anchorage 99516

Representative: *JIM JACKSON* (907, 278-3420)

Alternate: Vacant

ALASKA ASSOCIATION OF SOIL AND WATER CONSERVATION DISTRICTS

President: CHARLES GOFF, Box 10296, Fairbanks 99710

Vice-President: SCOTT SCHULTZ, P.O. Box 1284, Delta Junction 99737

Secretary-Treasurer: PAT MARQUIS, SR Box 550, Anchor Point 99556

ALASKA CENTER FOR THE ENVIRONMENT, 400 H St., Suite 4, Anchorage 99501 (907, 274-3621)

Nonprofit organization which functions as an advocacy and citizen organizing facility for Alaskan environmental activities. Founded: 1971.

Executive Directors: Administration, SUSAN LIBENSON; Issues, CLIFF EAMES; Hazardous Waste, KRISTINE BENSON

Publication: *Center News*

ALASKA CONSERVATION FOUNDATION, 430 W. 7th Ave., Suite 215, Anchorage 99501 (907, 276-1917)

A public "grassroots" foundation, supported by gifts and grants. It provides financial and technical support to conservation organizations based in Alaska. The Board of Trustees are primarily Alaskans. ACF began in early 1980. It is not a membership organization but lists its donors as "Friends."

President: DENNY WILCHER

Chairperson: SUE MATTHEWS

Vice-Chairperson: CINDY MARQUETTE

Secretary: MARILYN MILLER

Vice-President: JIM STRATTON

Treasurer: Vacant

ALASKA ENVIRONMENTAL LOBBY, INC., P.O. Box 22151, Juneau 99802-2151 (907, 586-2345)

A coalition of 19 environmental groups, and a citizens' lobbying effort of the Alaska state legislature. Fifteen volunteers per year spend a month in Juneau working on issues of concern to the environmental community, including land management, hazardous wastes, clean water, energy, budget for resource agencies, and many others.

Executive Director: GAIL GATTON

President: MARY CORE

Vice-President: BART KOEHLER

Secretary: MARCIA VANDERCOOK
Treasurer: BARBARA RUDIO

NATIONAL AUDUBON SOCIETY, Alaska-Hawaii Regional Office, 308 G. St., Suite 219, Anchorage 99501 (907, 276-7034)
The NAS is one of the largest and oldest wildlife conservation organizations in the U.S. A regional office in Anchorage, staffed by two professionals, coordinates society activities throughout Alaska and Hawaii. The society is working to help foster a better understanding and appreciation of our natural world. Special emphasis in this work is given to conserving Alaska and Hawaii's diverse wildlife populations and their habitats, and promoting sound management of our public lands. Membership: 2,550.
Regional Vice-President: DAVID R. CLINE

NORTHERN ALASKA ENVIRONMENTAL CENTER, 218 Driveway, Fairbanks 99701 (907, 452-5021)
Dedicated to the protection of the quality of the Alaskan environment through action and education. NAEC covers areas North of the Alaska Range and works closely with government agencies on land-use issues, such as the State Lands Disposal, implementation of the Alaska Lands Act, and the Arctic National Wildlife Refuge. The center is also concerned with wildlife, air and water quality, and many other issues. Founded: 1972. Membership: 600.
President: JANE ASPNES
Vice-President: MIKE PERRY
Secretary: DOUG FRUGE
Treasurer: WOODY BROOKS
Executive Director: REX BLAZER
Officer Manager: MARY ZALAR
Publication: *The Northern Line*
Editor: MARY ZALAR

SOUTHEAST ALASKA CONSERVATION COUNCIL, P.O. Box 021692, Juneau 99802 (907, 586-6942)
The SEACC is a coalition of thirteen grassroots and conservation groups. The SEACC is dedicated to ensuring maximum protection of Southeast Alaska's unique old growth forest; including wildlands, wildlife, water quality, fisheries, recreation opportunities, and the Southeast way of life. Membership: approximately 900. Founded: 1969.
President: LARRY EDWARDS, Box 6001, Sitka 99835 (747-8996)
Vice-President: REUBEN YOST, Box 85, Pelican 99832 (735-2252)
Secretary: JIM McGOWAN, 329 Harbor Dr., #201, Sitka 99835 (747-8650)
Treasurer: MARGARET CALVIN, Box 97, Sitka 99835 (747-3584)
Executive Director: BART KOEHLER
Publication: *RAVENCALL*
Editor: JULIE KOEHLER

TROUT UNLIMITED ALASKA (Rainbow Chapter)
Dedicated to the protection and enhancement of the cold water fishery resource.
President: ROBERT A. SHARRER, P.O. Box 453, Eagle River 99577 (907, 694-2737)

TRUSTEES FOR ALASKA, 725 Christensen Dr., Ste. 4, Anchorage 99501 (907, 276-4244)
Nonprofit, public interest environmental law firm working to ensure that Alaska's unique environmental values are not lost to future generations through irresponsible development or irrational public management. Primarily concerned with protection of Alaska's

environment and the wise management of Alaska's resources. Membershhip: approximately 750. Founded: 1974.
Executive Director: RANDALL WEINER
Staff Attorney: PATTI J. SAUNDERS
Project Attorney: LEONE HATCH
Board of Trustees: NANCY SIMEL, Chairperson; THOMAS DAHL; PAUL BINGHAM; EIVIN BRUDIE; ALISON HORTON; THOMAS ALBERT; VIRGINIA JOHNSON; JOHN McCONNAUGHY; ERIC MYERS; HEATHER NOBLE; BEVERLY THORNBURG; BILL PARKER; RON ZOBEL; COLLEEN BURGH; MARY CORE; DOUG ELLIOTT; WILLIAM HOLMAN; PETER MOORE; SCOTT HIGHLEYMAN; RANDY ROGERS

WILDLIFE SOCIETY ALASKA CHAPTER
President: CHARLES SCHWARTZ, 34828 Kalifornski Beach Rd., Suite B, Soldotna 99669 (907, 262-9368)
President-Elect: BUTCH YOUNG, 304 Lake St., Sitka 99835 (747-5449)
Secretary-Treasurer: CHRIS HUNDERTMARK, 34828 Kalifornski Beach Rd., Suite B, Soldotna 99669 (262-9368)

ARIZONA

GOVERNMENT AGENCIES

GOVERNOR: ROSE MOFFORD, Governor of Arizona, State House, Phoenix 85007 (602, 255-4331)

ARIZONA COOPERATIVE FISH AND WILDLIFE RESEARCH UNIT, U.S.D.I., 210 Biological Sciences East, University of Arizona, Tucson 85721 (602, 621-1959)
Leader: O. EUGENE MAUGHAN
Assistants: CHARLES D. ZIEBELL (621-1959); DR. NORMAN S. SMITH (621-1105)

ARIZONA GEOLOGICAL SURVEY, 845 North Park Ave., Suite 100, Tucson 85719 (602, 621-7906)
Develops, maintains, and disseminates information related to the geologic framework, geological hazards and limitations, and mineral and energy resources. Created: 1915, with redirected authority, 1977 and 1987.
Director and State Geologist: DR. LARRY D. FELLOWS (621-7906)
Publications: Fieldnotes; Circulars; Special Papers; Bulletins; Maps; Open-file Reports

DEPARTMENT OF ENVIRONMENTAL QUALITY, 2005 North Central Ave., Phoenix 85004 (602, 257-2300)
Director (Acting): RONALD L. MILLER, Ph.D. (257-6917)
Deputy Director: MICHAEL J. DOYLE (257-2301)
Assistant Directors: NORM WEISS, Office of Waste Programs (257-2318); WILLIAM SHAFER, Office of Water Quality (257-2305); WILLIAM WATSON (Acting), Office of Air Quality (257-2308); FRAN GONZALO, Office of Administration (257-2307)

GAME AND FISH DEPARTMENT, 2222 W. Greenway Rd., Phoenix 85023 (602, 942-3000)
Manages the wildlife resources of the state, including the enforcement of laws and Commission orders relating to wild animals, birds, and fish; also charged with enforcement of watercraft and off-road vehicle laws.
Commissioners: LARRY ADAMS, Chairman, Bullhead City; FRANCES W. WERNER, Tucson; THOMAS G. WOODS JR.,

Phoenix; PHILLIP W. ASHCROFT, Edgar; GORDON K. WHITING, Willcox
Director: TEMPLE A. REYNOLDS
Deputy Director: DUANE L. SHROUFE
Associate Director, Field Operations: LEE PERRY
Regional Coordinator: KELLY NEAL
Supervisors: MIKE YEAGER, Region I (Pinetop); TOM BRITT, Region II (Flagstaff); WES MARTIN, Region III (Kingman); DON WINGFIELD, Region IV (Yuma); TOM SPALDING, Region V (Tucson); DON TURNER, Region VI (Mesa)
Chief, Special Services Division: ROLAND H. SHARER
Branch Supervisors: JIM BURTON, Development and Maintenance; PETE EDGAR, Data Processing; RAY PERKINS, Engineering; RANDY KING, Finance and Accounting; WARNER POPPLETON, Funds Coordination; JOHN CARR, Planning and Evaluation; JOHN ALDER, Supply
Chief, Wildlife Management Division: BRUCE TAUBERT
Branch Supervisors: JIM DEVOS, Research; TICE SUPPLEE, Game; JOSEPH L. JANISCH, Fisheries; DON VANCE, Enforcement; TERRY JOHNSON, Nongame; DAVE DAUGHTRY, Audio-Visual
Chief, Information and Education Division: JAMES R. GRABAN
Education Coordinator: KERRY BALDWIN
Information Coordinator: WES KEYES
Publications Editor: Vacant

LAND DEPARTMENT, 1616 W. Adams St., Phoenix 85007 (602, 255-4621)
To administer trust lands of the state of Arizona and is the forestry and conservation office also. Established: 1915.
Commissioner, State Land: M.J. HASSELL
Deputy Commissioner, State Land: GLENDON E. COLLINS
Director, Contracts and Records Division: RICHARD B. OXFORD (255-4602)
Director, Administrative Services Division: LYNN LARSON (255-4634)
Director, Commercial Division: JIM SCHWARTZMANN (255-3666)
Director, Urban Planning Division: NICKI HANSEN (255-3671)
Director, Natural Resources Division: ROBERT E. YOUNT (255-4626)
Director, Resource Analysis Division: BILL BAYHAM (255-4061)
Director, Forestry Division: T. MIKE HART (255-4627)

OUTDOOR RECREATION COORDINATING COMMISSION, 800 W. Washington, Suite 415, Phoenix 85007 (602, 255-1996)
Established by executive order on October 1, 1964, and subsequently confirmed by legislature, to allocate funds of P.L. 88-578 (Land and Water Conservation Fund Act), the Arizona State Lake Improvement Fund, and Arizona Boating Law Enforcement and Safety Fund. Advises the Arizona State Parks Board on statewide planning and coordination for public outdoor recreation.
Chairman: JAMES COLLEY
Vice-Chairman: RICHARD HILEMAN
State Liaison Officer: WAYNE SHUYLER
Grants: LYLE A. BAIR
Planning: DON A. MYERS

STATE EXTENSION SERVICES
Director of Cooperative Extension Service: DR. ROY RAUSCHKOLB, Forbes Bldg., Rm. 301, University of Arizona, Tucson 85721 (602, 621-7209)
Extension Range Management Specialist: DR. GEORGE RUYLE, School of Renewable Natural Resources, College of Agriculture, Forbes Bldg., University of Arizona, Tucson 85721 (621-1384)
Extension Wildlife and Range Specialist: JOHN L. STAIR, School of

Renewable Natural Resources, College of Agriculture, Forbes Bldg., University of Arizona, Tucson 85721 (621-7269)

CITIZENS' GROUPS

ARIZONA WILDLIFE FEDERATION, 4330 N. 62nd St., #102, Scottsdale 85251 (602, 946-6160)
A representative statewide organization, affiliated with the National Wildlife Federation, primarily devoted to the wise use, conservation, aesthetic appreciation, and restoration of wildlife and other natural resources. Organized: 1923.
President: JACK SIMON, 6401 S. 44th St., Phoenix 85040 (835-0055)
Affiliate Representative: ACE PETERSON, Rt. #11, Box 50, Flagstaff 86004 (526-0368)
Alternate: RICK ERMAN, 3435 E. Windrose Dr., Phoeniz 85032 (971-2388)
Publication: Arizona Wildlife News
Editor: TONI ERMAN, 3453 E. Windrose Dr., Phoenix 85032

ARIZONA ASSOCIATION OF CONSERVATION DISTRICTS
President: PHILLIP (McD) HARTMAN, Rt. 2, Box 815, Maricopa 85239
Vice-President: RONALD (Corky) NARRAMORE, P.O. Box 9, Palo Verde 85343
Secretary-Treasurer: LUFKIN HUNT, Box 453, Pine 85544

ARIZONA BASS CHAPTER FEDERATION
An organization of Bassmaster chapters, affiliated with the Bass Anglers Sportsman Society, to fight pollution, assist state and national conservation agencies in their efforts and teach the young people of our country good conservation practices. Dedicated to the realistic conservation of our water resources.
President: RIC CRATTE, 10616 N. 60th Pl., Scottsdale 85254 (602, 998-9630)

ARIZONA CONSERVATION COUNCIL, Box 11312, Phoenix 85061
A council of statewide citizens' organizations representing a broad spectrum of general and special conservation interests, including outdoor recreation, wildlife management, scenic preservation, roadside development, wilderness, ecology, and planning. Organized: 1960.
Chairman: JOE ARNOLD, 1220 W., Higgland 85013
Vice-Chairman: JACK DOYLE, 4334 W. Griswold Rd., Glendale 85302
Secretary: DALE L. SLOCUM, 1213 E., Higgland 85014
Treasurer: L.V. YATES, 4750 N. 16th St., Higgland 85016 (602, 264-7052)

ARIZONA STATE PARKS, 800 W. Washington, Suite 415, Phoenix 85007 (602, 255-4174)
Programs include the: State Historic Preservation Office, which deals with the National and State Registers of Historic Places; Natural Areas Advisory Council, an advisory body to the Board on designation of natural areas to the Natural Areas Register; Hiking and Equestrian Trails Committee, an advisory body to the Board for the establishment of trails; Bicycle Task Force, an advisory body to the Board for the establishment of bicycle trails and education; Archaeology Advisory Commission, an advisory body to the Board for the protection of archaeological sites. Established: 1957.
Chairman: DUANE MILLER
Vice-Chairman: JONI BOSH
Secretary: WILLIAM G. ROE

Executive Director: KENNETH E. TRAVOUS
Deputy Director: COURTLAND NELSON

COMMISSION ON THE ARIZONA ENVIRONMENT, 1645 West
Jefferson, Suite 416, Phoenix 85007 (602, 255-2102)
An 11-member commission, representing environmental and conservation groups, the private sector, government, agencies, the educational community and other organizations. The commission is appointed by the Governor and confirmed by the Senate. An advisory council will advise the commission on natural resource related issues. The commission and council are advisory to the legislature and other governmental agencies on environmental and natural resources issues. Organized: 1965.
Commission Members: SUE LOFGREN (967-4156); ROBERT O. BUFFINGTON (749-3967); SCOTT R. BURGE (496-0025); DAN CAMPBELL (622-3861); MARYBETH CARLILE, Chair (881-3939); WILLIAM M. FISHER (451-0958); ALVIN W. GERHARDT (425-2714); DR. RAYMOND KARY (945-0009); MAXINE LAKIN (266-4501); RAYMOND D. REBERT (368-6080); ROBER FERLAND (229-5609)
Executive Director: ALICIA BRISTOW (255-2102)
Publications: Quarterly Reports; *Membership Directory; Directory of Arizona Environmental and Conservation Organizations; Environmental Fact Sheets*

WILDLIFE SOCIETY ARIZONA CHAPTER
President: NORRIS DODD, P.O. Box 2526, Pinetop 85935 (602, 367-0684)
Vice-President: SHERRY BARRETT, 1115 East Silver, Tuscon 85719 (629-5061)
Recording Secretary: ROSEMARY MAZAIKA, 325 Biology Science East, SRNR, University of Arizona, Tuscon 85721 (621-5239)
Secretary/Treasurer: HENRY J. MESSING, 17435 North 7th St., #2138, Phoenix 85022 (870-6774)

ARKANSAS

GOVERNMENT AGENCIES

GOVERNOR: BILL CLINTON, Governor of Arkansas, State Capitol, Little Rock 72201 (501, 371-2345)

DEPARTMENT OF PARKS AND TOURISM, One Capitol Mall,
Little Rock 72201 (501, 682-1511)
Develop, maintain, and operate 45 state parks; advertise and promote all of the state's recreation and travel potentials; provide accurate information on the state's scenic, recreational, cultural and historic attractions, and trails; manage the state's archives; provide interpretive services; provide technical assistance and grants to museums throughout the state; administration of the Land and Water Conservation Fund; and preparation of comprehensive outdoor recreation and implementation of the Statewide Comprehensive Outdoor Recreation Plan.
Director: JO LUCK WILSON (682-2535)
Director, Parks Division: RICHARD W. DAVIES (682-7743)
Director, Tourism Division: JOE DAVID RICE (682-1088)
Director, Administrative Services: R.L. CARGILE (682-2039)
Director, History Division: DR. JOHN L. FERGUSON (682-6900)
Assistant Director, Tourism Division: JUDY STOUGH (682-1120)
Manager, Historial Resources and Museum Services Section: BARBARA HEFFINGTON (682-6907)
State Trails Coordinator: KEN EASTIN (682-6947)
Outdoor Recreation Grants: BRYAN KELLAR (682-1301)

DEPARTMENT OF POLLUTION CONTROL AND ECOLOGY,
8001 National Dr., P.O. Box 9583, Little Rock 72219 (501, 562-7444); Construction Grants Division (562-8910)
To prevent, abate, and control all types of pollution and maintain the state's natural environment. Created in 1949 as the Water Pollution Control Commission; in 1965 became Pollution Control Commission when air division was added; present title Commission on Pollution Control and Ecology after solid waste and environmental preservation were included in 1971. Authority for hazardous waste regulation added in 1979.
Commissioners: JERRY HILL ; BRYCE MOBLEY, Chairman; JOE PASCALE, Vice-Chairman; STEVE WILSON; NORMAN WILLIAMS; EUGENE FARRELL; WILLIAM WRIGHT; JAKE LOONEY; EDWIN E. WADDELL; RANDY YOUNG; RICHARD MASON
Director: PAUL N. MEANS, JR.
Deputy Directors: RANDALL MATHIS; WILSON TOLEFREE
Chiefs: VINCE BLUBAUGH, Water Division; J.B. JONES, Air Division; MARK WITHERSPOON, Solid Waste Division; JOHN GIESE, Biologist; RICHARD THOMPSON, Chemist, Water; JOHN A. MITCHELL, Chemist, Air
Chief, Administration and Communications Division: ED MORRIS, Ph.D.
Chiefs: FLOYD DURHAM, Mining Division; MIKE BATES, Hazardous Waste Division; DOUG SZENHER, Coordinator, Communications; RICHARD CASSAT, Technical Services; LARRY WILSON, Construction Grants; JIM SHELL, Environmental Field Services; CHERYL TERAI, Counsel, Legal

FORESTRY COMMISSION, P.O. Box 4523, Asher Sta., 3821
W. Roosevelt Rd., Little Rock 72214 (501, 664-2531)
To prevent and suppress forest fires; control forest insects and diseases; grow and distribute forest planting stock; and collect and disseminate information concerning growth, utilization, and renewal of forests.
Commission Chairman: JAMES BIBLER
State Forester: EDWIN E. WADDELL
Deputy State Forester: BOBBY D. BUZBEE
Fire Control: ROBERT J. MCFARLAND
Forest Management: J. GARNER BARNUM
Fiscal Department: BOB C. CHAPMAN
Information and Education: JAMES E. GRANT, JR.
Special Projects: RANDALL L. LEISTER
Baucum Nursery: FLOYD HICKAM (945-3345)
Bluff City Nursery: J.L. FRANKLIN (685-2665)

GAME AND FISH COMMISSION, #2 Natural Resources Dr.,
Little Rock 72205 (501, 223-6300)
Purpose is the control, management, restoration, conservation, and regulation of wildlife, and wildlife resources of the State, including hatcheries, sanctuaries, refuges, reservations, and all property now owned, or used for said purposes. Established: 1915.
Commission Members: CHARLES J. AMLANER, JR. (575-3251); MICHAEL CORNWELL (495-2525); HAROLD IVES (673-1541); FRANK LYON, JR., Chairman (569-2747); TOMMY L. SPROLES (664-0505); BILL BREWER (239-8511); MAURICE LEWIS (234-4116)
Director: STEVE N. WILSON
Division Chiefs: BILLY WHITE, Federation Coordination and Support Services (223-6355); DAVID HERMAN, Enforcement (223-6384); RAY SEBREN, Fiscal (223-6341); ALLEN CARTER, Fisheries (223-6371); STEVE COLE, Wildlife Management (223-6359); STEPHEN R. WILSON, Information and Education (223-6403); P. DOUGLAS MAYS, Legal (223-6327); T.J. ROWELL, Real Estate (223-6319); RON BYRNS, Personnel (223-6317)

Publications: *Arkansas Game and Fish Magazine; Arkansas Outdoors Newsletter*
Editors: GREGG PATTERSON (223-6351); JIM LOW (223-6351)

NATURAL AND SCENIC RIVERS COMMISSION

To prepare surveys and recommendations to the governor and the legislature for the preservation of selected rivers in the state of Arkansas possessing outstanding natural, scenic, educational, geological, recreational, historic, fish and wildlife, scientific, and cultural values of great present and future benefit to the people. Authorized: 1979.
Chairman: ALICE ANDREWS, 3817 Compton, Little Rock 72205
Vice-Chairman: ROBIN SHADDOX, 2512 West Second Pl., Russellville 72801
Director: DONNA H. ETCHIESON, The Heritage Center, Suite 200, 225 E. Markham, Little Rock 72201 (501, 371-8134)

NATURAL HERITAGE COMMISSION, Suite 200, The Heritage Center, 225 E. Markham, Little Rock 72201 (501, 371-1706)

Responsible for system of natural areas; acquires and holds both lands and interests in land; maintains a registry of natural areas in other ownerships; and defends natural areas from adverse influences. Established: 1973.
Commission Members: JANE LUCKY, Chairman, McGehee; RALPH WILSON, Vice-Chairman, Osceola; ELLEN SHIPLEY, Secretary, Fayetteville; ELLEN NEAVILLE, Rogers; TOM CLARK, Conway; EDDIE HOLT, Crossett; ROBERT A. PIERCE, Little Rock; GODFREY WHITE, Osceola ; RAYMOND ABRAMSON, Clarendon
Executive Director: HAROLD K. GRIMMETT
Deputy Director: MINA MARSH
Coordinator, Environmental Applications: WILLIAM M. SHEPHERD
Coordinator, Research: KEN SMITH
Coordinator, Stewardship: BILL PELL
Publication: *Annual Report*

STATE EXTENSION SERVICES

Director of Extension Service: TED L. JONES, P.O. Box 391, Little Rock 72203 (501, 373-2575)
Extension Fisheries Specialist: D. LeROY GRAY, P.O. Box 391, Little Rock 72203 (373-2637)
Extension Wildlife Specialist: ROBERT A. PIERCE, P.O. Box 391, Little Rock 72203 (373-2636)
Extension Foresters: JAMES C. GEISLER, P.O. Box 391, Little Rock 72203 (373-2638); R. LARRY WILLETT, P.O. Box 3468, Monticello 71655 (460-1049); FRANK A. ROTH II, Rte. 3, Box 258, Hope 71801 (777-9702); R.S. BEASLEY, Head, Department of Forestry, University of Arkansas-Monticello, P.O. Box 3468, Monticello 71665 (460-1049)
Extension Fisheries Specialist: NATHAN M. STONE, Box 82, Pine Bluff 71601 (541-6614)
Extension Fisheries Specialist: LARRY W. DORMAN, P.O. Drawer D, Lonoke 72086 (676-3124)

STATE PLANT BOARD, 1 Natural Resources Dr., P.O. Box 1069, Little Rock 72203 (501, 225-1598)

Chairman: JOHN E. TULL
Director: GERALD KING

CITIZENS' GROUPS

ARKANSAS WILDLIFE FEDERATION, 7509 Cantrell Rd., #226, Little Rock 72207 (501, 663-7255)
A representative statewide organization, affiliated with the National Wildlife Federation, primarily devoted to the wise use, conservation, aesthetic appreciation, and restoration of wildlife and other natural resources. Organized: 1936.
President: PRICE HOLMES, P.O. Box 1300, Newport 72112
Executive Director: TERRY HORTON
Affiliate Representative: RALPH GILLHAM, 915 N Front Dr., Dardanelle 72834 (501, 229-3510)
Alternate: TERRY HORTON (501, 653-2492)
Publication: *Arkansas Out-of-Doors*
Editor: TERRY HORTON

ARKANSAS ASSOCIATION OF CONSERVATION DISTRICTS

President: MARY RATCLIFFE, P.O. Box 146, Sweet Home 72164
Vice-President: C.H. BROWN, Rt. 6, Box 64, Harrison 72601
Secretary: STERLIN HURLEY, P.O. Box 219, Clarksville 72830
Treasurer: HAROLD JONES, Rt. 1, Box 754, Lauaca 72941

ARKANSAS BASS CHAPTER FEDERATION

An organization of Bassmaster Chapters, affiliated with the Bass Anglers Sportsman Society, to fight pollution, assist state and national conservation agencies in their efforts and to teach the young people of our country good conservation practices. Dedicated to the realistic conservation of our water resources.
President: NORMAN STEPHENS, 1609 W. Gum, Rogers 72756 (636-9308)

OZARK SOCIETY, THE, P.O. Box 2914, Little Rock 72203

To promote the knowledge and enjoyment of the scenic and scientific resources (particularly free-flowing streams, wilderness areas, and unique natural areas) of the Ozark-Ouachita mountain region, and to help protect those resources for present and future generations. Members: 1,000. Established: 1962.
President: STEWART NOLAND
Publications: *The Pack and Paddle; Journal*

WILDLIFE SOCIETY ARKANSAS CHAPTER

President: JOE CLARK, Arkansas Game and Fish Commission, #2 Natural Resources Dr., Little Rock 72205 (501, 223-6359)
President-Elect: DANNY ADAMS, P.O. Box 8038, Arkadelphia 71923 (501, 246-5622)
Secretary-Treasurer: DOYLE SHOOK, AR Fish and Game Commission, #2 Natural Resources Dr., Little Rock 72205

CALIFORNIA

GOVERNMENT AGENCIES

GOVERNOR: GEORGE DEUKMEJIAN, Governor of California, State Capitol, Sacramento 95814 (916, 445-2841)

CALIFORNIA COOPERATIVE FISHERY RESEARCH UNIT, U.S.D.I., Fisheries Department, Humboldt State University, Arcata 95521 (707, 826-3268)

Leader: DR. ROGER A. BARNHART
Assistant Leader: DR. THOMAS J. HASSLER

DEPARTMENT OF EDUCATION, CONSERVATION EDUCATION SERVICE, 721 Capitol Mall, P.O. Box 944272, Sacramento 94244-2720

Created by the legislature in 1970 to provide statewide leadership and program services to local educational agencies and community groups. Consultant services, curricular materials, teacher workshops, community education programs, and program grants are offered.

Environmental-Energy Education Unit Manager: THOMAS P. SACHSE (916, 324-7187)

DEPARTMENT OF FOOD AND AGRICULTURE, 1220 N St., Sacramento 95814 (916, 445-9280)
To assure public health, safety and welfare, protects agriculture by administering, directing and enforcing the state's agricultural rules and regulations.
Director: JACK C. PARNELL (445-7126)
Chief Deputy Director: DANIEL D. HALEY (445-7126)
Deputy Directors: ROBERT FOX (445-8226); R. WILLIAM TRACY
Associate Director: REX MaGEE (323-6315)
Administrative Adviser: HERBERT L. COHEN (445-6429)
Regional Coordinator, Sacramento: RICHARD E. DEVOL (445-7944)
Legislative Coordinator: LUCINDA CHIPPONERI (322-4834)
Communications Officer: JANET WESSELL (445-8614)
Assistant Director, Plant Industry: ISI SIDDIQUI (445-5537)
Assistant Director, Inspection Services: EZIO DELFINO (455-4106)
Assistant Director, Animal Industry: PATTON L. SMITH, DVM (445-6506)
Assistant Director, Marketing Services: JED A. ADAMS (445-2491)
Assistant Director, Measurement Standards: DARRELL GUENSLER (366-5119)
Assistant Director, Fairs and Expositions: ESTER ARMSTRONG (924-2226)
Assistant Director, Pest Management: REX MaGEE (322-6315)

ENVIRONMENTAL AFFAIRS AGENCY, THE, P.O. Box 2815, Sacramento 95812 (916, 322-5840)
The Secretary of Environmental Affairs, a member of the Governor's Cabinet, serves as the Governor's principal advisor on environmental protection issues and oversees the activities of the Air Resources Board, Water Resources Control Board, and Waste Management Board. The Secretary is also Chairperson of the Air Resources Board.
Secretary, Environmental Affairs: JANANNE SHARPLESS (322-5840)
Chairwoman, Air Resources Board: JANANNE SHARPLESS
Deputy Secretary: JOHN DOYLE (322-5847)
Deputy Secretary: JOHN HUNTER (322-5844)
Assistant to the Secretary: CHARLES SHULOCK (324-8124)
Chief, Offshore Development: MICHAEL KAHOE (324-3706)
Senior Attorney and Administrator, Hazardous Substances Cleanup Arbitration Panel: KIRK OLIVER (324-6881)
Chief, Office of Hazardous Materials Data Management: STEPHEN HANNA (324-9924)

California Air Resources Board, P.O. Box 2815, Sacramento 95812 (916, 322-2990)
California's state agency responsible for the adoption and enforcement of the state's ambient air quality standards, and rules and regulations for the control of vehicular air pollution and toxic air contaminants throughout the state. Oversees efforts of 41 air pollution control districts that regulate emissions from industrial facilities. Conducts studies of the causes of air pollution and evaluates its effort upon human, plant, and animal life. Nine members comprise the board. Established: 1968.
Secretary, Environmental Affairs: JANANNE SHARPLESS (322-5840)
Chairwoman, Air Resources Board: JANANNE SHARPLESS
Executive Officer: JAMES D. BOYD (445-4383)
Chief Deputy Executive Officer: WILLIAM W. STYLE (322-2890)
Deputy Executive Officer: THOMAS CACKETTE (322-2892)
Assistant Executive Officer: MICHAEL H. SCHEIBLE (445-3335)

General Counsel, Office of Legal Affairs: DAVID NAWI (322-2884)
Chief, Office of External Affairs: WILLIAM C. LOCKETT (323-8711)
Chief, Legislative Office: SHEILA D. MARSEE (322-2896)
Public Information Officer: BILL SESSA (322-2990)
Chief, Administrative Services Division: WAYNE E. RODGERS (322-8198)
Chief, Monitoring and Laboratory Division: WILLIAM V. LOSCUTOFF (445-3742)
Chief, Compliance Division: JAMES J. MORGESTER (322-6022)
Chief, Mobile Source Division: K.D. DRACHAND (818, 575-6820)
Chief, Research Division: JOHN R. HOLMES, Ph.D. (445-0753)
Chief, Stationary Source Division: PETER D. VENTURINI (445-0650)
Chief, Technical Support Division: TERRY W. McGUIRE (322-5350)
Publication: *AiReview* magazine
Editor: WILLIAM L. SESSA, Communications Director

California Waste Management Board, 1020 9th St., Suite 300, Sacramento 95814 (916, 322-3330)
The CWMB was founded in 1972, and comprises nine public members; seven appointed by the Governor, two by the Legislature. The board is responsible for solid waste management and resource recovery.
Chairman: JOHN E. GALLAGHER
Vice-Chairman: JOHN P. MOSCONE
Board Members: SAM ARAKALIAN; PHILLIP A. BEAUTROW; GINGER BREMBERG: LES BROWN; JAMES W. CALLOWAY; E.L. (Skeet) VARNER
Chief Executive Officer: GEORGE T. EOWAN
Chief Deputy Executive Officer: HERBERT IWAHIRO
Deputy Executive Officer: ALAN A. OLDALL
Legislative Director: JO-ELLEN JACKSON
General Counsel: ROBERT F. CONHEIM
Publication: *California Waste Management* Bulletin
Editor: CHRIS PECK, Publication Information Officer

Water Resources Control Board, 901 P St., P.O. Box 100, Sacramento 95801-0100 (916, 445-3993)
To protect water quality and allocate water rights. These objectives are achieved through two action programs: water quality and water rights.
Chairman: W. DON MAUGHAN
Vice-Chairwoman: DARLENE E. RUIZ
Members: EDWIN H. FINSTER; ELISEO M. SAMANIEGO; DANNY WALSH
Executive Director: JAMES W. BAETGE
Chief Deputy Executive Director: JAMES R. BENNETT
Regional Board Executive Officers: BEN KOR, North Coast Region (707, 576-2220); STEVEN RITCHIE, San Francisco Bay Region (415, 464-1255); BILL LEONARD, Central Coast Region (805, 549-3147); ROBERT P. GHIRELLI, Los Angeles Region (213, 620-4460); WILLIAM CROOKS, Central Valley Region (916, 361-5600); OSSIAN BUTTERFIELD, Lahontan Region (916, 544-3481); ARTHUR SWAJIAN, Colorado River Basin Region (619, 346-7491); GERALD THIBEAULT, Santa Ana Region (714, 782-4130)

OFFICE OF PLANNING AND RESEARCH, 1400 Tenth St., Sacramento 95814 (916, 322-2318)
Primary areas of concentration are the development of environmental and related land use goals and policies; evaluation of state plans and programs, and administration of federal grants-in-aid to ensure consistency with statewide environmental goals and policies. Established: 1970.

Director: HUSTON T. CARLYLE, JR.
Deputy Director: JOHN OHANIAN

RESOURCES AGENCY, THE, 1416 Ninth St., Rm. 1311,
   Sacramento 95814 (916, 445-5656)
Responsible for ensuring an adequate and properly balanced
management of government functions related to California's natu-
ral environment.
Secretary, Resources: GORDON K. VAN VLECK
Undersecretary, Resources: TERRENCE M. EAGAN
Assistant Secretary, Administration/Finance: HAROLD F. WARAAS
Assistant to the Secretary: JO ANNE J. JACKSON
Assistant Secretary, Legal Affairs: CHRISTINE A. SPROUL
Deputy Secretary, Legislation: MARSHA M. JOHNSON
Assistant Secretary, Public Information: FRANK HUBBARD
Assistant Secretary, Federal/State Projects Coordinator: DR. GOR-
   DON F. SNOW
Deputy Secretary, Operations: MICHAEL D. McCOLLUM

California Coastal Commission, 631 Howard St., San
   Francisco 94105 (415, 543-8555)
A coastal management agency which carries out mandated policies
on coastal conservation and development through regulation and
planning programs. These policies deal with public access to the
coast, coastal recreation, the California marine environment,
coastal land resources, and coastal development of various types,
including power plant and other energy installation.
Executive Director: PETER DOUGLAS
Chief, Deputy Director: JAMES BURNS
Deputy Director for Coastal and Ocean Resources: TOM CRAN-
   DALL
Chief Staff Counsel: RALPH FAUST
Assistant Deputy Director for Energy and Ocean Resources: SUSAN
   HANSCH
Assistant Deputy Director for Land Use: STEVE SCHOLL
Legislative Liaison, Sacramento: BILL ALLAYAUD, 921-11th St.,
   Rm. 1200 (445-6067)

California Conservation Corps, 1530 Capitol Ave., Sacramento
   95814 (916, 445-0307)
The CCC was created in 1976 with a dual mission: the employment
and development of the state's youth, and the protection and
enhancement of California's natural resources. Some 20 million
hours of public service conservation work and emergency assistance have been provided by the corps in its first decade. More
than 2,000 young men and women will serve in the CCC during
1988.
Director: BUD SHEBLE
Chief Deputy Director: LISA LOUIE
Deputy Director: ANN MALCOLM
Regional Deputy Directors: RON PERRY; DAVID BOONE; PAUL
   CARRILLO
Administrative Officer: DICK BERNHEIMER

California Water Commission, 1416 Ninth St., Rm. 1104-4,
   Sacramento 95814 (445-8750)
Serves as a policy advisory body to the Director of Water Resources
on all California water resources matters. The nine-member citizen
commission provides a water resources forum for the people of the
state, acts as liaison between the legislative and executive branches
of state government, and coordinates federal, state, and local water
resources efforts. Created: 1913
Executive Officer and Chief Engineer: ORVILLE L. ABBOTT

Colorado River Board of California, 107 S. Broadway, Rm.
   8103, Los Angeles 90012 (213, 620-4480)
Created by the legislature in 1937 to protect California's rights and
interests in the water of the Colorado River System.
Executive Director: DENNIS B. UNDERWOOD

Department of Boating and Waterways, 1629 S St.,
   Sacramento 95814 (916, 445-6281)
Makes loans to public agencies and small businesses for small craft
harbor development and grants to public agencies for boat
launching facilities and floating restrooms, licenses yacht and ship
brokers and for-hire vessel operators, conducts a program of
boating safety and regulation, and grants funds to local entities for
boating law enforcement activities. Participates with the Corps of
Engineers and local agencies in the construction of beach erosion
control projects and assists local jurisdictions in obtaining the
greatest benefits available from federal beach erosion programs
and conducts a water hyacinth control program in the Sacramento-
San Joaquin Delta.
Director: WILLIAM H. IVERS
Assistant Director: BILL SATOW (445-9657)

Department of Conservation, 1416 Ninth St., Rm. 1320,
   Sacramento 95814 (916, 322-7683)
Helps to protect, conserve, and encourage informed development
of California's soil, mineral, geothermal, and petroleum resources,
and to promote the conservation of agricultural and open space
lands. The department also administers the California Beverage
Container Recycling and Litter Reduction Act. The State Mining and
Geology Board provides input for management and policy direction
of mineral resources, and the Beverage Container Recycling
Advisory Committee provides advice to the Director on all matters
relating to beverage container recycling.
Director: RANDALL M. WARD
Deputy Director: HOWARD A. SARASOHN
Chief, Division of Administration: Vacant
Assistant to the Director: SHIRLEY MITCHELL
State Oil & Gas Supervisor, Division of Oil & Gas: M.G. MEFFERD
State Geologist, Division of Mines and Geology: Vacant
Special Representative, State Mining and Geology Board: DEBO-
   RAH L. HERRMANN

Department of Fish and Game, 1416 Ninth St., Sacramento
   95814 (916, 445-3531)
Responsible for the protection and management of fish and wildlife
and threatened native plants in California. Enforces the laws
pertaining to fish and game and threatened native plants enacted
by the legislature and the regulations of the Fish and Game
Commission.
Director: PETER F. BONTADELLI (445-5095)
Chief Deputy Director: ROBERT C. FLETCHER (445-5250)
Deputy Director: PAUL T. JENSEN (445-5095)
Deputy Director: Vacant (445-5250)
Legislative Coordinator: VERN GOEHRING (445-9880)
Assistant Director, Administration: EDWARD O. WILLIS (445-
   4840)
Chief, Wildlife Management: E.G. HUNT (445-5561)
Chief, Wildlife Protection: R. DeWAYNE JOHNSTON (324-7243)
Chief, Marine Resources: AL PETROVICH (445-8386)
Chief, Environmental Services: DON LOLLOCK (445-1383)
Chief, Inland Fisheries: ROBERT RAWSTRON (445-8231)

Department of Forestry and Fire Protection, 1416 Ninth St.,
   P.O. Box 944246, Sacramento 94244-2460 (916, 445-
   9920)
The CDF is responsible for the fire protection, fire prevention,

maintenance and enhancement of the state's forest, range, and brushland resources, including enforcement of the Z'berg-Nejedly Forest Practice Act and other related forest and fire laws, forest pest control, contract fire protection, associated emergency services, and assistance in civil disasters and other non-fire emergencies. The CDF is also responsible for the administration of forest practice rules, forest advisory services and underwriting forest and fire research programs.

Director: JERRY PARTAIN
Chief Deputy Director: RICHARD J. ERNEST
Deputy for Fire Protection: RICHARD J. DAY
Deputy for Management Services: JOSEPH KEATING
Deputy for Resources: KENNETH L. DELFINO
Assistant Director for Public Affairs and Legislation: MARYN PITT
Assistant Director for Special Projects: ROY GRIMES
Chief, Support Services: SHELLEY MATEO
Chief, Personnel Services: LINDA DIANE JONES
Chief, Management and Systems Planning: BILL HOOKANO
Chief, Fire Control Operations: BILL TEIE

Department of Parks and Recreation, 1416 Ninth St., P.O. Box 942896, Sacramento 94296-0001 (916, 445-2358)
Responsible for the acquisition, preservation, development, interpretation, and operation of the state park system; also responsible for the administration of grants for recreation to local government and for development of the California Outdoor Recreation Resources Plan.
Director: HENRY R. AGONIA (324-9067)
Chief Deputy Director: LES McCARGO (445-0290)
Chief Deputy for Operations: JACK HARRISON (323-1171)
Deputy Director, Off Highway Motor Vehicle Recreation: LEON CHAUVET (445-0305)
Deputy Director of Administration: FRANK TORKELSON (445-8560)
Assistant Deputy Director, External Affairs: JACKIE DEUSCHLE (445-4624)
Resource Protection Division, Chief: RICHARD G. RAYBURN (445-7067)
Acquisition Division, Chief: KENNETH MITCHELL (445-9210)
Development Division, Chief: ROBERT D. CATES (445-4794)
Historic Preservation Office: KATHRYN GUALTIERE (445-8006)
Regional Directors: CARL CHAVEZ, Northern Region, Santa Rosa; RICHARD E. FELTY, Central Coast Region, Monterey; WILLIAM MONAGHAN, Inland Region; KEN JONES, Southern Region, San Diego; DEBORAH WELDON, San Simeon Region, San Simeon
Operations Headquarters Office: RON RAWLINGS (445-7090)
Office of Interpretive Services: KEITH DEMETRAK (445-9672)
Planning and Local Assistance, Chief: ROSS HENRY (445-0835)
Office of Off Highway Motor Vehicle Recreation: GERALD JOHNSON (322-9619)
Legislative Office: MARILYN OLSON (322-7396)
Legal Office: F.C. (Casey) BUCHTER (445-3653)
Office of Economic and Fiscal Affairs: ROBERTO VELLANOWETH (445-9060)

Department of Water Resources, 1416 Ninth St., P.O. Box 942836, Sacramento 94236-0001 (916, 445-9248)
The basic goal is to ensure that California's needs for water supplies, water-related recreation, fish and wildlife, hydroelectric power, prevention of damage and loss of life from floods and dam failures, and water-related environmental enhancement are met; and to ensure that the manner in which these needs are fulfilled is consistent with public desires and attitudes concerning environmental and social considerations.
Director: DAVID N. KENNEDY (445-6582)

Deputy Directors: JOHN P. CAFFREY; ROBERT G. POTTER; LAWRENCE A. MULLNIX
Assistant Director for Legislation: SALLE S. JANTZ
Office of Public Information and Communications, Chief: ANITA GARCIA-FANTE (445-4501)
District Chiefs: JAMES U. McDANIEL; Central District, Sacramento (445-5631); WAYNE S. GENTRY, Northern District, Red Bluff (916, 446-2248); LOUIS A. BECK, San Joaquin District, Fresno (209, 445-5222); CARLOS MADRID, Southern District, Los Angeles (213, 620-4108)
Division of Operations and Maintenance, Chief (Acting): JOHN R. EATON (445-2073)
Division of Design and Construction, Chief: JOHN H. LAWDER (445-6100)
Division of Energy, Chief: VIJU PATEL (445-6687)
Division of Planning, Chief: ARTHUR C. GOOCH (445-9610)
Division of Flood Management, Chief: G. DONALD MEIXNER (324-4784)
Division of Safety of Dams, Chief: VERNON H. PERSSON (445-7606)
Office of Water Conservation, Chief: (Acting) JONAS MINTON (322-9989)
Division of Land and Right of Way, Chief: DONALD E. OWEN (445-4284)

Energy Resources Conservation and Development Commission, 1516 Ninth St., Sacramento 95814 (916, 324-3298)
Established in 1975 to ensure continuation of a reliable supply of energy for California at a level consistent with the state's needs.
Chairman: CHARLES R. IMBRECHT
Executive Director: STEPHEN M. RHOADS
Deputy Executive Director: KENT G. SMITH
Vice-Chair: BARBARA CROWLEY
Commissioners: ROBERT MUSSETTER; WARREN D. NOTEWARE; RICHARD A. BILAS
Division Chiefs: DON WALLACE, Administrative Services; E. ROSS DETER, Energy Forecasting and Planning Division; MICHAEL S. SLOSS, Energy Efficiency and Local Assistance Division; DAVID L. MODISETTE, Energy Technology Division; ROBERT L. THERKELSEN, Energy Facilities Siting and Environmental Protection Division

Fish and Game Commission, 1416 Ninth St., P.O. Box 944209, Sacramento 94244-2090 (916, 445-5708)
Adopts fish, game, and plant regulations as authorized by the Fish and Game Code and sets policies for the Department of Fish and Game. Founded: 1870.
Commissioners: ALBERT C. TAUCHER, President, Long Beach; ROBERT A. BRYANT, Vice-President, Yuba City; JOHN A. MURDY III, Newport Beach; E.M. McCRACKEN, JR., Carmichael; BENJAMIN F. BIAGGINI, San Francisco
Executive Secretary: HAROLD C. CRIBBS

San Francisco Bay Conservation and Development Commission, 30 Van Ness Ave., Rm. 2011, San Francisco 94102 (415, 557-3686)
To implement a planning and regulatory program designed to conserve and use beneficially the environmental, economic, social, and aesthetic values of San Francisco Bay through carefully considered and democratically determined policies. Composed of 27 commissioners, representing the public and state, federal, and local governmental agencies. Created: 1965.
Chairman: ROBERT TUFTS
Executive Director: ALAN PENDLETON
Assistant Executive Director: RUSSELL ABRAMSON

Deputy Director: WILLIAM TRAVIS
Chief Planner: JEFFREY BLANCHFIELD
Chief of Permits: NANCY WAKEMAN

State Coastal Conservancy, 1330 Broadway, Suite 1100, Oakland 94612 (415, 464-1015)
A state agency using planning, land use conflict resolution, acquisition, and development techniques in the restoration, enhancement, and preservation of coastal resources. Program areas include agricultural preservation, lot consolidation, urban waterfront restoration, coastal resource enhancement, the reservation of significant resource sites, provision of public access, and assistance to nonprofit organizations.
Executive Officer: PETER GRENELL
Assistant Executive Officer: RONALD KUKULKA
Publications: *State Coastal Conservancy-Annual Report; Waterfront Age*
Editor: RASA GUSTAITIS

State Reclamation Board, 1416 Ninth St., Rm. 455-6, Sacramento 95814 (916, 445-9454)
Agency responsible for furnishing required local cooperation in federal flood control works in the central valley of California. The board also has significant authorities in controlling development in floodways and along streams within the central valley and in controlling local reclamation works. Created: 1911.
General Manager: RAYMOND E. BARSCH

Wildlife Conservation Board, 1416 Ninth St., Sacramento 95814 (916, 445-8448)
Acquires and develops lands and waters for wildlife conservation and related recreational purposes for the State Department of Fish and Game and in cooperation with local agencies. Founded: 1947.
Executive Officer: W. JOHN SCHMIDT
Assistant Executive Officer: ALVIN G. RUTSCH
Chief, Land Acquisition: JAMES V. SARRO
Board Members: Fish and Game Commission President, ALBERT C. TAUCHER; JESSE HUFF, Director, Department of Finance; PETER BONTADELLI, Director, Department of Fish and Game

SEA GRANT COLLEGE PROGRAM
Director: DR. JAMES J. SULLIVAN, California Sea Grant College Program, University of California San Diego, La Jolla 92093 (619, 534-4444)
Director, USC Sea Grant Program: DR. ROBERT FRIEDHEIM, Institute for Marine and Coastal Studies, University of Southern California, University Park, Los Angeles 90007 (213, 743-6840)
Coordinator, UC Marine Advisory Program: RONALD O. SKOOG, Cooperative Extension, University of California, Davis 95616 (916, 752-6191)
Director, USC Marine Advisory Program: JIM FAWCETT, Institute for Marine and Coastal Studies, University of Southern California, University Park, Los Angeles 90007 (213, 741-6068)

STATE EXTENSION SERVICES
Vice-President: KENNETH R. FARRELL, Agriculture and Natural Resources, Director, Cooperative Extension and Agricultural Experiment Station, University of California, 300 Lakeside Dr., 6th Fl., Oakland 94612-3560 (415, 987-0060)
Assistant Vice-President: LOWELL N. LEWIS, ANR Programs, Associate Director, Cooperative Extension and Agricultural Experiment Station, University of California, 300 Lakeside Dr., 6th Fl., Oakland 94612-3560 (415, 987-0026)
Dean: WILFORD R. GARDNER, College of Natural Resources,

Director, ANR Programs, University of California, Berkeley 94720 (415, 642-7171)
Dean: CHARLES E. HESS, College of Agricultural and Environmental Sciences, Director, ANR Programs, University of California, Davis 95616 (916, 752-1605)
Dean: EDWARD RHODE, Veterinary Medicine, University of California, Davis 95616 (916, 752-1360)
Dean (Acting): SEYMOUR D. VAN GUNDY, College of Natural and Agricultural Sciences, University of California, Riverside 92521 (714, 787-3101)
Director: KENNETH W. ELLIS, ANR Programs, North Central Region, 104 Cooperative Extension Headquarters, University of California, Davis 95616 (916, 752-8181)
Director: WILLIAM R. HAMBLETON, Director, ANR Programs, South Central Region, Kearney Agricultural Center, 9240 South Riverbend Ave., Parlier 93648 (209, 891-2566)
Director: ALLYN D. SMITH, Director, ANR Programs, Southern Region, 302 Cooperative Extension Bldg., University of California, Riverside 92521 (714, 787-3321)
Director: RICHARD D. TEAGUE, Director, ANR Programs, Northern Region, 102 Cooperative Extension Headquarters, University of California, Davis 95616 (916, 752-0570)

STATE LANDS COMMISSION, 1807 13th St., Sacramento 95814 (916, 322-4105)
Jurisdiction over and management responsibility for state-owned sovereign and congressional grant lands. Handles related land leases, exchanges, and transactions. Conducts oil, gas, geothermal, and other mineral leasing programs. Related activity involves boundary and ownership determination, granted lands administration, and maintaining land information system.
State Controllers: GRAY DAVIS; LT. GOVERNOR LEO T. McCARTHY
State Director, Finance: JESSE R. HUFF
Executive Officer: CLAIRE T. DEDRICK
Assistant Executive Officer: JAMES F. TROUT
Legislative Liaison: WILLIAM V. MORRISON (445-5303)
Chief Counsel: ROBERT C. HIGHT (322-2277)
Chief, Division of Research and Planning: DWIGHT E. SANDERS (322-7827)
Chief, Division of Land Management and Conservation: LANCE KILEY (445-1012)
Chief, Extractive Development: W.M. THOMPSON, 245 W. Broadway, Suite 425, Long Beach 90802 (213, 590-5243)

CITIZENS' GROUPS

CALIFORNIA NATURAL RESOURCES FEDERATION,
2830 Tenth St., Suite 4, Berkeley 94710 (415, 848-2211)
A representative statewide organization, affiliated with the National Wildlife Federation, primarily devoted to the wise use, conservation, aesthetic appreciation, and restoration of wildlife and other natural resources.
President: FRANK GEARY, 1825 Abraham Ct., Seaside 93955 (408, 394-5218)
Executive Director: RICHARD L. HUBBARD
Affiliate Representative: MIKE JOHNSON, 303 Reindollar Ave., Marina, CA 93933
Alternate: FRANK GEARY
Publication: CNRF Newsletter
Editor: JIM DAVIS, Box 2610, Bradley 93426

CALIFORNIA ACADEMY OF SCIENCES, Golden Gate Park, San Francisco 94118 (415, 221-5100)
Object is the exploration and interpretation of natural history. Maintains research collections and operates a museum-aquarium-planetarium complex to which one and one-half million visitors come each year. Membership: 23,500. Founded: 1853.
Chairman, Board of Trustees: JEFFERY W. MEYER
Vice-Chairmen: JOHN R. GREY; EUGENE A. SHURTLEFF
President: JAMES C. KELLEY
Vice-President: W.M. LAETSCH
Secretary: RICHARD J. BERTERO
Treasurer: JOHN W. LARSON
Director: FRANK H. TALBOT
Publications: *Academy Newsletter; Pacific Discovery*

CALIFORNIA ASSOCIATION OF RESOURCE CONSERVATION DISTRICTS
President: ERNEST WHITE, 21592 Gallagher Ave., Corning 96021 (916, 824-3177)
Vice-President: ELBERT REED, 1845 Bagpipe Way, San Jose 95121 (408, 274-0617)
Secretary-Treasurer: J. PETER LOUNSBURY, Star Route, Box 45A, Oro Grande 92368 (619, 245-8219)
Executive Director: BETTY HARRIS, 3830 U St., Sacramento 95817 (916, 739-6251)
Council Member: ROY RUTZ, 5800 Hackomiller Rd., Garden Valley 95633 (916, 333-4738)

CALIFORNIA BASS CHAPTER FEDERATION
An organization of Bassmaster Chapters, affiliated with the Bass Anglers Sportsman Society, to fight pollution, assist state and national conservation agencies in their efforts and teach the young people of our country good conservation practice. Dedicated to the realistic conservation of our water resources.
President: BERNIE KRONK, 954 Calle Angosta, Thousand Oaks 91360 (805, 498-4649/499-6650)

CALIFORNIA COMMITTEE OF TWO MILLION (CCO2M), P.O. Box 2046, San Francisco 94126 (415, 981-4134)
Statewide political action group linked with California Trout, Inc., dedicated to maintenance of free-flowing rivers and establishment of rational water resources development policy in California. Founded: 1969.
Chairman: RICHARD H. MAY
Secretary-Treasurer: H. L. JOSEPH, M.D.

CALIFORNIA FOREST PROTECTIVE ASSOCIATION, 1121 L St., Suite 307, Sacramento 95814 (916, 444-6592)
A nonprofit landowners' organization which promotes forest management and resource development and protection on private commercial timberlands. Organized: 1907. Incorporated: 1909.
Executive Vice-President: STEPHEN L. DEMARIA
Assistant Manager Director, Forest Resource Management: FRED LANDENBERGER
Legislative Advocate and Director of Economics and Taxation Services: RYAN HAMILTON
Director of Environmental Affairs: MATT R. ANDERSON

CALIFORNIA TRAPPERS ASSOCIATION, Rt. 2, Box 51, Adin 96006 (916, 299-3506)
Dedicated to encourage conservation, enhancement and scientific management of all our natural resources. Also to promote state and federal wildlife projects through volunteer skilled labor and financial contributions. Individual members: 1,160; 8 affiliated clubs (710 members). Incorporated: 1973. Founded: 1969.
President: SPENCER THOMAS

Vice-President: EARL SHELDON, 1628 Gate Ln., Paradise 95969 (877-7014)
Executive Secretary: DONALD L. STEHSEL, 2600 S. Third Ave., Arcadia 91006 (818, 446-3679)
Treasurer: TOM LAUSTALOT, 18907 Indian Creek Rd., Fort Jones 96032
Publications: *Fur Facts; Legislative Alerts*
Editor: GEORGE GAMBLE (707, 966-2513)

CALIFORNIA TROUT, INC., 870 Market St., #859, San Francisco 94102 (415, 392-8887)
Statewide organization of anglers dedicated to protection and restoration of wild trout, native steelhead, and their waters in California, and to the creation of high-quality angling adventures for the public to enjoy. Motto: "Keeper of the Streams." Membership: 3,200 individuals, 50 affiliated organizations. Founded: 1970.
President: RICHARD H. MAY
Vice-Presidents: ROY E. CRAWFORD; BARRETT W. McINERNEY
Secretary-Treasurer: WILLIAM NOBLE POST III
Publication: *Streamkeeper's Log*

CALIFORNIA WATERFOWL ASSOCIATION, 3840 Rosin Ct., Suite 100, Sacramento 95834 (1-800, 424-3825; out of state: 916, 648-1406)
A statewide nonprofit public benefit corporation whose principal objectives are the preservation, protection and enhancement of California's waterfowl resources and the recreational opportunities which they provide. The association directly represents the interests of over 100,000 sportsmen and conservationists throughout the state and indirectly represents the interests of millions of other Californians who are concerned with and benefit from these unique resources.
President: TIMOTHY EGAN
Senior Vice-President: BILL QUINN
Executive Director: TED BRYANT
Vice-Presidents: DANIEL CHAPIN, Governmental Affairs; BILL SHAW, Southern California; JEFF KERRY, Grasslands; TABER KOPAN, The Sacramento Valley; SCOTT PATTON, Financial Planning; RICH RADIGONDA, The Suisun Marsh
Secretary-Treasurer: BRIAN GARRETT
Research Biologist: DR. ROBERT McLANDRESS
Publication: *California Waterfowl*
Editor: PAT FREEMAN

CALIFORNIA WILDLIFE DEFENDERS, P.O. Box 2025, Hollywood 90078 (213, 663-1856)
A nonprofit association whose purpose is to eradicate the prejudice toward predators, especially coyotes; to acquaint the public with their role in the ecosystem; authored an ordinance banning the feeding of coyotes in order to restrict hillside residents who unknowingly exacerbated the urban coyote problem; has been instrumental in its enactment in several California cities and counties; authored brochure "How to Coexist with Urban Wildlife"; has obtained trapping restrictions in California and wildlife drinking facilities in hillside communities.
Director: LILA BROOKS
Associates: VIVIAN RYAN, La Crescenta; ALBERTA BURKE, Los Angeles; JUDY GARCIA, Tarzana
Publication: *Wildlife Alerts*

CALIFORNIA WILDLIFE FEDERATION, P.O. Box 1527, Sacramento 95812-1527 (916, 349-1813)
A nonprofit, statewide organization of councils, clubs, and individual members dedicated to promote the conservation, enhancement, scientific management and wise use of all our natural resources. Individual members: 11,200; 281 affiliated clubs (membership

16,800; nine state councils (membership 70,000+). Founded: 1952.
President: DONALD L. STEHSEL, 2600 S. 3rd St., Arcadia 91006 (818, 446-3679)
Vice-President: VIC SHADA, 5606 Franklin Blvd., Sacramento 95824 (916, 428-5184)
Secretary: CARL LARSON, 3077 Eastern Ave., A59, Sacramento 95821 (916, 488-1539)
Treasurer: DAN TICHENOR, 11478 Cull Canyon Rd., Castro Valley 94552 (415, 537-8440)
Director, Legislative and Governmental Affairs: JERRY UPHOLT, P.O. Box 1527, Sacramento 95812-1527 (916, 349-1813)
Publications: *California Wildlife; CWF Legislative Bulletins*
Editor: LYN BERNSTEIN

COALITION FOR CLEAN AIR, 309 Santa Monica Blvd., Suite 212, Santa Monica 90401 (213, 451-0651)
A statewide, nonprofit, tax-exempt organization dedicated to the eradication of air pollution. Founded: 1970.
President: JAN CHATTEN-BROWN, 631 Via de la Paz, Pacific Palisades 90272
Vice-President: MARK ABRAMOWITZ, 631 Via de la Paz, Pacific Palisades 90272
Treasurer: JACK NOVACK
Secretary: VIRGINIA FIELD, 4415 5th St., Riverside 92501
Program Director: MARK ABRAMOWITZ, 750 Marine St., #C, Santa Monica 90405-5656

COUNCIL FOR PLANNING AND CONSERVATION, Box 228, Beverly Hills 90213 (213, 276-3202)
Serves as a clearinghouse for information and gives inexperienced groups ready access to advice and assistance. Provides a center through which opportunities for southern California's environmental protection and enhancement may be communicated. Concerns include air and water quality, water supply, energy options, land use, transportation, coastal conservation, urban planning, housing, and public access to cable TV and telecommunications planning.
President and Executive Secretary: ELLEN STERN HARRIS
Treasurer/Secretary: SAM WEISZ
Vice-President: ALITA L. HANGER

ECOLOGY CENTER, 1403 Addison St., Berkeley 94702 (415, 548-2220)
A nonprofit, tax-exempt organization established to furnish support to conservation and environmental action efforts on a grassroots level through volunteer citizen work, unification of local group activities, and wider distribution of environmental information. Services provided as an environmental information center include telephone switchboard, library, bookstore, calendar of events and curbside pickup of newspapers, glass and metal containers, sponsorship of local farmer's market, and classes on organic gardening and other topics. Formed: 1969.
Project Coordinator: KATHY EVANS
Publication: *Ecology Center Newsletter*
Editor: SHARON SEIDENSTEIN

ELSA WILD ANIMAL APPEAL (California Chapter)
Regional branches of the Elsa Wild Animal Appeal concern themselves with wildlife matters, educational programs, liaison with other wildlife and governmental groups for the betterment of our natural environment and wildlife protection; coordinated through National Headquarters of EWAA; establish local volunteer corps to implement programs.
A.P. RASMUSSEN JR., P.O. Box 4572, North Hollywood 91607 (818, 761-8387)

Southern California Chapter
EVE RATTNER, 3139 Coachman Ct., Oceanside 92054

ENVIRONMENTAL DEFENSE CENTER, INC., 906 Garden St., Suite 2, Santa Barbara 93101 (805, 963-1622)
(Annual Meeting: January of each year, Santa Barbara)
A nonprofit public interest environmental law firm providing legal services on environmental issues facing California's central coast. The center currently is focusing much of its attention on the extensive oil development of the Santa Barbara channel and its resulting environmental and social impacts. Also represents client groups seeking protection of natural habitats, open space, trails and coastal access.
Chairman of the Board: CHASE MELLEN
Chief Counsel: PHILIP A. SEYMOUR
Staff Attorney: MARC CHYTILD
Publications: Quarterly Members' Report

FOREST LANDOWNERS OF CALIFORNIA, 3807 Pasadena Ave., Suite 100, Sacramento 95821-2815 (916, 972-0273)
A statewide organization affiliated with the National Woodland Owners Association, dedicated to wise management and multiple use of private forest lands in California. Membership: 270. Founded: 1970.
President: HAL BOWMAN
Executive Director: THOMAS P. KERR
Publication: *Forest Land Owner*
Editor: THOMAS P. KERR

FRIENDS OF THE SEA OTTER, P.O. Box 221220, Carmel 93922 (408, 625-3290)
A nonprofit organization dedicated to the protection and maintenance of a healthy population of southern sea otters, a threatened species, and their marine habitat along the central California coast. Encourages research and public education to develop a sound conservation program. Membership: 4,700. Founded: 1968.
President: MARGARET W. OWINGS, Big Sur (667-2254)
1st Vice-President: DR. ROBERT T. ORR, Larkspur
Executive Director: CAROL FULTON, Monterey (375-2051)
Staff Biologist: RACHEL SAUNDERS, Pacific Grove (375-4509)
Director Sea Otter Center: JO NIX (625-6887)
Membership Secretary: JULIA WENNER (649-5661)
Attorney: STUART SOMACH, Sacramento (916, 444-3900)
Advisory: ALAN BALDRIDGE; WILLIAM BRYAN; MILDRED BUCHSBAUM; DR. RALPH BUCHSBAUM; DR. WILLIAM FRANCIS; BOBBIE HARMS; DR. EMMET T. HOOPER; DR. GEORGE LINDSAY; JAMES MATTISON JR.; CHARLES MEHLERT; DR. KENNETH NORRIS; DR. ROBERT ORR; MARGARET OWINGS; DR. JOHN PEARSE; DR. JOHN PHILLIPS; NATHANIEL PRYOR REED; DR. JAMES W. ROTE; FERDINAND S. RUTH; DR. VICTOR B. SCHEFFER; JUDSON VANDEVERE; DR. EDWARD L. WALKER; DR. TOM WILLIAMS
Publication: *The Otter Raft*
Editor: CAROL FULTON (375-2051)

IZAAK WALTON LEAGUE OF AMERICA, INC. (California Division)
Organized: 1938.
President: LESTER KING, 1241 N. East St., #184, Anaheim 92806 (714, 525-3376)
Executive Secretary: HEIDI DUFFIELD, 1909 Carnegie Ln., #3, Redondo Beach 90278 (213, 318, 2086)

MONO LAKE COMMITTEE, P.O. Box 29, Lee Vining 93541
(619, 647-6595) (Annual Meeting: Labor Day Weekend,
Lee Vining)
Works toward preserving the scenic, biological, and scientific
values of Mono Lake and the Great Basin by limiting water
diversions to levels that are not environmentally destructive.
Encourages public interest in the natural history and preservation
of these lakes through slide programs and field trips.
Executive Director: MARTHA DAVIS (213, 477-8229)
Co-Chairs: ED GROSSWILER; SALLY GAINES
Treasurer: DAVE PHILLIPS
Secretary: HELEN GREEN
Los Angeles Office, 1355 Westwood Blvd., Suite 6, Los Angeles
90024 (213, 477-8229)
Sacramento Office, 909 12th St., #207, Sacramento 95814
(916, 448-1045)
Publication: *Mono Lake Newsletter*
Editor: LAUREN DAVIS

MOUNT SHASTA AREA AUDUBON SOCIETY, P.O. Box 530,
Mount Shasta 96067 (916, 926-4251/3900)
An associate member organization of the National Wildlife Federa-
tion to protect, enhance and enjoy the natural environment of the
Mount Shasta region, including its birds, wildlife, forests, moun-
tains, meadows, and waters. Membership: 337. Founded: 1971.
President: BETTE KOERNER, 907 W. Ream Ave., Mount Shasta
96067 (926-4251)
Vice-President: KERRY MAURO, 2220 Pack Tr., Mount Shasta
96067 (926-5132/926-2093)
Secretary: KAREN CODE, 838 Old McCloud Rd., Mount Shasta
96067 (926-4728)
Publication: *Endeavor Newsletter*
Editor: PHIL McCRACKEN, 1424 Timber Hills Rd., Mount Shasta
96067 (926-3581)

NONGAME WILDLIFE ADVISORY COMMITTEE, California
Department of Fish and Game, 1416 Ninth St., Sacramento
95814 (916, 445-5561)
Established by the Director of the Department of Fish and Game in
1975. The seven members, appointed by the Director of the
Department of Fish and Game, are requested to recommend
objectives, programs, and funding for nongame wildlife.
Chairman: RODOLFO RUIBAL, University of California, Dept. of
Biology, Riverside 92521 (714, 787-5929/5903)
Members: URSULA FAASII-LIAKOS; ROBERT HASSUR; LLOYD
TEVIS; PETER MOYLE
Publication: *Annual Report*

NORTHCOAST ENVIRONMENTAL CENTER, 879 Ninth St.,
Arcata 95521 (707, 822-6918)
A tax-exempt educational organization dedicated to illuminating the
relationships between humankind and the biosphere. Toward that
end, the center provides environmental information and referral
services to northwestern California and operates a library open to
the public. The center also conducts special projects, such as the
Adopt-a-Beach program. Established: 1971.
Coordinator: TIM McKAY
Publication: *ECONEWS*
Editor: SID DOMINITZ

PLANNING AND CONSERVATION LEAGUE, 909 12th St.,
Suite 203, Sacramento 95814 (916, 444-8726)
A nonprofit, nonpartisan corporation supported by 7,500 individual members and 120 affiliated organizations who, in order to
protect and conserve the quality of California's environment and
establish methods of planning that will contribute to the wise use of
resources, have joined together to seek state-level legislative
action. Founded: 1965.
President: GARY PATTON, 701 Ocean St., Santa Cruz 95060
(408, 425-2202)
Executive Director: DR. GERALD H. MERAL
Publication: *California Today*
Editor: DR. GERALD H. MERAL

SAVE SAN FRANCISCO BAY ASSOCIATION, P.O. Box 925,
Berkeley 94701 (415, 849-3053)
Nonprofit, tax-exempt organization dedicated to the protection and
enhancement of San Francisco Bay's many natural and public
values. Current priorities include: protecting wetlands, improving
water quality, providing shoreline parks and trails, preventing
unnecessary bay fill and preventing additional fresh water diversion
from the estuary. Membership: over 22,000. Established: 1961,
by MRS. CLARK KERR, MRS. CHARLES A. GULICK, and MRS.
DONALD H. McLAUGHLIN
President: DORIS SLOAN
Vice-Presidents: E. CLEMENT SHUTE; DONALD R. WEDEN; DAVID
M. FOGARTY
Secretary: FRANCES M. BRIGMANN
Treasurer: DEXTER S. CHAN
Publications: *The Baywatcher Newsletter;* Information fact sheets
Editor: DORIS SLOAN

STANFORD ENVIRONMENTAL LAW SOCIETY, Stanford Law
School, Stanford 94305 (415, 723-4421)
The society conducts original research in critical areas of environ-
mental and natural resource law. The results of this research are
then made available to the public in a series of practical, citizen-
oriented publications. Founded: 1969.
President: THOMAS S. WALDO
Publications: *ELS Handbook Series; ELS Law Annual*

TROUT UNLIMITED CALIFORNIA COUNCIL
A statewide council working for the protection and enhancement of
coldwater fishery resources.
Chairman: GARY WIDMAN, 28 Marinaro Cir., #31, Tiburon
94920 (415, 435-0360)
Membership Chairman: DAVID ARMOCIDO, P.O. Box 280, Arbuckle 95912 (916, 437-2375)

WILDLIFE SOCIETY WESTERN SECTION
President: JOHN KIE, 2081 E. Sierra Ave., Fresno 93710 (209,
487-5589)
President-Elect: ROBERT SCHMIDT, UC Hopland Field Station,
4070 University Rd., Hopland 95449 (707, 744-1424)
Secretary: MARTI J. KIE, 181 Orangewood Ave., Clovis 93612
(209, 298-3908)
Treasurer: MIKE CHAPEL, 106 Janet Way, Grass Valley 95949
(916, 265-4531)

COLORADO

GOVERNMENT AGENCIES

GOVERNOR: ROY ROMER, Governor of Colorado, State Capitol, Denver 80203 (303, 866-2471)

COLORADO COOPERATIVE FISH AND WILDLIFE RESEARCH UNIT, U.S.D.I., 201 Wagar Bldg., Dept. of Fishery and Wildlife Biology, Colorado State University, Ft. Collins 80523 (303, 491-5396)
Offers expertise and training facilities in fish and wildlife population ecology, habitat analysis, and conservation biology. environmental impact assessment and management alternatives. Organized: 1947.
Leader: DR. DAVID R. ANDERSON
Assistant Leaders: DR. ERIC P. BERGERSEN; DR. KENNETH P. BURNHAM

DEPARTMENT OF AGRICULTURE, 1525 Sherman St., Denver 80203 (303, 866-2811)
Strives to meet the increasingly complex needs of agriculture through work on marketing problems, technological changes in pest and insect control, and rapidly changing patterns in crop and livestock operations. Established: 1949.
Commission Chairman: NAOMI BENSEN
Commissioner: PETER R. DECKER
Deputy Commissioner: STEVEN W. HORN
Director, Animal Industry Division: DR. JAMES WILLIAMS
Director, Division of Inspection and Consumer Services: RONALD TURNER
Resource Analyst: DAVID CARLSON
Director, Plant Industry Division: ROBERT I. SULLIVAN
Market Development Section: JIM RUBINGH, Program Administrator
Brand Commissioner, Board of Stock Inspection Division: GARY SHAUN

DEPARTMENT OF EDUCATION, 201 E. Colfax Ave., State Office Building, Denver 80203
Conservation Education Services, jointly with the Division of Wildlife: KURT CUNNINGHAM (303, 866-6787)

DEPARTMENT OF HEALTH, 4210 E. 11th Ave., Denver 80220 (303, 331-4510)
The Office of Health and Environmental Protection has the responsibility for improving and protecting the health and environment for Colorado's citizens by: assuring a healthy working and living environment, protecting people against exposure to diseases, establishing preventive health services and providing a quality environment through air, waste, water, radiation, and other environmental protection activities.
Assistant Director for Health and Environmental Protection: THOMAS P. LOOBY
Executive Director: THOMAS M. VERNON, M.D.

DEPARTMENT OF NATURAL RESOURCES, 1313 Sherman, Rm. 718, Denver 80203 (303, 866-3311)
Responsible for mineral and energy, land, water, wildlife and park resources management for the state. Also responsible for major environmental conservation and management programs. Established: 1968.
Executive Director: HAMLET J. BARRY III
Deputy Director: DENNIS W. DONALD

Assistant Director: RONALD W. CATTANY
Assistant to the Director: LAURIE A. MATHEWS
Budget Officer: DEBORAH WAGNER
Human Resources Director: CINDY HORIUCHI
Director, Joint Review Process: STEVE NORRIS (866-3311)

Colorado Geologic Survey
Director: JOHN ROLD (866-2611)

Colorado Natural Areas Program
Director: DAVID KUNTZ (866-3311)

Division of Mined Land Reclamation
Director: FRED BANTA (866-3567)

Division of Mines
Director: FRED BANTA (866-3567)

Division of Parks and Outdoor Recreation, 1313 Sherman St., Rm. 618, Denver 80203 (866-3437)
Director: RONALD HOLLIDAY

Division of Water Resources
Director: JERIS DANIELSON (866-3581)

Division of Wildlife, 6060 Broadway, Denver 80216 (297-1192)
Director: Vacant

Oil and Gas Conservation Commission, Logan Tower Bldg., Suite 380, 1580 Logan St., Denver 80203
Director: WILLIAM SMITH (894-2100)

Soil Conservation Board (866-3351)
Director: DANIEL O. PARKER

State Board of Land Commissioners (866-3454)
President: ROWENA ROGERS

Water Conservation Board
Director: J. WILLIAM MCDONALD (866-3441)

OFFICE OF ENERGY CONSERVATION, 112 E. 14th Ave., Denver 80203 (303, 866-2507)
Established by Governor Richard D. Lamm in 1977 to promote conservation in the state and to help Coloradans use energy more efficiently.
Director: JUDY HARRINGTON
Periodical Publications: *EnergyTalk*
Editor: SHEILAH ROGERS

STATE EXTENSION SERVICES
A branch of Colorado State University. Conducts statewide noncredit educational programs off campus. Established: 1915.
Director of Extension: DR. KENNETH R. BOLEN, Colorado State University, Fort Collins 80523 (303, 491-6281)
Assistant Director, Agriculture and Natural Resource Programs: DR. W. DENNIS LAMM, Colorado State University, Fort Collins 80523 (491-6281)
Extension Wildlife Specialist, Animal Damage Control: WILLIAM F. ANDELT, Ph.D., Dept. of Fishery and Wildlife Biology, 109 Wagar, Colorado State University, Fort Collins 80523 (491-7093)
Extension Wildlife Specialist, Wildlife Management: DELWIN E. BENSON, Dept. of Fishery and Wildlife Biology, 109 Wagar, Colorado State University, Ft. Collins 80523 (303, 491-6411)

STATE FOREST SERVICE, Colorado State University, Ft. Collins 80523 (303, 491-6303)
Main responsibility: the environmental protection and management of approximately 8 million acres of private and state-owned forest land. Provides aid to all groups and individuals upon request. Founded: 1885.
State Forester: JAMES E. HUBBARD
Assistant State Forester: BILL WILCOX
Staff Forester, Information and Education: MIKEL (Mike) F. WAY
Nursery Manager: RANDY MOENCH (491-8429)
Staff Forester, Fire: RONALD J. ZELENY
Assistant Staff Forester, Insect and Disease: DAVE LEATHERMAN
Staff Forester, Forest Management: TOM OSTERMANN
Staff Forester, Community Forestry: PHIL HOEFER
Publication: *Colorado Forestry News*
Executive Editor: MIKE WAY

CITIZENS' GROUPS

COLORADO WILDLIFE FEDERATION, *1560 Broadway, Ste. 763, Denver 80202 (303, 830-2557)*
A representative statewide organization, affiliated with the National Wildlife Federation, primarily devoted to the wise use, conservation, aesthetic appreciation, and restoration of wildlife and other natural resources. Organized: 1952.
President: JOHN VOELKER, 12849 County Rd., 250, Durango 81301 (247-4209)
Executive Director: STEVE BLOMEKE
Affiliate Representative: TOM WARREN, 6755 Metropolitan St., Colorado Springs 80911 (392-9515)
Alternate: WALLY GALLAHER, 7387 Robb Ct., Arvada 80005 (420-5478))
Publication: Colorado Wildlife
Editor: KELLY LADYGA, 1560 Broadway, Suite 763, Denver 80202

COLORADO ASSOCIATION OF SOIL CONSERVATION DISTRICTS
President: RALPH G. CURTIS, P.O. Box 437, Saguache 81149 (W: 719, 589-6301/H: 655-2244)
Vice-President: CALISTA GRAVES, Star Route, Box 46, Model 81059 (384-4198)
Treasurer: DANIEL O. PARKER, 3000 Youngfield, Suite 163, Lakewood 80215 (303, 232-6242)
Council Member: LEON SILKMAN, 28494 Road 51 1/2, Burlington 80807 (719, 346-7612)

COLORADO BASS CHAPTER FEDERATION
An organization of Bassmaster Chapters, affiliated with the Bass Anglers Sportsman Society, organized to fight pollution, assist state and national conservation agencies in their efforts and to teach the young people of our country good conservation practices. Dedicated to the realistic conservation of our water resources.
President: SETH GOLDSTEIN, 6775 Pennsylvania Ave., Littleton 80122 (303, 797-7182)

COLORADO ENVIRONMENTAL COALITION, INC., 777 Grant St., #606, Denver 80203-3518 (303, 837-8701)
Citizens' coordinating council, employing paid staff & volunteers, engaged in education, study, and legislative action in such areas as pollution, wilderness, land-use planning, energy, water resources, mining, and urban problems. Membership: 35 organizations plus 1,000 individuals. Founded: 1964.
President: STEPHEN BONOWSKI

Director: ELIZABETH OTTO
Wilderness and Public Lands: KIRK KOEPSEL
Water and Timber: ROCKY SMITH
Publications: *The Colorado Environmental Report;* Newsletter
Editor: ELIZABETH OTTO

COLORADO MOUNTAIN CLUB, 2530 W. Alameda Ave., Denver 80219 (303, 922-8315)
To unite the energy, interest, and knowledge of the students, explorers and lovers of the mountains of Colorado; to collect and disseminate information regarding the Rocky Mountains in behalf of science, literature, art, and recreation; to stimulate public interest in our mountain area; to encourage the preservation of forests, flowers, fauna, and natural scenery; and to render readily accessible the alpine attractions of this region. Membership: 7,624. Founded: 1912.
President: GARY GRANGE
Corporate Secretary: MARGARET AULD
Office Manager: MARILYN MICKLICK
Treasurer: MIKE TABB
Accounting Manager: ELIZABETH TRUITT
Conservation Chairperson: ANNE VICKERY
Publication: *Trail and Timberline*
Editor: SALLY ROSS

COLORADO TRAPPERS ASSOCIATION
Associate of Fur Takers of America and National Trappers Association. Dedicated to the wise conservation and management of fur-bearing animals, the education of fur harvesters and public about fur-bearer management and the preservation of America's rich heritage in the harvest of wild furs.
President: MARVIN D. MILLER, 29201 Rainbow Hill Rd., Golden 80401 (303, 526-9207)
Vice-President: JIM JAY, Box 182, Wray 80758 (332-5124)
Secretary/Treasurer: DWIGHT COPPOCK, 8000 Massey Cir., Littleton 80123 (973-4063)
Director for Public Relations: JOE FRANKFURTER, 5741 E. 66th Ave., Commerce City 80022 (287-2032)
Director for Publications: Major L. BODDICKER, 4620 Moccasin Cr., La Porte 80535 (484-2768)
Publications: *Managing Rocky Mountain Furbearers; Colorado Trappers Association Journal; Fur and Wildlife; Fur Marketing and Trappers Supply Handbook; Product Marketing Handbook*
Editor: MAJ. L. BODDICKER

COLORADO WATER CONGRESS, 1390 Logan St., Suite 312, Denver 80203 (303, 837-0812)
To institute and advance programs for the conservation, development, protection and efficient utilization of the water resources of Colorado. Founded: 1958.
President: TOM GRISWOLD
Vice-President: DOUGLAS LOCKHART
Executive Director: RICHARD D. MacRAVEY
Publications: *Colorado Water Rights; Colorado Water Almanac & Directory; Water Intelligence Report; Water Legal News; Water Legislative Report; Water Financial News; Water Research News; Water Special Report; Water Quality News; Ground Water News; Water Conservation News; Colorado Laws Enacted of Interest to Water Users*

IZAAK WALTON LEAGUE OF AMERICA, INC. (Colorado Division)
President: KENNETH BORDEN, 6294 W. Exposition, Lakewood 80226 (719, 922-1081)
Secretary-Treasurer: HELEN V. STAMMEN, 1585 C1 Gatehouse Cir., Colorado Springs 80904 (303, 473-1105)

NATIONAL WILDLIFE FEDERATION NATURAL RESOURCES CLINIC
See National Wildlife Federation listing on page 85.

ROCKY MOUNTAIN BIGHORN SOCIETY (Colorado Order),
P.O. Box 1086, Denver 80201 (Annual meeting in Colorado: February).
The purpose of the society is to support the sound management of the Rocky Mountain Bighorn Sheep and its habitat and to promote the advancement and knowledge of the bighorn. Membership: 600. Founded: 1975.
President: TOM BROWN, 17130 W. 57th Pl., Golden 80403 (278-2502)
Vice-President: MARY CLYNCKE, 7190 S. Boulder Rd., Boulder 80303 (494-7727)
Treasurer: JOHN MURPHY, 13564 W. Virginia Dr., Lakewood 80228 (986-6911)
Secretary: TERRY SANDMEIER, 2821 W 64th Ave., Denver 80221

Area Representatives
Southeast: SANDY FULLER, 1345 9th St., Penrose 81240 (372-3777)
Southwest: GEORGE VAN DEN BERG, P.O. Box 157, Durango 81301
Northwest: DARYL ISER, 537 28 3/4 Rd., Grand Junction 81501 (242-5478)
Northcentral: GREG JUNGMAN, P.O. Box 1827, Dillon 80435 (468-5995)

TROUT UNLIMITED COLORADO COUNCIL, 1557 Ogden St., 3rd Fl., Denver 80218
A statewide council with 35 chapters working for the protection and enhancement of coldwater fishery resources.
President: BRUCE HOAGLAND, 370 Oneida St., Boulder 80303 (303, 494-6747)
1st Vice-President: CLAUDE GRAVES (259-5133)
Area Vice-Presidents: KEN PLANK, West Metro (985-4535); PAUL SEIPEL, East Metro (690-1115); NEILL PETERSON, Southwest (259-3247); GREG ASBURY, West (641-4439); BOB BUSH, Northeast (443-8966); DOUG HARDWICK, North Central (468-9130); FRED RASMUSSEN, South (539-2098); DON OLBERT, West Central (945-8831)
Membership Vice-President: DALE GARRON (694-2541)
Secretary: HERB JOHNSON (986-5636)
Treasurer: ROGER GREENE (337-1121)
Rocky Mountain Regional Vice-President: DEAN SWANSON (422-1564)
Administrative Director: DAVE TAYLOR (837-1908)
Resource Director: RICHARD HAMILTON (837-1908)
Administrative Assistant: ANN PALMQUIST (837-1908)

WILDLIFE SOCIETY COLORADO CHAPTER
President: DAVE WEBER, 6900 Warren Dr., Denver 80221 (303, 291-7231)
President-Elect: BOB STREETER, 832 Gregory Rd., Ft. Collins 80524 (493-8401)
Secretary: LINDA SIKOROWSKI, 824 E. 22nd Ave., Denver 80205 (291-7273)
Treasurer: DAVID FREDDY, P.O. Box 252, Kremmling 80459 (724-3433)

GOVERNMENT AGENCIES

GOVERNOR: WILLIAM A. O'NEILL, Governor of Connecticut, State Capitol, Hartford 06106 (203, 566-4840)

COUNCIL ON ENVIRONMENTAL QUALITY, Rm. 239, 165 Capitol Ave., Hartford 06106 (203, 566-3510)
Prepares annual reports to the Governor on the status of Connecticut's environment; receives and investigates citizen complaints pertaining to the environment; reviews environmental assessments of construction activities of state agencies. The council is composed of nine appointed members who serve without compensation. Established: 1971.
Chairman: GREGORY A. SHARP
Executive Director: KARL J. WAGENER
Publication: *Annual Report on the Status of Connecticut's Environment*

DEPARTMENT OF AGRICULTURE, 165 Capitol Ave., Rm. 273, State Office Bldg., Hartford 06106 (203, 566-4667)
Commissioner: KENNETH B. ANDERSEN
Deputy Commissioner: VINCENT R. MAJCHIER
Chief, Livestock Division: WILLIAM HARRINGTON
State Veterinarian: Vacant
Chief, Dairy Division: PAUL GOTTHELF
Chief, Marketing Division: KENNETH VIET
Chief, Canine Control Officer: FRANK A. INTINO
Chief, Agriculture Division: JOHN VOLK
Director, Farmland Preservation: MARY E. GOODHOUSE

DEPARTMENT OF ENVIRONMENTAL PROTECTION, State Office Bldg., 165 Capitol Ave., Hartford 06106 (203, 566-5599)
Created by the Connecticut General Assembly to conserve, protect and improve the state's environment and to manage the basic resources of air, water, and land for the benefit of present and future generations.
Commissioner, Environmental Protection: LESLIE CAROTHERS
Deputy Commissioner, Conservation and Preservation: DENNIS P. DeCARLI (566-4522)
Deputy Commissioner, Environmental Quality: JOHN W. ANDERSON (566-4856)
Director, Information and Education: WILLIAM DELANEY (566-5524)
Director, Planning/Coastal Area Management: ARTHUR ROCQUE (566-7404)
Director, Fisheries Bureau: ROBERT JONES (566-2287)
Director, Wildlife Bureau: PAUL HERIG (566-4683)
State Forester: PETER BABCOCK (566-5348)
Director, Office of State Parks and Recreation: RICHARD K. CLIFFORD (566-2304)
Director, Law Enforcement Bureau: ROBERT BUYAK (566-3978)
Assistant Deputy Commissioner, Environmental Quality: ROBERT MOORE (566-4007)
Director, Water Resources Unit: Vacant (566-7220)
Director, Water Compliance Unit: RICHARD BARLOW (566-3245)
Assistant Directors, Water Compliance Unit: MICHAEL HARDER (566-2719); ROBERT SMITH (566-2588)
Director, Radiation Control: KEVIN McCARTHY (566-5668)
Director, Air Compliance Unit: LEONARD BRUCKMAN (566-4030)
Director, Solid Waste Management Unit: CHARLES KURKER (566-3672)

Director, Hazardous Materials Management: STEPHEN HITCH-
COCK (566-4924)
Director, Land Acquisition and Management: CHARLES REED
(566-2904)
Publication: *Connecticut Environment*
Editor: ROBERT PAIER, Rm. 112, State Office Bldg., Hartford
06106 (566-3489)

STATE EXTENSION SERVICES

Dean, College of Agriculture and Natural Resources: DR. KIRUIN
KNOX, 1376 Storrs Rd., Box U-66, University of Connecticut,
Storrs 06268 (203, 486-2917)
Extension Environmentalist: DAVID R. MILLER, Ph.D., Box U-87,
University of Connecticut, Storrs 06268 (486-2839)
Wildlife Expert: JOHN S. BARCLAY, Ph.D., Box U-87, University of
Connecticut, Storrs, 06268 (486-2839)
Fisheries Expert: W.R. WHITWORTH, Ph.D., Prof. of Fisheries, Box
U-87, University of Connecticut, Storrs 06268 (486-2839)
Natural Resources Experts: HUGO H. JOHN, Ph.D., Prof. of Natural
Resources, Box U-87, University of Connecticut, Storrs 06268
(486-2839); DAVID B. SCHROEDER, Ph.D., Prof. of Plant
Pathology and Acting Head of Renewable Natural Resources
Dept., Box U-87; STEVE BRODERICK, Extension Forester,
Extension Center, Brooklyn 06234

CITIZENS' GROUPS

CONNECTICUT WILDLIFE FEDERATION, *27*
Washington St., Middletown CT 06457 (203, 347-
1291)
*A representative statewide organization, affiliated with the National
Wildlife Federation, primarily devoted to the wise use, conservation,
aesthetic appreciation, and restoration of wildlife and other natural
resources.*
*President: JOHN F. REILLY III, 14 Bishop Dr., Woodbridge
06525 (397-1480)*
*Secretary: MARTIN ROBERTS, 150 Buckingham St., Meridan
06450 (238-1342)*
Affiliate Representative: JOHN F. REILLY III
Alternate: BOB ABORN, 4 Jude Rd., Plainville 06062
Editor: Vacant

AMERICAN BASS ASSOCIATION OF CONNECTICUT, THE

An organization of the individual members and bass fishing clubs,
affiliated with the American Bass Association, Inc., dedicated to
protecting and enhancing the state's fishery resources; to promote
the sport of bass fishing, and to teach youngsters the fun of fishing
and instill in them an appreciation of the life-giving waters of
America.
President: ED METZGER, 131 Cedar Lake Rd., Deep River 06417
(203, 526-3472)

AUDUBON COUNCIL OF CONNECTICUT, Rt. 4, RR1, Box
171, Sharon 06069 (203, 364-0520)

The statewide organization of the National Audubon Society
initiates and supports programs to advance the protection and wise
use of the wildlife, plants, soil, water, and other natural resources of
Connecticut; encourages the exchange of information, cooperation,
and coordination among member organizations. Membership:
24,000. Organized: 1967.
President: MEADA EBINGER, 111 Mohawk Dr., Wallingford 06492
(203, 269-5114)
1st Vice-President: GEORGE LETIS, 173 Hunt L., East-Haven
06512

Secretary: CRAWFORD BENEDICT, P.O. 393, Newtown 06470
Treasurer: MICHAEL AURELIA, 72 Oak Ridge, Greenwich 06830
(203, 622-9297)
Publication: *Audubon Update*

BERKSHIRE-LITCHFIELD ENVIRONMENTAL COUNCIL, INC.,
P.O. Box 552, Lakeville 06039 (203, 435-2004)

Primarily concerned with energy, transportation, and land use
issues in the southern Berkshires. Membership: 1,000. Organized:
1970.
President: KARL A. STOECKER (435-0520)
Vice-Presidents: ROLLIN H. BATES; VICTORIA GIVOTOVSKY; ROB-
ERT C. TAPSCOTT; MIRIAM JONES
Chairman Executive Committee: JOHN BROCK
Secretary: NANCY BARNETT
Treasurer: ROLLIN H. BATES
Counsel: WILLIAM F. MORRILL
Publication: *BLEC News*

CONNECTICUT ASSOCIATION OF SOIL AND WATER
CONSERVATION DISTRICTS, INC.

President and Council Member: MORTIMER GELSTON, Maple Ave.,
East Haddam 06423 (203, 873-8495)
Vice-President: LARRY JOHNSTON, 31 Franklin St., Westport
06880 (226-9383)
Secretary-Treasurer: RAY CRAGIN, 102 Taine Rd., Burlington
06103 (688-7725)
PETER FABAR, Laurel Way, Winchester Center 06752 (567-
8188)

CONNECTICUT AUDUBON SOCIETY, 2325 Burr St., Fairfield
06430 (203, 259-6305)

Dedicated to helping people appreciate and conserve Connecticut's
natural resources through educational programs, sanctuary acqui-
sition and management, legislative action, and wildlife and natural
areas research. Membership: 18,000. Organized: 1898.
Chairman of Board: ROBERT R. LARSEN, Fairfield
President: DR. ROBERT B. BRAUN, Fairfield
Vice-Presidents: W. BRADLEY MOREHOUSE, Fairfield; JOHN E.
TIERNEY, Stratford
Central Regional Vice-President: ROGER HANLON, West Hartford
Western Regional Vice-President: GLORIA S. BARNES, Fairfield
Secretary: KATHERINE K. MICHELSEN, Fairfield
Treasurer: BERNARD F. MARTIN, Fairfield
Executive Director: SHERMAN KENT (527-8737)
Director, Field Studies/Ornithology: MILAN BULL
Director, Fairfield Regional Center: MILAN BULL
Operations Coordinator: MARILYN DUDA
Director, Youth Education: KATE SAUVAGE
Director, Sanctuary Operations: LOUIS J. BACCHIOCCHI
Director, Connecticut Audubon Environmental Center: DAVID
SUTHERLAND, Hartford (527-8737)
Director of Membership: JANE ANDAAS
Teacher/Naturalist: JAMES SIRCH
Director, Holland Brook Center, Glastonbury: KATE SAUVAGE
(633-8402)
Director, Communications and Adult Education: LAUREN BROWN,
Fairfield
Publications: *Connecticut Audubon Magazine;* Environmental White
Papers
Editor: EDWARD R. RICCIUTI

CONNECTICUT BASS CHAPTER FEDERATION

An organization of Bassmaster Chapters, affiliated with the Bass
Anglers Sportsman Society, to fight pollution, assist state and
national conservation agencies in their efforts and to teach the

young people of our country good conservation practices. Dedicated to the realistic conservation of our water resources.
President: WILLIAM PICCIRILLO, 13 Orangewood West, Derby 06418 (203, 735-3481)

CONNECTICUT FOREST AND PARK ASSOCIATION, INC., 16
Meriden Rd., Route 66, Middlefield, Middletown 06457-2945 (203, 346-2372)
A voluntary organization for conserving forests, scenery, wildlife, and developing natural resources and outdoor recreation.
President: GEORGE M. MILNE, Hebron
Vice-President: RUSSELL L. BRENNEMAN, Glastonbury
Treasurer: GORDON L. ANDERSON, East Hartford
Secretary-Forester/Executive Director: JOHN E. HIBBARD, Hebron
Publications: *Connecticut Woodlands; Connecticut Forest and Park Association Newsletter; The Connecticut Walk Book; Forest Trees of Southern New England*
Editor: JOHN E. HIBBARD
Director of Education and Development: LINDA RAPP

CONNECTICUT FUND FOR THE ENVIRONMENT, 152 Temple
St., New Haven 06510 (203, 787-0646); 32 Grand St., Hartford 06106 (203, 524-1639)
(Annual meeting: September, New Haven)
CFE was organized in 1978 to promote the safe utilization of Connecticut's resources. Since this time CFE has become a powerful public interest organization with over 3,000 members.
Director: SUZANNE LANGILLE MATTEI
President: BROOKS KELLEY, Ph.D.
Vice-President: WILLIAM CRONON, Ph.D.
Treasurer: ROBERT GRADOVILLE, Esq.
Secretary: ROBERT McLELLAN, M.D., M.P.H.
Publications: Newsletter; Fact Sheets
Editor: FAITH LARKIN

E-P EDUCATION SERVICES, INC., 15 Brittany Ct., Cheshire
06410 (203, 271-2756)
A nonprofit group formed in 1972 to promote environmental and population education in Connecticut and committed to assisting educators in the task of providing quality environmental education for the citizens of our state.
President and Executive Director: LARRY SCHAEFER
Vice-President: HARRY O. HAAKONSEN
Secretary: LINA ANN LAWALL
Treasurer: J. ROBERT BOUCHARD
Teaching Specialist: PATRICIA KRUKOWSKI
Resource Center Librarian: VIRGINIA EVITTS
Publication: Newsletter, Exchanges
Editor: LARRY SCHAEFER

LONG ISLAND SOUND TASKFORCE OF THE OCEANIC
SOCIETY, Stamford Marine Center, Magee Ave., Stamford 06902 (203, 327-9786)
A nonprofit, tax-exempt organization that focuses on marine conservation, education activities for the Long Island Sound region as a regional chapter of the Oceanic Society. Activities conducted by the Taskforce include: semi-annual conferences, a Sea Camp for young people, intertidal fields studies, courses, bi-monthly membership meetings, whale watch weekends, and a speaker's bureau. The taskforce is a member of the Citizens Advisory Committee of the Long Island Sound Study, The Connecticut Clean Water Coalition, and the Jay Coalition. Membership: 1,000.
President: KATHRYN H. CLARKE
Vice-President: GERARD CAPRIULO, Ph.D.
Chairman: ARTHUR GLOWKA
Executive Director: RICHARD SCHREINER

Publication: *Long Island Sound Study Update*
Editor: RICHARD SCHREINER

TROUT UNLIMITED CONNECTICUT COUNCIL
A statewide council with seven chapters working for the protection and enhancement of coldwater fishery resources.
Chairman: WILLIAM MRAZ, 384 Litchfield Rd., Watertown 06795 (203, 274-6443)
National Directors: NEIL KINGSNORTH, 1056 Main St., Woodbury 06798 (263-3597); LINDA MORGENS, Nathan Hale Dr., S. Norwalk 06854 (853-2933)

DELAWARE

GOVERNMENT AGENCIES

GOVERNOR: MICHAEL N. CASTLE, Governor of Delaware, Legislative Hall, Dover 19901 (302, 736-4101)

DEPARTMENT OF AGRICULTURE, 2320 S. DuPont Highway, Dover 19901 (302, 736-4811)
The DDA plays a key role in the state through management and support of this vital industry. Farmers, in particular, look to the department not only for assistance with their farm products, but also as a source of information on new markets and market opportunities. The DDA oversee Delaware's #1 industry.
Secretary: WILLIAM B. CHANDLER, JR.
Executive Assistant: MIKE OWENS
Director: ROLAND L. DERRICKSON
Communityt Relations Officer: TERRI HOPKINS

Resource Management Unit
Manager, Aglands Preservtion: MICHAEL McGRATH
State Forester, Forestry: WALT GABEL

Production Support and Promotion Unit
Managers: BILL SAMMONS, Marketing and Product Development; JEAN HAMILTON, Agriculture Products Grading; RICHARD GOERGER, Seed Laboratory; LINDA BRADLEY, Plant Industry
State Veterinarian, Poultry and Animal Health: H. WESLEY TOWERS

Consumer Protection Unit
Managers: EUGENE KEELEY, Weights and Measures; GRIER STAYTON, Pesticides Compliance; TERESA CRENSHAW, Agriculture Compliance Laboratory; H. DAVIS SHOCKLEY, Meat Inspection

DEPARTMENT OF NATURAL RESOURCES AND
ENVIRONMENTAL CONTROL, 89 Kings Highway, P.O. Box 1401, Dover 19903
Reorganized in 1970 to encompass the Board of Game and Fish Commissioners, Shell Fisheries Commission, State Park Commission, State Soil and Water Commission, and Water and Air Resources Commission.
Secretary: JOHN E. WILSON III (302, 736-4403)
Executive Assistant: DAVID S. HUGG III (736-3091)
Office of Information and Education: DAVID SMALL (736-4506)
Publication: *Delaware Conservationist*
Associate Editors NANCY I. ROLLI; KATHLEEN JAMISON; DONNA STACHECKI (736-4506)

Division of Air and Waste Management
Director: PHILLIP G. RETALLICK (736-4764)
Deputy Director: JUNE D. MacARTOR (736-4764)

Manager, Air Resources: ROBERT R. FRENCH (736-4791)
Manager, Waste Management: GARY A. MOLCHAN (736-3672)

Division of Water Resources
Director: R. WAYNE ASHBEE (736-4860)
Deputy Director: GERARD L. ESPOSITO (736-5722)
Manager, Technical Services: HARRY W. OTTO (736-4771)
Manager, Wetlands: WILLIAM F. MOYER (736-4691)
Manager, Surface Water Management: ROBERT ZIMMERMAN (736-5731)
Manager, Planning and Support: ROBERT H. MacPHERSON (736-5409)
Manager, Ground Water Management: ALAN J. FARLING (736-4762)

Division of Fish and Wildlife
Director: WILLIAM C. WAGNER II (736-5295)
Assistant Director, Federal Aid Coordinator: Vacant (736-5296)
Manager, Fisheries: CHARLES A. LESSER (736-3441)
Manager, Wildlife: H. LLOYD ALEXANDER JR. (736-5297)
Manager, Mosquito Control: CHESTER J. STACHECKI (736-4492)
Manager, Acquisition/Construction: RONAL W. SMITH (736-5296)
Manager of Enforcement: RODNEY L. HARMIC (736-3440)

Division of Parks and Recreation
Director: WILLIAM J. HOPKINS (736-4401)
Manager, Recreation Section: GLENN T. SMOOT (736-4413)
Manager, Parks Section: EARL R. FENTON (736-4702)
Manager, Technical Services: CHARLES SALKIN (736-5284)

Division of Soil and Water Conservation
Director: JOHN A. HUGHES (736-4411)
Manager, Drainage Operations: RICHARD T. SMITH (856-5488)
Manager, Beach Preservation: ROBERT D. HENRY (736-4411)
Manager, Conservation Districts: FREDERICK T. MOTT (736-4411)

GEOLOGICAL SURVEY, University of Delaware, Newark 19716 (302, 451-2833)
Founded in 1951 to study the geology, water, and other earth resources of Delaware; charged, also, to prepare reports, maps, and otherwise disseminate its findings, and to provide assistance in its area to other agencies and individuals.
State Geologist and Director: ROBERT R. JORDAN
Associate Director, Geology: THOMAS E. PICKETT
Associate Director, Hydrology: KENNETH D. WOODRUFF

SEA GRANT PROGRAM
Director, Delaware Sea Grant College Program: DR. CAROLYN THOROUGHGOOD, University of Delaware, Newark 19716 (302, 451-2841)
Executive Director: ANDREW T. MANUS, University of Delaware, Newark 19716 (302, 451-8062)

STATE EXTENSION SERVICE
Director of Extension Service: DR. RICHARD E. FOWLER, University of Delaware, Townsend Hall, Newark 19717-1303 (302, 451-2504)

CITIZENS' GROUPS

WILDLIFE FEDERATION OF DELAWARE, P.O. Box 8111, Newark 19711
A representative statewide organization, affiliated with the National Wildlife Federation, primarily devoted to the wise use, conservation, aesthetic appreciation, and restoration of wildlife and other natural resources.
President: JOHN CAMPANELLI, 70 Concord Creek Rd., Glen Mills, PA 19342 (215, 358-0430)
Secretary: MARY ANN PARASKIEWICZ, 1915 Windemere Ave., Wilmington 19804 (302, 998-7532)
Affiliate Representative: JOHN PARASKIEWICZ, 1915 Windmere Ave., Wilmington 19804 (302, 998-7532)
Alternate: JOHN WARREN, R.D. 1, Box 286, Smyrna 19977
Editor: JOHN CAMPANELLI

DELAWARE ASSOCIATION OF CONSERVATION DISTRICTS
President and Council Member: RICHARD B. WELDON, 1039 Red Lion Rd., New Castle 19720 (834-6434)
Vice-President: ROBERT WINKLER, R.D. 1, Box 168, Felton 19943 (302, 335-3351)
Secretary: DEAN C. BELT, 114 N. Dillwyn Rd., Windy Hills, Newark 19711 (451-2506)
Treasurer: DARIEL C. RAKESTRAW, R.D. 3, Box 247-A, Hockessin 19707 (366-5372)

DELAWARE BASS CHAPTER FEDERATION
An organization of Bassmaster Chapters, affiliated with the Bass Anglers Sportsman Society, to fight pollution, assist state and national conservation agencies in their efforts and to teach the young people of our country good conservation practices. Dedicated to the realistic conservation of our water resources.
President: BILL HUBBARD, 219 N. Walnut St., Milford 19963 (301, 742-3156/302, 422-7729)

DELAWARE MUSEUM OF NATURAL HISTORY, P.O. Box 3937, Wilmington 19807 (302, 658-9111)
To increase awareness and understanding of the diversity of life and the interdependence of all life forms including man through museum exhibits, programs, and research. Founded: 1957. Membership: 550.
Director: BARBARA H. BUTLER, Ph.D.
Malacology: RUDIGER BIELER, Ph.D.
Public Programming: RICHARD M. BUSCH, Ph.D.
Ornithology: GENE K. HESS
Public Relations: MARY JANE ARDEN
Publications: Nemouria; Musenews (DMNH Newsletter)
Editors: RUDIGER BIELER; MARY JANE ARDEN

DELAWARE NATURE EDUCATION SOCIETY, INC., Box 700, Hockessin 19707 (302, 239-2334)
To help preserve representative natural areas in Delaware, foster understanding and appreciation of conservation, natural science, and ecology through nature education programs, and provide now and in the future some pleasant environment in which to live, work, and enjoy life. Membership: 2,100. Founded: 1964.
President: BERNARD S. DEMPSEY
Vice-President: NANCY G. FREDERICK
Secretary: ROBERT D. VARRIN
Treasurer: M. DANIEL DAUDON
Executive Director: MICHAEL E. RISKA
Executive Secretary: JANICE B. TAYLOR
Publications: Newsletter; Wildflowers of Delaware and the Eastern Shore; Program brochures
Editors: CLAUDE E. PHILLIPS; LORRAINE M. FLEMING

DELAWARE WILD LANDS, INC., 303 Main St., Odessa 19730 (302-834-1332/378-2736)
A nonprofit charitable land conservancy actively engaged in acquiring areas on the Delmarva Peninsula for their natural resource values and for educational purposes; presently owns and

manages approximately 20,000 acres. Produced two films, "The Endangered Shore" and "Swamp," now available on loan or for purchase. Organized: 1961.
Executive Director: HOLGER H. HARVEY
President: EDWARD W. COOCH, JR.
Vice-Presidents: MRS. HENRY B. DUPONT; WILLIAM K. DUPONT
Secretary: EUGENE H. BAYARD
Treasurer: NATHAN HAYWARD III

DELMARVA ORNITHOLOGICAL SOCIETY, P.O. Box 4247, Greenville 19807

The purpose of this society shall be the promotion of the study of birds, the advancement and diffusion of ornithological knowledge, and the conservation of birds and their environment. Membership: 380. Organized: 1963.
President: HOWARD P. BROKAW, 2701 Montchanin Rd., Greenville 19807
Corresponding Secretary: JOSEPH BUDAY, 301-9 Harbor Dr., Claymont 19703
Publications: *Delmarva Ornithologist; DOS Flyer*
Editor: DR. LLOYD L. FALK, 123 Bette Rd., Lynnfield, Wilmington 19803

FORWARD LANDS, INC., 2800 Pennsylvania Ave., Wilmington 19806 (302, 655-2151)

A nonprofit organization dedicated to the preservation and conservation of our natural resources. Forward Lands promotes alternatives which demand intelligent land stewardship and planning by way of purchase, easements, bequests, or gifts. Current project: Scenic River and Road Project, Brandywine Creek Area. Established: 1964.
President: FRANCIS I. dUPONT
Vice-President: ARNOLD GOLDSBOROUGH
Treasurer: ROBERT F. KOKE
Secretary: PETER A. LARSON
Publications: *Forward Lands* Brochure; *Annual Report*

TROUT UNLIMITED DELAWARE CHAPTER (Part of Mid-Atlantic Council)

A statewide chapter dedicated to the protection and enhancement of the coldwater fishery resource.
President: TIM STULL, 1507 Clayton Rd., Wilmington 19805 (302, 429-8853)
Membership: MYRON S. HARDESTY, 78 White Clay Crescent, Newark 19711

DISTRICT OF COLUMBIA

GOVERNMENT AGENCIES

DEPARTMENT OF PUBLIC WORKS, 2000 14th St., NW, Washington 20009

Director: JOHN E. TOUCHSTONE (202, 939-8000)
Public Space Maintenance Administration, Administrator: ANNE W. HOEY (767-8512)
Water and Sewer Utility Administration, Administrator: WALLACE WHITE (767-7651)

STATE EXTENSION SERVICES

Director of Extension Service: DR. THORNELL K. PAGE, University of the District of Columbia, 901 Newton St., NE, Washington 20017 (202, 576-6993)
State Program Leader, Agriculture and Natural Resources: WIL-

LIAM EASLEY, DC Cooperative Extension Service, 901 Newton St., NE, Washington 20017 (576-6951)

CITIZENS' GROUPS

DISTRICT OF COLUMBIA CONSERVATION DISTRICT

Chairman and Council Member: LACY C. STREETER, 614 H St., NW, Rm. 1120, Washington 20001 (202, 727-7170)
District Manager: JAMES BUTLER, 614 H St., NW, Rm. LL18, Washington 20001 (727-7577)

FORCE (FRIENDS OF ROCK CREEK'S ENVIRONMENT), Rock Creek Park, National Park Service, National Capital Region, 5000 Glover Rd., NW, Washington 20015 (202, 426-6835/6832)

A voluntary support group to the park. Volunteers are retirees, scouts, intern students, singles, couples, single parents, or families who are involved in a variety of conservation and interpretive programs throughout the park. Projects completed in 1987 were removal of exotic plantlife (English Ivy, Kudzu), erosion control, trail repair, leading interpretive hikes, assisting with park photography, and assisting with costumed interpretation at Pierce Mill and Old Stone House. New members welcome. Membership: 50. Established: 1975.
FORCE/Volunteer Coordinator: CINDY DONALDSON
Superintendent, Rock Creek Park: ROLLAND SWAIN

POTOMAC APPALACHIAN TRAIL CLUB, 1718 N St., NW, Washington 20036 (202, 638-5306)

Maintains a network of trails, extending over 800 miles. Activities include publication of maps and guidebooks, mountaineering, ski-touring, construction and maintenance of trails, shelters, and cabins, and many conservation activities. Membership: 3,600. Founded: 1927.
President: WARREN SHARP
Supervisor of Trails: TOM FLOYD
General Secretary: SANDRA MARRA
Publications: *Potomac Appalachian*
Editor: LINDA KEYSER

TROUT UNLIMITED NATIONAL CAPITAL CHAPTER

Dedicated to the protection and enhancement of coldwater fishing resources.
President (Acting): SCOTT FALEY, 1706 New Hampshire Ave., NW, Washington 20009

WILDLIFE AND FORESTRY PROFESSIONAL INFORMATION EXCHANGE, Box 18028, Washington 20036 (202, 659-9510)

Nonprofit, membership organization of area natural resource professionals. Meets monthly to hear timely presentations and attend field trips. Provides an informal opportunity to exchange ideas and information on environmental issues, events, and careers. Founded: 1982.
President: DR. ALBERT M. MANVILLE (703, 237-3920)
Vice-President: KATHRYN R. TOLLERTON (202, 659-9510)
Executive Board: LISA PETERFREUND (703, 998-0494); JULIE DUNLAP (301, 997-7057); CHRIS CASSIDY (202, 546-8321); SANDY SCHOLAR (703, 237-3920); CINDY SHOGAN (202, 543-9389); CHRISTINE HAUGEN (301, 654-5821); HARRY TOLLERTON, Esq. (202, 667-5013); ROBERT J. SMITH (202, 667-0191)
Counsel: HARRY TOLLERTON, Esq. (202, 546-2237)

Publication: *The Environmental Network Newsletter*

WILDLIFE SOCIETY NATIONAL CAPITOL CHAPTER

President-Elect: JIM SWEENEY, USDA Forest Service, P.O. Box 96090, RP-E 1208, Washington 20090-6097 (703, 235-2756)

President: MATTHEW C. PERRY, Patuxent Wildlife Research Center, Laurel, MD 20708 (301, 498-0331)

Secretary-Treasurer: TERESA RAML, 1704 Woodtree Cir., Annapolis, MD (703, 235-8015)

FLORIDA

GOVERNMENT AGENCIES

GOVERNOR: BOB MARTINEZ, Governor of Florida, State Capitol, Tallahassee 32399-0001 (904, 488-4441)

DEPARTMENT OF AGRICULTURE AND CONSUMER SERVICES, State Capitol, Tallahassee 32301

Commissioner: DOYLE CONNER (904, 488-3022/376-1990)

Division of Forestry

Director: JOHN M. BETHEA
Assistant Director: HAROLD K. MIKELL
Chief, Fire Control: MICHAEL LONG
Chief, Forest Education: ROBERT McDONALD
Chief, Forest Management: W.R. HELM JR.

Soil and Water Conservation, P.O. Box 1269, Gainesville 32602 (904, 376-1990)

The department provides administrative legislative and promotional assistance to sixty-one Soil and Water Conservation Districts in Florida.

Council Chairman: LYNN HARRISON (813, 322-1188)
Chief, Bureau of Soil and Water Conservation: GLENN BISSETT

DEPARTMENT OF ENVIRONMENTAL REGULATION, 2600 Blair Stone Rd., Tallahassee 32399-2400 (904, 488-4805)

Chairman, Environmental Regulation Commission: ROBERT A. MANDELL

Secretary: DALE TWACHTMANN
Assistant Secretary: JOHN SHEARER
Information Director: WAYNE W. STEVENS (488-9334)
Director, Division of Water Management: RANDY ARMSTRONG (488-0130)
Director, Division of Water Facilities: HOWARD L. RHODES (487-1855)
Director, Division of Administrative and Technical: MIKE PEYTON (488-0876)
Director, Division of Waste Management: RICHARD WILKINS (488-0190)
Director (Acting), Division of Air Resources Management: STEVE SMALLWOOD (488-L344)
Publications: *Newsletter; Florida's Environment*
Editor: ROGER DOHERTY

DEPARTMENT OF NATURAL RESOURCES, Marjory Stoneman Douglas Bldg., Tallahassee 32303 (904, 488-1554)

Florida law charges the department with the "administration, supervision, development and conservation" of Florida's natural resources.

Executive Board: BOB MARTINEZ, Governor; JIM SMITH, Secretary of State; BOB BUTTERWORTH, Attorney General; GERALD A. LEWIS, Comptroller; BILL GUNTER, Treasurer; BETTY CASTOR, Commissioner of Education; DOYLE CONNER, Commissioner of Agriculture

Executive Director: TOM GARDNER
Assistant Executive Director: DON E. DUDEN
Director of Communications: RANDY LEWIS
Legal Office: TOM TOMASELLO, General Counsel

Division of Administration (904, 488-8587)

Director: MYRA WILLIAMS
Assistant Director: JOHN CHERRY
Chief, Bureau of Finance and Accounting: LARRY McGINNIS
Chief, Bureau of Management Systems & Services: BRENDA CLOTFELTER
Chief, Bureau of Purchasing: Vacant
Chief, Bureau of Office Operations: Vacant
Chief, Bureau of Personnel: ALYCE PARMER

Division of Marine Resources (904, 488-6058)

Director: EDWIN A. JOYCE, JR.
Chief, Bureau of Marine Research: KAREN STEIDINGER
Chief, Marine Resource Regulation & Development: JOHN SCHNEIDER
Chief, Bureau of Marketing & Extension Services: CHARLES THOMAS

Division of Beaches and Shores (904, 487-4469)

Director: KIRBY GREEN
Assistant Director: ANDREW GRAYSON
Chief, Bureau of Coastal Data Acquisition: HAL BEAN
Chief, Bureau of Coastal Engineering and Regulation: AL DEVEREAUX
Administrator, Office of Beach Erosion Control: LONNIE RYDER
Administrator, Office of Administration Enforcement: GILL HILL

Division of Law Enforcement (904, 488-6559)

Director: COL. D.N. ELLINGSEN
Marine Patrol Operations, Deputy Director: C.S. KIDD
Marine Patrol Support Services, Deputy Director: R.L. HEALY

Division of Resource Management (904, 488-3177)

Director: JEREMY CRAFT
Assistant Director: H.J. WOODARD
Chief, Bureau of Geology: WALTER SCHMIDT
Chief, Bureau of Aquatic Plant Research and Control: SHIRLEY FOX
Chief (Acting), Bureau of Mine Reclamation: RANDY BUSHEY

Division of State Lands

Director: PETE MALLISON
Deputy Directors: DIANA DARTLAND; ED CONKLIN
Chief, Bureau of Submerged Lands: CASEY FITZGERALD
Chief, Bureau of Survey and Mapping: TERRY WILKINSON
Chief, Bureau of Uplands: DEBORAH HART
Chief, Bureau of Aquatic Preserve: RUSS DANSER
Chief, Bureau of Sanctuaries and Research: DANIEL PENTON
Chief, Bureau of Land Acquisition: CHARLES HARDEE
Chief, Bureau of Appraisal: Vacant

Division of Recreation and Parks (904, 488-6131)

Supervises, administers, regulates, and controls the operation of state parks, including sites of historic significance; and administers the state's recreational land acquisition and development program.

Director: NEY C. LANDRUM
Chief, Office of Recreation Services: RICHARD FROEMKE

Chief, Bureau of Park Planning and Design: R. DOUGLASS STRICK-LAND
Deputy Director, Park Operations: ELLISON E. HARDEE
Chief, Office of Policy and Planning: ALBERT GREGORY
Chief, Bureau of Scientific and Technical Services: JAMES A. STEVENSON
Chief, Bureau of Construction: MIKE BULLOCK
Chief, Bureau of Park Operations, Region I: JAMES COOK
Deputy Director, Support Services: NEVIN G. SMITH
Chief, Bureau of Park Operations, Region II: C.W. HARTSFIELD, JR.
Chief, Bureau of Park Operations, Region III: JOSEPH F. KNOLL, JR.

FLORIDA COOPERATIVE FISH AND WILDLIFE RESEARCH UNIT, U.S.D.I. 117 Newins-Ziegler Hall, University of Florida, Gainesville 32611 (904, 392-1861)

Established in 1979 by cooperative agreement among the Fish and Wildlife Service, Florida Game and Fresh Water Fish Commission and University of Florida. Primary purpose is research, graduate education and extension activities integrating fish and wildlife ecology and management in Florida's unique ecosystems.
Leader: DR. WILEY M. KITCHENS
Assistant Leader (Wildlife): DR. H. FRANKLIN PERCIVAL
Assistant Leader (Fisheries): DR. CAROLE C. McIVOR

GAME AND FRESH WATER FISH COMMISSION, 620 S. Meridian St., Tallahassee 32399-1600 (904, 488-1960)

Commissioners: THOMAS L. HIRES, SR., Lake Wales; WILLIAM G. BOSTICK, JR., Auburndale; C. TOM RAINEY, D.V.M., Miami; MRS. GILBERT W. HUMPHREY, Miccosukee; DON WRIGHT, Orlando
Executive Director: ROBERT M. BRANTLY (488-2975)
Assistant Executive Director: ALLAN L. EGBERT (488-3084)
General Counsel: JAMES V. ANTISTA (487-1764)
Director, Division of Fisheries: SMOKIE HOLCOMB (488-4066)
Director, Division of Wildlife: FRANK MONTALBANO III (488-3831)
Director, Division of Law Enforcement: BRANTLEY GOODSON (488-6251)
Director, Office of Informational Services: DENNIS E. HAMMOND (488-4676)
Director, Division of Administrative Services: BILL SUMNER (488-6551)
Director, Office of Environmental Services: BRAD HARTMAN (488-6662)
Publication: *Florida Wildlife*
Editor: Vacant (488-5564)

MARINE LABORATORY, Florida State University, Rt. 1, Box 219A, Sopchoppy 32358 (SUNCOM 904, 644-4740)

Includes studies on the aquatic chemistry of pesticide wastes, oil pollution, and sewage on marine environments, chemistry of the marine atmosphere, coastal zone management, and analysis of shallow water marine communities.
Director: W. ROSS ELLINGTON

SEA GRANT COLLEGE

Director, SUS, Florida Sea Grant College Program: DR. JAMES C. CATO, Bldg. 803, Rm. 4, University of Florida, Gainesville 32611-0341 (904, 392-5870)
Sea Grant Extension Program Assistant Dean and Coordinator: MARION L. CLARKE, 117 Newins/Ziegler Hall, University of Florida, Gainesville 32611 (392-1837)
Associate Director, SUS, Florida Sea Grant College Program: DR. WILLIAM SEAMAN, Bldg. 803, Rm. 4, University of Florida, Gainesville 32611-0341 (392-5870)

Publications: *Marine Log; Florida Sea Grant SGEB-5* listing various publications available
Editors: LIN WELCH (392-2801); TOM LEAHY (392-2801)

SOUTH FLORIDA WATER MANAGEMENT DISTRICT, 3301 Gun Club Rd., P.O. Box 24680, West Palm Beach 33416-4680 (407, 686-8800/1-800-432-2045)

Responsible for local cooperation in the Federal-State Central and Southern Florida Flood Control Project. Goals include flood control, water supply, water quality, and environmental protection to sixteen counties in south Florida. Additional benefits are preservation of natural conditions in Everglades, land purchases under Save Our Rivers program, enhancement of wetlands, fish, wildlife, and waterfowl and public recreation.
Governing Board: NANCY ROEN, Chairman, Plantation; J.D. YORK, Vice-Chairman, Palm City; JOHN R. WODRASKA, Executive Director and Secretary
Members: NATHANIEL P. REED, Hobe Sound; OSCAR M. CORBIN, JR., Ft. Myers; JAMES F. GARNER, Ft. Myers; DORAN A. JASON, Key Biscayne; ARSENIO MILIAN, Miami; FRITZ STEIN, Belle Glade; MIKE STOUT, Windermere
Executive Council Members: JOHN WODRASKA, Executive Director; TILFORD CREEL, Deputy Executive Dirctor; BILL BRANNEN, Assistant Executive Dirctor; STEVE LIGHT, Policy Director; JOE MOORE, Budget Director; BONNIE KRANZER, Program Evaluation Director; K.C. MALONE, Senior Staff Analyst; JIM HARVEY, Director, Office of Resource Assistance; CATHY ANCLADE, Director, Office of Communications; STEVE WALKER, District Counsel; IRENE QUINCEY, Deputy District Counsel; JOHN LYNCH, Director, Office of Technical Services; BILL MALONE, Department Director, Land Management; FRED DAVIS, Deputy Department Director, Land Management; JIM YAGER, Department Director, Finance and Administration; ED HILL, Deputy Department Director, Finance and Administration; PETE RHOADS, Department Director, Resource Planning; LESLIE WEDDERBURN, Deputy Department Director, Resource Planning; DICK ROGERS, Department Director, Resource Control; FRED DAVIS, Deputy Department Director, Resource Control; JEANNE HALL, Deputy Department Director, Resource Control; JOE SCHWEIGART, Department Director, Resource Operations; ALAN HALL, Deputy Department Director, Resource Operations TOM MacVICAR, Deputy Director, Construction Management; BERNIE SCHATTNER, Deputy Department Director, Construction Management

STATE COOPERATIVE EXTENSION SERVICES

Director of Extension Service and Sea Grant Advisory Program: DR. JOHN T. WOESTE, 1038 McCarty Hall, University of Florida, Gainesville 32611 (904, 392-1761)
Extension Forester: MITCH FLINCHUM, 342B Newins Ziegler Hall, University of Florida, Gainesville 32611 (392-5420)
Coordinator of Sea Grant Science Programs: DR. MARION L. CLARKE, 117 Newins Ziegler Hall, University of Florida, Gainesville 32611 (392-1837)
Director, Center for Natural Resources Programs: DR. JOSEPH JOYCE, Center for Aquatic Weeds, University of Florida, 7922 NW 71st St., Gainesville 32606 (392-9613)
Extension Wildlife: DR. WAYNE MARION, 118 Newins-Ziegler Hall, University of Florida, Gainesville 32611 (392-5420)
Extension Fisheries: DR. CHARLES CICHRA, Fisheries and Aquaculture, 7922 NW 71st St., Gainesville 32606 (392-9617)

STATE DEPARTMENT OF HEALTH AND REHABILITATIVE SERVICES, State Health Office, 1317 Winewood Blvd., Tallahassee 32301 (904, 487-2705)

Prevention and Control Programs:

State Health Officer: CHARLES S. MAHAN, M.D.
Environmental Health Programs: EANIX POOLE
Epidemiology Program: WILLIAM J. BIGLER, Ph.D.
Environmental Hazards: THOMAS D. ATKESON

CITIZENS' GROUPS

FLORIDA WILDLIFE FEDERATION, P.O. Box 6870, Tallahassee 32314 (904, 656-7113)
A representative statewide organization, affiliated with the National Wildlife Federation, primarily devoted to the wise use, conservation, aesthetic appreciation, and restoration of wildlife and other natural resources. Organized: 1935.
Chairman: J. STEPHEN O'HARA, 1061 Holly Lane, Jacksonville, FL 32207 (904, 354-0624)
President: MANLEY FULLER
Affiliate Representative: TIM KEYSER, P.O. Box 92, Interlachen, FL 32048 (904, 684-4673)
Alternate: J. STEPHEN O'HARA,
Publication: Wildlife Notes
Editor: RICHARD FARREN, Rt. 5, Box 610, Tallahassee 32301

ENVIRONMENTAL INFORMATION CENTER OF THE FLORIDA CONSERVATION FOUNDATION, INC., 1191 Orange Ave., Winter Park 32789 (407, 644-5377)
A public, nonprofit, tax-exempt foundation engaged in environmental research and education pertaining to Florida. Incorporated: 1968.
President: DR. JOHN O. BLACKBURN, 221 Shell Point Rd., Maitland 32751 (407, 644-1269)
Vice-President: M.C. RIGANTE, 2115 Nela Ave., Belle Isle 32809 (855-1282)
Secretary/Treasurer: DEAN FLETCHER, 2405 Coolidge Ave., Orlando 32804 (423-7976)
Director, Environmental Information Center: WILLIAM M. PARTINGTON
Publications: *ENFO Newsletter; Build Your Own Solar Water Heater; Report of Investigation of Environmental Effects of Private Waterfront Canals; Sustainable Futures; Florida's Electric Future: Building Plentiful Supplies on Conservation; An Official's Guide to Florida Environmental Issues; Florida Calamity Calendar 1989; Solar Heating for Swimming Pools; The Untapped Oilfield, an Economist's Case for Public Action to Promote Energy Conservation*
Editor: GERALD GROW, ENFO, 809 Teague St., Tallahassee 32303

FLORIDA ASSOCIATION OF SOIL AND WATER CONSERVATION DISTRICT SUPERVISORS
Vice-President: GENE WELDON, 1900 Brumley Rd., Chuluota 32766 (305, 365-6034)
Vice-President: EARL CLARK, 827 Paddock Way, Casselberry 32707 (699-6560)
Secretary-Treasurer: WYMAN LONG, Rt. I, Box 3850, Palatka 32077 (904, 328-3471)

FLORIDA AUDUBON SOCIETY, 1101 Audubon Way, Maitland 32751 (407, 647-2615)
A statewide organization founded in 1900 to promote public interest, understanding, and protection of Florida wildlife, and the environment and habitats that support it.
Chairman of the Board: LEAH SCHAD, 1628 Boardman, West Palm Beach 33407
President: DR. BERNARD J. YOKEL

Senior Vice-President: CHARLES LEE
Vice-President, Science and Research: PETER C.H. PRITCHARD, Ph.D.
Vice-President, Ornithological Research: HERBERT W. KALE II, Ph.D.
Vice-President, Environmental Education: WENDY HALE
Treasurer/Secretary: ALAN STEINBERG, 7800 Red Rd., Miami 33143
Publication: *The Florida Naturalist*
Editor: PEGGY LANTZ

FLORIDA BASS CHAPTER FEDERATION
An organization of Bassmaster Chapters, affiliated with the Bass Anglers Sportsman Society, organized to fight pollution, assist state and national conservation agencies in their efforts and to teach young people of our country good conservation practices. Dedicated to the realistic conservation of our water resources.
President: WILLIE TOWNS, P.O. Box 52, Lake Hamilton 33851 (813, 439-2156)

FLORIDA DEFENDERS OF THE ENVIRONMENT, INC., Home Office, 1523 NW 4th St., Gainesville 32601 (904, 372-6965); Environmental Service Center, 102 West Third Ave., Tallahassee 32303 (904, 222-0433)
A nonprofit organization of scientists, attorneys, and other specialists who volunteer their expertise by researching and compiling data on potential threats to the Florida environment. This information is synthesized and provided to government, industry, citizen organizations, and news media in an unbiased, reliable format.
President: MARJORIE H. CARR 1523 NW 4th Street, Gainesville 32601 (904, 375-1544)
Vice-President: JOSEPH W. LITTLE, Esq.
Secretary: KATHERINE EWEL, Ph.D.
Treasurer: RICHARD HAMANN, Esq.
Suwannee River Coordinators: HELEN H. HOOD; JANE WALKER
Executive Director: NORMAN L. RICHARDS, Ph.D., 1523 NW 4th St., Gainesville 32601 (372-6965)
Apalachicola River Coordinator: STEVE LEITMAN, Environmental Service Center
Oklawaha River Coordinators: JOHN H. KAUFMANN, Ph.D.; MARJORIE H. CARR
Publication: *The Monitor*
Editor: KARLA BRANDT

FLORIDA FORESTRY ASSOCIATION, P.O. Box 1696, Tallahassee 32302 (904, 222-5646)
Nonprofit, trade-supported organization of industries, businesses and individuals who encourage the promotion, development and protection of forestry in Florida. Founded: 1923.
President: H. WYNDELL SAPP, P.O. Box 875, Cantonment 32533
President-Elect: WILLIAM K. COOK, P.O. Box 87, Callahan 32011
Vice-President: KELLEY R. SMITH, JR., P.O. Box 75, Bostwick 32007
Secretary-Treasurer: JOHN A. BEALL, P.O. Box 191, Tallahassee 32302
Executive Vice-President: WILLIAM CARROLL LAMB, C.A.E.
Publication: *Pines and Needles*
Editor: DEBRA OSBORNE

FLORIDA WILDLIFE SANCTUARY, 2600 Otter Creek Ln., Melbourne 32935 (305, 254-8843)
Receive injured wildlife and maintain complete hospital facilities; keep statistical data on all injuries, sickness, recovery dates of animals and birds. Have 64 environmental slide programs with narrated lectures available to state, county and civic organizations upon request. Membership: 2,300 including 91 associate clubs.

President: CARLTON O. TEATE
Vice-President: WILLIAM C. POTTER, 1380 Sarno Rd., Melbourne
    32935
Secretary: GLADYS TEATE
Treasurer: EMMETT MITCHELL, 1450 Morgan Dr., Merritt Island
    32952
Environmental Schedule Planning: ED WASHBURN, City Hall, City
    of Melbourne 32901
Publication: *The Coot Call*
Editor: LINDA ROGGENKAMP

IZAAK WALTON LEAGUE OF AMERICA, INC. (Florida Div.)
President: CARL KEELER, 4512A 86th Street Court W, Bradenton
    33529 (813, 792-8482)
Treasurer: BETTY KUCK, 18700 Rio Vista Dr., Jupiter 33458
    (746-4656)

MANASOTA-88, c/o Gloria Rains, 5314 Bay State Rd.,
    Palmetto 34221
Chairman: GLORIA RAINS (813, 722-7413)
Vice-Chairmen: REBECCA EGER, 324 W. Royal Flamingo Dr.,
    Sarasota 33578 (366-1765); RUSSELL G. FERNALD, 5920
    Gulf of Mexico Dr., Longboat Key 33548 (383-3834)
Publication: *The Manasota-88 Newsletter*
Editor: GLORIA RAINS

SANIBEL-CAPTIVA CONSERVATION FOUNDATION, INC., P.O.
    Drawer S, 3333 Sanibel-Captiva Rd., Sanibel 33957,
    Nature Center Office: (472-2329); Native Plant Nursery:
    (472-1932); Research Laboratory: (813, 395-0222)
The Conservation Foundation is a not-for-profit organization dedicated to the preservation of natural resources and wildlife habitat
on and around Sanibel and Captiva. Community programs include:
land acquisition, habitat management, advocacy, research, education, and wildlife assistance. Formed: 1967.
Executive Director: ERICK LINDBLAD
Publication: *Conservation Update*

SAVE THE MANATEE CLUB, 500 N. Maitland Ave., Maitland
    32751 (407, 539-0990)
A statewide organization founded 1981, by Governor Bob Graham
and singer/songwriter Jimmy Buffett, to promote public awareness
and education of the endangered West Indian manatee. Current
number of members on the committee are 10. Current number of
members in the Save The Manatee Club are over 16,000.
Chairman: JIMMY BUFFETT, c/o Margaritaville Store, 424A Flem-
    ing St., Key West 33040 (305-296-9089)
Vice-Chairman: PATRICK M. ROSE, St. Petersburg Marine Lab,
    Florida Department of Natural Resources, 100 8th Ave. SE, St.
    Petersburg 33701 (813, 896-8626)
Executive Director: JUDITH DELANEY VALLEE

WILDLIFE SOCIETY FLORIDA CHAPTER
President: LARRY PERRIN, Rt. 3 Box 5466, Crawfordville 32327
    (904, 488-6661)
President-Elect: DONALD PROGULSKE, Avon Park Air Force Range,
    Avon Park 33825 (813, 452-4119)
Secretary-Treasurer: FRED JOHNSON, 3991 SE 27th Ct., Okeec-
    bobee 34974 (813, 763-7469)

GEORGIA

GOVERNMENT AGENCIES

GOVERNOR: JOE FRANK HARRIS, Governor of Georgia, State
    Capitol, Atlanta 30334 (404, 656-1776)

DEPARTMENT OF AGRICULTURE, Agriculture Bldg., 19 Martin
    Luther King Dr., Capitol Square, Atlanta 30334 (404, 656-
    3600)
The department serves farmers and consumers in the state by
verifying and enforcing accuracy and quality of both product and
service in many areas including content of food products, seed,
fertilizer, pesticides, fuel, weights and measures and bedding, and
through testing and eradication of certain animal diseases and
pests.
Commissioner: TOMMY IRVIN, Rt. 1, Mt. Airy 30563
Assistant Commissioners: JIM BRIDGES, Administration (656-
    3608); A.T. BRAY, Legislative (656-3743); JOHN COBB,
    Animal Industry (656-3671); BILLY MOORE, Consumer Protec-
    tion Field Forces (656-3627); RON CONLEY, Entomology and
    Pesticides (656-4958); BILL TRUBY, Fuel and Measures (656-
    3605); CECIL SPOONER, General Field Forces (656-3665);
    DON ROGERS, Marketing (656-3680); ELMO WINSTEAD, Plant
    Industry (656-3633)
Publications: *Farmers and Consumers Market Bulletin; Consumer
    Services Newsletter; Georgia Agriculture*
Editors: TOBY MOORE, Rm. 226; BRENDA JAMES JONES, Rm.
    300; LISA RAY, Rm. 300

DEPARTMENT OF NATURAL RESOURCES, Floyd Towers East,
    205 Butler St., Atlanta 30334 (404, 656-3530)
Commissioner: J. LEONARD LEDBETTER (404, 656-3500)
Deputy Commissioner for Administration: PETE MCDUFFIE
Executive Assistant: LONICE C. BARRETT
Board Members: DOLAN E. BROWN, JR., Twin City; MARSHALL
    MITCHELL, Atlanta; J. LEONARD EUBANKS, Pelham; PAT
    EDWARDS, Barnesville; LINDA S. BILLINGSLEY, Atlanta; C.W.
    JACKSON, Cartersville; JOHN LANIGAN, Atlanta; WILL D. (Billy)
    HERRIN, Chairman, Savannah; J. WIMBRIC WALKER, McRae;
    FELKER W. WARD, JR., Atlanta; JAMES H. BUTLER, Vice-
    Chairman, Smyrna; GLENN E. TAYLOR, Atlanta; DONALD J.
    CARTER, Gainesville; C. TOM GRIFFITH Watkinsville; JAMES
    GRIFFIN, JR., Secretary, Albany
Environmental Protection Division, Assistant Director: HAROLD
    REHEIS
Air Quality Evaluation Section, Chief: WILLIAM D. ESTES
Land Reclamation Program, Manager: LEWIS TINLEY
Land Protection Branch, Chief: JOHN TAYLOR
Air Protection Branch, Chief: ROBERT H. COLLOM, JR.
Water Protection Branch, Chief: JACK C. DOZIER
Game and Fish Division, Director: LEON KIRKLAND
Law Enforcement, Chief: COL. STEVE BLACK
Game Management, Chief: TERRY KILE
Fisheries Management, Chief: MIKE GENNINGS
Coastal Resources Division, Director: DUANE HARRIS
Parks and Recreation Historic Sites Division, Director: RICK
    COTHRAN
Parks Operation Section, Chief: EWELL LYLE
Maintenance and Construction Section, Chief: DAVID FREEDMAN
Historic Preservation, Chief: DR. ELIZABETH LYON
Internal Consultant for Parks, Recreation, and Historic Sites:
    JAMES H. PITTMAN
Communications, Director: KAKI THURBER

FORESTRY COMMISSION, Box 819, Macon 31298-4599
(912, 744-3211)

To foster, improve, and encourage reforestation; to engage in research and other projects for better forestry practices; and to detect, prevent, and combat forest fires. Organized: 1925.

Board of Commissioners: JIM L. GILLIS, JR., Chairman, Soperton (912, 529-3212); DR. GLORIA SHATTO, Mount Berry, GA; ELEY C. FRAZER, Albany; FELTON DENNEY, Carrolton; ROBERT SIMPSON III, Lakeland

Director: JOHN W. MIXON (912, 744-3237)

Deputy Director: DAVID L. WESTMORELAND (912, 744-3237)

Personnel Officer: RANDALL PERRY (404, 656-3204)

Chief, Forest Protection: WESLEY WELLS (912, 744-3251)

Chief, Forest Management: LYNN HOOVEN (912, 744-3241)

Chief, Forest Education: WILLIAM R. LAZENBY (912, 744-3364)

Chief, Reforestation: JOHNNY BRANAN (912, 744-3354)

Chief, Forest Administration: GARLAND NELSON (912, 744-3231)

Chief, Forest Research: J. FRED ALLEN (912, 744-3353)

Publication: *Georgia Forestry*

Editor: HOWARD BENNETT

GEORGIA COOPERATIVE FISH AND WILDLIFE RESEARCH UNIT, U.S.D.I., School of Forest Resources, University of Georgia, Athens 30602 (404, 546-2234)

The unit is supported by the U.S. Fish and Wildlife Service, Georgia Department of Natural Resources, the University of Georgia. Fisheries and wildlife research, graduate education and training, technical assistance and extension are the main missions of the unit. Established: July 1, 1984.

Leader: MICHAEL J. VAN DEN AVYLE

Assistant Leader, Fisheries: VICKI S. BLAZER

Assistant Leader, Wildlife: MICHAEL J. CONROY

INSTITUTE OF NATURAL RESOURCES, University of Georgia, Rm. 13, Ecology Bldg., Athens 30602 (404, 542-1555)

Applied research in selected areas of natural resources management and policy: water, wildlife, forestry, energy, and climate. Established: 1964.

Director: RONALD M. NORTH

Associate Director, Wildlife Management: A. SYDNEY JOHNSON

Associate Director, Climate Program: GAYTHER L. PLUMMER

Associate Director, Energy Program: JACKIE SELLERS

Associate Director, Water Resources: KATHRYN J. HATCHER

Associate Director, Environmental Law: J. OWENS SMITH

Associate Director, Environmental Policy: JAMES L. REGENS

SEA GRANT PROGRAM

Director, Sea Grant Program: DR. MAC RAWSON, JR., University of Georgia, Ecology Bldg., Athens 30602 (404, 542-7671)

STATE EXTENSION SERVICES

Director of Extension Service: DR. C. WAYNE JORDAN, University of Georgia, Athens 30602 (404, 542-3824)

Head, Extension Forest Resources Dept.: DR. JOHN E. GUNTER (542-3446)

Wildlife Specialist: DR. JEFFERY J. JACKSON (542-3447)

Fisheries Specialist: DR. GEORGE W. LEWIS (542-1924)

STATE SOIL AND WATER CONSERVATION COMMISSION, P.O. Box 8024, Athens 30603 (404, 542-3065)

Established in 1937 under the Soil Conservation Districts Act to work with and assist the 40 Soil And Water Conservation Districts and their 370 District Supervisors throughout Georgia.

Chairman: J.M. (Bob) PLEMONS, P.O. Box 295, Ringgold 30736

Executive Director: F. GRAHAM LILES, JR.

Publications: *Conservation Commission Newsletter; Conservation Contact*

Editor: DENNIS HOPPER

CITIZENS' GROUPS

GEORGIA WILDLIFE FEDERATION, 1936 Iris Dr., Suite G, Conyers 30207-5046 (404, 929-3350)

A representative statewide organization, affiliated with the National Wildlife Federation, primarily devoted to the wise use, conservation, aesthetic appreciation, and restoration of wildlife and other natural resources. Organized: 1955.

President: GLENN REEVES, 3135 Embry Hills Dr., Atlanta 30341 (404, 455-8344)

Executive Director: JERRY McCOLLUM

Affiliate Representative: VIVIAN PRYOR, P.O. Box 186, Newington 30446 (912, 857-4562)

Alternate: B. DOUGLAS RITHMIRE, Rt. l, Box 317-A-l, Cedar Bluff, Al 35959

Publication: Georgia Wildlife

Editor: JERRY McCOLLUM

GEORGIA ASSOCIATION OF CONSERVATION DISTRICT SUPERVISORS

President: WILLARD KIMSEY, Rt. 6, Box 380, Toccoa 30577 (404, 886-3507)

Immediate Past President: ABE T. MINCHEW, JR., Rt. I, Axson 31624 (912, 422-3479)

Secretary-Treasurer: OLIN C. NEWBY, P.O. Box 321, Washington 30673 (404, 678-7790)

Council Member: SILAS S. ELLIOTT, 999 Elliott Rd., McDonough 30253 (404, 957-5383)

GEORGIA BASS CHAPTER FEDERATION

An organization of Bassmaster Chapters, affiliated with the Bass Anglers Sportsman Society, organized to fight pollution, assist state and national conservation agencies in their efforts, and to teach young people of our country's good conservation practices. Dedicated to the realistic conservation of our water resources.

President: LARRY S. LEWIS, 11575 Northgate Trail, Roswell 30075 (H:404, 993-6597/W:404, 526-6385)

GEORGIA CONSERVANCY, INC., THE, 8615 Barnwell Rd., Alpharetta 30201 (404, 642-4000)

To preserve areas of scenic, geologic, biologic, historic, or recreational importance in Georgia; to establish or aid in the establishment of nature reserves; and to develop programs of conservation education. Membership: 3,000. Chartered: 1967.

Chairman: ELIZABETH H. BARNETT

Executive Director: G. ROBERT KERR

Coastal Director: HANS NEUHAUSER, 711 Sandtown Rd., Savannah 31410 (912, 897-6462)

Vice-Chairmen: TONY COPE; ROBERT C. CABOT; LOUISE B. FRANKLIN; ROBERT A. BRADDY; STEPHEN O'DAY

Secretary: TEED LOWANCE

Treasurer: DOUGLAS COCKRILL

Publications: *The Georgia Conservancy Newsletter ; Georgia Waterline; A Guide to the Georgia Coast;* environmental education publications include *Magic from the Woods* by Mark Warren; *Earth Trek; A New Agenda*

GEORGIA ENVIRONMENTAL COUNCIL, P.O. Box 2388, Decatur 30031-2388 (404, 262-1967)

A statewide umbrella of organizations interested in environmental protection that seeks to facilitate the exchange of information among member organizations, to provide a forum for discussion of environmental issues of interest to the members, and to monitor state government activities.

President: BRYAN RIPLEY-MAGER (373-2938)

Secretary: LUCINDA HEADRICK (634-3481)

Publications: *Pre-Legislative Status Report; Status Reports;* Newsletter; *Directory of Environmental Groups in Georgia*

GEORGIA FORESTRY ASSOCIATION, INC., 40 Marietta St. NW, Suite 1020, Atlanta 30303-2806 (404, 522-0951)

Membership: 3,800. Founded: 1907.

President: BONNER JONES, Millegeville

Vice-President: LARRY WALKER, Olethorpe

Treasurer: BOB CHAMBERS, Atlanta

Executive Director: BOB IZLAR, Atlanta

Publication: *Tops*

Executive Editor: BOB IZLAR, Atlanta

Editor: LAURA NEWBERN, Atlanta

GEORGIA TRAPPERS ASSOCIATION, P.O. Box 335, Doerun 31744 (912, 782-5417)

An organization of Georgia trappers and friends of trappers, affiliated with Georgia Wildlife Federation and National Trappers Association, organized to protect the rights of trappers to trap, to coordinate a trappers education program with the Georgia Department of Natural Resources and to conserve and protect the natural resources of Georgia. Organized: 1979. Membership: 630.

President: TOM ETHRIDGE, P.O. Box 335, Doerun 31744

Vice-President: Vacant

Secretary-Treasurer: GRACE M. CONDER, P.O. Box 474, Brooklet 30415

General Organizer: TOMMY KEY, Rt. 2, Newnan 30623

NTA Director: RALPH GOODSON, P.O. Box 4398, Albany 31706

TROUT UNLIMITED GEORGIA COUNCIL

A statewide council with 11 chapters working for the protection and enhancement of coldwater fishing resources.

Council Chairman: WILLIAM B. CHITWOOD, 106 Riderwood Dr., Dalton 30721 (404, 272-2300)

National Directors: DON MABRY, 5346 Chantilly Terr., College Park 30349 (997-3189); FRANK RICHARDSON, 2595 Lake Capri Dr., Lithonia 30058 (482-8206); EARL WORSHAM, Worsham Brothers, 1401 W Paces Ferry Rd. NW, Suite E-2, Atlanta 30327 (262-2855)

WILDLIFE SOCIETY GEORGIA CHAPTER

President: RONNIE SHELL, Piedmont National Wildlife Refuge, Rt. 1, Box 670, Round Oak 31038 (912, 986-5441)

President-Elect: DAVID WALLER, 6157 Crestview Dr., Covington 30209 (404, 656-3522)

Secretary-Treasurer: EMILY JOE WENTWORTH, SE Cooperative Wildlife Dis. Study, Vet. Med. Bldg. 6, University of Georgia, Athens 30602 (404, 542-8791)

GUAM

GOVERNMENT AGENCIES

GOVERNOR: JOSEPH F. ADA, Governor of Guam, Executive Chambers, Agana 96910 (671, 472-8931/9)

DEPARTMENT OF AGRICULTURE, Agana 96910 (734-3941, 42, 43)

Charged with responsibility for the conservation and management of Guam's fish, wildlife, soil, and forestry resources together with development of agricultural and fishery production for food purposes. Founded: 1950.

Director: Vacant

Deputy Director: JOAQUIN N. NAPUTI

Aquatic and Wildlife Resources, P.O. Box 2950, Agana, Guam 96921 (734-3944-5)

Chief: HARRY T. KAMI

Assistant Chief: ROBERT D. ANDERSON

Wildlife Biologists: GARY J. WILES; PAUL CONRY; MICHAEL RITTER; ROBERT BECK

Fisheries Biologists: WAYNE KRUCKENBERG; ROBERT MYERS; GERALD DAVIES; GRETCHEN R. GRIMM

Public Information Officer: LILLIAN L. MARIANO

Program Coordinator: Vacant

Biological Aides: HERMAN Q. MUNA; ROBERT J. CRUZ; JESSE P. GUERRERO; OSCAR MATA; ESTHER E.C. ARCA; GLENN V. SAN NICOLAS

DIVISION OF FORESTRY AND SOIL RESOURCES, P.O. Box 2950, Agana 96910 (671, 734-3948)

Chief: CARLOS L.T. NOQUEZ

Management Forester : RODOLFO L. ANDO

Forester II: DAVID T. LIMTIACO

Fire Prevention Specialist: NOLAN J. HENDRICKS

ENVIRONMENTAL PROTECTION AGENCY, P.O. Box 2999, Agana 96910 (671, 646-8863/4/5)

Responsibilities include: the supervision, planning, and regulation of all new or modified wastewater sources; development and protection of potable water supplies; solid and hazardous waste management pesticide importation, distribution, and use; and air pollution sources. Additionally, the agency reviews all environmental assessments and impact statements and coordinates with other local agencies in reviewing environmental impacts of new subdivisions, zone changes, and other land use activities. Established: 1973.

Administrator: CHARLES P. CRISOSTOMO

Deputy Administrator: ROLAND B. SOLIVIO

Board Secretary: SANDRA L. CRISOSTOMO

Head, Air and Land Programs Division: JAMES L. CANTO

Head, Monitoring Division: KENNETH L. MORPHEW

Head, Water Programs Division: NARCISO G. CUSTODIO

Director, Pesticide Program: VIRGILIO L. OBIAS

Director, Solid and Hazardous Waste Program: JOSE L.G. TECHAIRA

Director, Air Pollution Control Program: DAWN D. CAHOON

Director, Drinking Water Program: ANGEL B. MARQUEZ

Director, Water Pollution Control Program: DOMINGO S. CABUSAO

Director, Groundwater Management Program: LARRY W. STRAIN

Head, Environmental Review Section: GARY L. STILLBERGER

Publications: *Annual Report;* List available on request.

EXTENSION SERVICES

Dean/Director of Extension Service (Acting): JOSE T. BARCINAS, College of Agriculture and Life Sciences, University of Guam, UOG Station, Mangilao 96923

Associate Dean of Extension Service (Acting): EDITH R. BLANKEN-FILD

Associate Director of Agricultural Experiment Station: JEFREN L. DEMETERIO

HAWAII

GOVERNMENT AGENCIES

GOVERNOR: JOHN D. WAIHEE, Governor of Hawaii, State Capitol, Honolulu 96813 (808, 548-5420)

DEPARTMENT OF AGRICULTURE, P.O. Box 22159, Honolulu 96822

Promotes the best use of Hawaii's agricultural resources. Concerned with the protection of agricultural lands and water and diversification of the state's agricultural economy. Functions include agricultural planning, agricultural credit, market development, plant and animal quarantine, plant and animal disease and pest control, meat and poultry inspection service, milk control, livestock and market reporting service, commodities grading, pesticide use enforcement, and enforcement of weights and measures standards.

Chairperson: YUKIO KITAGAWA (808, 548-7101)

Deputy to the Chairperson: SUZANNE D. PETERSON (548-7103)

Administrative Services Chief: ANN OSHIRO (548-7106)

Planning Program Administrator: PAUL SCHWIND, Ph.D. (548-7133)

Agricultural Loan Division Head: RICHARD MORIMOTO (548-7126)

Plant Industry Division Head: PO-YUNG LAI, Ph.D. (548-7119)

Animal Industry Division Head: Vacant (487-5351)

Marketing & Consumer Services Division Head: MASAO HANAOKA (548-7138)

Measurement Standards Division Head: GEORGE MATTIMOE, Ph.D. (548-7152)

DEPARTMENT OF HEALTH, Box 3378, Honolulu 96801 (548-2211)

Director of Health: JOHN C. LEWIN, M.D. (808, 548-6505)

Deputy Director for Environmental Health: BRUCE S. ANDERSON, Ph.D. (548-4139)

Health Education Officer: CHRISTINE LING (548-5886)

DEPARTMENT OF LAND AND NATURAL RESOURCES, Box 621, Honolulu 96809 (548-6550)

Chairman: WILLIAM W. PATY

Deputies to Chairman: LIBERT K. LANDGRAF; RUSSELL N. FUKUMOTO; MANABU TAGOMORI

Board Members: HERBERT Y. ARATA; JOHN Y. ARISUMI; HERBERT K. APAKA, JR.; J. DOUGLAS ING; MOSES W. KEALOHA

Natural Area Reserves System Commission, Chairman: DR. FRED KAMEMOTO, 1151 Punchbowl St., Honolulu 96813

Animal Species Advisory Commission, Chairman: DR. E. ALISON KAY

Heritage Conservation and Recreation Service Office (HCRS), Planner: KEIJI IKEZAKI

Aquaculture Development Program (ADP), Manager: JOHN S. CORBIN

Division of Aquatic Resources, 1151 Punchbowl St., Honolulu 96813 (548-4000)

Director: HENRY M. SAKUDA

Chief, Fisheries Branch: PAUL Y. KAWAMOTO

Division of Conservation and Resources Enforcement, 1151 Punchbowl St., Honolulu 96813 (548-5919)

Director: MAURICE M. MATSUZAKI

Division of Forestry and Wildlife, 1151 Punchbowl St., Honolulu 96813 (548-8850)

Administrator: CALVIN W.S. LUM, D.V.M.

Wildlife Chief: RONALD L. WALKER

Division of Land Management, P.O. Box 621, Honolulu 96809 (548-7517)

Land Management Administrator: MIKE SHIMABUKURO

Division of State Parks & Recreation, P.O. Box 621, Honolulu 96809 (548-7455)

State Parks Administrator: RALSTON H. NAGATA

Division of Water and Land Development, P.O. Box 373, Honolulu 96809 (548-7533)

Manager-Chief Engineer: MANABU TAGOMORI

ENVIRONMENTAL CENTER, Water Resource Research Center, University of Hawaii, 2550 Campus Rd., Honolulu 96822 (808, 948-7361)

To stimulate, expand, and coordinate education, research, and service efforts of the university related to ecological relationships, natural resources, and environmental quality, with special relation to human needs and social institutions, particularly with regard to the state. Established: 1970.

Director: L. STEPHEN LAU

Environmental Coordinator: JOHN T. HARRISON

Associate Environmental Coordinator: JACQUELIN N. MILLER

HAWAII COOPERATIVE FISHERY RESEARCH UNIT, U.S.D.I., 2538 The Mall, University of Hawaii, Honolulu 96822 (808, 948-8350)

Activities include research, graduate program teaching, and public service regarding inshore marine and inland waters with emphasis on native fishes and invertebrates.

Leader: DR. JAMES D. PARRISH

INSTITUTE OF MARINE BIOLOGY, University of Hawaii, P.O. Box 1346, Kaneohe 96744 (808, 247-6631)

Concerned with research in marine tropical biology and oceanography with emphasis on coral reef biology, aquaculture, fish endocrinology, and behavior of reef organisms. Provides research facilities for investigations in tropical marine biology.

Director: PHILIP HELFRICH

INSTITUTE OF TROPICAL AGRICULTURE AND HUMAN RESOURCES, College of Tropical Agriculture and Human Resources, University of Hawaii, 3050 Maile Way, Honolulu 96822 (808, 948-8131)

Plan and implement research and extension in agriculture, natural resources, and human resources relevant to Hawaii and the tropics, with emphasis on the Pacific and Asia. Organized: 1978.

Director: CHAUNCEY T. K. CHING, Ph.D.

Publications: Various research and extension publications
Editor: CHARLES J. DELUCA, University of Hawaii, 3050 Maile Way, Gilmore 121, Honolulu 96822 (948-7538)

OFFICE OF ENVIRONMENTAL QUALITY CONTROL

Office established by the State Legislature in 1970. Coordinates state governmental agencies in matters concerning environmental quality. Serves the governor in an advisory capacity on matters relating to environmental quality control.
Director: MARVIN T. MIURA, Ph.D., 465 S. King St., Rm. 104, Honolulu 96813 (808, 548-6915)

SEA GRANT PROGRAM

Director, Sea Grant College Program: DR. JACK R. DAVIDSON, University of Hawaii, 1000 Pope Rd., Rm. 222, Honolulu 96822 (808, 948-7031)
Director, Sea Grant Extension Service: BRUCE J. MILLER, 1000 Pope Rd., Rm. 205, Honolulu 96822 (948-8191); Marine Extension Agent, RAYMOND S. TABATA, Recreation and Tourism, 1000 Pope Rd., Rm. 217, Honolulu 96822 (948-8191); Information Specialist, PETER J. RAPPA, 1000 Pope Rd., Rm. 205, Honolulu 96822 (948-8191); Marine Extension Agent, HOWARD TAKATA, East Hawaii, Cooperative Extension Service, 875 Komohana St., Hilo 96720 (959-9155); Fisheries Specialist, DICK BROCK, 1000 Pope Rd., Rm. 210, Honolulu 96822 (948-8191); Communications Specialist, RICK KLEMM, 1000 Pope Rd., Rm. 200, Honolulu 96822 (948-7410); Marine Extension Agent, BARRY SMITH, Marine Lab., University of Guam, University of Guam Station, Mangilao 96913 (0011671); Ocean Recreation and Tourism Specialist, JAN AUYONG TITGEN, 1000 Pope Rd., Rm. 205, Honolulu 96822 (948-8191); Education Coordinator, CHRIS WOOLAWAY, 1000 Pope Rd., Rm. 205, Honolulu 96822 (948-8191)

WATER RESOURCES RESEARCH CENTER, University of Hawaii, Holmes Hall 283, 2540 Dole St., Honolulu 96822 (808, 948-7847)

To initiate, coordinate, and conduct research in hydrology, hydrogeology, hydrometeorology and agrohydrology, hydraulic and sanitary engineering, water quality and pollution, environmental aspects, and water-related socioeconomics and law for the university and the state. Established: 1964.
Director: DR. L. STEPHEN LAU
Publications: *Technical Report and Technical Memorandum Report* series; collected reprints; *Annual Report;* Workshop series; *Cooperative Report* series; Publications List; Project Bulletin; *Conference Proceedings*
Editor: FAITH N. FUJIMURA (948-8272)

CITIZENS' GROUPS

CONSERVATION COUNCIL FOR HAWAII, Box 2923, Honolulu 96802 (808, 941-4974)
A representative statewide organization, affiliated with the National Wildlife Federation, primarily devoted to the wise use, conservation, aesthetic appreciation, and restoration of wildlife and other natural resources.
Chairman: RICK SCUDDER, 707 Richards St., #803, Honolulu 96813 (531-2963)
Secretary: LINDA DAY, 1617 Keeaumoku St., #1507, Honolulu 96822 (531-2963)
Affiliate Representative: STEVEN L. MONTGOMERY, 94610 Palai St., Waipahu 96797 (676-4974)
Alternate: RICK SCUDDER

Publication: CCH Newsletter
Editor: RICK SCUDDER

HAWAII ASSOCIATION OF CONSERVATION DISTRICTS

President: LES WISHARD, JR., P.O. Box 1149, Kamuela 96743 (808, 882-7962)
Council Member: H. PETER L'ORANGE, P.O. Box 1719, Kailua-Kona 96740 (329-2334)
Secretary-Treasurer: LOREN MOCHIDA, P.O. Box 45, Kekaha 96752 (337-1562)

HAWAII AUDUBON SOCIETY, P.O. Box 22832, Honolulu 96822

For better understanding, appreciation, and conservation of Hawaii's native wildlife resources, especially its unique and endangered bird species and their associated ecosystems. Membership: 1,600. Founded: 1939.
(Note: Officers elected annually in December.)
President: BRUCE EILERTS
Publications: *'Elepaio; Hawaii's Birds;* checklists; postcards
Managing Editor: THANE PRATT
Scientific Editor: SHEILA CONANT

HAWAIIAN BOTANICAL SOCIETY, c/o Botany Dept., University of Hawaii, 3190 Maile Way, Honolulu 96822 (808, 948-8369/8072)

Objectives of society are: to advance the science of Botany in all of its applications; to encourage research in botany in all of its phases; to promote the botanical welfare of its members; and to develop the spirit of good fellowship and cooperation in botanical matters. The society is particularly interested in the preservation of the Hawaiian flora. Membership: 175. Founded: 1924.
President: RYLAN S.N. YEE
Vice-President: ISABELLA A. ABBOTT
Treasurer: DERRAL HERBST
Secretary: CHRISTA RUSSELL
Publication: *Newsletter of the Hawaiian Botanical Society*
Editor: C.W. SMITH

LIFE OF THE LAND, 19 Niolopa Pl., Honolulu 96817 (808, 595-3903)

Direct, aggressive action based on fact. A non-profit tax-exempted organization working on environmental issues facing the State of Hawaii. Concerned with land use, air, and water pollution, pesticides, energy consumption, and overdevelopment. Membership: 400. Founded: 1970.
President: CORINNE CHING
Vice-President: ART MORI
Secretary: ROGER ROACH
Treasurer: CHRISTINA B. MELLER
Executive Director: Vacant

OUTDOOR CIRCLE, THE, 200 N. Vineyard Blvd., #506, Honolulu 96817 (808, 521-0074)

A nonprofit organization whose purpose is to work for and develop a more beautiful state, freeing it from disfigurement, conserving and developing its natural beauty, and cooperating in educational and other efforts towards community welfare, health, sanitation, sightliness, and physical good order.
President: CAROLIE SIMONE
Vice-Presidents: SUSAN FRISTOE; LAURA THOMPSON; MRS. JAMES ANDERSON; BILLIE BEAMER
Treasurer: MIDGE TROXELL
Recording Secretary: LOUISE CALDWELL
Corresponding Secretary: MRS. WILLIAM FROOME

Publications: *Keep Hawaii Green; Majesty: The Exceptional Trees of Hawaii; Pua Nani: Hawaii is a Garden*

WILDLIFE SOCIETY HAWAII CHAPTER
President: JOHN R. HENDERSON, 1238 Kainui Dr., Kailua 96734 (808, 943-1225)
President-Elect: BRUCE R. EILERTS, 1541 Dominis St., #1107, Honolulu 96822 (474-5921)
Secretary: ANDY YUEN, 350 Aoloa St., C-209, Kailua 96743 (541-2749)
Treasurer: TIM SUTTERFIELD, 3430-A Alohea Ave., Honolulu 96816 (474-5923)

IDAHO

GOVERNMENT AGENCIES

GOVERNOR: CECIL D. ANDRUS, Governor of Idaho, State Capitol, Boise 83720 (208, 334-2100)

DEPARTMENT OF AGRICULTURE, P.O. Box 790, Boise 83701 (208, 334-3240)
Director: RICHARD R. RUSH
Administrator, Division of Plant Industries: DR. ROGER R. VEGA (334-2986)
Administrator, Division of Animal Industries: DR. GREG NELSON (334-3256)
Administrator, Division of Agricultural Inspections: LANE JOLLIFFE (334-2623)
Administrator, Division of Agricultural Development: RICK PHILLIPS (334-3240)

DEPARTMENT OF HEALTH AND WELFARE, Statehouse, Boise 83720
Responsible for water, air, solid, and hazardous waste pollution control for the state. Field offices are maintained in five locations to provide direct pollution prevention programs.
Director of Health and Welfare: RICH DONOVAN (208, 334-5500)
Administrator, Division of Environment: KENNETH BROOKS (334-5840)
Chief, Bureau of Water Quality: AL MURREY (334-5860)
Chief, Bureau of Hazardous Materials: CHERYL KOSHUTA (334-5879)
Chief, Bureau of Air Quality: JOHN LEDGER (334-5898)

DEPARTMENT OF LANDS, State Capitol Bldg., Boise 83720 (208, 334-3280)
The State Board of Land Commissioners is a constitutional board charged with administering the trust under which endowment lands are held. These lands were granted to the state at the time of statehood for the financial support of nine beneficiaries, the largest being the common schools.
State Board of Land Commissioners: GOV. CECIL D. ANDRUS, President (208, 334-2100); PETE T. CENARRUSA, Secretary of State (334-2300); JIM JONES, Attorney General (334-2400); JOE R. WILLIAMS, State Auditor (334-3100); JERRY L. EVANS, Superintendent of Public Instruction (334-3301); STANLEY F. HAMILTON, Director (334-3280)

DEPARTMENT OF WATER RESOURCES, Statehouse, Boise 83720
Administration of State Water Plan and Energy Plan; allocation and planning of water resources and energy programs and projects; permit and license procedures for water rights, dams and mine tailing impoundment structures, well construction, injection wells, and stream channel alterations.
Director: R. KEITH HIGGINSON (208, 334-7910)
Chairman of the Board: GENE M. GRAY (208, 642-3388)
Administrators: WAYNE T. HAAS, Policy and Planning Division; NORMAN C. YOUNG, Resources Administration Division
Publications: Water and Energy Information Bulletins; *Rules and Regulations; State Water Plan,* and *Currents*

FISH AND GAME DEPARTMENT, 600 S. Walnut, Box 25, Boise 83707 (208, 334-3700)
To preserve, protect, perpetuate, and manage all wildlife within state of Idaho; to make and declare such rules and regulations and to employ personnel necessary to administer and enforce the harvest of wildlife. Created by Initiative Measure in 1938.
Commission Members: NORMAN H. GUTH, Salmon (756-3279); LOUIS F. RACINE, JR., Pocatello (232-4727); FRED A. CHRISTENSEN, Nampa (467-2106); KEITH CARLSON, Lewiston (743-1031); RICHARD J. HANSEN, Bayview (683-2262)
Director: JERRY M. CONLEY (334-5159)
Assistant Director: KENNETH D. NORRIE (334-3771)
Chiefs: JERRY MALLET, Field Operations (334-3772); STEVEN BARTON, Administration (334-3782); FRANK NeSMITH, Enforcement (334-3736); GRANT CHRISTENSEN, Engineering (334-3730); DAVID L. HANSON, Fisheries (334-3791); TOM REINECKER, Wildlife (334-2920); TRACEY TRENT, Program Coordination (334-3180); WILLIAM H. (Bill) GOODNIGHT, Information and Education (334-3746)
Publication: *Idaho Wildlife*
Editor: DIANE RONAYNE (334-3748)

GEOLOGICAL SURVEY, Morrill Hall, Rm. 332, University of Idaho, Moscow 83843 (208, 885-7991)
To promote orderly, efficient, and complete development of Idaho's mineral resources. Conducts field investigations and laboratory studies; assists in preparation of geologic maps and derivative land use planning and geologic hazards maps; provides expertise to individuals and governmental and private groups in planning land use. Organized: 1919; reorganized under University of Idaho, July, 1984.
Director: ROBERT W. BARTLETT (885-7991)

IDAHO COOPERATIVE FISH AND WILDLIFE RESEARCH UNIT, U.S.D.I., College of Forestry, Wildlife and Range Sciences, University of Idaho, Moscow 83843 (208, 885-6336)
An interagency organization—federal, state, and university—which conducts research, graduate level training, and extension in the fisheries and wildlife fields. Organized 1963.
Leader: DR. J. MICHAEL SCOTT
Assistant Leaders: DR. THEODORE C. BJORNN; DR. JAMES L. CONGLETON

IDAHO STATE PARKS AND RECREATION, Statehouse Mail, 2177 Warm Springs, Boise 83720 (208, 334-2154)
To formulate and put into execution a long-range program for the acquisition, planning, protection, operation, maintenance, development, and wise use of parks; to provide state leadership in recreation.
Board Members: MONTE LATER, Chairman, St. Anthony (624-7434); REN THOMSON, Malad (766-2214); ROBERT G. THOMAS, Coeur d'Alene (664-9904); TOM NEAL, Moscow (882-2551); GLENN SHEWMAKER, Kimberly (423-4600)
Director: YVONNE FERRELL

STATE EXTENSION SERVICES

Director of Extension Service: HARRY R. GUENTHNER, University of Idaho, Moscow 83843 (208, 885-6639)

Extension Forester: RONALD MAHONEY, University of Idaho, Moscow 83843 (885-6356)

STATE SOIL CONSERVATION COMMISSION, 801 S. Capitol Blvd., Boise 83702 (208, 334-2148)

Coordinates programs and activities of Soil Conservation Districts in Idaho. Concerned with overall leadership and administration of districts in development, wise use, and conservation of soil and water and other closely related resources. Participates in the National Cooperative Soil Survey Program through employment of soil scientists and has been designated the state water quality management agency for private and state agricultural lands. Administers low-interest loan program for conservation improvements on private and public lands. Authorized: 1939.

Chairman: GRANT JONES, Holbrook Rt., Malad 83252 (766-2771)

Administrator: WAYNE R. FAUDE

CITIZENS' GROUPS

IDAHO WILDLIFE FEDERATION, 2405 Fifth St., Lewiston 83501 (208, 746-9046)
A representative statewide organization, affiliated with the National Wildlife Federation, primarily devoted to the wise use, conservation, aesthetic appreciation, and restoration of wildlife and other natural resources.
President: KENT HENDERSON
Affiliate Representative: KENT HENDERSON
Alternate: ERNEST BRATLEY
Publication: Idaho Wildlife News
Editor: JO PARRIS, P.O. Box 142, Pocatello 83204 (208, 232-0469)

IDAHO ASSOCIATION OF SOIL CONSERVATION DISTRICTS

President and Council Member: DELBERT WINTERFELD, P.O. Box 97, Swan Valley 83449 (208, 483-3683)

Vice-President: KEVIN FREDERIKSEN, Rt. 3, Box 181, Rupert 83350 (532-4518)

Secretary: ART BEAL, P.O. Box 23, Ola 83657 (584-3567)

Treasurer: FRANK WALKER, 5230 Walker Rd., Viola 83872 (875-0782)

Executive Assistant: AMOS GARRISON, 118 W. Franklin, Meridian 83642 (888-1592)

IDAHO ENVIRONMENTAL COUNCIL, P.O. Box 1708, Idaho Falls 83403

Founded to coordinate and stimulate the creative ideas, manpower, and financial resources of conservation-minded individuals and organizations to provide an increased understanding of modern man's impact upon his environment. Action, the objective, is based on information and research.

President: ALAN HAUSRATH (208, 336-4930)

Northern Idaho, Vice-President: DENNIS BAIRD (882-8289)

Southeastern Idaho, Vice-President: RALPH MAUGHAN (233-9553)

Publication: *IEC Newsletter*

Editor: JERRY JAYNE (523-6692)

IDAHO TRAPPERS ASSOCIATION, 354 W. 1st, N. Rexburg 83440 (208, 356-5796)

A statewide organization of trappers, affiliated with the IWF, FTA, and NTA. Promotes sound conservation legislation and administrative procedures that pertain to furbearer management, promotes trapper education, provides public education concerning the role of trapping as a necessary wildlife management tool, and defends Idaho's natural resources from waste.

President: JOHN P. SMITH

Vice-President: DONNA KELLY, 735 Amy Ln., Idaho Falls 83401 (522-6296)

Secretary: BARBARA SMITH, 8065 S. 1800, W. Rexburg 83440 (356-0582)

Treasurer: JONNIE JO SAWYER, 330 W. 1st, N., Rexburg 83440 (356-8179)

Publication: *The Trapper*

Editor: DON SHUMAKER, Box 337, Sutton, NE 68979 (402, 773-5454/773-4343)

Directors:

Region 1: JIM JOYCE, Rt. 2, Box 678, Blanchard 83804 (437-4052)

Region 2: DON JENNI, Box 384, Orosino 83544 (476-5768)

Region 3: WILLARD POLLOCK, Rt. 1, Box 1093-A, Nampa 83651 (459-2354)

Region 4: RICK UNDERWOOD, 603 N. Fir, Jerome 83338

Region 5: JOHN CONTOR, 587 W. 200, S. Blackfoot 83221 (785-5761)

Region 6: ROBERT GOKEY, Rt. 1, Box 10, Roberts 83444 (228-6561)

TROUT UNLIMITED IDAHO CHAPTER (North Idaho)

Dedicated to the protection and enhancement of the coldwater fishery resource.

President: DENNIS GLOE, 460 West Clayton Ave., Coeur d'Alene 83014

Idaho Panhandle Chapter: MIKE RUSKEY, P.O. Box 1289, Sandpoint 83864

WILDLIFE SOCIETY IDAHO CHAPTER

President: JOHN W. CONNELLY, Idaho Department of Fish and Game, 5205 South 5th, Pocatello 83201 (208, 232-4702)

Vice-President: JEROME HANSEN, Idaho Department of Fish and Game, 600 South Walnut, Boise 83712 (334-5057)

Secretary: SIGNE SATHER-BLAIR, HC 33 Box 3228, Boise 83706 (334-1931)

Treasurer: PAUL MOROZ, Boise National Forest, 1750 Front St., Boise 83702 (334-1516)

ILLINOIS

GOVERNMENT AGENCIES

GOVERNOR: JAMES R. THOMPSON, Governor of Illinois, State Capitol, Springfield 62706 (217, 782-6830)

DEPARTMENT OF AGRICULTURE, State Fairgrounds, Springfield 62706 (217, 782-2172)

Created in 1917 under the Civil Administrative Code and reorganized in 1974, to encourage and promote, in every practicable manner, the interests of agriculture.

Director: LARRY A. WERRIES

Superintendent, Plant Industries and Consumer Services: JIM ONKEN (782-3817)

Superintendent, Marketing: MICHAEL BAISE (782-6675)

Superintendent, Animal Industries: DR. PAUL DOBY (782-4944)

Superintendent, Administrative Services: RICHARD DAVIDSON

Superintendent, State Fair: MERLE MILLER (782-6661)

Superintendent, Natural Resources: JAMES BRIM (782-6297)

Publications: *True Facts; Illinois Agricultural Products; Ag Group Directory; Livestock Market News; Grain Market News; Annual Report; Ag Scene*

DEPARTMENT OF CONSERVATION, Lincoln Tower Plaza, 524 S. Second St., Springfield 62706 (217, 782-6302)

To conserve the natural and cultural resources of Illinois and to provide outdoor recreational opportunities. Founded: 1925.

Director: MARK FRECH (782-6302)

Assistant Director: KATHY SELCKE (782-6302)

Chief, Information Programs Section: CHARLES TAMMINGA (782-7454)

Director, Office of Administration: ROY MILLER (785-8552)

Associate Director, Planning and Development: JOHN COMERIO (782-1807)

Chief, Technical Services Division: ROBERT CORRIGAN (782-2605)

Chief, Planning and Information: EDWARD HOFFMAN (782-3715)

Director, Office of Land Management and Enforcement: JAY JOHNSON (785-8285)

Director, Office of Resource Management: JOHN A. TRANQUILLI (785-8285)

Chief, Land Management: RONALD HALLBERG (782-6752)

Chief, Concession and Lease Management: RON CHEZEM (782-0179)

Chief, Fisheries Division: MIKE CONLIN (782-6424)

Chief, Forest Resources Division: AL MICKELSON (782-2361)

Chief, Wildlife Resources Division: JAMES MOAK (782-6384)

Chief, Law Enforcement Division: LARRY CLOSSON (782-6431)

Chief, Natural Heritage Division: CARL BECKER (785-8774)

Publication: *Outdoor Highlights*

Editor: GARY THOMAS (782-7454)

DEPARTMENT OF ENERGY AND NATURAL RESOURCES, 325 W. Adams St., Rm. 300, Springfield 62704

Provides scientific inquiry, applied research, technology development, advice, and assistance to help residents, businesses, and government of Illinois understand and solve natural resource and energy issues and problems. Conducts applied environmental and economic research to guide the state's energy and natural resource policy decisions from an integrative perspective. The agency also provides energy conservation training and information and funds research, and development and demonstration of new energy technologies. Established: 1978.

Director: DON ETCHISON (217, 785-2800)

Director, Energy and Environmental Affairs Division: FRANK M. BEAVER (785-2009)

Chief, Illinois State Geological Survey Division: MORRIS W. LEIGHTON, 615 E. Peabody, Urbana 61820 (333-4747)

Chief, State Water Survey Division: RICHARD SEMONIN, 2204 Griffith Dr., Champaign 61820 (333-2211)

Chief, Illinois State Natural History Survey Division: LORIN NEVLING, 607 E. Peabody, Urbana 61820 (333-6880)

Director, State Museum Division: BRUCE McMILLAN, State Museum Bldg., Springfield 62706 (782-7386)

Publications: *Illinois Resources; Illinois Energy Data Review; The Living Museum; The Illinois Natural History Survey Reports*

Editors: GALE STEINHOUR, Dept. of Energy and Natural Resources, 325 W. Adams St., Rm. 300, Springfield 62704; G. DENNNIS CAMPBELL, Illinois State Museum, Springfield 62706; SHIRLEY McCLELLAN, Illinois Natural History Survey, Natural Resources Bldg., 607 E. Peabody, Champaign 61820

DEPARTMENT OF TRANSPORTATION, 2300 S. Dirksen Pkwy., Springfield 62764 (217, 782-5597)

Secretary: HARRY R. HANLEY

Director, Division of Highways: HAROLD W. MONRONEY (782-2151)

Chief, Bureau of Location and Environment: M.J. MACCHIO (782-1959)

Chief of Environment: J. PAUL BIGGERS (782-4770)

DIVISION OF WATER RESOURCES, 2300 S. Dirksen Pkwy., Springfield 62764 (217, 782-2152)

Director: DONALD R. VONNAHME

ILLINOIS ENVIRONMENTAL PROTECTION AGENCY, 2200 Churchill Rd., Springfield 62706 (217, 782-3397)

Responsible for implementing the environmental program for the state of Illinois. Administers a variety of programs to protect the air, land, and water.

Director: BERNARD P. KILLIAN

Manager, Public Information: CINDA SCHIEN (782-3397)

Division Managers: MICHAEL HAYES, Air Pollution Control (782-7326); JAMES PARK, Water Pollution Control (782-1654); ROGER SELBURG, Public Water Supplies (785-8653); WILLIAM CHILD, Land Pollution Control (782-6760); ROGER KANERVA, Environmental Programs (785-5735):

Publications: *Illinois Environmental Progress; Environmental Progress*

Editor: JOAN MURARO

NATURE PRESERVES COMMISSION, 524 S. Second St., Lincoln Tower Plaza, Springfield 62701-1787 (217, 785-8686)

State commission to oversee Illinois nature preserves system. Established by legislative act: 1963. Revised: 1981.

Chairman: CHARLES S. POTTER, JR., North American Wildlife Foundation, 102 Wilmot Rd., Suite 410, Deerfield 60015

Vice-Chairman: GEORGE BURGER, P.O. Box 194, Dundee 60118

Secretary: VALERIE SPALE, 10327 Elizabeth, Westchester 60153

Director: BRIAN D. ANDERSON

STATE EXTENSION SERVICES

Director of Extension Service (Acting): DR. DONALD L. UCHTMANN, 122 Mumford Hall, 1301 West Gregory Dr., University of Illinois, Urbana 61801 (217, 333-2660)

Extension Forester: THEODORE W. CURTIN, 219 Mumford Hall, 1301 W. Gregory Dr., University of Illinois, Urbana 61801 (333-2777)

Specialist in Outdoor Recreation and Sea Grant: ROBERT D. ESPESETH, 104 Huff Hall, University of Illinois, Champaign 61820 (333-1824); DR. PETER D. BLOOME, Assistant Director, Agriculture & Natural Resources, University of Illinois, 116 Mumford Hall, 1301 W. Gregory Dr., Urbana 61801 (333-9025)

Area Adviser, Marine Extension: CHRISTINE PENNISI, University of Illinois, Regional Office, 1010 Jorie Blvd., Suite 300, Oak Brook 60521 (312, 920-0760)

Associate Director: DR. ROBERT P. BENTZ, 116 Mumford Hall, 1301 W. Gregory Dr., University of Illlinois, Urbana 61801 (217, 333-9025)

STATE GEOLOGICAL SURVEY, Natural Resources Bldg., 615 E. Peabody Dr., Champaign 61820 (217, 333-4747)

A scientific and professional staff of 150 engaged in research and service of: environmental applications of geology, geochemistry, and minerals engineering; and the mineral resources of Illinois. Established in 1905 as an agency of the state government and an

allied agency of the University of Illinois, a division of Illinois Department of Energy and Natural Resources.
Chief: MORRIS W. LEIGHTON
Mineral Resources Group: J. JAMES EIDEL
General and Environmental Geology Group: KEROS CARTWRIGHT
Chemistry and Minerals Engineering Group: ROBERT A. GRIFFIN

STATE NATURAL HISTORY SURVEY DIVISION, 172 Natural Resources Bldg., 607 E. Peabody Dr., Champaign 61820 (217, 333-6880)
Conducts research on the protection and most intelligent use of the state's renewable natural resources to assure maximum sustained economic, educational, and recreational benefits. Organized: 1858.
Chief: LORIN I. NEVLING (333-6830)
Head, Botany and Plant Pathology Section: ANTON G. ENDRESS (333-6886)
Head, Aquatic Biology Section: ROBERT W. GORDEN (333-6889)
Head, Economic Entomology Section: WILLIAM G. RUESINK (333-6656)
Head, Faunistic Surveys and Insect Identification Section: WALLACE La BERGE (333-6846)
Head, Wildlife Research Section: GLEN C. SANDERSON (333-6870)
Natural History Survey River Laboratory, Box 599, Havana 62644 (309, 543-3950)
Sam A. Parr Fisheries Research Center, R.D. 1, Box 126, Kinmundy 62854 (618, 245-6348)
Natural History Survey Reservoir Laboratory, R.D. 1, Box 157, Sullivan 61951 (217, 728-4498)
Natural History Survey Laboratory, Ridge Lake, Fox Ridge State Park, Charleston 61920 (217, 345-6490) (Open May through September.)
Publications: Bulletin; Circular; Biological Notes; INHS Reports; Special Publications
Editor: AUDREY HODGINS (217, 244-0871)

CITIZENS' GROUPS

ILLINOIS WILDLIFE FEDERATION, *123 S. Chicago St., Rossville 60963 (217, 748-6365)*
A representative statewide organization, affiliated with the National Wildlife Federation, primarily devoted to the wise use, conservation, aesthetic appreciation, and restoration of wildlife and other natural resources.
President: FANNIE HILLS, Rt. 2, Box 365, Manito 61546 (217, 748-6365)
Affiliate Representative: TOM MILLS, 403 S. Chicago St., Rossville 60963 (217, 748-6040)
Alternate: BILL MURRY, P.O. Box 443, Sesser 62884 (618, 625-5454)
Publication: Illinois Wildlife
Editor: TOM MILLS

AUDUBON COUNCIL OF ILLINOIS
Composed of representatives of 13 National Audubon Chapters, the council's purpose is to coordinate efforts of the chapters on statewide environmental issues. Organized: 1973.
President: JAMES O. SMITH, R.R. 1, Box 327, Homer 61849 (217, 896-2079)
Director: MARGARET HOLLOWELL, 908 Arlene Ave., Bloomington 61701 (309, 662-1808)
Secretary: MARY HRUSKA, 117 W. Michigan, Urbana 61801 (217, 344-5919)

Treasurer: HELEN PARKER, 103 W. Delaware, Urbana 61801 (217, 367-3130)

EAST CENTRAL ILLINOIS FUR TAKERS, R.R. 2, Paxton 60957 (217, 379-4067)
State chapter of Fur Takers of America. Helps monitor fur-bearing wildlife populations in the state and helps conserve this renewable resource. Membership: 200. Founded: 1974.
President: GREG ANDERSON
Vice-President: JIM IIFT
Secretary-Treasurer: MIKE WILSON (949-5221)

ILLINOIS ASSOCIATION OF SOIL AND WATER CONSERVATION DISTRICTS
President: RUDY RICE, R.R. 1, DuQuoin 62832 (618, 542-4102)
Vice-President: LEE BUNTING, R.R. #1, Dwight 60420 (815, 934-5573)
Secretary: STAN HOWELL
Treasurer: CHARLES CURRY
Council Member: FLOYD BOHLEN, R.R. 2, Fithian 61844 (217, 776-2287)
Executive Director: JOHN OLSON, 3085 Stevenson Dr., Suite 305A, Springfield 62703 (217, 529-7788)

ILLINOIS AUDUBON SOCIETY, P.O. Box 608, Wayne 60184 (312, 584-6290)
Dedicated to the enjoyment and preservation of wildlife, and to the achievement of an ecologically sound environment. Chartered in 1897.
President: DR. G. TANNER GIRARD, Principia College, Elsah 62028
Vice-President: DAVID SCHUUR, Rt. 1, Box 21-A, Flat Rock 62427
Executive Director: WARREN R. DEWALT
Publications: *Illinois Audubon; The Cardinal News; Illinois Birds and Birding*
Editor: VERNON KLEEN

ILLINOIS BASS CHAPTER FEDERATION
An organization of Bassmaster Chapters, affiliated with the Bass Anglers Sportsman Society, organized to fight pollution, assist state and national conservation agencies in their efforts, and to teach the young people of our country good conservation practices. Dedicated to the realistic conservation of our water resources.
President: ROBERT KIRK, 102 Patton St., Pana 62557 (217, 562-2536)

ILLINOIS ENVIRONMENTAL COUNCIL, 313 W. Cook St., Springfield 62704 (217, 544-5954)
Coalition of environmental groups and individuals from throughout the state which have joined to lobby for effective environmental and conservation legislation. Membership: 50 groups. Founded: 1975.
Board of Directors: DONNA HRILJAC, President; KIM MAJERUS, Vice-President
Executive Director: VIRGINIA R. SCOTT
Business Manager: ROSELYN WALLIS
Publications: *IEC Bulletin; Action Alert*
Editor: VIRGINIA R. SCOTT

ILLINOIS NATURAL HERITAGE FOUNDATION, 320 South Third St., Rockford 61104 (815, 964-6666)
A nonprofit organization to protect Illinois's native flora and fauna, and to encourage wise stewardship of the natural resources that affect them. Organized: 1982.
President: EDWARD C. GARST
Secretary: LEE G. JOHNSON
Treasurer: GARY L. ANDERSON

Executive Director: GEORGE B. FELL

ILLINOIS PRAIRIE PATH, P.O. Box 1086, Wheaton 60189 (312, 665-5310)

To preserve natural areas and establish footpaths and other protected areas to be used for scientific, educational, and recreational p rposes by the public. Promotes development of a 55-mile path for bicycles, hikers, and horseback riders on former railroad right-of-way spanning DuPage County; extended Jan. 1972 into Kane County to Fox River Valley; extended Dec. 1979 4 ½ mi. into Cook County. Founded: 1963; incorporated: 1965. In 1971 designated part of National Trails System. Membership: 1,500.
President: F. PAUL MOORING (469-4289)
Vice-President: ROBERT HARGIS (668-7377)
Secretary: NANCY BECKER (544-7517)
Treasurer: JOAN B. HAMILL (584-3567)
Publications: Newsletter; *The Illinois Prairie Path, A Guide; Trail Map*
Editor: JEAN C. MOORING, 295 Abbotsford Ct., Glen Ellyn 60137 (469-4289)

IZAAK WALTON LEAGUE OF AMERICA, INC. (Illinois Division)
President: TIMOTHY REID, 230 W. 148th Pl., Dolton 60419 (312, 841-3732)
Secretary: KAREN SNEED, 17850 Ridgeland, Tinley Park 60477 (429-4725)

NATIONAL CAMPERS AND HIKERS ASSOCIATION, INC. (Illinois State Association)
To educate and assist local chapters in the preservation of the beauties of nature in Illinois; to educate and assist members in a campaign of safety in outdoor living; and to promote improvement in public camping and hiking areas where the need exists. Incorporated: 1962.
Presidents: GARY AND CHRIS BLUHM, 205 Sylvan Dr., Decatur 62521
State Directors: AMOS AND MARTHA WHITCOMB, 1009 W. Madison, Ottawa 61350
Conservation Directors: BURT AND RUTH ROBERTS, 901 Madison, Monticello 61856
Publication: *ISA Camper*

NATURAL LAND INSTITUTE, 320 S. Third St., Rockford 61104 (815, 964-6666)
A nonprofit organization to preserve natural areas in Illinois and elsewhere. Organized: 1958.
President: EDWARD C. GARST
Secretary: LEE G. JOHNSON
Treasurer: GARY L. ANDERSON
Executive Director: GEORGE B. FELL

OPEN LANDS PROJECT, 53 W. Jackson Blvd., Chicago 60604 (312, 427-4256)
Formed in 1963 as a committee of the Welfare Council of Metropolitan Chicago to promote "the preservation and protection of open and natural lands for conservation, recreation and scientific purposes." In 1968, the project was separately incorporated as a nonprofit organization.
President: H. JAMES FOX
Vice-President, Program: GEORGE DAVIS
Vice-President, Development: FRED BATES
Vice-President, Administration, and Secretary-Treasurer: GERALD B. FRANK
Director: GERALD ADELMANN
Publications: *Terrain; Open Lands Action*
Editor: CHRISTINE ESPOSITO

TROUT UNLIMITED ILLINOIS COUNCIL
A statewide council with three chapters working for the protection and enhancement of the coldwater fishery resources.
Chairman: JOE HAMMON, 2580 Forest View, River Grove 60304 (312, 751-4730)
National Director: MARSHALL FIELD, 333 West Wacker Dr., Chicago 60606

WILDLIFE SOCIETY ILLINOIS CHAPTER
President: STAN ETTER, 506 East 7th St., Gibson City 60936 (217, 784-4730)
Vice-President: RICHARD E. WARNER, 607 E. Peabody Dr., Champaign 61820 (333-5199)
Secretary-Treasurer: GARY POTTS, 129 North Kennedy Blvd., Vandalia 62471 (283-3070)

INDIANA

GOVERNMENT AGENCIES

GOVERNOR: EVAN BAYH, Rm. 210, Statehouse, Indianapolis 46204 (317, 232-4567)

DEPARTMENT OF NATURAL RESOURCES, 608 State Office Bldg., Indianapolis 46204
Chairman, Natural Resources Commission: JAMES LAHEY (317, 232-4020)
Chairman, Land, Forest, and Wildlife Resources Advisory Council: MAX LEWIS (232-4020)
Chairman, Water and Minerals Resources Advisory Council: JOSEPH SIENER (232-4020)
Director: JAMES M. RIDENOUR (232-4020)
Deputy Director, Bureau of Water and Minerals: THOMAS BRUNS (232-4020)
Deputy Director, Bureau of Lands, Forests, and Wildlife: JOHN T. COSTELLO (232-4020)
Deputy Director, Inter-Divisional Services: PAUL E. GREENWALT (232-4020)
Controller: JAMES VAUGHN (232-4020)
Head, Division of Enforcement: DOUGLAS PHELPS (232-4010)
Head Chief Engineer, Division of Engineering: HOWARD PEDIGO (232-4150)
State Entomologist, Head, Division of Entomology: JAMES CLARK (232-4120)
Head, Division of Fish and Wildlife: EDWARD HANSEN (232-4080)
State Forester, Head, Division of Forestry: JOHN F. DATENA (232-4105)
Head, Division of Information and Education: JAMES PARHAM (232-4200)
Head, Division of Land Acquisition: SAM PHIPPS (232-4050)
Head, Division of Museums and State Historic Sites: DR. LEE SCOTT THEISEN (232-1637)
Head, Division of Nature Preserves: JOHN BACONE (232-4052)
Head, Division of Oil and Gas: GARY FRICKE (232-4055)
Head, Division of Outdoor Recreation (Administers Land and Water Conservation Fund): GERALD PAGAC (232-4070)
Head, Division of Personnel: PAM KNOX HAMMERSLEY (232-4031)
Head, Division of Reservoir Management: G.T. DONCEEL (232-4060)
Head, Division of State Parks: WILLIAM C. WALTERS (232-4124)
Head, Division of Water: JOHN SIMPSON (232-4160)
Head, Division of Reclamation: RICHARD MCNABB (232-1555)
Head, Division of Accounting: THOMAS BARTON (232-4041)

Head, Division of Historic Preservation and Archaeology: RICHARD GANTZ

Head, Division of Purchasing: LARRY SLOAN

Head, Indiana Geological Survey: NORMAN HESTER

Head, Division of Soils: CHARLES McKEE

Head, Management Information Systems: REX BECKER

Publication: *Outdoor Indiana*

Editor: JAMES PARHAM

DIVISION OF SOIL CONSERVATION, Department of Natural Resources, FLX 1 Bldg., Rm. 101, Purdue University, West Lafayette 47907 (317, 494-8383)

Soil Conservation Board, Chairman: HAROLD H. WILSON

Director: CHARLES C. McKEE

STATE BOARD OF HEALTH, 1330 W. Michigan St., P.O. Box 1964, Indianapolis 46206-1964 (317, 633-0100)

State Health Commissioner: WOODROW A. MYERS, JR., M.D.

INDIANA DEPARTMENT OF ENVIRONMENTAL MANAGEMENT 105 S. Meridian St., P.O. Box 6015, Indianapolis 46206-6015 (317, 232-8603)

Commissioner: NANCY MALOLEY

Deputy Commissioner: DAVID WAGNER

Assistant Commissioner, Air Management: THOMAS RARICK

Assistant Commissioner, Water Management: CHARLES BARDON-NER

Assistant Commissioner, Solid and Hazardous Waste Management: JANE MAGEE

STATE EXTENSION SERVICES

Director of Extension Service: DR. HENRY A. WADSWORTH, Purdue University, West Lafayette 47907 (317, 494-8489)

State Extension Forester: BURNELL C. FISCHER, Dept. of Forestry and Natural Resources, Purdue University, West Lafayette 47907 (494-3584)

Extension Wildlife Specialist (and Sea Grant): HERBERT C. KRAUCH, JR., Dept. of Forestry and Natural Resources, Purdue University, West Lafayette 47907 (494-3586)

STATE GEOLOGICAL SURVEY, Department of Natural Resources, 611 N. Walnut Grove, Bloomington 47405 (812, 335-7636)

Conducts field and laboratory investigations and provides basic geologic information to the mineral industries, governmental agencies, and citizens of Indiana. Founded: 1869.

Director and State Geologist: NORMAN C. HESTER

Head, Mineral Resources and Data Management Branch: DONALD D. CARR (335-2687)

Head, Research and Project Development Branch: BRIAN D. KEITH (335-7428)

Head, Technical Services and Administration Branch: JOHN R. HILL (335-2862)

Head, Public Relations and Educational Services: JOHN R. HILL (335-7636)

Special Projects: GORDON S. FRASER (335-9350)

CITIZENS' GROUPS

INDIANA WILDLIFE FEDERATION, Box 283, Zionsville 46077 (317, 873-3915)

A representative statewide organization, affiliated with the National Wildlife Federation, primarily devoted to the wise use, conservation,

aesthetic appreciation, and restoration of wildlife and other natural resources.

President: EMILY KRESS, R.R. #1, Box 465, Parker City 47368 (317, 468-7410)

Secretary: NELDA CARPENTER, P.O. Box 108, Kennard 47351

Affiliate Representative: CHARLES SCHEFFE, P.O. Box 631, Seymour 47274 (812, 522-5369)

Alternate: EMILY KRESS

Publication: Hoosier Conservation

Editor: HERB KRAUCH, 148 Ivy Hill Dr., West Lafayette 47906 (317, 463-3673)

ACRES, INC., 1802 Chapman Rd., P.O. Box 141, Huntertown 46748 (219, 637-6264)

For acquisition and permanent preservation of natural areas in northeastern Indiana. Conducts a guided field-trip program and a program of films and lectures. Administers 20 nature preserves totalling more than 1,000 acres. Founded: 1960.

President: THEODORE H. HEEMSTRA

Vice-Presidents: ROBERT C. WEBER; ETHYLE R. BLOCH; JAMES M. BARRETT III

Secretary: MRS. THOMAS E. DUSTIN

Treasurer: JAMES SHEARER

Publication: *Acres*

ASSOCIATION OF GREAT LAKES OUTDOOR WRITERS, 301 Cross St., Sullivan 47882 (812, 268-6232)

A nonprofit professional association of outdoor communicators dedicated to perpetuate the great outdoors through the judicious use of the written and spoken word. Membership: approximately 320. Established: 1957.

President: EDWARD J. MAHONEY, 3343 Sherman, Springfield, IL 62703 (217, 529-3181)

Vice-President: COL. WILLIAM H. RADKE, 3320 Arthur Ave., Brookfield, IL 60513 (312, 485-0935)

Secretary-Treasurer: BILL BEEMAN 301 Cross, Sullivan, IN 47882 (812, 268-6232)

Chairman, Board of Directors: ROBERT KACZKOWSKI, 3137 W. Hilltop Ln., Franklin, WI 53132 (414, 761-0657)

Publication: *Aglow Horizons*

Editor: BILL BEEMAN (812, 268-6232)

ENVIRONMENTAL EDUCATION ASSOCIATION OF INDIANA, INC.

A statewide nonprofit organization dedicated to the wise use and management of natural resources through conservation education. Activities include an annual meeting, workshops, teaching materials, exhibits, and speakers. Founded: 1969.

President: HARRY NIKIDES, Division St., Rm. 103, Noblesville 46060 (317, 773-1406)

Vice-President: PETE FORTUNE, 2017 E. 54th St., Indianapolis 46220 (251-7918)

Secretary: SUE SCHLEMMER, R.R. 5, Box 181, LaGrange 46761 (463-3471)

Treasurer: DOUG WALDMAN, 11832 Kress Rd., Roanoke 46783 (672-3842)

Publication: *CREED Newsletter*

Editor: HOWARD MICHAUD, 301 E. Stadium Ave., W. Lafayette 47906

HOOSIER ENVIRONMENTAL COUNCIL, P.O. Box 1145, Indianapolis 46206-1145 (317, 636-8282)

To encourage and promote more aggressive environmental regulation and enforcement in the state of Indiana. The council objectives are as follows: facilitation of communication between environmental groups and individuals, coordination of action on current

environmental issues, educational programs and publications, and representation of the concerns of the membership before administrative officials and regulatory boards/agencies of the state and federal government.
President: ETHYLE BLOCH, 6340 Donna Dr., Ft. Wayne 46819 (219, 747-4450)
Executive Director: JEFFREY STANT, 22 E. Washington St., Victoria Center, Suite 316, Indianapolis 46204 (636-8282)
Treasurer: WILLIAM HAYDEN, 22 E. Washington St., Victoria Center, Suite 316, Indianapolis 46250 (636-8282)
Secretary: ROBERT G. PEDERSEN, 1202 Thorndale St., Indianapolis 46214 (317, 243-2476)
Publications: *Monitor; Boardwatch*
Editor: DONNA McCARTY, 4832 Guion Rd., Indianapolis 46254

INDIANA ASSOCIATION OF SOIL AND WATER CONSERVATION DISTRICTS, INC.
President: KENNETH J. WALLPE, R.R. 9, Box 67, Greensburg 47240 (812, 663-2512)
Vice-President: JERRY W. FREY, R.F.D. 1, Rossville 46065 (317, 379-2786)
Secretary: MICHAEL J. THOMAS, 9730 Fischer Rd., Evansville 47712 (812, 963-5069)
Treasurer: MIKE CLODFELTER, 105 Hilltop Ln., Greencastle 46135 (317, 653-6608)
Council Member: EARL BLANK, R.R. I, Box 390-A, Corydon 47112 (312, 952-2108)

INDIANA AUDUBON SOCIETY, INC., Mary Gray Bird
Sanctuary, R.R. 6, Connersville 47331 (317, 825-9788)
Works for the conservation of wildlife, especially birds. Members: 980. Organized: 1898. Incorporated: 1939.
President: SALLIE POTTER, 4305 Belt Ln., Martinsville 46151 (342-2382)
President-Elect: CARL WILMS, R. 6, Connersville 47331 (827-0908)
Secretary: BETTIE HALLER, 303 W. 10014, Valpraiso 46383
Treasurer: ROBERT G. MILLER, 710 N. Martin Ave., Muncie 47303 (284-3354)
Sanctuary Resident Supervisor: DENZEL BARRICKLOW, R.R. 6, Box 165, Connersville 47331 (825-9788)
Publications: *The Indiana Audubon; The Cardinal*
Editors: CHARLES E. KELLER, 2505 E. Maynard Drive, Indianapolis 46226 (786-5822); MARY GOUGH, 901 Maplewood Dr., New Castle 47362 (529-5225)

INDIANA BASS CHAPTER FEDERATION
An organization of Bassmaster Chapters, affiliated with the Bass Anglers Sportsman Society, organized to fight pollution, assist state and national conservation agencies in their efforts and to teach the young people of our country good conservation practices. Dedicated to the realistic conservation of our water resources.
President: LINUS HALLER, Rt. 31, Box 737, Terre Haute 47803 (812, 237-2479)

INDIANA FORESTRY AND WOODLAND OWNERS ASSOCIATION, 2505 Radcliffe Ave., Indianapolis 46227 (317, 888-8484)
A statewide organization affiliated with the National Woodland Owners Association, providing leadership and programs to advance forestry in Indiana. Membership: 2,000. Founded: 1977.
President: WILLIAM A. SIGMAN (638-7611)
Executive Director: MITCHELL (Gene) HASSLER
Publication: *LEAVES AND LIMBS*
Editor: BETTY DATENA (247-5302)

INDIANA STATE TRAPPERS ASSOCIATION, INC.
A statewide organization dedicated to the conservation, restoration, and wise use of wildlife and other renewable natural resources. Provides public education concerning the role of trapping in the management of wildlife. Founded: 1961. Membership: 265.
President: KEN BROSMAN, 828 Elm St., Huntington 46750 (812, 939-3215)
Vice-President: JERRY MILLER, R.R. I, 21 N. 300 W., Bluffton 46714
Secretary-Treasurer: KAREN MOSS, R.R. I, Box 57, Clay City 47841 (219, 369-1573)
Directors: ROBERT COATS, R.R. 1, Box 300, Portland 47371; JOHN DREIMAN, R.R. I, Box 179, Monroe City 47557; NELSON TEETERS, R.R. I, Box 140A, West Union 60180
Publication: *The Trapper*

IZAAK WALTON LEAGUE OF AMERICA, INC. (Indiana Division)
President: EMIL GARCIA, 3420 W. 40th Pl., Gary 46408 (219, 980-2612)
Secretary: CONNIE BYERS, 315 East Barkdol, Kokomo 46901 (317, 472-5758)
Publication: *The Hoosier Waltonian*
Editor: KAREN GRIGGS

WILDLIFE SOCIETY INDIANA CHAPTER
President: STEVE BACKS, c/o Patoka Fish and Wildlife Area, R.R. #1, Winslow 47598 (812, 849-4586)
President-Elect: GEORGE SEKETA, State Office Bldg., Rm. 607, Indianapolis 46204 (317, 232-4080)
Secretary-Treasurer: JOHN WADE, c/o Patoka Fish and Wildlife Area, R.R. #1, Winslow 47598

IOWA

GOVERNMENT AGENCIES

GOVERNOR: TERRY BRANSTAD, Governor of Iowa, State Capitol, Des Moines 50319 (515, 281-5211)

DEPARTMENT OF AGRICULTURE AND LAND STEWARDSHIP, AND DIVISION OF SOIL CONSERVATION, Wallace State Office Bldg., Des Moines 50319 (515, 281-5851)
Administers soil and water conservation district laws. Allocates state appropriations to 100 soil and water conservation districts for personnel, commissioners' expense, and cost-share program. Reviews watershed and RC & D project applications. Oversees erosion control law. Involved with water resources and nonpoint-source pollution control planning. Division licenses mine operations and administers federal surface mining and Abandoned Mine Land Program regulations.
State Soil Conservation Committee, Chairperson: KENNETH KASSEL, Rt. #2, Box 63, Ayrshire 50515; Vice-Chairperson, OLIVER EMERSON , Rt. 1, Box 100, Waterville 52170
Director: JAMES B. GULLIFORD
Assistant Director: KENNETH R. TOW

Bureaus
Field Services: Vacant (281-5258)
Financial Incentive Program: WILLIAM McGILL (281-6148)
Mines and Minerals: KENNETH R. TOW (281-6142)
Water Resource: DAN LINDQUIST (281-5564)

DEPARTMENT OF NATURAL RESOURCES, E. Ninth and Grand Ave., Wallace Bldg., Des Moines 50319-0034 (515, 281-5145)

Established July 1, 1986 with the merging of the following state agencies: Iowa Conservation Commission, Department of Water, Air and Waste Management; Iowa Geological Survey; and the resources/conservation functions of the Energy Policy Council. The seven-member Natural Resources Commission is a policy- and rule-setting authority over the Fish and Wildlife Division, Parks, Recreation and Preserves Division, and the Forestry Division; the eleven-member Environmental Protection Commission is the policy- and rule-setting authority over the Environmental Protection Division.

Director: LARRY J. WILSON

Deputy Director: ROBERT G. FAGERLAND

Natural Resource Commission Members: WILLIAM B. RIDOUT, Estherville; SAM KENNEDY III, Chairman, Clear Lake; DOUGLAS R. SMALLEY, Des Moines; JOHN D. FIELD, Hamburg; THOMAS E. SPAHN, Dubuque; RICHARD C. YOUNG, Waterloo; MARION J. PATTERSON, Cedar Rapids

Environmental Protection Commission Members: ROBERT W. SCHLUTZ, Chairman, Columbus Junction; CATHERINE DUNN, Dubuque; DONNA M. HAMMITT, Woodbine; CHARLOTTE MOHR, Eldridge; GARY C. PRIEBE, Algona; NANCYLEE A. SIEBENMANN, Cedar Rapids; RICHARD L. TIMMERMAN, Johnston; CLARK A. YEAGER, Ottuma

Coordination and Information Division

Administrator: JAMES COMBS

Information-Education Bureau, Chief: ROSS HARRISON

Iowa Conservationist, Editor: JULIE HOLMES

Government Liaison Bureau, Chief: MIKE MURPHY

Planning Bureau, Chief: ARNIE SOHN

Administrative Services Division

Administrator: STAN KUHN

Budget and Grants Bureau, Chief: MARK SLATTERLY

Finance Bureau, Chief: GENE GEISSINGER

Administrative Support Bureau, Chief: SANDY ADAMS

Licensing Bureau, Chief: JUDY PAWELL

Construction Services Bureau, Chief: TOM ALBRIGHT

Land Acquisition Bureau, Chief: JOHN BEAMER

Data Processing Bureau, Chief: JOE VAZQUEZ

Environmental Protection Division

Administrator: ALLAN STOKES

Surface and Groundwater Protection Bureau, Chief: DARRELL McALLISTER

Air Quality and Solid Waste Protection Bureau, Chief: PETE HAMLIN

Field Evaluation and Emergency Response Bureau, Chief: JOE OBR

Fish and Wildlife Division

Administrator: ALLEN FARRIS

Fisheries Bureau, Chief: JIM MAYHEW

Wildlife Bureau, Chief: RICHARD BISHOP

Law Enforcement Bureau, Chief: RICK McGEOUGH

Hunter Safety, Coordinator: SONNY SATRE

Parks, Recreation and Preserves Division

Administrator: MIKE CARRIER

Parks and Recreation Bureau, Chief: DOYLE ADAMS

Preserves and Ecological Services Bureau, Chief: DARRELL HO-WELL

Forests and Forestry Division

Administrator: BILL FARRIS

State Forests Management Bureau, Chief: JIM BULMAN

Forestry Services Bureau, Chief: MIKE BRANDRUP

Energy and Geological Resources Division

Administrator: LARRY BEAN

Energy Bureau, Chief: PHIL SVANOE

Geological Survey Bureau, Chief: DON KOCH

Waste Management Authority Division

Administrator: TERESA HAY

IOWA COOPERATIVE FISH AND WILDLIFE RESEARCH UNIT, U.S.D.I., 11 Science Hall II, Iowa State University, Ames 50011 (515, 294-3056)

Organized: 1935.

Leader: DR. PAUL A. VOHS

Assistant Leader, Wildlife: DR. ERWIN E. KLAAS

Assistant Leader, Fisheries: DR. JOHN S. RAMSEY

STATE EXTENSION SERVICES

Interim Director of Extension Service: RONALD C. POWERS, 110 Curtiss Hall, Iowa State University, Ames 50011 (515, 294-4576)

Extension Wildlife Conservationist: JAMES L. PEASE, 103 Science II, Iowa State University, Ames 50011 (294-7429)

Extension Forester: PAUL H. WRAY, 251 Bessey Hall, Iowa State University, Ames 50011 (294-1168)

CITIZENS' GROUPS

IOWA WILDLIFE FEDERATION, INC., Box 1222, Cedar Rapids 52406

A representative statewide organization, affiliated with the National Wildlife Federation, primarily devoted to the wise use, conservation, aesthetic appreciation, and restoration of wildlife and other natural resources.

President: LOREN FORBES, 7 Arbury Dr., Iowa City 52246 (319, 338-5385)

Affiliate Representative: B. JAMES MURPHY, JR., 2749 Balboa Dr., Dubuque 52001 (319, 582-5205)

Alternate: ROBERT MOORMAN, 1223 9th Ave., Ames 50010 (515, 232-1316)

Publication: Iowa Wildlife

Editor: MICHAEL T. MEYER, 1595 Atlantic, Dubuque 52001 (319, 588-1556)

IOWA ACADEMY OF SCIENCE, University of Northern Iowa, Cedar Falls 50614 (319, 273-2021)

To further the work of scientists, facilitate cooperation among them, and increase public understanding and appreciation of the importance and promise of the methods of science in human progress. A conservation section meets each year as part of an annual convention submitting papers dealing with all conservation happenings. Membership: 1,800. Organized: 1875.

President: PAUL CHRISTIANSEN (319, 895-8811)

President-Elect: RUTH SWENSON (515, 294-4729)

Executive Director: PAUL E. RIDER

Publications: *Journal of the Iowa Academy of Science; Iowa Science Teachers Journal; Iowa's Natural Heritage; IAS Bulletin* (Newsletter)

Editors: DRS. ROGER and MARILYN BACHMANN, Iowa State University (515, 294-8801); CARL BOLLWINKEL, Price Lab

School, University of Northern Iowa, Cedar Falls 50614 (319, 273-2021); PAUL E. RIDER, University of Northern Iowa, Cedar Falls 50614

IOWA ASSOCIATION OF SOIL AND WATER CONSERVATION DISTRICT COMMISSIONERS

President and Council Member: NORMAN KADING, Rt. 1, Box 66, Casey 50048 (515, 746-2696)

Vice-President: DANIEL BRUENE, R.R. 2, Box 84, Gladbrook 50635 (515, 473-2338)

Secretary: LINDA BINDNER, Rt. 1, Box 42, Marcus 50135 (712, 376-2577)

Treasurer: OLLIE KALDENBERG, Rt. 5, Albia 52531 (515, 932-2008)

Executive Director: Vacant, 2925 1/2 School, Des Moines 50311 (515, 266-2189)

IOWA BASS CHAPTER FEDERATION

An organization of Bassmaster Chapters, affiliated with the Bass Anglers Sportsman Society, organized to fight pollution, assist state and national conservation agencies in their efforts, and to teach the young people of our country good conservation practices. Dedicated to the realistic conservation of our water resources.

President: TOM BOWLER, 3282 Midway, Marion 52302 (319, 393-1481)

IOWA CONSERVATION EDUCATION COUNCIL, INC., c/o

Conservation Education Center, Rt. 1, Box 53, Guthrie Center 50115 (515, 747-8383)

To encourage and lead the development and practice of a widespread and effective conservation education program in Iowa. Founded: 1958.

Chairperson: PAUL REGNIER, Warren County Conservation Board, 1565 118th Ave., Indianola 50125 (961-6169)

Vice-Chairperson: DUANE TOOMSEN, Department of Education, Grimes State Office Bldg., Des Moines 50319 (281-3146)

Secretary: SHARON KAUFMAN, Clinton County Conservation Board, P.O. Box 161, Grand Mound 52751 (733-4386) (319, 847-7202)

Treasurer: JUDY LEVINGS, Box 132, State Center 50247 (483-2717)

Executive Committee Members: BOB RYE, Conservation Education Center, R.R. #1, Box 53, Guthrie Center 50115; MARK WAGNER, Jasper Co. Conservation Board, Courthouse Basement, Newton 50208; CARL BOLLWINKEL, University of Northern Iowa, Cedar Falls 50613 (319, 273-2414); DIANE HOLT, NE Hamilton Community School, Box 25, Blairsburg 50034

Publication: Newsletter

Editors: LINDA ZALETEL; CELE BURNETT

IOWA NATURAL HERITAGE FOUNDATION, Insurance Exchange Bldg., Suite 1005,, 505 Fifth Ave., Des Moines 50309 (515, 288-1846)

An independent, statewide, nonprofit corporation founded in 1979 by a broad-based group of leading Iowans concerned with the rapid depletion of the state's natural resources. It serves as a catalyst and facilitator in both the preservation and protection of Iowa's natural resources. Program emphasis on land protection, resource education, and long-range planning and research.

Chairman: WILLIAM J. FULTZ

Vice-Chairman: ROBERT MEIER

Secretary: RICHARD B. RAMSAY

Treasurer: HARRY C. JENSEN

Executive Director: GERALD F. SCHNEPF

Associate Director: MARK C. ACKELSON

Director of Development: SCOTT C. STEVENSON

Resourceful Farming Project Director: DUANE SAND

Wetlands for Iowa Program Director: BEN VAN GUNDY

Office Manager: SUSAN HOUGH

Administrative Support: CHERYL FLOYD

Publication: *Iowa Natural Heritage*

IOWA ORNITHOLOGISTS' UNION, 825 7th Ave., Iowa City 52240

For the study and protection of native birds and to promote fraternal relations among Iowa bird students. Membership: 500. Organized: 1923.

President: CAROL THOMPSON, 1116 Muscatine Ave., Iowa City 52240

Secretary: ANN BARKER, R.R. 3, Box 190, Davenport 52803

Treasurer: FRANCIS MOORE, 336 Fairfield St., Waterloo 50703

Publication: *Iowa Bird Life*

Editor: THOMAS H. KENT, 211 Richards, Iowa City 52240

IOWA TRAPPERS ASSOCIATION, INC., c/o Anna Marie Scalf, 123 North Madison Ave., Ottumwa 52501 (515, 682-3937)

(Spring and fall conventions and meetings held each year in various parts of the state.)

A nonprofit organization that works to continue the wise use and harvest of Iowa's renewable resource of furbearing animals. Cooperates with all recognized conservation agencies, law enforcement agencies, legislative committees, and provides input on the benefits and necessity of trapping. Membership: approximately 2,000. Founded: 1950.

President: THOMAS G. MONROE, 623 South Stone, Sigourney 52591 (622-2426)

Vice-President: RICHARD L. REGAN, R.R. 1, Box 77, Plymouth 50464 (696-5702)

Secretary: MARGARET L. SQUIER, 709 West Main Ave., Rockford 50468 (756-3565)

Treasurer: ANNA MARIE SCALF, 123 North Madison Ave., Ottumwa 52501 (682-3937)

Publication: *The Trapper and Predator Caller*

Editor: RICK FALER, P.O. Box 691, Greenville, PA 16125

IZAAK WALTON LEAGUE OF AMERICA (Iowa Division)

President: RICHARD PEER, Rt. #1, Donahue 52746 (319, 282-4636)

Executive Secretary: RICHARD VANDER HORN, 11 Columbia Ct., Davenport 52804 (326-0910)

WILDLIFE SOCIETY IOWA CHAPTER

President: WILLIAM R. CLARK, 124 Sciences II, Iowa State University, Ames 50010 (515, 294-5176)

President-Elect: ROBERT DOLAN, Iowa Department of Natural Resources, SCS Bldg., 912 7th St., Onawa 51040 (712, 423-2426)

Secretary-Treasurer: DOUGLAS REEVES, Iowa Department of Natural Resource Research Station, Boone 50036 (515, 432-2823)

KANSAS

GOVERNMENT AGENCIES

GOVERNOR: MIKE HAYDEN, Governor of Kansas, State House, Topeka 66612 (913, 296-3232)

GEOLOGICAL SURVEY, 1930 Constant Ave., Campus West, Kansas University, Lawrence 66046 (913, 864-3965)
Purpose is to research and develop mineral and water resources of Kansas and to study and report on their interactions with other sections of the state's economy. Founded: 1864.
Director and State Geologist: LEE C. GERHARD
Deputy Director: DON W. STEEPLES
Section Chief, Advanced Projects: JOHN C. DAVIS
Section Chief, Geologic Investigations: LAWRENCE L. BRADY
Section Chief, Geohydrology: MANOUTCH HEIDARI
Section Chief, Petroleum Research: W. LYNN WATNEY
Publications: Bulletin; Journals; Maps; Energy Series; Mineral Resources Series; Environmental Geology Series; Irrigation Series; Educational Series; Geology Series; Guidebook Series; Subsurface Geology Series; Series on Spatial Analysis; Chemical Quality Series; Ground Water Series

KANSAS BIOLOGICAL SURVEY, 2291 Irving Hill Rd., Campus West, Lawrence 66045 (913, 864-7725)
A research and development branch of the University of Kansas whose purpose is to survey and inventory the native plants and animals of Kansas, report on its findings, and develop and administer lands for the study and preservation of native animal and plant resources. Founded: 1959.
Director and State Biologist: DR. EDWARD MARTINKO
Associate Director: DR. FRANK deNOYELLES
Assistant Director: PAUL M. LIECHTI

KANSAS DEPARTMENT OF WILDLIFE AND PARKS, 900 Jackson St., Suite 502, Topeka 66612-1220 (913, 296-2281)
Charged with the conservation of state wildlife and fishery resources, provision of environmental services and habitat protection, and park development and management. Administers state boating law, hunter education programs, Land and Water Conservation Funds, and other related functions.
Secretary: ROBERT L. MEINEN,
Commission Members: EDWARD B. ANDERSON, Elkhart (316, 697-4311); WILLIAM A. ANDERSON, JR., Fairway (816, 842-2300); WILLIAM R. BROWNING, M.D., Madison (316, 437-2200); DR. GERALD W. TOMANEK, Hays (913, 625-9390); RONALD HOPKINS, Wichita (316, 262-8076); KATHY BROWN GEORGE, Junction City (913, 238-8565); RONALD A. VINE, Topeka (913, 295-3838)

Operations Office, Box 54A, Rt. 2, Pratt 67124-9599 (316, 672-5911)
Undersecretary: W. ALAN WENTZ, Ph.D.
Special Assistant, Operations: JOHN HERRON
Chief, Parks and Public Lands Division: Vacant
Chief, Fisheries and Wildlife Division: Vacant
Chief, Wildlife and Parks Law Enforcement: OMAR STAVLO
Training Officer, Wildlife and Parks Law Enforcement: FRANK HENDRICKS
Chief, Administrative Services: GEORGE E. AXLINE
Supervisor, Business Management and Planning: VERLYN EBERT
Supervisor, Engineering: NORMAN DAVIS

Supervisor, Licensing and Revenue: ROSE EWING
Federal Aid Coordinator: MIKE MARROW
Chief, Education and Public Affairs: MIKE COX
Coordinator, Wildlife Education Service: JOYCE HARMON DEPENBUSCH
Coordinator, Hunter Education, Boating Safety, Furharvester Education: ROB MANES
Publication: *Kansas Wildlife and Parks*
Editor: PAUL KOENIG

STATE AND EXTENSION FORESTRY, Kansas State University, Department of Forestry, 2610 Claflin Rd., Manhattan 66502 (913, 537-7050)
Provides technical forestry assistance to landowners, wood industries, and communities; conducts a tree distribution program, a tree improvement program, a rural fire protection program, and an extension forestry education program.
State Forester (Acting): LESTER R. PINKERTON
Foresters: RAYMOND G. ASLIN, Rural Fire Protection; KEITH D. LYNCH, Forest Management; JAMES J. NIGHSWONGER, Urban and Community Forestry; WILLIAM L. LOUCKS, Tree Improvement Program; LEONARD K. GOULD, Forest Utilization and Marketing; GARY G. NAUGHTON, Forest Resource Planning

STATE BOARD OF AGRICULTURE, 109 SW 9th St., Topeka 66612
Secretary: SAM BROWNBACK (913, 296-3556)

Division of Water Resources, 109 SW Ninth St., Suite 202, Topeka 66612
Chief Engineer-Director: DAVID L. POPE (913, 296-3717)
Assistant Chief Engineer: WAYLAND ANDERSON
Water Structures Section: GEORGE A. AUSTIN, Section Head
Water Appropriation Section: WARREN D. LUTZ, Section Head
Technical Services Section: JAMES O. BAGLEY, Section Head

STATE CONSERVATION COMMISSION, 109 SW Ninth St., Rm. 300, Topeka 66612 (913, 296-3600)
The SCC is directed by an eight-member board and has administrative responsibilities to provide leadership, direction, and support to the conservation districts, watershed districts and other special purpose districts of the state. It administers ten financial assistance programs with funds appropriated by the State Legislature. Created: 1937.
Executive Director: KENNETH F. KERN

STATE DEPARTMENT OF HEALTH AND ENVIRONMENT, Forbes Field, Bldg. 740, Topeka 66620
Secretary, Health and Environment: STANLEY C. GRANT (913, 296-1522)
Directors: JAMES A. POWER, Division of Environment (296-1535); KARL MUELDENER, Bureau of Water Protection (296-5500); JOHN IRWIN, Bureau of Air Quality and Radiation Control (296-1540); RON HAMMERSCHMIDT, Bureau of Environmental Remediation; DENNIS MURPHEY, Bureau of Waste Management (296-1593); ROBERT MOODY, Public Information (296-1531)

STATE EXTENSION SERVICES
Extension Specialist: F. ROBERT HENDERSON, Wildlife Damage Control, Department of Animal Sciences and Industry, 128 Call Hall, Kansas State University, Manhattan 66506 (913, 532-5654)
Extension Specialist: GEORGE C. HALAZON, Wildlife and Outdoor Recreation, Community Development Programs, 215 Umberger Hall, Kansas State University, Manhattan 66506 (532-5840)

WATER OFFICE, 109 SW Ninth St., Suite 200, Topeka 66612-1215 (913, 296-3185)
State water planning, policy, and coordination agency. Prepares state plan of water resources management, conservation, and development; reviews water laws, and recommends new or amendatory legislation. Administers the state water marketing program.
Director: JOSEPH F. HARKINS
Assistant Director: CLARK DUFFY

WILDLIFE AND PARKS COMMISSION
Chairman: DR. GERALD TOMANEK, 1503 Oakmont, Hays 67601
Secretary: ROBERT L. MEINEN, Department of Wildlife and Parks (formerly Kansas State Park and Resources Authority), 900 Jackson St., Rm. 502, Topeka 66612 (913, 296-2281)

CITIZENS' GROUPS

KANSAS WILDLIFE FEDERATION, INC., *P.O. Box 5711, Topeka 66605 (913, 266-6185)*
A representative statewide organization, affiliated with the National Wildlife Federation, primarily devoted to the wise use, conservation, aesthetic appreciation, and restoration of wildlife and other natural resources.
President: ROSS MANES, P.O. Box 371, Ellsworth 67439 (472-4576)
Executive Director: JERRY HAZLETT
Affiliate Representative: B.J. BRIGHTON, P.O. Box 1803, Manhattan 66502 (539-0482)
Alternate: SPENCER TOMB, 5321 Thompson, Manhattan 66502 (537-8265)
Publication: Kansas Sportsman
Editor: B.J. BRIGHTON

KANSAS ACADEMY OF SCIENCE
A nonprofit scientific organization, to increase, diffuse, and promote knowledge in various departments of science; interest young people in science and encourage them to consider science as their profession; aid the improvement of science teaching; and aid in development of the state's economic growth. Membership: 450. Founded: 1868.
President: DAN BOWEN, Department of Biology, Benedictine College, Atchison 66002 (913, 367-5340)
President-Elect: DAN MERRIAM, Department of Geology, Wichita State University, Wichita 67208 (316, 689-3140)
Vice-President: M. DUANE NELLIS, Department of Geography, Kansas State University, Manhattan 66506 (913, 532-6727)
Secretary: GAYLEN NEUFELD, Department of Biology, Emporia State University, Emporia 66801 (316, 343-1200/Ext. 5311)
Publication: *Transactions of the Kansas Academy of Science*
Editor: J. ROBERT BERG, Department of Geology, Wichita State University, Wichita 67208 (316, 689-3140)

KANSAS ADVISORY COUNCIL FOR ENVIRONMENTAL EDUCATION
Organized to promote and support effective environmental education in order to enhance awareness, knowledge, and concern about the environment among the citizens of Kansas. The advisory council is made up of representatives of over 68 public and private organizations, institutions, business organizations, and individuals. Organized: 1969.
President: EMMETT WRIGHT, Bluemont Hall, Kansas State University, Manhattan 66506 (913, 532-5550)
Vice-President: BARB STANLEY, Topeka School District, #501, 125 SE 27th St., Topeka 66605 (913, 233-2772)

Secretary: DR. J. ROBERT BERG, Department of Geology, Box 27, Wichita State University, Wichita 67208 (316, 689-3140)
Treasurer: RUTH GENNRICH, Museum of Natural History, University of Kansas, Lawrence 66045 (913, 864-4173)

KANSAS ASSOCIATION OF CONSERVATION DISTRICTS
President: SHEILA LEIKER, R.R. #1, Box 68, Victoria 67671
Vice-President: JOHN BROWN, R.R. #4, Box 94, Ft. Scott 66701
Secretary-Treasurer: J.D. CAMERON, R.R. #1, Box 87, Summerfield 66541

KANSAS BASS CHAPTER FEDERATION
An organization of Bassmaster Chapters, affiliated with the Bass Anglers Sportsman Society, organized to fight pollution, assist state and national conservation agencies in their efforts and to teach the young people of our country good conservation practices. Dedicated to the realistic conservation of our water resources.
President: DARRELL CROSSMAN, 6415 South West St., Wichita 67233 (H:316, 522-6217/W:316, 265-2915)

KANSAS ORNITHOLOGICAL SOCIETY
Formed to promote the study of ornithology, to advance the members in ornithological science, to promote conservation, and the appreciation of birds by the general public. Members: 430. Organized: 1949.
President: ELMER J. FINCK, Division of Biology, Kansas State University, Manhattan 66506 (913, 532-6629)
Vice-President: DAVID SEIBEL, 1446 Kentucky, Lawrence 66046 (913, 864-3178)
Recording-Corresponding Secretary: DWIGHT PLATT, Rte. 2, Box 209, Newton 67114 (316, 283-2500)
Membership Secretary: JANE HERSHBERGER, 18 Circle Dr., Newton 67114 (316, 283-5129)
Treasurer: EUGENE R. LEWIS, 1285 MacVicar, Topeka 66604 (913, 232-1847)
Librarian: RUTH FAUHL, 1923 Ohio St., Lawrence 66044
Business Manager: JOYCE WOLF, 2535 Arkansas, Lawrence 66044 (913, 749-3203)
Publications: *K.O.S. Bulletin; K.O.S. Newsletter*
Editors: JOHN L. ZIMMERMAN, Division of Biology, Kansas State University, Manhattan 66506 (913, 532-6659); SCOTT SELTMAN, R.R. 1, Box 36, Nekoma 67559 (913, 329-4411)

WILDLIFE SOCIETY KANSAS CHAPTER
President: JOE D. KRAMER, 2702 Buffalo Dr., Dodge City 67801 (316, 227-8609)
President-Elect: ROBERT CULBERSTON, P.O. Box 582, New Strawn 66839 (364-2282)
Secretary-Treasurer: KEITH SEXSON, 1229 Neosho, Emporia 66801 (342-0658)

KENTUCKY

GOVERNMENT AGENCIES

GOVERNOR: WALLACE G. WILKINSON, Governor of Kentucky, Commonwealth of Kentucky, State Capitol, Frankfort 40601 (502, 564-2611)

DEPARTMENT OF AGRICULTURE, Capital Plaza Tower, Frankfort 40601 (502, 564-4696)
The service, regulatory, and promotional agency for Kentucky's agriculture industry. Established: 1876.

Commissioner: WARD (Butch) BURNETTE

Director, Division of Communications: BRIAN GONNELLY (564-3394)

Publication: *Kentucky Agricultural News*

Editor: FAUN FISHBACK (564-3397)

DEPARTMENT OF FISH AND WILDLIFE RESOURCES, #1

Game Farm Rd., Frankfort 40601 (502, 564-3400)
Organized: 1944.
Commission Members: JAMES D. WILKERSON, JR., Louisville; DR. JAMES R. RICH, Covington; DAVID H. GODBY, Somerset; DR. ROBERT C. WEBB, Grayson; GEORGE E. WARREN, Henderson; DOUG HENSLEY, Hazard; MIKE BOATWRIGHT, Paducah; DR. JAMES C. SALATO, Columbia; CHARLES E. PALMER, JR., Lexington
Commissioner: DON R. McCORMICK
Deputy Commissioner: THOMAS A. YOUNG

Director, Division of Law Enforcement: PAUL OLIVER (564-3176)
Director, Division of Fisheries: PETER W. PFEIFFER (564-3596)
Coordinator, Dingell-Johnson Section: JAMES AXON (564-5448)
Superintendent, Fish Hatchery: DAN BREWER, R.D. 4, Morehead 40351 (606, 784-6872)
Director, Division of Conservation Education: W. KELLY HUBBARD, JR. (564-4762)
Director, Division of Wildlife: LAUREN E. SCHAAF (564-4406)
Coordinator, Pittman-Robertson Section: LYNN GARRISON (564-4406)
Superintendent, State Game Farm: DANNY WATSON (564-5448)
Director, Division of Engineering: BENNIE R. MAFFET (564-4762)
Director, Division of Public Relations: JOHN WILSON (564-4336)
Director, Division of Fiscal Control: REBECCA GAMES (564-4224)
Regional Directors: DAVID LOVELESS, Rt. 10, Box 271, Benton (527-3394); DONAN JENKINS, P.O. Box 74, Sturgis 42459 (333-2249); JOE BLAND, Department of Fish and Wildlife, Bowman Field, Louisville 40205 (588-4039); MAC WARREN, Rt. 3-B, Box 476, Springfield 40069 (606, 336-3012); BARTH JOHNSON, Rt. 2, Box 96, Butler 41006 (606, 428-3193); P. RAY FLOYD, P.O. Box 203, Stanford 40484 (606, 365-7615); TOMMY CANTRELL, Van Lear 41265 (606, 789-8366); GEORGE W. MARTIN, Box 46, Barbourville 40906 (606, 546-3222); CHARLES ASA HALE, HCR 75, Box 624, Wellington 40387 (606, 674-6228)
Publication: *Happy Hunting Ground*
Editor: JOHN WILSON (564-4336)

DEPARTMENT OF PARKS, 10th Fl., Capital Plaza Bldg.,

Frankfort 40601 (502, 564-2172)
Commissioner of Parks: RAPIER SMITH
Executive Assistant: JIM KENNEDY
Deputy Commissioners: JIM GOODMAN; BOB BENDER
Director, Resort Parks: BLUEFORD M. RICE
Director, Accommodations: J.W. YOUNG (564-6957)
Director, Recreational Parks and Historic Sites: ED HENSON (564-2172)
Director, Accounting: LOUIS TANDY (564-4264)
Director, Administrative Services and Budget: HUGH SMITH (564-6860)
Director, Food Service: BENNIE D. HAGER (564-3612)
Director, Golfing: HUMZEY YESSIN (564-6957)
Director, Personnel: W. GAYLE FAUST (564-4815)
Director, Planning: DONALD F. PENEGOR (564-4940)
Director, Planning, Construction and Maintenance: TOM ENGSTROM (564-3006)
Director, Construction: ARMOND RUSS (564-8110)
Director, Project Administration: JIM TRUE (564-3006)
Director, Accommodations: J.W. YOUNG (564-6957)

Director, Purchases: GLENN T. BUMPOUS (564-4590)
Director, Recreation: MIKE BRIEN (564-5410)
State Naturalist: CAREY TICHENOR (564-5410)
Director, Rangers: DAVID KING (564-4841)
Director, Customer Services: DAN GLASS (564-4841)
Publications: MARTI BOOTH (564-4841)

ENVIRONMENTAL QUALITY COMMISSION, 18 Reilly Rd., Ash

Annex, Frankfort 40601 (502, 564-2150)
A seven-member citizens advisory group whose members are appointed by the Governor. They advise the Governor and the Secretary of the Natural Resources and Environmental Protection Cabinet on environmental matters. They hold monthly public meetings on current environmental issues and regulations. Founded: 1973.
Chairperson: WILLIAM HORACE BROWN (633-4754)
Vice-Chairperson: W. HENRY GRADDY IV (606, 873-8033)
Secretary: KENT RIGGS (927-6921)
Executive Director: LESLIE A. COLE (564-2150)
Publication: *Kentucky's Environment* Newsletter

GEOLOGICAL SURVEY, 228 Mining and Mineral Resources

Bldg., University of Kentucky, Lexington 40506 (606, 257-5500)
Investigates the geology and mineral and water resources of Kentucky and makes this information available to the public. It is a research and service organization. Founded: 1854.
Director and State Geologist: DONALD C. HANEY
Assistant State Geologist: JOHN D. KIEFER
Coal and Minerals Section, Head: JAMES C. COBB
Stratigraphy and Petroleum Geology Section, Head: IAN M. JOHNSTON
Publications Section, Head: DONALD W. HUTCHESON
Water Resources Section, Head: JAMES S. DINGER
Computer Services Section, Head: STEVEN J. CORDIVIOLA
Publications: List available on request.

NATURAL RESOURCES AND ENVIRONMENTAL PROTECTION

CABINET, 5th Fl., Capital Plaza Tower, Frankfort 40601
(502, 564-3350)
Secretary: CARL H. BRADLEY
Deputy Secretary: CHARLES W. MARTIN
Office of Communications and Community Affairs: CHARLES PEARL, Director
Office of General Counsel: ART WILLIAMS
Division of Hearings: GORDON GOAD, Director
Division of Administrative Services: H. SCOTT HANKLA, Director

Department for Environmental Protection, 18 Reilly Rd.,

Frankfort 40601 (502, 564-2150)
Commissioner: DR. JAMES CORUM
Division of Air Pollution Control: WILLIAM EDDINS, Director
Division of Waste Management: DONALD F. HARKER, Director
Division of Water: JACK A. WILSON, Director
Division of Environmental Services: WILLIAM E. DAVIS, Director

Department for Natural Resources, 691 Teton Tr., Frankfort

40601 (502, 564-2184)
Commissioner: ROBERT F. KNARR
Division of Abandoned Lands: DAVID H. ROSENBAUM, Director
Division of Forestry: DONALD A. HAMM, Director
Division of Conservation: H. STANLEY HEAD, Director
Division of Water Patrol: CHARLES BROWNING, Director

Department for Surface Mining Reclamation and Enforcement, #2 Hudson Hollow, Frankfort 40601 (502, 564-6940)
Commissioner: C. THOMAS BENNETT
Division of Permits: SUSAN BUSH, Director
Division of Field Services: CARL CAMPBELL, Director

Environmental Quality Commission, Fort Boone Plaza, 18 Reilly Rd., Frankfort 40601 (502, 564-2150)
Chairman: W. HORACE BROWN
Executive Director: LESLIE COLE

Nature Preserves Commission, 407 Broadway, Frankfort 40601 (502, 564-2886)
Chairman: JON RICKERT
Director: RICHARD R. HANNAN

STATE EXTENSION SERVICES

Associate Director of Extension Service: SHIRLEY H. PHILLIPS, University of Kentucky, Lexington 40546 (606, 257-4302)
Extension Forestry: DR. DEBORAH B. HILL, University of Kentucky, Lexington 40546 (257-7610)
Wildlife Expert: DR. FRED SERVELLO, Dept. of Forestry, University of Kentucky, Lexington 40546 (257-8633)
Assistant Extension Director of Agriculture: DR. CURTIS ABSHER, University of Kentucky, Lexington 40546 (257-1846)
Chairman, Dept. of Forestry: DR. BART THIELGES, University of Kentucky, Lexington 40546 (257-7596)

CITIZENS' GROUPS

LEAGUE OF KENTUCKY SPORTSMEN, INC., P.O. Box 406, Ft. Thomas 41075 (606, 781-3464)
A representative statewide organization, affiliated with the National Wildlife Federation, primarily devoted to the wise use, conservation, aesthetic appreciation, and restoration of wildlife and other natural resources.
President: BOB SMITH, Rt. #2, Box 352, Butler 41006 (606, 635-5023)
Secretary: ROBERT DICKEY, 36 Grand Ave., Ft. Thomas 41075 (606, 781-3464)
Affiliate Representative: RON ELMORE, 35 Boone Lake, Walton 41094 (606, 485-7177)
Alternate: BOB SMITH
Publications: Newspaper; The Happy Hunting Ground
Editor: PHYLLIS G. ANDERSON, P.O. Box 409, Silver Grove 41085

KENTUCKY ACADEMY OF SCIENCE

To encourage scientific research, promote the diffusion of scientific knowledge, and unify the scientific interests of Kentucky. Membership: 720. Founded: 1914.
President: DR. LARRY GIESMANN, Dept. of Biology, Northern Kentucky University, Highland Heights 41076
Vice-President: RICHARD HANNAN, Kentucky Nature Preserves Commission, Frankfort 40601
President-Elect: DR. WILLIAM P. HETTINGER, JR., Ashland Petroleum Co., Ashland 41101
Secretary: DR. ROBERT O. CREEK, Dept. of Biological Sciences, Eastern Kentucky University, Richmond 40475
Treasurer: DR. MORRIS D. TAYLOR, Dept. of Chemistry, Eastern Kentucky University, Richmond 40475

Publication: *Transactions of the Kentucky Academy of Science*
Editor: DR. BRANLEY A. BRANSON, Dept. of Biological Sciences, Eastern Kentucky University, Richmond 40475

KENTUCKY ASSOCIATION FOR ENVIRONMENTAL EDUCATION (KAEE), Blackacre Nature Preserve, 3200 Tucker Station Rd., Jeffersontown 40299 (502, 456-3747)

Organized to promote and support formal and nonformal environmental education programs throughout the state. Promotes information sharing, research, and development of EE programs and activities. Annually sponsors a three-day conference.
Publication: Newsletter
Editor: ANN R. SEPPENFIELD, Rm. 1829, Dept. Education, Capital Plaza Tower, Frankfort 40601 (564-2672)

KENTUCKY ASSOCIATION OF CONSERVATION DISTRICTS

President: BILLY JOE MILES, R. 3, Owensboro 42301
Vice-President: JAMES LACY, Box 432, Campton 41301
Secretary-Treasurer: GARY STENGER, Rt. 2, Box 24, Morganfield 42437
Past President: JOHN CHISM, 1442 Lilly Ferry Rd., Winchester 40391

KENTUCKY AUDUBON COUNCIL

Associated with the National Audubon Society. Works to promote, foster, and encourage the conservation and preservation of all wildlife, plants, soils, water, air, and other natural resources for the benefit of all people. Organized: 1971.
President: HERB ZIMMERMAN, 1363 Tyler Park Dr., Louisville 40204 (502, 456-6126)
Vice-President: RUTH HOUSEK, 784 Marcella St., Versailles 40383 (606, 873-4964)
Secretary: TOM HICKS, 5304 Old Henderson Rd., Owensboro 42301
Treasurer: MAGGIE SELVIDGE, 904 North Dr., Hopkinsville 42240 (502, 886-8078)

KENTUCKY BASS CHAPTER FEDERATION

An organization of Bassmaster Chapters, affiliated with the Bass Anglers Sportsman Society, to fight pollution, assist state and national conservation agencies in their efforts and to teach the young people of our country good conservation practices. Dedicated to the realistic conservation of our water resources.
President: DAVE KIK, 6406 Mayfair Ave., Prospect 40059 (502, 228-1214)

KENTUCKY CONSERVATION COUNCIL, 4232 Lynnbrook Dr., Louisville 40220 (502, 451-3466)

Promotes public support of natural resources conservation, advocates effective public interest in protecting these resources, and encourages proper use of Kentucky's lands and waters to encourage the return of nature's balance for our social, economic, and aesthetic welfare. Founded: 1940. Membership: 125.
President: CONNIE QUINTAVALLE

KENTUCKY RESOURCES COUNCIL, P.O. Box 1070, Frankfort 40602 (502, 875-2428)

The KRC is a nonprofit, membership-based statewide organization dedicated to the conservation and prudent use of Kentucky's natural resources. The council comprises Kentuckians from all walks of life—urban dwellers, rural residents and farmers; river recreationists and community activists. This broad-based membership shares a common concern with the impact of natural resource development on our homes, health, and quality of life.
Director: TOM FITZGERALD

TROUT UNLIMITED KENTUCKY COUNCIL
A statewide council with four chapters working for protection and enhancement of the coldwater fishery resources.
Chairman: NORM OBERTO, 3312 High Hope Rd., Lexington 40502 (606, 293-4231)

WILDLIFE SOCIETY KENTUCKY CHAPTER
President: STEPHEN B. WHITE, Department of Biological Sciences, Murray State University, Murray 42071 (502, 762-6298)
President-Elect: STEVEN BLOEMER, Wildlife Management Section, Land Between The Lakes, Golden Pond 42231 (924-5602)
Secretary Treasurer: JEFF SOLE, Kentucky Department of Fish and Wildlife Resources, #1 Game Farm Rd., Frankfort 40601 (564-4858)

LOUISIANA

GOVERNMENT AGENCIES

GOVERNOR: BUDDY ROEMER, Governor of Louisiana, State Capitol, Baton Rouge 70804 (504, 342-7015)

DEPARTMENT OF AGRICULTURE, P.O. Box 94302, Baton Rouge 70804-9302 (504, 342-7011)
Commissioner: BOB ODOM
Assistant Commissioner, Office of Management and Finance: RICHARD ALLEN
Deputy Commissioner: JOHN COMPTON (295-8401)

DEPARTMENT OF AGRICULTURE AND FORESTRY, OFFICE OF FORESTRY, P.O. Box 1628, Baton Rouge 70821 (504, 925-4500)
Charged with: detection and suppression of wildfire on forest lands; providing technical management assistance to forest landowners; and dissemination of materials and information for education of the public. Established: 1944.
Commission Members: BURTON D. WEAVER, JR., Flora; JOHN SQUIRES, Shreveport; MICHAEL S. BAER, SR., Bogalusa; BOBBY GREEN, Monroe; BILLY W. WEAVER, Chairman, Robert; DR. THOMAS A. HANSBROUGH, Baton Rouge; VIRGINIA VAN SICKLE, Baton Rouge
State Forester (Acting): CARLTON S. HURST
Associate State Forester: W.D. MERCER
Chief, Forest Protection: Vacant (925-4500)
Chief, Forest Management: PAUL D. FREY (925-4500)
Chief, Prevention and Education: JAMES L. CULPEPPER (925-4500)
Chief, Reforestation: OLIN L. STUBBS (925-4515)

DEPARTMENT OF WILDLIFE AND FISHERIES, P.O. Box 98000, Baton Rouge 70898 (504, 765-2800)
Established as a part of state government to protect, conserve, and replenish the natural resources of the state, the wildlife of the state, including wild game and nongame quadrupeds or animals, game, oysters, fish, and other aquatic life.
Commission Members: DR. JACK T. CAPPEL, JR., Alexandria; WARREN POL, Baton Rouge; JAMES H. JENKINS, JR., Baton Rouge; DON HINES, Vice-Chairman, Bunkie; JOE PALMISANO, Chairman, Chauvin; NORMAN F. McCALL, Cameron; DALE VINET, Delcambre
Secretary: VIRGINIA VAN SICKLE (765-2803)
Deputy Secretary: A. KELL McINNIS III (765-2957)
Undersecretary: BETTSIE BAKER (765-2860)

Assistant Secretaries: ROBERT MISSO, Office of Wildlife (765-2806); Vacant, Office of Fisheries (765-2801)
Information and Education Division: BOB DENNIE, Administrator (765-2916)
Administrator, Division of Seafood: WILLIAM S. (Corky) PERRET (765-2370)
Administrator, Division of Inland Fisheries: BENNIE J. FONTENOT (765-2330)
Administrator, Division of Game: HUGH BATEMAN (765-2346)
Chief, Division of Enforcement: Vacant (765-2989)
Administrator, Division of Fur and Refuge: JOHNNIE TARVER (765-2811)
Publication: *Louisiana Conservationist*
Editor: BOB DENNIE

GEOLOGICAL SURVEY, P.O. Box G, University Sta., Baton Rouge 70893 (504, 342-6754)
Established by legislative act in 1934, is charged with conducting geologic investigations and preparing technical reports that will assist in finding and properly developing new reserves of natural resources in the state. Attention is being focused on those resources which are most critical to the future economic health of the state: oil and gas, lignite, groundwater, geothermal energy, and on coastal and land resources in areas of maximum human impact. Because it is not a regulatory organization, the Geological Survey is able to conduct studies from an objective viewpoint, thus ensuring that the results are useful to both the public and private sectors of the state.
Director: CHARLES G. GROAT
Assistant Director: Vacant

LOUISIANA COOPERATIVE FISH AND WILDLIFE RESEARCH UNIT, U.S.D.I., U.S. Fish and Wildlife Service, School of Forestry, Wildlife, and Fisheries, Rm. 124, Louisiana State University, Baton Rouge 70803 (504, 388-4179; FTS #687-0380)
Leader: CHARLES F. BRYAN
Assistant Leaders: ALAN D. AFTON; WILLIAM H. HERKE

OFFICE OF STATE PARKS, DEPARTMENT OF CULTURE, RECREATION AND TOURISM, P.O. Box 44426, Baton Rouge 70804 (504, 342-8111)
Created in 1934 to plan, design, construct, operate, and maintain the state's parks, natural areas, recreational facilities, and commemorative sites. Office has 14 parks or recreational areas, 13 commemorative sites, and one preservation area open to the public. Office is assisted by Parks and Recreation Commission, an advisory board appointed by the governor.
Assistant Secretary: LINTON ARDOIN

SEA GRANT COLLEGE PROGRAM
Director, Sea Grant Program: DR. JACK R. VAN LOPIK, Center for Wetland Resources, Louisiana State University, Baton Rouge 70803 (504, 388-6710)
Marine Advisory Program: RONALD E. BECKER, Associate Director, Sea Grant Program, Center for Wetland Resources, Louisiana State University, Baton Rouge 70803 (388-6345)

STATE EXTENSION SERVICES
Director of Extension Service: DENVER T. LOUPE, Ph.D., Louisiana State University Agricultural Center, Baton Rouge 70803 (504, 388-6083)
Specialist, Wildlife and Sea Grant: JAMES F. FOWLER, Ph.D., Louisiana State University Agricultural Center, Baton Rouge 70803 (388-2180)
Extension Forester: ALDEN MAIN, Ph.D., Knapp Hall, Rm. 265,

Louisiana State University Agricultural Center, Baton Rouge 70803 (388-4087)

Associate Specialist, Aquaculture: LARRY DE LA BRETONNE, JR., Knapp Hall, Rm. 202 A, Louisiana State University Agricultural Center, Baton Rouge 70803 (388-2180)

Specialist, Seafood Technology: MICHAEL W. MOODY, Ph.D., Knapp Hall, Rm. 202 D, Louisiana State University Agricultural Center, Baton Rouge 70803 (388-2180)

Specialist, Marine Resource Economics: KENNETH J. ROBERTS, Ph.D., Knapp Hall, Rm. 259, Louisiana State University Agricultural Center, Baton Rouge 70803 (388-2145)

Specialist, Forestry: ROBERT H. MILLS, Ph.D., Knapp Hall, Louisiana State University Agricultural Center, Baton Rouge 70803 (388-4087)

STATE OFFICE OF CONSERVATION, P.O. Box 94275, Capitol Sta., Baton Rouge 70804-9275 (504, 342-5540)
Commissioner: J. PATRICK BATCHELOR

STATE SOIL AND WATER CONSERVATION COMMITTEE, Louisiana State University, P.O. Drawer CS, Baton Rouge 70893 (504, 342-7543/342-7919)
To assist soil and water conservation districts in carrying out their powers and programs, to keep supervisors informed of activities of all districts, and to secure the cooperation and assistance of governmental agencies, state and federal, in the work of such districts. Established: 1938.
Chairman: A. LEE ALLEE, P.O. Box 108, St. James 70086
Vice-Chairman: TERRY SMITH
Secretary-Treasurer: EARL FONTENOT, JR.
Members: DR. H. ROUSE CAFFEY, Baton Rouge; TERRY SMITH, Jonesville; RICHARD B.S. NETTERVILLE, St. Joseph; BOB ODOM, Baton Rouge; WARREN J. HARANG, JR., Thibodaux
Executive Director: BRADLEY E. SPICER

CITIZENS' GROUPS

LOUISIANA WILDLIFE FEDERATION, INC., *337 S. Acadian Throughway, Baton Rouge 70806 (504, 344-6707)*
A representative statewide organization, affiliated with the National Wildlife Federation, primarily devoted to the wise use, conservation, aesthetic appreciation, and restoration of wildlife and other natural resources.
President: MRS. GEORGE ANN BERNARD, 110 Myrtle Oak, New Iberia 70560 (318, 365-6756)
Executive Director: RANDY P. LANCTOT
Affiliate Representative: WILSON J. THIBODEAUX, 3737 Beech St., Baton Rouge 70805 (504, 355-2717)
Alternate: RANDY P. LANCTOT
Publication: Louisiana Out of Doors
Editor: RANDY P. LANCTOT

AMERICAN LUNG ASSOCIATION OF LOUISIANA, INC., Suite 500, 333 St. Charles Ave., New Orleans 70130 (504, 523-LUNG) (Annual meeting July of each year, New Orleans)
A nonprofit citizens' agency and serving as the Louisiana unit of the national ALA, the organization has the prevention and control of lung diseases as its primary goal. Devotes considerable time to public education, social action, advocacy, and coordination aimed at prevention and control of air pollution. An "Action for Clean Air Clearinghouse" is maintained by the organization and consists of frequent mailings of data and notices to persons and institutions

concerned with air pollution throughout Louisiana. Incorporated: 1923.
Executive Director: W. FINDLEY RAYMOND
Volunteer Officers: BIBBY TATE, President; JUDITH A. HARRIS, M.D., Vice-President; BERNICE JACOBS, Treasurer

ELSA WILD ANIMAL APPEAL (Louisiana Chapter)
Regional branch of ELSA WILD ANIMAL APPEAL; concerned with wildlife matters, educational programs, liaison with other wildlife and governmental groups for the betterment of natural environment and wildlife protection; coordinated through EWAA National Headquarters; establishes local volunteer corps to implement programs.
LAURA LANZA, 1540 Chateau Cir., Lake Charles 70605 (318, 477-9782)

LOUISIANA ASSOCIATION OF CONSERVATION DISTRICTS
President: WARREN J. HARANG, JR., P.O. Box 629, Thibodaux 70301 (504, 447-3767)
Vice-President: STIRLING MELANCON, P.O. Box 361, Hahnville 70057 (504, 468-4411)
Secretary-Treasurer: CHARLES F. DUPUY, 100 N. Patton St., Marksville 71351 (318, 253-7603)

LOUISIANA BASS CHAPTER FEDERATION
An organization of Bassmaster Chapters, affiliated with the Bass Anglers Sportsman Society, to fight pollution, assist state and national conservation agencies in their efforts, and to teach the young people of our country good conservation practices. Dedicated to the realistic conservation of our water resources.
President: MIKE THOMAS, 125 Lawrence, Houghton 71037 (318, 949-8450)

LOUISIANA FORESTRY ASSOCIATION, P.O. Drawer 5067, Alexandria 71307 (318, 443-2558)
Trade-supported association whose purpose is the protection of the state's forest land and the promotion of the products derived therefrom. Membership: 2,300. Organized: 1947.
President: NORMAN E. WELCH, JR., Alexandria 71315
1st Vice-President: MERVIN G. PARKER, Ruston 71270
2nd Vice-President: ROBERT H. CROSBY III, Metairie 70002
3rd Vice-President: JOHN H. GERBER, DeRidder 70634
Treasurer: FRANK FOOTE, Alexandria 71301
Executive Director: CHARLES A. (Buck) VANDERSTEEN
Staff Forester: MARY S. LEACH
Publication: *Forests and People*
Information Coordinator and Editor: JOHN R. GORMLEY

WILDLIFE SOCIETY LOUISIANA CHAPTER
President: JERALD V. OWENS, Louisiana Department of Wildlife and Fisheries, P.O. Box 4004, Monroe 71211 (318, 343-4044)
President-Elect: ROBERT H. CHABRECK, 1821 Cloverdale Ave., Baton Rouge 70808 (388-4220)
Secretary-Treasurer: BENJAMIN N. TUGGLE, 110 Margaret Pl., Grambling 71245 (274-2499)

MAINE

GOVERNMENT AGENCIES

GOVERNOR: JOHN R. McKERNAN, JR., Governor of Maine, State House, Augusta 04333 (207, 289-3531)

DEPARTMENT OF AGRICULTURE, FOOD, AND RURAL RESOURCES, State House Station # 28, Augusta 04333
Commissioner: BERNARD W. SHAW (207, 289-3871)

DEPARTMENT OF CONSERVATION, State House Station #22, Augusta 04333 (207, 289-2211)
To preserve, protect, and enhance the land resources of the state of Maine; to encourage the wise use of the scenic, mineral, and forest resources; to ensure that coordinated planning for the future allocation of lands for recreational, forest production, mining, and other public and private uses is effectively accomplished; and to provide for the effective management of public lands. Created in 1973 including former state departments of forestry and parks and recreation.
Commissioner: ROBERT R. LaBONTA
Deputy Commissioner: SUSAN J. BELL
Assistant to the Commissioner: CATHERINE A. WARD
Director of Administrative Services: JANET E. WALDRON
Director, Maine Conservation Corps: KENNETH E. SPALDING
Assistant to the Commissioner, Public Information: MARSHALL T. WIEBE
Forests for the Future Program: JAMES CONNORS
Director, Division of Engineering and Realty: FRED BARTLETT

Bureau of Parks and Recreation (207, 289-3821)
Director: HERBERT HARTMAN
Director, Operations and Maintenance: STEVEN O. CURTIS
Supervisor, Planning and Research: THOMAS J. CIESLINSKI
Supervisor, Snowmobile Program: SCOTT RAMSAY
Supervisor, Allagash Wilderness Waterway: TIMOTHY CAVERLY
Supervisor, Boating Facilities: RICHARD SKINNER

Maine Forest Service (207, 289-2791)
Director: JOHN H. CASHWELL
State Entomologist: THOMAS MORRISON
State Supervisor, Forest Fire Operations: GEORGE BOURASSA
Director of Forest Management and Utilization: VLADEK KOLMAN
Administrative Assistant: THOMAS P. DRISCOLL

Maine Geological Survey, State House, Station #22, Augusta 04333 (207, 289-2801)
Director and State Geologist: WALTER A. ANDERSON
Director, Bedrock and Surficial Geology Division: WOODROW B. THOMPSON
Director, Marine Geology Division: JOSEPH T. KELLEY
Associate Director and Director, Hydrogeology Division: JOHN S. WILLIAMS
Director, Cartographic Division: ROBERT D. TUCKER

Bureau of Public Lands, State House, Station #22, Augusta 04333 (207, 289-3061)
Director: C. EDWIN MEADOWS, JR.
Resource Administrator: Vacant
Director, Land Management: LEIGH HOAR, JR.
Director of Planning: THOMAS DOAK

Land Use Regulation Commission, State House, Station 22, Augusta 04333 (207, 289-2631); In-state toll-free number: 1, 800, 452-8711)
Director: PAUL B. FREDERIC
Assistant to Director: JAMES ST. PIERRE
Supervisor, Development Review: GLORIA LeVASSEUR
Supervisor, Land Use Planning: FREDERICK W. TODD
Coordinator, Enforcement: SCOTT FOSTER

DEPARTMENT OF INLAND FISHERIES AND WILDLIFE, 284 State St., Station #41, Augusta 04333 (207, 289-2766) Organized: 1880.
Commissioner: WILLIAM J. VAIL (289-5202)
Deputy Commissioner: NORMAN E. TRASK (289-3371)
Advisory Council Members: ALANSON B. NOBLE, Otisfield (539-4027); WILLIAM SYLVESTER, Clayton Lake (435-6128); CARROLL YORK, West Forks (663-2201); NATHAN COHEN, Eastport (853-2754); F. PAUL FRINSKO, Portland (774-6291); F. DALE SPEED, Princeton (796-5155); JOHN CRABTREE, Warren (273-2465); DR. OGDEN SMALL, Caribou (498-6502)
Director, Bureau of Resource Management: FREDERICK B. HURLEY (289-5252)
Chief, Fishery Research and Management Division: PETER M. BOURQUE (289-5261)
Chief, Wildlife Research and Management Division: GARY G. DONOVAN (289-5252)
Director, Bureau of Warden Service: LARRY CUMMINGS (289-2766)
Director, Bureau of Administrative Service: PETER C. BRAZIER (289-5210)
Chief, Planning Division: KENNETH H. ANDERSON (289-3286)
Chief, Engineering and Realty Division: G. DONALD TAYLOR (289-5210)
Director, Licensing and Registration Division: VESTA C. BILLING (289-2043)
Rules and Regulations Officer: JANET F. POTTER (289-3371)
Director, Public Information and Education: W. THOMAS SHOENER (289-2871)
Publication: *Maine Fish and Wildlife Magazine*
Editor: W. THOMAS SHOENER

DEPARTMENT OF MARINE RESOURCES, State House, Station #21, Augusta 04333 (207, 289-2291)
Responsible for research, development, promotion, planning, and enforcement of laws relating to conservation of Maine's marine resources.
Commissioner: WILLIAM J. BRENNAN
Deputy Commissioner: E. PENN ESTABROOK
Director, Bureau of Marine Sciences: BRIAN M. MARCOTTE, Fisheries Research Station, West Boothbay Harbor 04575 (207, 633-5572)
Director, Bureau of Marine Development: HAROLD C. WINTERS
Chief, Bureau of Marine Patrol: ROBERT L. FOGG
Director, Bureau of Administration: ANNA M. STANLEY

MAINE ATLANTIC SEA RUN SALMON COMMISSION, P.O. Box 1298, Hedin Hall, Bangor 04401 (207, 941-4449)
Charged by the Maine legislature with the restoration and management of the Atlantic salmon in Maine waters. Established: 1948.
Commission Members: WILLIAM J. VAIL, Chairman, Augusta (289-3371); WILLIAM BRENNAN, Commissioner, Augusta (289-2291); JOSEPH SEWALL, Public Member, Old Town; PAUL FERNALD, Public Member, Brunswick; PETER WASS, Public Member, Cherryfield
Program Coordinator: EDWARD T. BAUM (941-4449)

MAINE COOPERATIVE FISH AND WILDLIFE RESEARCH UNIT, U.S.D.I., 240 Nutting Hall, University of Maine, Orono 04469 (207, 581-2870)

Provide graduate training and research experience in wildlife and fish ecology and management. Supported cooperatively by the University of Maine in Orono, Maine Department of Inland Fisheries and Wildlife, U.S. Fish and Wildlife Service, and the Wildlife Management Institute. Established: 1935.

Leader: DR. WILLIAM B. KROHN
Assistant Leader, Wildlife: Vacant
Assistant Leader, Fishery: DR. JOHN R. MORING, 310 Murray Hall, University of Maine, Orono 04469 (207, 581-2582)

SEA GRANT PROGRAM, Center for Marine Studies, DR. ROBERT E. WALL, Director, 14 Coburn Hall, University of Maine, Orono 04469 (207, 581-1434)

Director, Sea Grant Marine Advisory Program: DAVID J. DOW (581-1443)
Ira C. Darling Center: DR. LES WATLING, Director (Acting), Walpole 04575 (563-3146)
Sea Grant Research: DR. BRYAN PEARCE, Director (Acting), Center for Marine Studies, 14 Coburn Hall, University of Maine, Orono 04469 (581-1433)
Oceanography Program: DR. L. KENNETH FINK, JR., Program Coordinator, University of Maine, 14 Coburn Hall, Orono 04469 (581-1437)

STATE EXTENSION SERVICE

Program Leader, Natural Resources/Community Development: ROGER S. LEACH, 100 Winslow Hall, University of Maine, Orono 04469 (207, 581-3194)
Extension Foresters: MARVIN W. BLUMENSTOCK, 107 Nutting Hall, University of Maine, Orono 04469 (581-2892); JAMES F. PHILP, 261 Nutting Hall, University of Maine, Orono 04469; WILLIAM D. LILLEY, 105 Nutting Hall, University of Maine, Orono 04469
Extension Fisheries and Wildlife Specialist: DR. CATHERINE ELLIOTT, 234 Nutting Hall, University of Maine, Orono 04469 (581-2902)
Extension Environmental Specialist: DR. VAUGHN HOLYOKE, 414 Deering Hall, University of Maine, Orono 04469 (581-2941)

STATE SOIL AND WATER CONSERVATION COMMISSION, Deering Bldg., AMHI Complex, Station #28, Augusta 04333 (207, 289-2666)

To assist in the organization of soil and water conservation districts statewide; to develop and carry out a program of erosion and sediment control, flood control, water management, and proper land use; to coordinate the programs of districts with those of other state and federal agencies. Founded: 1941.

Members: L. HERBERT YORK, Chairman (778-3835); CHARLES PERKINS, Vice-Chairman (379-2921); ALBAN BOUCHARD (834-3237); ANNE FAVREAU (725-6944); DAVID BRIDGES (382-6221); FRANKLIN EGGERT (469-7516)
Ex-Officio Members: Vice-President, Research and Public Service, GREGORY N. BROWN, College of Life Sciences and Agriculture (581-7161); BERNARD SHAW, Commissioner, Department of Agriculture, Food, and Rural Resources (289-3871); ROBERT R. LaBONTA, Commissioner, Department of Conservation (289-2212); WILLIAM J. VAIL, Commissioner, Inland Fisheries and Wildlife (289-3371); DEAN C. MARRIOTT, Commissioner, Department of Environmental Protection; WILLIAM BRENNAN, Commissioner, Marine Resources (289-2291)
Advisory Member: CHARLES WHITMORE, State Conservationist, Soil Conservation Service (866-2132)
Chairman: L. HERBERT YORK

Executive Director: FRANK W. RICKER
Soil Scientist: DAVID ROCQUE
Secretary to Executive Director: JEAN TENNEY

CITIZENS' GROUPS

 NATURAL RESOURCES COUNCIL OF MAINE, 271 State St., Augusta 04330 (207, 622-3101)

A representative statewide organization, affiliated with the National Wildlife Federation, primarily devoted to the wise use, conservation, aesthetic appreciation, and restoration of wildlife and other natural resources.

President: JOHN LUND, 21 Second St., Hallowell 04347 (622-4843)
Executive Director: EVERETT B. CARSON
Affiliate Representative: DES FITZGERALD, R.F.D. 2, Box 378, Lincolnville 04849 (763-3970)
Alternate: EVERETT CARSON
Publication: Maine Environment
Editor: DORCAS MILLER

MAINE ASSOCIATION OF CONSERVATION COMMISSIONS (MACC), P.O. Box 831, Yarmouth 04096 (207, 846-3329)

A membership organization whose objectives are twofold: to assist Maine municipalities in establishing conservation commissions; to assist the existing 200 conservation commissions through technical assistance and educational programs. Membership: 120 commissions. Founded: 1970.

President: JACK DIRKMAN
Staff Director: BILL SERETTA
Publication: Newsletter; *Grass Roots*
Editor: BILL SERETTA

MAINE ASSOCIATION OF CONSERVATION DISTRICTS

President: WALTER SIMPSON, R.F.D. #4, Winslow 04902
Vice-President: RUDY DIONNE, Rt. 1, Box 1100, Madison 04950
Secretary: BERNARD SHAW, R.F.D. 1, Box H, Limestone 04750
Treasurer: NORRIS CONANT, R.F.D. 1, Box 619, Canton 04221

MAINE AUDUBON SOCIETY, Gilsland Farm, 118 U.S. Rt. 1, Falmouth 04105 (207, 781-2330)

Wildlife species and habitat protection and research; forest and marine ecosystem research; alternative energy research; environmental education for both children and adults, including courses, nature programs, day camp, teachers' curricula, and resource center; environmental advocacy public information program and environmental library; 100+ field trips throughout Maine and New England, as well as worldwide nature tours; store specializing in natural history books, binoculars; 15 sanctuaries; publish magazine seven times a year. Membership: 6,800. Founded: 1843.

Executive Director: THOMAS A. URQUHART
Publications: *Habitat: Journal of the Maine Audubon Society*
Editor: WILLIAM HANCOCK

MAINE BASS CHAPTER FEDERATION

An organization of Bassmaster Chapters, affiliated with the Bass Anglers Sportsman Society, organized to fight pollution, assist state and national conservation agencies in their efforts, and to teach young people of our country good conservation practices. Dedicated to the realistic conservation of our water resources.

President: ANDREW RAIO, Box 268, Mary Jane Rd., R.R. 1, West Buxton 04093 (207, 121-3215)

MAINE COAST HERITAGE TRUST, 167 Park Row, Brunswick 04011 (207, 729-7366)

To protect land that is essential to the character of Maine, in particular its coastline and islands. Provides free advisory services on open space protection to landowners, town officials, state and federal agencies, land trusts, and other private conservation organizations. Organized: 1970.

Chairman: HAROLD E. WOODSUM, JR., Athletic Director, Yale University Athletics Department, 402A Yale Station, New Haven, CT 06520 (203, 432-1414)

Treasurer: BENJAMIN R. EMORY

President: JAMES J. ESPY, JR.

Publications: *Directory of Maine Land Conservation Trusts; Annual Report;* Newsletter; Technical Bulletins

Editor: JAMES J. ESPY, JR.

MAINE ENVIRONMENTAL EDUCATION ASSOCIATION, INC., Chewonki Foundation, Wiscasset 04578 (207, 882-7323)

A nonprofit organization dedicated to promote environmental education (EE) in Maine by working for inclusion of K-12 EE in all schools, by providing methodological information and materials to teachers and parents, publishing a newsletter and by coordinating the work of organizations involved in EE. Founded: 1981.

President: DON HUDSON, Ph.D., Chewonki Foundation, Wiscasset 04578 (882-7323)

Vice-President: JULIE EASTMAN, P.O. Box 514, Camden 04843

Treasurer: ROGER BENNATTI, George Stevens Academy, Blue Hill 04614 (374-2808)

Secretary: MARY M.S. LANNON, Wiscasset 04578

Publication: *Connections*

Editor: MARY SEWALL HAMBLIN, R.R. 2, Box 107, Gorham 04038

SMALL WOODLAND OWNERS ASSOCIATION OF MAINE, INC., S. Gouldsboro 04678 (207, 963-2331)

A statewide nonprofit organization which pursues better understandings, skills, and directions in small woodland ownership/management under integrated use objectives.

President: PETER W. LAWRENCE, 5 Bond St., Portland 04102 (772-6863)

Vice-President: RICHARD LANGTON, 304-A Cross Point Rd., Edgecomb 04556 (882-6194)

Treasurer: VICTOR HAUGHTON, 60 Blueberry Cove, Yarmouth 04096 (846-4607)

Secretary: MARK MILLER, R.D. 2, Box 1886, Coopers Mills 04341 (549-7802)

Publications: Newsletter; *SWOAM NEWS*

Editor: ELINOR VASSEY

SPORTSMAN'S ALLIANCE OF MAINE, P.O. Box 2783, Augusta 04330 (207, 622-5503) (Annual meeting: third Saturday in September.)

A statewide nonprofit organization of sportsmen dedicated to hunting, fishing, trapping, protection of wildlife habitat, and conservation. Lobbies and works with state agencies on behalf of Maine Sportsmen. Membership: 9,000. Founded: 1975.

President: MIKE LEE

1st Vice-President: MATT SCOTT

2nd Vice-President: JOHN CHAREST

Secretary: CARLEEN COTE

Treasurer: WES SMITH

Executive Director: STEPHEN L. DUREN

Assistant Executive Director: SCOTT HALL

Publication: *SAM News*

Editor: STEPHEN L. DUREN

TROUT UNLIMITED MAINE COUNCIL

A statewide Council with 11 chapters working for the protection and enhancement of the coldwater fishery resources.

Chairman: JAMES WALKER, R.F.D., Brown Rd, Box 164B, Raymond 04071 (207, 428-3993)

National Director: DAVID BOWIE, 540 Duck Pond Rd., Westbrook 04092 (207, 854-9978)

WILDLIFE SOCIETY MAINE CHAPTER

President: WILLIAM B. KROHN, 4 Meadow Ln., Brewer 04412 (207, 581-2870)

President-Elect: STEVE OLIVERI, LURC, Department of Conservation, Augusta 04333 (289-2631)

Secretary-Treasurer: BARRY BURGASON, Maine Department of Inland Fish and Wildlife, Enfield 04433 (732-4131)

MARYLAND

GOVERNMENT AGENCIES

GOVERNOR: WILLIAM DONALD SCHAEFER, Governor of Maryland, State House, Annapolis 21404 (301, 269-3901)

AGRICULTURAL COMMISSION, Department of Agriculture, 50 Harry S. Truman Pkwy., Annapolis 21401 (301, 841-5782)

Established by law in 1969 and placed within the Department of Agriculture in 1973, the commission formulates and makes proposals for the advancement of Maryland agriculture by serving as an advisory body to the Secretary of Agriculture. Composed of seventeen members, one member is Vice-President of Agricultural Affairs at the University of Maryland; the remaining sixteen members are appointed by the Governor from nominations submitted by commodity and farm organizations to serve three-year terms.

Chairman: DREW STABLER

Vice-Chairman: W. SIMPSON DUNAHOO

Executive Secretary: LYNNE C. HOOT

CHESAPEAKE WILDLIFE HERITAGE, P.O. Box 1745, Easton 21601 (301, 822-5100)

A private, nonprofit conservation group working with private landowners in the Chesapeake Bay drainage system to build wetlands and upland habitats for game and nongame wildlife which will improve water quality in the Chesapeake Bay and its tributaries. Members: 350. Organized: 1983.

President: SCOTT BEATTY

Executive Director: THOMAS R. HUGHES, JR.

Habitat Biologists: JOHN E. (Ned) GERBER; MICHAEL ROBIN CLIFFORD

Research Biologist: ROLAND J. LIMPERT, Ph.D.

Secretary-Treasurer: DOTTIE HINER

DEPARTMENT OF AGRICULTURE, 50 Harry S. Truman Pkwy., Annapolis 21401 (301, 841-5700)

Created as a cabinet-level state agency in 1972, the department is charged with assisting soil conservation districts to protect state waters from agricultural nonpoint source pollution, overseeing numerous inspection, testing, grading, and marketing programs, mosquito control and gypsy moth control and forest pest management under various laws. The department also has responsibility for regulatory functions, such as pesticide applicators, weights and measures, nursery inspection, seed and turf regulation, certification, agricultural chemical and product registration.

Secretary: WAYNE A. CAWLEY, JR. (841-5880)

Deputy Secretary: ROBERT L. WALKER (841-5881)

Assistant Secretary, Office of Animal Health and Consumer Services: DR. ARCHIBALD B. PARK (841-5782)

Assistant Secretary, Office of Plant Industries and Resource Conservation: DR. CHARLES W. PUFFINBERGER (841-5870)

State Veterinarian: DR. HENRY A. VIRTS (841-5810)

Director, Marketing and Agricultural Development: HENRY SCHMIDT (841-5769)

Meat and Poultry Inspection Section: DR. STEPHEN WOLFORD (269-2033)

Counsel: CRAIG A. NIELSEN (841-5883)

Publications: List on request.

Editor: ANNE SIELING

DEPARTMENT OF NATURAL RESOURCES, Tawes State Office Bldg., Annapolis 21401 (301, 974 plus extension)

Secretary: TORREY C. BROWN, M.D. (Ext.3041)

Deputy Secretary: JOHN R. GRIFFIN (Ext. 3043)

Assistant Secretaries: JAMES PECK (Ext. 3548); VERNA E. HARRISON (Ext. 2255); DONALD MacLAUCHLAN (Ext. 2640); MICHAEL J. NELSON (Ext. 7947); HERBERT M. SACHS (Ext. 3547); JAMES DUNMYER (Ext. 2031)

Board of Review: JOHN W. NEUMANN, Chairman (974-2257)

Advisory Board: ERWIN C. HANNUM, Chairman (567-3661)

Public Affairs Director: ED MASON (Ext. 3988)

Licensing and Consumer Services (Acting): JACK ARNEY, Administrator (Ext. 3211)

Tidewater Administration: PAUL MASSICOT, Administrator (Ext. 2926)

Forest, Park, and Wildlife Services: JIM MALLOW, Director of Administration (Ext. 2870); GARY TAYLOR, Director of Wildlife (Ext. 3195); JIM ROBERTS, Director of Forestry (Ext. 3776); DAVE HATHWAY, State Parks and Forests (Ext. 3771)

Natural Resources Police Force: JACK T. TAYLOR, Superintendent (Ext. 3170)

Maryland Environmental Service: GEORGE PERDIKAKIS, Director (Ext. 3281)

Maryland Geological Survey: DR. KENNETH N. WEAVER, Director, 2300 St. Paul St., Baltimore 21218 (554-5500)

Power Plant Research Program: JAMES TEITT, Administrator (Ext. 2788)

Water Resources Administration: CATHERINE STEVENSON, Director (Ext. 3846)

Maryland Environmental Trust: H. GRANT DeHART, Executive Director, Suite 700, 118 N. Howard St., Baltimore 21201 (659-6440)

DEPARTMENT OF THE ENVIRONMENT, 2500 Broening Highway, Baltimore 21224 (301, 631-3000)

The Department of the Environment is charged with protection of the state's land, air, and water resources, to ensure the long-term protection of public health and quality of life. Inception: July 1, 1987.

Secretary: MARTIN W. WALSH, JR. (631-3084)

Deputy Secretary: THOMAS C. ANDREWS (631-3086)

Public Affairs Director: CHARLES WALKER

Assistant Secretary, Toxics Environmental Science and Health: DR. KATHERINE FARRELL (631-3851)

Assistant Secretary, Planning and Capital Programs: ROBERT PERCIASEPE (631-3121)

Assistant Secretary, Operations: RICHARD F. PECORA (631-3175)

Director, Air Management Administration: GEORGE P. FERRERI (631-3255)

Director, Waste Management Administration: RONALD NELSON (631-3304)

Director, Water Management Administration: J.L. HEARN (631-3567)

Director, Sediment and Stormwater Administration: EARL SHAVER (631-3553)

Director, Finance and Administration: CHARLES BRANNAN

Publications: *Monthly Regulatory Calendar; Annual Air Quality Data Report; Biennial Water Quality Report;* List of Potential Hazardous Waste Sites

SEA GRANT COLLEGE

Director: RICHARD N. JARMAN, Sea Grant College, University of Maryland, College Park 20742 (301, 454-5690)

STATE EXTENSION SERVICES

Director of Extension Service and Sea Grant Extension Program: DR. CRAIG S. OLIVER, University of Maryland, College Park 20742 (301, 454-3742)

Associate Director, Agricultural Programs and Marine Advisory Programs: RALPH J. ADKINS, University of Maryland, College Park 20742 (454-4848)

Extension Forester: JOHN F. KUNDT, Department of Horticulture, University of Maryland, College Park 20742 (454-6464)

STATE SOIL CONSERVATION COMMITTEE, 50 Harry S. Truman Pkwy., Annapolis 21401 (301, 841-5863)

A state agency established in 1937 to organize soil conservation districts and to establish policy, resolve problems to give guidance and assistance to districts. Membership includes representatives from the Department of Natural Resources, Department of Agriculture, Department of the Environment, Maryland Agricultural Commission, University of Maryland, Maryland Association of Soil Conservation Districts, and five soil conservation district supervisors. The committee is a unit of the Maryland Dept. of Agriculture.

Chairman: FLOYD ALLRED, JR. (658-4412)

Vice-Chairman: GEORGE H. GODFREY (438-3501)

Executive Secretary: LOUISE LAWRENCE (841-5863)

Publication: *SSCC Reporter Newsletter*

CITIZENS' GROUPS

 *MARYLAND:* Vacant

AMERICAN BASS ASSOCIATION OF MARYLAND, THE

An organization of the individual members and bass fishing clubs, affiliated with the American Bass Association, Inc., dedicated to protecting and enhancing the state's fishery resources; to promote the sport of bass fishing; and to teach youngsters the fun of fishing and instill in them an appreciation of the life-giving waters of America.

President: ED LOHR, 15401 Wembrough St., Colesville 20904 (301, 989-2507)

CHESAPEAKE BAY FOUNDATION, INC., 162 Prince George St., Annapolis, 21401 (301, 268-8816); Heritage Bldg., Suite 815, 1001 E. Main St., Richmond, VA 23219 (804, 780-1392); 214 State St., Harrisburg, PA 17101 (717, 234-5550)

A nonprofit membership organization established to promote the environmental welfare and proper management of Chesapeake Bay, including its tidal tributaries. The foundation operates three programs: environmental defense, environmental education, land preservation. Membership: 60,000. Organized: 1966.

Chairman: GODFREY A. ROCKEFELLER, Washington, DC

President: WILLIAM C. BAKER

Vice-Presidents: ANTHONY M. ZANE; ANN POWERS
Virginia Executive Director: JOSEPH H. MAROON
Pennsylvania Executive Director: THOMAS P. SEXTON III
Environmental Defense Director: JIM ROBERTSON
Educational Director: DONALD R. BAUGH
Director of Lands Program: SAUNDERS C. HILLYER
Attorneys: ANN POWERS; JIM ROBERTSON; PATRICK GARDNER, Annapolis
Scientists: STEVE BUNKER, Annapolis; WILLIAM GOLDSBOROUGH, Annapolis; STUART LEHMAN, Annapolis; JOLENE CHINCHILLI, Richmond; LEO SNEAD, Richmond
Grassroots: JAY SHERMAN, Annapolis; RUSS BAXTER, Richmond
Publications: *CBF Newsletter; CBF Annual Report; BayWatcher Bulletin; Homeowner Series*

COMMITTEE TO PRESERVE ASSATEAGUE ISLAND, INC., 616 Piccadilly Rd., Towson 21204 (301, 828-4520)

An independent, nonprofit, educational organization dedicated to preservation, understanding, and appreciation of Assateague Island, Maryland and Virginia, Chincoteague National Wildlife Refuge, and other coastal areas in mid-Atlantic region; protection of wetlands, wildlife, natural resources, water and environmental quality. Membership: 1,000+. Founded: 1970.
President: JUDITH C. JOHNSON
Vice-President: A. BLAKEMAN EARLY, 2212 Glasgow Rd., Alexandria, VA 22307 (703, 765-1268)
Treasurer: MARY ELLEN HASSLINGER, 313 Jody Way, Timonium 21093 (252-3387)
Secretary: REBECCA EBAUGH, 500 Woodlawn Rd., Baltimore 21210 (889-2905)
Publication: Newsletter

IZAAK WALTON LEAGUE OF AMERICA, INC. (Maryland Division)

President: WILLIAM ROULETTE III, P.O. Box 148, Tilghman 21671
Executive Secretary: THOMAS (Warren) FISHER, 6700 Needwood Rd., Derwood 20855 (301, 926-8713)

MARYLAND ASSOCIATION OF SOIL CONSERVATION DISTRICTS

President and Council Member: RICHARD W. WRIGHT, Rt. 2, Box 97, Delmar 21875 (301, 883-3533)
1st Vice-President: JOHN NICOLAI, 5410 Kerger Rd., Ellicott City 21043 (465-8310)
2nd Vice-President: GEORGE BISHOFF, Star Rt., Box 77, Friendsville 21531 (746-5502)
Secretary: ALAN R. HATTON, I16 S. Blvd., Salisbury 21801 (742-8373)
Executive Secretary: J.G. WARFIELD, 2115 Sand Hill Rd., Marriottsville 21104 (442-1755)
Treasurer: LORING T. SPARKS, 17422 Falls Rd., Upperco 21155 (374-4358)

MARYLAND BASS CHAPTER FEDERATION

An organization of Bassmaster Chapters, affiliated with the Bass Anglers Sportsman Society, to fight pollution, assist state and national conservation agencies in their efforts and to teach the young people of our country good conservation practices. Dedicated to the realistic conservation of our water resources.
President: KEN ANDREJAK, 21 Clara Cir., Glen Burnie 21061 (301, 760-9275/787-5332)

MARYLAND ENVIRONMENTAL TRUST, Suite 700, 118 N. Howard St., Baltimore 21201 (301, 333-6440)

Formed to conserve, improve, stimulate, and perpetuate the aesthetic, natural, health and welfare, scenic, and cultural qualities of Maryland's environment. Receives voluntary donations of conservation easements on rare or unique natural areas, farmland, scenic areas, watersheds, or other open spaces; presently administering 128 easements on 25,000 acres; works with local volunteers on recycling, community clean-ups, land use planning, and environmental education. Created by state legislature: 1967.
Chairman: BRICE M. CLAGETT, Holly Hill, Friendship 20758 (741-5587)
Vice-Chairman: JAMES B. WILSON, Rt. 3, Box 82, Cambridge 21613 (228-8260)
Secretary: ELLEN H. KELLY, 7214 Bellona Ave., Baltimore 21212 (377-0671)
Treasurer: MRS. THOMAS B. EASTMAN, 112 E. Lake Ave., Baltimore 21212 (323-2999)
Director: H. GRANT DeHART
Senior Planner: JODY M. ROESLER
Planner: JOHN C. WOLF
Publications: *Conservation Easements: To Preserve A Heritage* (1974, revised 1987); *MET Newsletter, Land Marks*
Editor: SHIRLEY L. MASSENBURG
Poster: Our Shores Survived The Winter of '77 ... Can They Survive Us? (1977)

MARYLAND FORESTS ASSOCIATION, 623 Shore Acres Rd., Arnold 21012 (301, 757-3581)

A nonprofit citizens organization for people interested in trees, forests, and forestry.
President: JACK BRODIE
Vice-President: JOHN FORMAN
Executive Director: HENRY DeBRUIN
Publications: *Crosscut;* educational brochures
Editor: HANK DeBRUIN, 623 Shore Acres Rd., Arnold 21012 (757-3581)

MARYLAND-NATIONAL CAPITAL PARK AND PLANNING COMMISSION, 6609 Riggs Rd., Hyattsville 20782 (301, 853-3300)

Established in 1927 by the General Assembly of the state of Maryland to provide for the orderly development of Montgomery and Prince George's Counties; and to provide a system of parks to serve the recreation needs of the residents of this bi-county region.
Vice-Chairman: NORMAN L. CHRISTELLER, 8787 Georgia Ave., Silver Spring 20907 (495-4605)
Chairman: JOHN W. RHOADS, 14741 Governor Oden Bowie Dr., Upper Marlboro 20870 (952-3560)
Executive Director (Acting): JOHN DOWNS, JR.
Secretary-Treasurer: A.E. NAVARRE
Montgomery County Planning Director: RICHARD TUSTIAN
Prince George's County Planning Director (Acting): MICHAEL PETRENKO
Montgomery County Director of Parks: DONALD K. COCHRAN
Prince George's County Director of Parks: HUGH ROBEY

MARYLAND ORNITHOLOGICAL SOCIETY, INC., Cylburn Mansion, 4915 Greenspring Ave., Baltimore 21209

Nonprofit statewide organization of 15 chapters. Aims to promote the knowledge, protection, and conservation of wildlife and natural resources; to foster appreciation of the natural environment; to establish educational and scientific projects to inform and enrich the public; to record, evaluate, and publish observations of birdlife in Maryland. Membership: 2,107. Organized: 1945.
President: ROBERT F. RINGLER, 6272 Pinyon Pine Ct., Eldersburg 21784
Vice-President: RICHARD DOLESH, 17800 Croom Rd., Brandywine 20613 (627-2270)

Secretary: PATRICIA J. MOORE, 24600 Woodfield Rd., Damascus
   20872 (253-2796)
Treasurer: EMILY D. JOYCE, 816 Oak Trail, Crownsville 21032
Executive Secretary: JOY ASO, 1250 4th St., SW, W-709, Washing-
   ton, DC 20024
Publications: *Maryland Birdlife; The Maryland Yellowthroat*
Editor: CHANDLER S. ROBBINS, Patuxent Wildlife Research Center,
   Laurel 20811 (498-0281)

NATURAL HISTORY SOCIETY OF MARYLAND, INC., THE,
   2643 N. Charles St., Baltimore 21218 (301, 235-6116)
Organized: 1929.
President: HERBERT S. HARRIS, JR. (531-4395)
Chairman, Board of Trustees: V. REV. J. MARK ODELL
Vice-Presidents: ARNOLD NORDEN; JEAN R. WORTHLEY
Recording Secretary: WILLIAM F. SEIP
Treasurer: T. MILTON OLER, JR.
Publications: *Bulletin of the Maryland Herpetological Society; News
   & Views; Maryland Naturalist*
Editors: HERBERT S. HARRIS, JR.; HAVEN KOLB; ARNOLD NOR-
DEN

TROUT UNLIMITED MARYLAND COUNCIL (Mid-Atlantic)
A statewide council with 8 chapters working for the protection and
enhancement of coldwater fishery resources.
Chairman: GUY TURENNE, 18011 Silver Leaf Dr., Gaithersburg
   20877 (301, 565-7588)
National Directors: JAMES W. GRACIE, 314B Crosby Rd., Baltimore 21228 (301, 788-4468); ROBERT BERLS, 2751 Uni-
   corn Ln., NW, Washington, DC 20015 (202, 244-2944);
   CHRIS FARRAND, 8500 Warde Terr., Potomac 20854 (202,
   659-8101); BARTON F. WALKER III, 1730 Bolton St., Baltimore 21217 (301, 669-1066)

WILDLIFE SOCIETY MARYLAND CHAPTER
President: THOMAS MATHEWS, 1034 Bedford St., Cumberland
   21502 (301, 777-7581)
President-Elect: BRAD BORTNER, 2321 Kaetzel Rd., Knoxville
   21758 (498-0305)
Secretary-Treasurer: MARILYN MAUSE, 9811 Tabor Rd., Myers-
   ville 21773 (356-5538)

MASSACHUSETTS

GOVERNMENT AGENCIES

GOVERNOR: MICHAEL S. DUKAKIS, Governor of
   Massachusetts, State House, Boston 02133 (617, 727-
   3600)

DEPARTMENT OF PUBLIC HEALTH, 150 Tremont St., Boston
   02111 (617, 727-2700)
The lead health agency in Massachusetts, responsible for promoting health and preventing disease and illness, regulating the state's
health care industry and contracting for and, in some cases,
providing direct health care services. Major offices within the
department include: Community Health Services, Environmental
Health, Health Care Systems, Local and Regional Health, Health
Resources, Legal Policy and Planning, the Center for Laboratories
and Communicable Disease Control Management Services, Public
Information and Health Education, and the Center for Health
Promotion and Environmental Disease Prevention.
Commissioner: DEBORAH PROTHROW-STITH, M.D. (727-2700)

Assistant Commissioner for Environmental Health: GERALD S.
   PARKER (727-7099)

DEPARTMENT OF PUBLIC WORKS, 10 Park Plaza, Boston
   02116 (617, 973-7500)
Commissioner: JANE F. GARVEY (973-7800)
Chief Engineer: ROBERT JOHNSON (973-7830)
Deputy Chief Engineer, Highway Engineering: MARIO H. TOCCI
   (973-7520)
Environmental Engineer: FRANK BRACAGLIA (973-7484)
Director (Acting), Transportation, Planning, and Development:
   GERALD ROURKE (973-7310)

EXECUTIVE OFFICE OF ENVIRONMENTAL AFFAIRS, Leverett
   Saltonstall Bldg., 100 Cambridge St., Boston 02202 (617,
   727-9800)
The chief environmental agency in the state and includes within the
office all state environmental agencies.
Secretary: JAMES S. HOYTE
Undersecretary: WILLIAM EICHBAUM
Coastal Zone Management: RICHARD F. DELANEY, Director (727-
   9530)
Conservation Services: JOEL A. LERNER, Director (727-1552)
Massachusetts Environmental Policy Act: STEVEN DAVIS, Director
   (727- 5830)
Water Resources Commission: ELIZABETH KLINE
Executive Coordinator: (727-9800)

Department of Food and Agriculture, 100 Cambridge St.,
   Boston 02202 (617, 727-3002)
Commissioner: AUGUST SCHUMACHER, JR.
Reclamation Board: MARGARET HAVEY, Secretary (727- 3035)

Animal Health
Director: MABEL OWEN (617, 727-3015)

Fairs
Director: STEPHEN QUINN (617, 727-3037)

Division of Agricultural Development
Director: WALTER LARMIE (617, 727-3018)

Bureau of Land Use
Chief: JAMES P. ALICATA (617, 727-0464)

Bureau of Markets
Chief: CRAIG RICHOV (617, 727-3018)

Division of Regulatory Services
Director: LEWIS F. WELLS (617, 727-6632)

Bureau of Pesticide
Chief: JEFFREY CARLSON (617, 727-7712)

Bureau of Plant Pest Control
Chief: Vacant (617, 727-3031)

Bureau of Farm Products
Chief (Acting): JAMES CASSIDY (617, 727-3018)

Bureau of Dairying
Chief: DAVID SHELDON (617, 727-3008)

Bureau of Milk Marketing
Chief: JOHN B. KELLEY (617, 727-3028)

Department of Environmental Management, 100 Cambridge St., Boston 02202 (617, 727-3163)
Commissioner: JAMES GUTENSOHN
Deputy Commissioner, Administration and Finance: KATHY PROSSER (727-2331)
Deputy Commissioner, Policy Development and Communications: SHELLEY BEEBY (727-3188)
Division of Planning and Development: ROBERT KUMOR, Deputy Commissioner (727-3160); DELORES BOOGDAMIAN, Chief, Legal Affairs (727-3160); RICHARD SUNDSTROM, Chief, Operations (727-3160); KATHERINE ABBOTT, Director, Natural Resource Planning (727-3160)
Office of Safe Waste Management: MICHAEL BROWN, Director (727-4293)
Water Resources: RICHARD THIBEDEAU, Director (727-3267)
Division of Forests and Parks: GILBERT A. BLISS, Director (727-3180)
Chief, Bureau of Recreation: CHARLES DANE (727-3180)
Chief, Bureau of Interpretive Services: ELLEN ROTHMAN (727-3180)
Bureau of Forest Development: THOMAS QUINK, Chief Forester (727-3180)
Bureau of Fire Control: ANTONIO CASTRO, Chief Fire Warden (727-3180)
Chief, Bureau of Shade Tree Management: JAMES MacARTHUR (727-3180)
Chief, Bureau of Urban Services: ROBERT FREEDMAN (727-3180)
Office of Acquisition and Construction: MARK CULLINAN, Chief Engineer (727-3174)
Division of Waterways: JOHN CAVANAUGH, Director (727-8893)

Department of Environmental Quality Engineering, One Winter St., Boston 02108 (617, 292-5856)
Commissioner: DANIEL GREENBAUM
Water Pollution Control: THOMAS C. McMAHON, Director (292-5646)
Air Quality Control: BRUCE K. MAILLET, Director (292-5592)
Water Supply: PATRICIA DEESE, Director (292-5570)
Division of Hazardous Waste: WILLIAM CASS, Director (292-5589)
Division of Solid Waste: L. JAMES MILLER, Director (292-5961)

Division of Wetlands and Waterways, One Winter St., Boston 02108 (617, 292-5516)
Director: GARY CLAYTON

Laboratories, 37 Shattuck St., Lawrence 01843 (682-5237)
Director: DR. JOHN DELANEY

Department of Metropolitan District Commission, 20 Somerset St., Boston 02108 (617, 727-5114)
Operates and maintains 19 swimming pools, 17 salt water beaches, 3 fresh water beaches, 23 skating rinks, and various other recreational facilities; also maintains a network of parkways and main traffic roadways and a police force for protection of its property and people using its facilities. Founded: 1919.
Commissioner: WILLIAM J. GEARY
Division of Recreation: LOU RODRIGUES, Director (727-9547)
Reservations and Historic Sites Unit: GARRET F. VAN WART, Director (727-2744)
Division of Parks Engineering and Construction: FRANCIS FAUCHER, Director (727-5264)
Division of Watershed Management: ILYAS BHATTI, Director (727-5274)
Division of Police: WILLIAM BRATTON, Superintendent (727-5520)
Secretary of the Commission: WILLIAM CHISHOLM (727-5204)

Environmental Quality Division
Director: JOSEPH McGINN, Principal Sanitary Engineer (727-2043)

Department of Fisheries, Wildlife and Environmental Law Enforcement, 100 Cambridge St., Boston 02202
Commissioner: WALTER E. BICKFORD (617, 727-1614)
Deputy Commissioner: ANTHONY M. RODRIGUEZ
Assistant Commissioner: CHRISTOPHER P. KENNEDY
Division of Marine Fisheries: PHILIP G. COATES, Director (727-3193)
Assistant Director, Research: W. LEIGH BRIDGES (727-3194)
Assistant Director, Sport Fisheries: RANDALL E. FAIRBANKS (727-3194)
Assistant Director, Commercial Fisheries: JAMES FAIR (727-3194)
Assistant Director, Administration: MICHAEL HENRY (727-3194)
Division of Fisheries and Wildlife: Vacant (727-3151)
Deputy Director, Administration: JOHN BUCKLEY
Deputy Director, Field Operations: CARL PRESCOTT, Westboro (366-4470)
Natural Heritage and Endangered Species: DR. THOMAS FRENCH, Assistant Director (727-3151)
Public Access Board: JOHN E. SHEPPARD, Director (727-1843)
Law Enforcement: ALLAN McGROARY, Director (727-3190)
Law Enforcement, Inland: VINCENT CARACCIOLO, Chief (508, 365-7239)
Law Enforcement, Coastal: SAM AMEEN, Chief (740-1163)
Law Enforcement, Boating Safety: FRED NATALONI, Chief (727-8761)
Law Enforcement, Boat, ATV Vehicle Registration: ALBAN LANDRY (727-3905)

MASSACHUSETTS COOPERATIVE FISHERY RESEARCH UNIT, U.S.D.I., 204 Holdsworth Hall, University of Massachusetts, Amherst 01003 (413, 545-0398; 545-2757; 545-2758)
Provides graduate training and research experience in fisheries ecology, population dynamics, genetics, and management. Supported cooperatively by the University of Massachusetts, Massachusetts Division of Fisheries and Wildlife, Massachusetts Division of Marine Fisheries, and the U.S. Fish and Wildlife Service. Established: 1963.
Leader: Vacant
Assistant Leader: BOYD E. KYNARD

MASSACHUSETTS COOPERATIVE WILDLIFE RESEARCH UNIT, U.S.D.I., University of Massachusetts, Amherst 01003 (413, 545-2757)
Provides graduate training and research experience in wildlife ecology and management. Supported cooperatively by the University of Massachusetts, Massachusetts Division of Fisheries and Wildlife, U.S. Fish and Wildlife Service, and the Wildlife Management Institute. Established: 1948.
Leader: DR. BECKY FIELD
Assistant Leader: Vacant

SEA GRANT COLLEGE PROGRAM
Director, Sea Grant College Program: CHRYSSOSTOMOS CHRYSSOSTOMIDIS, Massachusetts Institute of Technology, Bldg. E38, Rm. 302, Cambridge 02139 (617, 253-7042)
Coordinator, Sea Grant Program: DR. DAVID ROSS, Woods Hole Oceanographic Institution, Woods Hole 02543 (548-1400)
Marine Advisory Program: NORMAN DOELLING, Associate Director, Massachusetts Institute of Technology, Rm. E38-324, 77 Massachusetts Ave., Cambridge 02139

Publications: *A Citizen's Guide to Sources for Marine and Coastal Information in Massachusetts (1986); Marine-Related Research at MIT (1987-1988); MIT Sea Grant Quarterly Report*

STATE EXTENSION SERVICES

Associate Director of Cooperative Extension: ROBERT G. LIGHT, University of Massachusetts, Stockbridge Hall, Amherst 01003 (413, 545-4800)

Extension Foresters: CHRISTINE PETERSON, Department of Forestry, University of Massachusetts, Amherst 01003; DAVID KITTRIDGE, Department of Forestry, University of Massachusetts, Amherst 01003 (413, 545-2715)

Fish and Wildlife Specialist: DR. DON PROGULSKE, Department of Forestry, University of Massachusetts, Amherst 01003

CITIZENS' GROUPS

MASSACHUSETTS WILDLIFE FEDERATION, 295 E. Riding Dr., Carlisle 01741 (617, 369-3118)
A representative statewide organization, affiliated with the National Wildlife Federation, primarily devoted to the wise use, conservation, aesthetic appreciation, and restoration of wildlife and other natural resources.
President: *PAUL KRESS, 295 E. Riding Dr., Carlisle 01741 (369-3118)*
Secretary: *WILLIAM ANDRADE, 8 Williams St., Bedford 01730 (275-1808)*
Affiliate Representative: *WAYNE DAVIS, 18 Tamarack Rd., Reading 01867 (944-6432)*
Alternate: *PAUL KRESS*
Publications: *Massachusetts Wildlife Notes*
Editor: *DR. KALIL BOGHDAN, 12 School St., S. Hamilton 01982 (468-4398)*

ENVIRONMENTAL LOBBY OF MASSACHUSETTS (ELM), Three Joy St., Boston 02108 (617, 742-2553)
Lobbies for the passage of environmentally sound legislation on the state level and the effective implementation of state programs, i.e., Coastal Zone Management, farmland preservation and the Clean Air Act. Founded: 1898.
President: ANN ROOSEVELT
Treasurer: JOHN A. CRONIN
Executive Director: KELLY MCCLINTOCK
Director of Lobbying: JUDY A. SHOPE
Publication: *Legislative Bulletin*

MASSACHUSETTS ASSOCIATION OF CONSERVATION COMMISSIONS, Lincoln Filene Center, Tufts University, Medford 02155 (617, 381-3457)
Assists municipal conservation commissions in 351 cities and towns in Massachusetts in furthering the objectives of wetlands protection and conservation. Founded: 1961. Membership: 3,200.
President: TANIA ASSAYKEEN
1st Vice-President: ROBERT GRAY
2nd Vice-President: SARA SCHNITZER
3rd Vice-President: SALLY ZIELINSKI
Secretary: ROBERT CLARK
Treasurer: FREDERICK FAWCETT
Executive Director: CAROLINE SIMMONS

Publications: *Environmental Handbook for Massachusetts Conservation Commissioners,* 1985 Edition; Newsletter of the Association for members of conservation, commissions, associate members, government agencies, educational institutions, and organizations; Publications list available.

MASSACHUSETTS ASSOCIATION OF CONSERVATION DISTRICTS
President: ROBERT MURPHY, 307 Main St., North, Easton 02356 (617, 238-4208)
Vice-President: KATHERINE BECKER, 657 Burroughs Rd., Boxboro 01719 (263-8097)
Secretary: ADRIAN MEYER, E. Windsor Rd., Peru 01235 (655-8008)
Treasurer: HENRY JAESCHKE, West Rd., Adams 01220 (238-4208)
Council Member: ROBERT HATCH, 19 Pleasant St., Granby 01033 (413, 467-9820)
Executive Director: RITA KAPLAN, 78 Center St., (Arterial) Pittsfield 01201 (413, 443-1776)

MASSACHUSETTS AUDUBON SOCIETY, INC., S. Great Rd., Lincoln 01773 (617, 259-9500)
A nonprofit organization of 42,500 member households committed to the protection of the environment for people and wildlife. One of the oldest conservation organizations in the world and the largest in New England. Owns and protects 18,000 acres with 17 staffed sanctuaries across Massachusetts. Programming priorities: conservation, education, advocacy, and research. Founded: 1896.
President: GERARD A. BERTRAND
Chairman, Board of Directors: JOHN THORNDIKE
Publication: *Sanctuary*
Editor: JOHN HANSON MITCHELL

MASSACHUSETTS BASS CHAPTER FEDERATION
An organization of Bassmaster Chapters, affiliated with the Bass Anglers Sportsman Society, to fight pollution, assist state and national conservation agencies in their efforts and to teach young people of our country good conservation practices. Dedicated to the realistic conservation of our water resources.
President: BRUCE JOHNSON, #8 Notre Dame, Bedford 01730 (617, 275-1064/648-2750)

MASSACHUSETTS FORESTRY ASSOCIATION, P.O. Box 202, Princeton 01541 (508, 464-5821)
A voluntary nonprofit association dedicated to conservation, stewardship and advocacy of the forest land of Massachusetts. An educational organization offering information, workshops, conferences, publications and professional assistance. Begun in 1970 as the Massachusetts Land League, changed to present name in 1986.
President: EDWIN B. CADY, JR.
Vice-President: HOWARD F.R. MASON
Secretary-Treasurer: REXFORD V.N. BAKER
Director: ROBERT S. BOND
Administrative Assistant: PATRICIA DOWER

MASSACHUSETTS TRAPPER'S ASSOCIATION, INC., 155 Wiliams Rd., Concord 01742 (508, 369-5065)
Objectives are to develop leadership for the advancement of the interests of the trapper and the fur industry and to promote sound management for the conservation of fur-bearing animals. Founded: 1950.
President: DONALD GRAVES, Laurel St., Shelburne Falls 01370 (413, 297-0810)

Vice-President: BILL ANDRADE, 8 Williams St., Bedford 01730 (617, 275-1809)
Recording Secretary: TOM HAYES (508, 369-5065)
Treasurer: IRENE HAYES
Publication: *Fur Ever*
Editor: TOM HAYES

TROUT UNLIMITED MASSACHUSETTS/RHODE ISLAND COUNCIL

A statewide council with 13 chapters working for the protection and enhancement of the coldwater fishery resources.
Chairman: JOHN McCARTHY, 3370-10 Lafayette Rd., Portsmouth, NH 03802 (603, 926-7777)
National Directors: STEPHEN A. MESSIER, Vice-President, New England Region, 104 Sharon Ave., Pawtucket, RI 02860 (401, 724-0655); CHARLES OLCHOWSKI, 473 Main St., Green Field 01301 (413, 774-2218); GENE McKENNA, 132 Hayden Rowe St., Hopkington 01748 (617, 435-5560); RICHARD NICOLO, 1225 Charles St., North Providence, RI 02904 (401, 723-8765)

TRUSTEES OF RESERVATIONS, THE, 572 Essex St., Beverly 01915 (508, 921-1944)

The Trustees of Reservations is a land conservation organization dedicated to perserving properties of exceptional scenic, historic, and ecological value throughout Massachusetts. Membership: 5,700. Founded: 1891.
Chairman: HERBERT VAUGHN
President: HENRY R. GUILD, JR.
Vice-Presidents: PETER MADSEN; THOMAS L.P. O'DONNELL; HALL J. PETERSON; PRESTON SAUNDERS; NORTON Q. SLOAN
Secretary: ROGER B. HUNT
Treasurer: PETER THOMPSON
Director: FREDERIC WINTHROP, JR.
Deputy Director: DAVIS CHERINGTON
Deputy Director, Land Conservation: WESLEY WARD
Deputy Director, Development: ANN POWELL
Deputy Director, Publications: ELOISE HODGES
Publications: *Annual Report;* Newsletter; assorted publications relating to individual properties

MICHIGAN

GOVERNMENT AGENCIES

GOVERNOR: JAMES J. BLANCHARD, Governor of Michigan, State Capitol, Lansing 48913 (517, 373-3400)

DEPARTMENT OF AGRICULTURE, 4th Fl., North Ottawa Bldg., P.O. Box 30017, Lansing 48909 (517, 373-1050)
Director: DR. PAUL KINDINGER
Environmental Division Director: CHRISTINE LIETZAU (373-2620)
Communications Division Director: MARGARET R. COOKE (373-1104)

DEPARTMENT OF NATURAL RESOURCES, Box 30028, Lansing 48909 (Information: 517, 373-1220; Telephone Device for the Deaf (TDD): 517, 335-4623)
State agency for administration, including enforcement of laws and regulations, of the state's natural resources; for protecting environmental quality; and for enhancing recreational opportunities and quality. Derived from the Department of Conservation. Established 1921.
Natural Resources Commission: KERRY KAMMER, Clarkston (313, 625-7770); THOMAS J. ANDERSON, Southgate (313, 284-6889); DAVID D. OLSON, Marquette (906, 228-4830); MARLENE J. FLUHARTY, Mt. Pleasant (433-2101); O. STEWART MYERS, Bitely (616, 745-4889); RAYMOND POUPORE, Detroit (313, 961-1415); GORDON E. GUYER, East Lansing (517, 332-6227)
Director: DAVID F. HALES (373-2329)
Assistant to the Director: GREGORY A. LYMAN (373-0023)
Chief Administrative Officer: Vacant (373-2425)
Deputy Directors: DELBERT RECTOR, Environmental Protection (373-7917); JACK D. BAILS, Resource Management (373-0046)
Region I, Marquette: FRANK P. OPOLKA, Deputy Director (906, 228-6561)
Region II, Roscommon: JOHN M. MacGREGOR, Deputy Director (275-5151)
Region III, Lansing: MICHAEL D. MOORE, Deputy Director (322-1300)
Public Information Director (Acting): SUSAN E. HENRY (373-1214)
Economic Development Liaison: DONNA STINE (335-0940)
Director, Office of the Great Lakes: THOMAS D. MARTIN (373-3588)
Equal Employment Opportunity Executive: CORDREE McCONNELL (335-1582)
Commission and Legislative Liaison: BARBARA McLEOD (373-3216)
Permit Coordinator: MINDY KOCH (373-7917)
Management Specialist: DARREL J. ALLEN (373-2425)
Chief, Administrative Services Division: KENNETH L. HENDRICK (373-1187)
Chief, Air Quality Division: ROBERT P. MILLER (373-7023)
Chief, Fisheries Division: JOHN M. ROBERTSON (373-1280)
Chief, Forest Management Division: HENRY H. WEBSTER (373-1275)
Chief, Wildlife Division: KARL R. HOSFORD (373-1263)
Chief, Geological Survey Division: R. THOMAS SEGALL (334-6907)
Chief, Environmental Response Division: GARY E. GUENTHER (373-1947)
Chief, Waste Management Division: ALAN J. HOWARD (373-2730)
Chief, Real Estate Division: ROLAND HARMES, JR. (373-1246)
Chief, Law Enforcement Division: HERBERT BURNS (373-1230)
Mackinac Island State Park Commission: DAVID PAMPERIN (906, 847-3328)
Chief, Management Information Division: JULANE ALLEN (373-9510)
Chief (Acting), Office of Environmental Enforcement: JOHN M. SHAUVER (373-3503)
Chief, Land and Water Management Division: DENNIS J. HALL (373-1170)
Chief, Parks Division: JACK BUTTERFIELD (373-1270)
Chief, Personnel Division: NATHANIEL LAKE (373-1207)
Chief, Recreation Division: O.J. SCHERSCHLIGT (373-1660)
Chief, Surface Water Quality Division: PAUL D. ZUGGER (373-1949)
Chief, Office of Internal Audit: MARION HART (373-1188)
Chief, Office of Budget and Federal Aid: DENNIS R. ADAMS (373-1750)
Chief Hearings Officer: WILLIAM C. FULKERSON (335-4235)
General Manager, Office of State Exposition and Fairgrounds: BERNIE LENNON (313, 368-1000)
Director, Safety and Health: EARLE N. LATIMER (373-3937)

Chief, Office of Special Services: FRANK J. RUSWICK (373-1188)

Publications: *Michigan Natural Resources Magazine; Natural Resources Register*

Editors: NORRIS McDOWELL (373-9267); JEANETTE G. COWELS (373-1214)

Information Services Center: (373-1220)

DEPARTMENT OF PUBLIC HEALTH, 3423 N. Logan St., Box 30195, Lansing 48909 (517, 335-8022)

Began in 1873 and is the fifth oldest state health agency in the nation. The protection and improvement of the health of the people of Michigan is the statutory responsibility and purpose of the department. The state health department serves as the coordinator for the control and prevention of disease in Michigan.

Director, State Health (Acting): RAJ M. WIENER

MICHIGAN SEA GRANT COLLEGE PROGRAM, University of Michigan, 2200 Bonisteel Blvd., Ann Arbor 48109 (313, 763-1437)

To promote the understanding and wise use of the Great Lakes through research, education, and extension. Founded: 1969.

Director: DR. MICHAEL G. PARSONS, Michigan Sea Grant College Program, University of Michigan, IST Bldg., Rm. 4103, 2200 Bonisteel Blvd., Ann Arbor 48109 (313, 763-1437)

Assistant Director: RUSSELL A. MOLL, Michigan Sea Grant College Program, University of Michigan, 1st. Bldg., Rm. 4109, 2200 Bonisteel Blvd., Ann Arbor 48109 (313, 763-1437)

Program Leader, Sea Grant Extension: JOHN D. SCHWARTZ, Michigan Sea Grant College Program, Michigan State University, 334 Natural Resources Bldg. East Lansing 48824 (517, 353-9568)

Associate Director: DR. NILES R. KEVERN, Department of Fisheries and Wildlife, Michigan State University, 7 Natural Resources Bldg., East Lansing 48824 (517, 353-0647)

Publication: *Upwellings*

Editor: MARTHA WALTER (764-1138)

STATE EXTENSION SERVICES

Director of Extension Service: DR. W.J. MOLINE, 106 Agriculture Hall, Michigan State University, East Lansing 48824 (517, 355-2803)

Assistant Director, Natural Resources and Public Policy: ADGER B. CARROLL, 108 Agriculture Hall, Michigan State University, East Lansing 48824 (355-0118)

Extension Specialists: MELVIN R. KOELLING, Forestry Education, 121 Natural Resources Bldg., Michigan State University, East Lansing 48824 (355-0090); THEODORE HASKELL, Park Management, 131 Natural Resources Bldg., Michigan State University, East Lansing 48824 (353-5190); ECKHART DERSCH, Soil and Water Conservation, 326 Natural Resources Bldg., Michigan State University, East Lansing 48824 (355-3346); GLENN R. DUDDERAR, Wildlife Education, 8 Natural Resources Bldg., Michigan State University, East Lansing 48824 (355-7493); RUSSELL P. KIDD, Forestry, P.O. Box 507, Courthouse Annex, Roscommon 48653 (275-5043); DEAN SOLOMON, 3700 E. Gull Lake Dr., Hickory Corners 49060-9516

WATER RESOURCES COMMISSION, P.O. Box 30028, Lansing 48909 (517, 373-1949)

State surface and ground water pollution control programs.

Executive Secretary: PAUL D. ZUGGER

Assistant Executive Secretary: ALAN HOWARD

Commission Members: CHRISTINE LIETZAU, Representing Director, Department of Agriculture; CLEM LAY, Representing Industrial Management; THOMAS HOOGERHYDE, Representing Director, Department of Public Health; DELBERT RECTOR, Representing Director, Department of Natural Resources; FREDERICK L. BROWN, Representing Conservation Groups; JIM KOSKI, Representing Municipal Groups

CITIZENS' GROUPS

 MICHIGAN UNITED CONSERVATION CLUBS, INC., 2101 Wood St., Box 30235, Lansing 48909 (517, 371-1041)

A representative statewide organization, affiliated with the National Wildlife Federation, primarily devoted to the wise use, conservation, aesthetic appreciation, and restoration of wildlife and other natural resources.

President: WENDELL BRIGGS, 3747 Hordyk, NE, Grand Rapids 49505 (616, 361-1053)

Executive Director: THOMAS L. WASHINGTON

Affiliate Representative: JOHN EICHINGER, 92 Oakwood, Holland 49423 (616, 399-8140)

Alternate: GERALD GOODMAN, 1213 Lalley Rd., Ice Lake, Iron River 49935 (906, 265-2116)

Publication: *Michigan Out-of-Doors*

Editor: KENNETH S. LOWE

IZAAK WALTON LEAGUE OF AMERICA, INC. (Michigan Div.)

President: DAN SPALINK, 855 28th St., SE, Grand Rapids 49508 (616, 281-3026)

Secretary: SUSAN BINGHAM, 7117 Davison Rd., Davison 48423 (313, 658-1828)

MICHIGAN ASSOCIATION OF CONSERVATION DISTRICTS

President: FRANK BROWN, 10200 Garbow Rd., Middleville 49333 (616, 795-9834)

Vice-President: RUSSELL PARMELEE, 3259 18th St., Hopkins 49328 (793-3096)

Secretary-Treasurer: RICHARD COOPER, 5039 Indian Hill Rd., Honor 49640 (325-2175)

Executive Director: DEBRA A. BOGAR, 1405 S. Harrison, Suite 305, East Lansing 48823 (517, 337-6920)

MICHIGAN AUDUBON SOCIETY, 409 West E. Ave., Kalamazoo 49007 (616, 344-8648) Organized: 1904.

Executive Director: TERRY YONKER, 13609 Grace Dr., Eagle 48822

President: KAY DODGE, 2846 Northville Dr., NE, Grand Rapids 49505

Vice-President: JAMES LUDWIG, 310 South Burns, Essexville 48732

Secretary: KATHERINE STRASSBURG, 1225 Willow, Apt. 3, Grand Ledge 48837

Treasurer: TOM HENDRICKSON, 3804 North 168th, Holland 49423

Publications: *The Jack-Pine Warbler; The Michigan Audubon News; Audubon Newsletter*

Editors: CHRIS HULL, 1937 Sunnyside, Lansing 48910; BILL MEEK, 14150 Pangborn Rd., Rt. 3, Hemlock 48626

MICHIGAN BASS CHAPTER FEDERATION

An organization of Bassmaster Chapters, affiliated with the Bass Anglers Sportsman Society, organized to fight pollution, assist state and national conservation agencies in their efforts and to teach the young people of our country good conservation practice. Dedicated to the realistic conservation of our water resources.

President: DUANE ZACK, 1120 Dogwood, Portage 49081 (616, 323-6777/327-4137)

MICHIGAN NATURAL AREAS COUNCIL, University of
   Michigan, Botanical Gardens, 1800 N. Dixboro Rd., Ann
   Arbor 48105
Seeks to locate and study choice natural areas, prepares recommendations for their preservation under dedicated ownership, either public or private, and attempts to assure their perpetuity. Membership: 200. Founded: 1952.
Chairman: JAMES A. FOWLER, Cranbrook Institute of Science, 500 Lone Pine Rd., P.O. Box 801, Bloomfield Hills 48013
Vice-President: DR. GERARD T. DONNELLY, W.J. Beal Botanical Garden, Michigan State University, 412 Olds Hall, East Lansing 48824-1047
Secretary: HARVEY E. BALLARD, JR., The Nature Conservancy, Michigan Chapter, 2840 E. Grand River Ave., East Lansing 48823
Publication: *Michigan Natural Areas News,* natural area and endangered species information for Michigan
Editor: SUSAN CRISPIN, MNFI, Stevens T. Mason Bldg., P.O. Box 30028, Lansing (517, 373-1552)

MICHIGAN NATURE ASSOCIATION, 7981 Beard Rd., Box
   102, Avoca 48006 (313, 324-2626)
Purpose is to acquire and maintain nature sanctuaries that contain examples of Michigan's original flora and fauna. Holds title to 107 properties totaling 5,025 acres in 42 counties of Michigan. Available to public for nature education and appreciation. Membership: 1,400. Founded: 1952.
President: RICHARD W. HOLZMAN (548-5278)
Vice-President: NORMA LUDECKE (421-6422)
Executive Secretary-Treasurer: BERTHA A. DAUBENDIEK (324-2626)
Publications: *Members' Newsletter; MNA Sanctuary Guidebook; MNA--In Retrospect: A Celebration of 28 Years of Preserving Michigan's Wild and Rare Natural Lands 1960-1988*
Editor: BERTHA DAUBENDIEK, Box 102, Avoca 48006

SAFARI CLUB INTERNATIONAL MICHIGAN CHAPTER, 6915
   Georgetown, Hudsonville 49426
Goals are to educate the public, especially children, in the realm of conservation as it relates to the hunter. Especially concerned with environmental respect and the preservation of any endangered species. Founded: 1973. Membership: 200.
President: LEN VINING (616, 698-7440)
President-Elect: MERLE BARNABY
Secretary-Treasurer: DAN PRING (846-3787)
Assistant Secretary-Treasurer: Vacant
Education: ED HOEZEE (538-6000)
Program: DON LIPINSKI (453-7437)

TROUT UNLIMITED MICHIGAN COUNCIL
A statewide council with 25 chapters working for the protection and enhancement of the coldwater fishery resources.
Chairman: ALLEN PIENKOWSKI, 830 Merton, #102, Detroit 48203 (313, 354-8500 Ext. 3718)
National Directors: ALLEN PIENKOWSKI, Vice-President, Midwest Region, 830 Merton, Apt. 102, Detroit 48203 (313, 341-1915); H. RAND OSLUND, 7035 Alden Dr., West Bloomfield 48033 (313, 333-3330); DANIEL E. CROCKETT, 1334 Whites Rd., Kalamazoo 49008 (616, 382-1616)

WEST MICHIGAN ENVIRONMENTAL ACTION COUNCIL, 1432
   Wealthy SE, Grand Rapids 49506 (616, 451-3051)
   (Annual Meeting: May)
Provide leadership in environmental protection and preservation in west Michigan and throughout Michigan on issues such as public lands management, solid and hazardous waste management, energy conservation and oil recycling. Through the involvement of concerned volunteers, WMEAC has promulgated landmark environmental legislation and assured application of existing laws. Membership: 500 individuals, 30 organizations.
Executive Director: FRANK RUSWICK, JR.
Publication: *Action Issue*

WILDLIFE SOCIETY MICHIGAN CHAPTER
President: GARY A. DAWSON, Environmental Department, Consumers Power Company, 1945 W. Parnall Rd., Jackson 49201 (517, 788-2432)
President-Elect: LEONARD E. SCHUMANN, 1235 Primrose Ln., Dewitt 48820 (337-6652)
Secretary-Treasurer: ROBERT AHO, DNR North US-41, Baraga 49908

MINNESOTA

GOVERNMENT AGENCIES

GOVERNOR: RUDY PERPICH, Governor of Minnesota, State
   Capitol, St. Paul 55155 (612, 296-3391)

BOARD OF WATER AND SOIL RESOURCES, 90 West Plato,
   St. Paul 55107
Formed in 1987, under MRS ch. 110B to work with Soil and Water Conservation Districts and watershed districts throughout Minnesota and assist in their programs, also to administer statewide comprehensive local water planning statute.
Director: JAMES R. BIRKHOLZ (612, 296-3767)
Chairman: DONALD OGAARD, 705 5th St., Ada 56510

DEPARTMENT OF AGRICULTURE, 90 W. Plato Blvd., St. Paul
   55107 (612, 297-2200)
Enforces laws to protect the public health, promote family farming and marketing of farm products, conserve soil and water, and to prevent fraud and deception in the manufacture and distribution of foods, animal feeds, fertilizers, pesticides, seeds and other items. Established: 1919.
Commissioner: JAMES NICHOLS
Deputy Commissioner: ANNE KANTEN
Assistant Commissioner: HERB HALVORSON
Personnel Director: HAROLD FRANK (296-2323)
Accounting and Licensing Director: JOSEPH KOMRO (296-1577)
Agronomy Services Director: WILLIAM BULGER (296-1161)
Dairy and Livestock Director: WILLIAM COLEMAN (296-1586)
Family Farm Security Director: WAYNE MARZOLF (296-8435)
Food Inspection Director: TOM MASSO (296-2629)
Grain Inspection Director: EDWARD MOLINE (341-7190)
Laboratory Services Director: WILLIAM KRUEGER (296-3273)
Marketing Director: RALPH GROSCHEN (297-2223)
Planning Division Director: GERALD HEIL (296-1486)
Plant Industry Director: ART MASON (296-8448)
Agricultural Statistics Director: CARROLL ROCK (296-3896)
Board of Water and Soil Resources: JIM BIRKHOLZ (296-3767)

DEPARTMENT OF NATURAL RESOURCES, 500 Lafayette Rd., St. Paul 55155 (612, 296-6157)

Commissioner: JOSEPH N. ALEXANDER (296-2549)

Deputy Commissioner: STEVEN G. THORNE (296-2540)

Assistant Commissioner, Operations: RAY HITCHCOCK (296-5229)

Assistant Commissioner, Administration: EUGENE GERE (296-0533)

Assistant Commissioner, Planning and Special Programs: KAREN LOECHLER (297-1767)

Assistant to the Commissioner, Department Relations: JOHN GUENTHER

Deputy Attorney General: JIM SCHOESSLER, 520 Lafayette Rd., St. Paul 55101 (296-0693)

Director, Division of Enforcement: LEO HASEMAN (296-4828)

Director, Division of Fish and Wildlife: DR. LARRY R. SHANNON (297-1308)

Chief, Fisheries Section: RICHARD HASSINGER (296-0792)

Chief, Wildlife Section: ROGER HOLMES (296-3344)

Chief, Ecological Services Section: JOHN SKRYPEK

Director, Division of Forestry: GERALD ROSE (296-4484)

Assistant to the Commissioner, Departmental Relations: JOHN GUENTHER (296-5468)

Director, Division of Minerals: WILLIAM BRICE (296-4807)

Administrator, Bureau of Planning: VONNY HAGEN (296-6235)

Director, Division of Parks and Recreation: WILLIAM MORRISSEY (296-2270)

Director, Division of Waters: RON NARGANG (296-4810)

Director, Bureau of Information and Education: GAIL GENDLER (296-3336)

Administrator, Bureau of Real Estate Management: RODNEY SANDO (297-4931)

Director, Human Resources: MARY O'NEILL (296-6478)

Administrator, Bureau of Engineering: JOHN ERNSTER (296-2119)

Administrator, Field Service Bureau: NORMAN KORDELL (297-4906)

Controller: DOUG WATNEMO (296-9530)

Director, Regulatory and Legislative Services Unit: ANDY BREWER (296-0915)

Administrator, Financial Management: ALLEN YOZAMP (296-2188)

Administrator, License Bureau: MARGARET WINKEL (296-4507)

Director, Volunteer Services: RENEE VAIL (297-1448)

Administrator, Management Systems Bureau: GEORGE ROBERTS (296-0654)

Administrator, Office Services Bureau: RONALD WINKEL (297-2433)

Regional Administrators: ROBERT HANCE, Brainerd (218, 828-2613); JAMES SCHNEIDER, New Ulm (507, 354-2196); MERLYN WESLOH, Bemidji (218, 755-3955); JOHN CHELL, Grand Rapids (218, 327-4455); WILLIAM JOHNSON, Rochester (507, 285-7418); KATHLEEN WALLACE, Central Region (296-3572)

Executive Director, Environmental Education Board: JACKIE LIND (296-2368)

Director, Trails and Waterways: PAUL SWENSON (296-4822)

Director, Minnesota Conservation Corps: LARRY FONNEST (296-2144)

Training Director: CHERYL MAGNUSON-GIESE (296-4823)

Publication: *The Minnesota Volunteer*

Editor: ROBERT KRASKE (296-0900)

GEOLOGICAL SURVEY, University of Minnesota, 2642 University Ave., St. Paul 55114 (612, 627-4780)

Established in 1872 as a Geological and Natural History Survey, reconstituted in 1911 as the Minnesota Geological Survey to investigate the geology of the state, to describe, classify and map the geological formations, mineral and water resources and investigate all aspects of the geology affecting the environment.

Director: PRISCILLA C. GREW

Associate Director and Chief Geologist: GLENN B. MOREY

Program Manager: JOHN F. SPLETTSTOESSER

Publications: List available on request.

MINNESOTA SEA GRANT COLLEGE PROGRAM

A statewide program that supports research, extension and educational programs related to Lake Superior and the Great Lakes. Research areas include: environmental quality, fisheries, biotechnology, applied economics, water policy, and aquaculture.

Director, Sea Grant Institute: DONALD McNAUGHT, 116 Classroom Office Bldg., University of Minnesota, 1994 Buford Ave., St. Paul 55108 (612, 625-9288)

Director, Sea Grant Extension Program: DALE R. BAKER, University of Minnesota, 208 Washburn Hall, Duluth 55812 (218, 726-8106)

Publications: *The Seiche Newsletter; Lacustrine Lessons Newsletter*

Editors: ALICE TIBBETTS (612, 625-9790); KAREN PLASS (218, 726-8106); ANNETTE LARSON (612, 625-6781)

POLLUTION CONTROL AGENCY, 520 Lafayette Rd., St. Paul 55155 (612, 296-6300)

Administers the state statutes covering water pollution, air pollution, and solid and hazardous waste control. Established: 1967.

Chairman of the Board: KEITH H. LANGMO

Commissioner: GERALD L. WILLET (296-7301)

Deputy Commissioner: MICHAEL ROBERTSON (295-7303)

Assistant Commissioner: BARBARA LINDSEY SIMS (296-7305)

Director, Division of Water Quality: TIMOTHY SCHERKENBACH (296-7202)

Director, Division of Air Quality: J. MICHAEL VALENTINE (296-7331)

Director, Division of Hazardous Waste: RICHARD SVANDA (296-7282)

Director, Division of Groundwater and Solid Waste: RODNEY MASSEY (296-7777)

Regional Offices

MPCA, Brainerd: LARRY SHAW, Director, 1601 Minnesota St., Brainerd 56401 (218, 828-2492)

MPCA, Duluth: WAYNE GOLLY, Director, Duluth Government Svc. Ctr., Rm. 704, 320 W 2nd St., Duluth (218, 723-4660)

MPCA, Detroit Lakes: WILLIS MATTISON, Director, Lake Avenue Plaza, 714 Lake Ave., Suite 220, Detroit Lakes 56501 (218, 847-1519)

MPCA, Marshall: MARK JACOB, Director, RLC Bldg., 109 So. Fifth St., Marshall 56258 (507, 537-7146)

MPCA, Rochester: LARRY LANDHERR, Director, 2116 Campus Dr. SE, Suite 140, Rochester 55904 (507, 285-7343)

STATE EXTENSION SERVICES

Dean and Director of Minnesota Extension Service: PATRICK J. BORICH, University of Minnesota, 240 Coffey Hall, St. Paul 55108 (612, 624-2703)

Associate Director, Operations: DAN PANSHIN, 260F Coffey Hall (624-1773)

Natural Resources Program Leader: STEVEN B. LAURSEN, 260 Coffey Hall (624-9298)

Extension Specialists Aquaculture: ANNE KAPUSCINSKI, 130 Hodson Hall (624-2720); DAVID LANDKAMER, 138 Hodson Hall (624-2720)

Forest Products: LEWIS T. HENDRICKS, 206 Kaufert Lab. (624-

2790); FLOYD T. MILTON, North Cent. Experiment Sta., 1861 Highway 69 East, Grand Rapids 55744 (218, 327-4490); HARLAN D. PETERSEN, 202 Kaufert Lab. (624-3407); TIM LARSON, 24 Kaufert Lab.

Forest Resources: MELVIN J. BAUGHMAN, 102 Green Hall (624-0734); ROBERT HANSEN, 101 Green Hall (624-7222); CHARLES R. BLINN, 209 Green Hall (624-3788); HAROLD SCHOLTEN, 349 Green Hall (624-1746); CARL E. VOGT, 102 Green Hall (624-3639).

Harvesting: A. SCOTT REED, 175 University Rd., Cloquet 55720 (218, 879-4528)

Soils and Water Quality: JAMES L. ANDERSON, 503 Soils (625-8209); THOMAS HOLBACH, 216 Soils

Wildlife: JAMES R. KITTS, 216 Hodson Hall (624-3298)

Youth: LARRY KARELS, 340 Coffey Hall

Public Policy: STEVEN TAFT, 337-C

CITIZENS' GROUPS

 *MINNESOTA CONSERVATION FEDERATION, 1036-B, S. Cleveland Ave., St. Paul 55116 (612, 690-3077)*

A representative statewide organization, affiliated with the National Wildlife Federation, primarily devoted to the wise use, conservation, aesthetic appreciation, and restoration of wildlife and other natural resources.

President: RICHARD BUSS, 12110 210th St., Lakeville 55044 (469-5649)

Affiliate Representative: RICHARD BUSS

Alternate: CLARENCE TRUSHENSKI, 8401 Ivy Pl., Rice 56367 (252-4187)

Publication: Minnesota Out-of-Doors

Editor: DON J. DINNDORF, R.R. #3, St. Cloud 56301 (259-1498)

FRIENDS OF ANIMALS AND THEIR ENVIRONMENT, P.O. Box 7283, Minneapolis 55407

A nonprofit organization dedicated to preserving and protecting Minnesota's wildlife with emphasis on banning the use of the leghold trap and other trapping abuses in Minnesota. Believes it is time for wildlife and the public to receive priority over the sport and marginal income of trapping. Established: 1975.

Coordinators: HOWARD GOLDMAN, Issues, 2076 Goodrich Ave., St. Paul 55105 (690-4997); BOB WALIGORA, 2427 Tenth Ave. S., Minneapolis 55404 (872-1135)

Publication: Newsletter

FRIENDS OF THE BOUNDARY WATERS WILDERNESS, 1313 5th St., SE, Suite 329, Minneapolis 55414 (612, 379-3835)

Established to protect and preserve the wilderness character of northeastern Minnesota's Boundary Waters Canoe Area (BWCA) Wilderness and its surrounding integral areas in the international Quetico-Superior Ecosystem. Works on wilderness protection, acid rain, forestry issues, water quality, rivers protection, military overflights, and wildlife species, such as the wolf. Established: 1976. Membership: 2,000.

Executive Director: KEVIN PROESCHOLDT

Chairperson: HERBERT C. JOHNSON (370-0111)

Vice-Chair: GREG LAIS (379-3858)

Secretary: DAN ENGSTROM (624-7005)

Treasurer: JEFF EVANS (696-6742)

Publications: *BWCA Wilderness News;* occasional fact sheets; reports; action alerts

Editor: KEVIN PROESCHOLDT

IZAAK WALTON LEAGUE OF AMERICA, INC. (Minnesota Division), 525 Park St., #101, St. Paul 55103 (612, 221-0215)

President: AL LAYMAN, R.R. I, Box 78, Austin 55912 (296-5508)

Secretary: DOROTHY WALTZ, 2095 Delaware Ave., Mendota Heights 55118 (454-5889)

MINNESOTA ASSOCIATION OF SOIL AND WATER CONSERVATION DISTRICTS

President: CARL A. ANDERSON, Rt. 1, Box 127, Chokio 56221

Vice-President: DWAIN OTTE, 28937 Northfield Blvd., Randolph 55065

Secretary-Treasurer: KEN PEDERSEN, Fertile 56540

MINNESOTA BASS CHAPTER FEDERATION

An organization of Bassmaster Chapters, affiliated with the Bass Anglers Sportsman Society, organized to fight pollution, assist state and national conservation agencies in their efforts and to teach young people of our country good conservation practices. Dedicated to the realistic conservation of our water resources.

President: AL LIBERA, Rt. 1, Box 161, Deerwood 56444 (218, 678-2349)

MINNESOTA FORESTRY ASSOCIATION, 220 First Ave., NW, Rm. 210, Grand Rapids 55744 (218, 326-4200)

A nonprofit organization dedicated to promoting the high potential advantages of intensive scientific management of forests, woodlots and other renewable resources.

President: HOWARD E. OLSON, 2370 Lexington Ave., So., Apt. 109, Mendota Heights 55120 (612, 688-9320)

Vice-President: THOMAS W. HOUGHTALING, 4436 Norwood St., Duluth 58804 (218, 525-5621)

Past-President: LANSIN HAMILTON, R. 1, Box 61, Deerwood 56444 (218, 828-3963)

Secretary-Treasurer: STANLEY B. RINGOLD, P.O. Box 518, Coleraine 55722 (218, 245-3981)

Executive Director: JOHN R. SUFFRON, 12 Chisholm Tr., Grand Rapids 55744 (218, 326-4200)

Publication: *Minnesota Forests*

Editor: JOHN R. SUFFRON

Managing Editor: KATHLEEN PREECE

MINNESOTA HERPETOLOGICAL SOCIETY, James Ford Bell Museum of Natural History, 10 Church St. SE, University of Minnesota, Minneapolis 55455-0104 (612, 626-2030)

A nonprofit organization chartered for the conservation and preservation of reptiles and amphibians, through the education of the members and public as to the value of reptiles and amphibians.

Membership: 200. Founded: 1981.

President: ANN PORWOLL

Vice-President: JOHN MORIARTY

Secretary: KATHRYN ANDERSON

Treasurer: DELVIN JONES

Publications: *MHS Newsletter;* occasional papers of MHS

Editor: TOM SCHMITZ

MINNESOTA NATIVE PLANT SOCIETY, 220 Biological Sciences Center, 1445 Gortner Ave., University of Minnesota, St. Paul 55108

A nonprofit organization dedicated to education about native Minnesota flora and to its preservation and conservation. Membership: 245. Founded: 1982.

President: DAVID J. McLAUGHLIN (612, 333-8806)

Vice-President: MAY WRIGHT (429-7674)

Treasurer: RUTH PHIPPS (457-8908)

Secretary: WELBY SMITH (297-0373)

Publication: *Minnesota Plant Press*
Editor: ANITA F. CHOLEWA (625-0215)

MINNESOTA ORNITHOLOGISTS' UNION, James Ford Bell
Museum of Natural History, 10 Church St. SE, University
of Minnesota, Minneapolis 55455
Statewide organization contributing to scientific knowledge through
bird observations; stimulating public interest in birds; and working
to preserve bird life and bird habitat. Membership: 1,200. Founded
1937.
President: BOB HOLTZ, 2997 Chatsworth, St. Paul 55113
Vice-President: JO BLANICH, Box 96, Crosby 56441
Secretary: MARION CASHDOLLAR, 9400 Cedar Ave., # 102,
Bloomington 55420
Treasurer: ED KUEHNEL, 2731 Mackubin St., # 39, Roseville
55113
Publications: *The Loon; MOU Newsletter*
Editors: ROBERT B. JANSSEN, 10521 S. Cedar Lake Rd., #212,
Minnetonka 55343 (612, 546-4220); BETTE BELL, 5868
Pioneer Rd. S., St. Paul Park 55071

MINNESOTA WILDLIFE HERITAGE FOUNDATION, INC., 5701
Normandale Rd., Suite 325, Minneapolis 55424 (612,
925-1923)
Formed to promote the idea of charitable giving for conservation
purposes and to assist people in making charitable donations of
property for wildlife habitat.
President and Director: HUGH C. PRICE, 4424 Dunham Dr., Edina
55435 (925-2486)
Vice-President: ROBERT I. CHRISTENSEN, Christensen and Christensen Law Office, Suite 1300, 386 N. Wabasha St., St. Paul
55102
Secretary and Legal Counsel: LAURENCE F. KOLL, 633 Sunset Ln.,
Mendota Heights 55118 (291-9155)
Treasurer: MICHAEL W. TENNEY, C.P.A., 550 Midland Bank Bldg.,
401 Second Ave., So. Minneapolis 55401 (338-0589)

TROUT UNLIMITED MINNESOTA COUNCIL
A statewide council with eight chapters working for the protection
and enhancement of the coldwater fishery resources.
Chairman: BILL HAUGEN, Box 221, Rushford 55971
National Directors: GARY SOBOTTA, 942 NW 41st St., Rochester
55901 (507, 281-4073); DAVE KOLBERT, 4115 5th St., NW,
Rochester 55901 (612, 345-5355)

WILDLIFE EDUCATION PROGRAM FOR A LIVING FUTURE,
Bittner's Resort, Rt. 2, Box 225A, Bovey 55709 (218,
245-3049)
A nonprofit, independent extension of North American Wildlife Park
Foundation with several slide lectures, Mobile Wildlife Museum,
educational program, and teacher's workshops with wolves and
humans curriculum dedicated to understanding the predatory
animal; to inform people of its vital role within the balance of
nature; stress importance of preservation of total ecosystem;
promote realistic solutions for man and nature to coexist. Nationwide program available; special emphasis on predators, wolves,
historical relationship between man and wolves, and global perspective on the wolf of Minnesota.
Regional Coordinator: KARLYN ATKINSON BERG

WILDLIFE SOCIETY MINNESOTA CHAPTER
President: ED BOGGESS, 4929 Woodcrest, White Bear Lake
55110 (612, 296-3344)
President-Elect: AL BERNER, 123 2nd St., SW, Medelia 56062
(507, 642-8478)

Secretary-Treasurer: MIKE ZICUS, 102 23rd St., Bemidji 56601
(218, 755-2973)

MISSISSIPPI

GOVERNMENT AGENCIES

GOVERNOR: RAY MABUS, Governor of Mississippi, P.O. Box
139, Jackson 39205 (601, 359-3100)

DEPARTMENT OF AGRICULTURE AND COMMERCE, P.O. Box
1609, Jackson 39205 (601, 359-3639)
The department was created in 1906 to foster and promote the
business of agriculture. Duties include regulatory, consumer pro-
tection, marketing, and a wide range of service activities.
Commissioner: JIM BUCK ROSS
Director, Grain Inspection and Weighing Division: RALPH HOWELL
(762-8141)
Director, Consumer Protection Division: JOE HARDY (359-3648)
Director, Grain Warehouse Licensing: CHRIS SPARKMAN (359-
3643)
Director, Feed, Seed and Fertilizer Control: JOE HARDY (359-
3636)
Director, Division of Market Development: JEFF GIACHELLI (359-
6573)
Personnel Officer: MARY LYNN FAGAN (359-3658)
Director, Swine Protection Division: TOMMY HARRELL (359-
3656)
Information Officer: BILLY COX (359-3642)
Director, Accounting Division: TOM PRITCHARD (359-3652)
Director, Board of Animal Health: DR. HARVEY F. McCRORY (354-
6089)
Director, Farmers Market: TIP BISHOP (354-6552)
Director, Meat Inspection Division: DR. SAM COX (354-6581)
Director, Weights and Measures: BILL ELDRIDGE (359-3670)
Publication: *Mississippi Market Bulletin*
Editor: CHARLINDA SHACK (359-3657)

**DEPARTMENT OF NATURAL RESOURCES, BUREAU OF LAND
AND WATER RESOURCES,** Southport Mall, P.O. Box
10631, Jackson 39209 (601, 961-5200)
Administers Water Use Permitting Act of 1985, licensing of water
well drillers, the 1976 Ground Water Management Act, and the
1978 Dam Safety Act, inventories water resources, coordinates
water and land resources planning, and conducts reviews of
proposed water resources development. Organized: 1956.
Bureau Director: CHARLES T. BRANCH, P.E.
Chief, Division of Regional Water Resources: MARION G. STEWART,
JR. (961-5207)

**DEPARTMENT OF NATURAL RESOURCES, BUREAU OF
POLLUTION CONTROL,** P.O. Box 10385, Jackson 39209
(601, 961-5171)
Director, Bureau of Pollution Control: CHARLES H. CHISOLM

**DEPARTMENT OF NATURAL RESOURCES, BUREAU OF
RECREATION AND PARKS,** P.O. Box 10600, Jackson
39209 (601, 961-5099)
Created to provide outdoor recreation opportunities for Mississip-
pians and out-of-state guests. Of the 26 parks under commission
jurisdiction, 22 are classified as state recreation areas, and four as
historical and cultural sites. Established: 1936.
Commissioners: JOLLY McCARTY, Chairman; HENRY WEISS, Vice-

Chairman; THOMAS GOLDMAN; ROBERT C. TRAVIS; J.K. HURDLE; EARL BOYD; MARSHALL WATKINS

Executive Director: J.I. PALMER, JR. (961-5000)

Bureau Director: AUBREY D. ROZZELL (961-5240)

Publications: Newsletter; *The Resource;* information brochures

Editor: ELEANA TURNER

DEPARTMENT OF WILDLIFE CONSERVATION, Southport Mall, P.O. Box 451, Jackson 39205 (601, 961-5300)

The purpose of the DWC is to manage, conserve, develop, and protect Mississippi's wildlife and marine resources and their habitats to provide continuing recreational, economic, educational, ecological, aesthetic, social and scientific benefits for present and future generations.

Commissioners: S.T. RAYBURN, Chairman, lst Congressional District; CHAMP TERNEY, Vice-Chairman, 2nd Congressional District; MICHAEL GOFF, 3rd Congressional District; DAVID NEW, JR., 4th Congressional District; DR. HENRY K. HILLMAN, 5th Congressional District

Executive Director: VERNON BEVILL (961-5315)

Chief of Game: SETH MOTT (961-5338)

Chief of Fisheries: RON GARAVELLI (961-5341)

Hunter Safety Administrator: L.J. SMITH (961-5335)

Chief Law Enforcement Officer: DAN TULLOS (961-5312)

Director, Bureau of Administrative Services: WILLIAM Y. QUISEN-BERRY III (961-5322)

Director, Bureau of Fisheries and Wildlife: JACK HERRING (961-5311)

Director, Bureau of Marine Resources: DR. RICHARD LEARD (864-4602)

Publication: *MS Outdoors*

Editor: DAVID L. WATTS (961-5369)

FORESTRY COMMISSION, 301 N. Lamar St., Suite 300, Jackson 39201 (601, 359-1386)

Basic duties are forest protection against wildfire, insects and disease; operation of tree seedlings nurseries for reforestation; provision of forest resource management assistance to private landowners and creation of interest in forestry. Organized: 1926.

Commissioners: LANNY L. AUTRY; RICHARD BARGE; L.C. WHITE; GARY L. DEARMAN; WM. P. (Pat) WEBER; ARNOLD B. SMITH; CHARLES L. ROGERS, SR.; C.A. THIGPEN; WARREN THOMPSON

State Forester: R. SIDNEY (Sid) MOSS

Deputy State Forester-Services: CHARLES H. GREEN

Fiscal Officer: ROD SANDERS

Chief Management Forester: FREDDIE M. JORDAN

Chief Protection Forester: JAMES (Jim) BRIGHT

Information-Education Director: BILL COLVIN

Publications: *Inside The Bark; Forestry Forum Magazine*

Editors: JOE McDONALD; BILL COLVIN

GULF COAST RESEARCH LABORATORY, Ocean Springs 39564 (601, 875-2244)

Carries on research in marine biology, fisheries, geology, chemistry, and oceanography. Founded: 1947.

Director: HAROLD D. HOWSE

Assistant Director for Administration and Academic Affairs: DAVID W. COOK

Assistant Director for Fisheries Research and Management: THOMAS D. McILWAIN

Publications: Marine Briefs; Gulf Research Reports

Editors: HAROLD HOWSE; SUSAN GRIGGS

MISSISSIPPI COOPERATIVE FISH AND WILDLIFE RESEARCH UNIT, U.S.D.I., P.O. Drawer BX, Mississippi State University, Mississippi State 39762 (601, 325-2643)

Established March 10, 1978 and is sponsored by the U.S. Fish and Wildlife Service, Mississippi Department of Wildlife Conservation, Mississippi State University and the Wildlife Management Institute. Fisheries and wildlife research, graduate education, technical assistance and extension are the unit's main missions.

Leader: ROBERT J. MUNCY

Assistant Leader, Wildlife: EDWARD P. HILL III

Assistant Leader, Fisheries: L.E. (Steve) MIRANDA

SEA GRANT PROGRAM

Director: JAMES I. JONES, Ph.D., Mississippi-Alabama Sea Grant Consortium, Caylor Bldg., Gulf Coast Research Laboratory, P.O. Box 7000, Ocean Springs 39564-7000 (601, 875-9341)

Mississippi Sea Grant Advisory Services Program: C. DAVID VEAL, Ph.D., Leader, 4646 W. Beach Blvd., Suite 1-E, Biloxi 39531 (601, 388-4710)

Alabama Sea Grant Extension Services Program: WILLIAM HOSK-ING, Ph.D., Program Coordinator, Alabama Sea Grant Advisory Service, 3940 Government Blvd., No. 5, Mobile 36609 (205, 661-5004)

STATE DEPARTMENT OF HEALTH, P.O. Box 1700, Jackson 39215-1700

State Health Officer: ALTON B. COBB, M.D. (601, 960-7634)

Director of Environmental Health: JOE D. BROWN, P.E. (960-7518)

Director, Division of Epidemiology: F.E. THOMPSON, M.D. (960-7725)

STATE EXTENSION SERVICES

Director of Extension Service: DR. JAMES R. CARPENTER, Mississippi State University, Mississippi State 39762 (601, 325-3036)

Leader, Extension, Wildlife and Fisheries Department: Vacant, Box 5446, Mississippi State University, Mississippi State 39762 (325-3174)

Extension Wildlife Specialist: Vacant, Box 5446, Mississippi State University, Mississippi State 39762 (325-3174)

Area Extension Fisheries Specialist: MARTIN DAVID CROSBY, Delta Branch Experiment Station, P.O. Box 142, Stoneville 38776 (686-9311/ext. 302)

Extension Forestry: DR. THOMAS A. MONAGHAN, Leader, P.O. Box 5446, Mississippi State University, Mississippi State 39762 (325-3150)

Area Extension Fisheries and Wildlife Specialist: ROBERT M. DURBOROW, P.O. Box 142, Stoneville 38776 (696-9311/ext. 302)

Area Extension Wildlife and Forestry Specialist: Vacant, 1018 N. Gloster, Suite G, Tupelo 38801 (841-2293)

Area Extension Fisheries Specialist: PETER W. TAYLOR, P.O. Box 239, Belzoni 39038 (247-2915)

Area Extension Foresters: ANDREW W. EZELL, 3825 Ridgewood Rd., Jackson 39211 (982-6218); I. WINSTON SAVELLE, JR., 200 Caprenter Bldg., Hattiesburg 39401 (545-6161); TIMOTHY A. TRAUGOTT, 1241 Mound St., Grenada 38901 (226-2070)

STATE SOIL AND WATER CONSERVATION COMMISSION

Established in 1938 to handle elections of Soil and Water Conservation District Commissioners; to establish and administer qualification standards for district commissioners and officers; to study, classify and evaluate land use needs and problems in the state; to assist individual land owners, operators and organized groups, associations, or other agencies.

Chairman: M.C. SPARKS, JR., 1260 Mabry Rd., Lake Cormorant 38641

Executive Director: GALE MARTIN, P.O. Box 23005, Jackson 39225-3005 (601, 359-1281)

Publication: *Mississippi Association of Conservation Districts Newsletter*

Editor: GALE MARTIN, P.O. Box 23005, Jackson 39225-3005

CITIZENS' GROUPS

MISSISSIPPI WILDLIFE FEDERATION, *520 North President St., Jackson 39201 (601, 353-6922)*
A representative statewide organization, affiliated with the National Wildlife Federation, primarily devoted to the wise use, conservation, aesthetic appreciation, and restoration of wildlife and other natural resources.
President: FRANK SMITH, 366 Robin Rd., Granada 38901 (226-3141)
Executive Director: MIKE GOFF
Affiliate Representative: RAMON L. CALLAHAN, Suite 1321, Fed. Bldg., 100 W. Capitol St., Jackson 39269 (601, 965-5203)
Alternate: MIKE GOFF
Publication: Mississippi Out-of-Doors
Editor: JIM EWING

MISSISSIPPI ASSOCIATION OF CONSERVATION DISTRICTS, INC.

President: SIDNEY BRANCH, Rt. 1, Box 181A, Winona 38967
1st Vice-President: BOB WALES, Southern Station, Box 5051, Hattiesburg 39041
2nd Vice-President: JOHN OGLESBY, Box 205, Chatham 38731
Secretary-Treasurer: GALE MARTIN, P.O. Box 23005, Jackson 39225-3005

MISSISSIPPI BASS CHAPTER FEDERATION

An organization of Bassmaster Chapters, affiliated with the Bass Anglers Sportsman Society, organized to fight pollution, assist state and national conservation agencies in their efforts and to teach the young people of our country good conservation practices. Dedicated to the realistic conservation of our water resources.
President: TONY BYRD, 5417 Robbinson Road Extention, Jackson 39204 (601, 372-6754)

MISSISSIPPI FORESTRY ASSOCIATION, INC., 201 Realtors Bldg., 620 N. State St., Jackson 39202-3398 (601, 354-4936)

A nonprofit organization to conserve, develop, protect, and promote the forest and related natural resources of Mississippi for the best interest of this and succeeding generations. Composed of about 1,800 tree farmers, forest industries, equipment suppliers, and financial institutions. Organized: 1938.
President: GEORGE FAURE
Executive Vice-President: STEVE CORBITT
Publications: *The Voice of Forestry; Tree Talk*

WILDLIFE SOCIETY MISSISSIPPI CHAPTER

President: CHUCK HILL, 1207 Highland Dr., Picayune 39466 (601, 688-2047)
President-Elect: DALE H. ARNER, P.O. Drawer LW, Mississippi 39762 (325-2617)
Secretary-Treasurer: ELLEN GOETZ, 102 Erin Cove, Clinton 39056 (965-5506)

GOVERNMENT AGENCIES

GOVERNOR: JOHN ASHCROFT, Governor of Missouri, State Capitol, Jefferson City 65101 (314, 751-3222)

DEPARTMENT OF AGRICULTURE, P.O. Box 630, 1616 Missouri Blvd., Jefferson City 65101 (314, 751-4211)
Director: CHARLES E. KRUSE
Deputy Director: LESLIE M. (Jake) GREINER
Public Information Officer: F.M. (Mike) KRAEMER

DEPARTMENT OF CONSERVATION, P.O. Box 180, Jefferson City 65102-0180 (314, 751-4115) Organized: 1937.
Commissioners: JOHN POWELL, Rolla; RICHARD T. REED, East Prairie; JAY HENGES, Earth City; JEFF CHURAN, Chillicothe
Director: JERRY J. PRESLEY
Deputy Director: EDWIN H. GLASER
Assistant Director: KENNETH M. BABCOCK
Assistant Director: DAVID D. HURLBUT
General Counsel: ROBERT J. SWIFT, JR.
Internal Auditor: ROBBIE B. BRISCOE
Engineering Administrator: CHARLES E. HOOKER
Fiscal Administrator: AARON R. CHAPMAN
Public Affairs Administrator: JONATHAN D. POWERS
Operations Administrator: EVERETT E. CLARK
Personnel Administrator: ROGER E. PONDER
Environmental Administrator: DAN F. DICKNEITE
Natural History Administrator: JAMES H. WILSON
Education Administrator: DONALD K. HEARD
Land Acquisition Superintendent: RONALD E. THOMA
Publication: *Missouri Conservationist*
Editor: MALCOLM K. JOHNSON

Protection Division
Chief: ROBERT B. KING
Assistant Chiefs: Administration, RONALD L. GLOVER; Field, JOHN V. FRYE; Field, GLEN D. McCLOUD

Fisheries Division
Chief: JAMES P. FRY
Assistant Chiefs: Administration, STANLEY M. MICHAELSON; Hatcheries, M. LeROY HEMAN; Management, LEE C. REDMOND; Research, JAMES R. WHITLEY

Wildlife Division
Chief: OLIVER A. TORGERSON
Assistant Chiefs: Research, WAYNE R. PORATH; Administration, GEORGE P. DELLINGER; Wildlife Services, SAMUEL B. KIRBY; Land Management, JIM L. CHOATE
Agricultural Liaison Coordinator: RAYMOND D. EVANS

Forestry Division
State Forester: GERALD E. ROSS
Assistant State Foresters: Administration and Nursery, MARVIN D. BROWN; Staff, EUGENE L. BRUNK; Field, JAMES F. JOHNSON; Field, EDWARD A. KEYSER

DEPARTMENT OF NATURAL RESOURCES, P.O. Box 176, Jefferson City 65102 (314, 751-3332; 1-800-334-6946)
Director: FREDERICK A. BRUNNER, Ph.D., P.E. (751-4422)
Deputy Director: RON KUCERA (751-3195)
Policy Research Program: PAM WALKER, Director (751-3195)

Environmental Improvement and Energy Resources Authority: STEPHEN MAHFOOD, Director (751-4919)

Division of Energy: ROBERT JACKSON, Director (751-6856)

Residential Grants Services: ELDON HATTERVIG , Director (751-7056)

Energy Management Services: JACK DAYTON (751-7370)

Community Services: JUDIE DIDRIKSEN, Director (751-6757)

Division of Management Services: GARY HEIMERICKS, Director (751-3767)

Assistant Director: LaVERNE BRONDEL (751-3767)

Management Services, Budget and Program Analysis: RICK ANDERSON, Budget Director (751-3767)

Management Services, General Support Services: ED BAILEY, Director (751-2480)

Management Services, Management Information Services: MARCY KREMER, Director (751-2963)

Management Services, Personnel Services: GASTON de la TORRE, Director (751-2518)

Management Services, Financial Services: Vacant, Director (751-2561)

Management Services, Public Information Services: WILLIAM PALMER, Director (751-3443)

Division of Geology and Land Survey: JAMES H. WILLIAMS, Ph.D., Director and State Geologist, Box 250, Rolla 65401 (364-1752)

Assistant State Geologist and Assistant Director for Water Research and Planning: JERRY VINEYARD (364-1752)

Assistant Director, Land Survey and Dam Safety: ROBERT MYERS (364-1752)

Division of Environmental Quality: WILLIAM FORD, Director, P.O. Box 176, Jefferson City 65102 (751-4810)

Assistant Director, Division of Environmental Quality: JOHN YOUNG (751-8730)

Air Pollution Control Program, Staff Director: Vacant (751-7840)

Water Pollution Control Program, Staff Director: CHARLES STIEFERMANN (751-1300)

Land Reclamation Program, Staff Director: ROBERT CLARK (751-6778)

Soil and Water Conservation Program, Staff Director: DON WOLF (751-4932)

Laboratory Services Program, Director: JAMES LONG (751-7928); Environmental Emergency Response (634-2436)

Public Drinking Water, Director: JERRY LANE (751-5331)

Regional Office Program: HAROLD PATRICK, Director (751-1493)

Waste Management Program: NICK DiPASQUALE, Director (751-2747)

Jefferson City Regional Office, Administrator: BILL KESLER, P.O. Box 1368, Jefferson City 65102 (751-2729)

Kansas City Regional Office, Administrator: JAMES MCCONATHY, 4609 Norfleet, Independence 64055 (816, 353-5001)

Macon Regional Office, Administrator: CHARLES S. DECKER, P.O. Box 489, Macon 63552 (816, 385-2129)

Poplar Bluff Regional Office, Administrator: JAMES BURRIS, 948 Lester St., Poplar Bluff 63901 (785-0832)

St. Louis Regional Office, Administrator: DON MADDOX, 8460 Watson Rd., Suite 217, St. Louis 63119 (849-1313)

Springfield Regional Office, Administrator: JOHN NIXON, 1155 E. Cherokee, Springfield 65807 (417, 883-4033)

Division of Parks, Recreation and Historic Preservation: WAYNE GROSS, Director, P.O. Box 176, Jefferson City 65102 (751-2479)

Director, Field Operations Program: RUSS HARDING (751-2479)

Director, Historic Preservation Program: CLAIRE BLACKWELL (751-2479)

Director, Planning and Development Program: WILLIAM FARRAND (751-2479)

Director, Outdoor Recreation Assistance Program: DEIRDRE K. HIRNER (751-2479)

Director, Administration Program: Vacant

Publication: *Missouri Resource Review*

Editor: MICHAEL McINTOSH (751-3443)

MISSOURI COOPERATIVE FISH AND WILDLIFE RESEARCH UNIT, U.S.D.I., 112 Stephens Hall, University of Missouri, Columbia 65211 (314, 882-3634)

Established in 1985 by cooperative agreement among the Fish and Wildlife Service, Missouri Department of Conservation, University of Missouri, and Wildlife Management Institute. Primary purpose is research and graduate student education in wildlife conservation, aquatic ecology and fisheries management areas.

Leader: DR. CHARLES F. RABENI (882-3524)

Assistant Leader, Wildlife: DR. RONALD D. DROBNEY (882-9420)

Assistant Leader, Fisheries: DR. DAVID L. GALAT (882-3634)

STATE EXTENSION SERVICES

Director, Extension Service: DR. GAIL L. IMIG, University of Missouri, 309 University Hall, Columbia 65211 (314, 882-7754)

Extension Forester: JOHN P. SLUSHER, 1-34 Agriculture Bldg., University of Missouri, Columbia 65211 (882-4444)

CITIZENS' GROUPS

CONSERVATION FEDERATION OF MISSOURI, *728 W. Main St., Jefferson City 65101-1543 (314, 634-2322)*

A representative statewide organization, affiliated with the National Wildlife Federation, primarily devoted to the wise use, conservation, aesthetic appreciation, and restoration of wildlife and other resources.

President: CHARLES BELL, 2260 Country Ln., Columbia 65201 (449-5240)

Executive Director: ED STEGNER

Affiliate Representative: G. ANDY RUNGE, 123 E. Jackson, Mexico 65265

Alternate: ABE PHILLIPS, 41 South Central, Clayton 63105

Publication: Missouri Wildlife

Editor: CHARLES F. DAVIDSON

AUDUBON SOCIETY OF MISSOURI

A nonprofit, statewide society affiliated with National Audubon Society. Dedicated to preservation and protection of birds and all wildlife forms and habitat; to educate citizenry toward appreciation of the natural world; and to work for wise conservation practices related to people and wildlife. Organized: 1901.

President: RANDY WASHBURN, 2319 Gray Fox Terr., #D, Jefferson City 65101 (314, 636-2765)

Vice-President: JOANN GARRETT, 1680 Southwind Dr., Raymore 64083 (816, 322-1580)

Secretary: JEANNE BARR, 1416 Sylvan Ln., Columbia 65202 (314, 449-4063)

Treasurer: SYDNEY J. WADE, 2114 St. Louis Rd., Jefferson City 65101 (314, 635-0402)

Publication: *The Bluebird*

Editor: BILL CLARK, 3906 Grace Ellen Dr., Columbia 65202-1796 (314, 474-4510)

MISSOURI ASSOCIATION OF SOIL AND WATER CONSERVATION DISTRICTS

President: ART DUNCAN, Rt. 1, Box 162, Gideon 63848 (314, 396-5322)

Vice-President: BEN A. ROGERS, Russellville 65074 (496-3395)
Secretary-Treasurer: EUGENE EHLMANN, 3503 Ipswich Ln., St. Charles 63301 (724-5121)

MISSOURI BASS CHAPTER FEDERATION,

An organization of Bassmaster Chapters, affiliated with the Bass Anglers Sportsman Society, organized to fight pollution, assist state and national conservation agencies in their efforts and to teach the young people of our country good conservation practices. Dedicated to the realistic conservation of our water resources.
President: MIKE SIMMONS, 1008 W. Springfield, Union 63084 (314, 583-2500)

MISSOURI PRAIRIE FOUNDATION, P.O. Box 200, Columbia 65205

A nonprofit citizens' group organized in 1966 to ensure the preservation of native prairie along with associated plant and animal life by acquisition, management protection, control, and perpetuation of the prairie; to carry on educational programs; and to provide scientific research relative to native prairie.
President: JERRY OVERTON (816, 361-1700)
Vice-President: JOHN R. CLINE (314, 581-6566)
Secretary: WALLACE WEBER (417, 836-5883)
Treasurer: RANDY WASHBURN
Advisor to the Board: D.M. CHRISTISEN
Publications: *Missouri Prairie Journal; Prairie Zephyr Newsletter*
Editor: JUNE HUNZEKER, 6115 N. Michigan, Gladstone 64118

WILDLIFE SOCIETY MISSOURI CHAPTER

President: RUSS TITUS, Box 509, Rolla 65401 (314, 364-4221)
President-Elect: DAVE ERICKSON, Fish and Wildlife Res. Center, 1110 College Ave., Columbia 65210 (449-3761)
Secretary: LISA DEBRUYKERE, 633 Bent Oak, Lake St. Louis 63367 (625-1613)
Treasurer: ERNIE WIGGERS, Missouri Cooperative Fish and Wildlife Research Unit, 112 Stephens Hall, University of Missouri, Columbia 65111 (882-9423)

MONTANA

GOVERNMENT AGENCIES

GOVERNOR: STAN STEPHENS, Governor of Montana, State Capitol, Helena 59620 (406, 444-3111)

BUREAU OF MINES AND GEOLOGY, c/o Montana College of Mineral Science and Technology, Butte 59701 (406, 496-4180)
Established by law in 1919, to aid the development and wise use of the state's mineral, energy, and groundwater resources by geologic and hydrogeologic studies of their occurrence and potential.
Director and State Geologist: EDWARD T. RUPPEL

DEPARTMENT OF AGRICULTURE, Environmental Management Division, Agriculture and Livestock Bldg., Capitol Station, Helena 59620-0201 (406, 444-3144)
Director: KEITH KELLY
Deputy Director: W. RALPH PECK
Administrator, Environmental Management Division: GARY GINGERY (444-2944)
Administrator, Plant Industry Division: ROY BJORNSON (444-3730)

Administrator, Agricultural Development Division: MIKE MURPHY (444-2402)

DEPARTMENT OF FISH, WILDLIFE, AND PARKS, 1420 East Sixth, Helena 59620 (406, 444-2535)
Commission Members: ROBERT JENSEN, Chairman, Circle; DAN OAKLAND, Great Falls; JIM OLSON, Hamilton; DON BAILEY, Forsyth; BILL HOWELL, West Yellowstone
Director: JAMES W. FLYNN (444-3186)
Deputy Director: RICHARD L. JOHNSON (444-3186)
Associate Director: RON MARCOUX (444-3186)
Administrator, Field Services: EUGENE O. ALLEN (444-2602)
Administrator, Management Services: DAVE MOTT (444-4786)
Administrator, Fisheries: PAT GRAHAM (444-2449)
Administrator, Wildlife: ARNOLD OLSEN, Ph.D. (444-2612)
Administrator, Law Enforcement: ERWIN J. KENT (444-2452)
Administrator, Parks: DON HYYPPA (444-3750)
Administrator, Conservation Education: RON AASHEIM (444-2535)
Publication: *Montana Outdoors*
Editor: DAVE BOOKS (444-2474)

DEPARTMENT OF NATURAL RESOURCES AND CONSERVATION, 1520 East Sixth Ave., Helena 59620-2301 (406, 444-6699)
Created by the Executive Reorganization Act of 1971. Administers state-owned water projects; plans, regulates, or coordinates the development or use of other water, land, and energy resources; water-right adjudication; flood plain management; supervision, assistance and coordination for local conservation and grazing districts; energy facility siting; alternative energy grants; energy conservation; regulation of oil and gas production.
Director: LARRY FASBENDER
Deputy Director: DAVE DARBY
Chief Legal Counsel: DONALD D. MacINTYRE
Information Officer/Citizen Participation Advocate: JIM BOND
Board of Natural Resources and Conservation: CHARLES HASH; BILL SHIELDS, Chairman; CARROLL GRAHAM; JOAN TOOLE; DAN RIEDER; JERRY WIEDEBUSH; GILES GREGOIRE
Centralized Services Division: JOHN ARMSTRONG, Administrator (444-6700)
Conservation Districts Division: RAY BECK, Administrator (444-6667)
Oil and Gas Conservation Division: CHARLES G. MAIO, Administrator, 2535 St. Johns Ave., Billings 59102 (656-0040)
Board of Oil and Gas Conservation: JAMES C. NELSON, Chairman; ROBERT PENNER, Vice-Chairman; DONALD D. CECIL; GEORGE R. CROTTY; WARREN H. ROSS; ARNOLD G. HANSEN; DEAN A. SWANSON
Water Resources Division: GARY FRITZ, Administrator (444-6601)
Energy Division: VAN JAMISON, Administrator (444-6697)

DEPARTMENT OF STATE LANDS, Capitol Station, Helena 59620 (406, 444-2074)
State Board of Land Commissioners: GOV. TED SCHWINDEN, Chairman, Helena; ED ARGENBRIGHT, Superintendent of Public Instruction, Helena; VERNER BERTELSEN, Secretary of State, Helena; MIKE GREELY, Attorney General, Helena; ANDREA BENNETT, State Auditor; DENNIS HEMMER, Commissioner, Department of State Lands, Helena

ENVIRONMENTAL QUALITY COUNCIL, State Capitol, Helena 59620 (406, 444-3742)
Established as environment and natural resources research agency of state legislature to provide oversight of state agency programs. Council includes eight state legislators, four citizens appointed by

legislative leaders, and governor's representative as ex-officio non-voting.

Chairman, Senator: MIKE HALLIGAN

Executive Director: DEBORAH B. SCHMIDT

MONTANA COOPERATIVE FISHERY RESEARCH UNIT, U.S.D.I.,
Dept. of Biology, Montana State University, Bozeman 59717 (406, 994-3491)

Conduct applied research, train graduate students in fisheries and disseminate information; research specialties include fish ecology, habitat assessment, instream flow, population dynamics, species interactions, fisheries management.

Leader: DR. ROBERT G. WHITE

Assistant Leader: DR. WILLIAM R. GOULD (994-2450)

MONTANA COOPERATIVE WILDLIFE RESEARCH UNIT,
U.S.D.I., H.S. 107, University of Montana, Missoula 59812 (406, 243-5372/FTS: 585-3128)

Primarily engaged in short-term management-oriented studies of wildlife and habitat conducted by graduate students. Organized: 1950.

Leader: DR. BART W. O'GARA

Assistant Leader: DR. I.J. BALL

STATE DEPARTMENT OF HEALTH AND ENVIRONMENTAL SCIENCES, Cogswell Bldg., Capitol Station, Helena 59620 (406, 444-2544)

The agency is charged with responsibilities in the areas of disease control, laboratory services, dental health, maternal and child health, health education, vital records, inspection and licensing of medical facilities, emergency medical services, and environmental health. Specifically, the Environmental Sciences Division antici-pates, identifies and measures hazardous conditions, and attempts to secure compliance with statutes and rules relating to air and water pollution, food and consumer safety, solid and hazardous waste management, occupational health and radiation, subdivision development, and safe drinking water. Founded: 1901.

Director: JOHN J. DRYNAN, M.D.

Administrator, Division of Environmental Sciences: LARRY L. LLOYD

Administrator (Acting), Health Services: WARREN E. BRASS

STATE EXTENSION SERVICES
Director of Extension Service: JAMES R. WELSH, Montana State University, Bozeman 59717 (406, 994-3681)

CITIZENS' GROUPS

MONTANA WILDLIFE FEDERATION, P.O. Box 6537, Bozeman 59715 (406, 587-1713)

A representative statewide organization, affiliated with the National Wildlife Federation, primarily devoted to the wise use, conservation, aesthetic appreciation, and restoration of wildlife and other natural resources.

President: TONY SCHOONEN, Box 2, Ramsay 59748 (782-1560)

Executive Director: RICHARD C. DAY

Affiliate Representative: GORDON STEWART, 254 Fairview Dr., Kalispell 59901 (257-5627)

Alternate: KATHY HADLEY, 431 Boulder Rd., Deer Lodge 59722 (W:494-4572; H:846-1125)

Publication: Montana Wildlife

Editor: RICHARD C. DAY

MONTANA ASSOCIATION OF CONSERVATION DISTRICTS,
Helena 59601 (406, 443-5711)

President: ROBERT LANE, Box 97, Three Forks 59752 (285-6693)

Vice-President: LORENTS GROSFIELD, Melville Rt., Big Timber 59011 (537-4489)

Treasurer (Acting): EINAR HOVLAND, R.R. 1282, Great Falls 59401 (727-5045)

Council Member: JOHN TEIGEN, JR., Capitol Star Rt., Capitol 59324 (972-4587)

Executive Vice-President: PEGGY HAAGLUND, 1 S. Montana, Helena 59601 (443-5711)

Administrative Secretary: SUSAN DRAKE, 1 S. Montana, Helena 59601 (443-5711)

MONTANA BASS CHAPTER FEDERATION
An organization of Bassmaster chapters, affiliated with the Bass Anglers Sportsman Society, to fight pollution, assist state and national conservation agencies in their efforts, and teach the young people of our country good conservation practice. Dedicated to the realistic conservation of our water resources.

President: STEVE McGUIRE, 221 Garland St., Kalispell 59901 (406, 752-8164/752-4261)

MONTANA ENVIRONMENTAL INFORMATION CENTER, P.O.
Box 1184, Helena 59624 (406, 443-2520)

Overall purpose is to protect and enhance Montana's natural environment. Mobilizes citizens on significant resource issues to pressure for wise decisions on local, state and federal levels. Founded: 1973. Members: 1,000.

Executive Director: JIM JENSEN

President of Board of Directors: KIM WILSON

Vice-President of Board of Directors: CAROL FOX

Publications: *Down to Earth; The Capitol Monitor*

MONTANA LAND RELIANCE, P.O. Box 355, Helena, 59624 (406, 443-7027)

A private nonprofit organization protecting and conserving ecologi-cally and agriculturally significant land in Montana, as well as sharing knowledge of voluntary, private sector land conservation techniques. Pioneering ways to assure a legacy of responsibly managed land.

President: ALLEN BJERGO, 238 Wilcox Ln., Corvallis 59828 (961-4538)

Vice-President: DANA MILTON, M/F Ranch, 823 Highway 87 N., Roundup 59072 (323-1771)

Secretary-Treasurer: GEORGE OLSEN, Galusha, Higgens & Galu-sha, Box 1699, Helena 59601 (442-5520)

Development Director: WILLIAM H. DUNHAM

Financial Director: WILLIAM LONG

Lands Director: JAN KONIGSBERG

Publications: *Private Options: Tools and Concepts for Land Conser-vation* (monograph); *Annual Report*

MONTANA WILDERNESS ASSOCIATION, P.O. Box 635, Helena 59624 (406, 443-7350)

A nonprofit organization dedicated to the preservation and proper management of all public lands, including designated and de facto wilderness areas, national parks, national forests, wildlife refuges and BLM lands in Montana. MWA believes wilderness, wildlife, watershed protection and recreation are important aspects of multiple use management of public lands. Founded: 1958. Mem-bership: 1,200 individuals and families.

President: LOU BRUNO (226-9294)

Vice-President: SUSAN COTTINGHAM (449-7582)

Treasurer: NANCY McLANE (443-6047)

Program Director: JOHN GATCHELL
Administrative Director: SUSAN MILES BRYAN
Publications: *Wild Montana; Letter Be Wild; Wilderness Walks Program*
Editor: SUSAN MILES BRYAN

NORTHERN ROCKIES ACTION GROUP, INC., 9 Placer St., Helena 59601 (406, 442-6615)

A nonprofit, strategy and training center for citizen activists and social change organizations in Montana, Idaho and Wyoming. Through training sessions, on-site consulting, and publications, NRAG assists in strengthening citizen groups and increasing the professional skills of their staff and leaders. Skills-training provided include: organizing, financial management, all areas fundraising, management assistance, strategy development, and long range planning.

Executive Director: MICHAEL SCHECHTMAN
Fiscal Manager: JUDY HESTER
Field Consulting Staff: BEKI BRANDBORG; PAM MAVROLAS; MARSHALL MAYER
Special Project Staff: KATHY VAN HOOK; CLAUDIA KURIC; BOB ANDERSON

TROUT UNLIMITED MONTANA COUNCIL

A statewide council with 12 chapters working for the protection and enhancement of the coldwater fishery resource.
Chairman and National Director: BILL CAIN, #1 Bittersweet Dr., Butte 59701 (406, 723-5421)

WILDLIFE SOCIETY MONTANA CHAPTER

President: JOE BALL, Montana Cooperative Wildlife Research Unit, University of Montana, Missoula 59807 (406, 243-5372)
President-Elect: Vacant
Secretary-Treasurer: HARVEY NYBERG, Box 689, Malta 59538 (654-1641)

NEBRASKA

GOVERNMENT AGENCIES

GOVERNOR: KAY A. ORR, Governor of Nebraska, State Capitol, Lincoln 68509 (402, 471-2244)

DEPARTMENT OF AGRICULTURE, 301 Centennial Mall So., P.O. Box 94947, Lincoln 68509 (402, 471-2341)
Director: DR. ROY L. FREDERICK

DEPARTMENT OF ENVIRONMENTAL CONTROL, State House Sta., Box 98922, Lincoln 68509 (402, 471-2186)
Created by the Nebraska Environmental Protection Act in 1971. Administers and enforces rules and regulations, and monitors the quality of the environment in Nebraska.
Director: DENNIS GRAMS
Assistant Director: GEORGE LUDWIG
Secretary, State Environmental Control Council: DENNIS GRAMS
Chief, Land Quality Division: JACK SUKOVATY
Chief, Water Quality Division: GALE HUTTON
Chief, Air Quality Division: GENE ROBINSON
Public Information Officer: BRIAN C. McMANUS
Publication: *Environmental Update*
Editor: BRIAN C. McMANUS

DEPARTMENT OF WATER RESOURCES, State House Station, Box 94676, Lincoln 68509 (402, 471-2363)
Administers and enforces the state water laws and all matters pertaining to water rights, measuring and recording the flow of various streams and canals, approving plans and specifications for dam construction, inspection of dams, approving plans and specifications for construction activities in flood plains, and registration of wells.
Director: J. MICHAEL JESS
Assistant Director: THOMAS R. LAMBERSON
Chief, Operations Branch: ROBERT F. BISHOP
Chief, Engineering Branch: LUMIR C. KUBICEK
State Hydrologist: ANN S. BLEED
Publications: *Channels Newsletter; Biennial Report; Hydrographic Report*

GAME AND PARKS COMMISSION, 2200 N. 33rd St., P.O. Box 30370, Lincoln 68503 (402, 464-0641)
The commission has sole charge of state parks, game and fish and all things pertaining thereto, boating, and administration of the Land and Water Conservation Fund.
Commission Members: STAN JUELFS, Chairman; WAYNE ZIEBARTH; LAVERN SCHNEIDER; L. BRUCE WRIGHT; RICHARD COYNE; ALAN CRAMER; ELVIN ADAMSON
Director: REX AMACK
Assistant Directors: WILLIAM J. BAILEY; DALE R. BREE
Chiefs: LARRY MORRIS, Administration; WESLEY SHEETS, Fisheries; JACK HANNA, Budget and Fiscal; JIM SHEFFIELD, Engineering; JIM MacALLISTER, Information and Education; DON SCHAEPLER, Law Enforcement; HAROLD EDWARDS, Resource Services; KEN JOHNSON, Wildlife; CHARLES DUNCAN, State Parks; TED STUTHEIT, Historical Parks; JAMES J. CARNEY, Recreation Areas; PAUL HORTON, Outdoor Education; BRUCE SACKETT, Realty
Publication: *Nebraskaland Magazine*
Editors: LOWELL JOHNSON; JON FARRAR

District Offices

District I: Box 725, Alliance 69301 (308, 762-5605)
District II: Box 508, Bassett 68714 (402, 684-2921)
District III: Box 934, Norfolk 68701 (402, 371-4950)
District IV: R.D. 4, Box 36 North Platte 69101 (308, 532-6225)
District V: P.O. Box 30370, Lincoln 68503 (402, 464-0641)
Game and Parks Commission: State Office Bldg., 1313 Farnam, Omaha 68102 (402, 554-2144)
AK-Sar-Ben Aquarium: Rt. 1, Box 165, Gretna 68028 (402, 332-3901)

GEOLOGICAL SURVEY, Conservation and Survey Division, University of Nebraska, Lincoln 68588 (402, 472-3471)
The CSD has responsibilities to survey and describe Nebraska's natural resources including soil, water, geology, mineral resources and climate. Additionally, the division publishes studies which describe operations and production of leading industries in the state. Staff members also provide educational talks and materials to citizens.
Director: P.B. WIGLEY

NEBRASKA NATURAL RESOURCES COMMISSION, 301 Centennial Mall South, P.O. Box 94876, Lincoln 68509 (402, 471-2081)
The state agency responsible for comprehensive water resources planning, flood plain management, administration of state financial assistance for water resources, flood control, soil and water conservation; advisory and administrative responsibility for Natural Resources Districts throughout the state.

Chairman: CLIFFORD WELSH
Director: DAYLE E. WILLIAMSON

STATE EXTENSION SERVICES

Dean and Director of Cooperative Extension Service: DR. LEO E. LUCAS, University of Nebraska, Lincoln 68583-0703 (402, 472-2966)

State Forester: DR. GARY HERGENRADER, Department of Forestry, Fisheries and Wildlife, 102 Plant Industry Bldg., Institute of Agriculture and Natural Resources, Lincoln 68583 (472-1467)

Extension Forester: MICHAEL KUHNS, Department of Forestry, Fisheries and Wildlife, 107 Plant Industry Bldg., University of Nebraska, Lincoln 68583-0814 (472-5822)

Extension Wildlife Specialist: RON J. JOHNSON, Department of Forestry, Fisheries and Wildlife, 202 Natural Resources Hall, University of Nebraska-Lincoln, Lincoln 68583-0819 (472-6823)

Extension Vertebrate Pest Specialist: SCOTT E. HYGNSTROM, Department of Forestry, Fisheries and Wildlife, 202 Natural Resources Hall, University of Nebraska-Lincoln, Lincoln 68583-0819 (472-6822)

CITIZENS' GROUPS

NEBRASKA WILDLIFE FEDERATION, INC., 410 S. 11th St., Lincoln 68508 (402, 476-0581)
A representative statewide organization, affiliated with the National Wildlife Federation, primarily devoted to the wise use, conservation, aesthetic appreciation, and restoration of wildlife and other natural resources. Organized: 1970.
President: STEVE ROTHENBERGER, 2214 E. 4th, Fremont 68205
Executive Manager: MARLYN LOGAN
Affiliate Representative: DON LEU, 5105 Davenport St., Omaha 68132
Alternate: STEVE ROTHENBERGER
Publication: Prairie Blade
Editor: MARLYN LOGAN

IZAAK WALTON LEAGUE OF AMERICA, INC. (Nebraska Div.)

President: DAVID EISELE, 3801 Spruce St., Lincoln 68516 (402, 475-2252)
Secretary: ROGER EILERS, 4010 N. 15th St., Lincoln 68521 (435-8363)

NEBRASKA ASSOCIATION OF RESOURCES DISTRICTS

President: ELDEN WESELEY, Rt. 1, Oakland 68045 (402, 685-5956)
Vice-President: GERALD VAP, 1302 Norris Ave., McCook 69001 (W:308, 345-5011/H:345-6041)
Secretary-Treasurer: JOHN BURKHOLDER, Rt. 2, Holdrege 68949 (308, 995-8329)
Council Member: ROY STUHR, R.F.D. 1, McCool Junction 68401 (402, 724-2436)

NEBRASKA BASS CHAPTER FEDERATION

An organization of Bassmaster Chapters, affiliated with the Bass Anglers Sportsman Society, organized to fight pollution, assist state and national conservation agencies in their efforts and to teach the young people of our country good conservation practices. Dedicated to the realistic conservation of our water resources.
President: JOE CITTA, JR., 1518 Kozy Dr., Columbus 68601 (402, 563-2297/563-5355)

NEBRASKA ORNITHOLOGISTS' UNION, INC., University of Nebraska State Museum, W436 Nebraska Hall, Lincoln 68588-0514 (402, 472-6606)

To promote the study of ornithology and natural history in general by uniting the natural history students of Nebraska, both professional and amateur. To encourage the conservation of wildlife through scientific study and distribution of data. Membership: 200. Founded: 1899.

President and Newsletter Editor: THOMAS E. LABEDZ (H:423-1384)
Vice-President: DOUG G. THOMAS, 1035 Mississippi, Alliance 69301 (H:308, 762-1157)
Secretary: RUTH C. GREEN, 506 W. 31st. Ave., Bellevue 68005 (H:402, 292-0451)
Treasurer: ALICE KENITZ, HC 50 Box 38B, Gering 69341 (H:308, 436-2959)
Librarian: DR. M. ROSALIND MORRIS, 3018 O St., Lincoln 68510 (H:402, 435-3382)
Publication: *The Nebraska Bird Review*
Editor: RUSHTON G. CORTELYOU, 5109 Underwood Ave., Omaha 68132 (402, 556-7489)

WILDLIFE SOCIETY NEBRASKA CHAPTER

President: RICHARD L. NELSON, 1820 Cedarberry Rd., North Platte 69101 (308, 532-6225)
Vice-President: BRUCE TRINDLE, Rt. 4, Darberry Rd., Norfolk 68701 (402, 371-4950)
Secretary: DAVID CARLSON, 4030 Reed Dr., Grand Island 68801 (308, 381-5571)
Treasurer: GREG WINGFIELD, Rt. 4, Box 36, North Platte 69101 (308, 532-6225)

NEVADA

GOVERNMENT AGENCIES

GOVERNOR: RICHARD H. BRYAN, Governor of Nevada, State Capitol, Carson City 89710 (702, 885-5670)

BUREAU OF MINES AND GEOLOGY, University of Nevada, Reno 89557-0088 (702, 784-6691)
Does research on Nevada geology and mineral resources. Collects and disseminates information (including published maps and reports) on Nevada geology, mineral resources, base maps, and airphotos.
Director/State Geologist: JONATHAN G. PRICE

DEPARTMENT OF AGRICULTURE, 350 Capitol Hill Ave., P.O. Box 11100, Reno 89510 (702, 789-0180)
Executive Director: THOMAS W. BALLOW
Director, Division of Plant Industry: PHILLIP C. MARTINELLI
Director, Division of Animal Industry: JACK N. ARMSTRONG, DVM
Director, Division of Brand Inspection: STEPHEN J. MAHONEY

DEPARTMENT OF CONSERVATION AND NATURAL RESOURCES, Capitol Complex, Nye Bldg., 201 S. Fall St., Carson City 89710 (702, 885-4360)
Director: ROLAND D. WESTERGARD

Division of Water Resources
State Engineer: PETER G. MORROS (702, 885-4380)

Division of State Parks
Administrator: JOHN RICHARDSON (702, 885-4384)
Assistant Administrator: J. STEPHEN WEAVER
Chief of Planning and Development: Vacant

Division of State Lands
Administrator and State Land Registrar: PAMELA B. WILCOX (702, 885-4363)

Division of Forestry
State Forester: LOWELL V. SMITH, Capitol Complex (702, 885-4350)

Division of Conservation Districts
Administrator (Acting): PAMELA B. WILCOX (702, 885-4363)

State Environmental Commission
Chairman: MELVIN D. CLOSE
Executive Officer (Acting): LEWIS H. DODGION (702, 885-4670)

State Park Advisory Commission
Chairman: CLIFFORD SEGERBLOHM (702, 885-4384)

Division of Historic Preservation and Archeology
Deputy State Historic Preservation Officer: RONALD M. JAMES
Administrator: Vacant (702, 885-5138)

Division of Environmental Protection
Administrator: LEWIS H. DODGION (702, 885-4670)

DEPARTMENT OF WILDLIFE, Box 10678, Reno 89520 (702, 789-0500)
A regulatory and policy-making body; administers the laws, regulations and policies. Mission is the protection, propagation, restoring, introduction, transplanting and management of wildlife throughout the state.
Board of Wildlife Commissioners: KEITH L. LEE, Chairman; JOHN (Andy) LEITCH, Vice-Chairman; BRUCE K. KENT; LEONTINE (Tina) NAPPE; JOHN SWEETLAND; STEVEN BOIES
Director: WILLIAM A. MOLINI
Deputy Director: TERRY R. CRAWFORTH
Chief of Administrative Services: JAMES P. WENNER
Chief of Game: GEORGE TSUKAMOTO
Chief of Fisheries: PAT COFFIN
Chief of Enforcement: Vacant
Chief of Conservation Education: DAVID K. RICE
Chief of Habitat: ROBERT McQUIVEY
Regional Supervisors:
Region I: RICHARD T. HEAP, 380 W. B St., Fallon 89406 (423-3171)
Region II: LARRY BARNGROVER, 1375 Mt. City Highway, Elko 89801 (738-5332)
Region III: JOHN A. DONALDSON, 4747 W. Vegas Dr., Las Vegas 89108 (486-5127); Mail Address: State of Nevada, Mail Room Complex, Las Vegas 89158

STATE EXTENSION SERVICE
Associate Director of Extension Service: DR. ELWOOD MILLER
Extension Range Specialists: DR. WAYNE BURKHARDT; DR. SHERMAN SWANSON, Department of Range, Wildlife and Forestry, University of Nevada, 1000 Valley Rd., Reno 89512 (702, 784-4055)

CITIZENS' GROUPS

 NEVADA WILDLIFE FEDERATION, P.O.Box 71238, Reno 89570 (702, 825-5158)
A representative statewide organization, affiliated with the National Wildlife Federation, primarily devoted to the wise use, conservation, aesthetic appreciation, and restoration of wildlife and other natural resources.
President: PAULA J. DEL GIUDICE, P.O. Box 2783, Elko 89801 (702, 738-9709)
Secretary/Treasurer: GALE DuPREE, 216 E. Hampton Dr., Carson City 89701 (702, 887-7204)
Affiliate Representative: FRED E. WRIGHT, 1122 Greenbrae Dr., Sparks 89431 (702, 358-2206)
Alternate: PAULA J. DEL GIUDICE
Publication: Western Sportsmen
Editor: CHARLIE CRUNDEN, 5517 Heron Ave., Las Vegas 89107 (702, 870-1502)

NEVADA ASSOCIATION OF CONSERVATION DISTRICTS
President: JOE SICKING, 9475 Pasture Rd., Fallon 89406
Vice-President: STUART HARRINGTON, Rt. 1, Box 96-A, Lovelock 89419
Secretary-Treasurer: MORENA HEISER, 111 Sheckler Rd., Fallon 89406

WILDLIFE SOCIETY NEVADA CHAPTER
President: ROBERT J. TURNER, 4804 San Sebastian Ave., Las Vegas 89121 (702, 486-5127)
President-Elect: DONNA WITHERS, 6600 Wild Horse Rd., Las Vegas 89108 (486-5127)
Secretary-Treasurer: KENNETH WILKINSON, c/o Gallagher Hatchery, Ruby Valley 89833 (779-2231)

NEW HAMPSHIRE

GOVERNMENT AGENCIES

GOVERNOR: JUDD GREGG, Governor of New Hampshire, State House, Room 208, Concord 03301 (603, 271-2121)

COUNCIL ON RESOURCES AND DEVELOPMENT, c/o Office of State Planning, 2½ Beacon St., Concord 03301 (603, 271-2155)
The ten members on the council represent the state's development and resource agencies. The council conducts studies and presents recommendations concerning problems in the fields of environmental protection, natural resources and growth management; consults with, negotiates with, and obtains information from other state and federal agencies; offers guidance and recommendations to the Governor and council or the General Court; recommends disposition or lease of state-owned surplus real property; resolves differences or conflicts concerning development, resource management, and the implementation of the state tourism policy. Established: 1963.
Chairman: JOHN E. DABULIEWICZ, Director

DEPARTMENT OF AGRICULTURE, Caller Box 2042, Concord 03302-2042
Commissioner: STEPHEN H. TAYLOR (603, 271-3551)

DEPARTMENT OF ENVIRONMENTAL SERVICES, Waste Management Division, Health and Human Services Bldg., #8518, 6 Hazen Dr., Concord 03301 (603, 271-3503) The DES is a result of a legislatively mandated reorganization of state environmental agencies. Consists of four divisions as follows: Water Supply and Pollution Control Division; Waste Management Division; Water Resources Division; and Air Resources Division. Established: 1987.
Commissioner: ALDEN H. HOWARD
Assistant Commissioner: GEORGE A. MOLLINEAUX

Water Resources Division 64 North Main St., P.O. Box 2008, Concord 03301 (603, 271-3406)
Director: DELBERT F. DOWNING
Chairman: DELBERT F. DOWNING, Wetland Board; Water Resources Council; Water Well Board; Water Resources Bureau; Water Management Bureau; Maintenance Bureau

DEPARTMENT OF RESOURCES AND ECONOMIC DEVELOPMENT, P.O. Box 856, 105 Loudon Rd., Concord 03301
Advisory Commission: ZVI COHEN, Recreation; RALPH LABNON, Chairman, Public Relations; RICHARD HAMILTON; DAVID NOYES, Forestry; RICHARD BEAUDET, Agriculture
Commissioner: GEORGE C. JONES (603, 271-2411)
Director, Division of Forests and Lands: JOHN SARGENT (271-2214)
Director, Division of Economic Development: JOHN BURNS (271-2341)
Director, Division of Parks: WILBUR LA PAGE (271-3254)
Chief, Bureau of Off-Highway Recreational Vehicles: DOUGLAS EOUTE

Forest Fire Control
Chief, Fire Control Section: ROBERT NELSON (271-2217)
Forest Management Section, Chief: THOMAS MINER (271-3456)
State Forest Nursery Foreman: DANIEL DeHART (796-2323)
Forest Information and Planning Chief: J.B. CULLEN (271-3456)
Chief, Land Management Section: JAMES F. CARTER (271-3456)
Forest Insect and Disease Control: ALFRED C. AVERY, Chief (271-3457)
Urban Forester, Urban Forestry Center, Portsmouth: MARY K. REYNOLDS (431-6774)

FISH AND GAME DEPARTMENT, 2 Hazen Dr., Concord 03301 (603, 271-3421)
Commission Members: FRANK G. CLARK; GORDON FREEMAN, Secretary; JOHN R. MONSON, Chairman; ELLIS HATCH, JR.; GORDON WILDER; RICHARD PATCH; RICHARD PINNEY; JOSEPH OTTOLINI; JAMES C. PAINE, B.S. DVM, Vice-Chairman; MICHAEL BLAISDELL; JOHN R. CLARK
Executive Director: DONALD A. NORMANDEAU, Ph.D.
Chief, Inland and Marine Fisheries Division: DUNCAN McGINNIS
Chief, Game Management and Research Division: HOWARD C. NOWELL, JR.
Chief, Law Enforcement Division: HENRY P. MOCK
Chief, Maintenance and Construction Division: JOHN S. BOWYER, JR.
Chief, Marine Fisheries Division: JOHN NELSON
Business Administrator IV: LOIS SIMPSON
Business Administrator II: CHARLES BROOWN
Publication: *Fish and Game HIGHLIGHTS*
Editor/Program Planner III: DIXIE SHERROD

SEA GRANT PROGRAM
Director, UNH/UM Joint Sea Grant College Program: DR. JAY GRIMES, University of New Hampshire, Durham 03824 (603, 862-2996)
Project Leader, Sea Grant Extension Program: BRIAN DOYLE, NEC Admin. Bldg., University of New Hampshire, Durham 03824 (862-3460)
Communication and Information Coordinator: STEVE ADAMS, Marine Program Bldg., University of New Hampshire, Durham 03824 (862-2996)

STATE CONSERVATION COMMITTEE, Department of Agriculture, Caller Box 2042, Concord 03302-2042 (603, 271-3576)
The SCS consists of nine members. Four members represent state agencies and five are appointed. Duties are to offer assistance to supervisors of the ten conservation districts, to keep supervisors of each district informed of other district activities, and coordinate activities of the several districts. Established: 1945.
Members: DR. PETER HORNE, Director, Extension Service, University of New Hampshire (862-1520); DR. THOMAS FAIRCHILD, Director, Experiment Station, University of New Hampshire (862-1450); STEPHEN H. TAYLOR, Commissioner, Department of Agriculture; JOHN SARGENT, Director, Division of Forests and Lands Representing on the SCC; Commissioner, Department of Resources and Economic Development (271-2214); DAN TUTTLE; AUGUSE GOMES; STANLEY RASTALLIS; ROBERT PIERCE
Chairman: ROBERT M. BODWELL, Box 93, Sanbornton 03269 (603, 286-4986)

STATE EXTENSION SERVICES
Director of Extension Service: DR. PETER J. HORNE, University of New Hampshire, Taylor Hall, Durham 03824 (603, 862-1520)
Chairman, Department of Forest Resources: DR. HAROLD HOCKER, James Hall, University of New Hampshire, Durham 03824 (862-1020)
Extension Forester: STANLEY W. KNOWLES, Pettee Hall, University of New Hampshire, Durham 03824 (862-1029)
County Forest Management Supervisor: ROBERT L. EDMONDS, Pettee Hall, University of New Hampshire, Durham 03824 (862-1029)
Extension Wildlife Specialist: CHARLES A. BRIDGES, Pettee Hall, University of New Hampshire, Durham 03824 (862-1065)

CITIZENS' GROUPS

NEW HAMPSHIRE WILDLIFE FEDERATION, INC., *54 Portsmouth St., Box 239, Concord 03301 (603, 224-5953)*
A representative statewide organization, affiliated with the National Wildlife Federation, primarily devoted to the wise use, conservation, aesthetic appreciation, and restoration of wildlife and other natural resources.
President: TOM DECOSTER, 49 Birkdale, Bedford 03102 (668-4353)
Executive Director: Vacant
Affiliate Representative: TOM DECOSTER
Alternate: ERICK SAWTELLE, Lee Hook Rd., NewMarket 03857 (659-2627)
Publication: New Hampshire Wildlife
Editor: Vacant

AMERICAN BASS ASSOCIATION OF NEW HAMPSHIRE, THE
An organization of the individual members and bass fishing clubs, affiliated with the American Bass Association, Inc., dedicated to

protecting and enhancing the state's fishery resources; to promote the sport of bass fishing; and to teach youngsters the fun of fishing and instill in them an appreciation of the life-giving waters of America.
President: GEORGE BALLINGALL, 100 Holly Ave., Manchester 03103 (603, 668-5982)

AUDUBON SOCIETY OF NEW HAMPSHIRE, 3 Silk Farm Rd., P.O. Box 528B, Concord 03302-0516 (603, 224-9909)
Independent, statewide, nonprofit organization dedicated to the preservation, understanding and appreciation of New Hampshire's wildlife and other natural resources. Membership: 7,500. Founded: 1914.
President: ELIZABETH JANEWAY, RFD 1, Blackwater Rd., Contoocook 03229
Secretary: NORA TUTHILL, 18 Hobbs Rd., Kensington 03833
Treasurer: ARTHUR W. MUDGE, 14 South Main St., Box 231, Hanover 03755
Executive Director: D. DICKINSON HENRY, JR.
Education Director: JEFFREY SCHWARTZ
Director, Wildlife Programs: CAROL R. FOSS
Director, Environmental Affairs: JACQUELYN L. TUXILL
Director, Sanctuaries: STEPHEN R. WALKER
Director, Loon Preservation Committee: JEFFREY S. FAIR
Publications: *NH Audubon; NH Bird Records; Audubon Alert*
Editor: TOM McMILLAN

NEW HAMPSHIRE ASSOCIATION OF CONSERVATION COMMISSIONS, 54 Portsmouth St., Concord 03301 (603, 224-7867)
To provide technical assistance, regional workshops, field trips, and better communications among the state's 188 municipal conservation commissions as established by law. Membership: 188 towns and cities in NH and 1,176 conservation commissioners. Founded: 1970.
President: CYNTHIA M. IVEY, Waterville Valley
Vice-President: MARY JANE GRASTY, New Ipswich
Executive Director: MARJORY M. SWOPE
Secretary: GEORGE JONES III, Salem
Publications: *NH Conservation News; Handbook;* Factsheets; *Guide to the Designation of Prime Wetlands in New Hampshire;* Legislative Updates; Notices of Public Hearings
Editor: MARJORY M. SWOPE

NEW HAMPSHIRE ASSOCIATION OF CONSERVATION DISTRICTS
President: DAVID THOMPSON, LeBrecque St., Lincoln 03251 (603, 745-8821)
Vice-President: JOHN HODSDON, R.F.D. #2, Meredith 03253 (279-6126)
Secretary-Treasurer: STANLEY GRIMES, Buck St., Pembroke 03275 (485-9326)

NEW HAMPSHIRE BASS CHAPTER FEDERATION
An organization of Bassmaster Chapters, affiliated with the Bass Anglers Sportsman Society, organized to fight pollution, assist state and national conservation agencies in their efforts to teach the young people of our country good conservation practices. Dedicated to the realistic conservation of our water resources.
President: Vacant

NEW HAMPSHIRE NATURAL RESOURCES FORUM, Sky Farm, Box 341, Charlestown 03603
Shares information and strategies, explores and forms coalitions for specific projects, and fosters cohesiveness within the environmental community. Its members are both individuals and organizations who share a commitment for maintaining and improving the quality of New Hampshire's natural environment. Founded: 1983.
Coordinator: SHARON F. FRANCIS (603, 826-5865)
Chairman: STEPHEN BLACKMER
Vice-Chairman: SUSAN PASCHELL
Publications: *How Clean New Hampshire's Waters,* A study of the Clean Water Act, accomplishments and unmet needs; *Echoes in New Hampshire,* The Impact of Federal Energy Policy; *Conference Proceedings: Acid Rain '84; Tools for Community Water Supply Protection*

NEW HAMPSHIRE TIMBERLAND OWNERS ASSOCIATION, 54 Portsmouth St., Concord 03301 (603, 224-9699)
A statewide organization affiliated with the National Woodland Owners Association, dedicated to the promotion of wise forest management and the protection of forestry interests in New Hampshire. Membership: 1,150. Founded: 1911.
President: PHIL BRYCE
Executive Director: CHARLES R. NIEBLING
Publication: *TIMBER CRIER*
Editor: CHARLES R. NIEBLING

SEACOAST ANTI-POLLUTION LEAGUE, 5 Market St., Portsmouth 03801 (603, 431-5089)
To promote the wise use of natural resources of the seacoast region and to alert and educate the community and relevant government agencies of threats to the environment. The league has been particularly active as a legal intervenor in the Seabrook nuclear plant licensing proceedings. Membership: 800. Founded: 1969.
President: CHARLES PRATT
Vice-President: VIRGINIA CARL
Field Director: JANE DOUGHTY
Treasurer: JUNE DAIGNEAULT
Secretary: LINDA HASKINS
Publication: *SAPL News*

SOCIETY FOR THE PROTECTION OF NEW HAMPSHIRE FORESTS, 54 Portsmouth St., Concord 03301-5486 (603, 224-9945)
A voluntary, nonprofit organization dedicated to promoting the wise use of the renewable natural resources of New Hampshire. Membership: 9,000. Organized: 1901.
Chairman of the Board: HAROLD JANEWAY
President and Forester: PAUL O. BOFINGER
Secretary: JANET NIXON
Director of Policy: STEVE BLACKMER
Director of Finance and Administration: DAVID FREEMAN-WOOLPERT
Director of Forestry and Lands Stewardship: BRUCE A. HOVLAND
Publications: *Forest Notes; Action*
Editor: RICHARD OBER

SPACE: STATEWIDE PROGRAM OF ACTION TO CONSERVE OUR ENVIRONMENT, P.O. Box 392, Exeter 03833 (603, 778-1220)
A nonprofit organization working on its own behalf and to assist existing agencies achieve broad public support for legislation and programs which will save open space. Founded: 1968.
Chairman: PHILIP C. HEALD, Heald Rd., Wilton 03086 (878-1321)
Clerk: JOHN BARTO, Christian Mutual Bldg., 6 Loudon Rd., Concord 03301 (224-3863)
Treasurer: RICHARD KELLEY, Pow Wow River Rd., East Kingston 03827 (642-5566)
Public Affairs & Legislative Counsel: DALE L. ELLISON (778-1220)
Publication: *SPACE Newsletter, News from SPACE*

TROUT UNLIMITED NEW HAMPSHIRE COUNCIL
A statewide council with six chapters working for the protection and enhancement of the coldwater fishery resource.
Chairman and National Director: Vacant

NEW JERSEY

GOVERNMENT AGENCIES

GOVERNOR: THOMAS H. KEAN, Governor of New Jersey, State House, Office of the Governor, CN-001, Trenton 08625 (609, 292-6000)

DEPARTMENT OF AGRICULTURE, CN 330, Trenton 08625
Secretary: ARTHUR R. BROWN, JR.
Assistant Secretary of Agriculture: SAMUEL GARRISON (292-5530)
Executive Assistant to the Secretary: SHARON AINSWORTH (633-7794)
Director, Division of Rural Resources: RICHARD D. CHUMNEY (609, 292-5532)
Coordinator, Soil and Water Conservation Services: SAMUEL R. RACE (292-5540)
Director, Division of Administration: JOHN J. GALLAGHER, JR. (292-6931)
Director, Division of Animal Health: DR. SIDNEY R. NUSBAUM (292-3965)
Director, Division of Dairy Industry: WOODSON W. MOFFETT, JR. (292-5648)
Director, Division of Markets: JOHN J. REPKO (292-5536)
Director, Division of Plant Industry: WILLIAM W. METTERHOUSE (292-5441)
Director, Division of Regulatory Services: ROBERT C. FRINGER (292-5575)
Executive Director, State Agriculture Development Committee: DONALD D. APPLEGATE (984-2504)

DEPARTMENT OF ENVIRONMENTAL PROTECTION, 401 E. State St., CN 402, Trenton 08625 (609, 292-2885)
Commissioner (Acting): CHRISTOPHER J. DAGGETT
Deputy Commissioner: MICHAEL F. CATANIA
Assistant Commissioner for Regulatory and Governmental Affairs: ARTHUR R. KONDRUP (292-9289)
Assistant Commissioner for Management and Budget: DONALD A. DEIESU (292-2916)
Assistant Commissioner for Natural Resources: HELEN FENSKE (292-3541)
Office of Science and Research: ROBERT TUCKER, Director (984-6070)
Public Information Officer: JAMES M. STAPLES (292-2994)
Planning Group Director: LAWRENCE SCHMIDT (292-2662)

Division of Fish, Game, and Wildlife, CN 400, Trenton 08625 (292-2965)
Director: GEORGE P. HOWARD (292-9410)
Administrator of Marine Fisheries: BRUCE FREEMAN (292-1056)
Chief, Bureau of Marine Fisheries: BRUCE HALGREN (441-3289)
Chief, Bureau of Freshwater Fisheries: BRUCE PYLE (292-8642)
Chief, Bureau of Shellfisheries: GALE CRITCHLOW (292-1055)
Program Manager, Endangered and Nongame Species Program: JO ANN FRIER-MURZA (292-9101)
Chief, Law Enforcement: STEVEN HERB (292-9430)

Chief, Bureau of Wildlife Management: FRED CARLSON (292-6685)

Division of Coastal Resources, CN 401, Trenton 08625 (609, 292-2795)
Director: JOHN R. WEINGART
Chief, Bureau of Administration: HOWARD WOLF (609, 292-7915)
Chief, Bureau of Coastal Engineering and Construction: BERNARD J. MOORE (201, 286-6447)
Chief, Bureau of Tidelands: JAMES JOHNSON (609, 292-2573)

Division of Water Resources, CN 29, Trenton 08625
Director: GEORGE McCANN (609, 292-1637)

Division of Solid Waste Management, CN 414, Trenton 08628 (609, 292-0048)
Director: JOHN Z. CZAPOR

Division of Parks and Forestry, CN 404, Trenton 08625 (609, 292-2733)
Director: GREGORY A. MARSHALL
Deputy Director: CARL R. NORDSTROM (292-2773)
Assistant Director, State Parks Service: FRANK F. GUIDOTTI (292-2772)
Assistant Director, State Forestry Services and State Forester: OLIN WHITE (292-2520)
Chief, Bureau of Forest Fire Management and State Firewarden: DAVID HARRISON (292-2977)
Chief, Bureau of Forest Management: GEORGE H. PIERSON (292-2520)
Administrator, Office of New Jersey Heritage: NANCY ZERBE (292-2023)

Division of Hazardous Waste Management
Director: JOHN J. TRELA (609, 633-1408)

Division of Hazardous Site Mitigation
Director: ANTHONY J. FARRO (609, 984-2902)

Green Acres and Recreation Program, CN 412, Trenton 08625
Administrator: BONNIE HAMMERSTEDT (609, 588-3450)
Deputy Administrator: DENNIS DAVIDSON (588-3450)
Chief, Legal Services: ROBERT L. SOLAN (588-3461)
Chief, Outdoor Recreation Planning: ROBERT STOKES (588-3492)
Director, Division of Personnel: BARBARA GRABOWSKI (292-1898)
Director, Financial Management, Planning and General Services: RONALD S. TUMINSKI (292-9230)
Director, Environmental Awareness and Education Program: BEVERLY FEDORKA (633-1317)
Publication: *New Jersey Outdoors*
Editor: STEPHEN PERRONE (292-2477)

NEW JERSEY GEOLOGICAL SURVEY, CN 029, Trenton 08625 (609, 292-1185)
Founded in 1864 to study, evaluate, and prepare maps and reports on New Jersey's resources. In addition to a geologic map and information on the mineral industry and water resources, the survey provides geologic and ground water reports, geologic and topographic maps, ground and surface water monitoring, and other resource information. Established: 1864.
State Geologist: HAIG KASABACH
Chief, Bureau of Geology and Topography: RICHARD DALTON (292-2576)

Chief, Bureau of Ground Water Resource Evaluation: WAYNE R. HUTCHINSON (984-6587)

Chief, Bureau of Monitoring Management: ROBERT RUNYON (292-0427)

Chief, Bureau of Marine Water Classification and Analysis: WILLIAM EISELE (441-3400)

NEW JERSEY PINELANDS COMMMISSION, P.O Box 7, New Lisbon 08064 (609, 894-9342)

State planning and regulatory agency with jurisdiction over land use and development in the million acre Pinelands region; 52 municipalities in the state Pinelands area must revise local master plans and zoning ordinances to incorporate standards of regional conservation plan. Established: 1979.

Chairman: RICHARD SULLIVAN

Executive Director: TERRENCE D. MOORE

Assistant Director, Planning and Management: JOHN C. STOKES

Assistant Director, Development Review and Enforcement: WILLIAM F. HARRISON

Manager, Public Programs: ROBERT BEMBRIDGE

Educational Coordinator: BETSY CARPENTER

Publications: *The Pinelander Newsletter;* A list of reports and studies is available upon request.

Editor: ROBERT BEMBRIDGE

SEA GRANT PROGRAM

Director: WILLIAM G. GORDON, New Jersey Marine Science Consortium, Ft. Hancock 07732 (201, 872-1300)

Director: ALEX WYPYSZINSKI, New Jersey Sea Grant Marine Advisory Service, P.O. Box 231, Rutgers University/Cook College, New Brunswick 08903 (932-9636)

STATE EXTENSION SERVICES

Director, Rutgers Cooperative Extension: DR. JOHN L. GERWIG, Rutgers, The State University, New Brunswick 08903 (932-9306)

Specialist in Forest Resources: DR. MARK C. VODAK, Rutgers, The State University, New Brunswick 08903 (932-8993)

Specialist in Natural Resources: Vacant

STATE SOIL CONSERVATION COMMITTEE, Department of Agriculture, CN 330, Trenton 08625 (609, 292-5540)

A unit of state government administered by the state Dept. of Agriculture. Responsible for conservation of soil resources and control and prevention of soil erosion, prevention of damage by floodwater or sediment and conservation of water for agricultural purposes. Provides direction, leadership, standards, rules, funding and administrative assistance and coordinates local district conservation programs and is interagency with 12 members. Established: 1937.

Chairman: ARTHUR R. BROWN, JR.

Executive Secretary: SAMUEL R. RACE

CITIZENS' GROUPS

NEW JERSEY STATE FEDERATION OF SPORTSMEN'S CLUBS, P.O. Box 7065, Hackettstown 07840

A representative statewide organization, affiliated with the National Wildlife Federation, primarily devoted to the wise use, conservation, aesthetic appreciation, and restoration of wildlife and other natural resources.

President: MIKE GROSSMANN, 28 Mansion Terrace, Cranford 07016 (201, 276-2311)

Executive Director: BILL HOBOKAN, 311 Church St., Hackettstown 07840 (852-0600)

Affiliate Representative: JAMES BROOKER, 114 James Ave., Cranford 07016 (H:276-3677/W:354-1050)

Alternate: MIKE GROSSMANN

Publication: NJ Federated Sportsmen

Editor: RON JACOBSEN, 25 Glenside Dr., Budd Lake 07828

AMERICAN BASS ASSOCIATION OF NEW JERSEY, THE

An organization of the individual members and bass fishing clubs, affiliated with the American Bass Association, Inc., dedicated to protecting and enhancing the state's fishery resources; to promote the sport of bass fishing; and to teach youngsters the fun of fishing and instill in them an appreciation of the life-giving waters of America.

President: GEORGE HUTCHINSON, 302 Redstone Ridge, Deptford 08096 (609, 541-7183)

ASSOCIATION OF NEW JERSEY ENVIRONMENTAL COMMISSIONS, P.O. Box 157, Mendham 07945 (201, 539-7547)

Private, nonprofit environmental organization serving the state's municipal environmental commissions, environmental organizations, and individual members by providing training programs, publications, research, reference and liaison services. Membership: 2,000. Founded: 1969.

President: CANDACE M. ASHMUN

Treasurer: CARL BLUMENTHAL

Executive Director: SALLY DUDLEY

Publication: *ANJEC Report*

NEW JERSEY AGRICULTURAL SOCIETY, CN 331, Trenton 08625 (609, 394-7766) (Annual Meeting: April 26, 1989.)

Has continually worked to improve and promote agriculture in New Jersey. The society is charitable, nonprofit and conducts numerous educational programs to inform the non-farming public of agriculture's vital role in the economy of New Jersey. Society membership: 1,100. Founded: 1781.

President: EDWARD V. LIPMAN (201, 545-0079)

Vice-President: SEN. C. WILLIAM HAINES (609, 235-0400)

Secretary-Treasurer: ARTHUR R. BROWN, JR. (609, 292-3976)

Assistant Secretary-Treasurer: JOHN I. RIGOLIZZO, JR. (609, 768-0059)

Publication: *Harbinger*

Editors: CINDY K. EFFRON; JULIA T. FIRMAN, New Jersey Department of Agriculture, CN 330, Trenton 08625

NEW JERSEY ASSOCIATION OF CONSERVATION DISTRICTS

President: JOSEPH LOMAX, P.O. Box 9, Cape May Court House 08210 (609, 465-9857)

Ist Vice-President: LEWIS DONALDSON, Airport Rd., R.D. #3, Box 71C, Hackettstown 07840 (201, 852-2054)

2nd Vice-President: ROBERT B. OSTERGAARD, 1024 Broadway, West Long Branch 07764 (201, 222-9095)

Secretary: JOHN R. TRAINO, 191 Matlack Dr., Maple Shade 08052 (609, 726-1330)

Treasurer: KENNETH ROEHRICH, 451 Schooley's Mt. Rd., Hackettstown 07840 (201, 852-5787)

NEW JERSEY AUDUBON SOCIETY, P.O. Box 125, 790 Ewing Ave., Franklin Lakes 07417 (201, 891-1211)

Fosters environmental awareness and a conservation ethic among New Jersey citizens; protects New Jersey's birds, mammals, other animals, and plants, especially endangered and threatened species;

promotes preservation of New Jersey's valuable natural habitats. Membership: 10,000. Organized: 1897.
President: FRED L. DITMARS
Executive Director: THOMAS J. GILMORE
Director, Cape May Bird Observatory: PAUL KERLINGER, P.O. Box 3, Cape May Point 08212 (609, 884-2736)
Director, Rancocas Nature Center: KARL ANDERSON, R.D. 1, Rancocas Rd., Mt. Holly 08060 (609, 261-2495)
Director, Scherman and Hoffman Sanctuaries: RICHARD KANE, P.O. Box 693, Bernardsville 07924 (201, 766-5787)
Director, Lorrimer Sanctuary: GORDON SCHULTZE, Director, Owl Haven Nature Center, P.O. Box 125, 790 Ewing Ave., Franklin Lakes 07417 (201, 891-2185); ALICE FORSHEE, P.O. Box 26, Tennent 07763 (201, 780-7007)
Administrative Director: ROSANNE ASERO
Publications: *New Jersey Audubon;* Records of New Jersey Birds; *Peregrine Observer* (Journal of the Cape May Bird Observatory)
Editors: PETER DUNNE, P.O. Box 693, Bernardsville 07924 (201, 766-5787); RICHARD KANE, P.O. Box 693, Bernardsville 07924

NEW JERSEY BASS CHAPTER FEDERATION

An organization of Bassmaster Chapters, affiliated with the Bass Anglers Sportsman Society, organized to fight pollution, assist state and national conservation agencies in their efforts and to teach the young people of our country good conservation practices. Dedicated to the realistic conservation of our water resources.
President: TONY GOING, 77 Kenvil Ave., Succasunna 07876 (201, 554-6010)

NEW JERSEY CONSERVATION FOUNDATION, 300 Mendham Rd., Morristown 07960 (201, 539-7540)

A nonprofit, membership organization concerned with environmental education, issues related to land use and open-space acquisition and preservation through use of its revolving land fund. Formed in 1964 from the Great Swamp Committee of the North American Wildlife Foundation. Membership: 4,000.
President: ANTOINETTE C. BENTLEY
1st Vice-President: WILLIAM D. DANA, JR.
2nd Vice-President: DONALD B. JONES
Secretary: I. LLOYD GANG
Treasurer: RIMMER DE VRIES
Counsel: CLIFFORD W. STARRETT
Executive Director: DAVID F. MOORE
Publications: *Footprints; Environmental Bulletin; Farmland Forum*
Editor: PATRICIA J. BAXTER

NEW JERSEY FORESTRY ASSOCIATION, P.O. Box 51, Chatham 07928-0051 (609, 292-2532)

A statewide organization affiliated with the National Woodland Owners Association, Inc., formed to encourage the scientific management and perpetuation of woodlands in New Jersey. Membership: 400. Founded: 1975.
President: RICHARD WEST
Publication: *NJFA NEWSLETTER*
Editor: RON SHEAY

TROUT UNLIMITED NEW JERSEY COUNCIL

A statewide council with nine chapters for the protection and enhancement of the coldwater fishery resource.
Chairman: JIM WILCOX, Box 309, Oldwick 08858 (201, 236-9425)
National Director: JOHN MENZEL, 8 Suttie Ave., Piscataway 08854 (201, 463-0634)

WILDLIFE SOCIETY NEW JERSEY CHAPTER

President: MIRIAM DUNNE, R.D. 1, Box 288A, Belvidere 07823 (201, 637-4125)
Secretary: KATHLEEN CLARK, 222-A Hand Ave., Cape May Courthouse 08210 (609, 884-7550)
Treasurer: CINDY KEUNSTNER, 516 Newark Ave., Piscataway 08854 (609, 259-3346)

NEW MEXICO

GOVERNMENT AGENCIES

GOVERNOR: GARREY CARRUTHERS, Governor of New Mexico, State Capitol, Santa Fe 87503 (505, 827-3000)

DEPARTMENT OF AGRICULTURE, P.O. Box 30005, Dept. 3189, Las Cruces 88003-0005
Organized in 1955 to protect state's agriculture from importation of plant diseases and insects and help control those that gain entrance; to ensure products offered for sale meet quality standards as advertised and labeled; maintain inspection of agricultural products for interstate shipping; laboratory analyses of animal diseases and deaths on fee basis; promote state agricultural commodities; provide market news; conduct consumer service activities designated by law.
Office of the Director and Secretary: FRANK A. DUBOIS, Director and Secretary of Agriculture (505, 646-3007)
Head of Public Relations: LANA DICKSON (646-2804)
General Services Division: DR. CHARLES H. GREENE, Division Director (646-5340)
    State Chemist Laboratory: RICK JANECKA, State Chemist (646-3318)
    State Seed Laboratory: TERRY TURNER, State Seed Analyst (646-3407)
Agricultural and Environmental Services Division: BARRY PATTERSON, Division Director (646-3208)
Agricultural Programs and Resources Division: RONALD J. WHITE, Division Director (646-2642)
Marketing and Development Division: ROBERT TOBERMAN, Division Director (646-4929)
Standards and Consumer Services Division: FRED GERK, Division Director (646-1616)
Veterinary Diagnostic Services: DR. CLAIR HIBBS, Director (841-2576)
Publications: *Biennial Report; New Mexico Agricultural Statistics; New Mexico Agricultural Export Directory; Agricultural Trade in the Border Region—Structure of Government Offices; Temperature and Precipitation Probabilities, Growing Season Data, Degree Day Data and Design Temperatures*

ENERGY, MINERALS, AND NATURAL RESOURCES DEPARTMENT, Villagra Bldg., Santa Fe 87503 (505, 827-7834)

Provides for the preservation, development and management of the energy, minerals, and natural resources of New Mexico for the use, enjoyment, benefit, and security of its people.
Cabinet Secretary: TOM BAHR

Forestry Division, Villagra Building, P.O. Box 2167, Santa Fe 87503 (505, 827-5830)
Provides management and protection of New Mexico's renewable forest, rangeland, soil and water resources through professional forest, pest, fire, and land management; provides law enforcement

and administration, public education in conservation, and supports to enhance the environment and quality of resources to protect jobs, and maintain social and economic benefits.
State Forester: WILLIAM CHAPEL

Park and Recreation, Villagra Building, P.O. Box 1147, Santa Fe 87503 (505, 827-7465)
Provides and cares for the recreational resources, facilities, and opportunities, and promotes user safety on recreational land and water to benefit and enrich the lives of New Mexico residents and visitors alike.
Director: ELZA (Skeeter) PAUL

Energy Conservation and Management Division, 525 Camino de los Marquez, Santa Fe 87503 (505, 827-5990)
Administers state and federally funded energy conservation and alternative energy technology programs to state agencies, political subdivisions, regional organizations, nonprofit community service agencies and New Mexico energy consumers, by providing engineering and technical assistance, informational, financial and programmatic support.
Director: KERRY BOYD

Oil Conservation Division, Land Office Building, 310 Old Santa Fe Tr., P.O. Box 2088, Santa Fe 87503 (505, 827-5800)
Regulates and sets standards for operations related to the drilling and production of crude oil, natural gas and geothermal resources and promotes the development and conservation of these resources while ensuring the prevention of waste and protection. Care for the prevention of loss and contamination of freshwater supplies.
Director: BILL LeMAY

Mining and Minerals Division, 525 Camino de los Marquez, Santa Fe 87503 (505, 827-5970)
Provides for the study, development, and optimun production of the mineral and energy resources within the state, the reduction of hazards associated with these processes consistent with the conservation of these resources, the protection of public health, safety and the environment, and the economic well-being of the citizens.
Director: ERLING BROSTUEN

Administrative Services Division, 525 Camino de los Marquez, Santa Fe 87503 (505, 827-5925)
Provides clerical, recordkeeping, and administrative support to the department in the areas of personnel, budget, procurement and contracting, and administration of federal and state grants.
Director: GLORIA LITHGOW

ENVIRONMENTAL IMPROVEMENT DIVISION, P.O. Box 968, Santa Fe 87504-0968
To ensure an environment that in the greatest possible measure will confer optimum health, safety, comfort, and economic and social well-being on its inhabitants; will protect this generation, as well as those yet unborn, from health threats posed by the environment; and will maximize the economic and cultural benefits of a healthy people.
Director: MICHAEL J. BURKHART (505, 827-2850)
Community Services Bureau: BENITO GARCIA
Occupational Health and Safety Bureau: SAM ROGERS, Chief (827-2879)
Special Waste Bureau: NEIL WEBER, Chief (827-2939)
Air Quality Bureau: CUBIA CLAYTON (827-0042)
Program Support Bureau: PHIL MARTINEZ, Chief (827-2843)

Surface Water Quality Bureau: KATHLEEN SISNEROS, Chief (827-2792)
Ground Water Bureau: STUART CASTLE, Chief (Acting) (827-2778)
District Managers: TITO MADRID, District I (841-6580); MICHAEL BROWN, District II (473-3473); KEN SMITH, District III (524-6300); GARY McCASLIN, District IV (624-6046)

NEW MEXICO GAME AND FISH DEPARTMENT, Villagra Building, Santa Fe 87503 (505, 827-7899)
The State Game Commission and the Game and Fish Department are administratively attached to the Natural Resources Department. The authority of the State Game Commission is to develop policy for the Game and Fish Department.
Director: BILL MONTOYA
Assistant Directors: RICHARD McCLESKEY; WAIN EVANS
Secretary: TOM BAHR
Division Chiefs: DAN SUTCLIFFE, Game Management (Ext. 7885); TOM MOODY, Fish Management (Ext. 7905); JUDE GONZALES, Business Management (Ext. 7920); JIM VAUGHT, Field Operations (Ext. 7934); GERALD MARACCHINI, Public Affairs (Ext. 7911); DICK BROWN, Special Services (Ext. 7882)
Area Offices: Albuquerque, 3700 Osuna NE, Suite 611, Albuquerque 87109 (841-8881); Las Cruces, 401 North 17th St., Suite 4, Las Cruces 88005 (524-6090); Raton, York Canyon Rd., Box 1145, Raton 87740 (445-2311); Roswell, 1912 West 2nd St., Roswell 88201 (624-6135)
State Game Commission: GERALD MAESTAS, Chairman, Espanola; CHRISTINE DiGREGORIO, Gallup; DR. THOMAS P. ARVAS, Albuquerque; RICHARD ALLGOOD, Silver City; BOB JONES, Dell City, TX
Publication: *New Mexico Wildlife*
Editor: JEFF PEDERSON (Ext. 7916)

STATE BUREAU OF MINES AND MINERAL RESOURCES, Campus Station, Socorro 87801 (505, 835-5420)
Charged with investigation and reporting on all types of mineral resources and the geology of the state; responsible for conducting applied research on all types of mineral deposits for the purpose of finding, increasing production, utilization, and conservation of New Mexico's minerals. Created: 1927.
Director: FRANK E. KOTTLOWSKI
Environmental Geologists: JOHN W. HAWLEY; DAVID W. LOVE;
Publications: Bulletins; Circulars; Memoirs; Geologic Maps; New Mexico Geology
Editor: CAROL HJELLMING

STATE ENGINEER/INTERSTATE STREAM COMMISSION, Bataan Memorial Bldg., Santa Fe 87503 (505, 827-6160)
Administration, development, protection, and conservation of the water resources of the state of New Mexico.
State Engineer: S.E. REYNOLDS
General Counsel, Legal Services Division: PETER THOMAS WHITE
Chief, Technical Division: ELUID L. MARTINEZ
Chief, Water Rights Division: DAVID N. STONE
Interstate Stream Engineer: PHILIP B. MUTZ
Interstate Stream Commission Members: S.E. REYNOLDS, Secretary, Santa Fe; ALBERT E. UTTON, Chairman, Albuquerque; J. PHELPS WHITE III, Roswell; GEORGE BRANTLEY, Carlsbad; TRACY SEIDMAN, Wagon Mound; RICHARD C. JOHNSON, Silver City; SAMMIE SINGH, La Mesa; PETER A. CASADOS, El Guique; JACK D. COOK, Farmington

STATE EXTENSION SERVICES
Chief Administrative Officer: JOHN C. OWENS, New Mexico State University, Las Cruces 88003 (505, 646-3748)

Associate Dean and Director: ROBERT GILLILAND, New Mexico State University, Las Cruces 88003 (646-3015)

Extension Program Director: JERRY SCHICKEDANZ, New Mexico State University, Las Cruces 88003 (646-1154)

Extension Range Management Specialist: CHRIS ALLISON, Box 3-I, New Mexico State University, Las Cruces 88003 (646-1944)

Extension Wildlife Management Specialist: JAMES KNIGHT, Box 4901, New Mexico State University, Las Cruces 88003 (646-1164)

Extension Livestock Specialist: RON PARKER, Box 3AE, New Mexico State University, Las Cruces 88003 (646-1709)

Extension Entomologist: MIKE ENGLISH, Box 3AE, New Mexico State University, Las Cruces 88003 (646-2546)

CITIZENS' GROUPS

NEW MEXICO WILDLIFE FEDERATION, 3240-D Juan Tabo NE, Suite 10, Albuquerque 87111 (505, 299-5404)

A representative statewide organization, affiliated with the National Wildlife Federation, primarily devoted to the wise use, conservation, aesthetic appreciation, and restoration of wildlife and other natural resources.

President: FRED GROSS, JR., 9 La Rosa, White Rock 87544 (672-9151)

Office Manager: MARY REED

Affiliate Representative: BILL REED, P.O. Box 35, Sandia Park 87047 (281-3996)

Alternate: FRED GROSS, JR.

Publication: *New Mexico Outdoor Reporter*

Editor: MARY REED

NEW MEXICO ASSOCIATION OF SOIL AND WATER CONSERVATION DISTRICTS

President and Council Member: GRETCHEN SAMMIS, P.O. Box 227, Cimarron 87714 (505, 376-2398)

Vice-President: LOUIS OLIVER, Rt. 15, Box 925, San Lorenzo 88057 (536-9511)

Secretary: FRED ROMERO, Box 3901, Fairview Station, Espanola 87532 (753-4772)

NEW MEXICO BASS CHAPTER FEDERATION

An organization of Bassmaster Chapters, affiliated with the Bass Anglers Sportsman Society, organized to fight pollution, assist state and national conservation agencies in their efforts and to teach the young people of our nation good conservation practices. Dedicated to the realistic conservation of our water resources.

President: RON GILWORTH, Box 717, Socorro 87801 (505, 835-1140/835-1200)

TROUT UNLIMITED NEW MEXICO (Truchas Chapter)

Dedicated to the protection and enhancement of the coldwater fishery resource.

President: JOHN A. TALBOTT, P.O. Box 504, Santa Fe 87501

Contact: DONALD SPATZ, 8709 Aztec NE, Albuquerque 87111 (505, 299-0410)

National Director: RALPH TINGLE, 711 Camino Del Monte Sol, Santa Fe 87501

WILDLIFE SOCIETY NEW MEXICO CHAPTER

President: DONALD DELORENZO, 1210 Morning Dr., Santa Fe 87505 (505, 988-6926)

Vice-President: LEE OTTENI, 4113 Cherrydale Ct., NW, Albuquerque 87107 (842-3227)

Secretary-Treasurer: JAMES M. RAMAKKA, 39 Road 3118, Aztec 87410 (327-5344)

NEW YORK

GOVERNMENT AGENCIES

GOVERNOR: MARIO M. CUOMO, Governor of New York, State Capitol, Albany 12224 (518, 474-8390)

ADIRONDACK PARK AGENCY, P.O. Box 99, Ray Brook 12977 (518, 891-4050)

Created by state law in 1971 and charged with developing a State Land Master Plan for public land and a Private Land Use and Development Plan for private land within the six million acre Adirondack Park. Also, the agency administers the state's Wild Scenic and Recreational Rivers System Act and the Freshwater Wetlands Act within the park. The APA's two Adirondack Park Interpretive Centers (nature education centers) are scheduled to open at Paul Smiths and Newcomb Memorial Day Weekend, 1989. The agency's governing board consists of 11 members.

Chairman: HERMAN F. COLE, JR.

Executive Director: ROBERT C. GLENNON

Counsel: Vacant

Director, Planning: JOHN BANTA

Director, Regulatory Programs: WILLIAM J. CURRAN

Director, Adirondack Park Interpretive Programs: EDMUND E. LYNCH

Publications: *Newsline;* publications list available upon request.

Editor: LAURA M. VISCOME

DEPARTMENT OF AGRICULTURE AND MARKETS, 1 Winners Cir., Capital Plaza, Albany 12235 (518, 457-3880)

Promotes and regulates production, manufacturing, marketing, storing, and distribution of food. Supervises quality of plant materials, health of animals, and regulates dogs. Also, represents agricultural interests before NY Public Service Commission on siting of transmission lines and power plants. Founded in 1884 as the Dairy Commission.

Commissioner: DONALD S. BUTCHER

Director, Division of Animal Industry: DR. BRUCE WIDGER

Director, Division of Plant Industry: RONALD BARRETT; ROBERT J. MUNGARI

Division of Agricultural Support Services: KIM T. BLOT

Publication: *Ag-Line*

DEPARTMENT OF ENVIRONMENTAL CONSERVATION, 50 Wolf Rd., Albany 12233

Commissioner: THOMAS C. JORLING (518, 457-3446)

Assistant to the Commissioner: SUSAN L. BARBARISI (457-3446)

Executive Deputy Commissioner: LANGDON MARSH (457-6804)

Special Assistant to the Executive Deputy Commissioner: DEBRA ZIAMANDANIS (485-8934)

Deputy Commissioner and General Counsel: MARC GERSTMAN (457-4415)

Deputy Commissioner, Administration: RICHARD TORKELSON (457-6533)

Deputy Commissioner, Natural Resources: Vacant (457-6934)

Deputy Commissioner, Environmental Quality: DR. ROBERT DARRYL BANKS (457-5768)

Deputy Commissioner, Hazardous Waste: EDWARD O. SULLIVAN (457-1415)

Assistant Commissioner for Fish, Wildlife and Marine Resources: HERBERT E. DOIG (457-7435)

Assistant Commissioner for Public Affairs: MADELINE J. LEWIS (457-2390)

Assistant Commissioner for Human Resources and Affirmative Action: ELROI E. BAUMANN (457-7417)

Assistant Commissioner: ROBERT F. CROSS (457-6557)

Assistant Commissioner for Hearings: ROBERT FELLER (457-3468)

Special Assistants to the Commissioner: J. WINTHROP ALDRICH (457-6558); DR. ROBERTA WEISBROD (718, 482-4949); PETER DALTON (457-6610); ANNETTE VALENTI (457-9103); WILLIAM HANLON (457-2390); ELIZABETH POHANKA (457-3785)

Director of Land Resources Planning: CHARLES MORRISON (457-7433)

Deputy Counsel: JANICE CORR (457-4415)

Director, Division of Legal Affairs: Vacant (457-6724)

Chief, Bureau of Environmental Quality (Legal): MITCHELL GOROSKI (457-6695)

Chief, Bureau of Natural Resources (Legal): LARRY VERNON (457-6695)

Chief, Corporate Bureau: PHILIP WARDWELL (457-6695)

Chief, Legislation and Federal Liaison Unit: SUSAN WEBER (457-6696)

Director (Acting), Division of Environment Enforcement: DAVID MARKELL (457-4346)

Director, Law Enforcement: GEORGE FIRTH (457-5681)

Assistant Director, Law Enforcement: JOSEPH LYNCH (457-5680)

Assistant Director, Environmental Conservation Investigations: D. WAYNE BREWER (457-1002)

Director, Division of Regulatory Affairs: LOU CONCRA (457-7424)

Bureau of Energy: RONALD HARVEY (457-5915)

Bureau of Environmental Analysis: JEROME JENSEN (457-2224)

Bureau of Regulatory Management: GEORGE DANSKIN (457-2224)

Office of Human Resources Management and Affirmative Action:

Bureau of Personnel: JUDITH HOGUE, Director (457-3263)

Bureau of Labor Relations: WILMA DeLUCCO, Director (457-4155)

Bureau of Affirmative Action: FRANCISCO LOPEZ, Director (457-7187)

Agency Safety Director: JEAN C. EDOUARD (457-7404)

Director, Training: LINDA PARR (457-2524)

Office of Public Affairs: EDWARD S. FELDMANN, Associate Director (457-5400)

Director, Press Office: ARTHUR WOLDT (457-5400)

Public Information Officer: R.W. GRONEMAN (457-5400)

Director, Environmental Education Services: ROBERT E. BUDLIGER (457-3720)

Chief, Bureau of Audio-Visual Services: CLARK PELL (457-3678)

Chief, Bureau of Publications: MARY KADLECEK (457-2344)

Publications: *The Conservationist; Environmental Notice Bulletin; New York State Environment; Water Bulletin*

Managing Editor: JOHN DUPONT (457-5547)

Editors: ROBERT DeVILLENEUVE (457-2344); ARNOLD BAER (457-7463)

Division of Air Resources

Director (Acting): THOMAS ALLEN (518, 457-7230)

Associate Director: Vacant (457-5618)

Acid Rain Coordinator: DAVID SHAW (457-2823)

Director, Bureau of Technical Services: GERARD BLANCHARD (457-5385)

Bureau of Air Toxics: ROBERT MAJEWSKI (457-7688)

Bureau of Toxic Air Sampling: ARTHUR J. FOSSA (457-7454)

Director, Abatement Planning: EDWARD DAVIS (457-6379)

Director, Air Quality Surveillance: DONALD GOWER (457-3676)

Bureau of Impact Assessment and Meteorology: EDWARD BENNETT (457-7450)

Bureau of Source Control: JOHN DAVIS (457-5385)

Bureau of Air Research: S.T. RAO (457-3200)

Division of Hazardous Waste Remediation

Director: MICHAEL O'TOOLE (457-5861)

Division of Water

Director, Water Programs: DANIEL BAROLO (518, 457-6674)

Associate Director: SALVATORE PAGANO (457-6675)

Assistant Director: CHARLES GODDARD (457-0730)

Director, Bureau of Program Management: JACK McKEON (457-1684)

Director, Bureau of Hazardous Site Control: FRANK RICOTTA (457-8807)

Director, Bureau of Eastern Remedial Action: JOSEPH SLACK (457-4349)

Director, Bureau of Western Remedial Action: JACK WILSON (457-0414)

Director, Bureau of Construction Services: AL ROCKMORE (457-9280)

Division of Hazardous Substances Regulation

Director: N.G. KAUL (518, 457-6934)

Director, Bureau of Hazardous Wastes Facility Permitting: PAUL R. COUNTERMAN (457-9236)

Director, Bureau of Hazardous Wastes Program Development: JOHN E. LANOTTI (457-7267)

Director, Bureau of Hazardous Waste Operations: DAVID MAFRICI (457-3691)

Director, Bureau of Pesticide Management: MARILYN DuBOIS (457-7482)

Director, Bureau of Radiation: DR. PAUL MERGES (457-5915)

Division of Solid Waste

Director: NORMAN NOSENCHUCK (457-6603)

Assistant Director: DAVID H. KING (457-7111)

Chief, Bureau of Municipal Waste Permitting: DAVID R. O'TOOLE (457-2051)

Chief, Bureau of Facility Management: DAVID A. BLACKMAN (485-7732)

Chief (Acting), Bureau of Waste Reduction and Recycling: ROBERT P. McCARTY (457-7337)

Chief, Bureau of Resource Recovery: H. RICHARD KOELLING (457-7336)

Chief, Bureau of Program Resource Management: ALBERT H. MUENCH (457-2553)

Bureau of Spill Response: TOM QUINN (457-7469)

Emergency Operations: WILLIAM MINER (457-4107)

Bureau of Wastewater Facilities Operations: ARTHUR WARNER (457-5968)

Bureau of Flood Protection: JAMES KELLEY (457-3157)

Bureau of Technical Services and Research: ITALO CARCICH (457-7470)

Bureau of Wastewater Facilities Design: DANIEL HALTON (457-1067)

Bureau of Water Resources: RUSSELL MT. PLEASANT (457-1627)

Bureau of Water Quality Management: PHILIP DeGAETANO (457-3656)

Bureau of Monitoring and Assessment: PETER MACK (457-3495)

Bureau of Information and Bulk Storage: DANIEL CAMPBELL (457-7463)

Division of Construction Management
Director: WILLIAM LaROW (518, 457-3891)
Associate Director: ROBERT HAMPSTON (457-9226)
Assistant Director: FRED ESMOND (457-6252)
Bureau of Grants Administration: GEORGE WALLACE (457-3856)
Bureau of Metropolitan Projects: JAMES DEZOLT (457-9412)
Bureau of Program Management: WILLIAM STRYKER (457-3833)
Bureau of Technical Services: FRANK BOGEDAIN (457-3824)

Division of Fish and Wildlife
Director: KENNETH WICH (518, 457-5691)
Assistant Director: GERALD BARNHART (457-5691)
Chief, Bureau of Fisheries: BRUCE SHUPP (457-5420)
Chief, Bureau of Wildlife: GARY PARSONS (457-4480)
Chief, Bureau of Environmental Protection: JAMES COLQUHOUN
  (457-6178)

Division of Lands and Forests
Director: ROBERT BATHRICK (518, 457-2475)
Assistant Director: JAMES BEIL (457-2475)
Forest Resource Management Bureau: DANIEL WELLER (457-
  7370)
Real Property Services Bureau: JAMES WEST (457-7670)
Preserve Protection and Management Bureau: GARRY IVES (457-
  7433)
Forest Protection and Fire Management Bureau: EDWARD JACOBY
  (457-5740)
Land Resources Bureau: BARTON ZEH (457-7431)

Division of Marine Resources
Director: GORDON COLVIN (516, 751-7900)
Shellfisheries Bureau: PIETER VAN VOLKENBURG (751-7900)
Finfish and Crustaceans Bureau: JOHN POOLE (751-7900)
Marine Habitat Protection Bureau: KENNETH KOETZNER (751-
  7900)

Division of Mineral Resources
Director: GREGORY SOVAS (518, 457-9337)
Assistant Director: JOHN HARMON (457-9633)
Bureau of Resource Management and Development: ROBERT
  NORTON (457-9341)
Bureau of Oil and Gas Regulation: SANDRA BRENNAN (457-3682)

Division of Fiscal Management
Director: RICHARD LYNCH (518, 457-1141)
Assistant Director: WILLIAM BERNASKI (457-6341)
Assistant Director and Chief,
Bureau of Capital Projects: JOSEPH MARCY (457-6058)
Chief, Bureau of Revenue and Expenditure Accounts: WILLIAM
  AGRESTA (457-2809)
Chief, State Operations Budgeting: NANCY LUSSIER (457-7080)
Bureau of Purchasing: KEITH CALLAHAN (457-5490)
Bureau of Federal and Municipal Accounts: WILLARD WILSON
  (457-5317)

Division of Aviation
Director: VINCENT O'BRIEN (453-1807)

Division of Operations
Director: RONALD BERNHARD (518, 457-6310)
Assistant Director: Vacant (457-6310)
Recreation Bureau: FRANK FULLER (457-2500)
Electronics Bureau: WILLIAM FRENZ (457-3914)
Engineering Bureau: AL MIGNEAULT (457-1216)
Construction and Maintenance Bureau (Acting): ARTHUR STAN-
  TON (457-3559)

Office Services and Equipment Management Bureau: DAVID KEE-
GAN (457-2377)

**Division of Management Planning and Information Systems
Development**
Director: THOMAS TRACY (518, 457-6367)
Chief, Bureau of Management Planning: GRAHAM GREELEY (457-
  1148)
Chief, Bureau of Information Systems Development: THOMAS
DONOVAN (457-5724)

Regional Directors
Region 1: HAROLD BERGER, Bldg. 40, State University of New
  York, Stony Brook 11794 (516, 751-7900)
Region 2: CAROL ASH, Hunters Point Plaza, Long Island City
  11101 (718, 482-4900)
Region 3: PAUL KELLER, 21 S. Putt Corners Rd., New Paltz 12561
  (914, 255-5453)
Region 4: ELDRED RICH (Acting), 2176 Guilderland Ave., Schenec-
  tady 12306 (518, 382-0680)
Region 5: THOMAS R. MONROE, Ray Brook 12977 (518, 891-
  1370)
Region 6: THOMAS BROWN, 317 Washington St., Watertown
  13601 (315, 782-0100)
Region 7: WILLIAM KRICHBAUM, 615 Erie Boulevard West,
  Syracuse 13024-2400 (315, 426-7400)
Region 8: PETER BUSH (Acting), P.O. Box 57, Avon 14414 (716,
  226-2466)
Region 9: JOHN SPAGNOLI, 600 Delaware Ave., Buffalo 14202
  (716, 845-4560)

DEPARTMENT OF HEALTH, Tower Bldg., Empire State Plaza,
  Albany 12237
Director, Office of Public Health: LINDA RANDOLPH, M.D.
Director, Center for Environmental Health: WILLIAM M. STASIUK,
  Ph.D. (518, 458-6400)

ENVIRONMENTAL PROTECTION BUREAU, Department of Law,
  State of New York, 120 Broadway, New York City 10271
Institutes legal actions on behalf of the people of the state in cases
involving air and water pollution, protection of wildlife, and
protection of scenic and natural resources. Has responsibility for
enforcement of the Mason Law, which protects endangered species
of wildlife, as well as public nuisance actions to restrain pollution
and other environmental damage.
Assistant Attorney General in Charge: JAMES SEVINSKY (212,
  341-2451)
Environmental Engineer: PETER SKINNER (518, 474-4819)

GEOLOGICAL SURVEY, Cultural Education Center, Albany
  12230 (518, 474-5816)
It serves as a clearinghouse for information concerning bedrock
and surficial geology within the state. The survey conducts regular
mapping projects and investigations in basic, environmental, and
applied geology and publishes maps and reports of investigations.
Founded: 1836.
State Geologist and Chief Scientist: ROBERT H. FAKUNDINY
State Seismologist: WALTER MITRONOVAS (474-5817)
Oil and Gas Office Director: WILLIAM B. ROGERS (486-2020)
Engineering and Environmental Geology: ROBERT H. FICKIES
  (474-5810)

Publications: *New York State Geogram;* publications list of the New York State Geological Survey

MARINE SCIENCES RESEARCH CENTER, State University of New York, Stony Brook 11794 (516, 632-8700)

University-wide center to develop marine research, instructional programs and facilities for the State University of New York. Ongoing research projects are directed toward coastal oceanographic processes, marine environmental problems and management, and resources management. Among the center's organized units are the Living Marine Resources Institute, The Waste Management Institute, The Coastal Ocean Science, Management Alternatives Program, and the Flax Pond Laboratory.

Director (Acting): M.J. BOWMAN

Graduate Programs, Marine Environmental Sciences (M.S. degree) and Coastal Oceanography (Ph.D. degree): LAURA RICHARDSON (Ext. 8681)

Publications: *Technical Report Series; Graphical Report Series; Working Report Series; Special Report Series;* Newsletter; Collected reprints.

NEW YORK COOPERATIVE FISH AND WILDLIFE RESEARCH UNIT, Department of Natural Resources, Fernow Hall, Cornell University, Ithaca 14853 (607, 255-2839)

Primary purpose is field and laboratory research on management and conservation of a variety of fish and wildlife species, and graduate research training in fisheries and wildlife resources. Supported cooperatively by U.S. Fish and Wildlife Service, Cornell University, New York State Department of Environmental Conservation, and the Wildlife Management Institute. Wildlife Unit established: 1961. Fisheries: 1963. Combined: 1984.

Leader: DR. MILO E. RICHMOND (255-2151)

Assistant Leader, Wildlife: DR. RICHARD A. MALECKI (255-2839)

Assistant Leader, Fisheries: Vacant (255-2014)

OFFICE OF ENERGY CONSERVATION AND ENVIRONMENTAL PLANNING, New York State Dept. of Public Service, 3 Empire State Plaza, Albany 12223 (518, 474-1677)

Focal point for energy conservation and environmental matters involving the state's utilities. Evaluates, and testifies in formal proceedings on, environmental aspects of applications of the state's electric and gas utilities for certificates to build major transmission lines and major steam electric generating facilities. Regulates utility residential energy conservation program, involving home energy conservation audits and low-interest financing. Administers Electrical Conservation Investment Program which requires state's electric utilities to develop demand side management (i.e., conservation and load management) programs which defer the need to build new power plants. Established: 1970.

Director: DR. LAWRENCE DEWITT

ST. LAWRENCE-EASTERN ONTARIO COMMISSION, 317 Washington St., Watertown 13601 (315, 785-2461)

Created by the New York State Legislature in 1969 to preserve, enhance, and develop the scenic, historic, recreational and natural resources of the St. Lawrence River Valley and lands adjacent to eastern Lake Ontario. Duties include assisting units of local government in economic development of the tourism sector of the economy and in development of comprehensive land use plans. The Commission is further charged with reviewing development projects proposed within the area.

Chairmen: FRANCIS G. HEALEY; WILLIAM L. CURTIS, JR.

Secretary: PATRICIA C. MASON

Ex-Officio Members: NYS Dept. of Economic Development; NYS Dept. of Environmental Conservation; NYS Dept. of State

Executive Director: DANIEL J. PALM, Ph.D.

Legal Counsel: EDWARD H. COLE

Publication: Technical Reports

SEA GRANT PROGRAM

Director, New York Sea Grant Institute: DR. ROBERT E. MALOUF, Dutchess Hall, State University of New York, Stony Brook 11794-5001 (516, 632-6905)

Associate Director and Program Leader: DR. MICHAEL P. VOILAND, New York Sea Grant Extension Program, 12 Fernow Hall, Cornell University, Ithaca 14853-3001 (607, 255-2832)

Program Coordinator: DAVID WHITE, Sea Grant Extension Program, 52 Swetman Hall, SUNY at Oswego, Oswego 13126 (315, 341-3042)

STATE COOPERATIVE EXTENSION

Director of Cooperative Extension: DR. LUCINDA A. NOBLE, New York State College of Agriculture and Life Sciences, 103 Roberts Hall, Cornell University, Ithaca 14853-3001 (607, 255-2117)

General Fish and Wildlife, Chairman: DR. JAMES P. LASSOIE, Associate Professor, Dept. of Natural Resources, 117 Fernow Hall, Cornell University, Ithaca 14853-3001 (Ext. 2114)

Natural Resources Extension Programs and Department Extension, Leader: DR. DANIEL J. DECKER, Associate Professor, Department of Natural Resources, 124 Fernow Hall, Cornell University, Ithaca 14853-3001 (Ext. 2831)

Forest Resources and Land Use: DR. JAMES P. LASSOIE, Associate Professor, Dept. of Natural Resources, 117 Fernow Hall, Cornell University, Ithaca 14853-3001 (Ext. 2114)

STATE FISH AND WILDLIFE MANAGEMENT BOARD, Albany 12233

Membership composed of sportsmen, landowners, and local government representatives. State and regional boards assist the Department of Environmental Conservation in programs designed to improve resource management by landowners and increase public access to private lands. Established: 1958.

Chairman: ROGER H. COLE, 22 Birchwood Ln., Hartsdale 10530 (914, 761-2653)

Vice-Chairman: NEIL JOHNSON, R.D. 1, Box 249A, Mayville 14757 (716, 753-7603)

Secretary: KENNETH F. WICH, Fish and Wildlife Management Board, 50 Wolf Rd., Rm. 524, Albany 12233-4750 (518, 457-5690)

Regional Board Chairmen

Board 3: ROBERT EWALD, R.D. 1, Pinebush 12566 (914, 361-5069)

Board 4: DAVID McLEAN, Burlington Flats 13315 (607, 965-8084)

Board 5: KENNETH BURCH, R.D. #2, Granville 12832 (518, 632-5617)

Board 6: WILLIAM SMITH, Box 761, Belleville 13611 (315, 846-5017)

Board 7: GUST FREEMAN, 258 DuBois Rd., Ithaca 14850 (607, 273-2861)

Board 8: JOHN ANDREWS, R.D. #2, Box 42, Waterloo 13165 (315, 539-2820)

Board 9: JOHN LONG, Box 37, 821 Main St., Niagara Falls 14302 (716, 731-4002)

STATE OFFICE OF PARKS, RECREATION AND HISTORIC PRESERVATION, Empire State Plaza, Albany 12238 (518, 474-0456)

Operates 147 state parks, park preserves and recreational facilities, and 35 historic sites throughout the state outside of the forest preserves; preserves the state's historic heritage through the Division of Historic Preservation and administers the navigation and snowmobile laws through the Bureau of Marine and Recreational Vehicles.

Commissioner: ORIN LEHMAN

Deputy Commissioner for Administration and Fiscal Affairs: JOSEPH V. McCARTIN (474-0439)

Deputy Commissioner for Planning and Operations: IVAN VAMOS (474-0449)

Deputy Commissioner for Regional Administration: JOHN PRENDERVILLE

Assistant Commissioner for Recreation Services: GUS THOMPSON (474-0403)

Assistant Commissioner for Community and Governmental Affairs: BRIAN McLANE (474-0435)

Deputy Commissioner for Historic Preservation: JULIA STOKES (474-0468)

Executive Deputy Commissioner and Counsel: ALBERT CACCESE (474-0401)

Public Relations Officer: ROBERT J. ARNOLD (474-0447)

CITIZENS' GROUPS

NEW YORK STATE CONSERVATION COUNCIL, INC., 8 E. Main St., Ilion 13357-1899 (315, 894-3302)

A representative statewide organization, affiliated with the National Wildlife Federation, primarily devoted to the wise use, conservation, aesthetic appreciation, and restoration of wildlife and other natural resources.

President: HARRY PROBST, Rt. #1, Box 20, Ripley 14775 (716, 736-2465)

Secretary: FRANCIS E. HARTMAN, Star Route 1, Box 146, Sparrowbush 12780 (914, 856-6685)

Affiliate Representative: WILLIAM R. HILTS, 5115 Bear Rd., Sanborn 14132 (716, 731-9984)

Alternate: ROBERT A. BOICE, R.D. #2, Archer Rd., Watertown 13601 (315, 788-5868)

Publication: Conservation Council Comments

Editor: WILLIAM R. HILTS

ADIRONDACK COUNCIL, THE, P.O. Box D-2, Elizabethtown 12932 (518, 873-2240)

A nonprofit coalition of conservation organizations and individuals concerned about the future of the 6 million acre Adirondack Park. Programs include monitoring and influencing state programs in the park, helping to promote understanding of the park and the need to protect its very special character, and supporting and advancing positive programs to enhance the park and benefit its people. Founded: 1975. Individual membership: 8,000.

Chairman: KIM ELLIMAN

Vice-Chairmen: BARBARA GLASER; THOMAS D. THACHER II

Secretary: DEAN COOK

Treasurer: TIMOTHY L. BARNETT

Executive Director: CHARLES M. CLUSEN

Director, Park Protection: MICHAEL G. DiNUNZIO

Publications: *The Adirondack Council Newsletter; Let's Stop Acid Rain* (brochure); *Forever Wild* (brochure); *Adirondack Wildguide—A Natural History of The Adirondack Park* (book); *State of the Park* (Annual Report)

ADIRONDACK LAND TRUST, INC. P.O. Box D-2, Elizabethtown 12932 (518, 873-9239)

A nonprofit organization dedicated to preserving the agricultural, forest, and open space lands of northern New York state through education and the acquisition of conservation easements and other land protection devices. Founded: 1984.

Chairman: JAMES C. DAWSON, Birchwood Dr., Peru 12972 (643-9289)

Vice-Chairman: NEAL A. BROWN, Esq., 99 Park Ave., New York City 10016 (212, 818-9600)

Secretary: DANIEL P. McGOUGH, Lyons Falls Pulp and Paper Corp., Lyons Falls 13368 (315, 348-8411)

Treasurer: KIM ELLIMAN, 18 E. 74th St., New York City 10021 (212, 772-8850)

Executive Director: Vacant

Associate Director: THOMAS R. DUFFUS

Publications: *Developing a Land Conservation Strategy:* A Handbook for Land Trusts (1987)

ADIRONDACK MOUNTAIN CLUB, INC., THE, 174 Glen St., Glens Falls 12801 (518, 793-7737)

Chartered 1922 for purpose of promoting a forever wild concept for New York's Adirondack and Catskill Forest Preserve, to educate public interest in principles of conservation of natural resources, to sponsor outdoor recreation and educational programs consistent with conservation objectives, to encourage organization of local chapters of the club, to develop environmentally sound outdoor skills among recreationists, and to collect and publish information about the Adirondacks and Catskills. Membership: 10,000; twenty-seven chapters in NY, NJ, and PA.

President: JOSEPH DAWSON, 35 Lincoln Ave., Glens Falls 12801 (792-2328)

Executive Director: WALTER M. MEDWID

Associate Director: RICK STEVENS

North Country Director: JOHN JURCZYNSKI (523-3441)

Conservation Director: ROBERT LINCK

Publications: *Adirondacc Magazine; The Forest Preserve of New York State: A Handbook for Conservationists;* Guides to Adirondack Trails; Adirondack Canoe Waters, North Flow; Geology of the High Peaks Region and others; ADK hiking and canoeing guidebooks; natural history and cultural history books on the region; educational brochures series, and topographic maps.

Editor: NEAL BURDICK, 35 Woods Dr., Canton 13617

ASSOCIATION FOR THE PROTECTION OF THE ADIRONDACKS, THE, c/o Schenectady Museum, Nott Terrace Heights, Schenectady 12308 (518, 382-7890)

To protect the natural character of the state forest preserve lands as water-holding and regulating forests which serve as a home for wildlife and as wilderness recreation areas. Membership: 1,000. Organized: 1901.

Chairman: ARTHUR M. CROCKER

President: JAMES C. DAWSON, Birchwood Dr., Peru, NY 12972 (643-9289)

Vice-Presidents: BARBARA McMARTIN; PAUL SCHAEFER; WILLIAM P. DUNHAM; CLARENCE E. GALSTON; THOMAS L. COBB

Treasurer: DAVID L. NEWHOUSE

Secretary: MARYDE KING

Assistant Scretary: LYDIA M. SERRELL

Executive Director: DAVID H. GIBSON

CATSKILL CENTER FOR CONSERVATION AND DEVELOPMENT, INC., THE, Arkville 12406 (914, 586-2611)

A private, nonprofit organization founded in the belief that the beauty, history, culture and economy of the Catskill Mountains can only survive pressures of growth and change through the concern and action of an informed public. Sponsors programs, publications and projects relating to regional and local land use planning,

historic preservation, environmental resource management and open space preservation. Membership: 3,500. Founded: 1969.
President: WILLIAM R. GINSBERG
Vice-Presidents: DR. MADELEINE F. COUTANT; ROBERT L. BISHOP; GEDDY SVEIKAUSKAS
Secretary: WILLIAM B. RHOADS
Treasurer: RUTH REYNOLDS
Executive Director: THOMAS H. MINER
Publication: *Catskill Center Newsletter*
Editor: DIANE GALUSHA

ENVIRONMENTAL PLANNING LOBBY, 33 Central Ave., Albany 12210 (518, 462-5526)

A statewide coalition of organizations and individuals founded in 1969 and devoted to preservation and enhancement of the quality of the environment of New York State through the enactment of sound environmental legislation and its effective implementation. EPL maintains a full-time lobbyist and staff in Albany.
President: WARREN LIEBOLD
Executive Director: LAWRENCE G. SHAPIRO
Publications: *Annual Environmental Voters Guide; Albany Report;* periodic research reports; legislative alerts

FEDERATION OF NEW YORK STATE BIRD CLUBS, INC.

President: BERNA WEISSMAN, 15 Laurel Hill Rd., Dobbs Ferry 10522
Vice-President: CHAD COVEY, 49 So. Main St., New Berlin 13411
Treasurer: STANLEY R. LINCOLN, P.O. Box 362, Mt. Kisco 10549-0362
Recording Secretary: OIVIND JENSEN, 176-5 Meadowbrook West, N. Chili 14514
Corresponding Secretary: MARY ANN SUNDERLIN, 505 Bay Rd., Webster 14580
Publication: *The Kingbird*
Editor: PAUL DEBENEDICTIS, 306 Kensington Pl., Syracuse 13210

INSTITUTE OF ECOSYSTEM STUDIES, THE NEW YORK BOTANICAL GARDEN, Mary Flagler Cary Arboretum, Box AB, Millbrook 12545 (914, 677-5343)

Devoted to the understanding of ecosystem structure and function. "The program focus is on disturbance and recovery of northern temperate ecosystems." Education and research interests include wildlife management, biogeochemistry, landscape ecology, aquatic ecology, plant-animal interactions, microbial ecology, forest ecology, chemical ecology, and air and water pollution. Graduate program in ecological studies offered jointly with Yale University. Facilities include a 778-hectare arboretum, greenhouses, residences and dormitories, modern laboratories for analysis of organic and inorganic materials, library, herbarium, microcomputers, darkroom and Class A weather station.
Director: GENE E. LIKENS, Ph.D.
Administrator: JOSEPH S. WARNER, M.A.
Education Coordinator: ALAN R. BERKOWITZ, Ph.D.
Aquatic Ecologist: THOMAS S. BIANCHI, Ph.D.
Plant Ecologist: CHARLES D. CANHAM, Ph.D.
Aquatic Microbiologist: JONATHAN J. COLE, Ph.D.
Aquatic Ecologist: STUART E.G. FINDLAY, Ph.D.
Chemical Ecologist: CLIVE G. JONES, D.Phil.
Wildlife Ecologist: JAY B McANINCH, M.S.
Plant Ecologist: GARY M. LOVETT, Ph.D.
Terrestrial Ecologist: MARK J. McDONNELL, Ph.D.
Aquatic Ecologist: DAVID L. STRAYER, Ph.D.
Aquatic Ecologist: MICHAEL L. PACE, Ph.D.
Aquatic Ecologist: GEORGE B. McMANUS, Ph.D.
Plant Ecologist: STEWARD T.A. PICKETT, Ph.D.
Plant Ecologist: DAVID M. WOOD, Ph.D.
Biogeochemist: NINA M. CARACO, Ph.D.
Publications: Newsletter; periodic reports, and articles in scientific journals

IZAAK WALTON LEAGUE OF AMERICA, INC. (New York Div.)

President: STEPHEN CASTNER, 1594 Carroll Rd., Penn Yan 14527 (315, 536-3036)
Secretary: LESLIE MONOSTORY, 125 Euclid Dr., Fayetteville 13066 (315, 637-6735)

NEW YORK BASS CHAPTER FEDERATION

An organization of Bassmaster Chapters, affiliated with the Bass Anglers Sportsman Society, organized to fight pollution, assist state and national conservation agencies in their efforts and to teach the young people of our country good conservation practices. Dedicated to the realistic conservation of our water resources.
President: MIKE ZASULY, R.D. 1, Box 502, Montgomery, AL 12549 (914, 457-5996)

NEW YORK FOREST OWNERS ASSOCIATION, INC.

To unite the 500,000 owners of 11 million acres of forest land in New York to encourage the wise management of private woodland resources in N.Y.S. by promoting, protecting, representing and serving the interests of woodland owners. Membership: 1,200. Founded: 1962.
President: MARY SOONS McCARTY, 4300 East Ave., Rochester 14618 (716, 381-6373)
1st Vice-President: NORMAN A. RICHARDS, 156 Westminster Ave., Syracuse 13210
2nd Vice-President: RICHARD E. GARRETT, 1261 Apulia Rd., Lafayette 13984
Executive Secretary: RUTH J. THODE, P.O. Box 123, Boonville 13309

NEW YORK SOIL CONSERVATION DISTRICTS ASSOCIATION, INC.

President and Council Member: JOHN O'NEILL, Tannery Rd., Stony Creek 12878 (518, 696-2395)
Vice-President: Vacant
Secretary: EDMUND ARMSTRONG, Hervey St., Cornwallville 12418 (518, 622-3048)
Treasurer: ROBERT YUNKER, 4420 Covington Rd., Leicester 14481 (716, 382-3408)
Executive Vice-President: DALE CLARK, 1 Winners Cir., Capital Plaza, Albany 12235 (518, 457-7229)

NEW YORK STATE ASSOCIATION OF CONSERVATION COMMISSIONS, INC., 1304 Buckley Rd., Syracuse 13221 (315, 451-0268)

To promote establishment and help improve the workings of local conservation commissions and county environmental management councils, thereby fostering better municipal government in the area of environmental quality and management of natural resources. Membership: 100 commissions/councils. Founded: 1972.
President: PATRICIA McCONNELL, R.F.D. 2, Big Island Rd., Warwick 10990
Vice-President: JOY SQUIRES
Secretary: ANNE TROY BROWN
Treasurer: JACK LOVELAND
Publication: *NYSACC News*
Editor: ROBERT BELLANDI

SCENIC HUDSON, INC., 9 Vassar St., Poughkeepsie 12601 (914, 473-4440)

A nonprofit citizens' group dedicated to the preservation and improvement of natural, recreational, historic and scenic resources of the Hudson River Valley. Speakers' Bureau available to the public. Organized: 1963.

Chairman: ALEXANDER E. ZAGOREUS

Vice-Chairmen: RUDOLPH S. RAUCH III; DAVID S. SAMPSON; WARNE SMITH PRICE

Executive Director: KLARA SAUER

Publication: *Scenic Hudson News*

Editors: CAROL SONDHEIMER; KLARA SAUER

TROUT UNLIMITED NEW YORK COUNCIL

A statewide council with 28 chapters working for the protection and enhancement of the coldwater fishery resourcs.

Chairman and National Director: JEFF R. ROOT, Ph.D., R.D. 1, Box 106, East Nassau 12062 (518, 766-5222)

National Directors: FRANK VADALA, 2827 James St., Suite 210, Syracuse 13206 (315, 457-1200); J. LEON CHANDLER, 3736 Kellogg Rd., P.O. Box 5588, St. Cortland 13045 (607, 749-2324); GARDNER L. GRANT, 200 Mamaroneck Ave., Suite 405, White Plains 10601; OAKLEIGH THORNE, P.O. Box 556, Milbrook 12545 (212, 246-5070); ZANE J. McFADDEN, 28 Elm Hill Way, Camillus 13031 (315, 467-2604)

UPPER CATSKILL FUR TAKERS, Allen Rd., Jefferson 12093 (607, 652-6986)

State chapter of Fur Takers of America. Promotes conservation and perpetuation of fur-bearing animals in New York State through scientific management and regulated trapping, and educates the public in that regard.

President: VICTOR VAN STEENBURG, 71 Gilbert St., Oneonta 13820

Vice-President: TOM FISHER

Secretary: PAUL THAYER

Treasurer: JOHN FRANKL

WILDLIFE SOCIETY/NEW YORK CHAPTER, Wildlife Resources Center, Delmar 12054

President: ARTHUR JOHNSEN, R.D. #1, Box 111, Rensselaerville 12147 (518, 457-0697)

Vice-President: LAWRENCE JACKSON, 1423 High Point Rd., West Acres, Berne 12023 (474-1611)

Secretary: NAN CHADWICK, R.D. #1, Box 162, West Berne 12023 (234-4303)

Treasurer: JOHN I. GREEN, Department of Biology, St. Lawrence University, Canton 13617 (315, 379-5295)

NORTH CAROLINA

GOVERNMENT AGENCIES

GOVERNOR: JAMES G. MARTIN, JR., Governor of North Carolina, State Capitol, Raleigh 27603 (919, 733-4240)

DEPARTMENT OF AGRICULTURE, P.O. Box 27647, Raleigh 27611

Commissioner: JAMES A. GRAHAM (919, 733-7125)

DEPARTMENT OF NATURAL RESOURCES AND COMMUNITY DEVELOPMENT, P.O. Box 27687, Raleigh 27611 (919, 733-4984)

Secretary: S. THOMAS RHODES (733-4984)

Assistant Secretary for Natural Resources: MARY JOAN PUGH

Director of Public Affairs: DON FOLLMER

Forest Resources Director: HARRY F. LAYMAN (733-2162)

Environmental Management Director: R. PAUL WILMS (733-7015)

State Parks and Recreation Director: WILLIAM W. DAVIS (733-4181)

Land Resources: STEPHEN CONRAD (733-3833)

Wildlife Resources Commission, Executive Director: CHARLES R. FULLWOOD, JR. (733-3391)

Community Assistance: BOB CHANDLER (733-2850)

Soil and Water Conservation: DAVID R. SIDES, Director (733-2302)

Coastal Management: DAVE OWENS, Director (733-2293)

Division of Marine Fisheries: WILLIAM T. HOGARTH, Director, P.O. Box 769, Morehead City 28557 (726-7021)

Office of Water Resources: JOHN MORRIS, Director (733-4064)

NORTH CAROLINA COOPERATIVE FISH AND WILDLIFE RESEARCH UNIT, U.S.D.I., Box 7617, 4105 Gardner Hall, North Carolina State University, Raleigh 27695 (919, 856-4320)

Leader: MELVIN T. HUISH

SEA GRANT PROGRAM

Director, UNC Sea Grant College Program: DR. B.J. COPELAND, Box 8605, 105-1911 Bldg., North Carolina State University, Raleigh 27695-8605 (919, 737-2454)

Marine Advisory Program: JAMES D. MURRAY, UNC Sea Grant Program Marine Advisory Service, Box 8605, North Carolina State University, Raleigh 27695-8605 (737-2454)

SOIL AND WATER CONSERVATION COMMISSION, Dept. of Natural Resources and Community Development, 512 North Salisbury St., Raleigh 27611 (919, 733-2302)

The Soil and Water Conservation Commission of the Department of Natural Resources and Community Development has the power and duties to adopt rules and regulations to be followed in the development and administration of a Soil and Water Conservation Program in the 94 Soil and Water Conservation Districts of North Carolina.

Chairman: ALBERT F. TROUTMAN, JR., Rt. 1, Box 232, Aberdeen 28315 (281-3202)

Division Director: DAVID W. SIDES

District Programs Section Chief: CHARLES E. BULLOCK

STATE EXTENSION SERVICES

Director of Extension Service: DR. CHESTER D. BLACK, North Carolina State University, Box 7602, Raleigh 27695 (919, 737-2811)

Extension Forester: M.P. LEVI, North Carolina State University, Box 8003, Raleigh 27695 (737-3368)

Wildlife and Game Specialists: E.J. JONES, Extension Forestry Specialist, Wildlife, North Carolina State University, Box 8003, Raleigh 27695 (737-3386); GARY J. SAN JULIAN, Extension Wildlife Specialist, Zoology Dept., Box 7617, North Carolina State University, Raleigh 27695 (737-2741)

Extension Fisheries Specialist: J.A. RICE, Box 7617, North Carolina State University, Raleigh 27695 (737-2741)

WILDLIFE RESOURCES COMMISSION, Archdale Bldg., 512 N. Salisbury St., Raleigh 27611 (919, 733-3391) Organized: 1947.

Commission Members: ROBERT W. HESTER, Fairfield; EUGENE PRICE, Chairman, Goldsboro; HOWELL W. WOLTZ, Advance; EDDIE C. BRIDGES, Greensboro; WILLIAM H. McCALL, M.D., Asheville; ROBERT E. BARNHILL, JR., Vice-Chairman, Tarboro; ALLAN D. MILES, SR., 4545 Highway 29, Harrisburg 28075; R. REED ALLEN, JR., Lake Waccamaw; JOHN HAMRICK, JR., M.D.,

Shelby; M. WOODROW PRICE, Gloucester; STUART R. PAINE, Southern Pines; JOHN F. LENTZ, Ellerbe; DONALD ALLEN THOMPSON, Mount Gilead

Executive Director: CHARLES R. FULLWOOD

Assistant Director: RICHARD B. HAMILTON

Chief, Division of Conservation Education: A. SIDNEY BAYNES (733-7123)

Chief, Division of Wildlife Management: HAL S. ATKINSON, JR. (733-7291)

Chief, Division of Boating and Inland Fisheries: FRED HARRIS (733-3633)

Chief, Division of Administrative Services: CONNIE R. SPIVEY (733-4566)

Chief, Division of Enforcement: HAROLD RAGLAND (733-7191)

Publication: *Wildlife in North Carolina*

Publications Coordinator/Editor: JAMES W. DEAN (733-7123)

CITIZENS' GROUPS

 NORTH CAROLINA WILDLIFE FEDERATION, Box 10626, Raleigh 27605 (919, 833-1923)

A representative statewide organization, affiliated with the National Wildlife Federation, primarily devoted to the wise use, conservation, aesthetic appreciation, and restoration of wildlife and other natural resources.

President: NOLAN YOUNT, 819 4th Street Dr., NW, Hickory 28601 (704, 324-2859)

Executive Director: MICHAEL CORCORAN

Affiliate Representative: PHIL BRACEWELL, 235 16th Ave., NW, Hickory 28601 (704, 322-9112)

Alternate: NELL COPELAND, Rt. 15, Box 2781, Lexington 27292

Publication: Friend O'Wildlife

Editor: MICHAEL CORCORAN

CAROLINA BIRD CLUB, INC., P.O. Box 27647, Raleigh 27611

Nonprofit, educational, and ornithological organization to promote bird study and conservation. Affiliated local chapters. Membership: 900. Founded: 1937.

President: DR. SIDNEY A. GAUTHREAUX, JR., Department of Biological Sciences, 132 Long Hall, Clemson University, Clemson, SC 29634-1903

Headquarters Secretary: LAURA H. BECKER, Raleigh

Publications: *The Chat;* Newsletters

Editors: DR. H.T. HENDRICKSON, Department of Biology, UNC Greensboro, Greensboro 27412-5001 (919, 334-5391); CLYDE SMITH, JR., 2615 Wells Ave., Raleigh 27608 (919, 781-2637)

CONSERVATION COUNCIL OF NORTH CAROLINA, 307 Granville Rd., Chapel Hill 27514 (919, 942-7935)

To initiate, participate in and coordinate local, regional, state and national action in environmental and energy matters and in conservation and environmental education. Membership: 500; and over 45 member organizations. Organized: 1968.

President: MARY BETH EDELMAN, 7019 Old NC 86, Chapel Hill 27516

Vice-President: JANET HOYLE, P.O. Box 88, Glendale Springs 28629

Coordinator: SCOTT BREIDENBACH, 307 Granville Rd., Chapel Hill 27514

Publications: *Carolina Conservationist Newsletter; Legislative Bulletin*

Editor: LAVON PAGE, 5529 Earle Rd., Raleigh 27606

Editor and Lobbyist: BILL HOLMAN, 1024 Washington St., Raleigh 27605

NORTH CAROLINA ASSOCIATION OF SOIL AND WATER CONSERVATION DISTRICTS

President: WILLIAM V. GRIFFIN, 1505 Island Creek Rd., New Bern 28560 (919, 224-6951)

Vice-President: REBECCA RHYNE, 1213 Old Dallas Highway, Dallas 28034 (704, 922-3940)

Secretary: JAMES SPRUILL, Rt. 3, Box 223, Vanceboro 28586 (919, 244-0908)

Treasurer: RALPH C. TUCKER, 3029 E 14th St., Greenville 27858 (756-4126)

Council Member: WILLIAM G. SULLIVAN, Rt. 1, Mount Olive 28365 (919, 658-3518)

NORTH CAROLINA BASS CHAPTER FEDERATION

An organization of Bassmaster Chapters, affiliated with the Bass Anglers Sportsman Society, organized to fight pollution, assist state and national conservation agencies in their efforts and to teach the young people of our country good conservation practices. Dedicated to the realistic conservation of our water resources.

President: ED CANNON, 1105 Misty Wood Ln., Harrisburg 28075 (704, 547-8522/782-0962)

NORTH CAROLINA HERPETOLOGICAL SOCIETY

A nonprofit group formed in 1978 to promote an interest in and to educate members and the general public concerning the ecological importance and conservation of reptiles and amphibians.

President: WAYNE VAN DEVENDER, Department of Biology, Appalachian State University, Boone 28608 (704, 262-3025)

Vice-President: CARLTON HECKROTTE, Biology Department, ECU, Greenville 27858

Secretary: RODNEY WOODS, P.O. Box 29112, Charlotte 28229

Treasurer: DALE McGINNITY, Rt. 1, Box 6064, Willow Springs 27592

Advisor: ALVIN BRASWELL, N.C. State Museum of Natural Sciences, P.O. Box 27647, Raleigh 27611

Publication: *NC HERPS*

Editor: JEFF BEANE, North Carolina State Museum of Natural Sciences, P.O. Box 27647, Raleigh 27611

NORTH CAROLINA RECREATION AND PARK SOCIETY, INC., 436 N. Harrington St., Raleigh 27603 (919, 832-5868)

A nonprofit organization formed to promote the wise use of leisure and intelligent development of the state's recreation resources. An affiliate of National Recreation/Park Association. Membership: 1,700. Founded: 1944.

Executive Director: HUBERT HENDERSON, 436 N. Harrington St., Raleigh 27603

President: BETTY WILSON, Gaston County Park and Recreation Department, P.O. Box 801, Dallas 28034

Publication: *North Carolina Recreation and Park Review*

Editor: HUBERT HENDERSON, 436 N. Harrington, Raleigh 27603

TROUT UNLIMITED, NORTH CAROLINA COUNCIL

A statewide council with 14 chapters working for the protection and enhancement of the coldwater fishery resource.

Chairman: RICHARD FAYSSOUX, P.O. Box 1244, Drexel 28619

National Directors: G. RICHARD MODE, Vice-President, Southeast Region, 206 Woodlawn Dr., Morganton 28655 (704, 433-1162); ALEN BAKER, 13400 Hiwassee Rd., Huntersville 28078 (704, 875-1505)

WILDLIFE SOCIETY NORTH CAROLINA CHAPTER
President: PHIL DOERR, P.O. Box 7617, Raleigh 27695 (919, 737-2741)
President-Elect: ALLEN C. BOYNTON, 245 N. Anderson St., Morgantown 28655 (704, 433-8669)
Secretary: SUSAN L. ALLEN, 225 Winding Ridge Rd., Raleigh 27606 (919, 737-2741)
Treasurer: RICHARD C. YATES, Rt. 1, Box 327, New Hill 27562 (919, 362-3288)

NORTH DAKOTA

GOVERNMENT AGENCIES

GOVERNOR: GEORGE A. SINNER, Governor of North Dakota, State Capitol, Bismarck 58505 (701, 224-2200)

DEPARTMENT OF AGRICULTURE, State Capitol, Bismarck 58505
The North Dakota Department of Agriculture is the regulating and licensing agency for the agricultural industry in North Dakota.
Commissioner: KENT JONES (701, 224-2231)

DEPARTMENT OF HEALTH, Bismarck 58505
State pollution control programs.
State Health Officer: ROBERT M. WENTZ, M.D. (701, 224-2372)
Director, Division of Water Supply and Pollution Control: FRANCIS SCHWINDT (224-2354)
Director, Division of Environmental Engineering: DANA K. MOUNT (224-2348)
Director, Division of Food and Lodging: JACK LONG (224-2382)
Director, Division of Environmental Enforcement: WILLIAM J. DELMORE (224-3234)
Director, Division of Waste Management: MARTIN SCHOCK (224-2366)

GEOLOGICAL SURVEY, University Station, Grand Forks 58202-8156 (701, 777-2231)
Responsible for collecting and disseminating geologic information. Founded: 1895.
State Geologist (Acting): SIDNEY B. ANDERSON
Publication: Newsletter
Editor: JOHN P. BLUEMLE

INSTITUTE FOR ECOLOGICAL STUDIES, P.O. Box 8278, University Station, University of North Dakota, Grand Forks 58202 (701, 777-2851)
A nonprofit university research center devoted to ecology, policy analysis, and environmental biology. An interdisciplinary staff composed of university faculty, biologists, and associates conducts basic and applied research centering in the upper Midwest, trains graduate and post-graduate students, and provides technical services for government and corporate agencies, and the public. Established: 1965.
Director: RODNEY D. SAYLER
Assistant Director: Vacant
Publications: Natural Resource Management Bulletin; Contributions; research reports

PARKS AND RECREATION DEPARTMENT, 1424 W. Century Ave., Suite 202, Bismarck 58501 (701, 224-4887)
To preserve for public use North Dakota's many parks and areas of historic, natural, and recreational significance. Administration of

the Land and Water Conservation Funds available to ND, planning and promoting the development and use of recreational facilities. Organized: 1975.
Executive Director: DR. DOUGLAS K. EIKEN
Deputy Director: TIM MUELLER
Publication: Recreation Digest

STATE EXTENSION SERVICE, North Dakota State University, Box 5437, Fargo 58105 (701, 237-7173)
Assistant Director, Agriculture and Community Resource Development: DR. DUANE BERGLUND, North Dakota State University, Box 5437, Fargo 58105 (237-7173)
Extension Wildlife Specialist: TERRY A. MESSMER, Stevens Hall, North Dakota State University, Box 5517, Fargo 58105 (237-7950)

STATE FOREST SERVICE, First and Brander, Bottineau 58318 (701, 228-2277)
State Forester: LARRY KOTCHMAN (Ext. 290)
Deputy State Forester: WALTER PASICZNYK (Ext. 286)
Finance Officers: STEVEN PARKMAN (Ext. 232); JOHN VAN ELLS, Staff Forester (Ext. 248); RICHARD GILMORE, Staff Forester (Ext. 283)
Publication: The Prairie Forester

District Offices
District Foresters: ROBERT HARSEL, Box 604, Lisbon 58054 683-4323); THOMAS KARCH, Box 21-A, Forestry Dr., Bottineau 58318 (228-3700); MAURE SAND, 1303 E. Central, Bismarck 58505-0178 (224-4414)
Towner Nursery, Manager: ROY LAFRAMBOISE, SR 2, Box 13, Towner 58788 (537-5636)
Community Forestry Specialist: CRAIG FOSS, Box 219, Carrington 58421 (652-2951)
Insect and Disease Technician, RC&D: ARDEN TAGESTAD, Box 21A, Forestry Dr., Bottineau 58318 (228-2633)

STATE GAME AND FISH DEPARTMENT, 100 North Bismarck Expressway, Bismarck 58501 (701, 221-6300)
Commissioner: DALE HENEGAR
Deputy Commissioner (Acting): PAUL SCHADEWALD
Chief, Information-Education Division: TED UPGREN
Chief, Enforcement Division: RAY GOETZ
Chief, Fishery Division: JAMES RAGAN
Leader, Statewide Game Surveys: C.R. GRONDAHL
Leader, Statewide Lands and Development: ROBERT L. MORGAN
Publication: North Dakota Outdoors
Editor: HAROLD UMBER

STATE SOIL CONSERVATION COMMITTEE, State Hwy. Bldg., Capitol Grounds, Bismarck 58505 (701, 224-2650)
To organize soil conservation districts and provide for control and prevention of soil erosion; represent the state in soil conservation matters; accept P.L. 566 Small Watershed applications, assign planning priority; and administer the Surface Mining Reports Law; a soil survey program; a soil conservation technician grants program. Membership: seven voting members, five elected soil conservation district supervisors and two appointed by the Governor. Created: 1937.
Executive Secretary: BLAKE VANDER VORST

WATER COMMISSION, Bismarck 58505 (701, 224-2750)
Secretary and State Engineer: VERNON FAHY

CITIZENS' GROUPS

NORTH DAKOTA WILDLIFE FEDERATION, INC., *P.O. Box 7248, Bismarck 58502 (701, 222-2557)*
A representative statewide organization, affiliated with the National Wildlife Federation, primarily devoted to the wise use, conservation, aesthetic appreciation, and restoration of wildlife and other natural resources.
President: RICH CUNNINGHAM, R.R. #2, West Heart Estates, Bismarck 58501 (W:663-6445/H:258-6937)
Affiliate Representative: DUANE ANDERSON, 913 West Central, Minot 58701 (839-2971)
Alternate: RICHARD CUNNINGHAM
Publication: Flickertales
Editor: JANET HEISER

NORTH DAKOTA ASSOCIATION OF SOIL CONSERVATION DISTRICTS
President: WALLACE JACOBS, R.R. 1, Box 22, Amidon 58620 (701, 879-6255)
President-Elect: MAURICE ORN, R.R. 1, Box 304, Stirum 58069 (678-2738)
Secretary-Treasurer/Executive Vice-President: GARY PUPPE, Box 1601, Bismarck 58502 (223-8518)
Council Member: THILMER ISZLER, R.R. Box 23, Streeter 58483 (424-3655)

NORTH DAKOTA NATURAL SCIENCE SOCIETY, P.O. Box 8238, University Station, Grand Forks 58202-8238 (701, 777-2199)
Dedicated to the observation, recording, study, and preservation of all aspects of the natural history of the Great Plains. Membership: 300. Organized: 1967.
President: DR. JOHN P. BLUEMLE, ND Geological Survey, Box 8156, University Station, Grand Forks 58202-8156 (772-2231)
Secretary-Treasurer: DR. PAUL B. KANNOWSKI
Publication: *The Prairie Naturalist*
Editor: DR. PAUL B. KANNOWSKI

WILDLIFE SOCIETY NORTH DAKOTA CHAPTER
President: BILL BERG, J. Clark Salyer NWR, Box 66, Upham 58789 (701, 768-2548)
President-Elect: RANDY KREIL, 100 N. Bismarck Expressway, Bismarck 58501 (224-9870)
Secretary-Treasurer: ARLEN HARMONING, 100 N. Bismarck Expressway, Bismarck 58501 (221-6329)

OHIO

GOVERNMENT AGENCIES

GOVERNOR: RICHARD F. CELESTE, Governor of Ohio, State House, Columbus 43215 (614, 466-3555)

DEPARTMENT OF AGRICULTURE, 65 S. Front St., Columbus 43215 (614, 466-2732)
Administers the laws and regulations of agricultural activity. Provides inspection of foods, dairies, drugs, fertilizer, seeds, nursery stock, grain warehousing, labeling, meat, and administers plant and animal disease control programs, pesticide certification and applicator training and weights and measurers testing.
Director: STEVEN D. MAURER
Information Service: ALICE WALTERS (466-8798)

DEPARTMENT OF NATURAL RESOURCES, Fountain Square, Columbus 43224 (614, 265-6886)
Created to formulate and execute a long term comprehensive plan and program for the development and wise use of the natural resources of the state to the end that the health, happiness and wholesome enjoyment of life of the people of Ohio may be further encouraged. Established: 1949.
Director: JOSEPH J. SOMMER (265-6875)
Assistant Director: CHARLES E. MAUGER (265-6877)
Executive Assistant to Director for Legislative Affairs: F. MARTIN ROOKARD (265- 6889)
Deputy Director, Resource Management: ANNE WICKHAM (265-6882)
Deputy Director, Resource Protection: THOMAS L. SHERMAN (265-6888)
Deputy Director, Recreation Management: JOHN A. PIEHOWICZ (265-6845)
Office of Business and Administrative Services: Vacant (265-6833)
Office of Chief Engineer: STEVEN W. CARTER, Chief (265-6948)
Division of Civilian Conservation: EDWARD C. HINTON, JR., Chief (265- 6423)
Office of Employee Services: MICHAEL CANAVAN, Chief (265-6990)
Office of Litter Control: MARY WIARD, Chief (265-6333)
Office of Outdoor Recreation Services: MICHAEL D. CRADEN, Chief (265-6395)
Office of Public Information and Education: C. LYNN MALOWNEY, Chief (265-6789)
Division of Forestry: Vacant, Chief (265-6694)
Division of Geological Survey: Vacant, Chief (265-6605)
Division of Natural Areas and Preserves: RICHARD E. MOSELEY, JR., Chief (265-6453)
Division of Oil and Gas: MICHAEL BIDDISON, Chief (265-6917)
Division of Parks and Recreation: STANLEY SPAULDING, Chief (265-6561)
Division of Reclamation: TIMOTHY DIERINGER, Chief (265-6633)
Division of Soil and Water Conservation: LAWRENCE G. VANCE, Chief (265-6610)
Division of Water: ROBERT GOETTEMOELLER, Chief (265-6717)
Division of Watercraft: PAUL GREGORY, Chief (265-6480)
Division of Wildlife: CLAYTON LAKES, Chief (265-6300)

ENVIRONMENTAL PROTECTION AGENCY, P.O. Box 1049, 1800 Watermark Dr., Columbus 43266-0149 (614, 644-3020)
State regulatory agency with jurisdiction covering air, waste water, drinking water, hazardous waste, and land pollution control; maintains central office in Columbus and has five district offices. Established: 1972.
Director: RICHARD L. SHANK, Ph.D. (644-2782)
Assistant Director: STEVEN GROSSMAN (644-2782)
Deputy Director, Legal and Governmental Affairs: RICK SAHLI (644-2782)
Deputy Director, Technical and Remedial Programs: MAURY WALSH (644-2782)
Chief, Environmental Planning and Management: CARL WILHELM (644-2131)
Chief, Public Interest Center: ALLAN FRANKS (644-2160)
Chief, Division of Solid and Hazardous Waste Management: PAUL FLANIGAN (644-2917)
Chief, Division of Water Pollution Control: MATT TIN (644-2001)
Governmental Relations: VAUGHN LAUGHLIN (644-2782)

Chief, Division of Air Pollution Control: PATRICIA WALLING (644-2270)

Chief, Division of Public Drinking Water: STUART BRUNY (644-2752)

Emergency Response Coordinator: KEN SCHULTZ (644-2260)

Chief, Division of Water Quality Monitoring and Assessment: ANDREW TURNER (644-2856)

Chief, Division of Ground Water: GARY MARTIN (644-2905)

OHIO COOPERATIVE FISH AND WILDLIFE RESEARCH UNIT, U.S.D.I., Ohio State University, 1735 Neil Ave., Columbus 43210 (Wildlife: 614, 292-6112; Fisheries: 614, 292-8961)

Leader: DR. THEODORE A. BOOKHOUT

Assistant Leader, Wildlife: DR. JONATHAN R. BART

Assistant Leader, Fisheries: DR. BRUCE VONDRACEK

SEA GRANT PROGRAM AND CENTER FOR LAKE ERIE AREA RESEARCH (CLEAR)

Director: DR. JEFFREY M. REUTTER, Ohio State University, 1314 Kinnear Rd., Columbus 43212 (614, 292-8949)

The SGP is dedicated to the goal of promoting the understanding, development, utilization, and conservation of the ocean and coastal resources, specifically Lake Erie, through research, education, and advisory services. The program is administered by the Center for Lake Erie Area Research (CLEAR) within the College of Biological Sciences at the Ohio State University.

Publication: *Twine Line*

Editor: MARAN BRAINARD

STATE EXTENSION SERVICES

Director of Extension Service: DR. BOBBY D. MOSER, Ohio State University, 2120 Fyffe Rd., Columbus 43210 (614, 292-4067)

Assistant Director (Acting), Community and Natural Resource Development: DR. JOHN D. ROHRER, Ohio State University, 2120 Fyffe Rd., Columbus 43210 (292-8436)

Director (Acting), School of Natural Resources: DR. JOHN DISINGER, Ohio State University, 2021 Coffey Rd., Columbus 43210 (292-9884)

Extension Specialist, Forestry: RANDALL B. HEILIGMANN, Ohio State University, 2021 Coffey Rd., Columbus 43210 (292-9838)

Extension Specialist, Fish and Wildlife: DR. THOMAS M. STOCKDALE, Ohio State University, 2021 Coffey Rd., Columbus 43210 (292-9772)

Leader, Small Business and Natural Resources: GREGORY R. PASSEWITZ, Ohio State University, 2120 Fyffe Rd., Columbus 43210 (292-8436)

CITIZENS' GROUPS

LEAGUE OF OHIO SPORTSMEN, 3953 Indianola Ave., Columbus 43214 (614, 268-9924)

A representative statewide organization, affiliated with the National Wildlife Federation, primarily devoted to the wise use, conservation, aesthetic appreciation, and restoration of wildlife and other natural resources.

President: HERMAN DEITERS, 6787 Wells Rd., Anna 45302 (614, 628-2954)

Secretary: GEORGE A. LYNCH, 5649 Hunters Ridge Rd., Dayton 45431 (513, 253-2382)

Affiliate Representative: MATTHEW PRIBANIC, 1229 W. 33rd St., Lorain 44053 (216, 282-5928)

Alternate: MIKE PAVELSCHAK, 1501 West 40th St., Lorain 44053

Office Manager: MARILYN BROWN

Publication: Ohio Out-Of-Doors

Editor: JOHN DiFRANCO, P.O. Box 25651, Garfield Heights 44125

CENTRAL OHIO ANGLERS AND HUNTERS CLUB, P.O. Box 28224, Columbus 43228

Promotion of conservation and conservation education in all their phases, with a particular reference to land, air, and water; to promote good fellowship and good citizenship; to inculcate regard for the rights of others and respect for the obedience to law; to support a safe and effective conservation program for and by the state and nation.

President: SCOTT FURST, 8000 Walnut St., New Albany 43054 (614, 855-9022)

Vice-President: MIKE ANDRES, 5114 Bigelow Dr., Hilliard 43026 (876-4563)

Secretary: RICHARD De BROSSE, 1268 Republic Ave., Columbus 43211 (268-3996)

Treasurer: JERRY BANYOTS, 3543 Kroehler Dr., Hilliard 43026 (876-7001)

Directors: JOHN HOBBS, 3559 Blackbottom Ct., Columbus 43220 (876-8523); STEVE JAMES, 1948 Willow Run Rd., Grove City 43123 (871-4053); WARD MILLER, 5791 Safron, Galloway 43119 (878-0608)

DAWES ARBORETUM, THE, 7770 Jacksontown Rd., SE, Newark 43055 (614, 323-2355)

A nonprofit organization that promotes the planting of forest and ornamental trees, and promotes increased love and knowledge of trees, shrubs, and related subjects through a variety of classes and programs. Founded: 1929.

Chairman: JO DAWES HIGGINS, 102 Saddle Mountain Rd., Rome, GA 30161

Secretary: BEMAN D. YOUNG, 600 Main St., Watertown, WI 53094

Treasurer: SARAH DAWES HAUSER, 5099 Doral Ave., Columbus 43213

Director: DONALD R. HENDRICKS

Horticulturist: J. PAUL BOWLES

Naturalist and Educator: LORI A. TOTMAN

Superintendent of Maintenance: ARTHUR O. PATZNICK

Publication: *The Dawes Arboretum Newsletter*

Editor: ALAN D. COOK

ENVIRONMENTAL BOARD OF REVIEW, 236 E. Town St., Rm. 300, Columbus 43215 (614, 466-8950)

The Environmental Board of Review is an administrative board designed to review the actions of the Ohio EPA, and the various county boards of health charged with environmental jurisdiction in order to determine that the agencies' actions have been reasonable and lawful.

Chairman: JAMES L. BAUMANN

Vice-Chairman: RICHARD E. MIDDEN

Member: PETER A. PRECARIO

Executive Secretary: MARY J. OXLEY

IZAAK WALTON LEAGUE OF AMERICA, INC. (Ohio Div.)

President: RAY ZEHLER, 900 Moorman Rd., Hamilton 45013 (513, 868-3179)

Executive Secretary: EDWARD SCHEKELHOFF, 512 N. Sandusky, Tiffin 44883 (419, 447-7716)

OHIO ACADEMY OF SCIENCE, THE, 445 King Ave., Columbus 43201 (614, 424-6045) (Annual Meeting: 1989, April 28-30, Cuyahoga Community College, Western Campus, 11000 Pleasant Valley Rd., Parma 44130)

A Nonprofit organization designed to stimulate interest in the sciences, to promote research, to improve instruction in the sciences, to disseminate scientific knowledge; and to recognize high achievement in attaining these objectives. Membership: 1,650. Founded: 1891.

President: DR. DONALD L. WISE, Department of Biology, College of Wooster, Wooster 44691 (216, 263-2000)

Vice-President, Natural Resources: DR. DAVID TODD, Shawnee State University, 940 Second St., Portsmouth 45662 (614, 354-3205)

Secretary: RAYMOND F. JEZERINAC, Ohio State University Newark, University Dr., Newark 43055 (614, 366-3321)

Treasurer: ROBERT H. ESSMAN, Dept. of Genetics, Ohio State University, 1735 Neil Ave., Columbus 43210 (614, 292-8084)

Executive Officer: LYNN EDWARD ELFNER

Publications: *The Ohio Journal of Science; OAS News*

Editor: DR LEE MESERVE, Department of Biological Sciences, Bowling Green State University, Bowling Green 43403 (419, 372-8361/Ext. 2332)

OHIO ALLIANCE FOR THE ENVIRONMENT, 445 King Ave., Columbus 43201 (614, 421-7819)

A statewide nonprofit organization established in 1977 to provide leadership in resolving environmental conflicts, and to promote and support environmental education in Ohio. The alliance is a nonadvocacy organization working to establish channels of communication among diverse groups with environmental concerns and to provide balanced environmental information through conferences and publications.

President: DR. DAVID HICKCOX, Professor of Geography and Geology, Ohio Weslyan University, Delaware 43015 (614, 369-4431)

Vice-President: KATHLEEN STIMLER, Esq., Manager, State Government Relations, BF Goodrich Company, Corporate Headquarters, 3925 Embassy Parkway, Akron 44131 (216, 374-2962)

Secretary: JANE HAYNES, Editor, Newsletter, Ohio Alliance for the Environment, 2178 Castle Crest Dr., Worthington 43085 (614, 885-3735)

Treasurer: BARBARA PIKE, Administrative Secretary, Ohio Mining and Reclamation, 50 South Young St., Columbus 43215 (614, 228-6336)

Executive Director: IRENE PROBASCO

Publications: *Ohio Alliance for the Environment; OAE Newsletter*

Editor: JANE HAYNES

OHIO AUDUBON COUNCIL, INC., 3776 Wales Ave., NW, Massillon 44646

Associated with the National Audubon Society. Works to promote, foster, and encourage the conservation and preservation of all wildlife, plants, soil, water, air, and other natural resources for the benefit of all citizens. Organized: 1969.

President: CAROL AVRIL, 2966 Timbercrest Dr., Cincinnati 45238 (513, 662-4505)

Vice-President: CHUCK BUECHELE, 5055 Hahn Ave., Fairborn 45324 (513, 684-1857)

Past President: ALAN DOLAN, P.O. Box 935, Massillon 44648 (216, 832-2491)

Secretary: BETTY PUGH, 272 Whittier Dr., Lancaster 43130 (614, 653-5518)

Treasurer: JOHN F. GALLAGHER, 121 Larchmont Rd., Springfield 45503 (513, 323-0782)

OHIO BASS CHAPTER FEDERATION

An organization of Bassmaster Chapters, affiliated with the Bass Anglers Sportsman Society, organized to fight pollution, assist state and national conservation agencies in their efforts, and to teach the young people of our country good conservation practices. Dedicated to the realistic conservation of our water resources.

President: GARY RUSK, 1880 Lewis Center Rd., Box 625, Lewis Center 43035

OHIO BIOLOGICAL SURVEY, 980 Biological Sciences Bldg., Ohio State University, 484 W. 12th Ave., Columbus 43210 (614, 292-9645)

An inter-institutional organization of 68 Ohio colleges, universities, museums, and other organizations. Produces and disseminates scientific and technical information concerning the flora and fauna of the Ohio environment. Founded: 1912.

Chairman of the Advisory Board: DR. JERRY H. HUBSCHMAN, Wright State University

Executive Director: DR. CHARLES C. KING

Publications: Bulletins; Biological Notes; Informative Circulars

Editor: VEDA M. CAFAZZO

OHIO ENVIRONMENTAL COUNCIL, INC., Suite 300, 22 East Gay St., Columbus 43215-3113 (614, 224-4900)

A statewide federation of over 80 organizations and over l,500 individuals devoted to the preservation and enhancement of the quality of urban and natural environments in Ohio. Founded: 1969.

President: CHRISTINE CARLSON, c/o Kettering Foundation, 200 Commons Rd., Dayton 45459-2799 (800, 523-0078)

Vice-President: JOHN MARSHALL, 723 Oak St., Columbus 43205 (614, 221-1160)

Secretary: LOIS WHEALEY, 14 Oak St., Athens 45701, (614, 593-7668)

Treasurer: RICHARD HOLZ, 220 E. Weisheimer, Columbus 43214, (614, 462-2296)

Executive Director: STEPHEN SEDAM

Publications: *Environmental Hotline Newsletter; Ohio Legislative and Government Directory;* variety of other publications on critical environmental issues for Ohio.

OHIO FEDERATION OF SOIL AND WATER CONSERVATION DISTRICTS

President: NEVIN SMITH, 637 Township Rd. 46 N., Bellefontaine 43311 (513, 592-8122)

President-Elect: LYNN J. MEYER, 6623 Hankins Rd., Middletown 45042 (513, 539-8769)

Vice-President: ROBERT ROCKWELL, 60420 Sandy Ridge Rd., Barnesville 43713 (614, 425-2013)

Secretary-Treasurer: EDWARD ELLIOTT II, Box 66, Mt. Victory 43340 (513, 354-4581)

OHIO FORESTRY ASSOCIATION, INC., THE, 1301 Worthington Woods Blvd., Worthington 43085 (614, 846-9456)

To promote the welfare of the people and private enterprise of Ohio by improving, through education, the wise management of Ohio's forest resource. Sponsors annual forestry camp for youths 15-19; assists schools' conservation activities and edu ation; sponsors Paul Bunyan Forestry Exposition with Hocking Technical College; and coordinates American Tree Farm Program in Ohio. Members: 1,000. Founded: 1903.

Chairman of the Board: ANDY ADELMAN, Adelman and Clark Lumber Company, Rt. 93, McArthur 45651

President: ROY PALMER, Hocking Technical College, Rt. #1, Nelsonville 45764

Executive Director: RONALD C. CORNELL (614, 846-9456)

Publications: *Ohio Woodlands*

TROUT UNLIMITED OHIO
Dedicated to the protection and enhancement of the coldwater fishery resource.

President (Western Reserve Chapter): CHARLES CHLYSTA, 6790 Wall St., Ravenna 44266

President (Madmen Chapter): ELLIOTT JENNINGS, 5273 Bittersweet Dr., Dayton 45429

National Directors: KEITH C. RUSSELL, McDonald & Co., 2100 Central Nat'l Bank Bldg., Cleveland 44114; STEVEN RENKERT, P.O. Box 9240, Canton 44711 (216, 484-4887)

WATER MANAGEMENT ASSOCIATION OF OHIO, 445 King Ave., Columbus 43201 (614, 424-6106)
Goal is to promote and support the development, conservation, control, protection, and utilization of the water resources of Ohio for all beneficial purposes, to help coordinate interest in water programs among all interests, and to help create interest in the water resources of the state. Created: 1972. Membership: 325.

President: DAVID J. WILLIAMS (513, 579-0042)

Executive Vice-President: JOHN E. BARKER (513, 425-2644)

Immediate Past President: S.V. JACKSON (614, 349-2729)

Secretary-Treasurer: BEA CORNELIUS (513, 226-6295)

Publication: *Ohio Water Table*

Editor: DOUGLAS J. WETHERHOLT

WILDLIFE SOCIETY OHIO CHAPTER
President: THEODORE BOOKHOUT, Ohio Cooperative Wildlife Research Unit, Ohio State University, 1735 Neil Ave., Columbus 43224 (614, 292-6112)

President-Elect: DAVID RISLEY, Ohio Division of Wildlife, Fountain Square, Bldg. C, 4th Fl., Columbus 43224 (265-6330)

Secretary: KATHY SHIPLEY, Ohio Division of Wildlife, 8589 Horseshoe Rd., Ashley 43003 (747-2525)

Treasurer: ROMY MYSZKA, Soil Conservation Service, 200 N. High St., Rm. 522, Columbus 43215 (469-6980)

OKLAHOMA

GOVERNMENT AGENCIES

GOVERNOR: HENRY BELLMON, Governor of Oklahoma, State Capitol, Rm. 212, Oklahoma City 73105 (405, 521-2345)

CONSERVATION COMMISSION, 2800 N. Lincoln Blvd., Suite 160, Oklahoma City 73105 (405, 521-2384)
To assist and supervise conservation districts in carrying out conservation practices of all renewable natural resources. Created: 1938.

Chairman: E.F. COKER, Rt. 1, Granite 73547

Executive Director: MASON B. MUNGLE

Assistant Director: CAROL ROSS WOFFORD

Water Quality Program Director: JOHN HASSELL

Abandoned Mine Land Reclamation Director: MIKE KASTL

District Operations Coordinator: DR. DAN A. SEBERT

Publication: *Conservation Conversation Newsletter*

Information Representative: JIM MITCHELL

DEPARTMENT OF WILDLIFE CONSERVATION, 1801 N. Lincoln, P.O. Box 53465, Oklahoma City 73152 (405, 521-3851) Organized: 1909.

Commission Members: JOHN GIBBS, Chairman, Holdenville; JIM-MY HARREL, Vice-Chairman, Leedey; H.B. ATKINSON, Secretary, Midwest City; L.B. SELMAN, Tulsa; JOHN GROENDYKE, Enid; CARL PIERCEALL, Muskogee; K.E. PENNINGTON, Madill; ROY BOECHER, Kingfisher

Director: STEVEN ALAN LEWIS

Assistant Director: CHARLES WALLACE

Chief, Game Division: GREG DUFFY (521-2739)

Chief, Fisheries Division: KIM ERICKSON (521-3721)

Chief, Information-Education Division: DEAN GRAHAM (521-3855)

Chief, Law Enforcement Division: KENNETH VAN HOOZER (521-3719)

Radio Communications: HANK STOKES

Environmental Services: RICARDO GOMEZ

Publication: *Outdoor Oklahoma*

Editor: DEAN GRAHAM (521-3855)

OKLAHOMA COOPERATIVE FISH AND WILDLIFE RESEARCH UNIT, U.S.D.I., 404 Life Sciences West Bldg., Oklahoma State University, Stillwater 74078 (405, 744-6342)
Leader: PHILLIP J. ZWANK

Assistant Leader, Fishery: ALEXANDER V. ZALE

Assistant Leader, Wildlife: DAVID M. LESLIE, JR.

OKLAHOMA GEOLOGICAL SURVEY, University of Oklahoma, Rm. 163, 830 Van Vleet Oval, Norman 73019 (405, 325-3031)
To investigate and disseminate information on the geological formations of the state, with special reference to mineral resources. Investigations include geologic mapping, evaluation of metallic and nonmetallic mineral deposits, and studies of groundwater and fossil fuels, plus basic research and environmental studies. Founded: 1908.

Director: CHARLES J. MANKIN

Associate Director: KENNETH S. JOHNSON

Publications: Oklahoma Geology Notes; Bulletins, Circulars, Guidebooks, Geologic Map Series, Educational Publications Series, Hydrologic Atlases, Special Publications

Editor: LARRY N. STOUT

Promotion and Information Specialist: CONNIE G. SMITH

STATE BOARD OF AGRICULTURE, 2800 N. Lincoln Blvd., Oklahoma City 73105 (405, 521-3864)
The Oklahoma Department of Agriculture is principally a regulatory agency, but it is also a promotional and cooperative agency for segments of agriculture and forestry. Major divisions of the department are forestry, animal industry, plant industry, marketing, agriculture laboratory and the federal-state cooperative programs of animal damage control and agricultural statistics—or the crop and livestock reporting service—and international market development.

President and Commissioner: JACK CRAIG

Deputy Commissioner: CLIFFORD W. LeGATE (Ext. 202)

Administrative Assistant: CHARLES ANDERSON (Ext. 203)

Forestry Division: ROGER L. DAVIS, Director (Ext. 280)

Plant Industry Division: A.L. (Punk) BONNER, Director (Ext. 240)

Animal Industry Division: DR. ROBERT HARTIN, Director (Ext. 329)

Agricultural Laboratory: SUE CANNON, Director (Ext. 374)

Agricultural Statistics: BOB BELLINGHAUSEN, Director (525-9226)

Animal Damage Control: BERKELEY PETERSON, Director (521-4039)

Marketing Development Division: ANNA BELLE WIEDEMANN, Director (Ext. 236)

Information Officer: TONDA AMES (Ext. 209)

STATE DEPARTMENT OF HEALTH, 1000 Northeast Tenth, P.O. Box 53551, Oklahoma City 73152 (405, 271-5600) Environmental Assessment, Protection and Control.
Commissioner: JOAN K. LEAVITT, M.D.
Deputy Commissioner for Environmental Health Services: MARK S. COLEMAN
Chief, Water Facilities Engineering Service: GEORGE McBRYDE
Chief, Air Quality Service: JOHN DRAKE
Chief, Occupational Licensing Service: JOHN H. ARMSTRONG
Chief, Waste Management Service: DAMON WINGFIELD
Chief, Radiation and Special Hazards Service: J. DALE McHARD
Chief, Waste Water Construction Assistance: JON CRAIG
Chief, Health Education and Information Service: RICHARD M. GUNN
Chief, State Environmental Laboratory: JUDY DUNCAN

STATE EXTENSION SERVICES
Extension Forestry and Wildlife are a unit of the Oklahoma Cooperative Extension Service and the Department of Forestry, Division of Agriculture, Oklahoma State University. The unit was founded in 1946 to bring educational programs in these subject areas to citizens of the state of Oklahoma.
Director of Cooperative Extension Service: C.B. BROWNING, Oklahoma State University, Stillwater 74078 (405, 744-5398)
Extension Forester: STEVE ANDERSON, Oklahoma State University, Rm. 239, Agricultural Hall, Stillwater 74078 (Ext. 9431)
Associate Director of Cooperative Extension Service: DR. T. ROY BOGLE, Oklahoma State University, Rm. 139, Agricultural Hall, Stillwater 74078 (Ext. 5398)
Department Head, Forestry: ED MILLER, Oklahoma State University, Rm. 012, Agricultural Hall, Stillwater 74078 (Ext. 5437)

TOURISM AND RECREATION DEPARTMENT, 500 Will Rogers Memorial Bldg., Oklahoma City 73105 (405, 521-2409)
To promote Oklahoma, "America's Frontier Lake State," as a vacation destination for residents and travelers to the state; and to develop human and natural resources for the purpose of promoting tourism, recreation, wildlife preservation and environmental conservation. An annual industry conference is held each February. Founded: 1972.
Executive Director: GLENN SULLIVAN (521-2413)
Division of State Parks: TOM CREIDER (521-3411)
Division of Marketing Services: EUGENE DILBECK (521-2406)
Division of Lodges: TOM RICH (521-3988)
Division of Planning and Development: KRISTINA S. MAREK (521-2973)
Division of Administration: MICHAEL L. MOCCIA (521-2471)
Publications: *Oklahoma Today; Oklahoma Vacation Guide*
Editors: SUE CARTER (521-2496); TIM MILLER (521-2406)

CITIZENS' GROUPS

OKLAHOMA WILDLIFE FEDERATION, 4545 Lincoln Blvd., Suite 171, Oklahoma City 73105 (405, 524-7009)
A representative statewide organization, affiliated with the National Wildlife Federation, primarily devoted to the wise use, conservation, aesthetic appreciation, and restoration of wildlife and other natural resources.
President: MRS. ODIE McREYNOLDS, 1413 Hillcrest, Bartlesville 74003
Executive Director: JIM BENNETT
Affiliate Representative: MRS. ODIE McREYNOLDS
Alternate: DON COX, Star Route, Broken Bow 74728 (584-3351)

Publication: *Outdoor News*
Editor: DALE SMITH

IZAAK WALTON LEAGUE OF AMERICA, INC. (Oklahoma Div.)
President: BILL ALTMAN, 1905 E. 4th St., Stillwater 74074
Secretary: CATHARINE COE, 1003 West Scott, Stillwater 74075 (405, 372-4536)

OKLAHOMA ACADEMY OF SCIENCE, P.O. Box 53443, Oklahoma City 73152 (405, 271-2133)
To stimulate scientific research; to promote fraternal relationship among those engaged in scientific work in Oklahoma; to diffuse among the citizens of the state a knowledge of the various departments of science; and to investigate and make known the material, educational and other resources of the state. Founded: 1909. Membership: 875; professional, 100 libraries.
President: MARY CARPENTER, Ph.D., Oklahoma Medical Research Foundation, 825 NE 13th, Oklahoma City 73104
President-Elect: KENNETH E. CONWAY, Ph.D., Department of Botany and Plant Pathology, Oklahoma State University, Stillwater 74078-0285
Recording Secretary: LEO T. HALL, Ph.D., P.O. Box 2000, University Station, Phillips University, Enid 73702
Executive Secretary-Treasurer: DR. PAUL BUCK, P.O. Box 4424, Tulsa 74159-0424
Publications: *Proceedings-Oklahoma Academy of Science; Annals-Oklahoma Academy of Science; Transactions-Oklahoma Junior Academy of Science; CAS Newsletter*
Editor: GLENN W. TODD, Ph.D., Department of Botany and Microbiology, Oklahoma State University, Stillwater 74078 (624-5559)

OKLAHOMA ASSOCIATION OF CONSERVATION DISTRICTS
President: LEE ROY HUDSON, 906 W. Vivian, Hollis 73550 (405, 688-2974)
1st Vice-President: J. BERRY HARRISON, Rt. 3, Box 505, Ponca City 74601 (405, 765-6922)
2nd Vice-President: GEORGE STUNKARD, Rt. 1, Coweta 74429 (918, 486-5400)
3rd Vice-President: BILLY WILSON, P.O. Box 208, Kinita 74552 (918, 768-3542)
Treasurer: WAYNE SMITH, 506 N. Penn, Mangum 73554 (405, 782-3575)

OKLAHOMA BASS CHAPTER FEDERATION
An organization of Bassmaster Chapters, affiliated with Bass Anglers Sportsman Society, organized to fight pollution, assist state and national conservation agencies in their efforts, and to teach the young people of our country good conservation practices. Dedicated to the realistic conservation of our water resources.
President: DON LINDER, 2409 Cardinal, Ponca City 74604 (405, 762-3301/767-4793)

OKLAHOMA ORNITHOLOGICAL SOCIETY
Affiliated with National Audubon Society and the Oklahoma Wildlife Federation. Dedicated to the observation, study, and conservation of birds in Oklahoma. Membership: 600. Founded: 1950.
President: ALBERT HARRIS, Rt. 7, Box 62, Tahlequah 74464 (918, 456-2071)
Treasurer: BILL DIRCK, Box 65, Ada 74820 (405, 332-3266)
Secretary: FRANCES NEELD, 1219 Elder, Duncan 73533 (405, 255-2280)
Business Manager: BRUCE G. STEWART, P.O. Box 31, Fittstown 73460 (405, 777-2785)

Publications: *The Scissortail; The Bulletin of the Oklahoma Ornithological Society*
Editors: ROBERT and SUSAN CARL, Zoology Dept., University of Oklahoma, Norman 73019; JACK D. TYLER, Biology Dept., Cameron State University, Lawton 73501 (405, 248-2200)

TROUT UNLIMITED OKLAHOMA CHAPTER
A statewide chapter working for the protection and enhancement of the coldwater fishery resources.
President: RICHARD MEADORS, 4613 Zella Way, Piedmont 73078
National Director: Vacant

WILDLIFE SOCIETY OKLAHOMA CHAPTER
President: KENNETH L. GEE, Rt. 1, Box 339, Allen 74825 (405, 332-8070)
President-Elect: JOHN SKEEN, ODWC, P.O. Box 53465, Oklahoma City 73152 (521-3851)
Secretary: BILL BARTUSH, DEH, Fort Sill 73503 (351-4324)
Treasurer: DAN STINNETT, 3510 E. 23rd St., Tulsa 74114 (918, 581-7458)

OREGON

GOVERNMENT AGENCIES

GOVERNOR: NEIL GOLDSCHMIDT, Governor of Oregon, State Capitol, Salem 97310 (503, 378--3100)

DEPARTMENT OF AGRICULTURE, Salem 97310-0110
Director, Information Service: DALTON HOBBS (503, 378-3773)

Soil and Water Conservation Division, 635 Capitol St., NE, Salem 97310-0110
Supervises the organization and operation of soil and water conservation districts, approves or disapproves all projects, practices, personnel, budgets, contracts, regulations of Oregon's 45 districts, keeping the directors of each district informed of the experience of others. State administrative agency for nonpoint source water quality programs. Organized: 1939.
Administrator: GEORGE STUBBERT (503, 378-3810)
Soil and Water Conservation Commission/Members: CALVIN KRAHMER, Vice-Chairman, Rt. 4, Box 76, Cornelius 97113-9401 (357-6216); NOLA MILLHOUSER, 9220 Smith Rd., Monmouth 97361 (838-3903); ROBERT ELDER, Chairman, HC 64, Box 290, Paisley 97636-9704 (943-3230); BILL TODD, P.O. Box 176, Grass Valley 97029-0176 (333-2225); KEN MESSERLE, Rt. 1, Box 275, Coquille 97423-9750 (396-2273); KEVIN CAMPBELL, Box 475, Kimberly 97848 (934-2237); THOMAS STRAUGHAN, 1421 SW 45th Dr., Pendleton 97801 (278-0218)
Advisory Members: BENNO WARKENTIN, Soils Department, Oregon State University, Corvallis 97331-2213 (503, 754-2441); JACK P. KANALZ, SCS, 1220 SW 3rd Ave., 16th Fl., Portland 97204-2881 (221-2751); NORM GOETZE, Extension Hall, Oregon State University, Corvallis 97331-3611 (754-2711); GLEN STONEBRINK, ASCS, 1220 SW 3rd. Ave., 15th Fl., Portland 97204-2880 (221-2741); BOB BAUM, NACD, 831 Lancaster Dr., Suite 207, Salem 97301-2978 (363-0912); JOE BRUMBACH, OACD, 4260 Buckhorn Rd., Roseburg 97470-9406 (503, 673-3998)
Publication: *Oregon Natural Resources Conservation News*

DEPARTMENT OF ENVIRONMENTAL QUALITY, 811 SW Sixth Ave., Portland 97204
Regulates all pollution control programs in the State. Has jurisdiction over air quality; water quality; hazardous and solid waste management; subsurface and/or alternative on-site sewage facilities; and noise control. Created: 1969.
Director: FRED HANSEN (503, 229-5300)
Assistant to the Director: JOHN LOEWY (229-5327)
Principal Officers: NICK NIKKILA, Air Quality (229-5397); MICHAEL J. DOWNS, Environmental Cleanup Division (229-5254); STEPHANIE HALLOCK, Hazardous and Solid Waste (229-5356); RICHARD J. NICHOLS, Water Quality (229-5324); THOMAS R. BISPHAM, Regional Operations (229-5287)
Publication: *Recycling Newsletter; Beyond Waste;* Annual Reports
Editor: CAROLYN YOUNG

DEPARTMENT OF FISH AND WILDLIFE, 506 SW Mill St., Portland 97201; Mailing Address: P.O. Box 59, Portland 97207 (503, 229-5551)
Responsibilities include: management of fish and wildlife resources, and regulation of commercial and recreational harvest. Founded: 1975.
Commissioners: BOB JACOBSON; JIM VAN LOAN; R. GENE MORRIS; PHILLIP W. SCHNEIDER; KEN JERNSTEDT; FRED A. PHILLIPS II; JANE CAPIZZI
Director: RANDY FISHER (229-5406)
Deputy Director: ROLLIE ROUSSEAU (229-5247)
Assistant Director, Fisheries: HARRY H. WAGNER (229-5440)
Assistant Director, Wildlife: ROD INGRAM (229-5454)
Assistant Director, Field Operations: MIKE GOLDEN (229-5667)
Section Chiefs:
  Division of Habitat, Conservation and Planning: NANCY Mac HUGH (229-5433)
  Office of Public Affairs: BARBARA HUTCHINSON (229-5425)
  Assistant Director, Administrative Services: JOHN VAUGHN (229-5442)
  Engineering: FOLKERT MENGER (229-5695)
  Personnel: BARBARA DODD (229-5392)
  Realty: WAYNE RAWLINS (229-5249)
  Statistical Services: DALE CHRISTENSEN (229-5048)
Regional Supervisors:
  Region 1: RICHARD L. LANTZ (757-4186)
  Region 2: JAMES L. FESSLER (440-3353)
  Region 3: STEVE LEWIS (388-6363)
  Region 4: WARREN W. ANEY (963-2138)
  Region 5: RON BARTELS (573-6582)
  Region 6: NEAL COENEN (867-4741)
  Region 7: ROBERT R. MABEN (657-2008)
Publication: *Oregon Wildlife*
Editor: JAMES L. GLADSON (229-5435)

DEPARTMENT OF GEOLOGY AND MINERAL INDUSTRIES, 910 State Office Bldg., Portland 97201-5528 (503, 229-5580)
State Geologist: DONALD A. HULL
Publications: List available on request.

DEPARTMENT OF TRANSPORTATION, Transportation Bldg., Salem 97310 (503, 378-6388)
Director: ROBERT N. BOTHMAN
State Parks and Recreation Division: DAVID G. TALBOT (378-6305)
Environmental Section: EB ENGELMANN, Manager (378-8486)

OREGON COOPERATIVE FISHERY RESEARCH UNIT, U.S.D.I.,

Department of Fisheries and Wildlife, Oregon State University, Corvallis 97331 (503, 754-4531)
Leader: DR. CARL B. SCHRECK
Assistant Leader: DR. HIRAM W. LI

OREGON COOPERATIVE WILDLIFE RESEARCH UNIT, U.S.D.I.,

104 Nash Hall, Oregon State University, Corvallis 97331 (503, 754-4531)
Leader: DR. E. CHARLES MESLOW
Assistant Leader: DR. ROBERT G. ANTHONY

SEA GRANT PROGRAM

Director, Sea Grant College Program: WILLIAM Q. WICK, Administrative Services, Bldg. A320, Oregon State University, Corvallis 97331 (503, 754-2714)
Extension Sea Grant Program: BRUCE DeYOUNG, Program Leader, Agric. and Res. Economics, Bal E 240, Oregon State University, Corvallis 97331 (503, 754-4531)

STATE DEPARTMENT OF FORESTRY, 2600 State St., Salem 97310 (503, 378-2560)

Responsible for fire protection of 15 million acres of private and public forests; directs insect and disease management on 11 million acres of state and private forests; manages 786,000 acres of state-owned forests; provides forestry assistance to private forest landowners; enforces Oregon forest laws; provides forest marketing assistance, forestry information to schools, organizations, and individuals; and advises Governor and State Legislature on forestry matters. Established: 1911.
State Board of Forestry: Vacant
State Forester: JAMES E. BROWN (378-2511)
Deputy State Forester: THOMAS W. LANE (378-2507)
Associate State Forester: NEIL T. SKILL (378-2564)
Assistant State Forester, Administrative Services: STEVE JACKY (378-2104)
Assistant State Forester, Forest Management: J. MICHAEL BEYERLE (378-2539)
Assistant State Forester, Forest Protection: FRED R. ROBINSON (378-2551)
Fire Prevention Director: LEE LAFFERTY (378-2513)
Fire Control Division Executive Assistant: DOUGLAS J. COYLE (378-2517)
Public Affairs Director: JAMES G. FISHER (378-2562)
Insect and Disease Management Director: LeROY KLINE (378-2554)
Service Forestry Director: ROBERT MADSEN (378-2148)
Forest Management Staff Director: WILLIAM VOELKER (378-2552)
Forest Practices Director: RAY CRAIG (378-2494)
Forest Products Marketing Director: WALLACE RUTLEDGE (378-5557)
Board Members: TOM WALSH, Chairman, 3015 SW lst Ave., Portland 97201 (222-4375); JAMES E. BROWN, Secretary, 2600 State St., Salem 97310 (378-2511); JANET McLENNAN, 5252 SW Northwood Ave., Portland 97201 (230-5154); L.W. (Lynn) NEWBRY, 707 Valley View Rd., Talent 97540 (535-2362); RICHARD E. ROY, 900 SW 5th Ave., Suite 2300, Portland 97204 (294-9519); JOHN SHELK, P.O. Box 668, Prineville 97754 (447-6296); BARTE STARKER, P.O. Box 809, Corvallis 97339 (929-2477); PAT STRAUB, 2087 Orchard Heights Rd., Salem 97304 (585-4407)

Area Directors

Northwest Oregon: LEE OMAN, 801 Gales Creek Rd., Forest Grove 97116 (503, 357-2191)

Eastern Oregon: J. FRED GRAF, R.D. 2, Box 357, Prineville 97754 (447-5658)
Southern Oregon: CRAIG ROYCE, 1758 NE Airport Rd., Roseburg 97470 (440-3412)
Publication: *The Forest Log*
Editor: KATHY APLIN (378-2562)

STATE EXTENSION SERVICES

Director of Extension Service: O.E. SMITH, Oregon State University, Corvallis 97331 (503, 754-2713)
Coordinator, Forestry Extension: GEORGE W. BENGTSON, Peavy Hall 150, Oregon State University, Corvallis 97331 (754-2221)
Associate Directors, Extension County Programs: HAROLD KERR; TOM ZINN; ALBERTA B. JOHNSTON, Extension Hall 102, Oregon State University, Corvallis 97331 (754-2711)
Associate Director, Campus Programs: NORMAN GOETZE, Extension Hall 101, Oregon State University, Corvallis 97331 (754-2711)
Head, Fisheries and Wildlife: RICHARD A. TUBB, Nash Hall 104C, Oregon State University, Corvallis 97331 (754-4531)
Extension Wildlife Specialist: DAVID S. de CALESTA, Nash Hall 104E, Oregon State University, Corvallis 97331 (754-4586)

STATE MARINE BOARD, 3000 Market St., NE, 505, Salem 97310 (503, 378-8587)

Director: PAUL E. DONHEFFNER

WATER RESOURCES DEPARTMENT, 3850 Portland Rd., NE, Salem 97310 (503, 378-3739)

Created by the 1975 Oregon legislature when it consolidated the water responsibilities of other state agencies dating back to 1909, its purpose is to safeguard the citizens of Oregon and their interests through the protection, conservation and development of the state's water resources.
Director: WILLIAM H. YOUNG (378-2982)
Administrator, Resource Management Division: REBECCA KREAG (378-3671)
Administrator, Field Operations Division: JOHN BORDEN, Deputy Director (378-8128)
Administrator, Central Services Division: KEN WEESE (378-3741)

Water Resources Commission

WILLIAM R. BLOSSER, Chairman, Dayton (864-2282); HADLEY C. AKINS, Pendleton (278-0902/276-0669); DEIRDRE MALARKEY, Eugene (342-5078); CLIFF BENTZ, Ontario (889-5368); CLAUDE CURRAN, Ashland (482-6251); LORNA J. STICKEL, Portland (248-3182); JAMES HOWLAND, Corvallis (752-4271/753-3691)

CITIZENS' GROUPS

 * OREGON WILDLIFE FEDERATION, P.O. Box 3072, Portland 97208-3072 (503, 647-5796)*
A representative statewide organization, affiliated with the National Wildlife Federation, primarily devoted to the wise use, conservation, aesthetic appreciation, and restoration of wildlife and other natural resources.
President: BARBARA BREUNIG, 15045 NE Sacramento, #68, Portland 97230 (253-6540)
Executive Secretary: DAVE W. DORAN
Affiliate Representative: DAVE W. DORAN
Alternate: JOHN PLATT, Rt. 1. Box 546, Hillsboro 97123 (238-0667)

Publication: *Resource Review*
Editor: DR. LARRY L. SOWA, 18438 So. Holly Ln., Oregon City
97045 (655-4543)

ENVIRONMENTAL EDUCATION PROJECT, School of Education,
Portland State University, P.O. Box 751, Portland 97207
(503, 229-4721)
Nonprofit, educational organization seeking to create quality learning experiences by providing access to environmental education
resources and materials, conducting in-service and pre-service
teacher training workshops, and promoting cooperative efforts that
help people of the Northwest explore, understand, and celebrate
their relationship to the natural world. Founded: 1972.
Director: LARRY BEUTLER
Publication: *Clearing*
Editor: LARRY BEUTLER

**IZAAK WALTON LEAGUE OF AMERICA, INC. (Oregon
Division)**
To protect, perpetuate, and strive for renewal of Oregon's natural
resources, including the air, soil, woods, waters, and wildlife; to
promote means and opportunities for education of the public in
respect to such resources and the enjoyment and utilization
thereof. Membership: 1,319. Founded: 1930.
President: ELLIS ANTRIM, 1241 Cleveland Hill Rd., Roseberg
97470 (503, 672-2552)
Executive Secretary: DYAS RAWLINGS, 1825 NE 92nd Ave.,
Portland 97220 (255-2070)

**OREGON ASSOCIATION OF SOIL AND WATER
CONSERVATION DISTRICTS**
President: JOE BRUMBACH, 4260 Buckhorn Rd., Roseburg
97470 (503, 673-3998)
Vice-President: HAROLD LAMPI, Hamlet Route, Box 523, Seaside
97138 (738- 5998)
Treasurer: BEN CHRISTENSEN, 23888 Rowland Rd., Harrisburg
97446 (995-6857)

OREGON BASS CHAPTER FEDERATION
An organization of Bassmaster Chapters, affiliated with Bass
Anglers Sportsman Society, organized to fight pollution, assist state
and national conservation agencies in their efforts, and to teach the
young people of our country good conservation practices. Dedicated to the realistic conservation of our water resources.
President: BILL PORFILY, P.O. Box 643, Stanfield 97875 (503,
449-1327/4427)

OREGON ENVIRONMENTAL COUNCIL, INC., 2637 SW Water
Ave., Portland 97201 (503, 222-1963)
A coalition of environmental, conservation, recreation, health, and
labor organizations joined together to encourage citizen, legislative,
legal and administrative action toward the protection and restora-
tion of Oregon's environment, and the creation of communities
which reflect these values, through creative planning, education,
and wise stewardship. Membership: 70 organizations, 1,800
individuals. Organized: 1968.
President: ALLEN JOHNSON, 767 Williamette St., Suite 203,
Eugene 97401
Secretary: JIM OWENS, 3946 NE 37th, Portland 97212
Executive Director: JOHN A. CHARLES
Publication: *Earthwatch Oregon*

Publications Directors: MARY KYLE McCURDY; JEAN MEDDAUGH

OREGON NATURAL RESOURCES COUNCIL, Yeon Building,
Suite 1050, 522 Southwest Fifth Ave., Portland 97204
(503, 223-9001)
A nonprofit, tax-exempt statewide association of conservation,
sportsmen, recreation, commercial, and educational organizations
actively involved in citizen participation for wise use and steward-
ship of Oregon's public lands and waters, especially protection of
wilderness, wild rivers and other watershed and wildlife values.
Membership: 90 organizations, 3,000 individuals. Organized in
1972, and incorporated in 1974.
President: TOM SMITH
Vice-President: DAVID ATKIN
Executive Director: JAMES MONTEITH
Associate Director for Administration and Finance: NANCY DOTY
Associate Director for Conservation: ANDY KERR
Northeast Field Coordinator: TIM LILLEBO, Prairie City (820-
3714)
Ocean Campaign Coordinator: CAROL ALEXANDER
West-Central Field Coordinator: WENDELL WOOD
Publication: *Wild Oregon*
Editor: DAVID O'TOOLE

OREGON SMALL WOODLANDS ASSOCIATION, 1149 Court
St., NE, Salem 97301 (503, 588-0050)
A statewide organization affiliated with the National Woodland
Owners Association, Inc., dedicated to the protection, management,
use, and enhancement of Oregon's forest resources. Membership:
2,700. Founded: 1967.
President: PHIL KUHL (820-4495)
Executive Director: GARY M. CARLSON
Publication: *NORTHWEST WOODLANDS*
Editor: LORI D. RASOR (228-3624)

**OREGON STATE PUBLIC INTEREST RESEARCH GROUP
(OSPIRG),** 027 SW Arthur, Portland 97214 (503, 222-
9641) (Monthly Board of Directors Meetings.)
Provides advocacy, research, and information to consumers and
those interested in environmental protection since 1971. We work
on issues such as car buyer protection, landlord/tenant relations,
Oregon utility reform, toxic waste problems, and other consumer
issues affecting Oregonians. Membership: 30,000 students and
over 40,000 community members.
Chair of Board of Directors: MAUREEN KIRK
Publications: Consumer Guides; *Citizen Agenda Newsletter; OS-
PIRG Impact;* Newsletter; *Legislative Insider; Connection*

OREGON TROUT, INC., P.O. Box 19540, Portland 97219
(503, 244-2292)
A statewide organization that unites all concerned anglers and
individuals with the single purpose of preserving, protecting, and
restoring wild fish and their habitat in Oregon.
President: JIM WILLIAMS
Vice-President: RICHARD MACE
Treasurer: FLOYD ARMS
Secretary: LARRY CALLISTER
Executive Director: BILL BAKKE
Administrative Director: CALVIN P. COLE

TROUT UNLIMITED OREGON
A statewide council with four chapters working for the protection
and enhancement of the coldwater fishery resource.
Chairman and National Director: DAVE NOLTE, P.O. Box 7479,
Bend 97708 (503, 389-8149)

WILDLIFE SOCIETY OREGON CHAPTER
President: CHARLES BRUCE, Rt. 5, Box 325, Corvallis 97330 (503, 757-4186)
President-Elect: MARY WALTER, Rt. 5, Box 325, Corvallis 97330 (757-4186)
Secretary-Treasurer: GEOFF PAMPUSH, 1234 NE 12th, Portland 97210 (228-9561)

PENNSYLVANIA

GOVERNMENT AGENCIES

GOVERNOR: ROBERT P. CASEY, Governor of Pennsylvania, State Capitol, Harrisburg 17120 (717, 787-2500)

DEPARTMENT OF AGRICULTURE, 2301 N. Cameron St., Harrisburg 17110-9408 (717, 787-4737)
Responsible for the development of agriculture, marketing agricultural goods and upgrading the quality of farm and rural life. In addition to its consumer protection and regulatory services, the department is responsible for enforcing state laws, governing preservation of farmlands, monitoring farmland conversion, and cooperating with state-federal soil water conservation programs.
Secretary of Agriculture: BOYD E. WOLFF (787-4737)
Deputy Secretary, Regulatory Affairs: NEAL R. BUSS (787-3418)
Deputy Secretary, Administration: J. FRED KING (783-6985)
Deputy Secretary, Market and Economic Development: THOMAS P. FERGUSON (787-9125)
Executive Assistant to the Secretary: STEVE CRAWFORD (787-4626)

Bureaus
Animal Industry: MAX A. VANBUSKIRK, JR., VMD, Director (783-5301)
Amusement Rides and Attractions: NEIL CASHMAN, Director (787-2291)
Agricultural Development: PAUL HAUGHLAND, Director (783-8460)
Dog Law Enforcement: WILLIAM KENNEDY, Director (787-4833)
Foods and Chemistry: LEROY C. CORBIN, Director (787-4315)
Marketing Development: RON GASKILL, Director (787-4210)
Plant Industry: WALTER PEECHATKA, Director (787-4843)
Administrative Services: PETER DALINA, Director (787-4854)
Comptroller: ROSS E. STARNER (787-3105)
Press Office: GENE SCHENCK, Press Secretary (787-5085)
Standard Weights and Measures: JOHN YAHNER, Director (787-9089)
Pennsylvania State Farm Show: Vacant, Director (787-5373)
Government Donated Food: BARRY SHUTT, Director (787-2940)
Legal Counsel: JERRY OSBURN (787-8744)
Pennsylvania Agricultural Statistics Service: WALLACE EVANS, Director (787-3904)
Pennsylvania Horse Racing Commission: Vacant, Executive Secretary (787-1942)
Pennsylvania Harness Racing Commission: RICHARD SHARBAUGH, Executive Secretary (787-5196)
Publication: *Agriculture News Bulletin*

Regional Offices
Region I: LINDA FIELD, Director, Box 413, R.D. 4, Meadville 16335 (814, 336-6890)
Region II: THOMAS HERMAN, Director, Box 208, 675 Rose St., Williamsport 17701 (717, 327-3550)

Region III: FRANCIS McHUGH, Director, Rt. 92 South, Tunkhannock 18657 (717, 836-2181)
Region IV: CLAYTON WINEBARK, Director, 5349 William Flynn Hwy., Gibsonia 15044 (412, 443-1585)
Region V: THEODORE HOOVER, Director, 615 Howard Ave., Altoona 16601 (814, 946-7315)
Region VI: DAVID STETLER, Director, P.O. Box 419, Summerdale 17093 (717, 787-3400)
Region VII: ERNEST HECKMAN, Director, Rt. 113, Creamery, 19403 (215, 489-1003)

DEPARTMENT OF ENVIRONMENTAL RESOURCES, Communications Office, 9th Fl., Fulton Bldg., Box 2063, Harrisburg 17120 (717, 787-1323)
The DER mission is to ensure the wise use of Pennsylvania's natural resources; protect and restore the natural environment; protect public health and safety; provide opportunities for outdoor recreation; and enhance the quality of life for all Pennsylvanians. The DER will carry out its stewardship responsibilities in a fair and timely manner that both respects environmental values and is deserving of the public's trust.
Secretary: ARTHUR DAVIS (787-2814)
Comptroller: ROSS E. STARNER (787-3105)
Press Secretary, Press Office: JOHN H. WRIGHT (787-1323)
Director, Topographic and Geologic Survey: DR. DONALD HOSKINS (787-2169)
Deputy Secretary, Administration: GREGG ROBERTSON (787-7116)
Chief Counsel: KEITH WELKS, Director (787-4489)
Deputy Secretary, Environmental Protection: MARK M. McCLELLAN (787-5028)
Deputy Secretary, Public Liaison: R. DAVID MYERS (787-9580)
Special Deputy Secretary: PATRICK J. SOLANO (783-6387)
Deputy, Resources Management: JAMES R. GRACE (787-2869)
Dirctor, Bureau of Deep Mine Safety: THOMAS WARD (787-1376)
Director, Secretary's Office of Policy: FREDERICK G. CARLSON (783-1566)
Director, Office of Environmental Management: RICHARD M. BOARDMAN (787-4686)
Director, Office of Environmental Energy Management: GARY L. MERRITT (787-4686)
Director, Bureau of Mining and Reclamation: ERNEST GIOVANNITTI (787-5103)
Director, Bureau of Waste Management: JAMES P. SNYDER (787-9870)
Director, Bureau of Radiation Protection: THOMAS M. GERUSKY (787-2480)
Director, Bureau of Community Environmental Control: GLENN E. MAURER (787-9035)
Director (Acting), Bureau of Water Quality Management: DANIEL DRAWBAUGH (787-2666)
Director, Bureau of Air Quality Control: JAMES K. HAMBRIGHT (787-9702)
Director (Acting), Bureau of Forestry: JAMES NELSON (787-2703)
Director, Bureau of State Parks: WILLIAM C. FORREY (787-6640)
Director, Bureau of Water Resource Management: JOHN E. McSPARRAN (787-6750)
Director (Acting), Bureau of Water Projects: JAMES McNANEY (787-3411)
Chief Engineer, Office of Resources Management, Contracts and Engineering: J. DIXON EARLEY (783-8796)
Director, Bureau of Soil and Water Conservation: PAUL O. SWARTZ (787-5267)

FISH COMMISSION, P.O. Box 1673, Harrisburg 17105 (717, 657-4518) Organized: 1866.

President: LEON REED

Vice-President: DAVID COE

Commission Members: WILLIAM SABATOSE; JOAN PLUMLY; LEONARD A. GREEN; T.T. (Ted) METZGER, JR.; MARILYN BLACK; CALVIN J. KERN; J. WAYNE YORKS; ROSS J. HUHN

Executive Director: EDWARD R. MILLER (657-4515)

Director, Bureau of Education and Information: CHERYL K. RILEY (657-4518)

Chief Counsel and Director, Environmental Affairs: DENNIS T. GUISE (657-4545)

Director, Bureau of Administrative Services: ALLISON MAYHEW (657-4522)

Director, Bureau of Fisheries: DELANO GRAFF (814, 359-5169)

Director, Bureau of Property and Facilities Management: JAMES A. YOUNG (814, 359-5152)

Director, Bureau of Boating: JOHN F. SIMMONS (657-4538)

Director, Bureau of Law Enforcement: EDWARD W. MANHART (657-4542)

Publications: *Pennsylvania Angler; Boat Pennsylvania*

Editor: ARTHUR J. MICHAELS (657-4520)

Regional Law Enforcement Supervisors

Region I (Northwest): WALTER LAZUSKY, 1281 Otter St., Franklin 16323 (814, 437-5774)

Region II (Southwest): THOMAS QUALTERS, R.D. 2, Somerset 15501 (814, 445-8974)

Region III (Northeast): KERRY MESSERLE, Box 88, Sweet Valley 18656 (717, 477-5717)

Region IV (Southeast): ROBERT PERRY, Box 6, Elm 17521 (717, 626-0228)

Region V (North Central): PAUL SWANSON, Box 187, Fishing Creek Rd., Lamar 16848 (717, 726-6056)

Region VI (South Central): FRANK SCHILLING, R.D. #1, Box 848, Newville 17241 (717, 486-7087)

GAME COMMISSION, 2001 Elmerton Ave., Harrisburg 17110-9797 (717, 787-4250)

Organized: 1895.

Commission Members: C. DANA CHALFANT, President; ROY J. WAGNER, JR., Vice-President; CLAIR W. CLEMENS, Secretary; THOMAS P. GREENLEE; TAYLOR A. DOEBLER, JR.; DONALD R. CRAUL; EDWARD L. VOGUE, JR.; EDSON S. CRAFTS

Executive Director: PETER S. DUNCAN III

Deputy Executive Director: PAUL C. WEIKEL

Comptroller: ROSS E. STARNER (787-4492)

Director, Bureau of Administration: KENNETH L. HESS (787-5670)

Chief, Division of Personnel: ROBERT M. TOTH (787-7836)

Director, Bureau of Wildlife Management: DALE E. SHEFFER (787-5529)

Director, Bureau of Information and Education: LANTZ A. HOFFMAN (787-6286)

Assistant Director, Bureau of Information and Education: J. CARL GRAYBILL, JR. (787-6286)

Chief, Public Information Division: R. THEODORE GODSHALL (787-7015)

Chief, Hunter and Trapper Education Division: JAMES P. FILKOSKY (787-7015)

Chief, Audio-Visual Services Division: JOSEPH OSMAN (787-1434)

Chief, Exhibits and Visitor Center Division: GLENN H. HOY (964-3022)

Legislative Liaison: JOHN W. PLOWMAN, JR. (783-1076)

Director, Bureau of Land Management: JACOB I. SITLINGER (787-6818)

Director, Bureau of Law Enforcement: J. RICHARD FAGAN (787-5743)

Regional Directors

Northwest Region: JACK M. LAVERY, Franklin 16323 (814, 432-3187)

Southwest Region: DONALD C. MADL, Ligonier 15658 (412, 238-9523)

North Central Region: WILLIS A. SNEATH, Jersey Shore 17740 (717, 398-4744)

South Central Region: DAVID SLOAN, Huntingdon 16652 (814, 643-1831)

Northeast Region: BARRY L. WARNER, Dallas 18612-0220 (717, 675-1143)

Southeast Region: CHARLES J. WILLIAMS, Reading 19605-9791 (215, 926-3136)

Publication: *Pennsylvania Game News*

Editor and Chief, Paid Publications Division: ROBERT S. BELL

Assistant Editor and Chief, Paid Publications Division: ROBERT C. MITCHELL

PENNSYLVANIA COOPERATIVE FISH AND WILDLIFE RESEARCH UNIT, Ferguson Bldg., Pennsylvania State University, University Park 16802 (814, 865-4511)

Established in 1938 as a cooperative activity among The Pennsylvania State University, Pennsylvania Fish Commission, Wildlife Management Institute, Pennsylvania Game Commission, and the U.S. Fish and Wildlife Service. Areas of research are: the effects of natural and man-made forces on aquatic and terrestrial ecosystems, animal-habitat interactions, acid precipitation effects, fish and wildlife management, and health profiles of game animals. Graduate training is also provided.

Unit Leader: DR. ROBERT F. CARLINE

Associate Leaders: DR. DEAN E. ARNOLD, Fisheries; DR. GERALD L. STORM, Wildlife

Publication: Annual Report available on request.

PENNSYLVANIA ENERGY OFFICE, P.O. Box 8010, Harrisburg 17105 (717, 783-9981)

To insure energy security for the Commonwealth of Pennsylvania through planning, development, and conservation. PEO is the principal authority for development of energy policy and coordination of federal grant programs; also active in the areas of coal development, renewable energy, projects, utility reform, and energy conservation. Established: 1974.

Chairman: LT. GOV. MARK S. SINGEL

Executive Director: JAN H. FREEMAN (783-9981)

Deputy Director for Administration: Vacant (783-9981)

Deputy Director for Development: DANE BICKLEY (783-9981)

Deputy Director for Renewables: DAN DESMOND (783-9981)

Press Secretary: DARLENE CRAWFORD (783-9981)

General Counsel: ROGER CLARK (783-9981)

Associate Director for Fossil Fuels: RODERICK FLETCHER (783-9981)

Associate Director for Energy Development: JOHN MEMMI (783-9981)

Publications: List available on request.

STATE CONSERVATION COMMISSION, Department of Environmental Resources, Executive House, P.O. Box 2357, Second and Chestnut Sts., Harrisburg 17120 (717, 787-5267)

To establish policy for Pennsylvania's 66 local conservation districts. Programs administered by the commission include: a

$1,200,000 grant program, which provides funds to conservation districts for the employment of managerial and technical staff; a $4 million Chesapeake Bay Program, which provides technical and financial assistance to farmers to install soil conservation and nutrient management practices. Established: 1945.
Chairman: ARTHUR DAVIS
Executive Secretary: PAUL O. SWARTZ

STATE EXTENSION SERVICES

Dean and Director of Extension Service: LAMARTINE F. HOOD, Pennsylvania State University, 101 Ferguson Bldg., University Park 16802 (814, 865-2541)
Associate Director of Extension Service: DR. WAYNE SCHUTJER, 323 Agricultural Administration Bldg., Pennsylvania State University, University Park 16802 (863-3438)
Pesticides Coordinator: DR. WINAND K. HOCK, 419 Agricultural Administration Bldg., Pennsylvania State University, University Park 16802 (863-0263)
Wildlife Resource Specialist: DR. MARGARET BRITTINGHAM, 110 Ferguson Bldg., Pennsylvania State University, University Park 16802 (863-0401)

CITIZENS' GROUPS

PENNSYLVANIA FEDERATION OF SPORTSMEN'S CLUBS, INC., 2426 N. Second St., Harrisburg 17110 (717, 232-3480)
A representative statewide organization, affiliated with the National Wildlife Federation, primarily devoted to the wise use, conservation, aesthetic appreciation, and restoration of wildlife and other natural resources.
President: JAMES BIERY, JR., 3718 Vista Ter., Harrisburg 17111
Executive Director: DICK BRAME
Affiliate Representative: JAMES N. PRICE, Star Route, Tannersville 18372 (717, 629-0927)
Alternate: WENDELL Z. PETERSON, 1036 Rimrock Rd., Greensburg 15601
Publication: Pennsylvania Wildlife
Editor: JACK HUBLEY

AMERICAN BASS ASSOCIATION OF EASTERN PENNSYLVANIA

An organization of the individual members and bass fishing clubs, affiliated with the American Bass Association, Inc., dedicated to protecting and enhancing the state's fishery resources; to promote the sport of bass fishing; and to teach youngsters the fun of fishing and instill in them an appreciation of the life-giving waters of America.
President: JOE NORDON, 1205 McKean Rd., Ambler 19002 (215, 628-4024)

BRANDYWINE CONSERVANCY, INC., P.O. Box 141, Chadds Ford 19317 (215, 388-7601/459-1900)
A nonprofit organization providing model land use and environmental regulations for Pennsylvania municipalities, and land and historic site conservation and management assistance to landowners and conservation organizations, primarily in Pennsylvania and Delaware. Membership: 2,500. Founded: 1967.
Chairman: GEORGE A. WEYMOUTH
Executive Director: JAMES H. DUFF (Ext. 135)
Public Relations: JOHN SHEPPARD (Ext. 136)
Environmental Management Center Staff:
Director: H. WILLIAM SELLERS (Ext. 145)
Assistant Director: DAVID C. SWEET (Ext. 152)

Senior Planners: JOHN SNOOK (Ext. 187); JOHN GAADT (Ext. 188); DAVID D. SHIELDS (Ext. 142)
Publications: *The Catalyst; Environmental Currents; Environmental Management Handbook*

IZAAK WALTON LEAGUE OF AMERICA, INC. (Pennsylvania Div.)

President: PAUL H. KAUFFMAN, 806 E. 10th Ave., York 17402 (717, 755-8255)
Secretary: MARTHA SHAFFER, P.O. Box 35, Loganville 17342 (428-2883)

NATURAL LANDS TRUST, INC., AND PHILADELPHIA CONSERVATIONISTS, INC.,

1616 Walnut St., Suite 812, Philadelphia 19103-5308 (215, 732-0940)
Specializing in the management of open space for conservation purposes. The NLT-PC owns and/or manages more than 16,000 acres, and its staff of 542 persons provides professional planning, management, and information services for the permanent protection of natural and agricultural lands in the Mid-Atlantic region.
Planning and Management Center, Hildacy Farm, 1031 Palmers Mill Rd., Media 19063 (353-5587)
President: ANDREW L. JOHNSON
Vice-President: MICHAEL G. CLARKE
Director, Management: RICHARD STUDENMUND
Director, Planning: ANDREW PITZ
Director, Berks County, Pennsylvania: DENNIS G. COLLINS
Maryland, Mount Harmon Plantation, P.O. Box 65, Earleville 21919
Property Manager: ALLAN R. CHRISTOPHER (301, 275-8819)
Tour Coordinator: JANE V. CHRISTOPHER (301, 275-2721)
Youghiogheny River Field Office, P.O. Box 353, Friendsville 21531 (301, 387-7167)
Field Representative: KEITH A. ROBERTS

PENNSYLVANIA ASSOCIATION OF CONSERVATION DISTRICT DIRECTORS, INC.

President: FRANK MALINZAK, 1889 Rt. 22-322, Dauphin 17018 (717, 921-8715)
Vice-President: DAVID MANKAMYER, R.D. 7, Somerset 15501 (814, 445-8618)
Secretary: ROBERT WAGNER, 373 Scott Rd., Quarryville 17566 (717, 529-2831)
Treasurer: JAMES BEAR, R.D. #4, Box 788, Newville 17241 (717, 776-3964)
Council Member: WALTER R. ROSSMAN, R.D. 3, Box 310, Ebensburg 15931 (814, 472-6092)
Executive Director: PATRICIA W. DEVLIN, 121 South St., Harrisburg 17101 (717, 236-1006)
Chesapeake Bay Education Coordinator: ANNE H. SWAIM, 225 Pine St., Harrisburg 17101 (717, 236-1006)

PENNSYLVANIA BASS CHAPTER FEDERATION, INC.

An organization of Bassmaster Chapters, affiliated with the Bass Anglers Sportsman Society, organized to fight pollution, assist state and national conservation agencies in their efforts, and to teach the young people of our country good conservation practices. Dedicated to the realistic conservation of our water resources.
President: CHUCK BASSELL, 1269 Browntown Rd., Larimar 15647 (412, 564-4047)

PENNSYLVANIA CITIZENS' ADVISORY COUNCIL, 8th Fl., Rm. 816, Executive House, P.O. Box 2357, Harrisburg 17120 (717, 787-4527)

To review all state environmental laws and make suggestions for revision, modification, and codification thereof; study and review

the work of the Department of Environmental Resources; make recommendations for the improvement of the work of the department; report annually to the Governor and Legislature. Created by Act 275 of the PA General Assembly, 1971.
Chairperson: PAUL W. HESS, Ph.D., Hershey
Vice-Chairperson: ANNE MARTIN, Pittsburgh
Executive Director: MICHAEL D. KREMPASKY
Administrative Assistant to the Council: ANITA L. WASHINGTON

PENNSYLVANIA ENVIRONMENTAL COUNCIL, INC., (PEC),
225 S. 15th St., Philadelphia 19102 (215, 735-0966)
Nonprofit, nonpartisan, statewide membership organization, which strives to coordinate and strengthen the efforts of concerned groups and individuals to improve the quality of the environment in Pennsylvania. PEC forms coalitions to secure the passage and enforcement of effective environmental legislation and regulations. PEC also conducts research and holds conferences on environmental issues. Members: 1,500. Organized: 1969.
President: JOSEPH M. MANKO
Executive Director: JOANNE REDMOND DENWORTH
Publications and Television Programs: *Environmental Forum; Legislative Update; Pennsylvania's Environmental Laws, Rules, and Regulations At A Glance; Acid Rain in Pennsylvania; Municipal Waste Management; Hazardous Waste Management; Groundwater Protection; Growth Management*
Editor: BRIAN J. HILL

PENNSYLVANIA FORESTRY ASSOCIATION, THE, 410 E. Main
St., Mechanicsburg 17055
An independent, nonprofit conservation organization. The oldest of all state conservation and forestry associations. Dedicated to environmental improvement and wise use of natural resources. Membership includes a cross section of all groups and individuals interested in true conservation. Founded: 1886.
President: W.R. ROSSMAN, Pennsylvania Electric Company, 1001 Broad St., Johnstown 15907 (814, 533-8245)
Vice-President: RICHARD THORPE, Box 158, Rt. 1, Roaring Branch 17765
Secretary: WILLIAM S. CORLETT, 51 Fort St., Lemoyne 17043 (717, 737-7118)
Treasurer: PATRICK LANTZ, 361 Bethel Church Rd., New Cumberland 17070 (717, 787-2105)
Executive Director: Vacant
Publication: *Pennsylvania Forests*
Editor: ELLEN ROM, 209 A Ferguson Bldg., University Park 16802

PENNSYLVANIA RECREATION AND PARK SOCIETY, INC.,
723 South Atherton St., State College 16801 (814, 234-4272)
To promote quality recreation and park opportunities for all the citizens of the Commonwealth of Pennsylvania by actively involving professionals and citizens in recreation, park and conservation programs, by fostering and maintaining high standards of professional qualifications and ethics, and by providing quality educational opportunities. Membership: 1,400. Founded: 1935.
President: LAWRENCE E. BEST, Milton Hershey School, P.O. Box 830, Hershey 17033 (717, 534-3540)
President-Elect: DANIEL J. DINUNZIO, Carlisle Parks and Recreation Department, 415 Franklin St., Carlisle 17013 (717, 243-3318)
Secretary: SUZANNE MARK, Corporate Recreation Coord. Outdoor World, P.O. Box 447, Bushkill 18324 (717, 588-6661/Ext. 2321)
Treasurer: GARY SMITH, 519 North Houcks Rd., Harrisburg 17109 (717, 783-3317)
Executive Director: ROBERT D. GRIFFITH, Pennsylvania Recreation

and Park Society, Inc., 723 South Atherton St., State College 16801
Publication: *Pennsylvania Recreation and Parks*
Editor: VANILA S. TIERNEY

PENNSYLVANIA RESOURCES COUNCIL, INC., (formerly PA
Roadside Council), 25 West 3rd St. P.O. Box 88, Media 19063 (1-800, 346-4242)
Pennsylvania Resources Council is the oldest conservation organization in Pennsylvania. It works to promote recycling, fight litter, and protect scenic beauty. It also represents all of the major recycling groups in Pennsylvania as well as individuals, municipalities, and businesses involved in recycling, and is a state-wide citizen action organization. Organized: 1939.
President: ROBERT G. STRUBLE, JR. (793-1090)
Vice-Presidents: CAROLE RUBLEY (215, 524-3500); ROBERT B. McKINSTRY (215, 636-4669); FLORENCE THOMPSON (717, 784-6631)
Executive Director: RUTH H. BECKER
Publications: *PRC Newsletter; All About Recycling*

TROUT UNLIMITED PENNSYLVANIA COUNCIL
A statewide council with 52 chapters working for the protection and enhancement of the coldwater fishery resource.
Chairman: RICHARD TIETBOHL, 863 Hillside Dr., Camp Hill 17011 (717, 763-1737)
National Directors: CHRISTIAN LANTZSCH, Vice-Chairman, Mellon Bank, Spanich Tract Rd., Sewickley 15143 (412, 741-4741); ALBERT GRETZ, Box 19, Star Route, Oliveburg 15764 (814, 938-4331); HERBERT WEIGL, 13 N. Letort Dr., Carlisle 17013 (717, 245-2646)

WESTERN PENNSYLVANIA CONSERVANCY, 316 Fourth Ave.,
Pittsburgh 15222 (412, 288-2777)
A nonprofit citizens' organization dedicated to the conservation of forests, and waters. Membership: 16,000. Founded: 1932.
Chairman: JOSHUA C. WHETZEL, JR.
Vice-Chairman: FRANCIS B. NIMICK, JR.
President: JOHN C. OLIVER III
Vice-President and Counsel: THOMAS M. SCHMIDT
Secretary: M. GRAHAM NETTING
Treasurer: JARVIS B. CECIL
Administrative Officer, Assistant Secretary-Treasurer: CYNTHIA CARROW LOVEJOY
Director, Land Acquisition: ANTHONY P. SUPPA
Director, Natural Areas Program: PAUL G. WIEGMAN
Publications: *Conserve; Business Associate Newsletter*
Editor and Director, Public Relations and Membership: WILLIAM L. RANDOUR

WILDLANDS CONSERVANCY, (formerly Lehigh Valley
Conservancy), 601 Orchid Pl., Emmaus 18049-1637 (215, 965-4397)
A nonprofit, member-supported organization serving eastern Pennsylvania. Involved in land preservation and environmental education. Preserved over 5,500 acres of open space, much of it in cooperation with the Pennsylvania Game Commission. Operates nature preserves and sanctuaries with concomitant educational programs for students and families; develops and implements plans for stream greenway and other types of preservations; developing a curriculum (kindergarten through college) that teaches responsible watershed stewardship; and operates the Friends of the Parks, an advocacy group for Lehigh Valley parks. Founded: 1973.
President: THOMAS STONEBACK
Executive Director: THOMAS J. KERR

Director, Environmental Management: JOSEPH E. HOFFMAN
Publication: *Wildlands*

WILDLIFE SOCIETY PENNSYLVANIA CHAPTER
President: DANIEL A. DEVLIN, P.O. Box 1467, Harrisburg 17120 (717, 787-3444)
President-Elect: GORDON KIRKLAND, Shippensburg University, Shippensburg 17257 (532-1407)
Secretary-Treasurer: PETER DALBY, Clarion University, Biology Department, Clarion 16214

PUERTO RICO

GOVERNMENT AGENCIES

GOVERNOR: RAFAEL HERNANDEZ-COLON, Governor of Puerto Rico, La Fortaleza, San Juan 00901 (809, 721-7000)

DEPARTMENT OF AGRICULTURE, Box 10163, San Juan 00908 (809, 722-2120)
Secretary (Acting): HON. JUAN BAUZA SALAS
Undersecretary: HON. LUIS A. MEJIA MATTEI
Director: A. PEREZ VELEZ, Special Assistant to the Secretary (723-4517)
Land Use and Preservation Office, Box 10163, San Juan 00908

DEPARTMENT OF HEALTH (809, 722-2050)
Radiological Health Programs.
Secretary: JAIME RIVERA-DUEN, M.D.
Assistant Secretary for Environmental Health and Consumer Protection: JORGE CHIRIBOGA, M.D., Box 10427, Hato Rey 00922 (767-9264)

DEPARTMENT OF NATURAL RESOURCES, P.O. Box 5887, Puerta de Tierra Sta., San Juan 00906 (809, 724-8774/723-3090)
To protect, investigate, evaluate, and administer the natural resources of Puerto Rico, to derive maximum public benefits.
Founded: June 23, 1972.
Secretary of Natural Resources: JUSTO A. MENDEZ (723-3090)
Undersecretary: CRUZ MANUEL RODRIGUEZ (722-2540)
Assistant Secretary, Scientific Research Area: EDUARDO L. CARDONA (722-1429)
Assistant Secretary, Permits Eng.: RUTH D. CARRERAS (723-9752)

STATE EXTENSION SERVICES
Dean and Director: DR. JORGE L. RODRIGUEZ, University of Puerto Rico, Mayaguez 00708 (809, 833-7000)
State Leader, CRD Program: EFRAIN FIGUEROA, Extension Service
State Leader, Educational Program: MOISES CORDERO, Extension Service

SOIL CONSERVATION COMMITTEE OF PUERTO RICO
Executive Secretary: FILIBERTO MATIAS, Box 10163, Santurce 00908

SEA GRANT PROGRAM
Marine Education Program: ALIDA ORTIZ-SOTOMAYOR, Coordinator, Marine Education Center, Humacao University College, HUC Station, Humacao 00661 (809, 852-2525/Ext. 360)

CITIZENS' GROUPS

NATURAL HISTORY SOCIETY OF PUERTO RICO, INC., THE *GPO Box 1036, San Juan 00936*
A nonprofit organization affiliated with the National Wildlife Federation. Aims to encourage a greater awareness of the value of natural and cultural resources, coordinate conservation activities of concerned organizations, and promote legislation fostering conservation.
President: RENE COLON, Calle Barbe 504, Santurce 00912 (809, 727-8032)
Secretary: YUDIT de FEROINANOY, Apartabo 21701 UPR Station, Rio Piedras 00931 (763-9553)
Affiliate Representative: RENE COLON
Alternate: OSCAR MESORANA, Calle 8, Building 16, #8, Alturas De Torrimar, Guaynabo 00657 (720-5686)
Publication: ECOS
Editor: MARITZA ALVAREZ, Box 20258, Rio Piedras 00928 (W:765-8806/H:759-7173)

CONSERVATION TRUST OF PUERTO RICO, P.O. Box 4747, San Juan, Puerto Rico 00905 (809, 722-5834); Washington, DC Office: 499 South Capitol St., SW, Suite 103, Washington, DC 20024 (202, 554-0606) (Annual Meeting: December, Trust Offices, San Juan)
A Nonprofit educational and scientific trust created January 23, 1970 with the purpose of devoting its corpus and income to the preservation of the natural resources and the protection and enhancement of the total environment of the Island of Puerto Rico.
Trustees: GUILLERMO RODRIGUEZ BENITEZ, Chairman; JOSE ANGEL BORGES, San Juan; LUIS F. GUINOT, JR.
Executive Director: FRANCISCO JAVIER BLANCO
Assistant Director: JOSE L. BARRETO

PUERTO RICO ASSOCIATION OF SOIL AND WATER CONSERVATION DISTRICTS
President: EFRAIN de JESUS, Box 1894, Bayamon 00619 (809, 797-1255)
Vice-President: CARMELO RIVERA, Street 8-G15, University Gardens, Arecibo 00612
Secretary: ALFONSO DAVILA, 1237 Mariano Abril St., Rio Piedras 00924 (752-2778)
Treasurer: VOLTAIRE LOPEZ, Box 288, Mantati 00701 (854-2583)
Council Member: ISRAEL RIVERA, Box 288, Ponce 00933 (809, 837-2015)

RHODE ISLAND

GOVERNMENT AGENCIES

GOVERNOR: EDWARD D. DiPRETE, Governor of Rhode Island, State House, Providence 02903 (401, 277-2080)

DEPARTMENT OF ENVIRONMENTAL MANAGEMENT, 9 Hayes St., Providence 02908 (401, 277-2774)
The Department of Environmental Management's top priortities include: the preservation and protection of the environmental quality of Rhode Island. Air Pollution, water pollution, and waste disposal problems are handled by the DEM. The DEM develops, administers, and enforces programs designed to preserve and manage Rhode Island's forests, parks, farms, wildlife, fisheries, and

coastline. The DEM is also responsible for providing on the average of 750 full-time jobs for the people of Rhode Island.

Director: ROBERT L. BENDICK, JR. (Ext. 2771)

Chief Legal Counsel, Office of Legal Services: ANDRIENNE SOUTHGATE, 9 Hayes St., Providence 02908 (Ext. 2771)

Assistant Director, Operations: FRANK GEREMIA, 22 Hayes St., Providence 02908 (Ext. 6605)

Commander, Investigative Unit: MARY CAPPELLI, 9 Hayes St., Providence 02908 (Ext. 6768)

Chief, Division of Agriculture: JOHN LAWRENCE, 22 Hayes St., Providence 02908 (Ext. 2781)

Chief, Division of Water Resources: EDWARD SZYMANSKI, 83 Park St., Providence 277-3961

Chief, Division of Coastal Resources: JAMES T. BEATTIE, 22 Hayes St., Providence 02908 (Ext. 3429)

Chief, Division of Enforcement: ERNEST WILKINSON, 83 Park St., Providence (Ext. 2284)

Chief, Division of Fish and Wildlife: Vacant, Washington County Government Center, Wakefield 02879 (789-3094)

Chief, Division of Forest Environment: THOMAS DUPREE, R.F.D. #2, Box 851, North Scituate 02859 (647-3367)

Chief, Division of Parks and Recreation: WILLIAM HAWKINS, 22 Hayes St., Providence 02908 (Ext. 2635)

Assistant Director, Regulations: JAMES W. FESTER, 83 Park St., Providence (Ext. 2234)

Chief, Division of Air and Hazardous Materials: THOMAS GETZ, 75 Davis St., Providence 02908 (Ext. 2808)

Chief, Division of Groundwater and Freshwater Wetlands: STEPHEN G. MORIN, 83 Park St., Providence 02903 (277-2234)

Assistant Director, Administration: MALCOLM J. GRANT (Ext. 2771)

Chief, Office of Planning and Development: JUDITH BENEDICT, 22 Hayes St., Providence 02908 (Ext. 2776)

Chief, Office of Information and Education: FRANCES SEGERSON, 9 Hayes St., Providence 02908 (Ext. 6800)

Fiscal Management Officer, Office of Business Affairs: ROBERT SILVIA, 22 Hayes St., Providence 02908 (Ext. 6825)

Chief, Office of Employee Relations: MELANIE MOURADJIAN, 22 Hayes St., Providence 02908 (Ext. 2774)

DEPARTMENT OF TRANSPORTATION, 210 State Office Bldg., Providence 02903 (401, 277-2481)

Director: MATTHEW J. GILL, JR.

STATE EXTENSION SERVICES

Director of Cooperative Extension Service: DR. GERALD A. DONOVAN, University of Rhode Island, Kingston 02881 (401, 792-2474)

Associate Professor, Natural Resources Science: FRANCIS C. GOLET, Ph.D., University of Rhode Island, Kingston 02881 (Ext. 2370)

Professor, Natural Resources Science: JAMES H. BROWN, JR., College of Resource Development, University of Rhode Island, Kingston 02881 (Ext. 2370)

Associate Professor, Natural Resources Science: THOMAS P. HUSBAND, College of Resource Development, University of Rhode Island, Kingston 02881 (Ext. 2370)

STATE WATER RESOURCES BOARD, 265 Melrose St., Providence 02907 (401, 277-2217)

Chairman: A. JOSEPH MATTERA

CITIZENS' GROUPS

ENVIRONMENT COUNCIL OF RHODE ISLAND, INC.,
P.O. Box 8765, Cranston 02920

A representative statewide organization, affiliated with the National Wildlife Federation, primarily devoted to the wise use, conservation, aesthetic appreciation, and restoration of wildlife and other natural resources.

President: PAUL BEAUDETTE, 72 Sawyer Ave., Warwick 02818 (401, 884-2596)

Correspondence Secretary: KRISTINE STUART, 406 Stony Ln., North Kingstown 02852 (847-9196)

Affiliate Representative: GUY LEFEBVRE, 34 Taft Ave., Providence 02906 (232-6163)

Alternate: ROBERT RANDALL, 54 Highland Ave., Westerly 02891 (596-1073)

Publication: Conservation Update

Editor: EUGENIA MARKS, 34 Taft Ave., Providence 02906

AUDUBON SOCIETY OF RHODE ISLAND, 12 Sanderson Rd., Smithfield 02911 (401, 231-6444)

To focus attention on critical natural resource problems, provide leadership when conservation action is necessary, carry out a broad program of public conservation education, and preserve examples of unique natural areas and native wildlife habitat. Membership: 3,900. Organized: 1897.

President: IRVING M. LEVEN, Seekonk, MA

1st Vice-President: DR. DOUGLAS L. KRAUS, South Kingstown

2nd Vice-President: RICHARD BOWEN, Swansa, MA

Treasurer: SAMUEL H. HALLOWELL, JR., Providence

Secretary: ROBERT BUSHNELL, North Scituate

Executive Director: ALFRED L. HAWKES

Associate Director: HOBSON R.A. CALHOUN

Refuge Staff, Caratunk Wildlife Refuge: CLARE STONE, Director; Parker Woodland: JEAN PAUL FORCIER, Director

Education Program: CAROLYN A. CYR, Director

Publications and Advocacy: EUGENIA S. MARKS, Director

Membership Secretary: KAREN SULLIVAN

Properties Manager: JEAN PAUL FORCIER

Special Events Coordinator: JAMES E. OSBORN III

Secretaries: KAREN SULLIVAN; PRISCILLA SAYWARD

Publication: The Audubon Society of Rhode Island Report

Editor: EUGENIA S. MARKS

CONSERVATION LAW FOUNDATION OF RHODE ISLAND, Box 1943, Providence 02912

A nonprofit legal organization formed in 1975, which acts as a public interest overseer of state and local environmental issues. Provides private individuals and organizations facing environmental and land-use problems with legal aid.

Chairman: HAROLD WARD

RHODE ISLAND BASS CHAPTER FEDERATION

An organization of Bassmaster chapters, affiliated with the Bass Anglers Sportsman Society, to fight pollution, assist state and national conservation agencies in their efforts and teach the young people of our country good conservation of our water resources.

President: JOHN McELROY, 42 Nesbit, Providence 02906 (401, 751-2186)

RHODE ISLAND STATE ASSOCIATION OF CONSERVATION DISTRICTS

President and Council Member: ROBERT S. SWANSON, 11 Harcourt Ave., Wakefield 02879 (401, 783-9751)

Vice-President: JACK NELSON, Blue Flag Farm, W. Main Rd., Little Compton 02837 (635-4733)

Secretary-Treasurer: ROBERT HOWARD, Howard Ln., North Scituate 02857 (H:401, 934-0219/W:828-1660)

Administrative Secretary: CLAUDETTE DONNELLY, P.O. Box 1145, Hope Valley 02832 (539-7767)

SAVE THE BAY, INC., 434 Smith St., Providence 02908-3732

The state's largest citizens' environmental organization dedicated to protecting and maximizing the assets of Rhode Island's greatest natural resource--Narragansett Bay. Founded: 1970. Membership: 10,000.

President: CHRISTOPHER H. LITTLE (401, 456-1363)

Vice-Presidents: J. CHRISTOPHER POWELL (789-0281); ANNA F. PRAGER (789-9331); JOHN RECTOR (274-3541)

Secretary: PAUL A. BEAUDETTE (785-0400 Ext. 411)

Treasurer: NANCY LAPOSTA-FRAZIER (294-2183)

Chairman of the Board: DR. VINCENT ROSE (792-2262)

Executive Director: TRUDY COXE

Publications: *Save The Bay* Newspaper; *Beyond The Pipe Dream: New and Different Ways to Treat Sewage; Life, Liberty and the Pursuit of Energy; Septic Systems: A Homeowners Manual; Down the Drain; Toxic Discharges and the State of Pretreatment in Rhode Island (Vols. I and II); Helping the Land Save the Bay, A Land Use Manual; Saving Our Bays, Sounds and The Great Lakes: The National Agenda*

Editor: CHIP YOUNG

TROUT UNLIMITED RHODE ISLAND CHAPTER (Narragansett)

A statewide chapter, dedicated to the protection and enhancement of the coldwater fishery resources.

President: ROBERT LURIE, 492 Cumberland Ave., North Attleboro, MA 02760 (617, 695-3288)

SOUTH CAROLINA

GOVERNMENT AGENCIES

GOVERNOR: CARROLL A. CAMPBELL, JR., Governor of South Carolina, State House, Columbia 29211 (803, 758-3208)

DEPARTMENT OF AGRICULTURE, Wade Hampton Office Bldg., Box 11280, Columbia 29211 (803, 734-2210)

Administers more than 30 state laws relating to agriculture and the consumer. Represents the farmer in national, regional and state policy matters and is involved in programs of commodity promotion locally and internationally. Enforces regulatory programs affecting the consumer on a statewide basis. Created: 1904.

Commissioner: D. LESLIE TINDAL

Assistant Commissioner, Marketing Services: ROBERT B. ROGERS

Assistant Commissioner, Administrative Services: DAN W. RAMAGE

Assistant Commissioner, Consumer Services: CAROL FULMER

Assistant Commissioner, Laboratory Services: H.T. KELLY

Assistant Commissioner, Executive Affairs: MARSHALL H. FOSTER

Assistant to the Commissioner: WILLIAM HARRY BUSBEE

Public Information Director: REGINALD HALL

DEPARTMENT OF HEALTH AND ENVIRONMENTAL CONTROL, J. Marion Sims Bldg., 2600 Bull St., Columbia 29201

Commissioner: MICHAEL D. JARRETT (803, 734-4880)

Deputy Commissioner, Office of Environmental Quality Control: R. LEWIS SHAW (734-5360)

Publications: Update; *Environmental Quality*

Editors : THOMAS BERRY (758-5500); STEVE DAVIS (734-5360)

DEPARTMENT OF PARKS, RECREATION, AND TOURISM, Edgar A. Brown Bldg., 1205 Pendleton St., Columbia 29201

Executive Director: FRED P. BRINKMAN

Deputy Executive Director: JOHN W. LAWRENCE

Director, Planning Division: WILLIAM R. JENNINGS

Director, State Parks Division: RAY M. SISK

Director, Tourism Division: ROBERT G. LIMING

Director, Finance and Personnel Division: HARRIS B. CALDWELL

Director, Recreation Division: RONALD CARTER

DIVISION OF ENERGY, AGRICULTURE AND NATURAL RESOURCES, P.O. Box 11369, Office of the Governor, Columbia 29201

Director: JOHN N. McMILLAN (803, 734-0445)

FORESTRY COMMISSION, Box 21707, Columbia 29221 (803, 737-8800)

Provides basic forest fire protection on all state and private forest lands in South Carolina; assists landowners in proper management and utilization of forest lands; promotes forest fire prevention and other forestry practices through an information and education program; operates four forest tree nurseries and four state forests. Organized: 1927.

Commission Members: BORIS HURLBUTT, Chairman, Box 770, Walterboro 29488 (549-2506); WILLIAM D. BAUGHMAN, Vice-Chairman, P.O. Box 1950, Summerville 29484 (871-5000); DR. MAX LENNON, P.O. Box 992, Clemson 29631 (656-3413); JOHN E. BANKHEAD, Rt. 1, Richburg 29729 (482-3984); JOSEPH C. WOODARD, SR., Rt. 2, Box 204, Eastover 29044 (353-8587); HENRY F. FLOYD, P.O. Box 978, Pickens 29671 (878-4721); JOE P. SIMPSON, P.O. Box 128, Catawba 29704 (329-6653); GEORGE E. CALLAWAY, P.O. Box 477, Manning 29102 (435-8642); GROVER F. BOWERS, JR., P.O. Box 188, Luray 29932 (625-4251)

State Forester: LEONARD A. KILIAN, JR. (Ext. 202)

Staff Director: ROBERT J. GOULD (Ext. 203)

Executive Assistant: C. DEAN CARSON (Ext. 221)

Director, Field Operations Division: WRAY E. FREEMAN (Ext. 232)

Director, Administration Division: GILBERT BROWN (Ext. 240)

Director, Forest Engineering: JOHN M. SHIRER (Ext. 208)

Coastal Regional Forester: CHARLES JONES (Ext. 218)

Piedmont Regional Forester: J. HUGH RYAN (Ext. 219)

GEOLOGICAL SURVEY, Budget and Control Board, Harbison Forest Rd., Columbia 29210 (803, 737-9440)

The primary mission of the South Carolina Geological Survey is acquiring, interpreting, and distributing South Carolina geological data.

State Geologist: NORMAN K. OLSON

Publication: *South Carolina Geology*

SEA GRANT CONSORTIUM

A state agency that works with public research institutions to develop, secure funding, and deliver research, education, and extension programs that enhance both the utilization and conservation of coastal marine resources.

Director: MARGARET A. DAVIDSON, 287 Meeting St., Charleston 29401 (803, 727-2078)

Chairman: JAMES A. TIMMERMAN, JR., Ph.D., Marine Extension Program (727-2075)

Publications: *Coastal Heritage Newsletter; Estuary Bulletin;* coastal notes, fact sheets, other pamphlets, brochures, and educational materials

SOUTH CAROLINA COASTAL COUNCIL, Ashley Corporate Center, 4280 Executive Place North, Suite 300, Charleston 29405 (803, 744-5838)

A state agency charged with the dual responsibility of protecting the coastal environment while promoting responsible coastal development. The council is comprised of 18 members from across the state, backed by a staff of experts in marine biology, engineering, planning, and environmental law.

Chairman: SEN. JOHN C. HAYES III, Drawer 964, Rock Hill 29731 (327-7171)

Executive Director: H. WAYNE BEAM, Ph.D., Suite 1520, Capitol Center, Columbia 29201 (737-0880)

Deputy Director: CHRIS BROOKS

Permit Administrator: STEVE MOORE

Director of Planning: STEVE SNYDER

Publications: *Carolina Currents*

Editor: DONNA McCASKILL GRESS

SOUTH CAROLINA ENERGY OFFICE, P.O. Box 11405, Columbia 29211

Executive Director: JOHN F. CLARK (803, 734-1740)

Director of Technical Services: FRANK BARRETT

Director of Information and Special Projects: BARBARA GRISSOM

Administrative Assistant: KATHY NORBERG

STATE EXTENSION SERVICES

Dean and Director of Extension Service: DR. B.K. WEBB, Clemson University, Clemson 29634-0310 (656-3382)

Extension Forester: DR. G.D. KESSLER, Clemson University, Clemson 29634-1003 (656-2478)

Department Head, Aquaculture, Fisheries, and Wildlife, Extension Fish and Wildlife Specialist: D.L. ROBINETTE, 307 Long Hall, Clemson University, Clemson 29634-0362 (656-3117)

Extension Program Coordinator-Agriculture and Natural Resources Project Leader, Marine Extension Program: W.P. YATES, 108 Barre Hall, Clemson University, Clemson 29634-0310 (656-4422)

Extension Poultry Scientist: PETER SKEWES, 127 Poole Agriculture Center, Clemson University, Clemson 29634-0379

STATE LAND RESOURCES CONSERVATION COMMISSION, 2221 Devine St., Suite 222, Columbia 29205 (803, 734-9100)

Chairman: GLENN C. ALEXANDER

Executive Director: JOHN W. PARRIS

Deputy Director, Conservation Programs and Public Affairs: CHARLES A. LOGAN

Deputy Director, Administration and Regulatory Programs: CARY D. CHAMBLEE

Director, Public Information: BONNIE SCHNEIDER

Director, Conservation Districts: VON P. SNELGROVE

Director, Sediment and Erosion Control: MARK H. CORLEY

Director, Mining and Reclamation: PATRICK T. WALKER

Director, Dams and Reservoirs Safety: DR. GEORGE D. BALLENTINE

Director, Land Resource Planning: CHARLES F. COUSINS

Director, Soil Science: DR. ROBERT C. SOMERS

WATER RESOURCES COMMISSION, 1201 Main St., Suite 1100, Columbia 29201 (803, 737-0800)

To provide for planning, management and policy recommendations for the maximum beneficial use and conservation of the state's water resources. Created: 1967.

Chairman: ERICK B. FICKEN, Myrtle Beach

Executive Director: ALFRED H. VANG

Deputy Director: HANK STALLWORTH

Geology and Hydrology Division: CAMILLE RANSOM III, Chief

Attorney: PAUL LEAGUE

Surface Water Division: DANNY JOHNSON, Chief

Administrative Services Division: CHARLES MYERS

Research and Development Division: RICHARD E. ROUSE, Chief

Public Information and Editor of Newsletter: LINDA SMALL

Executive Assistant, Policy Development: ANN NOLTE

State Permit Coordinator: JEFFREY F. HAVEL, Biologist

Administrative Assistant: VIRGINIA KENDALL

Periodical Publications: *Palmetto Waters Newsletter; South Carolina Floodplain Management Newsletter*

WILDLIFE AND MARINE RESOURCES DEPARTMENT, Rembert C. Dennis Bldg., P.O. Box 167, Columbia 29202 (803, 734-3888)

The department was organized by the 1952 Regular Session of the legislature, and is charged by law to provide the public with the management, protection, research, conservation and preservation of the state's vital wildlife, marine and natural resources.

Commission Members: MARION BURNSIDE, Chairman, Hopkins (776-2842); CHARLES L. COMPTON, Vice-Chairman, Laurens (682-3169); JAMES O. THOMASON, Spartanburg (582-8277); THOMAS W. MILLER, Anderson (224-2536); LARRY C. OWEN, Easley (878-2883); G.B. STOKES, Florence (662-3291); REMBERT C. DENNIS, Moncks Corner (761-8111); JOHN DRUMMOND, Columbia (734-2797); L. EDWARD BENNETT, Springfield (258-3109); J.M. PENDARVIS, Estill (625-2362)

Executive Director: DR. JAMES A. TIMMERMAN, JR. (734-4007)

Assistant Executive Director: LARRY D. CARTEE (734-4008)

Director, Division of Administrative Services: JOHN B. REEVES (734-3975)

Director, Division of Conservation, Education, and Communications: PRESCOTT S. BAINES (734-3948)

Director, Division of Law Enforcement and Boating: WILLIAM K. CHASTAIN (734-4021)

Director, Division of Marine Resources: DR. PAUL A. SANDIFER (795-6350)

Director, Division of Game and Fresh Water Fisheries: BROCK CONRAD (734-3889)

Publications: *South Carolina Wildlife; The Resource*

Editors: JOHN DAVIS (734-3963); MIKE CREEL (734-3950); GAIL WRIGHT (734-3952)

CITIZENS' GROUPS

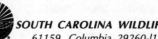

SOUTH CAROLINA WILDLIFE FEDERATION, P.O. Box 61159, Columbia 29260-l159 (803, 782-8626)

A representative statewide organization, affiliated with the National Wildlife Federation, primarily devoted to the wise use, conservation, aesthetic appreciation, and restoration of wildlife and other natural resources.

President: W. BURKE WATSON, JR., 722 W. Liberty St., Sumter 29150 (W:755-1281/H:481-8466)

Executive Director: ELIZABETH (Betty) H. SPENCE

Affiliate Representative: WALTER T. AHEARN, 4512 Oakwood Rd., Columbia 29206 (803, 787-1708)

Alternate: THURSTON CHAVIS, JR., 2147 Chapin Rd., Chapin 29036

Publication: *South Carolina Out-Of-Doors*
Editor: ELIZABETH (Betty) H. SPENCE

SOUTH CAROLINA ASSOCIATION OF CONSERVATION DISTRICTS

President: WALTER B. COUSINS, P.O. Box 463, Newberry 29108 (H:803, 276-1526/W:276-1522)

Vice-President: YANCEY A. McLEOD, JR., 1211 Adges Rd., Columbia 29205 (H:353-2522/W:771-6040)

Secretary: G.W. HORTON, Rt. 4, Box 182, Pageland 29728 (672-5312)

Treasurer: H.O. MULLINAX, Box 127, Donalds 29638 (H:456-2377/W:379-2785)

Council Member: DAVID L. ALLEN, Box 414, Hartsville 29550 (H:332-7494/W:332-8151)

SOUTH CAROLINA BASS CHAPTER FEDERATION

An organization of Bassmaster Chapters, affiliated with the Bass Anglers Sportsman Society, organized to fight pollution, assist state and national conservation agencies in their efforts, and to teach the young people of our country good conservation practices. Dedicated to the realistic conservation of our water resources.

President: JIM SESSIONS, 606 Plantation Cir., Conway 29526 (803, 365-9248/248-5261)

SOUTH CAROLINA FORESTRY ASSOCIATION, 4811 Broad River Rd., P.O. Box 21303, Columbia 29221 (803, 798-4170)

A nonprofit educational organization with a membership of timberland owners, pulpwood dealers, wood-using industries, equipment suppliers, and individuals interested in forest conservation and wise use of natural resources. Organized: 1968.

Chairman of the Board: WILLIAM C. SULLIVAN
President: ROBERT R. SCOTT
Publication: *South Carolina Forestry Journal*

TROUT UNLIMITED SOUTH CAROLINA COUNCIL

A statewide council dedicated to the protection and enhancement of the coldwater fishery resource.

Chairman: LARRY VICKERY, P.O. Box 793, Inman 29349
Director: DAVID D. ARMSTRONG, P.O. Box 10388, Greenville 29603 (803, 271-3609)

WILDLIFE SOCIETY SOUTH CAROLINA CHAPTER

President: ROBERT H. FOLK III, c/o Hurlbutt, Waldrop, and Folk, P.O. Box 779, Waltersboro 29488 (803, 549-2507)

Vice-President: JOSEPH HAMILTON, 250-B Bells Highway, Waltersboro 29488 (549-1008)

Secretary-Treasurer: CARROLL BELSER, 117-A Ste. Phillip St., Charleston 29403

SOUTH DAKOTA

GOVERNMENT AGENCIES

GOVERNOR: GEORGE S. MICKELSON, Governor of South Dakota, State Capitol, Pierre 57501 (605, 773-3212)

BOARD OF MINERALS AND ENVIRONMENT, Department of Water and Natural Resources, Joe Foss Bldg., Pierre 57501

The Board of Minerals and Environment was formed on July 1, 1981, and replaced the Board of Environmental Protection and some activities of the SD Conservation Commission. Responsible for establishing the rules and regulations to be administered by the Department of Water and Natural Resources relating to surface mining, mineral, oil and gas exploration, underground injection control, air, solid waste, and hazardous waste problems in the state.

Secretary of the Department: JOHN J. SMITH (773-3151)

Members: GRACE PETERSEN (224-5374); LEE M. McCAHREN (624-4449); CHARLES MICKEL (348-2527); RICHARD C. SWEETMAN (336-2928); GEORGE VALENTINE (224-6377); WILLIAM C. TAYLOR, JR. (336-3890); JOHN FITZGERALD (348-7250); WILBERT BLUMHARDT (285-6467); LINDA HILDE (256-9158)

DEPARTMENT OF AGRICULTURE, 445 E. Capitol, Sigurd Anderson Bldg., Pierre 57501 (605, 773-3375)

Secretary: JAY C. SWISHER

Conservation Division

Chairman, State Conservation Commission: VERNON SPARTZ, 712 Northeast 6th, Madison 57042 (256-2645)

Director: PETER ORWICK, 445 E. Capitol, Sigurd Anderson Bldg., Rm. 304, Pierre 57501 (773-3258)

DEPARTMENT OF WATER AND NATURAL RESOURCES, Joe Foss Office Bldg., Pierre 57501 (605, 773-3151)

Secretary: JOHN J. SMITH

Division of Water Development, Director: MARK E. STEICHEN (773-4216)

Division of Water Rights, Director and Chief Engineer: JOHN HATCH (773-3352)

Division of Geological Survey, Director and State Geologist: MERLIN TIPTON Science Center, University of South Dakota, Vermillion 57069 (677-5227)

Division of Land and Water Quality, Director: STEVE PIRNER (773-3351)

Division of Air Quality and Solid Waste, Director: JOEL SMITH (773-3153)

GAME, FISH AND PARKS DEPARTMENT, 445 East Capitol, Pierre 57501-3185 (605, 773 plus extension)

Commission Members: DR. R.L. LIUDAHL, Pierre; BOB ADRIAN, White River; DR. LARRY GUNNER, Martin; DR. WAYNE UNZICKER, Mitchell; JEREMIAH MURPHY, Sioux Falls; RICHARD MEYER, Sturgis; BERDETTE ZASTROW, Columbia; NEIL BIEN, Veblen

Department Secretary: RICHARD BERINGSON (Ext. 3718)

Director, Wildlife Division: ART TALSMA (Ext. 3381)

Assistant Director, Operations, Wildlife Division: WALLACE DAVIS (Ext. 3381)

Assistant Director, Technical Services, Division of Wildlife: GEORGE VANDEL (Ext. 3381)

Boating and Hunting Safety: WILLIAM SHATTUCK (Ext. 3630)

Staff Specialist, Fisheries: ROBERT HANTEN (Ext. 3384)

Staff Specialist, Game: RON FOWLER (Ext. 3385)

Staff Specialist, Land: DAVE McGUIGAN (Ext. 3385)

Staff Specialist, Enforcement: RONALD CATLIN (Ext. 3630)

Supervisor of Information and Education: CHUCK POST (Ext. 3485)

Director, Parks and Recreation: DOUG HOFER (Ext. 3391)

Coordinator, Inter-Agency: JOHN KIRK (Ext. 4196)

Animal Damage Control Supervisor: ALVIN MILLER (Ext. 4197)

Federal Aid Manager: DAVID HAMM (Ext. 4507)

Division Director of Custer State Park: ROLLIE NOEM (255-4515)

Director, Division of Administration: KEN ANDERSON (Ext. 3396)

Personnel Officer: CHERYL NELSON (Ext. 5246)

Executive Director, Foundation: JACK MERWIN (Ext. 3718)

Publication: *South Dakota Conservation Digest*
Editor: BRUCE COONROD (Ext. 3485)

SOUTH DAKOTA COOPERATIVE FISH AND WILDLIFE
RESEARCH UNIT, U.S.D.I., Department of Wildlife and Fisheries Sciences, South Dakota State University, Brookings 57007 (605, 688-6121)

Conducts fish and wildlife research and provides training for fishery and wildlife biologists. Cooperating Agents: South Dakota Department of Game, Fish and Parks, South Dakota State University, Fish and Wildlife Service, U.S.D.I., Wildlife Management Institute.
Leader: CHARLES R. BERRY, JR.
Assistant Leader, Wildlife: KENNETH F. HIGGINS
Assistant Leader, Fisheries: WALTER G. DUFFY

STATE EXTENSION SERVICES
Director of Extension: DR. RICHARD BATTAGLIA, South Dakota State University, P.O. Box 2207D, Brookings 57007 (605, 688-4792)
Extension Range Management Specialist: JAMES R. JOHNSON, West River Research and Extension Center, South Dakota State University, 801 San Francisco St., Rapid City 57701 (394-2236)

CITIZENS' GROUPS

SOUTH DAKOTA WILDLIFE FEDERATION, *812 N. Monroe, Pierre 57501 (605, 224-5360)*

A representative statewide organization, affiliated with the National Wildlife Federation, primarily devoted to the wise use, conservation, aesthetic appreciation, and restoration of wildlife and other natural resources.
President: MIKE McKERNAN, P.O. Box 43, Murdo 57550
Executive Director: ROGER PRIES
Affiliate Representative: LEO PETERS, Box 418, Britton 57430
Alternate: DENNIS ROEHER, Box 78, R.R. #1, Britton 57430
Publication: *South Dakota Out-of-Doors*
Editor: *ROGER PRIES*

AUGUSTANA RESEARCH INSTITUTE, Box 783, Augustana
College, Sioux Falls 57056 (605, 336-4912)
To provide research service to the northern Great Plains region by encouraging and conducting investigations of a pure and applied nature, seeking opportunities to examine technical, cultural, sociological, commercial, educational, political, and other needs of the region. Founded: 1973.
Chairman: DR. JOHN SORENSON
Vice-Chairman: HERB BOWDEN
Secretary: DR. DENNIS LARSON
Treasurer: DR. JAMES A. MEADER
Director of Research: DR. JAMES A. MEADER
Research Associate: NANCY NIEDRINGHAUS
Publication: *ARI News Bulletin*

IZAAK WALTON LEAGUE OF AMERICA, INC. (South Dakota
Div.)
President: DICK RASMUSSEN, 711 Franklin St., Rapid City 57701 (605, 342-3296)
Secretary: JO ANN HONERMAN, 1019 N. Duluth, Sioux Falls 57104 (338-2948)

SOUTH DAKOTA BASS CHAPTER FEDERATION
An organization of Bassmaster Chapters, affiliated with the Bass Anglers Sportsman Society, organized to fight pollution, assist state

and national conservation agencies in their efforts, and to teach young people of our country good conservation practices. Dedicated to the realistic conservation of our water resources.
President: GLENN IMBERI, 1308 S. 6th St., Aberdeen 57401 (605, 255-7400/225-1200)

SOUTH DAKOTA ORNITHOLOGISTS' UNION, Jocelyn Lee
Baker, 3220 Kirkwood Dr., Rapid City 57702
To encourage the study of birds in South Dakota, and to promote the study of ornithology by more closely uniting the students of this branch of natural science. Membership: 350. Founded: 1949.
President: JOCELYN LEE BAKER
Vice-President: REX RIIS, Fort Pierre 57532
Secretary: L.M. BAYLOR, 1941 Red Dale Dr., Rapid City 57702
Treasurer: NELDA HOLDEN, Rt. 4, Box 252, Brookings 57006
Publication: *South Dakota Bird Notes*
Editor: DAN TALLMAN, Box 740, Northern State College, Aberdeen 57401

SOUTH DAKOTA RESOURCES COALITION, P.O. Box 7020,
Brookings 57007 (605, 594-3558)
Seeks to promote the survival and integrity of water, energy, land, wildlife, and air resources along with justice in their allocation.
Chair: KAY HUNT, P.O. Box 390, Garretson 57030
1st Vice-Chair: DARRELL WELLS, R.R. 4, Box 233, Brookings 57006 (693-4357)
2nd Vice-Chair: Vacant
Secretary: LAWRENCE NOVOTNY, P.O. Box 7020, Brookings 57007 (692-6026/688-5467)
Treasurer: ROBERT ROBY, South Dakota Lung Association, 208 East 13th St., Sioux Falls 57102 (336-7222)
Publication: *ECO-Forum*
Editor: LINDA REDDER, 208 East 13th St., Sioux Falls 57102 (336-7222)

SOUTH DAKOTA STATE ASSOCIATION OF CONSERVATION
DISTRICTS
President: TIM REICH, 1007 Kingsbury, Belle Fourche 57717 (605, 892-4366)
Vice-President: CURTIS EGGERS, R.R. 10, Box 74, Sioux Falls 57104 (332-0718)
Secretary-Treasurer: DON PUEPPKE, R.R. 1, Box 45, Farmer 57336 (239-4572)
Council Member: DICK FOSSUM, R.R. 1, Box 39, Canton 57013 (987-5218)
Executive Secretary: ANNETTE SEVERSON, 116 N. Euclid, Pierre 57501 (224-0361)

WILDLIFE SOCIETY SOUTH DAKOTA CHAPTER
President: KEN HIGGINS, Box 2206, South Dakota State University, Brookings 57007 (605, 688-4779)
Vice-President: JOHN KOERNER, Sand Lake NWR, R.R. #1, Columbia 57433 (885-6320)
Secretary-Treasurer: CHUCK DIETER, South Dakota State University, Box 2206, Brookings 57007 (688-4739)

TENNESSEE

GOVERNMENT AGENCIES

GOVERNOR: NED R. McWHERTER, Governor of Tennessee, State Capitol, Nashville 37219 (615, 741-2001)

DEPARTMENT OF AGRICULTURE, P.O. Box 40627, Melrose Station, Ellington Agricultural Center, Nashville 37204 (615, 360-0103)
Commissioner: A.C. CLARK

DEPARTMENT OF CONSERVATION, 701 Broadway, Customs House, Nashville 37219 (615, 742-6758)
To plan, promote, protect, and conserve this state's natural, cultural, recreational and historical resources for the benefit of the people of the state of Tennessee.
Commission Members: VICTOR ASHE, Knoxville; JUDY SHUFORD, Franklin; IDA RILEY, Kingsport; DR. PHIL LAVELY, Martin; GRANVILLE HINTON, Savannah; MARTINE MADLINGER, Memphis; EARLWOOD BARDEN, Memphis; DR. WALLACE BIGBEE, McMinnville; STEVE BRUNSON, Moscow; LARRY M. WILSON, Memphis; JOHN HARDCASTLE, Nashville; MAY DEAN EBERLING, Nashville; MITCHELL MAGID, Nashville; HELEN CLARK, Johnson City; BETTY ANN TABATABAI, Memphis
Commissioner: ELBERT T. GILL, JR., 701 Broadway, Nashville (742-6747)
Deputy Commissioner: DR. TOM RIPLEY (742-6636)
Assistant Commissioners: GERALD McKINNEY (742-6745); ROY ASHLEY (742-6621)
State Forester: ROY ASHLEY (742-6621)
State Archaeologist, Division of Archaeology: GEORGE F. FIELDER JR. (742-6607)
Director, Division of Geology: DR. WILLIAM T. HILL (742-6691)
Director, Historical Commission: HERBERT HARPER (742-6719)
Director, Administrative Services: GENE NAIFEH (742-6574)
Director, Division of Parks and Recreation: GERALD McKINNEY (742-6745)
Director, Division of Internal Audit: MARVIN PINSON, Nashville (742-6514)
Director, Division of Facilities Management: ANNE MARTIN (742-6537)
Publication: *Tennessee Conservationist*
Editor: VALARY MARKS (742-6744)

ENERGY, ENVIRONMENT, AND RESOURCES CENTER,

University of Tennessee, 327 South Stadium Hall, Knoxville 37996-0710 (615, 974-4251)
Established in 1972 to serve as a focal point within the university for environmental and energy programs, to conduct research (energy, hazardous waste management, water quality, etc.), and assist clients (government, teachers, citizen interest groups, industrial firms) in solving environmental and energy problems.
Director: DR. E. WILLIAM COLGLAZIER
Associate Director: DR. ROBERT BOHM
Associate Director for Development: DR. LILLIAN CLINARD
Assistant Director for Information and Education: DR. SHEILA W. McCULLOUGH
Associate Director for Communications and Coordination: JOYCE FINNEY
Associate Director for Utility Studies: DR. DONALD ALVIC
Associate Director for Administrative Services: DR. HELEN HAFFORD
Librarian: ALAN B. JOHNS

STATE EXTENSION SERVICES
Dean of Extension Service: DR. M. LLOYD DOWNEN, Agricultural Extension Service, University of Tennessee, P.O. Box 1071, Knoxville 37901-1071 (615, 974-7114)
Professor and Head, Department of Forestry, Wildlife and Fisheries: DR. GEORGE T. WEAVER, P.O. Box 1071, Agricultural Extension Service, University of Tennessee, Knoxville 37901-1071 (974-7126)
General Fish and Wildlife Specialist: Vacant, Forestry, Wildlife & Fisheries, Agricultural Extension Service, P.O. Box 1071, University of Tennessee, Knoxville 37901-1071 (974-7252)

STATE SOIL CONSERVATION COMMITTEE, Tennessee Department of Agriculture, Ellington Agriculture Center, P.O. Box 40627, Nashville 37204 (615, 360-0108)
Chairman: DAVID HINTON, Rt. 6, Clarksville 37040 (647-6460); R.J. MASON, Member, Rt. 2, Niota 37826 (568-2470); BARRY LAKE, P.O. Box 107, Hickory Valley 38042 (901, 764-2909); SAM NICHOLSON, Rt. 2, Jefferson City 37760 (615, 397-7277/397-7400); TOBY WOODMORE, Rt. 3, Lebanon 37087 (615, 374-2201); DAN PASCHALL, Rt. 3, Cottage Grove 38224 (901, 782-3460); JIMMY C. BOND, Rt. 1, Denmark 38391 (901, 422-2084); ELBER T. GILL, Commissioner of Conservation, 701 Broadway, Nashville 37203; A.C. CLARK, Commissioner of Agriculture, Box 40627, Melrose Station, Nashville 37204
Executive Secretary: JOE D. RICHARDSON, Box 40627, Nashville, 37204 (360-0108/Ext. 268)

TENNESSEE COOPERATIVE FISHERY RESEARCH UNIT, U.S.D.I., Tennessee Technological University, Box 5114, Cookeville 38505 (615, 372-3093/3094)
Leader: DR. R. DON ESTES
Assistant Leader: DR. JAMES B. LAYZER

WATER QUALITY CONTROL BOARD, Department of Public Health, 150 9th Ave., N., Nashville 37203 (615, 741-2275)
State water pollution control program.
Technical Secretary: PAUL E. DAVIS

WILDLIFE RESOURCES AGENCY, P.O. Box 40747, Ellington Agricultural Center, Nashville 37204 (615, 781-6500)
Created to have full and exclusive jurisdiction of the duties and functions relating to wildlife and boating and to the management, protection, propagation and conservation of wildlife, including hunting and fishing. Organized: 1949.
Commission Members: CHARLES PEAVYHOUSE; TOMMY AKIN, Secretary; NORMA CROW, Chairman; RHEA R. BROWDER; TOMMY KNOWLES; WILLIAM J. CAMPBELL, Vice-Chairman; TOM HENSLEY; JOHNNY BELLIS; FRANK MADLINGER; ELBERT T. GILL, JR.
Executive Director: GARY MYERS (781-6552)
Assistant Director, Field Operations: RON FOX (781-6557)
Assistant Director, Staff Opertions: ALLEN S. GEBHARDT (781-6555)
Chief, Wildlife Management Division: LARRY MARCUM (781-6610)
Chief, Law Enforcement Division: BOB HARMON (781-6580)
Chief, Fish Management Division: WAYNE POLLOCK (781-6575)
Nongame/Endangered Species Manager: BOB HATCHER (781-6579)
Chief, Administrative Services Division: KEN TARKINGTON (781-6512)
Chief, Engineering Division: LES HAUN (781-6545)
Chief, Environmental Division: DAVID McKINNEY (781-6543)

Chief of Information: TIM HERGENRADER (781-6502)

Education Supervisor: DAVE WOODWARD (781-6538)

Staff Attorney: BROOKS GARLAND (781-6606)

Federal Aid Coordinator: EARL CUNNINGHAM (781-6560)

Chief, Personnel: JIM DILLARD (781-6594)

West Tennessee Regional Manager: HAROLD HURST (901, 423-5725)

Middle Tennessee Regional Manager: LARRY McGINN (615, 781-6622)

Cumberland Plateau Regional Manager: REID TATUM (615, 484-9571)

East Tennessee Regional Manager: BOB RIPLEY (615, 587-4670)

Publication: *Tennessee Wildlife*

Editor: TIM HERGENRADER

CITIZENS' GROUPS

TENNESSEE CONSERVATION LEAGUE, *1720 West End Ave., Suite 308, Nashville 37203 (615, 329-4230)*
A representative statewide organization, affiliated with the National Wildlife Federation, primarily devoted to the wise use, conservation, aesthetic appreciation, and restoration of wildlife and other natural resources.
President: DON BYERLY, 7821 Ramsgate Dr., Knoxville 37919 (693-6028)
Executive Director: ANTHONY J. CAMPBELL
Affiliate Representative: ANTHONY J. CAMPBELL
Alternate: ED THACKSTON, 2010 Priest Rd., Nashville 37215
Publication: Tennessee Out of Doors
Editor: DOUG MARKHAM

ENVIRONMENTAL ACTION FUND (EAF), PO Box 22421, Nashville 37202 (615, 244-4994)
A nonprofit, non-partisan union of citizen groups joined to preserve and protect Tennessee's natural resources and environmental health. EAF works for strong environmental legislative programs and policies. Organized in 1976.
President: JEAN NELSON, P.O. Box 2757, Nashville 37219
Secretary: NANCY GILLIAM, 303 Church St., Nashville 37219 (726-1766)
Treasurer: ANNE DAVIS, 28th Fl., First American Center, Nashville 37238 (742-6294)

TENNESSEE ASSOCIATION OF CONSERVATION DISTRICTS
President: JOE K. THOMAS III, Rt. 3, Box 257, Bristol 37620
Vice-President: JOHN CHARLES WILSON, 1415 Wilson Ln., Arlington 38002
Secretary-Treasurer: JOE JACK DEMENT, Rt. 2, Barlow Ln., Lascassas 37085 (615, 896-1099)

TENNESSEE BASS CHAPTER FEDERATION
An organization of Bassmaster Chapters, affiliated with the Bass Anglers Sportsman Society, organized to fight pollution, assist state and national conservation agencies in their efforts, and to teach the young people of our country good conservation practices. Dedicated to the realistic conservation of our water resources.
President: BOB JACKSON, 447 Shannon Dr., Hixson 37343 (615, 842-1964/751-5569)

TENNESSEE CITIZENS FOR WILDERNESS PLANNING, 130 Tabor Rd., Oak Ridge 37830 (615, 482-2153)
To develop plans concerning wilderness and natural areas; to communicate these plans to fellow citizens; and to act with local, state, and federal government representatives in establishing

policies for the preservation of optimum areas of wild lands and waters. Organized: 1966.
President: MARTHA KETELLE, 637 Kenesaw Ave., Knoxville 37919 (522-2443)
Vice-President: DICK AMBROSE, 308 East Dr., Oak Ridge 37830 (482-9229)
Secretary: ALICE RUNTSCH, 100 Lehigh Ln., Oak Ridge 37830 (483-1532)
Treasurer: CHARLES KLABUNDE, 219 E. Vanderbilt Dr., Oak Ridge 37830 (483-8055)
Executive Director: JENNY FREEMAN JOHNSON, 4600 Appleby Rd., Knoxville 37920 (577-5219)
Publication: *TCWP Newsletter*
Editor: LIANE B. RUSSELL

TENNESSEE ENVIRONMENTAL COUNCIL, 1719 West End Ave., Suite 227, Nashville 37203 (615, 321-5075)
To provide leadership, coordination, and information to all citizens and groups interested in environmental health, natural resources protection, and natural areas issues in Tennessee. Membership: 40 organizations and 1,100 individuals. Formed: 1970.
President: SHIRLEY CALDWELL-PATTERSON (321-5075)
Vice-President: JOEL SOLOMON (297-5550)
Secretary: JEAN NELSON (292-0900)
Treasurer: JAMES WEINBERG (244-3991)
Executive Director: JOHN SHERMAN
Publication: *PROTECT*
Editor: PAUL ELWOOD

TENNESSEE FORESTRY ASSOCIATION, 1720 West End Avenue, Nashville 37203 (615, 327-2473)
A nonprofit conservation group of about 600 woodland owners, public and private foresters, educators, and wood using companies, as well as individual citizens and allied businesses, encouraging the development and wise use of Tennessee's forest resources. Organized: 1951.
President: RAY ROZIER, Winchester
1st Vice-President: JOHN WOOD, Wickliffe, KY
Vice-Presidents: TIM McCALL, Maryville; RICHARD WINSLOW, Jasper; JIM WARMBROD, Jackson
Treasurer: MIKE WITT, Cookeville
Executive Director: JEFF DORAN, Nashville
Publications: *TreeLine Newsletter; Annual Meeting Magazine; Firing Line—Legislative*

TROUT UNLIMITED TENNESSEE COUNCIL
A statewide council with four chapters working for the protection and enhancement of the coldwater fishery resource.
Chairman and National Director: MARK LAMBERTH, 106 Scotch St., Hendersonville 37075 (615, 824-5140)

WILDLIFE SOCIETY TENNESSEE CHAPTER
President: DANIEL C. EAGAR, Department of Conservation, 701 Broadway, Nashville 37219-5237 (615, 742-6553)
President-Elect: RICK D. OWENS, Animal Damage Control, USDA, Suite 104, Brentwood 37027 (736-5095)
Secretary-Treasurer: ROBERT M. HATCHER, TWRA, Ellington Agric. Center, P.O. Box 40747, Nashville 37204 (360-0579)

TEXAS

GOVERNMENT AGENCIES

GOVERNOR: WILLIAM P. CLEMENTS, JR., Governor of Texas, State Capitol, Austin 78711 (512, 463-2000)

AGRICULTURAL EXTENSION SERVICE
Director of Extension Service: DR. ZERLE L. CARPENTER, Texas A&M University, College Station 77843 (409, 845-7967)
Extension Forester and Project Supervisor in Forestry: DR. MICHAEL J. WALTERSCHEIDT, Texas A&M University, College Station 77843 (845-1351)
Extension Fisheries Specialist and Project Supervisor in Wildlife and Fisheries: DONNY W. STEINBACH, Texas A&M University, College Station 77843 (845-7471)
Head, Department of Wildlife and Fisheries/Sciences: DAVID SCHMIDLY, Texas A&M University, College Station 77843 (845-5777)
Head, Department of Forestry: DR. JOHN C. LEE, Texas A&M University, College Station 77843 (845-5000)
Head, Department of Range Science: DR. JOSEPH L. SCHUSTER, Texas A&M University, College Station 77843 (845-5579)
Head, Department of Recreation and Parks: DR. THOMAS M. BONNICKSEN, Texas A&M University, College Station 77843 (845-7324)
Assistant Director for Agriculture and Natural Resoures: DR. WALTER J. WALLA, Texas A&M University, College Station 77843 (845-7980)

BUREAU OF ECONOMIC GEOLOGY, University of Texas at Austin, University Station, Box X, Austin 78713-7508 (512, 471-1534)
Functions as a state geological survey. Program includes basic research; application of geology to resources, conservation, and engineering problems; and publication of varied reports and maps. Maintains an extensive environmental mapping program. Established: 1909.
Director: W.L. FISHER
Deputy Director: E.C. BINGLER
Associate Director, Administration: D.C. RATCLIFF
Publications: University of Texas Publications; Report of Investigations; Geological Circulars; Special Publications; Environmental Geologic Atlases; *Geological Atlas of Texas;* Geological Quadrangle Maps; Guidebooks; Handbooks; Annual Reports; Mineral Resource Circulars; Miscellaneous Maps

DEPARTMENT OF AGRICULTURE, P.O. Box 12847, Capitol Station, Austin 78711 (512, 463-7476)
Established in 1907 by the Texas Legislature as a regulatory agency as well as a leader in marketing promotion for the industry.
Commissioner: JIM HIGHTOWER
Deputy Commissioner: MIKE MOELLER (463-7576)
Assistant Commissioners: BEN DELGADO (463-7597); RICK LOWERRE (463-7664)
Directors, Agricultural and Environmental Sciences Division: ELLEN WIDESS (463-7699); ALVIN ASHORN (463-7698)
Director, Consumer Services Division: SUSAN RALEIGH (463-7602)
Director, Marketing Division: JOHN VLCEK (463-7420)
Director, Seed Division: KENNETH BOATWRIGHT (463-7614)
Director, Special Programs: KIT SEAY (463-7452)

Publication: *Texas Gazette*

DEPARTMENT OF HEALTH, 1100 W. 49th St., Austin 78756 (512, 458-7111)
Created in 1879 to protect and promote the health of the people of Texas.
Commissioner of Health: ROBERT BERNSTEIN, M.D., F.A.C.P. (Ext. 7375)
Associate Commissioner, Environmental and Consumer Health Protection: DAVID M. COCHRAN (Ext. 7541)
Chief, Office of Environmental Analysis: MARTIN W. REYNOLDS (Ext. 7234)
Director, Shellfish Sanitation Control Division: RICHARD E. THOMPSON (Ext. 7510)
Chief, Bureau of Environmental Health: L. DON THURMAN (Ext. 7542)
Director, Water Hygiene Division: CHARLES R. MADDOX (Ext. 7533)

FOREST SERVICE, College Station 77843 (409, 845-2641)
To encourage and aid private land owners to practice multiple-use forestry; to protect private forest land against wildfire, insects and diseases; to inform public of the contribution that forests make. Part of The Texas A&M University system. Established: 1915.
Director: BRUCE R. MILES
Associate Director: JAMES B. HULL
Head, Forest Resource Development: EDWIN R. BARRON
Head, Reforestation Department: J.P. VAN BUIJTENEN, Ph.D. (845-1325)
Head, Fire Control Department: PATRICK A. EBARB, Lufkin (639-8100)
Head, Forest Products Department: DEWAYNE I. WELDON, Lufkin (639-8180)
Head, Information and Education Section: SAM D. LOGAN
Publication: *Texas Forest News*
Editor: JOHN F. SUDDATH

Area Foresters
Area I: STEPHEN W. ADAMS, P.O. Box 469, Linden 75563 (214, 756-5571)
Area II: D.JOE FOX, P.O. Drawer 1327, Henderson 75653 (214, 657-0511)
Area III: BOBBY R. YOUNG, Rt. 5, Box 3650, Lufkin 75901 (409, 875-4400)
Area IV: GARY M. LACOX, P.O. Box 336, Woodville 75979 (409, 283-3728)
Area V: JAMES T. BLOTT, Rt. 7, P.O. Box 151, Conroe 77304 (409, 273-2261)
Area VI: ROBERT F. FEWIN, Rt. 3, Box 216, Lubbock 79401 (806, 746-5801)

GUADALUPE-BLANCO RIVER AUTHORITY, P.O. Box 271, Seguin 78156-0271 (512, 379-5822)
Responsibility to develop, conserve, and protect the water resources within its ten county service area and to aid in the prevention of soil erosion and flooding. Actively engaged in water supply, irrigation, hydroelectric power generation, water and wastewater treatment and outdoor recreation operations. Established: 1935.
Board of Directors: KATHRYN CHENAULT, Secretary-Treasurer; HARRY ALEX FISH; E.T. SUMMERS, JR.; JOHN C. TAYLOR, Vice-Chairman; PRESTON A. STOFER; H.E. GUMBERT, JR., Chairman; HERBERT R. SCHNEIDER; WARREN P. KIRKSEY; JOSEPH P. KELLY
General Manager: JOHN H. SPECHT
Director of Planning and Development: DAVID WELSCH

Operations Manager: FRED BLUMBERG
Chief Engineer: THOMAS D. HILL
Controller: JAMES L. COOKSEY
Water Quality Services Supervisor: JAMES E. ARNST
Administrative Services Manager: CLARA FISCHER

PARKS AND WILDLIFE DEPARTMENT, 4200 Smith School
Rd., Austin 78744 (512, 389-4800)
Commission Members: CHUCK NASH, Chairman, San Marcos;
RICHARD R. MORRISON III, Vice-Chairman, Clear Lake City;
DELO H. CASPARY, Rockport; BOB ARMSTRONG, Austin;
GEORGE R. BOLIN, Houston; BEATRICE CARR PICKENS, Amarillo; WILLIAM L. GRAHAM, Amarillo; A.R. (Tony) SANCHEZ, JR.,
Laredo; HENRY C. BECK III, Dallas
Executive Director: CHARLES D. TRAVIS (389-4802)
Director, Administrative Services: ROY L. HOGAN (389-4803)
Director, Finance: JAMES E. DICKINSON (389-4816)
Director, Law Enforcement: CHESTER BURDETT (389-4845)
Director, Fisheries: GARY MATLOCK (389-4857)
Director, Wildlife: CHARLES ALLEN (389-4971)
Director, Parks: WILSON E. DOLMAN (389-4866)
Director, General Services: CARL WELGE (389-4950)
Director, Data Processing: RON ROSSBERG (389-4980)
Director, Information and Education: BRADY B. MAYO (389-4992)
Director, Resource Protection: SUSAN RIEFF (389-4864)
Publication: *Texas Parks and Wildlife Magazine*
Editor: DAVID BAXTER (389-4990)

SEA GRANT PROGRAM, Sea Grant College Program, THOMAS
J. BRIGHT, Texas A&M University, College Station 77843
(409, 845-3854)
Marine Advisory Program: MIKE HIGHTOWER, Program Coordinator and Deputy Director, Rm. 810, O&M Bldg., Texas A&M
University, College Station 77843 (845-3854)
Marine Information Service: AMY BROUSSARD, Associate Director
and Head, Texas A&M University at Galveston, Galveston
77553-1675 (740-4460)
Publications: *Texas Shores; Marine Education*
Editors: NORMAN MARTIN; AMY BROUSSARD

STATE SOIL AND WATER CONSERVATION BOARD, P.O. Box
658, Temple 76503 (817, 773-2250)
Executive Director: HARVEY DAVIS

TEXAS CONSERVATION FOUNDATION, P.O. Box 12845,
Capitol Station, Austin 78711 (512, 463-2196)
Established in 1969 by the Texas Legislature as trustee for gifts to
the state for the enhancement of Texas' system of parks, natural
and scientific areas, wildlife management areas, and historic sites.
Board Members: GEORGE LAMBERT BRISTOL, Chairman; MRS.
J.W. HERSHEY; FRED AGNICH; GARRY MAURO; C.D. TRAVIS;
CURTIS TUNNELL
Executive Director: JOHN HAMILTON

TEXAS GENERAL LAND OFFICE, Stephen F. Austin State
Office Bldg., Austin 78701
Serves as the custodian of approximately 22.5 million acres of
state-owned land of which 4.25 million acres is submerged coastal
land. Responsibilities include administering state land sales, trades
and leases; issuing land patents; protecting state land from
unlawful use; insuring compliance for mining claims, gas and oil
leases, pipeline easements, coastal easements and various other
permits; managing special projects relevant to the protection of the
state's coastal natural resources; and providing the public with
information pertaining to the state's land resources.
Commissioner: GARRY MAURO (512, 463-5256)

Chief Clerk: JACK GIBERSON (463-5254)
Senior Deputy Commissioner: JOHN HALL (463-5014)
General Counsel: JAMES M. PHILLIPS (463-5235)
Deputy Commissioner, Veteran's Land Board: DAVID GLOIER (463-5199)
Deputy Commissioner, Energy Resources: STEVE ROBERTS (463-5237)
Deputy Commissioner, Central Administration: JUDITH E. DALE
(463-5400)
Executive Secretary, Veteran's Land Board: JACK GIBERSON (463-5254)
Deputy Commissioner, Land Management: DAN RUIZ (463-5027)
Deputy Commissioner, Field Operations: ARNOLD GONZALES
(463-5280)
Deputy Commissioner, Data Services: JUNE MIDDLEBRROOKS
(463-5141)
Deputy Commissioner, Legal Services: DAN MILLER (463-5009)
Deputy Commissioner, Research and Fiscal Management: LEE
SOLSBERY (463-5081)
Deputy Commissioner, Asset Management: SPENCER REID (463-5236)
Director of Archives: MICHAEL HOOKS (463-5261)
Director of Records: SUSAN DORSEY (463-5260)

TEXAS WATER DEVELOPMENT BOARD, 1700 N. Congress,
Austin 78711; Mailing Address: P.O. Box 13231, Austin
78711 (512, 463-7847)
The agency of the state given primary responsibility for implementing the provisions of the constitution and laws relating to water
resources planning, water development, and data collection and
evaluation. The agency also administers the Texas Water Development Fund and the Water Assistance Fund, which provides financial
assistance to local governmental entities for the planning and
construction of water supply, wastewater treatment, and flood
control facilities, and the federal construction grants program for
municipal sewer facilities. Restructured: 1985.
Chairman: LOUIE WELCH
Vice-Chairman: STUART S. COLEMAN
Executive Administrator: M. REGINALD ARNOLD II (463-7847)
Deputy Administrator: SETH C. BURNITT (463-7850)
General Counsel: SUZANNE SCHWARTZ (463-7850)
Director of Planning: HERBERT W. GRUBB (463-7868)
Director, Construction Grants: C.R. MIERTSCHIN (463-7853)

Water Commission, P.O. Box 13087, Capitol Station, Austin
78711 (512, 463-8028)
Functions as administrator over state waters; the commission
authorizes the impoundment, storage, diversion and use of these
waters for beneficial purposes in the public interest through a
permit system and the adjudication process in compliance with
state laws; also grants permits for the disposal of wastewater and
solid wastes, approves plans and specifications for levees, issues
weather modification permits and supervises municipal water
districts. Created: 1913.
Commissioner: JOHN O. HOUCHINS (463-7901)
Chairman: PAUL HOPKINS (463-7909)
Commissioner: RALPH ROMING (463-7910)
Chief Clerk: MARY ANN HEFNER (463-7898)
Chief Hearings Examiner/General Counsel: JAMES K. ROURKE, JR.
(463-7875)
Executive Director: LARRY R. SOWARD (463-7791)

CITIZENS' GROUPS

SPORTSMEN CONSERVATIONISTS OF TEXAS, INC.,
311 Vaughn Bldg. 807 Brazos St., Austin 78701 (512, 472-2267)
A representative statewide organization, affiliated with the National Wildlife Federation, primarily devoted to the wise use, conservation, aesthetic appreciation, and restoration of wildlife and other natural resources.
President: TOM MARTINE, 720 Brazos, #900, Austin 78701
Executive Director: ALAN ALLEN
Affiliate Representative: TOM MARTINE
Alternate: ALAN ALLEN
Publication: *SCOT Wildlife News*
Editor: ALAN ALLEN

ASSOCIATION OF TEXAS SOIL AND WATER CONSERVATION DISTRICTS
President: CLYDE HALE, Rt. 4, Box 43-A, Sherman 75090 (H:214, 893-5646/W:892-9101 Ext. 525)
Vice-President: CHARLES (Buddy) CLARK, Box 126, Menard 76859 (915, 396-4457)
Treasurer: W.O. RICHARDS, Box 546, Paducah 79248 (806, 492-3333)
Council Member: GEORGE CASON, Rt. 1, Box 76, Eagle Lake 77434 (409, 234-2148)

BIG BEND NATURAL HISTORY ASSOCIATION, P.O. Box 68, Big Bend National Park 79834 (915, 477-2236)
A private nonprofit organization, whose main objectives are: to facilitate popular interpretation of the scenic, scientific and historical values of Big Bend, and to encourage research related to those values. To accomplish these goals, the association is authorized by the National Park Service to publish, print, or otherwise provide books, maps, and illustrative material on the Big Bend region. Fourteen member Board of Directors. Founded: 1956.
Executive Director: RICK L. LoBELLO
Chairman of the Board: JIM FRANCOIS
Publications: *El Paisano,* official park newspaper; sales catalog available on request.
Editor: RICK L. LoBELLO

NATIVE PLANT SOCIETY OF TEXAS, 1204 South Trinity St., Decatur 76234
A nonprofit organization dedicated to the education concerning, and promotion of conservation, preservation, and utilization of the native plants and the plant habitats of Texas. Founded: April, 1980; Membership: 1,160.
President: ANN MILLER GONZALEZ (512, 698-1868)
Secretary-Treasurer: BETTYE JANE DODDS (817, 627-2862)
President-Elect: SALLY WASOWSKI (214, 327-6220)
Vice-President, North Texas Region: LORRI DENNIS (214, 939-1780)
Vice-President, South Texas Region: WILLIAM WOLLER (512, 696-3186)
Vice-President, Central Region: MICHAEL J. KASPAR (512, 346-7734)
Vice-President, Coastal Region: STEPHEN M. YOUNG (713, 443-8731)
Vice-President, East Region: BRYAN H. THOMPSON (214, 595-0905)
Vice-President, Southwest Region: BURR WILLIAMS (915, 686-9632)
Vice-President, Panhandle Region: BRITT CANADA (915, 573-1359)

Publication: *Texas Native Plant Society News*
Editor: PATTY LESLIE, 328 Larchmont, San Antonio 78209 (512, 824-1235)

TEXAS BASS CHAPTER FEDERATION
An organization of Bassmaster Chapters, affiliated with the Bass Anglers Sportsman Society, organized to fight pollution, assist state and national conservation agencies in their efforts, and to teach the young people of our country good conservation practices. Dedicated to the realistic conservation of our water resources.
President: JACK DANIELS, P.O. Box 80401, Midland 79709 (915, 548-5348)

TEXAS COMMITTEE ON NATURAL RESOURCES, 5934 Royal Ln., Suite 223, Dallas 75230-3803 (214, 368-1791)
The TCONR is a nonprofit membership organization begun in 1968 to address environmental issues and promote a quality environment. The TCONR is administered by a board of 35 trustees. It is organized as an 'umbrella" to numerous volunteer issue task forces and serves as a network for environmental education. The TCONR addresses a broad range of issues, including forests and wilderness, land use, transportation, toxics, water, and wildlife.
Chairman: JANICE BEZANSON, 601 Westlake Dr., Austin 78757
Vice-Chairman: EVERETT HARDING, 233 Terrace Ct., East, Aledo 76008 (817, 441-9041)
Forestry Chairman: EDWARD C. FRITZ, 4144 Cochran Chapel Rd., Dallas 75209 (214, 352-8370)
Secretary: CHARLOTTE MONTGOMERY, 1703 North St., Nacogdoches (409, 564-8515)
Treasurer: HARVEY DAVIS, 2905 Lovers Ln., Dallas 75225 (214, 821-1968)
Executive Director: WILMA ANDERSON
Publication: *Conservation Progress*

TEXAS FORESTRY ASSOCIATION, P.O. 1488, Lufkin 75901 (409, 632-TREE)
Private, nonprofit, statewide organization promoting the conservation, fullest economic development, and utilization of forest and related resources. Organized: 1914.
President: BOB CURRIE, Rt. 1, Box 181, Kennard 75847
Executive Vice-President: RONALD H. HUFFORD

TEXAS WILDLIFE ASSOCIATION, 1635 NE Loop 410, Suite 108, San Antonio 78209 (512, 826-2904)
Texas Wildlife Association is a nonprofit corporation, formed to protect and promote the rights of Texas's wildlife managers, land operators, sportsmen and the state's wildlife resources. Current statewide membership is approximately 1,200. Formed: 1985.
President: GARY MACHEN (334-3712)
Vice-President: BOB NUNLEY, JR. (988-2752)
Secretary: DR. SAM L. BEASOM (595-3922)
Treasurer: MURPHY E. RAY, JR. (622-3363)
Publication: *Texas Wildlife Association Newsletter*
Publisher: FRED KING, 5214 Starkridge, Houston 77035 (713, 721-5919)

TROUT UNLIMITED TEXAS CHAPTER
Dedicated to the protection and enhancement of the coldwater fishery resource.
President: JAMES C. VYNALEK, HC67, Box 8C, Pleasanton 78064

WATERFOWL HABITAT ALLIANCE OF TEXAS, 1973 West Gray, Suite 6, Houston 77019 (713, 522-5025)
A nonprofit, educational organization of conservationists dedicated to preserving, reclaiming, and enhancing waterfowl habitat in Texas. Constructs varied projects on public and private land.

Coordinates statewide wood duck box program. Also known as WHAT Ducks. Organized: 1984. Membership: 2,000.
Chairman: RICHARD TINSLEY (880-2355)
Secretary: ROBERT JUNGMAN (951-5851)
Treasurer: W.G. ELLER (237-5228)
Executive Director: PINK LOGAN (530-4464)
Administrative Director: FRED KING
Publication: *Marsh Wings*

WILDLIFE SOCIETY TEXAS CHAPTER
President: BOBBY G. ALEXANDER, P.O. Box 17063, Austin 78760 (512, 389-4976)
President-Elect: RAY TELFAIR II, M&R Station, Rt. 10, Box 1043, Tyler 75707 (214, 566-2161)
Secretary-Treasurer: PENNY BARTNICKI, P.O. Box 17063, Austin 78760 (512, 389-4505)

UTAH

GOVERNMENT AGENCIES

GOVERNOR: NORMAN H. BANGERTER, Governor of Utah, State Capitol, Salt Lake City 84114 (801, 538-1000)

DEPARTMENT OF AGRICULTURE, 350 North Redwood Rd., Salt Lake City 84116 (801, 533-4100)
Commissioner: MILES (Cap) FERRY
Deputy Commissioner and Regulatory Services Director: EDISON STEPHENS
Administrative Services Director: RENEE MATSUURA
Agricultural Development and Conservation: JAMES CHRISTENSEN
Marketing Director: BRUCE J. RICHESON
Plant Industry, Director: VAN BURGESS
State Chemist: AHMAD SALARI
State Veterinarian: DR. MICHAEL MARSHALL
Information Officer: EL SHAFFER

STATE DEPARTMENT OF NATURAL RESOURCES, 1636 W. North Temple, Salt Lake City 84116-3156
Executive Director: DEE C. HANSEN (801, 538-7200)
Associate Director for Resource Management: MILO A. BARNEY
Associate Director for Energy and Minerals: RICHARD J. MITCHELL
Public Affairs Director: ALTON FRAZIER

Division of Wildlife Resources, 1596 W. North Temple, Salt Lake City 84116-3154 (801, 533-9333)
Wildlife Board Members: WARREN T. HARWARD, Richfield; HUGH H. HOGLE, Salt Lake City, Chairman; JOANN S. BOWNS, Cedar City; PAUL STRINGHAM, Vernal; ROBERT G. VALENTINE, Brigham City
Board of Big Game Control: BILL GEER, Salt Lake City, Chairman; NEWELL A. JOHNSON, Provo; GREG CUNNINGHAM, Fruita, CO; MERRELL R. MILLER, Salt Lake City; WILLIAM BURBRIDGE, Ogden
Director: BILL GEER
Assistant Director: TIMOTHY H. PROVAN
Chief, Field Services: JOHN SALEVURAKIS
Chief, Game Management: S. DWIGHT BUNNELL
Chief, Law Enforcement: PAUL WOODBURY
Chief, Information and Education: CATHERINE QUINN
Chief, Fiscal Management: JoANN STEWART
Chief, Fisheries Management: BRUCE SCHMIDT
Research Consultant: ROBERT HASENYAGER

Chief, Nongame Management: RANDALL D. RADANT
Chief, Resource Analysis: DARRELL H. NISH

Regional Supervisors:
Central Region: RODNEY JOHN, 1115 N. Main St., Springville 84663 (801, 489-5678)
Northern Region: JACK A. RENSEL, 515 E. 5300 South, Ogden 84405 (479-5143)
Northeastern Region: DONALD A. SMITH, 152 E. 100 North, Vernal 84078 (789-3103)
Southeastern Region: JOHN LIVESAY, 455 W. Railroad Ave., Price 84501 (637-3310)
Southern Region: F. CLAIR JENSEN, 622 N. Main St., Box 606, Cedar City 84720 (586-2455)

Oil, Gas, and Mining Division, 355 W. North Temple, 3 Triad Center, Suite 350, Salt Lake City 84180-1203 (801, 538-5340)
Established in 1955, whose purpose is to foster, encourage and promote sound conservation practices for oil and natural gas, and to protect correlative rights. Further responsibilities include the reclaiming of mined lands and "used" oil throughout the state.
Board of Oil, Gas, and Mining: CHARLES R. HENDERSON, Vernal; GREGORY P. WILLIAMS, Chairman, Salt Lake City; JOHN M. GARR, Salt Lake City; E. STEELE McINTYRE, Eureka; RICHARD B. LARSEN, Springville; JUDY LEVER, Salt Lake City; JAMES W. CARTER, Park City
Director: DR. DIANNE NIELSON

Division of Parks and Recreation, 1636 W. North Temple, Salt Lake City 84116-3156 (801, 538-7220)
Board Members: CLAYTON J. PARR, Salt Lake City; SIDNEY J. ATKIN, St. George; KENT D. TIBBITTS, Blanding; BLAIR FRANCIS, Woodruff; DR. WENDELL H. McGARRY, Chairman, Ephraim; LAVORN G. SPARKS, Provo; JACK A. BARNETT, Bountiful
Director: JERRY A MILLER
Development Services: JERRY HOVER
Program Specialist: SCOTT BEHUNIN
Supervisor, Central Region: DENNIS WEAVER (538-7337)
Supervisor, Southwest Region: ROY BIRRELL (586-4497)
Supervisor, Northern Region: JAY CHRISTIANSON (533-5127)
Supervisor, Southeast Region: MAX JENSEN (259-8151)

Division of State Lands and Forestry, 355 W. North Temple, 3 Triad Center, Suite 400, Salt Lake City 84180-1204 (801, 538-5508)
Board Members: FRANK NISHIGUCHI, Riverside; JAMES BOWNS, Cedar City; MAX WILLIAMS, Nephi; LORYN S. ROSS, Vice-Chairman, Myton; REED CHRISTENSEN, Helper; WILLARD H. GARDNER, Provo; CALVIN BLACK, Blanding; ROGER W. PEART, Chairman, Randolph; RULAND J. GILL, Bountiful
Director: PATRICK D. SPURGIN
Minerals Section Manager: EDWARD BONNER
Assistant Director/State Forester: DICK KLASON

Geological and Mineral Survey, 606 Black Hawk Way, Salt Lake City 84108-1280 (801, 581-6831)
Board Members: KENNETH R. POULSON, Salt Lake City; MILTON E. WADSWORTH, Salt Lake City; GREGORY FRANCIS, Salt Lake City; JOSEPH C. BENNETT, Salt Lake City; JO BRANDT, Salt Lake City; LAWRENCE REAVELEY, Chairman, Salt Lake City; SAMUEL C. QUIGLEY, Price
Director: GENEVIEVE ATWOOD

Division of Water Resources, 1636 W. North Temple, Salt Lake City 84116-3156 (801, 538-7230) Created: 1947.
Chairman, Board of Water Resources: WAYNE M. WINEGAR, Kaysville
Director: D. LARRY ANDERSON
Board Members: IRVIN A. HAWS, Vernal; ROY P. URIE, Cedar City; GEORGE BUZIANIS, Tooele; CLARK J. WALL, Richfield; PHILIP S. KNIGHT, Provo; O. EUGENE JOHANSEN, Castle Dale; CLAIR ALLEN, Cove

Division of Water Rights, 1636 W. North Temple, Salt Lake City 84116-3156 (801, 538-7240)
State Engineer/Director: ROBERT L. MORGAN
Directing Engineers: RICHARD HALL; LEE H. SIM; JAMES RILEY; KENT JONES; JERRY OLDS

Utah Energy Office, 355 West North Temple, 3 Triad Center, Suite 450, Salt Lake City 84180-1204 (801, 538-5428)
Director: RICHARD M. ANDERSON
Energy Conservation and Development Council: GREGORY PROBST, Salt Lake City; TED D. LEWIS, Salt Lake City; DARRELL G. RENSTROM, Ogden; ROBERT HUNTER, Ogden; RICHARD CLOWARD, Magna; JOHN P. REDD, Chairman, Salt Lake City; GLADE M. SOWARDS, Salt Lake City; JIM BINGHAM, Tremonton; DR. J. RAND THURGOOD, Salt Lake City; WILLIAM HOWELL, Price; CLARA PRICE, Vernal; GEORGE H. MIDDLETON, Loa; WILLIAM T. BARTON, West Valley

STATE EXTENSION SERVICES
Director Extension Service (and Sea Grant): DR. R. PAUL LARSEN, Vice-President, Utah State University, Logan 84322-4900 (801, 750-2200)
Extension Forester/Outdoor Recreation Specialist: FRED A. BAKER, College of Natural Resources, Utah State University, Logan 84322-5215 (Ext. 2550)
Wildlife Resource Specialist: GAR W. WORKMAN, College of Natural Resources, Utah State University, Logan 84322-5210 (Ext. 2461)
Range Resource Specialist: PAUL F. McCAWLEY, College of Natural Resources, Utah State University, Logan 84322-5230 (Ext. 2468)

STATE SOIL CONSERVATION COMMISSION, 350 N. Redwood Rd., Salt Lake City 84116 (801, 538-7120)
Assists Utah's 38 soil conservation districts (SCD) in encouraging land operators to implement measures and practices to: prevent soil deterioration; restore depleted soil; prevent flood damage; improve irrigation water efficiency; and to encourage non-point water pollution control programs. The commission has 12 members; 5 ex-officio, and 7 governor-appointed SCD members with their alternates. Created: 1938.
Chairman: MILES (Cap) FERRY
Executive: K.N. (Jake) JACOBSON

UTAH COOPERATIVE FISH AND WILDLIFE RESEARCH UNIT,
U.S.D.I., College of Natural Resource, Utah State University, Logan 84322-5210 (801, 750-2509/2511)
Purpose of the unit is to conduct research and training in all aspects of fishery and wildlife biology and management. Wildlife unit was established in 1935, fishery unit established 1962.
Unit Leader: DR. JOHN A. BISSONETTE (750-2511)
Assistant Leader, Fisheries: DR. TIM MODDE (750-2510)
Assistant Leader, Wildlife: DR. THOMAS C. EDWARDS, JR.
Fishery Biologist: DR. CHERYL COURTNEY

UTAH DEPARTMENT OF HEALTH, P.O. Box 16700, Salt Lake City 84116-0700 (801, 538-6111)
Executive Director: SUZANNE DANDOY, M.D., M.P.H.
Director, Division of Environmental Health: KENNETH ALKEMA (538-6421)
Director, Bureau of Water Pollution Control and Executive Secretary, Water Pollution Control Committee: DON A. OSTTER (538-6146)
Director, Bureau of Air Quality and Executive Secretary, Air Conservation Committee: BURNELL CORDNER (538-6108)
Director, Bureau of Solid and Hazardous Waste Management and Executive Secretary Solid and Hazardous Waste Committee: BRENT BRADFORD (538-6170)
Director, Bureau of Drinking Water/Sanitation and Executive Secretary, Safe Drinking Water Committee: GAYLE SMITH (538-6163)
Director, Bureau of Radiation Control: LARRY ANDERSON (538-6734)
Department of Health Public Information Officer: L. ROSS MARTIN (538-6339)

CITIZENS' GROUPS

 UTAH WILDLIFE FEDERATION, P.O. Box 15636, Salt Lake City 84115
A representative statewide organization, affiliated with the National Wildlife Federation, primarily devoted to the wise use, conservation, aesthetic appreciation, and restoration of wildlife and other natural resources.
President: VERL DAVIS, 254 S. Broadway, Tooele 84074 (801, 882-1755)
Affiliate Representative: GERALD GORDON, 120 N. 5th St., Tooele 84074 (882-2023)
Alternate: VERL DAVIS
Publication: Utah Wildlife News
Editor: VERL DAVIS

TROUT UNLIMITED UTAH
Dedicated to the protection and enhancement of the coldwater fishery resource.
President (Stonefly Society Chapter): CARL ANDREASON, 5968 S. 4000 W., Kearnesy 84228

UTAH ASSOCIATION OF SOIL CONSERVATION DISTRICTS
President: NORMAN CARROLL, P.O. Box 155, Orderville 84758
Vice-President: WESLEY PETERSON, Box 55, Hinckley 84563
Treasurer-Secretary: KENNETH R. CARDON, 1075 1/2 N. Main, Logan 84321

UTAH BASS CHAPTER FEDERATION
An organization of Bassmaster Chapters, affiliated with the Bass Anglers Sportsman Society, organized to fight pollution, assist state and national conservation agencies in their efforts, and to teach young people of our country good conservation practices. Dedicated to the realistic conservation of our water resources.
President: JERRY LITTLE, 181 Springhill Dr., No. Salt Lake City 84054 (801, 298-2500/292-4164)

UTAH NATURE STUDY SOCIETY
Promotes conservation and nature education through workshops and field trips for members; publicizes conservation problems and issues through meetings and its newsletter. Member of Utah Associated Garden Clubs. Organized: 1954.
President: ELDON ROMNEY, Salt Lake City

Secretary: MARIA DICKERSON, 323 S. 2nd West, Tooele 84074

Executive Secretary: STANLEY B. MULAIK, 1144 E. 3rd South St., Salt Lake City 84102

Publication: *Nature News Notes*

Editors: DOROTHEA D. MULAIK, 1144 E. 3rd South, Salt Lake City 84102; CATHERINE QUINN, 2220 Laird Way, Salt Lake City 84108

UTAH WILDERNESS ASSOCIATION, 455 E. 400 South, #306, Salt Lake City 84111 (801, 359-1337)

A nonprofit organization working on all public land issues in Utah. UWA focuses on BLM and Forest Service wilderness issues as well as resource planning and allocation of public lands. UWA publishes a regular newsletter, conducts seminars and produces educational and resource issue alerts to involve UWA members in resource issues. Membership: 650. Established: 1979.

Coordinator: DICK CARTER

Secretary: MARK McKEOUGH

Publication: *UWA Review*

Editor: MARGARET PETTIS

WILDLIFE SOCIETY UTAH CHAPTER

President: JIM KARPOWITZ, 2549 South 660 West #3, Price 84501 (801, 637-3310)

President-Elect: JERRAN T. FLINDERS, 401 WIDB, Brigham Young University, Provo 84602 (378-2322)

Secretary: JOHN FAIRCHILD, UDWR, 1596 West North Temple, Salt Lake City 84116 (533-9333)

Treasurer: BOB BENTON, 1621 E. 900 South, Salt Lake City 84105

VERMONT

GOVERNMENT AGENCIES

GOVERNOR: MADELEINE M. KUNIN, Governor of Vermont, Pavilion Office Bldg., Montpelier 05602 (802, 828-3333)

AGENCY OF NATURAL RESOURCES, 103 S. Main St., Waterbury 05677 (802, 244-7347)

Created: 1970.

Secretary: JONATHAN LASH (244-7347)

Assistant to the Secretary: PEG ELMER

Director, Environmental Conservation Planning: STEPHEN B. SEASE

Director, Administrative Services: ELSIE F. BEARD

State Geologist: CHARLES A. RATTE' (244-5164)

Director of Communications: NANCY BAZILCHUK (244-7347)

Department of Forests, Parks, and Recreation, Waterbury Complex, 10 South (244-8715)

Commissioner: MOLLIE BEATTIE

Director of Forests: CONRAD MOTYKA (244-8716)

Chief, Forest Resource Protection: H. BRENTON TEILLON

Chief, Forest Resource Management: M. BRIAN STONE

Director, State Parks and Lands: EDWARD KOENEMANN (244-8711)

State Naturalist: CHARLES JOHNSON

Chief, Park Operations: LARRY SIMINO

Director of Recreation: GEORGE PLUMB (244-8713)

Department of Environmental Conservation, Waterbury Complex, 1 South

Commissioner: PATRICK PARENTEAU (244-8755)

Director, Water Resources Operations: REGINALD A. LaROSA

Environmental Engineering Executive: WILLIAM C. BRIERLEY (244-8744)

Director, Water Quality: DAVID L. CLOUGH, (244-6951)

Director, Hazardous Waste Management: Vacant (244-8702)

Director, Permits and Compliance: GARY SCHULTZ (244-5674)

Director, Air Quality: RICHARD A. VALENTINETTI (244-8731)

Director, Solid Waste Management: ED LEONARD (244-7831)

Environmental Board, East State St., Montpelier 05602 (802, 828-3309)

Chairman: LEONARD WILSON

Executive Officer: STEPHANIE KAPLAN

Department of Fish and Wildlife, Waterbury Complex, 10 South (244-7331)

Commissioner: STEVE E. WRIGHT

Business Manager: JOSEPH HEALY

Director of Wildlife: BENJAMIN DAY, JR.

Director of Fisheries: ANGELO INCERPI

Director of Law Enforcement: ROGER WHITCOMB

Director of Information and Education: JOHN HALL

Fish and Wildlife Board Members: ROY BERKELEY; NORMAN CARTIER; JOHN LICCARDI, Chairman; MAURICE EATON; ROBERT HURST; BRUCE BATCHELDER; ARTHUR RYE

DEPARTMENT OF AGRICULTURE, 116 State St., Montpelier 05602

Created: 1908.

Commissioner: RONALD A. ALLBEE (802, 828-2430)

Deputy Commissioner: WILLIAM PAINE (828-2100)

Administrative Services: ELSIE W. LaFLAMME, Business Manager (828-2428)

Director, Agricultural Development Division: AMANDA LEGARE (828-2416)

Animal and Dairy Industries: DONALD F. GEORGE (828-2432)

Plant Industry, Laboratories, and Standards: PHILIP R. BENEDICT (828-2435)

State Veterinarian: DR. DAVID U. WALKER (828-2450)

Publications: *Agriview Newsletter;* List available on request.

DEPARTMENT OF HEALTH, P.O. Box 70, 60 Main St., Burlington 05402 (802, 863-7280)

Commissioner: ROBERTA R. COFFIN, M.D.

Director, Environmental Health Division: KENNETH M. STONE (863-7223)

OFFICE OF THE STATE GEOLOGIST, Agency of Natural Resources, 103 South Main St., Center Bldg., Waterbury 05676 (802, 244-5764)

Provides geological information services to citizens, industry, state, and federal agencies. Conducts continued geological research and field investigations in the state. Established: 1844.

State Geologist: DR. CHARLES RATTE

STATE EXTENSION SERVICES

Director of Extension Service (Interim): ROBERT E. HONNOLD, Morrill Hall, University of Vermont, Burlington 05405 (802, 656-2990)

Water Resource Specialist: LINDA G. MAREK, Aiken Center-Natural Resources, University of Vermont, Burlington 05405 (656-4057)

Program Leaders: DON J. McFEETERS, State Program Leader

(Acting), AG/CD/NR, Morrill Hall, Burlington 05405 (656-2992); DONALD R. WHAPLES, State 4-H Expansion and CRD Specialist, Extension Morrill Hall, Burlington 05405 (656-2991); ROBERT W. JACKSON, Special Programs Coordinator, Morrill Hall, Burlington 05405 (656-2992); THOMAS J. MCEVOY, Forest Management Specialist, Aiken Center - Natural Resources, Burlington 05405 (656-3258)

Publication: *Natural Resources Forum*

Department Chairman, Office of Information: MEG ASHMAN, Morrill Hall, University of Vermont, Burlington 05405 (656-3024)

STATE NATURAL RESOURCES CONSERVATION COUNCIL,
Agency of Natural Resources, 103 S. Main St., Center Bldg., Waterbury 05676
Chairman: WINSTON S. SEELEY, R.D. 3, Middlebury 05753
Executive Secretary: WILLIAM F. SNOW (802, 244-5764)

CITIZENS' GROUPS

VERMONT NATURAL RESOURCES COUNCIL, *9 Bailey Ave., Montpelier 05602 (802, 223-2328)*
A representative statewide organization, affiliated with the National Wildlife Federation, primarily devoted to the wise use, conservation, aesthetic appreciation, and restoration of wildlife and other natural resources.
Chairman: DICK MIXER, R.F.D. #1, Box 2340, Starksboro 05487 (434-2088)
Executive Director: R. MONTGOMERY FISCHER
Affiliate Representative: JEAN FLACK, R.D. #2, Enosburg Falls 05450
Alternate: R. MONTGOMERY FISCHER
Publication: Vermont Environmental Report
Editor: SUSAN CLARK

MERCK FOREST FOUNDATION, INC., Rupert 05768 (802, 394-7836)
A nonprofit educational organization providing outdoor living and work/study experiences. With 2,600 acres of fields and forests, 26 miles of hiking and ski trails, 11 overnight lean-to shelters, a natural science museum, and a variety of streams, ponds and mountain peaks, the Merck Forest offers a variety of year-round living and learning opportunities for individuals and organized groups. Information available on special programs, camping facilities and slide lectures.
President: MRS. ROBERT GREEN
Director: JOHN J. PARKER

TROUT UNLIMITED VERMONT COUNCIL
A statewide council with six chapters working for the protection and enhancement of the coldwater fishery resource.
Council Chairman: SYL STEMPEL, Box 308, Jonesville 05466 (802, 828-2868)
National Director: DR. PHILIP KELLEHER, 60 Manor Woods, Kennedy Dr., South Burlington 05403 (656-1997)
Atlantic Salmon Coordinator: ALAN ERDOSSY, Minister Brook Rd., Worcester 05682 (229-6234)

VERMONT ASSOCIATION OF CONSERVATION DISTRICTS
President and Council Member: WESLEY LARRABEE, R.F.D., Shoreham 05770 (802, 897-2626)
Vice-President: EDWARD POMAINVILLE, R.F.D. #1, Brandon 05733 (483-2225)

Secretary-Treasurer: DAVID STEVENS, Rt. 1, Wells River 05081 (757-2318)
Executive Director: MARY S. HOOPER, P.O. Drawer B, Montpelier 05602 (229-4982)

VERMONT AUDUBON COUNCIL
A statewide council consisting of nine chapters of the National Audubon Society, and one independent organization formed to advance the protection and wise use of wildlife and other natural resources of Vermont, and to encourage coordination and information exchange among its members.
President: ABBOTT FENN, P.O. Box 121, Middlebury 05753 (802, 545-2538)
Secretary: JUDITH DiMARIO, P.O. Box 512, Waitsfield 05673

VERMONT INSTITUTE OF NATURAL SCIENCE, Church Hill Rd., Woodstock 05091 (802, 457-2779)
A nonprofit organization formed to encourage the people of Vermont in their curiosity about the natural world, to investigate and publicize the special natural features of Vermont and to educate towards conserving and preserving the natural environment. Vermont Raptor Center, Living Museum of birds of prey, on VINS grounds. Membership: 5,650. Founded: 1972.
President: PETER ARNOLD
Vice-President: JUNE McKNIGHT
Secretary: FRANCESCA KEELER
Treasurer: FRANK THORNE
Director: SARAH B. LAUGHLIN
Education Director: JENEPHER LINGELBACH
Program Director: MARGARET BARKER
Research Director: CHRISTOPHER RIMMER
Publications: *Vermont Natural History; Vermont Institute of Natural Science Newsletter;* Records of Vermont Birds
Editor: SARAH B. LAUGHLIN

VIRGIN ISLANDS

GOVERNMENT AGENCIES

GOVERNOR: ALEXANDER FARRELLY, Governor of the Virgin Islands, Government House, Charlotte Amalie, St. Thomas 00801 (809, 774-0001)

COOPERATIVE EXTENSION SERVICE, University of Virgin Islands, R.R. #2, Box 10,000, Kingshill, St. Croix 00850
Vice-President, Research and Land Grant Affairs: DR. DARSHAN S. PADDA, R.R. #2, Box 10,000, Kingshill, St. Croix 00850 (809, 778-0246/DIALCOM: CVI040 (5825:CVI040)
Integrated Pest Management Coordinator, Pesticide Impact Liaison, Natural Resources Program Leader: DR. WALTER I. KNAUSENBERGER
Extension Specialist, Natural Resources: DR. P. JOY MICHAUD, Terrestrial Flora, Forage Legumes and Grasses

DEPARTMENT OF PLANNING AND NATURAL RESOURCES,
P.O. Box 4399, St. Thomas 00801 (809, 774-3320)
Responsible for: fish and wildlife; trees, vegetation and water resources; air and water pollution control; flood control; regulate sewers and sewage disposal; culture and the arts; libraries and museums; minerals and other natural resources; historical preservation; submerged lands; earth change permits and oil spill prevention and control. Established: 1968.
Commissioner: ALAN SMITH

Chief, Bureau of Environmental Enforcement: JOSEPH SUTTON
Director, Division of Fish and Wildlife: DENTON MOORE (775-6762)
Chief, Bureau of Fisheries: JAMES BEETS
Chief, Bureau of Wildlife: DAVID NELLIS
Director, Division of Natural Resources Management: FRANCINE LANG
Director, Coastal Zone Management: ROBERT PEDERSON
Publications: *Annual Report; Zone Management Notes (CZM Notes); Blue Book*

CITIZENS' GROUPS

 VIRGIN ISLANDS CONSERVATION SOCIETY, INC., P.O. Box 12379, St. Thomas 00801
A nonprofit organization affiliated with the National Wildlife Federation. Aims to encourage a greater awareness of the value of natural and cultural resources, to coordinate conservation activities of concerned organizations, and promote legislation fostering conservation. Organized: 1968.
President: LEONARD REED, Box 2426, St. Thomas 00802 (W:809, 774-3320/H:774-8278)
Executive Vice-President: ROY WATLINGTON, Box 2321, St. Thomas 00801 (776-7464)
Affiliate Representative: ROSEMARY E. GALIBER, Box 7464, St. Thomas 00801 (H:775-3220/W:774 2563)
Alternate: JOAN ELTMAN, Box 2998, Christiansted, St. Croix 08820
Editor: PAGE STULL, Box 284, St. Thomas 00801 (774-0300)

VIRGIN ISLANDS CONSERVATION DISTRICT
Chairman: MARIO GASPERRI, P.O. Box 969, Christiansted, St. Croix 00840

VIRGINIA

GOVERNMENT AGENCIES

GOVERNOR: GERALD L. BALILES, Governor of Virginia, State Capitol, Richmond 23219 (804, 786-2211)

COUNCIL ON THE ENVIRONMENT, 903 Ninth Street Office Bldg., Richmond 23219 (786-4500)
To implement the environmental policy of the Commonwealth as set forth in Virginia Code Section 10.1-1201, to promote the wise use of air, water, land and other natural resources, and to protect them from pollution, impairment or destruction. Council has fourteen members and a staff of twenty-one. Created: 1970.
Administrator: KEITH J. BUTTLEMAN
Chairman: MARIE RIDDER
Publications: List available on request.

DEPARTMENT OF AGRICULTURE CONSUMER SERVICES, P.O. Box 1163, Richmond 23209 (804, 786-3501)
Commissioner: S. MASON CARBAUGH
Director of Communication: B.J. ALTSCHUL, APR (786-2373)
Director of Policy Analysis and Development: Vacant (786-3539)
Publication: Bulletin
Editor and Publisher: B.J. ALTSCHUL, APR

DEPARTMENT OF CONSERVATION AND HISTORIC RESOURCES, Division of Parks and Recreation, 203 Governor St., Suite 306, Richmond 23219 (804, 786-2121)
The department mission is to conserve, protect, enhance, and advocate wise use of Virginia's unique natural, historic, recreational, scenic and cultural resources to maintain and improve the quality of life for present and future generations. The department is responsible for administrative support of various state collegial bodies including: the Board of Conservation and Historic Resources, the Virginia Cave Board, the Virginia Historic Landmarks Board, the Virginia Soil and Water Conservation Board, the Virginia War Memorial Board, the Public Beach Board, and the Virginia Outdoor Foundation. Created: 1985.
Director: B.C. LEYNES, JR. (786-6115)
Deputy Director: JERALD F. MOORE
Executive Assistant: LEON E. APP
Administrative Staff Manager: BONNIE S. GREENWOOD

Division of Administration, 203 Governor St., Richmond 23219
Director: ALBERT E. NEALE (786-0001)
ADP Director: ERIC W. KAPLAN
Fiscal Services Director: ROBERT J. DANDRIDGE, JR.
Human Resources Director: RONALD G. SHOWALTER

Division of Historic Landmarks, 221 Governor St., Richmond 23219
Director: H. BRYAN MITCHELL (786-3143)

Division of Natural Areas Conservation, 203 Governor St., Richmond 23219
Director: Vacant

Virginia Natural Heritage Program, Governor St., Richmond 23219
Program Director: MICHAEL L. LIPFORD (786-4554)

Division of Planning and Resource Development, 203 Governor St., Richmond 23219
Director: Vacant

Division of Soil and Water Conservation, 203 N. Governor St., Suite 206, Richmond 23219
Director: ROLAND B. GEDDES (804, 786-2064)

Division of State Parks, 203 Governor St., Richmond 23219
Commissioner: RONALD D. SUTTON (786-2132)

Board of Conservation and Historic Resources, 203 Governor St., Suite 302, Richmond 23219
Chairman: Vacant

Virginia Cave Board, 611 Third Ave., Farmville 23901
Chairman: DR. LYNN M. FERGUSON

Virginia Historic Landmarks Board, 221 Governor St., Richmond 23219
Chairman: Vacant

Public Beach Board, P.O. Box 339, Gloucester Point 23062
Chairman: BENJAMIN C. GARRETT III
Advisor: JACK E. FRYE

Virginia Soil and Water Conservation Board, 203 Governor St., Suite 206, Richmond 23219
Chairman: ROBERT E. WILKINSON (804, 786-2064)

Virginia War Memorial Board, 203 Governor St., Richmond 23219
Chairman: Vacant

DEPARTMENT OF GAME AND INLAND FISHERIES, 4010 W. Broad St., Box 11104, Richmond 23230 (804, 367-1000)
Board Members: OMAR W. BALL, JR., Powhatan; R. LEON McFILLEN, Rosslyn; LEWIS M. COSTELLO, Winchester; THOMAS C. LEGGETT, South Boston; WALTER P. CONRAD, JR., Chesapeake; ELI B. JONES, JR., Tazewell; LEON O. TURNER, Roanoke; JAMES S.G. DAVENPORT, Newport News; HENRY A. THOMAS, Alexandria (Chairman); FRANK T. SUTTON III, Richmond
Director: JAMES A. REMINGTON
Assistant Director: JOHN P. RANDOLPH
Chief, Law Enforcement Division: GERALD SIMMONS
Chief, Game Division: JACK W. RAYBOURNE
Chief, Fish Division: JACK M. HOFFMAN
Chief, Education Division: HARRY L. GILLAM
Chief, Administrative Services: SAM J. PUTT
Chief, Lands and Engineering Division: LARRY G. HART
Publication: *Virginia Wildlife*
Editor: HARRY L. GILLAM

DEPARTMENT OF HEALTH, James Madison Bldg., 109 Governor St., Richmond 23219 (804, 786-3561)
The department carries out protective and preventive public health services for all citizens of the Commonwealth and provides direct health care services to the indigent. Created: 1872
Health Commissioner: C.M.G. BUTTERY, M.D., M.P.H.
Deputy Commissioner for Administration: CYNTHIA A. CAVE, Ph.D. (Ext. 3563)
Deputy Commissioner for Community Health Services: ROBERT B. STROUBE, M.D., M.P.H. (Ext. 3575)
Deputy Commissioner for Health Care Services: EDWIN M. BROWN, M.D., M.P.H. (Ext. 3563)
Director, Division of Dental Health: JOSEPH M. DOHERTY, D.D.S. (Ext. 3556)
Director, Medical Examiner Division: DAVID K. WIECKING, M.D. (Ext. 3174)
Director, Division of Water Programs: ERIC BARTSCH (Ext. 1760)
Publication: *Virginia's Health*
Editor: BARBARA MITCHELL (Ext. 3551)

DEPARTMENT OF MINES, MINERALS AND ENERGY, 2201 West Broad St., Richmond 23220 (804, 367-0330)
Committed to enhancing the development and conservation of energy and mineral resources in a safe and environmentally sound manner in order to support a more productive economy in Virginia. Began activities in January 1985. Six operating divisions: Division of Mined Land Reclamation, regulates the operation of coal surface-mining activities, enforce the reclamation laws and regulations, and administers financial resources for reclaiming abandoned coal mining sites; Division of Mineral Resources, provides information on Virginia's geology, mineral resources, physical and cultural features; Division of Mines, enforces the coal mining laws of the Commonwealth to promote the safety and health of coal miners; Division of Energy, promotes the efficient use and conservation of energy and the use of alternative energy sources; Division of Mineral Mining, regulates the operation of non-coal mining activities for environmental protection and worker safety; Division of Gas and Oil, regulates the operation and reclamation of gas and oil extractions.
Director: O. GENE DISHNER

Division of Mined Land Reclamation, Drawer U, Big Stone Gap 24219
Commissioner: DANNY R. BROWN (703, 523-2925)

Division of Gas and Oil, P.O. Box 1416, Abingdon 24210
Oil and Gas Inspector: TOM FULMER (703, 628-8115)

Division of Mineral Mining, 7705 Timberlake Rd., Lynchbyrg 24502
Director: WILLIAM O. ROLLER (804, 239-0602)

Division of Mines, 219 Wood Ave., Big Stone Gap 24219
Chief: HARRY D. CHILDRESS (703, 523-0335)

Division of Mineral Resources, Box 3667, Charlottesville 22903
State Geologist: DR. ROBERT C. MILICI (804, 293-5121)

Division of Energy, 2201 West Broad St., Richmond, 23220
Director: SAM BIRD (804, 367-1310)

MARINE RESOURCES COMMISSION, P.O. Box 756, 2401 West Ave., Newport News 23607 (804, 247-2200)
This state agency holds regulatory jurisdiction over all commercial and sports fishing, marine fish, marine shellfish, and marine organisms in the tidal waters of Virginia. Holds permit jurisdiction on all projects involving use of state owned submerged lands and authority over use or development in vegetated and non-vegetated tidal wetlands and coastal primary sand dunes. Established: 1875.
Board Members: R. WAYNE BROWNING, Davis Wharf; RICHARD S. BRAY, Portsmouth; GEORGE S. FORREST, Poquoson; JOHN FREEMAN, Hampton; TIMOTHY G. HAYES, Richmond; JANE CARTER WEBB, Newport News; WILLLIAM A. HUDNALL, Heathsville; TED WOOL, Virginia Beach
Commissioner: WILLIAM A. PRUITT
Chief, Administration and Finance: ROBERT D. CRAFT
Chief, Law Enforcement: ROBERT J. MARKLAND
Chief, Habitat Management: NORMAN E. LARSEN
Chief, Fisheries Management: JACK G. TRAVELSTEAD
Publication: *Virginia Landings Bulletin*

NORTHERN VIRGINIA REGIONAL PARK AUTHORITY, 5400 Ox Rd., Fairfax Station 22039 (703, 352-5900)
To preserve open and wooded areas and provide outdoor recreation to meet the needs of a growing population. Founded: 1959.
Chairman: WALTER L. MESS
Executive Director: DARRELL G. WINSLOW

RESOURCE-USE EDUCATION COUNCIL
A volunteer, nonprofit organization, composed of members of the state and federal government, colleges and private industry working to promote the broad principle of environmental education. Founded: 1952.
Chairman: HELEN JETER, Soil Conservation Service, P.O. Box 10026, Richmond 23240 (804, 782-2457)
Secretary-Treasurer: HARRY L. GILLAM, Department of Game and Inland Fisheries, Box 11104, Richmond 23230 (367-1000)

SEA GRANT PROGRAM
Sea Grant Program Director: DR. WILLIAM L. RICKARDS, Virginia Graduate Marine Science Consortium, 170 Rugby Rd., Madison

House, University of Virginia, Charlottesville 22903 (804, 924-5965)

Marine Advisory Program: DR. WILLIAM DuPAUL, Virginia Institute of Marine Science, Gloucester Point 23062 (642-7164)

STATE EXTENSION SERVICES

Vice-Provost and Director of Extension Service: DR. M.R. GEASLER, Virginia Polytechnic Institute, Blacksburg 24061 (703, 961-6705)

Extension Specialist, 4-H Forestry Programs: WILLIAM A. McELFRESH, Virginia Polytechnic Institute, Blacksburg 24061 (961-5676)

Project Leader, Forestry Extension: ROBERT L. McELWEE, Ph.D., Virginia Polytechnic Institute, Blacksburg 24061 (961-5483)

Extension Wildlife Specialist: PETER T. BROMLEY, Ph.D., Virginia Polytechnic Institute, Blacksburg 24061 (961-5087)

Extension Fisheries Specialist: LOUIS A. HELFRICH, Ph.D., Virginia Polytechnic Institute & State University, Blacksburg 24061 (961-5059)

Sea Grant

Extension Seafood Technologist, GEORGE J. FLICK, JR., Ph.D.,

Dept. of Food Science and Technology, Virginia Polytechnic Institute, Blacksburg 24061 (961-6965)

STATE WATER CONTROL BOARD, 2111 N. Hamilton St., P.O. Box 11143, Richmond 23230 (804, 257-0056)

Established in 1946 for eliminating water pollution in Virginia; and effective July 1, 1972, for comprehensive development of Virginia's water resources.

Chairman: HENRY O. HOLLIMON, JR., Ruthville

Executive Director: RICHARD N. BURTON

VIRGINIA COOPERATIVE FISH AND WILDLIFE RESEARCH UNIT, U.S.D.I., 106 Cheatham Hall, Virginia Polytechnic Institute and State University, Blacksburg 24061 (703, 961-5927)

Founded in 1935 for training graduate students in fisheries and wildlife; teaching and extension in fisheries and wildlife biology. Cooperatively supported by U.S. Fish and Wildlife Service, Department of Game and Inland Fisheries, and Virginia Polytechnic Institute and State University.

Leader: DR. RICHARD J. NEVES

Assistant Leader: DR. MICHAEL R. VAUGHAN (961-5046)

Publications: Annual Reports; Research Publications

VIRGINIA OUTDOORS FOUNDATION, 221 Governor St., Richmond 23219 (804, 786-5539)

To preserve Virginia's natural, scenic, historic, scientific, open space, and recreational areas by means of private philanthropy. The foundation accepts gifts of cash, stock, real property, or open space easements to achieve its purpose. Created: 1966.

Executive Director: TYSON B. VAN AUKEN

CITIZENS' GROUPS

VIRGINIA WILDLIFE FEDERATION, 4602 D West Grove Ct., Virginia Beach 23455 (804, 464-3136)

A representative statewide organization, affiliated with the National Wildlife Federation, primarily devoted to the wise use, conservation, aesthetic appreciation, and restoration of wildlife and other natural resources.

President: PAUL A. SHRAUDER, 3006 Fleetwood Ave., SW, Roanoke 24015 (703, 774-7735)

Executive Secretary: DOROTHY TRAUB, 784 Glasgow Ct., Virginia Beach 23452 (804, 340-9056)

Affiliate Representative: RODGER SPRUILL, JR., 3204 E. Sewells Pt. Rd., Norfolk 23513 (804, 855-0645)

Alternate: PAUL A. SHRAUDER

Publication: Federation Record

Editor: JOSEPH A. HOEHLEIN, 3027 Bruin Dr., Chesapeake 23321 (804, 464-3136)

AMERICAN BASS ASSOCIATION OF VIRGINIA, THE

An organization of the individual members and bass fishing clubs, affiliated with the American Bass Association, Inc., dedicated to protecting and enhancing the state,s fishery resources; to promote the sport of bass fishinig; and to teach youngsters the fun of fishing and instill in them an appreciation of the life-giving waters of America.

President: GEORGE RODEHEAVER, 208 Cameron Ln., Charlottesville 22903 (804, 296-7821)

CONSERVATION COUNCIL OF VIRGINIA, P.O. Box 106, Richmond 23201

The council helps citizens and organizations who share a common concern for the wise use and reasonable protection of natural resources to participate effectively within Virginia's legislative and regulatory agency process. Membership: 50 organizations and 140 individuals. Established: 1969.

President: DAVID CHUSE, Rt. 1, Box 220, Castleton 22716 (703, 937-4919)

Vice-Presidents: TAMARA VANCE, 1010 Harris St., SW #1, Charlottesville 22901 (804, 977-2033); FRANKLIN FLINT, 2427 Indian Hill Rd., Lynchburg 24503 (804, 384-1254)

Secretary: STELLA KOCH, 1056 Manning St., Great Falls 22066 (703, 759-5453)

Treasurer: ELIZABETH ROGERS, 210 Queens Dr., West, Williamsburg 23185 (804, 229-3779)

Publication: *Newsletter*

Editor: MARY BARRETT, 3457 West Carey St., Richmond 23221 (804, 353-6776)

IZAAK WALTON LEAGUE OF AMERICA, INC. (Virginia Div.)

President: SAMUEL MASON, 205 Maple St., Fredericksburg 22405 (703, 373-4486)

Secretary: DR. FRANK FLINT, 2427 Indian Hill Rd., Lynchburg 24503 (804, 384-1254)

PIEDMONT ENVIRONMENTAL COUNCIL, P.O. Box 460, Warrenton 22186 (703, 347-2334); 1010 Harris St., Charlottesville 22901 (804, 977-2033)

A nonprofit organization formed to conserve natural resources and the pastoral landscape of a nine-county region of the Northern Virginia Piedmont. Public education and services to public officials and citizens, covering: land use; farmland retention; open space conservation; historic preservation; and rural planning legislation. Active statewide and federally on rural conservation issues. Organized: 1972.

Chairman: JAMES A. SAGERHOLM

Vice-Chairman: HOPE W. PORTER

President: ROBERT T. DENNIS

Director, Planning Services: KATHERINE L. IMHOFF

Director, Charlottesville Office: TAMARA A. VANCE

Staff Attorney: ARTHUR B. LARSON

Director, Environmental Education: CYNTHIA S. DeCANIO

Publications: *PEC Newsreporter;* Periodic books and special reports.

TROUT UNLIMITED VIRGINIA COUNCIL
A statewide organization with 14 chapters working for the protection and enhancement of the coldwater fishery resource.
Chairman: CHARLES E. HUDSON, P.O. Box 4786, Lynchburg 24512 (804, 384-0487)
National Director: CORBIN DIXON, Rt. 1, Box 12, Fisherville 22939 (703, 337-3818)

VIRGINIA ASSOCIATION OF SOIL AND WATER CONSERVATION DISTRICTS
President: JOHN H. BOLDRIDGE, Rt. 1, Box 161, Rixeyville 22737 (703, 937-5375)
Vice-President: H. EARL LONGEST, P.O. Box 727, Mechanicsville 23111 (804, 769-7879)
Secretary-Treasurer: EUGENE W. TAYLOR, Box 67, Rustburg 24588 (804, 332-5952)
Council Member: DON F. GROSS, Rt. 5, Box 82, Covington 24426 (H: 703, 962-1607/W: 962-3217)

VIRGINIA BASS CHAPTER FEDERATION
An organization of Bassmaster Chapters, affiliated with the Bass Anglers Sportsman Society, organized to fight pollution, assist state and national conservation agencies in their efforts, and to teach the young people of our country good conservation practices. Dedicated to the realistic conservation of our water resources.
President: PEE WEE POWERS, 14151 Pine St., Chester 23831 (804, 748-6099/743-6289)

VIRGINIA FORESTRY ASSOCIATION, 1205 E. Main St., Richmond 23219 (804, 644-8462)
An association of individuals, clubs, groups, industries and businesses, formed to encourage the development and wise use of Virginia's forest and related resources for the best interests of this and succeeding generations. Membership: 2,000. Organized: 1943.
President: A.L.C. NELSON, 2994 Peanut Ln., Mechanicsville 23111
Vice-President: ROBERT LUNDBERG, Stone Container Corp, P.O. Box 1009, Hopewell 23860
Treasurer: EARL LONGEST, Farm Credit Association, P.O. Box 727, Mechanicsville 23111 (804, 746-1252)
Executive Director: CHARLES F. FINLEY, JR.

VIRGINIA WILDFLOWER PRESERVATION SOCIETY, INC., P.O. Box 844, Annandale 22003
The VWPS and chapters throughout Virginia seek to further appreciation and conservation of Virginia's wild plants and habitats. Programs emphasize public education, protection of endangered species, habitat preservation, and encouragement of appropriate landscape use of native plants. Includes both amateurs and professionals. Membership brochures available. Active chapters are established throughout the state. Membership: 1,000. Established: 1982.
President: NICKY STAUNTON (703, 368-9803)
1st Vice-President: ANN REGN
2nd Vice-President: JAMES A. MINOGUE
Corresponding Secretary: DORNA KREITZ
Recording Secretary: ELIZABETH D. SMITH
Treasurer: JOHN WHITE
Chairmen: DOROTHY BLISS, Botany; FAITH CAMPBELL, Conservation; CRISTOL FLEMING, Education; PHOEBE WHITE, Membership; JENIFER BRADFORD, Publicity and Publications
Members-At-Large: NANCY ARRINGTON; JOCELYN ALEXANDER;

KEN WIERINGO; LARRY MORSE; REBECCA WHITE; JAMES R. TUGGLE
Publications: Bulletin; Chapter Newsletters; *Wildflower Conservation Guidelines;* Nursery Source List
Editor: ROY SEWARD

WILDLIFE SOCIETY, VIRGINIA CHAPTER
President: KAREN TERWILLIGER, P.O. Box 11104, Richmond 23230-1104 (804, 257-1000)
President-Elect: PETE BROMLEY, Department of Fish and Wildlife, VPI and SU, Blacksburg 24061 (703, 961-5087)
Secretary: MICHAEL FIES, 2221 Noon St., Staunton 24401 (703, 895-9005)
Treasurer: JIM BOWMAN, Rt. 3, Box 112, Broadway 22815 (703, 984-4101)

WASHINGTON

GOVERNMENT AGENCIES

GOVERNOR: BOOTH GARDNER, Governor of Washington, State Capitol, Olympia 98504 (206, 753-6780)

DEPARTMENT OF AGRICULTURE, 406 General Administration Bldg., Olympia 98504 (206, 753-5063)
Director: C. ALAN PETTIBONE (753-5050)
Deputy Director: MIKE SCHWISOW (753-5035)
Information Officer: MARY BETH LANG (586-6108)
Assistant Director, Chemical and Plant Division: ART LOSEY (753-5062)
Assistant Director, Agricultural Development Division: ART SCHEUNEMANN (753-5046)
Assistant Director, Livestock Services Division: MIKE WILLIS (753-5065)
Assistant Director, Commodity Inspection Division: J. ALLEN STINE (753-3786)
State Veterinarian: DR. ROBERT MEAD (753-5040)
Assistant Director, Dairy and Food Division: JIM WOMMACK (753-5042)

DEPARTMENT OF ECOLOGY, Olympia 98504 (206, 459-6000)
Charged with programs of air quality control, water pollution control, solid waste management, management of water resources, Model Litter Control Act, shoreline management, coastal zone management, noise, hazardous waste, and State Environmental Policy Act (SEPA). Created: 1970.
Director: ANDREA BEATTY RINIKER (459-6168)
Deputy Director, Programs: PHILLIP C. JOHNSON (459-6170)
Program Manager, Solid and Hazardous Waste: EARL TOWER (459-6316)
Program Manager, Water Quality: CAROL JOLLY (459-6143)
Deputy Director, Operations and Enforcement: MARC C. HORTON (459-6053)
Program Manager, Water Resources: HEDIA ADELSMAN (459-6056)
Assistant Director, Management and Support Services: STEVE HUNTER (459-6012)
Assistant Director, Nuclear Waste Management: TERRY HUSSEMAN (459-6670)
Program Manager, Air Programs: STU CLARK (459-6256)
Program Manager, Shorelands and Coastal Zone Management: D. RODNEY MACK (459-6777)

Program Manager, Hazardous Waste Clean Up: JOHN LITTLER (438-3007)

Program Manager, Central Operations: GREG SORLIE (459-6037)

Program Manager, Technical Services: DICK CUNNINGHAM (586-1826)

DEPARTMENT OF FISHERIES, 115 General Administration Bldg., Olympia 98504 (206, 753-6600)

Purpose is to protect, perpetuate and manage the marine food fish, shellfish, and anadromous food fish resources of the state. Created: 1890.

Director: JOSEPH R. BLUM (753-6623)

Deputy Director: JUDITH MERCHANT (753-6588)

Assistant to Director for Legislative and Constituent Relations: ED MANARY (753-3267)

Assistant Director, Management Services: Vacant (753-6517)

Assistant Director, Planning, Research and Harvest Management: GENE DIDONATO (753-5012)

Assistant Director, Marine Fish: MARK PEDERSEN (545-6592 or 753-6716)

Assistant Director, Shellfish: JUDITH FREEMAN (753-6749)

Assistant Director, Salmon: KAHLER MARTINSON (753-6631)

Assistant Director, Interjurisdictional Fisheries: ROBERT A. TURNER (753-6627)

Division Chief, Construction and Engineering: RUSSELL WEBB (753-6610)

Division Chief, Habitat Management: DUANE PHINNEY (753-3621)

Division Chief, Harvest Management: DENNIS AUSTIN (753-6629)

Division Chief, Salmon Culture: WILBUR ASHCRAFT (753-1876)

Assistant Director, Field Services: JAMES McKILLIP (753-6585)

Patrol Chief: JAMES McKILLIP (753-6585)

DEPARTMENT OF NATURAL RESOURCES, Public Lands Bldg., Olympia 98504 (206, 753-5327)

Board of Natural Resources: Governor BOOTH GARDNER, Olympia; DR. FRANK BROUILLET, Olympia; Commissioner BRIAN J. BOYLE, Olympia; DR. DAVID THORUD, Seattle; JAMES L. OZBUN, Pullman

Administrator: BRIAN J. BOYLE, Commissioner of Public Lands (753-5317)

Executive Assistant: JOHN L. CHAMBERS (753-5323)

Supervisor: ART STEARNS (753-5331)

Deputy Supervisors: PAT McELROY, State Lands (753-5308); TED PRICE, Proprietary (753-5308); LAURA ECKERT, Services (753-5308)

Division Managers

ARDEN OLSON, Forest Regulation and Assistance (753-5315)

KENNETH SOLT, Lands and Minerals (586-6382)

JOHN DeMEYER, Aquatic Lands (753-5326)

BILL LUNDBERG, Administrative Services (753-5310)

GRANT FREDRICKS, Engineering (753-2093)

KEN HOOVER, Fire Control (459-6900)

JACK HULSEY, Timber Sales (753-5334)

BOB EDWARDS, Management Services (753-1308)

RAYMOND LASMANIS, Geology and Earth Resources (459-6372)

HARRY ANDERSON, Forest Land Management (753-0671)

ROBERT B. HARPER, Director of Communications (753-5330)

TIM BOYD, Press Relations Officer (753-5330)

GENE NIELSEN, Central Area (206, 748-8616)

RYDER CHRONIC, Northeast Area (509, 684-5201)

HAROLD VILLAGER, Northwest Area (206, 856-0083)

JOHN CALHOUN, Olympia Area (206, 374-6131)

MIKE GRIGGS, South Puget Sound Area (206, 825-1631)

DONALD PLESS, Southeast Area (509, 925-6131)

JAN GANO, Southwest Area (206, 577-2025)

Publication: *Totem*

Editor: JULIANNE CRANE (753-5330)

DEPARTMENT OF WILDLIFE, 600 N. Capitol Way, Olympia 98504 (206, 753-5700)

Organized: 1933.

Commission Members: TERRY KARRO, Winthrop; JOHN McGLENN, Bellevue; DENNIS BARCI, Everett; DR. JAMES M. WALTON , Chairman, Port Angeles; NAT WASHINGTON, Ephrata; NORMAN RICHARDSON, Vice-Chairman, Yakima

Director: CURT SMITCH

Deputy Director: JERRY NEAL

Assistant Directors: CHRIS DRIVDAHL; CAL GROEN; JENENE FENTON

Special Assistant to the Director: RICHARD POELKER (753-5710)

Chief, Wildlife Enforcement: DANIEL WYCKOFF (753-5740)

Chief, Engineering: BOB DICE (753-5730)

Chief, Fisheries Management: JIM DESHAZO (753-5713)

Chief, Wildlife Management: JACK SMITH (753-5728)

Chief, Habitat Management: GENE TILLETT (753-3318)

Chief, Management Services: LEMBIT RATASSEP (753-5723)

Chief, Information and Education: JANET O'MARA (753-5707)

Publication: *Washington Wildlife*

Editor: BOB STEELQUIST (754-2645)

Regional Managers

BRUCE SMITH, N. 8702 Division St., Spokane 99218 (509, 456-4082)

RAY DUFF, P.O. Box 850, Ephrata 98823 (509, 754-4624)

LARRY POPEJOY, 2802 Fruitvale Blvd., Yakima 98902 (509, 575-2740)

JOAN KELLER, 16018 Mill Creek Blvd., Mill Creek 98012

BRUCE CRAWFORD, 5405 NE Hazel Dell, Vancouver 98663 (206, 696-6211)

MIKE KUTTEL, 905 E. Heron, Aberdeen 98520 (206, 533-9680)

OREGON AND WASHINGTON COLUMBIA RIVER GORGE COMMISSIONS, P.O. Box 100, North Bonneville 98639 (509, 427-8866)

Established by the state legislatures in the 1950s to preserve, develop, and protect the recreational, scenic, and historical areas of the Columbia River Gorge. The commissions are composed of five members from Oregon and six from Washington. Commission goals focus on achieving a balance between economic growth and environmental preservation.

Chairman: NANI WARREN, Portland, OR

Chairman: K.R. (Ken) POWELL, Camas, WA

Vice-Chairman: MASAMI ASAI, Hood River, OR

Vice-Chairman: DICK ADLARD, Stevenson, WA

Program Director: JEFFREY P. BRECKEL, Stevenson, WA

Publication: *Gorge Notes Newsletter*

Editor: SHERRIL NOSSUM ANDERSON

SEA GRANT PROGRAM

Director Sea Grant Program: LOUIE S. ECHOLS, University of Washington, 3716 Brooklyn Ave., NE, Seattle 98105 (206, 543-6600)

Sea Grant Advisory Program: MICHAEL A. SPRANGER, Program Leader for Advisory Program, University of Washington, 3716 Brooklyn Ave., NE, Seattle 98105 (206, 543-6600)

STATE CONSERVATION COMMISSION, PV-11, Olympia 98504 (206, 459-6227)

Assists, guides, and coordinates the programs of 48 conservation districts and encourages the cooperation and collaboration of the federal, state, regional, interstate and local public agencies which assist them; keeps the public informed of renewable natural resource conservation activities. Founded: 1939. Membership: 10.

Chairman: KENNETH M. BROOKS, 644 Old Eaglemount Rd., Port Townsend 98368 (206, 732-4917)

Executive Secretary: WAYNE REID

Western WA Field Representative: KAHLE JENNINGS (206, 459-6232)

Central WA Field Representative: THOMAS R. NEWCOMB (509, 786-2226)

Eastern WA Field Representative: RAY LEDGERWOOD (509, 332-3333)

Administrative Officer: ROBERT P. BOTTMAN (206, 459-6229)

Grants Officer: DENISE LIVINGSTON (206, 459-6141)

Communications Officer: RENEE GUILLIERIE (206, 459-6048)

STATE EXTENSION SERVICES

Assistant Director, Agriculture and Natural Resources: HARRY B. BURCALOW, Washington State University, Pullman 99164-6230 (509, 335-2837)

Extension Forester: DONALD HANLEY, College of Forest Resources, University of Washington, AR-10, Seattle 98195 (206, 545-4960)

Extension Forester: DAVID M. BAUMGARTNER, 131A Johnson Hall, Washington State University, Pullman 99164-6412 (335-2811)

Extension Range Management Specialist: BEN F. ROCHE, JR., 185 Johnson Hall, Washington State University, Pullman 99164 (335-3716)

Extension Vertebrate Pest Management Specialist: LEONARD ASKHAM, 131B Johnson Hall, Washington State University, Pullman 99164-6412 (335-2811)

STATE PARKS AND RECREATION COMMISSION, 7150 Cleanwater Ln., Olympia 98504-5711

To acquire, develop, improve, and maintain state parks and recreation areas. Involvement includes but is not limited to state parks, seashore conservation, water and boating safety, snowmobile safety, and natural and historic heritage interpretation. Established: 1912.

Director: JAN TVETEN (206, 753-5758)

Deputy Director: CLEVE PINNIX (753-5759)

Assistant Director, Operations: LYNN GENASCI (753-5761)

Assistant Director, Resources Development: TOM FRANCE (753-5767)

Assistant Director, Administrative Services: DENNIS SMITH (753-5766)

Chief, Personnel and Training: JAN MILLER (753-5760)

Public Affairs Administrator: JUDITH LERAAS (753-2027)

Chief, Environmental Coordination: DAVID W. HEISER (753-2016)

Regional Office Supervisors

Region I: JOHN JOHNS, 11838 Tilley Rd., S. Olympia 98502 (206, 753-7143)

Region II: TERRY DORAN, P.O. Box 487, Burlington 98233 (206, 755-9231)

Region III: ANGE TAYLOR, 2201 N. Duncan Dr., Wenatchee 98801 (509, 662-0420)

Region IV: GLEN REISWIG, Sacajawea Park Rd., R.R. 9, Box 2501, Pasco 99301 (509, 545-2315)

Region V: MORGAN BRASSFIELD, 1601 29th St., SE, Auburn 98002 (206, 931-3907)

WASHINGTON COOPERATIVE FISH AND WILDLIFE RESEARCH UNIT, U.S.D.I., U.S. Fish and Wildlife Service, School of Fisheries, University of Washington, Seattle 98195 (206, 543-6475/543-6476)

Leader: GILBERT B. PAULEY

Assistant Leader: GARY L. THOMAS

CITIZENS' GROUPS

 *WASHINGTON:* Vacant

MOUNTAINEERS, THE, 300 Third Ave., West, Seattle 98119 (206, 284-6310)

To explore, study, preserve, and enjoy the natural beauty of the Northwest. An outdoor club which supports protection of the Northwest environment. Membership: 11,000. Organized: 1906.

President: CARSTEN LIEN

Vice-President: DIANNE HOFF

Secretary: JIM JUNG

Treasurer: SHARON ROWLEY

Conservation Chair: BEV DAHLIN

OLYMPIC PARK ASSOCIATES, 13245 40th Ave., NE, Seattle 98125 (206, 364-3933)

Olympic Park Associates was founded in 1948, incorporated in 1949 in the State of Washington. It is dedicated to preservation of the integrity and wilderness of Olympic National Park and surrounding areas, as well as supporting wild land and wildlife habitat protection elsewhere in the nation. Membership: approximately 300.

President: POLLY DYER, Seattle, WA (364-3933)

Vice-President: TIM McNULTY, Quilcene, WA (765-3260)

Secretary: NORMAN WINN, Seattle, WA (624-8901)

Treasurer: JOHN W. ANDERSON, Seattle, WA (523-5043)

Publication: *Voice of the Wild Olympics*

Editor: SANDY MARVINNEY

TROUT UNLIMITED NORTHWEST STEELHEAD AND SALMON COUNCIL, P.O. Box 2137, Olympia 98507

A statewide council with 38 chapters working for the protection and enhancement of the coldwater fishery resources.

Northwest Executive Director: JERRY PAVLETICH, 2100 Bay Ave., Aberdeen 98520 (206, 533-3122)

President and Director: JACK RAY, 7019 Zangle Rd., Olympia 98506 (206, 753-2060)

Vice-President, Eastern Washington: CARL BABIAR, Rt. 1, Box 127, E. Leavenworth 98826 (509, 548-7414)

Vice-President, Western Washington: FRANK GAFFNEY, 5070 SW Waite, Seattle 98116 (206, 623-7361)

National Directors: BOB NOISEAU, 135 Brighten Pl., Kelso 98626 (206, 425-6002); GEORGE ENGLEDOW, 5942 95th SW, Olympia 98502 (206, 754-4450); LOYD STAFFORD, 17110 2nd Ave., SW, Seattle 98166 (206, 382-2418); DALE E. KNOWLTON, 2311 NE 6th Pl., Renton 98056 (206, 255-2258); BOB FUHRMAN, 20005 Poplar Way, Lynnwood 98056 (206, 776-3235)

Publication: *Trout and Salmon Leader*

Editor: BRIAN DIRKS, 111 SW 330th, #2002, Federal Way 98023 (206, 874-6478)

WASHINGTON ASSOCIATION OF CONSERVATION DISTRICTS

President and Council Member: HOWARD JAEGER, Sky Ranch, Kalama 98625 (206, 673-5338)

Vice-President: J. READ SMITH, Rt. 1, Box 69, St. John 99171 (509, 648-3922)

Secretary-Treasurer: ROBERT SCHMIDT, Rt. 1, Box 58, Rosalia 99170 (509, 523-4381)

WASHINGTON BASS CHAPTER FEDERATION

An organization of Bassmaster Chapters, affiliated with the Bass Anglers Sportsman Society, organized to fight pollution, assist state and national conservation agencies in their efforts, and to teach the young people of our country good conservation practices. Dedicated to the realistic conservation of our water resources.

President: MIKE CRANDELL, 17410 26 Dr., SE, Bothell 98012 (206, 485-5632)

WASHINGTON ENVIRONMENTAL COUNCIL, INC., 76 S. Main, P.O. Box 4445, Seattle 98104 (206, 623-1483)

Promotes citizen, legislative, and administrative action toward providing a better environment. Membership: 1,600. Established: 1967.

President: DAVID BRICKLIN, 1015 Fourth Pike Bldg., Seattle 98101 (459-1067)

Vice-President, Administration: Vacant

Vice-President, Legislative: Vacant

Vice-President, Liaison: Vacant

Secretary: Vacant

Treasurer: JOHN ANDERSON (523-5043)

Administrative Director: SUSAN ROBINSON

Publication: *WEC Alert*

WASHINGTON FARM FORESTRY ASSOCIATION, P.O. Box 7663, Olympia 98507 (206, 459-0984)

A statewide organization affiliated with the National Woodland Owners Association, established to promote good forest practice in managing non- industrial private forest lands for pleasure and profit. Membership: 2,100. Founded: 1967.

President: NELS HANSON (943-3875)

Executive Secretary: CHERYL L. STEWART

Publication: *NORTHWEST WOODLANDS*

Editor: LORI D. RASOR (503, 228-3624)

WASHINGTON STATE FORESTRY CONFERENCE, College of Forest Resources, University of Washington, Seattle 98195 (206, 545-4960/545-1928)

Association of individuals in public and private forestry whose purpose is to provide a public forum to promote the wise use and perpetuation of Washington's forest resources, disseminate information, and further communications and cooperation between all forestland users in the state of Washington.

President: DAVID B. THORUD

Vice-Presidents: J.D. MacWILLIAMS; ART STEARNS; JAMES C. GEISINGER

Secretary-Treasurer: ENNIS G. COOPER (782-7098)

President Emeritus: JAMES S. BETHEL

WASHINGTON WILDLIFE HERITAGE FOUNDATION, 32610 Pacific Hwy. S., Federal Way 98003 (206, 874-1800)

A nonprofit, tax-exempt organization dedicated to preserve, protect, enhance and perpetuate fish, wildlife, and natural resources in Washington state.

Chairman of the Board: TOM NELSON, 19524 75th Ave., SE, Snohomish 98290 (485-9019)

Vice-Chairman: HARVEY CHAUSSEE, 7635 159th Pl., NE, Redmond 98052 (885-4644)

Secretary: GREGG MacDONALD, P.O. Box 983, Issaquah 98027 (392-5455)

Treasurer: ALAN BOND, 11711 SE 8th St., Summit Bldg., Suite 310, Bellevue 98005 (453-1666)

Directors: JIM BROWN, 14107 NE 4th St., Bellevue 98007; LONNIE MARCHANT, 1017 W. Highway 12, Grandview 98027

Managing Director: LARRY MINKLER

WILDLIFE SOCIETY WASHINGTON CHAPTER

President: RICHARD E. FITZNER, Rt. 1, Box 1070, Benton City 99320 (509, 376-7179)

President-Elect: HARRIET ALLEN, 7025 Sandy Point Rd., Olympia 98506 (206, 586-1449)

Secretary-Treasurer: ROBERT EVERITT, Washington Department of Game, 16018 Mill Creek Blvd., Mill Creek 98012 (206, 775-1311)

WEST VIRGINIA

GOVERNMENT AGENCIES

GOVERNOR: GASTON CAPERTON, Governor of West Virginia, State Capitol, Charleston 25305 (304, 340-1600)

DEPARTMENT OF AGRICULTURE, State Capitol Bldg., Charleston 25305 (304, 348-2201)

Commissioner: GUS R. DOUGLASS

Assistant Commissioner: JOHN PERDUE

Plant Pest Control Division: DR. CHARLES C. COFFMAN, Director

State Forester (Acting): RALPH GLOVER

State Soil Conservation Committee

Executive Secretary: EDWARD BUMGARNER

DEPARTMENT OF NATURAL RESOURCES, 1800 Washington St., East, Charleston 25305 (304, 348-2754)

The objective is to provide a comprehensive program for the exploration, conservation, development, protection, enjoyment, and use of the natural resources of the state of West Virginia. The West Virginia Conservation Commission, formed in 1933, was the forerunner of the Department of Natural Resources, created by the legislature in 1961.

Commissioners: PATRICK J. DOFKA, Wheeling (242-7110); CARL R. SULLIVAN, Charles Town (725-8137); LAWRENCE DEITZ, Richwood (846-9261); WILLIAM C. WAGONER, Barboursville (736-1511); B.F. MITCHELL, Petersburg (257-4555); WILLIAM P. STAFFORD, Princeton (425-4991); CARL GAINER, Richwood (846-2551)

Director: RONALD R. POTESTA

Deputy Director: ROBERT K. PARSONS

Special Assistant to the Director: DENNIS H. TREACY

Executive Secretary: CHARLES W. LEWIS (348-3315)

Chief of Wildlife Resources: ROBERT L. MILES (348-2771)

Assistant Chief, Game Management: JAMES M. RUCKEL (348-2771)

Assistant Chief, Warmwater Fisheries: BERNARD F. DOWLER (348-2771)

Assistant Chief, Coldwater Fisheries: DONALD P. PHARES, Elkins (636-1767)

Assistant Chief, Special Projects: PETER E. ZURBUCH, Elkins (636-1767)

Assistant Chief, Biometrics and Planning: WALT KORDEK (636-1767)

Administrator, Office of Environmental and Regulatory Affairs: DENNIS H. TREACY

Chief of Law Enforcement: RICHARD M. HALL (348-2784)

Chief of Water Resources: DAVID W. ROBINSON (348-2107)
Public Information Officer: DIANNA YOUNG (348-3380)
Conservation Education/Litter Control: MAXINE SCARBRO (348-3370)
Publication: *Wonderful West Virginia*
Editor: ARNOUT C. HYDE JR. (348-9152)

GEOLOGICAL AND ECONOMIC SURVEY, Box 879, Morgantown 26507-0879 (304, 594-2331)

Charged with the responsibility of examining all geological formations and physical features of the state with particular emphasis on their economic importance, utilization and conservation, and preparing reports and maps of the geology and natural resources of West Virginia. Established: 1897.
Director and State Geologist: ROBERT B. ERWIN (Ext. 323)
Administration: ROBERT B. ERWIN, Director and State Geologist (Ext. 323); LARRY D. WOODFORK, Assistant State Geologist (Ext. 325)
Publications: Bulletins; Reports of Investigations; Circulars; Coal-Geology Bulletins; Environmental Geology Bulletins; Mineral Resources Series; River Basin Bulletins; Basic Data Reports; County Geologic Reports; Educational Series; State Park Bulletins; Field Trip Guides; Reprints; Special Listings; State Maps; County Maps; Topographic Maps; Geologic Quadrangle Maps; Hydrologic Maps; *Annual Report;* Newsletters
Editor: FRED C. SCHROYER (Ext. 211)

STATE EXTENSION SERVICES

Associate Vice-President, University Extension Public Service: DR. RACHEL TOMPKINS, West Virginia University, 817 Knapp Hall, Morgantown 26506 (304, 293-5691)
Extension Specialist, Forest Management: W.E. KIDD, JR., 325C Percival Hall, West Virginia University, Morgantown 26506 (293-4411)
Extension Specialist, Water Quality: DR. ROBERT E. ANDERSON, 508 Brooks Hall, West Virginia University, Morgantown 26506 (293-3911)
Division Leader, Agriculture, Forestry, and Community Development, Cooperative Extension Service: EDMOND B. COLLINS
Extension Specialist, Forestry: JOSEPH N. YEAGER, State 4-H Camp, P.O. Box 429, Weston 26452 (269-6681)
Extension Specialist, Wildlife: WILLIAM GRAFTON 307-B Percival Hall, West Virginia University, Morgantown 26506
Curriculum Designer, Wildlife: NORMA J. VENABLE, 408 Knapp Hall, Morgantown 26506 (293-4201)

CITIZENS' GROUPS

WEST VIRGINIA WILDLIFE FEDERATION, INC., *Box 275, Paden City 26159 (304, 455-3342/After 5 P.M.: 472-2171)*
A representative statewide organization, affiliated with the National Wildlife Federation, primarily devoted to the wise use, conservation, aesthetic appreciation, and restoration of wildlife and other natural resources.
President: CONNIE S. MILLER, P.O. Box 191, Paden City 26159 (455-3342)
Secretary: MARY JOE COOK, Rt. #4, Box 62B, Clintonville 24928 (392-5680)
Affiliate Representative: JIM KULPA, Rt. 2, Box 512, Wheeling 26003 (242-5069/232-6170)
Alternate: CONNIE S. MILLER

Publication: Wildlife Notes
Editors: JOHN MARTYS and PHIL LEINBACH, c/o Marbach Publications, P.O. Box 2928, Clarksburg 26301 (337-9166)

BROOKS NATURE CENTER, Oglebay Institute, Oglebay Park, Wheeling 26003 (304, 242-6855)

Oglebay Institute operates a variety of programs: resident nature summer camps for adults and Children; backpacking camp; resident environmental education programs; children's day camping; special workshops and weekends; exhibits; school programs; and also the A.B. Brooks Nature Center and Speidel Observatory.
Director, Nature Education: SUE B. STROYLS
Interpretive Naturalist: WILLIAM BEATTY
Environmental Education Specialists: GREG PARK; THOMAS SHEPHERD

IZAAK WALTON LEAGUE OF AMERICA, INC. (West Virginia Division)

President: MICHAEL HOFER, Rt. 3, Box 89A, Morgantown 26505 (304, 296-3392)
Secretary: MARIE CYPHERT, Box 1096, Morgantown 26507 (599-9237)

TROUT UNLIMITED WEST VIRGINIA COUNCIL

A statewide council with 10 chapters working for the protection and enhancement of coldwater fishery resources.
Chairman: GARY LANG, 6 Fox Ridge Ln., Elkins 26241 (304, 636-7642)
National Director: ERNEST NESTER, P.O. Box 235, Alloy 25002 (779-2706)

WEST VIRGINIA BASS CHAPTER FEDERATION

An organization of Bassmaster Chapters, affiliated with the Bass Anglers Sportsman Society, organized to fight pollution, assist state and national conservation agencies in their efforts, and to teach the young people of our country good conservation practices. Dedicated to the realistic conservation of our water resources.
President: RON GILLESPIE, 404 Grand Ave., Bridgeport 26330 (304, 842-4796)

WEST VIRGINIA HIGHLANDS CONSERVANCY, 1206 Virginia St., E., Suite 201, Charleston 25301

An organization devoted to the conservation and wise management of West Virginia's natural and historic resources. Active in wilderness preservation, river conservation, public lands management, mining, air and water quality, water resources management and a wide variety of other environmental and conservation issues. Established 1967.
President: JOHN C. PURBAUGH, 2502 Dudden Fork, Kenna 25248 (304, 342-6814)
Senior Vice-President: DAVID ELKINTON, Rt. 5, Box 228A, Morgantown 26505
Vice-President for State Affairs: RON SHIPLEY, 1126 Hickory Rd., Apt. D, Charleston 25314
Vice-President for Federal Affairs: SKIP DEEGANS, 2112 New Hampshire Ave., NW, Apt. 615, Washington, DC 20009
Treasurer: TOM MICHAEL, Rt. 2, Box 217, Lost Creek 26385
Secretary: MARY LOU NEWBERGER, Box 89, Looneyville 25259
Past President: JOE RIEFFENBERGER, Rt. 1, Box 523, Elkins 26241
Publication: *The Highlands Voice*
Editor: GARY WORTHINGTON, 118 Clark Ave., Fayetteville 25840
Membership Secretary: ADRIENNE WORTHY, Suite 201, 1206 Virginia St. E., Charleston 25301 (304, 343-2767)

WEST VIRGINIA SOIL AND WATER CONSERVATION DISTRICT SUPERVISORS ASSOCIATION
President: DELMER SCHELL, Box 5, Scherr 26726
Vice-President: FRANK GLOVER, 664 Villa Pl., Morgantown 26505
Secretary: ROBERT HOLLOWAY, 220 Stave Branch Rd., Fraziers Bottom 25082
Treasurer: J. ARTHUR McKEE, Rt. 3, Box 264-B, Bridgeport 26330

WILDLIFE SOCIETY WEST VIRGINIA CHAPTER
President: PAUL JOHANSEN, Rt. 3, Box 127, Elkins 26241 (304, 336-5880)
Vice-President: CURTIS TAYLOR, General Delivery, Jumping Branch 25969 (256-6947)
Secretary-Treasurer: JACK I. CROMER, Rt. 1, Box 224, Beverly 26241 (636-1767)

WISCONSIN

GOVERNMENT AGENCIES

GOVERNOR: TOMMY G. THOMPSON, Governor of Wisconsin, State Capitol, Madison 53707 (608, 266-1212)

DEPARTMENT OF AGRICULTURE, TRADE AND CONSUMER PROTECTION, P.O. Box 8911, 801 W. Badger Rd., Madison 53708 (608, 266-7100)
Secretary: HOWARD RICHARDS

DEPARTMENT OF NATURAL RESOURCES, Box 7921, Madison 53707 (608, 266-2621)
Responsibilities include: fish, wildlife, forest, and parks management, forest fire control, control of air and water pollution, solid-waste disposal, mining regulation, flood plain and shoreland zoning, water management and regulation, lake rehabilitation, and long-range planning in the broad fields of outdoor recreation and natural resources.
Natural Resources Board: HELEN M. JACOBS, Chair, Milwaukee; THOMAS D. LAWIN, Vice-Chair, Bloomer; STANTON P. HELLAND, Secretary, Wisconsin Dells; RICHARD A. HEMP, Mosinee; DONALD C. O'MELIA, Rhinelander; JOHN A. LAWTON, Madison; WILL LEE, Wisconsin Rapids
Secretary: C.D. BESADNY (266-2121)
Deputy Secretary: BRUCE B. BRAUN (266-2197)
Executive Assistant: LINDA BOCHERT (266-2243)

Bureau of Legal Services
Director: JAMES A. KURTZ (266-3695)

Office of Intergovernmental Programs
Director: PAULETTE J. HARDER (266-0836)

Bureau of Community Assistance
Director: MARJORIE DEVEREAUX (266-5896)

Office of Planning and Analysis
Administrator: RONALD SEMMANN (266-2252)

Bureau of Management and Budget
Director: JOSEPH P. POLASEK, JR. (266-2794)

Bureau of Finance
Director: CLARENCE L. GOLDSWORTHY (266-2951)

Division of Environmental Standards
Administrator: LYMAN F. WIBLE (266-1099)
Assistant Administrator: JAY G. HOCHMUTH (267-9521)
Office of Technical Services: LLOYD A. LUESCHOW, Director (266-6977)
Office of Wastewater Operation & Maintenance: THOMAS A. KROEHN, Director (267-7656)

Bureau of Solid Waste Management
Director: PAUL P. DIDIER (266-1327)

Bureau of Air Management
Director: DONALD F. THEILER (266-0603)

Bureau of Wastewater Management
Director: CARL J. BLABAUM (266-3910)

Bureau of Water Resources Management
Director: BRUCE J. BAKER (266-8631)

Bureau of Water Supply
Director: ROBERT M. KRILL (267-7651)

Division of Resource Management
Administrator: JAMES ADDIS (266-0837)
Assistant Administrator: CRAIG L. KARR (266-5782)

Bureau of Facilities Management
Director: HOWARD S. DRUCKENMILLER (266-2136)

Bureau of Fish Management
Director: DOUGLAS MORRISSETTE (266-7025)

Bureau of Wildlife Management
Director: STEVEN W. MILLER (266-2193)

Bureau of Endangered Resources
Director: RONALD F. NICOTERA (266-2625)

Bureau of Forestry
Director: JOSEPH M. FRANK (266-0842)

Bureau of Parks and Recreation
Director: DAVID L. WEIZENICKER (266-2185)

Bureau of Research
Director: KENT E. KLEPINGER (266-8170)

Division of Enforcement
Administrator: GEORGE E. MEYER (266-0015)
Assistant Administrator: KATHRYN A. CURTNER (266-7820)

Bureau of Law Enforcement
Director: RALPH E. CHRISTENSEN (266-1115)

Bureau of Water Regulation and Zoning
Director: ROBERT W. RODEN (266-8034)

Office of Environmental Enforcement
Director: JOHN L. LaFONTAINE (266-5848)

Bureau of Environmental Analysis and Review
Director: Vacant (266-0860)

Division of Management Services
Administrator: MARTIN HENERT (266-9980)
Assistant Administrator: MARILYN DAVIS (266-2272)

Bureau of Information and Education
Director: W. JEFFREY SMOLLER (266-2747)
Publication: *Wisconsin Natural Resources Magazine*
Editor: LARRY SPERLING, Box 7921, Madison 53707

Bureau of Information Management
Director: JANET PRICE (266-6897)

Bureau of Program Services
Director: RICHARD FOX (266-2452)

Bureau of Personnel
Director: DEBRA MARTINELLI (266-2048)

District Directors
Southern: JAMES HUNTOON, Madison (608, 275-3260)
Southeast: GLORIA L. McCUTCHEON, Milwaukee (414, 562-9510)
Lake Michigan: CHARLES E. HIGGS, Green Bay (414, 497-4038)
West Central: JAMES L. LISSACK, Eau Claire (715, 839-3711)
North Central: DALE T. URSO, Rhinelander (715, 362-7616)
Northwest: DAVID A. JACOBSON, Spooner (715, 635-4010)

DEPARTMENT OF PUBLIC INSTRUCTION, 125 S Webster St., P.O. Box 7841, Madison 53707 (608, 267-9266)
Promotes environmental education in public schools and supervises teacher preparation programs. Conducts workshops, provides consultant services to elementary and secondary schools, colleges and universities, and produces publications to aid in program development.
Supervisor of Environmental Education: DAVID C. ENGLESON

GEOLOGICAL AND NATURAL HISTORY SURVEY, University of Wisconsin Extension, 3817 Mineral Point Rd., Madison 53705 (608, 262-1705)
Created by the legislature in 1897, and has the responsibility to survey the state's geology, mineral, water, soil, plant, animal, and climate resources and to coordinate topographic mapping.
State Geologist and Director: MEREDITH E. OSTROM (263-7364)
Assistant Director: RONALD HENNINGS (263-7395)
Budgeting Specialist: KATHLEEN ZWETTLER (263-9418)

LAND AND WATER RESOURCES BUREAU, DEPARTMENT OF AGRICULTURE, TRADE AND CONSUMER PROTECTION, 801 W. Badger Rd., Madison 53713
Responsible for administering state soil and water conservation and farmland preservation programs.
Secretary: HOWARD C. RICHARDS
Bureau Director: JAMES JOHNSON (608, 267-9788)

SEA GRANT INSTITUTE
Director: DR. ROBERT A. RAGOTZKIE, University of Wisconsin, 1800 University Ave., Madison 53705 (608, 262-0905)
Represents a unique working partnership of federal, state, university and private sectors. UW Sea Grant is a statewide program that supports university-based research, education and public service activities related to the wise use and management of marine and Great Lakes issues. Established:1968.
Sea Grant Advisory Services: ALLEN H. MILLER
Communications Coordinator: STEPHEN WITTMAN

STATE EXTENSION SERVICES
Director of Cooperative Extension Programs: DR. PATRICK G.

BOYLE, University of Wisconsin Extension, 432 North Lake St., Madison 53706 (608, 262-3786)
Statewide Program Leader (Acting), Community, Natural Resource, and Economic Development: DR. ROBERT N. DICK, Rm. 625, 432 N. Lake St., Madison 53706 (262-1748)
Extension Forester: A. JEFF MARTIN, Ph.D., 111 Russell Laboratories, University of Wisconsin, Madison 53706 (262-0134)
Extension Wildlife Specialists: DR. ROBERT L. RUFF, Ph.D., 226 Russell Laboratories, University of Wisconsin, Madison 53706 (263-2071); DR. SCOTT CRAVEN, Ph.D., 215 Russell Laboratories, University of Wisconsin, Madison 53706 (263-6325)

WISCONSIN CONSERVATION CORPS, 30 W. Mifflin, Suite 406, Madison 53703-2558 (608, 266-7730)
The WCC provides work experience and personal development opportunities to young adults ages 18-25, and valuable conservation and other services to Wisconsin communities. Approximately 300 corps members annually work at three dozen rotating project sites throughout the state. Government agencies and nonprofit organizations are eligible to apply for WCC assistance. Created as an independent state agency in 1983.
Executive Director: WILLIAM A. BRAKKEN
Publications: *On Corps Newsletter; Biennial Report*

WISCONSIN COOPERATIVE FISHERY RESEARCH UNIT, U.S.D.I., College of Natural Resources, University of Wisconsin, Stevens Point 54481 (715, 346-2178)
Interagency organization—federal, state, and university—to carry out research, training, and extension in biology and management of fresh water fishery resources.
Leader: DR. DANIEL W. COBLE

WISCONSIN COOPERATIVE WILDLIFE RESEARCH UNIT, U.S.D.I., FWS, Department of Wildlife Ecology, 226 Russell Laboratories, University of Wisconsin, Madison 53706 (608, 263-6882)
Leader: DR. DONALD RUSCH

CITIZENS' GROUPS

 WISCONSIN WILDLIFE FEDERATION, Tranquil Acres, Reeseville 53579 (414, 927-3131)
A representative statewide organization, affiliated with the National Wildlife Federation, primarily devoted to the wise use, conservation, aesthetic appreciation, and restoration of wildlife and other natural resources.
President: JERRY LAUDON, 6248 Briarwood Ln., Waterford 53185 (414, 895-2630)
Secretary: ARTHUR HAGEMANN, 911 S. 15th Ave., Wausau 54401 (715, 845-2500)
Affiliate Representative: ROBERT LACHMUND, 3876 S. Hanson Ave., Milwaukee 53207
Alternate: ROBERT MILLER, 646 E. Division, Sparta 54656 (608, 269-2843)
Publication: Wisconservation
Editor: ROBERT A. LACHMUND

CITIZENS NATURAL RESOURCES ASSOCIATION OF WISCONSIN, INC.
To protect Wisconsin's natural resources through education, legislation, and the courts. The CNRA initiated and sponsored the action which resulted in the banning of DDT in Wisconsin and two years later in the United States. Recently, the CNRA has been concentrating on protecting and restoring native vegetation along Wisconsin's roads. Organized: 1951.

President: DAVID KOPITZKE, Rt. 1, Box 287, Richland Center 53581 (608, 538-3180)

Vice-President: LORRIE OTTO, 9701 N. Lake Dr., Milwaukee 53217 (414, 352-0734)

Secretary: KAY RILL, 1520 Bowen St., Oshkosh 54901

Treasurer: ETHEL PRINCL, 1240 S. 11th Ave., Wausau 54401

Councilors: CY KABAT, 4014 Lori Cr., Madison 53714; FRED OTT, 6537 Revere Ave., Wauwatosa 53221; JAN SCALPONE, 2033 Menominee Dr., Oshkosh 54901; LEONIE VRTILEK, 330 Ledgeview Ave., Fond du Lac 54935

Publications: *The CNRA Report; Wisconsin Roadsides*

Editor: JAN SCALPONE, 2033 Menominee Dr., Oshkosh 54901

IZAAK WALTON LEAGUE OF AMERICA, INC. (Wisconsin Division)

President: GARY WARD, Box 265, Benton 53803 (608, 759-6212)

Secretary: BARBRA W. GAREY, 12509 N. Woodberry Dr., Mequon 53092 (414, 242-0813)

TREES FOR TOMORROW, INC., 611 Sheridan Rd., Box 609, Eagle River 54521 (715, 479-6456/6457)

Original purpose to help reforest northern Wisconsin; currently conducts natural resource information and education programs on the social and economic significance of the environment. Founded: 1944.

President: JELMEN SWOBODA, Vice-President, Marketing, Wisconsin Public Service Corp, Green Bay 54307

Vice-President: LLOYD GODELL, James River Corporation, P.O. Box 790, Green Bay 54305

Secretary: LLOYD KOTH, Vice-President, Lionite Hardboard, P.O. Box 138, Phillips 54555

Treasurer: RONALD SCHULTZE, Wausau Insurance Company, 400 Westwood Dr., Wausau 54401

Executive Director: HENRY H. HASKELL

Publication: Newspaper: *Trees For Tomorrow's Northbound*

Editor: BRYAN PIERCE

TROUT UNLIMITED WISCONSIN COUNCIL

A statewide council with 22 chapters working for the protection and enhancement of coldwater fishery resources.

Chairman: RICHARD WACHOWSKI, 4500 North Shore Dr., St., Eau Claire 54701 (715, 835-4093)

National Directors: TOM FLESCH, N3079 Tomlinson Rd., Foynette 53955 (608, 241-3311/Ext. 3142); THOMAS SOPKOVICH, 810 East Fairy Chasm Rd., Milwaukee 53217 (414, 351-4011); JOHN CANTWELL, 2286 Mt. Olive Dr., Green Bay 54303 (715, 735-7703); ROBERT BOLZ, 411 Summit Rd., Madison 53704 (608, 249-6197)

WILDLIFE SOCIETY WISCONSIN CHAPTER

President: TOM HAUGE, P.O. Box 863, Madison 53701-0863 (608, 267-7857)

Vice-President: ALAN CROSSLEY, 459 Sidney St., Madison 53703 (275-3242)

Secretary-Treasurer: JOHN CARY, 1622 Jefferson, Madison 53711 (263-6710)

WISCONSIN ASSOCIATION FOR ENVIRONMENTAL EDUCATION, INC., 2428 Downy, Green Bay 54303 (414, 499-6500/497-3027)

Promotes environmental education in schools and other institutions and organizations in Wisconsin. Founded: 1962. Membership: 500.

Chairperson: RANDALL CHAMPEAU, CNR, University of Wisconsin-Stevens Point, Stevens Point 54481 (715, 346-2853/592-4619)

Vice-Chairperson: CARRIE MORGAN, 2428 Downy St., Green Bay 54303 (414, 499-6500/497-3027)

Secretary: MARTHA KRONHOLM, 105 Birch St., Vesper 54489 (715, 569-4195)

Treasurer: DEAN SAUERS, 3040 N. Canary, Appleton 54915

Publications: *Wisconsin Association for Environmental Education Bulletin; EE News*

Editors: JUDY KLIPPEL; ANNE HALLOWELL

WISCONSIN ASSOCIATION OF SOIL AND WATER CONSERVATION DISTRICTS

President: GEORGE NETTUM, 404 E. South St., Viroqua 54665 (608, 637-3236)

Vice-President: CONRAD NAPARALLA, Rt. 1, Box 146, Princeton 54968 (414, 295-3144)

Secretary-Treasurer: RICHARD MARKUS, Rt. 1, Potosi 53820 (608, 763-2332)

WISCONSIN BASS CHAPTER FEDERATION

An organization of Bassmaster Chapters, affiliated with the Bass Anglers Sportsman Society, organized to fight pollution, assist state and national conservation agencies in their efforts, and to teach young people of our country good conservation practices. Dedicated to the realistic conservation of our water resources.

President: GEORGE GOODSELL, Box 77, Dresbach 55930 (507, 643-6382)

WISCONSIN PARK AND RECREATION ASSOCIATION, 7000 Greenway, Suite 201, Greendale 53129 (414, 423-1210)

A nonprofit organization, with over 800 members state-wide affiliated with the National Recreation and Park Association, working with other groups and organizations to achieve the best in park services and recreational opportunities.

President: BOB RUNDLE, Greendale Park and Recreation, 7000 Greenway, Greendale 53129 (414, 423-0612)

Executive Vice-President: TRISHA PUGAL, 7000 Greenway, Suite 201, Greendale 53129 (414, 423-1210)

Treasurer: KENNETH VAN ES, Eau Claire Park and Recreation Department, 1300 1st Ave., Eau Claire 54703 (715, 839-5032)

Publications: *Impact Magazine; Leisure Line Newsletter*

Editors: CATHERINE SWANSON, Mt. Carmel Health Care Center, 5700 W. Layton Ave., Greenfield 53220 (414, 281-7200); TRISHA PUGAL

WISCONSIN SOCIETY FOR ORNITHOLOGY, INC., THE (Annual Convention: May 12-14, Madison)

To stimulate interest in and promote the study of birds in Wisconsin for a better understanding of their biology and basis for their preservation. Membership: 1,200. Founded: 1939.

President: JOHN H. IDZIKOWSKI, 2558 South Delaware, Milwaukee 53207 (414, 744-4818)

Vice-President: RANDY HOFFMAN, 305 5th St., Waunakee 53597 (608, 849-4502)

Secretary: CARL G. HAYSSEN, JR., 6917 N. Highway 83, Hartland 53029 (414, 966-2839)

Treasurer: GWYN TUTTLE GOY, 1430 CTH 6, La Crescent, MN 55947 (507, 895-4865)

Wisconsin Birder Hot Line: (414, 352-3857)

Publications: *Badger Birder; Passenger Pigeon*

Editors: MARY DONALD, 6918 N. Belmont Ln., Milwaukee 53217; STANLEY A. TEMPLE, Department of Wildlife Ecology, UW-Madison, Madison 53706

WISCONSIN WATERFOWLERS ASSOCIATION, INC., P.O. Box 792, Waukesha 53187-0792

A statewide nonprofit environmental/educational organization. Establishes, promotes, assists, and contributes to conservation, restoration and management of Wisconsin wetlands to perpetuate waterfowl and wildlife. Represents waterfowl enthusiasts via a unified statewide voice on Wisconsin migratory bird hunting regulations and conservation legislation benefiting the protection of wetlands. Educational programs and waterfowl hunting seminars. Membership: 4,000. Founded: 1984.

President: ROBERT A. KIECKHEFER, 340 E. Daphne Rd., Milwaukee 53217 (414, 352-3714)

Chairman of the Board: JERRY SOLSRUD, 1539 Milwaukee St., Delafield 53018 (414, 646-8768)

Secretary: RANDY KRENN, 2379 S. Logan Ave., Milwaukee 53207 (414, 744-0647)

Treasurer: JAMES C. BOLTON, JR., P.O. Box 7900, Madison 53707 (608, 252-4052)

Habitat Chairman: JOHN M. KEENER, 4821 Maher Ave., Madison 53716 (608, 222-6693)

Executive Director: KEN COOK, 12204 W. Blue Mound Rd., Wauwatosa 53226 (414, 778-0004)

Publication: *WWA Newsletter*

Editor: JIM WEIX, P.O. Box 292, Dousman 53118 (414, 965-3909)

WISCONSIN WOODLAND OWNERS ASSOCIATION, P.O. Box 285, Stevens Point 54481 (715, 341-4798)

A statewide organization affiliated with the National Woodland Owners Association, established to advance the interests of woodland owners and the cause of forestry in Wisconsin. Membership: 2,600. Founded: 1979.

President: RACHAEL L. JORDAN (608, 935-3833)

Executive Director: BETTY HAUGE

Publication: *WISCONSIN WOODLANDS*

Editor: GRACE W. WHITE (608, 233-5253)

WYOMING

GOVERNMENT AGENCIES

GOVERNOR: MIKE SULLIVAN, Governor of Wyoming, State Capitol, Cheyenne 82002 (307, 777-7434)

DEPARTMENT OF AGRICULTURE, 2219 Carey Ave., Cheyenne 82002 (307, 777-7321)

Commissioner: DON ROLSTON (777-6569)

Assistant Commissioner: ED ANDERSON (777-6570)

Manager, Standards and Consumer Services: WILLIAM H. HOVEY (777-6591)

Manager, Marketing Services: JUDI ADAMS (777-6581)

Manager, Special Services (Natural Resources): COLLIN FALLAT (777-6576)

DEPARTMENT OF HEALTH AND SOCIAL SERVICES, Division of Health and Medical Services, Hathaway Bldg., Cheyenne 82002 (307, 777-7121)

Administrator: R. LARRY MEULI, M.D.

ECONOMIC DEVELOPMENT AND STABLIZATION BOARD, Herschler Bldg., Cheyenne 82002 (307, 777-7284)

To investigate plans for development of any resource in the state, and attraction and development of any new industries into the state. To conduct studies and carry out activities including loans in connection with the conservation, storage, distribution, and use of water. To make studies of all mineral resources and present and future development. Created: 1985.

Executive Director: BILL BUDD (777-7287)

Publications: *Wyoming Economic Development Newsletter; Wyoming Minerals Yearbook; Wyoming Directory of Manufacturing and Mining*

ENVIRONMENTAL QUALITY DEPARTMENT, 122 W. 25th St., 4th Fl., Herschler Bldg., Cheyenne 82002 (307, 777-7937)

Responsible for the prevention, reduction and elimination of pollution and the preservation and enhancement of the air and water and reclamation of the land of Wyoming; established to plan the development, use, reclamation, preservation, and enhancement of the air, land, and water resources of the state. Established: 1973.

Council Members: JOHN CROW, Pinedale; JOHN C. DARRINGTON, Secretary, Gillette; FRED H. CARR, Casper; HAROLD L. BERGMAN, Laramie; VINCENT R. LEE, Vice-Chairman, Wilson; DAVID B. PARK, Casper; JOHN C. SCHIFFER, Chairman, Kaycee

Director: RANDOLPH WOOD

Management Services Supervisor: HAROLD A. ALLEN

Water Quality Administrator: WILLIAM L. GARLAND (777-7781)

Air Quality Administrator: CHARLES A. COLLINS (777-7391)

Land Quality Administrator: ROGER SHAFFER (777-7756)

Solid Waste Program Manager: DAVID A. FINLEY (777-7752)

GAME AND FISH DEPARTMENT, 5400 Bishop Blvd., Cheyenne 82002 (307, 777-7735)

To provide an adequate and flexible system for control, propagation, management, protection and regulation of Wyoming wildlife for the best public interest. Founded: 1939.

Commission Members: DONALD SCOTT, Torrington: O.R. (Bud) DAILY, Rawlins; NORMAN PAPE, Daniel; D.C. (Rusty) HOLLER, Sheridan; KENNETH BROWN, Worland; DENZEL COFFEY, Manville; EDWARD P. McCARTHY, Casper

Director: WILLIAM MORRIS

Assistant Directors: FRANCIS E. PETERA; DOUGLAS M. CROWE

Chief, Game Warden: REX M. CORSI (777-7604)

Chief, Fish Division: JOE WHITE (777-7686)

Chief, Habitat and Technical Services Division: ART REESE (777-6986)

Chief, Administrative and Fiscal Services Division: Vacant (777-5827)

District Game Supervisors: TOM TOMAN, Box 67, Jackson 83001 (733-2321); TERRY KILLOUGH, 2820 State Highway 120, Cody 82414 (527-7125); GARY SHORMA, Box 6249, Sheridan 82801 (672-7418); PHIL RIDDLE, 351 Astle, Green River 82935 (875-3223); JAY LAWSON, 528 S. Adams, Laramie 82070 (745-4046); JOHN TALBOTT, 260 Buena Vista, Lander 82520 (332-2688); TERRY CLEVELAND, 2800 Pheasant Dr., Casper 82604 (234-9185)

Chief, Information and Education Services Division: LARRY L. KRUCKENBERG (777-7735)

Manager, Information Section: AL LANGSTON (777-7735)

Manager, Education Section: DENNIS GUNTER (777-6988)

Project WILD Coordinator: JOE VOGLER (777-6993)

Hunter Education Coordinator: Vacant (777-6993)

Manager, Audio-Visual Section: DON MILLER (777-6991)

Special Publications: JUDY HOSAFROS (777-6958)

Publication: *Wyoming Wildlife*

Editor: CHRIS MADSON (777-7737)

GEOLOGICAL SURVEY OF WYOMING, THE, Box 3008, University Station, Laramie 82071 (307, 766-2286)

Activities include surface and subsurface geologic mapping; mineral, rock, and fossil investigations; natural resource and natural hazards investigations; and assistance in resources development. Established: 1933.

State Geologist: GARY B. GLASS

Deputy Director: W. DAN HAUSEL

Industrial Minerals Geologist: RAY E. HARRIS

Coal Geologist: RICHARD W. JONES

Petroleum Geologist: RODNEY H. De BRUIN

Stratigrapher: ALAN J. VER PLOEG

Geological Hazards Geologist: JAMES C. CASE

Publications: Memoirs; bulletins; reports of investigations; public information circulars; state and county maps; quarterly newsletter *(Wyoming Geo-Notes);* List of publications sent on request.

Editor: SHEILA ROBERTS

OFFICE OF INDUSTRIAL SITING ADMINISTRATION, State of Wyoming, 2301 Central Ave., Third Fl., Barrett Bldg., Cheyenne 82002 (307, 777-7368)

Administers Wyoming Industrial Development Information and Siting Act, which deals with the social, economic and environmental impacts of large-scale industrial development. Responsibilities consist of investigating, reviewing, processing and serving notice of permit applications. Established: 1975.

Council Members: TYLER DODGE, Wheatland; DAVID EVANS, Cheyenne; HAROLD MEIER, Casper; PAUL ANSELMI, Rock Springs; LaVERNA HENDRICKS, Glenrock; NANCY PETERNAL, Kemmerer; WILLIAM T. FULKERSON, Chairman, Gillette

Director: GARY G. BEACH (307, 777-7360)

RECREATION COMMISSION, 122 West 25th St., Herschler Bldg., Cheyenne 82002 (307, 777-7695)

Responsible for administering the Land and Water Conservation Fund Act, state parks, state recreation areas, historic sites, petroglyph site, archaeological site, markers and monuments, state archaeologist program, and snowmobile program. Formed: 1967.

Director: R.D. (Max) MAXFIELD, P.E. (Ext. 6310)

Assistant Director: GARY STEPHENSON (Ext. 6300)

Chief, State Parks Division: GARY THORSON (Ext. 6324)

Chief, Administration Division: GARY STEPHENSON (Ext. 6300)

State Archaeologist: MARK E. MILLER, Ph.D. (766-5564)

STATE BOARD OF LAND COMMISSIONERS, Herschler Bldg., Cheyenne 82002 (307, 777-7331)

Chairman: GOV. MIKE SULLIVAN

Secretary and Land Commissioner: HOWARD M. SCHRINAR

STATE CONSERVATION COMMISSION, 2219 Carey Ave., Cheyenne 82002 (307, 777-7323)

Purpose is to assist and guide 37 conservation districts within the state in the preparation and performance of soil and water conservation programs for the protection and wide use of Wyoming's nature resources. Organized: 1941.

Chairman: JOHN NILAND

Conservation Commission State Executive: BILL GENTLE

Wyoming State Conservation Commission Members: JOHN NILAND, Chairman, Herschler Bldg., Cheyenne 82002 (307, 777-7284); FORREST ALLEN, 5006 Powell Hwy., Cody 82414 (587-2038); RICHARD GRAY, Box 528, Moorcroft 82721 (756-3202); PETER HANSEN, Vice Chairman, Rt. 1, Box 106, Lusk 82225 (334-3827); BRYAN TARANTOLA, Box 2460, Jackson 83001 (733-7371); STEVE ADAMS, Box 98, Baggs 82321 (383-2277); DR. LEE BULLA, Dean, College of Agriculture, University of Wyoming, University Station, Laramie 82070

(766-4133); GEORGE CHRISTOPULOS, State Engineer, Herschler Bldg., Cheyenne 82002 (777-7354); ALBERT PROCTOR, Moorcroft 82721 (756-3282) President, Livestock Board; JOHN ORTON, Commissioner of Agriculture, 2219 Carey Ave., Cheyenne 82002 (777-7321)

Publications: *Wyoming Conservation News; Conservation District Directory*

Editor: BILL GENTLE

STATE EXTENSION SERVICES

Director: JAMES O. DeBEE, University Station, Box 3354, Laramie 82071 (307, 766-5124)

Extension Horticulturist and Forester: JAMES A. COOK, University Station, Box 3354, Laramie 82071 (766-2243)

Range Management Division, Head: BILL LAYCOCK, Box 3354, University Station, Laramie 82071 (766-5263)

Director (Acting), Communication Service: NORMAN (Skip) ROBERTS, University Station, Box 3315, Laramie 82071 (766-2379)

Publications: Journal articles; scientific abstracts; science monographs; research journals; bulletins; 4-H publications; regional publications

STATE FORESTRY DIVISION, 1100 West 22nd St., Cheyenne 82002 (307, 777-7586)

Has direction of all forestry matters within the jurisdiction of the state of Wyoming; management of state-owned forest land; coordinates fire protection on twenty-nine million acres of state and private rural lands; assists landowners in proper management and utilization of forested lands; and provides forestry information to schools, organizations and individuals. Organized: 1952.

State Forester: CARL E. JOHNSON

Deputy State Forester: BRYCE E. LUNDELL

Assistant State Forester, Fire Management: MICHAEL H. GAGEN

Assistant State Forester, Forest Management: HERBERT C. COTTRELL

WYOMING COOPERATIVE FISH AND WILDLIFE RESEARCH UNIT, U.S.D.I., University of Wyoming, Box 3166, University Station, Rm. 419, Biological Sciences Bldg., Laramie 82071 (307, 766-5415)

Conducts research under auspices of U.S. Fish and Wildlife Service and Wyoming Game and Fish Department in northern Rocky Mountain region. Organized: 1980.

Leader: DR. STANLEY H. ANDERSON

Assistant Leader, Fishery: DR. WAYNE A. HUBERT

Assistant Leader, Wildlife: DR. FREDERICK G. LINDZEY

CITIZENS' GROUPS

 WYOMING WILDLIFE FEDERATION, P.O. Box 106, Cheyenne 82003 (307, 637-5433)

A representative statewide organization, affiliated with the National Wildlife Federation, primarily devoted to the wise use, conservation, aesthetic appreciation, and restoration of wildlife and other natural resources.

President: TORY TAYLOR, Cross Brace Ranch, R.R. 31, Box 601, Dubois 82513 (455-2714)

Executive Director: MARCIA ROTHWELL

Affiliate Representative: JO LYN REEVES, 2215 Pennsylvania, Green River 82935

Alternate: TORY TAYLOR

Publication: The Pronghorn

Editor: MARCIA ROTHWELL

IZAAK WALTON LEAGUE OF AMERICA, INC. (Wyoming Div.)

To encourage the protection and wise use of our lands, our forests, our scenic and recreational areas, our waters, minerals, wildlife and other conservation and environmental values. Membership: 150.

President: RAYMOND G. JACQUOT, 1072 Empinado, Laramie 82070 (307, 742-2785)

Secretary: BRUCE WARD, 159 Aster, Casper 82604 (307, 234-6853)

POWDER RIVER BASIN RESOURCE COUNCIL, 23 N. Scott, Sheridan 82801 (307, 672-5809)

Nonprofit grassroots organization whose major purpose is to help Wyoming people work to prevent and alleviate environmental and agricultural problems. Major issues include coal leasing and mining, water development, toxics and hazardous wastes, and the agricultural financial crisis. Membership: 600. Founded: 1973.

Chairman: MELODY KUECKS, Converse County

Vice-Chairman: RONN SMITH, Sheridan County

Secretary: KATIE HUMPHRIS, Sheridan County

Treasurer: CAM FORBES, Sheridan County

Staff Director: CHESIE LEE

Publication: *Powder River Breaks*

TROUT UNLIMITED WYOMING

Dedicated to the protection and enhancement of the coldwater fishery resource.

Chairman and Director: EDWARD INGOLD, P.O. Box 2185, Jackson 83001 (307, 733-5261)

Council Staff Director: SUZANNE VAN GYTENBEEK, T.U. Wyoming, P.O. Box 4069, Jackson 83001 (733-1486)

WILDLIFE SOCIETY WYOMING CHAPTER

President: KEVIN HURLEY, 1032 Arapahoe, Thermopolis 82443 (307, 864-9375)

President-Elect: TOM RYDER, 1625 South Summit, New Castle 82701 (746-3655)

Secretary: BOB McCARTY, P.O. Box 424, Pinedale 82941 (367-4358)

Treasurer: STEVE BUSKIRK, Box 3166, University Station, Laramie 82070 (766-2357)

WYOMING ASSOCIATION OF CONSERVATION DISTRICTS

President and Council Member: RICHARD GRAY, Box 580, Moorecroft 82721 (307, 756-3202)

Vice-President: PETER HANSEN, Star Rt., Box 106, Lusk 82225 (334-3827)

Secretary-Treasurer: MARY LOU O'BLENESS, Box 24, Cheyenne 82003 (632-1533)

Executive Director: DEBI BRAMMER, 1750 Westland Rd., Rm. 167, Cheyenne 82001 (632-5716)

WYOMING OUTDOOR COUNCIL, INC., 201 Main St., P.O. Box 1449, Lander 82520 (307, 332-7031)

A statewide organization composed of groups and individuals working together to preserve the essential character of Wyoming, especially its natural resources. Serves as an active citizen lobby for sound environmental policies, monitors state and federal agencies. Organized: 1967.

President: KIM CANNON, P.O. Box 728, Sheridan 82801 (672-7491)

Vice-President: STUART THOMPSON, P.O. Box 18, Cora 82925 (367-2502)

Treasurer: LARRY MEANS, P.O. Box 1535, Lander 82520 (332-7474)

Director of Education: DR. A. DONN KESSELHEIM

Publications: *The Crossroads Monitor; Legislative Analysis; Frontline Report*

CANADIAN GOVERNMENT AGENCIES AND NATIONAL CITIZENS' GROUPS

GOVERNMENT AGENCIES

CANADIAN FORESTRY SERVICE, Agriculture Canada, Ottawa K1A 1G5 (819, 997-1107)
Acts as focus for forestry policy and related matters in Canada. The CFS undertakes research and development initiatives in the forest sector; encourages the transfer of technology from research to the provinces and industry; provides information, advice and technical services to governments, industry and the general public; supports research by science subventions; and participates in a number of international programs and organizations.
Associate Deputy Minister: JEAN CLAUDE MERCIER (Ext. 9192)
Assistant Deputy Ministers: DR. J.S. MAINI, Forestry Policy (Ext. 9195); TOM LEE, Forestry Opeations (Ext. 9290)
Director General, Policy, Planning, and Economics Directorate: PAUL HUNT (Ext. 9176)
Director, Planning: TIM BEZANSON (Ext. 9171)
Director, International Forestry Relations: G.A. STENEKER (Ext. 9180)
Director General, Forest Science Directorate: CARL WINGET (Ext. 9101)
Director, Research Coordination and Assessment: DR. LES CARLSON (Ext. 9117)
Director, Scientific Information and Survey: Vacant (Ext. 1107)
Director, Science Policy and Planning: DR. GRAHAM PAGE (Ext. 9327)
Chief, Scientific and Technical Publications Division: J. TOMLINSON (Ext. 9105)
Director General, Forestry Development Directorate: A. HUGHES (Ext. 9240)
Director (Acting), Forestry Development: JOHN FORSTER (Ext. 9242)
Director, Labour Market Development: JACK SMITH (Ext. 9256))
Director General, Industry, Trade, and Technology Directorate: W. CALOW (Ext. 9140)
Director, Industry: FRED JOHNSON (Ext. 9162)
Manager, Pulp and Paper: RICHARD GLANDON (Ext. 9161)
Director, Communications Division: N. HESELTINE (Ext. 9265)
Director, Economics Division: DOUG KETCHESON (Ext. 9151)
Manager, Personnel Unit: G. SAMSON-VERRAULT (Ext. 9280)
Director, Finance and Administration Directorate: D. BICKERTON (Ext. 9230)
Director, Finance: G. SEQUIN (Ext. 9210)
Director, Material Management and Administration: CLAUDE MENARD (Ext. 9200)
Director, Informatics: M. FARRINGTON (Ext. 9232)
Manager, Program Audits: G. MAIR (Ext. 9233)
Department Assistant: PAULINE MYRE, Office of the Minister of State Forestry and Mines, Killeany Bldg., 160 O'Connor St., Ottawa, Ontario K1A OE4

Regional Establishments
Director General: DR. R. DOBBS, Pacific Forstry Centre, Canadian Forestry Service, 506 West Burnside Rd., Victoria, British Columbia V8Z 1M5 (604, 388-0600)
Director General: A.D. KILL, Northern Forestry Centre, Canadian Forestry Service, 5320-122nd St., Edmonton, Alberta T6H 3S5 (403, 435-7210)
Director General: R. HAIG, Great Lakes Forestry Centre, Canadian Forestry Service, P.O. Box 490, 1210 Queen St., East, Saulte Ste. Marie, Ontario P6A 5M7 (705, 949-9461)
Director General: DR. F. POLLETT, Petawawa National Forestry Institute, Canadian Forestry Service, Chalk River, Ontario K0J IJ0 (613, 589-2880)
Director General: M. YVAN HARDY, Centre Forestier Des Laurentides, Service Canadian des Forets, 1055 rue du P.E.P.S., C.P. 3800, Ste-Foy, Quebec GIV 4C7 (408, 648-4991)
Director General: H. OLDHAM, Maritimes Forestry Centre, Canadian Forestry Service, P.O. Box 4000, MacKay Dr., Fredericton, New Brunswick E3B 5P7 (506, 452-3500)
Director General: J. MUNRO, Newfoundland Forestry Centre, Canadian Forestry Service, Building 304, Pleasantville, P.O. Box 6028, St. John's Newfoundland A1C 5X8 (709, 772-6019)

CONSERVATION AND PROTECTION, Place Vincent Massey, Hull, P.Q. (Mailing address: Ottawa, Ontario K1A OH3
Responsible for operational and research activities pertaining to Inland Waters Directorate, Canadian Wildlife Service, and Lands and Environmental Protection Directorate. In addition to four headquarters directorates there are regional establishments covering inland waters, wildlife, lands and environmental protection.
Assistant Deputy Minister: LORETTE GOULET (819, 997-1575)
Special Advisor to the ADM: GILLES LAMOUREUX (953-2969)
Director, Policy Branch: JIM MAXWELL (997-3157)

Lands
Responsible for investigating national aspects of land use in terms of management, research, planning, and environmental concerns.
Director (Acting): J. THIE (819, 997-1246)
Director, Land Resources & Data Systems Branch: J. THIE (997-1090)
Director, Land Use Policy and Research Branch: L.C. MUNN (997-1303)
Office of Program Planning and Evaluation: Vacant

Inland Waters
Responsible for planning and managing national and international water programs. Conducts research and gathers data related to inland waters and provides for the planning and administration of the Canada Water Act.
Director General: D.A. DAVIS (997-2019)
Director, Management Services: A.M. TIPPINS (997-2540)
Director, Research Coordination and Program Evaluation: J.E. SLATER (953-1523)
Director, Water Planning and Management Branch: R.L. PENTLAND (997-2071)
Director, Water Quality Branch: V. NIEMELA (997-1920)
Director, Water Resources Branch: D.R. KIMMETT (997-1508)
Director, National Hydrology Research Institute: T.M. DICK (306, 975-5718)

Canadian Wildlife Service
Administers Migratory Birds Convention Act, Canada Wildlife Act, Convention on International Trade in Endangered Species of Wild Fauna and Flora, and National Registry of Pesticides Residues in Wildlife Tissues. Carries out research throughout Canada on migratory birds, endangered species and other wildlife of national and international importance. Organized: 1947.
Director General: H.A. CLARKE (819, 997-1301)

Director, Management and Administration Branch: D.K. POLLOCK (997-1245)

Director, Migratory Birds Branch: DR. J.H. PATTERSON (997-2957)

Director, Wildlife Conservation and Environmental Quality Branch: J.A. KEITH (997-1092)

Senior Research Scientist, Migratory Birds Branch: DR. F.G. COOCH (953-1417)

Senior Scientist, Migratory Birds Branch: H. BOYD (953-1422)

Management and Administration Branch:

     Administrator, Convention on International Trade in Endangered Species: J.B. HEPPES (997-1840)

     Head, Scientific and Technical Publications: PATRICIA LOGAN (953-1413)

Migratory Birds Branch:

     Chief, Research and Co-ordination Division: Vacant

     Co-ordinator, Habitat: D.I. GILLESPIE (953-1421)

     Chief, Populations and Surveys Division: J.L. WENDT (953-1425)

     Chief, Regulations and Enforcement Division: J.A. STONER (953-1424)

     Co-ordinator, Endangered Species: T.C. DAUPHINE (953-1429)

     Head, Wildlife Toxicology Section: DR. D.B. PEAKALL (997-2780)

Regional Directors, Canadian Wildlife Service

Atlantic Region, DR. G.H. FINNEY, Canadian Wildlife Service, Environment Canada, P.O. Box 1590, Sackville, New Brunswick E0A 3C0 (506, 536-3025)

Ontario Region, S.G. CURTIS, Canadian Wildlife Service, Environment Canada, 1725 Woodward Dr., Ottawa, Ontario K1A 0E7 (613, 998-4693)

Pacific and Yukon Region, A.M. MARTELL, Canada Wildlife Service, Environment Canada, 5421 Robertson Rd., Delta, British Columbia V4K 3Y3 (604, 946-8546)

Quebec Region, J. CINQ-MARS, Canadian Wildlife Service, Environment Canada, 1141 Route de l'Eglise, P.O. Box 10100, Quebec G1V 4H5 (418, 694-3914)

Western and Northern Region, G. KERR, Canadian Wildlife Service, Environment Canada, 1000, 9942-108 St., Edmonton, Alberta T5K 2J5 (405, 425-2536)

Environmental Protection

Purpose is to formulate and take action to meet threats to environmental quality arising through adverse impacts of human activities. Priority responsibilities include toxic chemicals and acid rain and the on-going management of concerns such as hazardous wastes, chemicals in commerce, environmental impact assessment and environmental emergencies.

Director-Geneal: PETER HIGGINS (819, 997-1298)

Directors:

     Management and Emergencies Branch: GEORGE CORNWALL (997-2375)

     Industrial Programs Branch: D.G. KELLEY (994-2493)

     Technology Development and Technical Services Branch: F.G. HURTUBISE (994-2103)

     Commercial Chemicals Branch: GLENN ALLARD (997-1499)

     Environmental Analysis Branch: ALAIN JOLICOEUR (Acting) (953-2972)

Regional Directors

Atlantic: E. NORRENA (902, 426-3593)

Quebec: G. MEZZETTA (514, 283-7377)

Ontario: K. SHIKAZE (416, 973-5840)

Western and Northern: R.K. LANE (403, 468-8041)

Pacific and Yukon: B.A. HESKIN (604, 666-0064)

ENVIRONMENT CANADA, Ottawa, Ontario K1A 1G2

Minister: Hon. TOM McMILLAN (819, 997-1441)

Deputy Minister: GENEVIEVE SAINTE-MARIE (997-4203)

Parks

To acquire and develop representative areas of the country, for use by the public consistent with the preservation of such areas in their natural state; to preserve, restore and operate sites, and structures of importance to Canadian history including historic canals.

Assistant Deputy Minister: JIM D. COLLISON (819, 997-9525)

Director-General: GEORGE A. YEATES (994-1790)

Program Management Directorate: JANE ROSZELL, Director, Program Planning Analysis Branch (994-5792)

Director, National Parks Branch: PAT A. THOMSON (994-2657)

Director, National Historic Parks and Sites Branch: R.Y. SIMOND (Acting) (994-1808)

Director, Information Services: JIM SHEARON (997-3736)

Regional Directors

Western: STEVE KUN, 220 Fourth Ave., South East, Calgary, Alberta T2P 3H8 (403, 292-4444)

Prairie: D. HARPER, 457 Main St., Winnipeg, Manitoba R3B 1B4 (204, 949-2120)

Ontario: J.C. CHRISTAKOS, 111 Water St., East, Cornwall, Ontario K6H 6S3 (613, 933-7951)

Quebec: GILLES DESAULNIERS, 3 Rue Buade, C.P. 6060, Haute-Ville, Quebec G1R 4H5 (418, 648-4042)

Atlantic: W.C. TURNBULL, Historic Properties, Upper Water St., Halifax, Nova Scotia B3J 1S9 (902, 426-3405)

FISHERIES AND OCEANS, Ottawa, Ont. K1A 0E6

The Department of Fisheries and Oceans is responsible for fisheries development and management on both coasts, fisheries research, oceanography, hydrography, and the administration of small craft harbours.

Minister: JOHN FRASER (613, 992-3474)

General Inquiries (993-0600)

Deputy Minister, Fisheries and Oceans: DR. A.W. MAY (993-2200)

Associate Deputy Minister: K. STEIN (993-2400)

Assistant Deputy Minister, Atlantic Fisheries: L.S. PARSONS (993-0850)

Assistant Deputy Minister, Pacific and Freshwater Fisheries: A. LEFEBVRE-ANGLIN (990-0359)

Assistant Deputy Minister, Marketing and International Fisheries: DR. V. RABINOVITCH (993-0678)

Assistant Deputy Minister, Ocean Science and Surveys: Vacant (993-2741)

Director-General, Communications Directorate: DIXI LAMBERT (993-0991)

Director-General, Atlantic Operations: W.A. ROWAT (990-0140)

Director-General, Fisheries Research Directorate: DR. B.S. MUIR (990-0271)

Director-General, Operations Directorate (Pacific and Freshwater Fisheries): DR. J.C. DAVIS (990-0004)

Director-General, International Directorate: B. APPLEBAUM (993-1840)

Director-General, Economic and Commercial Analysis Directorate: R.W. CROWLEY (993-1914)

Director-General, Marketing: JOSHUA JOHN (993-2649)

Director, Fish Habitat Management Branch: DR. J.C. MacLEOD (990-0200)

Director, Resource Allocation Branch-Atlantic: MARY WALSH (990-0119)

Director General, Small Craft Harbours Branch: DR. K.T. BRODERSEN (993-3012)

Chairman, Fisheries Prices Support Board: Vacant

Chairman, Freshwater Fish Marketing Corporation: D.D. TANSLEY (993-2164)

Chairman, Canadian Saltfish Corporation: D.D. TANSLEY (993-2164)

Regions

Newfoundland, P.O. Box 5667, St. John's, Nfld. A1C 5X1 (709, 737-4417 or 737-4420)
Regional Director General: ERIC DUNNE

Scotia-Fundy, P.O. Box 550, Halifax, N.S. B3J 2S7 (902, 426-2581)
Director General: P. SUTHERLAND

Gulf, Memramcook Institute, P.O. Box 5030, St. Joseph, New Brunswick E1C 9B6 (506, 758-9044)
Director General: JEAN HACHE

Ontario, 3050 Harvester Rd., Burlington, Ontario L7N 3J1 (416, 637-4673)
Director General: W. FALKNER

Western, 501 University Crescent, Winnipeg, Manitoba R3T 2N6 (204, 949-5000)
Director General: DR. G. H. LAWLER

Pacific, 1090 West Pender St., Vancouver, B.C. V6E 2P1 (604, 666-6097)
Director-General, Fisheries Management: P.S. CHAMUT

Sea Lamprey Control Center, Huron St., Ship Canal P.O., Sault Ste. Marie, Ontario P6A 1P0
Director: DR. J. J. TIBBLES (705, 949-1102)

Fisheries Research Establishments, Northwest Atlantic Fisheries Centre, St. John's, Newfoundland A1C 5X1
  Director, Research and Resource Services: M.C. MERCER (709, 737-2027)
Marine Ecology Laboratory, P.O. Box 1006, Dartmouth, N.S. B2Y 4A2
  Director: DR. K.H. MANN (902, 426-3696)
Biological Station, St. Andrews, N.B. E0G 2X0
  Director: DR. R.H. COOK (506, 529-8854)
Arctic Biological Station, 555 Boulevard St., Pierre, Ste. Anne de Bellevue, Que. H9X 3R4
  Director: DR. A.W. MANSFIELD (514, 457-3660)
Freshwater Institute, 501 University Crescent, Winnipeg, Man. R3T 2N6
  Director-General: DR. G.H. LAWLER (204, 949-5000)
West Vancouver Laboratory, 4160 Marine Drive, Vancouver, B.C. V7V 1N6
  Head, Enrichment Research: DR. J.G. STOCKNER (604, 926-2614)
Pacific Biological Station, Dept. of Fisheries and Oceans, Nanaimo, B.C. V9R 5K6
  Director: Resource Services Branch: DR. R.J. BEAMISH (604, 758-5202)
Great Lakes Fisheries Research Branch, Canada Centre for Inland

Waters, 867 Lakeshore Rd., P.O. Box 5050, Burlington, Ont. L7R 4A6
Director: DR. R.L. THOMAS (416, 637-4568)

Ocean Science and Surveys, Ottawa, Ontario
Assistant Deputy Minister (Acting): DR. R.M. McMULLEN (613, 993-2741)
Director-General, Marine Sciences and Information Directorate: DR. N.J. CAMPBELL (613, 990-0298)
Dominion Hydrographer: S B. MacPHEE (613, 995-4413)
Director and Editor, Scientific Information and Publications: DR. J. WATSON (613, 990-0229)

Research Establishments
Atlantic Region, Director General: DR. A.R. LONGHURST, Bedford Institute of Oceanography, P.O. Box 1006, Dartmouth, Nova Scotia B2Y 4A2 (902, 426-3492)
Bayfield Laboratory for Marine Science and Surveys, 867 Lakeshore Rd., P.O. Box 5050, Burlington, Ontario L7R 4A6
  Director-General, Central Region: A. WALTON (416, 637-4339)
Pacific Region, Institute of Ocean Sciences, P.O. Box 6000, Sidney, British Columbia V8L 4B2
  Director General: DR. C.R. MANN (604, 656-8215)
Quebec Region, Ocean Science & Surveys, Gare Maritime Champlain, P.O. Box 15, 500, Quebec G1K 7Y7
  Director: DR. J. PIUZE (418, 648-7781)

CITIZENS' GROUPS

CANADIAN ARCTIC RESOURCES COMMITTEE, 111 Sparks St., 4th Fl., Ottawa, Ontario K1P 5B5 (613, 236-7379)
To ensure that important social, environmental, and economic ramifications of northern development are studied and analyzed before major decisions relating to northern Canada are made; to exchange information and viewpoints among the public, government, and industry; to develop better perspective on options available; and to inform the public. Founded: 1971.
Co-Chaired: ROBBIE KEITH; NANCY JAMIESON
Executive Director: JOHN MERRITT
Publications: *Northern Perspectives; Northern Decisions;* List of books on request.
Editors: ALAN SAUNDERS; ANN RAY

CANADIAN ENVIRONMENTAL LAW ASSOCIATION, 243 Queen St., West, 4th Fl., Toronto, Ontario M5V 1Z4 (416, 977-2410)
Nonprofit, independent, public interest legal group founded in 1971 to use current environmental laws to protect the environment and to promote better environmental legislation throughout Canada.
Counsels: MICHELLE SWENARCHUK; STEVEN SHRYBMAN; TOBY VIGOD
Publication: Newsletter, *The Intervenor*
Editor: BONNIE GIBSON WEISZ

CANADIAN FEDERATION OF HUMANE SOCIETIES, 30 Concourse Gate, Suite 102, Nepean, Ontario K2E 7V7 (613, 224-8072 (Annual general meeting: May-June.)
To prevent and suppress cruelty to, and suffering of animals and assist in the enforcement of all national, provincial, territorial or municipal laws respecting cruelty to, and suffering of animals. Incorporated August, 1957, 45 member humane societies from across Canada.

President: NANCY ERICKSON, Box 22, Site 14, R.R. 13, Thunder Bay, Ontario P7B 5E4 (807, 983-2008)
Executive Director: JAMES H. BANDOW
Publications: *Caring for Animals; Animal Welfare in Focus*
Editors: J.H. BANDOW; STEPHANIE BROWN

CANADIAN FORESTRY ASSOCIATION, 185 Somerset St., West, Suite 203, Ottawa, Ontario K2P 0J2 (613, 232-1815)
President: W.K. FULLERTON, Ottawa, Ontario
President-Elect: G.L. AINSCOUGH, Vancouver, British Columbia
Immediate Past-President: C.H. GEALE, Edmonton, Alberta
Vice-President: J.H. CAYFORD, Sault Ste. Marie, Ontario
Member-At-Large: DR. A. DICKSON, Fredericton, New Brunswick
Executive Director: A.D. HALL, Ottawa, Ontario
Publications: *What They Say About Forestry On The Hill; Proceedings of National Forest Congress 1986; Taxation and Private Land Forests and Woodlots in Canada*
Editor: A.D. HALL

CANADIAN INSTITUTE OF FORESTRY, 151 Slater St., Suite 1005, Ottawa, Ontario K1P 5H3 (613, 234-2242)
An independent, nonprofit association of professional foresters, forest scientists, and affiliates in Canada. Encourages wider understanding of problems in forestry, improves forestry practice, advances members in their knowledge of forestry, cultivates an esprit de corps within the profession, publishes The *Forestry Chronicle* in the interests of forestry. Membership: 2,350. Established: 1908.
President: CLAUDE GODBOUT, 992 Duchesneau, St. Foy, Quebec G1W 3W8
1st Vice-President: P.W. ACKHURST, 3950 Sunset Blvd., Vancouver, British Columbia V7R 3X9
Executive Director: J.H. CAYFORD, 151 Slater St., Suite 1005, Ottawa, Ontario K1P 5H3
Publication: *Forestry Chronicle*
Editor: I.C.M. PLACE, 3 Kitimat Crescent, Nepean, Ontario K2H 7G4
Production Manager: D.R. REDMOND, 643 Tillbury Ave., Ottawa, Ontario K2A 0Z9

CANADIAN NATIONAL SPORTSMEN'S SHOWS, 595 Bay St., Toronto, Ontario, Canada M5G 2C2 (416, 593-7333)
A national nonprofit corporation presenting 21 outdoor shows, and three magazines, including Outdoor Canada, relating to fishing, hiking, camping, boating, skiing and outdoor life exhibitions to the public from Vancouver to Halifax. Net proceeds are granted through the Canadian National Sportsmen's shows granting programs which are dedicated to support the enjoyment and preservation of Canada's outdoor heritage. Founded: 1948.
Chairman and Chief Executive Officer: NORMAN G. JAMES
Vice-Chairman and Chairman/Philanthropic: DR. WILLIAM J. WALSH

CANADIAN NATURE FEDERATION, 453 Sussex Dr., Ottawa, Ontario K1N 6Z4
Canada's national naturalists' organization promotes the understanding, appreciation and enjoyment of nature and the conservation of the environment so that the integrity of natural systems is maintained. Formed in 1971 from the Canadian Audubon Society. The CNF represents over 120 affiliated conservation groups and 20,000 individual members across the country.
President: DR. ROGER TAYLOR (1, 613, 238-6154)
Executive Director: PAUL GRISS (238-6154)
Coodinator of Conservation Programs: B. THERESA ANISKOWICZ, Ph.D.

Nature Canada Bookshop Manager: MAGGIE NIEMI (238-6154)
Publications: *Nature Canada Magazine;* Almanac and Nature Alert Newsletters
Managing Editor: BARBARA STEVENSON (238-6154)
Marketing/Membership Coordinator: RICHARD McCARRON (238-6154)

CANADIAN PARKS AND WILDERNESS SOCIETY, 69 Sherbourne St., Suite 313, Toronto, Ontario M5A 3X7 (416, 366-3494)
An educational, nonprofit, national citizens dedicated to the wise use of park resources, the establishment and proper management of national and provincial parks, and the promotion of park values within Canadian park systems. Membership: 1,500. Founded: 1963.
President: ROBERT PEART, 36 Government St., Victoria, British Columbia, V8V 2K3 (604, 384-9081)
Executive Director: ANGUS C. SCOTT (416, 366-3494)
Executive Assistant: MAGGIE PAWSON
Publication: *Park News*
Editor: DR. COLIN WOOD, University of Victoria, British Columbia (604, 721-7335)

CANADIAN SOCIETY OF ENVIRONMENTAL BIOLOGISTS, P.O. Box 962, Station F, Toronto, Ontario, Canada M4Y 2N9
A Canada-wide society of environmental biologists whose primary goals are: 1) the conservation of the natural resources of Canada, and the prudent management of these resources so as to minimize adverse environmental effects, 2) the interchange of ideas among environmental biologists, and 3) maintaining high professional standards in education, research and management related to natural resources and the environment. Founded: 1959.
President: JOHN LILLEY, 1003 Garland Terr., Sherwood Park, Alberta T8A 2R5 (403, 427-5792)
1st Vice-President: LEWIS COCKS, 66 Eaglemount Crescent, Winnipeg, Manitoba R3P 1X3 (H:204, 489-6965/W:895-6658)
2nd Vice-President: PAT RYAN, Department of Fisheries and Oceans, P.O. Box 5667, St. John's, Newfoundland A1C 5X1
Secretary-Treasurer: FRANK MAHER, 88 Westwood Ln., Richmond Hill, Ontario L4C 6Y2 (H:416, 886-1581/W:886-1581)
Managing Editor: CHRISTINE BRODIE, 8722 96 Ave., Apt. E, Edmonton, Alberta T6C 2B2 (H:403, 466-0130/W:427-2375)
Past President: GARY ASH, R.L. & L. Environmental Services Ltd., 17312 - 106 Ave., Edmonton, Alberta T5S 1H9

CANADIAN WILDLIFE FEDERATION, 1673 Carling Ave., Ottawa, Ontario K2A 3Z1 (613, 725-2191)
To foster understanding of natural processes so that people may live in harmony with the land and its resources for the long term benefit and enrichment of society; to maintain a substantial program of information and education based on ecological principles; to conduct or sponsor research and scientific investigation. Membership and supporters: 528,000. Founded: 1961.
President: DR. LOUIS LEMIEUX, Ottawa, Ontario
Vice-Presidents: LORNE YEO, Montague, Prince Edward Island; JIM HOOK, Kenora, Ontario RON GLADISH, Sherwood Park, Alberta
Executive Vice-President: KENNETH BRYNAERT
Treasurer: CARL SHIER, 828 Beresford Ave., Winnipeg, Manitoba R3L IK2 (204, 475-2822)
Secretary: BRIAN POPE, 40 Tay St., Whitehorse, Yukon Y1A 4M6 (W:403, 667-5365/H:668-3304)

Directors-At-Large

MONIKA BEHR, P.O. Box 132, Paradise, Nfld. A0A 2E0 (709, 576-4420

JOSEPH BRYANT, 447 Thessaly Cresent, Ottawa, Ontario KIH 5W7 (613, 731-4878)

PROF. PETER JACOBS, Universite de Montreal, Faculte de l'Amenagement, 5620 Avenue Darlington, Montreal, Quebec H3T 2TI (W:514, 343-7119/H:487-6947)

DR. YVES JEAN, C.P. 5030, St-Augustin, Quebec G3A 2A7 (W:418, 657-2262 Ext. 417/H:878-4047)

KEN LOUNSBURY, 465 Hixson St., Beamsville, Ontario L0R 1B0 (416, 563-7175)

THE HON. IRWIN McINTOSH, McIntosh Publishing Co. Ltd., Box 430, North Battleford, Saskatchewan S9A 2Y5 (W:306, 445-4401/H:445-4214)

DR. ROBERT MARTIN, 1474 Orchard Ave., Ottawa, Ontario K1H 7C7 (613, 731-3388)

DOUG OGSTON, P.O. Box 28, Lively, Ontario P0M 2E0 (705, 692-9614)

NESTOR ROMANIUK, 11921 St. Albert Trail, Edmonton, Alberta T5L 4G5 (403, 453-3270)

Directors

Alberta: JOHN GRAHAM, 6016-105 St., Edmonton, Alberta T6H 2N4 (403, 434-1198); DOUG RUMSEY, 41 Martin Close, Red Deer, Alberta T4n 5J8 (W:403, 342-8235/H:343-3126)

Manitoba: ROBERT BARTON, P.O. Box 387, Carberry, Manitoba R0K OH0; DON PORTER, 105 5th St., NW, Dauphin, Manitoba R7N 1J4 (204, 638-445)

New Brunswick: FRED WHEATON, 56 Drummond St., Moncton, New Brunswick E1A 2Z2 (W:506, 857-4231/H:382-3507); JAMES MARRINER, 190 Cameron St., Moncton, New Brunswick E1C 5Z2 (506, 857-2056/H: 386-7733)

NewFoundland and Labrador: RICHARD BOUZAN, 14 Fairhaven Pl., St. John's Newfoundland A1E 4S1 (709, 737-7263); MIKE BARRON, 80 The Blvd., Apt. 702, St. John's Newfoundland A1A 6V6

Nova Scotia: GERALD BLOM, 21 Litchfield Cres., Halifax, Nova Scotia B3P 2N4 (W:902, 422-7327/H:479-1096); E. ROBERT CROSS, 65 Havelock Cres., Dartmouth, Nova Scotia B2W 4T7 (902, 434-6998)

Ontario: CHARLES ALEXANDER, 3 Thunder Dr., Dryden, Ontario P8N 1V9 (807, 223-6336); JACK CRAIK, Box 1434, New Liskkeard, Ontario P0J 1P0 (705, 647-7143)

Prince Edward Island: PAUL A. GALLANT, P.O. Box 413, Souris, Prince Edward Island C0A 2B0 (902, 687-2382); LEO PETERS, P.O. Box 190, Winsloe, Prince Edward Island C0A 2H0 (902, 964-3431)

Quebec: LEO-PAUL QUINTAL, 12780 Des Forges, Trois, Rivieres, Quebec G9H 5E1 (W:819, 277-4391/H:376-0995); FERNAND GOUGEON, 67 Hebert St., Gatineau, Quebec J8P 6B6 (W:613, 998-3082/H:819, 643-2540)

Saskatchewan: DERREK STANLEY, R.R. No. 1, Tisdale, Saskatchewan S0E 1T0 (306, 873-5472); RUSS HANSON, 8925-19th Ave., North Battleford, Saskatchewan S9A 2V8 (306, 445-3374)

British Columbia: JOHN CARTER, R.R. No. 2, Shuswap Rd., Kamloops, British Columbia V2C 2J3 (W:604, 372-4471/H:573-3000); STEWART REEDER, 204 1560 Hillside Ave., Victoria, British Columbia V8T 5B8 (604, 592-6610)

Yukon Territory: DOUG PHILLIPS, 9 Klondike Rd., Whitehorse, Yukon Territory Y1A 3L8 (W:403, 667-5716/H:667-6358); LAWRENCE LEIGH, Yukon Fish and Game Association, 10 Redwood St., Whitehorse, Yukon Y1A 4B3 (W:403, 667-6401/H:633-4161)

Northwest Territories: JACK VAN CAMP, Research Associate Arctic

Institute of North America, The University of Calgary, 2500 University Dr., NW, Calgary, Alberta T2N 1N4 (403, 220-7515); GREG ROBERTSON, P.O. Box 1266, Yellowknife, Northwest Territories X1A 2N9 (403, 873-4818)

Publications: *Wildlife Update; International Wildlife; Ranger Rick Magazine; Wildlife Management; Role of Wildlife; Your Big Backyard; Biosphere; Key to Conservation; Together We Can Help Wildlife; Wildlife Needs You: Join Hands In Conservation*

DUCKS UNLIMITED, Canada, 1190 Waverley St., Winnipeg, Manitoba, R3T 2E2 (204, 477-1760)

An international, private, nonprofit conservation organization dedicated to the perpetuation and increase of North America's waterfowl resources through restoration, preservation and creation of prime breeding habitat in Canada. Development of this habitat on a multi-use concept benefits wildlife and the general environment and provides water for agriculture, domestic and recreational use. Founded 1938.

Chairman of the Board: ARTHUR L. IRVING, Irving Oil Limited, Golden Ball Bldg., P.O. Box 1421, Saint John, New Brunswick E2L 4K1 (506, 632-2000)

President of Executive Committee: DR. DUNCAN SINCLAIR, 155 Talbot St., West, Aylmer, Ontario, N5H 1J9 (519, 773-9234)

Vice-President: G.G. FRASER, Freedom Edmonton Ford, 7505-75th St., Edmonton, Alberta T6C 4H8 (403, 465-9411)

Secretary: ROLAND E. RIVALIN, Tupper and Adams, 4th Fl., 200 Portage Ave., Winnipeg, Manitoba R3C 3X2 (204, 942-0161)

Treasurer: H. (Graham) LeBOURVEAU, Clarkson and Gordon, 1300-707 7th Ave., SW, Calgary, Alberta T2P 3H6 (403, 290-4100)

Executive Vice-President: D.S. MORRISON

Chief Biologist: DR. T.G. NERAASEN

Chief Engineer: R.W. COLEY

Public Relations Manager: J.D. GILES

Contributor Services Manager: DAVID S. GRAY

Controller: L.J. WARREN

Corporate Counsel: G.R. KARASEVICH

Manager-Biological Services Group: DR. PATRICK CALDWELL

Pacific Regional Manager: RON W. COLEY

Central Regional Manager: B. FORBES, P.O. Box 4465, 1606-4th Ave., Regina, Saskatchewan S4P 3W7 (306, 569-0424)

Eastern Regional Manager: J. WAUGH, P.O. Box 430, 9 Havelock St., Amherst, Nova Scotia B4H 4A1 (902, 667-8726)

(Note: See U.S. DUCKS UNLIMITED)

HUNTSMAN MARINE SCIENCE CENTRE, THE, Brandy Cove, St. Andrews, New Brunswick E0G 2X0 (506, 529-8895)

A nonprofit educational and research centre founded in 1969, composed of 14 universities as well as private and government agencies. It provides laboratory, field and shipboard facilities for students and investigators in the marine and coastal sciences. In addition the laboratory operates a public aquarium and has accommodation for visiting scientists and students.

Chairman of the Board: DR. W.C. LEGGETT, Dean of Science, McGill University, 853 Sherbrooke St., W., Montreal, Quebec H3A 2T6

Director: DR. G. ROBIN SOUTH

INTERNATIONAL COUNCIL FOR BIRD PRESERVATION,
Canadian National Section

Protection of birds and their habitats in Canada, in their winter quarters in North and South America and off Canada's coasts, are among major concerns.

Chairman: RICHARD YANK, c/o Canadian Nature Federation, 453 Sussex Dr., Ottawa, Ontario, KIN 6Z4

NATURE CONSERVANCY OF CANADA, THE, 794A Broadview Ave., Toronto, Ontario M4K 2P7 (416, 469-1701)
A national, nonprofit organization, dedicated to the acquisition and preservation of ecologically significant natural land areas throughout Canada, in cooperation with governments, conservation groups, and individuals. Raises and contributes funds to support the conservation of natural area land. Founded: 1963.
Chairman: ROBIN W.W. FRASER
Executive Director: GERRY T. GLAZIER
Publications: *Annual Report;* Spring and Fall Newsletters

POLLUTION PROBE FOUNDATION, 12 Madison Ave., Toronto, Ontario M5R 2S1 (416, 926-1907)
To bring serious environmental problems to the attention of both those responsible and the public at large; to offer constructive suggestions to business and government about their role in maintaining and enhancing environmental quality; and to offer instructive suggestions which will help the individual citizen to live in harmony with his environment. Membership: 1,500. Established: 1969.
Executive Director: COLIN F.W. ISAACS
Pollution Probe Research Coordinator: PAMELA MILLAR (926-9876)
Ecology House Coordinator: GERALD COFFEY (967-0577)
Financial Coordinator: JO-ANN OPPERMAN (926-1043)
Chairman, Pollution Probe Foundation: SHERRY BRYDSON
Publication: *Probe Post: Canada's Environmental Magazine*
Editor: GAIL RICHARDSON (926-1647)

CANADIAN PROVINCIAL, TERRITORIAL AGENCIES AND CITIZENS' GROUPS

ALBERTA

GOVERNMENT AGENCIES

DEPARTMENT OF FORESTRY, LANDS, AND WILDLIFE, Main
Fl., North Tower, Petroleum Plaza, 9945-108 St.,
Edmonton, Alberta T5K 2G6
The overall responsibilities of the division are to manage the fish
and wildlife resources of the Province of Alberta for the benefit and
enjoyment of the people, and to promote legislation and programs
in support of this goal.
Minister, Forestry, Lands, and Wildlife: HON. LeROY FJORDBOT-
TEN (403, 427-3674)
Deputy Minister: F.W. McDOUGALL (427-3552)

Fish and Wildlife Division
Assistant Deputy Minister: L.J. COOKE (427-6749)
Executive Coordinator, Policy and Coordination: ERNIE J. PSIKLA
(427-6999)
Director, Operations: JIM R. NICHOLS (427-6735)
Director, Regulations Development: Vacant (427-6735)
Director, Enforcement Services: ROBERT ADAMS (427-6735)
Director, Program Support: TOM W. SMITH (427-6727)
Manager, Resource Economics and Assessment: MIKE MELNYK
(427-4771)
Manager, Administrative Services: M. MOHAN (427-0326)
Manager, License and Budget: GERALD JOY (427-6763)
Manager, Public Information and Extension: KEN CRUTCHFIELD
(427-6756)
Manager, Public Information: BOB STEVENSON (427-6767)
Director, Wildlife Management: ROBERT R. ANDREWS (427-6733)
Manager, Inventory, Fur, and Nongame Management: WILLIAM K.
HALL (427-6752)
Manager, Game Management: BRENT J. MARKHAM (427-9503)
Manager, Brooks Wildlife Centre: JIM ARCHER (362-4122)
Leader, Wildlife Resource Inventory Unit: HARRY STELFOX (427-
4192)
Leader, Fur Management Unit: ARLEN W. TODD (427-6750)
Leader, Nongame and Habitat Management: DOUG CULBERT
(427-4192)
Leader, Deer and Antelope Management Unit: WILLIAM M. GLAS-
GOW (427-4192)
Leader, Moose Management and Game Farming Unit: GERRY
LYNCH (427-6750)
Leader, Bird Game Management Unit: Vacant (427-6750)
Leader, Carnivore, Elk, and Problem Wildlife Management: JOHN
GUNSON (427-6750)
Director, Fisheries: TOM MILL (427-6730)
Manager, Sportfishing Management: ERNIE STENTON (427-6730)
Manager, Commercial Fisheries Management: KEN ZELT (427-
6730)
Manager, Fish Culture: TERRY McFADDEN (427-6730)
Director, Habitat Services: KEN AMBROCK (427-9505)
Manager, Habitat Assessment: BRUCE STUBBS (427-6734)

Regional Directors
Southern Region: DUANE RADFORD (381-5266)
Central Region: JIM B. STRUTHERS (340-5142)
Eastern Slopes Region: FRANK CARDINAL (845-8230)
Peace River Region: GERRY THOMPSON (624-6405)
Northeast Region: RAY MAKOWECKI (645-6313)

CITIZENS' GROUPS

ALBERTA FISH AND GAME ASSOCIATION, THE, 6924-104
St., Edmonton, Alberta T6H 2L7 (403, 437-2342)
To promote through education, lobbying, and programs, the
conservation and utilization of fish and wildlife and to protect and
enhance the habitat they depend upon. Established: 1908. Incorpo-
rated: 1946. Membership: 20,000.
President: JACK GRAHAM, 6016-105 St., Edmonton, Alberta T6H
2N4 (434-1198)
Senior Vice-President: DOUG RUMSEY, 41 Martin Close, Red Deer,
Alberta T4N 5J8 (343-3126/342-8235)
Vice-President: NIELS DAMGAARD, 127 MacEwan Glen Way, NW,
Calgary, Alberta T3K 2G6 (274-3422/248-0506)
Executive Director: LYLE FULLERTON, 6924-104th St., Edmonton,
Alberta T6H 2L7 (403, 437-2342)
Past President: NESTOR ROMANIUK, 11921 St. Albert Trail,
Edmonton, Alberta T5L 4G5 (453-3270)

Directors
Zone 1: BUB KLUMPH (Acting), Box 624, Magrath, Alberta T0K IJ0
(758-6381)
Zone 2: LOUISE NEILSEN, Box 399, High River, Alberta T0L IB0
(395-3743)
Zone 3: IKE JOHANNSON, Box 9, Site 15, R.R. 1, Innisfail, Alberta
T0M 1A0 (728-3831)
Zone 4: RICHARD THORNE, Box 2800, Edson, Alberta T0E 0P0
(723-5363)
Zone 5: CHARLOTTE DRAKE, Box 216, Grande Centre, Alberta
T0A 1T0 (594-4500/594-4401)
Zone 6: DARRYL SMITH, Box 1650, Valleyview, Alberta T0H 3N0
(524-4454/524-3864)
Publication: *Western Canada Outdoors*
Editor: STAN NOWAKOWSKI

ALBERTA TRAPPERS ASSOCIATION, Bag 7000, Edson AB,
T0E 0P0
Purpose is to help the trapper in all his problems. Cooperates with
all other trappers associations and government agencies for a
sensible conservation program. Humane trapping courses. Membership: 1,700. Founded: 1974.
President: FRED D. BEHRENS (403, 723-2209)
1st Vice-President: TED GANSKE, Box 1378, Bonnyville AB, T0A
0L0
2nd Vice-President: JIM ROBISON, Box 989, Whitecourt AB, T0E
2L0
Treasurer: ELAINE BOYKO, Box 121, Sexsmith AB, T0H 3C0
Secretary: SHANNON BEHRENS, Bag 7000, Edson AB, T0E 0P0
Publication: *The Alberta Trapper*
Editor: INEZ CURTIS, R.R. 2, Bluffton AB, T0C 0M0

ALBERTA WILDERNESS ASSOCIATION, Box 6398, Station D,
Calgary, Alberta T2P 2E1 (403,283-2025)
A nonprofit, charitable organization, founded in 1968 in an

attempt to retain the opportunity in Alberta for high quality non-motorized outdoor experience and to lobby for the retention of wilderness lands in the province.

President: VIVIAN PHARIS
Vice-President: BRIAN HOREJSI
Executive Director: DIANNE PACHAL
Treasurer: JANE KENNEDY
Publications: *Wilderness Alberta Newsletter;* List of other publications upon request.
Editor: JANE KENNEDY

DUCKS UNLIMITED, Canada, 302, 10335-172 St., Edmonton, Alberta T5S 1K9 (403, 489-2002)
Provincial Manager: GORDON EDWARDS
Provincial Biologist: GARY STEWART
Provincial Engineer: JIM WOHL

FEDERATION OF ALBERTA NATURALISTS, Box 1472, Edmonton, Alberta T5J 2N5 (403, 453-8629)
To increase Albertans' knowledge of natural history; foster creation of new natural history groups; promote natural areas; and provide a forum for discussion and means of taking action on environmental problems of concern to naturalists. Membership: 8 natural history societies. Founded: 1970.
President: ROBERT GARDNER
Treasurer: MARGOT HERVIEUX, 11445 - 125 St., Edmonton, Alberta T5M 0N1
Publication: *Alberta Naturalist*
Editor: DEREK JOHNSON, 7109 - 106 St., Edmonton, Alberta T6E 4V5

BRITISH COLUMBIA

GOVERNMENT AGENCIES

MINISTRY OF ENVIRONMENT, Parliament Bldgs., Victoria V8V 1X5 (604, 387-5429)
Is responsible for the preservation of a quality environment for all living resources, including man. Its mandate involves several management activities, many of which are interrelated, as well as cooperation with other provincial and federal agencies. The ministry, under its legislation, is responsible for the management of water resources (quality and quantity), air quality, freshwater sport fisheries, and wildlife. It also regulates waste disposal and pesticide use.
Associate Deputy Minister R. DALON (387-5429)
Assistant Deputy Minister: E.D. ANTHONY (387-9887)
Waste Management Branch Director: R.H. FERGUSON (387-9993)
Recreational Fisheries Branch Director: DR. D. NARVER (387-9507)
Wildlife Branch Director: J. WALKER (387-9731)
Water Management Branch Director: DR. D. KASIANCHUK (387-6989)
Pesticide Control Branch Director: DR. R.W. KOBYLNYK (387-9414)
Planning and Assessment Director: DR. J. O'RIORDAN (387-9669)
Conservation Officer Service: R.L. ALDRICH (387-9401)

MINISTRY OF TOURISM AND PROVINCIAL SECRETARY, 1117 Wharf St., Victoria V8V 2Z2
Minister: BILL REID, Rm. 323, Parliament Bldgs., Victoria, B.C. V8V 1X4 (604, 387-1201)
Deputy Minister: MELVIN H. SMITH, Q.C. (387-1727)

Director, Public Affairs: MIKE HUGHES (387-1428)
Assistant Deputy Minister, Development: JIM DOSWELL (387-6929)
Director, Community Development: RICK LEMON (387-0122)
Assistant Deputy Minister, Marketing: AD VAN HAAFTEN, 865 Hornby St., Vancouver, B.C. V6Z 2G3 (660-3230)
Director, Domestic Marketing: DON FOXGORD, 865 Hornby St., Vancouver, B.C. V6Z 2G3 (660-3754)
Director, United States Marketing: KARL CROSBY, 865 Hornby St., Vancouver, B.C. V6Z 2G3 (660-3754)
Manager, International Marketing: DONNA DORNIK, 865 Hornby St., Vancouver, B.C. V6Z 2G3 (660-3234)
Director, Marketing Services: DAVE HENDERSON, 865 Hornby St., Vancouver, B.C. V6Z 2G3 (660-2861/3231)
British Columbia Film Commissioner: DIANNE NEUFELD, 865 Hornby St., Vancouver, B.C. V6Z 2G3 (660-3235)
Executive Director, Management Services: EVELYN J. GREENE (387-1428)
Director, Financial Services: D. MARR HENDERSON (387-1428)
Director, Research: JIM LEE (387-1566/6780)
Director, Personnel: GARY LOAT (387-1428)

CITIZENS' GROUPS

BRITISH COLUMBIA WILDLIFE FEDERATION, 5659-176th St., Surrey, British Columbia V3S 4C5 (604, 576-8288)
The BCWF is a province-wide voluntary conservation organization representing British Columbians whose aims are: in cooperation with the general public, the media, government, industry, and special interest groups; to protect, enhance and promote the wise use of the environment for the benefit of present and future generations.
President: STU REEDER, 204-1560 Hillside Ave., Victoria, British Columbia V8T 5B8
Vice-Presidents: STEVE HEAD, 6085 Trent Dr., Prince George, British Columbia V2N 2G4; DICK PHILLIPS, 2070 Wesbrook Dr., Sidney, British Columbia V8L 4K1
Treasurer: DON STEBBING, 2107 East 37th Ave, Vancouver, British Columbia V5P 1G3
Past-President: JOHN CARTER, R.R. 2, Shuswap Rd., Kamloops, British Columbia V2C 2J3
Officer Manager: MRS. LORAYNE SWIFTS (576-8288)
Executive Director: CHARLIE CORNFIELD
Publication: *British Columbia Sportsman*
Editor: HENRY FREW

BRITISH COLUMBIA WATERFOWL SOCIETY, THE, 5191 Robertson Rd., Delta V4K 3N2 (604, 946-6980)
To further the conservation and management of waterfowl habitat in British Columbia. Operates the George C. Reifel Migratory Bird Sanctuary in Delta. Founded: 1961.
President: CRAIG RUNYAN
Vice-President: GEORGE H. REIFEL
Secretary: PEGGY McCUAIG
Treasurer: JAMES MORRISON
Staff Members: JOHN IRELAND; VARRI JOHNSON
Publication: *Marsh Notes;* Newsletter

CRESTON VALLEY WILDLIFE MANAGEMENT AUTHORITY, P.O. Box 640, Creston, British Columbia V0B 1G0 (604, 428-3260)
A unique joint provincial/federal/private agency, established 1967, to conserve, develop and manage remaining waterfowl habitat in a mountain valley. Broader purpose: demonstrate

cooperative wetland management in action. Operates a 17,000 acre wetland/upland complex, primarily as a waterfowl management area, with public recreation facilities (campground, trails, nature centre).

Chairman of the Management Authority: DENNIS MCDONALD (354-6347)

Area Manager: BRIAN G. STUSHNOFF (428-3260)

Publication: *Creston Valley Wildlife Management Area Annual Newsletter*

DUCKS UNLIMITED CANADA, Canada - British Columbia Operation, 954 A Laval Crescent, Kamloops; 954 A Laval Crescent, Kamloops V2C 5P5 (604, 374-8307, 8308)

An international, private, nonprofit conservation organization dedicated to the perpetuation and increase of North America's waterfowl resources through restoration, preservation and creation of prime breeding habitat in Canada. Development of this habitat on a multi-use concept benefits wildlife and the general environment and provides water for agricultural, domestic and recreational use. Founded: 1938.

Pacific Regional Manager: RON COLEY

Provincial Manager: T.K. SLATER

Provincial Biologist: ED HENNAN

Publications: *Ducks Unlimited; Conservator*

Editors: LEE D. SALBER, One Waterfowl Way at Gilmer Rd., Long Grove, IL 60047; SCOTT SMALLWOOD, 1190 Waverley St. Winnipeg, Manitoba R3T 2E2

FEDERATION OF BRITISH COLUMBIA NATURALISTS, 1200 Hornby St., Vancouver, British Columbia V6Z 2E2 (604, 687-3333)

To provide the naturalists of British Columbia with a unified voice in conservation matters, to encourage formation of natural history societies, to promote activities of interest to naturalists, and to endeavor to preserve our outdoors values. Organized: 1963.

President: JOSEPH LOTZKAR, 7195 Selkirk St., Vancouver V6P 6J4

Vice-President: DUANNE VAN DEN BERG, 12554 Grace St., Maple Ridge, V2X 5N2

Executive Secretary: ADELINE NICOL, 2590 Parker St., Vancouver V5K 2T3

Publication: *B.C. Naturalist*

Editor: JUDE GRASS

MANITOBA

GOVENMENT AGENCIES

DEPARTMENT OF BUSINESS DEVELOPMENT AND TOURISM, Travel Manitoba, Dept. 9245, 7-155 Carlton St., Winnipeg, Manitoba R3C 3H8

Coordinates visits to Manitoba by travel/outdoor editors; produces and distributes travel/outdoor literature and films.

Director of Promotions: GERRY TURENNE (204, 945-4131)

DEPARTMENT OF NATURAL RESOURCES, Legislative Bldg., Winnipeg R3C 0V8 (204, 945-3730)

The purpose of Manitoba Natural Resources is to encourage wise use of Manitoba's natural resources and preserve them for future generations.

Minister: HON. LEONARD HARAPIAK, 118 Legislative Bldg., Winnipeg R3C 0V8

Special Assistant: CHRISTINE BURTON (Ext. 4258)

Deputy Minister: DALE STEWART, 112 Legislative Bldg., Winnipeg R3C 0V8 (Ext. 3785)

Director of Lands Branch: R.W. WINSTONE, Box 2-1495, St. James St., Winnipeg R3H 0W9 (Ext. 6655)

Executive Director of Administrative Services Division: W.J. PODOLSKY, 500-191 Broadway Ave., Winnipeg R3C 4B2 (Ext. 4056)

Director, Surveys and Mapping Branch: D. CRANDALL, 1007 Century St., Winnipeg R3H 0W4 (Ext. 6613)

Regional Managers

Southeast Region: KEN HILL, Bldg. 3, 139 Tuxedo Blvd., Winnipeg R3N 0H6 (Ext. 7267)

Southwest Region: RAY ELKE, Box 10, 27-2nd Ave., SW, Dauphin, Manitoba R7N 3E5 (638-9111/Ext. 259)

Northwest Region: S.J. WILLIAMSON, Box 2550, The Pas R9A 1M4 (623-6411/Ext. 261)

Interlake Region: ED WONG, Box 50, Provincial Bldg., 20-1st St., Beausejour, Manitoba R0E 0C0 (268-1411/Ext. 285)

Western Region: RAY ELKE, Box 10, 27-2nd Ave., SW, Dauphin, Manitoba R7N 3E5 (638-9111/Ext. 259)

Whiteshell Regional Office: Rennie, Manitoba R0E 1R0 (369-5232)

Western Region: ED WONG, Box 50, Provincial Bldg., 20 First St., S., Beausejour, Manitoba R0E 0C0 (268-1411/Ext. 285)

Director, Fisheries Branch: W. HAYDEN, Box 20, 1495 St. James St., Winnipeg R3H 0W9 (Ext. 7814)

Director, Forestry Branch: DAVE RANNARD, 300-530 Kenaston Blvd., Winnipeg R3N 1Z4 (Ext. 7998)

Assistant Deputy Ministers: D. DOYLE, Box 50, 1495 St. James St., Winnipeg (Ext. 6826); R. GOULDEN, Assistant Deputy Minister (Acting), Box 47 (Ext. 6829)

Director, Wildlife Branch: ARTHUR HOOLE, 1495 St. James St., Box 24, Winnipeg R3H 0W9 (Ext. 7761)

Publications: *Resources News; Conservation Comment*

Editors: DONALD KEITH, GLEN SUGGETT, Manitoba Natural Resources, Public Information Services, Box 22, 1495 St. James St., Winnipeg, Manitoba R3H 0W9

CITIZENS' GROUPS

MANITOBA WILDLIFE FEDERATION, 1770 Notre Dame Ave., Winnipeg, Manitoba R3E 3K2 (204, 633-5967)

Promotes conservation, safety, and good sportsmanship. Manages the Habitat Trust fund which secures critical land to ensure habitat for wildlife. Membership: 147, affiliated associations with 17,400 members. Founded: 1944.

President: ROBERT BARTON

Vice-Presidents: DON ADAMS; JERRY MARYNIUK; RUDY USICK; LARRY MILIAN; GERRY WOOD; CONRAD McCLURE

Secretary: DARLENE MARSHALL

Treasurer: JOE McMULLAN

Publication: *Wildlife Crusader*

Managing Editor: DENIS CORNEAU

DUCKS UNLIMITED, Canada-Manitoba Operation, 5 - 1325 Markham Rd., Winnipeg R3T 4J6 (204, 269-6960)

Provincial Manager: R.A. WISHART

Provincial Biologist: D.A. SEXTON

MANITOBA NATURALISTS SOCIETY, 302-128 James Ave., Winnipeg R3B 0N8 (204, 943-9029)

Fosters an awareness and appreciation of the natural environment and an understanding of man's place therein; and lectures,

workshops, field trips on natural history topics. Membership: 2,500. Founded: 1920.
President: GEORGE HOLLAND (489-6539)
Secretary: JAN SCHULTZ (261-7865)
Publication: Bulletin
Editor: MARTY HELGERSON (475-2792)

WILDLIFE SOCIETY MANITOBA CHAPTER
President: KEN DE SMET, Box 206, Station L, Winnipeg, Manitoba R3H 0Z5, (204, 945-6301)
President-Elect: MARK MATTSON, Box 24, 1495 St. James St., Winnipeg, Manitoba (204, 945-6816)
Secretary-Treasurer: RICK WISHART, 11 Syracuse Cr., Winnipeg, Manitoba (204, 477-1760)

NEW BRUNSWICK

GOVERNMENT AGENCIES

DEPARTMENT OF NATURAL RESOURCES, P.O. Box 6000, Fredericton, New Brunswick E3B 5H1 (506, 453 plus local listing)
Minister: M. GREEN (Local: 2510)
Deputy Minister: B.J. WALKER, Fish and Wildlife (Local: 2501) Branch, P.O. Box 6000, Fredericton E3B 5H1 (453-2440)
Executive Director: B. MEADOWS
Director (Acting), Wildlife Management: JEFFREY R. PATCH
Director, Fish and Wildlife Enforcement: RICHARD MONROE
Director, Fish Management: M.A. REDMOND
Administrative Officer: D.L. LEGER

CITIZEN'S GROUPS

NEW BRUNSWICK WILDLIFE FEDERATION, 190 Cameron St., Moncton, New Brunswick E1C 5Z2 (506, 857-2056)
Promotes the wise use of renewable natural resources, with prime emphasis on education of the young. Affiliated with the Canadian Wildlife Federation. Founded: 1924.
President and Executive Director: JAMES MARRINER

NEWFOUNDLAND

GOVERNMENT AGENCIES

DEPARTMENT OF CULTURE, RECREATION AND YOUTH, P.O. Box 4750, St. John's, NewFoundland A1C 5T7
Minister: JOHN C. BUTT (709, 576-2810)
Deputy Minister: BOB JENKINS (576-2812)
Assistant Deputy Minister: J. INDER (576-3556)

Wildlife Division, Bldg. 810, Pleasantville, P.O. Box 4750, St. John's, NF A1C 5T7
Objective is to maintain the ecosystems upon which wildlife and people depend and to do so recognizing the values of the diversity and abundance of species; provide for the safe and sustainable use of wildlife both consumptive and non-consumptive; help create a social environment conducive to effective wildlife conservation.
Director: D.G. PIKE (576-2817)

Research and Management Branch
Chief of Operations: J. HANCOCK (576-2543)
Chief of Research and Development: E. MERCER (576-2540)
Senior Biologist, Moose: S. OOSENBRUG (576-2547)
Senior Biologist, Environmental Assessment: K. CURNEW (576-2548)
Senior Biologist, Caribou and Black Bear: S. MAHONEY (576-2542)
Senior Biologist, Labrador: S. LUTTICH (896-2732)
Regional Biologist, Eastern (Disease and Parasite Specialist): D. FONG (466-7449)
Regional Biologist, Central (Furbearer Specialist): O. FORSEY (651-2055)
Regional Biologist, Western (Small Game Specialist): W. SKINNER (686-2381)

Protection Branch
Chief, Wildlife Protection Officer: A. MacPHEE (709, 576-2647)
Regional Wildlife Protection Supervisor, Eastern: M. PARSONS (466-7449)
Regional Wildlife Protection Supervisor, Central: R. BURT (651-2055)
Regional Wildlife Protection Supervisor, Western: C. MALONEY (686-2371)
Regional Wildlife Protection Supervisor, Labrador: R. TRASK (896-2732)

Information & Education Branch
Chief: D. MINTY (709, 576-2630)
Hunter Education Co-ordinator: C. YATES (576-2630)
Trapper Education Coordinator: F. PHILLIPS (576-2630)
Salmonier Nature Park Manager: K. MOORE (521-2202)
Publications: *Newfoundland and Labrador Hunting and Trapping Guide; Trappers Newsletter; Newfoundland and Labrador Hunter Education Manual* Student and Instructor editions.

CITIZENS' GROUPS

NEWFOUNDLAND LABRADOR WILDLIFE FEDERATION (709, 364-8415) Affiliated Membership: 900.
President: MIKE BARRON, 80 The Blvd., Apt. 702, St. John's Newfoundland A1A 6V6
Secretary: FRANCES CLEARY, 14 Fairhaven Pl., St. John's A1E 4S1 (335-2226)

NORTHWEST TERRITORIES

GOVERNMENT AGENCIES

DEPARTMENT OF ECONOMIC DEVELOPMENT AND TOURISM, GOVERNMENT OF THE N.W.T., Box 1320, Yellowknife, NT X1A 2L9
Deputy Minister: DWIGHT NOSEWORTHY (403, 873-7115)
Director, Policy and Planning: ERIC CHRISTENSEN (873-7318)
Assistant Deputy Minister, Business Development: FRED KOE (873-7229)
Assistant Deputy Minister, Tourism: ALAN VAUGHAN (873-7115)

DEPARTMENT OF RENEWABLE RESOURCES, GOVERNMENT OF THE N.W.T., Yellowknife, NT X1A 2L9
Has broad responsibility for wildlife management and environmental protection in the Northwest Territories and provides assistance

to people dependent on these resources to harvest wildlife in a manner which will ensure continued availability of the resource.
Minister: RED PEDERSEN (403, 873-7959)
Deputy Minister: J.W. BOURQUE (873-7420)
Assistant Deputy Minister, Management: DAVID BRACKETT (920-6389)
Assistant Deputy Minister, Operations: BOB WOOLEY (920-6389)
Director, Wildlife Management: KEVIN LLOYD (873-7411)
Supervisor, Wildlife Population Management: SUSAN BONNYMAN (873-7769)
Supervisor, Habitat Management: PAUL GRAY (873-7765)
Director, Conservation Education: DOUG STEWART (920-8716)
Director, Forest Management: BOB LARSON (920-6405)
Supervisor, Resource Development: LEN COLOSIMO (873-7758)
Supervisor, Fur Management: RUS HALL (873-7771)
Supervisor, Conservation Education: EDWIN HALL (873-7134)
Director, Policy and Planning: RON LIVINGSTON (920-8046)
Director, Pollution Control: MEL SMITH (873-7654)
Director, Land Use Planning: IAN ROBERTSON (920-6118)
Regional Superintendent, Baffin: JIM NOBLE, Iqaluit X0A 0H0 (979-6246)
District Coordinator, Fort Smith: DON BOXER, Fort Smith X0E 0P0 (872-7337)
Regional Superintendent, Keewatin: ALEX ILLASIAK, Eskimo Point X0C 0E0 (819, 857-2828)
Regional Superintendent, Kitikmeot: DON VINCENT, Coppermine X0E 0E0 (403. 982-4201)
Regional Superintendent, Inuvik: JOHN BAILEY, Inuvik X0E 0T00 (979-7200)

CITIZENS' GROUPS

NORTHWEST TERRITORIES WILDLIFE FEDERATION RESEARCH ASSOCIATION
Affiliated with the Canadian Wildlife Federation.
President: JACK VAN CAMP, Arctic Institute of North America, The University of Calgary, 2500 University Dr., NW, Calgary, Alberta T2N 1N4 (403, 220-7515)

NOVA SCOTIA

GOVERNMENT AGENCIES

DEPARTMENT OF LANDS AND FORESTS, P.O. Box 698, Halifax, NS B3J 2T9 (902, 424-5935)
Charged with the administration of the Lands and Forests Act and various other statutes. Inherent in the legislation and incumbent upon the department are responsibilities pertaining to the productivity of the forests generally, the supply of forest products, the conservation of wildlife and the enhancement of recreational areas.
Minister: JACK MacISAAC (424-4037)
Administrative Assistant to Minister: PAT GORMAN (424-4047)
Deputy Minister: JOHN MULLALLY (424-4121)
Senior Director, Program Planning: J.D. SMITH (424-4103)
Senior Director, Administration: GARY E. RIX (424-6694)
Director, Financial Mangement: JAMES MORRISON (424-5990)
Coordinator, Air Services: L.D. CROCKER, Shubenacadie (758-3438)
Senior Director, Operations: R.G. MACGREGOR (424-5826)
Director, Forest Management, Private Lands: ARDEN L. WHIDDEN (424-5703)

Director, Forest Management, Crown Lands: DANIEL L. EIDT (424-7594)
Director, Forest Protection: EDWARD M. MacAULAY (758-2232)
Manager, Enforcement and Hunter Safety: E.W. (Casey) PENDERGAST (424-8925)
Director, Wildlife: MERRILL H. PRIME, Box 516, Kentville, B4N 3X3 (678-8921)
Director, Parks and Recreation: BARRY DIAMOND, R.R. 1, Belmont, Colchester County B0M IC0 (662-3030)
Senior Director, Forestry: D.J. (Dan) GRAHAM (424-3949)
Director, Rreforestation and Silviculture: R.E. BAILEY, Box 68, Truro B2N 5B8 (895-1591)
Director, Forest Resources Planning and Mensuration: F.R. WELLINGS, Truro (895-1591)
Supervisor, Wildlife Parks: E.R. PACE, Shubenacadie, Hants County (758-2040)
Senior Director (Acting), Land Services: C.A. STEEL (424-4267)
Director, Land Acquisition and Registry: J.D. BANCROFT (424-5481)
Director, Surveys: K. AUCOIN (424-3145)
Director, Extension Services: GERALD T. JOUDREY (424-4445)
Periodical Publications: *Nova Scotia Conservation; Nova Scotia Trappers Newsletter; Forest Times*
Editors: SANDY ANDERSON, JIM GUILD, P.O. Box 68, Truro B2N 5B8
Information Officer: BLAIN HENSHAW (424-5252)

CITIZENS' GROUPS

NOVA SCOTIA WILDLIFE FEDERATION, P.O. Box 654, Halifax, NS B3J 2T3
Affiliated with the Canadian Wildlife Federation. Aims to unite all conservation organizations in Nova Scotia, fosters appreciation of wildlife and habitat, promotes fish and game management, seeks enactment and enforcement of laws necessary to environmental controls, and preservation of wildlife resources. Membership: 6,000 (30 branches) plus 5 affiliated organizations. Established: 1930.
President: GERALD F. BLOM, 21 Litchfield Crescent, Halifax B3P 2N4 (902, 422-7327)
Vice-President: BOB CROSS, 65 Havelock Crescent, Dartmouth, B2W 4T7 (902, 434-6998)

DUCKS UNLIMITED CANADA, Canada—Eastern Canada Operation, 9 Havelock St., Amherst, NS B4H 3Z5 (902, 667-8726)
Regional Manager: JOHN WAUGH
Provincial Biologist: KEITH McALONEY
Constribution Services Representative: ALLAN GLOVER

NOVA SCOTIA FORESTRY ASSOCIATION, 64 Inglis Pl., Suite 202, Truro, Nova Scotia B2N 4B4 (902, 893-4653)
The Nova Scotia Forestry Association has since 1959, been an active part of forestry awareness and educational programs in the province. Programs such as Smokey Bear Wildlife Prevention Program, Woodsy Owl, Litter Prevention Program, and other school programs highlight the Association's work.
President: DAVID BRADSHAW
Past President: R.K. MacKINNON
Vice-President: CHARLES BAXTER, JR.
Secretary-Manager: ELIZABETH NORTHCOTT

ONTARIO

GOVERNMENT AGENCIES

MINISTRY OF NATURAL RESOURCES, Toronto, Ontario M7A 1W3

Provides opportunities for resource development and outdoor recreation for the continuous economic and social benefit of the people of Ontario and to administer, protect and conserve public lands and waters. The ministry's programs are concerned with the use of the physical resources of land, water, trees, fish, animals, and certain minerals for resource utilization and recreation.

Minister: VINCENT G. KERRIO (416, 965-1301)
Parliamentary Assistant: JAMES McGUIGAN (965-5676)
Deputy Minister: GEORGE TOUGH (965-2704)
Assistant Deputy Minister, Administration: MICHAEL R. GARRETT (965-7106)
Assistant Deputy Minister, N. Ontario: G.A. McCORMACK, 435 James St. S., P.O. Box 5000, Thunder Bay 'F' P7C 5G6 (807, 475-1271)
Budget and Program Analyst: L.O. KELLER, 435 James St. S., P.O. Box 5000, Thunder Bay 'F' P7C 5G6 (807, 475-1271)
Assistant Deputy Minister, S. Ontario: R.J. BURGAR (832-7193)
Operations Analyst: J. BARKER (832-7190)
Director Policy and Planning Secretariat: L.A. DOUGLAS (965-8422)

Administration Division

Supports, facilitates and evaluates the achievement of ministry objectives and targets by developing, coordinating, improving, and monitoring management processes to provide management with effective program planning, administrative and accounting controls, performance evaluation and accountability, and to supply analytical, and specialized support services to the ministry.

Assistant Deputy Minister: MICHAEL R. GARRETT (416, 965-7106)
Executive Coordinator, Finance and Administration Group: MICHELLE FORDYCE (965-6147)
Director (Acting), Communications Services: M.L. WELCH (965-3315)
Director, Legal Services: B.G. JONES (965-2748)
Director, Human Resources: R.M. GORDON (965-3828)

Finance and Administration Group

Executive Coordinator: MICHELLE FORYUCE (965-6147)
Director (Acting), Administrative Management: T. KURTZ (965-2711)
Director, Systems Services: J.A. QUEEN (416, 965-2750)
Director (Acting), Management Planning and Analysis: J. BYRNE (965-4143)
Director (Acting), Financial Resources: T. PIERRO (965-2761)
Director, Information Technology Planning: J.H. FINDEIS (965-6688)
Director, Internal Audit Services: A.A. WARD (965-4087)

Forest Resources Group

The Forest Resources manages for the production and harvest of timber and the provision of woodland for recreational purposes.
Executive Coordinator: J.F. GOODMAN (705, 945-6600)
Director (Acting), Forest Resources: G. OLDFORD (945-6612)
Director (Acting), Timber Sales: T.R. ISHERWOOD (945-6660)
General Manager, Ontario Tree Improvement and Forest Biomass Institute: D.P. DRYSDALE (832-7266)

Lands and Waters Group

Provides for the management of Crown lands and waters including the sale or lease of mining and surface rights to public lands; land acquisition; land use planning and coordination; surveying, mapping and remote sensing services; engineering and water management services; researching Indian land claims; and provides policy direction, and technical and financial assistance to Ontario's conservation authorities in their water and related resource management programs.

Executive Coordinator: R.J. VRANCART (416, 965-6046)
Director, Office of Indian Resource Policy: E.G. WILSON (965-6045)
Director, Land Management: S.E. YUNDT (965-1498)
Director, Surveys, Mapping and Remote Sensing: G. ZARZYCKI (733-8010)
Surveyor General for Ontario: S.B. PANTING (733-8010)
Associate Director, Ontario Centre for Remote Sensing: V. ZSILINSKY (733-8010)
Director, Conservation Authorities and Water Management: M.G. LEWIS (965-6287)

Outdoor Recreation Group

Responsible for managing Ontario's resources of fish, wildlife, provincial parks, and recreation areas in addition to planning and providing the wide variety of recreational opportunities afforded by these resources.

Executive Coordinator: R.M. CHRISTIE (416, 965-5661)
Chairman, Provincial Parks Council: L. BURRIDGES (519, 255-6731)
Coordinator, Provincial Parks Council: Vacant (965-2745)
Director, Parks and Recreational Areas: N.R. RICHARDS (965-5160)
Director, Fisheries: G.R. WHITNEY (965-5947)
Director, Wildlife: D.W. SIMKIN (965-4254)

Field Offices

Northern Ontario: Assistant Deputy Minister, G.A. McCORMACK, Ontario Government Bldg., 435 James St. So., P.O. Box 5000, Thunder Bay P7C 5G6 (807, 1271)
  Budget and Program Analyst: L.O. KELLER, 435 James St. S., P.O. Box 5000, Thunder Bay, 'F' P7C 5G6 (807, 475-1271)
Aviation and Fire Management Centre: P.O. Box 310, 747 Queen St. East, Sault Ste. Marie P6A 5L8
  Director: L.H. LINGENFELTER (705, 942-1800)
Northwestern Region: Regional Director, D.R. JOHNSTON, 810 Robertson St., Box 5160, Kenora P9N 3X9 (807, 468-3111)
North Central Region: Regional Director, G.P. ELLIOTT, 435 James St. S., P.O. Box 5000, Thunder Bay 'F' P7C 5G6 (807, 475-1261)
Northern Region: Regional Director, R.A. RILEY, 140 Fourth Ave., Box 3000, Cochrane P0L 1C0 (705, 272-7014)
Northeastern Region: Regional Director, M. KLUGMAN, 199 Larch St., Sudbury P3E 5P9 (705, 675-4120)
Southern Ontario: Assistant Deputy Minister, R.J. BURGAR (416, 832-7193)
  Operations Analyst: J. BARKER (832-7190)
Algonquin Region: Regional Director, Vacant, Brendale Sq., Box 9000, Huntsville P0A 1K0 (705, 789-9611)
Leslie M. Frost Natural Resources Centre: Dorset P0A 1E0
  Director: D.D. WHITE (705, 766-2451)
Eastern Region: Regional Director, J.R. OATWAY, Provincial Government Bldg., Concession Rd., Kemptville K0G 1J0 (613, 258-3413)
Central Region: Regional Director, A.S. HOLDER, 10670 Yonge St., Richmond Hill L4C 3C9 (416, 883-3256)

Southwestern Region: Regional Director, D.J. JOHNSTONE, 659 Exeter Rd., Box 5463, London N6A 4L6 (519, 661-2743)

Ministerial Agencies

Algonquin Forestry Authority, Chairman: P.I. ROCHE (705, 789-9647)

General Manager: W.J. BROWN, 222 Main St. West, P.O. Box 1198 Huntsville POA 1KO (705, 789-9647)

Mining & Lands Commissioner: G.H. FERGUSON, 700 Bay St., 24th Fl., Box 330, Toronto M5G 1Z6 (416, 965-1824)

NIAGARA ESCARPMENT COMMISSION, 232 Guelph St., Georgetown L7G 4B1 (416, 877-5191)
Maintains the Niagara Escarpment and land in its vicinity substantially as a continuous natural environment, and ensures only such development occurs as is compatible with that natural environment. Established: June, 1973, under the Niagara Escarpment Planning and Development Act.
Commission Members: G.H.U. BAYLY, Chairman; WILLIAM SMEATON; JOAN LITTLE; IVAN AITCHESON; JOHN ALEXANDER; HAROLD DAVIDSON; CAROL CURRIE; MURRAY BETTS; DOUGLAS THOMPSON; MARGARET CAPEL; GRACE CRONIN; ANNE REDISH; FRED GREENLAND; LYN MacMILLAN; JOSEPHINE MEEKER; JIM MONTGOMERY; JOSEPH NOONAN
Director: FRANK G. SHAW
Manager, Plan Administration: CECIL A. LOUIS
Manager, Development Control: KEITH C. JORDAN
Manager, Communications and Community Relations: RICHARD MURZIN
Information Officer: RILLA HEWER
Manager, Administration: SUSAN HERROLD

CITIZENS' GROUPS

ONTARIO FEDERATION OF ANGLERS AND HUNTERS, INC., THE, 169 Charlotte St., P.O. Box 28, Peterborough, Ontario K9J 6Y5 (705, 748-6324)
Purpose is to conserve Ontario's natural resources and promote ethical angling and hunting practices. Membership: 66,000. Incorporated: 1947. (705, 748-6324)
President: JACK CRAIK, Box 1434, New Liskeard P0J 1P0 (647-7143)
1st Vice-President: CHARLES ALEXANDER, 3 Thunder Dr., Dryden P8N 1V9 (807, 223-6336)
Executive Vice-President: RICK MORGAN, 169 Charlotte St., P.O. Box 28, Peterborough, Ontario K9J 6Y5 (748-6324)
Treasurer: JACK O'DETTE, 377 Bath Rd., Kingston K7M 2Y1 (613, 542-5615)
Publication: *The Angler and Hunter*
Editor: GARY BALL, Box 1541, Peterborough K9J 7H7 (748-3891)

ALGONQUIN WILDLANDS LEAGUE, 229 College St., Suite 206, Toronto, Ontario M5T 1R4 (416, 595-0443)
To educate the public to recognize the importance of protecting public parks in Ontario, particularly those of significant wilderness character; to encourage the establishment of additional wilderness park areas; and to promote their use in a manner appropriate for both recreation and scientific study. Founded: 1968.
President: HEATHER COOK, 111 Ashburnham Rd., Toronto, Ontario M6H 2K6 (653-7837)
1st Vice-President: PETER GARSTANG, 33 Rathnelly Ave., Toronto, Ontario M4V 2M8 (925-3927)

Publications: *Wildland News; Wilderness Now; Why Wilderness*

CONSERVATION COUNCIL OF ONTARIO, THE, Suite 202, 74 Victoria St., Toronto, Ontario M5C 2A5 (416, 362-2218)
Coordinates Provincial conservation associations. The Council is currently working on developingan Ontario Conservation Strategy which will improve the efficiency with the province addresses its environmental and resource problems. Membership: 33 organizations. Organized: 1952
President: GLENN HARRINGTON, Toronto
Vice-President: WENDY COOK, Toronto
Treasurer: DAVID EMBERLY, Cambridge
Publication: *Ontario Conservation News*

DUCKS UNLIMITED CANADA, Unit 10, 240 Bayview Dr., Barrie L4N 4Y8 (705, 726-3825)
Provincial Manager: M.J. BAIN

FEDERATION OF ONTARIO NATURALISTS, 355 Lesmill Rd., Don Mills M3B 2W8 (416, 444-8419)
Committed to protecting and increasing awareness of Ontario's natural areas and wildlife, and exerts influence to protect our natural environment. Membership: 12,000. 71 federated clubs across Ontario. Organized: 1931.
President: DOUGLAS THOMAS
1st Vice-President: MARY SMITH
2nd Vice-President: ED JOHNS
Secretary: DOUGLAS GEDDES
Treasurer: DAVE SUTTON
Executive Director: IAN KIRKHAM
Environmental Director: DON HUFF
Publication: *Seasons*
Editor: GAIL MUIR

JACK MINER MIGRATORY BIRD FOUNDATION, INC., P.O. Box 39, Kingsville, Ontario N9Y 2E8 (519, 733-4034/733-4650)
A nonprofit, tax deductible, public foundation inc. in both the U.S. and Canada. This sanctuary and its founder, Jack Miner have become internationally known as one of the earliest efforts in waterfowl conservation. Jack Miner pioneered the tagging of waterfowl in 1909. Awarded the OBE in 1943 for 'the greatest achievement in conservation in the British Empire'. Canada set aside the week of his birthday (April 10) as National Wildlife Week. Founded: 1904.
President: JASPER W. MINER
Vice-President: ROBERT T. KENNEDY
Secretary-Treasurer: KIRK W. MINER

ONTARIO FORESTRY ASSOCIATION, 150 Consumers Rd., Willowdale M2J 1P9 (416, 493-4565)
Promotes sound land use and the full development, protection, and utilization of Ontario's forest resources for maximum public advantage. Programs include Smokey Bear, Honour Roll of Ontario Trees, tree farming, forestry courses, land use/forest management advocacy, forestry publicity and historical data. Membership: 1,005. Founded: 1949.
President: R. BUNNEY, Dryden
1st Vice-President: R. STALEY, Vandorf
2nd Vice-President: J. DUNCANSON, Toronto
Executive Vice-President: J.D. COATS
Publication: *OFA Newsletter*
Editor: J.D. COATS

PRINCE EDWARD ISLAND

GOVERNMENT AGENCIES

DEPARTMENT OF COMMUNITY AND CULTURAL AFFAIRS,
P.O. Box 2000, Charlottetown C1A 7N8
Objectives are to conserve and manage wildlife, fish, and habitats on which they depend. Objectives are approached through coordinated biological, enforcement, education, and public relations programs.
Minister: GILBERT R. CLEMENTS (892-0311/Ext. 288)
Deputy Minister: KENNETH F. DESROCHES (892-0311/Ext. 287)
Director, Fish and Wildlife Division: ARTHUR SMITH (892-0311/Ext. 268)
Fisheries and Upland Game Biologist: ALAN GODFREY (892-0311/Ext. 302)
Waterfowl and Furbearer Biologist: RANDALL DIBBLEE (892-0311/Ext. 318)
Chief Conservation Officer: NELSON HURRY (892-0311/Ext. 271)
Publications: *Familiar Wildlife of P.E.I.; Tracks in the Snow; Wildlife and the Island; Patterns of the Pond; Island Woodland Plants: Our Land and Water*

CITIZENS' GROUPS

PRINCE EDWARD ISLAND WILDLIFE FEDERATION
Affiliated with the Canadian Wildlife Federation.
President: LEO PETERS, P.O. Box 190, Winsloe, Prince Edward Island C0A 2H0 (902, 964-3431)

QUEBEC

GOVERNMENT AGENCIES

DEPARTMENT OF RECREATION, FISH AND GAME, Place de la Capitale 150 East, St-Cyrille Blvd., Quebec City G1R 2B2
Minister: YVON PICOTTE (418, 643-6527)
Deputy Minister: PIERRE BERNIER (643-2207)
Assistant Deputy Minister, Regional Operations: MICHEL RENAUD (643-2207)
Director of Planning and Development: JACQUES AUGER (644-1361)
Director of Administration: PIERRE-A. BELANGER (643-2207)
Assistant Deputy Minister, Parks and Outdoors: BERNARD HARVEY (643-2207)
Executive Secretary: JEAN RIVET (643-2207)
Director of Information: PHILIPPE GAGNON (643-2984)
Director of Personnel: JACQUES RIVARD (643-6420)
Director of Municipal Programs: JEAN RIOUX (643-8969)

Fish and Game Branch
Director: GILES BARRAS (644-9376)
Wildlife Management Division: CHRISTIAN POTVIN (643-5539); CLAUDE BERNARD (643-5382)
Conservation Division Director: FRANCOIS DORLOT (643-8364)

Parks and Outdoor Branch
Directors: ANDRES MAGNY (644-2823); CONRAD DUBUC (Ext. 2210); GUY BUSSIERES (Ext. 5747)
Mont Sainte-Anne Park, Director: CLAUDE BRUNELLE (827-4423)
Zoological Garden, Director: PHILIPPE DEMERS (622-0312)
Aquarium, Director: PIERRE PAULHUS (659-5266)

CITIZENS' GROUPS

QUEBEC WILDLIFE FEDERATION, 319 Est, Rue St-Zotique Montreal, Quebec H2S 1L5 514, 271-2487/271-2488)
Membership: 300,000. Organized: 1945.
President: LEO-PAUL QUINTAL
Vice-President: CLAUDE MARCOUILLER
General Secretary: GUY LESAGE
General Treasurer: PIERRE FRENETTE
Past-President: JACQUES BERIAULT
Vice-President, Sector Number 1-East: Vacant
Vice-President, Sector Number 2-South: SALVADOR AZNAR
Vice-President, Sector Number 3-North-East: ROBERT PERRON
Vice-President, Sector Number 4-North-West: FERNAND GOUGEON
President of Researches Committee (CER): YVES JEAN

DUCKS UNLIMITED, Canada-Quebec Operation, STE 260-710 Bouvier St., Quebec City G2J 1A6
Provincial Manager: PATRICK PLANTE (418, 623-1650)
Provincial Biologist: J.P. LANIEL

PROVINCE OF QUEBEC SOCIETY FOR THE PROTECTION OF BIRDS, INC., 4832 de Maisonneuve Blvd. West, Montreal H3Z 1M5 (514, 937-0224)
Membership: 708. Organized: 1917.
President: BROOKE CLIBBON, 452 Victoria Ave., Westmount H3Y 2R4 (484-2774)
Hon. Secretary: BETSY BARBER, 4832 de Maisonneuve Blvd., West, Westmount H3Z 1M5 (937-0224)
Vice-President: RICHARD YANK, 566 Chester Rd., Beaconsfield H9W 3K1 (697-1997)
Vice-President: ETHEL FOGARTY, 240 36th Ave., Lachine H8T 2A3 (637-3256)
Hon. Treasurer: JIM CORISTINE, 114 Abbott Ave., Westmount H3Z 2J9 (631-3437)
Publications: *.Tchebec* (Annual Review) Field Check List of Birds in the Montreal Area; *In Search of Birds* (Intro to birds of Montreal Area); Monthly Newsletter
Editor: ETHEL FOGARTY, 240 36th Ave., Lachine H8T 2A3 (637-3256)

QUEBEC FORESTRY ASSOCIATION, INC., Association Forestiere Quebecoise, Inc., 110, 915 St. Cyrille Blvd., West, Quebec City, Quebec, Canada G1S 1T8 (418, 681-3588) (Annual Meeting: June, Quebec City)
A nonprofit organization dedicated to public education and to the protection of natural resources and environment. Founded: 1939.
Membership: 5,000. Operates les clubs 4-H du Quebec inc.
President: YVAN BASTIEN
1st Vice-President: YVES G. QUELLETTE
2nd Vice-President: WILLIAM H. JOURNAUX
Treasurer: JOHANNE DUMONT
Director General: ERIC LESSARD
Publication: *Foret Conservation*
Editor: ERIC LESSARD

STOP, Bibliotheque Atwater, Salle 1, 1200 Avenue Atwater, Montreal H3Z 1X4 (514, 932-7267)
Devoted to preserving and improving the quality of the physical and human environment and to promoting rational utilization of natural resources. Priority areas include acid rain, urban air pollution, sewage treatment, protection of rivers and rapids, solid waste, toxic waste, and environmental education. Membership: 500. Founded: 1970.
President: LYNNAE DUDLEY
Publication: *Stop Press*
Editor: DEREK MORTON

SASKATCHEWAN

GOVERNMENT AGENCIES

DEPARTMENT OF PARKS AND RENEWABLE RESOURCES,
3211 Albert St., Regina S4S 5W6
Minister: HON. COLIN MAXWELL, Rm. 340, Legislative Bldg., Regina S4S 0B3 (787-9130)
Deputy Minister: JOHN C. LAW (787-2930)
Assistant Deputy Minister, Support Services: LYLE G. LENSEN (787-2380)
Director, Administration: GRAHAM POWELL (787-8445)
Director, Human Resources Branch: B. MARR (787-2858)
Assistant Deputy Minister, Programs: DOUG CRESSMAN (787-5419)
Director (Acting), Management Services: SHARON COFFIN (787-2880)
Director, Integrated Resource Policy: G.W. PEPPER (787-7815)
Director, Construction Services: BRIAN WOODCOCK (787-2325)

Parks Branch
Director: ALAN G. APPLEBY (787-2846)
Operations, Executive Director: ROSS MACLENNAN (787-9079)
Director, Regional Parks Program: CLARK GABEL (787-2897)
Director, Communications: NOLAN MATTHIES (787-2322)
Southern Field Services Branch, Director: B. TETHER (787-2323)
Northern Field Services Branch, Director: D. HUNTER (953-2672)
Visitor Services Branch, Director: SHELLEEN VANDERMEY (787-3861)
Resource Lands Branch, Director: DOUG MAZUR (787-7796)

Regional Directors
Regina: MAE BOA, 3211 Albert St., Regina S4S 5W6 (787-2782)
Hudson Bay: F.R. FORD, Box 970, Hudson Bay S0E 0Y0 (865-2274)
Prince Albert: GUS MACAULEY, Box 3003, McIntosh Mall, Prince Albert S6V 6G1 (953-2899)
Meadow Lake: GLEN ROLLES, Box 580, Meadow Lake S0M 1V0 (236-5681)
Saskatoon: LEN ARNDT, 122-3rd Ave., N., Saskatoon S7K 2H6 (933-6240)
Melville: T.P. NELSON, 117-3rd Ave., Melville S0A 2P0 (728-4491)
Swift Current: D. NOBLE, 350 Cheadle St. W., Swift Current S9H 4G3 (773-1521)
La Ronge: ROSS DUNCAN, Box 5000, La Ronge S0J 1L0 (425-4231)

Forestry Branch, Box 3003, McIntosh Mall, Prince Albert S6V 6G1
Executive Director: PAUL BRETT (953-2222)

Director, Forest Operations: VICTOR BEGRAND (953-2444)
Director, Forest Management: W. BAILEY (953-2440)
Manager, Silviculture: M.T. LITTLE (953-2343)
Manager, Timber Management: J.A. BENSON (953-2442)
Manager, Forest Inventory: L. STANLEY (953-2247)
Manager, Regional Operations: F. FLAVELLE (953-2334)
Director, Forest Fire Management: W. RICHARDS (953-3473)

Fisheries, 3211 Albert St., Regina S4S 5W6
Director: PAUL NAFTEL (787-2884)
Resource Management Consultant: ALAN R. MURRAY (787-2950)
Data and Legal Services: HART HORN (787-2877)
Director, Wildlife: DENNIS SHERRATT (787-2309)

Regional Supervisor, DAVID PHILLIPS (787-2797)
Habitat Supervisor: SYD BARBER (787-2891)
Landowner Assistance Supervisor: CAM SCHEELHAASE (787-2886)
Population Allocation Supervisor: HUGH HUNT (787-9038)

CITIZENS' GROUPS

SASKATCHEWAN WILDLIFE FEDERATION
Affiliated with the Canadian Wildlife Federation.
Executive Director: ED BEGIN, Box 788, Moose Jaw, Saskatchewan S6H 4P5 (W:306, 692-7772/H:693-1343)

DUCKS UNLIMITED, Canada—Saskatchewan Operation, P.O. Box 4465, 1606-4th Ave., Regina S4P 3W7 (306, 569-0424)
A private, nonprofit conservation organization dedicated to preserving waterfowl by creating and restoring breeding habitat in Canada. This organization is funded by sportsmen of United States and Canada. Founded: 1938.
Provincial Manager: D.A. CHEKAY
Provincial Biologist: R.J. MacFARLANE
Central Regional Manager: C.B. FORBES
Publication: Newsletter

SASKATCHEWAN NATURAL HISTORY SOCIETY, Box 414, Raymore, S0A 3J0 (306, 746-4544)
Publishes a journal of natural history of the region and special publications on flora and fauna of the province and neighboring provinces; operates a nature bookshop; involved in sanctuaries, support conservation activities and nature education. Membership: 2,000. Founded: 1942.
President: DALE HJERTAAS, 14 Olson Place, Regina S4S 2J6
Vice-President: LORNE ROWELL, Box 639, Fort Qu'appelle S0G 1S0
Treasurer: WAYNE HARRIS, Box 414, Raymore S0A 3J0 (306, 746-4544)
Secretary: KATHY MEERES, 1125 4TH St., E., Saskatoon, S7H 1K7
Publications: *The Blue Jay; Blue Jay News*
Editor: SHEILA LAMONT, Box 414, Raymore S0A 3J0 (746-4544)

YUKON TERRITORY

GOVERNMENT AGENCIES

DEPARTMENT OF RENEWABLE RESOURCES, Box 2703,
Whitehorse Y1A 2C6
Deputy Minister: BILL KLASSEN (403, 667-5460)
Director, Fish and Wildlife: HUGH J. MONAGHAN (667-5715)
Chief, Wildlife and Management (Research and Habitat): MANFRED
HOEFS (667-5761)

Senior Big Game Biologist: BRIAN PELCHAT (667-5720)
Senior Small Game Biologist: DAVE MOSSOP (667-5766)

CITIZENS' GROUPS

YUKON FISH AND GAME ASSOCIATION
Affiliated with the Canadian Widlife Federation.
President: LAWRENCE LEIGH, 10 Redwood St., Whitehorse, Yukon
Territory Y1A 4B3 (W:403, 667-6401/H:633-4161)

COLLEGES AND UNIVERSITIES IN THE UNITED STATES AND CANADA

ALABAMA

Auburn University, School of Forestry, 108 M. White Smith Hall, Auburn University 36849 (205, 826-4000)
Forestry (B.S., M.S., Ph.D.), DR. EMMETT F. THOMPSON, Dean

ALASKA

University of Alaska, Fairbanks 99775-0990
Cooperative Wildlife Research Unit: DR. DAVID R. KLEIN, Leader (907, 474-7673)
Cooperative Fishery Research Unit: DR. JAMES B. REYNOLDS, Leader (474-7661)
Agriculture and Land Resource Management (M.S., Ph.D.), Vacant, Head (474-7083)
Dept. of Biology, Fisheries, and Wildlife: DR. ROBERT WEEDEN, Head
Program of Biology: DR. RONALD SMITH, Chairman (474-7542)
Program of Fisheries: DR. JAMES REYNOLDS, Chairman
Program of Wildlife: DR. ROBERT WEEDEN, Chairman
College of Natural Sciences: DR. KOLF JAYAWEERA, Dean (474-7608)

ARIZONA

Arizona State University, Tempe 85287
Wildlife (B.S.), Wildlife Management or Fisheries Management Options: DR. WENDELL L. MINCKLEY; DR. STUART G. FISHER; DR. ANDREW T. SMITH; DR. THOMAS E. MARTIN (602, 965-3571)
Agriculture (B.S., M.S.), Environmental Resources in Agriculture: DR. GEORGE SEPERICH, Center for Environmental Studies (602, 965-3585/2975): DR. DUNCAN T. PATTEN; DR. ROBERT D. OHMART; DR. PAUL C. MARSH

Northern Arizona University, Flagstaff 86011 (602, 523-3031)
Forestry (B.S., M.S., M.F.), DR. L.D. GARRETT, Dean

University of Arizona, Tucson 85721 (602, 621-7255)
School of Renewable Natural Resources: DR. EDGAR L. KENDRICK, Head (621-7257); DR. MALCOLM J. ZWOLINSKI, Associate Head (621-1755)
Cooperative National Park Resources Studies Unit: DR. DENNIS FENN, Leader (629-6886)
Forest-Watershed Mgt. (B.S., M.S., Ph.D.), DR. RICHARD HAWKINS
Watershed Hydrology (B.S., M.S., Ph.D.)
Natural Resources Recreation (B.S.)
Range Management (B.S., M.S., Ph.D.), DR. LAMAR SMITH
Renewable Natural Resources Studies (M.S., Ph.D.)
Wildlife, Fisheries, and Recreation Resources: DR. WILLIAM W. SHAW
Landscape Architecture (B.L.A., M.L.A.), MICHAEL DEETER
Cooperative Fish and Wildlife Research Unit: DR. O. EUGENE MAUGHAN, Leader (621-1959)

ARKANSAS

Arkansas State University, State University 72467 (501, 972-3082)
Department of Biological Sciences: DR. V. RICK MCDANIEL, Chairman
Biology (B.S., M.S.)
Botany (B.S.)
Wildlife Management (B.S.)
Zoology (B.S.)

Arkansas Tech University, Russellville 72801 (501, 968-0391)
Fisheries and Wildlife Biology (B.S.), BUFORD TATUM, Head
Recreation Administration (B.S.)
Park Administration (B.S.), DR. MICHAEL FREED

University of Arkansas at Little Rock, Little Rock 72204 (501, 569-3270)
Environmental Health Sciences (B.S.), DR. CARL R. STAPLETON, Director

University of Arkansas at Monticello, Monticello 71655 (501, 367-6811)
Forestry (B.S.)
Wildlife & Fisheries (B.S.), DR. R. SCOTT BEASLEY, Head, Department of Forest Resources
Biology (B.S.), ERIC SUNDELL, Head, Department of Natural Sciences

CALIFORNIA

California Polytechnic State University, San Luis Obispo 93407 (805, 546-0111)
Landscape Architecture (B.S.), Architecture (B.S., M.S.), City and Regional Planning (B.S.), MCRP
Architecture: W. MIKE MARTIN, Head
City and Regional Planning: WILLIAM A. HOWARD, Head
Landscape Architecture: GERALD L. SMITH, Head
School of Architecture and Environmental Design: GAR DAY DING, Dean
Natural Resources Management (B.S.), DR. NORMAN H. PILLSBURY, Head
Soil Science (B.S.), DR. BRENT G. HALLOCK, Head
Soil Conservation (M.S.)
School of Agriculture and Natural Resources: DR. LARK CARTER, Dean
Biological Sciences (B.S., M.S.), DR. V.L. HOLLAND, Head
Civil and Environmental Engineering (B.S.), PETER Y. LEE, Head
School of Engineering and Technology: WILLIAM F. HORTON, Dean

California State University, Chico 95929-0560 (916, 895-6408)
Areas of study include environmental education and interpretation, recreation and natural resource management, maintenance management, and planning and design.
Recreation and Parks Management (B.S., M.A.), DR. JAMES E. FLETCHER, Chairman; DR. JON K. HOOPER, Coordinator, Parks and Natural Resources Management Option

California State University, Sacramento 95819 (916, 454-6752)
Recreation and Leisure Studies with options in Recreation and Park Administration and in Therapeuic Recreation. (B.S., M.S.)
Biological Conservation (B.S., M.S.), DR. C. DAVID VANICEK
Environmental Studies (B.A.), VALERIE ANDERSON

Humboldt State University, Arcata 95521 (707, 826-3561)
College of Natural Resources: DR. RICHARD L. RIDENHOUR, Dean
Fisheries (B.S., M.S.), DR. GARY L. HENDRICKSON, Department Chairman
Forestry (B.S., M.S.), DR. WILLIAM J. SULLIVAN, Department Chairman
Natural Resources Planning and Interpretation (B.S., M.S.), DR. DAVID E. CRAIGIE, Department Chairman
Wildlife (B.S., M.S.), DR. DAVID W. KITCHEN, Department Chairman
Oceanography (B.S.), DR. JAMES A. GAST, Department Chairman
Range Management (B.S.), DR. NORMAN E. GREEN, Department Chairman
Watershed Management (M.S.), DR. WILLIAM J. SULLIVAN, Department Chairman
Cooperative Fishery Research Unit (M.S.), DR. ROGER A. BARNHART, Leader
Experiment Station, Pacific Southwest Forest and Range Station: DR. ROBERT T. ZIEMER, Project Leader

San Jose State University, San Jose 95192 (408, 277-2000)
Wildlife Zoology; Wildlife Management (B.A.), DR. LEON C. DOROSZ, Chairman
Environmental Studies (B.A.) in Environmental Studies with a concentration in the Social Sciences or Humanities; (B.A.) in Environmental Studies with a concentration in the Natural Sciences; (B.S.) in Environmental Studies with a concentration in Environmental Technology or Management; (B.A.) in Environmental Studies with a Multiple Subject Credential; Minor degrees in Energy Resource Management and Environmental Studies; Solar Energy Studies; Master of Science in Environmental Studies: DR. DONALD AITKEN, Environmental Studies Program Coordinator

University of California, Berkeley 94720 (415, 642-0376)
Forestry and Resource Management (B.S., M.S., Ph.D.), JOE R. MCBRIDE, Chairman
Range Management (M.S., Ph.D.)
Wildlife (Ph.D.)
Natural Resources (B.S., M.S., Ph.D.), DR. WILFORD GARDNER, Dean

University of California, Davis 95616 (916, 752-6586)
Wildlife and Fisheries Biology (B.S.), DANIEL W. ANDERSON, Chairman
Environmental Studies: C. GOLDMAN, Chairman
Range and Wildlands Science (B.S.), J.W. MENKE, Major Advisor
Graduate Group in Ecology (M.S., Ph.D.), T.C. FOIN, Chairman
Institute of Ecology: P.J. RICHERSON, Director
Cooperative National Park Resources Studies Unit: S.D. VEIRS, JR., Leader
Graduate Group in Range and Wildlands Science: R. MERTON LOVE, Chairman
Resource Sciences, Atmospheric Science, Environmental Planning and Management, Environmental Toxicology, Soil and Water Science, (B.S.), C.E. HESS, Dean, College of Agr. and Envir. Sci.

University of California, Los Angeles 90024 (213, 825-4321)
Analysis and Conservation of Ecosystems: DR. HARTMUT WALTER
Geography, Biogeography, and Resource Management (M.A., Ph.D.), DR. CHARLES F. BENNETT
Environmental Engineering (B.S., M.S., Ph.D.), DR. RICHARD L. PERRINE
Environmental Science and Engineering (D. Env.), DR. WILLIAM GLAZE
Environmental Systems Engineering (B.S., M.S., Ph.D.), DR. MICHAEL K. STENSTROM

University of California, Riverside 92521 (714, 787-4551)
Environmental Science (B.S., B.A.), DR. JOHN LETEY, JR., Chairman, Environmental Sciences Division (787-5105); PETER H. DIAGE, Advisor in Environmental Sciences (787-3850)

University of California, Santa Barbara 93106 (805, 961-2968)
Environmental Studies (B.A.), DAVID BROKENSHA, Chairperson

University of California, Santa Cruz 95064 (408, 429-2634)
Environmental Studies (B.A.), DR. GARY LEASE, Chairperson
Environmental Studies Library and Resource Center (408, 429-4270)

University of Southern California, Los Angeles 90089-0231 (213, 743-7517)
Environmental Engineering Program (M.S.) in Environmental Engineering; (Ph.D.) in Engineering (Environmental Engineering): MIHRAN S. AGBABIAN, Director
Environmental Social Sciences Program: undergraduate certificate program administered through the Division of Social Sciences and Communication: DR. DONALD LEWIS, Dean of the Division; JOSEPH KERTES, Assistant Dean for Student Affairs
Courses are offered at undergraduate and graduate level in Marine Biology, Marine Ecology, Geological and Biological Oceanography (B.S., M.S., Ph.D.) in Biological Sciences and Geological Sciences: DR. NORMAN ARNHEIM, Chairman, Biological Sciences; DR. ROBERT H. OSBORNE, Chairman, Geological Sciences

COLORADO

Colorado State University, Fort Collins 80523 (303, 491-1101)
Dean: DR. JAY M. HUGHES
Assistant Dean: DR. DONALD L. CREWS
Cooperative Fish and Wildlife Research Unit: DR. DAVID R. ANDERSON, Leader
Forestry and Natural Resources (B.S., M.S., Ph.D.), DR. JAY M. HUGHES, Dean
Fishery and Wildlife (B.S., M.S., Ph.D.), DR. ROBERT S. COOK, Head
Forest and Wood Sciences (B.S., M.F., Ph.D.) DR. A. ALLEN DYER Head
Range Science (B.S., M.S., Ph.D.), DR. HAROLD GOETZ, Head
Recreation Resources and Landscape Architecture (B.S., M.S., Ph.D.), DR. GLENN HAAS, Head
Earth Resources (B.S., M.S., Ph.D.), DR. HAROLD S. BOYNE, Head
Environmental Philosophy (M.A.), DR. HOLMES ROLSTON, Graduate Advisor
Natural Resource Ecology Laboratory: DR. ROBERT G. WOODMANSEE, Director

Colorado University Environmental Center, Campus Box 207, University of Colorado, Boulder 80309 (303, 492-8308)
The Environmental Center as a major campus organization which educates students and the community on environmental issues through our conferences, programs, newsletters and library. We house the largest campus recycling program in the country, and various activist groups: Animal Rights, Ecological Living, Legislative Watchdog, Wilderness Study, and Rainforest Action Group. Organized: 1970.
Director: ROZ McCLELLAN (492-8309)
Recycling Director: JACK DeBELL (492-8307)
Chair of Environmental Board: LYNN BUHLIG (492-8308)
Publications: *CU Environmental Review; Rainforest Action Group* (RAG) Bulletin
Editor: KIM MATTHEWS

Natural Resources Law Center, University of Colorado School of Law, Campus Box 401, Boulder 80309-0401 (303, 492-1286)
Conducts research on natural resources law and policy, including water, public lands, minerals, Indian law, etc. Sponsors conferences and workshops and hosts visiting scholars. Publishes books, research papers, and *Resource Law Notes* newsletter. Founded in 1981 as function of University of Colorado School of Law.
Director: LAWRENCE J. MacDONNELL
Conference Coordinator: KATHERINE TAYLOR
Secretary: BETTY BUTLER

CONNECTICUT

Connecticut College, New London 06320 (203, 447-1911)
Human Ecology Program (B.A.), PROF. SALLY TAYLOR, Director

University of Connecticut, Box U-87, 1376 Storrs Rd., WBY, Rm. 308, Storrs 06268 (203, 486-2840)
Department of Natural Resources Management and Engineering, (B.S., M.S.) in Natural Resources with emphasis in Forestry, Fisheries, Wildlife, Biometeorology, Watershed Hydrology, Remote Sensing, Soil and Water Conservation, Natural Resources Engineering, etc. Joint Ph.D. program with affiliated departments. DR. DAVID B. SCHROEDER, Acting Head

University of New Haven, 300 Orange Ave., West Haven 06516 (203, 934-6321)
Dept. of Biology and Environmental Studies: PROF. HENRY E. VOEGELI, Chairman, Environmental Engineering (M.S.), Occupational Safety & Health (A.S., B.S.), Environmental Science (M.S.)

Yale University, School of Forestry and Environmental Studies, 205 Prospect St., New Haven 06511 (203, 432-5100)
Forestry & Environmental Studies (D.F., M.F., M.F.S., M.E.S., Ph.D.), JOHN C. GORDON, Dean

DISTRICT OF COLUMBIA

Georgetown University Law Center, 600 New Jersey Ave., NW, Washington 20001
Dean: ROBERT PITOFSKY

George Washington University, Washington 20052 (202, 994-1000)
Environmental Law (J.D., L.L.M., S.J.D.), ARNOLD W. REITZE, JR., Director and Professor of Law (994-6908)
Environmental Studies (B.A., B.S.), Environmental & Resource Policy (M.A.), Environmental Science (M.S.), HENRY MER-

CHANT, Chairman, Committee on Environmental Studies and Associate Professor of Biology (994-7123)
Environmental Engineering (M.S., D.Sc.), RAYMOND R. FOX, Chairman, Department of Civil, Mechanical and Environmental Engineering and Professor of Engineering and Applied Science (994-6749)
Environmental Management (MEA), BARRY SILVERMAN, Associate Professor of Engineering Administration (994-6433)

George Washington University National Law Center, 720 20th St., NW, Washington 20052
Dean: JACK FRIEDENTHAL

University of DC (Van Ness Campus), Washington 20008 (202, 282-7370)
Dept. of Environmental Science: A. JOSE JONES, Chairperson, Programs: (B.S.) Environmental Science; (A.S.) Marine Science; (A.S.) Air Quality Management; (A.S.) Water Quality Management; (B.S.) Geoscience/Earth Science; (B.S.) Horticulture

DELAWARE

University of Delaware, Newark 19717 (302, 451-2526)
College of Agricultural Sciences: DR. DONALD F. CROSSAN, Dean
Dept. of Entomology & Applied Ecology (B.S., M.S.), DR. ROLAND ROTH, Acting Chairperson

FLORIDA

Florida State University, Tallahassee 32306 (904, 644-2525)
Anthropology (B.S., M.S., Ph.D.), DR. J.A. PAREDES, Chairman
Biological Science (B.S., M.S. Ph.D.), DR. LAWRENCE G. ABELE, Chairman
Chemical Physics (M.S., Ph.D.), DR. S.A. SAFRON, Chairman
Chemistry (B.S., M.S., Ph.D.), DR. ROBLEY J. LIGHT, Chairman
Computer Science (B.S., M.S., Ph.D.), DR. ABRAHAM KANDEL, Chairman
Geography (B.S., M.S., Ph.D.), DR. PATRICK O'SULLIVAN, Chairman
Geology (B.S., M.S., Ph.D.), DR. J.F. TULL, Chairman
Geophysical Fluid Dynamics (Ph.D.), DR. RICHARD L. PFEFFER, Program Director
Mathematics (B.S., M.S., Ph.D.), DR. RALPH D. McWILLIAMS, Chairman
Meteorology (B.S., M.S., Ph.D.), DR. DAVID W. STUART, Chairman
Oceanography (M.S., Ph.D.), DR. WILTON STURGES, Chairman
Physics (B.S., M.S., Ph.D.), DR. DONALD ROBSON, Chairman
Psychology (B.S., M.S., Ph.D.), DR. MICHAEL RASHOTTE, Chairman
Statistics (B.S., M.S., Ph.D.), DR. JAYARAM SETHURAMAN, Chairman
Program in Medical Sciences, DR. ROBERT H. REEVES, Director
Program in Medical Technology, DR. JOHN HOZIER, Director
Program in Molecular Biophysics (Ph.D.), DR. WILLIAM F. MARZLUFF, Program Director
Center for Biomedical and Toxicological Research, DR. E.A. FERNALD, Executive Director; DR. ROY C. HERNDON, Director of Research; FRANK UNGER, Technical Director
Center for Aquatic Research and Resource Management, DR. ROBERT J. LIVINGSTON, Director
Center for Polar Desert Research, DR. IMRE FRIEDMAN, Director

University of Florida, Gainesville 32611 (904, 392-1791)
School of Forest Resources and Conservation: DR. ARNETT C. MACE, JR., Director (392-1791)

Fisheries and Aquaculture (M.F.R.C., M.S., Ph.D.), DR. JEROME V. SHIREMAN, Chairman (376-0732)

Forestry (B.S.F., M.F., Ph.D.), DR. C.P. PAT REID, Chairman (392-1850)

Wildlife and Range Sciences (B.S.F.R.C., M.F.R.C., M.S., Ph.D.), DR. MICHAEL COLLOPY, Chairman (392-4851)

Cooperative Fish and Wildlife Research Unit: DR. WILEY KITCHENS, Leader (392-1861)

Center for Natural Resources: DR. JOSEPH JOYCE, Director (392-7622)

Center for Aquatic Weeds: DR. JOSEPH JOYCE, Director (376-0732)

University of Miami, Rosenstiel School of Marine and Atmospheric Science, 4600 Rickenbacker Causeway, Miami 33149 (305, 361-4000)

Dean: DR. CHRISTOPHER G.A. HARRISON

Biology and Living Resources (M.S., Ph.D.)

Marine and Atmospheric Chemistry (M.S., Ph.D.)

Marine Geology and Geophysics (M.S., Ph.D.)

Meteorology and Physical Oceanography (M.S., Ph.D.)

Marine Affairs (B.A., M.A.)

Marine Science/Biology, Marine Science/Chemistry, Marine Science/Geology, Marine Science/Physics (B.S.)

University of West Florida, Department of Biology, Pensacola 32514-5751 (904, 474-2746)

Biology (B.S., M.S.)

Coastal Zone Studies (M.S.)

GEORGIA

Emory University, Atlanta 30322 (404, 329-6292)

Biology (terrestrial ecology; systems ecology) (M.S., Ph.D.)

Georgia College, Milledgeville 31061 (912, 453-4246)

Aquatic Ecology, option (B.S., M.S.), DR. DAVID J. COTTER, Head

Environmental Science, options Air Quality and Water Quality Control (B.S.), DR. DAVID J. COTTER, Coordinator

Georgia Institute of Technology, Atlanta 30332 (404, 894-3776)

Environmental Resources Center: DR. BERND KAHN, Director

University of Georgia, Faculty of Environmental Ethics, 106 Peabody Hall, Athens 30602 (404, 542-2823)

Cooperative Fish and Wildlife Research Unit: DR. MICHAEL J. VAN DEN AVYLE, Leader (542-5260)

Forestry (B.S.F.R., M.S., M.F.R., Ph.D.), L.A. HARGREAVES, JR., Dean (542-4744)

Wildlife (B.S., M.S., Ph.D.), DR. R. LARRY MARCHINTON (542-3932)

Fisheries (B.S., M.S., Ph.D.), DR. ROBERT E. REINERT (542-1477)

Institute of Natural Resources: DR. RONALD M. NORTH, Director (542-1555)

Institute of Ecology: DR. RONALD PULLIAM, Director (542-2968)

Faculty of Environmental Ethics: DR. FREDERICK FERRE, Director (542-2823)

Cooperative National Park Service Research Unit: DR. SUSAN POWER BRATTON, Leader (542-2968)

University of Georgia Marine Institute, Sapelo Island 31327 (912, 485-2221)

Concerned with research into the system-ecology, biology, chemistry, and geology of the salt marshes, barrier islands and nearshore zone of the Georgia coast. Organized: 1953.

Director: JAMES J. ALBERTS

HAWAII

University of Hawaii, 2538 The Mall, Honolulu 96822 (808, 948-8350)

Cooperative Fishery Research Unit: DR. JAMES D. PARRISH, Leader

IDAHO

Idaho State University, Pocatello 83209 (208, 236-3765)

Ecology (B.S.), ROD R. SEELEY, Chairman

University of Idaho, Moscow 83843 (208, 885-6441)

Forestry, Wildlife and Range Sciences (Ph.D.), DR. JOHN C. HENDEE (885-6442)

Forest Resources (B.S., M.F., M.S.), DR. CHARLES R. HATCH (885-7952)

Fish and Wildlife Resources (B.S., M.S.), DR. ERNEST D. ABLES (885-6434)

Range Resources (B.S., M.S.), DR. KENDALL JOHNSON (885-6536)

Wildland Recreation Management (B.S., M.S.), DR. WILLIAM J. McLAUGHLIN (885-7911)

Forest Products (B.S., M.F., M.S.), DR. ALI A. MOSLEMI (885-6126)

Cooperative Fish and Wildlife Research Unit: DR. J. MICHAEL SCOTT, Leader (885-6336)

Cooperative Park Studies Unit: DR. GERALD WRIGHT, Project Leader, Biology (885-7990); DR. GARY MACHLIS, Project Leader, Sociology (885-7129)

Wilderness Research Center: DR. EDWARD GARTON, Director (Acting) (885-7426)

ILLINOIS

Bradley University, Peoria 61625 (309, 676-7611)

Biology (B.S., B.A., M.S.), B.J. MATHIS, Chairman

Environmental Science (Interdepartmental) (B.S.), B.J. MATHIS, Chairman of Coordinating Committee

Eastern Illinois University, Charleston 61920 (217, 581-3011)

Environmental Biology (B.S., M.S.), WILLIAM WEILER, Chairperson, Environmental Biology Studies Comm. (581-2928)

Botany (B.S., M.S.), T.M. WEIDNER, Chairman (581-3624)

Zoology (B.S., M.S.), RICHARD FUNK, Chairman (581-3126)

Southern Illinois University, Carbondale 62901 (618, 453-2121)

Forestry (B.S., M.S.), DR. DWIGHT R. McCURDY, Chairperson, Forest Resource Management (B.S., M.S.) (453-3341)

Forestry Recreation (B.S., M.S.)

Cooperative Wildlife Research Lab. (M.S., Ph.D.), DR. ALAN WOOLF, Director (536-7766)

Cooperative Fisheries Research Lab (M.S., Ph.D.), DR. ROY C. HEIDINGER, Director (536-7761)

Plant and Soil Science (B.S., M.S.), DR. DONALD J. STUCKY, Chairperson (453-2496)

University of Illinois, at Urbana-Champaign, Urbana 61801 (217, 333-1000)

Forestry (B.S., M.S., Ph.D.), GARY ROLFE, Head

Wildlife Research Section, Natural History Survey: DR. GLEN C. SANDERSON, Head

Landscape Architecture (B.L.A., M.L.A.), VINCENT J. BELLAFIORE, Head

Institute for Environmental Studies: ROGER A. MINEAR, Director

Urban and Regional Planning (B.A., M.U.P., Ph.D.), LEWIS D. HOPKINS, Head

Ecology, Ethology, and Evolution (B.A.), GEORGE O. BATZLI, Head

Civil Engineering (B.S., M.S., Ph.D.), WILLIAM J. HALL, Head

Geography (B.S., M.S., Ph.D.), GEOFFREY HEWINGS, Head

Western Illinois University, Macomb 61455 (309, 298-1266/298-1546)

Wildlife (B.S., M.S.), DR. THOMAS C. DUNSTAN

Fisheries (B.S., M.S.), DR. LARRY A. JAHN

INDIANA

Ball State University, Muncie 47306 (317, 285-5780)

Natural Resources (B.S., M.A., M.S.), DR. CHARLES O. MORTENSEN, Chairman

Option I, Natural Resource Studies, Advisor: DR. TIMOTHY F. LYON (Ext. 5783)

Option II, Natural Resources Interpretation and Public, Advisors: DR. CHARLES O. MORTENSEN (Ext. 5780); DR. CLYDE W. HIBBS (Ext. 5786)

Option III, Outdoor Recreation Management, Advisor: DR. CLYDE W. HIBBS (Ext. 5786)

Option IV, Environmental Protection, Advisors: DR. THAD GODISH (Ext. 5782); DR. H. FRED SIEWERT (Ext. 5790)

Option V, Land Resource Management, Advisors: DR. B. THOMAS LOWE (Ext. 5785); DR. JAMES R. COOPER (Ext. 5788); DR. JOHN R. PICHTEL (Ext. 5791)

Departmental Minor in Natural Resources, Advisor: DR. CHARLES O. MORTENSEN (Ext. 5780)

Departmental Minor In Energy Resources, Advisor: DR. B. THOMAS LOWE (Ext. 5785)

Teaching Minor in Conservation and Environmental Studies, Advisor: DR. CLYDE W. HIBBS (Ext. 5786)

Indiana State University, Terre Haute 47809 (317, 237-2261)

Conservation (B.S., M.S., Ph.D.), DR. WILLIAM BROOKS; DR. KAMLESH LULLA; DR. JOHN E. OLIVER

Ecology and Wildlife (B.S., M.S., Ph.D.), DR. MARION T. JACKSON; DR. JOHN O. WHITAKER, JR.; DR. GEORGE S. BAKKEN; DR. WILLIAM CHAMBERLAIN

Indiana University, Bloomington 47405 (812, 335-9485)

School of Public and Environmental Affairs (B.S., M.P.A., M.S.E.S., Ph.D.), CHARLES F. BONSER, Dean; DANIEL E. WILLARD, Director

Environmental Programs include: Bachelor of Public Affairs degree, concentrations in Environmental Science; Masters of Public Affairs, concentration in Environmental Policy; Master of Science in Environmental Science with concentrations in Applied Ecology, Chemistry, Geology, Hazardous Waste, and Water Resources; Master of Science in Environmental Science and Doctor of Jurisprudence combined program.

Purdue University, West Lafayette 47907

Department of Forestry and Natural Resources: DR. DENNIS C. Le MASTER, Head (317, 494-3591)

Forest Management (B.S.F., M.S., Ph.D.)

Forest Products (B.S.F., M.S., Ph.D.)

Forest Recreation (B.S.F., M.S., Ph.D.)

Urban Forestry (B.S.F., M.S., Ph.D.)

Wildlife Management (B.S.F., M.S., Ph.D.)

Wildlife Science (B.S., M.S., Ph.D.)

Fisheries Science (B.S., M.S., Ph.D.)

For information on undergraduate programs, contact: DR. F.H. MONTAGUE, Director of Student Services (494-3630)

For information on graduate programs, contact: DR. PHILLIP E. POPE, Director of Graduate Studies (494-3593)

IOWA

Iowa State University, Ames 50011

Forestry (B.S., M.S., Ph.D.), DR. STEVEN E. JUNGST, Chairman (515, 294-1166)

Cooperative Wildlife Research Unit: DR. PAUL A. VOHS, Leader (294-3056)

Fisheries, Wildlife Biology and Animal Ecology (B.S., M.S., Ph.D.), DR. BRUCE W. MENZEL, Chairman (294-6148)

Landscape Architecture (B.L.A.), (M. Land. Arch.), ALBERT J. RUTLEDGE, Chairman 294-5676)

University of Iowa, Iowa City 52242 (319, 353-2121)

Environmental Engineering Program, Division of Energy Engineering (M.S., Ph.D.), DR. RICHARD DAGUE, Program Director

Preventive Medicine and Environmental Health (M.S., Ph.D.), DR. KEITH R. LONG, Environmental Program Director

KANSAS

Emporia State University, Emporia 66801 (316, 343-1200/Ext. 5623)

Ecology and Wildlife Biology (with emphasis in aquatic ecology and wildlife management) (B.S., M.S.), DR. CARL W. PROPHET; DR. THOMAS A. EDDY; DR. DWIGHT L. SPENCER

Kansas State University, Manhattan 66506 (913, 532-6011)

Wildlife (B.S., M.S., Ph.D.), DR. ROBERT J. ROBEL

Landscape Architecture (B.L.A.), THOMAS A. MUSIAK

Range Management (B.S., M.S., Ph.D.), DR. CLENTON OWENSBY

Natural Resources Conservation and Use (B.S.), DR. MICHEL D. RANSOM

Regional and Community Planning: DR. VERNON P. DEINES

Konza Prairie Research Natural Area: DR. THEODORE M. BARKLEY

Fisheries (B.S., M.S., Ph.D.), DR. HAROLD E. KLAASSEN

Pre-Forestry and Park Resource Management (B.S.), DR. TED T. CABLE

University of Kansas, Lawrence 66045 (913, 864-4301)

Systematics and Ecology (B.S., M.A., Ph.D.), HANS-PETER SCHULTZE, Chairman (864-3763)

Environmental Studies (with options in Ecology and Field Biology; Environmental Impact Analysis; Environmental Health; Geology and Meteorology; Water Resources; Environment and Land-Use Analysis) (B.A., B.G.S.), FRANK DENOYELLES , Director

Kansas Applied Remote Sensing (KARS) Program (with emphasis in Natural Resources Management): EDWARD A. MARTINKO, Director (864-4775)

Experimental and Applied Ecology (with emphasis in aquatic ecology and population biology of small mammals and plants) (M.A., Ph.D.), KENNETH B. ARMITAGE, Director; W. DEAN KETTLE, Associate Director, Facilities

KENTUCKY

Eastern Kentucky University, 204 Bennington Ct., Richmond 40475 (606, 622-1531)

Wildlife Management (B.S., M.S.), DR. M. PETE THOMPSON; DR. CHARLES ELLIOTT; DR. ROBERT FREDERICK

Environmental Resources (B.S.), DR. M. PETE THOMPSON
Fisheries Management (B.S., M.S.), DR. BRANLEY A. BRANSON
Marine Biology (B.S.), DR. GUENTER SCHUSTER
Applied Ecology (M.S.), DR. SANFORD JONES
Lillie Woods Research Natural Area: DR. WILLIAM MARTIN

Georgetown College, Georgetown 40324 (502, 863-8088)
Environmental Science (B.S.), DR. THOMAS SEAY

Morehead State University, Morehead 40351 (606, 783-2111)
Environmental Science (with options in Ecology; Geology; Chemistry and Physics; or Social Sciences and Economics; a minor is also available) (B.S.), DR. JERRY F. HOWELL, JR. (783-2952)
Biology (with emphasis on Fish and Wildlife), (B.S., M.S.), DR. GERALD L. DEMOSS (783-2944)

Murray State University, Murray 42071 (502, 762-3011)
Wildlife and Fisheries (B.S., M.S), DR. STEPHEN B. WHITE, Wildlife (762-6298); DR. TOM J. TIMMONS, Fisheries (762-6185)

University of Kentucky, Lexington 40546 (606, 257-7596)
Forestry (B.S., M.S., M.S.F.), DR. BART A. THIELGES, Chairman
Publication: *Natural Resources Newsletter*
Editor: DR. ALLAN J. WORMS, Dept. of Forestry, University of Kentucky, Lexington, 40546-0073

University of Louisville, Louisville 40292 (502, 588-6731)
Water Resources Laboratory (M.S., Ph.D.)
Fisheries (M.S., Ph.D.), DR. WILLIAM D. PEARSON, Professor; DR. JAMES THORP, Director

LOUISIANA

Louisiana State University, Baton Rouge 70803 (504, 388-4131)
Cooperative Fish and Wildlife Research Unit: DR. CHARLES F. BRYAN, Leader
Assistant Leaders: DR. ALAN D. AFTON; DR. WILLIAM H. HERKE
Forestry (B.S., M.S., Ph.D.)
Wildlife (M.S.)
Fisheries (M.S)
Wildlife & Fisheries Sciences (Ph.D.), DR. STANLEY B. CARPENTER, Director, School of Forestry, Wildlife, and Fisheries

Louisiana Tech University, Ruston 71272 (318, 257-4985)
Forestry (B.S.), J. LAMAR TEATE, Director, School of Forestry

McNeese State University, Department of Agriculture, Lake Charles 70609 (318, 437-5690) DR. ROBERT L. RUMSEY; DR. HAROLD AYMOND, Head

Northwestern State University, Natchitoches 71497 (318, 357-5375)
To educate people in the art, skill and science of wildlife management; to prepare people for management of natural resources at the professional entry levels.
Wildlife Management (B.S.), DR. ARTHUR S. ALLEN, Director

Tulane University, New Orleans 70118 (504, 865-5546)
Environmental Biology (ecology and systematics) (B.S., M.S., Ph.D.)
Cell Biology and Comparative Physiology (B.S., M.S., Ph.D.)
Developmental Biology (B.S., M.S., Ph.D.), Molecular Biology (B.S., M.S., Ph.D.), DR. ARTHUR WELDEN, Chairman

MAINE

College of the Atlantic, 105 Eden St., Bar Harbor 04609 (207, 288-5015)
The College of the Atlantic is a fully accredited four-year residential college. Students are attracted to its excellent programs in Marine Biology, Environmental Studies and Ecology, Environmental Design, Public Policy, Education and selected Humanities. Under 200 students. Awards a Bachelor of Arts in Human Ecology.
President: LOUIS RABINEAU
Vice-President: CHARLES HESSE
Provost: STEVE KATONA
Director of Admission: MELVILLE COTE
Director of Summer Programs: THEODORE KOFFMAN

University of Maine, Orono 04469 (207, 581-1110)
College of Forest Resources, Dean: DR. FRED B. KNIGHT (581-2840)
Forest Resources (B.S., M.F., M.S., Ph.D.), DR. THOMAS J. CORCORAN, Chairman Department of Forest Management (581-2846); DR. MICHAEL S. GREENWOOD, Chairman, Department of Forest Biology (581-2838)
Wildlife Management (B.S., M.S., M.W.C., Ph.D.), DR. RAY B. OWEN, JR., Chairman, Department of Wildlife (581-2863)
Cooperative Fish and Wildlife Research Unit: DR. WILLIAM B. KROHN, Leader

University of Maine at Fort Kent, Fort Kent 04743 (207, 834-3162)
Environmental Studies Program (B.S.), DR. EBERHARD THIELE, Director

Unity College, Unity 04988
Environmental Sciences (A.A.S., B.S.) (207, 948-3131)
Freshwater Fisheries: A. JIM CHACKO
Marine Fisheries: DAVID STAFFORD POTTER
Wildlife: ERIC ANDERSON; PHILLIP MASON
Botany: SUSAN GAWLER
Forestry: GRANT ESTELL
Geology: JERRY CINNAMON
Chemistry: ROBERT M. HAWTHORNE, JR.
Computer Sciences: CLIFF SHAFFER
Mathematics: BARRY WOODS

MARYLAND

The Johns Hopkins University, Baltimore 21218 (301, 338-8000)
Environmental Engineering (M.S.E., Ph.D.), CHARLES O'MELIA
Environmental Health Sciences (M.S., Ph.D., Sc.D.), GARETH M. GREEN
Natural Resources, Environmental Economics (M.S., Ph.D.), M. GORDON WOLMAN; JOHN BOLAND
Waterfowl Biology (M.S., Ph.D., Sc.D.), WILLIAM J.L. SLADEN

University of Maryland Baltimore County, Catonsville 21228 (301, 455-2261)
Biological Sciences (B.S.), DR. RONALD E. YASBIN, Professor and Chair, Dept. of Biological Sciences

University of Maryland College Park, College Park 20742 (301, 454-3311)
Agricultural and Resource Economics (B.S., M.S., Ph.D.), DR. DARRELL HUETH, Chairman
Agronomy (B.S., M.S., Ph.D.), DR. M. KENNETH AYCOCK, Chairman

Animal Sciences Graduate Program (M.S., Ph.D.), DR. D.S. WES-
THOFF, Chairman

Civil Engineering (B.S., M.S., Ph.D.), DR. JAMES COLVILLE, Chairman

Conservation and Resource Development Program (B.S.), DR. G.R.
GIBSON, Coordinator

Entomology (B.S., M.S., Ph.D.), DR. ALLEN STEINHAUER, Chairman

Geography (B.S., M.S., Ph.D.), DR. K.E. COREY, Chairman

Recreation (B.A., M.A., Ed.D., Ph.D.), DR. FRED N. HUMPHREY,
Chairman

Agricultural and Extension Education: DR. MERL E. MILLER,
Chairman (Acting), (M.S.),

University of Maryland Eastern Shore, Princess Anne 21853
(301, 651-2200)

Natural Sciences (B.S., M.S., Ph.D.), DR. JAMES A. ADAMS,
Chairman

Environmental Scientist: GIAN GUPTA

Coastal Ecology Research Center: DR. TERRY BASHORE; DR.
CLEMENT COUNTS

Marine, Estuarine, and Environmental Sciences Program: DR.
STEVE REBACH

University of Maryland, Frostburg State University, Consortium,
Frostburg 21532

Biology (B.S., M.S.), DR. WAYNE A. YODER, Chairman, Biology
Dept., Frostburg State University

Wildlife and Fisheries (B.S) DR. JAMES H. HOWARD, Wild-
life/Fisheries Program Coordinator, Biology Dept., Frostburg
State University

Wildlife and Fisheries (M.S., Ph.D.), DR. KENT FULLER, Head,
Appalachian Environmental Laboratory, University of Maryland,
Frostburg State University

University of Maryland System, The, Center for Environmental
and Estuarine Studies, Cambridge 21613 (301, 228-
9250)

Director and Professor (Acting): DR. THOMAS C. MALONE

Associate Director for Administration: WILLIAM L. OUTHOUSE

Associate Director for Educational Affairs: DR. ROBERT E. MENZER

Horn Point Environmental Laboratories, Cambridge 21613 (228-
8200)

Head and Professor: DR. DENNIS L. TAYLOR

Chesapeake Biological Laboratory, Solomons 20688 (326-4281)

Head and Professor: DR. KENNETH R. TENORE

Appalachian Environmental Laboratory, Frostburg 21532 (689-
3115)

Head and Principal Agent: PROF. KENT B. FULLER

MASSACHUSETTS

Harvard University, 212B Pierce Hall, Cambridge 02138
(617, 495-2833)

Harvard and Radcliffe students may concentrate in Engineering
Sciences with an environmental sciences emphasis. Courses on
environmental topics are offered by the Departments of Biology,
Economics, Earth and Planetary Sciences, and the Division of
Applied Sciences. Graduate students may also take degrees in
Engineering Sciences with an environmental emphasis, and
Harvard also offers a one year program in Forest Sciences
located at the Harvard Forest in Petersham.

Massachusetts Institute of Technology, Rm. 3-234,
Cambridge 02139 (617, 253-7753)

Environmental Council: c/o DR. LOUIS MENAND, Office of the
Provost

Northeastern University, Department of Health, Sport, and
Leisure Studies, 360 Huntington Ave., Boston 02115
(617, 437-2000)

Vertebrate Ecology and Systematics (B.S., M.S., Ph.D.), DR. GWI-
LYM S. JONES, Curator, Museum of Natural History (437-
2851)

Salt Marsh Ecology (B.S., M.S., Ph.D.), DR. ERNEST RUBER (437-
2260)

Marine Biology (B.S., M.S., Ph.D.), DR. KENNETH SEBENS, Director,
Marine Science and Maritime Studies Center (581-7370)

Outdoor Recreation/Education (B.S., M.S.,Ed.D.), GEORGE ATKIN-
SON, Program Coordinator (437-3153)

Tufts University, Medford 02155 (617, 381-3211)

Environmental Engineering, Environmental Health, and Hazardous
Materials Management Programs (Civil Engineering Depart-
ment) (M.S.), and joint programs with Department of Urban and
Environmental Policy

LINFIELD C. BROWN, Chair

University of Massachusetts, Amherst 01003 (413, 545-
2665) DR. DONALD G. ARGANBRIGHT, Head

Educational Programs: Wildlife and Fisheries Biology (B.S., M.S.,
Ph.D.); Natural Resource Studies (B.S.); Forestry (B.S., M.S.,
Ph.D.); Wood Science and Technology (B.S., M.S., Ph.D.); U.S.
Fish and Wildlife Service

Coopertative Fishery Research Unit: DR. HENRY BOOKE, Leader
(545-2757); DR. BOYD KYNARD, Assistant Leader

Cooperative Wildlife Research Unit: DR. REBECCA FIELD, Leader
(545-2757)

U.S. Forest Service Cooperative Wildlife Research Unit: DR. RICH-
ARD M. DEGRAAF, Leader (549-0520)

Landscape Architecture and Regional Planning: DR. MEIR GROSS,
Head (545-2255)

Landscape Architecture Program: DR. ANN MARSTON (545-
2255)

Regional Planning Program: DR. LARRY KLAR (545-2255)

Arboriculture and Park Management: H. DENNIS RYAN (545-
2255)

Environmental Design Program: DR. JOHN AHERN (545-2222)

Williams College, Box 632, Williamstown 01267 (413, 597-
2346)

Center for Environmental Studies, Coordinate Program: DAVID P.
DETHIER, Director (Acting)

MICHIGAN

Central Michigan University, Department of Biology, Mt.
Pleasant 48859 (517, 774-3227)

Fisheries (B.S., M.S.), DR. HERBERT L. LENON (Ext. 3531)

Wildlife (B.S., M.S.), DR. JOHN N. KRULL (Ext. 3412)

Eastern Michigan University, Ypsilanti 48197 (313, 487-
1849)

Biology (B.S., M.S.), DR. HERBERT H. CASWELL, JR., Head (487-
4242)

Ecosystems Biology Concentration: DR. PATRICK C. KANGAS,
Advisor, Undergraduate Program (487-1174); DR. DALE C.
WALLACE, Advisor, Graduate Program (484-0212)

Conservation, Resource Use: DR. PATRICK C. KANGAS (487-
1174)

Kresge Environmental Education Center: BEN CZINSKI, Resident
Manager (664-1461)

Co-op Forestry Program: DR. PATRICK C. KANGAS (487-1174)

Geography and Geology (B.S., M.S.), DR. ELWOOD J. C. KURETH, Head (487-0218)

Ferris State University, Big Rapids 49307 (616, 592-2307)
Industrial and Environmental Health Management (B.S.), GEORGE J. HENSLEY, Program Director

Michigan State University, East Lansing 48824 (517, 355-1855)
Forestry (B.S., M.S., Ph.D.)
Park and Recreation Resources (B.S., M.S., Ph.D.), DR. PHYLLIS FORD, Chairperson
Fisheries and Wildlife (B.S., M.S., Ph.D.), DR. NILES R. KEVERN, Chairperson
Resource Development (B.S., M.S., Ph.D.), DR. JON BARTHOLIC, Chairperson

Michigan Technological University, School of Forestry and Wood Products, Houghton 49931 (906, 487-2454)
Forestry (B.S., M.S., Ph.D.), W.E. FRAYER, Dean
Undergraduate concentrations and graduate programs in forest management science, forest biology and ecology, wildlife biology and ecology, wood and fiber utilization.

Northern Michigan University, Marquette 49855 (906, 227-2500)
Department of Geography Earth Science, Conservation, and Planning (B.A., B.S., M.A.T.), D. ALFRED N. JOYAL III, Head

University of Michigan, Ann Arbor 48109-1115 (313, 764-2550)
Resource Ecology and Management (B.S.F., M.F., Ph.D.), BURTON V. BARNES, Coordinator
Resource Policy and Behavior (B.S., M.S., Ph.D.), STEVEN L. YAFFEE, Coordinator
Landscape Architecture and Planning (B.S.L.A., M.L.A.), TERRY J. BROWN, Coordinator
Urban, Technological and Environmental Planning (Ph.D.), KAN CHEN, Director

Wayne State University, Detroit 48202 (313, 577-2876)
Department of Biological Sciences (B.A., B.S., M.S., Ph.D.), ALBERT SIEGEL, Interim Chair Chairman
Courses offered in such subjects as Limnology, Bioecology, Ornithology, Mammalogy, Natural Resource Management, Biogeography, Natural History of Vertebrates, Animal Behavior, Population Genetics, Population Ecology, Microbial Ecology, Aquatic Plants, Phycology

Western Michigan University, Kalamazoo 49008 (616, 387-2716)
Environmental Studies Program (An interdisciplinary under graduate program which is designed to provoke thought about humanity, our relationship to society and to the natural environment): DR. JOHN COOLEY, Director
Institute of Public Affairs (Provides interdisciplinary research, technical assistance, and educational programs for Government agencies and community organizations): RUDY ZIEHL, Director
Science for Citizens Center (Facilitates interaction between citizens and scientists in developing programs which meet the scientific and technological information needs of citizens and their communities; assists citizens and citizen groups reach informed decisions and participate in the policymaking process on science-related issues): DR. DONALD J. BROWN, Director

MINNESOTA

Bemidji State University, Bemidji 56601 (755-2000)
Center for Environmental Studies (B.S., M.A.), STEVEN A. SPIGARELLI, Director (755-2910)
The Center for Environmental Studies, founded in 1968, is a research and teaching unit directed to understanding our physical, biological, and social environment, and to preventing its deterioration. The center conducts laboratory and field studies, both internally and externally funded, and offers baccalaureate and master's degree programs.

University of Minnesota, St. Paul 55108 (612, 624-1234)
College of Natural Resources (B.S., M.F., M.S., Ph.D.), DR. RICHARD A. SKOK, Dean
Department of Forest Products (B.S., M.S., Ph.D.), DR. JAMES BOWYER, Head (624-4292)
Department of Forest Resources (B.S., M.F., M.S., Ph.D.), DR. ALAN R. EK, Head (624-3400)
Recreation Resource Management Curriculum (B.S.), DR. TIMOTHY B. KNOPP, Coordinator (624-3400)
Department of Fisheries and Wildlife (B.S., M.S., Ph.D.), DR. IRA L. ADELMAN, Head (624-3600)
Office of Student Affairs: JOHN V. BELL, Assistant Dean (M.S.) (624-6768)

University of Minnesota Technical College, Crookston 56716 (218, 281-6510)
Offers broadly-oriented natural resource majors which prepare students for entry level technician positions after two years of study. Practical and field instruction is emphasized leading to an Associate of Applied Sciences degree.
Natural Resources Conservation, and Park and Recreational Area Management: DANIEL SVEDARSKY, Head; PHILIP BAIRD; THOMAS FEIRO

MISSISSIPPI

Mississippi State University, Drawer FR, Mississippi State 39762 (601, 325-2952)
Forest Resources (B.S., M.S., M.F., Ph.D.), DR. WARREN S. THOMPSON, Dean
Fisheries (B.S., M.S., Ph.D.), DR. ROBERT D. BROWN, Head (325-2615)
Forestry (B.S., M.S., M.F., Ph.D.), DR. DOUGLAS P. RICHARDS, Head (325-2948)
Wildlife (M.S., Ph.D.), DR. ROBERT D. BROWN, Head (325-2615)
Wood Science and Technology (B.S., M.S., Ph.D.), DR. MICHAEL E. HITTMEIER, Head (325-2119)

University of Southern Mississippi, Hattiesburg 39401 (601, 266-7011)
Aquatic Biology (M.S., Ph.D.), DR. GORDON GODSHALK
Aquatic Ecology: DR. JEAN W. WOOTEN; DR. FREDDIE G. HOWELL
Fisheries Biology (M.S., Ph.D.), DR. STEPHEN T. ROSS
Marine Biology (M.S., Ph.D.), DR. R. S. PREZANT; DR. JAMES B. LARSEN; DR. GARY ANDERSON
Zoology (M.S., Ph.D.), DR. J.W. CLIBURN
Recreation Planning and Resources Management (B.S., M.S.), DR. L. CHARLES BURCHELL
Resource Management and Environmental Planning (B.S., M.S., Ph.D.), DR. ROBERT W. WALES

MISSOURI

University of Missouri, Columbia 65211 (314, 882-6446)
School of Forestry, Fisheries and Wildlife (B.S., M.S., Ph.D.), DR. ALBERT R. VOGT, Director; DR. JOHN R. JONES, Director of Graduate Studies (882-3543)
Cooperative Fish and Wildlife/Research Unit: DR. CHARLES RABENI, Leader (882-3524); DR. RONALD DROBNEY, Assistant Leader, Wildlife (882-9420)

MONTANA

Montana State University, Department of Biology, Bozeman 59717 (406, 994-4548)
Fish and Wildlife Program (B.S., M.S., Ph.D.)
Program Director: DR. ROBERT L. ENG
Assistant Director: DR. HAROLD PICTON
Cooperative Fishery Research Unit: DR. ROBERT G. WHITE, Leader; DR. WILLIAM R. GOULD III, Assistant Leader
Wildlife (B.S., M.S., Ph.D.), DR. ROBERT L. ENG

University of Montana, Missoula 59812 (406, 243-5521)
Forestry (B.S., B.S.R.C., M.S., M.S.R.C., M.F., Ph.D.), DR. SIDNEY FRISSELL, Dean
Forestry Recreation (B.S., M.S.)
Range Management (B.S., M.S.)
Wildlife Biology Program (B.S., M.S.), DR. LEE METZGAR, Director
Montana Forest and Conservation Experiment Station: DR. SIDNEY FRISSELL, Director
Mission Oriented Research Program: DR. ROBERT PFISTER, Director (243-6582)

University of Montana School of Law, Missoula 59812
Dean: J MARTIN BURKE

NEBRASKA

University of Nebraska, Institute of Agriculture and Natural Resources, Lincoln 68583 (402, 472-7211)
Range Management (B.S., M.S., Ph.D.), JAMES STUBBENDIECK, 349 Keim Hall (472-1519); CHARLES BUTTERFIELD, 333 Keim Hall (472-1583); LOWELL E. MOSER, 352 Keim Hall (472-1558); BRUCE ANDERSON, 353 Keim Hall (472-6237); STEVEN S. WALLER, 347 Keim Hall (472-1541); ROBERT MASTERS, 362 Plant Science (472-1546); JAMES T. NICHOLS, JOSEPH BRUMMER, West Central Research and Extension Center, North Platte 69101 (308, 532-3611); PAT REECE, Panhandle Research and Extension Center, Scottsbluff 69361 (308, 632-1242)
Wildlife Management (B.S., M.S., Ph.D.), RONALD M. CASE, 204 Natural Resources Hall (472-6825); BOB KUZELKA, 110 Plant Industry (472-7527); RONNIE J. JOHNSON, 202 Natural Resources Hall (472-6823); JULIE SAVIDGE, 202 Natural Resources Hall (472-2043); SCOTT HYGNSTROM, 202 Natural Resources (472-6822)
Fisheries Management (B.S., M.S., Ph.D.), EDWARD PETERS, 203 Natural Resources Hall (472-6824); GARY HERGENRADER, 103 Plant Industry (472-1467)
Forestry: MICHAEL KUHNS, 107 Plant Industry (472-5822); JAMES BRANDLE, 002 Plant Industry (472-6626); STEVEN ERNST, 104 Plant Industry (472-6633); STEVEN RASMUSSEN, North East Research and Extension Center, Concord 68728 (402, 584-2261); WILLIAM LOVETT, 12 Plant Industry (472-6640); DOAK NICKERSON, Panhandle Research and Extension Center, Scottsbluff 69361-0224 (308, 632-1238); DENNIS ADAMS, Southeast Research and Extension Center,

Lincoln 68583-0714 (472-3645); SCOTT DEWALD, South-central Research and Extension Center, Clay Center 68933-0066 (402, 762-3535); MARK HARRELL, 007 Plant Industry (472-6635); RICH LODES, Southeast Research and Extension Center, Lincoln 68583-0714 (472-3645); DAVE MOOTER, Southeast Research and Extension Center, Lincoln 68583 (444-7804); JON WILSON, Westcentral Research and Extension Center, North Platte 69101-9495 (308, 532-3611); RICH STRAIGHT, Lower Loup, NRD, Ord 68862-0210 (308, 728-3221); TOM SCHMIDT, 12 Plant Industry (472-6637); TOM WARDLE, 12 Plant Industry (472-6636)

NEVADA

University of Nevada, 1000 Valley Rd., Reno 89512 (702, 784-4000)
Department of Range, Wildlife and Forestry: DR. GERALD F. GIFFORD, Chairman
Forestry (B.S., M.S.), DR. LEON J. BUIST; DR. ROGER F. WALKER
Wildlife Management (B.S., M.S.), DR. JOEL BERGER
Range Management (B.S., M.S.), DR. ROBERT NOWAK; DR. J. WAYNE BURKHARDT; DR. SHERMAN R. SWANSON; DR. ROBIN J. TAUSCH; DR. PAUL T. TUELLER; DR. FREDERICK F. PETERSON
Interdisciplinary Hydrology (B.S., M.S., Ph.D.), DR. JOHN C. GUITJENS; DR. GERALD F. GIFFORD; DR. WATKINS W. MILLER; CLARE N. MAHANNAH

NEW HAMPSHIRE

Antioch Univeresity (New England Graduate School), 103 Roxbury St., Keene 03431 (603, 357-3122)
The Antioch/New England Graduate School offers innovative programs in Environmental Studies and Resource Management and Administration. The M.S.T. degree in Environmental Studies is a field-oriented program that stresses professional preparation in natural history, teaching, communication, and administration. Elementary education, biology, and general science certifications are available. The M.S. degree in Resource Management and Administration integrates environmental science, natural resources policy, and administration. Students are prepared for policy positions in the environmental field.
Department of Environmental Studies, Co-Chairpersons: DR. TY MINTON; DR. MITCHELL THOMASHOW

University of New Hampshire, Durham 03824
Department of Forest Resources (603, 862-1020) HAROLD HOCKER, Chairman
Wildlife Ecology (B.S., M.S.), DR. WILLIAM MAUTZ, Program Coordinator
Forest Resources (B.S., M.S.), DR. TED HOWARD, Program Coordinator
Environmental Conservation (B.S.), DR. JOHN CARROLL, Program Coordinator
Soil Science (B.S., M.S.), DR. ROBERT HARTER, Program Coordinator
Water Resources Management (B.S.) DR. W.B. BOWDEN, Program Coordinator

NEW JERSEY

Glassboro State College, Glassboro 08028 (609, 863-7347)
Conservation and Environmental Education (M.A.), GARY PATTERSON, Advisor
Pinelands Institute for Natural and Environmental Studies, (P.I.N.E.S.) of Glassboro State College, GARY PATTERSON,

COLLEGES AND UNIVERSITIES IN THE UNITED STATES AND CANADA

Director, 120-13 Whitesbog Rd., Browns Mills 08015 (893-1765)

Montclair State College, Upper Montclair 07043 (201, 893-5258)
Environmental Studies (M.A.), DR. W. AUGUSTUS RENTSCH, Student Advisor; DR. DAVID K. ROBERTSON, Director

Rutgers University, Cook College, P.O. Box 231, New Brunswick 08903 (201, 932-9236)
Forestry (B.S., M.S.), DR. LEONARD J. WOLGAST, Head
Agriculture, Environmental Sciences, Conservation, Wildlife Fisheries Science (B.S., M.S., Ph.D.), DR. IAN MAW, Director of Resident, Instruction
Landscape Architecture (B.S.), PROF. ROY H. DeBOER, Head
Wildlife (B.S., M.S., Ph.D.), DR. LEONARD J. WOLGAST

Stockton State College, Pomona 08240 (609, 652-1776)
Conferences, Seminars, and Community Services: MICHAEL ROSE, Director (Ext. 4607)
Division of Natural Sciences and Mathematics: DONALD PLANK (Ext. 4546)
Biology (B.A., B.S.), ROSALIND HERLANDS, Program Coordinator
Chemistry (B.A., B.S.), ED PAUL, Program Coordinator
Environmental Studies (B.A., B.S.), GEORGE ZIMMERMANN, Program Coordinator
Marine Science (B.A., B.S.), STU FARRELL, Program Coordinator

NEW MEXICO

New Mexico State University, Head, Fishery and Wildlife Sciences, Box 30003, Dept. 4901, Las Cruces 88003 (505, 646-1544)
Range Science (B.S., M.S., Ph.D.), Dept. of Animal and Range Sciences: DR. BOBBY J. RANKIN, Department Head (646-2514); DR. KIRK McDANIEL (646-1191); DR. JERRY L. HOLECHEK (646-1649); DR. M. KARL WOOD (646-1041); DR. CHRIS ALLISON (646-1944); DR. REX D. PIEPER (646-4435); DR. RELDON F. BECK (646-3537); DR. GARY B. DONART (646-2518); DR. KELLY ALLRED (646-1042)
Fishery & Wildlife Sciences (B.S., M.S.), DR. CHARLES A. DAVIS, Department Head (646-1544); DR. RICHARD A. COLE (646-1346); DR. VOLNEY W. HOWARD, JR. (646-1217); DR. JAMES E. KNIGHT (646-1164); DR. S.D. SCHEMNITZ (646-1136); DR. ROBERT TAFANELLI (646-1929); DR. PAUL R. TURNER (646-1707); DR. RAUL VALDEZ (646-3719)

NEW YORK

Cornell University, Ithaca 14853 (607, 2556-1000/255-2298)
Department of Natural Resources (B.S., M.S., Ph.D.), DR. JAMES P. LASSOIE, Chairman
Fisheries and Aquatic Sciences: DR. WILLIAM YOUNGS (255-5469)
Environmental Conservation and Ethics: DR. RICHARD A. BAER (255-7797)
Forest Science: DR. JAMES P. LASSOIE (255-2298)
Wildlife Science: DR. AARON N. MOEN (255-3182)
Natural Resources Extension: DR. DANIEL J. DECKER (255-2114)

Rachel Carson College, State University of New York at Buffalo, Buffalo 14261 (716, 636-2245)
An undergraduate, interdisciplinary, academic, and residential program in environmental studies and activities.
Director of the College: LEE S. DRYDEN, Ph.D. (636-2245)

State University, College of Environmental Science and Forestry, Syracuse 13210
President: ROSS S. WHALEY (315, 470-6681)
Regional Campuses: Cranberry Lake 12927; Newcomb 12852; Tully 13159; Wanakena 13695; Warrensburg 12885
Faculty of Landscape Architecture (B.L.A., M.L.A.), RICHARD HAWKS, Chair (470-6541)
Faculty of Paper Science and Engineering (B.S., M.S., Ph.D.), LELAND R. SCHROEDER, Chair (470-6502)
Faculty of Environmental Studies (B.S., M.S., Ph.D.), ROBERT D. HENNIGAN, Chair (470-6636)
Faculty of Wood Products Engineering (B.S., M.S., Ph.D.), LEONARD A. SMITH, Chair (470-6880)
Faculty of Forest Engineering (B.S., M.S., Ph.D.), ROBERT H. BROCK, JR., Chair (470-6633)
Faculty of Chemistry (B.S., M.S., Ph.D.), ANATOLE SARKO, Chair (470-6824)
Faculty of Environmental and Forest Biology (B.S., M.S., Ph.D.), ROBERT L. BURGESS, Chair (470-6741)
Faculty of Forestry (B.S., M.S., Ph.D.), B.G. BLACKMON, Chair (470-6536)
Forest Technician Program (A.A.S.), RICHARD W. MILLER, Director (848-2566)
Office of Nonresident Programs: ROBERT C. KOEPPER, Dean (470-6891)
Adirondack Ecological Center: WILLIAM F. PORTER, Director (470-6798)
Empire State Paper Research Institute: LELAND SCHROEDER, Director (470-6502)
Polymer Research Institute: ISRAEL CABASSO, Director (470-6857)
N.C. Brown Laboratory for Ultrastructure Studies: WILFRED A. COTE, JR., Director (470-6877)
U.S. Forest Service Unit: ROWAN ROWNTREE, Project Leader (470-6729)
Cellulose Research Institute: TORE E. TIMELL, Director (470-6851)
Institute of Environmental Policy and Planning: RICHARD C. SMARDON, Director (470-6576)
Great Lakes Research Consortium:
Co-Directors: RICHARD C. SMARDON; ROBERT G. WERNER (470-6804)

State University of New York at Cortland, Cortland 13045 (607, 753-2011) JAMES M. CLARK, President
Recreation and Environmental Interpretation: DR. ANDERSON B. YOUNG, Chair (753-4941)
Environmental Sciences concentration for majors in Biology, Geology, Chemistry, or Physics: DR. HUBERT KEEN, Coordinator (753-2716)

State University of New York at Buffalo, Research Program in Environment and Society, Department of Sociology, 470A Park Hall, SUNY Buffalo, Amherst 14261 (716, 636-2595)
Conducts research focusing on the relationship between environment and society. Special expertise in studies of environmental beliefs, values, perceptions, opinions, attitudes. The Program also conducts research on Environmental Policy, Planning and Management and on Quality of Life; advises local, regional and state agencies on matters relating to Environmental Management and Quality of Life; acts as a center for academic and citizen information on Environmental Policy and Management, and Quality of Life research.
Director: DR. LESTER W. MILBRATH (636-2595)
Co-Director: DR. RUSSELL STONE (636-2441)

NORTH CAROLINA

Duke University, Durham 27706 (919, 684-2421)
School of Forestry and Environmental Studies (graduate programs only) (M.F., M.E.M., A.M., M.S., Ph.D.), DR. GEORGE F. DU-TROW, Dean
Forest Resource Management: DR. WILLIAM J. STAMBAUGH
Resource Ecology: DR. CURTIS J. RICHARDSON
Ecotoxicology: DR. RICHARD T. DiGIULIO
Water Resources: DR. KENNETH H. RECKHOW
Air Resources: DR. KENNETH R. KNOERR
Resource Economics and Policy: DR. ROBERT G. HEALY

North Carolina State University, Campus Box 7617, Raleigh 27695-7617 (919, 737-2741)
Cooperative Fish and Wildlife Unit: MELVIN T. HUISH, Leader, Raleigh 27695-7617 (737-2631)
Forestry (B.S., M.S., Ph.D.), DR. ART COOPER, Head, Raleigh 27695-8002 (737-2891)
Recreation Resources Administration (B.S., M.S.), DR. P.S. REA, Head, Raleigh 27695-8004 (737-3276)
Conservation (B.S.), DR. H. JOSEPH KLEISS, Raleigh 27695-7619 (737-2643); DR. LEROY C. SAYLOR, Coordinator, Raleigh 27695-8001 (737-2883)
Fisheries and Wildlife Sciences (B.S., M.S., Ph.D.), RICHARD L. NOBLE, Coordinator
Landscape Architecture (E.D.L., M.LAR.), ARTHUR SULLIVAN, Head, Raleigh 27695-7701 (739-2204)

University of North Carolina, Chapel Hill 27599 (919, 962-2211)
Institute for Environmental Studies: DR. RICHARD N.L. ANDREWS, Director (966-2358)
Environmental Sciences and Engineering: DR. WILLIAM H. GLAZE, Chairman (966-1171)
Air and Industrial Hygiene: DR. DAVID LEITH (966-3851)
Environmental Chemistry and Biology: DR. FREDERIC K. PFAEN-DER (966-3842)
Environmental Management and Protection: DR. ALVIS G. TURNER (966-3850)
Water Resources Engineering: DR. PHILIP C. SINGER (966-3865)
Ecology (M.S., Ph.D.), DR. SETH R. REICE, Chairman (962-1270)
Marine Sciences: DR. DIRK FRANKENBERG, Chairman (962-1252)

NORTH DAKOTA

North Dakota State University, Stevens Hall, Fargo 58105 (701, 237-7087)
Wildlife and Fisheries Biology Option in Zoology (B.S., B.A., M.S., Ph.D.), DR. J.W. GRIER; DR. J.J. PETERKA; DR. G. NUECHTER-LEIN, Advisors

University of North Dakota, Grand Forks 58202 (701, 777-2621)
Fishery Research Unit (B.S., M.S., Ph.D.), DR. BRUCE A. BARTON, Leader
Wildlife (B.S., M.S., Ph.D.), DR. RICHARD D. CRAWFORD, Coordinator

OHIO

Antioch College, Yellow Springs 45387 (513, 767-7331)
Biology: ROBERT BIERI; WALTER TULECKE
Geology: PETER TOWNSEND; WALT TULECKE
Environmental Studies: ROBERT BIERI; PETER TOWNSEND; WALT TULECKE

Environmental Interpretation: RALPH RAMEY
Chemistry: KAREN BRITO
Physics and Solar Energy/Alternative Technology: CHARLES TAY-LOR

Bowling Green State University, Bowling Green 43403 (419, 372-8207)
Environmental Baccalaureate Programs (B.S.), Education (Environmental Education)
(B.S.) Arts and Sciences (Environmental Science)
(B.S.) Health and Human Services (Environmental Health) (B.A.) Arts and Sciences (Environmental Policy and Analysis) THOMAS B. COBB, Director, Center for Environmental Programs
Undergraduate Environmental Programs and Services: JUSTINE MAGSIG, Assistant Director and Program Advisor, Center for Environmental Programs

Miami University, 122 Boyd Hall, Oxford 45056 (513, 529-5811)
Institute of Environmental Sciences (M.E.S.), GENE E. WILLEKE, Director
Architecture (B.E.D., M.A.), ROBERT ZWIRN, Department Chairman
Geography (A.B., M.A., M.A.T.), RICHARD V. SMITH, Department Chairman
Botany (A.B., B.S., M.A., M.S., M.A.T., Ph.D.), ROY C. BROWN, Department Chairman
Chemistry (A.B., B.S., M.S., Ph.D.), JAMES A. COX, Department Chairman
Zoology (A.B., B.S., M.A., M.S., Ph.D.), ROBERT SHERMAN, Department Chairman

Ohio State University, 2021 Coffey Rd., Columbus 43210 (614, 292-2265)
School of Natural Resources (B.S., M.S., Ph.D.), DR. JOHN F. DISINGER, Director (Acting)
Cooperative Wildlife and Fishery Research Unit (B.S., M.S., Ph.D.), DR. THEODORE A. BOOKHOUT, Leader
Dept. of Landscape Architecture (B.L.A., M.L.A.), DOUGLAS S. WAY, Chairman
Dept. of Zoology, College of Biological Sciences Fisheries Biology (B.S., M.S., Ph.D)
Wildlife Biology (B.S., M.S., Ph.D.), DR. JOHN L. CRITES, Chairman

Shawnee State University, 940 Second St., Portsmouth 45662 (614, 354-3205)
Natural Science (B.S.)
Recreation Leadership (A.A.S.), DAVID TODT, Coordinator (355-2239)
Pre-Forestry (A.A. or A.I.S.), DR. PAUL CRABTREE, Advisor (355-2251)
Health, Physical Education and Recreation (A.A.), HARRY WEIN-BRECHT, Head (355-2219)

University of Akron, Akron 44325 (216, 375-7991/657-2815)
Center for Environmental Studies: Interdisciplinary program involves (B.S., M.S.) in Arts and Sciences, Engineering, Education: DR. JIM L. JACKSON, Director

OKLAHOMA

Oklahoma State University, Stillwater 74074 (405, 624-5000)
Cooperative Fishery Unit: DR. EUGENE MAUGHAN, Leader
Wildlife (B.S., M.S. Ph.D.), Vacant

Cooperative Wildlife Research Unit: DR. EUGENE MAUGHAN, Leader (Acting)
Wildlife (B.S., M.S., Ph.D.)
Range Management (B.S., M.S., Ph.D.), DR. PAUL SANTELMANN, Head; Agronomy-Range Management (B.S., M.S., Ph.D.), DR. STANLEY B. CARPENTER, Head, Forestry (B.S., M.S.)

OREGON

Northwestern School of Law, Lewis and Clark College, 10015 SW Terwilliger Blvd., Portland 97219
Dean: STEPHEN KANTER (503, 244-1181/Ext. 600); MARY E. KING, Editor-in-Chief, Environmental Law (503, 244-1181/Ext. 701)

Oregon State University, Corvallis 97331 (503, 754-0123)
Cooperative Fishery Research Unit: DR. CARL B. SCHRECK, Leader
Forestry, including Forest Recreation (B.S., M.S., Ph.D.), DR. CARL H. STOLTENBERG, Dean
Fisheries and Wildlife (B.S., M.S., Ph.D.), DR. RICHARD A. TUBB, Head
Cooperative Wildlife Research Unit: DR. E. CHARLES MESLOW, Leader
Rangeland Resources (B.S., M.S., Ph.D.), DR. WILLIAM KRUEGER, Head

University of Oregon School of Law, Eugene 97403 (503, 686-3823)
Dean: MAURICE J. HOLLAND
Western Natural Resources Law Clinic Directors: MICHAEL D. AXLINE; JOHN E. BONINE

PENNSYLVANIA

Drexel University, Philadelphia 19104 (215, 895-2000)
Civil Engineering (Water Resources) (M.S.), Environmental Studies Institute, HERBERT E. ALLEN, Director
Environmental Engineering (M.S., Ph.D.)
Environmental Science (B.S., M.S., Ph.D.)
For Environmental Engineering and Science, specialized study is available in Air Pollution Control, Water Quality Control, Hazardous Wastes Technology, Occupational Health, Environmental Toxicology, Environmental Health, Environmental Planning and Management, Environmental Chemistry, and Environmental Assessment.

Pennsylvania State University, University Park 16802
Forest Resources (B.S., M.S., M.F.R., Ph.D.), DR. ALFRED D. SULLIVAN, Director, 102 Ferguson Bldg. (814, 865-7541)
Landscape Architecture (B.S.), DR. NEIL PORTERFIELD, Head, 210 Engineering Unit D (865-9511)
Environmental Pollution Control (M.S., M.E.P.C., M. ENG.), DR. RICHARD F. UNZ, Chairman, 226 Fenske Laboratory (865-1415)
Civil Engineering, Environmental Engineering (B.S., M.S.), DR. MICHAEL S. BRONZINI, Head, 212 Sackett Bldg. (865-8391)
Environmental Resource Management (B.S.), DR. HERSCHEL ELLIOTT, Coordinator, 213 Ferguson Bldg. (865-6942)
Ecology (M.S., Ph.D.), DR. EDWARD BELLIS, Chairman, 311 Mueller Laboratory (865-3942)
Earth Sciences (B.S.), DR. CHARLES THORNTON, 540 Deike Bldg. (865-7791)
Wildlife Science (B.S.), DR. ROBERT BROOKS, 319 Forest Resources (863-1596)

Slippery Rock University, Slippery Rock 16057 (412, 794-2510)
Parks and Recreation (B.S., M.S.), DR. J.W. SHINER, Chairman
Environmental Sciences (B.S.), DR. W.G. SAYRE, Program Director
Environmental Studies (B.S.), DR. BEVERLY BUCHERT, Coordinator
Environmental Education (B.S., M.Ed.), DR. CRAIG CHASE, Coordinator

University of Pennsylvania, Department of Landscape Architecture and Regional Planning, Philadelphia 19104-6311 (215, 898-6591)
Landscape Architecture (M.L.A., Ph.D.); Regional Planning (M.R.P., Ph.D.), ANNE WHISTON SPIEN, Chairman

University of Pittsburgh, Pittsburgh 15260 (412, 624-4141)
Ecology (M.S., Ph.D.), Pymatuning Laboratory of Ecology, Linesville, DR. RICHARD T. HARTMAN, Director; DR. ALBERT E. CHUNG, Chairman, Dept. Biological Sciences
Environmental Health (M.P.H., M.S., D.Sc.), DR. RAYMOND SELTSER, Dean, Graduate School of Public Health

Wilkes College, Wilkes-Barre 18766
Department of Earth and Environmental Sciences
The department offers degree programs and conducts research in both the earth (meteorology, geology, oceanography, and astronomy) and environmental (air and water quality, hydrology, and land use) sciences. DR. JAMES BOHNING, Chairman (717, 824-4651 Ext. 4614)

RHODE ISLAND

Brown University, Providence 02912 (401, 863-3449)
HAROLD R. WARD, Director, Center for Environmental Studies

Rhode Island School of Design, Providence 02903 (401, 331-3511)
Landscape Architecture (B.L.A.), emphasis in Design and Cultural Land Use Planning: MICHAEL EVERETT, Head

University of Rhode Island, Department of Natural Resources Science, Kingston 02881 (401, 792-2495)
Wildlife (M.S.), DR. WILLIAM R. WRIGHT, Chairman

SOUTH CAROLINA

Clemson University, Clemson 29634-0919 (803, 656-5572)
Environmental Engineering (M.Engr., M.S., Ph.D.), DR. T.M. KEINATH, Head
Forestry (M.F., M.S., Ph.D.), DR. MICHAEL A. TARAS, Head
Wildlife and Fisheries Biology (M.S.), DR. D. LAMAR ROBINETTE, Head

University of South Carolina, Columbia 29208 (803, 777-2692)
Marine Science Program (B.S., M.S., Ph.D.), DR. BRUCE C. COULL, Director
Baruch Institute Field Laboratory: DR. DENNIS M. ALLEN, Assistant Director, P.O. Box 1630, Georgetown 29442 (546-3623)
Belle W. Baruch Institute for Marine Biology and Coastal Research: DR. F. JOHN VERNBERG, Director (777-5288)

SOUTH DAKOTA

South Dakota State University, P.O. Box 2206, Brookings 57007-1696 (605, 688-6121)
Cooperative Fish and Wildlife Research Unit: DR. CHARLES R. BERRY, Leader
Wildlife and Fisheries Sciences (B.S., M.S.), DR. CHARLES G. SCALET, Head

TENNESSEE

Tennessee Technological University, Cookeville 38505 (615, 528-3013)
Wildlife Management (B.S.)
Wildlife and Fisheries Biology (M.S.), DR. WINSTON SMITH; DR. ERIC L. MORGAN; DR. M.J. HARVEY; DR. R. DON ESTES; DR. JAMES LAYZER
Tech Aqua Biological Station: DR. C.B. COBURN, JR.

University of the South, Sewanee 37375 (615, 598-5931)
Natural Resources (B.S.), PROF. D. BRANDRETH POTTER, Chairman, Dept. of Forestry and Geology

University of Tennessee, Knoxville 37901 (615, 974-7126)
Forestry, Wildlife and Fisheries Science (B.S., M.S.), DR. GEORGE T. WEAVER, Head
Ecology (M.S., Ph.D.), DR. DEWEY L. BUNTING, Director

Vanderbilt University, Box 6304-Station B, Nashville 37235 (615, 322-2697)
Environmental and Water Resources Engineering (B.E., B.S., M.E., M.S., Ph.D.), EDWARD L. THACKSTON, Chairman

TEXAS

University of North Texas, Institute of Applied Sciences, NT Box 13078, Denton 76203 (817, 565-2694)
A research unit in the Department of Biological Sciences whose primary research activities are oriented towards land and water resources. Research includes aquatic toxicology, surface and ground water quality, archeology, remote sensing, and geographic information systems. Over 100 scientists, support staff, and graduate and undergraduate students are involved in these activities. DR. KENNETH L. DICKSON, Director, IAS; DR. JOHN RODGERS, Associate Director, IAS, Program Director, Environmental Systems; DR. FARIDA SALEH, Program Director, Trace Analysis Laboratory/Research Scientist; DR. REID FERRING, Program Director, Archaeology/Research Scientist; DR. KATHLEEN GILMORE, Archaeology Research Scientist; DR. SAMUEL F. ATKINSON, Program Director, Remote Sensing and GIS/ Research Scientist

Rice University, Houston 77251 (713, 527-8101)
Environmental Science and Engineering (B.A., M.E.S., M.E.E., M.S., Ph.D.), C.H. WARD, Chairman
Biology (B.S., M.A., Ph.D.), RAYMOND GLANTZ, Chairman (B.A., B. Arch., M. Arch., M. Arch. in Urban Design, D. Arch.), School of Architecture, O. JACK MITCHELL, Dean

Stephen F. Austin State University, School of Forestry, Nacogdoches 75962-6109 (409, 568-3301) (B.S.F., M.S., M.S.F., D.F., Ph.D. all programs)
Forestry (Ph.D.), DR. KENT T. ADAIR, Dean
Forest Recreation Management (Ph.D) DR. MICHAEL LEGG
Forest Game Management (Ph.D.), DR. JAMES C. KROLL
Wood Science (D.F.), DR. MALCOLM MacPEAK
Forest Fire Management (Ph.D.), DR. HERSHEL C. REEVES

Environmental Science (Ph.D.), DR. KENNETH WATTERSON
Forest Pest Management (Ph.D.), DR. DAVID KULHAVY
Forest Hydrology (Ph.D.), DR. MINGTEH CHANG
Conservation Education, DAVID KNOTTS, Coordinator
Forest Ecology, DR. M. VICTOR BILAN
Biometrics, DR. DAVID LENHART

Texas A & M University, College Station 77843 (713, 845-3711)
Forest Sciences (B.S., M.S., M. Agr., Ph.D.), DR. J. CHARLES LEE, Head
Range Science (B.S., M.S., M. Agr., Ph.D.), DR. J.L. SCHUSTER, Head
Recreation and Parks (B.S., M.S., M. Agr., Ph.D.), DR. THOMAS BONNICKSEN, Head
Wildlife and Fisheries Sciences (B.S., M.S., M. Agr., Ph.D.), DR. DAVID J. SCHMIDLY, Head

Texas Christian University, Fort Worth 76129 (817, 921-7271)
Environmental Sciences (B.S., M.S.), DR. LEO NEWLAND, Director

Texas Tech University, Lubbock 79409 (806, 742-2841)
Range Management (B.S.), Range Science (M.S., Ph.D.)
Wildlife Management (B.S.), Wildlife Science (M.S., Ph.D.), DR. HENRY A. WRIGHT, Chairman

University of Houston, Houston 77004 (713, 749-3171)
Environmental Engineering Program (M.S., Ph.D.), DR. DENNIS A. CLIFFORD, Program Director (Ion Exchange and Membrane Processes) (749-3171); DR. JAMES M. SYMONS, Drinking Water Treatment (749-1703); DR. JACK V. MATSON, Hazardous Waste Management (749-1348); DR. GERALD E. SPEITEL, Biological Processes & Groundwater Pollution (749-4583); DR. FRANK WORLEY, CHE Air Pollution; DR. JERRY ROGERS, CE Water Resources (749-4476); DR. OSMAN GHAZZALY, CE Permeability of Clay Liners; DR. FRANK M. TILLER, CHE Filtration and Thickening; DR. H. WILLIAM PRENGLE, JR., CHE Chemical Oxidation; DR. C. VIPULANDAN, CE Waste Encapsulation; DR. BRIAN S. MIDDLEDITCH, Biophys Organic Analysis; DR. SANFORD GAINES, Law Environmental Liability; DR. DONALD FOX, Optometry Neurotoxicology

UTAH

Utah State University, Logan 84322 (801, 750-1000)
Utah Cooperative Fishery and Wildlife Research Unit: DR. JOHN A. BISSONETTE, Leader; DR. TIM MODDE, Assistant Leader, Fisheries; DR. TOM C. EDWARDS, Assistant Leader, Wildlife; DR. CHERYL COURTNEY, Fishery Biologist
Forest Resources (B.S., M.S., Ph.D.), DR. RICHARD F. FISHER, Head
Range Science (B.S., M.S., Ph.D.), DR. JOHN C. MALECHEK, Head
Fisheries and Wildlife (B.S., M.S., Ph.D.), DR. JOSEPH A. CHAPMAN, Head
Geography (B.S.), DR. DERRICK THOM, Head
Landscape Architecture (B.L.A., M.L.A., B.S., M.S.), CRAIG JOHNSON, Head
Division of Environmental Engineering (M.S., Ph.D.), DR. RONALD CHARLES SIMS, Head
College of Natural Resources: DR. THADIS W. BOX, Dean; DR. FREDERIC H. WAGNER, Associate Dean

VERMONT

Johnson State College, Department of Environmental and Health Sciences, Johnson 05656 (802, 635-2356)
Ecology (B.S.), Wildlife Ecology and Forest Ecology: DR. JOHN WRAZEN
Aquatic Ecology: DR. ROBERT GENTER
Environmental Science (B.S.), DR. PAUL ABAJIAN
Environmental Studies (B.A.), DR. MARGARET OTTUM, Program Director
Babcock Nature Preserve: DR. JOHN WRAZEN, Director

University of Vermont, Burlington 05405 (802, 656-4280)
School of Natural Resources: DR. LAWRENCE K. FORCIER, Dean; DR. DONALD H. DEHAYES, Interium Associate Dean
Forestry (B.S., M.S.), DR. JOHN R. DONNELLY
Wildlife and Fisheries Biology Program (B.S., M.S.), DR. DAVID H. HIRTH
Recreation Management (B.S.), DR. ROBERT E. MANNING
Resource Economics (B.S.), DR. ALPHONSE H. GILBERT
Natural Resources Planning (M.S.), DR. THOMAS R. HUDSPETH
The Environmental Program: DR. CARL H. REIDEL, Director, Environmental Studies (B.S., B.A.)
Water Resources Research Center: DR. ALAN W. McINTOSH, Interium Director

Vermont Law School, Environmental Law Center, South Royalton 05068 (802, 763-8303)
Dean: DOUGLAS M. COSTLE
Environmental Law Center (M.S.L., J.D.), DR. RICHARD O. BROOKS, Director

VIRGIN ISLANDS

University of the Virgin Islands, St. Thomas 00802 (809, 776-9200)
St. Thomas Campus: Marine Biology Major (B.A., B.S.), WILLIAM MacLEAN, Ph.D., Vice-President, Academic Affairs (Ext. 1472); MARY LOU PRESSICK, Ph.D., Coordinator, Ecological Research Center, Caribbean Research Institute (Ext. 1252); FRANK L. HEIKKILA, Ed.D., Chair, Division of Science and Mathematics (Ext. 1360); TERESA TURNER, Ph.D., Coordinator, Marine Biology Program (Ext. 1215)

VIRGINIA

Ferrum College, Ferrum 24088 (703, 365-2121)
Agriculture (A.S., B.S.), agricultural education, agricultural economics, agronomy, animal science, dairy science, horticulture, and poultry science: DR. WILLIAM MOORE
Environmental Studies (A.S., B.S.), aquatic ecology, botany, environmental chemistry, environmental management, field and laboratory technician, fish and wildlife biology, forestry and wildlife services, general (pre-graduate studies sequence), pollution control, terrestrial ecology, and field zoology: DR. JOSEPH D. STOGNER
Forestry and Wildlife Services (B.S.), RONALD T. STEPHENS
Leisure Services (B.S., B.A.), THOMAS N. HICKMAN
Recreation (A.A.), DR. DEMPSY HENSLEY

Institute of Marine Science, College of William and Mary, Gloucester Point 23062 (804, 642-7000)
A state institution, founded in 1940, for providing research, advisory services, and education for the public and for state and federal agencies responsible for managing marine resources.
Dean-Director: FRANK O. PERKINS (642-7102)

Associate Director for Research: ROBERT J. BYRNE (642-7102)
Associate Dean: MAURICE P. LYNCH (642-7105)
Associate Director for Finance and Administration: PAUL V. KOEHLY (642-7003)
Assistant Directors: MICHAEL CASTAGNA (787-3280); ROBERT J. HUGGETT (642-7236); BRUCE J. NEILSON (642-7204); ROBERT J. ORTH (642-7392); L. DONELSON WRIGHT (642-7267)
Assistant to the Director: A.H. (Hank) HUMPHREYS, JR. (642-7107)
Librarian: SUSAN BARRICK (642-7114)
Advisory Services Director: WILLIAM D. DUPAUL (642-7164)
Center for the Study of Estuarine Management and Policy, Co-Directors: N. BARTLETT THEBERGE; CARL HERSHNER (642-7109)

Virginia Polytechnic Institute and State University, 324 Cheatham Hall, Attn: Peggy Quarterman, Blacksburg 24061 (703, 231-5481)
School of Forestry & Wildlife Resources: DR. JOHN F. HOSNER, Director
Department of Forestry (B.S., M.S., Ph.D.), DR. ROBERT E. ADAMS, Head (231-5482)
Department of Forest Products (B.S., M.S., Ph.D.), DR. GEZA IFJU, Head (231-5330)
Department of Fisheries and Wildlife Sciences (B.S., M.S., Ph.D.), DR. GERALD H. CROSS, Head (231-5573)
Cooperative Fish and Wildlife Unit: RICHARD J. NEVES, Leader (231-5927)
Center for Environmental Studies: DR. JOHN CAIRNS, JR., Director (231-5538)

WASHINGTON

Huxley College of Environmental Studies, Division of Western Washington University, Bellingham 98225 (206, 676-3520)
Principally a two-year, upper division program and (M.S.) program; (B.A., B.S.) Environmental Studies; (M.S., Environmental Science; also cooperative programs, (M.S.) Applied Biology; (M.S.) Behavioral Toxicology. DR. JOHN C. MILES, Dean. Undergraduate concentrations in Social Assessment and Policy, Environmental Education, Environmental Science; Graduate tracks in Wildlife Toxicology, Applied Ecology, Environmental Chemistry
Associated Research Institutes: Institute of Wildlife Toxicology, DR. RONALD J. KENDALL, Director
Institute for Watershed Studies, DR. DAVID F. BRAKKE, Director

Institute for Environmental Studies, University of Washington, FM-12, Seattle 98195 (206, 543-1812)
The Institute for Environmental Studies was established by the University of Washington in 1972 to develop undergraduate and graduate environmental curricula, to encourage interdisciplinary research, and to develop public service programs.
Director: PROF. CONWAY B. LEOVY
Assistant Director: V. CRANE WRIGHT
Associate Director: PROF. P.D. BOERSMA
Publications: *Northwest Environmental Journal; Environmental Outlook*
Editors: GORDON H. ORIANS; POLLY DYER

University of Washington, Seattle 98195 (206, 543-6475)
Washington Cooperative Fishery Research Unit: GILBERT B. PAULEY, Unit Leader
College of Forest Resources (B.S., M.F.R., M.S., Ph.D.), DAVID B. THORUD, Dean; DALE COLE, Associate Dean, Research

Forest Resources Management Division: ROBERT G. LEE, Chairman

Forest Products and Engineering Division: GERALD F. SCHREUDER, Chairman

Center for Urban Horticulture: HAROLD TUKEY, Director

Center for Quantitative Science in Forestry, Fisheries, and Wildlife: E. DAVID FORD, Director

Wildlife Conservation, Advisors: STEPHEN D. WEST; DAVID A. MANUWAL

Graduate School of Public Affairs (M.P.A.), CHRISTOPHER K. LEMAN, Coordinator of the Concentration in Environmental Policy and Natural Resources Management (543-4920)

Washington State University, Pullman 99164

Wildlife and Wildland Recreation Management (B.S.)

Forest and Range Management (B.S., M.S.)

Wildlife Biology (B.S., M.S.), DR. FREDERICK F. GILBERT, Chairman, Dept. of Natural Resource Sciences (509, 335-6166)

Environmental Science and Regional Planning Program (B.S., M.S.), DR. H.H. CHENG, Chairman (335-8536)

Landscape Architecture (B.S.), DR. H. PAUL RASMUSSEN, Chairman, Dept. of Horticulture and Landscape Architecture (335-9502)

WEST VIRGINIA

Shepherd College, Shepherdstown 25443 (304, 876-2511)

Park Administration (B.S.), DR. CHARLES A. HULSE, Head

West Virginia University, Morgantown 26506 (304, 293-2941)

Division of Forestry (B.S., M.S., Ph.D.)

Forest Resources (B.S.F., M.S., Ph.D.), DR. JACK E. COSTER, Director

Recreation and Parks Management (B.S.R., M.S.)

Wood Industries (B.S.F., M.S., Ph.D.)

Wildlife Management (B.S., M.S., Ph.D.)

Cooperative Fish and Wildlife Research Unit, Leader: DR. JOSEPH MARGRAF

Assistants: PAT BROWN; SUE PERRY

Fisheries and Wildlife (B.S., M.S., Ph.D), DAVID E. SAMUEL; EDWIN D. MICHAEL; ROBERT L. SMITH; ROBERT C. WHITMORE; WILLIAM N. GRAFTON

WISCONSIN

University of Wisconsin-Eau Claire, Eau Claire 54701 (715, 836-4166)

Biology (B.S., M.S.), DR. VICTOR CVANCARA, Chairman

Geography (B.S.), DR. INGOLF VOGELER, Chairman

University of Wisconsin-Green Bay, Green Bay 54311-7001 (414, 465-2121)

Regional Analysis (B.S., B.A.), DR. DONALD A. GANDRE, Chairman

Human Biology (B.S., B.A.), College of Human Biology, DR. JOSEPH MANNINO, Chairman

Natural and Applies Sciences (B.S.), DR. HAROLD J. DAY, Chairman

Public and Environmental Administration (B.S., B.A.), DR. MICHAEL KRAFT, Chairman

Richter Natural History Museum: DR. ROBERT HOWE, Curator

Environmental Science (M.S.), DR. PAUL SAGER, Coordinator

University of Wisconsin, Madison 53706 (608, 262-1234)

Wildlife Ecology (B.S., M.S., Ph.D.), ROBERT L. RUFF, Chairman

Forestry (B.S., M.S., Ph.D.), DR. RONALD L. GIESE, Chairman

Landscape Architecture (B.S., M.S.), EVELYN HOWELL, Chairman

College of Agricultural and Life Sciences: LEO M. WALSH, Dean

School of Natural Resources: DONALD R. FIELD, Associate Dean

Soils: JOHN MURDOCK, Chairman

Rural Sociology: DORIS SLESINGER, Chairman

Agricultural Economics: EDWARD V. JESSE, Chairman

Institute for Environmental Studies, Water Resources Management (M.S.); Environmental Monitoring (M.S., Ph.D.); Land Resources (M.S., Ph.D.); Energy Analysis and Policy (M.S.); Environmental Studies (B.S.), ARTHUR SACKS, Director (Acting)

University of Wisconsin, Stevens Point 54481 (715, 346-0123)

Forestry (B.S., M.S.), DR. ROBERT ENGELHARD

Wildlife (B.S., M.S.), DR. JAMES HARDIN

Resources Management (B.S., M.S.), DR. MICHAEL GROSS

Cooperative Fishery Unit (M.S.), DR. DANIEL W. COBLE, Leader

Water Science (B.S., M.S.), DR. GERALD NIENKE

Soil Science (B.S., M.S.), DR. AGA RAZUI

College of Natural Resources: DR. ALAN HANEY, Dean; DR. RICHARD WILKE, Associate Dean

WYOMING

University of Wyoming, P.O. Box 3166, Laramie 82071

Wildlife and Fisheries Biology and Management (B.S., M.S., Ph.D.), DR. MARK S. BOYCE, Chairman (307, 766-5373)

Range Management (B.S., M.S., Ph.D.), DR. WILLIAM LAYCOCK, Head (766-5263)

Cooperative Fish and Wildlife Research Unit: DR. STANLEY H. ANDERSON, Leader (766-5415)

CANADA

Acadia University, Wolfville, Nova Scotia BOP IXO (902, 542-2201)

Wildlife, Fisheries, Aquatic Biology, Marine Ecology, Mammalogy, Animal Behavior, Ornithology (B.Sc., B.Sc. Hon. M.Sc.), FRANCIS E. SCHWAB; PETER C. SMITH; J. SHERMAN BLEAKNEY; GRAHAM R. DABORN; THOMAS B. HERMAN

Recreation Management (B.A., B.Sc.), JUDE HIRSCH; GLYN BISSIX

Environmental Science (B.Sc., Hon., M.Sc.), D.A. STILES

Lakehead University, School of Forestry, Thunder Bay, Ontario P7B 5E1 (807, 343-8511)

Forestry (H.B.Sc.F.); Forest Technology Diploma (M.Sc.F.), DR. J.K. NAYSMITH, Director

Wildlife: DR. HAROLD G. CUMMING (Ext. 8280)

University of Alberta, Faculty of Agriculture and Forestry, 2-14 Agriculture Forestry Center, Edmonton, Alberta T6G 2P5 (403, 432-4931)

Agriculture (B.Sc., M.Ag., M.Sc., Ph.D.); Forestry (B.Sc., M.Sc., Ph.D.); Agricultural Engineering (B.Sc., M.Sc., M.Eng.); Agricultural Business Management (B.Sc.); Food Science (B.Sc., M.Sc., M.Eng., Ph.D.), E.W. TYRCHNIEWICZ, Dean

Forest Science (B.Sc., M.Sc., Ph.D.), J.A. BECK, Chairman (432-2356)

Animal Science (B.Sc., M.Ag., M.Sc., Ph.D.), M.A. PRICE, Chairman (432-3235)

Agricultural Engineering (B.Sc., M.Sc., M.Eng.,), J.J. LEONARD, Chairman (432-4251)

Plant Science (B.Sc., M.Sc., Ph.D.), K.G BRIGGS, Chairman (432-3239)

Rural Economy (B.Sc., M.Ag., M.Sc., Ph.D.), W.E. PHILLIPS, Chairman (432-4228)

Soil Science (B.Sc., M.Ag. M.Sc., Ph.D.), W.B. McGILL, Chairman (432-3242)

Entomology (B.Sc., M.Sc., Ph.D.), B.K. MITCHELL, Chairman (432-3237)

Food Science (B.Sc., M.Sc., M.Eng., Ph.D.), F.H. WOLFE, Chairman (432-5188)

University of British Columbia, 2075 Main Mall, Vancouver V6T 1W5

Agricultural Sciences, Faculty: DR. JAMES F. RICHARDS, Dean

Resource Ecology, Resource Management Science: DR. L.M. LAVKULICH, Chairman

Botany Department: DR. A.D.M. GLASS, Head

Civil Engineering Department: DR. W. OLDHAM, Head

Forestry, Faculty: DR. R.W. KENNEDY, Dean

Geography Department: DR. D. LEY, Head

Graduate Studies, Faculty: DR. P. SUEDFELD, Dean

Oceanography Department: DR. P.H. LeBLOND, Head

Westwater Research Centre: PROF. A.H.J. DORCEY, Director (Acting)

Zoology Department: DR. G.G.E. SCUDDER, Head

University of Guelph, Guelph N1G 2W1 (519, 824-4120)

Zoology (B.Sc., M.Sc., Ph.D.) (Aquatic Sciences, Parasitology, Wildlife Biology, Wildlife Management, Behaviour, Environmental Physiology)

Marine Biology: J. BALLANTYNE; S. COREY; D.E. GASKIN; D.H. LYNN; J.C. ROFF; K. RONALD

Fisheries Biology: DRS. E.K. BALON; F.W.H. BEAMISH; D.L.G. NOAKES; J.F. LEATHERLAND; D.E. STEVENS; H.R. MacCRIMMON; G.J. VANDERKRAAK

Wildlife Ecology: DRS. R.J. BROOKS; J.P. BOGART; J. FRYXELL; P. YODZIS; D.M. LAVIGNE; A.L.A. MIDDLETON; V.G. THOMAS; T.D. NUDDS

Wildlife Ethology: DRS. E.D. BAILEY; G.A. BUBENIK; D.L.G. NOAKES

Wildlife Diseases: DRS. R.C. ANDERSON; M. BEVERLEY-BURTON; P.T.K. WOO

Wildlife Management: D.M. LAVIGNE; V.G. THOMAS; T.D. NUDDS

Fisheries Science: E.K. BALON; J.F. LEATHERLAND; F.W.H. BEAMISH; H.R. MacCRIMMON

Universite Laval, Quebec

Forestry (B.S., M.S., Ph.D.)

Sciences, Biology Department (B.S., M.S., Ph.D.) in Wildlife Management

Agriculture (M.S., Ph.D.) in Plant Biology

University of Manitoba, Winnipeg, Manitoba R3T 2N2

Natural Resources Institute: DR. WALTER R. HENSON, Director; PROF. THOMAS J. HENLEY, Assistant Director; DR. RICHARD K. BAYDACK, Associate Professor; PROF. DAVID A. YOUNG, Associate Professor; DR. MERLIN SHOESMITH, Adjunct Professor; DR. SUZANNE BAYLEY, Adjunct Professor; DR. WAYNE COWAN, Adjunct Professor; DR. WAYNE EVERETT, Adjunct Professor; DR. GEORGE HOCHBAUM, Adjunct Professor

University of New Brunswick, Forest Resources, Bag Service 44555, Fredericton, NB E3B 6C2

Forestry (B.Sc.F., M.Sc.F., Ph.D.), G.L. BASKERVILLE, Dean

Biology (B.Sc., M.Sc., Ph.D.), R.T. RIDING, Chairman

Wildlife Specialists: T.G. DILWORTH; DANIEL KEPPIE

University of Regina, Regina, Saskatchewan S4S 0A2

Wildlife, Animal Behavior, Animal and Plant Ecology (B.Sc., B.Sc. Hon., M.Sc., Ph.D.), DR. GEORGE J. MITCHELL; DR. ALINA WALTHER; DR. DIANE M. SECOY; DR. WILLIAM CHAPCO

University of Saskatchewan, Saskatoon S7N 0W0 (306, 966-4944)

Plant Ecology (B.S.A., M. Sc., Ph.D.), DR. R.E. REDMANN; DR. J. ROMO; DR. W. ARCHIBOLD; B. PYLYPEC; DR. B.L. HARVEY, Chairman, Department of Crop Science and Plant Ecology

Plant Taxomony: DR. V.L. HARMS

University of Toronto, Toronto M5S 1A1 (416, 978-6152)

Forestry (B.Sc.F., M.Sc., Ph.D.), DR. J. ROD CARROW, Dean

York University, Faculty of Environmental Studies, 4700 Keele St., North York, Ontario M3J 1P3 (416, 736-5252)

Environmental Studies (graduate programs) (M.E.S.), EDWARD S. SPENCE, Dean; ANNEMARIE GALLAUGHER, Coordinator, External Liaison

FISH AND GAME COMMISSIONERS AND DIRECTORS OF THE UNITED STATES AND CANADA

This is a listing of fish and game administrators of the United States and Canada. Additional conservation personnel are listed under the individual states and provinces.

UNITED STATES

Alabama Div. of Game and Fish, 64 N. Union St., Montgomery 36130 (205, 261-3465)
Director: CHARLES D. KELLEY

Alaska Dept. of Fish and Game, P.O. Box 3-2000, Juneau 99802 (907, 465-4100)
Commissioner: DR. DON W. COLLINSWORTH

Arizona Game and Fish Dept., 2222 W. Greenway Rd., Phoenix 85023 (602, 942-3000)
Director: TEMPLE A. REYNOLDS

Arkansas Game and Fish Commission, #2 Natural Resources Dr., Little Rock 72205 (501, 223-6300)
Director: STEVE N. WILSON

California Dept. of Fish and Game, 1416 9th St., Sacramento 95814 (916, 445-3531)
Director: PETE BONTADELLI

Colorado Div. of Wildlife, 6060 Broadway, Denver 80216 (303, 297-1192)
Director: PERRY D. OLSON

Connecticut Dept. of Environmental Protection, State Office Bldg., 165 Capitol Ave., Hartford 06115 (203, 566-5599)
Deputy Commissioner: DENNIS DeCARLI

Delaware Div. of Fish and Wildlife, P.O. Box 1401, Dover 19903 (302, 736-5295)
Director: WILLIAM C. WAGNER, II

District of Columbia Dept. of Conservation and Regulatory Affairs, Environmental Control Division/Fisheries, 5010 Overlook Ave., SW, Washington, DC 20032 (202, 767-7370)
Director: Vacant

Florida Game and Freshwater Fish Commission, Farris Bryant Bldg., 620 S. Meridian, Tallahassee 32399 (904, 488-1960)
Executive Director: ROBERT M. BRANTLY

Florida Department of Natural Resources, 3900 Commonwealth Blvd., Tallahassee, FL 32399
Executive Director: THOMAS E. GARDNER (904, 488-1554)

Georgia State Game and Fish Div., Floyd Towers East, Suite 1366, 205 Butler St., SE, Atlanta 30334 (404, 656-3530)
Director: LEON A. KIRKLAND

Guam Dept. of Agriculture, Agana 96910 (734-3941)
Director: ELIZABETH P. TORRES

Hawaii Div. Aquatic Resources, 1151 Punchbowl St., Honolulu 96813 (808, 548-4000)
Director: HENRY M. SAKUDA

Idaho Fish and Game Dept., 600 S. Walnut, Box 25, Boise 83707 (208, 334-5159)
Director: JERRY CONLEY

Illinois Dept. of Conservation, Lincoln Tower Plaza, 524 S. Second St., Springfield 62701-1787 (217, 782-6302)
Director: MARK FRECH

Indiana Div. of Fish and Wildlife, 607 State Office Bldg., Indianapolis 46204 (317, 232-4080)
Head: EDWARD HANSEN

Iowa Dept. of Natural Resources, Wallace State Office Bldg.,East Ninth and Grand Ave., Des Moines 50319 (515, 281-8666)
Director: LARRY WILSON

Kansas Dept. of Wildlife and Parks, Box 54A, R.R. 2, Pratt 67124 (316, 672-5911)
Secretary: ROBERT L. MEINEN

Kentucky Dept. of Fish and Wildlife Resources, #1 Game Farm Rd., Frankfort 40601 (502, 564-3400)
Commissioner: DON R. McCORMICK

Louisiana Department Wildlife and Fisheries, P.O. Box 15570, Baton Rouge 70895 (504, 925-3617)
Secretary: VIRGINIA VAN SICKLE

Maine Dept. of Inland Fisheries and Wildlife, 284 State St., Station #41, Augusta 04333 (207, 289-2766)
Commissioner: WILLIAM VAIL

Maryland Dept. of Natural Resources, Tawes State Office Bldg., Annapolis 21401 (301, 269 plus extension)
Assistant Secretary: DONALD MacLAUCHLAN (Ext. 3776)
Tidewater Administration, Administrator: LEE ZENI (Ext. 2926)

Massachusetts Dept. of Fisheries, Wildlife and Environmental Law Enforcement, Div. of Fisheries and Wildlife, 100 Cambridge St., Boston 02202 (617, 727-3151)
Directors: WAYNE MacCALLUM (Acting); PHILIP G. COATES, MA Div. of Marine Fisheries (617, 727-3193)

Michigan Dept. of Natural Resources, Stevens T. Mason Bldg., Box 30028, Lansing 48909 (517, 373-2329)
Director: DR. DAVID F. HALES

Minnesota Dept. of Natural Resources, 500 Lafayette Rd., St. Paul 55155-4020 (612, 296-6157)
Commissioner: JOSEPH N. ALEXANDER
Chief of Wildlife: ROGER HOLMES (Ext. 3344)
Division of Wildlife: DR. LARRY R. SHANNON

Mississippi Dept. of Wildlife Conservation, P.O. Box 451, Jackson 39205 (601, 961-5315)
Director: W. VERNON BEVILL

Missouri Dept. of Conservation, 2901 N. Ten Mile Dr., P.O. Box 180, Jefferson City 65102 (314, 751-4115)
Director: JERRY J. PRESLEY

Montana Dept. of Fish, Wildlife, and Parks, 1420 E. Sixth Ave., Helena 59620 (406, 444-3186)
Director: JAMES FLYNN

Nebraska Game and Parks Commission, P.O. Box 30370, 2200 N. 33rd, Lincoln 68503 (402, 464-0641)
Director: REX AMACK

Nevada Dept. of Wildlife, Box 10678, Reno 89520 (702, 789-0500)
Director: WILLIAM A. MOLINI

New Hampshire Fish and Game Dept., 34 Bridge St., Concord 03301 (603, 271-3421)
Executive Director: DONALD NORMANDEAU

New Jersey Div. of Fish, Game, and Wildlife, CN 400, Trenton 08625 (609, 292-9410)
Director: GEORGE P. HOWARD

New Mexico, Natural Resources Dept., Villagra Bldg., Santa Fe 87503 (505, 827-7899)
Secretary: LEO GRIEGO
Game and Fish Department, Director, BILL MONTOYA

New York Div. of Fish and Wildlife, 50 Wolf Rd., Albany 12233 (518, 457-5691)
Director: KENNETH WICH

Assistant Commissioner for Fish, Wildlife, and Marine Resources: HERBERT E. DOIG (519, 457-7435)

North Carolina Wildlife Resources Commission, Archdale Bldg., 512 N. Salisbury St., Raleigh 27611 (919, 733-3391)
Executive Director: CHARLES FULLWOOD

North Dakota State Game and Fish Dept., 100 North Bismarck Expressway, Bismarck 58501 (701, 221-6300)
Commissioner: DALE HENEGAR

Ohio Div. of Wildlife, Fountain Square, Columbus 43224 (614, 265-6300)
Chief: CLAY H. LAKES

Oklahoma Dept. of Wildlife Conservation, 1801 N. Lincoln, P.O. Box 53465, Oklahoma City 73152 (405, 521-3851)
Director: STEVEN A. LEWIS

Oregon Dept. Fish and Wildlife, Box 59, Portland 97207 (503, 229-5551)
Director: RANDY FISHER

Pennsylvania Fish Commission, P.O. Box 1673, Harrisburg 17105 (717, 657-4518)
Executive Director: EDWARD R. MILLER

Pennsylvania Game Commission, 2001 Elmerton Ave., Harrisburg 17110-9797 (717, 787-4250)
Executive Director: PETER S. DUNCAN, III

Puerto Rico Dept. of Natural Resources, P.O. Box 5887, Puerta De Tierra, San Juan 00906 (809, 722-8774)
Secretary: ALEJANDRO SANTIAGO-NIEVES

Rhode Island Dept. of Environmental Management, Div. of Fish and Wildlife, Washington County Government Center, Wakefield 02879 (401, 789-3094)
Chief: JOHN STOLGITIS

South Carolina Wildlife & Marine Resources Dept., Rembert C. Dennis Bldg., Box 167, Columbia 29202 (803, 734-3888)
Executive Director: DR. JAMES A. TIMMERMAN, JR.

South Dakota Dept. of Game, Fish and Parks, Sigurd Anderson Bldg., 445 E. Capitol, Pierre 57501-3185 (605, 773-3718)
Secretary: RICHARD J. BERINGSON

Tennessee Wildlife Resources Agency, Box 40747, Ellington Agricultural Center, Nashville 37204 (615, 781-6552)
Executive Director: GARY T. MYERS

Texas Parks and Wildlife Dept., 4200 Smith School Rd., Austin 78744 (512, 389-4800)
Executive Director: CHARLES D. TRAVIS

Utah State Div. of Wildlife Resources, 1596 WN Temple, Salt Lake City 84116 (801, 533-9333)
Director: WILLIAM GEER

Vermont Fish and Game Dept., 103 S. Main Street, 10 South, Waterbury 05676 (802, 244-7331)
Commissioner: STEPHEN E. WRIGHT

Virginia Dept. of Game and Inland Fisheries, 4010 W. Broad St., Box 11104, Richmond 23230 (804, 257-1000)
Executive Director: JAMES A. REMINGTON

Washington Dept. of Fisheries, 115 General Administration Bldg., Olympia 98504 (206, 753-6623)
Director: JOSEPH R. BLUM

Washington Dept. of Wildlife, 600 N. Capitol Way, Olympia 98504 (206, 753-5700)
Director: CURT SMITCH

West Virginia Div. of Wildlife Resources, 1800 Washington St., E., Charleston 25305 (304, 348-2771)
Chief: ROBERT MILES

Wisconsin Dept. of Natural Resources, Box 7921, Madison 53707 (608, 266-2621)
Secretary: C.D. BESADNY

Wyoming Game and Fish Dept., 5400 Bishop Blvd., Cheyenne 82002 (307, 777-7631)
Director: WILLIAM MORRIS

CANADA

Alberta Dept. of Public Lands and Wildlife, Petroleum Plaza, 9945-108 St., Edmonton T5K 2C9
Associate Minister: DON SPARROW, Director of Wildlife, Fish and Wildlife Div., Dept. of Energy and Natural Resources, Petroleum Plaza, South Tower, 9945-108 St., Edmonton, T5K 2C9; R. (Bob) ANDREWS (403, 427-6733)
Assistant Deputy Minister: LES COOKE (427-6749)

British Columbia Ministry of the Environment, Parliament Bldgs., Victoria V8V 1X5
Minister: BRUCE STRACHAN
Deputy Minister: THOMAS JOHNSON (604, 387-1161)
Assistant Deputy Minister, Environmental Management Division, E.D. ANTHONY (387-1161)
Director, Wildlife Branch: J.H.C. WALKER
Director, Fisheries Branch: DR. D. NARVER (387-6049)

Manitoba Dept. of Natural Resources: Natural Resources Division, Rm. 302, Legislative Bldg., Winnipeg R3C 0V8
Minister: HON. JACK PENNER, 215 Legislature Bldg., Winnipeg R3C-0V8
Deputy Minister: D. STEWART, P.O. Box 22, 1495 St. James St., Winnipeg R3H 0W9 (204, 944-6829)
Assistant Deputy Minister: RICH GOULDEN
Director (Acting), Wildlife Branch: LORNE COLPITTS (204, 944-7761)

New Brunswick Dept. of Natural Resources, Fish and Wildlife Branch, Centennial Bldg., P.O. Box 6000, Fredericton E3B 5H1
Minister: MORRIS GREEN (Local, 2510)
Deputy Minister: B.J. WALKER (Local, 2510)
Director: B. MEADOWS (Local, 2510)

Newfoundland Dept. of Culture, Recreation and Youth, Wildlife Div.
Minister: JOHN C. BOTT (709, 576-2810)
Deputy Minister: ROBERT JENKINS (576-2812)

Newfoundland Dept. of Fisheries, P.O. Box 4750, St. John's A1C 5T7
Director: D.G. PIKE (737-2817)

Nova Scotia Dept. of Lands and Forests, Wildlife Div., Toronto Dominion Bank Bldg., 1791 Barrington St., P.O. Box 698, Halifax B3J 2T9
Minister: JOHN A. MacISAAC (902, 424-4037)
Deputy Minister: JOHN MULLALLY (424-4121)
Director: M.H. PRIME (678-8921)

Ontario Ministry of Natural Resources, Outdoor Recreation Group, Whitney Block, Queen's Park, Toronto M7A 1W3
Minister: VINCENT G. KERRIO (416, 965-1301)
Deputy Minister: GEORGE TOUGH (965-2704)
Wildlife Director: DON W. SIMKIN (416, 965-4252)

Prince Edward Island Community and Cultural Affairs, 11 Kent St., P.O. Box 2000, Charlottetown C1A 7N8
Minister: HON. GILBERT R. CLEMENTS
Deputy Minister: KENNETH F. DESROCHES

Quebec Ministere Du Loisir, De La Chasse Et De La Peche, 150 est boul, St.-Cyrille, Quebec City, Quebec G1R 4Y1
Minister: YVON PICOTTE
Sous-Minister: GEORGE ARSENAULT (418, 643-2207)
Director, Fish and Game Branch: MARC GAUVIN

Saskatchewan Park and Renewable Resources, Legislative Bldg., Regina S4S 5W6
Minister: HON. COLIN MAXWELL (306, 565-2833)
Deputy Minister: DOUGLAS CRESSMAN (565-2930)
Director, Fisheries Branch: PAUL NAFTEL (565-2884)
Director, Wildlife Branch: DENNIS SHERRATT (565-2886)

Northwest Territory Dept. of Renewable Resources, Legislative Bldg., Yellowknife X1A 2L9

Minister: TITUS ALLOOLOO
Deputy Minister: J.W. BOURQUE
Chief, Wildlife Management Division: KEVIN LLOYD
Yukon Dept. Renewable Resources, Wildlife Branch, P.O. Box 2703, Whitehorse, Yukon Territory Y1A 2C6

Minister: DAVID PORTER
Deputy Minister: BILL KLASSEN
Chief of Wildlife Management: MANFRED HOEFS

STATE EDUCATION AGENCY COORDINATORS FOR ENVIRONMENTAL EDUCATION

ALABAMA: DONNA BENTLEY, Education Specialist Science/Environmental, Alabama Department of Education, 111 Colesium Blvd., Montgomery 36109 (205, 261-2746)

ALASKA: VERDELL JACKSON, Program Manager, Vocational Education, Alaska Department of Education, Pouch F, Juneau 99811 (907, 465-2980)

ARKANSAS: BILL FULTON, Science and Environmental Education Supervisor, Coordinator, Economic, Energy, #4 State Capitol Mall, Arkansas Department of Education, Arch Ford Bldg., Rm. 404-B, Little Rock 72201 (501, 682-4471)

CALIFORNIA: THOMAS P. SACHSE, Science, Environmental Unit Administrator, Environmental/Energy Educatiion, P.O. Box 944272, Sacramento 94244-2720 (916, 324-7187)

COLORADO: GEORGE A. EK, JR., Coordinator, Conservation Education Services CDE/DOW, Colorado Department of Education, State Office Bldg., 201 E. Colfax, Denver 80203 (303, 866-5000)

CONNECTICUT: DR. SIGMUND ABELES, Science Consultant, Connecticut Department of Education, P.O. Box 2219, Hartford 06145 (203, 566-4825)

DELAWARE: DAVID S. HUGG, III, Executive Assistant, Department of Natural Resources and Environmental Control, 89 Kings Highway, P.O. Box 1401, Dover 19903

FLORIDA: C. RICHARD TILLIS, Director, Special Programs and Projects, Florida Department of Education, Knott Bldg., Tallahassee 32301 (904, 488-6790)

GEORGIA: JAMES R. WILSON, Education Consultant, Science (K-8), Georgia Department of Education, State Office Bldg., Atlanta 30334 (404, 656-2575)

HAWAII: JOHN W. HAWKINS, Education Specialist-Environmental Education, Hawaii Department of Education, 189 Lunalilo Home Rd., 2nd Fl., Honolulu 96825 (808, 395-9252)

IDAHO: KAREN UNDERWOOD, Consultant, Proficiency Testing, Idaho Department of Education, 650 W. State St., Boise 83720 (208, 334-2281)

ILLINOIS: DON RODERICK, Educational Consultant, Illinois State Board of Education, 100 North First St., Springfield 62777 (217, 782-2826)

INDIANA: JOE E. WRIGHT, Environmental Science Education Consultant, Division of Curriculum, Indiana Department of Education, Rm. 229, State House, Indianapolis 46204 (317, 269-9641)

IOWA: DUANE TOOMSEN, Environmental Education Consultant, Curriculum Division, Iowa Department of Public Instruction, Grimes Office Bldg., Des Moines 50319 (515, 281-3146)

KANSAS: DR. RAMONA J. ANSHUTZ, Science and Mathematics Consultant, Kansas Department of Education, 120 East 10th, Topeka 66612 (502, 564-2672)

KENTUCKY: ANN R. SEPPENFIELD, Environmental Education Consultant, Kentucky Department of Education, Rm. 1829, Capitol Plaza Tower, Frankfort 40601 (502, 564-2672)

LOUISIANA: DR. JAMES E. BARR, Supervisor, Science, Energy, and Environmental Education, Louisiana Department of Education, P.O. Box 94064, Baton Rouge 70804-9064 (504, 342-1136)

MAINE: PETER DUMONT, Conservation Education Consultant, Maine State Department of Educational and Cultural Services, State House Station #23, Augusta 04333 (207, 289-2512)

MARYLAND: MARY ANN BREARTON, Science Specialist, Department of Education, 200 West Baltimore St., Baltimore 21201 (301, 659-2319); GARY HEATH, Environmental Science Specialist, Department of Education, 200 W. Baltimore St., Baltimore 21201 (301, 659-2322)

MICHIGAN: MOZELL P. LANG, Science Specialist, Michigan Department of Education, P.O. Box 30008, Lansing 48909 (517, 373-4223)

MINNESOTA: JOHN C. MILLER, Environmental Education Specialist, Minnesota Department of Education, 644 Capitol Square Bldg., St. Paul 55101 (612, 296-4069)

MISSISSIPPI: MICHAEL G. CAROTHERS, Mississippi Department of Education, P.O. Box 771, Jackson 39205 (601, 359-3997)

MISSOURI: DR. ROBERT M. TAYLOR, Director, Health, Physical Education, Safety, and Science, Missouri Department of Elementary and Secondary Education, P.O. Box 480, Jefferson 65102 (314, 751-4608)

MONTANA: SPENCER SARTORIUS, Specialist, Outdoor-Health-PE Education, Office of Public Instruction, Capitol Bldg., Helena, MT 59620 (406, 444-4434); BOB BRIGGS, Environmental Science Specialist, Education, Montana Office of Public Instruction, State Capitol Bldg., Helena, MT 59620 (406, 444-4439)

NEBRASKA: JIM WOODLAND, Science Consultant, Nebraska Department of Education, P.O. Box 94987, Lincoln 68509 (402, 471-4329)

NEW HAMPSHIRE: WILLIAM B. EWERT, Consultant, Science Education, New Hampshire Department of Education, 101 Pleasant St., Concord 03301 (603, 271-2632)

NEW JERSEY: WILLIAM BURCAT, Director of General Education Services, New Jersey Department of Education, Division of School Programs, 225 W. State St., Trenton 08625 (609, 292-8777)

NEW MEXICO: B.K. GRAHAM, Science and Conservation Consultant, New Mexico Department of Education, State Education Bldg., Santa Fe 87503 (505, 827-6579)

NEW YORK: BARRY W. JAMASON, Coordinator, Environmental Education, New York State Department of Education, Rm. 314H, Albany 12234 (518, 474-5890)

NORTH CAROLINA: CLINTON L. BROWN, Assistant Director, Division of Science, North Carolina Department of Public Instruction, Raleigh 27611 (919, 733-3694)

NORTH DAKOTA: CHARLES DeREMER, Director, Curriculum and NDN, North Dakota Department of Public Instruction, State Capitol, Bismarck 58505 (701, 224-2514)

OHIO: DR. JOHN HUG, Environmental Education Consultant, Division of Elementary and Secondary Education, Ohio Department of Education, 65 S. Front St., Rm. 1005, Columbus 43266-0308 (614, 466-2211)

OKLAHOMA: DORIS K. GIGSBY, Science Specialist, Oklahoma Department of Education, Oliver Hodge Bldg., 2500 N. Lincoln, Oklahoma City 73105 (405, 521-3361)

OREGON: RAYMOND E. THIESS, Specialist, Science/Energy/Environment Education, Oregon Department of Education, 700 Pringle Parkway, SE, Salem 97310 (503, 373-7898)

PENNSYLVANIA: DR. DEAN R. STEINHART, Director, Office of Environmental Education, Pennsylvania Department of Education, 333 Market St., 8th Floor, Harrisburg 17126-0333 (717, 783-6994)

RHODE ISLAND: JAMES L. HARRINGTON, Consultant, Program Development, Rhode Island Department of Education, 22 Hayes St., Providence 02908 (401, 277-2821)

SOUTH CAROLINA: E. LYNN TALTON, Science and Environmental

Education Consultant, South Carolina Department of Education, 803 Rutledge Bldg., Columbia 29201 (803, 734-8390)

SOUTH DAKOTA: JAMES HAUCK, Science Director, South Dakota Department of Elementary and Secondary Education, Kneip Bldg., Pierre 57501 (605, 741-2851)

TENNESSEE: DR. J. PADGETT KELLY, Director, Conservation Education, C-3/300 Cordell Hull Bldg., Nashville 37219

TEXAS: DR. JOSEPH J. HUCKESTEIN, Director, Science/Environmental Education, Texas Education Agency, 1701 N. Congress Ave., Austin 78701 (512, 469-9556)

UTAH: R. LAMAR ALLRED, Science Educational Specialist, Utah State Office of Education, 250 East 500 South, Salt Lake City 84111 (801, 533-5965)

VERMONT: ALAN KOUSEN, Science Consultant, Science, Energy, and Environmental Education, Vermont Department of Education, State Office Bldg., Montpelier 05602 (802, 828-3111)

VIRGINIA: DR. DAVID M. ANDREWS, Supervisor of Science, Virginia Department of Education, Science Service, P.O. Box 6Q, Richmond (804, 225-2651)

WASHINGTON: DAVID KENNEDY, Program Administrator for Curriculum, Office of the State Superintendent of Public Instruction, Old Capitol Bldg., Olympia 98504 (206, 753-6757); TONY ANGELL, Supervisor, Environmental Education Programs, 17011 Meridian Ave., North #16, Seattle, WA 98133 (206, 542-7671)

WEST VIRGINIA: LLOYD C. CULBERSON, Science Coordinator, West Virginia Department of Education, Capitol Complex, Rm. B-330, Bldg., 6, Charleston 25305 (304, 348-7805)

WISCONSIN: DAVID C. ENGLESON, Supervisor, Environmental Education, Wisconsin Department of Public Instruction, P.O. Box 7841, Madison 53707 (608, 267-9266)

WYOMING: DR. WILLIAM M. FUTRELL, Coordinator, Science/Mathematics/Environmental Education, Wyoming Department of Education, 241 Hathaway Bldg., Cheyenne 82002 (307, 777-6247)

NATIONAL WILDLIFE REFUGES IN THE UNITED STATES

The special mission of the National Wildlife Refuge System is to provide, preserve, restore, and manage a national network of lands and waters sufficient in size, diversity, and location to meet society's needs for areas where the widest possible spectrum of benefits associated with wildlife and wildlands is enhanced and made available. The National Wildlife Refuges are administered by the U.S. Fish and Wildlife Service.

ALABAMA

Bon Secour: JEROME T. CARROLL, P.O. Box 1650, Gulf Shores 36542 (205, 968-8623)

Choctaw: DOUGLAS BAUMGARTNER, Mgr., Box 808, 2704 Westside College Ave., Jackson 36545 (205, 246-3583)

Eufaula: JERRY L. WILSON, Rt. 2, Box 97-B, Eufaula 36027 (205, 687-4065)

Wheeler (Blowing Wind Cave; Fern Cave; Watercress Darter): TUCK STONE, Mgr., Box 1643, Decatur 35602 (205, 353-7243)

ALASKA

Alaska Maritime (Alaska Peninsula Unit; Bering Sea Unit; Churchi Sea Unit; Gulf of Alaska Unit; Alevtian Islands Unit): JOHN L. MARTIN, Mgr., 202 W. Pioneer Ave., Homer 99603 (907, 235-6546)

Alaska Peninsula: RONALD HOOD, Mgr., P.O. Box 277, King Salmon 99613 (907, 246-3339)

Arctic: GLEN W. ELISON, Mrg., Box 20, 101 12th Ave., Fairbanks 99701 (907, 456-0250)

Innoko: PHILLIP J. FEIGER, Mgr., General Delivery, McGrath 99627 (907, 524-3251)

Izembek: ROBIN WEST, Mgr., Box 127, Cold Bay 99571 (907, 532-2445)

Kanuti: Vacant, Mgr., Box 20, 101 12th Ave., Fairbanks 99701 (907, 456-0329)

Kenai: DANIEL DOSHIER, Mgr., P.O. Box 2139, Soldotna 99669 (907, 262-7021)

Kodiak (NWR): JAY BELLINGER, Mgr., 1390 Buskin River Rd., Kodiak 99615 (907, 487-2600)

Koyukuk: MIKE NUNN, Mgr., P.O. Box 287, Galena 99741 (907, 656-1231)

Nowitna: Vacant, Mgr., P.O. Box 287, Galena 99741 (907, 656-1231)

Selawik: JERRY STROEBELE, Mgr., P.O. Box 270, Kotzebue 99752 (907, 442-3799)

Tetlin: DAVE STEARNS, Mgr., P.O. Box 155, Tok 99780 (907, 883-5312)

Togiak: DAVE FISHER, Mgr., P.O. Box 270, Dillingham 99576 (907, 842-1063)

Yukon Delta: RON PERRY, Mgr., P.O. Box 346, Bethel 99559 (907, 543-3151)

Yukon Flats: LOU SWENSON, Mgr., Box 20, 101 12th Ave., Fairbanks 99701 (907, 456-0440)

ARIZONA

Buenos Aires: WAYNE SHIFFLETT, Mgr., P.O. Box 109, Sasabe 85633 (602, 823-4251)

Cabeza Prieta: DAVE STANBROUGH, Mgr., Box 418, Ajo 85321 (602, 387-6483)

Cibola: WESLEY V. MARTIN, Mgr., Box AP, Blythe, CA 92225 (602, 857-3253)

Havasu: JIM GOOD, Mgr., Box A, Needles, CA 92363 (619, 326-3853)

Imperial: ARNOLD W. NIDECKER, III, Mgr., Box 72217, Martinez Lake 85365 (602, 783-3371)

Kofa: MILTON K. HADERLIE, Mgr., Box 6290, Yuma 85364 (602, 783-7861)

San Bernardino: BENJAMIN ROBERTSON, Mgr., R.R. #1, Box 228 R, Douglas 85607 (602, 364-2104)

ARKANSAS

Big Lake: DONALD J. KOSIN, Mgr., Box 67, Manila 72442 (501, 564-2429)

Felsenthal: ROBERT J. BRIDGES, Mgr., Box 1157, Crossett 71635 (501, 364-3167)

Holla Bend: MARTIN D. PERRY, Mgr., Box 1043, 115 S. Denver St., Russellville 72801 (501, 968-2800)

Wapanocca: PAUL GIEDRON, Mgr., P.O. Box 279, Turrell 72384 (501, 343-2595)

Cache River: DALE GUTHRIE, Mrg., P.O. Box 279, Turrell 72384 (501, 343-3595)

White River: MARVIN T. HURDLE, Mgr., Box 308, 321 W. 7th St., De Witt 72042 (501, 946-1468)

CALIFORNIA

Cibola: See Arizona

Havasu: See Arizona

Imperial: See Arizona

Kern (Hopper Mountain; Pixley; Seal Beach; Blue Ridge; Bitter Creek): THOMAS J. CHARMLEY, Mgr., Box 219, Delano 93216-0219 (805, 725-2767)

Klamath Basin Refuges:

(Bear Valley, OR; Tule Lake; Clear Lake; Klamath Forest, OR; Lower Klamath (OR and CA); Upper Klamath, OR): ROGER D. JOHNSON, Mgr., Rt. 1, Box 74, Tulelake 96134 (916, 667-2231)

Modoc: EDWARD C. BLOOM, Box 1610, Alturas 96101 (916, 233-3572)

Sacramento (Butte Sink; Colusa; Delevan; Sutter; Willow Creek; Wildlife Management Area; Lurline): EDWARD J. COLLINS, Mgr., Rt. 1, Box 311, Willows 95988 (916, 934-2801)

Salton Sea (Tijuana Slough; Coachela Valley): GARY KRAMER, Mgr., Box 120, Calipatria 92233 (619, 348-5278)

San Francisco Bay (Antioch Dunes; Ellicott Slough; Farallon; Humboldt Bay; Salinas Lagoon; San Pablo Bay; Castle Rock): RICHARD A. COLEMAN, Mgr., Box 524, Newark 94560 (415, 792-0222)

San Luis (Kesterson; Merced; Grasslands; Wildlife Management Area; East Grasslands): GARY R. ZAHM, Mgr., Box 2176, Los Banos 93635 (209, 826-3508)

COLORADO

Arapaho (Bamforth, WY; Pathfinder, WY; Hutton Lake, WY): EUGENE C. PATTEN, Mgr., Box 457, Walden 80480 (303, 723-8557)

Browns Parks: JERRE GAMBLE, Mgr., 1318 Highway 318, Maybell 81640 (303, 365-3613)

Alamosa/Monte Vista: MELVIN T. NAIL, Mgr., Box 1148, Alamosa 81101 (303, 589-4021)

CONNECTICUT

Salt Meadow: See Rhode Island

Connecticut Coastal: See Rhode Island

DELAWARE

Bombay Hook: PAUL D. DALY, Mgr., Rt. 1, Box 147, Smyrna 19977 (302, 653-9345)

Prime Hook: GEORGE F. O'SHEA, Rt. 1, Box 195, Milton 19968 (302, 684-8419)

FLORIDA

Chassahowitzka (Cedar Keys; Pinellas; Crystal River; Egmont Key; Passage Key; Lower Suwannee): PATRICK HAGAN, Mgr., Rt. 2, Box 44, Homosassa 32646 (904, 382-2201)

Florida Panther: TODD LOGAN, Mgr., P.O. Box 158, Naples 33939 (813, 261-4477)

J.N. (Ding) Darling (Caloosahatchee; Island Bay; Matlacha Pass; Pine Island): ALBERT R. HIGHT, Mgr., 1 Wildlife Dr., Sanibel 33957 (813, 472-1100)

Lake Woodruff: LEON I. RHODES, Mgr., Box 488, DeLeon Springs 32028 (904, 985-4673)

Lower Suannee (Cedar Keys): JIM C. JOHNSON, Mgr., P.O. Box 1193C, Chiefland 32626 (904, 493-0238)

Merritt Island (Pelican Island; St. Johns): STEPHEN R. VEHRS, Mgr., Box 6504, Titusville 32780 (407, 867-0667)

National Key Deer (Great White Heron; Crocodile Lake; Key West): DEBORAH G. HOLLE, Box 510, Big Pine Key 33043 (305, 872-2239)

St. Marks: JOE D. WHITE, Mgr., Box 68, St. Marks 32355 (904, 925-6121)

St. Vincent: JERRY L. HOLLOMAN, Mgr., Box 447, Apalachicola 32320 (904, 653-8808)

Arthur R. Marshall Loxahatchee (Hobe Sound): BURKETT S. NEELY, JR., Rt. 1, Box 278, Boynton Beach 33437 (407, 732-3684)

GEORGIA

Okefenokee: JOHN D. SCHROER, Mgr., Rt. 2, Box 338, Folkston 31537 (912, 496-7366)

Piedmont: RONNIE L. SHELL, Mgr., Round Oak 31038 (912, 986-5441)

Savannah Coastal Refuges (Blackbeard Island; Harris Neck; Pinckney Island, SC; Savannah; Tybee; Wassaw; Wolf Island): JOHN P. DAVIS, Mgr., Box 8487, Savannah 31412 (912, 944-4415)

HAWAII

Hawaiian and Pacific Islands Complex: JERRY LEINECKE, Mgr., P.O. Box 50167, 300 Ala Moana Blvd., Honolulu 96850 (808, 541-1201)

Hawaiian Wetlands and Remote Islands Complex (Baker Island; Jarvis Island; Rose Atoll; Howard Island; Hawaiian Island; James C. Campbell; Kakahaia; Pearl Harbor; Hanalei; Juleia): STEWART FEFER, Mgr., P.O. Box 50167, 300 Ala Moana Blvd., Honolulu 96850 (808, 541-1201)

Johnston Atoll: DOUGLASS J. FORSELL, Biologist, P.O.Box 396, APO San Francisco, CA 96305-5000 (808, 422-0531/Ext. 3182)

IDAHO

Deer Flat: JAMES R. MESSERLI, Mgr., Box 448, Nampa 83651 (208, 467-9278)

Kootenai: LARRY D. NAPIER, Mgr., HCR 60, Box 283, Bonners Ferry 83805 (208, 267-3888)

Southeast Idaho Refuge Complex: CHARLES S. PECK, JR., Mgr., Federal Bldg., Rm. 142, 250 S. 4th Ave., Pocatello 83201 (208, 236-6833)

Bear Lake: GERALD L. DEUTSCHER, Mgr., 370 Webster, Box 9, Montpelier 83254 (208, 847-1757)

Camas: JACK L. RICHARDSON, Mgr., HC69. Box 1700, Hamer 83425 (208, 662-5423)

Grays Lake: EUGENE C. BARNEY, Mgr., HC70, Box 4090, Wayan 83285 (208, 574-2755)

Minidoka: Vacant, Mgr., Rt. 4, P.O. Box 290, Rupert 83550 (208, 436-3589)

ILLINOIS

Chautauqua (Mercdosia): GLEN MILLER, Mgr., Rt. 2, Havana 62644 (309, 535-2290)

Crab Orchard: NORREL F. WALLACE, Mgr., Box J, Carterville 62918 (618, 997-3344)

Mark Twain: ROBERT H. STRATTON, JR., Mgr., 311 North 5th St., Suite 100, Great River Plaza, Quincy 62301 (217, 224-8580)

Brussels District: GEORGE N. PEYTON, Mgr., Box 142, Brussels 62013 (618, 883-2524)

Clarence Cannon: See Missouri

Louisa District: See Iowa

Upper Mississippi River National Wildlife and Fish Refuge: See Minnesota

Savanna District: LARRY A. WARGOWSKY, Mgr., P.O. Bldg., Savanna 61074 (815, 273-2732)

INDIANA

Muscatatuck: LELAND E. HERZBERGER, Mgr., Rt. 7, Box 189A, Seymour 47274 (812, 522-4352)

IOWA

De Soto: GEORGE E. GAGE, Mgr., Rt. 1, Box 114, Missouri Valley 51555 (712, 642-4121)

Upper Mississippi River National Wildlife and Fish Refuge: See Minnesota

McGregor District: JOHN R. LYONS, P.O. Box 460, McGregor 52157 (319, 873-3423)

Mark Twain: See Illinois

Wapello District: WAYNE STANLEY, Mgr., Rt. 1, Wapello 52653 (319, 523-6982)

Union Slough: JOHN GUTHRIE, Mgr., Rt. 1, Box 52, Titonka 50480 (515, 928-2523)

KANSAS

Flint Hills: DAVID WISEMAN, Mgr., Box 128, Hartford 66854 (316, 392-5553)

Kirwin: MILTON STRUTHERS, Mgr., R.R. 1, Box 103, Kirwin 67644 (913, 543-6673)

Quivira: JAMES McCOLLUM, Mgr., Rt. 3 Box 48A, Stafford 67578 (316, 486-2393)

KENTUCKY

Reelfoot: See Tennessee

LOUISIANA

Catahoula: ERIC SIPCO, Mgr., P.O. Drawer LL, Jena 71342 (318, 992-5261)

D'Arbonne (Upper Ouachita): LEE R. FULTON, Mgr., Box 3065, Monroe 71201 (318, 325-1735)

Lacassine (Shell Keys): BOBBY W. BROWN, Mgr., Rt. 1, Box 186, Lake Arthur 70549 (318, 774-2750)

Sabine: JOHN R. WALTHER, Mgr., MRH 107, Hackberry 70645 (318, 762-3816)

Bogue Chitto (Breton; Delta): STEPHEN K. JOYNER, Mgr., 1010 Gause Blvd., Bldg. 936, Slidell 70458 (504, 646-7554)

Tensas River: GEORGE CHANDLER, Mgr., Rte. 2, Box 295, Tallulah 71282 (318, 574-2664)

MAINE

Moosehorn (Cross Island; Franklin Island; Seal Island; Carlton Pond WPA): DOUGLAS M. MULLEN, Mgr., Box X, Calais 04619 (207, 454-3521)

Petit Manan: THOMAS GOETTEL, P.O. Box 279, Milbridge 04658 (207, 546-2124)

Pond Island: See Massachusetts

Rachel Carson: See Massachusetts

MARYLAND

Blackwater (Martin; Susquehanna): DON R. PERKUCHIN, Mgr., Rt. 1, Box 121, Cambridge 21613 (301, 228-2677)

Eastern Neck: HAROLD C. OLSEN, Mgr., Rt. 2, Box 225, Rock Hall 21661 (301, 639-7056)

Patuxent: HAROLD O'CONNOR, Laurel 20708 (301, 498-0214)

MASSACHUSETTS

Great Meadows (John Hay, NH; Oxbow; Wapack, NH): ED MOSES, Mgr., Weir Hill Rd., Sudbury 01776 (617, 443-4661)

Parker River (Monomoy; Pond Island, ME; Nantucket; Thacher Island; Massasoit): JOHN L. FILLIO, Mgr., Northern Blvd., Plum Island, Newburyport 01950 (617, 465-5753)

Rachel Carson: ANDREW FRENCH, Mgr., Rt. 2, Box 751, Wells, ME 04090 (207, 646-9226)

MICHIGAN

Seney (Huron; Harbor Island): DONALD FRICKIE, Mgr., Seney 49883 (906, 586-9851)

Shiawassee (Michigan Islands; Wyandotte): THOMAS F. PRUSA, Mgr., 6975 Mower Rd., Rt. 1, Saginaw 48601 (517, 777-5930)

MINNESOTA

Agassiz: JOSEPH KOTOK, Mgr., Middle River 56737 (218, 449-4115)

Big Stone: JAMES HEINECKE, Mgr., 25 NW 2nd St., Ortonville 56278 (612, 839-3700)

Minnesota Valley: EDWARD S. CROZIER, Mgr., 4101 E. 80th St., Bloomington 55420 (612 854-5900)

Minnesota Wetlands Complex: ROLLIN SIEGFRIED, Mgr., Rt. 1, Box 76, Fergus Falls 56537 (218, 739-2291)

Morris Wetland Management District: ALFRED RADTKE, Mgr., Rt. 1, Box 208, Mill Dam Rd., Morris 56267 (612, 589-1001)

Fergus Falls Wetland Management District: Vacant, Mgr., Rt. 1, Box 76, Fergus Falls 56537 (218, 739-2291)

Litchfield Wetland Management District: SAMMY J. WALDSTEIN, Mgr., 305 N. Sibley, Litchfield 55355 (612, 693-2849)

Detroit Lakes Wetland Management District: HOWARD A. LIPKE, Mgr., Rt. 3, Box 47D, Detroit Lakes 56501 (218, 847-4431)

Rice Lake (Mille Lacs; Sandstone): JOHN LINDELL, Mgr., Rt. 2, McGregor 55760 (218, 768-2402)

Sherburne: THOMAS LARSON, Mgr., Rt. 2, Zimmerman 55398 (612, 389-3323)

Tamarac: DAROLD WALLS, Mgr., R.R., Rochert 56578 (218, 847-2641)

Upper Mississippi River Complex: See Wisconsin

Upper Mississippi River National Wildlife and Fish Refuge (MN, WI, IL, IA): JIM LENNARTSON, Mgr., 51 E. 4th St., Winona, MN 55987 (507, 452-4232)

Winona District: ROBERT DRIESLEIN, Mgr., 51 E. 4th St., Winona, MN 55987 (507, 454-7351)

MISSISSIPPI

Mississippi Sandhill Crane: JOE W. HARDY, JR., Mgr., Box 699, Gautier 39553 (601, 497-6322)

Noxubee: JIMMIE L. TISDALE, Mgr., Rt. 1, Box 142, Brooksville 39739 (601, 323-5548)

Yazoo: (Hillside; Mathews Brake; Morgan Brake; Panther Swamp): TIM WILKINS, Mgr., Rt. 1, Box 286, Hollandale 38748 (601, 839-2638)

MISSOURI

Annada District (Under Mark Train - See Illinois): ROSS ADAMS, Mgr., P. O. Box 88, Annada 63330 (314, 847-2333)

Mingo: GERALD L. CLAWSON, Mgr., Rt. 1, Box 103, Puxico 63960 (314, 222-3589)

Squaw Creek: RONALD BELL, Mgr., Box 101, Mound City 64470 (816, 442-3187)

Swan Lake: KEN GRANNEMAN, Mgr., Box 68, Sumner 64681 (816, 856-3323)

MONTANA

Benton Lake: ROBERT L. PEARSON, Mgr., Box 450, Black Eagle 59414 (406, 727-7400)

Bowdoin: GENE SIPE, Box T, Malta 59538 (406, 654-2863)

Charles M. Russell (Hailstone; Halfbreed Lake; Lake Mason; Nichols Coulee; Warhorse; UL Bend): JOHN FOSTER, Mgr., Box 110, Lewistown 59457 (406, 538-8706)

Fort Peck Wildlife Station: FRANCIS MAISS, Mgr., Box 166, Fort Peck 59223 (406, 526-3464)

Jordan Wildlife Station: BRADLEY KNUDSEN, Mgr., Box 63, Jordan 59337 (406, 557-6145)

Sand Creek Wildlife Station: MARK HEISINGER, River Route, Roy 59471 (406, 464-5181)

Medicine Lake (Lamesteer): EUGENE STROOPS, HC51, Box 2, Medicine Lake 59247 (406, 789-2305)

National Bison Range (Nine-Pipe; Pablo): JON M. MALCOLM, Mgr., Moiese 59824 (406, 644-2211)

Northwest Montana WMD (Swan River): RAYMOND L. WASHTAK, Mgr., 780 Creston Hatchery Rd., Kalispell 59901 (406, 755-7870)

Lee Metcalf: MARGARET ANDERSON, Mgr., Box 257, Stevensville 59870 (406, 777-5552)

Red Rock Lakes: BARRY REISWIG, Mgr., Monida Star Rt., Box 15, Lima 59739 (406, 276-3347)

Bowdoin (Black Coulee; Creedman Coulee; Hewitt Lake; Lake Thibadeau): GENE SIPE, Mgr., Box J, Malta 59538 (406, 654-2863)

NEBRASKA

Crescent Lake (North Platte): ROYCE HUBER, Mgr., HC-68, Box 21, Ellsworth 69340 (308, 762-4893)

De Soto: See Iowa

Fort Niobrara: ROBERT M. ELLIS, Mgr., Hidden Timber Rt., Valentine 69201 (402, 376-3789)

Valentine: LEONARD L. McDANIEL, Mgr., Hidden Timber Rt., Valentine 69201 (402, 376-3789)

Rainwater Basin Wetland Management District: ALAN K. TROUT, Mgr., Box 1686, Kearney 68847 (308, 236-5015)

NEVADA

Sheldon: See Oregon

Desert National Wildlife Range (Moapa Valley; Pahranagat; Amargosa Pupfish Station; Ash Meadows): DAVID J. BROWN, Mgr., 1500 N. Decatur Blvd., Las Vegas 89108 (702, 646-3401)

Ruby Lake: DANIEL L. PENNINGTON, Mgr., Ruby Valley 89833 (702, 779-2237)

Stillwater (Anaho Island; Fallon): RONALD M. ANGLIN, Mgr., Box 236, 1510 Rio Vista Rd., Fallon 89406 (702, 423-5128)

NEW HAMPSHIRE

Wapack: JOHN HAY, See Massachusetts

NEW JERSEY

Edwin B. Forsythe (Brigantine; Barnegat Divisions): DAVID L. BEALL, Mgr., Great Creek Rd., Box 72, Oceanville 08231 (609, 652-1665)

Great Swamp: WILLIAM KOCH, Mgr., Pleasant Plains Rd., R.D. 1, Box 152, Basking Ridge 07920 (201, 647-1222)

Killcohook: See Pennsylvania

Supawna Meadows: See Pennsylvania

NEW MEXICO

Bitter Lake: LEMOYNE B. MARLATT, Mgr., Box 7, Roswell 88201 (505, 622-6755)

Bosque del Apache: PHILLIP NORTON, Mgr., Box 1246, Socorro 87801 (505, 835-1828)

San Andres: PATTI HOBAN, Box 756, Las Cruces 88001 (505, 382-5047)

Sevilleta: THEODORE M. STANS, Mgr., General Delivery, San Acacia 87831 (505, 864-4021)

Grulla: See Texas

Las Vegas: JOE B. RODRIGUEZ, Mgr., Rt. 1, Box 399, Las Vegas 87701 (505, 425-3581)

Maxwell: JERRY FRENCH, Mgr., Box 276, Maxwell 87728 (505, 375-2331)

NEW YORK

Iroquois: DON TILLER, Mgr., P.O. Box 517, Casey Rd., Alabama 14003 (716, 948-9154)

Montezuma: GRADY E. HOCUTT, Mgr., 3395 Rt. 5/20 East, Seneca Falls 13148 (315, 568-5987)

Wertheim (Amagansett; Lido Beach; Seatuck Elizabeth A. Mortn; Conscience Point Oyster Bay; Target Rock): TOM STEWART, Mgr., P.O. Box 21, Shirley 11967 (516, 286-0485)

NORTH CAROLINA

Alligator River NWR (Currituck; Pea Island): JOHN T. TAYLOR, P.O. Box 1969, Manteo 27954 (919, 473-1131)

Great Dismal Swamp: See Virginia

Mackay Island: WILLIAM H. HEGGE, P.O. Box 31, Knotts Island 27950 (919, 429-3100)

Mattamuskeet (Cedar Island; Swanquarter; Pungo): LARRY R. DITTO, Mgr., Rt. 1, Box N-2, Swanquarter 27885 (919, 926-4021)

Pee Dee: MIKE CANADA, Mgr., Box 780, Wadesboro 28170 (704, 694-4424)

NORTH DAKOTA

Arrowwood (Chase Lake; Slade): DAVID STEARNS, Mgr., R.R. 1, Pingree 58476 (701, 285-3341)

Long Lake: STEVE KNODE, Mgr., Moffit 58560 (701, 387-4397)

Valley City Wetland Management District: DONALD G. HULTMAN, R.R. 1, Valley City 58072 (701, 845-3466)

Audubon (Lake Ilo): DAVID G. POTTER, Mgr., R.R. 1, Coleharbor 58531 (701, 442-5474)

Des Lacs (Lake Zahl): DELANO PIERCE, Mgr., Box 578, Kenmare 58746 (701, 385-4046)

Crosby Wetland Management District: TIM K. KESSLER, Mgr., Box 148, Crosby 58730 (701, 965-6488)

Lostwood: KAREN A. SMITH, Mgr., R.R. 2, Box 98, Kenmare 58746 (701, 848-2722)

Devils Lake Wetland Management District (Lake Alice; Sullys Hill National Game Preserve): MICHAEL R. McENROE, Mgr., Box 908, Devils Lake 58301 (701, 662-8611)

J. Clark Salyer: ROBERT HOWARD, Mgr., Upham 58789 (701, 768-2548)

Kulm Wetland Management District: ROBERT VANDENBERGE, Mgr., Box E, Kulm 58456 (701, 647-2866)

Tewaukon: FRED G. GIESE, Mgr., R.R. 1, Cayuga 58013 (701, 724-3598)

Upper Souris: DEAN KNAUER, Mgr., R.R. 1, Foxholm 58738 (701, 468-5467)

OHIO

Ottawa (Cedar Point; West Sister Island): MICHAEL TANSY, Mgr., 14000 W. State, Rt. 2, Oak Harbor 43449 (419, 898-0014)

OKLAHOMA

Salt Plains: RODNEY F. KREY, Mgr., Rt. 1, Box 76, Jet 73749 (405, 626-4794)

Sequoyah: RONALD S. SULLIVAN, Mgr., Rt. 1, Box 18A, Vian 74962 (918, 773-5251)

Tishomingo: Vacant, Mgr., Rt. 1, Box 151, Tishomingo 73460 (405, 371-2402)

Washita (Optima): JON BROCK, Mgr., Rt. 1, Box 68, Butler 73625 (405, 664-2205)

Wichita Mountains Wildlife Refuge: ROBERT A. KARGES, Mgr., Rt. 1, Box 448, Indiahoma 73552 (405, 429-3221)

OREGON

Sheldon-Hart Mountain (Sheldon): MARVIN R. KASCHKE, Mgr., P.O. Box 111, Rm. 308, US P.O. Bldg., Lakeview 97630 (503, 947-3315)

Hart Mountain: MICHAEL N. FISHER, P.O. Box 111, Rm. 308, US P.O. Bldg., Lakeview 97630 (503, 947-3315)

Columbian White-tailed Deer: See Washington

Klamath Forest and Upper Klamath: See California

Lewis and Clark: See Washington

Malheur: GEORGE CONSTANTINO, Mgr., P.O. Box 245, Princeton 97721 (503, 493-2323)

Umatilla (Cold Springs; McKay Creek; McNary; Toppenish): MORRIS C. LEFEVER, Mgr., P.O. Box 239, Umatilla 97882 (503, 922-3232)

Western Oregon Refuge Complex: PALMER SEKORA, Mgr., Rt. 2, Box 208, Corvallis 97333 (503, 757-7236)

William L. Finley (Ankeny; Bandon Marsh; Cape Meares; Oregon Islands; Three Arch Rocks): DANIEL L. BOONE, Mgr., Rt. 2, Box 208, Corvallis 97333 (503, 757-7236)

Baskett Slough: RALPH L. LETTENMAIER, Mgr., 10995 Highway 22, Dallas 97338 (503, 623-2749)

PENNSYLVANIA

Erie: THOMAS MOUNTAIN, Mgr., R.D. 1, Wood Duck Ln., Guy Mills 16327 (814, 789-3585)

Tinicum National Environmental Center (Killcohook, NJ): RICHARD F. NUGENT, Mgr., Suite 104, Scott Plaza, Supawna Meadows, NJ (See New Jersey)

PUERTO RICO

Caribbean Islands (Cabo Rojo; Culebra; Desecheo; Green Cay, Virgin Islands; Buck Island, Virgin Islands): JAMES P. OLAND, Mgr., Box 510, Carr. 301, KM 5.4, Boqueron 00622 (809, 851-7279)

RHODE ISLAND

Ninigret (Block Island; Sachuest Point; Salt Meadow, CT; Trustom Pond): CHARLES BLAIR, Mgr., Box 307, Charlestown 02813 (401, 364-9124)

Stewart B. McKinney: JAMES MUNSON, Mgr., U.S. Federal Bldg., Rm. 210, 915 Lafayette Blvd., Bridgeport 06604 (203, 579-5617)

SOUTH CAROLINA

Cape Romain: GEORGE R. GARRIS, Mgr., 390 Bulls Island Rd., Awendaw 29429 (803, 928-3368)

Carolina Sandhills: RON SNYDER, Mgr., Rt. 2, Box 330, McBee 29101 (803, 335-8401)

Pee Pee: See North Carolina

Santee: GLENN W. BOND, JR., Mgr., Rt. 2, Box 66, Summerton 29148 (803, 478-2217)

Pinckney Island: See Georgia

SOUTH DAKOTA

Lacreek: ROLF H. KRAFT, Mgr., HWC 3, Box 14, Martin 57551 (605, 685-6508)

Lake Andes (Karl E. Mundt): WILLIAM WILSON, Mgr., R.R. #1, Box 77, Lake Andes 57356 (605, 487-7603)

Madison Wetland Management District: DAVID L. GILBERT, Mgr., Box 48, Madison 57042 (605, 256-2974)

Sand Lake (Pocasse): JOHN KOERNER, Mgr., R.R. 1, Box 25, Columbia 57433 (605, 885-6320)

Waubay: RICHARD GILBERT, Mgr., R.R. 1, Box 79, Wauba 57273 (605, 947-4521)

TENNESSEE

Cross Creeks: VICKI C. GRAFE, Mgr., Rt. 1, Box 229, Dover 37058 (615, 232-7477)

Hatchie (Lower Hatchie): MARVIN L. NICHOLS, Mgr., Box 187, Brownsville 38012 (901, 772-0501)

Reelfoot (Lake Isom): DONALD TEMPLE, Mgr., Rt. 2, Hwy. 157, Union City 38261 (901, 538-2481)

Tennessee: CARRELL L. RYAN, Mgr., Box 849, Paris 38242 (901, 642-2091)

TEXAS

Anahuac (Moody): DOMENICK R. CICCONE, Mgr., Box 278, Anahuac 77514 (409, 267-3337)

McFaddin (Texas Point): JIM KRAKOWSKI, Mgr., Box 278, Anahauc 77514 (409, 971-2909)

Aransas (Matagorda): J. BRENT GIEZENTANNER, Mgr., Box 100, Austwell 77950 (512, 286-3559)

Attwater Prairie Chicken: STEPHEN LABUDA, JR., Mgr., Box 518, Eagle Lake 77434 (409, 234-3021)

Brazoria (Big Boggy): RONALD G. BISBEE, Mgr., Box 1088, Angleton 77515 (409, 849-6062)

San Bernard: JACK CRABTREE, Mgr., Box 1088, Angleton 77515 (409, 964-3639)

Laguna Atascosa: ARTHUR R. RAUCH, Mgr., Box 450, Rio Hondo 78583 (512, 748-3607)

Santa Ana: NITA M. FULLER, Mgr., Rt. 1, Box 202A, Alamo 78516 (512, 787-3079)

Buffalo Lake: JOHNNY BEALL, Mgr., Box 228, Umbarger 79091 (806, 499-3382)

Hagerman: JAMES M. WILLIAMS, Mgr., Rt. 3, Box 123, Sherman 75090 (214, 786-2826)

Muleshoe (Grulla, NM): DON CLAPP, Mgr., Box 549, Muleshoe 79347 (806, 946-3341)

Lower Rio Grande Valley: ROBERT W. SHUMACHER, Mgr., Rt. 1, Box 202A, Alamo 78516 (512, 787-3079)

UTAH

Fish Springs: CHARLES DARLING, Mgr., P.O. Box 568, Dugway 84022 (801, 522-5353)

Ouray (Bear River Migratory Bird Refuge): KEITH S. HANSEN, 1680 W. Hwy. 40, Rm. 1220, Vernal 84078 (801, 789-0351)

VERMONT

Mississquoi: ROBERT A. ZELLEY, Mgr., R.F.D. 2, Swanton 05488 (802, 868-4781)

VIRGINIA

Back Bay (Plum Tree Island): ANTHONY LEGER, Mgr., 4005 Sandpiper Rd., P.O. Box 6286, Virginia Beach 23456 (804, 721-2412)

Eastern Shore of VA (Fisherman Island): SHERMAN W. STAIRS, Mgr., R.F.D. 1, Box 122B, Cape Charles 23310 (804, 331-2760)

MacKay Island, VA: See North Carolina

Chincoteague (Wallops Island): Vacant, Mgr., Box 62, Chincoteague 23336 (804, 336-6122)

Great Dismal Swamp (Nansemond): LLOYD CULP, Mgr., 3216 Desert Rd., P.O. Box 349, Suffolk 23434 (804, 986-3705)

Mason Neck (Featherstone; Marumsco): J. FREDRICK MILTON, Mgr., 14416 Jefferson Davis Hwy., Suite 20A, Woodbridge 22191 (703, 690-1297)

Presquile: BARRY BRADY, Mgr., Box 620, Hopewell 23860 (804, 458-7541)

WASHINGTON

Columbia (Saddle Mountain): DAVID E. GOEKE, Mgr., 44 S. 8th Ave., P.O. Drawer F, Othello 99344 (509, 488-2668)

Ridgefield: (Pierce Ranch; Steigerwald Lake): BRUCE WISEMAN, Mgr., 301 N. Third, P.O. Box 457, Ridgefield 98642 (206, 887-41106)

Conboy Lake: HAROLD E. COLE, JR., Mgr., P.O. Box 5, Glenwood 98619 (509, 364-3410)

Willapa: JAMES A. HIDY, Mgr., HC01, Box 910, Ilwaco 98624 (206, 484-3482)

Columbian White-tailed Deer: RICHARD VETTER, Mgr., P.O. Box 566 C, Cathlamet 98612 (206, 795-3915)

McNary: Vacant, Mgr., Box 308, Burbank 99323 (509, 547-4942)

Nisqually San Juan Islands: WILLARD B. HESSELBART, Mgr., 100 Brown Farm Rd., Olympia 98506 (206, 753-9467)

Dungeness (Protection Island; Washington Island): NANCY CURRY, Mgr., P.O. Box 698, Sequim 98382 (206, 457-8792)

Toppenish: Vacant, Mgr., Rt. 1, Box 1300, Toppenish 98948 (509, 865-2405)

Turnbull: DANIEL BOONE, Mgr., Rt. 3, Box 385, Cheney 99004 (509, 235-4723)

Umatilla: See Oregon

WISCONSIN

Horicon (Gravel Island; Fox River; Green Bay): DICK BIRGER, Mgr., Rt. 2, Mayville 53050 (414, 387-2658)

Necedah: THOMAS S. SANFORD, Mgr., Star Rt., West, Box 386, Necedah 54646 (608, 565-2551)

Upper Mississippi River Complex: RICHARD BERRY, P.O. Bldg., Box 415, LaCrosse 54601 (608, 784-3910)

Upper Mississippi River National Wildlife and Fish Refuge (La Crosse District): RICHARD A. STEINBACH, Mgr., Rm. 208, P.O. Bldg., Box 415, La Crosse 54601 (608, 783-6451)

Trempealeau: ROBERT BARTELS, Mgr., Rt. 1, Trempealeau 54661 (608, 539-2311)

WYOMING

Bamforth: See Colorado

Hutton Lake: See Colorado

Pathfinder: See Colorado

National Elk Refuge: JOHN E. WILBRECHT, Mgr., Box C, Jackson 83001 (307, 733-9212)

Seedskadee: FRAN MAISSE, Mgr., P.O. Box 67, Green River 82935 (307, 875-2187)

Regional Directors:

Region 1: Vacant, Director, Lloyd 500 Bldg., Suite 1692, 500 NE Multnomah St., Portland, OR 97232 (503, 231-6118)

Region 2: MICHAEL J. SPEAR, Director, Box 1306, Albuquerque, NM 87103 (505, 766-2321)

Region 3: JAMES C. GRITMAN, Director, Federal Bldg., Fort Snelling, Twin Cities, MN 55111 (612, 725-3563)

Region 4: JAMES W. PULLIAM, JR., Director, Richard B. Russell Federal Bldg., 75 Spring St., SW, Atlanta, GA 30303 (404, 331-3588)

Region 5: RONALD LAMBERTSON, Director, One Gateway Center, Suite 700, Newton Corner, MA 02158 (617, 965-5100)

Region 6: GALEN A. BUTERBAUGH, Director, 134 Union Blvd., Lakewood, CO.; P.O. Box 25486, Denver Federal Center, Denver, CO 80225 (303, 236-7920)

Region 7: WALTER STIEGLITZ, Director, 1011 East Tudor Rd., Anchorage, AK 99503 (907, 786-3542)

NATIONAL FORESTS IN THE UNITED STATES

The National Forests are administered by the Forest Service.

ALABAMA

Conecuh, Talladega, and Tuskegee National Forests: JOE J. BROWN, Supervisor, National Forests in Alabama, 1765 Highland Ave., Montgomery 36107 (205, 832-4470)

ALASKA

Chugach National Forest: DALTON DuLAC, Supervisor, 201 E. Ninth Ave., Suite 206, Anchorage 99501 (907, 271-2500)

Tongass-Chatham Area National Forest: Vacant, Supervisor, 204 Siginaka Way, Sitka 99835 (907, 747-6671)

Tongass-Ketchikan Area National Forest: MIKE LUNN, Supervisor, Federal Bldg., Ketchikan 99901 (907, 225-3101)

Tongass-Stikine Area National Forest: Vacant, Supervisor, Box 309, Petersburg 99833 (907, 772-3841)

ARIZONA

Apache-Sitgreaves National Forest: NICK W. McDONOUGH, Supervisor, Federal Bldg., Box 640, Springerville 85938 (602, 333-4301)

Coconino National Forest: NEIL R. PAULSON, Supervisor, 2323 E. Greenlaw Ln., Flagstaff 86004 (602, 527-7400)

Coronado National Forest: ROBERT B. TIPPECONNIC, Supervisor, 300 W. Congress, Tucson 85701 (602, 629-6483)

Kaibab National Forest: LEONARD A. LINDQUIST, Supervisor, 800 South 6th St., Williams 86046 (602, 635-2681)

Prescott National Forest: COY JEMMETT, Supervisor, 344 S. Cortez, Prescott 86303 (602, 445-1762)

Tonto National Forest: JAMES L. KIMBALL, Supervisor, 2324 E. McDowell Rd., P.O. Box 5348, Phoenix 85010 (602, 225-5200)

ARKANSAS

Ouachita National Forest: MIKE CURRAN, Supervisor, Box 1270, Federal Bldg., Hot Springs National Park 71902 (501, 321-5202)

Ozark and St. Francis National Forests: LYNN C. NEFF, Supervisor, 605 West Main, Box 1008, Russellville 72801 (501, 968-2354),

CALIFORNIA

Angeles National Forest: GEORGE A. ROBY, Supervisor, 701 N. Santa Anita Ave., Arcadia 91006 (818, 574-1613)

Cleveland National Forest: MICHAEL J. ROGERS, Supervisor, 880 Front St., San Diego 92188 (619, 557-5050)

Eldorado National Forest: JERALD N. HUTCHINS, Supervisor, 100 Forni Rd., Placerville 95667 (916, 622-5062)

Inyo National Forest: DENNIS W. MARTIN, 873 North Main St., Bishop 93514 (619, 873-5841)

Klamath National Forest: ROBERT L. RICE, Supervisor, 1312 Fairlane Rd., Yreka 96097 (916, 842-6131)

Lassen National Forest: DICK HENRY, Supervisor, 55 S. Sacramento St., Susanville 96130 (916, 257-2151)

Los Padres National Forest: ARTHUR J. CARROLL, Supervisor, 6144 Calle Real, Goleta 93117 (805, 683-6711)

Mendocino National Forest: DANIEL C. CHISHOLM, 420 E. Laurel St., Willows 95988 (916, 934-3316)

Modoc National Forest: DOUGLAS G. SMITH, Supervisor, 441 N. Main St., Alturas 96101 (916, 233-5811)

Plumas National Forest: MARY J. COULOMBE, Supervisor, 159 Lawrence St., Box 11500, Quincy 95971-6025 (916, 283-2050)

San Bernardino National Forest: RICHARD STAUBER, Supervisor, 1824 S. Commeercenter Cir., San Bernardino 92408-3430 (714, 383-5588)

Sequoia National Forest: JAMES A. CRATES, Supervisor, 900 W. Grand Ave., Porterville 93257 (209, 784-1500)

Shasta-Trinity National Forest: ROBERT R. TYRREL, Supervisor, 2400 Washington Ave., Redding 96001 (916, 246-5222)

Sierra National Forest: JAMES L. BOYNTON, Supervisor, Federal Bldg., 1130 O St., Rm. 3017, Fresno 93721 (209, 487-5155)

Six Rivers National Forest: JAMES L. DAVIS, JR., Supervisor, 507 F St., Eureka 95501 (707, 442-1721)

Stanislaus National Forest: BLAINE L. CORNELL, Supervisor, 19777 Greenley Rd., Sonora 95370 (209, 532-3671)

Tahoe National Forest: GERI B. LARSON, Supervisor, Highway 49, Nevada City 95959 (916, 265-4531)

COLORADO

Arapaho and Roosevelt National Forests: RAYMOND O. BENTON, Supervisor, 240 W. Prospect St., Fort Collins 80526 (303, 224-1100)

Grand Mesa, Uncompahgre, and Gunnison National Forests: RAYMOND J. EVANS, Supervisor, 2250 Highway 50, Delta 81416 (303, 874-7691)

Pike and San Isabel National Forests: JACK A. WEISSLING, Supervisor, 1920 Valley Dr., Pueblo 81008 (303, 545-8737)

Rio Grande National Forest: JAMES B. WEBB, Supervisor, 1803 West Highway 160, Monte Vista 81144 (303, 852-5941)

Routt National Forest: JERRY E. SCHMIDT, Supervisor, 29587 W. US40, Suite 20, Steamboat Springs 80487 (303, 879-1722)

San Juan National Forest: WILLIAM SEXTON, Supervisor, Federal Bldg., 701 Camino Del Rio, Durango 81301 (303, 247-4874)

White River National Forest: TOM HOOTS, Supervisor, Old Federal Bldg., Box 948, Glenwood Springs 81602 (303, 945-2521)

FLORIDA

Apalachicola, Ocala, and Osceola National Forests: ROBERT T. (Bob) JACOBS, Supervisor, National Forests in Florida, City Centre Bldg., 227 No. Bronough St., Suite 4061, Tallahassee 32301 (904, 681-7265)

GEORGIA

Chattahoochee and Oconee National Forests: Vacant, Supervisor, 508 Oak St., NW, Gainesville 30501 (404, 536-0541)

IDAHO

Boise National Forest: DAVE RITTERSBACHER, Supervisor, 1750 Front St., Boise 83702 (208, 334-1516)

Caribou National Forest: PAUL R. NORDWALL, 250 S. 4th Ave., Suite 282, Federal Bldg., Pocatello 83201 (208, 236-6700)

Challis National Forest: JACK C. GRISWOLD, Supervisor, P.O. Box 404, Challis 83226 (208, 879-2285)

Clearwater National Forest: FREDERICK L. TREVEY, Supervisor, 12730 Highway 12, Orofino 83544 (208, 476-4541)

Idaho Panhandle National Forests: WILLIAM E. MORDEN, Supervisor, 1201 Ironwood Dr., Coeur d'Alene 83814 (208, 765-7223)

Nez-perce National Forest: TOM KOVALICKY, Supervisor, Rt. 2, Box 475, Grangeville 83530 (208, 983-1950)

Payette National Forest: VETO J. (Sonny) LASALLE, Supervisor, Forest Service Bldg., Box 1026, McCall 83638 (208, 634-8151)

Salmon National Forest: RICHARD T. HAUFF, Supervisor, Forest Service Bldg., Salmon 83467 (208, 756-2215)

Sawtooth National Forest: ROLAND M. STOLESON, Supervisor, 2647 Kimberly Rd., East, Twin Falls 8330-7976 (208, 737-3200)

Targhee National Forest: JOHN E. BURNS, 420 N. Bridge St., P.O. Box 208, St. Anthony 83445 (208, 624-3151)

ILLINOIS

Shawnee National Forest: KENNETH D. HENDERSON, Supervisor, 901 S. Commercial St., Harrisburg 62946 (618, 253-7114)

INDIANA

Wayne-Hoosier National Forest: FRANCIS J. VOYTAS, Supervisor, 811 Constitution Ave., Bedford 47421 (812, 275-5987)

KENTUCKY

Daniel Boone National Forest: RICHARD H. WENGERT, Supervisor, 100 Vaught Rd., Winchester 40391 (606, 745-3100)

LOUISIANA

Kisatchie National Forest: DANNY W. BRITT, Supervisor, 2500 Shreveport Hwy., Pineville 71360 (318, 473-7160)

MAINE

White Mountain National Forest: See New Hampshire

MICHIGAN

Hiawatha National Forest: R. KENNETH. HOLTJE, Supervisor, 2727 N. Lincoln Rd., Escanaba 49829 (906, 786-4062)

Huron-Manistee National Forest: JERRY W. McCORMICK, Supervisor, 421 S. Mitchell St., Cadillac 49601 (616, 775-2421)

Ottawa National Forest: DAVID H. MORTON, Supervisor, East U.S. 2, Ironwood 49938 (906, 932-1330)

MINNESOTA

Chippewa National Forest: WILLIAM F. SPINNER, Supervisor, Cass Lake 56633 (218, 335-2226)

Superior National Forest: CLAY C. BEAL, Supervisor, Box 338, Duluth 55801 (218, 720-5322)

MISSISSIPPI

Bienville, Delta, Desoto, Holly Springs, Homochitto, and Tombigbee National Forests: L.W. (Bud) BRADDOCK, Supervisor, National Forests in Mississippi, 100 W Capital St., Suite 1141, Jackson 39269 (601, 965-5486)

MISSOURI

Mark Twain National Forest: B. ERIC MORSE, Supervisor, 401 Fairgrounds Rd., Rolla 65401 (314, 364-4621)

MONTANA

Beaverhead National Forest: RONALD C. PRICHARD, Box 1258, 610 N. Montana St., Dillon 59725 (406, 683-3900)

Bitterroot National Forest: ROBERT S. MORGAN, Supervisor, 316 N. 3rd St., Hamilton 59840 (406, 363-3131)

Custer National Forest: DAVID A. FILIUS, Supervisor, Box 2556, Billings 59103 (406, 657-6361)

Deerlodge National Forest: FRANK E. SALOMONSEN, Supervisor, Federal Bldg., Box 400, Butte 59703 (406, 496-3400)

Flathead National Forest: EDGAR B. BRANNON, JR., Supervisor, Box 147, 1935 3rd Ave., E., Kalispell 59901 (406, 755-5401)

Gallatin National Forest: ROBERT S. GIBSON, Supervisor, Federal Bldg., Box 130, Bozeman 59771 (406, 587-6701/585-5011)

Helena National Forest: ERNIE NUNN, Supervisor, Federal Bldg., Drawer 10014, Helena 59626 (406, 449-5201)

Kootenai National Forest: JAMES F. RATHBUN, Supervisor, 506 Highway 2W, Libby 59923 (406, 293-6211)

Lewis and Clark National Forest: J. DALE GORMAN, Supervisor, Box 871, 1101 15th St., N., Great Falls 59403 (406, 791-7700)

Lolo National Forest: ORVILLE L. DANIELS, Supervisor, Bldg. 24, Ft. Missoula, Missoula 59801 (406, 329-3750)

NEBRASKA

Nebraska National Forest: ROBERT L. STORCH, Supervisor, 270 Pine St., Chadron 69337 (308, 432-3367)

NEVADA

Humboldt National Forest: BOBBY JOE GRAVES, Supervisor, 976 Mountain City Hwy., Elko 89801 (702, 738-5171)

Toiyabe National Forest: R.M. (Jim) NELSON, Supervisor, 1200 Franklin Way, Sparks Way 89431, (702, 355-5331)

NEW HAMPSHIRE

White Mountain National Forest: MICHAEL B. HATHAWAY, Supervisor, Federal Bldg., 719 Main St., Box 638, Laconia 03247 (603, 524-6450)

NEW MEXICO

Carson National Forest: JOHN C. BEDELL, Supervisor, Forest Service Bldg., Box 558, Taos 87571 (505, 758-6200)

Cibola National Forest: CHESTER P. SMITH, Supervisor, 10308 Candelaria, NE, Albuquerque 87112 (505, 275-5207)

Gila National Forest: DAVID W. DAHL, Supervisor, 2610 N. Silver St., Silver City 88061 (505, 388-8201)

Lincoln National Forest: JAMES R. ABBOTT, Supervisor, Federal Bldg., 11th and New York, Alamogordo 88310 (505, 437-6030)

Santa Fe National Forest: MAYNARD T. ROST, Supervisor, Pinon Bldg., 1220 St. Francis Dr., Box 1689, Santa Fe 87504 (505, 988-6940)

NORTH CAROLINA

Croatan, Nantahala, Pisgah, and Uwharrie National Forests: BJORN DAHL, Supervisor, National Forests in North Carolina, Post & Otis Sts., Box 2750, Asheville 28802 (704, 257-4200)

OHIO

Wayne National Forest: HAROLD L. GODLEVSKE, Supervisor, 3527 10th St., Bedford, IN 47421 (DD-8-332-4340)

OREGON

Deschutes National Forest: NORM ARSENEAULT, Supervisor, 1645 Highway 20 East, Bend 97701 (503, 388-2715)

Fremont National Forest: ORVILLE D. GROSSARTH, Supervisor, 524 North G St., Lakeview 97630 (503, 947-2151)

Malheur National Forest: MARK BOCHE, Supervisor, 139 NE Dayton St., John Day 97845 (503, 575-1731)

Mt. Hood National Forest: DAVE MOHLA, Supervisor, 2955 Division St., Gresham 97030 (503, 666-0700)

Ochoco National Forest: TERRY SOLBERG, Supervisor, Box 490, Federal Bldg., Prineville 97754 (503, 447-6247)

Rogue River National Forest: STEVEN W. DEITEMEYER, Supervisor, Federal Bldg., 333 W. 8th St., Box 520, Medford 97501 (503, 776-3600)

Siskiyou National Forest: RONALD J. McCORMICK, Supervisor, Box 440, Grants Pass 97526 (503, 479-5301)

Siuslaw National Forest: TOM L. THOMPSON, Supervisor, Box 1148, Corvallis 97339 (503, 757-4480)

Umatilla National Forest: JAMES LAWRENCE, Supervisor, 2517 SW Hailey Ave., Pendleton 97801 (503, 276-3811)

Umpqua National Forest: ROBERT J. DEVLIN, Supervisor, Box 1008, Roseburg 97470 (503, 672-6601)

Wallowa Whitman National Forests: ROBERT RICHMOND, Supervisor, Box 907, Baker 97814 (503, 523-6391)

Willamette National Forest: MICHAEL A. KERRICK, Supervisor, Box 10607, Eugene 97440 (503, 687-6521)

Winema National Forest: LEE F. COONCE, Supervisor, 2819 Dahlia, Klamath Falls 97601 (603, 883-6714)

PENNSYLVANIA

Allegheny National Forest: DAVID J. WRIGHT, Supervisor, 222 Liberty St., BOX 847, Warren 16365 (814, 723-5150)

PUERTO RICO

Caribbean National Forest: BERNIE RIOS, Supervisor, Call Box 25000, Rio Piedras 00928-2500 (809, 753-4335)

SOUTH CAROLINA

Francis Marion and Sumter National Forests: DONALD W. ENG, Supervisor, 1835 Assembly St., Box 2227, Columbia 29202 (803, 765-5222)

SOUTH DAKOTA

Black Hills National Forest: DARREL L. KENOPS, Supervisor, R.R. I, Custer 57730-9504 (605, 673-2251)

TENNESSEE

Cherokee National Forest: DONALD L. ROLLENS, Supervisor, 2800 N. Ocoee St., NW, Box 2010, Cleveland 37320 (615, 476-9700)

TEXAS

Angelina, Davy Crockett, Sabine, and Sam Houston National Forests: WILLIAM M. LANNAN, Supervisor, National Forests in Texas, Homer Garrison Federal Bldg., 701 N. 1st St., Lufkin 75901 (409, 639-8501)

UTAH

Ashley National Forest: DUANE G. TUCKER, Supervisor, Ashton Energy Center, 1680 W. Highway 40, Suite 1150, Vernal 84078 (801, 789-1181)

Dixie National Forest: HIGH C. THOMPSON, Supervisor, 82 N. 100 E. St., P.O. Box 580, Cedar City 84720 (801, 586-2421)

Fishlake National Forest: J. KENT TAYLOR, Supervisor, 115 East 900 North, Richfield 84701 (801, 896-4491)

Manti-LaSal National Forest: GEORGE A. MORRIS, Supervisor, 599 West Price River Dr., Price 84501 (801, 637-2817)

Uinta National Forest: DON T. NEBEKER, Supervisor, 88 West 100 North, Provo 84601 (801, 377-5780)

Wasatch-Cache National Forest: DALE BOSWORTH, Supervisor, 8230 Federal Bldg., 125 S. State St., Salt Lake City 84138 (801, 524-5030)

VERMONT

Green Mountain National Forest: STEPHEN C. HARPER, Supervisor, Federal Bldg., 151 West St., P.O. Box 519, Rutland 05701-0519 (802, 773-0300)

VIRGINIA

George Washington National Forest: GEORGE W. KELLY, Supervisor, P.O. Box 233, Harrison Plaza, Harrisonburg 22801 (703, 433-2491)

Jefferson National Forest: Vacant, Supervisor, Rm. 954, 210 Franklin Rd., SW, Roanoke 24001 (703, 982-6270)

WASHINGTON

Colville National Forest: ED SCHULTZ, Supervisor, 695 S. Main, Colville 99114 (509, 684-3711)

Gifford Pinchot National Forest: ROBERT WILLIAMS, Supervisor, 6926 E. 4th Plain Blvd., Vancouver 98660 (206, 696-7500)

Mt. Baker-Snoqualmie National Forest: J.D. MacWILLIAMS, Supervisor, 1022 First Ave., Seattle 98104 (206, 442-5400)

Okanogan National Forest: WILLIAM D. McLAUGHLIN, Supervisor, 1240 South Second, Okanogan 98840 (509, 422-2704)

Olympic National Forest: TED C. STUBBLEFIELD, Supervisor, Box 2288, Olympia 98507 (206, 753-9534)

Wenatchee National Forest: SONNY O'NEAL, Supervisor, Box 811, Wenatchee 98801 (509, 662-4335)

WEST VIRGINIA

Monongahela National Forest: JIM PAGE, Supervisor, USDA Bldg., Sycamore St., Box 1548, Elkins 26241-1548 (304, 636-1800)

WISCONSIN

Chequamegon National Forest: JOHN C. WOLTER, Supervisor, 1170 4th Ave., South, Park Falls 54552 (715, 762-2461)

Nicolet National Forest: JAMES S. BERLIN, Supervisor, Federal Bldg., 68 S. Stevens, Rhinelander 54501 (715, 362-3415)

WYOMING

Bridger-Teton National Forest: BRIAN STOUT, Supervisor, Forest Service Bldg., 340 N. Cache, Box 1888, Jackson 83001 (307, 733-2752)

Bighorn National Forest: LLOYD D. TODD, Supervisor, 1969 S. Sheridan Ave., Sheridan 82801 (307, 672-0751)

Medicine Bow National Forest: GERALD G. HEATH, 605 Skyline Dr., Laramie 82070 (307, 328-0471)

Shoshone National Forest: STEPHEN P. MEALEY, Supervisor, 225 West Yellowstone Ave., Box 2140, Cody 82414 (307, 527-6241)

NATIONAL PARKS IN THE UNITED STATES

The National Parks are administered by the National Park Service, United States Department of the Interior, Washington, DC 20240.

ALASKA

Denali National Park: ROBERT C. CUNNINGHAM, Supt., P.O. Box 9, McKinley Park 99755 (907, 683-2294)

Gates of the Arctic National Park: ROGER J. SIGLIN, Supt., P.O. Box 74680, Fairbanks 99707 (907, 452-5363)

Glacier Bay National Park: MARVIN JENSEN, Supt., Gustavus 99826 (907, 697-2232)

Katmai National Park: RAY BANE, Supt., P.O. Box 7, King Salmon 99613 (907, 246-3305)

Kenai Fjords National Park: ANNA J.O. CASTELLINA, Supt., P.O. Box 1727, Seward 99664 (907, 224-3874)

Kobuk Valley National Park: ALAN O. ELIASON, Supt., P.O. Box 287, Kotzebue 99752 (907, 442-3890)

Lake Clark National Park: ANDREW HUTCHISON, Supt., P.O. Box 61, Anchorage 99513 (907, 781-2205)

Wrangell-St. Elias National Park: RICHARD H. MARTIN, Supt., P.O. Box 29, Glenn Allen 99588 (907, 822-5235)

ARIZONA

Grand Canyon National Park: RICHARD W. MARKS, Supt., P.O. Box 129, Grand Canyon 86023 (602, 638-7888)

Petrified Forest National Park: EDWARD L. GASTELLUM, Supt., Petrified Forest National Park 86028 (602, 524-6228)

ARKANSAS

Hot Springs National Park: ROGER GIDDINGS, Supt., P.O. Box 1860, Hot Springs 71901 (501, 624-3383)

CALIFORNIA

Lassen Volcanic National Park: GILBERT E. BLINN, Supt., Mineral 96063 (916, 595-4444)

Redwood National Park: DOUGLAS G. WARNOCK, Supt., 1111 Second St., Crescent City 95531 (707, 464-6101)

Sequoia and Kings Canyon National Parks: JOHN H. DAVIS, Supt., Three Rivers 93271 (209, 565-3341)

Yosemite National Park: JOHN M. MOREHEAD, Supt., P.O. Box 577, Yosemite National Park 95389 (209, 372-4461)

Channel Islands National Park: WILLIAM H. EHORN, Supt., 1901 Spinnaker Dr., Ventura 93001 (805, 644-8157)

COLORADO

Mesa Verde National Park: ROBERT C. HEYDER, Supt., Mesa Verde National Park 81330 (303, 529-4465)

Rocky Mountain National Park: JAMES B. THOMPSON, Supt., Estes Park 80517 (303, 586-2371)

FLORIDA

Biscayne National Park: JAMES A. SANDERS, Supt., P.O. Box 1369, Homestead 33030 (305, 247-2044)

Everglades National Park: MICHAEL V. FINLEY, Supt., P.O. Box 279, Homestead 33030 (305, 247-6211)

HAWAII

Haleakala National Park: DONALD W. REESER, Supt., P.O. Box 369, Makawao, Maui 96768 (808, 572-9177)

Hawaii Volcanoes National Park: HUGO H. HUNTZINGER, Supt., Hawaii National Park 96718 (808, 967-7311)

KENTUCKY

Mammoth Cave National Park: FRANKLIN D. PRIDEMORE, Supt., Mammoth Cave 42259 (502, 758-2251)

MAINE

Acadia National Park: JOHN A. (Jack) HAUPTMAN, Supt., P.O. Box 177, Bar Harbor 04609 (207, 288-3338)

MICHIGAN

Isle Royale National Park: THOMAS C. HOBBS, Supt., 87 North Ripley St., Houghton 49931 (906, 482-3310)

MINNESOTA

Voyageurs National Park: RUSSELL W. BERRY, JR., Supt., P.O. Box 50, International Falls 56649 (218, 283-9821)

MONTANA

Glacier National Park: H. GILBERT LUSK, Supt., West Glacier 59936 (406, 888-5441)

NEVADA

Great Basin National Park: ALBERT J. HENDRICKS, Supt., Baker 89311 (702, 234-7331)

NEW MEXICO

Carlsbad Caverns National Park: RICHARD B. SMITH, Supt., 3225 National Parks Hwy., Carlsbad 88220 (505, 885-8884)

NORTH DAKOTA

Theodore Roosevelt National Park: CHARLES M. (Mack) SHAVER, Supt., P.O. Box 7, Medora 58645 (701, 623-4466)

OREGON

Crater Lake National Park: ROBERT E. BENTON, Supt., P.O. Box 7, Crater Lake 97604 (503, 594-2211)

SOUTH DAKOTA

Wind Cave National Park: ERNEST W. ORTEGA, Supt., Hot Springs 57747 (605, 745-4600)

Badlands National Park: IRVIN L. MORTENSON, Supt., P.O. Box 6, Interior 57750 (605, 433-5361)

TENNESSEE

Great Smoky Mountains National Park: RANDALL R. POPE, Supt., Gatlinburg 37738 (615, 436-5615)

TEXAS

Big Bend National Park: JAMES W. CARRICO, Supt., Big Bend National Park 79834 (915, 477-2251)

Guadalupe Mountains National Park: KAREN WADE, Supt., HC 60, Box 400, Salt Flat 79847-9400 Carlsbad 88220 (915, 828-3351)

UTAH

Arches National Park: PAUL D. GURAEDY, Supt., c/o Canyonlands National Park, 446 S. Main St., Moab 84532 (801, 259-8161)

Bryce Canyon National Park: ROBERT W. REYNOLDS, Supt., Bryce Canyon 84717 (801, 834-5322)

Canyonlands National Park: HARVEY D. WICKWARE, Supt., 446 South Main St., Moab 84532 (801, 259-7165)

Capitol Reef National Park: MARTIN C. (Marty) OTT, Supt., Torrey 84775 (801, 425-3871)

Zion National Park: HAROLD L. GRAFE, Supt., Springdale 84767 (801, 772-3256)

VIRGINIA

Shenandoah National Park: WILLIAM WADE, Supt., Luray 22835 (703, 999-2243)

VIRGIN ISLANDS

Virgin Islands National Park: RICHARD H. MAEDER, Supt., P.O. Box 7789, Charlotte Amalie, St. Thomas 00801 (809, 775-2050)

WASHINGTON

Mount Rainier National Park: NEAL G. GUSE, Supt., Tahoma Woods, Star Route, Ashford 98304 (206, 569-2211)

North Cascades National Park: JOHN REYNOLDS, Supt., 800 State St., Sedro Woolley 98284 (206, 855-1331)

Olympic National Park: ROBERT S. CHANDLER, Supt., 600 E. Park Ave., Port Angeles 98362 (206, 452-4501)

WYOMING

Grand Teton National Park: JACK E. STARK, Supt., P.O. Drawer 170, Moose 83012 (307, 733-2880)

Yellowstone National Park: ROBERT D. BARBEE, Supt., P.O. Box 168, Yellowstone National Park 82190 (307, 344-7381)

NATIONAL SEASHORES IN THE UNITED STATES

The National Seashores are administered by the National Park Service, United States Department of the Interior, Washington, DC 20240.

CALIFORNIA
Point Reyes National Seashore: JOHN L. SANSING, Supt., Point Reyes 94956 (415, 663-8522)

FLORIDA
Canaveral National Seashore: SIBBAL SMITH, Supt., P.O. Box 6447, Titusville 32782-6447 (305, 867-0634)
Gulf Islands National Seashore: JERRY A. EUBANKS, Supt., P.O. Box 100, Gulf Breeze 32561 (904, 932-5302)

GEORGIA
Cumberland Island National Seashore: KENNETH O. MORGAN, Supt., P.O. Box 806, Saint Marys 31558 (912, 882-4336)

MARYLAND
Assateague Island National Seashore: ROGER K. RECTOR, Supt., Rt. 2, Box 294, Berlin 21811 (301, 641-1441)

MASSACHUSETTS
Cape Cod National Seashore: HERBERT OLSEN, Supt., South Wellfleet 02663 (617, 349-3785)

MISSISSIPPI
Gulf Islands National Seashore: See Florida

NEW YORK
Fire Island National Seashore: NOEL J. PACHTA, Supt., 120 Laurel St., Patchogue 11772 (516, 289-4810)

NORTH CAROLINA
Cape Lookout National Seashore: WILLIAM A. HARRIS, Supt., P.O. Box 690, Beaufort 28516 (919, 728-2121)
Cape Hatteras National Seashore: THOMAS L. HARTMAN, Supt., Rt. 1, Box 695, Manteo 27964 (919, 473-2111)

TEXAS
Padre Island National Seashore: JOHN D. HUNTER, JR., Supt., 9405 South Padre Island Dr., Corpus Christi 78418 (512, 937-2621)

BUREAU OF LAND MANAGEMENT DISTRICTS IN THE UNITED STATES

The Bureau of Land Management Districts supervised by each state office are listed below.

ALASKA
 Anchorage District: JOHN J. RUMPS, Mgr., 6881 Abbot Loop., Anchorage 99507 (907, 267-1246)
 Glennallen District: GENE R. TERLAND, Mgr., P.O. Box 147, Glennallen 99588 (907, 267-1369)
 Arctic District: M. THOMAS DEAN, Mgr., 1541 Gaffney Rd., Fairbanks 99703 (907, 356-5130)
 Kobuk District: ROGER A. BOLSTAD, Mgr., 1541 Gaffney Rd., Fairbanks 99703 (907, 356-5384)
 Steese/White Mountain District: DONALD E. RUNBERG, Mgr., 1541 Gaffney Rd., Fairbanks 99703 (907, 356-5367)

ARIZONA
 Arizona Strip District: G. WILLIAM LAMB, Mgr., 390 North, 3050 East, St. George, UT 84770 (801, 673-3545)
 Phoenix District: HENRY R. BISSON, Mgr., 2015 W. Deer Valley Rd., Phoenix 85027 (602, 863-4464)
 Safford District: RAY A. BRADY, Mgr., 425 E. 4th St., Safford 85546 (602, 428-4040)
 Yuma District: J. DARWIN SNELL, Mgr., 2450 Fourth Ave., P.O. Box 5680, Yuma 85364 (602, 726-6300)

CALIFORNIA
 Bakersfield District: ROBERT D. RHEINER, JR., Mgr., 800 Truxton Ave., Rm. 302, Bakersfield 93301 (805, 861-4191)
 California Desert District: GERALD E. HILLIER, Mgr., 1695 Spruce St., Riverside 92507 (714, 351-6386)
 Susanville District: C. REX CLEARY, Mgr., 705 Hall St., Susanville 96130-3730 (916, 257-5381)
 Ukiah District: ALFRED W. WRIGHT, Mgr., 555 Leslie St., P.O. Box 940, Ukiah 95482 (707, 462-3873)

COLORADO
 Canon City District: DONNIE R. SPARKS, Mgr., 3170 E. Main St., P.O. Box 311, Canon City 81212 (303, 275-0631)
 Craig District: WILLIAM PULFORD, Mgr., 455 Emerson St., Craig 81625 (303, 824-8261)
 Grand Junction District: RICHARD FREEL, Mgr., 764 Horizon Dr., Grand Junction 81506 (303, 243-6552)
 Montrose District: ALAN L. KESTERKE, Mgr., 2465 S. Townsend, Montrose 81401 (303, 249-7791)

EASTERN STATES (All states bordering and east of the Mississippi River)
 Jackson District: Vacant, Mgr., 300 Woodrow Wilson Dr., Suite 326, Jackson, MS 39213 (601, 960-4405)
 Milwaukee District: BERT RODGERS, Mgr., P.O. Box 631, Milwaukee, WI 53201-0631 (414, 291-4400)

IDAHO
 Boise District: J. DAVID BRUNNER, Mgr., 3948 Development Ave., Boise 83705 (208, 334-1582)
 Burley District: JOHN S. DAVIS, Mgr., Rte. 3, Box 1, Burley 83318 (208, 678-5514)
 Coeur d'Alene District: FRITZ U. RENNEBAUM, Mgr., 1808 N. Third St., Coeur d'Alene 83814 (208, 765-7356)
 Idaho Falls District: LLOYD H. FERGUSON, Mgr., 940 Lincoln Rd., Idaho Falls 83401 (208, 529-1020)
 Salmon District: JERRY W. GOODMAN, Mgr., P.O. Box 430, Salmon 83467 (208, 756-2201)
 Shoshone District: JOHN M. IDSO, Mgr., 400 West 'F' St., P.O. Box 2B, Shoshone 83352 (208, 886-2206)

MONTANA (Also North Dakota and South Dakota)
 Butte District: JAMES A. MOORHOUSE, Mgr., 106 N. Parkmont, P.O. Box 3388, Butte, MT 59702 (406, 494-5059)
 Dickinson District: WILLIAM F. KRECH, Mgr., P.O. Box 1229, Dickinson, ND 58602 (701, 225-9148)
 Lewistown District: WAYNE W. ZINNE, Mgr., Airport Rd., Lewiston, MT 59457 (406, 538-7461)
 Miles City District: MATTHEW MILLENBACH, Mgr., West of Miles City, P.O. Box 940, Miles City, MT 59301 (406, 232-4331)

NEVADA
 Battle Mountain District: TERRY PLUMMER, Mgr., P.O. Box 1420, Battle Mountain 89820 (702, 635-5181)
 Carson City District: JAMES W. ELLIOTT, Mgr., 1535 Hot Springs Rd., Suite 300, Carson City 89701 (702, 882-1631)
 Elko District: RODNEY HARRIS, Mgr., P.O. Box 831, Elko 89801 (702, 738-4071)
 Ely District: KENNETH WALKER, Mgr., Star Route 5, Box 1, Ely 89301 (702, 289-4865)
 Las Vegas District: BEN COLLINS, Mgr., 4765 Vegas Dr., P.O. Box 26569, Las Vegas 89126 (702, 388-6403)
 Winnemucca District: FRANK C. SHIELDS, Mgr., 705 E. 4th St., Winnemucca 89445 (702, 623-3676)

NEW MEXICO (Also Kansas, Oklahoma, and Texas)
 Albuquerque District: ROBERT DALE, Mgr., P.O. Box 6770, Albuquerque 87197-6770 (505, 766-8281)
 Las Cruces District: JIM FOX, Mgr., 1800 Marquess, P.O. Box 1420, Las Cruces 88004-1420 (505, 525-8228)
 Roswell District: FRANCIS R. CHERRY, JR., Mgr., 1717 W. Second St., P.O. Box 1397, Roswell 88201-1397 (505, 622-9042)
 Tulsa District: JAMES F. SIMS, Mgr., 9522-H East 47th Pl., Tulsa, OK 74145 (918, 581-6480)

OREGON (Also Washington)
 Burns District: JOSHUA L. WARBURTON, Mgr., 74 S. Alvord St., Burns 97720 (503, 573-5241)
 Coos Bay District: Vacant, Mgr., 333 S. Fourth St., Coos Bay 97420 (503, 269-5880)
 Eugene District: MELVIN D. CLAUSEN, Mgr., 1255 Pearl St., P.O. Box 10226, Eugene 97401 (503, 687-6651)
 Lakeview District: JERRY ASHER, Mgr., 1000 Ninth St., S., P.O. Box 151, Lakeview 97630 (503, 947-2177)
 Medford District: Vacant, Mgr., 3040 Biddle Rd., Medford 97504 (503, 776-4173)
 Prineville District: JAMES L. HANCOCK, Mgr., P.O. Box 550, Prineville 97754 (503, 447-4115)
 Roseburg District: MEL BERG, Mgr., 777 NW Garden Valley Blvd., Roseburg 97470 (503, 672-4491)
 Salem District: VAN W. MANNING, Mgr., 1717 Fabry Rds., SE, Salem 97302 (503, 399-5643)
 Spokane District: JOSEPH BUESING, Mgr., E. 4217 Main Ave., Spokane, WA 99202 (509, 456-2570)
 Vale District: WILLIAM C. CALKINS, Mgr., 100 Oregon St., P.O. Box 700, Vale 97918 (503, 473-3144)

UTAH
 Cedar City District: MORGAN S. JENSEN, Mgr., 176 East D.L. Sargent Dr., Box 724, Cedar City 84720 (801, 586-2401)
 Moab District: GENE NODINE, Mgr., 82 East Dogwood, P.O. Box 970, Moab 84532 (801, 259-6111)
 Richfield District: DONALD L. PENDLETON, Mgr., 150 E. 900 North, P.O. Box 768, Richfield 84701 (801, 896-8221)

Salt Lake District: DEANE H. ZELLER, Mgr., 2370 S. 2300 West, Salt Lake City 84119 (801, 524-6761)

Vernal District: DAVID E. LITTLE, Mgr., 170 S. 500 East, Vernal 84078 (801, 789-1362)

WYOMING (Also Nebraska)

Casper District: JAMES W. MONROE, Mgr., 1701 East 'E' St., Casper 82601 (307, 261-5101)

Rawlins District: RICHARD BASTIN, Mgr., 1300 Third St., P.O. Box 670, Rawlins 82301 (307, 324-7171)

Rock Springs District: DONALD SWEEP, Mgr., Hwy. 191 North, P.O. Box 1869, Rock Springs 82902-1869 (307, 382-5350)

Worland District: CHET CONARD, Mgr., 101 South 23rd St., P.O. Box 119, Worland 82401 (307, 347-9871)

PERIODICALS OF INTEREST

Acid Rain Abstracts
Acid Rain Index
Bowker A&I Publishing
245 West 17th St.
New York, NY 10011
Bimonthly; $395.00 per year

Atlantic Salmon Journal, The
Atlantic Salmon Federation
1435 St. Alexandre, Suite 1030
Montreal, Quebec H3A 2G4
Quarterly

BioCycle Journal of Waste Recycling
The J G Press, Inc., Box 351
Emmaus, PA 18049

Boston College Environmental Affairs Law Review
(formerly Environmental Affairs)
Boston College Law School
885 Centre St.
Newton Centre, MA 02159
Quarterly; $22.00 per year

Catalyst for Environment/Energy
274 Madison Ave.
New York, NY 10016
Periodically; $16.00 for four consecutive issues

Conservation Foundation Letter
The Conservation Foundation
1250 24th St., NW
Washington, DC 20037
Bimonthly

Earth Island Journal
Earth Island Institute
300 Broadway, Suite 28
San Francisco, CA 94133
Quarterly

Ecology Law Quarterly
University of California
Boalt Hall School of Law
Berkeley, CA 94720
Quarterly (Personal subscriptions)
$26.00 per volume/year U.S. subscribers
$30.00 per volume/year foreign
Institutional subscriptions:
$40.00 per volume/year U.S. subscribers
$44.00 per volume/year foreign

Ecology USA
CJE Associates
237 Gretna Green Ct.
Alexandria, VA 22304-5602
Biweekly; $77.00 per year

Endangered Species Technical Bulletin
Division of Endangered Species
and Habitat Conservation
U.S. Fish and Wildlife Service
Washington, DC 20240

Endangered Species UPDATE
School of Natural Resources
The University of Michigan
Ann Arbor, MI 48109-1115
Annually; $15.00 per year (U.S.)
$18.00 per year (foreign)

Environment Abstracts
Bowker A&I Publishing
245 West 17th St.
New York, NY 10011
Monthly; $1,050.00 per year

Environment Index and Abstracts Annual
Bowker A&I Publishing
245 West 17th St.
New York, NY 10011
Annually; $495.00 per year

Environment Outlook
Institute for Environmental Studies
University of Washington, FM-12
Seattle, WA 98195
Monthly (except July and August)

Environment Report
Trends Publishing, Inc.
National Press Bldg.
Washington, DC 20045
Semi-monthly; $460.00 per year

Environment Reporter
Bureau of National Affairs, Inc.
1231 25th St., NW
Washington, DC 20037

Environmental Ethics
Environmental Philosophy, Inc.
The University of Georgia
Athens, GA 30602
Quarterly; $18.00 per year (individual)
$36.00 per year (institution)

Environmental Law Journal
Northwestern School of Law
Lewis and Clark College
10015 SW Terwilliger Blvd.
Portland, OR 97219
Quarterly

Environmental Law Reporter
Environmental Law Institute
1616 P St., NW, Suite 200
Washington, DC 20036
Monthly

Environmental Science and Technology
American Chemical Society

1155 16th St., NW
Washington, DC 20036
Monthly; $55.00 per year (individual)
$192.00 per year (institution)

Groundwater Newsletter
Water Information Center, Inc.
124 East Bethpage Rd.
Plainview, NY 11803
(516, 249-7634)
Semi-monthly; $167.00 per year (U.S.)
$187.00 per year (foreign)

Harvard Environmental Law Review
Harvard Law School
Cambridge, MA 02138 (617, 495-3110)
Semi-annually (winter and summer)
$20.00 per year (U.S.)
$23.00 per year (foreign surface mail)
$35.00 per year (foreign air mail)

High Country News
Box 1090, Paonia, CO 81428
Biweekly; $24.00 per year (individual)
$34.00 per year (institution)

Hunting Ranch Business
P.O. Box 35603
Houston, TX 77235-5603
Monthly; $59.50 per year

Land Letter
W.J. Chandler Associates
1511 K St., NW, Suite 1100
Washington, DC 20005
Biweekly; $165.00 per year

Land Use Planning Report
Business Publishers, Inc.
951 Pershing Dr.
Silver Spring, MD 20910
Biweekly; $185.50 per year
Includes lst class postage

Landscape Journal
The University of Wisconsin Press
114 N. Murray St.
Madison, WI 53715
Semi-annually
$18.00 (individual); $40.00 (institution)

Mother Earth News
P.O. Box 70
Hendersonville, NC 28793
Bimonthly

National Wetlands Newsletter
Environmental Law Institute
1616 P St., NW
Washington, DC 20036
Bimonthly

Natural Resources Journal
University of New Mexico School of Law
1117 Stanford, NE
Albuquerque, NM 87131

Quarterly; $22.00 per year (U.S.)
$24.00 per year (foreign)

Northwest Environmental Journal;
    The Journal of Environmental Policy and
    Research for Northwestern North America
Institute for Environmental Studies (FM-12)
University of Washington
Seattle, WA 98195
Semi-annually
$22.00 (U.S. and Canada) $32.00 (library)
$34.00 (foreign)

Organic Gardening Magazine
Rodale Press, Inc.
33 E. Minor St.
Emmaus, PA 18098
Monthly; $13.97 per year (U.S. and U.S.possessions)

Pollution Abstracts
Cambridge Scientific Abstracts
7200 Wisconsin Ave.
Bethesda, MD 20814

Pollution Control Guide; Energy Management;
    Regulation Reports; Federal Energy Guidelines;
    Energy Resources Tax Reports
Commerce Clearing House, Inc.
4025 W. Peterson Ave.
Chicago, IL 60646

Public Lands Restoration Task Force
    Riparian Enhancement Teams
812 SW Washington St., Suite 1105
Portland, OR 97205 (503, 248-9132)

Resource Recycling
P.O. Box 10540
Portland, OR 97210
$27.00 per year (seven times)
(503, 227-1319)

Restoration and Management Notes
The University of Wisconsin Press
114 N. Murray St.
Madison, WI 53715
Semi-annually
$14.00 (individual); $41.00 (institution)

Salar Newsletter
The Atlantic Salmon Federation
1435 St. Alexandre, #1030
Montreal, Quebec H3A 2G4
Quarterly

Water Newsletter/R & D News
Water Information Center, Inc.
125 East Bethpage Rd.
Plainview, NY 11803
(516, 249-7634)
Bimonthly; $127.00 per year (U.S.)
$147.00 per year (foreign)

World Rivers Review
International Rivers Network
300 Broadway, Suite 28

San Francisco, CA 94133-3312
(415, 788-3666)
Bimonthly

DIRECTORIES OF INTEREST

CALIFORNIA ENVIRONMENTAL DIRECTORY: A GUIDE TO ORGANIZATIONS AND RESOURCES

Order from California Institute of Public Affairs, P.O. Box 10, Claremont, CA 91711. This is the only systematic guide available to state and federal government agencies, university programs, major associations, and selected local and regional agencies in California (nearly 1,000 listings in all) that are concerned with protecting the environment and managing natural resources. Regular price $40.00. Special price for public, academic, and governmental libraries and for nonprofit public-interest associations ordering on letterhead: $25.00. Fourth edition.

CONGRESSIONAL DIRECTORY, 1987-1988

For sale by Superintendent of Documents, U.S. Government Printing Office, Washington, DC 20402. Lists information concerning the current Congress, including a biography of each member, committee memberships, officials of federal departments and agencies, governors of states and territories, foreign diplomats, and members of the press, radio, and television galleries. Cloth-bound edition, $20.00; clothbound with thumb index, $25.00; paperback edition, $15.00.

CONGRESSIONAL STAFF DIRECTORY, 1989

Box 62, Mt. Vernon, VA 22121. Contains information concerning the 101st Congress, including Members and their biographies, election results, office staffs in Washington and in districts and states, assignment of Members and staff to committees and subcommittees, 12,900 cities and counties and their congressional districts, 3,500 staff biographies, key-word subject index, and 19,000-name index of individuals. Single copy: $50.00.

DIRECTORY OF NATURAL SCIENCE CENTERS ENVIRONMENTAL, 1984

Published by National Science for Youth Foundation, 763 Silvermine Rd., New Canaan, Ct 06840. (203, 966-5643) The directory lists over 1,100 centers located throughout the United States, Canada, and the Virgin Islands. Each center is listed together with its address, telephone number, business hours and admission fees. The buildings, acreage, and any special features are also included. Single copy: $15.00 plus $2.50 for postage and handling.

DIRECTORY OF ENVIRONMENTAL GROUPS IN NEW ENGLAND

Environmental Protection Agency, Regiona l, Rm. 2203, John F. Kennedy Federal Bldg., Boston, MA 02203 MICHAEL R. DELAND, Regional Administrator

FEDERAL STAFF DIRECTORY, 1989

Box 62, Mt. Vernon, VA 22121. Published by Congressional Staff Directory, Ltd. Lists 28,000 Executive Branch officials by name, title, addresse, and phone number. Includes the White House, all departments and independent agencies, regulatory bodies, advisory organizations and regional offices outside the Washington area.

Also includes biographies of 2,400 key officials, key-word subject index, and index of individuals. Single copy: $50.00.

JUDICIAL STAFF DIRECTORY, 1989

Published by Congressional Staff Directory, Ltd., P.O. Box 62, Mt. Vernon, VA 22121. Contains listings of all federal courts and their judges and staffs. Also includes magistrates, court clerks and deputies, probation officers, and U.S. Attorneys and U.S. Marshals and their staffs. Includes the Supreme Court and other national courts, the federal circuit, district, and bankruptcy courts, committees of the Judicial Conference, the Department of Justice, 12,900 cities and counties and their circuit and district courts, maps of judicial districts, indexes of judges by appointing Presidents and by years of appointment, tables of judicial nominations and vacancies, court workload and case statistics, biographies of judges and key staff, and index of individuals. Single copy: $50.00.

NEW ENGLAND FIELD GUIDE TO ENVIRONMENTAL EDUCATION FACILITIES AND RESOURCES, THE

The directory lists over 175 organizations, including nature centers, museums, environmental education centers, sanctuaries, national parks, and state and regional organizations. It features a great deal of information about each organization, including programs, facilities, membership, staffing, budgets, internships, and more. It also is fully indexed, and includes cumulative statistics and appendices. Single copy $16.00 plus $1.50 postage and handling from New England Field Guide, Antioch/NE Graduate School, 103 Roxbury St., Keene, NH 03431

UNITED STATES AND THE GLOBAL ENVIRONMENT, THE: A GUIDE TO AMERICAN ORGANIZATIONS CONCERNED WITH ENVIRONMENTAL ISSUE

Order from California Institute of Public Affairs, P.O. Box 10, Claremont, CA 91711. It provides profiles - most of which run from several hundred to over 2,000 words - of 125 private and governmental groups that have significant international activities in environmental protection and natural resource management. Single copy: $25.00

WORLD DIRECTORY OF ENVIRONMENTAL ORGANIZATIONS, 1989.

California Institute of Public Affairs, P.O. Box 10, Claremont, CA 91711. Published for the Sierra Club, in cooperation with the International Union for Conservation of Nature and Natural Resources (IUCUNR). Still the only detailed reference of its kind. 'A much-needed source and a contribution to international communication.' 288 pages. Third edition. Please call for price. (714, 624-5212)

WORLD ENVIRONMENTAL DIRECTORY, 1989

Published by Business Publishers, Inc., 951 Pershing Dr., Silver Spring, MD 20910.
Comprehensive 1,000-page volume that actually is 13 directories in one. Includes approximately 60,000 listings of pollution control product manfacturers and consultants, conservation and environmental organizations, federal and state government agencies, attorneys with environmental interests, environmental education programs, databases, and funding sources. Published annually. Single copy: $125.00, 5th edition.

CONSERVATION/ENVIRONMENT OFFICES OF FOREIGN GOVERNMENTS

Afghanistan—Said Ahmad Gulabzol, Minister, Ministry of Interior Affairs, Kabul
Rector, Faculty of Science, Zoological Dept., Kabul University, Kabul

Argentina: Minister Guillermo E. Gonzalez, Director, Servicio Agrario Internacional, Ministerio de Economia, Secretaria de Agricultural, Ganaderia y Pesca Av.Paseo Colon 984, 1305 Buenos Aires (Phone: 362-5111/1705-1161)

Australia—Department of Arts, Sport, Tourism, and Environment, GPO Box 787, Canberra ACT 2601 (062, 68-9411)
Associate Secretary for Environment: Mr. P.J. Galvin (062, 46-7563)

Austria—Dr. Kurt Steyrer, Federal Minister for Health & the Environment, Stubenring 1, Vienna A1010

Bahamas, The—Ministry of Agriculture, Trade and Industry, Fisheries and Cooperatives Department of Agriculture, P.O. Box N-3028, Nassau, Bahamas (809, 323-1777)
Minister, The Honourable Ervin Knowles, M.P., Permanent Secretary, Colin Deane

Bangladesh—Maj. Gen. (Retd) Mahmudul Hassan, Minister of Agriculture, Government of the Peoples Republic of Bangladesh, Dhaka, Bangladesh (W:404282/404314; H:604784/6050006)
Minister of State: Mr. A.B.M. Ruhul Amin Howlader (W:405634/H:407239)
Secretary, Ministry of Agriculture: Mr. M.A. Syed (W:404273/H:406774)
Mr. N.A. Katebi, Chief Conservator of Forests, Ministry of Agriculture, Bangladesh Secretariat, Dhaka (W:605845/H:401260)

Barbados—Caribbean Conservation Association, Savannah Lodge, The Garrison, St. Michael; The Barbados National Trust, Independence Square, Bridgetown, St. Michael

Belgium—Mrs. Miet Smet, Secretary of State for Environment and Social Emancipation, Wetstraat, 56 B - 1040 Brussels, Belgium (Tel: 02/ 230 49 85; 02/230 50 93)

Benin—Codja Gandonou, Minister of Rural Development and Cooperative Action, Cotonou

Bolivia—Lic. Jose Justiniano, Minister of Agriculture and Rural Affairs, P.O. Box 8561, La Paz, Bolivia (36-1348)

Botswana—Director of Wildlife and Tourism, P.O. Box 131, Gaborone
Mr. K. Ngwamotsouko, Permanent Secretary, Ministry of Commerce and Industry, Private Bag 004, Gaborone

Brazil—Dr. Paulo Nogueira Neto, Secretaria Especial do Meio Ambiente, Ministerio do Interior, Esplanada dos Ministerios, Brasilia Dr. Paulo Nogueira Neto, Secretaria Especial do Meio Ambiente (SEMA) SEPN Quadra 510 lote 8 Edf. Cidade Cabo Frio, Brasilia DF Brasil 70750 (011-55-61) 274.94.85
Minister of Urban, Housing and Environment Sr. Deni Scwartz, SEP Quadra 505 Bloco B, Brasilia DF Brasil 70069 (011-55-61) 274.15.12

Bulgaria—Committee For Environment Protection at the Council of Ministers, 2 Benesh Sq., Sofia 1000

Burkina Faso—Minister of Popular Defense and Security, Commander, Lingani Boukary, Jean-Baptiste Minister of Secondary and Higher Education and Scientific Research, Ouedraogo Oumarou Clement Minister of Cooperative and Rural Action, Captain Sedego Laurent Minister of Primary amd Mass Education, Tiendrebeogo Alice Minister of Equipment, Captain Kambou Daprou Minister of Works of Social Security and Public Affairs, Naboho Kanidoua Minister of Finance, Sanogho Bintou State Secretary of Housing and Urbanism, Traore Moise State Secretary for Social Action, Sara Elie State Secretary for Secondary Education, Boleho Quemidoun Jules

Burma—U Tun Wai, Minister of Health and Information, Rangoon

Canada—Honourable Tom McMillan, M.P., P.C., Minister of the Environment, 10 Wellington St., Ottawa, Ontario K1A 0H3 (819, 997-1441)

Central African Republic—Mr. Basile Erepe, Minister in charge of Agriculture and Livestock; Mr. Raymond Mbitikon, Minister in charge of Waters, Forests, Hunting, Fishing and Tourism

Chad—Commandant Roasngar, Membre du C.S.M., Ministre du Developpement Agricole et Pastoral et des Calamites Naturelles, Ndjamena

Chile—General Jorge Veloso B., Minister of National Resources Ministry of National Resources, Av. Libertador B. O'Higgins, 280 SANTIAGO

China—Chuang-huan Chiu, Minister, Ministry of the Interior, 107 Roosevelt Rd., Sec. 4, Taipei, Taiwan, Republic of China
National Wildlife Protection Association of the Republic of China, Yu-yang Wang, Director, 3rd Fl., 180 Roosevelt Rd., Sec. 5, Taipei, Taiwan, Republic of China

Colombia—Instituto Nacional de los Recursos Naturales y del Ambiente Diagonal 34 N1. 5-18 (Inderena), Director, Calle 26 No.13B-47, Bogota, D.E. Señor doctor Director Inderena Carrera 14 N°25A-66 Bogata

Costa Rica—Servicio Nacional de Parques, Ministerio de Agricultura y Ganaderia, Apartado Postal 10094, San José Departamento de Conservacion y Reforestación, Instituto Constarricense de Electricidad, Apartado Postal 10032, San

José Asociación Costarricense para la Conservación de la Naturaleza (Ascona) Apartado, Postal 3099, San José, Costa Rica

Czechoslovakia—State Commission for Science, Technology and Investments, Division of Environmental Protection, Slezská 9, 120 29 Praha 2-Vinohrady (275-7777) Association for the Preservation of Nature, Nerudova 31, 110 00 Praha 1 - Malá Strana

Denmark—Lone Dybkjaer, Minister of the Environment, Slotsholmsgade 12 DK-1216, Copenhagen K

Ecuador—Ingeniero Diego Tamariz, Ministro De Energia Y Minas: Ministro De Energia Y Minas, Santa Prisca 223 Quito (523-028 / 570-034)

El Salvador—Señor Ministro, Ministerio del Interior, Centro de Gobirno, San Salvador, El Salvador; Señor Director, Dirección General de Recursos Naturales Renovables, Ministerio de Agricultura y Ganadería Blvd. Los Héroes y 21 Calle Poniente, San Salvador, El Salvador; Sr. Presidente, Asociación Amigos de la Tierra, Edificio Comercial Apt. 616, San Salvador, El Salvador; Señor Gerente, Instituto Salvadoreño de Turismo, Calle Rubén Darío 619, San Salvador

Ethiopia—Wildlife Conservation Dept., P.O. Box 386, Ras Desta Damtew Ave., Addis Ababa

Fiji—Ministry of Urban Development, Housing and Social Welfare, Mr. Peter Nacuva, Permanent Secretary, Government Bldgs., Suva

Finland—Ministry of the Environment, Kirkkokatu 12, 00170 Helsinki 17, Mr. Kaj Barlund; Minister of the Environment; Ministry of the Environment, Department for Environmental Protection and Nature Conservancy, Mr. Olli Ojala, Head of Department, Council for Environmental Protection, Secretary General, Mr. Martti Markkula

France—Brice Lalonde, Secretary of State to the Prime Minister, responsible for the Environment, 14 Boulevard du Gal Leclerc, 92521 Neuilly-sur-Seine, France

Germany, Federal Republic of—Federal Ministry of Food, Agriculture and Forestry (BML), Ignaz Kiechle, Minister, Rochusstr. 1, 5300 Bonn Federal Ministry for the Environment, Nature Conservation and Nuclear Safety (BMU), Prof. Dr. Klaus Topfer, Minister Adenaverallee 4, 5300 Bonn

German Democratic Republic—Deputy Prime Minister, Dr. Hans Reichelt Minister for Environmental Protection and Water Management, DDR-1040 Berlin, Schiffbauerdamm 15

Ghana—Ministry of Lands and Natural Resources, Dept. of Game and Wildlife, P.O. Box 212 ACCRA

Great Britain—Minister of State, Dept. of The Environment Minister For Housing and Planning: The Rt. Hon. John Gummer, Mp Minister for Environment, Countryside and Water, Theearlof Caithness Minister for Local Government, Micharl Howard, Esq, Qc, Mp (01-212-3434) Secretary of State for the Environment, 2 Marsham St., London SW1P 3EB

Guatemala—Direccioń General de Servicios Pecuarios Avenida La Reforma, 8-60, zona 9, Edificio Galerías, Reforma, Guatemala City Ministerio de Agricultura, Ganadería y Alimentación Palacio Nacional, Guatemala City

Guinea—Dr. Camara Kekoura, Minister of Forests and Fisheries, Conakry

Guyana—Dr. Noel Blackman, Minister of Health and Public Welfare, Upper Brickdam, Georgetown

Haiti—René Destin, Minister of Agriculture, Natural Resources and Rural Development, Damien Gustave Menager, Minister of Agriculture

Honduras—Ministry of Natural Resources, Prof. Rodrigo Castillo, Minister, Ministerio de Recursos Naturales, Blvd. Miraflores Tegucigalpa, Honduras, C.A. (504, 32-8723) Vice-Minister: Ing. Jose Montenegro (Natural Resources) Vice-Minister: Ing. Agronomo Luis Alonzo Quezada (Agriculture and Livestock)

Iceland—Ministry of Culture and Education, Minister, Hverfisgata 26, Reykjavik: Minister: Mr. Birgir Isleifur Gunnarsson

India—Ministry of Agriculture, Dept. of Agriculture, Division of Forestry, G.S. Dhillon, Indian Forest Service, Inspector General of Forests, Krishi Bhavan, New Delhi IIOOOI Ministry of Environment and Forests, Bhajan Lal National Committee on Environmental Planning and Coordination, Dept. of Science and Technology, Dr. Ashok Khosla, Secretary, Technological Bhavan, New Mehrauli Rd., New Delhi IIOOII

Indonesia—Syafii MANAN, Director, Directorate of Nature Conservation, Directorate General of Forest Protection and Nature Conservation, Department of Forestry, Jalan Ir. H. Juanda No. 9, Bogor - West Java, Indonesia

Ireland—The Secretary, Department of Agriculture, Kildare Street, Dublin 2, Ireland; The Secretary, Department of the Environment, Custom House, Dublin

Israel—Environmental Protection Service, Dr. Uri Marinov, Director, Ministry of The Interior, P.O. Box 6158, Jerusalem 91061 Israel Nature-Reserves Authority, Mr. A. Yaffe, Director, Hanatziv 16, Tel-Aviv (02-660-15)

Italy—Minister of the National Patrimony: Vincenzo Bono Parrino, Minister for Ecology: Giorgio Ruffolo

Ivory Coast—Vincent Pierre Lokrou , Ministre des Eaux et Forets: CCFLEXts, B.P. v. 94, Abidjan Ivory Coast Abidjan

Jamaica—Hon. Dr. Percival Broderick, Minister for Agriculture, P.O. Box 480, Hope Gardens, Kingston 6 Hon. Alva Ross, Speaker of the House of Representatives, Gordon House, 81 Duke St., Kingston National Resources and Conservation Department, P.O. Box 305, 53 Molynes Rd., Kingston 10

Japan Mr. Toshio Horiuchi, Director General of Environment Agency, 1-2-2 Kasumigaseki, Chiyoda-ku Tokyo 100 (03, 581-3351)

Jordan—Marwan Al-Hmoud, Minister, Ministry of Agriculture, P.O. Box 2099, Amman Minister of Agriculture, P.O. Box 2099, Amman, Jordan; Mr. Yusuf Hamdan Al Jaber, Minister of Municipal and Rural Affairs and the Environment, P.O. 1799, Amman, Jordan; Royal Society for the Conservation of Wildlife, Jebel Amman, Fifth Circle, Amman, Jordan

Kenya—Permanent Secretary, Ministry of Tourism and Wildlife, Utalii House, Box 30027, Nairobi
Permanent Secretary, Ministry of Environment and Natural Resources, Kencom House, Box 30126, Nairobi
Ministry of Tourism and Wildlife, Utalii Hse, Box 30027, Nairobi
Ministry of Environment and Natural Resources, Kencom Hse, Box 30126, Nairobi

Korea—Conservation Division, Forectry Administration Bureau, Office of Forestry Administration, Seoul, Korea
Forestry Administration Bureau, Office of Forestry Administration, Seoul, Korea
Planning and Coordination Bureau, Air Quality Management Bureau and Water Quality Management Bureau, Office of Environment Administration, Seoul,
National Environment Protection Institute, Seooul, Korea
Office of Cultural Property Maintenance, Seoul, Korea

Kuwait—Faisal Abdul Razaq Al-Khalid, Minister of Commerce and Industry, P.O. Box 2944 Safat Kuwait, Arabian Gulf 13030

Lebanon—Joseph El Hachem, Minister of Housing and Cooperatives and Public Health Adel Osseiran, Minister of Agriculture

Lesotho—J. R. L. Kotsokoane, Minister, Ministry of Agriculture, P.O. Box MS 24, Maseru

Liberia— Forestry Development Authority, P.O. Box 3010, Sinkor, Monrovia, Libera Ministry of Agriculture, Sinkor, Monrovia

Luxembourg—M. Benny Berg, Minister of Public Health; M. Robert Krieps, Minister of Environment, 57-90, bd de la Petrusse, Luxembourg-Ville, G.D.

Madagascar—Josph Randrianasolo, Ministre de la Production Animale et des Eaux et Forets Antananarivo

Malawi—The Secretary for Forestry and Natural Resources, P.O. Box 350, Capital City, Lilongwe 3

Malaysia—Datuk Amar Stephen Yong, Minister of Science Technology and Environment; Ministry of Science Technology and Environment, Oriental Plaza, Jalan Parry, Kuala Lumpur; Nik Mohd, Amin bin Nik Abu Bakar, Secretary General, Ministry of Science, Technology & Environment; S.T. Sundram, Director General, Division of Environment (DOE); Gurmit Singh, President, Environmental Protection Society

Mali—Services for Waters and Forests, rue Testard, Bamako

Malta—Natural Resources—The Hon. Michael Falzon - Minister for Development of Infrastructure, BELT-IS-SEBH; Environment: The Hon. Ugo Mifsud Boinnici - Minister of Education, Lascaris - Valletta

Mauritania—Doctor Oumar Ba, Minister of Rural Development, P.O. Box 366, Nouakaott

Mauritius—Permanent Secretary, Ministry of Agriculture, Fisheries and Natural Resources, Port Louis

Mexico—Secretariat of Urban Development and Ecology, Undersecretary of Ecology. Mr. Sergio Reyes Lujan, (Subsecretario do Ecologia) Rio Elba # 20, 16 piso, 06500 Mexico, D.F.

Morocco—Abderrahmane Boufettass, Rabat 60263) Minister of Housing, Urban Development, and Environment, Rabat; Tahar Masmoudi, Minister of Trade, Rabat-65951; Mohamed Bouamoud, Minister of Transportation, Rabat-73420; Mohamed Labied, Minister of Handicrafts and Social Affairs, Rabat-21625; Moussa Saaadi, Minsiter of Tourisme Rabat-60905

Nepal—National Parks and Wildlife Conservation Office, Chief, Birendra b. Shah, Banejnor, Kathmandu Kathmandu

Netherlands—Ministry of Housing, Physical Planning and Environment, Director-General for the Environment ir. M.E.E. Enthoven ,(mailing address: P.O. Box 450, 2260 MB Leidschendam, The Netherlands) Dokter Van der Stamstraat 2, Leidschendam (31-70-209367)
Ministry of Agriculture and Fisheries, Director for Nature, Environment and Wildlife Management, Drs. J.B. Pieters (mailing address: P.O. Box 20401, 2500 EK the Hague, The Netherlands) Bezuidenhoutseweg 73, the Hague. Responsible for nature conservation and wildlife management. (31-70-792603)
Ministry of Transport and Public Works, Ir. E. van Marle, Director, Office of Foreign Relations, Rijkswaterstaat, P.O. Box 20906, 2500 EX The Hague, Koningskade 4, 2500 EX The Hague. Responsible for surface water management. (31-70-745745)

New Zealand—David McDowell, Director-General, (designate) Department of Conservation, Box 10-420, Wellington Environmental Council, Chairman, Dr. J. A. Hayward, Executive Officer, K. Ryan, P.O. Box 10382, Wellington Blakeley, Secretary, Ministry for the Environment, Box 10-362, Wellington

Niger—Son Excellence, Mr. Attaher Darkoye, Ministre de l'Hydraulique et de l'Environnement Niamey—Republique du Niger
Directeur, du Service des Eaux et Foretŝts,. Niamey

Nicaragua—Instituto Nicaraguense De Recursos Naturales y Del Ambiente (IRENA) Servicio De Parques Nacionales Y Fauna Silvestre KM 12 1/2 Carretera Norte, Managua, Nicaragua

Nigeria—Dr. Kalu I. Kalu, Commissioner for Economic Development and Reconstruction, Lagos; Maj. Gen., Nasko Commissioner for Agriculture and Rural Development, 34/36 Ikoyi Rd., Lagos S.L. Edu, Chief, President and Trustee, Nigerian Conservation Foudation, Mainland Hotel, 1st Fl., P.O. Box 467, Lagos M.G. Nasko, Major-General, Honourable Minister of Agriculture and Rural Development, Federal Secretariat, Ikoyi, Lagos Dr. Kalu I. Kalu, Honourable Minister of National Planning, Federal Secretariat, Ikoyi, Lagos

Norway—Ministry of Environment, (Myntgaten 2, Oslo) P.O. Box 8013, Dep., N-0030, Oslo I
Norges Naturvernforbund (Norwegian Wildlife Organization), Pilestr. 41B, N-0166 Oslo I

Oman—Ministry of Environment and Water, P.O. Box 323, Muscat, Oman (696-444) H.H. Sayyid Shabib Bin Taimur Bin Faisal Al Said, Minister H.E. Maj. Gen. Bakheet Bin Said Al Sanfari, Under Secretary

Pakistan—Mr. Sartaj Aziz, Minister, Government of Islamic Republic of Pakistan, Ministry of Food, Agriculture, Cooperatives, and Local Government, Islamabad Mr. Mohammad Siddique, Secretary, Government of Islamic Republic of Pakistan, Ministry of Food, Agriculture, and Cooperatives, Islamabad

Panama—His Excellency Ing. manuel Balbino Moreno, Ministerio de Desarrollo Agropecuario, Apartado 5390, Panamá 5

Paraguay—Ing. Agr. Hernando Bertoni, Minister of Agriculture and Husbandry, Pte. Franco y 14 de Mayo, Asuncion

Peru—Ministry of Agricultural, Remigio Morales-Bermudez, Lima Ministry of Fisheries, Romulo Leon, Lima, National Office of Evaluation of Natural Resources:-O.N.E.R.N., Office of the Prime Minister, Lima

Philippines—Department of Natural Resources, Environment and Energy, Fulgencio Factoran, Jr., Secretary, Diliman, Quezon City; Parks and Wildlife Commission, Quezon Memorial Park, Quezon City

Poland—Waldemar Michna, Minister, Ministry for Environmental Protection and Natural Resources, 00-922 Warsaw, Ul. Wawelska 52/54 30 Janusz Zurek, Director, Institute of Environmental Protection 02-078 Warsaw, U1. Krzywickiego 9

Portugal—Carlos Alberto Martins Pimenta, Secretaria de Estado do Ambiente e Recursos Naturais, Rua do Seculo, 51, 1200 Lisboa

Qatar—Minister of Industry and Agriculture, Sheikh Faisal Bin Thani Al-thani, P.O. Box 1966, Doha, Arabian Gulf

Romania—National Council for Science and Technology, Ioan Ursu, President, Str. Roma No. 3234, Bucharest

Rwanda—Director, Office Rwandaise du Tourisme et des Parcs Nationaux, B.P. 905, Kigali

Saudi Arabia—H.E. Dr. Abdul Rahman Al Al-Sheikh, Minister of Agriculture and Water, Riyadh Ministry of Agriculture and Water, Airport Rd., Riyadh 11195
Director General of Animal Resoures: Dr. Saleh Abdul Aziz al-Muzaini
Range and Animal Development Organization, P.O. Box 322, Sakakah, Saudi Arabia
Meteorology and Environmental Protection Administration, Makarona St., P.O. Box 1358, Jeddah, Saudi Arabia
Chairman: Abdul Bin al-Qeen
Director General: Rumaih Mansour al-Rumaih

Senegal—Ministry of Rural Development, Cheikh Cissokho, Minister, Dakar

Sierra Leone—Chief Conservator of Forests, Ministry of Agriculture and Forestry, Youji Bldg., Brookfields, Freetown

Singapore—Minister for Environment, Ministry of Environment, 40, Scotts Road, Environment Building, Singapore 0922

Somalia—Ministry of Tourism Headed by Mohamed Omar Jess, Mogadisho

South Africa—The Director-General, Department of Water Affairs and Forestry and Environmental Conservation. Private Bag X313, Pretoria, 0001

Spain—Instituto Nacional para la Conservacion de la Naturaleza (ICONA), Ministerio de Agricultura, Gran Via de San Francisco, 85 Madrid 28005 7 (266-8200)
Instituto Nacional Para La Conservacion De la Naturaleza (I.C.O.N.A.) Director: Ilmo. Sr. D. Santiago Marraco Solana
Subdireccion: ACUTE General de Recursos en Regimen Especial. Subdirector General: Ilmo. Sr. D. Jose Antonio Novas Garcia
Subdireccióň General de Recursos Naturales Renovables Subdirector General: Ilmo Sr. D. Comse Morillo Fernandez
Subdireccióň General de Proteccion de la Naturaleza. Subdirector General: Ilmo Sr. D. Comse Morillo Fernandez
Subdireccióň General de Protección de la Naturaleza. Subdirector General Ilmo Sr. D. Fernando Estirado Gomez

Sri Lanka—Ministry of State, Department of Wildlife Conservation, Director, Wildlife Conservation, Trans Work House, Lower Chattam St., Colombo-I Sri Lanka

Sudan—Dr. Ali Fadlh, Minister, Ministry of Health, Khartoum

Swaziland—Permanent Secretary, Ministry of Agriculture, P.O. Box 162, Mbabane, Swaziland, Southern Africa; Mr. T.E. Reilly, Manager, Mlilwane Game Sanctuary, P.O. Box 33, Mbabane Tel: 61037

Sweden—Valfrid Paulsson, Director General, National Board for Environmental Protection, Box 1302, S-171 25 Solna 1

Switzerland—Federal Office for the Environment, the Forest, and the Landscape, Hallwylstr. 4, 3003 Bern; Swiss Federal Office for Land-Use Planning, Bundesrain 20, 3003 Bern

Syria—Dr. Mahamad Ghabbash, Minister of Agriculture and the Agrarian Reform, Damascus; Dr. Mohamad Harba, Minister of the Interior; Mr. Kamel Elbaba, Minister of Electricity

Tanzania—Ministry of Natural Resources and Tourism, Clock Tower Branch Bldg., Ind. Ave., Box 9372, Dar Es Salaam

Thailand—Dr. Choompol Swasdiyakorn, Secretary-General, National Research Council, 196 Phaholoyothin Rd. Bangkok 10900; Mrs. Chutamanee Eimsupan, Director, Research Promotion, Division, National Research Council, 196 Phaholyothin Rd. Bangkok 10900; Mr. Somchit Saenhorm, Chief of Library and Documentary Services, National Research Council, 196 Phaholyothin Rd. Bangkok 10900; Mr. Chumni Boonyophas, Director-General, Royal Forestry Department, Phaholyothin Rd., Bangkok 10900

Togo—Mr. Koffi Kadanga Walla, Minister of Rural Development

Trinidad and Tobago—Permanent Secretary, Ministry of Agriculture, Attn: Conservator of Forests, St. Clair Cicle, Port of Spain, Trinidad, W.I.; Dr. B.S. RAMDIAL, Conservator of Forest and wildlife, Ministry of Agriculture, Forestry Division, Port-of-Spain

Turkey—Offfice of the Prime Minister, Directorate General for Environmental Affairs, Ataturk Bulvari 143, Bakanliklar-Ankara
Director General: Muzaffer Evirgen
Assistant Director General: Kazim Ceylan

Uganda—Permanent Secretary, Ministry of Tourism and Wildlife Resources, P.O. Box 4241, Kampala
Permanent Secretary, Ministry of Agriculture P.O. Box 102, Entebbe
Permanent Secretary, Ministry of Animal Industry and Fisheries, P.O. Box, 7003, Kampala
Permanent Secretary, Ministry of Environment Protection, P.O. Box 8147, Kampala

Union of Soviet Socialist Republics—State Committee on Science and Technology, 11 Gorkey St., Moscow State Committee for Science and Technology, II Gorby St., Moscos 103905

United Arab Emirates—His Excellency Sheikh Mubarak Bin Mohammed Al-nahyan, Minister of the Interior, Abu Dhabi

The Republic of Cameroon—Salou Hayatou, Minister of Plan and Territorial Development, Ministry of Agriculture, Yaounde, Mr. Tonke Jean-Baptiste Centre for Forestry Research, Nkolbisson, Yaounde, Chief of Centre: Grison Francois, Wildlife School, Garoua, Director: Aloo Aloo; P.O. Box 271, Garoua, Cameroon

Uruguay—Ministerio de Industria y Energia, Rincón 747, Montevideo

Venezuela—Ministry of Agriculture, Direcion de Recursos Naturales Renovables, Torre Norte, Centro Simon Bolivar, Caracas; Ministry of Environment & Natural Resources, Torre Sur, Centro Simón Bolívar, Caracas

Yugoslavia—Federal Committee for Agriculture, Bulevar Avnoja No. 104, 11070 Novi Beograd

Zaire—Mr. Pendje Demodeto Yako, Commissaire, d'Etat Aux. Affaires Foncieres, Environment ET Conservation De La Nature, Kinshasa. Real Property, Environment, Nature Conservation

Zambia—Ministry of Water and Natural Resources, Department of National Parks and Wildlife Service, J.C.N. Zyambo, Director, P.O. Box Private, Bag 1, Chilanga

SOURCES OF AUDIO-VISUAL MATERIALS OR INFORMATION ON CONSERVATION AND ENVIRONMENTAL TOPICS

American Society of Mammalogists, Mammal Slide Library, 1907 Monument Canyon Dr., Grand Junction, CO 81503. Catalogs available.

A selected list of filmstrips on the conservation of natural resources, by Conservation Education Association. The Interstate, 19-27 N. Jackson St., Danville, IL 61832.

Association Films Inc., 866 Third Ave., New York, NY 10022. Sales, rental, free loan. Catalogs available.

Berlet Films, 1646 Kimmel Rd., Jackson, MI 49201 (517, 784-6969) Sales, rental. Free catalog available.

Bullfrog Films, Oley, PA 19547 (800, 543-3764) Films and videos rented and sold worldwide to educational institutions. Programs come with study guide with suggested activities, research topics, debate subjects, and bibliographies. Free catalogue available.

Contemporary films/McGraw-Hill, Eastern Region: Princeton-Hightstown Rd., Hightstown, NJ 08520; Mid-Continent: Manchester Rd., Manchester, Mo 63011; Western Region: 8171 Redwood Hgwy., Novato, CA 94947. Sales, rental. Free catalogs.

Critical index of films on man and his environment, by Conservation Education Association. The Interstate, 19-27 N. Jackson St., Danville, IL 61832.

Environmental Images, Inc., 300 I St., NW, Suite 101, Suite 325, Washington, DC 20036 (202, 675-9100) Films, videotapes, and slides.

Environmental Film Service, National Association of Conservation Districts, 408 E. Main, P.O. Box 855, League City, TX 77573. Catalog available.

Environment Film Review, Environment Information Center, Inc., Film Reference Dept., 292 Madison Ave., New York, NY 10017.

Films and Research for an Endangered Environment, Ltd., 201 N. Wells, Suite 1735, Chicago, IL 60606 (312, 782-1376) Film presentation available on request.

Georgia Department of Natural Resources, Film Unit, 270 Washington St., Atlanta, GA 30334. Free loan and sales. Free film catalog available upon request.

Index to Environmental Studies-Multimedia. National Information Center for Educational Media, University of Southern California, University Park, Los Angeles, CA 90007. Catalog available.

International Film Bureau, Inc., 332 S. Michigan Ave., Chicago, IL 60604. Sales, rental. Free catalog.

Media Network, 121 Fulton St., 5th Fl., New York, NY 10038 (212, 619,3455). Offers a computerized database of several thousand titles of films, videotapes and slideshows by phone and by mail.

Modern Talking Picture Service, 500 Park St., No., St. Petersburg, FL 33709 (813, 541-6763) Free catalogs available.

Montana Department of Fish and Game Motion Picture Production—Conservation Education Bureau, Montana Outdoors Building, 930 Custer Ave., Helena, MT 59601. Brochure upon request.

National Audiovisual Center, National Archives and Records Service, General Services Administration, Washington DC 20409. Handles audio-visual materials produced by or for U.S. Government. Sales, rental, free loan. Free catalogs.

South Carolina Wildlife and Marine Resources Dept., Film Dept., P.O. Box 167, Columbia, SC 29202. Catalog available.

Tennessee Dept. of Conservation, Division of Information and Education, 2611 West End Ave., Nashville, TN 37203. Film catalog and list of publications available upon request to Tennessee residents and organizations only.

U.S. Department of Agriculture films: available from film libraries of the 50 state land grant universities (see also U.S. Forest Service below). Catalogs available from university film libraries.

U.S. Department of the Interior films: catalogue available by writing Office of Public Affairs, U.S. Department of the Interior, 18th & C St. NW, Washington, DC 20240. Free.

U.S. Forest Service films: available through regional offices or private contractors. Free catalogs. Addresses: Alaska Region, Federal Office Bldg., P.O. Box 1628, Juneau 99802. California Region, 630 Sansome St., San Francisco 94111. Eastern Region, 633 W. Wisconsin Ave., Milwaukee, WI 53203. Intermountain Region, 324 25th St., Ogden, UT 84401. Northern Region, Federal Bldg., Missoula, MT 59801. Pacific Northwest Region, 319 S.W. Pine St., P.O. Box 3623, Portland, OR 97208. Rocky Mountain Region, Cromars, 1200 Stout St., Denver, CO 80204. Southern Region, 1720 Peachtree Rd., NW, Atlanta, GA 30309. Southwestern Region, Federal Bldg., 517 Gold Ave., SW, Albuquerque, NM 87102

Washington Department of Natural Resources, Public Information Office, Public Lands Bldg., Olympia, WA 98504. Catalog available.

West Wind Productions, Inc., P.O. Box 3532, Boulder, CO 80307, (303) 443-2800. 16mm films and video. Sales, rental. Free catalog available.

Wyoming Game and Fish Dept., Attn: Film librarian, Cheyenne, WY 82002. Catalog available.

Yaker Environmental Systems, Inc., P.O. Box 18, Stanton, NJ 08885 (201, 735-7056) Environmental computer software sales. Free catalog.

PUBLICATIONS INDEX

Title of Publication	Organization	Page

SUBJECT INDEX*

National Wildlife Federation

Staff for this Book

Dr. Jay D. Hair
President

Joel T. Thomas
General Counsel

Alric H. Clay
Senior Vice President,
Administration

William W. Howard, Jr.
Senior Vice President,
Conservation Programs

Francis A. DiCicco
Vice President,
Financial Affairs

Lynn A. Greenwalt
Vice President,
Resources Conservation

John W. Jensen,
Vice President,
Development

S. Douglas Miller
Vice President,
Research and Education

Kenneth S. Modzelewski
Vice President,
Promotional Activities

Larry J. Schweiger
Vice President,
Affiliate and Regional Programs

Stephanie C. Sklar
Vice President,
Public Affairs

Sue Sandmeyer
Director,
Educational Outreach Division

Rue Gordon
Editor,
Conservation Directory

Leslie Eichner LeFranc
Cover Design

Working for the Nature of Tomorrow.

NATIONAL WILDLIFE FEDERATION
1400 Sixteenth Street, N.W., Washington, D.C. 20036-2266